Factor Analysis of Data Matrices

Factor Analysis
of Data Matrices

PAUL HORST
University of Washington

HOLT, RINEHART AND WINSTON, INC.
New York   Chicago   San Francisco   Toronto   London

Copyright © 1965 by Holt, Rinehart and Winston, Inc.

Library of Congress Catalog Card Number: 65–12814
23733—0215
Printed in the United States of America

TO THE MEMORY OF MY TEACHER

Louis Leon Thurstone

Preface

It is perhaps unfortunate that most if not all books on factor analysis have been written by psychologists or by persons whose academic identification is closely related to psychology. By the same token, it may also be unfortunate that this book has been written by a psychologist. I can only say that in writing it I have tried to write as a scientist rather than as a psychologist, although for illustrative material I have drawn heavily from the discipline with which I am most familiar. The growing interest of other disciplines in the theories and techniques of factor analysis attest to the universal applicability of the more fundmental concepts underlying factor analytic methodology. Nevertheless, the historical accident by which psychologists initiated the development of factor analysis procedures may account for some of the philosophical and even occult overtones which tend to obscure the more fundamental objectives of the methodology.

It is particularly unfortunate that Charles Spearman's narrow and highly specialized two-factor theory of intelligence set the pattern and direction for much of the factor analytical work that has followed. Although the extension of Spearman's general factor concept to the multidimensional common factor concept of Thurstone represented an important advance, it still preserves the dominating status of specific factors alien to principles of parsimony so essential to scientific methodology in general. Unless and until a much more adequate epistemological foundation can be fashioned to support the dominant status of specific factors, the communality issue will persist as a center of controversy or at best as an interesting intellectual pastime. It is true that an uneasy truce on the communality issue can be reached via the attribute-scaling route, as suggested in Chapter 15. But this purely formal mathematical reconciliation has not yet led to a fundamental epistemological rapprochement essential for a more general or comprehensive philosophy of science.

Fortunately, however, in spite of the specific factor controversy, the fundamental contributions of factor analytic methodology are emerging in many disciplines with a wide variety of data. This is true because all scientists in all disciplines who investigate the relationships among two or more variables must utilize at least the rudiments of factor analytic methodology, however crudely, naively, or innocently. I can scarcely hope to escape the charge by some of my most esteemed colleagues of treating the communality problem cavalierly, casually, and perhaps with less than complete competence. However, I cannot escape the conviction that the contributions of factor analytic methodology to the sciences as a whole must vary inversely with the amount of emphasis placed on specific factors in the theories and models of factor analysis.

Perhaps factor analysis has had its most popular appeal as a device for generating plausible and acceptable taxonomies in disciplines where these have been traditionally confused and unsatisfactory. Certainly psychology and other social science disciplines qualify in this respect. It is interesting to observe, however, that even in the taxonomically more secure physical sciences, the fundamental objectives of the factor techniques are finding areas of application. These objectives have to do, of course, with reducing the dimensionality of an empirically specified set of variables. Labels seem to play a fundamental role in providing emotional security for all human beings, including scientists, and therefore the taxonomic function of factor analysis procedures probably needs no justification. However, it is in parsimonious description of natural phenomena that factor analysis has more fundamental and universal significance. This role or objective of factor analysis seems to be most apparent when one considers the techniques primarily from the point of view of the matrix of experimental data. I have tried to emphasize throughout the book that the covariance matrices cannot provide or generate information not latent or manifest in the data matrices.

Perhaps the overriding consideration in writing this book has been to present factor analysis as a methodology applicable to all the sciences. To some the presentation may seem austere and lacking in emotional appeal. To a degree this manner of presentation has been deliberate. I have tried to adhere closely to the algebraic and arithmetic essentials of the factor analytic techniques and thus to avoid as much as possible the ritualistic overgrowths which have tended to conceal its more fundamental characteristics.

It is my hope that the book will prove useful as both a textbook and a reference work. I believe a number of the methods I have presented are new and have not previously appeared in published texts on factor analysis. Modifications and, I hope, useful variations of previously published methods have also been included. In general, I have attempted to present most of the factoring methods as special cases of the rank reduction theorem. Notable exceptions will be recognized in the Jacobi-type solutions.

The first part of the book presents the background for the chapters which follow. Chapter 1 purports to be a nontechnical introduction to the nature and areas of application of the factor analytic procedures. The next two chapters present the elementary concepts of matrix algebra used in the later chapters. These two chapters are largely a condensation of my *Matrix Algebra for Social Scientists*. The matrix notation and concepts provide a simple, efficient, and powerful machinery for handling the type of data characteristic of the social sciences and more particularly the concepts and procedures of factor analysis. The notation and concepts are essentially simple and easy to grasp, and there seems to be little reason why those who wish to use the factor techniques should not readily acquire a working knowledge of simple matrix notation and operations. Chapter 4 is a more technical exposition of the foundations of factor analysis procedures.

The chapters in Part II present the more traditional factor analysis models, together with modifications and innovations of them. The chapters in Part III present variations of the Jacobi methods, together with more novel and less conventional methods.

Part IV is concerned with problems of metric, including both scale and origin. Considerations of metric lead naturally to a recognition that formally the entity and attribute modes of the two-mode data matrix are indistinguishable. These considerations lead also to a more detailed analysis of the multimode data matrix. The chapter on image analysis is less closely related to the other topics; however, since it provides a scale-free solution, it seems appropriate to include it in this part.

The first three chapters in Part V deal with the simple structure solutions and transformations. Less consideration is given to oblique or nonorthogonal transformations than some might wish. However, the completely analytical oblique solutions presented thus far still leave much to be desired. I have therefore tried to give most attention to methods which appear to be most useful in the analysis of empirical data. The last chapter is rather tenuously related to the others. It deals with the solution of factors core matrices. The emphasis is largely on the transformation of the data matrix to the factor score matrix; and it is primarily this formal aspect which might justify its inclusion.

The chapters in Part VI deal with a number of different special topics. Chapter 21 considers the higher order factor models and relates these higher order general factors to first-order general factor loadings and general factor scores. A somewhat more systematic treatment of factor-type models is attempted than is typical of current texts. Chapter 22 touches on the important problem of measure as it relates to factor analysis, but I claim no definitive treatment of this difficult and inadequately developed topic. Chapter 23 introduces the role of factor analysis in prediction and presents multiple regression analysis as a special case of lower rank matrix approximation. Chapter 24 extends the concept of factor analysis to multiple sets of variables, of which canonical analysis is a special case.

I regard as one of the most important features of this book the Appendix of Fortran II computer programs, which have been written for most of the methods presented in the book. These should prove useful to persons who

wish to apply the methods, whether or not they are interested in their rationale
or more theoretical aspects. It is assumed that most persons interested in
factor analysis will have computer facilities available. Most of the methods
presented are not practical for desk calculators except when the number of
variables is small. I do not pretend that the computer programs are optimal
or highly sophisticated. It is quite possible that nonfunctional statements
introduced in early stages of some of the programs have not all been eliminated. For this I apologize, but the worst that such statements can do is to
act as red herrings for those who might wish to follow the rationale of the program statements. For each program I have included the required subroutines,
even though they are repeated in other programs. Although this adds to the
bulk of the Appendix, it should make the programs easier to use than if the
subroutines were presented separately. I have also repeated with each program the data used in the corresponding numerical illustrations in the text
so that those who wish to punch a program deck may check output against
that in the book. The format statements are the same for input data as in the
data listed. Except for the first program I have not used variable format
statements.

The plan of the methods chapters—those after Part I—is as follows.
First, the characteristics of the methods are described in order to assist users
in selecting a suitable method. Next, the computational equations and
computational instructions are presented for those interested in following
the arithmetic operations. These are followed by numerical examples to
illustrate the procedure and results. The final section of each of these chapters
presents the appropriate mathematical rationale and proofs.

I have mentioned the use of matrix notation and indicated that it is
much more efficient than scalar notation. I have also introduced some
notational conventions and some nontraditional terminology. This I have
done partly in an attempt to improve upon traditional notation and terminology. In addition, I have found it helpful to invent new terms for concepts
which are important for the handling of data matrices as distinguished from
abstract mathematical matrices. I have tried to confine myself almost exclusively to algebraic notation and concepts and to avoid the indiscriminate
commingling of trigonometric and geometric symbolic systems with the
algebraic. This I have done with the full recognition that the literature of
factor analysis intermingles the three systems freely and, in my opinion, at
the expense of simplicity and clarity.

Although the computer programs can be used with a minimum of background, to profit most from this book the user should have a knowledge of
third-term high school algebra and an introductory course in statistics which
includes the product moment correlation coefficient. He should be able to
read and understand Chapters 2 and 3. To do this, a working knowledge of
my *Matrix Algebra for Social Scientists* would be helpful. A college course in

matrix algebra or linear algebra would also be adequate. However, such courses usually include much more material than is necessary or useful for this book.

This book can be used as a text at the upper division undergraduate level and at the graduate level. It is appropriate for students in any of the sciences —social, biological, or physical. Although the illustrations have been largely drawn from psychology, courses in this area are not prerequisite to an understanding of the text. A beginning course in psychology might be helpful, however.

If the text is used in undergraduate classes, the mathematical sections at the ends of the chapters will doubtless be omitted. These sections can be utilized in graduate classes and seminars. There will be no dearth of exercises, as data from other classes and projects and from other disciplines can be substituted for those provided in the Fortran programs in the Appendix. Some assistance may be required with respect to format statements for persons with no knowledge of programing, since the input format statements in the programs refer specifically to the data accompanying the program listings in the Appendix.

It is difficult to give due credit and thanks to the many persons from whose work I have drawn. Among those who have provided unusual stimulation are Messrs. Ledyard Tucker, Louis Guttman, Chester Harris, and Henry Kaiser. I do not pretend, however, that we agree on all issues, and I assume full responsibility for the points of view presented. I must also thank Dr. David Dekker, director of the Computer Center at the University of Washington, and members of his staff who cooperated with me in the lengthy and arduous task of preparing the Fortran computer programs. I also acknowledge the financial support provided by the National Institutes of Health and the Office of Naval Research. In particular, I wish to thank Dr. Glenn Bryan of the Office of Naval Research, who made possible a series of high-level working conferences on factor analysis. These conferences and my association with the conferees provided a great source of stimulation and encouragement in the preparation of this book. It must be evident that the preparation of the manuscript for this book required much painstaking typing. For this work I have to thank Misses Helen Ranck and Fern Thomas. Finally, I wish to acknowledge the great amount of time and effort which my wife has contributed to this book. She was responsible for the card punching involved in the preparation of the computer programs, as well as for much detail work required in the many submissions, corrections, and retrievals of the programs during the protracted debugging operations. She assumed much of the editorial responsibility for the last two drafts of the manuscript, carefully checking the numerous tables and equations and their referencing in the text. She also read both the galley proofs and the page proofs, assumed major responsibility for the index, and in many other ways contributed to the preparation of the book. It is inevitable, however, that with all these acknowledgements I alone assume responsibility for errors and deficiencies, both major and minor, which still remain.

P.H.

Seattle, Washington
June 1965

Contents

Preface

PART I. Introductory Background

PART III.   Matrix Factoring Methods—B

PART IV.   Categories, Origin, and Scale

PART V. Transformation Problems and Methods

PART VI. Special Problems

Part I

Introductory Background

Chapter 1

The Role of Factor Analysis in Science

Over the past 30 years a good many books have been written on the subject of factor analysis. Charles Spearman is probably responsible for the term. At the turn of the century he formulated a theory of intelligence which has been designated the two-factor theory of intelligence. His hypothesis was that intelligent behavior could be accounted for in terms of a general factor of intelligence and a number of specific factors, presumably independent of one another.

Spearman (1927) was concerned with objective techniques for the verification of his theory. The concept of the correlation coefficient came to be extremely useful and central to much of statistical theory and applications. By applying correlational procedures to the data obtained from psychological tests, Spearman attempted to verify his hypothesis of the two-factor theory of intelligence.

As it turned out, Spearman's so-called two-factor theory was soon found to be inadequate to account for the relationships among various measures of human performance. Others found it necessary to hypothesize factors other than the general and specific factors. These were called group factors. Later, however, Thurstone (1947), in extending the work of Spearman, designated what he called common factors. These were so named because they were regarded as existing in two or more measured variables within a set. In any case, the term factor stuck, and factors came to be thought of as hypothetical variables which in various combinations accounted for or explained the variations in various kinds of human behavior.

Actually, it was Thurstone who gave the name factor analysis to the type of statistical and computational activity which constitutes the subject matter of this book. It is perhaps unfortunate that this particular choice of phrase should have been made to comprehend the kind of activity to which it traditionally and currently refers. The word factor has well-established meaning in mathematics and in lay terminology. Even in the kinds of operations and calculations involved in what are usually referred to as factor analytic studies,

3

it would be more appropriate to use the term factor in the mathematical sense in which it is usually employed, rather than in the sense in which factor analysts, beginning with Thurstone, have used the term. Factor analysts have traditionally used the word factor to mean some sort of theoretical or hypothetical variable, whereas mathematicians use it to mean one of a number of things which when multiplied together give a product.

We shall see in the development of the subject in the following chapters that in the kind of work referred to as factor analysis we are very much concerned with finding things which, when multiplied together, give some specified product. Although we shall use the term factor in much the sense the traditional factor analysts use it, in deference to long-established usage, we shall attempt to make the distinction between the two uses of the word where ambiguity might arise.

One might also discuss at length the use of the word analysis and its appropriateness in describing the kind of activity that factor analysts engage in. Certainly the word can mean a wide variety of things in a wide variety of disciplines. In fact, the variety of ways in which the term is used, both in technical and lay terminology, is so great that it has become almost meaningless. In any case it is probably fair to say that for most factor analysts the term refers merely to specific computational procedures.

It is probable that many of the investigators in the field of factor analysis would object to this characterization of their use of the term. They may well insist that they are engaged in a much higher order of scientific and cerebral activity than that involved in a prespecified pattern of computational operations. Many would insist that they are attempting to get at the fundamental realities and truths of mental activity or human behavior, or perhaps even more philosophically fundamental concepts. Unfortunately, much of the literature of factor analysis is cluttered with a sort of occult and mystical terminology which obscures the true significance and value of factor analytic activities. Before considering the kinds of activities that factor analysts have been concerned with, it may be instructive to direct our attention to some more fundamental concepts involved in scientific investigation in general.

1.1 Data and Science

Scientific activity, in general, must be concerned in some way with data. In discussing the relationships between science and data we shall consider first, the nature of scientific investigation, and second, certain basic concepts of scientific investigation.

1.1.1 The Nature of Scientific Investigation. Scientific investigation may be distinguished from speculative or philosophical investigation in that for the former some kind of observational data is required. In philosophical or speculative investigation such data are not required. A good example of this is mathematics, which might be regarded as a special branch of philosophy. In mathematics we are concerned with abstract relations among abstract concepts. In particular, these concepts may be numbers, but they need not necessarily be so. Even if they are numbers they can be abstract numbers without reference to any objects in the physical world.

Certainly in scientific investigation we do use mathematics, and perhaps, unfortunately, we do not use it nearly as extensively as we should. Mathematics provides a method of rigorous formulation and verbalization of hypotheses which presumably we wish to investigate or verify in our scientific investigations. We shall not attempt here to give a sophisticated and scholarly treatment of the subject of scientific investigation and the philosophy of science. We shall only point out some of the practical and often overlooked essentials of a good scientific investigation, with particular reference to the relationship of factor analysis to scientific experimentation.

It will be noted that we have used the word experiment in connection with scientific investigation. Often it is said that a scientific experiment consists essentially in holding all variables constant except one, and then controlling the variation of this variable to see what happens to another variable. This, for example, is what has come to be known as experimental psychology.

It is unfortunate that so narrow a use of the term experimental method has persisted in the literature and in the procedures of many scientific investigators. The essence of scientific investigation is that some more or less clearly defined procedure be specified for making observations on things that vary. One may be interested in the average summer precipitation of rainfall in a number of geographical areas and the average wheat yield in those same geographical areas. On the other hand, our primary concern may be the amount of fertilizer of a specified kind applied to a given region and also the wheat yield. One may be interested not only in this particular region but also in a number of other regions. More particularly, one might wish to vary the amount of fertilizer in various plots of ground and subsequently observe the wheat yield in these various plots. This latter type of interest might be called experimental, in that one exercises control over one of the variables—namely, the amount of fertilizer per plot. The former might be called observational, in that one has no control over the amount of rainfall, but nevertheless one can observe it.

Perhaps we wish to study the blood pressure of a particular individual. We might, for example, record his blood pressure and his heart rate over a number of days. Or, instead of recording his heart rate, we may give him successive doses of adrenalin in varying amounts over a period of days. In the first case our interest centers on heart rate and blood pressure; in the second case it centers on adrenalin injection and blood pressure. In the first case we presumably exercise no control over either heart rate or blood pressure, but in the second case we do exercise control over the amount of adrenalin injected.

From a scientific point of view, the first pair of variables may be just as interesting or valid to study as the second. It is sometimes maintained that because the adrenalin injection is controlled by the investigator, we have a higher order of scientific investigation than in the other example, because in the latter the investigator exercises no control over the things he observes. It cannot be too strongly emphasized, however, that scientific investigation is not restricted to sets of observations in which control is exercised over some of the things which are being observed. This is not a necessary characteristic of scientific investigation. A necessary characteristic is, however, that observations and recordings of events be made as a basis for further scientific activity. Whether or to what extent the things being observed are under the control of the experimenter has nothing to do with the scientific quality of the investigation.

Unfortunately, many psychologists and perhaps most experimental psychologists do not recognize this fact. This is not to say that the control of certain events in a scientific experiment is not desirable—in many cases it may be very desirable and important. It may be a crucial aspect of a particular kind of experiment or investigation. But it is not the control feature that makes the experiment scientific.

In the examples we have given we have referred to the pairs of things on which the investigator's interest centers. In the first case, the interest centers in rainfall and crop yield. In the second case, it centers in fertilizer and crop yield; in the third case, blood pressure and heart rate. And in the fourth case, adrenalin injection and heart rate are the variables under study.

The fact that in all these cases there are two things of primary interest does satisfy one of the essential characteristics of scientific investigation. Presumably the implication in the first example is that there would be some relationship between rainfall and crop yield. There is an implicit assumption that the more rainfall—within limits—the better the crop yield. There is also the implicit assumption that the more fertilizer applied to a plot of ground, the better the crop yield. We have, then, the concept of the relationship between two things which may vary. In the case of blood pressure and heart rate, also, we may be concerned with the relationship of concomitant or sequential variation of the two. This is true also in the case of adrenalin injection and blood pressure. Again, the implication is that there may be some relationship between the amount of adrenalin injected and the blood pressure. For the time being we say nothing about the kinds of relationships or how they will be measured. It is enough to say that unless one is concerned with determining whether or not there is a relationship between two or more things which vary, his interest is not scientific. It would be purely clerical or on a verbal or descriptive level.

So far the examples we have used are from agriculture and physiology, and we have made no reference to variables or the kinds of things one might find interesting in the behavior of people. We have avoided "psychology" in choosing examples. The term factor analysis had its origin with psychologists, and they have been far more interested in the kinds of activities which factor analysts engage in than have other disciplines, but this is largely by coincidence. Actually, there is no more reason why psychologists should be interested in factor analysis than physiologists, meteorologists, economists, or investigators from other disciplines.

As a matter of fact, we shall see, when we get into the various types of factor analytic procedures and problems, that the kinds of things we are concerned with are basically the kinds of things that mathematicians are interested in. Factor analysis is sometimes described as a branch of statistical science. Actually, this characterization reflects a lack of appreciation of the fundamental characteristics of sophisticated factor analytic procedures. The fundamental concepts of factor analysis are primarily mathematical. It would be more appropriate to say that factor analysis is a branch of mathematics and that statistical analysis is a branch of factor analysis. This statement will come as a shock to many factor analysts who have not recognized its fundamental characteristics and who have been diverted by more or less irrelevant detail which has cluttered the literature over the years.

It is interesting, however, that the use of factor analysis is becoming increasingly more widespread in a large number of disciplines, both scientific and applied, particularly because factor analysis has had something of a checkered career. It started with great fanfare in the early thirties, and then for some years considerable disillusionment followed the early interest and applications. The recurrence of interest, however, attests to the fundamental importance of this particular approach to scientific problems, and it is probable that the interest and application of factor analytic techniques will spread to more disciplines and be used increasingly by a large number of persons in business, industry, education, and research.

In order to understand the implications of factor analytic techniques for the solution of scientific and practical problems, let us investigate in more detail some of the basic concepts of scientific investigation so that we can see how these fit into factor analytic theory and application.

1.1.2 Basic Concepts of Scientific Investigation. In the first example of the foregoing section, we referred to various geographical areas in which rainfall and crop yield were observed. We also mentioned various plots in which the amount of fertilizer applied differed from one plot to another. In the second example, we referred to a number of different days on which recordings were made of a person's blood pressure and heart rate. We also referred to the number of days in which he was given various dosages of adrenalin. In both of these examples, we have a number of things which differ from one another in some specified way. In the first case, we have several geographical areas which differ with respect to the rainfall and crop yield, and in the second case, we have a number of days which differ with respect to the blood pressure and heart rate of the individual and the amount of adrenalin injected.

We shall call the geographical areas and the days *entities*. These are the things which differ with respect to the observations made. A rather fundamental notion, then, in any scientific investigation is the concept of entities. More specifically, the concept of a number of *different* entities should be emphasized.

In books on statistics the term *observations* is commonly used incorrectly. For example, one might read that there are 20 observations in an experiment. This might involve a group of 20 entities, such as geographical areas or persons on which observations are made. But the entities themselves are not the observations. The common practice of using the term observations when referring to the entities on which the observations are made frequently leads to confusion.

Another important feature of the examples we have given has to do with the particular aspects of the entities that we are concerned with. For example, in the first case, we are interested in rainfall and crop yield. These we may call *attributes* of the entities. In the second case, we are interested in heart rate and blood pressure of the individuals on whom the measurements are taken. These we may call attributes of the individuals. In general, then, any scientific investigation must consist not only of a number of entities with respect to which observations of some kind are made, but also of observations with respect to some specified attributes, characteristics, qualities, or whatever we wish to call them. We shall use the term attributes or *variables*. A scientific investigation, then, must consist of observations on a group of entities with respect to particular attributes or variables.

Suppose now that instead of the previous example in which we took the blood pressure and heart rate of a person for a number of successive days, we have taken blood pressure and heart rate for each of a group of persons on a single day. In this case, we would have a number of entities on which we have observations with respect to several attributes or variables. Suppose also that for each member of the group of entities or persons we have taken measures of blood pressure on a number of successive days. Analogously, for the example using geographical locations as entities and rainfall and crop yield as variables, we may observe the values of these variables for the different entities not only for one year but also for each of a number of years.

We shall refer to these different years or these different days as different *occasions*. We see, then, that we may have a set of observations on a number of different entities with respect to a number of different variables or attributes on a number of different occasions.

We have now outlined a system in which we may have attributes of entities on a number of different occasions. Here we have three different modes or categories with respect to which we may characterize a system. Ordinarily, in scientific investigations, it has been customary to consider only two categories or modes. These have usually been treated as entity by attribute systems. For example, if we have a single individual, as in the earlier example cited, on whom we have made a number of different osbervations over a period of time with respect to several or more attributes, then the individual himself may be regarded as the system and the successive days or time intervals may be called entities. More recent formulations of the basic constructs required to describe a system have, however, emphasized the value of keeping the concept of occasions separate from the concept of entities. It seems, therefore, that in a scientific investigation of a system, the trend will be to include not only the concepts of attributes and entities but also that of occasions.

Although the concepts of entities, attributes, and occasions seem to be a minimal set of concepts for the scientific investigation of a system, it may be instructive to inquire whether there are other concepts which may be required for more complete investigations.

We may, for example, in the case of the entities whose blood pressure and heart rate were being observed over successive days, include a fourth category which we might designate the *evaluator* category. We may have a group of individuals consisting of physicians, laboratory technicians, nurses, or combinations of all of these, each of whom makes a separate recording on the basis of his observations for each of the variables on each of the individuals. Or the evaluators may be different types of instruments used to measure or record blood pressure and heart rate. This may seem to be a rather belabored procedure for proliferating the number of categories or modes relevant to the investigation of a particular system. Nevertheless, much of the work in psychometrics may appropriately involve a number of different evaluators.

We have still another mode or category which in psychological work has received considerable attention without, unfortunately, an appropriate recognition of how it fits into the general scheme or structure of systems analysis. This may be called the *condition* category. Suppose, for example, that we have administered a personality or attitude questionnaire consisting of a number of items—that is, attributes or variables—to a number of individuals, or entities. We may administer the same instrument to the same individuals on a number of occasions. However, we may instruct the entities responding to each item in the questionnaire that they respond to the questionnaire first as they feel it applies to themselves. Then we may tell them to respond as they wish it would apply to themselves. Next we may request that they respond again as they think the average person would. We may in this way generate the number of different instructions under which the subjects or entities respond to the questionnaire.

It should be observed that this mode or category is quite different from that of evaluators. We might have not only instructions to a particular subject to respond to the questionnaire under the various sets of instructions but we may also have a number of different evaluators, including the subject himself, indicating how he thinks the subject would respond to the questionnaire under each of the different conditions.

Therefore, some systems, to be satisfactorily and completely characterized, may well take into account observations or recordings for a number of different entities on a number of different attributes on a number of different occasions by a number of different evaluators with respect to a number of different conditions or instructions.

We have implied, in our discussion of the various modes or categories which are fundamental to the investigation of a system, that numbers or quantities are in some way involved. Certainly in the case of wheat yield we have a number of bushels per acre, and in the case of rainfall we imply some kind of measure, such as number of inches per summer. Also, in the case of blood pressure and heart rate, a measure is implied—we have some quantitative or numerical values implied in terms of pressure and number of beats per second. Even in the case of the questionnaire to which the individuals respond for each of the 60 items with *yes* or *no*, we may assign a 1 or a 0, according to whether the person answers the item *yes* or *no*.

We see, then, that a central concept in the scientific investigation of a system is that of measurement or quantification. We shall take the position that the scientific investigation of any system must yield numbers of some kind which may then be analyzed and manipulated according to specified computational or mathematical models. These numbers may be of a wide variety and kind. For a particular variable, they may be binary measures— that is, simply 1 and 0. These are also called *dichotomous* measures. We shall not concern ourselves in this book with number systems and the kinds of measures which are appropriate or possible in science. For example, we shall not concern ourselves with the questions of whether we are dealing with interval scales or with ratio scales or with cardinal or ordinal numbers. All we insist upon is that the observations or records which are obtained in the scientific investigation be numerical rather than verbal. We may have adjectival descriptions resulting from the observations, but before these can be subject to scientific treatment, they must be quantified. For example, we may have response alternatives of *yes* or *no*. These must be converted to 1 or 0, or to some other pair of two numbers.

1.2 The Data Matrix

It should be emphasized that the basic concepts we have discussed in the previous section are such that theoretically, at least, we have a number of possibilities for each mode. That is, we have a number of different members of the entity mode, the attribute mode, the occasion mode, the evaluator mode, and the condition mode. An element of the system, therefore, will consist of a number which is characterized by a single member from each of the modes within the system. That is, we may have the number 3 which is the measure of, say, the fourth entity on the third attribute during the fifth occasion under the second condition by the fourth evaluator. The number of elements in a system would therefore be the product of the number of members in each mode. It can readily be seen the observations such as we have discussed can be recorded as tables of numbers. These we shall call *data matrices*. In Chapters 2 and 3 we shall consider in detail the characteristics of matrices. The familiar type of data matrix and the one which has been most worked with is that in which the system consists of only two modes, the entities and the attributes. As a matter of fact, most of our treatment in the following chapters, and certainly factor analysis as it has been conducted traditionally, is restricted mainly to the two-mode system. However, it is of interest to consider in more detail the nature of the various modes within a system.

1.2.1 The Entity Mode. One may define the entities within a system in a wide variety of ways. For example, the entity for the case of wheat yield and rainfall may be defined as the geographical area comprising one of a number of counties in the system. On the other hand, it may be defined as one of a number of states in the United States. Or, it might be defined as a particular restricted plot or section in a group of plots or sections defined geographically for purposes of studying the relationships between rainfall and wheat yield. In a sociological study, one might define entities in terms of census tracts within a city or alternately, as one of a group of cities. As in the case of the agricultural example, one might also define an entity as the group of persons residing within one county of a number of counties.

In the case of psychological investigations, the entities are usually persons or in the case of experimental psychology, animals such as rats, dogs, monkeys and so on. Here there seems to be no particular problem in defining entities. Sometimes, however, as in the agricultural and sociological examples, great care must be taken in specifying or defining a single entity within the set. In the case of chemical research, the entities presumably would be specifically defined batches of physical material which are to be subjected to chemical analysis. In physiological research, the entities may be complete physiological organisms, such as persons or animals. On the other hand, they may also be specifically defined physiological specimens from a given individual or even groups of individuals, such as blood samples, urine samples, fragments of specified kinds of tissue, and so on. There may be great latitude in the definition or delimiting of an entity within a system, but these definitions must be formulated in such a way that they are not confused with other modes

tests so that the alternate forms were not mutually interchangeable. That is, the sets must be essentially different from one another in some respect.

It should be evident from the discussion that the status of the categorical sets of entities, attributes, and occasions is in a sense somewhat more fundamental and general than that of the evaluators and condition sets. It is even possible that further methodological investigation and research would indicate that the concepts of evaluators and conditions might be incorporated as special cases of the entity or attribute categories.

1.2.6   Measures. We have pointed out that an element of a system consists of a number which is identified in terms of one member from each of the categorical sets included within the system. We have also said that these numbers may be of a wide variety of kinds. In particular, they may be binary numbers. The question of how these numbers are obtained, how they are processed after they are obtained, and so on, is beyond the scope of this book. However, it is important to point out that the subject of quantification of observations and the transformation of measures is of great importance, and the value of the results of a scientific investigation may depend heavily on the manner in which the numbers were generated.

The problem of metric is concerned primarily with the problems of scaling and origin. A more subtle problem is that of nonlinear or functional transformations of numbers, as distinguished from scale and origin transformations. Functional transformations may involve a variety of nonlinear transformations such as polynomial, logarithmic, trigonometric, exponential, and other more involved combinations of these types of transformations. The question, for example, of whether the difference between 2 and 3 is the same as the difference between 6 and 7 may or may not be important, depending on the particular model one is using. The problems involved and the implications of transformations of variables in terms of what is to be done with the transformed variables require much more research.

1.3   Combination of Matrix Categories

We have pointed out that most of the work of factor analysis has concerned itself with two-category sets—entities and attributes. A great deal of the work in factor analysis has consisted, for example, in taking a number of different measures on a number of different entities and then, on this matrix of numbers, applying certain computational routines. We may take, for example, the case of a number of different psychological tests which have been administered to a number of different people. Here we have a test score for each of the tests for each of the individuals. The problem of what we do with these measures and what considerations shall guide us in treating them is considered in more detail later on. We shall restrict our attention for the time being to the two-category-set type of analysis, since the mathematical and computational models for sets beyond two have not been thoroughly developed. First let us consider the entity category and how we may get two-category systems in which this is one of the sets.

1.3.1 Two Categories Involving Entities. The most obvious combination of the two sets involving entities is one in which we have a number of different variables evaluated for a number of different entities. This is the traditional case, and the example of measurements of meteorological variables and agricultural yields for a number of different geographical areas during one year is typical. Typical also is the case in which we have a number of physiological measures taken on one day for each of a number of individuals or a number of different psychological tests administered on one day to a number of different individuals. Examples of this kind could be multiplied in many areas of investigation.

We may, however, also have a data matrix in which we have entities as one set and occasions as another set of categories. Here we may have administered a test to a group of individuals on one day, and then repeated the same test on a number of different occasions. Or we may have a group of individuals who are learning a skill such as typewriting, and we record their performance for each of a number of successive days or weeks. This is the familiar example which may yield a learning curve for each of a number of different individuals. As a matter of fact, in any discipline in which we have a number of different entities and are interested in only a single variable but wish to study change over a period of time, we start with the entity-occasion data matrix.

Next let us consider the entity-condition, two-set category system. Here we may ask each member of a group of individuals to respond to a single item or stimulus element under a number of different instructional sets. These may be as he would normally respond, as he would ideally respond, as he thinks his mother would respond, as he thinks his best friend would respond, and so on. Here, then, we have the entity and condition categorical sets as the basis of the data matrix.

1.3.2 The Two-Category Set Involving Attributes. We may, for a single entity, have a number of different attributes over a number of different occasions. This brings us back to one of the first examples we considered at the beginning of this chapter—the case in which we took physiological measures on a single individual over a number of days. Formally, the individual could be considered as the universe from which a sample of entities, namely, occasions, was drawn. In any case, here we have a single individual or member from the categorical set of entities, and we investigate the data matrix which has a measure for each of a number of variables on each of a number of successive occasions.

We may also consider a single entity or subject for each of a number of different attributes—for example, items on a questionnaire—and ask the subject to respond to each item as he thinks the ideal person, the average person, he himself, and so on, would respond. Here we have the combination of conditions and attributes for a single entity.

The model which considers a single entity as a system may have considerable value for clinical psychology and medicine in general, where a great deal of interest centers around the individual person. Much criticism has been leveled at statistical studies involving groups of individuals to the neglect of the single individual. The sentimental critic objects that a person is being treated as a number or as a statistic. It is interesting to point out that the statistical model which can be used upon groups of individuals can also be used upon a single individual by appropriately selecting the categorical sets which one wishes to investigate. The categorical sets of occasions, variables, and conditions may be investigated with respect to a single individual. These provide free rein to the investigator who insists that he is interested not in people in the mass, but rather in individuals or isolated members of the group. The basic concepts and appropriate methodological techniques are now available to those who want to investigate the individual as a whole and not merely as a single statistic in a vast group of individuals. They can now conduct scientific research on a single individual without resorting to crystal ball methods.

1.3.3   Occasions as One of a Two-set Category System. We have considered the combinations of entities and attributes with occasions. We also note that for a single entity and a single attribute one may measure the reactions of this entity on this attribute over a number of different occasions and under a number of different conditions. One may, for example, ask the individual to respond to a given stimulus element under a number of different response sets on repeated occasions. Other possibilities readily come to mind.

We see, therefore, that a great many interesting possibilities are offered by extending the categorical sets beyond the traditional entity-attribute systems. We shall now turn our attention to the relationship of factor analysis to these concepts.

1.4   Objectives of Factor Analysis

We have seen in the previous section how one may combine any two-category sets to yield a matrix of measures. That is, one obtains a table of numbers such that a given number represents the value of one of the members of one set and one of the members of the other set. This is true no matter what the sets are, and as we have pointed out, the most common application has been to the entity-attribute sets.

In any case, factor analysis procedures typically begin with a table of numbers made up of a two-category set. Specifically, we may have for each of a number of persons a test score for each of a number of tests. We can thus visualize a rectangular table in which the columns represent tests and the rows represent people. The primary concern of the factor analytic techniques is to investigate such a table of measures, irrespective of what the two-category sets consist of or how the numbers were arrived at. A primary concern of factor analysis with such a table of numbers is to determine whether the table may be simplified in some way.

1.4.1 Dimensionality of the System.

In general, the question is whether a smaller number of variables than is represented in the table of numbers could adequately account for the quantities in the table. This implies two things: first, that some of the numbers might be slightly changed so that the description of the resulting table would be greatly simplified, and second, that the numbers in the simplified or slightly altered table could be expressed as linear combinations of a table of numbers which had many fewer variables in it than the first. One objective of factor analysis is to find another table of numbers from which the first may be approximately reconstructed, but whose dimensionality is less that that of the first. In general, the dimensionality of the table may be regarded as the number of variables or number of entities, whichever is the smaller.

This objective of factor analysis is arrived at by certain computational procedures which yield numerical values corresponding to each of the variables and a smaller number of so-called factors. Thus we derive a matrix of measures whose rows correspond to the attributes of the original data matrix. The nmbuer of columns is much smaller than the number of rows. The smaller the number of factors yielded by the analysis, other things being equal, the more we have simplified the description of the data. The methods by which we arrive at such a table are the sujebct of this book.

1.4.2 The Primary Variables of a System.

The table or matrix of numbers that we get from a factor analysis of a two-category-set data matrix may consist of a very small number of factors, and if other appropriate criteria are satisfied, we may say that the set of observations has been greatly simplified without a loss of essential information. However, one of the characteristics of the factor analytic procedures and some of the basic mathematical concepts underlying them is that if one finds such a matrix of so-called factor loadings from a data matrix, then it is also true that an infinite number of such sets exists, each of which is equally useful in reproducing or accounting for the data in the original two-category data matrix.

The problem, then, is to determine which of these infinite numbers of sets should be used as the primary set of factor loadings. Any of these solutions implies a set of "factor" scores so that the score of an entity on a particular attribute could be approximately obtained as a linear function of the smaller number of factor scores if one knew what these factor scores were. For every observed measure for each attribute for a given entity, the factor loading matrix indicates what combination of the factor scores is required to make up the observed measure for that particular attribute.

For example, one might have measures on a large number of physiological variables for a number of individuals. Factor analysis would then conceivably enable him to say that there is a much smaller number of basic physiological variables. By taking various combinations of these relatively small numbers of physiological variables, we could determine the value of each of the larger number of variables without actually measuring it. We may, for example, have 40 or 50 different physiological measures and only 10 different basic physiological variables. If we knew what the measures of these 10 were for a particular individual, our analysis would show us how to weight them so that we could estimate the value of each of the 40 different physiological variables for that individual. The factor analytic procedures also enable us to get estimates of the measures of these primary or basic variables in addition to the factor loading matrix, that is, the matrix which tells us how to combine the primary measures to estimate the observed measures for all of the variables. When we say that we weight the underlying variables to estimate the observed variables, we imply linear combinations of the primary measures. Factor analysis procedures to date have used the linear combinations rather than nonlinear relationships.

In any case, some objective method of choosing the "best" set of underlying factor variables and factor loadings or weights is required, so that we need not decide arbitrarily which of these infinite numbers of sets is the best to use.

This involves the concept of simple structure which was introduced by Thurstone (1947). However, as Thurstone described it, the concept of simple structure enables one to select that set of factor loading weights which, according to the investigator, made the best sense, from an infinite number of sets. In the field of psychology, Thurstone talked about psychological sense. He said that the simple structure type of factor analysis solution made better psychological sense than certain other alternative types of solutions which accounted equally well for the observed data matrix. He then called this particular set of underlying variables the primary variables of the set.

The concept can be extended to all disciplines. For example, Thurstone (1947) conducted a factor analysis to show how the concept of simple structure could apply to simple geometrical concepts. He took a group of boxes of varying sizes and measured the height, width, and depth of each. He then formed certain combinations of height, width, and depth—both linear and nonlinear—so that altogether he had about 30 different measures. He then factor analyzed these measures, and found that there were three underlying dimensions to the system. This was a clear verification of the first objectives of factor analysis, because he knew beforehand that there should be only three dimensions in the system of measures which can be obtained from the dimensions of a box.

Just what these three underlying variables were was not clear in Thurstone's (1947) original factor analysis. It was not until after he had applied the procedures which resulted in what he called simple structure that he was able to see that the primary factors of the set of attributes on these boxes were height, width, and depth. This further verified the validity of his methods in that it showed how, by applying a mechanical or routine computational procedure to a set of measures, one came out with results which made common sense. It was known in advance that one knew these results should be achieved if the methods were valid. However, Thurstone pointed out that in most cases in science we do not know the underlying primary variables of the system under investigation. This is particularly true in psychology, sociology, and other social sciences, and probably in most of the biological sciences. Whether or not and to what extent it is true in the physical sciences is difficult to tell at this point, because physical scientists seem to have gotten along very well to date without the techniques of factor analysis. However, it is quite possible that the techniques could be usefully applied in chemistry and perhaps in other physical sciences.

Even though Thurstone emphasized that the factor analytic results should make common sense to the competent and experienced investigators in the field, others took the point of view that what made sense to one investigator did not necessarily make sense to another, and that what made psychological, anthropological, sociological, or physiological sense depended on whose opinion was taken as the criterion. This led to a somewhat more objective definition of the second aim of factor analysis, namely, that of *factorial invariance*.

1.4.3 Factorial Invariance. Even Thurstone (1947) had gone beyond his notion or criterion of psychological sense and maintained that if the criterion of simple structure was employed in arriving at a factor analysis solution, then one achieved what he called factorial invariance. By this he meant that the results which one obtained from the simple structure analysis were relatively invariant from one sample of entities and from one sample of attributes to another.

Mathematicians had favored a particular type of factor analysis known as the principal axis method, which was based on certain theorems of hyperspatial analytic geometry. However, despite the elegant mathematical properties of this type of solution, one of the big disadvantages is that the results of the analysis may differ considerably from one sample of individuals to another for the same variables. That is, the factor scores required one set of linear combinations to reproduce the observed variables when the analysis was applied to one set of individuals and another combination when it was applied to another set.

It was also found that these factor loadings, which indicate the saturation or concentration of a particular factor in a particular attribute, varied according to the particular group of attributes which were included in a factor analysis study. For example, one might include a particular mathematics test with a set of tests to be given to a group of individuals. A factor analysis on the tests might find that the mathematics test had loadings of 0.6, 0.3, 0.5, and 0.01 on factors 1, 2, 3, and 4, respectively. At another time, when the mathematics test was included with other tests the factor loadings might be 0.3 on the first, 0.2 on the second, and 0.5 on the other two. Certainly these could not be the same factors as those discovered in the first analysis with the first group of tests, or the factor loadings would be the same.

This idea that the factor loadings depend on the particular group of individuals included in that analysis and on the particular set of attributes was not acceptable to a number of scientists who insisted that stability or invariance of results was desirable in a scientific methodology. It was found, however, by Thurstone and others, that if Thurstone's simple structure criteria were used to determine the solution from among the infinite number of possible solutions, there was less tendency for this variation of factor loadings from one set of entities to another or from one set of attributes to another to be found. Therefore, in addition to the objective of reducing the dimensionality of a matrix of observations, the second objective of factor analysis is to find a particular method of analysis and reduction of dimensions which will yield relatively stable and invariant results, irrespective of the sample of entities and the sample of attributes which are used.

This discussion has dealt only with the entity-attribute sets of categories. The same logic can also be applied to any pair of categorical sets which we discussed in Section 1.3.

So far we have indicated as the primary objectives of factor analysis the reduction of dimensionality of a matrix of measures and the achievement of invariance with respect to particular samples of members from categorical sets which might be involved in the analysis. These appear to be rather broad objectives, and many may question their practical value. We may inquire then into the more practical values of these objectives. Essentially it is our position that the ultimate purpose of science is the prediction and control of natural events. Therefore, it appears that we should be able to link the objectives of factor analysis to this broad objective.

1.4.4   Factor Analysis and Prediction.   Later we shall consider in more detail the applications of factor analytic techniques to problems of statistical prediction, and outline a number of different applications to statistical prediction procedures. It is not the purpose of this book to go extensively into the methods of multivariate prediction, since this subject has been extensively treated in textbooks on the subject. Suffice it to say that the conventional least squares method of multiple rectilinear prediction from a set of independent variables to a set of dependent variables can be shown to be a special case of the more generalized formulation of factor analytic theory which is developed in this book.

One of the important roles of factor analysis in multivariate prediction has to do with the problem of degrees of freedom. Without going into detail, we can say that if it is desired to predict one or more criteria from a number of predictor variables, it is necessary to have many more entities than variables in order to solve for stable regression weights. In general, however, it is relatively easy to collect a very large number of variables on a relatively small number of entities. For example, if one considers each item in a personality questionnaire as a single variable in which the score may be either 1 or 0, he may, in several hours of testing time on several hundred individuals, get measures on many hundreds of items or variables. One may regard these as predictor variables and attempt to see how they may be used to predict success in some criterion variable, such as success in college or on a job. Investigations have indicated that it is very difficult to collect a set of variables, no matter how large, which cannot be shown to be some linear combination of a relatively small number of underlying variables—say, 30. The problem, however, is that if one were to select any subset of less than 30 from many hundreds of conceivable variables, it would be very difficult to tell whether or not he had chosen those 30 which best represented the underlying 30 in the set. The chances are that any *a priori* selection would yield a subset such that it, in turn, could be reproduced by a much smaller set of underlying variables. Therefore, factor analytic techniques are useful in reducing the dimensionality of a large set of predictor variables so that the number of underlying variables can be relatively small—say, 30—compared to the number of entities. These underlying variables may now be used to estimate the criterion variables by appropriate statistical techniques.

This approach, contrary to others, does not capitalize on a small number of degrees of freedom in evaluating regression coefficients on a particular sample. On one sample one may well get a perfect estimate of the criterion variables for that sample, but if he applied these regression weights to a new sample, he would, in general, find that the criterion variables for the new sample would be poorly estimated. As a matter of fact, in the prediction problem our primary interest is not with what we can predict for the experimental sample, because the criterion variables are already available. Our only legitimate interest is to see how accurately we can predict the criterion variables on the new sample. This introduces the concept of control. We wish to predict what will happen on the criterion variables as accurately as possible, so that we may take appropriate action—such as avoiding courses or careers in which success is apt to be minimal, or selecting those criterion activities in which reasonable expectations of success are indicated.

As a matter of fact, in the factor analytic approach to the prediction problem, we do not actually solve for the underlying variables of a set of predictor variables for a given experimental sample of entities and then use these predictor variables to determine the regression constants which will be used on later samples to estimate other variables. We determine indirectly, by algebraic methods, the weights which, if applied to the original variables, would give the same results as a much smaller set of weights applied to the underlying variables.

In many cases it may be necessary actually to reduce the number of predictor variables from a particular potential set which we wish to use for predictive purposes. In these cases, then, we must have some method of deciding which of the variables to reject. It may very well be that for administrative purposes we shall have only a very small fraction of time and resources available to us compared with time and resources available in the experimental sample of entities. This may be especially true when we have a large number of psychological variables including inventory items for a large number of persons for whom we wish to predict success in jobs or educational areas. It may also be true in other fields. For example, in the case of meteorological prediction, it may be that we can collect a very large number of meteorological variables for each of a number of meteorological entities, such as geographical areas, and we may work out a multiple prediction system on the basis of the methods indicated in the previous paragraph. We may find, however, that the collection and analysis of such variables is far too costly and time-consuming to be used as a continuing basis of weather forecasting, and we might find that a much smaller group of variables would be almost as efficient. This is the problem of predictor selection.

It is possible to select by factor analytic means a much smaller group of variables which is just as efficient in predicting criterion or dependent variables as a much larger group. Many methods are available for predictor selection, but, in general, these have not used the factor analytic techniques and are deficient in that they capitalize on chance error. Methods which have attempted to avoid this weakness often go to the other extreme and discard variables which would be useful in prediction. It is only recently that the factor analytic techniques have been applied to the problem of predictor selection. The techniques for increasing the degrees of freedom in the system of predictor variables and those for actually selecting predictor variables are very closely related. For the latter procedure one must first use the method which reduces the dimensionality of the set and then find the simple structure solution. This solution is used as a basis for the selection of the variables which actually will be used in the prediction procedure.

1.4.5 Facilitation of Interpretation.

Some have insisted that factor analysis should facilitate interpretation of the phenomena of the particular science or discipline one is investigating. This point has been touched upon in the preceding section where we have discussed the notion of common sense as viewed by the authorities in a particular discipline. There seems to be a general feeling even yet among many persons that the definition and isolation of the primary variables of the science in some objective fashion should be useful apart from the predictive value of the variables. There may be some value to the notion that the primary variables be defined and labeled, so that in general they have much the same meaning to all of the investigators in the field. Certainly the verbal ambiguities which characterize most of the social sciences are serious deterrents to scientific progress. A great deal of time is involved in semantic squabbles and in questions as to whether such and such variables really do exist, whether they are important, and so on. Perhaps, therefore, a case can be made for the role of factor analysis as a purely classificatory or labeling methodology.

For example, in psychology, the pioneering work of Thurstone resulted in redefining intelligence, not as a unidimensional or a single-variable phenomenon, but rather as multidimensional in character. His studies indicated, at least to his own satisfaction and that of many others, that intelligence consisted of a number of different dimensions. Some of these have been tentatively designated verbal intelligence, word fluency, number ability, spacial ability, perceptual ability, rote memory, inductive reasoning, and deductive reasoning. Much controversy still exists over whether or not these are the most useful dimensions of intelligence or adaptive human behavior and whether they are sufficiently inclusive. Nevertheless, the notion of an objective procedure for labeling independent kinds of abilities which go to make up intelligent behavior has much in its favor.

It is also possible that in physiology one might apply the concepts of factor analysis as a basis for an objective determination of what will be regarded as the primary physiological variables. This notion can also be extended to other disciplines in which the crucial variables are poorly defined. Nevertheless, it is probable that the emphasis on this aspect of factor analysis—namely, its role in classification or taxonomy—has a limited and superficial role and has done much to retard more fundamental applications to the problems of prediction.

1.5 Applications of Factor Analysis

It might be of interest to close this chapter with a brief discussion of the kinds of applications which have been or could be made in the various scientific disciplines.

1.5.1 Psychology. It is in the field of psychology that factor analysis had its beginning and where by far the greatest amount of theoretical and applied work has been done. However, as indicated in the beginning of this chapter, there is no particular reason why the techniques and objectives of factor analysis are more applicable to psychological data and psychological phenomena than they are to the phenomena of other scientific disciplines. Perhaps the individual or human being, as a reacting organism, is more complex than lower forms of biological organisms and the purely physiological aspects of biological organisms in general. It is certainly true that the human organism, as a reacting entity, is much more complex than the entities with which the physicist and chemist deal.

It may be for this reason that psychologists have felt the need of a methodology which would enable them to come to grips with the problem of defining the crucial variables of human behavior. Certainly the labels which have been applied to psychological variables are vast in number. It is not unreasonable to assume that the factor analytic techniques will have a salutary effect on purging the psychological literature of much of the confusing and beclouding verbiage with which it is burdened and which threatens to crush it if this semantic proliferation continues. In any case, the factor analytic techniques have been extensively applied in psychology to study such things as specialized abilities and aptitudes, personality and temperament traits, the analysis of interests, and many other areas.

The factor analytic techniques have also been applied to problems of learning. The conventional methods of treating learning curve data can be shown to discard much of the information in a set of learning data for a number of entities. For mental ailments and the study and analyses of psychoses, also, the factor analytic techniques, in recent years, have been extensively used. They promise to lead to a useful restructuring of the conventional categories of mental illness. The validity and usefulness of these traditional categories are being seriously questioned.

1.5.2 Political Science. In the field of political science, the factor analytic techniques probably have a most useful role to play in the future. In the past they have been applied to the voting behavior of members of Congress or various deliberating bodies, in which case the members are the entities and the issues on which they have voted, the variables. A factor analysis of data obtained in this way can yield, with appropriate analyses, an indication of the primary variables and characteristics of the individuals who do the voting. In this way, one may then predict how these persons will vote on various issues in the future. In any case, it is probable that the applications of factor analysis to many problems in political science have not yet made a beginning, compared to the potentialities of the method.

1.5.3   Medicine. It is only recently that medical science is becoming interested in the applications of the factor analytic techniques to problems of diagnosis. This interest is rapidly increasing and with the advent of high-speed electronic computers, medical colleges over the country are beginning to apply these computers to the analysis of their data. Demands for more effective and higher capacity factor analysis programs applicable to the high-speed computers are already in evidence. It is probable that factor analytic techniques can make an important contribution to more efficient diagnoses and prognoses, on both an entity group and a single entity basis.

1.5.4   Other Disciplines. It is not our purpose to explore in detail the possibilities of factor analysis for all of the disciplines in which it might be applicable. However, it may be useful to name a few of them.

In sociology, particularly, the factor analytic techniques have been used fairly extensively in the study and simplification of the description of socio-logical entities such as census tracts, cities, or other geographical entities. The techniques also have been found useful in the comparative studies of racial groups with respect to cultural variables.

In business and industry too, the techniques are beginning to be used to a considerable extent. In the field of market research and advertising, the factor analytic techniques are useful in simplifying the factors which influence consumers to make their decisions in buying various products. The techniques have been used in personnel work in industry, particularly in the case of job analysis procedures in which job evaluation is required as a basis for rate-setting, promotion, and so forth. Job evaluations are typically based on the evaluation of a job in terms of a number of different factors. Factor analytic techniques have been used to simplify and reduce to a few primary factors a large number of variables which have been regarded by supervisors as important for success in the job. The factor analytic techniques are useful in reducing the vast number of variables in terms of which people want to describe their jobs, and in establishing standard terminology.

It is surprising that in anthropology the factor analytic techniques have been less extensively used in recent years than in other fields. In this area they could be extremely useful, as has been shown by the extensive work of Carl Pearson. As a matter of fact, it was Pearson (1901) who suggested what has come to be known as the *principal axis technique* on certain anthro-pological data.

In education, as in psychology, factor analytic techniques have been used extensively. In the field of educational psychology, particularly, where the problems are closely related to those of psychology, the factor analytic techniques have been most extensively used. Their use in and extension to problems of learning and programed research have hardly begun. It is probable that the applications in this field will increase rapidly.

Another general field in which the factor analytic techniques might be extremely useful, and in which they have not yet been extensively applied, is that of economics. One example is the case of stock market prices. Here we have stocks as entities and days as occasions. An analysis of a matrix of stock prices over a period of time could yield useful results both from the point of view of characterizing particular stocks in terms of a few basic factors and as a basis for the prediction of stock market prices.

Many other applications of factor analysis will doubtless be found in the future. Because the role of factor analysis is so fundamental in systematic scientific investigations of all kinds, its use will probably be greatly extended and accelerated as the techniques are improved and methods of analysis become more generally feasible because of the availability of high-speed computers.

Chapter 2

Simple Matrix Concepts

We saw in Chapter 1 that all scientific investigations must in some way be based on tables of numbers which are obtained from observations on entities with respect to different attributes. We saw also how these observations may be repeated on a number of different occasions and under different conditions or sets of instructions. These observations, we learned, may be made by a number of different individuals or a number of different kinds of recording instruments.

We indicated that factor analysis is concerned with certain fundamental types of operations on tables of numbers obtained from such observations. We have repeatedly referred to these tables of numbers as matrices. Factor analysis, both in its more restricted traditional sense and in some of the more general extensions and applications which we shall consider in this text, is most efficiently treated from the point of view of a branch of mathematics called matrix algebra. It is important, therefore, that we become familiar with some of the more fundamental concepts of matrix algebra both as a language and as a tool for dealing with these matrices of observations which are the raw material for factor analytic procedures and operations.

This branch of mathematics has traditionally been presented as a rather advanced course in the mathematical curricula of colleges and universities. Also in textbooks on mathematics it usually has been introduced after the traditional topics of algebra, analytic geometry, trigonometry, and introductory courses in differential and integral calculus. It is unfortunate that the treatment of the subject has been assigned this chronological sequence in the presentation of mathematical topics. There are many fundamental and useful topics in the field of matrix algebra which can be readily grasped and utilized by those who have no more than a good knowledge of high school algebra. These topics are particularly useful in factor analytic concepts and computational procedures. We shall therefore devote this and the next chapter to a discussion of those elementary principles of matrix algebra which presuppose no more than a good working knowledge of high school algebra, and which are most useful for the analysis of the types of data with which the sciences typically deal. These principles are particularly helpful in the social and biological sciences, in which the number of variables or attributes can be extremely large. The number of entities or observations in these two sciences are also typically very large compared to those with which the physical scientists have been accustomed to dealing. We shall therefore first give a brief introduction to the concept of the matrix as it relates to the data with which science concerns itself.

2.1   Introduction

2.1.1   Definition of a Matrix.   A somewhat oversimplified definition of a matrix is a table of numbers or symbols which stand for numbers. This table, by definition, has both rows and columns of numbers or symbols in it. Figure 2.1.1 is an example of a table of numbers with both rows and columns which may be regarded as a matrix.

$$
\begin{array}{ccc}
4 & 3 & 1 \\
6 & 2 & 5 \\
1 & 3 & 4 \\
7 & 9 & 5
\end{array}
$$

Fig. 2.1.1

2.1.2   Sources of Matrices.   We may have two general types of matrices with respect to their source or origin. First, as we saw in Chapter 1, we get matrices from scientific observations of entities with respect to certain attributes and other categorical sets or modes. These we shall call *data matrices*, to indicate that they constitute the observed data on the basis of which scientific research is conducted. Other types of matrices are obtained by performing certain specified calculations or computations on data matrices.

It is the subject of this and the next chapter to indicate the various types of operations which we may perform upon data matrices. These new matrices we shall call *derived matrices*. The line of distinction between data matrices and derived matrices may not always be sharply drawn—for example, sometimes we may have matrices of observations which require further processing before they are subject to the kinds of operations which result in what we have called derived matrices. Nevertheless, the distinction seems to be useful in a discussion of the handling of observed data in terms of matrix notation and operations.

2.1.3   The Meaning of Rows and Columns of Data Matrices.   It is convenient to have a convention or stated procedure, even though it is arbitrary, for designating the rows and columns of a data matrix. Although we do not adhere to the convention rigorously, we shall say that usually the rows of the data matrix are taken as entities. This means that each individual row of the data matrix is regarded as a separate entity. Each column of the data matrix is regarded as an attribute or variable unless otherwise specified.

This convention is not important in the mathematical treatment of matrices because mathematicians are not ordinarily concerned with data matrices as such. Their treatment is usually on a more abstract level; therefore, they have not concerned themselves with the different categorical sets or modes to which we referred in Chapter 1. We shall not adopt a convention with respect to other categorical modes, since by far the largest part of our discussion will be restricted to the entity and attribute modes.

2.1.4 Interchangeability of Rows and Columns. Ordinarily in data matrices the serial order in which entities or rows are presented is not of significance. We may have the entities in alphabetical order, if they are persons, but this is just a convention and has no particular relevance for the analysis of the data. Similarly, we may have attributes in alphabetical order of the names of the attributes—for example, if they are test scores, we may have arithmetic, language, reading, and so on. For purposes of analysis, the columns of the data matrix may be arranged in any order convenient to the investigator. However, in the case of derived matrices, one may have less latitude in the selection of the order in which both the rows and the columns are arranged.

2.1.5 Exceptions to Interchangeability of Rows and Columns. When we consider a two-category data matrix in which we have entities and occasions, as in the example given in Chapter 1, it may be desirable to regard occasions as variables. In this case, there would be a compelling logic to the order in which the occasions were arranged. Presumably the temporal sequence in which the observations were made would indicate the order. Similarly, if we are dealing with a two-category set of variables and occasions for a single entity, the entity might be regarded as the population and the separate occasions for this entity might be regarded as a set of quasi-entities in which again the serial order would normally be dictated by the chronological sequence in which the observations were made.

2.1.6 Reciprocal Nature of Entities and Attributes. It can be seen from the discussion in Chapter 1 that it is up to the experimenter to specify which are entities and which are attributes in his particular model. It is surprising how much confusion and ambiguity may result in the execution of a scientific investigation simply because the investigator does not clearly define his entities and attributes.

The formal rules of matrix algebra, which will be presented later in this and the following chapter, do not concern themselves with the distinction between entities and attributes or, for that matter, any of the other possible categorical sets in a data model. The rules and principles of operation and computation specified by the formal system of matrix algebra recognize only the existence of one or more categorical sets. They have no way of indicating what the different categorical sets are. This is a scientific problem, and the specification of the categorical sets by the investigator is part of his model and is relevant to the interpretations issuing from the analyses of the data.

2.1.7   Scientific Prediction and Data Matrices.   All scientific predictions must be based on data matrices. Those which are not cannot be accorded the status of scientific predictions. Factor analysis in its broader and generalized sense may be regarded as comprehending scientific prediction as a special case. In scientific prediction the attributes are usually subdivided into two sets. One of these sets is called the *predictor subset* of variables and the other the *criterion subset*. These are also sometimes called, respectively, the *independent* and the *dependent variables*.

2.1.8   Criterion Attributes.   Criterion attributes or variables are those which we wish to predict. These may be crop yield, success in college, success on the job, the weather, or any one of a vast number of things which seem important to human beings. In general, criterion attributes are important as such or, as we sometimes say, socially significant. They are also usually costly to assess. For example, it may be very costly from the point of view of time and money to find out how successful a person can be as a physician. Furthermore, criterion attributes are usually not currently available. These are things which one wants to predict or estimate for some future time.

A data matrix may have more than one criterion attribute. For example, we may have not only success in college but also success in each of a number of different college course areas. Similarly we may have not only success in a job in general but also success in each of a number of kinds of jobs.

2.1.9   Predictor Attributes.   Predictor attributes are those we predict with. These are not necessarily important in themselves, and are usually relatively easy to assess. Furthermore, they are also currently available at the time one wishes to make the prediction. Examples of predictor attributes are rainfall, degree-days of temperature, or scores on a number of different tests. They could be heart rate, blood pressure, and so on. In all of these cases we might assume that these so-called predictor variables are available as of a given time, and we wish to use them to predict some criterion variables such as crop yield, health, or success in college or on a job at some later date.

2.1.10 The Prediction Formulas. The predictor attributes, to be useful for prediction, must have some kind of relationship with the criterion attributes or variables. If both of these sets are available in a specific data matrix for a group of entities, matrix algebra is useful in helping us to find these relationships with respect to the particular sample of entities. The assumption of science is that under certain specified restrictions these relationships will hold approximately in the future with other groups of entities. Factor analysis includes as a special case the determination of these relationships and their applications to prediction.

2.1.11 Kinds of Entities. We have implied in the previous subsection that there are two types of entities. These are first, those on which we perform an analysis to find the relationship between the predictor and the criterion attributes, and second, those on which we apply the knowledge gained on one set of entities to another set for which only the predictor and not the criterion variables are available. For convenience we may call the first type of entities the experimental entities, and the second type the administrative entities. Factor analysis concerns itself with both types of entities. That is, it is concerned with obtaining certain results on one group of entities and then applying the formulas derived from the first group to a second or subsequent group.

2.2 Matrix Notation

One of the big advantages in the application of matrix algebra to the analysis of data matrices and to factor analysis in particular is that it utilizes a particular notational system which has great simplicity and efficiency for indicating many kinds of complicated operations.

2.2.1 Showing That a Table of Numbers Is to Be Treated as a Matrix. If a table of numbers is designated as a matrix, it is subject to a well-defined set of operations. It is therefore convenient to have a conventional system of notation to indicate that a table of numbers is to be regarded as a matrix. A table may be so designated by enclosing it in one of the following: double ruling, parentheses, or brackets on each side. These three methods are indicated in Figs. 2.2.1, 2.2.2, and 2.2.3.

$$\left\| \begin{array}{ccc} 4 & 3 & 1 \\ 6 & 2 & 5 \\ 1 & 3 & 4 \\ 7 & 9 & 5 \end{array} \right\|$$

FIG. 2.2.1

$$\begin{pmatrix} 5 & 9 & 12 & 14 \\ 6 & 8 & 13 & 5 \\ 14 & 3 & 2 & 10 \\ 15 & 16 & 9 & 11 \end{pmatrix}$$

FIG. 2.2.2

$$\begin{bmatrix} 4 & 3 & 1 \\ 6 & 2 & 5 \\ 1 & 3 & 4 \\ 7 & 9 & 3 \end{bmatrix}$$

FIG. 2.2.3

As we shall see, it is important to keep a clear distinction between rows and columns. It is convenient ordinarily to write a series of numbers in a row rather than in a column, because it takes up less space. Sometimes a row of numbers is enclosed in braces to indicate that it should be regarded as a column. For example, one might have a row of numbers which are supposed to represent an attribute for each of a number of different entities. This would violate the convention that rows should be entities and columns attributes. We may therefore enclose the row in braces to indicate that it is meant to be a column. This notation is indicated in Fig. 2.2.4.

$$\{4 \quad 3 \quad 5 \quad 7\}$$

FIG. 2.2.4

In this text we shall ordinarily use the convention of enclosing a table of numbers in brackets to show that it is a matrix.

2.2.2   Specifying the Size of a Matrix. The number of rows and columns in a matrix is called its *order*. We may use the term *dimensions* to mean the same thing as order.

The number of rows is usually mentioned first. We say that the order of a matrix with four rows and three columns is 4 × 3. The height of a matrix is the number of rows and the width is the number of columns. If a matrix has more rows than columns we call it a *vertical matrix*. If it has more columns than rows we call it a *horizontal matrix*.

2.2.3   The Numbers in a Matrix. A single number or measure in a matrix is called an *element* of the matrix. It may also be called a *coordinate* of the matrix or simply an *entry* of the matrix. In specifying a particular element in a matrix, its row position is usually mentioned first and its column second. Thus, an element in the third row and the second column would be referred to as the element in the (3,2) position in the matrix. The number of elements in a matrix is obviously the product of its height by its width.

It is convenient to have a special name for the elements in a square matrix whose row and column positions are the same. This set of elements we call the *principal diagonal* of the matrix.

2.2.4 Using a Letter to Stand for a Number. A letter with double numerical subscripts may be used to indicate the elements in a matrix. The first number in the subscript generally refers to its row position and the second to its column position. Figure 2.2.5 is an example of a matrix whose elements are indicated by letters with numerical subscripts.

$$\begin{bmatrix} a_{11} & a_{12} & a_{13} \\ a_{21} & a_{22} & a_{23} \\ a_{31} & a_{32} & a_{33} \\ a_{41} & a_{42} & a_{43} \end{bmatrix}$$

FIG. 2.2.5

A letter element may have letter subscripts to designate any row and any column location. This scheme is shown in Fig. 2.2.6.

$$\begin{bmatrix} a_{11} & \cdots & a_{1j} & \cdots & a_{1m} \\ \cdots & \cdots & \cdots & \cdots & \cdots \\ a_{i1} & \cdots & a_{ij} & \cdots & a_{im} \\ \cdots & \cdots & \cdots & \cdots & \cdots \\ a_{n1} & \cdots & a_{nj} & \cdots & a_{nm} \end{bmatrix}$$

FIG. 2.2.6

We see that one of the elements has subscripts i and j. This means that this is the element in the ith row and the jth column of the matrix.

2.2.5 Using a Letter to Stand for a Matrix. A single letter may be used to stand for an entire matrix. This simplifies algebraic manipulations and the description of computational formats or procedures. The order of the matrix represented by a single letter may be indicated verbally, such as m by n or *3* by *4*.

A single letter standing for a matrix may carry double subscripts to indicate its order. Usually the first subscript will be its height and the second its width.

One must be careful when using subscripts in this way to specify that they indicate the order of the matrix. There can be ambiguity as to whether the subscripts mean location of the element in the matrix or order of the matrix. Usually this must be made clear by verbal specification.

2.3   Kinds of Matrices

We shall describe and name a number of different kinds of matrices which are commonly used in factor analysis so that when appropriate this terminology can be used in later chapters of the book.

2.3.1   The General Rectangular Matrix.

We may speak of any matrix which has more rows than columns as a rectangular matrix. It may also be called an oblong matrix to indicate that, in general, the number of rows and columns is not the same. The data matrix is usually a rectangular or oblong matrix. Ordinarily it is vertical rather than horizontal. This means that usually it has more rows than columns. Exceptions to this will be pointed out where they occur.

2.3.2   The Square Matrix.

A square matrix is obviously one whose width and height are the same. The square matrix is very rarely a data matrix. In some types of research the data matrix may be square. In the behavioral sciences square matrices are usually derived from data matrices.

2.3.3   The Symmetric Matrix.

A symmetric matrix is a special case of a square matrix in which corresponding elements of corresponding rows and columns are equal. In a symmetric matrix a we have $a_{ij} = a_{ji}$. Figure 2.3.1 is an example of a symmetric matrix.

$$\begin{bmatrix} 11 & 4 & 3 \\ 4 & 15 & 10 \\ 3 & 10 & 17 \end{bmatrix}$$

FIG. 2.3.1

Symmetric matrices play an important role in factor analysis. A symmetric matrix is sometimes written with only the principal diagonal and the elements either above or below it. This is incorrect and can lead to confusion with another type of matrix indicated in the following section.

2.3.4   The Diagonal Matrix.

The diagonal matrix is a special case of a symmetric matrix in which all nondiagonal elements are 0. It may be written without entries in the nondiagonal positions. The diagonal elements of a diagonal matrix may be written unambiguously with a single subscript to indicate their position. Figure 2.3.2 is an example of a diagonal matrix with numerical elements.

$$\begin{bmatrix} 15 & 0 & 0 \\ 0 & 12 & 0 \\ 0 & 0 & 0 \end{bmatrix}$$

Fig. 2.3.2

Figure 2.3.3 is an example of a diagonal matrix with letter elements.

$$\begin{bmatrix} a_1 & & \\ & a_2 & \\ & & \cdots \\ & & & a_n \end{bmatrix}$$

Fig. 2.3.3

In this book the following symbols are usually used to indicate diagonal matrices: D, d, Δ, δ.

2.3.5 The Scalar Matrix. This is a special case of a diagonal matrix in which all the diagonal elements are equal. Its letters are used to indicate number elements. The same letter may be used without subscripts for each diagonal position. Figure 2.3.4 is an example of a scalar matrix with numerical elements.

$$\begin{bmatrix} 3 & 0 & 0 \\ 0 & 3 & 0 \\ 0 & 0 & 3 \end{bmatrix}$$

Fig. 2.3.4

Figure 2.3.5 is an example of a scalar matrix with letter elements.

$$\begin{bmatrix} a & 0 & 0 \\ 0 & a & 0 \\ 0 & 0 & a \end{bmatrix}$$

Fig. 2.3.5

2.3.6   The Identity Matrix. This type of matrix is a special case of the scalar matrix in which the diagonal elements are all unity. The identity matrix serves the same function in matrix algebra as the number 1 serves in ordinary or scalar algebra. In this book the identity matrix will be indicated by *I* and not by 1, as in some texts. The order of an identity matrix may be indicated verbally or by a subscript. Figure 2.3.6 is an example of a third-order identity matrix.

$$\begin{bmatrix} 1 & 0 & 0 \\ 0 & 1 & 0 \\ 0 & 0 & 1 \end{bmatrix}$$

FIG. 2.3.6

This type of matrix can be indicated simply by I_3.

2.3.7   The Sign Matrix. The sign matrix differs from the identity matrix in that some of the diagonal elements may be -1. The sign matrix is not used extensively in traditional articles and texts on matrix algebra. It is, however, important in factor analysis and in the analysis of data matrices from the behavioral sciences. We therefore give it a special symbol, which is simply *i*. Figure 2.3.7 is an example of a third-order sign matrix.

$$\begin{bmatrix} -1 & 0 & 0 \\ 0 & 1 & 0 \\ 0 & 0 & -1 \end{bmatrix}$$

FIG. 2.3.7

2.3.8   The Skew-Symmetric Matrix. This matrix has zeros in the principal diagonal. Corresponding elements above and below the diagonal are equal in absolute magnitude and opposite in sign. In a skew-symmetric matrix we say that a_{ij} is equal to $-a_{ji}$. Figure 2.3.8 is an example of the skew-symmetric matrix.

$$\begin{bmatrix} 0 & -3 & 4 \\ 3 & 0 & -6 \\ -4 & 6 & 0 \end{bmatrix}$$

FIG. 2.3.8

2.3.9   The Triangular Matrix. A square matrix with only 0 elements above the main diagonal is called a *lower triangular matrix*. A square matrix with only zeros below the main diagonal is called an *upper triangular matrix*. For either upper or lower triangular matrices it is not necessary to write in the 0 elements. For this reason it is important to write in elements both above and below the diagonal of a symmetric matrix; otherwise, it might be confused with the triangular matrix. Figure 2.3.9 is an example of a lower triangular matrix.

$$\begin{bmatrix} 6 & 0 & 0 \\ 3 & 4 & 0 \\ 5 & 2 & 6 \end{bmatrix} \quad \text{or} \quad \begin{bmatrix} 6 & & \\ 3 & 4 & \\ 5 & 2 & 6 \end{bmatrix}$$

FIG. 2.3.9

Figure 2.3.10 is an example of an upper triangular matrix.

$$\begin{bmatrix} 2 & 5 & 7 \\ 0 & 3 & 6 \\ 0 & 0 & 7 \end{bmatrix} \quad \text{or} \quad \begin{bmatrix} 2 & 5 & 7 \\ & 3 & 6 \\ & & 7 \end{bmatrix}$$

FIG. 2.3.10

2.3.10 The Partial Triangular Matrix. A vertical matrix with 0 for each element whose column number is greater than its row number is called a *lower partial triangular matrix*. A horizontal matrix with 0 for each element whose row number is greater than its column number is called an *upper partial triangular matrix*. Triangular and partial triangular matrices play an important role in both traditional and more general types of factor analysis. Figure 2.3.11 is an example of a lower partial triangular matrix.

$$\begin{bmatrix} 6 & 0 & 0 \\ 3 & 4 & 0 \\ 5 & 2 & 6 \\ 2 & 8 & 9 \\ 9 & 5 & 8 \end{bmatrix}$$

FIG. 2.3.11

Figure 2.3.12 is an example of an upper partial triangular matrix.

$$\begin{bmatrix} 2 & 5 & 7 & 9 & 4 & 8 \\ 0 & 3 & 6 & 5 & 5 & 2 \\ 0 & 0 & 7 & 8 & 4 & 9 \end{bmatrix}$$

FIG. 2.3.12

2.3.11   The Binary Matrix. This is a matrix all of whose elements are either 0 or 1. This is a common type of data matrix in the social sciences. Figures 2.3.13 is an example of a binary matrix.

$$\begin{bmatrix} 0 & 1 & 1 & 0 \\ 0 & 0 & 1 & 0 \\ 1 & 1 & 1 & 0 \\ 0 & 0 & 1 & 1 \\ 1 & 1 & 0 & 1 \end{bmatrix}$$

FIG. 2.3.13

A *permutation matrix* is a special case of a binary matrix in which each row and column has a single 1 in it. It is therefore a square matrix. The permutation matrix plays an important part in rearranging the order of the rows and/or columns in a matrix. Figure 2.3.14 is an example of a fourth-order permutation matrix.

$$\begin{bmatrix} 0 & 1 & 0 & 0 \\ 0 & 0 & 1 & 0 \\ 1 & 0 & 0 & 0 \\ 0 & 0 & 0 & 1 \end{bmatrix}$$

FIG. 2.3.14

An *elementary matrix* is one which has all 0 elements save a single element which is 1. This matrix is designated by e_{ij}, which means that the element in the ith row and jth column is 1 and all others are 0.

2.3.12   The Null Matrix. This is the matrix all of whose elements are 0. It is indicated by a 0 and the dimensionality must be specified. The null matrix serves the same function in matrix algebra as 0 does in scalar algebra. Figure 2.3.15 is an example of a 4 by 3 null matrix.

$$\begin{bmatrix} 0 & 0 & 0 \\ 0 & 0 & 0 \\ 0 & 0 & 0 \\ 0 & 0 & 0 \end{bmatrix}$$

FIG. 2.3.15

2.3.13   The Vector. A vector is a special kind of matrix with only one row or column. The order of a vector is indicated by a single number which is the number of elements in it. However, it is also necessary to specify whether it is a row or a column vector. A letter designation for an element of a vector need carry only a single subscript to indicate its position in the vector. Figure 2.3.16 is an example of a vector with numerical elements.

$$[10 \quad 12 \quad 13 \quad 14]$$

FIG. 2.3.16

This is a row vector. Figure 2.3.17 is an example of a column vector with letter elements.

$$\begin{bmatrix} b_1 \\ b_2 \\ b_3 \\ b_4 \end{bmatrix}$$

FIG. 2.3.17

2.3.14   The Unit Vector. This is a vector all of whose elements are 1. A column unit vector is indicated by 1 and a row unit vector by 1'. The order of a unit vector may be indicated verbally, by means of a subscript, or by the context in which it is used. Figure 2.3.18 is an example of a row unit vector.

$$[1 \quad 1 \quad 1 \quad 1 \quad 1]$$

FIG. 2.3.18

Unit vectors are used extensively in the analysis of data matrices and in factor analysis.

2.3.15   The Binary Vector. This vector is a special case of a binary matrix with only one row or column. Figure 2.3.19 is an example of a row binary matrix.

$$[0 \quad 1 \quad 0 \quad 0 \quad 1 \quad 1 \quad 0]$$

FIG. 2.3.19

An *elementary vector* is a special case of a binary vector in which all elements are 0 except one, and that is 1. An elementary vector is indicated by the symbol e_i. The subscript indicates the location in which the unit element is located. The elementary vector is used extensively in the application of matrix algebra to data matrices and to factor analysis. It serves much the same role as does the Kronecker delta in scalar algebra. Figure 2.3.20 gives examples of elementary row and column vectors.

$$[0 \quad 1 \quad 0 \quad 0] \qquad \begin{bmatrix} 0 \\ 0 \\ 1 \end{bmatrix}$$

FIG. 2.3.20

2.3.16 The Null Vector. This is a vector all of whose elements are 0. It is indicated by a 0 together with the specification of its order. This specification may be either verbal or indicated by the use of a subscript. If a 0 is used to indicate a null vector, a prime is used to indicate a row vector; otherwise, it is a column vector.

2.3.17 The Scalar Quantity. This is a matrix with only one row and one column. It is the kind of matrix familiar to most persons. The scalar quantity can be distinguished from a matrix by a particular style of type or, for a particular problem, by verbal definition of notation. The use of a particular type font for distinguishing a scalar from a matrix will not be used in this text.

2.4   Transpose of a Matrix

In matrix algebra we have a concept which is not needed in scalar algebra. This is known as *matrix transposition*. It is an important type of operation although when it is applied to scalar quantities it does not alter these quantities. Before discussing matrix transposition we shall consider several concepts which are preliminary to our use of the term.

2.4.1 Equality of Matrices. Two matrices are said to be equal if and only if the elements of one matrix are equal to the corresponding elements of the other. Therefore, matrices cannot be equal unless their orders are the same. A necessary though not sufficient condition for two matrices to be equal is that their heights and widths be the same.

2.4.2 The Natural Order of a Matrix. We need a concept which is not required in formal mathematical discussions of matrix algebra. This is the *natural order* of the matrix. In this book the natural order of a data matrix is said to be that for which the rows are entities and the columns are attributes. This is a convenient convention to help us keep in mind which categorical set is which in the manipulation of data matrices. Matrices which are not data matrices will usually be considered in natural order if they are vertical. The natural order of a vector, unless otherwise specified, will be the column form. Exceptions to this will be pointed out where they occur.

In general, square matrices which are not data matrices do not have their natural order defined. The only square matrix to be assigned a natural order is the triangular type matrix. Its natural order will be taken as the lower triangular form.

2.4.3   The Transpose of a Matrix. The transpose of a matrix is a matrix in which the rows are written as columns and the columns as rows. Therefore, the *ij*th element of the matrix becomes the *ji*th element of its transpose. The order of the transpose of a matrix is the reverse of the order of the matrix. Figure 2.4.1 shows on the left the natural order of a matrix and on the right its transpose.

$$\begin{bmatrix} 3 & 2 \\ 2 & 1 \\ 7 & 9 \end{bmatrix} \quad \begin{bmatrix} 3 & 2 & 7 \\ 2 & 1 & 9 \end{bmatrix}$$

FIG. 2.4.1

2.4.4   The Natural Order and the Transpose. The transpose of the natural order data matrix has attributes for rows and entities for columns, unless otherwise specified. The transpose of a natural order rectangular matrix is usually a horizontal matrix, since the natural order of a data matrix is usually a vertical matrix.

2.4.5   The Symbol for the Transpose. If a letter stands for a matrix, it is primed to indicate its transpose. For example, a' is the transpose of a. If the natural order of a matrix is defined, the letter representing it is un-primed to indicate that it is in the natural order. The double subscript notation, in which the first subscript stands for row and the second for column, may also be reversed to indicate the transpose. Figure 2.4.2 shows on the left a natural order matrix with the subscripts of the elements in the conventional order. On the right is shown the transpose of this matrix with the subscripts reversed.

$$a = \begin{bmatrix} a_{11} & a_{12} \\ a_{21} & a_{22} \\ a_{31} & a_{32} \end{bmatrix} \quad a' = \begin{bmatrix} a_{11} & a_{21} & a_{31} \\ a_{12} & a_{22} & a_{32} \end{bmatrix}$$

FIG. 2.4.2

In general, when we deal with matrices, we use a single letter to represent a matrix so that we do not have to be concerned with the subscripts of the elements to indicate their positions in the matrix. It is only on special occasions that we shall use the individual elements of a matrix in the development or description of a procedure.

2.4.6 The Transpose of a Transpose. If the transpose of a matrix is transposed, the original matrix is restored. This result is expressed in the following equation.

$$(a')' = a \qquad\qquad (2.4.1)$$

2.4.7 Transpose of Common Kinds of Matrices. The transpose of a vertical matrix is horizontal, and vice versa. The transpose of a square matrix is a square matrix. The transpose of a lower triangular matrix is an upper triangular matrix, and vice versa. The same rule holds for partial triangular matrices. The transpose of all symmetric matrices is the same as the original matrices. This includes general symmetric matrices and diagonal, scalar, identity, and sign matrices. Obviously, it also includes scalar quantities. This is the reason that matrix transposition does not affect scalar quantities.

2.4.8 The Transpose of a Vector. The column vector is written without the prime. Its transpose is a row vector. The prime symbol used on a letter which represents a vector means a row vector unless otherwise specified. This is the reason that in the preceding section we used a prime on the unit vector when it was written as a row vector.

2.5 Supermatrices

Another concept which is not applicable in scalar algebra is that of supermatrices.

2.5.1 Definition of a Supermatrix. A matrix whose elements are scalar quantities is called a *simple matrix* to distinguish it from a supermatrix. A *supermatrix* is one in which one or more of its elements are themselves simple matrices. All matric elements in a given row of a supermatrix must have the same number of simple rows, and all matric elements in a given column of a supermatrix must have the same number of simple columns. The order of a supermatrix is determined by the number of simple matrices in the rows and columns of the supermatrix.

2.5.2 Partitioned Matrices. Supermatrices may be constructed from simple matrices by partitioning between certain rows and columns. This means that we separate successive sets of columns or successive sets of rows by spaces or by dotted, broken, or fine hairlines. Figure 2.5.1 is an example of a matrix which has been partitioned by rows and columns. This is a 2×2 supermatrix.

$$a = \begin{bmatrix} 2 & 4 & | & 5 & 1 \\ 3 & 7 & | & 3 & 2 \\ \hline 6 & 1 & | & 4 & 7 \\ 5 & 7 & | & 2 & 5 \end{bmatrix}$$

FIG. 2.5.1

The concept of the partitioning of matrices is most important in the analysis of data matrices, and we shall give considerably more attention to the concept than it ordinarily receives in discussions of matrix algebra.

2.5.3 The Natural Order of a Supermatrix. If the natural order of a supermatrix is to be defined, it must be done in terms of the natural order of its simple form. We cannot determine by looking at a supermatrix with letter elements which stand for matrices the simple order of that supermatrix, unless the simple orders of the matric elements are also specified.

2.5.4 Symmetric Partitioning. Symmetric partitioning is accomplished by partitioning between corresponding rows and columns. Therefore, only square matrices can be partitioned symmetrically. In a symmetrically partitioned matrix, the diagonal submatrices of the resulting supermatrix are all square. The orders of corresponding matric elements above and below the diagonal of a symmetrically partitioned square matrix are the mutual transposes of one another. Figure 2.5.2 shows a symmetrically partitioned square matrix.

$$\begin{bmatrix} 4 & | & 8 & 2 & | & 7 & | & 8 \\ \hline 3 & | & 6 & 1 & | & 4 & | & 8 \\ 2 & | & 1 & 5 & | & 7 & | & 7 \\ \hline 7 & | & 4 & 2 & | & 7 & | & 7 \\ \hline 9 & | & 3 & 7 & | & 3 & | & 6 \end{bmatrix}$$

FIG. 2.5.2

2.5.5 Symmetrically Partitioned, Symmetric Simple Matrices. In this matrix all diagonal matric elements are symmetric simple matrices. Corresponding nondiagonal matric elements are mutual transposes of one another. In this sense there is a difference between a square and a symmetric matrix. In the first instance, it will be recalled that only the orders of corresponding matric elements were mutual transposes; while in the case of a symmetrically partitioned, symmetric simple matrix, the actual corresponding matric elements are mutual transposes. Figure 2.5.3 is an example of a symmetrically partitioned, symmetric simple matrix.

$$a = \left[\begin{array}{cc|cc} 4 & 3 & 2 & 7 \\ 3 & 6 & 1 & 4 \\ \hline 2 & 1 & 5 & 2 \\ 7 & 4 & 2 & 7 \end{array}\right]$$

FIG. 2.5.3

2.5.6 *The General Diagonal Supermatrix.* This may have for matric diagonal elements any kind of simple matrices, including vectors and scalar quantities. All of the nondiagonal matric elements will be null. Figure 2.5.4 is an example of a diagonal supermatrix whose diagonal elements are unit vectors.

$$D_1 = \left[\begin{array}{c|c|c} 1 & 0 & 0 \\ 1 & 0 & 0 \\ \hline 0 & 1 & 0 \\ 0 & 1 & 0 \\ 0 & 1 & 0 \\ \hline 0 & 0 & 1 \\ 0 & 0 & 1 \end{array}\right]$$

FIG. 2.5.4

2.5.7 *The Partial Triangular Matrix as a Supermatrix.* The partial triangular matrix may be partitioned to yield a triangular matrix and a rectangular matrix. In such a partitioning, the first matric element becomes the triangular matrix and the next matric element, a rectangular matrix. Figure 2.5.5 is an example of a partial triangular matrix partitioned to yield submatrices.

$$\left[\begin{array}{ccc|cc} 3 & 4 & 7 & 6 & 8 \\ 0 & 2 & 1 & 2 & 5 \\ 0 & 0 & 5 & 4 & 9 \end{array}\right]$$

FIG. 2.5.5

2.5.8 Type 1 Supervectors. A partitioned simple vector is called a *type 1 supervector*. A column type 1 supervector has simple column vectors for elements. A row type 1 supervector has simple row vectors for elements. Figure 2.5.6 is an example of a type 1 column supervector whose vector elements are simple column vectors.

$$V = \begin{bmatrix} V_1 \\ V_2 \\ \cdots \\ V_n \end{bmatrix}$$

FIG. 2.5.6

Figure 2.5.7 is a numerical example of a type 1 row supervector. The elements of this supervector are themselves simple row vectors.

$$V' = [1 \quad 3 \mid 4 \quad 6]$$

FIG. 2.5.7

2.5.9 Matrices Expressed as Supervectors with Vector Elements. By partitioning a simple matrix between each column we have a row supervector which we call a *type 2 supervector*, each of whose elements is a simple column vector. In the same way we may partition a simple matrix between rows so that the matric elements of this type 2 supervector are now simple rows, but the vector itself is in column form. Therefore a matrix may be expressed as a column supervector whose elements are row vectors, or a row supervector whose elements are column vectors. It is convenient to represent matrices as special types of supervectors when we come to discuss matrix multiplication. Equation 2.5.1 is an example of a type 2 row supervector whose elements are column vectors.

$$a = [a_{.1} \quad a_{.2} \quad \cdots \quad a_{.m}]_n \tag{2.5.1}$$

Here $a_{.i}$ means the ith column of a. Equation 2.5.2 is an example of a type 2 column supervector whose elements are row vectors.

$$a = \begin{bmatrix} a_{1.}' \\ a_{2.}' \\ \cdots \\ a_{n.}' \end{bmatrix}_m \tag{2.5.2}$$

Here $a_{i.}'$ means the ith row vector of a.

2.5.10   Equality of Supermatrices. Two supermatrices are said to be equal if and only if their simple forms are equal to one another. Thus two supermatrices may be equal even though they are of different superorder. We shall see, however, that certain further restrictions must be placed on supermatrices other than on their simple order if we are to apply the rules of matrix algebra to them.

2.5.11   Type 3 Supervectors. If a vector has one or more of its elements as a matrix, it is called a *type 3 supervector*. A type 3 supervector may be constructed by partitioning a simple matrix either between rows or between columns, but not both.

2.6   Transpose of the Supermatrix

2.6.1   Transpose of the General Supermatrix with Matric Elements. In transposing a matrix whose matric elements are simple matrices, we use the same procedure as in transposing simple matrices. That is, we write rows for columns or columns for rows. In addition to this, however, we must also transpose each of the matric elements. Figure 2.6.1 is an example of a supermatrix with numerical elements.

$$A = \begin{bmatrix} 1 & 6 & 1 & 8 \\ 2 & 3 & 3 & 7 \\ 4 & 5 & 4 & 6 \\ \hline 7 & 2 & 9 & 3 \\ 3 & 4 & 7 & 5 \\ \hline 3 & 1 & 2 & 8 \end{bmatrix}$$

Fig. 2.6.1

Figure 2.6.2 is an example of the transpose of this supermatrix.

$$A' = \begin{bmatrix} 1 & 2 & 4 & 7 & 3 & 3 \\ 6 & 3 & 5 & 2 & 4 & 1 \\ \hline 1 & 3 & 4 & 9 & 7 & 2 \\ 8 & 7 & 6 & 3 & 5 & 8 \end{bmatrix}$$

Fig. 2.6.2

Figure 2.6.3 is an example of a supermatrix whose elements are indicated by letters representing matric elements.

$$A = \begin{bmatrix} a_{11} & a_{12} \\ a_{21} & a_{22} \\ a_{31} & a_{32} \end{bmatrix}$$

FIG. 2.6.3

Figure 2.6.4 is an example of the transpose of this supermatrix.

$$A' = \begin{bmatrix} a_{11}' & a_{21}' & a_{31}' \\ a_{12}' & a_{22}' & a_{32}' \end{bmatrix}$$

FIG. 2.6.4

2.6.2   Transpose of a Symmetrically Partitioned, Symmetric Simple Matrix. This transposition must yield the supermatrix which was transposed. Since the diagonal elements are symmetric submatrices, their transposes are the same as the original order. The corresponding supra- and infradiagonal matric elements of a symmetrically partitioned, symmetric simple matrix are mutual transposes. Therefore, writing rows as columns and transposing each matric element would yield the same corresponding element as in the original matrix.

2.6.3   Transpose of a Diagonal Supermatrix. In the general case, the diagonal matric elements must be transposed and the null nondiagonal elements must also be transposed. If the diagonal matric elements are simple diagonals, then the transpose of the diagonal supermatrix is the same as the original matrix.

2.6.4   Transpose of Type 1 Supervectors. Here the column supervector becomes a row supervector with row vector elements. The row supervector becomes a column supervector with column vector elements. Figure 2.6.5 is an example of a type 1 column supervector and its transpose.

$$V = \begin{bmatrix} V_1 \\ V_2 \\ \cdots \\ V_n \end{bmatrix} \qquad V' = [V_1' \quad V_2' \quad \cdots \quad V_n']$$

FIG. 2.6.5

2.6.5   Transpose of a Simple Matrix Expressed as a Type 2 Supervector. The type 2 column supervector becomes a row supervector with its row vector elements transposed to column vector elements. The row supervector becomes a column type 2 supervector with its column vector elements transposed to row vector elements.

Equations 2.6.1 and 2.6.2 indicate a type 2 column supervector and its transpose which is a type 2 row supervector.

$$a = \begin{bmatrix} a_{1.}' \\ a_{2.}' \\ \cdots \\ a_{n.}' \end{bmatrix}_m \tag{2.6.1}$$

$$a' = [a_{1.} \quad a_{2.} \quad \cdots \quad a_{n.}]_m \tag{2.6.2}$$

Equations 2.6.3 and 2.6.4 indicate a type 2 row supervector and its transposition to a type 2 column supervector.

$$a = [a_{.1} \quad a_{.2} \quad \cdots \quad a_{.m}]_n \tag{2.6.3}$$

$$a' = \begin{bmatrix} a_{.1}' \\ a_{.2}' \\ \cdots \\ a_{.m}' \end{bmatrix}_n \tag{2.6.4}$$

It can be seen that if one substitutes the rows and columns of simple matrices for these letter subscripts we have the simple case of a matrix transposition as indicated in Section 2.4.

It will be noted that the dot precedes the subscript if the vector is a column from the natural order of the matrix. The dot comes after the subscript if the vector was taken from a row of the natural order of the matrix. Whether or not the vector is written as a row or column is indicated by whether or not the symbol standing for the vector has a prime. If it has a prime it is a row; if it does not have a prime it is a column, irrespective of whether it came from a row or a column of the natural order of the matrix.

2.6.6   *Transpose of Type 3 Supervector.* In this case the column vector becomes a row with matric elements transposed. The row vector becomes a column with matric elements transposed. Figures 2.6.6 and 2.6.7 indicate for numerical elements a type 3 row vector and its transposition to a type 3 column vector.

$$T' = \begin{bmatrix} 3 & 2 & 4 & \bigm| & 5 & 2 \\ 0 & 6 & 1 & \bigm| & 3 & 5 \\ 0 & 0 & 2 & \bigm| & 1 & 6 \end{bmatrix}$$

FIG. 2.6.6

$$T = \left[\begin{array}{ccc} 3 & 0 & 0 \\ 2 & 6 & 0 \\ 4 & 1 & 2 \\ \hline 5 & 3 & 1 \\ 2 & 5 & 6 \end{array}\right]$$

FIG. 2.6.7

2.7 Addition and Subtraction of Matrices

2.7.1 Addition of Simple Matrices. The sum of two matrices is defined as a matrix, each element of which is the sum of the corresponding elements of the two. If $a + b = c$ with elements a_{ij}, b_{ij}, and c_{ij}, respectively, then $a_{ij} + b_{ij} = c_{ij}$. Therefore, only matrices of equal order can be added together and the order of the sum is equal to the order of the matrices. The sum of any number of matrices is a matrix, each element of which is the sum of corresponding elements of all the matrices. Figure 2.7.1 is an example of the sum of two matrices.

$$\begin{bmatrix} 4 & 6 \\ 3 & 7 \\ 2 & 5 \end{bmatrix} + \begin{bmatrix} 3 & 2 \\ 6 & 4 \\ 3 & 6 \end{bmatrix} = \begin{bmatrix} 4+3 & 6+2 \\ 3+6 & 7+4 \\ 2+3 & 5+6 \end{bmatrix} = \begin{bmatrix} 7 & 8 \\ 9 & 11 \\ 5 & 11 \end{bmatrix}$$

FIG. 2.7.1

Figure 2.7.2 is an example of the sum of three matrices.

$$\begin{bmatrix} 6 & 5 \\ 4 & 3 \end{bmatrix} + \begin{bmatrix} 2 & 4 \\ 3 & 5 \end{bmatrix} + \begin{bmatrix} 7 & 9 \\ 6 & 4 \end{bmatrix} = \begin{bmatrix} 6+2+7 & 5+4+9 \\ 4+3+6 & 3+5+4 \end{bmatrix} = \begin{bmatrix} 15 & 18 \\ 13 & 12 \end{bmatrix}$$

FIG. 2.7.2

2.7.2 Some Simple Laws of Addition. The associative law of addition is given by

$$(a + b) + c = a + (b + c) \tag{2.7.1}$$

This means that we can add first the matrices a and b, and then to this sum add the matrix c. Or we can add first the matrices b and c, and then add to this sum the matrix a.

The commutative law of addition is given by

$$a + b = b + a \qquad (2.7.2)$$

This means that the sequence in which we arrange matrices to be added together is immaterial. These two laws of addition are important because not all of the simple laws which hold for scalar algebra hold for matrix algebra.

2.7.3 Subtraction of Simple Matrices. Subtraction may be regarded as a special case of addition where the signs of all elements in the matrix to be subtracted are reversed. Then both the associative and the commutative laws of addition hold also for subtraction. Figure 2.7.3 is an example of the difference between two matrices.

$$\begin{bmatrix} 4 & 6 & 3 \\ 9 & 2 & 11 \end{bmatrix} - \begin{bmatrix} 5 & 9 & 2 \\ 8 & 3 & 5 \end{bmatrix} = \begin{bmatrix} 4-5 & 6-9 & 3-2 \\ 9-8 & 2-3 & 11-5 \end{bmatrix} = \begin{bmatrix} -1 & -3 & 1 \\ 1 & -1 & 6 \end{bmatrix}$$

Fig. 2.7.3

2.7.4 Addition and Subtraction. Any number of matrices may be combined by addition of some and subtraction of others. The associative and commutative laws hold for addition and subtraction of any number of matrices. Figure 2.7.4 is an example of the addition and subtraction of matrices.

$$\begin{bmatrix} 2 & 3 \\ 5 & 7 \end{bmatrix} - \begin{bmatrix} 1 & 7 \\ 4 & 3 \end{bmatrix} - \begin{bmatrix} 3 & 6 \\ 7 & 5 \end{bmatrix} + \begin{bmatrix} 4 & 8 \\ 7 & 8 \end{bmatrix}$$
$$= \begin{bmatrix} 2-1-3+4 & 3-7-6+8 \\ 5-4-7+7 & 7-3-5+8 \end{bmatrix} = \begin{bmatrix} 2 & -2 \\ 1 & 7 \end{bmatrix}$$

Fig. 2.7.4

2.7.5 Addition and Subtraction of Supermatrices. The sum or the difference of two supermatrices is a supermatrix, each of whose matric elements is the sum or the difference of corresponding elements of the two matrices. Supermatrices may be added or subtracted, therefore, if and only if they have the same superorder and corresponding matric elements are of the same order.

2.7.6 The Transpose of a Sum or a Difference. The transpose of a sum or a difference of simple matrices is equal to the sum or the difference of their transposes.

$$[a + b]' = a' + b' \tag{2.7.3}$$

An example of this rule is given for matrices with numerical elements in Fig. 2.7.5.

$$\left(\begin{bmatrix} 1 & 2 \\ 3 & 4 \end{bmatrix} - \begin{bmatrix} 2 & 1 \\ 1 & 2 \end{bmatrix} \right)' = \begin{bmatrix} -1 & 1 \\ 2 & 2 \end{bmatrix}' = \begin{bmatrix} -1 & 2 \\ 1 & 2 \end{bmatrix}$$

$$\begin{bmatrix} 1 & 2 \\ 3 & 4 \end{bmatrix}' - \begin{bmatrix} 2 & 1 \\ 1 & 2 \end{bmatrix}' = \begin{bmatrix} 1 & 3 \\ 2 & 4 \end{bmatrix} - \begin{bmatrix} 2 & 1 \\ 1 & 2 \end{bmatrix} = \begin{bmatrix} -1 & 2 \\ 1 & 2 \end{bmatrix}$$

FIG. 2.7.5

Another example of this rule is

$$[a - b]' = a' - b' \tag{2.7.4}$$

The transpose of a sum or a difference of supermatrices is equal to the sum or the difference of their transposes.

2.7.7 Sums and Differences of Special Kinds of Matrices.
The sum of any number of diagonal matrices is a *diagonal matrix.*
The sum of any number of scalar matrices is a *scalar matrix.*
The sum of any number of symmetric matrices is a *symmetric matrix.*
The sum of a matrix and its transpose is a *symmetric matrix.*
Figure 2.7.6 is an example of the sum of a matrix and its transpose.

$$\begin{bmatrix} 3 & 2 & 2 \\ 1 & 4 & 1 \\ 2 & 3 & 5 \end{bmatrix} + \begin{bmatrix} 3 & 1 & 2 \\ 2 & 4 & 3 \\ 2 & 1 & 5 \end{bmatrix} = \begin{bmatrix} 6 & 3 & 4 \\ 3 & 8 & 4 \\ 4 & 4 & 10 \end{bmatrix}$$

FIG. 2.7.6

The difference between a square matrix and its transpose is a *skew-symmetric matrix.* Figure 2.7.7 is an example of the difference between a matrix and its transpose.

$$\begin{bmatrix} 3 & 4 & 2 \\ 6 & 1 & 0 \\ 1 & 9 & 5 \end{bmatrix} - \begin{bmatrix} 3 & 6 & 1 \\ 4 & 1 & 9 \\ 2 & 0 & 5 \end{bmatrix} = \begin{bmatrix} 0 & -2 & 1 \\ 2 & 0 & -9 \\ -1 & 9 & 0 \end{bmatrix}$$

FIG. 2.7.7

2.8   Vector Multiplication

2.8.1   The Minor Product of Two Vectors. In the minor product of two vectors, the left factor is a row vector and is called the *prefactor*. The right factor is a column vector and is called the *postfactor*. The column vector is said to be premultiplied by the row vector and the row vector is said to be postmultiplied by the column vector.

The minor product of two vectors is a scalar quantity which is the sum of products of corresponding elements of the two vectors.

$$V_a'V_b = [a_1 \quad a_2 \quad \cdots \quad a_n]\begin{bmatrix} b_1 \\ b_2 \\ \cdots \\ b_n \end{bmatrix} = a_1b_1 + a_2b_2 + \cdots + a_nb_n \quad (2.8.1)$$

Figure 2.8.1 is a numerical example of the minor product of two vectors.

$$[3 \quad 4 \quad 7]\begin{bmatrix} 2 \\ 6 \\ 1 \end{bmatrix} = (3 \times 2) + (4 \times 6) + (7 \times 1) = 37$$

Fig. 2.8.1

The minor product of two vectors is sometimes called the *scalar product* or *inner product*. Because of the definition, the minor product of two vectors is defined only for vectors of equal order.

2.8.2   Transpose of a Minor Product of Two Vectors. This is equal to the minor product, since it is a scalar quantity. It is also equal to the product of the transposes in reverse order.

$$(V_a'V_b)' = V_b'V_a \quad (2.8.2)$$

2.8.3   The Major Product of Two Vectors. In the major product of two vectors, a column vector is postmultiplied by a row vector or a row vector is premultiplied by a column vector.

In a major product of two vectors, the product is a matrix in which the *ij*th element is the product of the *i*th element of the prefactor and the *j*th element of the postfactor.

$$V_aV_b' = \begin{bmatrix} a_1 \\ a_2 \\ \cdots \\ a_n \end{bmatrix}[b_1 \quad b_2 \quad \cdots \quad b_m] = \begin{bmatrix} a_1b_1 & a_1b_2 & \cdots & a_1b_m \\ a_2b_1 & a_2b_2 & \cdots & a_2b_m \\ \cdots & \cdots & \cdots & \cdots \\ a_nb_1 & a_nb_2 & \cdots & a_nb_m \end{bmatrix} \quad (2.8.3)$$

Figure 2.8.2 is a numerical example of the major product of two vectors.

$$\begin{bmatrix} 2 \\ 4 \\ 3 \end{bmatrix} [1 \quad 3 \quad 2 \quad 4] = \begin{bmatrix} 2 \times 1 & 2 \times 3 & 2 \times 2 & 2 \times 4 \\ 4 \times 1 & 4 \times 3 & 4 \times 2 & 4 \times 4 \\ 3 \times 1 & 3 \times 3 & 3 \times 2 & 3 \times 4 \end{bmatrix} = \begin{bmatrix} 2 & 6 & 4 & 8 \\ 4 & 12 & 8 & 16 \\ 3 & 9 & 6 & 12 \end{bmatrix}$$

Fig. 2.8.2

In the major product of two vectors the rows are proportional to one another and the columns are also proportional to one another.

The order of the major product of two vectors is the height of the prefactor and the width of the postfactor. For a major product of two vectors to exist, no restrictions are placed on the order of either vector. The major product of two vectors has also been called the simple product, but this does not seem to be a good designation.

2.8.4 Transpose of a Major Product. The transpose of the major product of two vectors is equal to the product of the transposes in reverse order.

$$(V_a V_b')' = V_b V_a' \tag{2.8.4}$$

2.8.5 The Product of a Vector by its Transpose. The minor product of a vector by its transpose is called the *minor product moment* of the vector. It is the sum of squares of the elements of the vector. Figure 2.8.3 is a numerical example of the minor product moment of a vector.

$$[1 \quad 3 \quad 2] \begin{bmatrix} 1 \\ 3 \\ 2 \end{bmatrix} = 1 + 3^2 + 2^2 = 1 + 9 + 4 = 14$$

Fig. 2.8.3

The major product of a vector by its transpose is called the *major product moment* of the vector. This is a symmetric matrix. An example of the major product of a vector is

$$V_a V_a' = \begin{bmatrix} a_1 \\ a_2 \\ \dots \\ a_n \end{bmatrix} [a_1 \quad a_2 \quad \cdots \quad a_n] = \begin{bmatrix} a_1^2 & a_1 a_2 & \cdots & a_1 a_n \\ a_2 a_1 & a_2^2 & \cdots & a_2 a_n \\ \dots & \dots & \dots & \dots \\ a_n a_1 & a_n a_2 & \cdots & a_n^2 \end{bmatrix} \tag{2.8.5}$$

2.8.6 Undefined Products of Vectors. A row vector cannot be multiplied by a row vector nor a column vector by a column vector. One of the factors must be a row and the other must be a column. These prohibitions on the multiplication of vectors are arbitrary and are imposed by the definition of vector multiplication. We could define products of row by row or column by column vectors. As a matter of fact, for computational purposes, we sometimes arrange the formats so that the two vectors which are to be multiplied together to get a scalar product are both in row or column form. This is merely for mechanical convenience.

2.8.7   The Commutative Law. The factors of a major product of vectors can be commuted only if they are of the same order. However, the product is then a scalar rather than a matrix.

The factors of a minor product of vectors can be commuted, but the product is then a matrix rather than a scalar. Vector multiplication is not commutative. The noncommutativity of vector multiplication is indicated by Fig. 2.8.4.

$$V_a V_b' \neq V_b' V_a$$
$$V_b V_a' \neq V_a' V_b$$

Fig. 2.8.4

2.8.8   Minor Products of Type 1 Supervectors. The minor product of two type 1 supervectors can be expressed if they are of the same superorder and their corresponding subvectors are of the same order. The minor product of two type 1 supervectors is the sum of the minor products of the corresponding subvectors. Figure 2.8.5 is an example of the minor product of type 1 supervectors.

$$V_a'V_b = [2 \quad 3 \mid 1 \quad 7 \quad 5] \begin{bmatrix} 2 \\ 1 \\ - \\ 2 \\ 1 \\ 3 \end{bmatrix} = [2 \quad 3] \begin{bmatrix} 2 \\ 1 \end{bmatrix} + [1 \quad 7 \quad 5] \begin{bmatrix} 2 \\ 1 \\ 3 \end{bmatrix}$$

$$= [2 \times 2 + 3 \times 1] + [1 \times 2 + 7 \times 1 + 5 \times 3] = 7 + 24 = 31$$

Fig. 2.8.5

2.8.9   The Major Product of Type 1 Supervectors. No restrictions are placed on the superorders of either factor or on the orders of their subvectors.

The *ij*th matric element of the product of two type 1 supervectors is the product of the *i*th column subvector of the prefactor postmultiplied by the *j*th row subvector of the postfactor.

The product is a supermatrix in which the number of matric rows is the superorder of the prefactor and the number of matric columns is the superorder of the postfactor. Figure 2.8.6 is a numerical example of the major product of type 1 supervectors.

$$V_a V_b' = \begin{bmatrix} 2 \\ 3 \\ \overline{2} \\ 4 \\ 1 \end{bmatrix} [3 \quad 1 \quad 2 \,|\, 2 \,|\, 2 \quad 3 \quad 5 \quad 1]$$

$$= \begin{bmatrix} \begin{bmatrix} 2 \\ 3 \end{bmatrix} [3 \quad 1 \quad 2] & \begin{bmatrix} 2 \\ 3 \end{bmatrix} [2] & \begin{bmatrix} 2 \\ 3 \end{bmatrix} [2 \quad 3 \quad 5 \quad 1] \\ \begin{bmatrix} 2 \\ 4 \\ 1 \end{bmatrix} [3 \quad 1 \quad 2] & \begin{bmatrix} 2 \\ 4 \\ 1 \end{bmatrix} [2] & \begin{bmatrix} 2 \\ 4 \\ 1 \end{bmatrix} [2 \quad 3 \quad 5 \quad 1] \end{bmatrix}$$

$$= \begin{bmatrix} 6 & 2 & 4 & 4 & 4 & 6 & 10 & 2 \\ 9 & 3 & 6 & 6 & 6 & 9 & 15 & 3 \\ \hline 6 & 2 & 4 & 4 & 4 & 6 & 10 & 2 \\ 12 & 4 & 8 & 8 & 8 & 12 & 20 & 4 \\ 3 & 1 & 2 & 2 & 2 & 3 & 5 & 1 \end{bmatrix}$$

FIG. 2.8.6

2.8.10 Transpose of the Major Product of Two Type 1 Supervectors.
This is equal to the product of the transposes in reverse order.

2.8.11 Special Vector Products.
2.8.11a. THE UNIT VECTOR. The minor product of a unit vector with a general vector is the sum of the elements in the latter.

$$1'V_x = V_x'1 = \Sigma X \tag{2.8.6}$$

A numerical example is given in Fig. 2.8.7.

$$[1 \quad 1 \quad 1] \begin{bmatrix} 3 \\ 4 \\ 7 \end{bmatrix} = [3 \quad 4 \quad 7] \begin{bmatrix} 1 \\ 1 \\ 1 \end{bmatrix} = 3 + 4 + 7 = 14$$

FIG. 2.8.7

The minor product moment of a unit vector is the order of the vector.

$$1_n'1_n = n \tag{2.8.7}$$

The major product of a unit vector postmultiplied by a general vector is a matrix all of whose rows are equal. See Fig. 2.8.8.

$$\begin{bmatrix} 1 \\ 1 \\ 1 \end{bmatrix} \begin{bmatrix} 3 & 4 & 7 \end{bmatrix} = \begin{bmatrix} 3 & 4 & 7 \\ 3 & 4 & 7 \\ 3 & 4 & 7 \end{bmatrix}$$

Fig. 2.8.8

The major product of a unit vector premultiplied by a general vector is a matrix all of whose columns are equal.

$$V_a 1' = \begin{bmatrix} a_1 & a_1 & \cdots & a_1 \\ a_2 & a_2 & \cdots & a_2 \\ a_n & a_n & \cdots & a_n \end{bmatrix} \tag{2.8.8}$$

The major product of two unit vectors is a matrix all of whose elements are 1. See Fig. 2.8.9.

$$\begin{bmatrix} 1 \\ 1 \\ 1 \end{bmatrix} \begin{bmatrix} 1 & 1 & 1 & 1 \end{bmatrix} = \begin{bmatrix} 1 & 1 & 1 & 1 \\ 1 & 1 & 1 & 1 \\ 1 & 1 & 1 & 1 \end{bmatrix}$$

Fig. 2.8.9

2.8.11b ELEMENTARY VECTORS. The minor product of an elementary vector by a unit vector is 1.

$$e_i'1 = 1'e_i = 1 \tag{2.8.9}$$

The minor product of an elementary vector and a general vector is the ith element of the general vector.

$$e_i'V = V'e_i = V_i \tag{2.8.10}$$

A numerical example is given in Fig. 2.8.10.

$$\begin{bmatrix} 0 & 1 & 0 & 0 \end{bmatrix} \begin{bmatrix} 5 \\ 4 \\ 6 \\ 2 \end{bmatrix} = 4$$

Fig. 2.8.10

The minor product of an elementary vector with another elementary vector is 0. A numerical example is given in Fig. 2.8.11.

$$[0 \quad 1 \quad 0 \quad 0]\begin{bmatrix} 1 \\ 0 \\ 0 \\ 0 \end{bmatrix} = 0 \times 1 + 1 \times 0 + 0 \times 0 + 0 \times 0 = 0$$

FIG. 2.8.11

The major product of an elementary vector with a general vector where the elementary vector is the prefactor is a matrix all of whose rows are zeros except the ith row, which is the vector.

The major product of an elementary vector with a general vector, where the elementary vector is the postfactor, is a matrix all of whose columns are zeros except the jth, which is the vector.

The major product of two elementary vectors is an elementary matrix. The location of the unit element in the elementary matrix is in the row corresponding to the unit element in the prefactor and in the column corresponding to the unit element in the postfactor.

$$e_i e_j' = e_{ij} \tag{2.8.11}$$

A numerical example is given in Fig. 2.8.12.

$$\begin{bmatrix} 0 \\ 1 \\ 0 \\ 0 \end{bmatrix} [1 \quad 0 \quad 0] = \begin{bmatrix} 0 & 0 & 0 \\ 1 & 0 & 0 \\ 0 & 0 & 0 \\ 0 & 0 & 0 \end{bmatrix}$$

FIG. 2.8.12

2.9 Matrix Multiplication

In defining the product of two matrices a and b, we shall first express these as type 2 supervectors.

2.9.1 Matrices Expressed as Type 2 Supervectors. Let a be expressed both as a type 2 row and a type 2 column supervector:

$$a = [a_{.1} \quad a_{.2} \quad \cdots \quad a_{.m}]_n \tag{2.9.1}$$

$$a = \begin{bmatrix} a_{1.}' \\ a_{2.}' \\ \cdots \\ a_{n.}' \end{bmatrix}_m \tag{2.9.2}$$

Then its transpose can be expressed as a type 2 column vector and also a type 2 row vector:

$$a' = \begin{bmatrix} a_{.1}' \\ a_{.2}' \\ \cdots \\ a_{.m}' \end{bmatrix}_n \tag{2.9.3}$$

$$a' = [a_{1.} \quad a_{2.} \quad \cdots \quad a_{n.}]_m \tag{2.9.4}$$

Let b be expressed both as a type 2 row supervector and a type 2 column supervector:

$$b = [b_{.1} \quad b_{.2} \quad \cdots \quad b_{.s}]_t \tag{2.9.5}$$

$$b = \begin{bmatrix} b_{1.}' \\ b_{2.}' \\ \cdots \\ b_{t.}' \end{bmatrix}_s \tag{2.9.6}$$

Then its transpose can be expressed as both a type 2 column and a type 2 row vector:

$$b' = \begin{bmatrix} b_{.1}' \\ b_{.2}' \\ \cdots \\ b_{.s}' \end{bmatrix}_t \tag{2.9.7}$$

$$b' = [b_{1.} \quad b_{2.} \quad \cdots \quad b_{t.}]_s \tag{2.9.8}$$

2.9.2 The Product ab as the Minor Product of Type 2 Supervectors.

The product of two matrices can be expressed in minor product form. The product of two matrices expressed as the minor product of type 2 supervectors is the sum of major products of simple vectors. The first vector of a term in the sum comes from the corresponding column vector of the prefactor:

$$ab = [a_{.1} \quad a_{.2} \quad \cdots \quad a_{.m}]_n \begin{bmatrix} b_{1.}' \\ b_{2.}' \\ \cdots \\ b_{t.}' \end{bmatrix}_s \tag{2.9.9}$$

$$ab = [a_{.1}b_{1.}' + a_{.2}b_{2.}' + \cdots + a_{.m}b_{t.}']_{ns} \tag{2.9.10}$$

Figures 2.9.1, 2.9.2, and 2.9.3 give an example of the product of the two matrices expressed as the minor product of type 2 supervectors.

$$(a_{.1})(a_{.2})$$

$$a = \begin{bmatrix} 2 & 1 \\ 3 & 5 \\ 6 & 1 \end{bmatrix} \qquad b = \begin{bmatrix} 1 & 2 \\ 3 & 1 \end{bmatrix} \begin{matrix} (b_1.') \\ (b_2.') \end{matrix}$$

FIG. 2.9.1

$$(a_{.1} \quad b_{.1}') \qquad (a_{.2} \quad b_{.2}')$$

$$ab = \begin{bmatrix} 2 \\ 3 \\ 6 \end{bmatrix} [1 \quad 2] + \begin{bmatrix} 1 \\ 5 \\ 1 \end{bmatrix} [3 \quad 1]$$

FIG. 2.9.2

$$ab = \begin{bmatrix} 2 & 4 \\ 3 & 6 \\ 6 & 12 \end{bmatrix} + \begin{bmatrix} 3 & 1 \\ 15 & 5 \\ 3 & 1 \end{bmatrix} = \begin{bmatrix} 5 & 5 \\ 18 & 11 \\ 9 & 13 \end{bmatrix}$$

FIG. 2.9.3

2.9.3   The Product of Two Matrices Expressed as the Major Product of Type 2 Vectors. This major product is expressed by the following:

$$ab = \begin{bmatrix} a_1.' \\ a_2.' \\ \cdots \\ a_n.' \end{bmatrix} [b_{.1} \quad b_{.2} \quad \cdots \quad b_{.s}]_t \qquad (2.9.11)$$

$$ab = \begin{bmatrix} a_1.'b_{.1} & a_1.'b_{.2} & \cdots & a_1.'b_{.s} \\ a_2.'b_{.1} & a_2.'b_{.2} & \cdots & a_2.'b_{.s} \\ \cdots & \cdots & \cdots & \cdots \\ a_n.'b_{.1} & a_n.'b_{.2} & \cdots & a_n.'b_{.s} \end{bmatrix} \qquad (2.9.12)$$

The product of the matrices expressed as the major product of type 2 vectors is a matrix of minor products of vectors. The ijth element is the minor product of the ith row of the prefactor postmultiplied by the jth column of the postfactor. A numerical example of the product of two matrices expressed as the major product of type 2 supervectors is given in Figs. 2.9.4 and 2.9.5.

$$ab = \begin{bmatrix} [2 \;\; 1]\begin{bmatrix}1\\3\end{bmatrix} & [2 \;\; 1]\begin{bmatrix}2\\1\end{bmatrix} \\[2ex] \hline [3 \;\; 5]\begin{bmatrix}1\\3\end{bmatrix} & [3 \;\; 5]\begin{bmatrix}2\\1\end{bmatrix} \\[2ex] \hline [6 \;\; 1]\begin{bmatrix}1\\3\end{bmatrix} & [6 \;\; 1]\begin{bmatrix}2\\1\end{bmatrix} \end{bmatrix}$$

FIG. 2.9.4

$$ab = \begin{bmatrix} 2 \times 1 + 1 \times 3 & 2 \times 2 + 1 \times 1 \\ 3 \times 1 + 5 \times 3 & 3 \times 2 + 5 \times 1 \\ 6 \times 1 + 1 \times 3 & 6 \times 2 + 1 \times 1 \end{bmatrix} = \begin{bmatrix} 5 & 5 \\ 18 & 11 \\ 9 & 13 \end{bmatrix}$$

FIG. 2.9.5

2.9.4 Reversing the Order of the Factors. The minor product of two matrices with the order of the factors reversed is shown below.

$$ba = [b_{.1} \quad b_{.2} \quad \cdots \quad b_{.s}]_t \begin{bmatrix} a_{1.}' \\ a_{2.}' \\ \cdots \\ a_{n.}' \end{bmatrix}_m \tag{2.9.13}$$

$$ba = [b_{.1}\, a_{1.}' + b_{.2}\, a_{2.}' + \cdots + b_{.s}\, a_{n.}']_{tm} \tag{2.9.14}$$

The major product of two matrices with the order of the factors reversed is shown below.

$$ba = \begin{bmatrix} b_{1.}' \\ b_{2.}' \\ \cdots \\ b_{t.}' \end{bmatrix}_s [a_{.1} \quad a_{.2} \quad \cdots \quad a_{.m}]_n \tag{2.9.15}$$

$$ba = \begin{bmatrix} b_{1.}'a_{.1} & b_{1.}'a_{.2} & \cdots & b_{1.}'a_{.m} \\ b_{2.}'a_{.1} & b_{2.}'a_{.2} & \cdots & b_{2.}'a_{.m} \\ \cdots & \cdots & \cdots & \cdots \\ b_{t.}'a_{.1} & b_{t.}'a_{.2} & \cdots & b_{t.}'a_{.m} \end{bmatrix} \tag{2.9.16}$$

2.9.5 Dimensions of Factors and Their Products. If the product ab exists, then m and t must be equal or the number of columns of a and the number of rows of b must be the same. If the product ba exists, then s and n must be equal or the number of columns of b and the number of rows of a must be the same.

The order of a product of two matrices is the height of the prefactor and the width of the postfactor.

The height of the prefactor and the width of the postfactor are called the *distinct orders* or *dimensions* of the matrix factors in a product. The width of the prefactor and the height of the postfactor are called the *common order* or *dimension* of the factors in a product. The rules of order for matrix multiplication may be indicated by subscript notation:

$$a_{xy}b_{yz} = c_{xz} \tag{2.9.17}$$

In using this subscript notation to indicate order or dimensionality, one must be careful to specify these subscripts to indicate order rather than to indicate the position of an element in a matrix. Since we restrict our use of symbols for actual elements in the matrix to a minimum, this dual use of subscript notation should not prove confusing.

2.9.6 The Commutative Law and Matrix Multiplication. Both of the products ab and ba exist only if the order of a and b' are the same. Even if ab and ba exist, they are not, in general, equal. Therefore the commutative law does not, in general, hold for matrix multiplication.

2.9.7 The Associative Law of Matrix Multiplication. The product of more than two matrices may be formed by finding successively the products of any two adjacent factors.

$$(ab)c = a(bc) \tag{2.9.18}$$

The order restriction on more than two factors and their products may be indicated by subscript notation:

$$u_{ab}v_{bc}w_{cd}x_{de} = y_{ae} \tag{2.9.19}$$

2.9.8 The Associative Law and Algebraic Checks. The product of two matrices may be checked by the associative law:

$$(ab)1 = a(b1) \tag{2.9.20}$$

The multiplication may also be checked thusly:

$$1'(ab) = (1'a)b \tag{2.9.21}$$

2.9.9 The Distributive Law of Matrix Multiplication. The distributive law of matrix multiplication is expressed by the following:

$$a(b_1 + b_2 + \cdots + b_n) = ab_1 + ab_2 + \cdots + ab_n \tag{2.9.22}$$

$$(b_1 + b_2 + \cdots + b_n)a = b_1a + b_2a + \cdots + b_na \tag{2.9.23}$$

A numerical example is given in Figs. 2.9.6–2.9.8.

$$a = \begin{bmatrix} 1 & 2 \\ 2 & 1 \end{bmatrix} \quad b = \begin{bmatrix} 3 & 1 \\ 4 & 2 \end{bmatrix} \quad c = \begin{bmatrix} 4 & 1 \\ 2 & 1 \end{bmatrix}$$

FIG. 2.9.6

$$\underset{a}{\begin{bmatrix} 1 & 2 \\ 2 & 1 \end{bmatrix}} \underset{b+c}{\begin{bmatrix} 7 & 2 \\ 6 & 3 \end{bmatrix}} = \begin{bmatrix} 19 & 8 \\ 20 & 7 \end{bmatrix}$$

FIG. 2.9.7

$$\underset{ab}{\begin{bmatrix} 11 & 5 \\ 10 & 4 \end{bmatrix}} + \underset{ac}{\begin{bmatrix} 8 & 3 \\ 10 & 3 \end{bmatrix}} = \begin{bmatrix} 19 & 8 \\ 20 & 7 \end{bmatrix}$$

FIG. 2.9.8

2.9.10 The Distributive Law and Algebraic Checks. The distributive law may be used for checking the addition or subtraction of matrices:

$$(a + b)1 = a1 + b1 \tag{2.9.24}$$

The distributive law may also be used for checking the addition or subtraction of matrices by using rows of column sums:

$$1'(a + b) = 1'a + 1'b \tag{2.9.25}$$

2.9.11 The Transpose of the Product of Any Number of Matrices. This is the product of their transposes in reverse order:

$$a = a_1 a_2 \cdots a_n \tag{2.9.26}$$

$$a' = a_n' \cdots a_2' a_1' \tag{2.9.27}$$

2.10 Special Matrix Products

It is convenient to see how the rules for matrix multiplication are simplified for special types of matrices and vectors.

2.10.1 The Product of a Matrix and Its Transpose. If the natural order of a matrix is premultiplied by its transpose, the product is called the *minor product moment* of the matrix. The minor product moment of a matrix is symmetrical.

$$(a'a)' = a'a \tag{2.10.1}$$

A numerical example of the minor product moment of a matrix is given in Fig. 2.10.1.

$$\begin{bmatrix} 3 & 1 & 2 \\ 1 & 4 & 2 \end{bmatrix} \begin{bmatrix} 3 & 1 \\ 1 & 4 \\ 2 & 2 \end{bmatrix} = \begin{bmatrix} 14 & 11 \\ 11 & 21 \end{bmatrix}$$

$$a' \qquad\qquad a \qquad\qquad a'a$$

FIG. 2.10.1

If the natural order of a matrix is postmultiplied by its transpose, the product is called the *major product moment* of the matrix. The major product moment of a matrix is symmetrical.

$$(aa')' = aa' \tag{2.10.2}$$

A numerical example is given in Fig. 2.10.2.

$$\begin{bmatrix} 3 & 1 \\ 1 & 4 \\ 2 & 2 \end{bmatrix} \begin{bmatrix} 3 & 1 & 2 \\ 1 & 4 & 2 \end{bmatrix} = \begin{bmatrix} 10 & 7 & 8 \\ 7 & 17 & 10 \\ 8 & 10 & 8 \end{bmatrix}$$

$$a \qquad\qquad a' \qquad\qquad aa'$$

FIG. 2.10.2

2.10.2 Inequality of Major and Minor Product Moments of Matrices. In general, the major and minor product moments of matrices are not equal.

$$aa' \neq a'a \tag{2.10.3}$$

The order of the minor product moment of a matrix is equal to the width of the matrix. The order of the major product moment of a matrix is equal to its height.

2.10.3 The Product of a Symmetric Matrix Pre- and Postmultiplied by a Matrix and Its Transpose. This is a symmetric matrix. If we let s be a symmetric matrix, this rule is indicated by

$$(asa')' = asa' \tag{2.10.4}$$

2.10.4 Square Products of Matrices. Given the matrices x and y, assume that the products $x'y$ and yx' exist. Then we have the following conclusions: $x'y$ is a square matrix; yx' is a square matrix; x and y are of the same order; the products $y'x$ and xy' exist.

The products $x'y$ and $y'x$ are called the *minor products* of the matrices. The products xy' and yx' are called the *major products*.

2.10.5 The Trace of a Matrix.

The sum of the diagonal elements of a square matrix is called the *trace* of a matrix. The trace of a matrix is equal to the trace of its transpose. The trace of the sum of matrices is the sum of their traces. The trace of the minor product of two matrices is equal to the trace of the major product.

$$tr\ ab' = tr\ b'a \tag{2.10.5}$$

The trace of a major product moment of a matrix is equal to the trace of the minor product moment of the matrix.

$$tr\ D_{aa'} = tr\ D_{a'a} \tag{2.10.6}$$

The trace of a product of two matrices is the sum of products of corresponding elements of the two matrices.

The trace of a product moment of a matrix is the sum of squares of its elements.

2.10.6 Products Involving Vectors.

In premultiplication of a matrix by a vector, the vector must be a row vector whose order is the height of the matrix. The product is a row vector whose order is the width of the matrix. A diagrammatic example is given in Fig. 2.10.3.

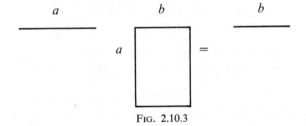

Fig. 2.10.3

In postmultiplication of a matrix by a vector, the vector must be a column whose order is the width of the matrix. The product is a column whose order is the height of the matrix. A diagrammatic example is given in Fig. 2.10.4.

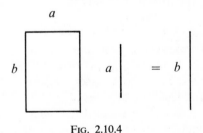

Fig. 2.10.4

In pre- and postmultiplication of a matrix by a vector, the prefactor must be a row vector and the postfactor must be a column vector.

2.10.7 Multiplication of a Matrix by a Unit Vector. Premultiplication of a matrix by a unit vector gives a row vector whose elements are the sums of corresponding column elements of the matrix. A numerical example is given in Fig. 2.10.5.

$$[1 \quad 1 \quad 1] \begin{bmatrix} 2 & 4 \\ 3 & 2 \\ 1 & 3 \end{bmatrix} = [6 \quad 9]$$

FIG. 2.10.5

Postmultiplication of a matrix by a unit vector gives a column vector whose elements are the sums of corresponding row elements of the matrix. A numerical example is given in Fig. 2.10.6.

$$\begin{bmatrix} 2 & 4 \\ 3 & 2 \\ 1 & 3 \end{bmatrix} \begin{bmatrix} 1 \\ 1 \end{bmatrix} = \begin{bmatrix} 6 \\ 5 \\ 4 \end{bmatrix}$$

FIG. 2.10.6

Pre- and postmultiplication of a matrix by a unit vector is a scalar which is the sum of all elements in the matrix. A numerical example is given in Fig. 2.10.7.

$$[1 \quad 1 \quad 1] \begin{bmatrix} 2 & 4 \\ 3 & 2 \\ 1 & 3 \end{bmatrix} \begin{bmatrix} 1 \\ 1 \end{bmatrix} = 15$$

FIG. 2.10.7

2.10.8 Multiplication of a Matrix by an Elementary Vector. Premultiplication of a matrix by an elementary vector gives a row vector which is the row vector of the matrix corresponding to the unit element in the elementary vector.

$$e_i' X = X_{i.}'$$
$$(2.10.7)$$

A numerical example is given in Fig. 2.10.8.

$$[0 \quad 1 \quad 0 \quad 0]\begin{bmatrix} 1 & 3 & 5 \\ 2 & 6 & 4 \\ 5 & 7 & 6 \\ 4 & 3 & 2 \end{bmatrix} = [2 \quad 6 \quad 4]$$

FIG. 2.10.8

Postmultiplication of a matrix by an elementary vector gives a column vector which yields the column of the matrix corresponding to the position of the unit element in the elementary vector.

$$Xe_i = X_{.i} \tag{2.10.8}$$

A numerical example is given in Fig. 2.10.9.

$$\begin{bmatrix} 1 & 3 & 5 \\ 2 & 6 & 4 \\ 5 & 7 & 6 \\ 4 & 3 & 2 \end{bmatrix}\begin{bmatrix} 0 \\ 0 \\ 1 \end{bmatrix} = \begin{bmatrix} 5 \\ 4 \\ 6 \\ 2 \end{bmatrix}$$

FIG. 2.10.9

Pre- and postmultiplication of a matrix by two elementary vectors gives a scalar which is the element from the row of the matrix corresponding to the position of the unit element in the prefactor and from the column corresponding to the position of the unit element in the postfactor.

$$e_i' X e_j = X_{ij} \tag{2.10.9}$$

A numerical example is given in Fig. 2.10.10.

$$[0 \quad 1 \quad 0 \quad 0]\begin{bmatrix} 1 & 2 & 3 \\ 2 & 6 & 4 \\ 5 & 7 & 6 \\ 4 & 3 & 2 \end{bmatrix}\begin{bmatrix} 0 \\ 0 \\ 1 \end{bmatrix} = 4$$

FIG. 2.10.10

2.10.9   Products Involving Diagonal Matrices. If a matrix is premultiplied by a diagonal matrix, each element in the ith row of the product is the corresponding element in the matrix multiplied by the ith element of the diagonal matrix.

$$\begin{bmatrix} D_1 & 0 & \cdots & 0 \\ 0 & D_2 & \cdots & 0 \\ \cdots & \cdots & \cdots & \cdots \\ 0 & 0 & 0 & D_n \end{bmatrix} \begin{bmatrix} a_{11} & a_{12} & \cdots & a_{1m} \\ a_{21} & a_{22} & \cdots & a_{2m} \\ \cdots & \cdots & \cdots & \cdots \\ a_{n1} & a_{n2} & \cdots & a_{nm} \end{bmatrix} = \begin{bmatrix} D_1 a_{11} & D_1 a_{12} & \cdots & D_1 a_{1m} \\ D_2 a_{21} & D_2 a_{22} & \cdots & D_2 a_{2m} \\ \cdots & \cdots & \cdots & \cdots \\ D_n a_{n1} & D_n a_{n2} & \cdots & D_n a_{nm} \end{bmatrix}$$

(2.10.10)

A numerical example is given in Fig. 2.10.11.

$$\begin{bmatrix} 3 & 0 & 0 \\ 0 & 2 & 0 \\ 0 & 0 & 4 \end{bmatrix} \begin{bmatrix} 2 & 4 & 3 & 1 \\ 6 & 2 & 5 & 2 \\ 2 & 3 & 4 & 1 \end{bmatrix} = \begin{bmatrix} 6 & 12 & 9 & 3 \\ 12 & 4 & 10 & 4 \\ 8 & 12 & 16 & 4 \end{bmatrix}$$

FIG. 2.10.11

If a matrix is postmultiplied by a diagonal matrix, each element in the jth column of the product is the corresponding element from the matrix multiplied by the jth element of the diagonal matrix.

$$\begin{bmatrix} a_{11} & a_{12} & \cdots & a_{1m} \\ a_{21} & a_{22} & \cdots & a_{2m} \\ \cdots & \cdots & \cdots & \cdots \\ a_{n1} & a_{n2} & \cdots & a_{nm} \end{bmatrix} \begin{bmatrix} D_1 & 0 & \cdots & 0 \\ 0 & D_2 & \cdots & 0 \\ \cdots & \cdots & \cdots & \cdots \\ 0 & 0 & \cdots & D_m \end{bmatrix} = \begin{bmatrix} a_{11}D_1 & a_{12}D_2 & \cdots & a_{1m}D_m \\ a_{21}D_1 & a_{22}D_2 & \cdots & a_{2m}D_m \\ \cdots & \cdots & \cdots & \cdots \\ a_{n1}D_1 & a_{n2}D_2 & \cdots & a_{nm}D_m \end{bmatrix}$$

(2.10.11)

A numerical example is given in Fig. 2.10.12.

$$\begin{bmatrix} 2 & 3 & 6 \\ 1 & 5 & 2 \\ 4 & 2 & 3 \end{bmatrix} \begin{bmatrix} 2 & 0 & 0 \\ 0 & 4 & 0 \\ 0 & 0 & 3 \end{bmatrix} = \begin{bmatrix} 4 & 12 & 18 \\ 2 & 20 & 6 \\ 8 & 8 & 9 \end{bmatrix}$$

FIG. 2.10.12

If a matrix is pre- and postmultiplied by a diagonal matrix, the ijth element of the product is the corresponding element from the matrix multiplied by the ith diagonal element of the prefactor and the jth diagonal element of the postfactor.

$$\begin{bmatrix} D_1 & 0 & \cdots & 0 \\ 0 & D_2 & \cdots & 0 \\ \cdots & \cdots & \cdots & \cdots \\ 0 & 0 & \cdots & D_n \end{bmatrix} \begin{bmatrix} a_{11} & a_{12} & \cdots & a_{1m} \\ a_{21} & a_{22} & \cdots & a_{2m} \\ \cdots & \cdots & \cdots & \cdots \\ a_{n1} & a_{n2} & \cdots & a_{nm} \end{bmatrix} \begin{bmatrix} d_1 & 0 & \cdots & 0 \\ 0 & d_2 & \cdots & 0 \\ \cdots & \cdots & \cdots & \cdots \\ 0 & 0 & \cdots & d_m \end{bmatrix}$$

$$= \begin{bmatrix} D_1 d_1 a_{11} & D_1 d_2 a_{12} & \cdots & D_1 d_m a_{1m} \\ D_2 d_1 a_{21} & D_2 d_2 a_{22} & \cdots & D_2 d_m a_{2m} \\ \cdots & \cdots & \cdots & \cdots \\ D_n d_1 a_{n1} & D_n d_2 a_{n2} & \cdots & D_n d_m a_{nm} \end{bmatrix}$$

(2.10.12)

A numerical example is given in Fig. 2.10.13.

$$\begin{bmatrix} 2 & 0 & 0 \\ 0 & 3 & 0 \\ 0 & 0 & 4 \end{bmatrix} \begin{bmatrix} 2 & 3 \\ 1 & 5 \\ 4 & 2 \end{bmatrix} \begin{bmatrix} 1 & 0 \\ 0 & 5 \end{bmatrix} = \begin{bmatrix} 2 \times 2 \times 1 & 2 \times 3 \times 5 \\ 3 \times 1 \times 1 & 3 \times 5 \times 5 \\ 4 \times 4 \times 1 & 4 \times 2 \times 5 \end{bmatrix} = \begin{bmatrix} 4 & 30 \\ 3 & 75 \\ 16 & 40 \end{bmatrix}$$

Fig. 2.10.13

2.10.10 Products in Which All Factors are Diagonal. The product of any number of diagonal matrices is a diagonal matrix whose ith element is the product of the ith elements of the matrices.

$$D_a D_b \cdots D_z = D_c \qquad (2.10.13)$$

A numerical example is given in Fig. 2.10.14.

$$\begin{bmatrix} 3 & 0 & 0 \\ 0 & 1 & 0 \\ 0 & 0 & 2 \end{bmatrix} \begin{bmatrix} 4 & 0 & 0 \\ 0 & 3 & 0 \\ 0 & 0 & 2 \end{bmatrix} \begin{bmatrix} 1 & 0 & 0 \\ 0 & 2 & 0 \\ 0 & 0 & 4 \end{bmatrix} = \begin{bmatrix} 12 & 0 & 0 \\ 0 & 6 & 0 \\ 0 & 0 & 16 \end{bmatrix}$$

Fig. 2.10.14

All diagonal matrices of the same order are commutative with one another for multiplication.

$$D_a D_b D_c = D_b D_a D_c = D_c D_b D_a = D_a D_c D_b = D_b D_c D_a = D_c D_a D_b \qquad (2.10.14)$$

2.10.11 Powers of Diagonal Matrices. Any power of a diagonal matrix with no vanishing diagonal elements is obtained by raising each diagonal element to the corresponding power. For example,

$$\begin{bmatrix} a_1 & 0 & \cdots & 0 \\ 0 & a_2 & \cdots & 0 \\ \cdots & \cdots & \cdots & \cdots \\ 0 & 0 & \cdots & a_n \end{bmatrix} = \begin{bmatrix} a_1{}^k & 0 & \cdots & 0 \\ 0 & a_2{}^k & \cdots & 0 \\ \cdots & \cdots & \cdots & \cdots \\ 0 & 0 & \cdots & a_n{}^k \end{bmatrix} \qquad (2.10.15)$$

The inverse of a diagonal matrix with no vanishing diagonal elements is obtained by taking the reciprocal of each diagonal element.

$$D_a{}^{-1} = \begin{bmatrix} a_1{}^{-1} & 0 & \cdots & 0 \\ 0 & a_2{}^{-1} & \cdots & 0 \\ \cdots & \cdots & \cdots & \cdots \\ 0 & 0 & \cdots & a_n{}^{-1} \end{bmatrix} = \begin{bmatrix} \dfrac{1}{a_1} & 0 & \cdots & 0 \\ 0 & \dfrac{1}{a_2} & \cdots & 0 \\ \cdots & \cdots & \cdots & \cdots \\ 0 & 0 & \cdots & \dfrac{1}{a_n} \end{bmatrix} \qquad (2.10.16)$$

A numerical example is given in Fig. 2.10.15.

$$
\begin{bmatrix} 2 & 0 & 0 \\ 0 & 4 & 0 \\ 0 & 0 & 1 \end{bmatrix}^{-1} = \begin{bmatrix} .5 & 0 & 0 \\ 0 & .25 & 0 \\ 0 & 0 & 1 \end{bmatrix}
$$

Fig. 2.10.15

Any power of a diagonal matrix is obtained by taking the same power of each diagonal element.

$$
D_a^{-1/2} = \begin{bmatrix} a_1^{-1/2} & 0 & \cdots & 0 \\ 0 & a_2^{-1/2} & \cdots & 0 \\ \cdots & \cdots & \cdots & \cdots \\ 0 & 0 & \cdots & a_n^{-1/2} \end{bmatrix} = \begin{bmatrix} \dfrac{1}{\sqrt{a_1}} & 0 & \cdots & 0 \\ 0 & \dfrac{1}{\sqrt{a_2}} & \cdots & 0 \\ \cdots & \cdots & \cdots & \cdots \\ 0 & 0 & \cdots & \dfrac{1}{\sqrt{a_n}} \end{bmatrix} \quad (2.10.17)
$$

A numerical example is given in Fig. 2.10.16.

$$
\begin{bmatrix} 4 & 0 & 0 \\ 0 & 16 & 0 \\ 0 & 0 & 9 \end{bmatrix}^{-1/2} = \begin{bmatrix} .5 & 0 & 0 \\ 0 & .25 & 0 \\ 0 & 0 & .33 \end{bmatrix}
$$

Fig. 2.10.16

2.10.12 Matrix Products Involving Scalar Matrices. If a matrix is pre- or postmultiplied by a scalar matrix, each element of the matrix is multiplied by the scalar diagonal constant. A numerical example is given in Fig. 2.10.17.

$$
\begin{bmatrix} 4 & 2 & 1 \\ 3 & 1 & 6 \\ 2 & 4 & 7 \\ 1 & 3 & 1 \end{bmatrix} \begin{bmatrix} 2 & 0 & 0 \\ 0 & 2 & 0 \\ 0 & 0 & 2 \end{bmatrix} = \begin{bmatrix} 8 & 4 & 2 \\ 6 & 2 & 12 \\ 4 & 8 & 14 \\ 2 & 6 & 2 \end{bmatrix}
$$

Fig. 2.10.17

A scalar matrix is commutative only with square matrices.

2.10.13 Products Involving Scalar Quantities. Multiplication of any matrix by a scalar quantity consists of multiplying each element of the matrix by the scalar. A numerical example is given in Fig. 2.10.18.

$$2\begin{bmatrix} 4 & 3 & 7 \\ 4 & 2 & 1 \\ 3 & 1 & 4 \\ 4 & 3 & 2 \end{bmatrix} = \begin{bmatrix} 8 & 6 & 14 \\ 8 & 4 & 2 \\ 6 & 2 & 8 \\ 8 & 6 & 4 \end{bmatrix}$$

Fig. 2.10.18

All scalar quantities commute with all matrices and with one another. If a and b are scalars, and x and y are matrices which are conformable for multiplication, this rule is indicated by Fig. 2.10.19.

$$abxy = baxy = axby = bxay = bxya = xbya = xayb = xyab$$

Fig. 2.10.19

2.10.14 Multiplication by Identity Matrices.
Multiplication of a matrix by an identity matrix leaves the matrix unchanged.

$$IA = AI = A \tag{2.10.18}$$

Identity matrices commute only with square matrices.
Any power of an identity matrix is the identity matrix:

$$I^k = I \tag{2.10.19}$$

2.10.15 Multiplication by the Sign Matrix.
Premultiplication of a matrix by a sign matrix changes the signs of the elements in the rows corresponding to the -1's.

$$\begin{bmatrix} 1 & 0 & 0 \\ 0 & -1 & 0 \\ 0 & 0 & 1 \end{bmatrix}\begin{bmatrix} 4 & 2 \\ 2 & 1 \\ 3 & 4 \end{bmatrix} = \begin{bmatrix} 4 & 2 \\ -2 & -1 \\ 3 & 4 \end{bmatrix}$$

Fig. 2.10.20

Postmultiplication of a matrix by a sign matrix changes the signs of the elements in the columns corresponding to the -1's.

$$\begin{bmatrix} 4 & 3 & 1 \\ 3 & 5 & 2 \\ 3 & 1 & 6 \end{bmatrix}\begin{bmatrix} 1 & 0 & 0 \\ 0 & -1 & 0 \\ 0 & 0 & -1 \end{bmatrix} = \begin{bmatrix} 4 & -3 & -1 \\ 3 & -5 & -2 \\ 3 & -1 & -6 \end{bmatrix}$$

Fig. 2.10.21

Pre- and postmultiplication of a square matrix by the same sign matrix leaves the principal diagonal unchanged.

$$\begin{bmatrix} 1 & 0 & 0 & 0 \\ 0 & -1 & 0 & 0 \\ 0 & 0 & 1 & 0 \\ 0 & 0 & 0 & -1 \end{bmatrix} \begin{bmatrix} 4 & 2 & 3 & 4 \\ 2 & 3 & 7 & 1 \\ 3 & 7 & 4 & 2 \\ 4 & 1 & 2 & 2 \end{bmatrix} \begin{bmatrix} 1 & 0 & 0 & 0 \\ 0 & -1 & 0 & 0 \\ 0 & 0 & 1 & 0 \\ 0 & 0 & 0 & -1 \end{bmatrix}$$

$$= \begin{bmatrix} 4 & 2 & 3 & 4 \\ -2 & -3 & -7 & -1 \\ 3 & 7 & 4 & 2 \\ -4 & -1 & -2 & -2 \end{bmatrix} \begin{bmatrix} 1 & 0 & 0 & 0 \\ 0 & -1 & 0 & 0 \\ 0 & 0 & 1 & 0 \\ 0 & 0 & 0 & -1 \end{bmatrix} = \begin{bmatrix} 4 & -2 & 3 & -4 \\ -2 & 3 & -7 & 1 \\ 3 & -7 & 4 & -2 \\ -4 & 1 & -2 & 2 \end{bmatrix}$$

FIG. 2.10.22

A sign matrix raised to a positive or a negative even power yields the identity matrix.

$$i^k = i^{-k} = I \qquad (2.10.20)$$

A numerical example is given in Fig. 2.10.23.

$$\begin{bmatrix} 1 & 0 & 0 \\ 0 & -1 & 0 \\ 0 & 0 & -1 \end{bmatrix} \begin{bmatrix} 1 & 0 & 0 \\ 0 & -1 & 0 \\ 0 & 0 & -1 \end{bmatrix} = \begin{bmatrix} 1 & 0 & 0 \\ 0 & 1 & 0 \\ 0 & 0 & 1 \end{bmatrix}$$

FIG. 2.10.23

A sign matrix raised to a positive or a negative odd power is the same sign matrix.

$$i^k = i^{-k} = i \qquad (2.10.21)$$

A numerical example is given in Fig. 2.10.24.

$$\begin{bmatrix} 1 & 0 & 0 \\ 1 & -1 & 0 \\ 0 & 0 & -1 \end{bmatrix}^3 = \begin{bmatrix} 1 & 0 & 0 \\ 0 & -1 & 0 \\ 0 & 0 & -1 \end{bmatrix} \begin{bmatrix} 1 & 0 & 0 \\ 0 & -1 & 0 \\ 0 & 0 & -1 \end{bmatrix} \begin{bmatrix} 1 & 0 & 0 \\ 0 & -1 & 0 \\ 0 & 0 & -1 \end{bmatrix}$$

or

$$\begin{bmatrix} 1 & 0 & 0 \\ 0 & -1 & 0 \\ 0 & 0 & -1 \end{bmatrix}^3 = \begin{bmatrix} 1 & 0 & 0 \\ 0 & 1 & 0 \\ 0 & 0 & 1 \end{bmatrix} \begin{bmatrix} 1 & 0 & 0 \\ 0 & -1 & 0 \\ 0 & 0 & -1 \end{bmatrix} = \begin{bmatrix} 1 & 0 & 0 \\ 0 & -1 & 0 \\ 0 & 0 & -1 \end{bmatrix}$$

FIG. 2.10.24

2.10.16   Multiplication by a Permutation Matrix. If a matrix is premultiplied by a permutation matrix, its columns are interchanged in the same way as the columns of an identity matrix were interchanged to obtain the permutation matrix. See Fig. 2.10.25.

$$\begin{bmatrix} 0 & 0 & 1 & 0 \\ 0 & 1 & 0 & 0 \\ 0 & 0 & 0 & 1 \\ 1 & 0 & 0 & 0 \end{bmatrix} \begin{bmatrix} 2 & 4 & 1 \\ 3 & 2 & 3 \\ 1 & 4 & 5 \\ 6 & 5 & 2 \end{bmatrix} = \begin{bmatrix} 1 & 4 & 5 \\ 3 & 2 & 3 \\ 6 & 5 & 2 \\ 2 & 4 & 1 \end{bmatrix}$$

Fig. 2.10.25

Any permutation matrix pre- or postmultiplied by its transpose gives the identity matrix.

$$\pi\pi' = I \tag{2.10.22}$$

$$\pi'\pi = I \tag{2.10.23}$$

A numerical example is given in Fig. 2.10.26.

$$\underbrace{\begin{bmatrix} 0 & 0 & 1 & 0 \\ 0 & 1 & 0 & 0 \\ 0 & 0 & 0 & 1 \\ 1 & 0 & 0 & 0 \end{bmatrix}}_{\pi} \underbrace{\begin{bmatrix} 0 & 0 & 0 & 1 \\ 0 & 1 & 0 & 0 \\ 1 & 0 & 0 & 0 \\ 0 & 0 & 1 & 0 \end{bmatrix}}_{\pi'} = \underbrace{\begin{bmatrix} 1 & 0 & 0 & 0 \\ 0 & 1 & 0 & 0 \\ 0 & 0 & 1 & 0 \\ 0 & 0 & 0 & 1 \end{bmatrix}}_{I}$$

Fig. 2.10.26

Any permutation matrix pre- or postmultiplied by a unit vector yields the same unit vector.

$$\pi 1 = 1 \tag{2.10.24}$$

$$1'\pi = 1' \tag{2.10.25}$$

2.10.17   Multiplication by an Elementary Vector. A matrix postmultiplied by an elementary vector gives the ith column vector of the matrix.

$$ae_i = a_{.i} \tag{2.10.26}$$

A matrix premultiplied by an elementary vector gives the jth row of the matrix:

$$e_j'a = a_{j.}' \tag{2.10.27}$$

2.10.18   The Powers of a Matrix. A square matrix may be raised to any power which is a positive whole number by multiplying the matrix by itself the number of times indicated by the exponent.

The laws of exponents for scalars hold for square matrices.

$$a^x a^y = a^{x+y}$$ (2.10.28)

$$[a^x]^y = a^{xy}$$ (2.10.29)

Chapter 3

Matrix Structure and Solutions

In the previous chapter we became familiar with a particular notation and terminology of matrix algebra and also with the operations of transposition, partitioning, addition, subtraction, and multiplication. In this chapter we shall turn our attention to further aspects of matrices and matrix operations which are useful in factor analysis.

3.1 Orthogonal Matrices

3.1.1 Orthogonal Vectors. Two vectors are said to be orthogonal to one another if their minor product is 0.

$$V_1'V_2 = 0 \tag{3.1.1}$$

3.1.2 Normal Vectors. A vector is said to be normal if its minor product moment is 1. An example of a normal vector is given in Fig. 3.1.1.

$$\begin{bmatrix} \dfrac{1}{\sqrt{3}} & \dfrac{1}{\sqrt{3}} & \dfrac{1}{\sqrt{3}} \end{bmatrix} \begin{bmatrix} \dfrac{1}{\sqrt{3}} \\ \dfrac{1}{\sqrt{3}} \\ \dfrac{1}{\sqrt{3}} \end{bmatrix} = 1$$

FIG. 3.1.1

Any vector V may be transformed into a normal vector U by

$$U = \frac{V}{\sqrt{V'V}} \tag{3.1.2}$$

74

3.1.3 Definition of Orthogonal Matrices. A vertical matrix X is said to be orthogonal if its minor product moment is a diagonal matrix. If X is an orthogonal matrix,

$$X'X = D \qquad (3.1.3)$$

An example of the minor product moment of an orthogonal matrix is given by Fig. 3.1.2.

$$X = \begin{bmatrix} 1 & 1 \\ 1 & 2 \\ 1 & -3 \end{bmatrix}$$

$$X'X = \begin{bmatrix} 1 & 1 & 1 \\ 1 & 2 & -3 \end{bmatrix} \begin{bmatrix} 1 & 1 \\ 1 & 2 \\ 1 & -3 \end{bmatrix} = \begin{bmatrix} 3 & 0 \\ 0 & 14 \end{bmatrix}$$

FIG. 3.1.2

3.1.4 Orthonormal Matrices. An orthonormal matrix is one whose minor product moment is the identity matrix. If Q is an orthonormal matrix,

$$Q'Q = I \qquad (3.1.4)$$

3.1.5 The Major Product Moment of a Vertical Orthonormal Matrix Q. The major product moment of a vertical orthonormal matrix cannot be an identity matrix. We have the inequality

$$QQ' \neq I \qquad (3.1.5)$$

The major product moment of an orthonormal matrix is a symmetric *idempotent matrix.* An idempotent matrix is one which, when raised to any power, is the matrix itself. This is indicated by the following equation, in which the exponent n is a positive integral value.

$$(QQ')^n = QQ' \qquad (3.1.6)$$

3.1.6 Square Orthogonal Matrices. If X is a square orthogonal, but not orthonormal, matrix such that $X'X$ is a diagonal matrix, then XX' cannot be diagonal. Figure 3.1.3 is an example of the major and minor product moment of a square orthogonal matrix.

$$X = \begin{bmatrix} \sqrt{2} & -\dfrac{1}{2} \\ \sqrt{2} & +\dfrac{1}{2} \end{bmatrix}$$

$$X'X = \begin{bmatrix} 4 & 0 \\ 0 & \dfrac{1}{2} \end{bmatrix} = D$$

$$XX' = \begin{bmatrix} \dfrac{9}{4} & \dfrac{7}{4} \\ \dfrac{7}{4} & \dfrac{9}{4} \end{bmatrix}$$

FIG. 3.1.3

If Q is a square orthonormal matrix such that $Q'Q = I$, then also $QQ' = I$. A numerical example is given in Figs. 3.1.4 and 3.1.5.

$$Q'Q = \begin{bmatrix} \dfrac{1}{\sqrt{2}} & \dfrac{1}{\sqrt{2}} \\ \dfrac{-1}{\sqrt{2}} & \dfrac{1}{\sqrt{2}} \end{bmatrix} \begin{bmatrix} \dfrac{1}{\sqrt{2}} & \dfrac{-1}{\sqrt{2}} \\ \dfrac{1}{\sqrt{2}} & \dfrac{1}{\sqrt{2}} \end{bmatrix} = \begin{bmatrix} 1 & 0 \\ 0 & 1 \end{bmatrix}$$

FIG. 3.1.4

$$QQ' = \begin{bmatrix} \dfrac{1}{\sqrt{2}} & \dfrac{-1}{\sqrt{2}} \\ \dfrac{1}{\sqrt{2}} & \dfrac{1}{\sqrt{2}} \end{bmatrix} \begin{bmatrix} \dfrac{1}{\sqrt{2}} & \dfrac{1}{\sqrt{2}} \\ \dfrac{-1}{\sqrt{2}} & \dfrac{1}{\sqrt{2}} \end{bmatrix} = \begin{bmatrix} 1 & 0 \\ 0 & 1 \end{bmatrix}$$

FIG. 3.1.5

An infinite number of square orthonormal matrices of order m exist.

3.1.7 Special Types of Square Orthonormal Matrices. The sign matrix i is a square orthonormal matrix.

The permutation matrix π is a square orthonormal matrix.

If we let V be a vector, then a square orthonormal matrix is given by

$$A = I - \frac{2VV'}{V'V} \tag{3.1.7}$$

An example of this type of square orthonormal matrix is Fig. 3.1.6.

$$\left[\begin{pmatrix} 1 & 0 & 0 \\ 0 & 1 & 0 \\ 0 & 0 & 1 \end{pmatrix} - 2\frac{\begin{pmatrix} 1 & 1 & 1 \\ 1 & 1 & 1 \\ 1 & 1 & 1 \end{pmatrix}}{3} \right] = \begin{bmatrix} \frac{1}{3} & -\frac{2}{3} & -\frac{2}{3} \\ -\frac{2}{3} & \frac{1}{3} & -\frac{2}{3} \\ -\frac{2}{3} & -\frac{2}{3} & \frac{1}{3} \end{bmatrix}$$

FIG. 3.1.6

3.1.8 Products of Orthonormal Matrices. The product of any number of square orthonormal matrices is a square orthonormal matrix.

Given the major product moment $Z = XY'$ of the vertical orthonormal matrices X and Y, the following equalities are true:

$$(Z'Z)^n = Z'Z \qquad (3.1.8)$$

$$(ZZ')^n = ZZ' \qquad (3.1.9)$$

Neither of the product moments of the minor product of two vertical orthonormal matrices has simple properties.

Pre- or postmultiplication of a rectangular orthonormal matrix by a square orthonormal matrix yields a rectangular orthonormal matrix.

3.1.9 Products of Matrices. Suppose we are given the matrix equation $XY = Z$. There then exist an infinite number of pairs of factors $X_i Y_i$ whose product is Z. Let a be square orthonormal.

$$XY = Z \qquad (3.1.10)$$

$$Xa = X_i \qquad (3.1.11)$$

$$a'Y = Y_i \qquad (3.1.12)$$

$$X_i Y_i = Z \qquad (3.1.13)$$

If a nonhorizontal matrix X is postmultiplied by a square orthonormal matrix a, the major product moment of the product is the same as the major product moment of X.

$$Y = Xa \qquad (3.1.14)$$

$$YY' = Xaa'X' \qquad (3.1.15)$$

$$YY' = XX' \qquad (3.1.16)$$

If a nonhorizontal matrix X is premultiplied by a square orthonormal matrix Q, the minor product moment of the product is the same as the minor product moment of X. The proof is analogous to that of the major product moment.

If a symmetric matrix S is either the major or minor product moment of a matrix, it is also the major or minor product moment of each of an infinite number of matrices.

If we pre- or postmultiply a matrix X by a square orthonormal matrix to get another matrix, the trace of either product moment of the second matrix will be the same as the trace of either product moment of X. Thus if a and b are orthonormal matrices, and we have

$$Xa = Y \tag{3.1.17}$$

$$bX = Z \tag{3.1.18}$$

the following relationships hold:

$$1'D_{x'x}1 = 1'D_{y'y}1 \tag{3.1.19}$$

$$1'D_{xx'}1 = 1'D_{zz'}1 \tag{3.1.20}$$

If a matrix X is postmultiplied by a square orthonormal matrix a to get a matrix Y, the sum of the squares of the column sums of X and Y are equal:

$$(1'X)(X'1) = (1'Y)(Y'1) \tag{3.1.21}$$

If a matrix X is premultiplied by a square orthonormal matrix b to get a matrix Z, the sum of the squares of row sums of X and Z are equal:

$$(1'X')(X1) = (1'Z')(Z1) \tag{3.1.22}$$

3.1.10 Matrices Orthogonal to One Another.

If any orthogonal matrix X is partitioned into a type 3 row vector, the submatrices are mutually orthogonal. Suppose we indicate this partitioning by

$$X = [X_1 \quad X_2 \quad \cdots \quad X_s] \tag{3.1.23}$$

Then we obtain

$$\begin{bmatrix} X_1'X_1 & X_1'X_2 & \cdots & X_1'X_s \\ X_2'X_1 & X_2'X_2 & \cdots & X_2'X_s \\ \cdots & \cdots & \cdots & \cdots \\ X_s'X_1 & X_s'X_2 & \cdots & X_s'X_s \end{bmatrix} = \begin{bmatrix} D_1 & 0 & \cdots & 0 \\ 0' & D_2 & \cdots & 0 \\ \cdots & \cdots & \cdots & \cdots \\ 0' & 0' & \cdots & D_s \end{bmatrix} \tag{3.1.24}$$

Two matrices, Y_1 and Y_2, may be orthogonal to one another even though neither is an orthogonal matrix.

A number of orthogonal matrices of equal height cannot be mutually orthogonal to one another if the sum of their widths is greater than their height.

The major product moment of a vertical matrix cannot be a diagonal matrix.

3.2 Rank of a Matrix

One of the fundamental concepts in factor analysis and in the various special cases of factor analysis, such as multiple regression and discriminant function analysis, is the concept of rank. The definition of the rank of a matrix is ordinarily given in terms of determinants. We do not use the concept of determinants in this book. Before defining the rank of the matrix we shall first consider some simple propositions about the factors of a matrix.

3.2.1   The Factors of a Matrix.   Any matrix can be expressed as the product of two factors whose common order is not greater than the smaller order of the matrix. An infinite number of such pairs of factors exist, as shown in Section 3.1.9.

Some matrices may be expressed as the major product of two matrices. This also may be done with any one of infinitely many pairs of such products.

3.2.2   Definition of Rank.   The rank of a matrix is the smallest common order among all pairs of matrices whose product is the matrix.

3.2.3   The Maximum Rank of a Matrix.   By definition, the rank of a matrix cannot be greater than the smaller of the number of columns or rows which do not have all 0 elements. The rank of the data matrix cannot be greater than the number of columns or rows, whichever is less.

3.2.4   Basic Matrices.   A basic matrix is one whose rank is equal to its smaller order. This means that a basic matrix cannot be expressed as the product of two matrices whose common order is less than the smaller order of the matrix. Data matrices are usually basic.

3.2.5   Types of Basic Matrices.   The following types of matrices are always basic: orthogonal matrices, including rectangular and square matrices; orthonormal matrices, including rectangular, square, and permutation matrices; diagonal matrices, including general diagonal matrices; scalar matrices, identity matrices, and sign matrices; and triangular matrices, including the square triangular and the partial triangular matrix. This assumes that none of the diagonal elements of diagonal and triangular matrices is 0 and that none of the diagonal elements of the triangular submatric elements of the partial triangular matrix is 0.

3.2.6   Minimum Rank of a Supermatrix.   The rank of a supermatrix cannot be less than the rank of its submatric element of highest rank.

3.2.7   The Rank of a Product of Matrices. The rank of the product of two or more matrices cannot be greater than the rank of the factor of lowest rank.

The rank of the product of two matrices cannot be less than the sum of their ranks less their common order.

3.2.8   Rank of Special Kinds of Products. The maximum rank of a product of two basic matrices cannot be greater than the smallest of the three dimensions. The maximum possible rank for the product of two horizontal matrices is the height of the prefactor.

The maximum possible rank for the major product of two basic matrices is their common order.

The rank of the product of two vertical basic matrices cannot be greater than the width of the postfactor.

The rank of the product of two basic matrices cannot be less than the sum of the smaller dimensions of each less their common order.

The rank of the major product of basic matrices cannot be less than their common order.

The rank of a minor product of two basic matrices cannot be less than the sum of their distinct orders less their common order.

The product of two vertical basic matrices is a basic matrix. The product of two horizontal basic matrices is a basic matrix.

3.2.9   Ranks of Products Involving Square Basic Matrices. If any basic matrix is pre- or postmultiplied by a square basic matrix, the product is basic.

If a matrix of rank r is pre- or postmultiplied by a square basic matrix, the product is of rank r.

3.2.10   Rank of a Product Moment. The rank of a major or minor product moment of a matrix is the rank of the matrix itself. The major product moment of a vertical matrix cannot be basic.

3.2.11   The Rank of a Sum of Matrices. The rank of a sum of any number of matrices cannot be greater than the sum of their ranks.

The rank of the sum of two matrices cannot be less than the absolute value of the difference between their ranks.

3.3   Finding the Rank of a Matrix

3.3.1   The Triangular Factors of a Matrix. Any matrix pre- and post-multiplied by suitable permutation matrices may be expressed as the major product of triangular type matrices. The common order of the triangular type factors is the rank of the matrix.

3.3.2   Special Case of a Basic Matrix. A matrix may be reduced a row and a column at a time to a matrix with 0 rows and 0 columns, if the leading diagonal for the part of the reduced matrix not consisting of 0 rows and 0 columns is distinct from 0. In general, we have

$$_iX - {_iL} = {_{i+1}X} \tag{3.3.1}$$

$$_iL = \frac{_iX_{.i}\,X_{i.}'}{_iX_{ii}} \tag{3.3.2}$$

This leads to the expression of X as a product of triangular type factors, as indicated below, in which D_a is a diagonal matrix.

$$X_{nm} = T_{nm}D_a^{-1}T_{mn}' \tag{3.3.3}$$

3.3.3   The Special Case of Nonbasic Matrices. If a matrix is nonbasic, the partial triangular factoring yields two partial triangular factors.

3.3.4   The Product of a General Matrix and Permutation Matrices. Any matrix may be reduced successively to one with 0 rows and 0 columns by operations of the type indicated below, in which X_{ab} is the largest element in the matrix or of any particular residual matrix.

$$Y = X - \frac{X_{.b}\,X_{a.}'}{X_{ab}} \tag{3.3.4}$$

By appropriate selection of permutation matrices π_L and π_R, we can always find the triangular factors in which r is the rank of X_{nm}:

$$\pi_L X_{nm}\pi_R = T_{nr}T_{rm}' \tag{3.3.5}$$

3.4   The Basic Structure of a Matrix

In this section we shall develop a concept which is not generally used by mathematicians. This is indeed surprising because of its importance for factor analysis and for the analyses of data matrices in general, and also as an abstract mathematical concept.

3.4.1   Definition of the Basic Structure of a Matrix. We let the matrices P and Q be defined by

$$P'P = I_{rr} \tag{3.4.1}$$

$$Q'Q = I_{rr} \tag{3.4.2}$$

This means that they are orthonormal matrices. We let Δ be a diagonal matrix. Any matrix X can be expressed as the product of three matrices:

$$X = P\Delta Q' \tag{3.4.3}$$

The right side of Eq. 3.4.3 is called the *basic structure* of the matrix. The P and Q' matrices are called the *left* and *right basic orthonormals*, respectively, of X. Δ is called the *basic diagonal* of X.

3.4.2   The Basic Structure of a Nonbasic Matrix.   Every nonbasic matrix may be expressed as a major product of basic matrices Y and Z, each of which may be expressed as the product of its basic structure factors. This is indicated in the following equations, where the F and H matrices are orthonormal.

$$X_{nm} = Y_{nr} Z_{rm} \tag{3.4.4}$$

$$Y_{nr} = H_1 \Delta_Y H_2' \tag{3.4.5}$$

$$Z_{mr} = F_1 \Delta_Z F_2' \tag{3.4.6}$$

Therefore, any nonhorizontal matrix may be expressed as the product, from left to right, of a nonhorizontal orthonormal by a diagonal by a nonvertical orthonormal matrix.

3.4.3   The Basic Diagonal.   The signs of the basic diagonal elements of a matrix may, without loss of generality, all be taken as positive.

The basic diagonal elements of a matrix may, without loss of generality, be taken in descending order of magnitude from upper left to lower right.

The basic diagonal of a matrix is unique for any given matrix.

Any nonhorizontal matrix may be expressed as the product, from left to right, of a nonhorizontal orthonormal, a diagonal, and a nonvertical orthonormal, where the diagonal has all positive elements in descending order of magnitude from upper left to lower right. The order of this diagonal is the rank of the matrix.

If the basic diagonal of a matrix includes sets of equal elements, only the submatrices from the basic orthonormal vectors not corresponding to these sets are unique.

3.4.4   The Basic Structure of the Product Moment Matrix.   Let the basic structure of the matrix X be given by

$$X = P\Delta Q' \tag{3.4.7}$$

The minor product moment of X is given by

$$X'X = Q\Delta^2 Q' \tag{3.4.8}$$

The major product moment of X is given by

$$XX' = P\Delta^2 P' \tag{3.4.9}$$

If we let $\partial = \Delta^2$, the power of any minor product is given by

$$(X'X)^n = Q \, \partial^n Q' \tag{3.4.10}$$

The power of any major product moment is given by

$$(XX')^n = P \, \partial^n P' \tag{3.4.11}$$

3.4.5 Matrices with the Same Orthonormals.

The major and minor products of matrices with the same basic orthonormals are symmetric matrices. If a and b have the same basic orthonormals,

$$a = P\Delta_a Q' \tag{3.4.12}$$

$$b = P\Delta_b Q' \tag{3.4.13}$$

$$ab' = ba' \tag{3.4.14}$$

$$a'b = b'a \tag{3.4.15}$$

Product moment matrices with the same basic orthonormals are commutative with respect to multiplication.

$$S_a = Q \, \partial_a Q' \tag{3.4.16}$$

$$S_b = Q \, \partial_b Q' \tag{3.4.17}$$

$$S_a S_b = S_b S_a \tag{3.4.18}$$

3.4.6 Special Exponents of Gramian Matrices.

A Gramian matrix is one which can be expressed as the product moment of a matrix. Therefore, all product moment matrices are Gramian matrices.

Any power of a Gramian matrix is given by a matrix with the same orthonormals as the original matrix and the corresponding power of the basic diagonal. Let the basic structure of S be given by

$$S = Q \, \vartheta Q' \tag{3.4.19}$$

Then the ath power of S is given by

$$S^a = Q \, \partial^a Q' \tag{3.4.20}$$

The inverse of a basic Gramian matrix S is given by

$$S^{-1} = Q \, \partial^{-1} Q' \tag{3.4.21}$$

3.4.7 The Basic Diagonal and Traces Involving Product Moments.

The sum of the elements in the basic diagonal of a product is the same as the trace of the product moment. Let the basic structure of the minor product moment of X be given by

$$X'X = Q \, \partial Q' \tag{3.4.22}$$

Then the trace of the minor product moment of X is given by

$$tr\,X'X = 1'\,\partial 1 \tag{3.4.23}$$

The trace of any power of a product moment matrix $X'X = Q\,\partial Q'$ is given by

$$tr(XX')^n = tr(X'X)^n = 1'\,\partial^n 1 \tag{3.4.24}$$

3.4.8   Pre- or Postmultiplication by a Square Orthonormal Matrix.
If a matrix is pre- or postmultiplied by a square orthonormal matrix, the basic diagonal of the product is the same as that of the original matrix.

3.5   The Inverse of a Matrix

3.5.1   The General Inverse and the Basic Structure.
The inverse b of a matrix a is defined as a matrix such that the product of the two is equal to the identity matrix.

A concept which is not generally used in mathematics and which has only recently been discussed by a limited group of mathematicians is the concept of the *general inverse*. This is sometimes called the *pseudo inverse*. The general inverse of a matrix X is defined in terms of its basic structure. Suppose we indicate the basic structure of X thusly:

$$X = P\Delta Q' \tag{3.5.1}$$

We define the general inverse of X as:

$$Y' = Q\Delta^{-1}P' \tag{3.5.2}$$

The major product of a matrix X and its general inverse Y' is the major product moment of its left basic orthonormal.

$$XY' = PP' \tag{3.5.3}$$

The minor product of a matrix and its general inverse is the major product moment of its right basic orthonormal.

$$Y'X = QQ' \tag{3.5.4}$$

If X is a basic matrix, the minor product of this matrix with its general inverse is the identity matrix.

$$Y'X = I \tag{3.5.5}$$

3.5.2   The Inverse of a Square Basic Matrix.
A square basic matrix is said to have a *regular inverse* or merely an *inverse*. In this case we have the relations

$$XY' = I \tag{3.5.6}$$

$$Y'X = I \tag{3.5.7}$$

The notation for the regular inverse of a square basic matrix is indicated by

$$XX^{-1} = I \tag{3.5.8}$$

$$X^{-1}X = I \tag{3.5.9}$$

3.5.3 Inverse of the Product of Square Basic Matrices.
The inverse of the product of any number of square basic matrices is the product of their inverse in reverse order.

$$(abcd)^{-1} = d^{-1}c^{-1}b^{-1}a^{-1} \tag{3.5.10}$$

3.5.4 Inverses of Special Types of Matrices.
The inverse of a square orthonormal matrix is the transpose of this matrix:

$$Q^{-1} = Q' \tag{3.5.11}$$

The general inverse of a vertical orthonormal matrix is its transpose.
If P is an orthogonal matrix, its minor product moment is a diagonal matrix:

$$P'P = D \tag{3.5.12}$$

Its general inverse, then, is

$$Y' = D^{-1}P' \tag{3.5.13}$$

3.5.5 The Inverse of an Upper Triangular Matrix.
We let T' be an upper triangular matrix. We then write T':

$$T' = D_T + t' \tag{3.5.14}$$

We define further matrices:

$$-D_T^{-1}t' = v \tag{3.5.15}$$

$$D_T^{-1} = D_u \tag{3.5.16}$$

The inverse B of T' may then be solved by

$$[v \mid D_u]\begin{bmatrix} B \\ \hline I \end{bmatrix} = B \tag{3.5.17}$$

3.5.6 Solution for the Inverse of a Square Basic Matrix.
Let X be a square basic matrix. We express it in terms of its triangular factors:

$$X = T_L T_u \tag{3.5.18}$$

We define the type 3 column supervector a:

$$a = \begin{bmatrix} X \\ \hline I \end{bmatrix} \tag{3.5.19}$$

We then indicate the triangular factoring of a:

$$a = \left[\frac{T_L}{T_u^{-1}} \right] T_u \tag{3.5.20}$$

The inverse of X is then given by

$$X^{-1} = T_u^{-1} T_L^{-1} \tag{3.5.21}$$

This is the product of the triangular factors in reverse order.

3.5.7 Solution of the Inverse of a Basic Product Moment Matrix.

Let X be a product moment matrix expressed in terms of its triangular factors:

$$X = TT' \tag{3.5.22}$$

The triangular factoring of a is shown below.

$$a = \left[\frac{X}{I} \right] = \left[\frac{TT'}{T'^{-1} T'} \right] \tag{3.5.23}$$

Then the regular inverse of X is:

$$X^{-1} = T'^{-1} T^{-1} \tag{3.5.24}$$

This is the product of the triangular factors in reverse order.

3.5.8 Solution for the Product of a Matrix by the Inverse of a Square Basic Matrix.

We indicate this product by a:

$$a = X^{-1} Y \tag{3.5.25}$$

The triangular factors of X are

$$X = T_L T_u \tag{3.5.26}$$

We now define matrices as

$$T_u = D_T + t' \tag{3.5.27}$$

$$v = -D_T^{-1} t' \tag{3.5.28}$$

$$w = D_T^{-1} T_L^{-1} Y \tag{3.5.29}$$

The solution for a is

$$[v \mid w] \left[\frac{a}{I} \right] = a \tag{3.5.30}$$

3.5.9 Solution for the General Inverse of a Vertical Basic Matrix.

If X is a vertical basic matrix, its general inverse can be calculated by

$$Y' = (X'X)^{-1}X' \tag{3.5.31}$$

This does not require the calculation of a basic factor.

3.5.10 The Major Product Moment of the Left Orthonormal of a Vertical Basic Matrix.

We define the basic structure of the matrix X:

$$X = P\Delta Q' \tag{3.5.32}$$

Then the major product moment of its left orthonormal is given by

$$PP' = X(X'X)^{-1}X' \tag{3.5.33}$$

Suppose we define a type 3 column supervector:

$$G = \left[\frac{X'X}{X} \right] \tag{3.5.34}$$

We define the minor product moment of X as the major product moment of its triangular factor:

$$X'X = TT' \tag{3.5.35}$$

We then indicate the triangular factoring of the matrix G:

$$G = \left[\frac{T}{Z} \right] T' \tag{3.5.36}$$

The major product moment of the left orthonormal is now given by Eq. 3.5.37, in which Z is taken from the left factor of G.

$$ZZ' = X(X'X)^{-1}X' \tag{3.5.37}$$

If Z is defined as in the previous sentence, it is a vertical orthonormal matrix. Its minor product moment is the identity matrix:

$$Z'Z = I \tag{3.5.38}$$

This method of solving for Z is sometimes referred to as the *Gram-Schmidt orthogonalization* of a matrix. As a matter of fact, the method traditionally given is somewhat different from this, and relies more heavily on scalar algebra notation than on matrix notation.

3.5.11 Solution for the General Inverse of a Nonbasic Matrix.

If X is nonbasic, we may consider the partial triangular factoring:

$$X = uv' \tag{3.5.39}$$

Then the general inverse as defined in Section 3.5.1 can be shown to be given by

$$Y' = v(v'v)^{-1}(u'u)^{-1}u' \qquad (3.5.40)$$

3.5.12   The Regular Inverse of Special Sums of Matrices. Let A be a square basic matrix and u and v be vertical basic matrices. We define X:

$$X = (A + uv') \qquad (3.5.41)$$

The inverse of X can be shown to be

$$X^{-1} = A^{-1} - A^{-1}u(I + v'A^{-1}u)^{-1}v'A^{-1} \qquad (3.5.42)$$

If u and v are vectors, the inverse of X can be shown to be

$$X^{-1} = A^{-1} - \frac{A^{-1}uv'A^{-1}}{1 + v'A^{-1}u} \qquad (3.5.43)$$

Let a and b be square basic matrices. We define X:

$$X = a^{-1} - (a + b)^{-1}ba^{-1} \qquad (3.5.44)$$

We define Y:

$$Y = a^{-1} - ba^{-1}(a + b)^{-1} \qquad (3.5.45)$$

With these definitions we can prove the relations expressed by

$$X = (a + b)^{-1} \qquad (3.5.46)$$

$$Y = (a + b)^{-1} \qquad (3.5.47)$$

These equations are useful in certain factor analytic models.

3.5.13   The Inverse of a Second Order Simple Matrix. We indicate the matrix a in terms of its elements:

$$a = \begin{bmatrix} a_{11} & a_{12} \\ a_{21} & a_{22} \end{bmatrix} \qquad (3.5.48)$$

Then the inverse of a is given by

$$a^{-1} = \begin{bmatrix} a_{22} & -a_{12} \\ -a_{21} & a_{11} \end{bmatrix} \frac{1}{a_{11}a_{22} - a_{12}a_{21}} \qquad (3.5.49)$$

3.6   Inverse of a Supermatrix

3.6.1   Conditions Required for the Regular Inverse of a Supermatrix. The simple form of the matrix must be square and basic. The supermatrix must be a symmetrically partitioned simple matrix. The diagonal submatrices must be basic.

3.6.2 The Inverse of a Second Order Supermatrix.

Let the supermatrix A be

$$A = \begin{bmatrix} A_{11} & A_{12} \\ A_{21} & A_{22} \end{bmatrix} \tag{3.6.1}$$

The submatric elements A_{11} and A_{22} are assumed square and basic. Then the inverse of A is given by

$$A^{-1} = \begin{bmatrix} A_{11}^{-1} + A_{11}^{-1}A_{12}M_2^{-1}A_{21}A_{11}^{-1} & -A_{11}^{-1}A_{12}M_2^{-1} \\ -M_2^{-1}A_{21}A_{11}^{-1} & M_2^{-1} \end{bmatrix} \tag{3.6.2}$$

in which M_2 is given by

$$M_2 = A_{22} - A_{21}A_{11}^{-1}A_{12} \tag{3.6.3}$$

An alternative solution for the inverse of the supermatrix A is given by

$$A^{-1} = \begin{bmatrix} M_1^{-1} & -M_1^{-1}A_{12}A_{22}^{-1} \\ -A_{22}^{-1}A_{21}M_1^{-1} & A_{22}^{-1} + A_{22}^{-1}A_{21}M_1^{-1}A_{12}A_{22}^{-1} \end{bmatrix} \tag{3.6.4}$$

in which M_1 is given by

$$M_1 = A_{11} - A_{12}A_{22}^{-1}A_{21} \tag{3.6.5}$$

The above formulas for the inverse of the supermatrix are most useful when one or both of the diagonal matrix elements are diagonal or when the nondiagonal matric elements A_{12} and A_{21} are vectors.

3.6.3 The Case When One Diagonal Is a Scalar Quantity.

We indicate an ith order matrix:

$$A_i = \begin{bmatrix} A_{i-1} & v_i \\ u_i' & a_{ii} \end{bmatrix} \tag{3.6.6}$$

We define the vectors

$$A_{i-1}^{-1}v_i = V_i \tag{3.6.7}$$

$$u_i' A_{i-1}^{-1} = U_i' \tag{3.6.8}$$

and the scalar

$$M_i = a_{ii} - U_i'V_i \tag{3.6.9}$$

We may then indicate the inverse of the matrix A_i:

$$A_i^{-1} = \begin{bmatrix} A_{i-1}^{-1} + \dfrac{V_iU_i'}{M_i} & \dfrac{-V_i}{M_i} \\ \dfrac{-U_i'}{M_i} & \dfrac{1}{M_i} \end{bmatrix} \tag{3.6.10}$$

This equation may be used iteratively for i from values 1 to n, where n is the order of the matrix to be inverted. This will yield the inverse of the matrix of order n.

3.6.4 The Inverse of a Lower Order Matrix from a Higher Order.
Suppose we let A_n be a matrix of order n. We indicate its inverse by

$$B = A_n^{-1} \tag{3.6.11}$$

We indicate the matrix A_n after deletion of the last row and last column by A_{n-1}. The inverse of this matrix with the last row and last column deleted can now be expressed by

$$B - \frac{B_{.n} B_{n.}'}{B_{nn}} = \begin{bmatrix} A_{n-1}^{-1} & 0 \\ 0 & 0 \end{bmatrix} \tag{3.6.12}$$

Suppose we wish to find the inverse of the matrix $A_{(ki)}$ obtained by deleting the kth row and the ith column from the A_n matrix. This inverse can be shown to be given by

$$B - \frac{B_{.k} B_{i.}'}{B_{ik}} = A_{(ki)}^{-1} \tag{3.6.13}$$

It will be noted that this equation leaves the kth column and ith row with all zeros. If we compress this matrix to eliminate this column and row, we have the inverse of the matrix obtained by deleting the kth row and the ith column from A_n.

3.7   The General Rank Reduction Theorem

This theorem plays an important role in most factor analytic models as well as in multiple regression models, which are special cases of factor analytic models.

3.7.1 The Reduction Equation.
We indicate order by subscripts. Suppose we have given a matrix X_{Nn} whose rank is defined by

$$X_{Nn} = X_{Nr} X_{rn} \tag{3.7.1}$$

Suppose also we have given arbitrary basic matrices X_{ns} and X_{sN}. We assume that s is less than or equal to r. We consider now:

$$Y_{Nn} = X_{Nn} - (X_{Nn} X_{ns})(X_{sN} X_{Nn} X_{ns})^{-1}(X_{sN} X_{Nn}) \tag{3.7.2}$$

We assume that the triple product has a regular inverse. We designate Eq. 3.7.2 the general rank reduction equation. The arbitrary basic matrices are designated the right and left arbitrary multipliers, respectively.

3.7.2 The Orthogonality Equations. From the rank reduction equation in the preceding section we have

$$X_{sN} Y_{Nn} = 0 \tag{3.7.3}$$

$$X_{Nn} X_{ns} = 0 \tag{3.7.4}$$

3.7.3 The Minimum Rank of the Product of Two Matrices. The rank of the product of any two matrices cannot be less than the sum of their ranks less their common order. These rules are given in Section 3.2.7 and are repeated here since they are required in the proof of the rank theorem.

3.7.4 The Rank Theorem. It can be proved that the rank of Y in Eq. 3.7.2 is precisely $r - s$.

3.7.5 Special Cases of the Rank Reduction Theorem. Suppose we let the arbitrary multipliers be given by the elementary vectors:

$$X_{sN} = e_i' \tag{3.7.5}$$

$$X_{ns} = e_j \tag{3.7.6}$$

The rank reduction equation now takes the form of

$$Y_{Nn} = X_{Nn} - X_{Nn} e_j (e_i' X_{Nn} e_j)^{-1} e_i' X_{Nn} \tag{3.7.7}$$

or, more simply,

$$Y = X - \frac{X_{.j} X_{i.}'}{X_{ij}} \tag{3.7.8}$$

This will be recognized as the general form for finding the rank of a matrix given by Eq. 3.3.4.

Suppose we let the original matrix be indicated by

$$X_{Nn} = X'X \tag{3.7.9}$$

We then indicate the basic structure of this matrix by

$$X'X = Q\delta Q' \tag{3.7.10}$$

We indicate the arbitrary multipliers by

$$X_{sN} = Q_{.1}' \tag{3.7.11}$$

$$X_{ns} = Q_{.1} \tag{3.7.12}$$

Then the rank reduction equation reduces to

$$Y = X'X - \delta_1 Q_{.1} Q_{.1}' \tag{3.7.13}$$

Suppose now we let the original matrix be given by

$$X_{Nn} = r \tag{3.7.14}$$

in which r is a correlation matrix.

We indicate the arbitrary matrices by

$$X_{sN} = 1' \tag{3.7.15}$$

$$X_{ns} = 1 \tag{3.7.16}$$

Then the rank reduction equation reduces to

$$Y = r - \left(\frac{r1}{\sqrt{1'r1}} \right) \left(\frac{1'r}{\sqrt{1'r1}} \right) \tag{3.7.17}$$

As we shall see, this equation is used in one of the factor analysis models.

3.8   Solving Linear Equations

Much of the work in factor analysis consists in the solution of linear equations. We shall therefore indicate how matrix algebra may be applied to a solution of various classes of equations.

3.8.1   The Matrix Form of Linear Equations.   Most scientific problems in the human sciences are concerned with predicting criterion variables from predictor variables. Suppose we let X_{Nn} be a matrix of known predictor measures of N entities for n variables. We let Z_{Nm} be a matrix of known criterion measures of m different criteria for each of the N entities. a_{nm} is a matrix of unknown vectors of predictor weights for estimating the m different criteria from the predictors. The fundamental matrix equation is given by

$$X_{Nn}a_{nm} - Z_{Nm} = \varepsilon_{Nm} \tag{3.8.1}$$

The matrix X may be one of four different types; namely, square and basic, vertical and basic, horizontal and basic, or nonbasic. First we shall consider the general inverse solution. We let the basic structure of X be given by

$$X = P\Delta Q' \tag{3.8.2}$$

and its general inverse by

$$Y' = Q\Delta^{-1}P' \tag{3.8.3}$$

The general inverse solution for the unknown matrix a is given by

$$a = Y'Z \tag{3.8.4}$$

3.8.2   The Case When X is Square and Basic.   This is the traditional mathematical case. The solution is given by

$$a = X^{-1}Z \tag{3.8.5}$$

This solution is exact, so that we have

$$Xa = Z \qquad (3.8.6)$$

3.8.3 *The Case When X is Vertical and Basic.* This is the usual case for data matrices in the social sciences. The general inverse solution for the a matrix is given by

$$a = (X'X)^{-1}X'Z \qquad (3.8.7)$$

This solution satisfies Eq. 3.8.8 and minimizes the trace of $\varepsilon'\varepsilon$.

$$X'\varepsilon = 0 \qquad (3.8.8)$$

3.8.4 *The Horizontal Basic Matrix X'.* This case has an infinite number of solutions. However, the general inverse solution is given by

$$a = X(X'X)^{-1}Z \qquad (3.8.9)$$

This solution is exact and minimizes the trace of $a'a$.

3.8.5 *The Case When X is Nonbasic.* This case is encountered with derived matrices and with certain advanced problems in factor analysis. We shall assume the rank of X to be given by

$$X = uv' \qquad (3.8.10)$$

Then the general inverse solution for the unknown matrix a is given by

$$a = v(v'v)^{-1}(u'u)^{-1}u'Z \qquad (3.8.11)$$

This solution minimizes the traces $a'a$ and $\varepsilon'\varepsilon$.

If the rank r of X is known, we can define the supermatrices:

$$X = \begin{bmatrix} X_{rr} & X_{rt} \\ X_{sr} & X_{st} \end{bmatrix} \qquad (3.8.12)$$

$$G_L = [I_{rr} \quad 0_{rs}] \qquad (3.8.13)$$

$$G_R = \begin{bmatrix} I_{rr} \\ \hline 0_{tr} \end{bmatrix} \qquad (3.8.14)$$

Here $r + s$ and $r + t$ are the height and the width, respectively, of X. Then, if X_{rr} is basic, the general inverse solution of a is given by

$$a = X_{rn}'(X_{rn}X_{rn}')^{-1}X_{rr}(X_{Nr}'X_{Nr})^{-1}X_{Nr}'Z \qquad (3.8.15)$$

where

$$X_{rn} = [X_{rr} \quad X_{rt}] \quad \text{and} \quad X_{Nr} = \begin{bmatrix} X_{rr} \\ X_{sr} \end{bmatrix} \qquad (3.8.16)$$

Chapter 4

Matrix Factoring and Approximation

We saw in Chapter 1 that any scientific investigation must yield a table of numbers consisting of measures of two or more different attributes for each of a number of different entities. Any factor analysis study must begin with such a table of numbers.

4.1 Essential Characteristics of Factor Analysis

In this chapter we shall consider in broad outline the essential characteristics and problems of factor analysis techniques. We saw in Chapters 2 and 3 that, beginning with a table of numbers or a matrix which stands for a table of numbers, we can perform certain well-defined and systematic operations which yield interesting and useful results. In this chapter we shall see that the methods of matrix algebra are admirably adapted to the operations and techniques of factor analysis.

As a matter of fact, most factor analysis techniques can be much more simply and effectively set forth in terms of matrix notation than in terms of the ordinary scalar notation which is used in most books and articles on factor analysis. Actually, once having become acquainted with the simple rules of matrix algebra, we find that many of the topics and developments presented in terms of scalar algebra in factor analysis textbooks turn out to be obvious or trivial in terms of matrix notation.

4.1.1 The Data Matrix. All scientific procedures which deal with experimental data must begin with a data matrix. Factor analysis is no exception. In a sense it is more general than other models of data analysis, such as analysis of variance and multiple regression. Actually, these latter techniques may be shown to be special cases of generalized factor analysis methods. In Chapter 23 we show, for example, that the conventional procedures of multiple regression analysis are special cases of factor analysis in its broadest sense.

94

Let us begin by considering a data matrix with N entities and n attributes. This matrix of experimental data, which we call x, is regarded as being a sum of two other matrices. One of these, which in some sense we shall regard as a matrix of true measures, we shall call u. We need not now define what we mean by true measures. The u matrix we regard as relevant and systematic. The other, a matrix of error measures, we call e. These are measures which in some sense we regard as irrelevant or random or unsystematic. This most general equation for a data matrix is expressed:

$$x = u + e \qquad (4.1.1)$$

One of the main difficulties in getting accustomed to matrix notation is learning to think of a symbol as a whole table of numbers, so that when a symbol is defined in terms of its order one can visualize its appearance if the numbers were written out in full. Once you can visualize the dimensions of the matrices involved in a factor analysis model, the equations and their meanings should not be difficult to understand.

In the beginning of this text, therefore, considerable emphasis will be placed on simply learning what the symbols mean in terms of numbers of entities and numbers of attributes. To enable you to visualize Eq 4.1.1, it is illustrated diagrammatically in Fig. 4.1.1.

FIG. 4.1.1

Here we see that the x matrix, the u matrix, and the e matrix are all the same size. As you learned in Chapter 2, matrices must have the same dimensions if they are to be added together.

4.1.2   The Approximation Matrix. In factor analysis and in other techniques of scientific analysis, the main interest centers around the u matrix or the matrix of systematic measures. This matrix is regarded in some way as being simpler than the x matrix of observed measures.

In Chapter 3 we became familiar with a fundamental concept by which we can characterize the simplicity of a matrix—namely, the concept of rank. Factor analysis studies are therefore concerned with the problems of determining the u matrix in such a way that it will closely resemble the x matrix and still have a much lower rank than the x matrix. Most matrices of experimental data are basic; that is, the rank is equal to the smaller dimension, which usually will be the number of attributes or the width of the matrix.

It should be observed at the outset that most treatments of factor analysis do not, however, begin with a consideration of the x matrix as such and the determination of the u matrix. These treatments usually begin with correlation matrices derived from the x matrix. This approach has led to much misunderstanding because the analyses applied to the correlation matrix sometimes imply that there is more information in the correlation matrix than in the data matrix x. This can never be the case. For this reason, as well as for others, it is much better to focus attention first on the data matrix, as such, in considering the problems and techniques of factor analysis.

We saw in Chapter 3 that if a matrix is nonbasic it can be expressed as the major product of two basic matrices. We learned also that the common order of these two basic matrices is the rank of the product. We shall therefore focus attention on the determination of the matrix factors whose product is the u matrix and whose common order is less than the smaller order of the data matrix. The right-hand factor is called the *factor loading matrix*, and the left-hand factor the *factor score matrix*.

4.1.3 The Factor Loading Matrix.

The factor loading matrix we shall call a_u. We shall also consider the error matrix as made up of a major product of basic matrices, of which the left factor will be an error factor score matrix and the right factor an error factor loading matrix. The entire factor loading matrix can be regarded as a supermatrix with two matric elements; namely, the a_u factor loading submatrix and the a_e factor loading submatrix.

$$a = (a_u, a_e) \tag{4.1.2}$$

The diagram indicating the dimensions for this supermatrix is given by Fig. 4.1.2.

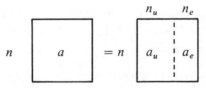

FIG. 4.1.2

Here we see that the entire a matrix is square, that is, of order n. It is partitioned vertically into two submatrices whose widths are, respectively, n_u and n_e. The matrix a is basic and therefore its submatrices a_u and a_e are also basic.

4.1.4 The Factor Score Matrix.

The factor score matrix is also partitioned into two submatrices; namely, the y_u and the y_e submatrices:

$$y = (y_u, y_e) \tag{4.1.3}$$

The dimensions of these matrices are illustrated in Fig. 4.1.3.

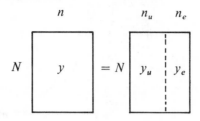

Fig. 4.1.3

The matrix y and hence y_u and y_e are basic.

Having defined the supermatrix involving the factor loading submatrices and the factor score supermatrix involving the factor score submatrices, we can see now how the systematic u matrix and the error matrix are made up in terms of these submatrices. The u matrix, expressed as the major product of the systematic factor score matrix and the transpose of the systematic factor loading matrix, is given by

$$u = y_u a_u' \tag{4.1.4}$$

The meaning of Eq. 4.1.4 is illustrated diagrammatically by Fig. 4.1.4.

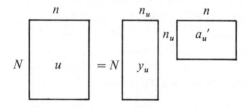

Fig. 4.1.4

Obviously, the rank of u, the systematic matrix, is n_u since it is the common order of the basic matrices on the right of Fig. 4.1.4.

The error matrix is then given by

$$e = y_e a_e' \tag{4.1.5}$$

Here y_e is the error factor score matrix. It is postmultiplied by the transpose

of the error factor loading matrix. The matrix e is shown as a major product
of these two error matrices with common order n_e in Fig. 4.1.5.

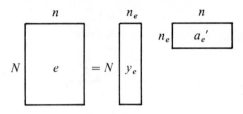

FIG. 4.1.5

We have seen then how a data matrix may be broken up into two parts:
a true or sytematic matrix of measures and an error matrix of measures.
These two matrices may be regarded as major products of factor score and
factor loading matrices, the sum of whose ranks adds up to the rank of
the experimental data matrix.

We shall next consider two fundamental concepts underlying all factor
analysis procedures which can lay claim to scientific and mathematical
respectability. Both of these have been briefly outlined in Chapter 3. We
shall now discuss them in more detail so that we may better understand their
applicability to the factor analysis of experimental data in the sciences. The
first of these involves the rank reduction theorem. The other involves the
concept of the basic structure of a matrix. The basic structure concept, as it
applies to factor analysis procedures and to matrix approximation by lower
rank matrices, turns out to be a special case of the rank reduction theorem.
Since the rank reduction theorem is in a sense more general than the basic
structure concept, we shall consider it first. The simpler but less accurate
methods of factor analysis are based on the rank reduction theorem and do
not utilize the basic structure concepts.

4.2   The Rank Reduction Theorem

The rank reduction procedure ordinarily begins with any matrix of real
numbers. In the case of factor analysis, we can begin with the data matrix
or we can calculate a covariance or correlation matrix from the data matrix,
and then apply the rank reduction methods to this.

4.2.1   The Data Matrix. To emphasize the fact that the data matrix
provides all the information available, and to keep as close to the data as
possible, we shall first consider the application of the rank reduction theorem to the data matrix. We shall begin with the inequality

$$N \gtrless n \gtrless r \gtrless s \tag{4.2.1}$$

in which the symbols are used to represent the orders of certain matrices. We let the rank of the data matrix x be defined by

$$x_{Nn} = x_{Nr} x_{rn} \qquad (4.2.2)$$

We use subscripts here to indicate the orders of the matrices involved. The first subscript, as you recall, indicates the number of rows, and the second, the number of columns. According to Eq. 4.2.2, the data matrix x is of rank r. This may or may not be equal to n. In any case, it will not be larger.

4.2.2 The Arbitrary Matrices.

Without considering for the present what these arbitrary matrices are and where they come from, we shall go back to our matrix reduction theorem of Chapter 3 and see how it can be used to factor the x matrix. The product of the data matrix postmultiplied by the right arbitrary matrix x_{ns} is given by

$$x_{Nn} x_{ns} = x_{Ns} \qquad (4.2.3)$$

This, of course, yields a matrix with N rows and s columns. The product of the data matrix premultiplied by the left arbitrary matrix, namely, x_{sN}, is given by

$$x_{sN} x_{Nn} = x_{sn} \qquad (4.2.4)$$

This yields a matrix of s rows and n columns.

4.2.3 The Triple Product.

Next we consider the triple product:

$$x_{sN} x_{Nn} x_{ns} = x_{ss} \qquad (4.2.5)$$

in which we have the data matrix premultiplied by the left arbitrary matrix and postmultiplied by the right arbitrary matrix to give a square matrix of order s. We recall from Chapter 3 that no restrictions are placed on these arbitrary multipliers, except that the triple product given by Eq. 4.2.5 must have a regular inverse. If the matrix does have a regular inverse, then it can be factored into the major product of two triangular factors:

$$x_{ss} = t_L t_R' \qquad (4.2.6)$$

On the right of Eq. 4.2.6, t_L means a lower triangular matrix, and t_R' means an upper triangular matrix.

4.2.4 The Product Matrices.

We define a factor score matrix of order $N \times s$, which is the product of the matrix obtained in Eq. 4.2.3 postmultiplied by the inverse of the upper triangular factor of Eq. 4.2.6.

$$y_{Ns} = x_{Ns} t_R'^{-1} \qquad (4.2.7)$$

We next consider the product:

$$a_{sn} = t_L^{-1} x_{sn} \tag{4.2.8}$$

This is a factor loading matrix which is given by the matrix obtained in Eq. 4.2.4 premultiplied by the inverse of the left triangular factor of Eq. 4.2.6. These two matrices given by Eqs. 4.2.7 and 4.2.8 will correspond to the systematic factor score matrix and the systematic factor loading matrix discussed in the previous section. You will note, however, that a_{sn} as given in Eq. 4.2.8 is horizontal, since it has s rows and n columns and therefore, according to Eq. 4.2.1, cannot be vertical. The product of these two matrices may now be subtracted from the original score matrix to yield the residual matrix e_{Nn}:

$$e_{Nn} = x_{Nn} - y_{Ns} a_{sn} \tag{4.2.9}$$

This error or residual matrix corresponds to the e matrix discussed in the previous section.

4.2.5 The Residual Matrix. Let us express the rank of this residual matrix by a major product of matrices:

$$e_{Nn} = e_{Ng} e_{gn} \tag{4.2.10}$$

in which g is the rank of the residual matrix. According to the matrix reduction theorem, we know that the rank of the residual matrix is given exactly by

$$g = r - s \tag{4.2.11}$$

It is precisely the rank of the data matrix less the common order s of the arbitrary matrices. We also know that the factor loading matrix given by Eq. 4.2.8 is orthogonal to the error matrix on the right:

$$E_{Nn} a_{sn}{}' = 0 \tag{4.2.12}$$

and that the factor score matrix given by Eq. 4.2.7 is orthogonal to this residual matrix on the left:

$$y_{Ns}{}' E_{Nn} = 0 \tag{4.2.13}$$

We see now that we have a general method for breaking up a data matrix into two matrices, the sum of whose ranks is equal to the rank of the data matrix. It must be observed that the success of this method depends entirely on the selection of the arbitrary matrices, and only if these are fortunately chosen will the residual matrix given by Eq. 4.2.9 have elements small enough to be regarded as error. Some of the methods of factor analysis discussed in subsequent chapters will consider procedures for selecting these arbitrary matrices.

4.2.6 The Product Moment Matrix. As we pointed out previously, it has been common practice to work with a covariance or correlation matrix derived from the data matrix in most factor analysis studies. To indicate briefly the application of the matrix reduction theorem to such a product moment matrix, we indicate the latter by

$$c_{nn} = x_{Nn}'x_{Nn} \tag{4.2.14}$$

We assume the rank of c to be given by

$$c_{nn} = c_{nr}c_{nr}' \tag{4.2.15}$$

in which the common order on the right is r. We note that the prime is used on the right factor rather than the method of subscript reversal to indicate that it is the transpose of the other.

We next form the product of the arbitrary matrix with the covariance matrix to get the product c_{ns} in

$$c_{nn}x_{ns} = c_{ns} \tag{4.2.16}$$

In this case, since c is symmetric, we need only one arbitrary matrix and its transpose. We form the triple product of pre- and postmultiplying the matrix c by the arbitrary matrix and its transpose:

$$x_{ns}'c_{nn}x_{ns} = c_{ss} \tag{4.2.17}$$

Here the left multiplier is the transpose of the right arbitrary multiplier.

We can now factor the symmetric matrix c_{ss} into the major product moment of a triangular matrix:

$$c_{ss} = tt' \tag{4.2.18}$$

Then the factor loading matrix is

$$a_{ns} = c_{ns}t'^{-1} \tag{4.2.19}$$

Here a_{ns} is simply the matrix c_{ns} postmultiplied by the inverse of the transpose of the triangular factor t. If we let $\tilde{c}$ be the approximation to the c matrix, it is expressed as the major product moment of the factor loading matrix:

$$\tilde{c}_{nn} = a_{ns}a_{ns}' \tag{4.2.20}$$

The residual matrix then is

$$E_{nn} = c_{nn} - \tilde{c}_{nn} \tag{4.2.21}$$

and its rank is

$$E_{nn} = E_{ng}E_{ng}' \tag{4.2.22}$$

The rank g is the common order of the major product moment on the right, and is precisely s less than the rank of c_{nn}. According to the matrix reduction theorem, this factor loading matrix must be orthogonal to the residual matrix:

$$E_{nn}a_{ns} = 0 \tag{4.2.23}$$

Since the approximation matrix and the covariance matrix are both symmetric, the residual matrix E must be symmetric. Therefore this residual matrix is also orthogonal to the factor loading matrix on the left:

$$a_{ns}'E_{nn} = 0' \qquad (4.2.24)$$

It is important to know how well any particular selection of the arbitrary matrix can yield an approximation to the covariance matrix. For example, Eq. 4.2.21 shows that the trace of the residual matrix is equal to the trace of the covariance matrix less the trace of the minor product moment of the factor loading matrix. The variance accounted for by the factor loading matrix is given directly by the trace of the minor product moment of the factor loading matrix. The problem in matrix approximation is to find an arbitrary matrix which will make this trace as large as possible, so that the trace of the residual will be a minimum for any specified rank s of the approximation matrix $\tilde{c}$ given in Eq. 4.2.20.

4.2.7 Special Cases of Arbitrary Matrices. The determination of the arbitrary matrices, so that the systematic approximation matrix of specified rank will be as close to the data or covariance matrix as possible, is one of the essential objectives of factor analysis methodology. The arbitrary matrices are selected or determined in various ways. One of the simplest methods is to use vectors for the arbitrary matrices. When vectors are used, the matrix reduction theorem is applied successively to the first residual matrix and to later residual matrices with the use of other arbitrary vectors. These methods will be outlined in detail in later chapters.

A special case of the arbitrary matrix is an elementary vector which is used in determining the rank of a matrix. When an elementary vector is used with successive residual matrices, we have the typical triangular factoring described in Section 3.3. We shall see, however, that more general methods are available. We may select arbitrary matrices whose common orders are the numbers of factors or the rank of the approximation matrix assumed in the investigation.

4.3 Basic Structure Solution

We have indicated that the extent to which matrix reduction techniques are useful in finding approximation matrices of lower rank for the data matrices depends on how fortunately the arbitrary matrices are chosen. We have also shown that the basic structure concept can be used as a basis for selecting the arbitrary matrices in the matrix reduction theorem.

4.3.1 Characteristics of the Approximation. It may truly be said that the basic structure concept is the very foundation of the more well-recognized factor analysis procedures. It is important because it yields the best least square approximation to a matrix for any specified rank.

We begin with the data matrix x expressed in terms of its basic structure, as defined in Chapter 3,

$$x = P\Delta Q' \tag{4.3.1}$$

in which Δ is a diagonal matrix, P is a nonhorizontal orthonormal matrix, and Q' a nonvertical orthonormal matrix.

These definitions of P and Q imply

$$P'P = I \tag{4.3.2}$$

$$Q'Q = I \tag{4.3.3}$$

If x is also basic, as it usually will be in the case of a data matrix, then Q will be a square orthonormal matrix, and we have

$$QQ' = I \tag{4.3.4}$$

We next express the orthonormal matrix P as a partitioned matrix consisting of P_u and P_e:

$$P = (P_u, P_e) \tag{4.3.5}$$

We now regard P_u as the systematic factor score submatrix and P_e as the error factor score matrix.

Similarly, we partition the diagonal Δ matrix:

$$\Delta = \begin{bmatrix} \Delta_u & 0 \\ 0 & \Delta_e \end{bmatrix} \tag{4.3.6}$$

The matrix Q' is also partitioned by rows:

$$Q' = \begin{bmatrix} Q_u' \\ Q_e' \end{bmatrix} \tag{4.3.7}$$

Next we define the factor loading matrices. First, a_u is given by

$$a_u = Q_u \Delta_u \tag{4.3.8}$$

In a similar way we define the error factor loading matrix a_e:

$$a_e = Q_e \Delta_e \tag{4.3.9}$$

We can now express the systematic and the error matrices u and e, which we considered in Section 4.1:

$$u = P_u a_u' \tag{4.3.10}$$

$$e = P_e a_e' \tag{4.3.11}$$

The residual matrix e is then the difference between the data matrix and the estimate of it:

$$e = x - u \qquad (4.3.12)$$

One great advantage of the basic structure concept is that we have a simple and exact relationship expressing the sums of squares of the residual elements as functions of the basic diagonal submatrix Δ_e.

$$tre'e = tr\Delta_e^2 \qquad (4.3.13)$$

We have then, that for any specified rank approximation to x, the sum of the squares of the residuals is precisely equal to the sum of the squares of the basic diagonals involved in the last submatrix of Δ given by Eq. 4.3.6. We know that this is the best least square approximation to the data matrix x for any specified rank of u.

Further interesting and useful relationships are

$$P_u'e = 0 \qquad (4.3.14)$$

$$ea_u = 0 \qquad (4.3.15)$$

$$P_u'P_e = 0 \qquad (4.3.16)$$

$$a_u'a_e = 0 \qquad (4.3.17)$$

Equation 4.3.14 shows that the matrix of error residuals is orthogonal to the matrix of systematic factor scores.

Equation 4.3.15 shows that the matrix of errors is orthogonal to the systematic factor loading matrix a_u.

That the systematic factor scores and the error factor scores are orthogonal to one another, that is, uncorrelated, is shown by Eq. 4.3.16.

That the systematic factor loading matrix and the error factor loading matrix are orthogonal to one another is shown by Eq. 4.3.17.

It can be proved that this solution for the factor score and factor loading matrices is a special case of the matrix reduction theorem. We merely substitute the matrix Q_u for x_{ns}, the right arbitrary factor:

$$x_{ns} = Q_u \qquad (4.3.18)$$

For the left arbitrary factor x_{sN} we substitute the transpose of the systematic factor score matrix P_u:

$$x_{sN} = P_u' \qquad (4.3.19)$$

4.3.2   The Covariance Solutions.   Let us now consider the same basic structure analysis applied to the covariance matrix given by the minor product moment of the score matrix:

$$c = x'x \qquad (4.3.20)$$

The basic structure form of c, according to Chapter 3, is

$$c = Q\Delta^2 Q' = Q\delta Q' \qquad (4.3.21)$$

Here, of course, we have lost the left orthonormal P. This is convenient in the actual solution for the basic structure factors.

We now use as the right arbitrary factor the matrix Q_u:

$$x_{ns} = Q_u \qquad (4.3.22)$$

Then the triple product matrix x_{ss} becomes simply $\Delta_u{}^2$:

$$x_{ss} = \Delta_u{}^2 \qquad (4.3.23)$$

We define the factor loading matrix for the systematic factors as previously:

$$a_u = Q_u \Delta_u \qquad (4.3.24)$$

Then the approximation to the covariance matrix is given by the major product moment of this factor loading matrix:

$$\tilde{c} = a_u a_u' \qquad (4.3.25)$$

The residual or difference between the observed and the approximation covariance matrix is

$$E = c - \tilde{c} \qquad (4.3.26)$$

It can be shown, then, that the basic structure of this residual matrix is

$$E = Q_e \Delta_e{}^2 Q_e' \qquad (4.3.27)$$

This residual matrix has some interesting properties. Both the trace and the sums of squares of elements are simple properties of the error part of the diagonal matrix. The trace of the residual matrix is simply the trace of the square of this diagonal:

$$trE = tr\Delta_e{}^2 \qquad (4.3.28)$$

The sum of the squares of the residuals, or the trace of the square of the residual matrix, is the sum of the squares of the δ's for the error part:

$$trE^2 = tr\delta_e{}^2 \qquad (4.3.29)$$

The basic orthonormal and diagonal matrices are closely related to what the mathematician calls latent roots and vectors. These are also called characteristic roots and vectors as well as eigenvalues and eigenvectors. We shall, however, in this book adhere mainly to the use of the term *basic structure*, since in some respects it is a more general and useful concept than related ones used by the mathematician. Much of this book is concerned with finding approximations to matrices in terms of these basic structure factors, because these give the best least square fit to the data matrix for any specified number of factors.

4.3.3   Kinds of Solutions.   At this time we shall indicate only briefly the different types of solutions which we shall consider in subsequent chapters. One of the types of solutions consists of finding one factor loading vector at a time, determining a residual matrix, and from this residual matrix finding another factor loading vector, and so on. Another method which is not so commonly used, but which has advantages in certain cases, also consists in finding one factor loading vector at a time. This method does not, however, require the actual calculation of residual matrices.

A second type of solution consists in estimating the number of factors or the rank of the matrix required to approximate the data matrix, and then solving for all of the factors at once. All of the methods involving the basic structure solution require iteration procedures which more and more closely approximate the true basic structure factors. The multiple factor types of solutions start with a set of rough approximations to the factors and proceed to get closer approximations by successive iterations.

Two such types of solutions will be discussed in Chapter 8. The first of these consists of a procedure such that each approximation to the factor loading matrix is an orthogonal matrix, in the sense that the factor vectors are orthogonal to one another. This method does not become a special case of the rank reduction procedure, however, until the final factor loading matrix has been determined to a specified degree of accuracy. The other simultaneous factor procedure for the basic structure solution also consists of taking a first approximation to the factor loading matrix, and then solving for successively closer approximations to the basic structure solution. This method, however, provides that each factor loading matrix approximation is a special case of the rank reduction method, so that if its major product moment were used to estimate the correlation matrix, no matter how poor the approximation, the residual matrix would nevertheless have a rank precisely equal to the difference between the rank of the correlation matrix and the number of factors postulated.

A third type of solution makes no assumptions about the number of factors required to approximate the data matrix adequately. The complete basic structure is obtained by successive approximations, but the complete solution is not available until all of the factors have been solved for. In these procedures one usually gets all factors at once, including many more than are usually required for typical experimental investigations.

A fourth type of solution resembles the single factor solution in that only one factor at a time is obtained. However, after each factor is obtained, instead of getting a residual matrix the original matrix is reduced in order by one. This method has the advantage that the order of the matrix upon which the operations are being performed is successively reduced as factors are solved for.

4.4   Indeterminateness of Factors

So far we have discussed the factor score and the factor loading matrix as though these were unique. We know, however, that if a matrix can be expressed as a major product of two factors, it can also be expressed as a major product of an infinite number of pairs of factors.

4.4.1   Square Orthonormal Transformations. Let us consider, therefore, how we may start with any particular factor loading matrix a_u and postmultiply it by any conformable square orthonormal matrix q:

$$a_q = a_u q \tag{4.4.1}$$

We may then also postmultiply the P_u or systematic factor score matrix by this same square orthonormal matrix:

$$P_q = P_u q \tag{4.4.2}$$

It is easy to prove that

$$P_u a_u' = P_q a_q' \tag{4.4.3}$$

Here, then, we have the major product of two pairs of factor score and factor loading matrices which are identical. Since there is an infinite number of q's of a given order, there would be an infinite number of pairs satisfying Eq. 4.4.3 on the right. Therefore, the systematic matrix can be expressed in an infinite number of ways by various choices of q:

$$u = P_q a_q' \tag{4.4 4}$$

Similarly, we see that the approximate matrix $\tilde{c}$ can be expressed in an infinite number of ways by major product moments of a_q matrices:

$$\tilde{c} = a_q a_q' \tag{4.4.5}$$

4.4.2   Square Basic Transformations. We have seen that by square orthonormal transformations we can get an infinite number of solutions either to the approximation data matrix or the estimate of the covariance matrix. However, we have a more general case. For example, let us consider

$$a_g = a_u g \tag{4.4.6}$$

Here we get the transformed factor loading matrix a_g by postmultiplying a_u, the basic structure factor loading matrix, by a square basic matrix g, conformable to a_u.

Next we may postmultiply the systematic factor score matrix by the transpose of the inverse of this g matrix:

$$P_u(g^{-1})' = P_g \tag{4.4.7}$$

We see again that the major product of the factor score and the factor loading matrices determined by the basic structure solution is equal to the major product of these transformed matrices:

$$P_u a_u' = P_g a_g' \tag{4.4.8}$$

Therefore, the approximation matrix u is also equal to the product moment of these two transformed matrices:

$$u = P_g a_g' \tag{4.4.9}$$

Since g may be any square basic matrix whose order is equal to the rank of the approximation, this approximation can be expressed by any one of an infinite number of products.

Suppose we define a symmetric matrix s by the inverse of the minor product moment of the g transformation matrix:

$$(g'g)^{-1} = s \tag{4.4.10}$$

Because of the definition of s and the definition of a_g, we see that the approximation to the covariance matrix $\tilde{c}$ is given by

$$\tilde{c} = a_g s a_g' \tag{4.4.11}$$

We see, then, that fundamentally we have two problems in factor analysis. The first problem is to find the best approximation of specified rank to the data matrix or some matrix derived from it; the second is to find the factors of this approximation matrix from all possible pairs which shall best satisfy certain criteria or desired objectives. Chapters 17–19 are concerned with the problem of determining these transformation matrices for the factor loading and factor score matrices obtained by matrix reduction or basic structure procedures.

4.5 Kinds of Matrices

We have outlined briefly the concepts of matrix approximation by lower rank matrices, and have indicated that these operations may be performed on data matrices and on matrices derived from them. We shall now consider in more detail the types of matrices to which factor analyses may be applied.

4.5.1 Data Matrices. It would seem, as indicated previously, that the most natural matrix to begin with is the actual data matrix, since this represents the observations which have been made with respect to attributes on specific groups of entities. In many cases it may not be desirable or feasible, however, to factor directly the matrix of raw data observations. This is the case if the various attributes or variables are not measured in comparable units or from comparable origins of measurements. One problem, then, is to determine a suitable origin for each variable. Usually we consider a deviation matrix with means of 0.

$$x = \left[I - \frac{1\,1'}{N} \right] X \qquad (4.5.1)$$

Here the matrix on the left is the deviation score matrix, and the matrix on the right is a raw score matrix which has been centered by columns by means of the matrix in brackets. This is simply a way of indicating in matrix notation that the means are subtracted from the columns of the raw scores.

Usually in factor analysis it is customary, for want of a better or more rational procedure, to deal with standard scores rather than deviation scores.

$$z = x D_\sigma^{-1} \qquad (4.5.2)$$

Here the deviation score matrix x is postmultiplied by the inverse of the diagonal matrix of the standard deviations. This is the way of indicating in matrix notation the z or normal scores whose standard deviations are 1 and whose means are 0.

It is usually possible to arrange factoring procedures, if they are to be done on data matrices, in such a way that it is not actually necessary to calculate either the deviation score matrix x or the standardized score matrix z. Usually, the computations can be organized in such a way as to operate directly on the raw score matrix, yet yield factor solutions which would have been obtained if the computations had been carried out directly with the z score matrix. In general, however, it is customary to work with product moment or covariance matrices.

4.5.2 Covariance Matrices.

For some problems, such as learning data, for which natural units are available, the product moment of the raw score matrix is appropriate:

$$G = \frac{X'X}{N} \qquad (4.5.3)$$

One of the advantages in working with product moment matrices is that for basic structure type solutions the left orthonormal disappears in the product moment, leaving only the right orthonormal and the basic diagonal to solve for.

For some types of problems it may be desirable to work with the covariance rather than the correlation matrix. The covariance matrix is simply the product moment of the deviation score matrix divided by the number of cases:

$$c = \frac{x'x}{N} \qquad (4.5.4)$$

In actual computation, however, it is not necessary to calculate the deviation matrix in order to get the covariance matrix. This can be computed by formula

$$c = G - MM'$$ (4.5.5)

where the last term on the right is the major product moment of the vector of means for the raw score matrix.

The most common matrix to which factor analysis has been applied in the past is the correlation matrix itself. This matrix has the advantage that, at least for a particular sample, the measures may be regarded as comparable in units and origins. A great deal of theoretical and experimental work still remains to be done on the problem of units and origins of measurement, but until these have been worked out, it is probable that most of the factor analysis procedures will be applied to the correlation matrix.

The correlation matrix is simply the minor product moment of the standard score matrix z divided by the number of cases:

$$r = \frac{z'z}{N}$$ (4.5.6)

Here again, however, the most convenient computational procedure is not to calculate the standard score matrix first and then get its minor product moment. Computationally, one would calculate the covariance matrix as in Eq. 4.5.5 and then pre- and postmultiply this covariance matrix by a diagonal whose elements are the reciprocals of the square roots of the diagonal of the c matrix:

$$r = D_c^{-1/2} c D_c^{-1/2}$$ (4.5.7)

It will be shown in Chapters 15 and 16, however, that some methods of factor analysis are independent of the particular scale used, so that analyses carried out on the covariance matrix and the correlation matrix will be equivalent.

4.5.3 Part Covariance Matrices.

Sometimes it is convenient to work with only a part of the correlation matrix in finding factor solutions. It may be that for some reason measures on a particular subset, say x, may be more readily available than for a subset y. For example, the subset x may have been obtained prior to y. We can indicate a partitioning of the matrix z:

$$z = [z_x, \quad z_y]$$ (4.5.8)

If we calculate a correlation matrix from this partitioned score matrix, it may be expressed by

$$r = \begin{bmatrix} r_{xx} & , & r_{xy} \\ r_{yx} & , & r_{yy} \end{bmatrix}$$ (4.5.9)

Sometimes, in order to save computing labor or for other reasons, we may have available only the nondiagonal submatrix, that is, r_{xy}. Factoring methods are available whereby the factor loadings on both the x and the y set may be estimated from this correlation matrix. Certain limitations are imposed, however, on the interpretation of these factors when determined in this way.

On the other hand, we may have available the r_{xx} and the r_{xy} matrices, but not the matrix of intercorrelations among the y variables. With these two submatrices several alternative methods of factoring, which will be considered in Chapter 11, are available.

4.6 The Problem of Metric

We have already mentioned that factor analyses can be performed on raw data matrices or that these measures may be modified with respect to origin and scale. The problem of metric is one which needs further research, both theoretical and experimental.

4.6.1 The Problem of Origin.
In many scientific investigations in which data matrices are obtained for a wide variety of attributes, the origins of measurement may be quite arbitrary. There may be no clearly defined 0 point for some of the variables. On the other hand, it may be that for some variables the origins may have some natural logical basis. In the physical sciences logical origins are perhaps more common than in the social or biological sciences. Particularly in the social sciences, the kinds of measures used are not such that a 0 value means that there is absolutely none of a particular attribute in the entity or that negative values mean there is less than nothing of this attribute in the entity.

For convenience it has been common, as indicated previously, to work with modified data matrices in which, for a particular sample, the means are subtracted from the raw score variables so that the new means are all 0. These 0 origins do not in many cases have adequate theoretical justification. For example, if another sample were obtained, the means might be quite different and the analysis performed on this second sample might well give different results.

The problem of determining rational or logical origins for various kinds of measures is one which has not been systematically or extensively explored in the social sciences. It is possible that the factor analysis problem could be defined in such a way that a rational or logical origin could be solved for.

4.6.2 The Problem of Scale.
Just as in the case of origin, it is also true that for most experimental data matrices the units of measurement are arbitrary. They are often functions of the particular kinds of measuring instruments or operations used for quantifying measures of the attributes. These may vary widely from one attribute to another, as in the case of test

scores, physiological measures, and so on. As in the case of origin, it is not common to have natural units which are absolute in any real sense. It is customary in factor analysis and in other models to normalize the measures for a particular sample so that the standard deviations of the new measures are all 1. This again is arbitrary, since for another sample the standard deviations might be quite different.

The problem of determining units which are independent of the sample is an important one. Fortunately, certain rationales and techniques in factor analysis now make it possible to factor a matrix in such a way that the results are independent of the scale. Even though the rationales of the methods may be challenged, they are at least objective, and a method of analysis which is independent of scale may be regarded as defining the appropriate scaling of the variables. A method of factoring which is independent of both origin and scale would be highly desirable.

In the chapters which follow we shall consider various methods of finding lower rank approximations to data, covariance, and correlation matrices as well as a number of rationales and procedures for getting optimal solutions.

Part II

Matrix Factoring Methods—A

Chapter 5

The Centroid Method

The centroid method is one of the best known and most frequently used methods of factor analysis. It is so named because of certain analogies to mechanical principles, but this need not concern us here. As a matter of fact, we shall emphasize the method as a special case of more general methods discussed in Chapter 4, rather than follow its traditional and perhaps somewhat misleading historical treatment.

The centroid method has a number of variations. Thurstone, who originated this technique of factor analysis, provided some of the methods. Others also have introduced major and minor variations into the rationale and computational procedures.

It must be admitted that the centroid methods of factor analysis do not hold today the important position in factor analysis technology that they did in the years before the advent of the high-speed computer. These methods constitute only rough approximations to some of the more elegant, efficient, and currently more popular procedures which will be discussed in later chapters. Nevertheless, where only desk computers are available and in some cases where the high-speed computers are available, the methods may still be useful. As a matter of fact, their approximation to the more accurate methods is often close and the computational time required is considerably less in most cases.

In the following sections we shall outline some of the more useful and practical centroid-type methods of factor analysis. First, however, we shall indicate some of the distinguishing characteristics of these techniques.

5.1 Characteristics of the Method

We shall consider four essential characteristics of the method. First, a single vector at a time of factor loadings is solved for. Second, the methods are a special case of the rank reduction method. Third, the methods are approximations to the basic structure solution. Fourth, the solution for the factor loading vectors is not, in general, unique.

114

5.1.1 One Vector at a Time. As indicated in Chapter 4, some of the methods of factor analysis consist of getting, in sequence, the factor loading vectors of the correlation matrix, while other methods yield by successive approximations all of the factor loading vectors at one time. While the centroid method permits the solution for any specified number of factor vectors to be obtained simultaneously, in practice it is better to solve for them sequentially.

5.1.2 Special Case of Rank Reduction Methods. As is true of most matrix factoring methods, the centroid methods utilize the rank reduction procedures discussed in Chapter 3. You may recall that these procedures guarantee that for each factor extracted, the rank of the corresponding residual matrix is reduced by one. Thus, if the original correlation matrix is basic—which, in general, it will be—the rank of the residual matrix will be equal to the number of variables less the number of factors extracted.

The centroid methods may be applied to either covariance or correlation matrices. In actual practice, however, they are usually applied to correlation matrices, as is true of most of the methods of factor analysis.

You recall that the rank reduction procedure involves what we have called the right and left arbitrary matrices. In the centroid method these arbitrary matrices are either unit or sign vectors. The unit vector is, of course, a special case of the sign vector in which all of the elements have a positive sign. Thus, all of the elements of the vectors are either $+1$ or -1. The left multiplier is always a row vector and the right multiplier is its transpose. The correlation matrix traditionally constitutes the matrix which is operated on by the arbitrary vectors.

5.1.3 Approximation to Basic Structure Solution. The centroid methods may properly be regarded as simplified approximations to the basic structure solution for a correlation matrix, although in his development of the centroid methods of factor analysis Thurstone did not explicitly recognize them as such. In the basic structure solution it will be recalled that the residual variance remaining after the extraction of each factor is a minimum or that the variance accounted for by a given factor is a maximum. The sign vector for each factor is chosen so that the triple product, from left to right, of its row form by the correlation or residual matrix by the column form is a maximum. This is analogous to finding a general normal vector which in such a triple product yields a maximum scalar quantity. Such a vector (as indicated in Chapter 3) is the first vector of the basic orthonormal of the correlation or residual matrix.

It is, however, much easier computationally to find a sign vector yielding such a maximum than to find the basic orthonormal vector. As will be seen in later sections of this chapter, the problem of finding a sign vector such that the triple product is a maximum is tantamount to finding a sign vector such that, when the correlation or residual matrix is multiplied by it, the elements of the resulting vector have the same signs as corresponding elements of the sign vector. We shall also see that this resulting vector is proportional to the factor loading vector.

5.1.4 Nonuniqueness of the Method.

As indicated in the previous paragraphs, the arbitrary multipliers are sign vectors. The methods for determining these sign vectors depend on the particular variations of the centroid methods which are being used. The particular sign vector corresponding to a factor vector depends both on the original approximation to the sign vector and on the method for finding successive approximations to these vectors. In the methods we shall consider, the initial selection of the sign vector is always a unit vector. The procedure for selecting successive approximations to the sign vector which we shall use will be unique—except in the case of ties, which will be rare. Therefore, the problem of uniqueness need not concern us for the methods outlined in the following sections.

5.2 Kinds of Solutions

We shall consider three types of solutions for the centroid method. In the first of these, 1 is used for the diagonal elements of the correlation matrix. In the second, estimates of what are known as communalities are used. In the third type, iterative solutions for unknown diagonal elements are required.

5.2.1 Unity in the Diagonal.

It is customary in books on factor analysis to introduce the subject of communality early in the discussion and to attempt to define the concept in both theoretical and computational terms. A great deal of controversy still exists over the concept of communality itself and a great many troublesome problems are involved, not only in giving a precise mathematical definition for it but also in finding a practical and useful computational solution for factor analysis models which utilize the communality concept. We shall introduce this concept in more detail in a later chapter.

At this point we shall consider communality only in terms of its implications for the arithmetical solution of the factor loadings. In a later chapter we shall see that some of the factor models assume the variance of a matrix of measures to consist of three types, namely, common factor variance, error variance, and specific factor variance. The common factor variance is called the communality. If we do not assume specific factor variance, the factor analytic solution begins by taking the correlation matrix with unity in the diagonals, solving for a factor loading vector, extracting this factor loading vector from the matrix to get a residual, and proceeding in this way to solve for successive factor loadings and corresponding residual matrices. In these solutions one is not concerned about the problem of specific factor variance.

5.2.2 Communality Estimates in the Diagonal.

The solutions which assume specific factors in addition to common factors begin by replacing the unit diagonal elements in the correlation matrix with what are called communality estimates. In general, these substitute values in the diagonal are smaller than 1. Many different methods have been proposed for estimating these values. The most common is to substitute the largest absolute nondiagonal value in the corresponding column of the correlation matrix for the unit element. A factor loading vector is then solved for, after which a residual matrix is calculated. In this residual matrix, the diagonal element is again replaced by the largest absolute nondiagonal value in the column of the residual matrix. For each subsequent residual correlation matrix, this same procedure of substituting for the diagonal the largest absolute nondiagonal value in the column is followed.

One of the advantages claimed for the substitution of communality estimates in the diagonal of the correlation matrix is that, in general, one can account for the intercorrelations of the matrix with a smaller number of factors than if 1 is used. The purposes and objectives of a particular factor analytic study determine largely which model and which particular type of solution should be used.

5.2.3 Iterative Solution for Communalities.

The method of successive communality estimates in successive residual matrices is the simplest and most frequently used procedure for the models assuming specific factors. It is possible, however, to set up a computational procedure which gives better estimates of the diagonal values. Here diagonal elements are found for a particular correlation matrix such that the matrix can be most accurately approximated by the major product moment of a factor loading matrix with a specified number of factors. The number of factors is presumably much less than the number of variables.

From a computational and empirical point of view, it is enough to regard what has been called the communality problem as nothing more than one of determining the diagonal values of a correlation or covariance matrix so as to satisfy this criterion of a minimum lower rank approximation. More specifically, we may therefore regard the communality problem as an effort to find a lower rank major product moment matrix which best approximates the nondiagonal elements of the correlation matrix without concern for the diagonal elements.

5.3   Unity in the Diagonal

5.3.1   Characteristics of the Solution.   When the factor analysis is performed on the correlation matrix with 1 in the diagonal, the solution has a number of characteristics which distinguish it from those solutions employing optimal diagonal elements. In general, the computations are simpler, the number of factors required for a specified accuracy of approximation are greater, the proportion of the variance of each variable accounted for by all the factors is less than or equal to its total variance, and the total variance accounted for by all factors is a maximum.

The computational procedures are simpler for both desk and electronic computers. Straightforward matrix procedures, both notationally and computationally, are readily available. Furthermore, the checking of the computations can be set up mechanically more elegantly and simply.

In general, the number of factors required is more for 1's in the diagonal than for methods with communalities in the diagonal. In cases where the intercorrelations or covariances are very low compared to the variances, one may require a much larger number of factors to account for both the variances and covariances, if unit diagonals are used rather than optimal diagonal values. Such examples are found in the case of personality-type items or items from questionnaires where, in general, the correlations among the items may be quite low. Furthermore, it is often the case that one can tell much more readily when to stop factoring with the optimal diagonal method than with the unit method. For the former, there is usually a sharper cutoff point between those factors which contribute significantly to the variance of the set and those factors which do not.

When 1 is used in the diagonal, one can be sure that for each variable the total amount of variance accounted for is always less than or equal to the original variance. This is referred to as proper variance. Strange as it may seem, certain of the procedures for optimizing the diagonals, if used indiscriminately, can yield factor loading matrices which account for a greater amount of variance for some variables than that which exists in the original variables. This means that negative residual variances may be obtained which, of course, are difficult to interpret. True, there are procedures for preventing this type of inconsistency or absurdity from occurring, but they are not incorporated in the more common methods of factor analysis.

While it is possible in optimal diagonal methods for some of the variances accounted for to be greater than the original variances, in general, the sum total of variance accounted for by the unit diagonal procedure is greater for a specified number of factors than it is by the optimal diagonal method. This is true even though in the unit diagonal method, the variance taken into account for each variable is never greater and is usually less than its total variance. If one is concerned, therefore, with accounting for the maximum variance of the system with the minimum number of factors rather than accounting for only the best approximation to the correlations with the minimum number of factors, 1 should be used in the diagonals.

We are now ready to consider the actual procedures for calculating a centroid factor loading matrix from a correlation matrix with 1 in the diagonal. To do this, we shall first present the computational equations necessary for this solution. Next, the computational instructions for carrying out the computations will be outlined. Finally, a numerical example illustrating the method will be presented.

Fortran II computer programs are provided in the Appendix for the methods outlined in this and subsequent chapters. The data following each program have yielded the output presented in the corresponding numerical examples throughout the book.

5.3.2   Computational Equations.

We shall first define the notation to be used and then present the equations on which the computational routines are based.

5.3.2a   DEFINITION OF NOTATION

$_0R$ is the original correlation matrix.

$_kR$ is the kth residual correlation matrix.

$_kD$ is a diagonal matrix of the diagonal elements of $_kR$.

$_k\rho$ is the kth residual matrix with zeros in the diagonal.

$_0V_{.k}$ is an arbitrary sign vector.

$_iV_{.k}$ is the ith approximation to the sign vector for the kth residual matrix.

$_iW_{.k}$ is the vector obtained by multiplying $_k\rho$ by $_iV_{.k}$.

α_i is the location containing the element with the largest absolute value in $_iW_{.k}$ which is different in sign from the corresponding element in $_iV_{.k}$.

e_{α_i} is an elementary vector with the unit in the α_i position.

$_k\rho_{.\alpha_i}$ is the $\alpha_i th$ column of $_k\rho$.

$_iV_{\alpha_ik}$ is the α_ith element of $_iV_{.k}$.

$V_{.k}$ is the final sign vector for the kth residual matrix, that is, the sign vector when the signs in corresponding elements of $_iW_{.k}$ and $_iV_{.k}$ are all the same.

$a_{.k}$ is the vector of factor loadings for the kth factor.

5.3.2b   COMPUTATIONAL EQUATIONS

$$_k\rho = {}_kR - {}_kD \tag{5.3.1}$$

$$_0V_{.k} = 1 \tag{5.3.2}$$

$$_0W_{.k} = {}_k\rho_0 V_{.k} \tag{5.3.3}$$

$$_{i+1}V_{.k} = {}_iV_{.k} - 2e_{\alpha_i} {}_iV_{\alpha_ik} \tag{5.3.4}$$

$$_{i+1}W_{.k} = {}_iW_{.k} + 2{}_k\rho_{.\alpha_i i}V_{\alpha_i k} \tag{5.3.5}$$

$$w_{.k} = W_{.k} + {}_kDV_{.k} \tag{5.3.6}$$

$$_kL = V_{.k}'w_{.k} \tag{5.3.7}$$

$$S_k = \frac{1}{\sqrt{{}_kL}} \tag{5.3.8}$$

$$a_{.k} = w_{.k}S_k \tag{5.3.9}$$

$$_k\lambda = a_{.k}'a_{.k} \tag{5.3.10}$$

$$_{k+1}R = {}_kR - a_{.k}a_{.k}' \tag{5.3.11}$$

$$W_{.1} = R1 \tag{5.3.12}$$

$$L_1 = 1'R1 \tag{5.3.13}$$

$$a_{.1} = \frac{R1}{\sqrt{1'R1}} \tag{5.3.14}$$

5.3.3 Computational Instructions.

5.3.3 Computational Instructions. The major part of the computational procedures consists of the solution for the sign vector corresponding to the factor loading vectors. We start with the correlation matrix whose diagonal elements have been replaced by zeros, as in Eq. 5.3.1.

We shall consider the general case where this matrix may be either the original correlation matrix in which the prescript k is 0 or where it is a residual correlation matrix in which the prescript k indicates the particular residual matrix. Whatever the value of k, we take the first approximation to the sign vector V as the unit vector. This is indicated by Eq. 5.3.2.

Next we calculate the vector W, as in Eq. 5.3.3, which is the product of the matrix ρ postmultiplied by the unit vector. This, of course, is simply a column vector whose elements are the sums of corresponding row elements of the correlation matrix, exclusive of the diagonal elements.

We now examine the W vector given by Eq. 5.3.3 to see which of these elements is different in sign from the corresponding elements of the V or unit vector. In general, these will all be different for the first approximation to V, namely, the unit vector. We therefore find the one which is largest in absolute value in the W vector. We call this position α_1.

We next consider an elementary vector with the unit in the α_1 position, multiply this by the α_1 element of the V vector, and subtract twice the resulting vector from the V vector to give us a new V vector, as in Eq. 5.3.4. Obviously, this amounts merely to changing the sign of the element in the α_1 position of the V vector from $+1$ to -1. It is helpful, however, to write the relationship between the new and the old V vectors in this form so as to clarify the computational procedure.

Next we multiply the α_1 column of the ρ matrix by the α_1 element of the V vector and add twice the resulting column to the W vector to get a new W vector, as indicated in Eq. 5.3.5. In this case, of course, the α_1 element of the V vector will be simply 1.

We now have new V and W vectors where i in the prescripts of V and W in Eqs. 5.3.4 and 5.3.5, respectively, is 1. We compare the signs of corresponding elements in the new V and W vectors to see which of these corresponding elements have different signs. For all of those elements having differing signs, we consider the position of that one which is largest in absolute value in the W vector. This we call the α_2 position.

We calculate a new V vector by Eq. 5.3.4 simply by changing the sign of the current α_2 element of the V vector. We then get a new W vector by using Eq. 5.3.5 exactly as we did to get the first W vector, except that now the α_2 column of the ρ matrix and the α_2 element of the current V vector are involved. This element of the V vector will determine whether we add or subtract twice the α_2 column of the ρ matrix.

Again we compare signs of corresponding elements of the current V and the current W vectors, and identify the position of the element largest in absolute value in W with sign different from that in V. This we call the α_3 position. This procedure, in which we change the sign of an element in the V vector and calculate a new W vector, continues until all of the elements of the current W vector and the current V vector have the same signs for corresponding elements.

When all corresponding elements of the W and V vectors have the same sign, we add to the W vector a vector of the diagonal elements of $_kR$, whether this is the original correlation matrix or a residual matrix. These elements take the signs of the corresponding elements of the final V vector. This is indicated by Eq. 5.3.6.

The second term on the right-hand side of this equation is simply the V vector premultiplied by the diagonal matrix of the diagonal element of R, which is, of course, a vector of the diagonal elements with the signs of the corresponding elements of V assigned to them. This then gives us a vector which in Eq. 5.3.6 is designated as $w_{.k}$.

We next get a scalar quantity L, which is the minor product of the final V vector by the w vector. This is shown in Eq. 5.3.7. It is clear that this minor product is identical to the sum of the absolute values of the elements in w. Since the elements in w have the same signs as the V vector, the minor product of the right hand side of Eq. 5.3.7 amounts merely to making all signs in w positive and adding the elements.

Next we calculate a scalar which is the reciprocal square root of the value calculated in Eq. 5.3.7. This is indicated by S in Eq. 5.3.8.

We then multiply each element of the w vector by the scalar S, which gives the column of factor loadings for the kth factor. This is indicated in Eq. 5.3.9.

Equation 5.3.10 gives a value we call λ, which is the minor product moment of the factor loading vector $a_{.k}$ or simply the sums of squares of these elements. This value gives us the amount of variance accounted for by the kth factor loading. It may be used as a criterion to determine how many factors are to be extracted.

For the unit diagonal method we may take as a rough rule of thumb that when λ is greater than 1, the corresponding factor loading vector is retained. If it is 1 or less, we may assume that it is not large enough to justify retaining the factor, since the factor accounts for no more variance than that accounted for by any one variable. In general, we should expect a factor to account for somewhat more of the total variance than that accounted for by any of the single variables in the system. This criterion may in general be expected to give an upper limit to the required number of factors.

If λ in Eq. 5.3.10 is greater than 1, we may proceed to find the next residual matrix, as indicated by Eq. 5.3.11. Here we see that the major product moment of the factor loading matrix $a_{.k}$ is calculated and the result subtracted from a current residual matrix $_kR$ to give the next residual matrix $_{k+1}R$. These computations may be made with a desk computer in two steps: first, calculate the major product moment matrix of the factor vector $a_{.k}$ and second, subtract this matrix from $_kR$. The computations can also be made by putting each element of R in the lower register and subtracting from it the corresponding product of the appropriate elements from $a_{.k}$. If the computations are made by an electronic computer, the operations will in general be of this second kind.

It should be observed that for most matrices of intercorrelations of aptitude or intelligence tests, the intercorrelations, in general, are positive and therefore the $_0W$ vector in Eq. 5.3.3 will have all of its elements positive. Since the $_0V$ vector is a unit vector, the signs of V and W will be the same. Therefore, the steps indicated by Eqs. 5.3.4 and 5.3.5, which for residual matrices

TABLE 5.3.1   Correlation Matrix and First Factor Loading Vector

1.000	.829	.768	.108	.033	.108	.298	.309	.351
.829	1.000	.775	.115	.061	.125	.323	.347	.369
.768	.775	1.000	.272	.205	.238	.296	.271	.385
.108	.115	.272	1.000	.636	.626	.249	.183	.369
.033	.061	.205	.636	1.000	.709	.138	.091	.254
.108	.125	.238	.626	.709	1.000	.190	.103	.291
.298	.323	.296	.249	.138	.190	1.000	.654	.527
.309	.347	.271	.183	.091	.103	.654	1.000	.541
.351	.369	.385	.369	.254	.291	.527	.541	1.000
3.728								
0.659	0.684	0.730	0.617	0.542	0.588	0.637	0.606	0.708

may require many iterations, will be eliminated. The computation of the first factor loading, then, is much simpler.

In this case, we first get a vector of the sums of rows of the correlation matrix, as in Eq. 5.3.12. Next we sum this W vector, as in Eq. 5.3.13, to get the scalar L_1 and finally, we multiply this W vector by the reciprocal square root of the L_1 scalar to get the first factor loading vector $a_{.1}$, as in Eq. 5.3.14. It will be seen that the L scalar is simply the sum of all of the elements in the correlation matrix, including the diagonals.

5.3.4 Numerical Example.
To illustrate the method, we use a ninth-order correlation matrix.

Table 5.3.1 shows the original correlation matrix together with the first factor loading vector at the bottom of the table.

Table 5.3.2 shows the first residual matrix, followed by the successive V and W vectors. The second factor loading vector is at the bottom of the table.

TABLE 5.3.2   First Residual Matrix, Successive V and W Vectors, and Second Factor Loading Vector

0.565	0.378	0.287	−0.299	−0.324	−0.279	−0.122	−0.091	−0.116
0.378	0.533	0.276	−0.306	−0.309	−0.277	−0.112	−0.067	−0.115
0.287	0.276	0.468	−0.178	−0.190	−0.191	−0.169	−0.171	−0.132
−0.299	−0.306	−0.178	0.620	0.302	0.264	−0.144	−0.191	−0.068
−0.324	−0.309	−0.190	0.302	0.706	0.391	−0.207	−0.238	−0.130
−0.279	−0.277	−0.191	0.264	0.391	0.655	−0.184	−0.253	−0.125
−0.122	−0.112	−0.169	−0.144	−0.207	−0.184	0.594	0.268	0.076
−0.091	−0.067	−0.171	−0.191	−0.238	−0.253	0.268	0.632	0.111
−0.116	−0.115	−0.132	−0.068	−0.130	−0.125	0.076	0.111	0.498
1.000	1.000	1.000	1.000	−1.000	1.000	1.000	1.000	1.000
0.083	0.086	−0.087	−1.223	−0.706	−1.436	−0.180	−0.157	−0.239
1.000	1.000	1.000	1.000	−1.000	−1.000	1.000	1.000	1.000
0.642	0.639	0.294	−1.751	−1.488	−1.436	0.188	0.350	0.012
1.000	1.000	1.000	−1.000	−1.000	−1.000	1.000	1.000	1.000
1.239	1.252	0.650	−1.751	−2.091	−1.963	0.476	0.731	0.147
2.017								
0.457	0.452	0.283	−0.601	−0.709	−0.663	0.271	0.346	0.164

Table 5.3.3 gives the second residual matrix, followed by the successive V and W vectors. The third factor loading vector is at the bottom of the table.

Table 5.3.4 gives the fourth residual matrix and the successive V and W vectors.

TABLE 5.3.3 Second Residual Matrix, Successive V and W Vectors, and Third Factor Loading Vector

0.356	0.172	0.157	−0.024	−0.000	0.024	−0.246	−0.249	−0.191
0.172	0.328	0.148	−0.035	0.011	0.024	−0.235	−0.224	−0.189
0.157	0.148	0.387	−0.008	0.010	−0.003	−0.246	−0.269	−0.178
−0.024	−0.035	−0.008	0.259	−0.124	−0.135	0.019	0.017	0.031
−0.000	0.011	0.010	−0.124	0.204	−0.080	−0.015	0.007	−0.014
0.024	0.024	−0.003	−0.135	−0.080	0.215	−0.004	−0.024	−0.017
−0.246	−0.235	−0.246	0.019	−0.015	−0.004	0.521	0.174	0.032
−0.249	−0.224	−0.269	0.017	0.007	−0.024	0.174	0.513	0.055
−0.191	−0.189	−0.178	0.031	−0.014	−0.017	0.032	0.055	0.472
1.000	1.000	1.000	1.000	1.000	1.000	−1.000	1.000	1.000
0.135	0.142	0.104	−0.297	−0.174	−0.206	−0.521	−0.861	−0.535
1.000	1.000	1.000	1.000	1.000	1.000	−1.000	−1.000	1.000
0.633	0.589	0.642	−0.331	−0.189	−0.158	−0.868	−0.861	−0.644
1.000	1.000	1.000	1.000	1.000	1.000	−1.000	−1.000	−1.000
1.014	0.968	0.999	−0.392	−0.161	−0.125	−0.932	−0.971	−0.644
1.000	1.000	1.000	−1.000	1.000	1.000	−1.000	−1.000	−1.000
1.062	1.037	1.014	−0.392	0.087	0.145	−0.970	−1.004	−0.705
1.281								
0.456	0.439	0.451	−0.209	0.094	0.116	−0.479	−0.488	−0.378

TABLE 5.3.4 Third Residual Matrix and Successive V and W Vectors

0.148	−0.029	−0.048	0.072	−0.043	−0.029	−0.027	−0.026	−0.018
−0.029	0.135	−0.050	0.057	−0.030	−0.027	−0.024	−0.010	−0.023
−0.048	−0.050	0.184	0.087	−0.032	−0.055	−0.029	−0.050	−0.008
0.072	0.057	0.087	0.215	−0.104	−0.111	−0.081	−0.085	−0.049
−0.043	−0.030	−0.032	−0.104	0.195	−0.091	0.030	0.053	0.022
−0.029	−0.027	−0.055	−0.111	−0.091	0.201	0.051	0.032	0.027
−0.027	−0.024	−0.029	−0.081	0.030	0.051	0.291	−0.060	−0.150
−0.026	−0.010	−0.050	−0.085	0.053	0.032	−0.060	0.275	−0.130
−0.018	−0.023	−0.008	−0.049	0.022	0.027	−0.150	−0.130	0.328
1.000	1.000	1.000	1.000	1.000	1.000	1.000	1.000	−1.000
−0.112	−0.090	−0.169	−0.118	−0.238	−0.256	0.009	−0.016	−0.328
1.000	1.000	1.000	1.000	1.000	−1.000	1.000	1.000	−1.000
−0.055	−0.035	−0.060	0.104	−0.057	−0.256	−0.093	−0.080	−0.383
1.000	1.000	1.000	1.000	1.000	−1.000	−1.000	1.000	−1.000
−0.000	0.014	−0.001	0.266	−0.117	−0.358	−0.093	0.039	−0.083
1.000	1.000	1.000	1.000	−1.000	−1.000	1.000	1.050	−1.000
0.085	0.074	0.063	0.475	−0.117	−0.177	−0.153	−0.067	−0.126
1.000	1.000	1.000	1.000	−1.000	−1.000	−1.000	−1.000	−1.000
0.138	0.093	0.162	0.645	−0.223	−0.241	−0.034	−0.067·	0.134
1.000	1.000	1.000	1.000	−1.000	−1.000	−1.000	−1.000	1.000
0.102	0.047	0.147	0.548	−0.180	−0.187	−0.333	−0.326	0.134
0.514								

In each of the first three tables the minor product moment of the factor loading vector is given immediately before the corresponding vector. In the fourth table this is less than 1; hence, the computations are terminated and the fourth factor loading vector is not displayed.

5.4   Optimizing the Diagonal Elements or Communality Estimates

We shall next consider the centroid method which assumes specific factors and is concerned only with a best approximation to the correlation coefficients, irrespective of the diagonal elements.

5.4.1   Characteristics of the Solution.
The characteristics of this type of solution will be discussed in terms of the simplicity of the computations, the number of factors required, the type of variances to be expected, and the amount of variance accounted for.

As indicated in the discussion of characteristics of the unit diagonal solution, the computations for this method of optimal diagonals or communalities is somewhat more complicated and not as straightforward. The problem of maintaining simple and mechanical computational checks is a little more difficult.

The number of factors required to account for the correlation coefficients, irrespective of the diagonal elements, is fewer, in general, than for the previous method. The difference between the number of factors required for the two methods is a function of the average size of the absolute values of the correlation coefficients. The smaller this average size, the fewer will be the number of factors required for this method.

The usual methods for estimating the diagonal elements make it possible to have the proportion of total variance accounted for greater than 100 per cent for some of the variables in the set. This phenomenon has been described in the literature as the Heywood (1931) case. Occasionally, the use of communality models with the centroid method yields communalities greater than 1, particularly if a large number of factor vectors are calculated.

The total amount of variance accounted for by this method is, in general, less than for the method which has unit diagonal elements. The extent to which it is less is again a function of the average size of the correlation coefficients. The smaller these are, the less will be the total amount of variance accounted for.

5.4.2   Computational Equations.

5.4.2a   DEFINITION OF NOTATION
$_k d_j$ is the largest absolute value in column j of ρ.
$_k d$ is a diagonal matrix of the $_k d_j$.

$_k d_L$ is the largest value in $_k d$.

All other symbols are the same as in Section 5.3.2a.

5.4.2b THE EQUATIONS. The computational equations for the communality method are essentially the same as for the unity method. For convenience they are repeated below together with the necessary modifications.

$$_k\rho = {}_k R - {}_k D \tag{5.4.1}$$

$$_k d_j = |_k\rho_{Lj}| \tag{5.4.2}$$

$$_k d = \begin{bmatrix} _k d_1 & \cdots & 0 \\ \cdots & \cdots & \cdots \\ 0 & \cdots & _k d_n \end{bmatrix} \tag{5.4.3}$$

$$_0 V_{.k} = 1 \tag{5.4.4}$$

$$_0 W_{.k} = {}_k\rho \, _0 V_{.k} \tag{5.4.5}$$

$$_{i+1} V_{.k} = {}_i V_{.k} - 2e_{\alpha_i i} V_{\alpha_i k} \tag{5.4.6}$$

$$_{i+1} W_{.k} = {}_i W_{.k} + 2_k\rho_{.\alpha_i i} V_{\alpha_i k} \tag{5.4.7}$$

$$w_{.k} = W_{.k} + {}_k d V_{.k} \tag{5.4.8}$$

$$_k L = V_{.k}' w_{.k} \tag{5.4.9}$$

$$_k S = \frac{1}{\sqrt{_k L}} \tag{5.4.10}$$

$$a_{.k} = w_{.k} \, _k S \tag{5.4.11}$$

$$C = \frac{tr\rho^2}{n(n-1)} - \frac{1}{N} \tag{5.4.12}$$

5.4.3 *Computational Instructions.* This method begins essentially the same as the unit diagonal method. First, we consider the ρ matrix as defined by Eq. 5.4.1, which gives the correlation or kth residual matrix with the diagonal elements subtracted. Therefore, ρ is the same as R, except that the diagonal elements are 0.

Next we consider a scalar quantity for each column or row of the ρ matrix in Eq. 5.4.1, which is the absolute value of the largest absolute value in that column. The notation for this is indicated in Eq. 5.4.2.

We then define a diagonal matrix of these largest absolute elements, as indicated in Eq. 5.4.3. Here we have a diagonal matrix of the largest absolute values of each column in the correlation matrix, exclusive of the diagonal.

We define the arbitrary V vector as the unit vector, as in the previous method. This is shown by Eq. 5.4.4.

Similarly, we define the first W vector as the sum of the row elements of the ρ matrix. This is shown in Eq. 5.4.5.

The procedure for finding a V and a W vector with the same sign by successively altering a sign of the V vector is indicated by Eqs. 5.4.6 and 5.4.7. This procedure is exactly the same as in Section 5.3.3.

The essential difference in the two methods comes in the next step, which is to get the w vector. Here, to get the final w vector, which has the same signs as the current V vector, we add not the diagonal elements of the correlation matrix but rather the elements defined by Eq. 5.4.3, namely, the largest non-diagonal elements in each of the columns. It should be emphasized that these elements take the signs of the corresponding elements in the final V vector, irrespective of what signs they had originally. This is indicated by the second term on the right-hand side of Eq. 5.4.8. This term is simply the final V vector premultiplied by the diagonal matrix defined in Eq. 5.4.3.

As in the previous method, we now calculate the sums of the absolute values of the w vector given in Eq. 5.4.8. This is indicated in Eq. 5.4.9 as the minor product of the V vector and the w vector.

The scalar $_kS$ is then calculated as the reciprocal square root of $_kL$. This is shown in Eq. 5.4.10.

As in Section 5.3.3, we also calculate the factor loading vector by multiplying each element in w by the scalar S. This is indicated in Eq. 5.4.11.

The procedure for getting residual matrices is identical to the previous method. However, the criterion for determining the number of factors needed cannot be the same, since this method is much less efficient in accounting for the total variance of the system. Therefore, we are not justified in assuming that a factor should account for more variance than a single variable. One convenient procedure is to factor until the average square residual of the $_k\rho$ matrix is less than some specified value. This value may be, for example, $1/N$ where N is the sample size. This is indicated by C in Eq. 5.4.12.

In general, it should be noted that the two methods of analysis may actually give similar results if the number of variables is very large and if the average of the original intercorrelations is not too small. If the sums of the absolute values of the correlation coefficients for each column are much larger than 1, for example, greater than 10, then one might better use 1 in the diagonal, as in Section 5.3.3.

5.4.4 Numerical Example. Using the same data as in Section 5.3.4, we shall illustrate the method for communality estimates.

Table 5.4.1 gives the first factor loading vector.

TABLE 5.4.1 First Factor Loading Vector

0.656	0.682	0.720	0.577	0.512	0.560	0.602	0.570	0.656

TABLE 5.4.2   First Residual Matrix, Successive V and W Vectors, and Second Factor Loading Vector

−0.431	0.381	0.295	−0.271	−0.303	−0.260	−0.097	−0.065	−0.079
0.381	−0.465	0.284	−0.278	−0.288	−0.257	−0.087	−0.041	−0.078
0.295	0.284	−0.518	−0.144	−0.164	−0.165	−0.137	−0.139	−0.087
−0.271	−0.278	−0.144	−0.333	0.340	0.303	−0.098	−0.146	−0.009
−0.303	−0.288	−0.164	0.340	−0.263	0.422	−0.170	−0.201	−0.082
−0.260	−0.257	−0.165	0.303	0.422	−0.314	−0.147	−0.216	−0.076
−0.097	−0.087	−0.137	−0.098	−0.170	−0.147	−0.362	0.311	0.133
−0.065	−0.041	−0.139	−0.146	−0.201	−0.216	0.311	−0.325	0.168
−0.079	−0.078	−0.087	−0.009	−0.082	−0.076	0.133	0.168	−0.430
1.000	1.000	1.000	1.000	−1.000	1.000	1.000	1.000	1.000
0.209	0.212	0.071	−0.983	−0.446	−1.240	0.048	0.072	0.053
1.000	1.000	1.000	1.000	−1.000	−1.000	1.000	1.000	1.000
0.728	0.726	0.402	−1.589	−1.291	−1.240	0.342	0.504	0.205
1.000	1.000	1.000	−1.000	−1.000	−1.000	1.000	1.000	1.000
1.269	1.283	0.689	−1.589	−1.971	−1.845	0.538	0.796	0.223
0.454	0.457	0.271	−0.530	−0.658	−0.623	0.233	0.304	0.107

TABLE 5.4.3   Second Residual Matrix, Successive V and W Vectors, and Third Factor Loading Vector

−0.206	0.174	0.173	−0.030	−0.005	0.023	−0.203	−0.203	−0.128
0.174	−0.209	0.160	−0.036	0.013	0.028	−0.194	−0.181	−0.127
0.173	0.160	−0.073	−0.000	0.014	0.003	−0.200	−0.222	−0.116
−0.030	−0.036	−0.000	−0.281	−0.009	−0.028	0.026	0.016	0.048
−0.005	0.013	0.014	−0.009	−0.433	0.012	−0.017	−0.001	−0.011
0.023	0.028	0.003	−0.028	0.012	−0.388	−0.001	−0.026	−0.009
−0.203	−0.194	−0.200	0.026	−0.017	−0.001	−0.055	0.240	0.108
−0.203	−0.181	−0.222	0.016	−0.001	−0.026	0.240	−0.093	0.135
−0.128	−0.127	−0.116	0.048	−0.011	0.009	0.108	0.135	−0.012
1.000	1.000	1.000	1.000	1.000	1.000	1.000	−1.000	1.000
0.207	0.199	0.255	−0.045	−0.002	0.055	−0.722	−0.242	−0.371
1.000	1.000	1.000	1.000	1.000	1.000	−1.000	−1.000	1.000
0.612	0.587	0.656	−0.096	0.031	0.058	−0.722	−0.722	−0.586
1.000	1.000	1.000	1.000	1.000	1.000	−1.000	−1.000	−1.000
0.869	0.841	0.888	−0.191	0.054	0.076	−0.937	−0.992	−0.586
1.000	1.000	1.000	−1.000	1.000	1.000	−1.000	−1.000	−1.000
0.929	0.913	0.888	−0.191	0.071	0.131	−0.988	−1.023	−0.682
0.424	0.414	0.415	−0.089	0.033	0.060	−0.460	−0.473	−0.305

Tables 5.4.2 and 5.4.3 give the residual matrices, the successive V and W vectors, and the second and third factor vectors.

Table 5.4.4 gives the third residual matrix.

TABLE 5.4.4   Third Residual Matrix

-0.179	-0.001	-0.003	0.008	-0.019	-0.002	-0.008	-0.003	0.001
-0.001	-0.171	-0.012	0.001	-0.001	0.004	-0.004	0.015	-0.001
-0.003	-0.012	-0.172	0.037	0.000	-0.021	-0.009	-0.025	0.011
0.008	0.001	0.037	-0.008	-0.006	-0.022	-0.015	-0.027	0.020
-0.019	-0.001	0.000	-0.006	-0.001	0.010	-0.002	0.015	-0.001
-0.002	0.004	-0.021	-0.022	0.010	-0.004	0.026	0.002	0.009
-0.008	-0.004	-0.009	-0.015	-0.002	0.026	-0.211	0.023	-0.033
-0.003	0.015	-0.025	-0.027	0.015	0.002	0.023	-0.223	-0.010
0.001	-0.001	0.011	0.020	-0.001	0.009	-0.033	-0.010	-0.093

5.5   Iterative Solution for Diagonals

The iterative solutions for the diagonals, where communalities are assumed, take on a wide variety of forms. The one we shall describe seems to be as simple and straightforward as any available. It begins with the correlation matrix with 1 in the diagonals.

5.5.1   Characteristics of the Solution.

The problem of determining a product moment matrix of specified rank which will best fit the nondiagonal elements of the correlation matrix is extremely complex mathematically. The solution can be indicated mathematically, but very complicated non-linear equations are involved and their solution requires successive iterations. As a matter of fact, the proofs of convergence are not, in general, available.

Essentially, the characteristics of the solution are similar to the one described in Section 5.3.3, except that the computational operations must go through a number of cycles and therefore the solution takes much longer. The number of factors required to account for the intercorrelations to a specified degree of accuracy is probably not much different for most cases of experimental data than that case in which the successive estimates of the communalities are the highest nondiagonal elements. In the iterative solution one can impose the condition that no communality shall exceed 1. We shall impose this restriction on the solution presented in the following section. As in the case of the less exact solution, the amount of variance accounted for with optimal diagonal elements will not, in general, be as great as for the solution with 1 in the diagonals.

5.5.2   Computational Equations.

In general, the notation and the computational equations are similar to the method with 1 in the diagonals.

TABLE 5.5.1 Successive Communality Estimates

0.942 8	0.916 1	0.991	0.998	0.991	0.998	0.998	0.991	0.991
0.883 7	0.855 2	0.911	0.997	0.940	0.949	0.994	0.982	0.987
0.835 6	0.821 3	0.841	0.990	0.842	0.886	0.969	0.926	0.962
0.820 6	0.816 4	0.803	0.988	0.773	0.842	0.958	0.901	0.951
0.816 5	0.817 5	0.783	0.973	0.726	0.787	0.898	0.767	0.891
0.819 5	0.823 6	0.773	0.973	0.704	0.766	0.815	0.683	0.891
0.813 4	0.821 7	0.763	0.923	0.685	0.738	0.748	0.638	0.690
0.819 4	0.828 8	0.762	0.923	0.686	0.739	0.678	0.619	0.582
0.821 4	0.832 9	0.760	0.923	0.686	0.740	0.652	0.631	0.538
0.805 3	0.825 10	0.737	0.788	0.663	0.694	0.618	0.625	0.514
0.807 3	0.833 11	0.732	0.709	0.668	0.682	0.609	0.635	0.512
0.813 3	0.842 12	0.731	0.661	0.681	0.682	0.608	0.645	0.515
0.818 3	0.849 13	0.729	0.632	0.694	0.685	0.608	0.652	0.517
0.822 3	0.855 14	0.728	0.614	0.704	0.688	0.608	0.657	0.519
0.825 3	0.858 15	0.726	0.603	0.712	0.690	0.608	0.660	0.521
0.828 3	0.861 16	0.725	0.596	0.718	0.691	0.608	0.662	0.522
0.829 3	0.863 17	0.723	0.591	0.722	0.692	0.608	0.663	0.522
0.830 3	0.864 18	0.722	0.588	0.725	0.693	0.608	0.663	0.523
0.831 3	0.865 19	0.722	0.586	0.727	0.693	0.608	0.664	0.523
0.832 3	0.866 20	0.721	0.585	0.728	0.693	0.608	0.664	0.523
0.832	0.866	0.721	0.584	0.729	0.693	0.608	0.664	0.524

5.5.3 Computational Instructions. We begin with 1 in the diagonals of the correlation matrix, and factor this matrix by the method of Section 5.3.3 until the average of the squared elements of the residual matrix $_k\rho$ is less than some specified value, say, the reciprocal of the sample size.

Next we calculate the diagonal of the major product moment of the factor loading matrix, and substitute it in the diagonal of the correlation matrix.

This matrix is then again factored by the method of Section 5.3.3 until the residuals satisfy the specified tolerance.

This procedure is continued until successive sets of diagonals or communalities are sufficiently close.

5.5.4 Numerical Example. We present a numerical example using the same data as in the two previous sections.

Table 5.5.1 gives the vectors of the successively calculated diagonal matrices obtained from the iterative solutions for the factor loading matrices, together with the number of factors extracted for each iteration and the number of the iteration.

Table 5.5.2 gives the factor loading matrix for the final solution. This table may be compared with the factor loadings obtained by the methods of the previous two sections.

Table 5.5.3 gives the final residual matrix.

TABLE 5.5.2   Final Factor Loading Matrix

0.658	0.690	0.712	0.569	0.517	0.558	0.594	0.573	0.654
0.462	0.462	0.253	−0.506	−0.679	−0.616	0.222	0.313	0.089
0.430	0.420	0.388	−0.066	0.027	0.039	−0.453	−0.488	−0.297

TABLE 5.5.3   Final Residual Matrix

0.000	−0.020	0.016	−0.004	−0.005	0.009	−0.001	−0.003	0.008
−0.020	0.000	0.004	−0.016	0.007	0.009	0.001	0.012	0.002
0.016	0.004	0.000	0.021	−0.002	−0.019	−0.007	−0.026	0.013
−0.004	−0.016	0.021	0.000	0.000	−0.001	−0.007	−0.017	0.023
−0.005	0.007	−0.002	0.000	0.000	0.001	−0.006	0.021	−0.015
0.009	0.009	−0.019	−0.001	0.001	0.000	0.013	−0.005	−0.007
−0.001	0.001	−0.007	−0.007	−0.006	0.013	0.000	0.023	−0.016
−0.003	0.012	−0.026	−0.017	0.021	−0.005	0.023	0.000	−0.006
0.008	0.002	0.013	0.023	−0.015	−0.007	−0.016	−0.006	0.000

5.6   Mathematical Proofs

5.6.1 The Maximizing Sign Vector. It was pointed out in Section 5.1 that all of the centroid methods are based on the rank reduction theorem and use sign vectors as the arbitrary matrices. It was also stated that the procedure, in general, for determining the sign vector is such as to obtain a maximum for the triple product in the matrix reduction equation. We shall now prove that each of these successive sign changes, as outlined in the computational procedure, does actually increase the value of this triple product.

We begin with the correlation matrix as a function of the ρ matrix and its diagonal terms:

$$R = \rho + D_R \qquad (5.6.1)$$

We consider next the scalar quantity L which is the triple product of the row V vector by the correlation matrix by the column V vector:

$$V'RV = L = \max. \qquad (5.6.2)$$

The problem is to make this value a maximum.

Next we consider the factor loading vector a:

$$a = \frac{RV}{\sqrt{V'RV}} \qquad (5.6.3)$$

This shows the factor loading vector as the correlation matrix postmultiplied by the V vector, and the product divided by the square root of the L scalar as defined in Eq. 5.6.2.

From Eqs. 5.6.1 and 5.6.2 we can express the scalar L as a function of the V vector, the ρ matrix, and the diagonal matrix D. This is given in Eq. 5.6.4.

$$L = V'(\rho + D)V \qquad (5.6.4)$$

If we multiply out the right-hand side of Eq. 5.6.4, we get

$$L = V'\rho V + V'DV \qquad (5.6.5)$$

Notice that the second term on the right-hand side of Eq. 5.6.5 is independent of the signs in the elements of the V vector. Irrespective of the signs of these elements, this term is simply the sum of the terms of the diagonal elements. Therefore, changes in the signs of the elements of V can change only the first term on the right-hand side of Eq. 5.6.5, and we shall direct our attention to this term. We shall designate it by μ:

$$\mu = V'\rho V \qquad (5.6.6)$$

We assume now that we start with some arbitrary sign vector V which is an approximation to the one which would yield maximum L in Eq. 5.6.2. We define the W vector as the product of the ρ matrix postmultiplied by the optimal V vector:

$$W = \rho V \qquad (5.6.7)$$

We consider also some ith approximation to this W vector and the corresponding μ_i:

$$_iW = \rho\,_iV \tag{5.6.8}$$

$$\mu_i = {}_iV'\rho\,_iV \tag{5.6.8a}$$

Suppose now that in Eq. 5.6.8 the kth element of W and the kth element of V are different in sign. We shall prove that if we change the sign of the kth element in V to get a new V, namely, $_kV$, the corresponding μ_k will be larger than μ_i.

First consider the matrix form for expressing the relationship between $_kV$ and $_iV$:

$$_kV = (_iV - 2e_k\,_iV_k) \tag{5.6.9}$$

This is simply a method of showing that we subtract twice the kth element of $_iV$ multiplied by the sign of this kth element to change its sign. This appears to be a complicated way to indicate the sign change, but it will be useful in the subsequent proof.

We express μ_k as a function of ρ and $_kV$, as given by the right-hand side of Eq. 5.6.9, by

$$\mu_k = (_iV' - 2e_k'\,_iV_k)\rho(_iV - 2e_k\,_iV_k) \tag{5.6.10}$$

If we expand the right-hand side of Eq. 5.6.10, we get

$$\mu_k = {}_iV'\rho\,_iV - 2\,_iV'\rho_{.k}\,_iV_k - 2\rho_{.k}'\,_iV\,_iV_k + \rho_{kk} \tag{5.6.11}$$

But since the two middle terms of the right-hand side of Eq. 5.6.11 are scalars and mutual transposes, they are equal. It is clear that these terms are equal to the kth element of the $_iW$ vector:

$$_iV'\rho_{.k} = \rho_{.k}\,_iV = {}_iW_k \tag{5.6.12}$$

We also note that, since by definition the diagonal elements of ρ are 0, ρ_{kk} is also 0:

$$\rho_{kk} = 0 \tag{5.6.13}$$

Because of Eqs. 5.6.12 and 5.6.13, we can rewrite Eq. 5.6.11 as

$$\mu_k = {}_iV'\rho\,_iV - 4\,_iW_k\,_iV_k \tag{5.6.14}$$

But the first term in the right-hand side of Eq. 5.6.14 is precisely the value of μ_i in Eq. 5.6.8a. Hence, we may rewrite Eq. 5.6.14 as

$$\mu_k = \mu_i - 4\,_iW_k\,_iV_k \tag{5.6.15}$$

Since we have by hypothesis that the sign of the kth element of $_iV$ and the kth element of $_iW$ are different, we know that their product must be negative and that therefore the second term on the right-hand side of Eq. 5.6.15 must be negative. Consequently, μ_k will be exactly four times the absolute value of the kth element of $_iW$ greater than the value of μ_i. It is for this reason that in the procedures for solving for the V vector we always choose the largest element in W which is different in sign from its corresponding element in V in determining the α_k position. This means that we always increase μ by the maximum amount possible with a single sign change.

5.6.2 Centroid Method as a Special Case of the Rank Reduction Theorem.

We shall now show that the centroid method discussed in Section 5.3 is a special case of the rank reduction theorem. The other methods are approximations to it. The second method is a rough approximation which cannot be expressed algebraically, due to the method of selecting the diagonal elements. The third method, in which the diagonals are solved for iteratively, is an exact special case of the rank reduction method for each new set of diagonal elements.

We start with a slight modification of Eq. 5.3.5:

$$_{i+1}W_{.k} = {_i}W_{.k} - 2\,_k\rho_{.\alpha_i}\,_iV_{\alpha_i k} \tag{5.6.16}$$

The two equations differ only with respect to sign. For convenience in computer programing the sign changes in Section 5.3 are made first with V then with W rather than vice versa as in this development. From this equation we can substitute for the first term on the right-hand side of Eq. 5.6.16 and get

$$_{i+1}W_{.k} = {_k}\rho V_{.k} - 2\,_k\rho_{.\alpha_i}\,_iV_{\alpha_i k} \tag{5.6.17}$$

This is because each W vector is the product of the ρ matrix times the corresponding V vector.

We also know that the α_i column of the ρ matrix has been obtained from this matrix by postmultiplying it by an e_i vector. Therefore, we can rewrite Eq. 5.6.17:

$$_{i+1}W_{.k} = {_k}\rho(V_{.k} - 2\,_k e_{\alpha_i}\,_iV_{\alpha_i k}) \tag{5.6.18}$$

The relationship of the $_{i+1}W$ vector as a function of the ρ matrix and the $_{i+1}V$ vector is expressed:

$$_{i+1}W_{.k} = {_k}\rho\,_{i+1}V_{.k} \tag{5.6.19}$$

We repeat the w vector indicated in Eq. 5.3.6 as

$$w_{.k} = W_{.k} + {_k}DV_k \tag{5.6.20}$$

Because of Eq. 5.6.19, we can rewrite Eq. 5.6.20 in the form of

$$w_{.k} = {_k}\rho V_{.k} + {_k}DV_{.k} \tag{5.6.21}$$

Factoring out the V vector on the right of the right-hand side of Eq. 5.6.21, we have

$$w_{.k} = ({_k}\rho + {_k}D)V_{.k} \tag{5.6.22}$$

But because of the definition of the D matrix of Eq. 5.3.1, we can rewrite Eq. 5.6.22:

$$w_{.k} = {}_kRV_{.k} \tag{5.6.23}$$

We also have Eq. 5.3.9 repeated as

$$a_{.k} = w_{.k} S_k \tag{5.6.24}$$

Using Eq. 5.3.8, we can therefore write

$$a_{.k} = \frac{w_{.k}}{\sqrt{{}_kL}} \tag{5.6.25}$$

But because of Eq. 5.3.7, we can also write

$$a_{.k} = \frac{w_{.k}}{\sqrt{V_{.k}'w_{.k}}} \tag{5.6.26}$$

Because of Eqs. 5.6.23 and 5.6.26, we can write

$$a_{.k} = \frac{{}_kRV_{.k}}{\sqrt{V_{.k}'{}_kRV_{.k}}} \tag{5.6.27}$$

We repeat Eq. 5.3.11 as

$${}_{k+1}R = {}_kR - a_{.k}a_{.k}' \tag{5.6.28}$$

If we substitute Eq. 5.6.27 in Eq. 5.6.28, we get

$${}_{k+1}R = {}_kR - RV_{.k}(V_{.k}'RV_{.k})^{-1}V_{.k}'R \tag{5.6.29}$$

This will be recognized as the special case of the rank reduction theorem in which the V vector and its transpose constitute the arbitrary matrices. Therefore, we see that each residual matrix has a rank exactly one less than the rank of the matrix preceding it.

5.6.3 Minor Product of Sign and Factor Matrices.

In general,

$${}_{k-1}R - \frac{{}_{k-1}RV_{.k}V_{.k}'{}_{k-1}R}{V_{.k}'{}_{k-1}RV_{.k}} = {}_kR \tag{5.6.30}$$

Because of Eq. 5.6.30, it can be shown that

$${}_{k+i}R = {}_{k-1}RM_i \tag{5.6.31}$$

where M_i can be solved for from Eq. 5.6.30.

In general,

$$\frac{{}_{k+i}RV_{.(k+i+1)}}{\sqrt{V_{.(k+i+1)}'{}_{k+i}RV_{.(k+i+1)}}} = a_{.(k+i+1)} \tag{5.6.32}$$

But from Eq. 5.6.30,

$$V_{.k}'{}_k R = 0 \tag{5.6.33}$$

From Eqs. 5.6.31–5.6.33,

$$V_{.k}' a_{.(k+i+1)} = 0 \tag{5.6.34}$$

for $i = 0$ to $m - k - 1$, where m is the number of factors.

Because of Eq. 5.6.34,

$$V'a = t \tag{5.6.35}$$

where t is a lower triangular matrix, and V and a are the $n \times m$ sign and factor matrices, respectively.

Chapter 6

Grouping Methods

We have seen how one of the types of factor analysis techniques consists of utilizing sign vectors, special cases of which may be unit vectors. Another model assumes we can estimate in advance of the analysis which particular variables measure approximately the same factor and may therefore be grouped together for purposes of analysis. These methods in their simplest form assume that each of the variables in a particular group are of equal importance in determining the factor loading vector corresponding to the group. Actually, the computational procedures can be applied to any arbitrary groupings for any number of subsets of variables.

6.1   Characteristics of the Grouping Methods

The grouping methods we shall consider are special cases of the rank reduction theorem, and the arbitrary matrices in the matrix reduction equation will have binary elements.

6.1.1   Special Case of Matrix Reduction Theorem.   Some minor variations of grouping methods are not special cases of the rank reduction theorem. These we shall not outline. Holzinger and Harman (1941) have proposed such a method known as the *bifactor method.* This procedure does not yield a rank reduction of the original correlation matrix for each factor extracted, although with appropriate modifications it can be made to do so.

6.1.2   The Arbitrary Matrices.   The arbitrary matrices in the grouping method, as we shall see, may be either vectors or matrices. As in the case of the centroid method, these arbitrary matrices are mutual transposes of one another, the left multiplier being the horizontal form of the matrix and the right multiplier the vertical form. In all of the grouping methods, however, the elements in the arbitrary multipliers are either 1 or 0. The unit elements in the arbitrary matrices serve to isolate or group the particular variables regarded as belonging to a set.

As with the centroid method, Thurstone (1947) is primarily responsible for the development of the grouping methods. Others have also contributed to the computational procedures and other variations of these methods. Thurstone apparently did not recognize the grouping methods as special cases of the rank reduction theorem and, as in the case of the centroid methods, it was Guttman (1944) who pointed out the rank reduction characteristics of these methods.

6.2   Kinds of Grouping Methods

There are two major kinds of grouping methods, one of which was designated by Thurstone as the *group centroid method* and the other as the *multiple group method*.

6.2.1   Group Centroid Methods.
Although Thurstone described only one type of group centroid method, we shall consider two variations or elaborations of this method which have certain advantages. In one of these the arbitrary vector is simply a binary vector and its transpose. In the other, the arbitrary vector is a weighted sum of a binary vector and a unit vector.

6.2.2   Multiple Group Method.
The multiple group method of factor analysis differs essentially from the group centroid methods in that the arbitrary matrices contain more than one binary vector. The multiple group method is better known than even the simple group centroid method described by Thurstone and much better known than the group centroid method involving also the unit vector.

6.3   Group Centroid with Binary Vector

For the group centroid method which utilizes only a binary vector and its transpose for the arbitrary matrices, we shall discuss the characteristics of the method and give the necessary computational equations, the computational instructions, and a numerical example.

6.3.1   Characteristics of the Method.
This method of factor analysis, like the centroid method, solves for a single factor loading vector at a time. After each factor vector is solved for, its major product moment is subtracted from the correlation matrix or the current residual to give a subsequent residual correlation matrix. Then another factor loading vector is obtained from the last residual matrix. One proceeds until, according to some criterion, enough factors have been extracted.

Another characteristic of this method is that the computational equations are extremely simple. The method is the simplest of all the mathematically respectable methods of factor analysis. Its greatest advantage is, perhaps, with small matrices or for rapid preliminary analyses, when high-speed computers are not available and it is necessary to use desk computers. The method, however, can be used with high-speed computers, and it may have definite advantages even with a very large number of variables.

A limitation of the group centroid method with binary vectors is that no completely satisfactory objective procedures are available for determining which of the elements in the binary vector should be 1 and which should be 0. In other words, no purely objective methods are available to determine which variables should be grouped together in the original correlation matrix or in any subsequent residual matrix. It is true that in a modification of this method, called the *bifactor method* of Holzinger and Harman (1941), certain criteria are specified for determining the unit elements in the binary vector. These are not, however, as completely objective as in the case of the centroid method, in which the determination of the $+1$ and -1 in the arbitrary vector is entirely mechanical.

6.3.2 Computational Equations.

The notation for the computational equations for the group centroid method with binary vector, and the equations, are given now.

6.3.2a DEFINITION OF NOTATION

$_iR$ is the correlation matrix when $i = 0$ and the ith residual matrix when i is greater than 0.

$f_{.i}$ is the binary or grouping vector corresponding to the ith factor.

$W_{.i}$ is the sum of the columns of $_{i-1}R$ corresponding to the unit elements in $f_{.i}$.

L_i is the sum of the intercorrelations, including the self correlations, of the variables corresponding to the unit elements of $f_{.i}$.

$a_{.i}$ is the factor loading vector for the ith factor.

6.3.2b THE EQUATIONS.

As indicated, the computations for this method of factor analysis are much simpler than for the centroid method. The computational equations are, therefore, fewer. These are

$$W_{.i} = {}_{i-1}Rf_{.i} \qquad (6.3.1)$$

$$L_i = f_{.i}'W_{.i+1} \qquad (6.3.2)$$

$$S_i = \frac{1}{\sqrt{L_i}} \qquad (6.3.3)$$

$$a_{.i} = W_{.i}S_i \qquad (6.3.4)$$

$$_iR = {}_{i-1}R - a_{.i}a_{.i}' \qquad (6.3.5)$$

6.3.3   Computational Instructions. The first step in the computational procedure consists of determining the first binary vector. This means that one must decide which of the variables one wishes to group together in solving for the first factor vector. If one has some *a priori* hypothesis or can on the basis of previous research determine which should be grouped together, this is all to the good. As a matter of fact, it has been proposed by Guttman and others that a factor analysis is not justified unless one does have an *a priori* hypothesis concerning variables which are presumed to measure the same factor. This, of course, means that one has an hypothesis about the number and kinds of factors involved in a particular domain which he may be investigating.

Even if such an hypothesis is available, one must still decide which group of variables to consider first. This method of factor analysis is not independent of the order in which the binary vectors corresponding to the group are used in determining successive factor loading vectors.

Holzinger and Harman (1941) have proposed that one begin with the two variables which have the highest correlation in the original correlation matrix and then proceed to add variables as follows. The third variable added will be the one such that the ratio of the average of the three correlations among each other to the average of the correlations of these three with all the others is a maximum. In this way one proceeds to add variables to the group until the ratio reaches a specified value. This method has certain disadvantages. First, one cannot be sure that the two variables having the highest correlation will provide the best starting point and second, there is no clear-cut criterion of when to stop adding variables to the group.

A method which is more objective is as follows. We determine the standard deviation of each column of correlation coefficients, exclusive of the diagonal. We then find the variable with the largest standard deviation. To the mean of the column of correlations for this variable, we add some constant, for example, 0.5 times the standard deviation. We find all correlations which are larger than this sum. The binary vector whose unit elements correspond to these variables is then taken as the first binary vector.

Having selected a binary vector, either by the objective method outlined or by some *a priori* or rational considerations, we designate this vector as $f_{.1}$ and calculate a $W_{.i}$, as indicated in Eq. 6.3.1. This equation means simply that all columns of the correlation matrix corresponding to the unit elements in the binary vector f are added together.

Next we premultiply the W vector given in Eq. 6.3.1 by the binary vector f to get the scalar quantity L. This is indicated in Eq. 6.3.2 for the ith factor loading vector or in this particular case, for the first factor loading vector. Here, of course, $_{i-1}R$ is the correlation matrix. Equation 6.3.2, it may be seen, then gives us simply the sum of all intercorrelations involving the variables corresponding to the unit elements in the binary vector.

The next step is to get the reciprocal square root of this sum of intercorrelations, as indicated in Eq. 6.3.3.

Now, we multiply each element of the W vector obtained from Eq. 6.3.1 by the scalar quantity obtained in Eq. 6.3.3. This is indicated in Eq. 6.3.4. The result is the first factor loading vector $a_{.1}$.

We then calculate the first residual matrix $_1R$ as indicated in Eq. 6.3.5, in which the prescript i is 1. This is obtained by subtracting the major product moment of the factor loading vector from the correlation matrix. As in the centroid method, one may first get the major product moment matrix of the first factor loading vector and then subtract this matrix from the correlation matrix or he may perform the operation simultaneously on the desk calculator. If high-speed computers are programed for the calculation, one would not perform the two-stage operation, but would indicate the simultaneous computations for the residuals.

Having obtained the first residual matrix, one may now use some objective method such as the one first indicated for determining the second binary vector $f_{.2}$. Or, if he has an hypothesis as to the groupings of variables beforehand, he may apply the corresponding binary vector directly to the first residual correlation matrix to get $W_{.2}$, as indicated in Eq. 6.3.1. Proceeding through the five steps, one obtains a second residual matrix. These cycles are continued until enough factors have been extracted.

How many factors to remove depends in part on whether 1 or estimates of communalities are used in the diagonals. The problem of what to use in the diagonals is exactly the same as in the case of the centroid method. One may use 1 in the diagonals and then proceed to factor until the minor product moment of the current factor loading vector is equal to or less than 1. The assumption here is implicit that if a factor does not account for more variance than any single variable, it should not be retained.

There is an essential difference, however, between this and the centroid method. Generally, in the centroid method each succeeding factor accounts for less of the variance than a preceding one, so that one may assume in a general way that the factors are extracted in terms of their importance. This is not necessarily true in the group centroid method because of the arbitrariness in the grouping procedures. If, of course, one has an *a priori* hypothesis as to the number of factors in the system and, therefore, the number of groups, and has set up the successive f or binary vectors according to this hypothesis, then the number of factors to be extracted is determined beforehand. One may examine the final residual matrix to see whether its residuals are small enough to be regarded as negligible. If one uses communality estimates in the diagonals, he may also factor until the residuals are sufficiently small. It must be admitted that tests of significance to determine the number of factors are in a most unsatisfactory state, and the question may well be raised whether it is worthwhile or necessary to strive for exact tests of significance.

6.3.4 Numerical Example. We give now, using the same data as in the centroid method, a numerical example of the group centroid method with binary vectors. In this example, the binary vectors are chosen by the objective method just outlined, which begins with the standard deviations for the vectors of correlation or residual matrices.

Table 6.3.1 is interpreted as follows. The first row has only one entry which is the sum of squares of factor loadings for the first factor and indicates the amount of variance accounted for by this factor. The second row also has only one entry and gives the number of the variable, in this case variable number 1, whose correlations with the remaining variables have the largest standard deviation. The third row gives the numbers of the variables whose correlations with variable 1 exceed the mean of all other correlations with variable 1 by some specified constant times the standard deviation, in this case 0.5. These are the variables 1, 2, and 3. They generate the first binary vector by means of which the first factor loading vector is calculated. This vector is given in the fourth row of the table. The remaining rows of the table give the first residual correlation matrix obtained by subtracting the major product moment of the first factor loading vector from the correlation matrix.

TABLE 6.3.1   Computations for First Factor Vector and First Residual Matrix

3.031								
1								
1 2 3								
0.933	0.936	0.914	0.178	0.107	0.169	0.330	0.333	0.397
0.129	−0.044	−0.085	−0.058	−0.067	−0.050	−0.010	−0.002	−0.020
−0.044	0.124	−0.080	−0.051	−0.040	−0.033	0.015	0.035	−0.003
−0.085	−0.080	0.165	0.109	0.107	0.083	−0.005	−0.033	0.022
—0.058	−0.051	0.109	0.968	0.617	0.596	0.190	0.124	0.298
−0.067	−0.040	0.107	0.617	0.988	0.691	0.103	0.055	0.211
−0.050	−0.033	0.083	0.596	0.691	0.971	0.134	0.047	0.224
−0.010	0.015	−0.005	0.190	0.103	0.134	0.891	0.544	0.396
−0.002	0.035	−0.033	0.124	0.055	0.047	0.544	0.889	0.409
—0.020	−0.003	0.022	0.298	0.211	0.224	0.396	0.409	0.842

Table 6.3.2 has the same meaning as Table 6.3.1 except that now the operations are applied to the first residual matrix to yield the second factor loading vector. The last rows of the table give the second residual matrix.

Table 6.3.3 is analogous to the first two and gives the third factor loading vector. In addition, it also includes a single entry line at the bottom which

TABLE 6.3.2 Computations for Second Factor Vector and Second Residual Matrix

```
2.381
5
4 5 6
```

−0.068	−0.048	0.115	0.840	0.885	0.870	0.165	0.087	0.283
0.125	−0.048	−0.077	−0.001	−0.008	0.009	0.002	0.004	−0.000
−0.048	0.122	−0.075	−0.011	0.003	0.008	0.023	0.039	0.011
−0.077	−0.075	0.152	0.012	0.005	−0.017	−0.024	−0.043	−0.010
−0.001	−0.011	0.012	0.262	−0.127	−0.135	0.052	0.051	0.061
−0.008	0.003	0.005	−0.127	0.206	−0.079	−0.043	−0.022	−0.039
0.009	0.008	−0.017	−0.135	−0.079	0.214	−0.009	−0.029	−0.022
0.002	0.023	−0.024	0.052	−0.043	−0.009	0.864	0.530	0.350
0.004	0.039	−0.043	0.051	−0.022	−0.029	0.530	0.881	0.384
−0.000	0.011	−0.010	0.061	−0.039	−0.022	0.350	0.384	0.762

gives the sum of squares of the fourth factor loadings. The computations for this factor are not shown. This number is less than 1.0 and the computations are therefore terminated. Actually, since according to the third line of the three tables all variables have been included in computations for the first three factors, the computations should in any case be terminated at this point.

TABLE 6.3.3 Computations for Third Factor Vector and Third Residual Matrix

```
1.699
8
7 8 9
```

0.002	0.033	−0.035	0.073	−0.046	−0.027	0.777	0.800	0.667
0.125	−0.048	−0.077	−0.001	−0.007	0.009	−0.000	0.002	−0.002
−0.048	0.121	−0.073	−0.014	0.004	0.009	−0.003	0.013	−0.011
−0.077	−0.073	0.150	0.015	0.003	−0.018	0.003	−0.016	0.013
−0.001	−0.014	0.015	0.257	−0.123	−0.133	−0.005	−0.008	0.012
−0.007	0.004	0.003	−0.123	0.204	−0.080	−0.007	0.015	−0.008
0.009	0.009	−0.018	−0.133	−0.080	0.214	0.012	−0.008	−0.004
−0.000	−0.003	0.003	−0.005	−0.007	0.012	0.260	−0.092	−0.169
0.002	0.013	−0.016	−0.008	0.015	−0.008	−0.092	0.241	−0.149
−0.002	−0.011	0.013	0.012	−0.008	−0.004	−0.169	−0.149	0.318
0.429								

6.4 Group Centroid with Binary and Unit Vectors

We shall now consider in detail a modification of the group centroid method which is not as well known as the method just discussed.

6.4.1 Characteristics of the Method. This method of factor analysis differs in several respects from the previous method. First, no residual matrices are calculated. Second, instead of using only a binary vector as the arbitrary vector in the matrix reduction equation, this arbitrary vector is a linear combination of a binary vector and a unit vector.

Specifically, the particular linear combination of the binary and unit vectors is determined in such a way that all variables which are assumed not to represent a given factor will have factor loadings for that factor which sum to 0. The rationale for this procedure is that the variables not belonging to the group should have negligible loadings in this factor. It is, in general, not possible to impose the condition that all of their loadings will be 0 by means of this simple linear combination of binary and unit vectors, but it is possible to determine the linear combination so that their sum will be 0. The computational procedure satisfies this restriction.

6.4.2 Computational Equations. In this method of factor analysis, the computations are somewhat more complex than in the previous method which utilizes only a binary vector. Let us then define the notation required and list the computational equations.

6.4.2a DEFINITION OF NOTATION

R is the correlation matrix.

V is a vector of row sums of R.

$f_{.i}$ is a binary vector.

$U_{.i}$ is the sum of columns of R corresponding to the unit elements in $f_{.i}$.

α is the sum of the elements in V.

b_i is the sum of the elements in $U_{.i}$.

c_i is the sum of the eleemnts in $U_{.i}$ corresponding to the unit elements in $f_{.i}$.

g_i is a scalar which makes the sums of the factor loadings corresponding to the zeros in f_1 equal to 0.

$W_{.i}$ is a vector proportional to the ith factor loadings.

$a_{.i}$ is the factor loading vector for the ith factor.

6.4.2b THE EQUATIONS

$$V = R1 \qquad\qquad (6.4.1)$$

$$U_{.i} = Rf_{.i} \qquad\qquad (6.4.2)$$

$$\alpha = 1'V \qquad\qquad (6.4.3)$$

$$b_i = 1'U_{.i} \tag{6.4.4}$$

$$c_i = f_{.i}' \, U_{.i} \tag{6.4.5}$$

$$g_i = \frac{b_i - c_i}{\alpha - b_i} \tag{6.4.6}$$

$$L_i = g_i{}^2\alpha - 2g_ib_i + c_i \tag{6.4.7}$$

$$S_i = \frac{1}{\sqrt{L_i}} \tag{6.4.8}$$

$$W_{.i} = U_{.i} - gV \tag{6.4.9}$$

$$a_{.i} = W_{.i} \, S_i \tag{6.4.10}$$

6.4.3 Computational Instructions. In computing factor loading vectors based on this procedure, the same considerations with reference to the choice of diagonal elements apply as in the cases of the centroid method and the group centroid method with binary vectors. In outlining the computational procedures we shall assume that 1 has been used in the diagonals, although we could substitute the largest nondiagonal element in each column.

The first step is to calculate the column vector whose elements are the corresponding row sums of the correlation matrix. This is indicated by Eq. 6.4.1.

We assume that the f_1 vector has been determined by some *a priori* method or by the objective procedure described in the previous section. We calculate the vector U with $i = 1$ as in Eq. 6.4.2. This is the correlation matrix multiplied by the f vector or simply a vector of the sums of columns of the correlation matrix corresponding to the unit elements in the f or binary vector.

Next we calculate the sum of those elements in the V vector defined in Eq. 6.4.1, as indicated in Eq. 6.4.3. This is α. It is simply the minor product of the V vector and the unit vector.

Then we calculate the sum of the elements in the U vector. This is the scalar quantity b given in Eq. 6.4.4. It is, of course, the minor product of the unit vector and the U vector.

The scalar quantity c, which is the minor product of the binary vector f and the U vector, is next calculated, as indicated in Eq. 6.4.5. It can be readily verified that this scalar c is simply the sum of all of the intercorrelations involving only the variables corresponding to the unit elements in the binary vector.

The scalar quantity g, given in Eq. 6.4.6, is now calculated. This is the ratio of two differences. The numerator is the value b given in Eq. 6.4.4 minus the value c given in Eq. 6.4.5. The denominator is the value α given in Eq. 6.4.3 minus the value b given in Eq. 6.4.4.

Having calculated the four scalar quantities given in Eqs. 6.4.3–6.4.6, we now calculate the scalar quantity L as given in Eq. 6.4.7, which is a function of these four scalar quantities.

In Eq. 6.4.8 we calculate the reciprocal square root of the L value given in Eq. 6.4.7, and designate this as S.

We next calculate a $W_{.1}$ vector, as indicated in Eq. 6.4.9. This is obtained by subtracting from the U vector of Eq. 6.4.2 g times the V vector of Eq. 6.4.1, where g is the value given in Eq. 6.4.6.

In Eq. 6.4.10 we have the ith factor loading vector, namely, $a_{.i}$, which is the $W_{.i}$ vector calculated in Eq. 6.4.9, multiplied by the scalar S_i calculated in Eq. 6.4.8.

The successive f vectors may be selected according to some hypothesis or they may be obtained as was the first vector, except that in determining a given f vector, variables included in any previous f vectors are excluded from consideration.

The f vectors are each applied to the original correlation matrix rather than to residual matrices. The solution for factor vectors may continue until each variable has been included in a subgroup corresponding to an f vector.

6.4.4 Numerical Example. In the numerical example, we use the same data as in the previous section.

Table 6.4.1 is interpreted as follows. The first row has 1 for each variable which has not yet been included in a binary grouping vector. At the beginning of the computations this, of course, includes all of the variables. The second row includes only one number and indicates the number of the variable not yet included in a binary vector for which the corresponding column of correlations has the largest standard deviation. The third row gives the numbers of the variables whose correlations with the variable indicated in the second row exceed the mean of all correlations with that variable by at least 0.5 times the standard deviation of those correlations. The fourth row gives the first factor loading vector. It will be noted that the sum of the factor loadings for the variables not included in the binary vector is 0. The last line of the table has only a single number, 1.000, which means that at least one of the variables in the set has not yet been included in a binary vector.

The interpretation of Table 6.4.2 is similar to that of Table 6.4.1. The first line indicates that all but the first three variables have not yet been included in a binary vector. The second line indicates that variable 5 has the largest standard deviation of correlations among those variables not yet included in a binary vector. The third row indicates that of those variables not yet included in a binary vector, variables 4, 5, and 6 are the only ones whose correlations with variable 5 exceed the mean of the correlations involving variable 5 by more than 0.5 times their standard deviation. It should be noted that while the self correlation of a variable is excluded in calculating the mean

and standard deviation of its correlations with other variables, it is nevertheless included among those variables whose correlations exceed the mean by
some specified constant times the standard deviation. This guarantees that
it will be included in the binary vector which it generates. The fourth line
gives the second factor loading vector. The last line is simply 1.000 and means
that at least one variable has not already been included in a binary vector.

Table 6.4.3 is interpreted in the same way as the two preceding tables with
the exception of the fifth line. This includes the number 0, which means that
no variables remain which have not already been included in a binary vector.
Therefore, the computations are terminated.

TABLE 6.4.1 Computations for First Binary Vector and Corresponding Factor Vector

1.000	1.000	1.000	1.000	1.000	1.000	1.000	1.000	1.000
1								
1 2 3								
0.888	0.878	0.824	−0.100	−0.153	−0.096	0.092	0.114	0.143
1.000								

TABLE 6.4.2 Computations for Secondary Binary Vector and Corresponding Factor Vector

0.000	0.000	0.000	1.000	1.000	1.000	1.000	1.000	1.000
5								
4 5 6								
−0.120	−0.105	0.067	0.811	0.875	0.854	0.037	−0.043	0.165
1.000								

TABLE 6.4.3 Computations for Third Binary Vector and Corresponding Factor Vector

0.000	0.000	0.000	0.000	0.000	0.000	1.000	1.000	1.000
8								
7 8 9								
0.072	0.100	0.018	0.013	−0.114	−0.089	0.781	0.811	0.666
0.000								

6.5 The Multiple Group Method

Perhaps one of the simplest and most useful techniques of factor analysis
is what has come to be known as the *multiple group method*, first developed
by Thurstone (1947). Thurstone pointed out that certain essential features

of the method had been anticipated by Holzinger (1944), and indicated in what respects the multiple group methods differ from the procedure outlined by Holzinger. Subsequently, Guttman (1952) showed that both the methods of Holzinger and Thurstone are special cases of a general method of matrix factoring outlined earlier by Guttman. Guttman also implies that if adequate hypotheses as to the simple structure factor loading of the variables are available, the laborious operations of rotation to simple structure may be largely circumvented by the multiple group method. These operations are discussed in Chapters 18 and 19.

6.5.1 *Characteristics of the Method.*

As indicated, the multiple group method is a special case of the rank reduction theorem, and in this respect it is like all of the methods we have considered so far. It differs essentially, however, from all of the centroid methods and the two group centroid methods in that some hypothesis as to the total number of factors to be extracted is adopted before the computations begin. The factors are then all solved for simultaneously. The calculation of residual matrices is generally avoided.

In the multiple group method, the dimensions of the arbitrary matrix correspond, respectively, to the number of variables and to the number of factors postulated. It is recalled that, according to the matrix reduction theorem, the residual matrix resulting from the application of such arbitrary multipliers must yield one of rank equal to the rank of the correlation matrix minus the number of factors postulated.

The arbitrary factor matrices in the multiple group method consist of a binary data matrix and its transpose. Obviously, the premultiplier is the horizontal form of the matrix and the postmultiplier is the vertical form. The binary matrix consists of binary vectors, each of which serves to group the variables into subsets according to the unit elements in the vector. As in the case of the group centroid method, it is not necessary that the unit elements in the vectors of the binary matrix be mutually exclusive. That is, certain variables may be included in more than one of the factors. However, it is better to restrict the overlapping as much as possible.

The problems involved in selecting the binary matrix in the multiple group method are the same as those involved in selecting the binary vectors in the group centroid methods. Guttman (1952) has pointed out that a factor analysis study, like any scientific investigation, should begin with certain initial hypotheses and should proceed to test these hypotheses. The implication for factor analysis is that one should have an hypothesis as to the primary variables in the particular domain under investigation, and should include measures of these variables in his data matrix. This point of view seems to be similar to that of Thurstone's (1947), although Thurstone's rotational procedures have not, in general, presupposed any knowledge of the primary factors in the system to be investigated. Harman (1960) has suggested that a preliminary cluster analysis of the correlation matrix may provide a basis for the grouping of the variables. However, since cluster analysis procedures are, in general, not objective, it is perhaps better to depend on some *a priori* or even arbitrary hypotheses concerning the way variables should be grouped in setting up the binary matrix. As a matter of fact, we may appropriately call the binary matrix the factor loading hypothesis matrix, in which the unit elements indicate the tests assumed to measure a particular factor, and the 0 elements, those which do not measure that factor. Lacking adequate hypotheses, one may use the procedure suggested in Section 6.4 to construct the binary hypothesis matrix. This, it will be recalled, requires the calculation of standard deviations of the vectors of the correlation matrix.

While it is not usually necessary in the multiple group method to calculate residual matrices, it may sometimes be desirable to do so. We may calculate a factor matrix based on some binary matrix. The major product moment of the factor matrix may then be subtracted from the correlation matrix to yield a residual matrix. If the residual elements are too large, one may then, by objective or other methods, apply a second binary arbitrary matrix to the residual matrix to solve for further factors.

6.5.2 *Computational Equations.* The notation we shall require for the computational equations for the multiple group method differs a little from that used in the previous methods. The procedure can be indicated more simply.

6.5.2a DEFINITION OF NOTATION

R is the correlation matrix.
f is the binary hypothesis matrix.
t is a lower triangular matrix.
a is the factor loading matrix.

6.5.2b COMPUTATIONAL EQUATIONS. The computational equations for the multiple group method are simpler than for other methods, although their meaning may be a little more involved.

$$W = Rf \tag{6.5.1}$$

$$S = f'W = f'Rf \tag{6.5.2}$$

$$tt' = S \tag{6.5.3}$$

$$a = Wt'^{-1} \tag{6.5.4}$$

$$\begin{bmatrix} t \\ a \end{bmatrix} t' = \begin{bmatrix} S \\ W \end{bmatrix} \tag{6.5.5}$$

6.5.3 Computational Instructions. We begin with a binary hypothesis matrix *f* obtained in some suitable manner. The problem of communalities, or what elements to use in the diagonal, is just as relevant as in the previous methods. One may use, in each of the diagonal positions of the correlation matrix, the highest absolute nondiagonal values in the corresponding column instead of the unit elements. However, since no residual matrices are calculated, one must follow through with these estimates rather than revise them for each successive residual. In the following, we shall assume the diagonal elements to be 1.

Equation 6.5.1 gives a matrix *W* which is the product of the correlation matrix postmultiplied by the binary matrix. This simply means that each column of *W* is the sum of those columns of *R* indicated by the positions of the unit elements in the corresponding *f* or binary matrix.

Next we premultiply the *W* matrix obtained in Eq. 6.5.1 by the transpose of the binary matrix *f*. This product we can recognize as the triple product in the matrix reduction formula in which the transpose of *f* is the arbitrary premultiplier and *f* is the postmultiplier.

Equation 6.5.3 shows that the matrix *S* calculated in Eq. 6.5.2 can be expressed as the major product moment of a lower triangular matrix. This was pointed out in Section 3.3.

Equation 6.5.4 shows that to obtain the factor loading matrix *a*, the matrix *W* obtained in Eq. 6.5.1 is postmultiplied by the inverse of the upper triangular matrix obtained from Eq. 6.5.3.

For computational purposes, it may be simpler to base the computations on a supermatrix, as indicated in Eq. 6.5.5. Here the right-hand side of the equation is a type 3 column supervector in which the first element is the *S* matrix obtained by Eq. 6.5.2, and the second element is the *W* matrix obtained by Eq. 6.5.1. The left-hand side of Eq. 6.5.5 indicates the partial triangular factoring of this matrix. Here we factor out the upper triangular matrix *t'*. This leaves the lower element of the submatrix as the factor loading matrix *a*.

6.5.4 Numerical Example. The same correlation matrix is used as in the previous examples.

Table 6.5.1 gives the transpose of the hypothesis matrix *f*.

Table 6.5.2 gives the *W'* matrix. This is the product of the correlation matrix premultiplied by the transpose of the binary hypothesis matrix.

TABLE 6.5.1   Transpose of Binary Hypothesis Matrix

1	1	1	0	0	0	0	0	0
0	0	0	1	1	1	0	0	0
0	0	0	0	0	0	1	1	1

Table 6.5.3 gives the triple product matrix S given by Eq. 6.5.2. This is the matrix of Table 6.5.2 postmultiplied by the hypothesis matrix whose transpose is given in Table 6.5.1.

Table 6.5.4 gives in the lower section the factor loading matrix a indicated by Eqs. 6.5.4 and 6.5.5. The calculation of this matrix is obtained by the partial triangular factoring of the supermatrix whose first element is given by Table 6.5.3 and whose second element is given by the transpose of Table 6.5.2. The upper section of Table 6.5.4 gives in the diagonal and supra-diagonal elements the upper triangular factor t' of the matrix S of Table 6.5.3. Note that the infradiagonal elements are the same as the corresponding elements of S. This is a consequence of the Fortran computer program.

TABLE 6.5.2   Product of Correlation Matrix Premultiplied by Transpose of Binary Hypothesis Matrix

2.597	2.604	2.543	0.495	0.299	0.471	0.917	0.927	1.105
0.249	0.301	0.715	2.262	2.345	2.335	0.577	0.377	0.914
0.958	1.039	0.952	0.801	0.483	0.584	2.181	2.195	2.068

TABLE 6.5.3   Triple Product of Correlation Matrix Postmultiplied by Hypothesis Matrix and Premultiplied by its Transpose

7.744	1.265	2.949
1.265	6.942	1.868
2.949	1.868	6.444

TABLE 6.5.4   Triangular Factor of Triple Product and Multiple Group Factor Loading Matrix

2.783	0.455	1.060
1.265	2.595	0.534
2.949	1.868	5.036
0.933	−0.068	0.002
0.936	−0.048	0.033
0.914	0.115	−0.035
0.178	0.840	0.073
0.107	0.885	−0.046
0.169	0.870	−0.027
0.330	0.165	0.777
0.333	0.087	0.800
0.397	0.283	0.667

Table 6.5.5 gives the residual matrix obtained by subtracting the major product moment of the factor loading matrix a from the correlation matrix R.

It is important to note that the factor loading vectors obtained in this section and in Section 6.3 are exactly the same. The group centroid and the multiple group method must yield the same results if the same binary hypothesis vectors are used in the same order for both methods. This fact does not seem to be well known. It may be noted that the methods of Sections 6.3 and 6.4 did actually for this set of data choose the same binary vectors and in the same order. If the method of Section 6.4 is used to choose the vectors of the binary hypothesis matrix of Section 6.5 one cannot, however, always be sure that these will be the same as those chosen by the method of Section 6.3.

TABLE 6.5.5　Residual Correlation Matrix

0.125	−0.048	−0.077	−0.001	−0.007	0.009	−0.000	0.002	−0.002
−0.048	0.121	−0.073	−0.014	0.004	0.009	−0.003	0.013	−0.011
−0.077	−0.073	0.150	0.015	0.003	−0.018	0.003	−0.016	0.013
−0.001	−0.014	0.015	0.257	−0.123	−0.133	−0.005	−0.008	0.012
−0.007	0.004	0.003	−0.123	0.204	−0.080	−0.007	0.015	−0.008
0.009	0.009	−0.018	−0.133	−0.080	0.214	0.012	−0.008	−0.004
−0.000	−0.003	0.003	−0.005	−0.007	0.012	0.260	−0.092	−0.169
0.002	0.013	−0.016	−0.008	0.015	−0.008	−0.092	0.241	−0.149
−0.002	−0.011	0.013	0.012	−0.008	−0.004	−0.169	−0.149	0.318

6.6　Mathematical Proofs

Here we shall present mathematical rationales for the computational procedures outlined in the previous sections.

6.6.1　The Group Centroid Method with Binary Vector.

We shall prove that the method outlined for the group centroid method is a special case of the rank reduction theorem. Let

$$W_{.i} = {}_{i-1}Rf_{.i} \tag{6.6.1}$$

$$L_i = f_{.i}'W_{.i} \tag{6.6.2}$$

$$S_i = \frac{1}{\sqrt{L_i}} \tag{6.6.3}$$

$$a_{.i} = W_{.i}S_i \tag{6.6.4}$$

$${}_iR = {}_{i-1}R - a_{.i}a_{.i}' \tag{6.6.5}$$

From Eqs. 6.6.1 and 6.6.2

$$L_i = f_{.i}'{}_{i-1}Rf_{.i} \tag{6.6.6}$$

From Eqs. 6.6.3, 6.6.4, and 6.6.6,

$$a_{.i} = \frac{_{i-1}Rf_{.i}}{\sqrt{f_{.i}'\,_{i-1}Rf_{.i}}} \tag{6.6.7}$$

From Eqs. 6.6.5 and 6.6.7,

$$_iR = {}_{i-1}R - {}_{i-1}Rf_{.i}(f_{.i}'\,_{i-1}Rf_{.i})^{-1}f_{.i}'\,_{i-1}R \tag{6.6.8}$$

It can be seen that Eq. 6.6.8 is a rank reduction form.

6.6.2 A Group Centroid Method Using Linear Combination of a Binary and Unit Vector.

First, we shall show that this method is a special case of the rank reduction solution. We shall also show that the value of g calculated as in Eq. 6.4.6 is such that the sum of the factor loadings for the variables corresponding to zeros in the f binary vector is exactly 0.

Given the vector

$$Y = f - g1 \tag{6.6.9}$$

where f is a binary vector and g is a scalar. Let

$$a = \frac{RY}{\sqrt{Y'RY}} \tag{6.6.10}$$

and

$$E = R - aa' \tag{6.6.11}$$

Substituting Eq. 6.6.10 into Eq. 6.6.11,

$$E = R - RY(Y'RY)^{-1}Y'R \tag{6.6.12}$$

which is the rank reduction form. Now determine g so that

$$(1-f)'a = 0 \tag{6.6.13}$$

This means that the sum of the elements in a corresponding to the zeros in f is 0. From Eqs. 6.6.10 and 6.6.13,

$$(1-f)'RY = 0 \tag{6.6.14}$$

From Eqs. 6.6.9 and 6.6.14,

$$(1-f)'R(f-g1) = 0 \tag{6.6.15}$$

From Eq. 6.6.15,

$$1'Rf - f'Rf - g(1'R1 - 1'Rf) = 0 \tag{6.6.16}$$

Let

$$\alpha = 1'R1 \tag{6.6.17}$$

$$b = 1'Rf \tag{6.6.18}$$

$$c = f'Rf \tag{6.6.19}$$

From Eqs. 6.6.16–6.6.19,

$$g = \frac{b - c}{\alpha - b} \tag{6.6.20}$$

The four preceding equations are equivalent respectively to Eqs. 6.4.3–6.4.6. Let

$$L = Y'RY \tag{6.6.21}$$

From Eqs. 6.6.9 and 6.6.21,

$$L = f'Rf - 2g1'Rf + g^2 1'R1 \tag{6.6.22}$$

From Eqs. 6.6.17–6.6.20 and 6.6.22,

$$L = g^2\alpha - 2gb + c \tag{6.6.23}$$

This is the same as Eq. 6.4.7. Let

$$V = R1 \tag{6.6.24}$$

$$U = Rf \tag{6.6.25}$$

$$W = U - gV \tag{6.6.26}$$

From Eqs. 6.6.9, 6.6.10, and 6.6.17–6.6.26,

$$a = \frac{W}{\sqrt{L}} \tag{6.6.27}$$

which is equivalent to Eq. 6.4.10 in Section 6.4.2.

6.6.3 The Multiple Group Method. Next we show that the computational method outlined in Section 6.4 does yield a special case of the rank reduction theorem.

6.6.3a THE MULTIPLE GROUP METHOD IS A RANK REDUCTION FORM. Let

$$W = Rf \tag{6.6.28}$$

$$tt' = f'Rf \tag{6.6.29}$$

$$a = Wt'^{-1} \tag{6.6.30}$$

$$E = R - aa' \tag{6.6.31}$$

Substituting Eq. 6.6.30 into Eq. 6.6.31,

$$E = R - Wt'^{-1}t^{-1}W' \tag{6.6.32}$$

$$E = Rf(tt')^{-1}f'R \tag{6.6.33}$$

From Eqs. 6.6.29 and 6.6.32,

$$E = Rf(f'Rf)^{-1}f'R \qquad (6.6.34)$$

which is a rank reduction form.

6.6.3b $f'a$ WITH a AS DEFINED IN SECTION 6.6.3a IS LOWER TRIANGULAR. From Eq. 6.6.30,

$$f'a = f'Wt'^{-1} \qquad (6.6.35)$$

From Eqs. 6.6.28 and 6.6.35,

$$f'a = f'Rft'^{-1} \qquad (6.6.36)$$

From Eqs. 6.6.29 and 6.6.36,

$$f'a = t \qquad (6.6.37)$$

Chapter 7

Basic Structure Successive Factor Methods

By far the most popular and the most frequently used factor analysis methods for the modern high-speed computers are those which are based on the basic structure of a correlation or data matrix. These principles of basic structure, as you recall, were discussed in Chapter 3. In Chapter 4 we indicated several variations of the basic structure methods.

We have, for convenience, divided these classifications into two general methods. The first of these consists of solving for a single factor vector at a time, that is, extracting one factor before another is solved for. The second general type of method consists of solving for a factor loading matrix iteratively, so that all the factor loading vectors to be solved for are obtained simultaneously. This second group of methods consists of two types, as indicated in Chapter 4—first, those methods which solve for only the most important factor loadings or those which account for most of the variance and second, those which solve for all of the factor loadings at one time, whether or not they are important.

The basic structure methods have been commonly designated by names such as the principal axis method, the eigenvalue-eigenvector method, the principal components method, the characteristic root and vector method, and the latent root and vector method. These techniques imply concepts which involve hyperspatial geometry, advanced statistics, and concepts of matrix theory which are considerably more involved and more specialized than those required for an understanding of factor analytic techniques. Since they also imply a familiarity with mathematical concepts and vocabulary which we have not introduced into this book, we shall usually prefer the term *basic structure*. Again, it should be emphasized that the methods of analysis discussed in this chapter, as all methods we have discussed, imply lower rank approximations to the data matrices.

The name of Harold Hotelling (1933) is most often associated with the type of basic structure solution which we shall consider in this chapter. He developed what is known as the *principal components method* of factor analysis, which is essentially the same as the methods we shall describe. Mathematicians much earlier had set forth all of the properties and characteristics of the method of principal components which Hotelling developed, but it was he who first applied them to the analysis of psychological data.

Thurstone (1947), in his development of the centroid method, utilized the principal components method as a final step. It should be noted, however, that the method used by Thurstone was different from that of Hotelling. Thurstone first solved for a centroid matrix and then found the basic structure of the centroid factor loading matrix, whereas Hotelling found the basic structure factor matrix directly from the correlation matrix.

7.1 Characteristics of the Methods

We shall now consider in more detail some of the essential characteristics of the basic structure successive factor methods. As we have said, the methods consist of solving for one factor at a time. The methods yield a least square solution for any given factor and involve an iterative type solution for each factor vector. The solution is a rank reduction type of solution for any iteration of any factor vector. Finally, each factor accounts for the maximum variance possible for a single factor.

7.1.1 One Factor at a Time. The methods of factor analysis discussed in this chapter are similar to the centroid and the group centroid methods in that a single factor vector is solved for before the second and subsequent vectors are solved for. The effect of a given factor is removed from the correlation matrix before the next factor is solved for. The method differs in this important respect from the multiple group method discussed in Chapter 6. Here you will recall that all of the factors were solved for simultaneously, and that some hypothesis was required as to the number of factors necessary to give a satisfactory approximation to the correlation matrix.

7.1.2 Least Square Solution. The basic structure successive factor methods are least square solutions in this sense: for each factor loading vector calculated, the solution is such that when its major product moment is subtracted from the correlation or appropriate residual matrix, a residual correlation matrix results whose sum of squared elements is a minimum. The major product moment of each factor loading vector solved for results in the best rank 1 approximation to the current residual matrix. It will be recalled that the major product moment of a vector is a rank 1 matrix. The centroid methods of analysis do not have this property, although in general they give reasonably good approximations to the basic structure factors. The group centroid method of analysis does not in general provide even an approximate least square solution for the residual matrix until the last factor has been removed.

7.1.3   Iterative Solution.   Like the centroid method, the basic structure successive factor method requires an iterative solution for each factor vector. A first approximation to the factor loading vector is required, and then, by successive iterations, better approximations to the correct factor loading vector are obtained. These methods differ essentially from the centroid methods in that the former are concerned with the solution for a sign vector which yields a maximum scalar when the matrix is post- and premultiplied by the sign vector and its transpose, respectively. The methods differ essentially from the group centroid solutions in that the latter are not iterative. The group centroid methods, it will be recalled, are based on the selection of a binary vector by means of which the factor loading vector is solved for directly without successive iterations.

7.1.4   Rank Reduction at Each Iteration.   Most methods of factor analysis yield rank reduction factor vectors. This means that if the major product moment of a factor vector is subtracted from the matrix from which it was derived, the residual matrix is of rank one less than the preceding matrix.

The methods described in this chapter have the further characteristic that for any factor vector being iteratively solved for, any iteration to that vector is a rank reduction vector. In this respect they are different from the methods of solution proposed by Hotelling (1933), which have been recommended in texts and commonly used by investigators. The Hotelling method does not in general yield a factor loading vector which at any iteration to the final vector is a rank reduction vector.

7.1.5   Maximum Variance of Factor Vectors.   All of the basic structure solutions which we shall consider in this and the next two chapters are such that the first factor loading vector accounts for the maximum variance of the set of variables which can be accounted for by a single factor. The next factor solved for accounts for the maximum variance not previously accounted for, and so on. This is true in the exact mathematical sense only if the iterations for each vector have been carried far enough.

7.1.6   Orthogonality of Solutions.   In all exact basic structure type solutions, the factor loading vectors are mutually orthogonal to one another. Therefore, these particular types of basic structure solutions involving successive factor vector solutions also must yield mutually orthogonal factor loading vectors if carried out to enough iterations. It is often stated that the centroid, the group centroid, and the multiple group methods of factor analysis yield orthogonal factors. This statement is ambiguous because it does not indicate in what sense the factors are orthogonal. Certainly it can be shown that the factor loading vectors obtained by the centroid, group centroid, and multiple group methods are not in general mutually orthogonal to one another. It is true, however, that in the centroid methods the factor loading vectors usually approach mutual orthogonality. Only for the basic structure type solutions are the factor loading vectors mutually orthogonal in the sense that the sums of cross products of factor loadings for any two factors are 0.

A simpler way to state the condition is that for the basic structure type solution, the minor product moment of the factor loading matrix is diagonal. The minor product moment of the centroid matrix approaches a diagonal matrix, but the nondiagonal elements, although in general small, are not all 0. Neither do the multiple group and the group centroid methods yield factor loading matrices whose minor product moments are diagonal matrices.

One of the chief advantages of the principal axis or basic structure methods is the fact that the minor product moment matrix is diagonal. This greatly simplifies solutions for factor score matrices, which are discussed in Chapter 20.

7.1.7 The Diagonal Elements. As in previous methods of factor analysis, we must decide what values to use in the diagonals of the correlation matrix. The characteristics of the methods discussed above apply strictly only if 1 is used in the diagonal. One may, however, use other diagonal elements as indicated, for example, in Chapter 5. As a matter of fact, it is possible to select diagonal elements other than 1 and still obtain exact basic structure solutions. However, the problem of selecting such values and the interpretation of the results may be troublesome.

Lawley (1940, 1942) has discussed a method known as the method of maximum likelihood, which does solve for the unknown diagonals. It is, in a most general sense, a principal axis type of solution. Methods of Rao (1955), very similar to those of Lawley, also solve for unknown diagonal elements and are basic structure type solutions. These solutions, however, raise considerable question as to their meaning and appropriateness with regard to the data matrix as distinguished from the correlation matrix. This problem involves the concept of communalities. There is still a great deal of controversy about the general issue of communalities and how they should be solved for—if at all—and what interpretations are implied by the various solutions.

7.2 Kinds of Solutions

In this chapter we shall discuss two general types of solutions involving the calculation of one factor vector at a time. The first of these requires calculations of successive residual matrices and the second does not.

7.2.1 Solution with Residual Matrix. By far the most common type of solution for the basic structure factor vector calls for the calculation of a residual matrix after each factor vector. This method is similar to the centroid method, in which the major product moment of a given factor is subtracted from the original or the current residual correlation matrix to find a new residual matrix from which the next factor loading vector is obtained. In this respect, this type of solution is similar to both the centroid and the group centroid methods of analysis.

7.2.2 Solution without Residual Matrix. A method due to Tucker (1944), much less commonly used, calculates a single vector at a time but does not require that a residual matrix be computed before calculating the next factor loading vector. The residual matrices are implicit in this method of solution but are not actually calculated.

7.3 Solution with Residual Matrix

We shall now consider in detail the type of solution which requires the residual matrix. First, we shall consider the characteristics of the method; then we shall present the computation equations, outline the computational instructions, and finally, give a numerical example.

7.3.1 Characteristics of the Method. As indicated, the method discussed here requires that successive approximations to the factor loading vector be calculated. It also requires the calculation of successive residual matrices. One of the advantages of the method is that one may observe the size of the residual elements as a basis for deciding how many factors to remove. However, this is not too important in basic structure solutions because, for each factor loading vector, one knows exactly how much of the total variance has been accounted for, and this bears a direct relationship to the squares of the elements in the residual matrix.

It is true, in general, that the more computations involved, the greater the amount of cumulative decimal error in a computational procedure. This is particularly true when a set of calculations is recorded to a lesser degree of decimal accuracy than that provided by the computing machines, and these truncated values are then used in further calculations. This, of course, is what happens when one calculates a residual matrix and records it in order to calculate another factor vector from it. For very large matrices requiring calculation of a large number of factor vectors, the final factor vectors may be in considerable error.

Another important consideration in a computational procedure is that of storage requirements, whether this is on computational worksheets or whether it is in the core storage, drums, tapes, or disks of high-speed computers. Interesting enough, the problem of storage requirements for desk calculators is rather different from those of high-speed electronic computers. In the residual method of analysis by a desk machine, one requires a separate worksheet for each residual matrix. The recording of these residual matrices may involve error in the transcription from the calculator dials to the paper. On the other hand, the electronic high-speed computers have, in general, the advantage of being able to write over previous computations. For example, with the electronic computer, calculations for a residual matrix may be written over a previous residual or correlation matrix so that additional space is not required.

In summary, one may say that the residual matrix method has the disadvantage of losing decimal accuracy both with desk computers and with high-speed computers. It has the disadvantage of requiring more worksheets and more recordings with desk computers, while with the high-speed computers it has the advantage of preserving some storage space because of the write-over capability of the computer.

7.3.2   Computational Equations

7.3.2.a   DEFINITION OF NOTATION.

$_kR$ is the kth residual correlation matrix if k is greater than 0. It is the correlation matrix if $k = 0$.

$Q_{.k}$ is the kth vector of the right basic orthonormal of $_0R$.

$_0V_{.k}$ is an arbitrary vector not orthogonal to $Q_{.k}$.

$_iD_k$ is the ith approximation to the kth diagonal of the basic diagonal of $_0R$.

D_k is the kth diagonal of the kth basic diagonal of $_0R$.

$D_{(k)}$ is a diagonal matrix of the first k elements of the basic diagonal of $_0R$.

$_ia_{.k}$ is the ith approximation to the kth factor loading vector.

$a_{.k}$ is the kth factor loading vector.

$a_{(k)}$ is a matrix of the first k factor loading vectors.

H is the tolerance limit or degree of accuracy required in comparing two successive approximations to $a_{.k}$.

G_k is the amount of variance accounted for by the first k factors.

P is a previously set tolerance limit.

7.3.2b   COMPUTATIONAL EQUATIONS

$$_1U_{.1} = {_0R}\,{_0V_{.1}} \tag{7.3.1}$$

$$_1L_1 = {_0V_{.1}'}\,{_1U_{.1}} \tag{7.3.2}$$

$$_1D_1 = \sqrt{_1L_1} \tag{7.3.3}$$

$$_1a_{.1} = \frac{_1U_{.1}}{_1D_1} \tag{7.3.4}$$

$$_{i+1}U_{.1} = {_0}R \, {_i}a_{.1} \tag{7.3.5}$$

$$_{i+1}L_1 = {_i}a_{.1}' \, {_{i+1}}U_{.1} \tag{7.3.6}$$

$$_{i+1}D_1 = \sqrt{_{i+1}L_1} \tag{7.3.7}$$

$$_{i+1}a_{.1} = \frac{_{i+1}U_{.1}}{_{i+1}D_1} \tag{7.3.8}$$

$$H = \left| \frac{_{i+1}D_1}{_iD_1} - 1 \right| \tag{7.3.9}$$

$$a_{.1} = {_{i+1}}a_{.1} \tag{7.3.10}$$

$$_{i+1}D_1 = D_1 \tag{7.3.11}$$

$$_1R = {_0}R - a_{.1} \, a_{.1}' \tag{7.3.12}$$

$$_0V_{.k}' \, Q_{.k} \neq 0 \tag{7.3.13}$$

$$_{i+1}U_{.k} = {_{k-1}}R \, {_i}a_{.k} \tag{7.3.14}$$

$$_{i+1}L_k = {_i}a_{.k}' \, {_{i+1}}U_{.k} \tag{7.3.15}$$

$$_{i+1}D_k = \sqrt{_{i+1}L_k} \tag{7.3.16}$$

$$_{i+1}a_{.k} = \frac{_{i+1}U_{.k}}{_{i+1}D_k} \tag{7.3.17}$$

$$H = \left| \frac{_{i+1}D_k}{_iD_k} - 1 \right| \tag{7.3.18}$$

$$a_{.k} = {_{i+1}}a_{.k} \tag{7.3.19}$$

$$D_k = {_{i+1}}D_k \tag{7.3.20}$$

$$_kR = {_{k-1}}R - a_{.k} \, a_{.k}' \tag{7.3.21}$$

$$G_k = \sum_{i=1}^{k} D_i \tag{7.3.22}$$

$$P \leq \frac{G_k}{tr \, {_0}R} \tag{7.3.23}$$

$$a_{(k)} = (a_{.1} \cdots a_{.k}) \tag{7.3.24}$$

$$Q_{(k)} = a_{(k)} \, D_{(k)}^{-1/2} \tag{7.3.25}$$

7.3.3 Computational Instructions. In this method of factor analysis, one begins with some arbitrary factor vector which may be a very rough approximation to the one being solved for. The only restriction to be placed on this vector is that it must not be orthogonal to the factor loading vector to be solved for. The first factor loading vector, as indicated in Chapter 4, is proportional to the first column of the left basic orthonormal of the correlation matrix. The closer the approximation vector to the correct vector, the fewer are the iterations required for the solution of the factor vector.

We may take the unit vector as the approximation vector. We have indicated this by $_0V$ rather than by the symbol 1, since it does not have to be the unit vector. One begins by multiplying the correlation matrix by the arbitrary vector, as indicated by Eq. 7.3.1. If this arbitrary vector is taken as the unit vector, the resulting U vector is simply a column vector of the row sums of the correlation matrix.

Next we have the minor product of the U vector by the arbitrary vector, as indicated by Eq. 7.3.2, to get a scalar quantity designated as L. Here the prescript means this is a first approximation, and the postscript means this refers to the first factor loading vector. Again, if the arbitrary vector $_0V$ is the unit vector, the L scalar is simply the sum of all of the elements of the correlation matrix.

Next we take the square root of the scalar L calculated by Eq. 7.3.2 to get the scalar D, with the appropriate pre- and post-subscripts, as in Eq. 7.3.3.

We then divide the U vector obtained in Eq. 7.3.1 by the scalar D obtained in Eq. 7.3.3. This is indicated in Eq. 7.3.4, and gives the first approximation to the factor loading vector.

We are now ready to calculate a second approximation to the first factor loading vector. This is done by using the first approximation to the first factor loading vector and going through the cycles from Eq. 7.3.1 to 7.3.4.

The general procedure then is as follows. To get the $i + 1$ approximation to the first factor loading vector, we postmultiply the correlation matrix by the ith approximation to the factor loading vector, as indicated in Eq. 7.3.5, to get a U vector.

We then get the minor product moment of this U vector by the ith approximation to the first factor loading vector to give the $i + 1$ approximation to the L_1 scalar quantity, as indicated by Eq. 7.3.6.

Then we take the square root of this L scalar to get the $i + 1$ approximation to the D scalar, as indicated in Eq. 7.3.7.

Next we divide the $i + 1$ approximation to the U vector by the D quantity just calculated, as in Eq. 7.3.8. This now gives us the $i + 1$ approximation to $a_{.1}$, the first factor loading vector. For each approximation to the factor loading vector, we check to see how close it is to the desired vector. If two successive D scalars were exactly equal, we would know that two successive approximations to the first factor loading vector would also be equal. (This is true provided the first basic diagonal is different from the second basic diagonal. As a matter of fact, in most cases of experimental data, this will be the case.) We could check to see whether two successive approximations to the first factor loading vector were equal, element for element, within the number of decimal places carried. It is much simpler, however, merely to check these D scalar quantities.

Ideally, the ratio of two successive D's should be equal to 1. However, we allow ourselves a certain tolerance limit and consider the ratio of the last D calculated to the immediately preceding D, from which we subtract the number 1, as in Eq. 7.3.9. It can be proved that, for any except the first D, this ratio can never be less than 1, and therefore the difference given by Eq. 7.3.9 must be equal to or greater than 0. We may arbitrarily set some tolerance limit such that this difference is not greater than 0.0001. We continue the cycles from Eqs. 7.3.1 to 7.3.9 until the quantity H is small enough.

We then take as the final value for the factor loading vector $a_{.1}$ the $i + 1$ approximation to this factor loading vector, as indicated by Eq. 7.3.10.

We also let the $i + 1$ approximation to the D scalar represent the final value of the D scalar, as indicated in Eq. 7.3.11. This quantity D_1 is now the approximation to the first basic diagonal of the correlation matrix.

We next calculate the first residual matrix, as indicated in Eq. 7.3.12. This is the residual correlation matrix obtained by subtracting the major product moment of the first factor loading vector from the correlation matrix.

We next select an arbitrary vector not orthogonal to the second basic orthonormal vector of the correlation matrix. From Section 3.4, we know that this second orthonormal vector is now the basic orthonormal vector corresponding to the first basic diagonal of the residual matrix. In Eq. 7.3.13, we indicate that the first approximation to the kth loading factor vector shall not be orthogonal to the kth basic orthonormal vector of the correlation matrix. It is not difficult to select such a vector, but it may be difficult to select one which is close to the kth basic orthonormal vector. It is convenient and usually satisfactory to use the unit vector for the first approximation.

To get the $i + 1$ approximation, then, to the kth factor loading vector, we multiply the $k - 1$ residual of the correlation matrix by the ith approximation to the kth factor loading vector. This is indicated in Eq. 7.3.14.

To get the $i + 1$ approximation to the L scalar for the kth factor loading vector, we get the minor product moment of the ith approximation to the kth factor loading vector and the $i + 1$ approximation to the $U_{.k}$ vector, as indicated in Eq. 7.3.15.

To get the $i + 1$ approximation to the D scalar for the kth factor, we take the square root of the scalar in the previous step, as indicated in Eq. 7.3.16.

To get the $i + 1$ approximation to the kth factor loading vector, we divide the $i + 1$ approximation to the $U_{.k}$ vector found in Eq. 7.3.14 by the D scalar found in Eq. 7.3.16, as indicated in Eq. 7.3.17.

We next check to see whether this $i + 1$ approximation to the kth factor loading vector is sufficiently close. This is done by taking the ratio of the $i + 1$ approximation to the D scalar to the ith approximation to this D scalar and subtracting 1 from it, as indicated in Eq. 7.3.18. If this difference is sufficiently small, we designate the $i + 1$ approximation to the $a_{.k}$ vector as the vector itself, as indicated in Eq. 7.3.19.

We also indicate the $i + 1$ approximation to the D_k scalar as the acceptable value of the D_k scalar, as indicated in Eq. 7.3.20.

Next we calculate the kth residual matrix, as indicated in Eq. 7.3.21. This is obtained by subtracting the major product moment of the kth factor loading vector from the $k - 1$ residual matrix.

After the calculation of a given factor loading vector, one must determine whether enough factors have been extracted. A criterion referred to in earlier chapters is that the sum of the squares of the factor loading vector should account for more of the total variance than any of the single variables in the set. This is an easy criterion to apply, and means simply that the minor product moment of the factor loading vector should be greater than 1. Since each successive factor loading vector in the basic structure or principal axis method accounts for no more, and usually for less, variance than the preceding one, one may continue until the minor product moment of the factor loading vector is equal to or less than 1. In this case, the vector would be discarded.

Often, however, one may have an idea as to what proportion of the total variance of the system he wants to account for with the factors extracted. Each of the final D scalars corresponding to each of the factor loading vectors is, as has been said, the corresponding diagonal for the basic diagonal of the factor loading matrix. It can also be proved that this scalar is precisely the variance accounted for by the corresponding factor loading vector. A convenient method for determining whether enough factors have been extracted is to specify the proportion of total variance to be accounted for. The total variance is usually the number of variables in the correlation matrix, since this is the sum of the diagonal terms.

One may then calculate the scalar constant G, as given in Eq. 7.3.22, which is the cumulative sum of the final D values from 1 to k, the number of factor vectors currently solved for. This quantity gives the total variance accounted for by the first k factors.

One may now take the ratio of the G scalar in Eq. 7.3.22 to the trace of the correlation matrix and compare it with the percentage of variance to be accounted for which has been previously specified. This is indicated in Eq. 7.3.23. If this ratio is less than the criterion percentage, one proceeds to compute further factors, as indicated in Eqs. 7.3.13–7.3.21. When the criterion is reached, the factoring may be stopped.

We may now assemble the factor loading matrix as the matrix from the k vectors solved for. This is indicated by Eq. 7.3.24. The parentheses around the subscript of a mean that this matrix includes all k of the vectors.

It is sometimes desirable to calculate the matrix of the first k vectors of the basic orthonormal of the correlation matrix. This can be done by means of

Eq. 7.3.25. This equation simply means that the factor loading matrix is postmultiplied by the reciprocal square root of a diagonal matrix made up of the D values, calculated as previously outlined. This, of course, amounts to dividing each of the elements of a vector by the square root of the corresponding D value. It can be proved from this method of calculation, and from the fact that the column vectors of a_k are mutually orthogonal, that the minor product moment of this Q matrix is the identity matrix.

7.3.4 Numerical Example. The following numerical example begins with the correlation matrix used in Chapters 5 and 6.

Table 7.3.1 gives in the first row the first factor loading vector and in successive rows the first residual matrix. Tables 7.3.2 and 7.3.3 give the same data for the second and third factors and the corresponding residual matrices.

Table 7.3.4 gives the fourth factor vector, the number of iterations for each factor, and the basic diagonals corresponding to the factors. It is seen that the fourth basic diagonal is 0.474. Since this is less than 1, the fourth factor is discarded.

TABLE 7.3.1   First Factor Vector and First Residual Matrix

0.715	0.739	0.772	0.557	0.465	0.520	0.640	0.614	0.715
0.489								
0.301	0.455							
0.216	0.205	0.404						
−0.291	−0.297	−0.158	0.689					
−0.300	−0.283	−0.154	0.377	0.783				
−0.264	−0.259	−0.163	0.336	0.467	0.730			
−0.160	−0.150	−0.198	−0.108	−0.160	−0.143	0.590		
−0.130	−0.107	−0.203	−0.159	−0.195	−0.216	0.261	0.622	
−0.160	−0.159	−0.167	−0.030	−0.079	−0.081	0.069	0.102	0.489

TABLE 7.3.2   Second Factor Vector and Second Residual Matrix

−0.496	−0.482	−0.300	0.647	0.742	0.691	−0.078	−0.165	0.034
0.242								
0.062	0.222							
0.067	0.060	0.314						
0.031	0.015	0.036	0.271					
0.068	0.075	0.068	−0.103	0.233				
0.080	0.074	0.044	−0.111	−0.046	0.252			
−0.199	−0.188	−0.222	−0.057	−0.102	−0.089	0.584		
−0.212	−0.186	−0.253	−0.053	−0.073	−0.103	0.248	0.595	
−0.144	−0.143	−0.157	−0.051	−0.104	−0.104	0.072	0.107	0.487

TABLE 7.3.3   Third Factor Vector and Third Residual Matrix

−0.348	−0.319	−0.405	−0.071	−0.184	−0.192	0.588	0.622	0.368
0.121								
−0.049	0.121							
−0.074	−0.069	0.150						
0.006	−0.008	0.007	0.266					
0.004	0.016	−0.006	−0.116	0.199				
0.013	0.013	−0.033	−0.124	−0.081	0.215			
0.006	0.000	0.016	−0.015	0.007	0.024	0.238		
0.004	0.012	−0.001	−0.009	0.042	0.017	−0.118	0.208	
−0.016	−0.026	−0.008	−0.025	−0.036	−0.033	−0.145	−0.122	0.352

TABLE 7.3.4   Fourth Factor Vector, Number of Iterations, and Basic Diagonals

0.030	0.057	−0.009	−0.107	0.118	0.131	0.285	0.166	−0.565
7	8	8	16					
3.749	2.050	1.331	0.474					

7.4   Solution without Residuals

In this section we shall first discuss essential characteristics of the method. The computational equations will be presented then, after which the computational instructions and a numerical example will be given.

7.4.1   Characteristics of the Solution.   The solution to be presented requires successive approximations for each of the factor vectors. Except for decimal accuracy, the solution, if carried to the same number of iterations, gives the same results as in the method just outlined. It is essentially different from the previous solution in that no residual matrices are required. Although no exact proof of the assertion has been worked out, it seems clear that the accumulation of decimal error in this method is less than in the previous method. This is true whether the computations are carried out by desk calculators or by electronic computers. However, the storage requirements for the computations are somewhat more for the electronic computers than in the method previously described. The reason for this is that, with the previous method, one can write out each factor loading vector as it is finally calculated, and it need not be retained in storage for further calculations. When using an electronic computer, it is, of course, possible to write the vector on scratch tape, but it must be brought back into core storage for further calculation. This method of computation, therefore, requires not only the correlation matrix but also all previously calculated factor vectors in the computation of the current factor vector. The previous method, on the other hand, requires no consideration of previously calculated factor vectors in the calculation of a current factor vector. However, for the method without residuals the number of worksheets required, if desk calculators are used, is considerably less than for the previous method. In summary, the current method requires no writing down of residual matrices on separate worksheets for desk computers, but it does require that successively calculated factor vectors be retained in storage for further computations if electronic computers are used.

7.4.2 Computational Equations.

7.4.2a. DEFINITION OF NOTATION. The definition of the basic notation involved in the computational equations for this method is the same as for the previous method; therefore, no new symbols will be required except those introduced in the computational equations. Such symbols are defined in terms of symbols already defined in Section 7.3.2.

7.4.2b THE EQUATIONS. The computational equations required when no residual matrices are calculated are a little more involved than when residual matrices are calculated.

$$_1U_{.1} = {_0R}\,_0V_{.1} \tag{7.4.1}$$

$$_1L_1 = {_0V_{.1}}'\,_1U_{.1} \tag{7.4.2}$$

$$_1D_1 = \sqrt{_1L_1} \tag{7.4.3}$$

$$_1a_{.1} = \frac{_1U_{.1}}{_1D_1} \tag{7.4.4}$$

$$_{i+1}U_{.1} = {_0R}\,_ia_{.1} \tag{7.4.5}$$

$$_{i+1}L_1 = {_ia_{.1}}'\,_{i+1}U_{.1} \tag{7.4.6}$$

$$_{i+1}D_1 = \sqrt{_{i+1}L_1} \tag{7.4.7}$$

$$_{i+1}a_{.1} = \frac{_{i+1}U_{.1}}{_{i+1}D_1} \tag{7.4.8}$$

$$H = \left| \frac{_{i+1}D_1}{_iD_1} - 1 \right| \tag{7.4.9}$$

$$a_{.1} = {_{i+1}a_{.1}} \tag{7.4.10}$$

$$G_1 = {a_{.1}}'\,a_{.1} \tag{7.4.11}$$

$$_1W_{.2} = {a_{.1}}'\,_0V_{.2} \tag{7.4.12}$$

$$_1U_{.2} = {_0R}\,_0V_{.2} - a_{.1}\,_1W_{.2} \tag{7.4.13}$$

$$_1L_2 = {_0}V_{.2}'\,{_1}U_{.2} \tag{7.4.14}$$

$$_1D_2 = \sqrt{_1L_2} \tag{7.4.15}$$

$$_1a_{.2} = \frac{_1U_{.2}}{_1D_2} \tag{7.4.16}$$

$$_iW_{.2} = a_{.1}'\,{_i}a_{.2} \tag{7.4.17}$$

$$_{i+1}U_{.2} = {_0}R\,{_i}a_{.2} - a_{.1}\,{_i}W_{.2} \tag{7.4.18}$$

$$_{i+1}L_2 = {_i}a_{.2}'\,{_{i+1}}U_{.2} \tag{7.4.19}$$

$$_{i+1}D_2 = \sqrt{_{i+1}L_2} \tag{7.4.20}$$

$$_{i+1}a_{.2} = \frac{_{i+1}U_{.2}}{_{i+1}D_2} \tag{7.4.21}$$

$$H = \left| \frac{_{i+1}D_2}{_iD_2} - 1 \right| \tag{7.4.22}$$

$$a_{.2} = {_{i+1}}a_{.2} \tag{7.4.23}$$

$$G_2 = a_{.2}'\,a_{.2} \tag{7.4.24}$$

$$T_2 = G_1 + G_2 \tag{7.4.25}$$

$$C = \frac{T_2}{tr\,{_0}R} - P \tag{7.4.26}$$

$$a_{(k-1)} = (a_{.1} \cdots a_{.k-1}) \tag{7.4.27}$$

$$_1W_{.k} = a_{(k-1)}'\,{_0}V_{.k} \tag{7.4.28}$$

$$_1U_{.k} = {_0}R\,{_0}V_{.k} - a_{(k-1)}\,{_1}W_{.k} \tag{7.4.29}$$

$$_1L_k = {_0}V_{.k}'\,{_1}U_{.k} \tag{7.4.30}$$

$$_1D_k = \sqrt{_1L_k} \tag{7.4.31}$$

$$_1a_{.k} = \frac{_1U_{.k}}{_1D_k} \tag{7.4.32}$$

$$_iW_{.k} = a_{(k-1)}'\,{_i}a_{.k} \tag{7.4.33}$$

$$_{i+1}U_{.k} = {_0}R\,{_i}a_{.k} - a_{(k-1)}\,{_i}W_{.k} \tag{7.4.34}$$

$$_{i+1}L_k = {_i}a_{.k}'\,{_{i+1}}U_{.k} \tag{7.4.35}$$

$$_{i+1}D_k = \sqrt{_{i+1}L_k} \tag{7.4.36}$$

$$_{i+1}a_{.k} = \frac{_{i+1}U_{.k}}{_{i+1}D_k} \tag{7.4.37}$$

$$H = \left| \frac{{}_{i+1}D_k}{{}_iD_k} - 1 \right| \tag{7.4.38}$$

$$a_{.k} = {}_{i+1}a_{.k} \tag{7.4.39}$$

$$G_k = a_{.k}{}' a_{.k} \tag{7.4.40}$$

$$T_k = T_{k-1} + G_k \tag{7.4.41}$$

$$C = \frac{T_k}{tr\,{}_0R} - P \tag{7.4.42}$$

$$Q_{(k)} = a_{(k)}\, D_{(k.)}{}^{-1/2} \tag{7.4.43}$$

7.4.3 Computational Instructions.

The computational procedure for this method begins, as in the previous method, with a first approximation to the factor loading vector. As in the former case, this approximation must not be orthogonal to the first basic orthonormal vector of the correlation matrix or, in traditional mathematical terms, to the eigenvector corresponding to the largest eigenvalue. For this method the calculation of the first factor loading vector is the same as for the previous method. For the sake of completeness, it will be repeated briefly.

The correlation matrix is multiplied by the first approximation vector, ${}_0V_{.1}$, to give the first approximation to the $U_{.1}$ vector, as in Eq. 7.4.1. The ${}_1L_1$ scalar quantity is also calculated, as in Eq. 7.4.2. Its square root is calculated in Eq. 7.4.3 to give the scalar ${}_1D_1$.

The first approximation to the first vector factor is given in Eq. 7.4.4 by dividing the first U vector by the D scalar. To get the $i + 1$ approximation to the U vector, the correlation matrix is postmultiplied by the ith approximation to the first factor vector, as in Eq. 7.4.5. The $i + 1$ approximation to the L scalar is given by Eq. 7.4.6. The $i + 1$ approximation to the D_1 scalar is given by Eq. 7.4.7. The $i + 1$ approximation to the $a_{.1}$ vector is given by Eq. 7.4.8 in the usual manner.

The check to see whether or not the approximation is close enough in terms of the ${}_{i+1}D$ value and the ith D value is given in Eq. 7.4.9.

If the H value is small enough, according to the degree of tolerance established, the first factor vector is given as the $i + 1$ approximation, as indicated in Eq. 7.4.10.

We may calculate the sum of the squares of the elements of the first factor loading vector, as in Eq. 7.4.11.

The calculation for the second and succeeding vectors now proceeds differently from that of the previous section. We do not calculate a residual matrix. Instead, we take an approximation to the second factor loading vector. For convenience, we take this as the unit vector. This is ${}_0V_{.2}$ in Eq. 7.4.12. We calculate the W scalar, which is the minor product moment of the first factor loading vector by this V vector. In this particular case, it is simply the sum of the elements. It will be noted that the subscript notation on W is that for a vector from a matrix, even though in this case it is a scalar. The reason is that for later calculations it does become a vector from a matrix.

The next step is to calculate the first approximation to the $U_{.2}$ vector in two stages. This is indicated on the right-hand side of Eq. 7.4.13. The first term on the right-hand side is simply the correlation matrix postmultiplied by this first approximation vector which, as in the previous case, is the column sum of row elements. The second vector, which is subtracted from this first term, is the first factor vector multiplied by the scalar calculated in Eq. 7.4.12.

With this new definition of the first approximation to the U vector, we now calculate the first approximation to the second L scalar exactly as in the previous method, according to Eq. 7.4.14.

The D scalar is also calculated in the previous manner, as in Eq. 7.4.15.

The first approximation to the second factor loading vector is calculated as previously, as in Eq. 7.4.16.

In general, the $i + 1$ approximation to the second factor loading vector is calculated as follows. First, we calculate the ith approximation to the scalar quantity $_iW_{.2}$, as indicated in Eq. 7.4.17. This is the minor product moment of the first factor loading vector and the ith approximation to the second factor loading vector.

We now calculate the $i + 1$ approximation to $U_{.2}$ by Eq. 7.4.18. This again consists of two parts. The first part consists of the correlation matrix multiplied by the ith approximation to the factor loading vector. From this is subtracted the first factor loading vector times the scalar $_iW_{.2}$ calculated in Eq. 7.4.17.

Having given the $_{i+1}U_{.2}$ vector, we then calculate the $i + 1$ approximations to the L and D scalar quantities, as indicated in Eqs. 7.4.19 and 7.4.20. Similarly, the $i + 1$ approximations to the $a_{.2}$ vector is calculated as in Eq. 7.4.21, which is analogous to previous calculations.

The test of convergence is given in Eq. 7.4.22. If the convergence is close enough, we then take the $i + 1$ approximation for $a_{.2}$, as indicated in Eq. 7.4.23.

We now calculate a second G value, as in Eq. 7.4.24, which is the minor product moment, or sum of squares of elements, of the second factor loading vector.

We calculate a scalar which is the sum of the G_1 for the first factor vector and G_2 for the second factor vector, as indicated in Eq. 7.4.25. This gives us the amount of variance accounted for by the first two factors.

We take the ratio of this scalar quantity to the trace of the correlation matrix, as indicated in Eq. 7.4.26, to see whether the percentage of variance accounted for is large enough. If so, we have extracted enough factors. If not, we go on to calculate further factors.

Subsequent computations are a little more involved than for getting the first or second factor vectors, but they can be generalized for any k factors as follows.

We indicate a matrix of $(k-1)$ factor loading vectors already calculated as in Eq. 7.4.27, in which the subscript $(k-1)$ enclosed in parentheses means that the matrix includes all $(k-1)$ vectors.

Next we calculate a first approximation to a W vector, as indicated in Eq. 7.4.28, which is the transpose of the matrix of previously calculated factor vectors, postmultiplied by the 0 approximation to the factor loading vector. Again we take this approximation to be the unit vector. Each element in $_1W_{.k}$, then, is the sum of the elements in the corresponding factor loading vector.

Next we calculate the first approximation to the $U_{.k}$ vector, as indicated in Eq. 7.4.29. This involves two vectors, the first of which is the correlation matrix postmultiplied by the $_0V$ unit vector. The second vector is a little more involved, however. It is the matrix of previously calculated factor loading vectors postmultiplied by the W vector calculated in Eq. 7.4.28. This vector, as indicated, is subtracted from the first term on the right of Eq. 7.4.29 to give the first approximation to the $U_{.k}$ vector.

The calculations for the scalars L and D and for the first approximation to the kth factor loading vector are the same as previously given. They are given here in Eqs. 7.4.30–7.4.32, respectively.

We are now ready to consider successive approximations to the kth factor loading vector. We define the approximation to the $W_{.k}$, as in Eq. 7.4.33. This is the transpose of the matrix made up of the first $k-1$ factor loading vectors postmultiplied by the ith approximation to the kth factor vector. It will be seen that this vector has $k-1$ elements in it. As a matter of fact, the computation for the second factor loading matrix had only one element in it, or $2-1$, and therefore was a scalar quantity.

The $i+1$ approximation to the $U_{.k}$ vector is indicated by Eq. 7.4.34. Here the first term on the right is the correlation matrix postmultiplied by the ith approximation to the $a_{.k}$ vector. The second term is the matrix of the first $k-1$ factor vectors, already solved for, postmultiplied by the W vector calculated in Eq. 7.4.33.

The $i+1$ approximations to the L and D scalar quantities and the $i+1$ approximation to the kth factor loading vector are given in Eqs. 7.4.35–7.4.37, respectively. These are analogous to the calculations for the first and second factor loading vectors.

The check to see whether the approximations are close enough is the same as previously, as indicated in Eq. 7.4.38. If they are close enough, we then, as before, let the kth factor loading vector be equal to the $i+1$ approximation, as in Eq. 7.4.39.

We now calculate the scalar quantity G_k, as indicated in Eq. 7.4.40, which is the minor product moment of the kth factor loading vector. This gives the amount of variance accounted for by this vector.

We add this scalar quantity to the T scalar calculated in previous computations, as indicated in Eq. 7.4.41. This gives the cumulative amount of variance accounted for by all of the factor vectors currently calculated.

We now test the ratio of this total variance accounted for to the total variance or trace of the correlation matrix, as indicated in Eq. 7.4.42, to see if we have accounted for the desired percentage of variance. If not, we may assume that additional factors are required and proceed as indicated in Eqs. 7.4.27–7.4.42. When the total number of factors desired has been solved for, we may calculate the corresponding basic orthonormals of the factor loading matrix, as indicated in Eq. 7.4.43, which is the same as in the preceding method.

7.4.4 Numerical Example. The method is applied to the same correlation matrix as in the previous examples. Table 7.4.1 gives the matrix of four factor loading vectors. The two rows at the bottom of the table give, respectively, the number of iterations for each factor and the corresponding basic diagonals. These latter, it will be recalled, indicate the amount of variance accounted for by the corresponding factor.

TABLE 7.4.1 Matrix of Column Factor Loading Vectors,
Number of Iterations for Each Factor,
and Variance Accounted For By Each

0.715	−0.496	−0.348	0.030
0.739	−0.482	−0.319	0.057
0.772	−0.300	−0.405	−0.009
0.557	0.647	−0.071	−0.107
0.465	0.742	−0.184	0.118
0.520	0.691	−0.192	0.131
0.640	−0.078	0.588	0.285
0.614	−0.165	0.622	0.166
0.715	0.034	0.368	−0.565
7	8	8	16
3.749	2.050	1.331	0.474

7.5 Mathematical Proofs

7.5.1 The Residual Solution. Let $_0V$ be an arbitrary vector not orthogonal to the first basic orthonormal vector of R. Consider the equations

$$_1U = R\,_0V \qquad (7.5.1)$$

Let

$$_1L = {_0V'}\,{_1U} \tag{7.5.2}$$

$$_1D = \sqrt{_1L} \tag{7.5.3}$$

$$_1a = \frac{_1U}{_1D} \tag{7.5.4}$$

$$_2U = R\,{_1a} \tag{7.5.5}$$

$$_2L = {_1a'}\,{_2U} \tag{7.5.6}$$

$$_2D = \sqrt{_2L} \tag{7.5.7}$$

$$_2a = \frac{_2U}{_2D} \tag{7.5.8}$$

$$_3U = R\,{_2a} \tag{7.5.9}$$

$$_3L = {_2a'}\,{_3U} \tag{7.5.10}$$

$$_3D = \sqrt{_3L} \tag{7.5.11}$$

$$_3a = \frac{_3U}{_3D} \tag{7.5.12}$$

From Eqs. 7.5.11 and 7.5.12

$$_3a = \frac{_3U}{\sqrt{_3L}} \tag{7.5.13}$$

From Eqs. 7.5.10 and 7.5.13,

$$_3a = \frac{_3U}{\sqrt{_2a'\,{_3U}}} \tag{7.5.14}$$

From Eqs. 7.5.9 and 7.5.14,

$$_3a = \frac{R\,{_2a}}{\sqrt{_2a'\,R\,{_2a}}} \tag{7.5.15}$$

From Eqs. 7.5.8 and 7.5.15,

$$_3a = \frac{R\,{_2U}}{\sqrt{_2U'\,R\,{_2U}}} \tag{7.5.16}$$

From Eqs. 7.5.5 and 7.5.16,

$$_3a = \frac{R^2\,{_1a}}{\sqrt{_1a'\,R^3\,{_1a}}} \tag{7.5.17}$$

From Eqs. 7.5.4 and 7.5.17,

$$_3a = \frac{R^2\,{_1U}}{\sqrt{_1U'\,R^3\,{_1U}}} \tag{7.5.18}$$

From Eqs. 7.5.1. and 7.5.18,

$$_3a = \frac{R^3\,_0V}{\sqrt{_0V'\,R^5\,_0V}} \tag{7.5.19}$$

In general, then,

$$_ia = \frac{R^i\,V}{\sqrt{_0V'\,R^{2i-1}\,_0V}} \tag{7.5.20}$$

Let

$$R = Q\,\delta\,Q' \tag{7.5.21}$$

be the basic structure of R.
Then

$$R^i = Q\,\delta^i\,Q' \tag{7.5.22}$$

Let

$$Y = Q'\,_0V \tag{7.5.23}$$

From Eqs. 7.5.20 –7.5.23,

$$_ia = \frac{Q\,\delta^i\,Y}{\sqrt{Y'\,\delta^{2i-1}\,Y}} \tag{7.5.24}$$

From Eq. 7.5.24,

$$_ia = \frac{Q_{.1}\,\delta_1{}^i\,Y_1 + Q_{)1(}\,\delta_{)1(}{}^i\,Y_{)1(}}{\sqrt{Y_1{}^2\,\delta_1{}^{2i-2} + Y_{)1(}'\,\delta_{)1(}{}^{2(i-1)}\,Y_{)1(}}} \tag{7.5.25}$$

where the subscript $)1($ means that the first vector or scalar has been excluded.
   Write Eq. 7.5.25 as

$$_ia = \frac{Q_{.1}\,\delta_i{}^i\,Y_1 + \varepsilon_1}{\sqrt{Y_1{}^2\,\delta_1{}^{2i-1} + \varepsilon_2}} \tag{7.5.26}$$

Assume i so large that ε_1 and ε_2 are negligible compared to the first terms in the corresponding expression, as i increases without limit.

$$_ia \to \frac{Q_{.1}\,\delta_i{}^i\,Y_1}{\sqrt{Y_1{}^2\,\delta_1{}^{2i-1}}} \tag{7.5.27}$$

or

$$_ia \to Q_{.1}\,\delta_i{}^{1/2} \tag{7.5.28}$$

where the right of Eq. 7.5.28 is the basic structure definition of the factor loading vector.

7.5.1a.   PROOF OF RESIDUAL.   Consider

$$_1R = {}_0R - a_{.1}\,a_{.1}' \tag{7.5.29}$$

From Eqs. 7.5.21, 7.5.28 and 7.5.29,

$$_1R = Q\delta Q' - Q_{.1}\,\delta_1\,Q_{.1}'$$ (7.5.30)

From Eq. 7.5.30,

$$_1R = Q_{)1(}\,\delta_{)1(}\,Q_{)1(}'$$ (7.5.31)

Equation 7.5.31 shows that the first residual has as its largest basic diagonal δ_2, hence the iterated solution for $a_{.2}$ will approach $Q_{.2}\,\delta_2^{1/2}$, which is the basic structure definition of $a_{.2}$.

In the same way we can prove that the kth residual matrix has δ_{k+1} as the largest basic diagonal, and hence the iterated solution converges to $a_{.(k+1)}$.

7.5.1b. PROOF OF RANK REDUCTION SOLUTION. It can be shown from Eq. 7.5.15 that the general solution for the $i+1$ approximation to the kth factor loading vector is

$$_{i+1}a_{.k} = \frac{R\,_ia_{.k}}{\sqrt{_ia_{.k}'R\,_ia_{.k}}}$$ (7.5.32)

We write

$$_{k+1}R = {_k}R - {_{i+1}}a_{.k}\,{_{i+1}}a_{.k}'$$ (7.5.33)

From Eqs. 7.5.32 and 7.5.33,

$$_{k+1}R = {_k}R - {_k}R\,_ia_{.k}\,(_ia_{.k}'\,_kR\,_ia_{.k})^{-1}\,_ia_{.k}'\,_kR$$ (7.5.34)

which is the familiar rank reduction form.

7.5.2 The Nonresidual Method.
Consider

$$_1R = {_0}R - a_{.1}\,a_{.1}'$$ (7.5.35)

and in general,

$$_kR = {_{k-1}}R - a_{.k}\,a_{.k}'$$ (7.5.36)

Let

$$a_{(k-1)} = (a_{.1}\,\cdots\,a_{.k-1})$$ (7.5.37)

From Eqs. 7.5.35–7.5.37,

$$_{k-1}R = {_0}R - a_{(k-1)}\,a_{(k-1)}'$$ (7.5.38)

Let

$$_{i+1}U_{.k} = {_{k-1}}R\,_ia_{.k}$$ (7.5.39)

From Eqs. 7.5.38 and 7.5.39,

$$_{i+1}U_{.k} = (_0R - a_{(k-1)}\,a_{(k-1)}')\,_ia_{.k}$$ (7.5.40)

Let

$$_iW_{.k} = a_{(k-1)}'\,_ia_{.k}$$ (7.5.41)

From Eqs. 7.5.40 and 7.5.41,

$$_{i+1}U_{.k} = {_0R}\,_ia_{.k} - a_{(k-1)}\,_iW_{.k} \tag{7.5.42}$$

which is the same as computational Eq. 7.4.34 in Section 7.4. The remainder of the computations for $a_{.k}$ are the same as the residual method, hence the convergence and rank reduction proofs for that method hold here.

Chapter 8

Simultaneous Basic Structure Methods

With one exception, all of the methods which we have considered so far require the calculation of one factor vector at a time. The exception is the multiple group method, which was discussed in Chapter 6. This method, you recall, begins with a binary matrix for the arbitrary matrix.

The simultaneous basic structure methods discussed in this chapter have not been commonly used and are not well known. However, the principles underlying them are useful for very large data matrices such as are obtained from personality, interest, or other types of inventory instruments in which a large number of individual items are correlated. A method presented by Horst (1937) many years ago may be regarded as the forerunner of the methods to be discussed in this chapter. However, that method is now superseded by those outlined in the following sections.

8.1 Characteristics of the Solutions

Among the most important distinguishing characteristics of the simultaneous basic structure methods are the following: first, a prespecified number of factors is simultaneously solved for. Second, the methods yield least square solutions. Third, the solution for the factor matrix is iterative. And fourth, the cumulative decimal error is relatively small.

8.1.1 Prespecified Number of Factors Simultaneously Solved for.
In the methods outlined below, one must determine in advance the number of factors he wishes to solve for. This may be done on some *a priori* or rational basis if the investigator has hypotheses with reference to the number of distinct dimensions of the system or domain which he is exploring. This, of course, is similar to criteria used in determining the number of factors in the multiple group method of factor analysis discussed in Chapter 6.

However, the simultaneous basic structure methods are appropriate for very large sets of variables if high-speed computers are available. If one has an hypothesis as to the upper limit of the number of factors in the system, he may specify a number of factors somewhat in excess of those which he really expects to find significant in the set. For example, if one has a set of intercorrelations of, let us say, 200 or more personality or interest items, one may assume that the number of significant or systematic factors in the set is no more than, perhaps, 15 or 20. One may set up the computations for several more factors than he expects to use, and discard those which are not significant.

8.1.2 Least Square Solution.

Like all basic structure solutions, those outlined in the following paragraphs give factor loading matrices such that if the major product moment of the factor loading matrix is subtracted from the correlation matrix, the sum of squares of the elements in the residual matrix is a minimum. In the simultaneous basic structure methods, however, one is not concerned with how small the residuals are, because once the number of factors to be taken out has been determined, the residual variance is automatically predetermined. Another corollary of the least square characteristics of the solution is that for the specified number of factors, these factors account for the maximum variance possible for that number.

8.1.3 Iterative Solutions.

Like all basic structure methods which explicitly or implicitly involve solutions for the basic diagonals of the correlation or data matrix, these solutions must be iterative. There is no exact algebraic solution to the factor loading vectors. One begins with some approximation, however crude, to the factor loading matrix, and by successive iterations converges toward the basic structure solution involving the largest basic diagonals and corresponding basic structure vectors.

8.1.4 Minimal Cumulative Decimal Error.

In the methods previously discussed which require residual matrices to be calculated, one loses decimal accuracy in the calculation of the residual matrix and the subsequent calculation of the corresponding factor vector based on each residual matrix. As was pointed out in Chapter 7, the successive factor vector solution, which does not require the calculation of residual matrices, does gain in decimal accuracy. Although no exact proof has been developed, it seems reasonable to assume from the method of calculation that even less decimal error is involved in the methods outlined here. This is because the computational procedure involved in the iterations is self-corrective, so that if either computational or decimal errors occur in a given iteration, these tend to be corrected in subsequent iterations.

8.1.5 Number of Computations Required.

The number of computations required may, in general, be greater than those required for methods previously discussed. This is certainly true for the basic structure methods discussed in Chapter 7, if the total number of iterations for all factors solved for is equal in both methods. In many cases, however, one may be satisfied with a smaller number of iterations for the simultaneous methods considered here than for the methods discussed in Chapter 7. This is because in methods described in this section one may have only a relatively small number of approximations and get a rather poor approximation to the exact basic structure solution, but it may nevertheless be a good approximation to some orthonormal transformation of the exact solution. In this case the factors would still account for about the same amount of variance as if they were the exact basic structure solution. The reason for this is indicated in Section 4.4.

8.2   Kinds of Solutions

We shall discuss two major types of solutions in which a prespecified number of the basic structure factors are solved for simultaneously. One of these we designate as the *rank reduction method* and the other as the *orthogonalization method*.

8.2.1   The Rank Reduction Method. This method of simultaneous basic structure solution is analogous to the methods discussed in Chapter 7 in that, for any iteration, the current approximation to the factor loading matrix is a rank reduction solution. This means that for any degree of approximation, after the first rough arbitrary approximation, the residual obtained by subtracting the major product moment of the approximate factor matrix from the correlation matrix has a rank equal to that of the correlation matrix less the number of factors.

8.2.2   The Orthogonalization Method. The essential characteristic of this simultaneous basic structure method is that in each approximation to the factor loading matrix, the factor vectors are all orthogonal to one another. In this sense each factor loading matrix approximation is similar to the final basic solution, in which by definition all the factor loading vectors are mutually orthogonal.

8.3   The Rank Reduction Method

As in the discussion of previous methods, we shall consider the rank reduction method first in terms of more detailed characteristics of the solution. We shall then present the computational equations and outline the computational instructions. Finally, a numerical example will be presented.

8.3.1   Characteristics of the Solution. As indicated in the previous section, any approximation to the factor loading matrix after the first rough arbitrary approximation is a rank reduction solution. It may be, of course, a very poor approximation in the least square sense. Even though an early approximation is a rank reduction matrix, its major product moment may be a poor approximation to the correlation matrix. On the other hand, if the first approximation was reasonably good, it is quite possible that a relatively small number of iterations will be adequate. For example, one may have a very good hypothesis as to the number of factors in the system and as to which variables are the best measures of these factors. One may then use the corresponding binary grouping matrix, as in the multiple group method, for the first approximation. This may well result in a good second or third approximation to the basic structure factor loading matrix, depending, of course, on how accurate the hypothesis as to the grouping of the variables is.

One of the disadvantages of the rank reduction method is particularly relevant to its use with high-speed computers. For the method currently programed, a slightly greater core storage is required than for the orthogonalization method. However, this increase is not great when compared to the total number of storage requirements.

8.3.2 Computational Equations.

8.3.2a DEFINITION OF NOTATION

R is the correlation matrix.

E is a first approximation to the factor loading matrix.

t is a triangular matrix.

$_i a$ is the ith approximation to the basic structure factor loading matrix of m factor vectors.

H is the criterion of convergence.

G_i is the ith approximation to the variance accounted for by the m factors in the basic structure factor loading matrix.

D_{i^s} is a diagonal matrix of the diagonal elements of the matrix S defined in the following equations.

P is a prespecified tolerance limit.

8.3.2b THE EQUATIONS

$$_0 a = E \tag{8.3.1}$$

$$_1 b = RE \tag{8.3.2}$$

$$_1 S = {_1 t} \, {_1 t'} = E'RE \tag{8.3.3}$$

$$\begin{matrix} _1 t \\ _1 a \end{matrix} \, {_1 t'} = \begin{bmatrix} _1 S \\ _1 b \end{bmatrix} \tag{8.3.4}$$

$$_1 a = {_1 b} \, {_1 t'}^{-1} \tag{8.3.5}$$

$$_i b = R \, {_{i-1} a} \tag{8.3.6}$$

$$_iS = {}_it\ {}_it' = {}_ib'_{i-1}a \tag{8.3.7}$$

$$\begin{bmatrix} _it \\ _ia \end{bmatrix} _it' = \begin{bmatrix} _iS \\ _ib \end{bmatrix} \tag{8.3.8}$$

$$_ia = {}_ib\ {}_it'^{-1} \tag{8.3.9}$$

$$_iD = D_{iS}{}^{1/2} \tag{8.3.10}$$

$$G_i = 1'D1 \tag{8.3.11}$$

$$H = \left| \frac{G_{i-1}}{G_i} - 1 \right| - P \tag{8.3.12}$$

8.3.3 Computational Instructions. First, one must decide how many factors are to be solved for so that some rough approximation to the factor matrix may be selected as a starting point. We designate this beginning matrix as in Eq. 8.3.1, in which we use the 0 prescript on a and indicate this as E. As just indicated, one may start with the E matrix as a binary matrix made up as in the multiple group method. If one can make a reasonable guess as to a single variable for each factor which is presumed to measure that factor, then one may consider a set of e_i vectors corresponding to these variables. This set would then constitute the matrix E, which has a single 1 in each column and zeros in all the rows except those corresponding to the variables which have been selected as measuring each of the factors postulated in the set. An even simpler method than this assumes that each of the first m variables, where m is the number of factors to be solved for, is linearly independent and that each is a sufficiently close approximation to one of the desired factors, irrespective of how good this approximation is.

This means, then, that the E matrix, in Eq. 8.3.1, is simply a binary matrix in which the first m rows constitute an identity submatrix and the remaining rows constitute a null submatrix. Since even error variance or unsystematic variance will ensure that for most experimental cases the m columns of the correlation matrix are basic, one is reasonably safe in using this latter method as a selection of the E matrix. As a matter of fact, the only necessary restriction on the vectors of the E matrix is that none of them be orthogonal to any of the first m vectors of the basic orthonormal of R. This restriction is not difficult to satisfy in the case of experimental data. However, the greater the departure of all the E vectors from orthogonality with any of the first basic orthonormal vectors of the correlation matrix, the fewer approximations will be required.

We assume the E matrix to be selected in the manner just indicated. We now multiply the correlation matrix by this binary matrix, as indicated in Eq. 8.3.2. The matrix on the left of this equation, $_1b$, is then simply the first m columns of the correlation matrix. It can be readily seen that the E matrix, consisting of an upper submatrix which is I and a lower submatrix which is null, does in fact isolate the first m columns of R in this fashion.

The next step is to premultiply the matrix found in Eq. 8.3.2 by the transpose of the E matrix, as indicated in Eq. 8.3.3. This gives an S matrix which is simply the matrix of the intercorrelations of the first m variables of the set. As indicated in the middle expression of this equation, the S matrix may be expressed as a major product moment of a lower triangular matrix.

We now use the matrix calculated in Eq. 8.3.2 together with the matrix calculated in Eq. 8.3.3 to yield a supermatrix, or type 3 supervector, as indicated in Eq. 8.3.4. The right-hand side of this equation has the S matrix of Eq. 8.3.3 as the upper matric element and the b matrix of Eq. 8.3.2 as the lower matric element.

We next carry out a triangular factoring of this matrix, as indicated on the left side of Eq. 8.3.4. This gives us as the left-hand partial triangular factor a supermatrix, or type 3 supervector, whose upper matric element is the lower triangular factor of the S matrix. The lower matric element, $_1a$, is the first approximation to the factor loading matrix a. We designate this as the first approximation, since the binary matrix E was designated as the 0 approximation. The reason for this use of subscripts is that $_1a$ is now a rank reduction matrix while the matrix E is not.

From Eq. 8.3.4, it can readily be verified that the $_1a$ factor loading approximation matrix can be obtained as in Eq. 8.3.5. It is possible, first, to factor the matrix S given in Eq. 8.3.3 into its triangular factors, then to calculate the inverse of the upper triangular factor t', and next to postmultiply the matrix b given in Eq. 8.3.2 by this inverse, as indicated in the right-hand side of Eq. 8.3.5. However, if the method implied in Eq. 8.3.4 is used, one can avoid the computation of the inverse of the triangular matrix.

Equation 8.3.6 shows how to get a second approximation to the b matrix. The original correlation matrix is postmultiplied by the current approximation to the factor loading matrix to give a subsequent b matrix.

We now consider the current factor loading matrix a premultiplied by the transpose of the b matrix just solved for, which gives us another symmetric matrix $_iS$, as indicated in Eq. 8.3.7. This matrix may be expressed as the major product moment of its triangular factor $_it$.

The next step is to construct the type 3 supervector, with the S matrix as the upper element and the b matrix as the lower element, as shown in Eq. 8.3.8. The left-hand side of this equation shows the supervector as the product of its partial triangular factor postmultiplied by the upper triangular factor of the S matrix.

Equation 8.3.9. shows the alternative method for solving for the ith approximation to the factor loading matrix. This consists of postmultiplying the b matrix by the inverse of the transpose of the lower triangular factor of the matrix S.

TABLE 8.3.1   Values of G Scalar for Successive Iterations

15.156556	19.100759	20.041658	20.122123	20.168801	20.200170	20.218481	20.229753	20.237152	20.242136
20.245502	20.247763	20.249269	20.250266	20.250922	20.251352	20.251633	20.251817	20.251936	20.252014
20.252065	20.252098	20.252119	20.252134	20.252142	20.252148	20.252152	20.252155	20.252156	20.252157

TABLE 8.3.2   First Four Basic Diagonal Elements and Matrix of Column Factor Loading Vectors

3.749069	2.049528	1.330791	0.474420
0.716585	−0.492676	0.350313	−0.029991
0.739871	−0.478086	0.321565	−0.056186
0.772825	−0.295709	0.406330	0.009356
0.555553	0.648894	0.067520	0.104755
0.463263	0.744045	0.180803	−0.115590
0.517682	0.693617	0.188445	−0.129935
0.640534	−0.079586	−0.587515	−0.287422
0.614925	−0.165978	−0.621122	−0.164958
0.715013	0.033679	−0.368561	0.565009

After the first and successive approximations to the S matrix, we calculate a diagonal matrix which is the reciprocal square root of the diagonal of this S matrix, as indicated in Eq. 8.3.10.

The diagonal matrix in Eq. 8.3.10 is an approximation to the basic diagonal of the correlation matrix. Since the solution converges toward this basic diagonal, eventually the left-hand term of Eq. 8.3.10 must, for some iteration, be equal to this diagonal within some specified degree of decimal accuracy.

We calculate the sum of these values, as indicated in Eq. 8.3.11, to see how they change from one approximation to the next.

The first test we make is for the value of $i = 2$, as indicated in Eq. 8.3.12. Here we have on the left side a function of the ratio of two successive G values and the tolerance limit P. We take the ratio of the preceding approximation to G to the current approximation and subtract 1 from it. From the absolute value of this difference we subtract the tolerance value P to get H. If the H value is greater than 0, we continue the iteration through the cycles indicated by Eqs. 8.3.6–8.3.12. Otherwise, the current value of $_i a$ is taken as the factor loading matrix.

8.3.4 Numerical Example.

For a numerical example we use the same correlation matrix as in the previous chapter.

The arbitrary factor matrix is taken as a binary matrix which isolates the first four columns of the correlation matrix.

The first b matrix is simply the first four columns of the correlation matrix. The matrix $_1 S$ gives the intercorrelations of the first four variables.

Table 8.3.1 gives the values of the G scalar for the successive iterations.

Table 8.3.2 gives in the first row the basic diagonal values corresponding to the factor vectors. These also indicate the variance accounted for by each factor. The fourth factor may be discarded since the value is less than 1. The remainder of the table gives the factor loading matrix.

A more accurate method of testing the convergences would be to get the sum of squares of elements for each approximation to the factor loading matrix. This sum of squares would tell us precisely at each approximation how much of the variance would be accounted for by this approximation. This value must increase with each approximation, which is not the case of the G value in Eq. 8.3.11. However, the two values must converge to the same value as the number of iterations increases. Therefore, it is simpler to use the D value, since fewer calculations are required.

8.4 The Orthogonalization Method

As in the previous example, we shall indicate in this section first the essential characteristics of the method. Then we shall present computational equations, give computational instructions, and, finally, display a numerical example.

8.4.1   Characteristics of the Method. One of the most distinguishing characteristics of this method is that it does not yield an exact rank reduction matrix for each of the approximations to the factor loading matrix. In this respect it is different from most of the methods we have considered. It is analogous to the method proposed by Hotelling (1933) referred to in the previous chapter. In that method each successive approximation to a U vector is divided by the largest absolute value of an element in that vector. As pointed out in Chapter 7, Hotelling's procedure is also not an exact rank reduction method for each approxiamtion. In his method, each iteration provides a vector which is only proportional to the approximations to the factor loading vector. It still requires multiplication by a scalar constant to make it a rank reduction vector.

The method of this section requires less storage than the one discussed in the preceding section. This advantage is more important for large matrices when electronic computers are used, in which case, of course, immediate access storage is always at a premium. The essential difference between this and the previous method is that the matrix designated S in the previous method is not required here. The difference in storage requirements, however, is not particularly great since the order of this S matrix is equal to the number of factors. This usually will be small compared to the number of variables, particularly if their number is large.

The most important characteristic of this method is that the successive approximations yield orthonormal matrices. Each approximation yields a matrix whose minor product moment is an identity matrix. This means, of course, that the column vectors are normalized and that they are all mutually orthogonal.

There is some similarity to the method in Section 7.4, which does not require the calculation of residual matrices. In that case, each approximation to a current factor loading vector is also orthogonal to each of the previously calculated vectors. This is a consequence of the method of solution.

Like the method discussed in the previous section of this chapter, the procedure we shall outline here is also self-correcting. As a matter of fact, most of the iteration methods are self-correcting. However, since no residual matrices are employed by this method, one gains additional decimal accuracy over those methods requiring the calculation of residual matrices. It is difficult to say which of the two methods discussed in this chapter achieves the greater advantage with respect to decimal accuracy.

8.4.2   Computational Equations.

8.4.2a   DEFINITION OF NOTATION
    E is the first approximation to the factor loading matrix.
    $_jQ_{.1}$ is the jth approximation to the ith basic orthonormal vector of R.

$_jD_i$ is the jth approximation to the ith basic diagonal element of R.

G_j is the jth approximation to the variance accounted for by the m factors.

$Q_{(m)}$ is the matrix of the first m columns of the basic orthonormal of R.

$_jQ_{(i)}$ is the jth approximation to the first i columns of the basic orthonormal of R.

D is the basic diagonal of R.

a is the factor loading matrix.

P is a prespecified tolerance limit.

8.4.2b THE EQUATIONS

$$_1A = RE \tag{8.4.1}$$

$$_1C_1 = {_1A_{.1}}'\,_1A_{.1} \tag{8.4.2}$$

$$_1D_1 = \sqrt{_1C_1} \tag{8.4.3}$$

$$_1Q_{.1} = \frac{_1A_{.1}}{_1D_1} \tag{8.4.4}$$

$$_1Q_{(i-1)} = (_1Q_{.1} \cdots\, _1Q_{.i-1}) \tag{8.4.5}$$

$$_1W_{.i} = {_1Q_{(i-1)}}'\,_1A_{.i} \tag{8.4.6}$$

$$_1U_{.i} = {_1Q_{(i-1)}}\,_1W_{.i} \tag{8.4.7}$$

$$_1b_{.i} = {_1A_{.i}} - {_1U_{.i}} \tag{8.4.8}$$

$$_1C_i = {_1b_{.i}}'\,_1b_{.i} \tag{8.4.9}$$

$$_1D_i = \sqrt{_1C_i} \tag{8.4.10}$$

$$_1Q_{.i} = \frac{_1b_{.i}}{_1D_i} \tag{8.4.11}$$

$$G_1 = \sum\,_1D_i \tag{8.4.12}$$

$$_jA = R\,_{j-1}Q_{(m)} \tag{8.4.13}$$

$$_jC_1 = {_jA_{.1}}'\,_jA_{.1} \tag{8.4.14}$$

$$_jD_1 = \sqrt{_jC_1} \tag{8.4.15}$$

$$_jQ_{.1} = \frac{_jA_{.1}}{_jD_1} \tag{8.4.16}$$

$$_jQ_{(i-1)} = (_jQ_{.1} \cdots\, _jQ_{.i-1}) \tag{8.4.17}$$

$$_jW_{.i} = {_jQ_{(i-1)}}'\,_jA_{.i} \tag{8.4.18}$$

$$_jU_{.i} = {_jQ_{(i-1)}}\,_jW_{.i} \tag{8.4.19}$$

$$_jb_{.i} = {_jA_{.i}} - {_jU_{.i}} \tag{8.4.20}$$

$$_jC_i = {_jb_{.i}'} \, {_jb_{.i}} \tag{8.4.21}$$

$$_jD_i = \sqrt{_jC_i} \tag{8.4.22}$$

$$_jQ_{.i} = \frac{_jb_{.i}}{_jD_i} \tag{8.4.23}$$

$$G_j = \sum {_jD_l} \tag{8.4.24}$$

$$H = \left| \frac{G_{j-1}}{G_j} - 1 \right| - P \tag{8.4.25}$$

$$a = Q_{(m)} \, D_{(m)}^{1/2} \tag{8.4.26}$$

8.4.3   Computational Instructions. This method, like the previous one, begins with some arbitrary matrix E, as indicated in Eq. 8.4.1, which is used as a postmultiplier of the correlation matrix. The same considerations which were discussed in the previous section for the selection of the E matrix apply equally well here. We shall therefore assume, for the sake of simplicity, that the E matrix is the one which isolates the first m columns of the correlation matrix. This assumes that we know the maximum number of factors we wish to solve for.

The left-hand side of Eq. 8.4.1 gives the $_1A$ matrix, which in this case is simply the first m columns of the correlation matrix.

Next we calculate the minor product moment of the first vector of this A matrix, as indicated in Eq. 8.4.2. We designate this by C, with appropriate subscripts. This is simply the sum of squares of elements in the first column of the A matrix or, in this particular case, the sum of squares of the correlations involving the first variable. This includes also the diagonal elements.

In both methods discussed in this chapter we assume the use of unity in the diagonals of the correlation matrix, although the methods do not depend on the use of 1. As a matter of fact, everything which has been said in previous chapters about the use of communalities applies to these methods of computation.

The next step is to calculate the square root of the scalar calculated in Eq. 8.4.2, as in Eq. 8.4.3.

The vector on the left of Eq. 8.4.1 is now divided by the scalar quantity calculated in Eq. 8.4.3 to yield the first approximation to the $Q_{.1}$ vector. This is the first approximation to the first basic orthonormal vector of the correlation matrix, even though it may be a very poor one.

The next step is indicated in Eq. 8.4.5. In this equation and those that follow, we shall assume the first value of i to be 2. In this particular case then, the left-hand side of Eq. 8.4.5 is simply the vector calculated in Eq. 8.4.4.

The next step is to calculate the vector indicated in Eq. 8.4.6. Notice that on the right-hand side of this equation we have the transpose of the matrix indicated in Eq. 8.4.5, postmultiplied by the vector $_1A_{.i}$ which is the second vector of the matrix in Eq. 8.4.1. In this case, of course, it is simply the second column of the correlation matrix. For the case of $i = 2$, this yields on the left-hand side of Eq. 8.4.6 a scalar quantity designated as the first approximation to $W_{.2}$.

Next we calculate Eq. 8.4.7. This is the Q matrix of Eq. 8.4.5 postmultiplied by $W_{.i}$ of Eq. 8.4.6 to give the $_1U_{.i}$ vector.

The next step is to calculate Eq. 8.4.8. On the right side of this equation we have two terms. The first of these is the second vector of the A matrix, and from it is subtracted the first approximation to the $U_{.i}$ vector. This gives us the first approximation to a vector $b_{.2}$.

We next calculate the minor product moment or sum of squared elements of the vector just calculated, as in Eq. 8.4.9. This is indicated as a scalar C.

We take the square root of this scalar as indicated in Eq. 8.4.10 to get a scalar D which is a first approximation to the second basic diagonal.

We now get a first approximation to $Q_{.2}$, as indicated in Eq. 8.4.11, by dividing the vector obtained in Eq. 8.4.8 by the scalar obtained in Eq. 8.4.10.

We repeat this cycle of operations for $i = 2$ to $i = m$, where m is the number of factors hypothesized. It will be seen that each time we go through the cycle, the matrix on the left of Eq. 8.4.5 is increased by one vector, so that when $i = 3$, it has two vectors, and so on. When $i = m$, this matrix has one less vector than the number of factors.

In the same way, each time i increases, the vector W on the left of Eq. 8.4.6 has one more element in it, so that for $i = 3$, it will have two elements in it. It always has in it one element less than the value of i for the $Q_{.i}$ vector being solved for.

When we have completed all of the steps for the first approximation to the Q or basic orthonormal matrix, we calculate the scalar G_1, as indicated in Eq. 8.4.12. This is simply the sum of the D values calculated in the successive applications of Eq. 8.4.10. It is an estimate of the sum of the basic diagonals for the first m factors, even though for the first cycle it may be a very poor estimate.

Let us now consider the computational procedure for the jth approximation to the first m vectors of the basic orthonormal and for the first m basic diagonal elements. We take the case for $j = 2$ and subsequent values. Here we start with Eq. 8.4.13. We multiply the correlation matrix by the current approximation to the Q matrix and thus get the next approximation to the A matrix.

We then get the next approximation to the first Q vector, as in Eqs. 8.4.14–8.4.16.

Equation 8.4.14 gives the minor product moment of the first vector in the jth approximation to the A matrix.

Equation 8.4.15 gives the square root of the value just obtained and is the jth approximation to the first basic diagonal.

Finally, we get the jth approximation to the $Q_{.1}$ vector, as in Eq. 8.4.16. This is the first vector of the A matrix calculated in Eq. 8.4.13 divided by the scalar calculated in Eq. 8.4.15. It is readily verified that this is a normalized vector.

Having calculated the first Q vector for the jth approximation to the basic orthonormal and its corresponding basic diagonal, we are now ready to calculate the second and subsequent basic orthonormal vectors and basic diagonals for the jth approximation.

First we consider the jth approximation to the first $i - 1$ orthonormal vectors, as indicated in Eq. 8.4.17.

We then calculate the W vector, indicated in Eq. 8.4.18, which, as shown on the right, is the transpose of the Q matrix given in Eq. 8.4.17 post-multiplied by the ith vector of the A matrix in Eq. 8.4.13.

Next we calculate the $_jU_{.i}$ vector of Eq. 8.4.19. This is the matrix of Eq. 8.4.17 postmultiplied by the vector of Eq. 8.4.18.

We now calculate the jth approximation to the $b_{.i}$ vector, as indicated on the right of Eq. 8.4.20. Here we have two terms, the first of which is the ith vector of the jth approximation to A. From this is subtracted the $_jU_{.i}$ vector of Eq. 8.4.19.

We calculate the next C scalar quantity as the minor product moment of the vector calculated in Eq. 8.4.20 or simply the sum of the squares of its elements. This is given in Eq. 8.4.21.

The next step is to calculate the square root of the scalar in Eq. 8.4.21. This is the jth approximation to the ith basic diagonal.

The jth approximation to the ith basic orthonormal vector is calculated as in Eq. 8.4.23. This is the vector calculated in Eq. 8.4.20 divided by the scalar calculated in Eq. 8.4.22.

We now calculate the jth approximation to the amount of variance accounted for by the m factors by Eq. 8.4.24. This is the sum of the jth approximation to the basic diagonal elements calculated by means of Eqs. 8.4.21 and 8.4.22.

In Eq. 8.4.25, we take the absolute value of the difference between the ratio of the preceding and current approximations to G and 1, and subtract from this the tolerance limit P to get H. If H is positive, we go on to further approximations in order to reach the desired degree of accuracy.

When the criterion in Eq. 8.4.25 is satisfied, we may assume that the approximations to the first m basic orthonormal vectors and the first m basic diagonals is sufficiently close, and we then calculate a final factor loading matrix a, as in Eq. 8.4.26. This is the final approximation to the first m basic orthonormal vectors, postmultiplied by the square root of a diagonal matrix made up of the first m basic diagonal elements given by Eq. 8.4.22 for the current values of D from 1 to m.

8.4.4 Numerical Example. We assume that the same matrix as in the previous numerical example is used for this solution. We also take the same arbitary matrix E as in that example, which gives for the first A matrix the first m or the first four columns of the correlation matrix.

Table 8.4.1 gives the successive G values which are the estimates of the total variance accounted for by the four factors.

The first row of Table 8.4.2 gives the first four basic diagonals of the correlation matrix. These indicate the variance accounted for by the corresponding factor. The remainder of the table gives the four factor loading vectors. As in the preceding method the last factor may be discarded.

8.5 Mathematical Proofs

8.5.1 The Rank Reduction Solution.
Consider

$$A_1 = Ra_0 \tag{8.5.1}$$

where R is the correlation or covariance matrix and a_0 is an m-wide arbitrary matrix such that no column vector is orthogonal to any of the first m basic orthonormal vectors of R.

$$t_1 t_1' = a_0' A_1 \tag{8.5.2}$$

$$a_1 = A_1 t_1'^{-1} \tag{8.5.3}$$

$$A_2 = Ra_1 \tag{8.5.4}$$

$$t_2 t_2' = a_1' A_2 \tag{8.5.5}$$

In general,

$$A_i = Ra_{i-1} \tag{8.5.6}$$

$$t_i t_i' = a_{i-1}' A_i \tag{8.5.7}$$

$$a_i = A_i t_i'^{-1} \tag{8.5.8}$$

Consider

$$E = R - a_i a_i' \tag{8.5.9}$$

It is clear from Eqs. 8.5.6–8.5.8, in 8.5.9, that

$$E = R - Ra_{i-1}(a_{i-1}'Ra_{i-1})^{-1}a_{i-1}'R \tag{8.5.10}$$

and hence a_i is always a rank reduction matrix for $i > 0$.

TABLE 8.4.1 Successive Estimates by Rows of Variance Accounted for by Four Factors

3.213556	5.421704	6.990548	7.349413	7.455889	7.520461	7.554278	7.572571	7.583493	7.590453
7.595014	7.598027	7.600018	7.601330	7.602190	7.602754	7.603122	7.603362	7.603518	7.603620
7.603686									

TABLE 8.4.2 Basic Diagonals and Factor Loading Matrix

3.749069	2.049527	1.330791	0.474299
0.716587	−0.492754	0.350241	−0.030237
0.739873	−0.478158	0.321495	−0.057594
0.772826	−0.295800	0.406287	0.011908
0.555550	0.648880	0.067615	0.118871
0.463260	0.744005	0.180912	−0.121273
0.517680	0.693575	0.188547	−0.137016
0.640534	−0.079450	−0.587527	−0.283343
0.614926	−0.165835	−0.621146	−0.167508
0.715013	0.033764	−0.368556	0.560333

8.5.1a PROOF OF CONVERGENCE TO BASIC STRUCTURE.

Now from Eqs. 8.5.6 and 8.5.8,

$$a_2 = Ra_1\, t_2'^{-1} \tag{8.5.11}$$

From Eqs. 8.5.3 and 8.5.11,

$$a_2 = RA_1\, t_1'^{-1} t_2'^{-1} \tag{8.5.12}$$

From Eqs. 8.5.1 and 8.5.12,

$$a_2 = R^2 a_0\, t_1'^{-1} t_2'^{-1} \tag{8.5.13}$$

or in general,

$$a_i = R^i a_0 (t_1'^{-1} \cdots t_i'^{-1}) \tag{8.5.14}$$

It can be proved that the product of upper triangular matrices is an upper triangular matrix. Hence, we let

$$T_i'^{-1} = t_1'^{-1} \cdots t_i'^{-1} \tag{8.5.15}$$

Equation 8.5.15 in Eq. 8.5.14 gives

$$a_i = R^i a_0\, T_i'^{-1} \tag{8.5.16}$$

or

$$a_i = R(R^{i-1} a_0) T_1'^{-1} \tag{8.5.17}$$

Since the a_i are rank reduction forms, we can write from Eq. 8.5.17,

$$T_i T_i' = (a_0' R^{i-1}) R (R^{i-1} a_0) \tag{8.5.18}$$

or

$$T_i T_i' = a_0' R^{2i-1} a_0 \tag{8.5.19}$$

We let

$$R = Q\delta Q' \tag{8.5.20}$$

so that

$$T_i T_i' = a_0\, Q\delta^{2i-1} Q' a_0 \tag{8.5.21}$$

Let

$$Q' a_0 = \begin{bmatrix} Q_a' & a_0 \\ Q_b' & a_0 \end{bmatrix} = \begin{bmatrix} M_a \\ M_b \end{bmatrix} \tag{8.5.22}$$

From Eqs. 8.5.21 and 8.5.22,

$$T_i T_i' = M_a' \delta_a^{2i-1} M_a + M_b' \delta_b^{2i-1} M_b \tag{8.5.23}$$

From Eqs. 8.5.17, 8.5.20, and 8.5.22,

$$a_i = (Q_a\, \delta_a^{\,i} M_a + Q_b\, \delta_b^{\,i} M_b) T_i'^{-1} \tag{8.5.24}$$

From Eq. 8.5.23,

$$\delta_a^{(1/2)-i} M_a'^{-1} T_i T_i' M_a^{-1} \delta_a^{(1/2)-i} = I + (\delta_a^{(1/2)-i} M_a'^{-1} M_b' \delta_b^{i-(1/2)})$$
$$(\delta_b^{i-(1/2)} M_b\, M_a^{-1} \delta_a^{(1/2)-i}) \tag{8.5.25}$$

Let

$$\mu = \delta_b{}^{i-(1/2)} M_b \, M_a{}^{-1} \delta_a{}^{(1/2)-i} \tag{8.5.26}$$

From Eqs. 8.5.25 and 8.5.26, we can write

$$\delta_a{}^{(1/2)-i} M_a'{}^{-1} T_i \, T_i' M_a{}^{-1} \delta_a{}^{(1/2)-i} = I + M'{}^{-1} \mu' \mu M^{-1} \tag{8.5.27}$$

or if i is sufficiently large, we may ignore the last term on the right of Eq. 8.5.27 and write

$$T_i \, T_i' = M_a' \delta_a{}^{2i-1} M_a \tag{8.5.28}$$

or

$$T_i'{}^{-1} = M_a{}^{-1} \delta_a{}^{(1/2)-i} h' \tag{8.5.29}$$

where h is a square orthonormal.
Substituting Eq. 8.5.29 into Eq. 8.5.24 gives

$$a_i = Q_a \, \delta_a{}^{1/2} h' + Q_b \, \delta_b{}^{1/2} \mu h' \tag{8.5.30}$$

or if i is sufficiently large,

$$a_i = Q_a \, \delta_a{}^{1/2} h' \tag{8.5.31}$$

This proves that the method converges toward the basic structure solution save for an orthonormal transformation h.

We next prove that the solution must converge toward the basic structure solution so that h in Eq. 8.5.31 approaches the identity . We rewrite Eq. 8.5.31:

$$a_i = Q \Delta h_0' \tag{8.5.32}$$

where

$$\Delta = \delta^{1/2} \tag{8.5.33}$$

and where the subscript a has been dropped but the order implied by it is retained. Consider now Eqs. 8.5.6–8.5.8 and 8.5.32, where now we let $a_0 = a_i$, and we get

$$a_0 = Q \Delta h_0' \tag{8.5.34}$$

$$t_0 \, t_0' = h_0 \, \Delta^4 h_0' \tag{8.5.35}$$

$$t_0 = h_0 \, \Delta^2 h_1' \tag{8.5.36}$$

where h_1 is the orthonormal which makes t_0 triangular. In general, we have

$$a_i = Q \Delta h_i' \tag{8.5.37}$$

$$t_i \, t_i' = h_i \, \Delta^4 h_i' \tag{8.5.38}$$

$$t_i = h_i \, \Delta^2 h_{i+1}' \tag{8.5.39}$$

and from Eq. 8.5.39,

$$t_{i+1} \, t_{i+1}' = t_i' t_i \tag{8.5.40}$$

Now we prove that

$$e_1' t' t e_1 \geqq e_1' t t' e_1 \tag{8.5.41}$$

From Eq. 8.5.41,

$$t_{.1}'t_{.1} \gtrless t_1. \, t_1.'$$ (8.5.42)

but because t is lower triangular, we have from Eq. 8.5.42,

$$t_{11}^2 + \sum_{i=2}^{m} t_{i1}^2 \gtrless t_{11}^2$$ (8.5.43)

Thus, each iteration of the type Eq. 8.5.40 must yield a larger element in its first diagonal position than the previous one until all remaining elements in the first column vanish. In the same way succeeding diagonals must increase until the elements below in the same column vanish. Thus, all elements below the diagonal must eventually vanish so that the t becomes diagonal. Since the transformations are all square orthonormal, we have

$$t = \Delta^2$$ (8.5.44)

The proof does not indicate precisely what happens in the computations, because as a_i approaches $Q\Delta h$, h also approaches I.

8.5.2   The Orthogonal Solution.

Given the matrix A, consider

$$Q_{.1} = A_{.1}\sqrt{A_{.1}'A_{.1}}$$ (8.5.45)

Let

$$Q_{(i-1)} = (Q_{.1} \cdots Q_{.(i-1)})$$ (8.5.46)

$$W_i = Q_{(i-1)}'A_{.1}$$ (8.5.47)

$$b_{.i} = A_{.i} - Q_{(i-1)} \, W_{.i}$$ (8.5.48)

$$Q_{.i} = b_{.i}\sqrt{b_{.i}'b_{.i}}$$ (8.5.49)

Equation 8.5.47 in Eq. 8.5.48 gives

$$b_{.i} = A_{.i} - Q_{(i-1)} \, Q_{(i-1)}'A_{.i}$$ (8.5.50)

or

$$b_{.i} = (I - Q_{(i-1)} \, Q_{(i-1)}')A_{.i}$$ (8.5.51)

Let i take in turn the values 2, 3, and so on. From Eqs. 8.5.45 and 8.5.51,

$$b_{.2} = \left(I - \frac{A_{.1} A_{.1}'}{A_{.1}'A_{.1}}\right)A_{.2}$$ (8.5.52)

From Eqs. 8.5.45, 8.5.49, and 8.5.52,

$$Q_{.1}'Q_{.2} = 0$$ (8.5.53)

and in general,

$$Q_{.i}'Q_{.j} = 0$$ (8.5.54)

for all $i < j$. Hence, by the method of calculation,

$$Q_{(i)}'Q_{(i)} = I_i \tag{8.5.55}$$

8.5.2a PROOF OF CONVERGENCE
Consider now

$$_LA = R_L Q_{(m)} \tag{8.5.56}$$

where L is the number of the approximation. Orthogonalize A in Eq. 8.5.56 as in Eqs. 8.5.45–8.5.49. As the process is repeated, $_LQ_{.1}$ approaches $Q_{.1}$. But $_LQ_{.2}$ is orthogonal to $_LQ_{.1}$; hence, as $_LQ_{.1}$ approaches $Q_{.1}$, $_LQ_{.2}$ approaches $Q_{.2}$, and so on with the succeeding vectors.

Part III

Matrix Factoring Methods—B

Chapter 9

Jacobi-Type Solutions

Most of the methods of factor analysis we have considered so far are based on the rank reduction theorem and require the multiplication of the correlation matrix by certain specified vectors. One of the variations of the group centroid method differs from the others in that the rank of the matrix is not reduced by the number of factors solved for. In this chapter we shall discuss a different type of method.

9.1   Characteristics of the Methods

The methods we shall discuss now are basic structure solutions. Therefore, it is possible to select the factors accounting for the maximum variance. They are essentially different from the other methods in rationale and computational procedure. The differences and similarities will be discussed in the following paragraphs.

9.1.1   Single Parameter Orthonormal Operations. Perhaps the most important characteristic of these methods is that the solution involves repeated operations with a one-parameter, square orthonormal matrix, as distinguished from repeated matrix by vector multiplication. Successive applications of the orthonormal matrices gradually transform the correlation matrix to its basic diagonal matrix, while at the same time an identity matrix is transformed to the basic orthonormal of the correlation matrix.

9.1.2   Iterative Solutions. Like all other basic structure methods involving the solution for basic diagonals, these solutions must be iterative or consist of a series of successive approximations. The total number of computations involved in a solution cannot be predicted in advance, because there is no rational algebraic solution to the basic diagonal elements or roots of a matrix. The reason for this will not be discussed in detail in this book, but it relates to the fact that polynomials of degree higher than four do not have rational solutions for the roots.

9.1.3 Large Decimal Error Accumulation. Another characteristic of the methods of this chapter is that the solutions are not self-correcting for the successive approximations. This means that each cycle of computations accumulates decimal error and passes it on to the next cycle. Therefore, if one has a very large number of variables, the accumulation of decimal inaccuracy may be fairly large.

9.2 Kinds of Methods

We shall discuss two variations of the method which involve repeated operations with a single parameter square orthonormal matrix. One of these is an iterative solution involving one-parameter orthonormal transformations, or what is sometimes known as binary rotations, which solves for all the basic diagonals and orthonormal vectors at once. The other is a method which involves the same type of orthonormal transformations of the original matrix, but the basic diagonals and corresponding orthonormal vectors are solved for in order of magnitude.

9.2.1 Simultaneous Method. The first method we shall consider involves the construction of a one-parameter, square orthonormal matrix such that when the correlation matrix is pre- and postmultiplied by that matrix and its transpose, respectively, some specified nondiagonal element in the resulting triple product is 0. A similar transformation on this product is then performed by another square orthonormal matrix, which results in making some other nondiagonal element 0. The process continues until all nondiagonal elements of the final product matrix are 0. Since this final product has been arrived at by pre- and postmultiplication of only basic square orthonormal matrices and their transposes, it can be regarded as having been obtained by pre- and postmultiplication by a single square orthonormal matrix and its transpose. If this process is continued until all nondiagonal elements are 0, the resulting diagonal matrix must be the basic diagonal of the correlation matrix, as is shown in Section 9.5.1.

9.2.2 Successive Method. This second method also consists of pre- and postmultiplying the correlation matrix by basic orthonormal matrices, but these are first applied repeatedly until all nondiagonal elements of the first row and column are 0 and the first diagonal is the first basic diagonal. After this transformation has been completed, one then operates similarly on the second row and column to get the second basic diagonal. It may not be necessary to get all of the principal axis factor loading matrices of the correlation matrix. In this case one finds only the specified number of basic diagonals and corresponding orthonormal vectors that are desired in the final factor loading matrix.

9.3   Simultaneous Method

The method we shall discuss now is perhaps the oldest of all methods of factor analysis. It has its foundation in the work of the mathematician Jacobi (1846). As a matter of fact, he developed the general method long before the subject of factor analysis, as such, was seriously considered. Although Kelley (1935) independently discovered the same method, it is now commonly referred to as the Jacobi method. Until very recently also it has been the method most commonly used on high-speed electronic computers. It is the first method used with electronic computers to find the principal axis or basic structure factors. This application was made by Wrigley and Neuhaus (1952).

9.3.1   Characteristics of the Method.

One of the distinguishing characteristics of this method is that, as traditionally used, none of the factor loading vectors is solved for until all are solved for. The method as used with the high-speed computers solves iteratively for all of the factor vectors simultaneously as well as for the basic diagonals or eigenvalues of the correlation matrix.

Solutions are arrived at, as just indicated, by repeated applications of orthonormal transformations to the correlation matrix and to subsequent matrices which have already been transformed by previous orthonormal matrices. The essential characteristic of these orthonormal matrices is that all of the elements in the diagonal are 1 except two—for example, the ith and the jth elements. All of the nondiagonal elements are 0 except two, namely, the one in the ith row and jth column and the one in the jth row and the ith column. These elements which are distinct from 1 and 0, respectively, are functions of a single scalar. The two diagonal elements are equal in absolute value as are also the nondiagonal elements. The latter are obtained by taking the square root of 1 minus the square of the diagonal element. The signs are determined by the sign of the ijth element in the current covariance matrix.

The method is sometimes called the *sine-cosine method* because the two by two matrix, which may be isolated from the orthonormal matrix, is a well-known matrix for a rigid rotation of axes in analytic gemoetry, in which the diagonals are the sine of an angle and the nondiagonals are the cosine, with opposite signs.

These single parameter elements are determined in such a way that when pre- and postmultiplied by the orthonormal and its transpose, the resulting covariance matrix has zeros in its ith row and jth column and in its jth row and ith column. Furthermore, the transformations have the characteristic that the new matrix differs from the old only in that the ith row and ith column and the jth row and jth column have been altered. All other elements in the matrix are the same as they were before the transformation.

An important property of the method is that the sum of squares of non-diagonal elements of the current covariance matrix is always less than the corresponding sum of the preceding matrix by an amount equal to twice the square of the element which was made 0. This is proved in Section 9.5.2.

Another important characteristic of this method is that the number of one-parameter, orthonormal transformation matrices required to bring the matrix into complete diagonal form cannot be predicted. As a matter of fact, this number may be very large. In general, the method has not been much used with desk computers because of this great unpredictability in the number of transformations required and because of the large number of total computations needed.

Another reason why the method has not been extensively used with desk computers is that it is difficult to set up a neat mechanical routine for computations. The method consists essentially of successively altering two rows and two columns of the covariance matrix. To set up computational worksheets so that this may be done seems to be impossible without wasting a great deal of paper and getting into bulky worksheet routines. This is no handicap to electronic computers, however, because as we have indicated previously, one can readily write over previous computations. The locations in storage for the new computations can be placed directly over old ones, wiping out the old computations. This is not feasible for worksheet operations with desk calculators because it is not convenient to erase previous calculations and write others in their place if a great deal of overwriting is required.

9.3.2   Computational Equations.

9.3.2a   DEFINITION OF NOTATION

$_1R$ is the correlation matrix.

$_LA$ is the $_L$th binary transformation matrix.

$_LQ$ is the $_L$th approximation to the basic orthonormal of $_0R$.

$_LR_{ij}$ is the element in the ith row and jth column of $_LR$.

S is the sign of $_LR_{ij}$.

9.3.2b   THE EQUATIONS

$$_LA = I + (S\,_L\alpha_{ij} - 1)e_i\,e_i' - S\,_L\beta_{ij}\,e_i\,e_j' + {_L\beta_{ij}}\,e_j\,e_i' + (_L\alpha_{ij} - 1)e_j\,e_j' \qquad (9.3.1)$$

$$_{L+1}Q = (_1A\,_2A\,\cdots\,_LA) \qquad (9.3.2)$$

$$_{L+1}R = {_LA'}\,_LR\,_LA \qquad (9.3.3)$$

$$_Ld_{ij} = {_LR_{ii}} - {_LR_{jj}} \qquad (9.3.4)$$

$$_LK_{ij} = \frac{_Ld_{ij}}{\sqrt{_Ld_{ij}{}^2 + 4\,_LR_{ij}{}^2}} \qquad (9.3.5)$$

$$_L\alpha_{ij} = \sqrt{\frac{1 + {_LK_{ij}}}{2}} \tag{9.3.6}$$

$$_L\beta_{ij} = \sqrt{1 - {_L\alpha_{ij}}^2} \tag{9.3.7}$$

$$_{L+1}R_{ii} = \frac{_LR_{ii} + {_LR_{jj}}}{2} + \tfrac{1}{2}\sqrt{_Ld_{ij}^{\,2} + 4\,_LR_{ij}^{\,2}} \tag{9.3.8}$$

$$_{L+1}R_{ij} = 0 \tag{9.3.9}$$

$$_{L+1}R_{jj} = {_LR_{jj}} + {_LR_{ii}} - {_{L+1}R_{ii}} \tag{9.3.10}$$

$$_{L+1}R_{ik} = S\,_L\alpha_{ij}\,{_LR_{ik}} + {_L\beta_{ij}}\,{_LR_{jk}} \tag{9.3.11}$$

$$_{L+1}R_{jk} = {_L\alpha_{ij}}\,{_LR_{jk}} - S\,_L\beta_{ij}\,{_LR_{ik}} \tag{9.3.12}$$

$$_{L+1}R_{km} = {_LR_{km}} \tag{9.3.13}$$

$$_0Q = I \tag{9.3.14}$$

$$_{L+1}Q_{.i} = S\,_L\alpha_{ij}\,{_LQ_{.i}} + {_L\beta_{ij}}\,{_LQ_{.j}} \tag{9.3.15}$$

$$_{L+1}Q_{.j} = {_L\alpha_{ij}}\,{_LQ_{.j}} - S\,_L\beta_{ij}\,{_LQ_{.i}} \tag{9.3.16}$$

$$_{L+1}Q_{.k} = {_LQ_{.k}} \qquad k \neq i, j \tag{9.3.17}$$

$$d_i = |_{L+1}R_{ii} - {_LR_{ii}}| \tag{9.3.18}$$

$$H = d_{i\,\max} - P \tag{9.3.19}$$

9.3.3 Computational Instructions.

We begin by defining a square orthonormal matrix, as indicated in Eq. 9.3.1. The prescript L in this equation means that it is the Lth such matrix which has been constructed.

Let us now examine the right-hand side of this equation in detail. The first term is simply the identity matrix. The second term is a scalar times the major product of an elementary vector, which means that it places an element in the ith diagonal position of A. The scalar 1, which is subtracted from the product of the sign S and a scalar α, to be defined, means that the 1 in the diagonal of A is replaced by the $S\alpha$ scalar. We assume j greater than i and consider the third term in this equation. This is simply the major product of an e_i by an e_j vector multiplied by a scalar $-S\beta$. This means that in the matrix A we place the scalar $-S\beta$ in the ith row and jth column. In the fourth term we have the major product of an e_j by an e_i vector multiplied by the scalar β, which means that we place β in the jth row and ith column of the matrix A. Finally, the last term means that we place the scalar α in the jth diagonal position of A. We specify now that $\alpha^2 + \beta^2 = 1$. It can then readily be verified that the matrix in Eq. 9.3.1 is an orthonormal matrix.

We next define the matrix $_LQ$ in Eq. 9.3.2 which is the product of matrices of the type in Eq. 9.3.1.

Now we consider the iterative Eq. 9.3.3 in which a new R matrix is obtained by the triple product of the previous R matrix premultiplied by a corresponding A' and postmultiplied by A. In this way it should be clear that every R matrix has been obtained from a previous one by orthonormal pre-and post-multiplication, and therefore that any R matrix can be obtained from the original R matrix by a pre- and postorthonormal transformation of the Q matrix given by Eq. 9.3.2.

We now consider the calculation of the α and β scalars in Eq. 9.3.1. We use the prescript L on these equations to indicate that this is for the Lth transformation or cycle, but in the discussion which follows we begin with $L = 1$.

We define a scalar $_Ld_{ij}$ as indicated in Eq. 9.3.4. This is obtained by subtracting the jth diagonal element of $_LR$ from the ith diagonal element. Our first task is to make the ijth and the jith elements in the next R equal to 0. Subsequent operations will accomplish this. Proof will be presented in Section 9.5.1.

We define a K scalar as in Eq. 9.3.5. Here we divide the scalar d obtained in Eq. 9.3.4 by the square root of its square plus four times the square of the element in the ith row and jth column of the R matrix.

We now define the α scalar in terms of this K scalar, as in Eq. 9.3.6.

Since the sum of the squares of α and β is equal to 1, we calculate β as in Eq. 9.3.7.

It is not necessary to go through the actual matrix multiplication operations of Eq. 9.3.3 to get the next R matrix. As a matter of fact, the Jacobi method in general is not well adapted to description by matrix notation.

We next calculate the diagonal element R_{ii} of the new R matrix, as indicated in Eq. 9.3.8. This diagonal element is the average of the ith and jth diagonal elements of the previous matrix to which the term on the right side is added. It is interesting to note from this equation that the new ith diagonal element can never be less than the old one. If the ijth element in the old matrix is 0, then according to the definition of d_{ij} given in Eq. 9.3.4, the new ith diagonal element would be exactly the same as the old.

We need not calculate the new ijth element because our method of calculation guarantees that this will be 0, as indicated in Eq. 9.3.9.

The jth diagonal element can be very simply calculated, as in Eq. 9.3.10. Here we subtract the new ith diagonal element from the sum of the previous i and j diagonal elements.

Next we consider the calculation of the remaining new elements which involve the ith and the jth variable. We let k take all values distinct from i and j. In Eq. 9.3.11 we show the value of the new R_{ik} element. This is the product of the sign S times the α scalar given in Eq. 9.3.6 times the previous R_{ik} value, plus the β scalar given in Eq. 9.3.7 times the previous R_{jk} value.

The R_{jk} values are calculated as in Eq. 9.3.12. These are obtained by getting the product of the α scalar times the previous R_{jk} scalar, and subtracting from it S times the β scalar times the previous R_{ik} value. All remaining elements of the new R matrix are the same as before. This is indicated in Eq. 9.3.13, where k and m are any values distinct from i and j.

In general, one continues these operations, always selecting a nondiagonal value in the current R matrix which is distinct from 0 as the basis for calculating the new α and β scalars in Eqs. 9.3.6 and 9.3.7. The question of which one of these elements to select as a basis for calculating the α and β scalars may have several answers. The most common procedure is to start with $i = 1$ and $j = 2$, that is, with the correlation between the first and second variables. Then in the next R matrix one uses the first and third, and so on, until one has reached the last variable in the first row. It should be observed, however, that the values in this first row of succeeding R matrices do not remain 0, but that they will be changed. The procedure is usually to go to the second and third variables of the current R matrix and proceed to the end of the second row for successive R matrices. This procedure is continued until one has used the correlation of the n and $n - 1$ variables in the current R matrix. One can then start over with the first and second columns and continue through this cycle.

One may also select each time the largest nondiagonal from the current R matrix. In general, this would tend to require fewer iterations, since for each successive covariance matrix the sum of squares of nondiagonal elements is reduced by twice the square of the largest nondiagonal of the preceding matrix. This procedure increases the ith diagonal element and reduces the jth. The objective is to make the increase as large as possible. Other things being equal, Eq. 9.3.8 shows that the larger the nondiagonal element, the larger will be the new ith diagonal of the new R. This is because of the R_{ij}^2 term under the radical in the right-hand term of the right side of Eq. 9.3.8.

However the nondiagonal is selected, the problem of getting the basic orthonormal still remains; this is done as follows. We let $_0Q$ be the identity matrix as indicated in Eq. 9.3.14.

Using Eq. 9.3.2 we may calculate the ith vector of $_{L+1}Q$ by means of Eq. 9.3.15.

The jth vector of $_{L+1}Q$ is calculated by Eq. 9.3.16.

The kth vector of $_{L+1}Q$, where k is distinct from i and j, is the same as the kth vector of $_LQ$; this is indicated by Eq. 9.3.17.

The absolute value of the difference between $_{L+1}R_{ii}$ and $_LR_{ii}$ is found for all values of i, as indicated in Eq. 9.3.18.

A tolerance limit P is set, as indicated in Eq. 9.3.19. When this is reached, the computations cease.

9.3.4 Numerical Example.

We shall not give here a complete numerical example calculated by the method first outlined for use with a desk calculator. This would be far too clumsy and laborious.

A complete solution, calculated on a computer, for the simultaneous Jacobi method is shown in the following table. The same matrix of intercorrelations is used as in the previous chapters.

Table 9.3.1 gives results obtained by taking $i = 2$ to $n - 1$ and $j = i + 1$ to n for each $_LA$ matrix. The first row gives the basic diagonals of the correlation matrix and the body of the table gives by rows the corresponding principal axis factor loading vectors.

TABLE 9.3.1   Complete Jacobi Solution for Basic Diagonals and Principal Axis Factor Matrix

3.749	2.050	1.331	0.474	0.383	0.347	0.285	0.212	0.169
0.717	0.740	0.773	0.556	0.463	0.518	0.640	0.615	0.715
0.493	0.478	0.296	−0.649	−0.744	−0.694	0.080	0.166	−0.034
0.350	0.322	0.406	0.068	0.181	0.188	−0.588	−0.621	−0.369
−0.030	−0.056	0.009	0.102	−0.115	−0.129	−0.288	−0.165	0.566
−0.010	−0.047	0.087	0.484	−0.185	−0.252	0.115	−0.070	−0.151
0.002	−0.034	0.013	−0.092	−0.135	0.156	0.358	−0.399	0.087
0.067	0.032	−0.124	0.093	−0.353	0.324	−0.115	0.108	−0.033
−0.204	−0.143	0.355	−0.063	−0.090	0.078	−0.029	0.069	−0.014
−0.272	0.304	−0.029	0.020	−0.018	−0.001	0.003	−0.023	0.004

9.4   Successive Method

Another procedure, as already indicated, is to operate only on the first row until all of the elements except the diagonal in the first row and column are 0 in the current R matrix. Since this consists of successive orthonormal transformations, this final diagonal element in the first position must be a root of the original correlation matrix or one of its basic diagonals. The procedure outlined guarantees that it is also the largest. This procedure enables one to get the largest root and corresponding basic orthonormal vector by the Jacobi method, without going to the trouble of getting all of the roots. One can then operate on the next and succeeding rows and columns until all but the diagonals are 0.

Since the computational equations and instructions are essentially the same as for the simultaneous method, they will not be repeated.

9.4.1   Numerical Example. Table 9.4.1 gives results obtained by choosing the nondiagonal elements so as to make all nondiagonal elements of a given row and column 0 before proceeding to the next row and column operations. Only the first three principal axis vectors are calculated. The first row gives the square roots of the basic diagonals and the next three rows give the three corresponding principal axis vectors.

TABLE 9.4.1   Jacobi Solution for First Three Principal Axis Factor Vectors

1.936	1.432	1.154						
0.718	0.741	0.773	0.554	0.462	0.517	0.641	0.615	0.715
−0.491	−0.477	−0.294	0.649	0.745	0.694	−0.080	−0.166	0.034
−0.351	−0.322	−0.407	−0.067	−0.180	−0.188	0.587	0.621	0.369

9.5   Mathematical Proofs

9.5.1   Iterated One-Parameter Orthonormal Transformation.   Consider a symmetric matrix

$$R = \begin{bmatrix} R_{11} & R_{12} \\ R_{12} & R_{22} \end{bmatrix} \tag{9.5.1}$$

and an orthonormal matrix

$$A = \begin{bmatrix} \alpha & -\sqrt{1-\alpha^2} \\ \sqrt{1-\alpha^2} & \alpha \end{bmatrix} \tag{9.5.2}$$

Let the basic structure of R be

$$R = Q\delta Q' \tag{9.5.3}$$

Determine α in Eq. 9.5.2 so that

$$A'RA = D \tag{9.5.4}$$

where D is diagonal.

But

$$Q'RQ = \delta \tag{9.5.5}$$

hence, $A = Q$.   Expanding Eq. 9.5.4, we have

$$\begin{bmatrix} A_{.1}' \\ A_{.2}' \end{bmatrix} R(A_{.1}, A_{.2}) = \begin{bmatrix} D_1 & 0 \\ 0 & D_2 \end{bmatrix} \tag{9.5.6}$$

or

$$\begin{bmatrix} A_{.1}' \\ A_{.2}' \end{bmatrix} R(A_{.1}, A_{.2}) = \begin{bmatrix} A_{.1}'RA_{.1} & A_{.1}'RA_{.2} \\ A_{.2}'RA_{.1} & A_{.2}'RA_{.2} \end{bmatrix} \tag{9.5.7}$$

From Eqs. 9.5.6 and 9.5.7,

$$A_{.1}'RA_{.2} = 0 \tag{9.5.8}$$

From Eqs. 9.5.2 and 9.5.8,

$$(\alpha, \sqrt{1-\alpha^2}) \begin{bmatrix} R_{11} & R_{12} \\ R_{12} & R_{22} \end{bmatrix} \begin{bmatrix} -\sqrt{1-\alpha^2} \\ \alpha \end{bmatrix} = 0 \tag{9.5.9}$$

From Eq. 9.5.9, we have

$$-\alpha\sqrt{1 - \alpha^2}(R_{11} - R_{22}) = (1 - 2\alpha^2)R_{12} \qquad (9.5.10)$$

Let

$$d = R_{11} - R_{22} \qquad (9.5.11)$$

Finally, from Eqs. 9.5.10 and 9.5.11,

$$\alpha^4 - \alpha^2 + \frac{R_{12}^2}{d^2 + 4R_{12}^2} = 0 \qquad (9.5.12)$$

From Eq. 9.5.12,

$$\alpha^2 = \frac{1 \pm \sqrt{\dfrac{d^2}{d^2 + 4R_{12}^2}}}{2} \qquad (9.5.13)$$

Let

$$K = \sqrt{\frac{d^2}{d^2 + 4R_{12}^2}} \qquad (9.5.14)$$

From Eqs. 9.5.13 and 9.5.14,

$$\alpha = \sqrt{\frac{1 + K}{2}} \qquad (9.5.15)$$

From Eq. 9.5.15,

$$\sqrt{1 - \alpha^2} = \sqrt{\frac{1 - K}{2}} \qquad (9.5.16)$$

and from Eq. 9.5.2, using Eqs. 9.5.15 and 9.5.16,

$$A = \begin{bmatrix} \sqrt{\dfrac{1 + K}{2}} & -\sqrt{\dfrac{1 - K}{2}} \\ \sqrt{\dfrac{1 - K}{2}} & \sqrt{\dfrac{1 + K}{2}} \end{bmatrix} \qquad (9.5.17)$$

From Eq. 9.5.7,

$$\delta_1 = A_{11}'RA_{11} \qquad (9.5.18)$$

$$\delta_2 = A_{12}'RA_{12} \qquad (9.5.19)$$

From Eq. 9.5.18,

$$\delta_1 = \alpha^2 R_{11} + 2\alpha\sqrt{1 - \alpha^2}R_{12} + (1 - \alpha^2)R_{22} \qquad (9.5.20)$$

From Eqs. 9.5.17 and 9.5.20,

$$\delta_1 = \frac{1 + K}{2}R_{11} + 2\sqrt{\frac{1 + K}{2}}\sqrt{\frac{1 - K}{2}}R_{12} + \frac{1 - K}{2}R_{22} \qquad (9.5.21)$$

Finally, from Eqs. 9.5.14 and 9.5.21,

$$\delta_1 = \frac{R_{11} + R_{22}}{2} + \tfrac{1}{2}\sqrt{d^2 + 4R_{12}^2} \tag{9.5.22}$$

Now

$$\delta_1 + \delta_2 = R_{11} + R_{22} \tag{9.5.23}$$

Hence,

$$\delta_2 = R_{11} + R_{22} - \delta_1 \tag{9.5.24}$$

Consider a larger matrix

$$_1R = \begin{bmatrix} R_{11} & \cdots & R_{1n} \\ \cdots & \cdots & \cdots \\ R_{1n} & \cdots & R_{nn} \end{bmatrix} \tag{9.5.25}$$

We can consider a general binary orthonormal of the order of Eq. 9.5.25 and of the form

$$_1A = I + (\alpha - 1)e_i\,e_i' - \beta e_i\,e_j' + \beta e_j\,e_i' + (\alpha - 1)e_j\,e_j' \tag{9.5.26}$$

where

$$\beta = \sqrt{1 - \alpha^2} \tag{9.5.27}$$

Let

$$_2R = {}_1A'\,_1R\,_1A \tag{9.5.28}$$

and

$$d = R_{ii} - R_{jj} \tag{9.5.29}$$

$$K = \frac{d}{\sqrt{d^2 + 4R_{ij}^2}} \tag{9.5.30}$$

$$\alpha = \sqrt{\frac{1 + K}{2}} \tag{9.5.31}$$

$$\beta = \sqrt{\frac{1 - K}{2}} \tag{9.5.32}$$

Then we can show from Eqs. 9.5.26–9.5.32 that

$$_2R_{ii} = \frac{_1R_{ii} + _1R_{jj}}{2} + \tfrac{1}{2}\sqrt{d^2 + 4\,_1R_{ij}^2} \tag{9.5.33}$$

$$_2R_{jj} = {}_1R_{jj} + {}_1R_{ii} - {}_2R_{ii} \tag{9.5.34}$$

$$_2R_{ij} = 0 \tag{9.5.35}$$

and for k distinct from i and j

$$_2R_{ik} = \alpha\,_1R_{ik} + \beta\,_1R_{jk} \tag{9.5.36}$$

$$_2R_{jk} = \alpha\,_1R_{jk} - \beta\,_1R_{ik} \tag{9.5.37}$$

and for m distinct from i and j

$$_2R_{km} = {}_1R_{km} \tag{9.5.38}$$

Equations 9.5.33 and 9.5.34 show that

$$_2R_{ii} > {}_1R_{ii} \tag{9.5.39}$$

if

$$R_{ij}^2 > 0 \tag{9.5.40}$$

Considering a particular $_2R_{ij}$ in Eq. 9.5.28 distinct from 0, we can use it to construct a new $_2A$ as in Eq. 9.5.26, and write

$$_3R = {}_2A'\,_2R\,_2A \tag{9.5.41}$$

We continue until all $_LR_{ij}$ vanish, in which case we cannot increase $_LR_{ii}$. At this point,

$$_LR = D \tag{9.5.42}$$

where D is diagonal.

In general,

$$_{L+1}R = {}_LA'\,_LR\,_LA \tag{9.5.43}$$

Let

$$_LQ = ({}_1A \cdots {}_LA) \tag{9.5.44}$$

From Eqs. 9.5.43 and 9.5.44,

$$_{L+1}R = {}_LQ'\,_LR\,_LQ \tag{9.5.45}$$

$_LQ$ is orthonormal, hence, from Eq. 9.5.42,

$$D = \delta \tag{9.5.46}$$

9.5.2 Convergence to Diagonal Form.

Let

$$R = \begin{bmatrix} R_{11} & \cdots & R_{1n} \\ \cdots & \cdots & \cdots \\ R_{1n} & \cdots & R_{nn} \end{bmatrix} \tag{9.5.47}$$

$$d = R_{ii} - R_{jj} \tag{9.5.48}$$

$$K = \frac{d}{\sqrt{d^2 + 4R_{12}^2}} \tag{9.5.49}$$

$$\alpha = \sqrt{\frac{1 + K}{2}} \tag{9.5.50}$$

$$\beta = \sqrt{\frac{1 - K}{2}} \tag{9.5.51}$$

$$A = I + (\alpha - 1)e_i e_i' - \beta e_i e_j' + \beta e_j e_i' + (\alpha - 1)e_j e_j' \qquad (9.5.52)$$

$$\rho = A'RA \qquad (9.5.53)$$

We prove that

$$tr(R - D_R)^2 - tr(\rho - D_\rho)^2 = 2R_{ij}^2 \qquad (9.5.54)$$

From Eqs. 9.5.47–9.5.53,

$$A'A = I \qquad (9.5.55)$$

From Eqs. 9.5.54

$$tr(R^2 - 2D_R R + D_R^2) - tr(\rho^2 - 2D_\rho \rho + D_\rho^2) = 2R_{ij}^2 \qquad (9.5.56)$$

From Eq. 9.5.56,

$$tr(R^2 - D_R^2) - tr(\rho^2 - D_\rho^2) = 2R_{ij}^2 \qquad (9.5.57)$$

From Eqs. 9.5.53 and 9.5.55,

$$trR^2 = tr\rho^2 \qquad (9.5.58)$$

From Eqs. 9.5.57 and 9.5.58,

$$trD_\rho^2 - trD_R^2 = 2R_{ij}^2 \qquad (9.5.59)$$

From Eqs. 9.5.52 and 9.5.53,

$$\rho_{LL} = R_{LL} \qquad \text{for } L \neq i, j \qquad (9.5.60)$$

$$\rho_{ii} = \frac{R_{ii} + R_{jj} + \sqrt{d^2 + 4R_{ij}^2}}{2} \qquad (9.5.61)$$

$$\rho_{jj} = \frac{R_{ii} + R_{jj} - \sqrt{d^2 + 4R_{ij}^2}}{2} \qquad (9.5.62)$$

From Eqs. 9.5.59 and 9.5.60,

$$2R_{ij}^2 = (\rho_{ii}^2 + \rho_{jj}^2) - (R_{ii}^2 + R_{jj}^2) \qquad (9.5.63)$$

From Eqs. 9.5.61 and 9.5.62,

$$\rho_{ii}^2 + \rho_{jj}^2 = \frac{(R_{ii} + R_{jj})^2 + d^2 + 4R_{ij}^2}{2} \qquad (9.5.64)$$

From Eqs. 9.5.48 and 9.5.64,

$$\rho_{ii}^2 + \rho_{jj}^2 = \frac{R_{ii}^2 + 2R_{ii} R_{jj} + R_{jj}^2 + R_{ii}^2 - 2R_{ii} R_{jj} + R_{jj}^2 + 4R_{ij}^2}{2}$$

$$= R_{ii}^2 + R_{jj}^2 + 2R_{ij}^2 \qquad (9.5.65)$$

Substituting Eq. 9.5.65 in 9.5.63,

$$2R_{ij}^2 = 2R_{ij}^2 \qquad (9.5.66)$$

Chapter 10

Order Reduction Methods

All of the methods we have considered so far consist of operations on the correlation or covariance matrix. These operations may consist of successive approximations, for example, in the case of the centroid and basic structure types of solutions, or they may consist of a predetermined number of operations, for example, in the group centroid and multiple group methods. A common characteristic of all of these methods is that the operations, whether prespecified or iterative, always take place on either the correlation matrix or residual matrices of the same order obtained from it. The two methods we shall discuss in this chapter proceed through major successive cycles as did the other methods, but they differ essentially from them in several important aspects.

10.1 Characteristics of the Methods

We shall discuss briefly the common characteristics of these methods and then take up each in more detail.

10.1.1 Basic Structure Solution. Like all but the centroid and grouping methods, the methods we shall now consider are of the basic structure type. They yield factor loading vectors which are proportional to the basic structure orthonormal vectors and the proportionality constants are the square roots of the corresponding basic diagonals.

10.1.2 Iterative Solutions. Like all of the basic structure methods, the solutions require sets of successive approximation computational cycles. Since it is not mathematically possible, in general, to solve for the basic diagonals of a matrix by rational algebraic solutions, all basic structure solutions require iterative solutions for the basic diagonals. Most of these methods require iterative computations on the correlation matrix or the residual correlation matrices.

10.1.3 Successive Order Reduction. The methods we consider now consist of operations on successively lower order matrices. Each major cycle of

211

computations operates on a matrix of order one less than the previous cycle. Some advantage is to be gained by reducing the size of the matrix with each cycle, although it is not always clear whether or not this advantage is offset by other additional computations required. It depends somewhat on the number of factors to be solved for and on the size of the original matrix.

10.1.4 Single Factor Solution at a Time. Both of the methods under consideration solve for a single factor at a time, rather than proceeding to iterate to all of the factors at once, as in the methods of Chapter 8. However, the two methods differ essentially in the procedures for arriving at the successive factors. These will be discussed in more detail later.

10.1.5 Nonresidual Solutions. The methods differ essentially from previous basic structure residual solutions in that residuals of the original correlation matrix are not required. In the basic structure residual methods of Chapter 7, each residual matrix is obtained by removing a basic orthonormal vector and its corresponding basic diagonal from the preceding residual matrix.

10.1.6 Specified Number of Factors. Both of the methods under consideration are like most of the previous methods in that one may solve for only a limited number of factor vectors. The methods differ from some of the previous methods, such as the multiple group and the simultaneous factor solution methods, in that one need not decide in advance how many factors he will solve for. One can judge from the size of the basic diagonals, which indicate the proportion of variance accounted for by corresponding factors, the number of factors to remove.

10.2 Kinds of Methods

There are at least three different kinds of methods which involve major cycles of computations on successively lower order matrices. Two of these maintain the symmetry of the matrices which are operated on and the other does not. We shall consider only the first two.

10.2.1 The Partial Reduction Method. The first method we shall consider is similar to the successive factor solution methods considered in Chapter 7 in that one solves for one basic diagonal or eigenvalue at a time in descending order of magnitude. Therefore, the computations need be carried only far enough to include the eigenvalues considered important. Furthermore, the calculations resulting in any specified number of eigenvalues yield also the corresponding basic orthonormal vectors of the original correlation matrix.

10.2.2   The Tridiagonal Solution.   The other solution we shall consider is essentially different from the first in that the correlation matrix is first transformed by successive orthonormal transformations to tridiagonal form, that is, all but the diagonal and bordering diagonal elements are 0. The tridiagonal matrix has the same eigenvalues as the correlation matrix.

10.3   The Partial Reduction Method

10.3.1   Characteristics of the Method.   The partial type of solution consists of a series of orthonormal transformations on the correlation matrix such that the first transformation results in making all but the diagonal element of the first row and column 0. The next transformation makes all but the diagonal element of the second row and column 0. In this way one proceeds by successive transformations to clear successive rows and columns, leaving only diagonal elements. These diagonal elements turn out to be the basic diagonals of the correlation matrix in order of magnitude.

In order to arrive at these orthonormal transformations one must, however, solve for the largest basic diagonal and the corresponding orthonormal vector of the current transformed correlation matrix at each stage. This involves an unpredictable number of operations, as in the methods of Chapters 7–9. One may therefore require a large number of iterations at any point before having the necessary values to reduce the order of the matrix by one, that is, to clear out another row and column of the matrix. The chief advantage of the method is that at each cycle one need take into account only the part of the matrix in which rows and columns have not been cleared, and since this is one less each time, the number of operations for each iteration for a basic diagonal is less than for the preceding basic diagonal.

This method does not, for each major cycle of operations, yield a basic orthonormal vector of the correlation matrix, even though it yields the largest remaining basic diagonal. However, by simple predictable operations, one can utilize the vectors already solved for to solve for those basic orthonormal vectors of the correlation matrix whose corresponding basic diagonals have already been solved for.

10.3.2   Computational Equations.

10.3.2a   DEFINITION OF NOTATION

$_1R$ is the correlation matrix.

δ_i is the ith eigenvalue of $_1R$.

$Q_{.i}$ is the ith eigenvector of $_1R$.

$_LR$ is a matrix derived from $_1R$ in which all but the diagonal elements of the first $L - 1$ rows and columns are 0.

$_L\rho$ is a matrix of all but the first $L - 1$ rows and columns of $_LR$.

$_L Q_{.L}$ is the first eigenvector of $_L\rho$.
$Q_{(k)}$ is the first k eigenvectors of $_1 R$.
$\delta_{(k)}$ is the first k eigenvalues of $_1 R$.
$a_{(k)}$ is the matrix of principal axis factor loadings.

10.3.2b THE EQUATIONS

$$_1 R \,_1 Q_{.1} = \delta_1 \,_1 Q_{.1} \tag{10.3.1}$$

$$\alpha_{11} = 1 - \,_1 Q_{11} \tag{10.3.2}$$

$$_1 U = \frac{_1 Q_{.1} - e_1}{\sqrt{\alpha_{11}}} \tag{10.3.3}$$

$$K_1 = \frac{\delta_1 - \,_1 R_{11}}{2\alpha_{11}} \tag{10.3.4}$$

$$_1 V = \frac{K_1 \,_1 Q_{.1} - \,_1 R_{.1}}{\sqrt{\alpha_{11}}} + g_1 e_1 \tag{10.3.5}$$

$$_2 R = \,_1 R - \,_1 U_1 V' - \,_1 V_1 U' \tag{10.3.6}$$

$$_L\rho \,_L Q_{.L} = \delta_L \,_L Q_{.L} \tag{10.3.7}$$

$$\alpha_{LL} = 1 - \,_L Q_{LL} \tag{10.3.8}$$

$$_L U = \frac{_L Q_{.L} - e_L}{\sqrt{\alpha_{LL}}} \tag{10.3.9}$$

$$K_L = \frac{\delta_L - \,_L\rho_{LL}}{2\alpha_{LL}} \tag{10.3.10}$$

$$_L V = \frac{K_L \,_L Q_{.L} - \,_L\rho_{.L}}{\sqrt{\alpha_{LL}}} + g_L e_L \tag{10.3.11}$$

$$_{L+1} R = \,_L R - \,_L U_L V' - \,_L V_L U' \tag{10.3.12}$$

$$Q_{.1} = \,_1 Q_{.1} \tag{10.3.13}$$

$$_{(L-1)L} Y = e_L - \,_L U \alpha_{LL} \tag{10.3.14}$$

$$\alpha_{(L-1)L} = \,_{L-1} U' \,_{(L-1)L} Y \tag{10.3.15}$$

$$_{(L-2)L} Y = \,_{(L-1)L} Y - \,_{L-1} U \alpha_{(L-1)L} \tag{10.3.16}$$

$$\alpha_{(L-k)L} = \,_{L-k} U' \,_{(L-k)L} Y \tag{10.3.17}$$

$$_{(L-k-1)L} Y = \,_{(L-k)L} Y - \,_{L-k} U \alpha_{(L-k)L} \tag{10.3.18}$$

$$Q_{.L} = \,_{1L} Y \tag{10.3.19}$$

$$a_{(k)} = Q_{(k)} \delta_{(k)}^{1/2} \tag{10.3.20}$$

10.3.3 Computational Instructions. The computational procedure for this method begins with an arbitrary vector such as a unit vector or an e_i vector. We find by the method of Chapter 7 a first basic diagonal and the first orthonormal vector of the correlation matrix, as indicated in Eq. 10.3.1. We do not, however, calculate the corresponding factor loading vector and subtract its major product moment from the correlation matrix, as in the conventional method.

We now proceed as follows. First, we calculate a scalar quantity as in Eq. 10.3.2. This α value is obtained, as indicated, by subtracting from 1 the first element of the $Q_{.1}$ vector. It will be noted that we use a prescript 1 on this scalar and on the corresponding vector of Eq. 10.3.1. This is because we shall use a prescript later for basic orthonormal vectors which are orthonormal vectors of certain transformations of the correlation matrix and not of the correlation matrix itself. We note that any factor loading vector may be equally well represented by changing all of its signs. The major product moment of a factor loading vector is independent of simultaneous sign changes of all of its elements. This is simply because the major product moment of the vector squares a -1, which makes it positive. We are therefore at liberty to reverse the signs of the elements of any factor loading vector if it suits our convenience.

We take then that set of signs which makes the first element of $Q_{.1}$ negative. This means that the value under the radical on the right of Eq. 10.3.3 is never less than 1. It will be 1 only if Q_{11} is 0, which in general it will not be.

Next we consider a vector U with the prescript 1 to indicate it is a first-cycle computation, as in Eq. 10.3.3. It will be seen that this vector, except for its first element, is proportional to the basic orthonormal vector solved for in Eq. 10.3.1. The proportionality constant is the reciprocal of the square root of the value calculated in Eq. 10.3.2.

We next calculate the scalar indicated in Eq. 10.3.4. This is obtained by subtracting from the first basic diagonal the first element of the correlation matrix and dividing the quantity by two times the scalar obtained in Eq. 10.3.2.

Next we calculate a vector designated as V and indicated in Eq. 10.3.5. This equation consists of first multiplying the $Q_{.1}$ vector by the scalar K of Eq. 10.3.4, second, subtracting from this the first column of the correlation matrix, and third, dividing this difference vector by the square root of the α quantity calculated in Eq. 10.3.2.

It will be noted that there is a second term on the right-hand side of Eq. 10.3.5 which has a single nonvanishing element in the first position. This is indicated by the e_1 vector multiplied by the scalar g_1. In further calculations the first element of the V vector will not be required; therefore, we are not concerned with the value of this g_1 scalar and we do not, in general, calculate the first value of the V vector given in Eq. 10.3.5. This means then that we use only the last $n - 1$ values of the $Q_{.1}$ vector and that we do not use the diagonal term of the first column of the correlation matrix. The equation has been written in its present form for completeness.

We now calculate a residual matrix, as indicated in Eq. 10.3.6. Here we subtract from the correlation matrix two major vector products. The first is the U vector of Eq. 10.3.3 postmultiplied by the transpose of the V vector in Eq. 10.3.5. The second is the transpose of this major vector product. This gives a matrix $_2R$ with zeros in the first row and column, except for the diagonal which is now the basic diagonal δ_1 of Eq. 10.3.1. We know by the method of computation that this must be the case, and therefore in Eq. 10.3.6 we do not calculate the first row and column of $_2R$. This means that in our calculations we do not need the first element of the V vector of Eq. 10.3.5 or the U column of Eq. 10.3.3. This is the reason we do not need to calculate the g_1 scalar on the right-hand side of Eq. 10.3.5.

We now consider Eq. 10.3.7. Here we use subscripts L on the symbols to indicate the Lth cycle of computations. For example, let us assume that $L = 2$. Here the ρ matrix with the L prescript is simply the part of $_2R$ in Eq. 10.3.6 with the first row and the first column deleted. We then consider the solution for its first basic diagonal and its corresponding basic orthonormal vector. This may be obtained by using a unit vector as the first approximation and proceeding in the conventional fashion to iterate to the largest basic diagonal and corresponding basic orthonormal vector.

It should be clear that the computations in Eq. 10.3.7 for $L = 2$ ignore the first row and column of the matrix, since these are known to be 0, except the diagonal which is δ_1. Similarly, we may regard the $Q_{.L}$ vector as a vector of full order in which the first element is 0. This way of interpreting the matrices and vectors will be convenient in the later computations.

We then go through Eqs. 10.3.8–10.3.12 for $L = 2$. These are precisely the same as in Eqs. 10.3.2–10.3.6. As in these equations, we must remember to take the signs of the basic orthonormal vector so that the Lth element of $_LQ_{.L}$ is negative, and gives a value which is not less than 1 in Eq. 10.3.8.

As in the case of Eq. 10.3.5, we do not, in Eq. 10.3.11, need to calculate the scalar g_L on the right-hand side of the equation in the right-hand term because we shall not need this Lth element of the V matrix. Remember that according to our interpretation, all elements above this Lth, or in this case the second position, are 0.

In the computation of the next reduced matrix we have Eq. 10.3.12. This is now analogous to Eq. 10.3.6. We know by the method of computation that except for the diagonal elements, the first and second rows and columns for $L = 2$ are all 0, and the first and second diagonal elements are the first and second basic diagonals of the correlation matrix, respectively. For $L = 2$, Eq. 10.3.12 gives us the third transformed matrix. However, here we need not be concerned with the first and second rows of $_2R$ on the right side of this equation, since we know what they will be. Similarly, we need not be concerned with the first and second elements of the U and V vectors, since these are involved in the first two rows and columns of the matrix on the left in Eq. 10.3.12, whose values are already known.

For $L = 2$ then, we get the $_3R$ matrix as a special case in Eq. 10.3.12, and we go on to $L = 3$ in Eq. 10.3.7. Here the ρ matrix is the same as the R matrix on the left of Eq. 10.3.12, except that we have eliminated the first two rows and columns. We consider now the solution for the first basic diagonal and the first basic orthonormal of this submatrix.

We proceed through cycles of the type given by Eqs. 10.3.7–10.3.12 until the sum of the basic diagonals solved for is sufficiently large to account for the amount of variance desired.

It will be seen that the major part of the computational work is involved in equations of the type (10.3.7), in which we must solve iteratively for the largest basic diagonal of the current ρ matrix and its corresponding vector. As in the traditional case, the number of iterations required will be determined by how close the largest basic diagonal is to the next largest and how good an approximation the unit or other arbitrary vector is to the first basic orthonormal vector.

Once we have decided that the total amount of variance accounted for by the currently calculated basic diagonals is adequate, we are ready to calculate the corresponding eigenvectors. It should be recalled that the Q vectors calculated in equations of the type (10.3.7) are not the eigenvectors of the correlation matrix but rather of the reduced matrices resulting from operations of the type indicated by Eqs. 10.3.8–10.3.12. The actual eigenvectors are functions of these Q vectors, as we shall see.

We begin with Eq. 10.3.13. This indicates that the first eigenvector is actually given by Eq. 10.3.1. This is, of course, because the solution begins with the original correlation matrix and therefore does yield the eigenvector corresponding to the largest eigenvalue. The eigenvectors we shall now calculate are functions of the U vectors given by Eq. 10.3.9, which, as is seen, are proportional to the Q vectors given by Eq. 10.3.7 with the exception of the first element.

We now define certain Y vectors which are used in calculating the Q vectors of the basic orthonormal of the correlation matrix. Equations 10.3.14–10.3.18 indicate the calculations for the Y vector. Let us take first the case of $L = 2$. The first Y vector denoted by appropriate prescript, which in this case would be 12, is simply an e_L vector, that is, a vector with the unit in the Lth position, from which is subtracted the corresponding $_LU$ vector of Eq. 10.3.9, multiplied by the corresponding α scalar of Eq. 10.3.8. In this particular case, the e_L vector would be an e_2 vector and $_LU$ and α_{LL} would be, respectively, $_2U$ and α_{22}.

We would note immediately that for $L = 2$ our computations are now finished because of Eq. 10.3.19. In this case, the first of the prescripts for Y would be 1, since Eq. 10.3.19 shows that when this prescript becomes 1, we have the eigenvector $Q_{.2}$ of the correlation matrix.

If, however, the L is more than 2, we go to Eq. 10.3.15. Here we calculate a new α scalar, which is the minor product of the $_{L-1}U$ vector of the type calculated in Eq. 10.3.9 and the Y vector calculated in Eq. 10.3.14.

With the vector and scalar calculated in Èqs. 10.3.14 and 10.3.15, respectively, we now go on to calculate a second Y vector, as indicated in Eq. 10.3.16. This will be seen to be a linear function of the previously calculated Y vector and the U vector used in the calculation of Eq. 10.3.15 multiplied by the scalar quantity calculated in that equation.

This set of operations is continued, as indicated in Eqs. 10.3.17 and 10.3.18, until the first prescript of the Y vector on the left side of Eq. 10.3.18 becomes 1.

Equation 10.3.19 then shows that this Y vector is the Lth eigenvector of the correlation matrix.

Equation 10.3.20 is the matrix of principal axis factor loading vectors, which is simply the matrix of corresponding eigenvectors postmultiplied by the square root of the diagonal matrix of corresponding eigenvalues.

10.3.4   Numerical Example. In this numerical example we use the same data as in the previous chapter.

Since we are already familiar with several methods for getting the largest basic diagonal and corresponding eigenvector from a symmetric matrix, these computations will not be presented.

Table 10.3.1 gives the data for the first factor loading vector. The number 6 in the upper left-hand corner is the number of iterations taken for the first factor. The number immediately below is the first eigenvalue of the correlation matrix. The first row is the corresponding basic orthonormal vector. The body of the table is the correlation matrix. The last row is the first principal axis factor loading vector and is, of course, proportional to the first row.

Table 10.3.2 gives the computations for the second factor loading vector. The body of the table is the first reduced-order matrix. The first number in the upper left corner is the number of iterations. The second number is the first eigenvalue of the reduced matrix and also the second eigenvalue of the correlation matrix. The first row is the corresponding eigenvector of the reduced matrix. The last row is the second principal axis factor loading vector.

Table 10.3.3 is analogous to Table 10.3.2. The body of the table is the second reduced matrix. The upper left-hand numbers are, respectively, the number of iterations and the third eigenvalue of the correlation matrix. The first and last rows are, respectively, the first eigenvector of the reduced matrix and the third principal axis factor loading vector.

Table 10.3.4 is analogous to Tables 10.3.2 and 10.3.3. It can be seen that

TABLE 10.3.1 Data and Computations for First Factor Loading Vector

6								
3.749								
0.3688	0.3808	0.3983	0.2887	0.2412	0.2692	0.3306	0.3172	0.3694
1.0000	0.8290	0.7680	0.1080	0.0330	0.1080	0.2980	0.3090	0.3510
0.8290	1.0000	0.7750	0.1150	0.0610	0.1250	0.3230	0.3470	0.3690
0.7680	0.7750	1.0000	0.2720	0.2050	0.2380	0.2960	0.2710	0.3850
0.1080	0.1150	0.2720	1.0000	0.6360	0.6260	0.2490	0.1830	0.3690
0.0330	0.0610	0.2050	0.6360	1.0000	0.7090	0.1380	0.0910	0.2540
0.1080	0.1250	0.2380	0.6260	0.7090	1.0000	0.1900	0.1030	0.2910
0.2980	0.3230	0.2960	0.2490	0.1380	0.1900	1.0000	0.6540	0.5270
0.3090	0.3470	0.2710	0.1830	0.0910	0.1030	0.6540	1.0000	0.5410
0.3510	0.3690	0.3850	0.3690	0.2540	0.2910	0.5270	0.5410	1.0000
0.7140	0.7374	0.7713	0.5589	0.4671	0.5213	0.6401	0.5141	0.7152

TABLE 10.3.2   Computations for Second Factor Loading Vector

10
2.046

0.2419	0.1107	−0.5248	−0.5788	−0.5504	−0.0303	0.0332	−0.1176	0.0347
0.3259	0.0975	−0.2512	−0.2291	−0.2185	−0.1449	−0.1083	−0.1588	
0.0975	0.3202	−0.0901	−0.0810	−0.1018	−0.1695	−0.1822	−0.1403	
−0.2512	−0.0901	0.8322	0.5078	0.4680	0.0200	−0.0415	0.1094	
−0.2291	−0.0810	0.5078	0.9030	0.5882	−0.0395	−0.0834	0.0525	
−0.2185	−0.1018	0.4680	0.5882	0.8512	−0.0253	−0.1081	0.0469	
−0.1449	−0.1695	0.0200	−0.0395	−0.0253	0.6957	0.3565	0.1826	
−0.1083	−0.1822	−0.0415	−0.0834	−0.1081	0.3565	0.7092	0.2044	
−0.1588	−0.1403	0.1094	0.0525	0.0469	0.1826	0.2044	0.6104	
−0.4949	−0.4838	−0.3024	0.6463	0.7407	0.6900	−0.0762	−0.1622	

TABLE 10.3.3 Computations for Third Factor Loading Vector

5
1.333

0.2451	0.0818	0.1992	0.1952	−0.5772	−0.6139	−0.3814		−0.3686
0.2891	0.0383	0.0563	0.0288	−0.1504	−0.1793	−0.1024		
0.0383	0.3128	−0.0448	−0.0579	−0.0650	−0.0611	−0.0503		
0.0563	−0.0448	0.3158	0.0295	−0.1322	−0.1063	−0.1191		
0.0288	−0.0579	0.0295	0.3195	−0.1134	−0.1298	−0.1164		
−0.1504	−0.0650	−0.1322	−0.1134	0.6876	0.3588	0.1610		
−0.1793	−0.0611	−0.1063	−0.1298	0.3588	0.7138	0.2027		
−0.1024	−0.0503	−0.1191	−0.1164	0.1610	0.2027	0.5649		
0.3453	0.3230	0.4036	0.0714	0.1851	0.1926	−0.5885	−0.6227	

TABLE 10.3.4 Computations for Fourth Factor Loading Vector

18
0.474

0.1392	−0.2052	−0.2205	−0.3848	−0.2165	0.8337		0.1695
0.3032	−0.0656	−0.0765	−0.0056	0.0034	−0.0109		
−0.0656	0.2711	−0.0101	−0.0046	0.0325	−0.0343		
−0.0765	−0.0101	0.2849	−0.0007	−0.0069	−0.0414		
−0.0056	−0.0046	−0.0007	−0.3238	−0.0371	−0.0807		
0.0034	0.0325	−0.0069	−0.0371	0.2832	−0.0603		
−0.0109	−0.0343	−0.0414	−0.0807	−0.0603	0.4042		
0.0303	0.0574	−0.0112	−0.1118	0.1200	0.1323		−0.5631

the eigenvalues or basic diagonals and the factor loading vectors agree closely with those found in Chapters 7 and 8.

10.4   The Tridiagonal Solution

It will be recalled that in the previous section we reduced successively the order of the correlation matrix until the desired number of factor loading vectors was obtained. In this method of solution we first get the entire matrix into tridiagonal form before finding any of the eigenvalues. We shall also consider several other important characteristics of the method.

10.4.1   Characteristics of the Method. This method, like the previous ones, is based on the calculation of certain orthonormal matrices. The correlation matrix is, in effect, successively multiplied on the right by such matrices and on the left by their transposes. In this respect, it is similar to the method discussed in the previous section and also to the Jacobi method, which proceeds by successive orthonormal transformations of the correlation matrix.

The method is similar to the previous one also in that for each successive cycle we have one lower order symmetric matrix to deal with. However, the orthonormal transformations are of such a nature that instead of wiping out a row and column, exclusive of the diagonal, we retain also a nonvanishing element adjacent to the diagonal. It can be seen, therefore, that if by successive orthonormal transformations we wipe out each time a row and column (except for the diagonal term and the one immediately below and to the right of the diagonal), eventually we must have a matrix which is of tridiagonal form. The number of operations involved in this type of reduction is completely predictable.

To arrive at the tridiagonal form the solutions are simpler than for the order reduction method described in the previous section. They are somewhat more complex, however, after the reduction to tridiagonal form has taken place. It is interesting to note that it is much more difficult to reduce a matrix by orthonormal transformations to diagonal form than to tridiagonal form. Once the matrix has been reduced to tridiagonal form, it is still something of a problem to solve for the eigenvalues and even more difficult to solve for the eigenvectors, which we need for the principal axis factor loading vectors. We must still solve for the desired number of basic diagonal elements of the tridiagonal matrix, then for as many of the corresponding eigenvectors as we wish to retain. Finally, we must use these eigenvectors, together with computations involved in the tridiagonal reduction, to get the basic structure vectors of the correlation matrix.

It would seem that for a given eigenvalue of a tridiagonal matrix it would be simple to calculate the corresponding eigenvector. The algebra looks deceptively simple. However, Wilkinson (1958) has pointed out that the obvious procedures are not satisfactory. He has suggested an approach which he reports gives good results, but others have not been uniformly successful with his method.

10.4.2. Computational Equations.

10.4.2a DEFINITION OF NOTATION

$_1R$ is the correlation matrix.

δ_i is the ith eigenvalue of $_1R$.

$Q_{.i}$ is the ith eigenvector of $_1R$.

$Q_{(k)}$ is the first k eigenvectors of $_1R$.

$\delta_{(k)}$ is the first k eigenvalues of $_1R$.

$a_{(k)}$ is the matrix of k principal axis factor loading vectors.

10.4.2b THE EQUATIONS

$$\alpha_1^2 = {}_1R_{.1}'\,{}_1R_{.1} - {}_1R_{11}^2 \tag{10.4.1}$$

$$\beta_1 = \sqrt{2}\sqrt{1 - \frac{{}_1R_{12}}{\alpha_1}} \tag{10.4.2}$$

$$\alpha_1\,{}_1R_{12} < 0 \tag{10.4.3}$$

$$_1U = [({}_1R_{.1} - {}_1R_{11}\,e_1)/\alpha_1 + e_2]/\beta_1 \tag{10.4.4}$$

$$_1P = {}_1R\,{}_1U \tag{10.4.5}$$

$$K_1 = \tfrac{1}{2}\,{}_1U'\,{}_1P \tag{10.4.6}$$

$$_1V = {}_1P - K_1\,{}_1U \tag{10.4.7}$$

$$_2R = {}_1R - {}_1V\,{}_1U' - {}_1U\,{}_1V' \tag{10.4.8}$$

$$_2R_{11} = {}_1R_{11} \tag{10.4.9}$$

$$_2R_{12} = \alpha_1 \tag{10.4.10}$$

$$_2R_{1(2+i)} = 0 \tag{10.4.11}$$

$$\alpha_L^2 = {}_LR_{.L}'\,{}_LR_{.L} - {}_LR_{(L-1)L}^2 - {}_LR_{LL}^2 \tag{10.4.12}$$

$$\beta_L = \sqrt{2}\sqrt{1 - \frac{{}_LR_{(L-1)L}}{\alpha_L}} \tag{10.4.13}$$

$$\alpha_L\,{}_LR_{(L-1)L} < 0 \tag{10.4.14}$$

$$_LU = [({}_LR_{.L} - {}_LR_{L-1}\,e_{L-1} - {}_LR_{LL}\,e_L)/\alpha_L + e_{L+1}]/\beta_L \tag{10.4.15}$$

$$_LP = {}_LR\,{}_LU \tag{10.4.16}$$

$$K_L = \tfrac{1}{2}\,{}_LU'\,{}_LP \tag{10.4.17}$$

$$_LV = {}_LP - K_L \, {}_LU \tag{10.4.18}$$

$$_{(L+1)}R = {}_LR - {}_LV \, {}_LU' - {}_LU \, {}_LV' \tag{10.4.19}$$

$$_{L+1}R_{LL} = {}_LR_{LL} \tag{10.4.20}$$

$$_{L+1}R_{L(L+1)} = \alpha_L \tag{10.4.21}$$

$$_{L+1}R_{L(L+1+i)} = 0 \tag{10.4.22}$$

$$A_L = {}_{L+1}R_{LL} \tag{10.4.23}$$

$$B_L = {}_{L+1}R_{L(L+1)} \tag{10.4.24}$$

$$\alpha_{(L-1)j} = {}_{L-1}U'Z_{.j} \tag{10.4.25}$$

$$_{L-1}Y_{.j} = Z_{.j} - {}_{L-1}U\alpha_{(L-1)j} \tag{10.4.26}$$

$$\alpha_{(L-2)j} = {}_{L-2}U' \, {}_{L-1}Y_{.j} \tag{10.4.27}$$

$$_{L-2}Y_{.j} = {}_{L-1}Y_{.j} - {}_{L-2}U\alpha_{(L-2)j} \tag{10.4.28}$$

$$\alpha_{(L-k)j} = {}_{L-k}U' \, {}_{L-k+1}Y_{.j} \tag{10.4.29}$$

$$_{L-k}Y_{.j} = {}_{L-k+1}Y_{.j} - {}_{L-k}U\alpha_{(L-k)j} \tag{10.4.30}$$

Continue until

$$_1Y_{.j} = Q_{.j} \tag{10.4.31}$$

Then

$$a_{(k)} = Q_{(k)} \, \delta_{(k)}^{1/2} \tag{10.4.32}$$

10.4.3 Computational Instructions. The first part of the computations involved in this method are those which reduce the correlation matrix to tridiagonal form. This has also been called the *codiagonal form* by Wilkinson (1958). The method is similar to one developed by Householder and Bauer (1959). It is much more subject to the accumulation of decimal error than methods described in Chapter 8.

We begin with the correlation matrix $_1R$. We then calculate a scalar α, as indicated in Eq. 10.4.1. This is the minor product moment of the first column of the correlation matrix, exclusive of the diagonal term.

We next define a scalar quantity, β, as in Eq. 10.4.2. This is obtained by taking the square root of 1 minus the ratio of $_1R_{12}$ to α_1, and multiplying by the square root of 2.

In calculating this scalar, we must always be sure that the inequality in Eq. 10.4.3 is satisfied. This means that the sign of α must be different from that of the R_{12} element. Then the second radical in Eq. 10.4.2 is never less than 1 because the ratio is always negative, since the two scalars involved are of opposite sign.

We now calculate a U vector, as indicated in Eq. 10.4.4. The first term in the expression in parentheses is simply the first column of $_1R$, the correlation matrix. We subtract from this vector its first element, as indicated, so that the vector in parentheses has 0 for its first element. This vector is then divided by the square root of the quantity given in Eq. 10.4.1, namely, the square root of α^2, where, it is recalled, the sign is opposite to that of the R_{12} element of the correlation matrix. We note now that the resulting vector has a unit element added to it in the second position, and that the entire vector now enclosed in brackets is divided by the scalar calculated in Eq. 10.4.2.

Next we calculate a vector indicated by Eq. 10.4.5. The P vector is simply the correlation matrix postmultiplied by the vector calculated in Eq. 10.4.4.

We next calculate the scalar quantity in Eq. 10.4.6. This expression is one half the minor product of the vector calculated in Eq. 10.4.5 by the vector calculated in Eq. 10.4.4. It should be noted in passing that the first element of the vector in Eq. 10.4.4 must be 0 by the method of calculation. However, the first element in Eq. 10.4.5 is not 0. Nevertheless, it is not necessary to calculate this first element, as we shall see later.

We now calculate a V vector as in Eq. 10.4.7. This is the P vector calculated in Eq. 10.4.5, after subtracting from it the U vector calculated by Eq. 10.4.4 multiplied by the scalar calculated in Eq. 10.4.6. Here again we leave the first element of V blank, which in effect makes it 0.

We now consider Eq. 10.4.8. This gives on the left the first reduced matrix. It will be noted in Eq. 10.4.8 that the right-hand side consists of subtracting a major product of two vectors and its transpose from the correlation matrix. The vectors involved in the major product are calculated in Eqs. 10.4.4 and 10.4.7, respectively. It should be observed, however, that we need not calculate the first row and column of $_2R$ in Eq. 10.4.8 because these values are already known from the method of computing the vectors V and U. It is for this reason that in the computations we do not calculate the first element of V.

The values in the first row and column in the right-hand side of Eq. 10.4.8 are given by Eqs. 10.4.9–10.4.11, respectively. From Eq. 10.4.9 we see that the first diagonal element of the reduced matrix in Eq. 10.4.8 is the same as the first diagonal element of the matrix $_1R$. In Eq. 10.4.10 we see that the elements in the first row and second column, and the first column and second row, are the square roots of the value calculated in Eq. 10.4.1. Here, the sign of α is given to the value. Finally, we see that all of the elements in the first row and column after the first two are 0, as indicated in Eq. 10.4.11.

We are now ready to consider the general form of the procedure for reducing the correlation matrix to tridiagonal form. We begin with Eq. 10.4.12. We calculate first the α^2 quantity analogous to the one in Eq. 10.4.1 for the correlation matrix. For any particular reduced matrix with the prescript L analogous to $_2R$ in Eq. 10.4.8, we calculate the sums of squares of the elements in the Lth column or row, minus the square of the diagonal element and the square of the element next to the diagonal. This means, for example, that we calculate the sum of squares of all elements in the row to the right of the diagonal. It can be seen by the method of computation that all of the remaining elements to the right of the diagonal or above the diagonal, with the exception of the one immediately adjacent, are 0.

The β scalar for the Lth cycle is calculated as in Eq. 10.4.13. Here the computation is exactly analogous to that of Eq. 10.4.2, except that now we are dealing with the element immediately adjacent to the Lth diagonal element.

As indicated in Eq. 10.4.14, we take the square root of α^2 in Eq. 10.4.12 different in sign from the element, $_LR_{(L-1)L}$, adjacent to the diagonal.

The Lth U vector is calculated as in Eq. 10.4.15. Here on the right-hand side the expression in parentheses is simply the vector of all elements in the Lth column of $_LR$ below the diagonal. The vector in parentheses is then divided by α_L from Eq. 10.4.12. To this vector we add 1 to the $L + 1$ position as indicated by the last term in brackets on the right side of Eq. 10.4.15. The entire expression in brackets is then divided by the β value calculated in Eq. 10.4.13.

We next calculate the Lth P vector as in Eq. 10.4.16. It can be shown from Eq. 10.4.15 that all elements of $_LU$, including the diagonal and above, are 0. In Eq. 10.4.16 we then require that only the elements of P beyond the L position be calculated, the rest being left 0.

We calculate a K scalar constant as in Eq. 10.4.17. This is comparable to the constant calculated in Eq. 10.4.6.

Next we calculate a V vector as in Eq. 10.4.18, where now we are utilizing the Lth vectors calculated in Eqs. 10.4.15 and 10.4.16, and the scalar constants calculated in Eq. 10.4.17.

Finally, we calculate the next reduced matrix as in Eq. 10.4.19. This equation is comparable to Eq. 10.4.8 except that now, to get the next reduced matrix, we use only the rows and columns after the first L rows and columns of the current reduced matrix. By the method of computations we know that the elements in the Lth row and column of the $L + 1$ reduced matrix are given by Eqs. 10.4.20–10.4.22, respectively. Equation 10.4.20 means that the Lth diagonal of the current and the reduced matrix are the same. The elements immediately below and to the right of the ith diagonal indicated by Eq. 10.4.21 are given by Eq. 10.4.12. Equation 10.4.22 means that all other values in the Lth row and column of the reduced $L + 1$ matrix are 0.

We continue through the cycles indicated by Eqs. 10.4.12–10.4.19, letting L take in turn the values from 2 to $n - 1$. At this point we have calculated the tridiagonal form of the reduced matrix.

We now define scalar constants as in Eq. 10.4.23. Here A_L is the Lth diagonal element of the reduced or the tridiagonal matrix.

Next we consider Eq. 10.4.24. Here B_L is the Lth bordering diagonal or nondiagonal element of the tridiagonal matrix.

We may now calculate the δ_i's from the A and B values of Eqs. 10.4.23 and

10.4.24 by the method of Ortega and Kaiser (1963). A further simplification by Horst indicated in the corresponding Fortran program enables one to get the eigenvalues in order of magnitude so that only those desired need be calculated.

Since no elegant, uniformly successful computational method exists at this writing, the reference to Wilkinson's (1958) procedure is offered for calculating the eigenvectors of the tridiagonal matrix corresponding to the calculated eigenvalues.

The computations for the eigenvectors of the correlation matrix, in terms of the eigenvector Z of the tridiagonal matrix, must now be accomplished as functions of the U vectors calculated by means of equations of the type (10.4.15).

We first consider Eq. 10.4.25 for the jth eigenvector of the correlation matrix. We start with the jth Z vector which is the eigenvector of the co-diagonal matrix corresponding to its jth eigenvalue. Equation 10.5.25 gives the scalar quantity α as the minor product of the final U vector (say, the $L-1$) and the $Z_{.j}$ vector.

Equation 10.4.26 calculates a Y vector as a linear function of this Z vector, the corresponding U vector, and the scalar quantity calculated in Eq. 10.4.25.

Next, the scalar quantity in Eq. 10.4.27 is calculated from the corresponding $_{L-2}U$ vector and the Y vector calculated in Eq. 10.4.26.

The next Y vector is calculated as in Eq. 10.4.28. This $_{L-2}Y$ vector is a linear function of the previously calculated Y vector, the $_{L-2}U$ vector, and the scalar quantity calculated in Eq. 10.4.27.

The general equation for the calculation of the α scalar quantity is given by Eq. 10.4.29.

The general equation for the Y vector is indicated by Eq. 10.4.30.

These operations proceed until $L-k$ is equal to 1, and the Y vector becomes identical to the jth eigenvector of the correlation matrix, as indicated by Eq. 10.4.31.

Equations of the type (10.4.25)–(10.4.31), of which Eqs. 10.4.29 and 10.4.30 are the general forms, are used for each $Z_{.j}$ value to calculate the corresponding $Q_{.j}$ vector of the original correlation matrix. Once these have been calculated, we calculate the factor loading matrix as in Eq. 10.4.32. Here, as usual, we simply multiply the matrix of the first k eigenvectors of the correlation matrix by the square root of the δ matrix of the corresponding eigenvalues.

10.4.4 Numerical Example. The same correlation matrix is used as in the previous section. Only the solution for the eigenvalues is presented.

The first row of Table 10.4.1 gives the diagonal elements of the tridiagonal matrix. The second row gives the nondiagonal elements. The third row gives the eigenvalues, which are also the eigenvalues of the correlation matrix. These are the same, within decimal error, as those calculated in Chapter 9.

TABLE 10.4.1   Elements and Eigenvalues of Tridiagonal Matrix

1.00000	2.63583	2.06416	1.53266	0.33746	0.40077	0.30308	0.37777	0.34826
0.00000	−1.26845	−0.92017	−0.42144	0.30745	−0.09397	0.07683	0.02404	−0.00568
3.74906	2.04946	1.33079	0.47434	0.38237	0.34727	0.28547	0.21219	0.16893

10.5 Mathematical Proofs

10.5.1 The Partial Reduction Method.

Let

$$_1R = {}_1Q\delta\,{}_1Q' \tag{10.5.1}$$

$$_1U = \frac{{}_1Q_{.1} - e_1}{\sqrt{1 - {}_1Q_{11}}} \tag{10.5.2}$$

$$_1W = I - {}_1U\,{}_1U' \tag{10.5.3}$$

From Eqs. 10.5.1–10.5.3,

$$_1W'\,{}_1W = I \tag{10.5.4}$$

Let

$$_2R = {}_1W'\,{}_1R\,{}_1W \tag{10.5.5}$$

From Eqs. 10.5.2 and 10.5.3,

$$_1W e_1 = {}_1Q_{.1} \tag{10.5.6}$$

From Eqs. 10.5.5 and 10.5.6,

$$e_1'\,{}_2R = {}_1Q_{.1}'\,{}_1R\,{}_1W \tag{10.5.7}$$

From Eq. 10.5.1,

$$_1Q_{.1}'\,{}_1R = \delta_1\,{}_1Q_{.1}' \tag{10.5.8}$$

From Eqs. 10.5.7 and 10.5.8,

$$e_1'\,{}_2R = \delta_1\,{}_1Q_{.1}'\,{}_1W \tag{10.5.9}$$

But from Eqs. 10.5.4, 10.5.6, and 10.5.9,

$$e_1'\,{}_2R = \delta_1\,e_1' \tag{10.5.10}$$

From Eq. 10.5.10,

$$_2R_{11} = \delta_1 \tag{10.5.11}$$

and

$$_2R_{.j} = 0 \qquad \text{for } j > 1 \tag{10.5.12}$$

Let

$$c_1 = \frac{{}_1U'\,{}_1R\,{}_1U}{2} \tag{10.5.13}$$

$$_1V = {}_1R\,{}_1U - c_1\,{}_1U \tag{10.5.14}$$

From Eqs. 10.5.3, 10.5.5, 10.5.13, and 10.5.14,

$$_2R = {}_1R - {}_1U\,{}_1V' - {}_1V\,{}_1U' \tag{10.5.15}$$

From Eqs. 10.5.1 and 10.5.2,

$$_1R\,{}_1U = \frac{\delta_1\,{}_1Q_{.1} - {}_1R_{.1}}{\sqrt{1 - {}_1Q_{11}}} \tag{10.5.16}$$

From Eqs. 10.5.12, 10.5.13, and 10.5.16,

$$c_1 = \frac{\delta_1 - 2\delta_1 \, _1Q_{11} + \, _1R_{11}}{2(1 - \, _1Q_{11})} \qquad (10.5.17)$$

From Eqs. 10.5.2, 10.5.14, and 10.5.16,

$$_1V = \frac{\delta_1 \, _1Q_{.1} - \, _1R_{.1}}{\sqrt{1 - \, _1Q_{11}}} - \frac{c_1(_1Q_{.1} - e_1)}{\sqrt{1 - \, _1Q_{11}}} \qquad (10.5.18)$$

or

$$_1V = \frac{(\delta_1 - c_1) \, _1Q_{.1} - \, _1R_{.1}}{\sqrt{1 - Q_{11}}} + \frac{c_1 e_1}{\sqrt{1 - Q_{11}}} \qquad (10.5.19)$$

Now from Eq. 10.5.17,

$$\delta_1 - c_1 = \frac{\delta_1 - \, _1R_{11}}{2(1 - \, _1Q_{11})} = K_1 \qquad (10.5.20)$$

From Eqs. 10.5.18 and 10.5.20,

$$_1V = \frac{K_1 \, _1Q_{.1} - \, _1R_{.1}}{\sqrt{1 - \, _1Q_{11}}} + \frac{c_1 e_1}{\sqrt{1 - \, _1Q_{11}}} \qquad (10.5.21)$$

Because of Eqs. 10.5.11 and 10.5.12, we can write

$$_2R = \begin{bmatrix} _1\delta & 0' \\ 0 & _2\rho \end{bmatrix} \qquad (10.5.22)$$

where $_1\delta = \delta_1$ and the roots of $_2R$ are the same as those of $_1R$ because of Eqs. 10.5.4 and 10.5.5. The second eigenvector of $_2R$ has 0 for its first element and the remaining elements are the same, respectively, as those of the first eigenvector of $_2\rho$. We may then calculate the first eigenvector and corresponding root of $_2\rho$. We augment the eigenvector with an initial 0 and call this $_2Q_2$. We then write

$$_2U = \frac{_2Q_{.2} - e_2}{\sqrt{1 - \, _2Q_{22}}} \qquad (10.5.23)$$

also

$$_2W = I - \, _2U \, _2U' \qquad (10.5.24)$$

Then

$$_2W' \, _2W = \, _2I \qquad (10.5.25)$$

We now let

$$_3R = \, _2W' \, _2R \, _2W \qquad (10.5.26)$$

Then, analogous to Eq. 10.5.10, we have

$$e_2'\,_3R = \delta_2\,e_2'$$

(10.5.27)

We let

$$c_2 = \frac{\delta_2 - 2\delta_2\,_2Q_{22} + \,_2R_{22}}{2(1 - \,_2Q_{22})}$$

(10.5.28)

and

$$K_2 = \frac{\delta_2 - \,_2R_{22}}{2(1 - \,_2Q_{22})}$$

(10.5.29)

and

$$_2V = \frac{K_2\,_2Q_{.2} - \,_2R_{.2}}{\sqrt{1 - \,_2Q_{22}}} + \frac{c_2\,e_2}{\sqrt{1 - \,_2Q_{22}}}$$

(10.5.30)

Then, by the methods of Eqs. 10.5.13–10.5.15,

$$_3R = \,_2R - \,_2U\,_2V' - \,_2V\,_2U'$$

(10.5.31)

In general, we have

$$_LR = \begin{bmatrix} _{L-1}\delta & 0' \\ 0 & _L\rho \end{bmatrix}$$

(10.5.32)

where

$$_{L-1}\delta = \begin{bmatrix} \delta_1 & \cdots & 0 \\ \cdots & \cdots & \cdots \\ 0 & \cdots & \delta_{L-1} \end{bmatrix}$$

(10.5.33)

$$_LR = \,_LQ\delta\,_LQ'$$

(10.5.34)

where $_LQ._L$ is the Lth eigenvector of $_LR$. Its first $k - 1$ elements are 0 and the remaining elements are, respectively, the same as those of the first eigenvector of $_L\rho$. Then δ_L is the largest eigenvalue of $_L\rho$. Also,

$$_LU = \frac{_LQ._L - e_L}{\sqrt{1 - \,_LQ_{LL}}}$$

(10.5.35)

$$K_L = \frac{\delta_L - \,_LR_{LL}}{2(1 - \,_LQ_{LL})}$$

(10.5.36)

$$_LV = \frac{K_L\,_LQ._L - \,_LR._L}{\sqrt{1 - \,_LQ_{LL}}} + \frac{c_L\,e_L}{\sqrt{1 - \,_LQ_{LL}}}$$

(10.5.37)

$$_{L+1}R = \,_LR - \,_LU\,_LV' - \,_LV\,_LU'$$

(10.5.38)

$$_{L+1}R = \begin{bmatrix} _L\delta & 0' \\ 0 & _{L+1}\rho \end{bmatrix}$$

(10.5.39)

Since according to Eq. 10.5.10,

$$e_L'{}_{L+1}R = \delta_L e_L' \tag{10.5.40}$$

we need not calculate the Lth element of $_LV$ in the determination of $_{L+1}\rho$ in Eqs. 10.5.38 and 10.5.39. Hence, we do not need c_L in Eq. 10.5.37. We remember, of course, that all of the elements preceding $_LV$ are 0. Therefore, we calculate only the first eigenvalue and vector of $_L\rho$. In getting $_{L+1}R$ then, we have to use Eq. 10.5.38 on only the $_L\rho$ of $_LR$, and even then we ignore the first row and column of $_L\rho$ because of Eq. 10.5.40, since we have already calculated δ_L.

Since any eigenvector of a Gramian matrix may always without loss of generality be multiplied by -1, we take the signs of $_LQ._L$ so that $_LQ_{LL}$ is negative. Therefore, the denominators of Eqs. 10.5.35–10.5.37 can never be less than 1.

We may proceed until the sum of the δ_i solved for indicates that enough of the variance has been accounted for. We then solve for the eigenvectors of $_1R$ in terms of the successive $_LU$ vectors. We let

$$_LM = {}_1W {}_2W \cdots {}_LW \tag{10.5.41}$$

From equations of the type (10.5.26), we have

$$_{L+1}R = {}_LW' {}_LR {}_LW \tag{10.5.42}$$

From Eqs. 10.5.41 and 10.5.42, we have

$$_{L+1}R = {}_LM' {}_1R {}_LM \tag{10.5.43}$$

From Eqs. 10.5.39 and 10.5.43,

$$\begin{bmatrix} {}_L\delta & 0' \\ 0 & {}_{L+1}\rho \end{bmatrix} = \begin{bmatrix} {}_LM_{(L)}' \\ {}_LM_{(n-L)}' \end{bmatrix} {}_1R[{}_LM_{(L)}, \quad {}_LM_{(n-L)}] \tag{10.5.44}$$

where the subscripts enclosed in parentheses mean inclusions of the first L and last $n - L$ columns of $_LM$, respectively.

From Eq. 10.5.44,

$$_L\delta = {}_LM_{(L)}' {}_1R {}_LM_{(L)} \tag{10.5.45}$$

It is well known that

$$_LM_{(L)} = Q_{(L)} \tag{10.5.46}$$

where $Q_{(L)}$ is the matrix of the first L eigenvectors of $_1R$. We have, therefore,

$$Q._i = {}_LMe_i \tag{10.5.47}$$

From Eqs. 10.5.41 and 10.5.47,

$$Q._i = ({}_1W {}_2W \cdots {}_LW)e_i \tag{10.5.48}$$

But because of Eq. 10.5.24,

$$_LW = I - {_LU}{_LU'} \tag{10.5.49}$$

and for $L > i$, we have

$$_LU'e_i = 0 \tag{10.5.50}$$

since the first $L - 1$ elements of $_LU$ are 0.

Hence, from Eqs. 10.5.48 and 10.5.50,

$$Q_{.i} = ({_1W} \cdots {_iW})e_i \tag{10.5.51}$$

From Eq. 10.5.51 and equations like (10.5.24), we have

$$Q_{.i} = (I - {_1U_1}U') \cdots (I - {_{i-1}U_{i-1}}U')(I - {_iU_i}U')e_i \tag{10.5.52}$$

From Eq. 10.5.35, we get

$$_iU'e_i = -\sqrt{1 - {_iQ_{ii}}} \tag{10.5.53}$$

We test

$$\alpha_{ii} = -\sqrt{1 - {_iQ_{ii}}} \tag{10.5.54}$$

$$_{(i-1)i}Y = e_i - {_iU}\alpha_{ii} \tag{10.5.55}$$

$$\alpha_{(i-1)i} = {_{i-1}U'}{_{(i-1)i}Y} \tag{10.5.56}$$

$$_{(i-2)i}Y = {_{(i-1)i}Y} - {_{i-1}U}\alpha_{(i-1)i} \tag{10.5.57}$$

and, in general,

$$\alpha_{(i-k)i} = {_{i-k}U'}{_{(i-k)i}Y} \tag{10.5.58}$$

$$_{(i-k-1)i}Y = {_{(i-k)i}Y} - {_{i-k}U}\alpha_{(i-k)i} \tag{10.5.59}$$

It can readily be verified from Eqs. 10.5.52–10.5.59 that

$$Q_{.i} = {_{1i}Y} \tag{10.5.60}$$

where $_{1i}Y$ is obtained by Eqs. 10.5.58 and 10.5.59.

10.5.2 The Tridiagonal Solution.

Given the correlation matrix $_1R$, let

$$_1U = \frac{_1R_{.1} - e_{11}R_{11} + e_2\alpha_1}{\pm\sqrt{2\alpha_1(\alpha_1 - {_1R_{12}})}} \tag{10.5.61}$$

where

$$\alpha_1^2 = {_1R_{.1}'}{_1R_{.1}} - {_1R_{11}^2} \tag{10.5.62}$$

Let

$$_1W = I - {_1U_1}U' \tag{10.5.63}$$

It can be shown from Eqs. 10.5.61–10.5.63 that

$$_1W'\,_1W = I \tag{10.5.64}$$

Let

$$_2R = \,_1W'\,_1R\,_1W \tag{10.5.65}$$

From Eq. 10.5.61,

$$_1U_1 = 0 \tag{10.5.66}$$

From Eqs. 10.5.61–10.5.65, it can be shown that

$$_2R_{11} = \,_1R_{11} \tag{10.5.67}$$

$$_2R_{12} = \pm\sqrt{\alpha_1{}^2} \tag{10.5.68}$$

and for i greater than 2,

$$_2R_{1i} = 0 \tag{10.5.69}$$

From Eq. 10.5.61,

$$_1U = \frac{(_1R_{.1} - \,_1R_{11}\,e_1)/\alpha_1 + e_2}{\sqrt{2}\sqrt{1 - (_1R_{12}/\alpha_1)}} \tag{10.5.70}$$

We take the sign of α_1 to be different from $_1R_{12}$. Again consider

$$_2U = \frac{(_2R_{.2} - \,_2R_{12}\,e_1 - \,_2R_{22}\,e_2)/\alpha_2 + e_3}{\sqrt{2}\sqrt{1 - (_2R_{23}/\alpha_2)}} \tag{10.5.71}$$

where

$$\alpha_2{}^2 = \,_2R_{.2}'\,_2R_{.2} - \,_2R_{12}{}^2 - \,_2R_{22}{}^2 \tag{10.5.72}$$

Let

$$_2W = I - \,_2U\,_2U' \tag{10.5.73}$$

Again from Eqs. 10.5.71–10.5.73, we can prove that

$$_2W'\,_2W = I \tag{10.5.74}$$

and now

$$_2U_1 = \,_2U_2 = 0 \tag{10.5.75}$$

We let

$$_3R = \,_2W'\,_2R\,_2W \tag{10.5.76}$$

Then we can show that

$$_3R_{11} = \,_2R_{11} = \,_1R_{11} \tag{10.5.77}$$

$$_3R_{22} = \,_2R_{22}$$

$$_3R_{23} = \pm\sqrt{\alpha_2{}^2} \tag{10.5.78}$$

Now also

$$_3R_{1i} = 0 \qquad \text{for } i > 2 \tag{10.5.79}$$

$$_3R_{2i} = 0 \qquad \text{for } i > 3 \tag{10.5.80}$$

In general,

$$\alpha_L{}^2 = {}_LR._L{}' {}_LR._L - {}_LR_{(L-1)L}{}^2 - {}_LR_{LL}{}^2 \qquad (10.5.81)$$

$$\beta_L = \sqrt{2}\sqrt{1 - ({}_LR_{L(L+1)}/\alpha_L)} \qquad (10.5.82)$$

where the signs of α_L and ${}_LR_{L(L+1)}$ are different.

$${}_LU = \frac{({}_LR._L - {}_LR_{(L-1)L}\, e_{L-1} - {}_LR_{LL}\, e_L)/\alpha_L + e_{L+1}}{\beta_L} \qquad (10.5.83)$$

Also

$${}_LW = I - {}_LU\, {}_LU' \qquad (10.5.84)$$

$${}_LW'\, {}_LW = I \qquad (10.5.85)$$

and

$${}_LU_1 = \cdots = {}_LU_L = 0 \qquad (10.5.86)$$

$${}_{L+1}R = {}_LW'\, {}_LR\, {}_LW \qquad (10.5.87)$$

and

$${}_1R_{ii} = \cdots = {}_LR_{ii} \qquad (10.5.88)$$

for $i = 1$ to $L - 1$, and

$${}_LR_{ij} = 0 \qquad (10.5.89)$$

for $i \le L$ and $j > i + 1$.

Since ${}_LR$ is symmetric,

$${}_LR_{ji} = {}_LR_{ij} \qquad (10.5.90)$$

Hence, this sequence of operations makes ${}_LR$ a tridiagonal form for $L = n - 2$ where n is the order of ${}_1R$. The transformation is orthonormal because of Eqs. 10.5.84 and 10.5.87.

To get ${}_{L+1}R$ from ${}_LR$, we let

$$K_L = \tfrac{1}{2} {}_LU'\, {}_LR\, {}_LU \qquad (10.5.91)$$

and

$${}_LV = {}_LR\, {}_LU - K_L\, {}_LU \qquad (10.5.92)$$

Then we can show that

$${}_{L+1}R = {}_LR - {}_LV\, {}_LU' - {}_LU\, {}_LV' \qquad (10.5.93)$$

It is noted that because of Eq. 10.5.86, Eq. 10.5.93 operates on only the last $n - L$ rows and columns of ${}_LR$.

If we let $Z_{(k)}$ be the matrix of these latent vectors, we may then solve for the latent vectors of ${}_1R$ by the method of the preceding section, except that now we calculate $n - 1$ of these ${}_LU$ vectors and proceed as follows. We let

$$M = (I - {}_1U_1U')\cdots(I - {}_{n-2}U_{n-2}U') \qquad (10.5.94)$$

Then

$$Q_{(k)} = MZ_{(k)} \qquad (10.5.95)$$

From Eqs. 10.5.94 and 10.5.95, we write

$$\alpha_{(n-2)j} = {}_{n-2}U'Z_{.j} \tag{10.5.96}$$

$$_{(n-2)j}Y = Z_{.j} - {}_{n-2}U\alpha_{(n-2)j} \tag{10.5.97}$$

$$\alpha_{(n-3)j} = {}_{n-3}U'{}_{(n-2)j}Y \tag{10.5.98}$$

$$_{(n-3)j}Y = {}_{(n-2)j}Y - {}_{n-3}U\alpha_{(n-3)j} \tag{10.5.99}$$

$$\alpha_{(n-k)j} = {}_{n-k}U'{}_{(n-k+1)j}Y \tag{10.5.100}$$

$$_{(n-k)j}Y = {}_{(n-k+1)j}Y - {}_{n-k}U\alpha_{(n-k)j} \tag{10.5.101}$$

and continue until

$$_{1j}Y = Q_{.j}' \tag{10.5.102}$$

Chapter 11

Solutions from Incomplete Covariance Matrices

There are several types of factor analysis solutions which do not utilize all of the intercorrelations of the variables involved in the data matrix. These solutions are employed in several kinds of situations. For example, it may be that one has not gone to the trouble of calculating all of the intercorrelations in a complete set of variables. Or it may be that for some of the intercorrelations only rough estimates are available.

11.1 Characteristics of the Solution

The types of solutions involved in the cases where incomplete correlation matrices are used do not in general make optimal use of the data. On the other hand, these methods can result in considerable computational economy.

11.1.1 Nonoptimal Use of Data. The methods generally may be used when certain of the intercorrelations must be only estimated rather than accurately calculated and when some of the others may not be calculated at all. However, a more typical situation occurs when one does not want to go to the time, trouble, or expense of calculating all of the intercorrelations or covariances available from the set of raw data. One of the methods to be discussed involves a sequential type of solution which begins with one of the conventional solutions on a subset of variables. The analysis may be completed for the remaining variables by short-cut procedures which discard much of the information, but the results are nevertheless considered to give sufficiently accurate estimates of the factor loadings for the additional variables.

11.1.2 Computational Economy. Perhaps one of the chief advantages of the methods to be discussed is that considerable time and computational cost may be saved by these short-cut methods which do not utilize all of the

237

information. As a matter of fact, we have seen that in general the amount of time and labor involved in most of the models for calculating factor loading vectors increases roughly in proportion to the square of the number of variables involved. It is frequently the case that the types of computational routines considered in the previous chapters may be applied to a limited set of variables. From this limited solution one may then get estimates of factor loading vectors on additional variables, perhaps several times or more greater in number than the initial set, with a relatively small amount of additional computation.

11.2 Kinds of Solutions

In the following sections we shall consider three different types of solutions based on incomplete covariance or correlation matrices. For all of these three methods, we begin with a symmetrically partitioned covariance matrix which yields a second-order supermatrix. The solutions then make certain assumptions concerning which of the submatrices in the supermatrix are actually or theoretically available and therefore which of them will be utilized in the solution of the factor loading vectors.

11.2.1 The R_{xy} Matrix. The first method we shall consider is based on the assumption that only the intercorrelations in the nondiagonal submatrix of the supermatrix will be utilized. This method is closely related to what Tucker (1958) called the *interbattery method* of factor analysis. The solution we shall discuss is similar to his solution, but the derivation differs in certain details.

11.2.2 Solution Involving Two Submatrices. Two other types of solutions we shall consider involve two of the submatrices of the partitioned correlation matrix. One of these is a symmetric diagonal submatrix and the other is a nondiagonal submatrix. For example, if we indicate one subset of variables as the x set and another subset of variables as the y set, then the intercorrelations used in the factor analysis solution involve the intercorrelations of the x set among themselves and the intercorrelations of the x set with the y set. The solution does not involve the intercorrelations of the variables in the y set.

It may be of interest to consider an example from a practical situation for which one may require this type of solution. Suppose we have administered a large set of psychological and aptitude tests to a group of entering freshmen at a university. We then have available the intercorrelations of these variables among themselves. This we may call the x set.

After the students enter the university, they take a wide variety of courses. Some take courses in certain areas and some in other areas which may or may not overlap the first areas. For example, some may take courses in psychology, sociology and mathematics; others, courses in mathematics, history and anthropology; and so on. In any case, the number of persons taking courses in a specific area would in general not be all of the people who took the original tests.

Nevertheless, for a subset of individuals one could get the correlation of the tests with their grades in a particular college course. In this way one could get estimates of the correlation of a particular college course area grade with the psychological test scores. True, these would not be based on all of the cases on which the intercorrelations of the test scores were based, but they may be used as estimates of what the correlations would have been had all of the persons taking the test also taken a course in, for example, anthropology.

If one is concerned with establishing prediction formulas for estimating grades in various college course areas from a set of measures taken previous to entrance, one could build up a submatrix of intercorrelations of test scores with college grades for a number of different course areas.

We shall call the grades for the various course areas the y set of variables. We may then calculate a matrix of intercorrelations for the x variables or the psychological tests, and also the correlations of the x tests with the y variables or college course area grades. If now one selects a set of y variables, that is, a set of college course areas, perhaps as many as 30, 40, or 50, listed in a college catalogue, it may be possible to get fairly large numbers of persons who have taken courses in each of the areas and thus get fairly stable correlations for grades in each course area with the psychological tests.

We have, however, a somewhat different situation when we attempt to get the intercorrelations of the y variables. For example, it may be that very few people who take courses in mathematics or in physics also take courses in history. Perhaps the number would be only 10 or 20, or even fewer, so that we would not want to use intercorrelations based on such a small number of cases.

We shall consider two types of solutions involving a diagonal and a nondiagonal submatrix of the partitioned correlation matrix. One of these is what may be called the *simultaneous solution* and the other a *two-stage solution*.

In the simultaneous solution we utilize both the diagonal submatrix and a nondiagonal submatrix in a single set of computational operations or in each of successive sets of computational operations.

In the two-stage type of solution we have, typically, the situation in which a factor analysis may already be available on one set of variables which we call the x set. This set of variables may actually be a set of predictor or independent variables, as indicated in the foregoing example, and the y set may be a set of criterion or dependent variables, as given in the same example.

For another example of the two-stage solution, we may have a set of variables which has been partitioned or divided into two sets on the basis of other considerations. We may already have a factor analysis on the first set of variables, and we wish to make optimal use of the factor loading matrix to estimate the factor loadings on the remaining y variables. Here we utilize the factor loading matrix in the first set and the intercorrelations of the first set with the second set to get an estimate of the factor loading vectors in the second set.

11.3 The R^{xy} Matrix

We shall first consider the solution involving only the intercorrelations of the x set of variables with the y set. Here we may simply not have gone to the trouble of calculating the intercorrelations of the x set and the intercorrelations of the y set. Or even if they are available, we may decide, because of limited time or facilities, to perform the factor analysis only with the correlations of the x set with the y set.

11.3.1 Characteristics of the Solution. The solution we shall consider has at least three distinguishing characteristics. It is a basic structure solution; it is maximally economical from a computational point of view; and it makes minimal use of data.

While it is possible to develop rationales for solutions other than a basic structure type solution, there seems to be little justification for doing so, since the basic structure solution has the characteristic of accounting for the intercorrelations in the R_{xy} matrix as accurately as possible in the least square sense with any specified number of factors. We may therefore use the procedures already discussed in previous basic structure type solutions, introducing certain modifications because of the fact that the matrix we are factoring is not symmetrical.

This method, using only the nondiagonal matrix, can result in great computational economy if either the x or the y set of variables is very small. The amount of time required in the solution is roughly a function of the number of variables in the smaller of the two sets of variables. On the other hand, the adequacy of the solution varies inversely with the number of variables in the smaller set. For example, if there were only one variable in the smaller set, it would not be possible to get more than one factor loading vector out of the solution, and even here the data would be overfitted.

In any case, it must be obvious, by the method of solution and the rationale underlying it, that any factor analysis based on the nondiagonal submatrix alone must give factor loadings only in factors which are common to the two sets of variables.

In particular, if the x set of variables were uncorrelated with the y set, then the R_{xy} would be a null matrix. This would mean that there are no factors in common between the two sets, and therefore no factor loading vectors other than 0 would be possible.

On the other hand, the number of x variables may be relatively small. These may have low intercorrelations among themselves and relatively substantial intercorrelations with the y variables. Then the x set might be regarded as what are sometimes called *marker* variables. These are relatively pure factor tests, as determined by previous research or competent rationale. For example, in the case of personality variables one may segregate in the first set a number of different items or different subsets of items, each of which is presumed to measure a different personality trait. In such cases one might proceed to do a factor analysis on the nondiagonal submatrix with some assurance that the factor loadings involved in the y variables would have meaning with reference to information gained in previous research or based on some sort of rational or plausible theory.

However, the method does make minimal use of the data available, if all measures are available on all cases represented in both sets of variables. One may, for example, have 20 variables in one set and 100 variables in another. In this case, the nondiagonal submatrix of intercorrelations would be 20×100. But the set of 100 y variables implies a large matrix of intercorrelations which would not be utilized at all in the solution.

11.3.2   Computational Equations

11.3.2a   DEFINITION OF NOTATION

R_{xy} is the correlation of the set of x variables with the y variables.

S is the minor product moment of R_{xy}.

Δ is the basic diagonal of R_{xy}.

$_xQ$ is the left basic orthonormal matrix of R_{xy}.

$_yQ'$ is the right basic orthonormal matrix of R_{xy}.

$\Delta_{(k)}$ includes the first k elements of Δ.

$_xQ_{(k)}$ includes the first k vectors of $_xQ$.

$_yQ_{(k)}$ includes the first k vectors of $_yQ$.

$_xa_{(k)}$ includes the first k factor loading vectors of the x variables.

$_ya_{(k)}$ includes the first k factor loading vectors of the y variables.

$a_{(k)}$ is the matrix of k factor loading vectors of both the x and the y sets.

11.3.2b   THE EQUATIONS

$$S = R_{xy}R_{yx} \tag{11.3.1}$$

$$_xQ\Delta^2{}_xQ' = S \tag{11.3.2}$$

$$_yQ\Delta = R_{yx}{}_xQ \tag{11.3.3}$$

$$a_{(k)} = \begin{bmatrix} {}_x Q_{(k)} \\ {}_y Q_{(k)} \end{bmatrix} \Delta_{(k)}{}^{1/2} = \begin{bmatrix} {}_x a_{(k)} \\ {}_y a_{(k)} \end{bmatrix} \qquad (11.3.4)$$

$$_x D_y D = \Delta \qquad (11.3.5)$$

$$_x a_{(k)} = {}_x Q_{(k)} {}_x D_{(k)} \qquad (11.3.6)$$

$$_y a_{(k)} = {}_y Q_{(k)} {}_y D_{(k)} \qquad (11.3.7)$$

$$_x D = \left[\frac{n_x}{n_y} \right]^{1/4} \Delta^{1/2} \qquad (11.3.8)$$

$$_y D = \left[\frac{n_y}{n_x} \right]^{1/4} \Delta^{1/2} \qquad (11.3.9)$$

11.3.3 Computational Instructions. The computational procedures in this method of analysis are simple and straightforward. We begin with Eq. 11.3.1. Here we let the symbol S represent the minor product moment of the nondiagonal correlation matrix R_{xy}. It should be noted that the use of the subscripts x and y is entirely arbitrary. We indicate the smaller of the sets as x and the larger as y. If the number is equal, then the distinction need not be made and it is immaterial which set we call x and which we call y. It is obvious, however, that if the x set is smaller than the y set, then Eq. 11.3.1 gives the minor product moment of the nondiagonal submatrix of intercorrelations. For example, if we have only 20 variables in the x set, then the order of the S matrix in Eq. 11.3.1 is only 20×20.

We now consider the basic structure solution of the S matrix, as indicated in Eq. 11.3.2. This matrix may be factored by any of the basic structure or principal axis methods previously considered. We thus get the vectors of the basic orthonormal matrix $_x Q$ and the basic diagonal Δ^2.

Next we perform the calculations indicated in Eq. 11.3.3. Here we have on the right-hand side the R_{yx} matrix postmultiplied by the basic orthonormal of the S matrix in Eq. 11.3.2. As in previous methods, we may stop the factoring before all the basic orthonormal vectors are calculated.

The criteria of how many of the Δ and the Q vectors to solve for are not the same, however, as in previous methods. In general, this method of analysis cannot be expected to account for nearly as large a proportion of the total variance of all of the variables as the methods previously discussed, which utilize all of the intercorrelations. No good criteria of how many factors to take out of this nonsymmetric covariance or correlation matrix have been worked out. As a matter of fact, there has been very little discussion of this point. Perhaps the best criterion is the trace of the product moment of the residual matrix of R_{xy}. Although the residual matrix itself may never be calculated, the trace of its product moment may be shown to be equal to the trace of S less the sum of the currently calculated Δ_i^2. This difference gives the sum of squared residuals. Its mean may be used to compare the variance of the residual correlations with the sampling variance of a correlation of 0 in a sample of size N. The problem of how many factors to take out of the nonsymmetric matrix is considered by Tucker (1958).

A solution for the complete factor loading matrix based on the calculation of k factor loading vectors is indicated in Eq. 11.3.4. Here, as previously, the subscript k enclosed in parentheses means that the matrix referred to has k columns. The left side of this equation means that this is the factor loading matrix involving both the x and the y sets of variables. The expression in the middle means that the selected basic orthonormal vectors of R_{yx} are multiplied by the square root of the corresponding basic diagonals to give the factor loading submatrices for the x and the y sets indicated in the right-hand side of Eq. 11.3.4.

It should be observed that the $_yQ$ matrix on the left of Eq. 11.3.3 is the left basic orthonormal of the matrix R_{yx} just as $_xQ'$ is its right basic orthonormal. This is clarified in the proof at the end of this chapter. From the middle term in Eq. 11.3.4, it is clear that the factor loading matrix is an orthonormal matrix, since it consists of submatrices which are themselves orthonormal. The postmultiplication by a diagonal does not affect the orthogonality of this type 3 column supervector made up of two nonhorizontal orthogonal submatrices.

Alternative solutions are also possible. It will be seen in Eq. 11.3.2 that we have used Δ^2 as the basic diagonal of the x matrix. It is possible to express Δ as the product of two other diagonal matrices which are not in general equal. One may then choose to distribute or divide this diagonal as follows.

First, consider Eq. 11.3.5. Here one may define two diagonal matrices as on the left side of the equation. This product is the basic diagonal of R_{yx}.

One may then consider Eq. 11.3.6 as the factor loading matrix for the x variables. Here the left basic orthonormal of Eq. 11.3.2 is postmultiplied by the diagonal corresponding to the x variables.

To get the y factor loading matrix we consider Eq. 11.3.7. Here the left basic orthonormal of R_{yx} is postmultiplied by the $_yD$ diagonal.

The question of how to determine the diagonal matrices on the left of Eq. 11.3.5 depends on how one wishes to distribute the variance accounted for by the solution between the two sets. It should be clear that the variance accounted for by the x set is simply the sum of squares of the $_xD$ values, and the variance accounted for by the y set is the sum of the squares of the $_yD$ values. One might wish to distribute these proportions roughly as the number of variables. In this case $_xD$ and $_yD$ would be given, respectively, by Eqs. 11.3.8 and 11.3.9, in which n_x and n_y are the number of variables in the x and the y sets.

11.3.4 Numerical Example. In this numerical example we consider only a set of intercorrelations of x with y variables. We use the method indicated by Eqs. 11.3.6–11.3.9 to distribute the variance between the two sets in proportion to the number of variables.

Table 11.3.1 gives the intercorrelation of a set of y variables (rows) with a set of x variables (columns).

Table 11.3.2 gives the minor product moment of the matrix in Table 11.3.1 as indicated by Eq. 11.3.1.

TABLE 11.3.1   Intercorrelations of y Variables with x Variables

0.108	0.125	0.238	0.626
0.298	0.323	0.296	0.249
0.309	0.347	0.271	0.183
0.351	0.369	0.385	0.369
0.492	0.468	0.446	0.271
0.555	0.525	0.523	0.185
0.425	0.381	0.396	0.279

TABLE 11.3.2   Minor Product Moment of R_{yx} Matrix

1.04986	1.03005	1.01078	0.68246
1.03005	1.01633	0.99564	0.68859
1.01078	0.99564	0.99519	0.74245
0.68246	0.68859	0.74245	0.80903

TABLE 11.3.3   Basic Diagonal of Minor Product Moment of R_{yx}

3.58188	−0.00000	0.00000	−0.00003
−0.00003	0.28369	0.00000	−0.00000
0.00001	0.00000	0.00393	0.00000
−0.00001	−0.00000	−0.00000	0.00091

Table 11.3.3 gives the basic diagonal matrix, Δ^2, of the matrix in Table 11.3.2. This is the Δ^2 in Eq. 11.3.2.

Table 11.3.4 gives the left basic orthonormal of Table 11.3.2 which is the same as the left orthonormal of R_{xy}. This is the $_xQ$ of Eq. 11.3.2. The matrices in Tables 11.3.3 and 11.3.4 were calculated by a Jacobi-type method described in Chapter 9.

Table 11.3.5 gives the factor loading column vectors for the x variables.

These are calculated from the matrices given by Eqs. 11.3.2, 11.3.6, and 11.3.8.

Table 11.3.6 gives the factor loading column vectors for the y variables. These are calculated by Eqs. 11.3.3, 11.3.7 and 11.3.9.

The computations were carried out to four factors. An examination of the basic diagonal elements of Table 11.3.3 indicates, however, that two factors doubtless would have been adequate.

TABLE 11.3.4   Left Basic Orthonormal of R_{xy}

0.53275	−0.33847	0.24947	0.73443
0.52625	−0.27852	−0.76326	−0.25083
0.52633	−0.06490	0.58746	−0.61126
0.40275	0.89647	−0.10041	0.15510

TABLE 11.3.5   Factor Loading Column
Vectors of x Variables

0.637	−0.215	0.054	0.111
0.629	−0.177	−0.166	−0.038
0.630	−0.041	0.128	−0.092
0.482	0.569	−0.022	0.023

TABLE 11.3.6   Factor Loading Column Vectors
of y Variables

0.419	0.748	0.039	−0.003
0.489	0.021	−0.107	−0.030
0.471	−0.086	−0.216	0.017
0.612	0.133	−0.023	−0.085
0.713	−0.131	0.002	0.088
0.771	−0.319	0.121	−0.100
0.625	−0.040	0.091	0.118

11.4   Simultaneous Solution for Two Submatrices

We shall next consider a solution which involves not only the submatrix of correlations of an x set with a y set, but one which also involves intercorrelations of the x set. In this example it is arbitrary which we call x and which we call y. The solution involves one symmetric submatrix and one nonsymmetric submatrix. We assume that no previous factor analyses have been performed on a subset of the variables.

11.4.1   Characteristics of the Method. This method, like the previous one and like most of the methods in this book, involves a basic structure solution. It requires, however, certain preliminary operations on the submatrices before the basic structure solution is applied. The method is somewhat more complex computationally than the previous one and the one which is to follow.

The method is more efficient in the utilization of data than the one described previously. We may have the kind of situation discussed at the beginning of this chapter in which we cannot get stable estimates of the intercorrelations of one of the sets, such as college course grades. We can get only the intercorrelations of the x set and estimates of the intercorrelations of the x set with the y set.

The method is particularly adapted to the case in which only an approximate estimate of the correlations of one set of variables with the other is available. But even though this may be the most appropriate application of the method, it may be used when both sets of measures are available on all cases. For example, we may have a set of marker variables which we call the x set and a number of other variables whose factor composition is unknown.

11.4.2   Computational Equations

11.4.2a   DEFINITION OF NOTATION

R_{xx} is the matrix of correlations for the x variables.

R_{yx} is the matrix of correlations of the y with the x variables.

t_x is the lower triangular factor of R_{xx}.

$a_{(k)}$ is the principal axis factor loading matrix for k factors.

11.4.2b   THE EQUATIONS

$$\begin{bmatrix} t_x \\ R_{yx}t_x'^{-1} \end{bmatrix} t_x' = \begin{bmatrix} R_{xx} \\ R_{yx} \end{bmatrix} \tag{11.4.1}$$

$$S = t_x't_x + (t_x^{-1}R_{xy})(R_{yx}t_x'^{-1}) \tag{11.4.2}$$

$$Q\Delta^2 Q' = S \tag{11.4.3}$$

$$a_{(k)} = \begin{bmatrix} {}_xa_{(k)} \\ {}_ya_{(k)} \end{bmatrix} = \begin{bmatrix} t_x \\ R_{yx}t_x'^{-1} \end{bmatrix} Q_{(k)} \tag{11.4.4}$$

11.4.3   Computational Instructions. The computational instructions for this procedure will not be given in minute detail because they involve procedures discussed at some length in other models presented in earlier chapters.

We begin with the solution indicated in Eq. 11.4.1. On the right-hand side of the equation we have the type 3 column supervector involving two submatrices. The first of these is the submatrix of intercorrelations of the x

variables among themselves, and the second submatrix is the matrix of inter-correlations of the y variables with the x variables. The left-hand side of this equation indicates a partial triangular factoring of this supermatrix, as in Section 3 of Chapter 8.

As can be seen, this partial triangular factoring results in another type 3 supervector which has the following characteristics. The first submatrix of the partial triangular factor is the lower triangular factor of the first matric element R_{xx} on the right of Eq. 11.4.1. The lower matric element is the lower matric element R_{yx} on the right-hand side of Eq. 11.4.1, postmultiplied by the inverse of the upper triangular factor of the matric element R_{xx}. As indicated in the previous discussions of triangular factoring, it is possible first to get the lower triangular factor of only the symmetric part of the supermatrix, that is, the upper matric element, and then to calculate its inverse and postmultiply the lower element by this inverse. However, as pointed out in earlier chapters, partial triangular factoring automatically accomplishes this objective, and therefore it is a simpler computational procedure.

The next step is to calculate the minor product moment of the type 3 supervector on the left of Eq. 11.4.1. As can readily be seen, this is the sum of two products. The first term on the right of Eq. 11.4.2 is the minor product moment of the lower triangular factor of R_{xx}. The second term is the lower matric element of the partial triangular factor in Eq. 11.4.1 premultiplied by its transpose.

As indicated in the left-hand expression of Eq. 11.4.3, we calculate the basic structure factors of the S matrix. Again, this can be accomplished by any of the methods previously indicated for basic structure solutions. The factoring can be carried out to as many factors as desired.

As in the previous sections, one would not in general carry out the factoring until all of the variance has been accounted for. As in those cases, the total variance which can be accounted for is the trace of the matrix S on the left-hand side of Eq. 11.4.2. In general, this will not be as great as the total variance of both the x and the y sets of variables. However, it can be expected to be greater than the total variance in the model of the previous section. There are no clear guidelines, but rarely would one be likely to account for more than 90–95 per cent of the variance indicated by the trace of the matrix S in Eq. 11.4.2.

The final set of computations required is indicated in Eq. 11.4.4. Here we show on the right-hand side that the partial triangular factor on the left of Eq. 11.4.1 is postmultiplied by the first k basic orthonormal vectors solved for in Eq. 11.4.3, to give the factor loading matrix of k factors. This solution gives the factor loading vectors both for the x set and for the y set, as indicated in the middle expression of Eq. 11.4.4.

It should be observed that the solution indicated by Eq. 11.4.4 is the left basic orthonormal of the partial triangular factor in Eq. 11.4.1 postmultiplied by its basic diagonal. This solution for the factor loadings is also an orthogonal solution; therefore, the factor vectors are mutually orthogonal to one another.

It might be interesting to point out aspects of the rationale of this method which are brought out more fully at the end of this chapter. It can be shown that if one takes the major product moment of the partial triangular factor on the left of Eq. 11.4.1, one gets back a correlation matrix whose first diagonal submatric element is precisely the intercorrelations of the x variables, whose nondiagonal elements are precisely the intercorrelations of the x with the y variables and whose lower diagonal term is an estimate of the intercorrelations of the y variables. This estimate can be shown to be the best least square estimate of the covariance of the y variables among themselves, where these estimates are based on the intercorrelations of the x variables and the correlations of the x with the y variables.

The question of whether this is the best possible solution from the data available, assuming that the intercorrelations of the y variables cannot be calculated, has not yet been answered. As a matter of fact, it may well be that even better estimates in some least square sense would be available for some specified number of factor loading vectors. It is clear, however, that the method of solution does give the best fit to the total correlation matrix if one takes as an estimate of the y intercorrelations the one just indicated.

11.4.4 Numerical Example.
The numerical example includes four x variables and eight y variables.

Table 11.4.1 is in two sections. The upper part gives the intercorrelations of the x variables and the lower part the intercorrelations of the y variables with the x variables.

Table 11.4.2 gives the partial triangular factoring of Table 11.4.1. The upper section gives the lower triangular factor of the upper part of Table 11.4.1, and the lower part is the lower part of Table 11.4.1 postmultiplied by the transpose of the inverse of the upper part, as indicated in Eq. 11.4.1.

Table 11.4.3 gives the minor product moment of Table 11.4.2, as indicated in Eq. 11.4.2.

Table 11.4.4 gives the basic structure solution for Table 11.4.3. The upper part is the basic diagonal and the lower part is the left basic orthonormal. These are the Δ^2 and Q matrices of Eq. 11.4.3.

Table 11.4.5 is the final factor loading matrix for both the x and the y variables and is also sectioned into parts, the upper part being for the x variables and the lower part for the y variables. It is obtained by postmultiplying Table 11.4.2 by the matrix in the lower part of Table 11.4.4, and is the left basic orthonormal of Table 11.4.2 postmultiplied by the basic diagonal of the matrix in Table 11.4.2. It is obtained as indicated by Eq.

11.4.4. Although all four factor vectors have been calculated, the first two are probably adequate.

TABLE 11.4.1 Intercorrelations of x Variables, and of y Variables with x Variables

1.000	0.829	0.768	0.108
0.829	1.000	0.775	0.115
0.768	0.775	1.000	0.272
0.108	0.115	0.272	1.000
0.033	0.061	0.205	0.636
0.108	0.125	0.238	0.626
0.298	0.323	0.296	0.249
0.309	0.347	0.271	0.183
0.351	0.369	0.385	0.369
0.492	0.468	0.446	0.271
0.555	0.525	0.523	0.185
0.425	0.381	0.396	0.279

TABLE 11.4.2 Lower Partial Triangular Factor of Table 11.4.1

1.000			
0.829	0.559		
0.768	0.247	0.591	
0.108	0.046	0.301	0.946
0.033	0.060	0.279	0.577
0.108	0.063	0.236	0.571
0.298	0.136	0.057	0.205
0.309	0.162	−0.011	0.154
0.351	0.140	0.137	0.300
0.492	0.108	0.070	0.203
0.555	0.116	0.115	0.090
0.425	0.051	0.096	0.213

TABLE 11.4.3 Minor Product Moment of Partial Triangular Factor

3.340	0.946	0.722	0.637
0.946	0.476	0.242	0.252
0.722	0.242	0.623	0.677
0.637	0.252	0.677	1.804

TABLE 11.4.4 Basic Diagonal and Left
Orthonormal of Table 11.4.3

4.108	0.000	−0.000	0.001
0.001	1.689	−0.000	−0.001
−0.000	−0.000	0.257	−0.004
−0.000	−0.001	−0.004	0.189
0.861	−0.404	−0.130	0.281
0.266	−0.083	−0.054	−0.959
0.264	0.262	0.928	−0.001
0.344	0.873	−0.344	0.039

TABLE 11.4.5 Factor Loading Column Vectors
for x and y Variables

0.861	−0.404	−0.130	0.281
0.862	−0.381	−0.138	−0.304
0.883	−0.176	0.435	−0.023
0.510	0.857	−0.062	0.023
0.316	0.558	0.053	−0.026
0.369	0.511	0.005	−0.008
0.378	0.062	−0.064	−0.039
0.359	−0.007	−0.112	−0.063
0.479	0.144	−0.029	−0.024
0.541	−0.012	−0.074	0.043
0.570	−0.125	−0.003	0.048

11.5 The Two-Matric Element, Two-Stage Solution

This method is similar to the one just discussed in that it starts with the same matrices, namely, the matrix of intercorrelations of the subset of x variables and the matrix of intercorrelations of these x variables with another set of y variables. It is essentially different, however, from the previous solution in that the factor analysis is performed in two stages. We first get the factor analysis of the x variables, and from this we estimate the factor loading matrix of the y variables.

11.5.1 Characteristics of the Method. This method is a combination of a basic structure and a multiple regression solution. The computational procedures are simple and utilize all of the available correlations. It is particularly appropriate when only an approximation to the nondiagonal submatrix is available.

The solution consists essentially of a basic structure factor analysis of that subset of data for which intercorrelations are available. Once having obtained the factor loading matrix for the x variables, one then proceeds by multiple regression methods to estimate the factor loading submatrix of the y variables from the factor loading matrix of the x variables, and the intercorrelations of the x variables with the y variables.

The solution is even simpler computationally than the one in the previous section. In that section the basic structure factors of a matrix whose order was the same as the number of variables in the x set was required. Here we also require the basic structure vectors of the matrix of this order. However, we do not require the triangular factoring of a supermatrix whose smaller order is the same as the x set. The set of multiple regression computations required is of a lower order of complexity because the number of factors is in general much less than the number of variables in the x set.

The method does utilize all of the data presumed to be available, that is, the intercorrelations of one set of variables and the correlations of this set with another set. The procedure, however, tends to give better approximations to the intercorrelations of the x set than to the correlations of the x with the y set. This is not in general the case with the previous method, which tends to distribute errors of approximation over both of the submatrices.

Like the previous method, this method is most appropriate for the case in which we can get only approximations to the correlations of the y with the x set because of conditions described in the example at the beginning of this chapter. In such cases it is usually not feasible to get intercorrelations of a y set of variables because the number of cases available for any two pairs of variables is too small to give stable results. However, the method is computationally and formally applicable to any case in which we have a set of x and a set of y variables, and in which we have not calculated the intercorrelations of the y set. A particular example, as previously mentioned, may be the situation in which we have already available a factor loading matrix on a particular set of variables and we have the correlation of this set with some other set. We may then avoid the necessity of going through a complete factor analysis for both sets by the method outlined here.

11.5.2 Computational Equations

11.5.2a DEFINITION OF NOTATION

R_{xx} is the correlation matrix for the x variables.

R_{yx} is the correlation matrix for the y with the x variables.

a_x is the principal axis factor loading matrix for the x variables.

a_y is the estimated factor loading matrix for the y variables.

11.5.2b THE EQUATIONS

$$Q\delta Q' = R_{xx} \tag{11.5.1}$$

$$a_x = Q\delta^{1/2} \tag{11.5.2}$$

$$a_y = R_{yx}(Q\delta^{-1/2}) \tag{11.5.3}$$

$$a_y = R_{yx}[a_x(a_x'a_x)^{-1}] \tag{11.5.4}$$

11.5.3 Computational Instructions. We begin by considering Eq. 11.5.1. Here we assume the intercorrelations of the x variables and the basic structure of these variables to be available.

From the basic structure of these variables we can, of course, in the usual way, calculate the factor loading matrix for any number of factors, as in Eq. 11.5.2. But the method does not depend on the assumption that the basic structure factor loading solution is available. It may also start with a centroid, multiple group, or other factor loading matrix for the x variables. In this case the solution will be a little more complex.

Having given, however, the basic structure factor loading matrix as indicated in Eq. 11.5.2, and also, in the process, the basic orthonormal of the R_{xx} matrix, we now calculate the factor loading matrix for the y variables. This is indicated in Eq. 11.5.3. Here we postmultiply the matrix of intercorrelations of the y variables with the x variables by the basic orthonormal matrix indicated in Eq. 11.5.1, and then postmultiply this product by the reciprocal square root of the basic diagonal of R_{xx} indicated in Eq. 11.5.1. The resulting matrix a_y well satisfies the condition that having given the factor loading matrix for the x variables, as in Eq. 11.5.2, the major product moment of the matrices on the right of Eqs. 11.5.2 and 11.5.3 give the best approximation in the least square sense to the matrix of correlations of the y with the x variables. It should be noted, however, that the matrix y is not in general an orthogonal matrix.

We have indicated that if the factor loading matrix for the x variables is not a basic structure or an orthogonal matrix, a somewhat more complicated procedure is required. When we refer to the factor loading matrix as being orthogonal, we must remember that this means its minor product moment is a diagonal matrix. Many writers refer to methods such as the centroid, multiple group, and group centroid as giving orthogonal factors. However, this is misleading because these methods do not yield orthogonal factor loading matrices.

If the matrix of factor loadings for the x variables is in fact not orthogonal, the least square solution for the factor loading matrix of the y variables is indicated in Eq. 11.5.4. Here we have somewhat more involved computations on the right-hand side of the equation. We notice, going from right to left, that we have first the inverse of the minor product moment of the factor loading matrix for the x variables. This is postmultiplied into the factor loading matrix for the x variables. The product is then postmultiplied into the correlation matrix of the y with the x variables. This type of solution is well known to be a least square solution, and the product in the bracketed part of the right-hand side of Eq. 11.5.4 is known as the general inverse of the matrix a_x. It is also of interest to note that the matrix in parentheses on the right-hand side of Eq. 11.5.3 is also the transpose of the general inverse of the matrix in Eq. 11.5.2. It can be shown that if we go through the operations indicated by the brackets in Eq. 11.5.4, then for this special case of the factor loading matrix we get the matrix indicated in the parentheses on the right-hand side of Eq. 11.5.3.

We need not concern ourselves here with the problem of how many factors to extract, because presumably this question has been answered in the calculations considered in Eq. 11.5.2. Here the same criteria, in general, as considered in previous chapters, are applicable to the factoring of the correlation matrix for the x variables in Eq. 11.5.1. For example, one may factor this matrix until the current basic diagonal is equal to or less than 1, or until the total variance accounted for by the basic diagonals is a prescribed proportion of the total variance of the x set.

11.5.4   Numerical Example. We shall use the same correlation matrix of nine variables as in earlier chapters and assume that the first three principal axis factors are available as given in those chapters.

Table 11.5.1 gives a matrix of correlations of three y variables with the nine x variables.

The first row of Table 11.5.2 gives the first three basic diagonal elements of the nine x variables as found in the solutions from previous chapters. The next nine rows give the first three principal axis factor loading vectors as found by previous solutions. The last three rows give the factor loadings for the three y variables as solved for by Eq. 11.5.3.

TABLE 11.5.1   Correlations of y Variables with x Variables

0.492	0.468	0.446	0.271	0.180	0.225	0.399	0.407	0.471
0.555	0.525	0.523	0.185	0.147	0.179	0.262	0.296	0.437
0.425	0.381	0.396	0.279	0.191	0.245	0.356	0.394	0.429

11.6   Mathematical Proofs

11.6.1.   The R_{xy} Method

Consider the nondiagonal correlation submatrix R_{xy} and its basic structure

$$R_{xy} = {}_xQ\Delta\,{}_yQ' \tag{11.6.1}$$

TABLE 11.5.2   First Three Basic
Diagonals and Factor Loading Column
Vectors of x and y Variables

3.749	2.050	1.331
0.717	0.493	0.350
0.740	0.478	0.322
0.773	0.296	0.406
0.556	−0.649	0.068
0.463	−0.744	0.181
0.518	−0.694	0.188
0.640	0.080	−0.588
0.615	0.166	−0.621
0.715	−0.034	−0.369
0.597	0.105	−0.048
0.565	0.186	0.112
0.544	0.046	−0.060

Without loss of generality, assume R_{xy} horizontal. Then

$$R_{xy}R_{yx} = {}_xQ\Delta^2{}_xQ'$$ (11.6.2)

and from Eqs. 11.6.1 and 11.6.2,

$${}_yQ\Delta = R_{yx}{}_xQ$$ (11.6.3)

Hence for any rank approximation to R_{xy} we take, say, the k largest Δ's and corresponding ${}_xQ$ and ${}_yQ$ vectors, respectively, so that we may write

$$\begin{bmatrix} {}_xa_{(k)} \\ {}_ya_{(k)} \end{bmatrix} = \begin{bmatrix} {}_xQ_{(k)} \\ {}_yQ_{(k)} \end{bmatrix} \Delta_{(k)}{}^{1/2}$$ (11.6.4)

Since the solution is a basic structure solution, it is the best least square approximation of rank k to R_{xy}. Because of Eq. 11.6.4, we have

$${}_ya_{(k)}\,{}_xa_{(k)}' = {}_xQ_{(k)}\,\Delta_{(k)}\,{}_yQ_{(k)}'$$ (11.6.5)

We wish to distribute the accounted for variance between the x and y sets in proportion to the number of variables n_x and n_y, respectively, in each. We then let

$${}_xD_{(k)} = \left[\frac{n_x}{n_y}\right]^{1/4} \Delta_{(k)}{}^{1/2}$$ (11.6.6)

$${}_yD_{(k)} = \left[\frac{n_y}{n_x}\right]^{1/4} \Delta_{(k)}{}^{1/2}$$ (11.6.7)

and

$$_xa_{(k)} = {_x}Q_{(k)} {_x}D_{(k)} \tag{11.6.8}$$

$$_ya_{(k)} = {_y}Q_{(k)} {_y}D_{(k)} \tag{11.6.9}$$

From Eqs. 11.6.6–11.6.9, we have

$$_xa_{(k)} {_y}a_{(k)} = {_x}Q_{(k)} \Delta_{(k)} {_y}Q_{(k)}' \tag{11.6.10}$$

But the right-hand side of Eq. 11.6.10 is the same as the right-hand side of Eq. 11.6.1 except for the subscripts (k). This shows that Eqs. 11.6.8 and 11.6.9 give the same estimate of R_{xy} as Eq. 11.6.4.

To show that the variance accounted for by Eqs. 11.6.8 and 11.6.9 is proportional to n_x and n_y, respectively, we prove simply that

$$\frac{tr \; {_x}a_{(k)}' \, {_x}a_{(k)}}{tr \; {_y}a_{(k)}' \, {_y}a_{(k)}} = \frac{n_x}{n_y} \tag{11.6.11}$$

From Eqs. 11.6.8 and 11.6.9, in (11.6.11),

$$\frac{tr \; {_x}D_{(k)}^{\,2}}{tr \; {_y}D_{(k)}^{\,2}} = \frac{n_x}{n_y} \tag{11.6.12}$$

From Eqs. 11.6.6 and 11.6.7, in (11.6.12),

$$\frac{\left[\dfrac{n_x}{n_y}\right]^{1/2} tr\Delta_k}{\left[\dfrac{n_y}{n_x}\right]^{1/2} tr\Delta_k} = \frac{n_x}{n_y} \tag{11.6.13}$$

From Eq. 11.6.13, we have the identity

$$\frac{n_x}{n_y} = \frac{n_x}{n_y} \tag{11.6.14}$$

11.6.2   The (R_{xx}, R_{xy}) Simultaneous Method

Consider the symmetrically partitioned correlation matrix

$$R = \begin{bmatrix} R_{xx} & R_{xy} \\ R_{yx} & R_{yy} \end{bmatrix} \tag{11.6.15}$$

Suppose we do not have available R_{yy}. The best least square estimate of R_{yy} from R_{xx} and R_{xy} is well known to be

$$\tilde{R}_{yy} = R_{yx} R_{xx}^{-1} R_{xy} \tag{11.6.16}$$

We let

$$t_x t_x' = R_{xx} \tag{11.6.17}$$

indicate the triangular factoring of R_{xx}.

We now write

$$\tilde{R} = \begin{bmatrix} R_{xx} & R_{xy} \\ R_{yx} & \tilde{R}_{yy} \end{bmatrix} \tag{11.6.18}$$

as an estimate of R in Eq. 11.6.15. From Eqs. 11.6.16–11.6.18, we have

$$\tilde{R} = \begin{bmatrix} t_x \\ R_{yx}t_x'^{-1} \end{bmatrix} (t_x', t_x^{-1}R_{xy}) \tag{11.6.19}$$

Let

$$b = \begin{bmatrix} t_x \\ R_{yx}t_x'^{-1} \end{bmatrix} \tag{11.6.20}$$

and let the basic structure of b be

$$b = P\Delta Q' \tag{11.6.21}$$

The best lower rank, say k, approximation to the factor matrix a will then be

$$b_{(k)} = P_{(k)} \Delta_{(k)} Q_{(k)}' \tag{11.6.22}$$

where the (k) means the k largest basic diagonals. First we solve for $Q_{(k)}$ and $\Delta_{(k)}$ in Eq. 11.6.22 by considering the minor product moment of b. From Eq. 11.6.21,

$$b'b = Q\Delta^2 Q' \tag{11.6.23}$$

From Eqs. 11.6.20 and 11.6.23,

$$t_x't_x + t_x^{-1}R_{yx}'R_{yx}t_x'^{-1} = Q\Delta^2 Q' \tag{11.6.24}$$

We let the principal axis factors be

$$a = P\Delta \tag{11.6.25}$$

From Eqs. 11.6.20, 11.6.21 and 11.6.25, we have

$$a = \begin{bmatrix} t_x \\ R_{yx}t_x'^{-1} \end{bmatrix} Q = P\Delta \tag{11.6.26}$$

or for the k largest Δ

$$a_{(k)} = \begin{bmatrix} t_x \\ R_{yx}t_x'^{-1} \end{bmatrix} Q_{(k)} = P_{(k)} \Delta_{(k)} \tag{11.6.27}$$

Let

$$\rho_{(k)} = P_{(k)} \Delta_{(k)}^2 P_{(k)}' \tag{11.6.28}$$

Then from Eqs. 11.6.20–11.6.22 and 11.6.25–11.6.27, $\rho_{(k)}$ is the best least square approximation of rank k to

$$\tilde{R} = \begin{bmatrix} R_{xx} & R_{xy} \\ R_{yx} & S \end{bmatrix} \tag{11.6.29}$$

where

$$S = {}_yP_{(k)}\, \Delta_{(k)}{}^2\, {}_yP_{(k)}{}' \tag{11.6.30}$$

in which ${}_yP_{(k)}$ is defined by

$$P_{(k)} = \begin{bmatrix} {}_xP_{(k)} \\ {}_yP_{(k)} \end{bmatrix} \tag{11.6.31}$$

and Eq. 11.6.30 gives the solution for S which enables us to get the best least square approximation of rank k to Eq. 11.6.28.

11.6.3 The Two Submatrices with Two-Stage Solution
Consider the correlation supermatrix

$$R = \begin{bmatrix} R_{xx} & R_{xy} \\ R_{yx} & R_{yy} \end{bmatrix} \tag{11.6.32}$$

Suppose we have already solved for the first k factor loading vectors of R_{xx}, say a_x, so that in

$$R_{xx} - a_x a_x{}' = \varepsilon_{xx} \tag{11.6.33}$$

the residuals may be assumed sufficiently small. In particular, let a_x be the best rank k approximation to R_{xx}.

Let us then consider the solution for the factor loading matrix a_y for the y variables and of the same width as a_x. We consider

$$a_x a_y{}' - R_{xy} = \varepsilon_{xy} \tag{11.6.34}$$

where we wish to determine a least square or general inverse solution for a_y. The solution is well known to be

$$a_y = R_{yx}\, a_x (a_x{}'a_y)^{-1} \tag{11.6.35}$$

If in particular a_x is a basic structure solution, then

$$a_x = {}_xQ_{(k)}\, {}_x\delta_{(k)}{}^{1/2} \tag{11.6.36}$$

where

$$R_{xx} = {}_xQ\, {}_x\delta\, {}_xQ' \tag{11.6.37}$$

and from Eqs. 11.6.35 and 11.6.36,

$$a_y = R_{yx}\, {}_xQ_{(k)}\, {}_x\delta_{(k)}{}^{-1/2} \tag{11.6.38}$$

Chapter 12

Factoring the Data Matrix

All of the methods we have considered so far assume that we have a correlation or covariance matrix on which to apply the factor analysis techniques. These methods are by far the most commonly used and best known. As a matter of fact, most of factor analytic theory has been based on the correlation matrix. It is perhaps unfortunate that this is the case, because there is a tendency to lose sight of the fact that the correlation matrix can yield no more information than is provided in the data from which it was derived. From this point of view, as indicated in Chapter 4, there are definite advantages in starting both theoretical and computational discussions from the data matrix and keeping as closely to the data matrix as possible.

12.1 Characteristics of the Methods

The essential characteristics of the methods which we shall discuss in this chapter are that no product moment computations are required and that the solutions yield simultaneously the factor score and the factor loading vectors.

12.1.1 No Product Moment Computations Required. In the procedures described in this chapter, the factoring is performed directly on the data matrix or, preferably, on a matrix derived from it, such as a normalized score matrix in which the means of the variables are 0 and the standard deviations are all equal. As a special case, the standard deviations may all be 1.

The advantages of these methods derive in part from the computational labor avoided in the calculation of covariance or correlation matrices. On the other hand, the time saved is not a net saving because the computations that apply to the correlation matrix, once it is derived, may proceed more rapidly than those applied directly to the data matrix.

12.1.2 Simultaneous Solutions for Factor Loading and Factor Score Matrices. The solutions provided in this chapter yield both a factor loading and a factor score matrix. The major product of these two matrices is then the approximation to the data matrix. If one is interested in obtaining factor scores on the particular sample under consideration as well as getting a factor loading matrix, the methods of this chapter have advantages over those previously discussed. However, as we shall see in Chapter 20, it is always possible to calculate a factor score matrix as a function of a factor loading matrix and the data matrix itself. It is therefore not necessary to employ the methods outlined below whenever one desires factor score matrices as well as factor loading matrices.

12.2   Kinds of Methods

It is possible to adapt almost any of the methods we have previously considered for calculating factor loading matrices from covariance or correlation matrices to the data matrices themselves. We shall not, however, consider the application of more than several of the types of methods previously considered to the data matrix directly. Those we shall consider are the centroid method, the basic structure method yielding a single factor at a time, and the basic structure method yielding all factors simultaneously.

12.2.1   The Centroid Method. The application of the centroid method to the data matrix involves essentially the same principles as those used in Chapter 5 in applying it to the correlation or covariance matrix. In the methods of Chapter 5, it will be recalled that one is concerned with finding a sign vector such that if the correlation or residual matrix is premultiplied by its transpose and postmultiplied by the vector, a scalar of maximum positive value results. In applying these methods to the data matrix, one is concerned with the determination of two such sign vectors. One of these would be the left multiplier for the data matrix and the other the right multiplier. One then attempts to find sign vectors such that the triple product yields a maximum positive scalar. This objective is sought both for an original data matrix and for successive residual data matrices.

12.2.2   Basic Structure Single Factor Solution. It will be recalled that in Chapter 7 we considered an iterative method of solution which yields in order of basic diagonal magnitude the basic structure factor loading vectors. Two such procedures were considered, one in which a residual matrix was calculated after each factor loading and another in which no residual matrices were calculated.

The method we shall consider in this section does calculate a residual data matrix each time a factor loading vector and a factor score vector are calculated. It is similar to the centroid method in that it is an iterative procedure and one does not know how many iterations will be required. As in all basic structure methods, this depends in part on the relative magnitude of successive basic diagonal elements. A characteristic of all of the methods which are based on factoring the data matrix is that one cannot conveniently assume communalities rather than total variances.

12.2.3   Basic Structure Simultaneous Factor Method. In Chapter 8 we considered how the basic structure solution for the factor loading vectors could be obtained simultaneously by suitable iteration processes so that the solution converges at the same time toward all of the basic structure factor loading vectors desired. This same principle may be employed directly on the data matrix. In this procedure one converges simultaneously to all of the factor loading vectors and all of the factor score vectors. The iterations at each cycle give both the approximate factor loading and factor score vectors.

12.3   The Centroid Method

12.3.1   Characteristics of the Method. The centroid method applied to the data matrix is a special case of the rank reduction method. It proceeds by calculating a factor loading vector and a factor score vector so that when the major product of these vectors is subtracted from the score matrix, the residual is reduced in rank by one over the preceding matrix. Therefore, as factor score and factor loading vectors are calculated successively and their major product subtracted from the current residual score matrix, the rank of the resulting residual score matrix is always reduced by one.

While it would be possible to develop methods whereby successive factor loading and factor score vectors could be obtained without calculating residual matrices, it appears that any such method would require more time and trouble than the procedure of getting one pair of factor loading and factor score vectors at a time.

The solution outlined in the following paragraphs is fairly simple from a computational point of view, just as is the centroid method applied to the correlation matrix. Although successive iterations to the sign vector are required, one may well expect that the total number of iterations made to determine a sign vector for a given factor would not be more than about half the number of variables. Furthermore, as in the case of the correlation matrix in which the centroid method is used, the operations used to make successive estimates of the sign vector are comparatively simple numerical operations, consisting primarily of addition and subtraction.

12.3.2   Computational Equations

12.3.2a   DEFINITION OF NOTATION

$_{kL}V$ is the kth approximation to the left sign vector.

$_{kR}V$ is the kth approximation to the right sign vector.

$_kZ$ is the kth residual matrix from the data matrix, Z being the data matrix for $k = 1$.

$Y_{.i}$ is the factor score vector for the ith factor.

$a_{.i}$ is the factor loading vector for the ith factor.

12.3.2b THE EQUATIONS

$$_{1L}V = 1 \tag{12.3.1}$$

$$_{1R}V = 1 \tag{12.3.2}$$

$$_{1L}U = Z\,_{1R}V \tag{12.3.3}$$

$$_{1L}W = -D_{1LV}\,_{1L}U \tag{12.3.4}$$

$$_{1L}W_{r_1} \quad \text{is largest element in } _{1L}W \tag{12.3.5}$$

$$_{2L}V = {}_{1L}V - 2\,_{1L}V_{r_1}\,e_{r_1} \tag{12.3.6}$$

$$_{2R}U = 0 + 2\,_{2L}V_{r_1}\,Z_{r_1.} \tag{12.3.7}$$

$$_{1R}W = -D_{1RV}\,_{2R}U \tag{12.3.8}$$

$$_{1R}W_{c_1} \quad \text{is largest element in } _{1R}W \tag{12.3.9}$$

$$_{2R}V = {}_{1R}V - 2\,_{1R}V_{c_1}\,e_{c_1} \tag{12.3.10}$$

$$_{2L}U = {}_{1L}U + 2\,_{2R}V_{c_1}\,Z_{.c_1} \tag{12.3.11}$$

$$_{2L}W = -D_{2LV}\,_{2L}U \tag{12.3.12}$$

$$_{2L}W_{r_2} \quad \text{is largest element in } _{2L}W \tag{12.3.13}$$

$$_{3L}V = {}_{2L}V - 2\,_{2L}V_{r_2}\,e_{r_2} \tag{12.3.14}$$

$$_{3R}U = {}_{2R}U + 2\,_{3L}V_{r_2}\,Z_{r_2.} \tag{12.3.15}$$

$$_{2R}W = -D_{2RV}\,_{3R}U \tag{12.3.16}$$

$$_{2R}W_{c_2} \quad \text{is largest element in } _{2R}W \tag{12.3.17}$$

$$_{3R}V = {}_{2R}V - 2\,_{2R}V_{c_2}\,e_{c_2} \tag{12.3.18}$$

$$_{3L}U = {}_{2L}U + 2\,_{3R}V_{c_2}\,Z_{.c_2} \tag{12.3.19}$$

$$_{kL}W = -D_{kLV}\,_{kL}U \tag{12.3.20}$$

$$_{kL}W_{r_k} \quad \text{is largest element in } _{kL}W \tag{12.3.21}$$

$$_{(k+1)L}V = {}_{kL}V - 2\,_{kL}V_{r_k}\,e_{r_k} \tag{12.3.22}$$

$$_{(k+1)R}U = {}_{kR}U + 2\,_{(k+1)L}V_{r_k}\,Z_{r_k.} \tag{12.3.23}$$

$$_{kR}W = -D_{kRV}\,_{(k+1)R}U \tag{12.3.24}$$

$$_{kR}W_{c_k} \quad \text{is largest element in } _{kR}W \tag{12.3.25}$$

$$_{(k+1)R}V = _{kR}V - 2\,_{kR}V_{c_k}\,e_{c_k} \tag{12.3.26}$$

$$_{(k+1)L}U = _{kL}U + 2\,_{(k+1)R}V_{c_k}\,Z_{.c_k} \tag{12.3.27}$$

Continue until all $_{kL}W$ and $_{kR}W$ are negative.

$$_{(k+1)L}V = _{L}V_{.1} \tag{12.3.28}$$

$$_{(k+1)R}U = _{R}U_{.1} \tag{12.3.29}$$

$$_{(k+1)R}V = _{R}V_{.1} \tag{12.3.30}$$

$$_{(k+1)L}U = _{L}U_{.1} \tag{12.3.31}$$

$$\alpha_1 = \sqrt{\frac{n}{_{L}U_{.1}'\,_{L}U_{.1}}} \tag{12.3.32}$$

$$\beta_1 = _{R}U_{.1}'\,_{R}V_{.1} \tag{12.3.33}$$

$$\gamma_1 = \frac{1}{\alpha_1\,\beta_1} \tag{12.3.34}$$

$$Y_{.1} = _{L}U_{.1}\,\alpha_1 \tag{12.3.35}$$

$$a_{.1} = _{R}U_{.1}\,\gamma_1 \tag{12.3.36}$$

$$_2Z = _1Z - Y_{.1}\,a_{.1}' \tag{12.3.37}$$

$$\alpha_i = \sqrt{\frac{n}{_{L}U_{.i}'\,_{L}U_{.i}}} \tag{12.3.38}$$

$$\beta_i = _{R}U_{.i}'\,_{R}V_{.i} \tag{12.3.39}$$

$$\gamma_i = \frac{1}{\alpha_i\,\beta_i} \tag{12.3.40}$$

$$Y_{.i} = _{L}U_{.i}\,\alpha_i \tag{12.3.41}$$

$$a_{.i} = _{R}U_{.i}\,\gamma_i \tag{12.3.42}$$

$$_{i+1}Z = _iZ - Y_{.i}\,a_{.i}' \tag{12.3.43}$$

12.3.3 Computational Instructions. The computational procedure for the centroid method applied to the data matrix is a little more involved than for its application to the correlation matrix. This is due to the lack of symmetry of the data matrix. This method, like the other methods to be considered for factoring the data matrix directly, is most suitable for cases in which the number of attributes or variables is about the same as the number of entities or cases.

One begins with approximations to the right and left sign vectors which are to be applied to the score matrix. A number of different methods are available for determining the original sign vectors, but it is convenient to begin with unit vectors for both the left and the right vectors, as indicated in Eqs. 12.3.1 and 12.3.2.

A left U vector is then calculated, as in Eq. 12.3.3. This is simply the vector of row sums of the score matrix Z which presumably has been put in standard measures. Equation 12.3.3 shows that the Z matrix is postmultiplied by the first right-hand sign vector, namely, the unit vector, to give this first left-hand U vector.

The next step is to examine the U vector calculated in Eq. 12.3.3 to see which elements have signs different from those in the corresponding left-hand vector given by Eq. 12.3.1. In this particular case, the vector is a unit vector. Therefore, we determine which is the largest negative value.

The right-hand side of Eq. 12.3.4 indicates that we multiply each element in the U vector by the negative of the corresponding element of the V vector. Actually, we need not go through these operations, but Eq. 12.3.4 is a convenient way of showing algebraically that we are determining those elements which are opposite in sign for the two vectors.

We then determine the largest element in the W vector. This is, of course, a positive value because of Eq. 12.3.4. We designate this the r_1 element of W, as indicated in Eq. 12.3.5.

We now indicate a second left-hand V vector, as in Eq. 12.3.6. This is simply the left unit vector of Eq. 12.3.1 with the r_1 element changed to -1.

Next we calculate a right-hand U vector, as indicated in Eq. 12.3.7. The first implied right-hand U vector, namely, $_{1R}U$, is 0 because the sums of columns add up to 0 if the scores are standard measures. We also give this two prescripts. According to Eq. 12.3.7, we take as the U vector twice the r_1 row of the Z matrix multiplied by the r_1 element of the current left-hand V vector.

We then symbolically multiply each element in the U vector of Eq. 12.3.7 by the negative of the corresponding element of the right-hand V vector, as indicated in Eq. 12.3.8. This we call the $_{1R}W$ vector. All elements in this vector whose corresponding elements in the V and the U vectors are different in sign will be positive. We then find the location of the largest element in the W vector and call this the c_1 position, as indicated in Eq. 12.3.9. We use the letter c to stand for column.

We next indicate the calculation of a new right-hand sign vector, as in Eq. 12.3.10. As can be seen by the right-hand side of this equation, we simply change the sign of the element of V in the c_1 position.

Now we calculate a new left-hand U vector, as indicated in Eq. 12.3.11. This is obtained by adding to the current U vector twice the c_1 column vector of the data matrix multiplied by the sign of the corresponding element of the current right-hand V vector. It will be remembered that multiplication by elements in V vectors is simply multiplication by either plus or minus 1.

Next we find the largest element in the current left-hand U vector which is largest in absolute value and different in sign from the corresponding element in the left V vector, by means of Eq. 12.3.12. This is the largest positive element in $_{2L}W$.

We call the position of the largest positive element the r_2 position. This is indicated by Eq. 12.3.13.

We alter the sign of the r_2 element of the left V vector, as indicated in Eq. 12.3.14.

Next we calculate a third U vector for the right-hand U, as in Eq. 12.3.15, by adding to the current right-hand U vector twice the r_2 row of the Z matrix multiplied by the r_2 element in the current left V vector.

In the same way we proceed to alter an element of the right V vector and then calculate a third left U vector, as indicated in Eqs. 12.3.16–12.3.19.

Equations 12.3.20–12.3.22 indicate in the same way how we change the sign in the r_k row of the current left V vector to get the $k + 1$ approximation to this vector.

Equation 12.3.23 shows how we get the $k + 1$ right U vector from the kth right U vector.

The calculation of the $k + 1$ right V vector and the $k + 1$ left U vector is indicated in Eqs. 12.3.24–12.3.27.

These routines are continued until the signs of the right V vector are the same as the signs of the corresponding elements in the right U vector, and the signs of the left V vector are the same as the signs of the corresponding elements in the left U vector.

Now we consider a $k + 1$ left V vector as the final $_L V$ vector for the first factor. This is indicated in Eq. 12.3.28.

Similarly, we take the $k + 1$ right U vector as the right U vector, as in Eq. 12.3.29.

We do the same for the $k + 1$ right V vector and the $k + 1$ left U vector. This is indicated in Eqs. 12.3.30 and 12.3.31.

We now calculate a scalar quantity α_1 as in Eq. 12.3.32. This is obtained by getting the sums of squares of the vector elements in Eq. 12.3.31, dividing the number of elements by this sum of squares, and taking the square root of the ratio, as indicated in Eq. 12.3.32.

We next calculate a scalar quantity β_1, as indicated in Eq. 12.3.33. This is simply the minor product of the right U vector and the right V vector, as indicated on the right of the equation. The product is actually the triple product of the left V vector by the data matrix Z by the right V vector. This is the scalar quantity which we have set out to maximize by our method of computation, and which we prove is a maximum in Section 12.6.

Next we calculate a scalar quantity γ_1, as indicated in Eq. 12.3.34. This is simply the reciprocal of the product of the scalars α and β calculated in Eqs. 12.3.32 and 12.3.33.

Now we calculate a vector $Y_{.1}$, which is the left U vector multiplied by the scalar α calculated in Eq. 12.3.32. This is the first vector of factor scores, given by Eq. 12.3.35.

Next we calculate the first factor loading vector, as in Eq. 12.3.36. This is the right U vector multiplied by the scalar γ calculated in Eq. 12.3.34.

We now calculate a residual $_2Z$ matrix, as in Eq. 12.3.37. This is the original data matrix from which the major product of the factor score and factor loading vectors for the first factor has been subtracted.

The procedure outlined above is then applied to the first residual matrix, or $_2Z$.

In general, the α scalar for the ith factor is calculated as in Eq. 12.3.38. This is obtained by dividing the number of elements in the left U vector for the ith factor by the sums of squares of these elements and taking the square root of the ratio.

The β scalar for the ith factor is simply the minor product of the right U vector for the ith factor and the right V vector for the ith factor, as in Eq. 12.3.39.

The γ scalar for the ith factor is the reciprocal of the product of the α and β scalars. This is indicated in Eq. 12.3.40.

The ith factor score vector is calculated as indicated in Eq. 12.3.41. This is the left U vector for the ith factor multiplied by the corresponding α scalar quantity calculated in Eq. 12.3.38.

The ith factor loading vector is calculated as in Eq. 12.3.42. Here the right U vector for the ith factor is multiplied by the corresponding scalar calculated in Eq. 12.3.40.

Each successive residual matrix is calculated as in Eq. 12.3.43, in which the

TABLE 12.3.1   Data Matrix

0.128	0.181	0.421	0.506	0.857	0.746	0.280	0.178	0.246
0.764	0.740	0.563	−0.387	−0.293	−0.202	0.261	0.281	0.043
−0.030	−0.046	0.014	0.147	−0.109	−0.135	0.640	0.682	0.661
−0.280	−0.351	−0.326	−0.023	−0.109	−0.186	0.083	0.091	−0.654
−0.336	−0.306	−0.429	−0.542	−0.006	−0.153	−0.428	0.056	−0.124
−0.276	−0.324	−0.271	−0.370	−0.225	0.035	0.129	−0.446	−0.124
0.057	−0.070	−0.016	0.006	0.152	−0.441	−0.166	−0.354	−0.033
−0.010	−0.140	0.326	−0.004	−0.258	−0.091	−0.410	−0.200	−0.101
−0.303	0.227	−0.014	0.029	−0.102	−0.125	−0.086	−0.106	−0.074
0.086	0.057	−0.003	0.161	0.073	0.134	−0.082	−0.067	−0.009
0.164	0.106	−0.124	0.234	−0.002	0.227	−0.072	0.025	0.156
0.036	−0.074	−0.142	0.242	0.023	0.192	−0.148	−0.119	0.011

major product moment of the ith factor score vector and the ith factor loading vector is subtracted from the ith residual matrix.

12.3.4   Numerical Example. A numerical example is given here.

Table 12.3.1 is a data matrix of twelve cases and nine variables. This data matrix yields the same correlation matrix used in Chapters 5–10.

Table 12.3.2 is the standardized data matrix, that is, a matrix in which the means are 0 and the variances 1.

The first two rows of Table 12.3.3 give, respectively, the first W vector and the corresponding Y vector for the first factor loading. The last two rows of this table give, respectively, the first V vector and the corresponding U vector for the first factor.

The first two rows of Table 12.3.4 give, respectively, the final W vector and corresponding Y vector for the first factor. It will be noted that the signs of corresponding elements of W and Y are the same. The last two rows of the table give, respectively, the final V vector and corresponding U vector for the first factor. Here also corresponding elements of the two vectors have the same sign.

Table 12.3.5 gives the matrix of column factor loading vectors. All nine factors have been calculated although the first three are perhaps adequate.

Table 12.3.6 gives the matrix of column factor score vectors. It is to be noted that, for this model of data matrix factoring, it is probably more difficult to tell when to stop factoring than for the two methods which follow.

TABLE 12.3.2   Standardized Data Matrix

0.444	0.627	1.458	1.754	2.967	2.585	0.970	0.616	0.853
2.648	2.563	1.950	−1.341	−1.015	−0.700	0.904	0.976	0.150
−0.104	−0.159	0.049	0.510	−0.378	−0.468	2.217	2.378	2.291
−0.970	−1.216	−1.129	−0.079	−0.378	−0.645	0.287	0.312	−2.266
−1.164	−1.060	−1.485	−1.878	−0.021	−0.530	−1.483	0.190	−0.429
−0.956	−1.122	−0.938	−1.282	−0.779	0.121	0.447	−1.565	−0.429
0.198	−0.242	−0.055	0.021	0.526	−1.528	−0.575	−1.244	−0.114
−0.035	−0.485	1.129	−0.014	−0.894	−0.316	−1.421	−0.705	−0.349
−1.050	0.786	−0.048	0.101	−0.354	−0.433	−0.298	−0.377	−0.256
0.298	0.197	−0.010	0.558	0.253	0.464	−0.284	−0.240	−0.031
0.568	0.367	−0.429	0.811	−0.007	0.786	−0.250	0.081	0.541
0.125	−0.256	−0.492	0.839	0.079	0.665	−0.513	−0.422	0.039

12.4   The Basic Structure Single Factor Method

This method for calculating factor loadings directly from the data matrix is different in several respects from the other two methods considered in this chapter.

TABLE 12.3.3 Initial W and Y Vectors, and V and U Vectors for First Factor

1.000	1.000	1.000	1.000	−1.000	1.000	1.000	1.000	1.000	1.000	1.000	1.000
12.274	6.134	6.336	−6.084	−7.862	−6.505	−3.014	−3.089	−1.929	1.205	2.470	0.064

1.000	1.000	1.000	1.000	1.000	1.000	1.000	1.000	1.000
2.329	2.120	2.971	3.757	0.042	1.061	2.966	−0.379	0.858

TABLE 12.3.4 Final W and Y Vectors and V and U Vectors for First Factor

1.000	1.000	1.000	−1.000	−1.000	−1.000	−1.000	−1.000	−1.000	1.000	1.000	1.000
12.274	6.134	6.336	−6.084	−7.862	−6.505	−3.014	−3.089	−1.929	1.205	2.470	0.064

1.000	1.000	1.000	1.000	1.000	1.000	1.000	1.000	1.000
7.957	6.678	5.053	6.264	3.799	6.663	6.087	6.779	7.687

12.4.1   Characteristics of the Method. Like the centroid method discussed in the previous section, this method calculates a single factor loading vector and a single factor score vector at a time, after which is calculated another factor score and factor loading vector, and so on. The method is also similar to the centroid method in that it is a rank reduction solution.

TABLE 12.3.5   Matrix of Factor Loading Column Vectors

0.806	−0.148	0.139	0.303	0.367	0.037	−0.274	−0.071	0.237
0.676	−0.073	0.299	0.104	0.167	0.237	0.035	0.222	−0.277
0.512	0.117	0.533	0.323	−0.255	−0.015	0.036	0.231	0.158
0.634	0.634	−0.077	−0.368	−0.189	0.048	−0.479	0.302	−0.079
0.385	0.408	−0.389	0.373	−0.042	0.241	0.203	−0.382	−0.119
0.675	0.524	−0.404	−0.075	0.467	0.211	0.276	0.080	0.198
0.617	−0.502	0.079	−0.477	−0.297	0.226	0.240	−0.151	0.040
0.687	−0.973	−0.517	0.070	−0.237	−0.500	0.000	−0.000	0.000
0.779	0.013	0.337	−0.253	0.019	−0.485	−0.036	−0.231	−0.158

TABLE 12.3.6   Matrix of Factor Score Column Vectors

2.127	1.927	−1.236	0.818	−1.913	0.237	1.781	−0.325	0.410
1.063	−2.435	2.283	1.780	1.294	1.519	−0.406	1.124	0.051
1.098	−0.751	0.091	−1.780	−1.294	−1.519	0.406	−1.124	−0.051
−1.054	−0.796	−1.581	−0.493	−1.102	1.564	−0.932	0.482	1.076
−1.363	−0.164	−0.794	0.493	1.102	−1.564	0.932	−0.482	−1.076
−1.128	0.033	0.607	−1.639	0.801	0.282	1.255	−0.966	1.435
−0.522	0.241	0.811	0.761	−0.579	0.843	−1.918	−1.931	−0.718
−0.535	0.681	0.763	0.901	−0.179	−1.227	0.027	1.447	1.435
−0.334	0.004	0.194	−0.023	−0.043	0.102	0.635	1.449	−2.153
0.209	0.360	−0.233	0.097	0.275	0.191	−0.416	0.166	−0.102
0.428	0.251	−0.363	−0.461	1.077	−0.261	−0.669	0.140	−0.457
0.011	0.647	−0.541	−0.454	0.561	−0.168	−0.696	0.018	0.149

Therefore, for any approximation to a given factor loading vector and the corresponding factor score vector, the major product of these vectors subtracted from the current residual matrix reduces the rank by exactly 1.

The method is essentially different from the centroid method in that it is a basic structure solution, so that each factor loading vector is a basic structure factor loading vector, and each factor score vector is the corresponding column of the left basic orthonormal of the data matrix. Therefore, each factor accounts for the maximum variance in the matrix from which it is determined.

12.4.2 Computational Equations

12.4.2a DEFINITION OF NOTATION

$_iZ$ is the ith residual data matrix. It is the data matrix if $i = 1$.

$_0U_{.1}$ is an arbitrary vector not orthogonal to the first row vector of the right basic orthonormal of $_iZ$.

$Y_{.i}$ is the ith column vector of basic structure factor scores.

$a_{.i}$ is the ith column vector of basic structure factor loadings.

12.4.2b THE EQUATIONS

$$_1V_{.1} = {}_1Z\,_0U_{.1} \tag{12.4.1}$$

$$_1\alpha_1 = \sqrt{{}_1V_{.1}'\,_1V_{.1}} \tag{12.4.2}$$

$$_1Y_{.1} = \frac{{}_1V_{.1}}{{}_1\alpha_1} \tag{12.4.3}$$

$$_1U_{.1}' = {}_1Y_{.1}'\,_1Z \tag{12.4.4}$$

$$_kV_{.1} = {}_1Z\,_{k-1}U_{.1} \tag{12.4.5}$$

$$_k\alpha_1 = \sqrt{{}_kV_{.1}'\,_kV_{.1}} \tag{12.4.6}$$

$$_kY_{.1} = \frac{{}_kV_{.1}}{{}_k\alpha_1} \tag{12.4.7}$$

$$_kU_{.1}' = {}_kY_{.1}'\,_1Z \tag{12.4.8}$$

$$\frac{{}_{k-1}\alpha_1}{{}_k\alpha_1} > P \tag{12.4.9}$$

$$Y_{.1} = {}_kY_{.1} \tag{12.4.10}$$

$$a_{.1} = {}_kU_{.1} \tag{12.4.11}$$

$$_2Z = {}_1Z - Y_{.1}\,a_{.1}' \tag{12.4.12}$$

$$_kV_{.i} = {}_iZ\,_{k-1}U_{.i} \tag{12.4.13}$$

$$_k\alpha_i = \sqrt{{}_kV_{.i}'\,_kV_{.i}} \tag{12.4.14}$$

$$_kY_{.i} = \frac{{}_kV_{.i}}{{}_k\alpha_i} \tag{12.4.15}$$

$$_kU_{.i}' = {}_kY_{.i}'\,_iZ \tag{12.4.16}$$

$$\frac{{}_{k-1}\alpha_i}{{}_k\alpha_i} > P \tag{12.4.17}$$

$$Y_{.i} = {}_kY_{.i} \tag{12.4.18}$$

$$a_{.i} = {}_kU_{.i} \tag{12.4.19}$$

$${}_{i+1}Z = {}_iZ - Y_{.i}\, a_{.i}' \tag{12.4.20}$$

$$G_i = \sum_{i=1}^{i} \alpha_i \tag{12.4.21}$$

Continue until

$$\frac{G_i}{n} = P \tag{12.4.22}$$

12.4.3 Computational Instructions. The solution begins with the data matrix, presumably in normalized form. We select some arbitrary U vector whose order is the same as the width of the Z matrix. In particular, this may be an e_i vector or an e_1 vector. The Z matrix is postmultiplied by this vector, as in Eq. 12.4.1, to yield a first approximation to a V vector for the first factor loading. Equations 12.4.1–12.4.12 involve the computations for the first factor score and factor loading vectors, and hence the postsubscript 1 is used.

If we use an e_1 vector for the U vector in Eq. 12.4.1, the resulting V vector is simply the first column of the Z matrix.

We calculate a first approximation to an α_1 scalar, as in Eq. 12.4.2. This is simply the square root of the sums of squares of the elements of the V vector calculated in Eq. 12.4.1.

The V vector calculated in Eq. 12.4.1 is then divided by the α scalar calculated in Eq. 12.4.2, as indicated in Eq. 12.4.3. This is the first approximation to the Y vector, which is the first approximation to the first factor score vector.

The factor score matrix is then premultiplied by the Y vector calculated in Eq. 12.4.3 to give the row vector U calculated in Eq. 12.4.4. This is the first successive approximation to a $U_{.1}$ vector.

Next a cycle of four operations is calculated for a second approximation. In general, four sets of operations are required for each approximation involving a factor score and a factor loading vector. These are indicated for the kth approximation in Eqs. 12.4.5–12.4.8.

In Eq. 12.4.5, the kth approximation to the V vector is obtained by postmultiplying the Z matrix by the $k - 1$ approximation to the U vector.

Next, we calculate the kth approximation to the α scalar as in Eq. 12.4.6. This is the square root of the sum of squares of elements of the V vector calculated in Eq. 12.4.5.

In Eq. 12.4.7, we indicate the kth approximation to the Y vector. This is the kth approximation to the V vector divided by the kth approximation to the α scalar.

Equation 12.4.8 indicates the kth approximation to the U vector as the Z matrix premultiplied by the kth approximation to the Y vector calculated in Eq. 12.4.7.

This iteration procedure should eventually result in two successive α's which are close enough to be regarded as equal. Therefore at each approximation we make the test indicated in Eq. 12.4.9. Here we take the ratio of the immediately preceding α to the current α. If this ratio is greater, say, than some proportion such as .999, indicated by P in the equation, we may assume that our iterations have proceeded far enough.

We then let the kth approximation to the Y vector be the first factor score vector, as indicated in Eq. 12.4.10. We also let the kth approximation to the U vector be the first factor loading vector, as indicated in Eq. 12.4.11.

We are now ready to calculate the first residual matrix. This is indicated in Eq. 12.4.12. We subtract the major product of the first factor score vector and the first factor loading vector, as indicated on the right-hand side of Eq. 12.4.12, from the matrix $_1Z$.

We then operate on this residual matrix $_2Z$, given by Eq. 12.4.12, in the same way that we operated on the original data matrix by means of Eqs. 12.4.1–12.4.11.

In general, the kth approximation to the ith V vector is given by Eq. 12.4.13. This is the ith residual matrix postmultiplied by the $k - 1$ approximation to the ith vector.

The kth approximation to the α scalar for the ith factor is the square root of the product moment of the V vector calculated in Eq. 12.4.13. This is indicated by Eq. 12.4.14.

The kth approximation to the factor score vector for the ith factor is given in Eq. 12.4.15. This is the V vector calculated in Eq. 12.4.13, divided by the α scalar calculated by Eq. 12.4.14.

The kth approximation to the U vector for the ith factor is given in Eq. 12.4.16. This is obtained by premultiplying the ith residual Z matrix by the vector obtained in Eq. 12.4.15.

We now take the ratio of the previous α scalar to the current α scalar to see whether this exceeds some proportion P, such as .999. If it does not exceed this proportion, we continue the cycle of operations indicated by Eqs. 12.4.13–12.4.16 until Eq. 12.4.17 does exceed the chosen tolerance limit.

We then let the kth approximation to the factor score vector Y be the factor score vector, as indicated in Eq. 12.4.18.

Similarly, we let the kth approximation to the U vector be the ith factor loading vector, as indicated in Eq. 12.4.19.

We then calculate the $i + 1$ residual matrix as indicated in Eq. 12.4.20. This we obtain by subtracting the major product of the ith factor score vector by the ith factor loading vector from the current residual matrix, namely, the ith residual matrix.

In order to determine at what point we have extracted enough factors, we may specify some proportion of the total variance which we wish to account for. The α scalar is the amount of variance accounted for by the corresponding ith factor loading vector. We therefore keep a cumulative sum of the α's solved for, as indicated in Eq. 12.4.21. This G scalar gives the total amount of variance we have accounted for by i factors.

If the ratio of this G scalar to the total number of variables exceeds some prespecified proportion P as indicated in Eq. 12.4.22, the computations cease. Otherwise, we continue the cycle from Eqs. 12.4.13–12.4.21 until the criterion given in Eq. 12.4.22 is satisfied.

12.4.4 Numerical Example. We use the same numerical example for the data matrix as in the previous section. The computations have been carried to four factors.

The first two rows of Table 12.4.1 give, respectively, the number of iterations for each factor, and the basic diagonal or amount of variance accounted

TABLE 12.4.1   Number of Iterations, Basic
Diagonals, and Column Factor Loading
Vectors

4	20	20	20
3.747	2.050	1.341	0.475
0.707	−0.505	−0.353	0.031
0.730	−0.490	−0.324	0.056
0.767	−0.308	−0.408	−0.009
0.566	0.639	−0.070	−0.111
0.475	0.737	−0.181	0.117
0.530	0.684	−0.186	0.135
0.641	−0.092	0.589	0.285
0.612	−0.178	0.625	0.164
0.716	0.021	0.366	−0.564

TABLE 12.4.2   Matrix of Column Factor
Score Vectors

1.956	1.937	−0.615	0.915
1.289	−2.680	−0.713	1.006
1.126	−0.343	2.850	−0.939
−1.133	0.244	0.689	2.527
−1.396	0.019	0.509	−0.204
−1.127	0.101	0.312	0.200
−0.492	−0.171	−0.701	−0.966
−0.458	−0.361	−1.101	−1.071
−0.308	−0.123	−0.174	−0.214
0.183	0.337	−0.496	−0.111
0.401	0.365	−0.181	−0.643
−0.040	0.676	−0.379	−0.500

for by each factor. The main body of the table gives the column factor loading vectors. An upper limit of 20 iterations was set for each factor. It is seen that the fourth basic diagonal is .475, or less than 1. Therefore, this factor should probably be discarded.

Since the data matrix yields the same correlation matrix as the one used in Chapters 5–9, and the solution yields basic structure or principal axis factors, they should be the same as the corresponding factor vectors found in Chapters 7–10. A comparison indicates that within limits of the iteration and tolerance limits used, they are the same.

Table 12.4.2 gives the column factor score vectors.

12.5   Basic Structure with Simultaneous Factor Solution

The method we shall next consider is analogous to the one outlined in Section 8.3. Here we recall that all of the factors were solved for simultaneously.

12.5.1   Characteristics of the Solution.   Like the previous solution, the method is a basic structure solution in that the factor score matrix consists of vectors from the left basic orthonormal of the data matrix corresponding to the largest basic diagonals, and the factor loadings are basic structure or principal axis factors. Like all basic structure solutions, the solution is iterative in that the number of operations cannot be predicted in advance.

Like the multiple group method and other methods in which all factors are solved for simultaneously, one specifies in advance the number of factors he intends to solve for. As for all of these methods, it is desirable to have some indication of what the maximum number of factors in the set might be. This information is sometimes available on the basis of previous experience or on the basis of hypotheses made in selecting the variables which are to be factor analyzed.

The method is a rank reduction type solution in the sense that the major product of the factor score and factor loading matrices yields a residual which is precisely of rank equal to that of the original matrix less the number of factors. This is true irrespective of which particular iteration one uses as the approximation to the factor score and factor loading matrices.

Like the two previous methods discussed in this chapter, the computational procedure yields both factor score and factor loading vectors. The method differs essentially from these two methods, however, in that no residual matrices are calculated and that the factor score and the factor loading vectors are solved for simultaneously for a specified number of factors. For this reason there is less cumulative decimal error in this method than in the two preceding methods in which residual matrices are calculated. The procedure is self-correcting for errors due to computational error, machine malfunction, or decimal error.

12.5.2 Computational Equations

12.5.2a DEFINITION OF NOTATION

Z is a normalized score matrix with variances of $1/N$.

$_0a$ is an arbitrary matrix of width k, the number of assumed factors.

Y is the basic structure factor score matrix.

12.5.2b THE EQUATIONS

$$_1W = Z\,_0a \tag{12.5.1}$$

$$_1S = {}_1W'\,_1W = {}_1t_1t' \tag{12.5.2}$$

$$_1U = Z'\,_1W \tag{12.5.3}$$

$$\begin{bmatrix} _1t \\ _1a \end{bmatrix}_1t' = \begin{bmatrix} _1S \\ _1U \end{bmatrix} \tag{12.5.4}$$

$$_iW = Z\,_{i-1}a \tag{12.5.5}$$

$$_iS = {}_iW'\,_iW = {}_it\,_it' \tag{12.5.6}$$

$$_iU = Z'\,_iW \tag{12.5.7}$$

$$\begin{bmatrix} _it \\ _ia \end{bmatrix}_it' = \begin{bmatrix} _iS \\ _iU \end{bmatrix} \tag{12.5.8}$$

$$_iD = D_{iS} \tag{12.5.9}$$

$$_id = {}_iD^{1/2} \tag{12.5.10}$$

$$G_i = 1'\,_id1 \tag{12.5.11}$$

$$\left[\frac{G_{i-1}}{G_i} - 1 \right] < P \tag{12.5.12}$$

$$a = {}_ia \tag{12.5.13}$$

$$Y = {}_iW_id^{-1} \tag{12.5.14}$$

12.5.3 Computational Instructions.

We begin with some crude approximation to the factor loading matrix. We specify in advance the number of factors to be solved for. We indicate the first approximation to the factor loading matrix by $_0a$, as indicated in Eq. 12.5.1. In particular, this may simply be a type 3 column supervector, as indicated in Section 8.3, where the upper submatrix is an identity matrix and the lower submatrix is a null matrix.

As indicated in Eq. 12.5.1, the score matrix is postmultiplied by this approximation matrix to give the W matrix. If this approximation matrix has been chosen with its upper matric element as the identity matrix, then W is composed of the first k columns of the score matrix Z.

As in the selection of approximation vectors or matrices previously discussed, the most important consideration is that none of the vectors of the a matrix be orthogonal to any of the first k basic orthonormal vectors of the right orthonormal of Z. But as in previous cases, it would be difficult to select vectors which are orthogonal, even though they might be nearly so. As in the previous cases also, the greater the departure from orthogonality of the a vectors to the first k vectors in the right orthonormal of Z, the fewer iterations will be required.

The next step is indicated in Eq. 12.5.2, which is the minor product moment of the matrix W calculated in Eq. 12.5.1. The right-hand expression of this equation shows that the matrix S may be considered as the major product moment of a triangular matrix.

The next step is to calculate a U matrix, as in Eq. 12.5.3. Here we premultiply the W matrix of Eq. 12.5.1 by the transpose of the data matrix Z.

We now consider a type 3 supervector as in Eq. 12.5.4. The right-hand side of this equation has, as the upper matric element, the product moment matrix, calculated in Eq. 12.5.2. For the lower element, we have the U matrix calculated in Eq. 12.5.3. The left-hand side of this equation indicates a partial triangular factoring of this supermatrix. The resulting partial triangular factor on the left has for the upper element the lower triangular factor of the S matrix. The lower element is the first approximation to the factor loading matrix a.

It will be recalled that this is similar to the procedure in Section 8.3, in which the computational procedures for the triangular factoring have been outlined. As in that case, it would be possible to solve first for the triangular factor of the S matrix, get the inverse of the lower triangular factor, and postmultiply the U matrix by the transpose of this inverse to give the approximation to the factor loading matrix. However, this is not necessary since these operations are automatically taken care of in the partial triangular factoring of the supermatrix.

The general form of the iterative solution may now be indicated. Having given the $i-1$ approximation to the factor loading matrix, we postmultiply the score matrix by it, as indicated in Eq. 12.5.5. This gives the ith approximation to the W matrix.

Then we take the minor product moment of this W matrix, as indicated in Eq. 12.5.6. Here we also indicate by the expression on the right of the equation the triangular factoring of the product moment matrix S.

The ith approximation to the W matrix is now used as a postmultiplier for the transpose of the Z matrix, as indicated in Eq. 12.5.7. This gives the ith approximation to the U matrix.

We now set up a supermatrix as indicated in Eq. 12.5.8. Here on the right-hand side the upper element is the product moment matrix S calculated in Eq. 12.5.6, and the lower element is the matrix U calculated in Eq. 12.5.7.

The left-hand side of this equation indicates the partial triangular factoring of the supermatrix. This gives as the upper element the lower partial triangular factor of the S matrix and as the lower element the ith approximation to the factor loading matrix.

We now consider a diagonal matrix as indicated in Eq. 12.5.9. This is made up of the diagonal elements of the current S matrix calculated by Eq. 12.5.6.

In Eq. 12.5.10, we indicate another diagonal matrix which is the square root of the diagonal matrix in Eq. 12.5.9. The diagonal matrix d in Eq. 12.5.10 is the ith approximation to the squares of the first k basic diagonals of the Z matrix. It is, in fact, an approximation to the basic diagonal elements of the correlation matrix corresponding to the score matrix. If the iterations are carried far enough, two successive d matrices given by Eq. 12.5.10 will be equal within specified limits of decimal accuracy. Rather than testing the individual elements, however, we take their sum as indicated in Eq. 12.5.11.

In Eq. 12.5.12, we take the ratio of the preceding G scalar to the current G scalar. We then subtract 1 from it. Equation 12.5.12 indicates the absolute value of the difference between this ratio and 1. We may specify that the absolute value of this difference shall not exceed some value P, such as 0.00001. When the criterion given in Eq. 12.5.12 is satisfied, we let the factor loading matrix be the current ith approximation, as indicated in Eq. 12.5.13.

At this point we may also regard the ith approximation to the W matrix as giving column vectors proportional to the factor score vectors. These must, however, be divided by their corresponding d values, as indicated by Eq. 12.5.14. Here we postmultiply the ith W matrix by the inverse of the diagonal matrix given by Eq. 12.5.10.

TABLE 12.5.1   First Approximation to Basic
Diagonals and First Four Column Factor
Loading Vectors

1.000	0.599	0.591	0.946
1.000	0.000	0.000	−0.000
0.829	0.559	0.000	−0.000
0.768	0.247	0.591	0.000
0.108	0.046	0.301	0.946
0.033	0.060	0.279	0.577
0.108	0.063	0.236	0.571
0.298	0.136	0.057	0.205
0.307	0.160	−0.012	0.149
0.351	0.139	0.137	0.300

12.5.4   Numerical Example. We use the same data matrix as in the two preceding sections.

The first row of Table 12.5.1 gives the first approximation to the first four basic diagonals or eigenvalues. The body of the table gives the first approximation to the first four column factor loading vectors. The zero approximation to these vectors was simply the set of e_1, e_2, e_3, and e_4 binary vectors.

TABLE 12.5.2   Second Approximation to Basic Diagonals and First Four Column Factor Loading Vectors

2.907	0.228	0.715	0.734
0.897	−0.397	−0.067	0.052
0.899	0.088	−0.235	−0.155
0.876	−0.079	0.207	−0.411
0.298	0.311	0.716	0.344
0.198	0.391	0.732	0.123
0.270	0.337	0.687	0.208
0.526	0.327	−0.107	0.360
0.525	0.350	−0.245	0.389
0.587	0.278	0.100	0.292

TABLE 12.5.3   Final Approximation to Basic Diagonals and First Four Column Factor Loading Vectors

3.749	2.049	1.341	0.464
0.717	−0.498	0.343	−0.029
0.740	−0.482	0.315	−0.067
0.773	−0.301	0.403	0.028
0.554	0.649	0.082	0.243
0.462	0.742	0.194	−0.179
0.517	0.691	0.199	−0.186
0.643	−0.069	−0.590	−0.232
0.615	−0.155	−0.629	−0.186
0.716	0.041	−0.366	0.497

The first row of Table 12.5.2 gives the second approximation to the first four eigenvalues. The body of the table gives the second approximation to the first four column factor loading vectors.

The computations were terminated after twelve iterations. Table 12.5.3 gives the final basic diagonals and column factor loading vectors. Since these are basic structure vectors, they should agree with those of the previous section. Presumably they are as close as the iteration and tolerance limits used in both cases permit.

12.6 Mathematical Proofs

12.6.1 The Centroid Method

12.6.1a PROOF THAT THE COMPUTATIONAL METHOD YIELDS MAXIMUM TRIPLE PRODUCT

Consider the data matrix Z and the sign vectors $_LV$ and $_RV$ such that

$$\beta = {}_LV'Z{}_RV \tag{12.6.1}$$

Let

$$_LU = Z{}_RV \tag{12.6.2}$$

$$_RU' = {}_LV'Z \tag{12.6.3}$$

Assume that

$$_LV_{r_1}{}_LU_{r_1} < 0 \tag{12.6.4}$$

This means that the elements in Eq. 12.6.4 are different in sign. Let

$$_{1L}V = {}_LV - 2{}_LV_{r_1}e_{r_1} \tag{12.6.5}$$

$$_1\beta = {}_{1L}V'Z{}_RV \tag{12.6.6}$$

From Eqs. 12.6.5 and 12.6.6,

$$_1\beta = ({}_LV' - 2{}_LV_{r_1}e_{r_1}')Z{}_RV \tag{12.6.7}$$

or

$$_1\beta = {}_LV'Z{}_RV - 2{}_LV_{r_1}Z_{r_1.}'{}_RV \tag{12.6.8}$$

But

$$Z_{r_1.}'{}_RV = {}_LU_{r_1} \tag{12.6.9}$$

Equations 12.6.1 and 12.6.9 in (12.6.8) give

$$_1\beta = \beta - 2{}_LV_{r_1}{}_LU_{r_1} \tag{12.6.10}$$

Because of Eqs. 12.6.4 and 12.6.10,

$$_1\beta > \beta \tag{12.6.11}$$

That is, $_1\beta$ exceeds β by exactly twice the absolute value of $_LU_{r_1}$.

In the same way, we may assume

$$_RV_{c_1}{}_RU_{c_1} < 0 \tag{12.6.12}$$

and let

$$_{1R}V = {}_RV - 2{}_RV_{c_1}e_{c_1} \tag{12.6.13}$$

$$_1\beta = {}_LV'Z{}_{1R}V \tag{12.6.14}$$

We may show by the same method that

$$_1\beta = \beta - 2\,_RV_{c_1}\,_RU_{c_1} \tag{12.6.15}$$

or

$$_1\beta > \beta \tag{12.6.16}$$

We have from Eq. 12.6.5, equations of the type

$$_{(k+1)L}V = {}_{kL}V - 2\,_{kL}V_{r_k}\,e_{r_k} \tag{12.6.17}$$

From Eq. 12.6.17 and equations like (12.6.3),

$$_{(k+1)R}U = {}_{kR}U - 2\,_{kL}V_{r_k}\,Z_{r_k}. \tag{12.6.18}$$

Also from Eq. 12.6.13, we have equations of the type

$$_{(k+1)R}V = {}_{kR}V - 2\,_{kR}V_{c_k}\,e_{c_k} \tag{12.6.19}$$

and from Eq. 12.6.19 and equations like (12.6.2),

$$_{(k+1)L}U = {}_{kL}U - 2\,_{kR}V_{c_k}\,Z_{.c_k} \tag{12.6.20}$$

Hence the computational procedure alters progressively and alternately the V and the U vectors until corresponding elements in $_RV$ and $_RU$ have the same signs, and so also for $_LV$ and $_LU$. At this point, β is also a maximum.

12.6.1b   PROOF OF RANK REDUCTION FORM

Let

$$_LU = {}_1Z\,_RV \tag{12.6.21}$$

$$_RU' = {}_LV'\,_1Z \tag{12.6.22}$$

$$\alpha = \sqrt{\frac{n}{{}_LU'_LV}} \tag{12.6.23}$$

$$\beta = {}_RU'_RV \tag{12.6.24}$$

$$\gamma = \frac{1}{\alpha\beta} \tag{12.6.25}$$

$$Y = {}_LU\alpha \tag{12.6.26}$$

$$a = {}_RU\gamma \tag{12.6.27}$$

$$_2Z = {}_1Z - Ya' \tag{12.6.28}$$

From Eqs. 12.6.21–12.6.27 in (12.6.28),

$$_2Z = {}_1Z - {}_1Z\,_RV({}_LV'Z\,_RV)^{-1}\,_LV'\,_1Z \tag{12.6.29}$$

which is a rank reduction form.

12.6.2   The Basic Structure Single Factor Method

12.6.2a   PROOF OF RANK REDUCTION FORM
Let

$$_kV = {}_iZ_{(k-1)}U \qquad (12.6.30)$$

$$_k\alpha = \sqrt{{}_kV'{}_kV} \qquad (12.6.31)$$

$$_kY = \frac{{}_kV}{\alpha} \qquad (12.6.32)$$

$$_kU' = {}_kY'{}_iZ \qquad (12.6.33)$$

$$_{i+1}Z = {}_iZ - {}_kY{}_kU' \qquad (12.6.34)$$

From Eqs. 12.6.32 and 12.6.33,

$$_kY{}_kU' = \frac{{}_kV{}_kY'{}_iZ}{\alpha} \qquad (12.6.35)$$

From Eqs. 12.6.31, 12.6.32, and 12.6.35,

$$_kY{}_kU' = \frac{{}_kV{}_kY'{}_iZ}{{}_kV'{}_kY} \qquad (12.6.36)$$

From Eqs. 12.6.30 and 12.6.36,

$$_kY{}_kU' = {}_iZ_{k-1}U({}_{k-1}U'{}_iZ'{}_iZ_{k-1}U)^{-1}{}_{k-1}U'{}_iZ'{}_iZ \qquad (12.6.37)$$

or dropping the subscripts involving k in Eq. 12.6.37 and substituting in Eq. 12.6.34,

$$_{i+1}Z = {}_iZ - {}_iZU[(U'{}_iZ'){}_iZU]^{-1}(U'{}_iZ'){}_iZ \qquad (12.6.38)$$

which is the matrix reduction form with the arbitrary left and right multipliers, respectively, of $U'{}_iZ'$ and U.

12.6.2b   PROOF OF CONVERGENCE TO BASIC STRUCTURE FORM
Let

$$_1V = Z_0U \qquad (12.6.39)$$

$$_1Y = \frac{{}_1V}{\sqrt{{}_1V'{}_1V}} \qquad (12.6.40)$$

$$_1U' = {}_1Y'Z \qquad (12.6.41)$$

$$_2V = Z_1U \qquad (12.6.42)$$

$$_2Y = \frac{{}_2V}{\sqrt{{}_2V'{}_2V}} \qquad (12.6.43)$$

$$_2U' = {}_2Y'Z \qquad (12.6.44)$$

From Eqs. 12.6.39–12.6.41,

$$_1U = \frac{Z'Z_0U}{\sqrt{_0U'Z'Z_0U}} \tag{12.6.45}$$

From Eqs. 12.6.42–12.6.44,

$$_2U = \frac{Z'Z_1U}{\sqrt{_1U'Z'Z_1U}} \tag{12.6.46}$$

or in general,

$$_{k+1}U = \frac{Z'Z_kU}{\sqrt{_kU'Z'Z_kU}} \tag{12.6.47}$$

Let

$$c = Z'Z \tag{12.6.48}$$

Eq. 12.6.48 in Eq. 12.6.47 gives

$$_{k+1}U = \frac{c_kU}{\sqrt{_kU'c_kU}} \tag{12.6.49}$$

From equations like (12.6.49),

$$_kU = \frac{c^k_0U}{\sqrt{_0U'c^{2k-1}_0U}} \tag{12.6.50}$$

Let

$$c = Q\delta Q' \tag{12.6.51}$$

Then

$$c^k = Q\delta^k Q' \tag{12.6.52}$$

Let

$$Q'_0U = W \tag{12.6.53}$$

From Eqs. 12.6.52 and 12.6.53, in (12.6.50),

$$_kU = \frac{Q\delta^k W}{\sqrt{W'\delta^{2k-1}W}} \tag{12.6.54}$$

From Eq. 12.6.54,

$$\frac{_kU}{\delta_1^{1/2}} = \frac{Q(\delta^k/\delta_1^k)W}{\sqrt{W'(\delta^{2k-1}/\delta_1^{2k-1})W}} \tag{12.6.55}$$

Assume

$$\delta_1 > \delta_{1+i} \tag{12.6.56}$$

Then for k sufficiently large,

$$\frac{\delta_{1+i}^k}{\delta_1^k} W_{1+i} \to 0 \tag{12.6.57}$$

$$\frac{\delta_{1+i}^{\ 2k-1}}{\delta_1^{\ 2k-1}} \, W_{1+i}^{\ 2} \to 0 \tag{12.6.58}$$

and we may write from Eq. 12.6.55,

$$\frac{_kU}{\delta_1^{1/2}} = \frac{Qe_1 W_1}{\sqrt{W_1^{\ 2}}} \tag{12.6.59}$$

or

$$_kU = Q_{.1}\,\delta_1^{1/2} \tag{12.6.60}$$

Let

$$_1Z = P\delta^{1/2}Q' \tag{12.6.61}$$

From equations like (12.6.30), we have

$$_{k+1}V = {}_1Z\,{}_kU \tag{12.6.62}$$

From Eqs. 12.6.60–12.6.62,

$$_{k+1}V = P\delta^{1/2}Q'Q_{.1}\,\delta_1^{1/2} \tag{12.6.63}$$

or

$$_{k+1}V = P_{.1}\,\delta_1 \tag{12.6.64}$$

Assume within specified decimal tolerance that

$$_{k+1}V = {}_kV \tag{12.6.65}$$

From Eqs. 12.6.30, 12.6.31, and 12.6.65,

$$_kY = P_{.1} \tag{12.6.66}$$

From Eqs. 12.6.33, 12.6.60, and 12.6.66,

$$_2Z = P\delta^{1/2}Q' - P_{.1}\,\delta^{1/2}Q_{.1}' \tag{12.6.67}$$

or

$$_{i+1}Z = P_{)i(}\,\delta_{)i(}^{1/2}Q_{)i(}' \tag{12.6.68}$$

where the reverse parentheses mean exclusion of the first i basic orthonormal vectors and basic diagonals.

12.6.3   The Basic Structure Simultaneous Factor Method
Consider

$$_iW = Z_{\,i-1}a \tag{12.6.69}$$

$$_iS = {}_iW'\,{}_iW = {}_it\,{}_it' \tag{12.6.70}$$

$$_iU = Z'\,{}_iW \tag{12.6.71}$$

$$\begin{bmatrix} {}_it \\ {}_ia \end{bmatrix} {}_it' = \begin{bmatrix} {}_iS \\ {}_iU \end{bmatrix} \tag{12.6.72}$$

From Eqs. 12.6.69 and 12.6.70,

$$_iS = {}_{i-1}a'Z'Z_{i-1}a \tag{12.6.73}$$

From Eqs. 12.6.69 and 12.6.71,

$$_iU = Z'Z_{i-1}a \tag{12.6.74}$$

Let

$$Z'Z = R \tag{12.6.75}$$

From Eq. 12.6.75, in Eqs. 12.6.73 and 12.6.74, respectively,

$$_1S = {}_{i-1}a'R_{i-1}a \tag{12.6.76}$$

$$_iU = R_{i-1}a \tag{12.6.77}$$

From Eqs. 12.6.72, 12.6.76, and 12.6.77, it is seen that this method gives the same solution as in Section 3 of Chapter 8. Hence it is both a basic structure and rank reduction solution.

Part IV

Categories, Origin, and Scale

Chapter 13

The Problem of Origin

13.1 Kinds of Origin Problems

In the factor analysis techniques previously discussed, we have expressly or implicitly assumed that we begin with either a correlation matrix or a matrix of standardized measures. In the latter case the means of the columns are 0 and their variances 1.

We have indicated in Chapter 4 that the results of a factor analysis are dependent on the selection of both scale and origin for each of the variables. We have pointed out that for some variables, such as height, weight, time, volume, and many physiological and other variables, there is a natural origin which means that when the value of the variable is 0, none of that attribute exists for a particular entity.

We have also indicated that in psychology and many other disciplines we may have measures in which it is difficult, if not impossible, to specify the true zero point for the particular attribute. For example, in psychological measures the score is frequently the number of items which are answered correctly. If the items are very difficult and are administered to a group of first-grade children, perhaps none of the children will get any of the items correct. If these items are supposed to measure some kind of intelligence, we certainly may not assume that some of the children have no intelligence because they got none of the items correct.

The problem of determining the zero points for a particular group of measures on a number of entities is usually solved by subtracting the mean from each variable, so that the resulting measures indicate the deviation of each of the individuals from the mean of the group.

We also pointed out in Chapter 4 that the scale of one attribute may be quite different from that of another. For example, a difference between a score of 5 and a score of 10 on a test may not be comparable to the difference between scores of 5 and 10 on another test, because the one test may have many more items in it than the other, and the items in the former may be much more or much less difficult.

In this chapter, however, we shall not consider the problem of scaling the variables. It will be recalled that usually they are scaled so that the standard deviations are all equal to 1. The more general problem of scaling and its effect on factor analysis will be considered in Chapter 15. In this chapter we shall be concerned with problems of origin as they relate to factor analysis results.

We have in general three kinds of origin problems for a data matrix of raw measures. The first of these we may call the major transformation problem; the second, the minor transformation problem; the third, the double transformation problem.

13.1.1   The Major Transformation Problem. If we have a vertical data matrix having more entities than attributes, the major transformation procedure consists of premultiplying the raw data matrix on the left by a matrix whose order is equal to the major dimension of the vertical matrix. The typical major transformation procedure for a data matrix consists simply of subtracting the mean of each column vector from every element in the column.

We can see, however, that this amounts to premultiplying the matrix by a special kind of matrix:

$$x = \left(I - \frac{1\,1'}{N} \right) X \tag{13.1.1}$$

Here we use X on the right of the equation to represent the raw score matrix. The x on the left represents the deviation score matrix. The order of the unit vector is N. The matrix in parentheses may be called a centering matrix because its premultiplication into the raw score matrix results in the x matrix whose elements are centered by columns.

It is easy to see from Eq. 13.1.1 that if we premultiply both sides of this equation by the row unit vector, we must get a null row vector. This is because premultiplication of the matrix in parentheses by the unit vector yields the null vector, and therefore the left-hand side of Eq. 13.1.1 must vanish.

We can show very simply that this matrix operation on the raw score matrix is the same as if we had subtracted the mean of each column of the raw score matrix from each element of the corresponding column. We indicate the computation of the vector of column means by

$$M' = \frac{1'\,X}{N} \tag{13.1.2}$$

This is the raw score matrix premultiplied by a row unit vector and divided by the number of rows. This is, of course, the conventional definition of a vector of means.

The subtraction of the mean of each column from each of the elements in that column is indicated by Eq. 13.1.3.

$$x = X - 1M' \tag{13.1.3}$$

It can readily be seen, by multiplying out the right-hand side of Eq. 13.1.1 and using Eq. 13.1.2, that Eq. 13.1.3 results.

It may not always be true, however, that we wish to perform our analysis upon the deviation score matrix indicated in Eq. 13.1.3. Instead of subtracting the mean of each column from the raw score matrix, we may wish to subtract other constants from the columns.

This case is indicated by

$$U = X - 1V' \qquad\qquad (13.1.4)$$

Here we may have a general vector of values V in which each element in the V vector may be different. Some of the elements may be positive and some negative. If we have a set of measures taken from arbitrary origins and if we have a good rationale for determining what the natural origins should be, we may adjust the matrix as in Eq. 13.1.4 so that the attributes of the matrix U on the left may be regarded as being measured from the natural origins of the attributes.

An example of natural origins occurs in learning data. One may, for example, have a group of subjects who are learning a skill such as typewriting. Measures of proficiency for a group of subjects may be taken at weekly intervals. A speed score of 40 words per minute during the third week would be meaningful when compared with a speed score of 60 the fifth week. One may therefore construct a data matrix in which the rows are entities or persons, and the columns are scores made at successive time intervals. To take deviation measures for each of the successive time intervals rather than retain the original measures may lose precisely the information that one is interested in studying.

13.1.2 The Minor Transformation. We may have a type of origin problem less common than the one considered in the previous paragraphs. This may be called a minor transformation. Here the data matrix is multiplied on the right by a centering matrix whose order is the minor order or width of the data matrix. Such a transformation is

$$W = X\left(I - \frac{1\,1'}{n}\right) \qquad\qquad (13.1.5)$$

Here we have the raw score matrix X, postmultiplied by the centering matrix in parentheses. This operation produces the matrix W on the left side of Eq. 13.1.5, whose rows sum to 0. It is easy to see that if we postmultiply both sides of Eq. 13.1.5 by a column unit vector, the result must be a null vector. This is because the centering matrix postmultiplied by the unit vector yields a null vector.

Let us now see what this type of operation means. We indicate a column vector of row means by Eq. 13.1.6. Let

$$m = \frac{X1}{n} \tag{13.1.6}$$

We see that now the mean of each row is subtracted from each element in the corresponding row of the original matrix:

$$W = X - m1' \tag{13.1.7}$$

If we multiply out the right-hand side of Eq. 13.1.5 and substitute from the left of Eq. 13.1.6, we get Eq. 13.1.7.

We may well ask why one should wish to center a matrix on the right in this fashion. One may have reason to believe that only the deviations of scores from a person's own mean are of significance. Certain models used in the measurement of personality traits result in right-centered data matrices.

It may be that instead of subtracting the mean from each row of a data matrix, we wish to subtract some other value. For example, we may have a series of blood pressure readings over a period of time for a number of individuals. It may be thought that the significant measure is not the absolute blood pressure at any interval, but rather its deviation from the blood pressure during a given condition of the individual, such as when he is resting or when he first gets up in the morning.

In this case, then, a different value may be subtracted from each of the row observations for the individuals:

$$W = X - v1' \tag{13.1.8}$$

Here v is a vector which may represent some base state for each of the individuals, and its elements may vary from one individual to the next.

In any case, the results of the factor analysis will be influenced by the right-centering type of operation or the generalization of it indicated in Eq. 13.1.8.

13.1.3 The Double Transformation.

In the previous discussion of the minor transformation we assumed that no major or left transformation had been performed on the data matrix. Perhaps the more common case involving the minor transformation or right-centering of the data matrix occurs when there has previously been a major or left-centering transformation also. It is perhaps most common to center a data matrix on the right after it has been converted to a deviation score matrix whose column means are 0.

The case of the doubly centered matrix is indicated by

$$z = \left(I - \frac{1\,1'}{N} \right) X \left(I - \frac{1\,1'}{n} \right) \tag{13.1.9}$$

Here we have the raw score matrix premultiplied by a centering matrix and postmultiplied by another centering matrix. It must be observed, however, that these are not in general the same centering matrices, since the number of entities is not usually the same as the number of attributes. The number of entities is ordinarily greater than the number of attributes. Then the order of the left-centering matrix will be larger than that of the right-centering matrix. This is indicated by the scalar quantities used to divide the major product moment of the unit vectors in the parentheses. It will be noticed that on the left this is N, indicating the number of cases, and on the right it is n, indicating the number of variables.

Let us now define a matrix or scalar quantity α:

$$\alpha = \tfrac{1}{2}\frac{1'X1}{Nn} \qquad (13.1.10)$$

This, we see, is obtained by taking the sum of all of the elements in the raw score matrix, and dividing it by the product of the number of entities by the number of attributes, and then taking one half this ratio. Obviously then, the value of α is simply one half the average value of all of the elements in the data matrix.

We next define a row vector as:

$$_M V' = M' - \alpha 1' \qquad (13.1.11)$$

We use a prescript M for the V vector, which is simply the M vector of Eq. 13.1.2 from each element of which has been subtracted the scalar α given in Eq. 13.1.10.

We define another V vector with a prescript m:

$$_m V = m - \alpha 1 \qquad (13.1.12)$$

This is obtained by subtracting from each element of the vector of row means defined in Eq. 13.1.6, the α scalar calculated in Eq. 13.1.10.

We now define a z matrix:

$$z = X - 1_M V' - {}_m V 1' \qquad (13.1.13)$$

This is obtained by subtracting from the raw score matrix two major products of vectors. The first of these is the unit vector postmultiplied by the vector calculated in Eq. 13.1.11, and the second is the vector calculated in Eq. 13.1.12, postmultiplied by the unit row vector. It can be proved from Eqs. 13.1.9–13.1.12 that this yields a matrix which is both left- and right-centered. This means that the sums of both rows and columns are 0.

It should be observed that the same results could have been obtained by first performing a left-centering, as in Eq. 13.1.3, and then performing a right-centering on the resulting matrix, as in Eq. 13.1.7. In this case, however, the right-centering would have been performed on the x matrix calculated in Eq. 13.1.3, rather than on the raw score matrix calculated in Eq. 13.1.7.

As in the previous examples, one may also have a more rational basis for subtracting a particular scalar from each element in a column and a particular scalar from each element in a row. This model is now indicated.

$$y = X - 1\,_G V' - \,_G v 1' \tag{13.1.14}$$

Here the V vector and the v vector in the terms on the right side of the equation consist of such elements.

In all of the three cases indicated, if the constants subtracted produce right or left-centering or both, the analysis is somewhat simpler than if general scalars are subtracted, as in Eqs. 13.1.4, 13.1.8 and 13.1.14.

13.2   Ipsative Measures

We shall next consider a special type of data matrix which is a special case of the minor and double transformation types, just considered. These are sometimes called *ipsative measures*.

There is a rather large class of problems in psychology which involves ipsative measures. These measures do not purport to be comparable from one individual to another for a given attribute, but only for different measures of the same individual. That is, the measures indicate the relative order of magnitude of the variable for a particular individual. For that individual the origin of the measures may be quite arbitrary. Measures such as these are known as ipsative, as distinguished from normative measures which do indicate for a particular variable the differences among individuals. This general problem has been extensively treated by Clemans (1956) in a doctoral dissertation.

First we shall consider how in psychology we may obtain matrices of data which are ipsative or which merely indicate from some arbitrary origin for each person his value on each of the variables in the set.

13.2.1   *Definition of Ipsative Measures.*   We begin by giving a more general mathematical definition of ipsative measures than is commonly used. We have seen that by a right-centering type of operation in which the row means are subtracted from each element in a row, we get a matrix the row sums of which are 0. We could now arbitrarily add some constant or scalar to each of the rows of this resulting matrix so that the rows would add up to a constant instead of 0.

Next let us look at the problem in a different way. Suppose that we have a matrix of raw measures obtained in some particular manner, which we shall discuss in more detail later. Suppose, however, that this matrix exhibits the characteristic that the sum of rows all add up to the same constant, say c:

$$X1 = c1 \qquad (13.2.1)$$

This equation indicates that the data matrix postmultiplied by the unit vector is equal to some constant times the unit vector.

Suppose now we perform a left-centering operation on this matrix, which amounts to putting it in deviation form by columns so that the sums of all columns are 0.

$$x = \left(I - \frac{1\,1'}{N}\right)X \qquad (13.2.2)$$

Recall that this operation simply subtracts the mean of each column from each element in that column.

We now prove that the resulting matrix x has the properties of a right-centered matrix:

$$x1 = 0 \qquad (13.2.3)$$

This means that the sums of rows of the resulting matrix are all 0.

The proof is as follows. From Eq. 13.2.2, we can write

$$x1 = X1 - \frac{1(1'X1)}{N} \qquad (13.2.4)$$

Here we simply expand the right side of Eq. 13.2.2.

Because of Eq. 13.2.1, we can write

$$1'X1 = c1'1 = cN \qquad (13.2.5)$$

This means that the sum of the elements in the X matrix is the constant c times the number of entities N.

If we substitute Eqs. 13.2.1 and 13.2.5 in Eq. 13.2.4, we get

$$x1 = c1 - c1 = 0 \qquad (13.2.6)$$

This proves that the sums of rows are 0 for the matrix in Eq. 13.2.2.

To state the case simply, if we have a matrix whose row elements add up to the same constant and we perform a left-centering operation on this matrix, the resulting matrix is such that its row elements also add up to 0. While many of the matrices we deal with in psychology are not directly of the right-centered type whose rows add up to 0, nevertheless, when they are left-centered or put in deviation form, the rows are also in deviation form or have the property of right-centered matrices.

13.2.2   Sources of Ipsative Measures.   We shall now consider a number of different ways in which ipsative matrices can arise. We shall use the term ipsative to cover any set of measures with entity rows and column attributes such that the row sums add up to the same constant, whether this constant is 0 or different from 0.

One type of model which involves the ipsative matrix is the differential prediction model. In this model we attempt to predict in which of a number of activity variables a person would be most likely to be superior. The question, however, is not what his score or performance would be in each of the criterion variables as compared with other persons in the sample, but how good he would be in each criterion measure relative to his performance in each of the other criteria.

It can be shown in methods developed by Horst (1954) that a solution of such a problem results from the following operations. We require a matrix of intercorrelations of predictor with criterion variables. This may or may not be a matrix on which the correlations for all pairs of variables are based on all the cases. Usually it will not be, as we have seen in Chapter 11. In any case, suppose we have such a correlation matrix in which the rows are correlations of a given predictor variable with all the criterion variables or in which a column is the correlation of a given criterion variable with all the predictor variables. If we take such a matrix and perform a right-centering operation upon it, we then have a resulting matrix whose rows add up to 0. By means of methods which are beyond the scope of this text, we then use this right-centered matrix, together with other data, to derive a matrix of prediction weights to apply to the predictor variables, so as to give the best differential prediction of success in the criterion variables.

Another source of ipsative measures comes from what is known as the forced choice type of psychological inventory. Here the subject is presented with pairs or groups of items. He is instructed to indicate which of these is most like him, which he most agrees with, or some other instruction which requires him to mark only one of each pair or group. If these scales are properly constructed, they have the advantage that the subject is choosing among the two or more items on the basis of two or more different traits, rather than on the basis of some single dimension, such as social desirability. Examples of such inventories are the Edwards Personal Preference Schedule and the Kuder Preference Record.

One of the characteristics of these measures is that normally the items are paired or grouped in such a fashion that the total of each person's score on each scale is a constant. That is, if the inventory is scored, say, for 15 different traits or measures, the sum of each person's measures will add up to the same constant. This means, then, that if a set of measures is transformed to deviation measures by a left-centering operation, the sum of rows of the resulting matrix will be 0.

Another source of ipsatized measures may occur when it is desired to determine experimentally the properties of ipsative, as distinguished from normative, measures. Wright (1957) administered the Edwards Personal Preference Schedule to a group of individuals. The items in the schedule were also prepared in a rating scale format so that each item was presented singly, and the same subjects were requested to respond on a rating scale which indicated the extent to which the item applied to them. It was then possible to get a score for each of the traits presumably measured by the scale by means of an appropriate scoring key. The problem was to see how the results of this kind of format compared with those of the forced choice, after the rating scale measures had been ipsatized by means of a right-centering operation.

Another type of ipsatization seems to occur, in part, with self-appraisal inventories of the interest, personality, and temperament type, even though the items are not in paired or forced choice format. There is evidence to indicate that if a person is presented with a set of items or statements in which he is asked to indicate how well each statement applies to him, he engages in a sort of self-ipsatizing operation. In other words, he tends to adopt some sort of an average of all of the items as they apply to him, and then indicate which of the items is above and which below his own average for all of the items in the set. There seems to be a tendency to adjust oneself to the particular set in a relative rather than an absolute sense. This appears to be a special case of a general phenomenon in which it is easier to make comparative judgments rather than absolute judgments.

In any case, factor analyses of items of this kind seem to give results which indicate that a sort of partial ipsatization has been taking place, even though not a complete right-centering type of operation.

13.2.3   Characteristics of Ipsative Matrices.

The effect of either right or left-centering of a matrix on the rank of this matrix is of considerable importance. It is especially so when ipsative measures are used as predictor variables. If, as is usually the case, there are more entities than attributes, then the ipsative matrix, after left-centering or conversion to deviation form, is reduced to a rank one less than its width.

This can be seen from Eq. 13.1.5. We learned in Chapter 3 that the product of any two matrices cannot be greater than the rank of the factor of smaller rank. If the matrix in Eq. 13.1.5 is vertical, the right-centering matrix in parentheses will be of the same order as the width of the data matrix. Its rank, however, will be one less than its order; otherwise, it would not be orthogonal to the unit vector. It can also be proved that it is of rank only one less by showing that it cannot be orthogonal to any other than the unit vector.

As already indicated, ipsative measures, whether derived from experimental or from computational procedures, cannot be normative in the sense that one person can be compared with another with respect to a single variable. This is, of course, because some arbitrary constant has been added or subtracted from all scores of each subject measured. Since this is not in general the same constant for all subjects, the resulting measures are not comparable from one subject to another. This limitation of ipsative measures is often overlooked. Frequently, persons are erroneously compared with one another with respect to ipsative measures.

13.3 Basic Structure and the Problem of Origin

We have indicated in Section 13.1 that in general the factor analytic results will vary for a given data matrix according to what is done about the problem of origin. The importance of this is not as widely recognized as it should be. We shall therefore examine the effect of row and column origin transformations on the basic structure characteristics of the data matrix.

In the following discussion, we shall not be concerned with whether the scale units are the same for each of the variables in the set. We shall assume for the time being that some sort of rational or natural scaling is available or that the variables have been scaled in terms of standard deviation or equal variance units. The problem of scale will be considered in more detail in Chapter 15, even though the influence of scaling on basic structure is currently not well understood.

In the following sections we shall consider four cases. The first of these assumes that we have a left-centered matrix in equal standard deviation units and that we have already available the basic structure solution for the corresponding correlation or normative covariance matrix. On the basis of this solution we wish to determine the basic structure of the raw covariance matrix, that is, the covariance matrix of the data matrix prior to left-centering.

The second case assumes that we have the basic structure factors of the covariance matrix prior to left-centering, and we wish to find the basic structure matrices of the correlation matrix as functions of the basic structure factors of the raw covariance matrix.

The third case assumes that the deviation or normative data matrix has also been centered on the right. We shall investigate the basic structure of the minor product moment ipsative covariance matrix of this ipsative data matrix as a function of the basic structure factors of the correlation or normative covariance matrix.

In the fourth case we have the basic structure of the covariance matrix obtained from the ipsative data matrix, and from this we wish to calculate the basic structure of the correlation or normative covariance matrix.

We shall now consider some relationships among the four types of covariance matrices.

13.4   Basic Structure of Raw Covariance Matrix from Correlation Matrix

13.4.1   Computational Equations

13.4.1a   DEFINITION OF NOTATION

X is the raw score matrix.

x is the deviation score matrix.

M' is the vector of means.

C is the normative covariance matrix.

G is the raw covariance matrix.

Q is the basic orthonormal of C.

H is the basic orthonormal of G.

δ is the basic diagonal of C.

ϕ is the basic diagonal of G.

13.4.1b   THE EQUATIONS

$$x = \left(1 - \frac{1\,1'}{N}\right) X \tag{13.4.1}$$

$$x = P\Delta Q' \tag{13.4.2}$$

$$M' = \frac{1'X}{N} \tag{13.4.3}$$

$$C = x'x = Q\delta Q' \tag{13.4.4}$$

$$G = X'X = H\phi H' \tag{13.4.5}$$

$$v = Q'M \tag{13.4.6}$$

If $L = 1$,

$$_1 Y_L = v'v + \delta_1 \tag{13.4.7}$$

$$_1 y_L = \delta_1 \tag{13.4.8}$$

If $L > 1$,

$$_1 Y_L = \delta_{L-1} \tag{13.4.9}$$

$$_1 y_L = \delta_L \tag{13.4.10}$$

$$_k Z_L = \frac{_k Y_L + {_k}y_L}{2} \tag{13.4.11}$$

$$_k F_L = \sum_{i=1}^{n} \frac{v_i^2}{\delta_i - {_k}Z_L} + 1 \tag{13.4.12}$$

If $|_k F_L| - P < 0$,

$$\phi_L = {_k}Z_L \tag{13.4.13}$$

If $_kF_L < 0$,

$$_{k+1}y_L = {_k}Z_L \qquad (13.4.14)$$

$$_{k+1}Y_L = {_k}Y_L \qquad (13.4.15)$$

If $_kF_L > 0$,

$$_{k+1}Y_L = {_k}Z_L \qquad (13.4.16)$$

$$_{k+1}y_L = {_k}y_L \qquad (13.4.17)$$

$$f_{.i} = (\delta - \phi_i I)^{-1}v \qquad (13.4.18)$$

$$H = Q(fD_{f'f}^{-1/2}) \qquad (13.4.19)$$

$$a_G = H\phi^{1/2} \qquad (13.4.20)$$

13.4.2 Computational Instructions. We begin with a score matrix X, and for the sake of simplicity we assume that the attributes all have unit standard deviations. We then apply a left-centering matrix as in Eq. 13.4.1. This, as we know, simply subtracts the mean of each of the attributes from every element in that vector.

Next we indicate the basic structure of this standard score matrix x, as in Eq. 13.4.2. The right-hand side is the product, from left to right, of the left orthonormal by the basic diagonal by the right orthonormal.

The means of the columns of the X matrix are indicated in Eq. 13.4.3. This is simply a row vector of the means of the variables.

The covariance minor product moment of the matrix in Eq. 13.4.2 is given by Eq. 13.4.4. Obviously, the left basic orthonormal disappears and the diagonal δ is the square of Δ in Eq. 13.4.2.

Equation 13.4.5 is not a computational equation but is given to indicate the minor product moment of X in terms of its basic structure. The basic orthonormals are H and H', respectively, and the basic diagonal is ϕ. We assume that the Q and the δ matrices in Eq. 13.4.4 have been calculated according to one of the basic structure methods of factor analysis indicated in previous chapters. The problem now is to find the basic structure factors of the G matrix as a function of the known basic structure factors.

First, we calculate the v vector as in Eq. 13.4.6. This vector is the transpose of the Q matrix calculated in Eq. 13.4.4, postmultiplied by the vector of means calculated in Eq. 13.4.3.

To solve for the ϕ_L elements of ϕ we proceed as follows.

If $L = 1$ we calculate a scalar $_1Y_1$ as the sum of the minor product moment of v in Eq. 13.4.6 and the first element of δ, namely, δ_1, as shown in Eq. 13.4.7.

We then set a scalar $_1y_L$ equal to δ_1 as indicated in Eq. 13.4.8.

If L is greater than 1, we set $_1Y_L$ equal to δ_{L-1}, as in Eq. 13.4.9, and we set $_1y_L$ equal to δ_L, as shown in Eq. 13.4.10.

In any case, as shown in Eq. 13.4.11, we set a scalar $_kZ_L$ equal to the average of $_kY_L$ and $_ky_L$, where the latter two are determined iteratively, as we shall show shortly, for k going from 1 to some prespecified iteration limit.

We substitute $_kZ_L$ given by Eq. 13.4.11 in Eq. 13.4.12 to get $_kF_L$.

If $_kF_L$ is sufficiently close to 0, as indicated by some tolerance limit P, we take $_kZ_L$ as the value of ϕ_L, as shown in Eq. 13.4.13.

If $_kF_L$ is negative, we set a new y equal to $_kZ_L$ and the new Y will be the same as the previous one, as shown in Eqs. 13.4.14 and 13.4.15.

If $_kF_L$ is positive, we set the new Y equal to the current Z and the new y is the same as the previous one, as shown in Eqs. 13.4.16 and 13.4.17.

Once all of the ϕ's have been solved for, we solve for vectors which are proportional to the vectors of H given in Eq. 13.4.5 by means of Eq. 13.4.18. This gives the solution for the ith column of an f matrix. As will be seen on the right of this equation, the v vector defined by Eq. 13.4.6 is premultiplied by the inverse of a diagonal matrix. This diagonal matrix for the ith column of the f matrix is obtained by subtracting from the δ matrix of Eq. 13.4.4 the ϕ_i already solved for.

The f vector solved for in Eq. 13.4.18 is then normalized, as indicated by the product in parentheses on the right of Eq. 13.4.19. In addition, the normalized f matrix must also be premultiplied by the Q matrix solved for in Eq. 13.4.4 to yield the H matrix of Eq. 13.4.19.

To get the principal axis factor loading matrix for the G matrix in Eq. 13.4.5, the H matrix calculated in Eq. 13.4.19 must be postmultiplied by the square root of the diagonal matrix of ϕ values. This is indicated in Eq. 13.4.20.

13.4.3   Numerical Example

In this example we shall use the same correlation matrix as in previous chapters. The vector of means used to generate the raw covariance matrix is given in Table 13.4.1.

We shall present the three covariance matrices—raw, normative and ipsative as well as their basic structures. The ipsatizing vector in the last two examples was taken as the unit vector divided by $\sqrt{n}$.

Table 13.4.2 gives the raw covariance matrix G which was obtained by adding the major product moment of the vector in Table 13.4.1 to the correlation matrix.

The first row of Table 13.4.3 gives the basic diagonal elements ϕ of the raw covariance matrix. The body of the table gives the basic orthonormal H of the raw covariance matrix in Table 13.4.2. These were calculated from G by a method in Chapter 9, as were also Tables 13.4.5 and 13.4.7.

Table 13.4.4 repeats for convenient reference the correlation matrix R.

The first row of Table 13.4.5 gives the basic diagonal elements δ of the correlation matrix R. The body of the table gives the basic orthonormal matrix Q of R.

TABLE 13.4.1 Vector of Means of Data Matrix

-0.4	-0.3	-0.2	-0.1	-0.0	0.1	0.2	0.3	0.4

TABLE 13.4.2 Raw Covariance Matrix G

-0.4	-0.3	-0.2	-0.1	-0.0	0.1	0.2	0.3	0.4
1.16000	0.94900	0.84800	0.14800	0.03300	0.06800	0.21800	0.18900	0.19100
0.94900	1.09000	0.83500	0.14500	0.06100	0.09500	0.26300	0.25700	0.24900
0.84800	0.83500	1.04000	0.29200	0.20500	0.21800	0.25600	0.21100	0.30500
0.14800	0.14500	0.29200	1.01000	0.63600	0.61600	0.22900	0.15300	0.32900
0.03300	0.06100	0.20500	0.63600	1.00000	0.70900	0.13800	0.09100	0.25400
0.06800	0.09500	0.21800	0.61600	0.70900	1.01000	0.21000	0.13300	0.33100
0.21800	0.26300	0.25600	0.22900	0.13800	0.21000	1.04000	0.71400	0.60700
0.18900	0.25700	0.21100	0.15300	0.09100	0.13300	0.71400	1.09000	0.66100
0.19100	0.24900	0.30500	0.32900	0.25400	0.33100	0.60700	0.66100	1.16000

TABLE 13.4.3 Basic Diagonals ϕ and Basic Orthonormal H of Raw Covariance Matrix

3.75072	2.18721	1.72066	0.50400	0.40746	0.34773	0.28544	0.22741	0.16937
0.37762	0.45666	0.17015	0.04074	0.00506	0.00084	0.11851	-0.45801	-0.62802
0.38813	0.41650	0.12300	0.02755	0.10607	0.06037	0.05831	-0.24569	0.76246
0.40369	0.29841	0.19922	-0.08977	-0.03480	-0.04380	-0.21507	0.79846	-0.11536
0.28681	-0.34966	0.29652	0.09157	-0.80422	0.10769	0.18423	-0.04775	0.06773
0.23789	-0.41259	0.35441	0.10045	0.29603	0.24950	-0.66799	-0.20104	-0.03115
0.26485	-0.40862	0.30373	0.02755	0.48419	-0.24399	0.60225	0.11329	-0.01920
0.32623	-0.12108	-0.44122	0.49806	-0.06532	-0.61914	-0.21504	-0.04648	0.01284
0.31173	-0.10407	-0.52983	0.26521	0.11557	0.68133	0.20372	0.13054	-0.06949
0.36221	-0.20973	-0.36750	-0.80740	-0.03244	-0.11623	-0.07552	-0.13262	-0.00460

TABLE 13.4.4 Normative Covariance or Correlation Matrix R

1.00000	0.82900	0.76800	0.10800	0.03300	0.10800	0.29800	0.30900	0.35100
0.82900	1.00000	0.77500	0.11500	0.06100	0.12500	0.32300	0.34700	0.36900
0.76800	0.77500	1.00000	0.27200	0.20500	0.23800	0.29600	0.27100	0.38500
0.10800	0.11500	0.27200	1.00000	0.63600	0.62600	0.24900	0.18300	0.36900
0.03300	0.06100	0.20500	0.63600	1.00000	0.70900	0.13800	0.09100	0.25400
0.10800	0.12500	0.23800	0.62600	0.70900	1.00000	0.19000	0.10300	0.29100
0.29800	0.32300	0.29600	0.24900	0.13800	0.19000	1.00000	0.65400	0.52700
0.30900	0.34700	0.27100	0.18300	0.09100	0.10300	0.65400	1.00000	0.54100
0.35100	0.36900	0.38500	0.36900	0.25400	0.29100	0.52700	0.54100	1.00000

TABLE 13.4.5   Basic Diagonals δ and Basic Orthonormal Q of Correlation Matrix

3.74907	2.04953	1.33079	0.47442	0.38261	0.34740	0.28533	0.21215	0.16870
0.37009	0.34414	−0.30364	0.04349	0.01542	0.00399	−0.12630	−0.44249	−0.66221
0.38211	0.33393	−0.27878	0.08123	0.07647	−0.05713	−0.06068	−0.31066	0.74085
0.39915	0.20657	−0.35222	−0.01294	−0.14028	0.02245	0.23294	0.77085	−0.07157
0.28690	−0.45323	−0.05853	−0.14862	−0.78182	−0.15550	−0.17400	−0.13710	0.04754
0.23932	−0.51976	−0.15671	0.16644	0.29930	−0.22904	0.66174	−0.19627	−0.04304
0.26733	−0.48451	−0.16335	0.18680	0.40810	0.26448	−0.60582	0.16939	−0.00176
0.33081	0.05559	0.50930	0.41816	−0.18573	0.60692	0.21552	−0.06236	0.00760
0.31760	0.11592	0.53843	0.23892	0.11339	−0.67780	−0.20136	0.15045	−0.05702
0.36926	−0.02350	0.31947	−0.82141	0.24394	0.14790	0.06259	−0.03072	0.00889

TABLE 13.4.6   Ipsative Covariance Matrix ρ

0.56570	0.37915	0.28859	−0.29896	−0.32607	−0.28030	−0.12196	−0.09141	−0.11474
0.37915	0.53459	0.28004	−0.30752	−0.31363	−0.27885	−0.11252	−0.06896	−0.11230
0.28859	0.28004	0.47548	−0.18007	−0.19919	−0.19541	−0.16907	−0.17452	−0.12585
−0.29896	−0.30752	−0.18007	0.62037	0.30426	0.26504	−0.14363	−0.19007	−0.06941
−0.32607	−0.31363	−0.19919	0.30426	0.71615	0.39593	−0.20674	−0.23419	−0.13652
−0.28030	−0.27885	−0.19541	0.26504	0.39593	0.65770	−0.18396	−0.25141	−0.12874
−0.12196	−0.11252	−0.16907	−0.14363	−0.20674	−0.18396	0.59437	0.26793	0.07559
−0.09141	−0.06896	−0.17452	−0.19007	−0.23419	−0.25141	0.26793	0.63348	0.10915
−0.11474	−0.11230	−0.12585	−0.06941	−0.13652	−0.12874	0.07559	0.10915	0.50281

TABLE 13.4.7 Basic Diagonals d and Basic Orthonormal q of Ipsative Covariance Matrix ρ

2.08395	1.33155	0.48297	0.38347	0.34929	0.28534	0.21507	0.16904	−0.00000
−0.39228	0.30627	−0.04279	−0.01569	0.00150	−0.12549	0.44869	−0.64965	0.33334
−0.38541	0.28215	−0.07309	−0.07283	−0.04748	−0.06101	0.28349	0.75083	0.33334
−0.26670	0.35823	0.04678	0.15209	0.03581	0.23107	−0.77588	−0.08622	0.33334
0.40533	0.06788	0.18405	0.77628	−0.18170	−0.17375	0.13256	0.05212	0.33333
0.48304	0.16394	−0.16644	−0.29888	−0.20860	0.66065	0.17497	−0.03241	0.33334
0.44111	0.17168	−0.16513	−0.38436	0.29794	−0.60680	−0.18124	−0.00148	0.33334
−0.09835	−0.50431	−0.37720	0.22433	0.61827	0.21600	0.05703	0.01119	0.33333
−0.15311	−0.53508	−0.24311	−0.12428	−0.65532	−0.20398	−0.17536	−0.05301	0.33328
−0.03365	−0.31090	0.83691	−0.25666	0.13948	0.06331	0.03572	0.00862	0.33333

TABLE 13.4.8 Basic Diagonal Elements ϕ and Basic Orthonormal H' as Determined from Basic Structure of R

3.75072	2.18720	1.72065	0.50401	0.40746	0.34773	0.28544	0.22742	0.16938
0.3776	0.3882	0.4037	0.2868	0.2380	0.2648	0.3262	0.3117	0.3622
0.4566	0.4165	0.2984	−0.3497	−0.4127	−0.4086	−0.1211	−0.1041	−0.2097
0.1701	0.1230	0.1992	0.2965	0.3544	0.3037	−0.4412	−0.5298	−0.3675
0.0408	0.0276	−0.0897	0.0915	0.1005	0.0275	0.4980	0.2652	−0.8074
−0.0050	−0.1061	0.0348	0.8042	−0.2960	−0.4842	0.0653	−0.1156	0.0325
0.0008	0.0604	−0.0438	0.1077	0.2495	−0.2440	−0.6192	0.6813	−0.1162
−0.1185	−0.0584	0.2151	−0.1843	0.6679	−0.6023	0.2150	−0.2037	0.0755
0.4580	0.2457	−0.7984	0.0477	0.2011	−0.1133	0.0465	−0.1306	0.1326
0.6281	−0.7624	0.1153	−0.0677	0.0312	0.0192	−0.0129	0.0695	0.0046

Table 13.4.6 gives the ipsative covariance matrix calculated from the correlation matrix by the equation $\rho = [I - (1\ 1'/n)]R[I - ((1\ 1'/n)]$.

The first row of Table 13.4.7 gives the basic diagonal elements of the ipsative correlation matrix ρ. The body of the table gives the basic orthonormal matrix q of ρ.

The first row of Table 13.4.8 gives the basic diagonal elements ϕ of the raw covariance matrix as calculated by Eqs. 13.4.7–13.4.17. The body of the table gives the basic orthonormal H' as calculated from Eqs. 13.4.18 and 13.4.19. Note that this matrix is the transpose of the one in Table 13.4.3. The values in the two tables agree within limits of decimal accuracy.

13.5 The Normative Covariance Basic Structure from the Raw Covariance Basic Structure

13.5.1 Computational Equations

13.5.1a DEFINITION OF NOTATION
The notation is the same as in the previous section.

13.5.1b THE EQUATIONS

$$V = H'M \tag{13.5.1}$$

$$_1Y_n = \phi_n \tag{13.5.2}$$

$$_1y_n = 0 \tag{13.5.3}$$

$$_1Y_L = \phi_L \tag{13.5.4}$$

$$_1y_L = \phi_{L+1} \tag{13.5.5}$$

$$_kZ_L = \frac{_kY_L + _ky_L}{2} \tag{13.5.6}$$

$$_kF_L = \sum_{i=1}^{n} \frac{V_i^2}{\phi_i - _kZ_L} - 1 \tag{13.5.7}$$

$$W_{.L} = H(\phi - \delta_L I)^{-1} V \tag{13.5.8}$$

$$Q_{.L} = \frac{W_{.L}}{\sqrt{W_{.L}' W_{.L}}} \tag{13.5.9}$$

13.5.2 Computational Instructions
First we calculate the vector V of Eq. 13.5.1. This is the vector of means premultiplied by the right orthonormal of the raw covariance matrix G.

Equations 13.5.2 and 13.5.3 give the limits of the normative basic diagonal

TABLE 13.5.1 Basic Diagonals δ and Basic Orthonormal Q' as Determined from G

3.74907	2.04952	1.33077	0.47442	0.38262	0.34740	0.28533	0.21215	0.16871
-0.3701	-0.3821	-0.3991	-0.2869	-0.2392	-0.2674	-0.3308	-0.3176	-0.3693
-0.3442	-0.3339	-0.2066	0.4532	0.5197	0.4846	-0.0556	-0.1159	0.0235
-0.3037	-0.2787	-0.3522	-0.0586	-0.1567	-0.1633	0.5093	0.5384	0.3195
-0.0435	-0.0812	0.0129	0.1486	-0.1664	-0.1868	-0.4182	-0.2389	0.8214
0.0154	0.0765	-0.1403	-0.7818	0.2993	0.4081	-0.1858	0.1134	0.2440
0.0039	-0.0571	0.0224	-0.1555	-0.2291	0.2644	0.6069	-0.6778	0.1479
0.1263	0.0606	-0.2329	0.1739	-0.6618	0.6058	-0.2156	0.2013	-0.0626
-0.4425	-0.3106	0.7709	-0.1371	-0.1962	0.1693	-0.0623	0.1504	-0.0307
-0.6622	0.7409	-0.0715	0.0476	-0.0431	-0.0017	0.0075	-0.0570	0.0089

δ_n. Equations 13.5.4 and 13.5.5 give the limits of the normative basic diagonals for δ_L where L is less than n.

Equation 13.5.6 gives the kth approximation to the Lth basic diagonal δ_L.

To solve for the Lth basic diagonal of $_1\delta_L$, we use Eq. 13.5.7 iteratively, as we used Eq. 13.4.12 to solve for ϕ_L. We note, however, that the last term on the right in Eq. 13.4.12 is $+1$, whereas it is -1 for Eq. 13.5.7.

Having solved for the δ's, we substitute these in Eq. 13.5.8 to solve for a vector proportional to the Lth vector of Q, the basic orthonormal of the correlation or normative covariance matrix.

Equation 13.5.9 shows the normalization of the $W_{.L}$ vector of Eq. 13.5.8 to give the Lth vector of Q.

13.5.3   Numerical Example

The first row of Table 13.5.1 gives the basic diagonal elements δ of the correlation matrix R as calculated by Eqs. 13.5.1–13.5.7. The body of the table gives the basic orthonormal Q' of R as calculated by Eqs. 13.5.8 and 13.5.9. Note that this matrix is the transpose of the one in Table 13.4.5. The values in the two tables agree within limits of decimal accuracy.

13.6   The Ipsative Covariance Basic Structure from the Normative Covariance Basic Structure

13.6.1   Computational Equations

13.6.1a   DEFINITION OF NOTATION

R is the normative covariance matrix.

Q is the basic orthonormal of R.

δ is the basic diagonal of R.

ρ is the ipsative covariance matrix.

q is the basic orthonormal of ρ.

d is the basic diagonal of ρ.

V is a normal vector whose order is the same as R.

The relation between ρ and R is given by $\rho = (I - VV')R(I - VV')$.

13.6.1b   THE EQUATIONS

$$U = Q'V \tag{13.6.1}$$

$$W = \delta^{1/2}U \tag{13.6.2}$$

$$_1Y_n = \delta_n \tag{13.6.3}$$

$$_1y_n = 0 \tag{13.6.4}$$

$$_1Y_L = \delta_L \tag{13.6.5}$$

TABLE 13.6.1   Basic Diagonals d and Basic Orthonormal q' as Determined from Basic Structure of R

2.08395	1.33155	0.48296	0.38347	0.34928	0.28534	0.21506	0.16903	0.00002
0.3923	0.3854	0.2667	−0.4053	−0.4830	−0.4411	0.0983	0.1531	0.0336
0.3062	0.2821	0.3583	0.0679	0.1640	0.1717	−0.5043	−0.5351	−0.3109
−0.0428	−0.0731	0.0468	0.1841	−0.1664	−0.1651	−0.3772	−0.2431	0.8369
−0.0157	−0.0728	0.1521	0.7763	−0.2988	−0.3844	0.2243	−0.1243	−0.2567
0.0015	−0.0475	0.0359	−0.1817	−0.2085	0.2979	0.6183	−0.6553	0.1395
0.1255	0.0611	−0.2310	0.1738	−0.6606	0.6069	−0.2160	0.2041	−0.0633
−0.4487	−0.2835	0.7758	−0.1325	−0.1750	0.1813	−0.0570	0.1754	−0.0357
−0.6496	0.7508	−0.0862	0.0521	−0.0324	−0.0015	0.0112	−0.0530	0.0086
0.5171	0.2582	−0.0732	0.2448	0.5206	0.2746	0.2746	0.4190	0.0571

$$_1 y_L = \delta_{L+1} \tag{13.6.6}$$

$$_k Z_L = \frac{_k Y_L + _k y_L}{2} \tag{13.6.7}$$

$$_k F_L = \sum_{i=1}^{n} \frac{W_L{}^2}{\delta_i - _k Z_L} - 1 \tag{13.6.8}$$

$$q._L = Q(\delta - d_L I)^{-1} U g \tag{13.6.9}$$

13.6.2 Computational Instructions

Equation 13.6.1 defines a vector U which is the product of the right ortho-normal matrix of R postmultiplied by the ipsatizing vector V.

Equation 13.6.2 defines a vector W which is the product of the U vector in Eq. 13.6.1 premultiplied by the square root of the basic diagonal of R.

Equations 13.6.3–13.6.6 give the first approximations to the limits of the basic diagonals of ρ, the ipsatized covariance matrix.

Equation 13.6.7 gives the kth approximation to the Lth basic diagonal of ρ.

The iteration procedure for getting successively smaller bounds for the d's is the same as in the two previous methods, except that now Eq. 13.6.8 is the iteration equation. It is of the same form as in the previous two methods. In this case the 1 is subtracted on the right as in Eq. 13.5.7.

Equation 13.6.9 gives the calculations for the $q._L$ vectors of the basic orthonormal q of ρ. The factor g on the extreme right is a normalizing scalar.

13.6.3 Numerical Example

The first row of Table 13.6.1 gives the basic diagonal elements d of the ipsative matrix ρ as calculated from Eqs. 13.6.1–13.6.8. The body of the table gives the basic orthonormal q' of ρ as calculated from Eq. 13.6.9. Note that this matrix is the transpose of the one in Table 13.4.7. The values in both tables agree within limits of decimal accuracy, except for the last line of Table 13.6.1. This discrepancy is due to the error in the last basic diagonal which should be 0 instead of .00002.

13.7 The Normative Covariance Basic Structure from the Ipsative Basic Structure

13.7.1 Computational Equations

13.7.1a DEFINITION OF NOTATION

The notation is the same as in Section 13.6.1.

13.7.1b THE EQUATIONS

$$U = RV \tag{13.7.1}$$

$$W = q'U \tag{13.7.2}$$

$$\alpha = V'U \tag{13.7.3}$$

$$_1Y_1 = \frac{d_1 + n}{2} \tag{13.7.4}$$

$$_1y_1 = d_1 \tag{13.7.5}$$

$$_1Y_L = d_{L-1} \tag{13.7.6}$$

$$_1y_L = d_L \tag{13.7.7}$$

$$_kZ_L = \frac{_kY_L + _ky_L}{2} \tag{13.7.8}$$

$$_kF_L = \sum_{L=1}^{n-1} \frac{W_L{}^2}{d_L - {}_kZ_L} + {}_kZ_L - \alpha \tag{13.7.9}$$

$$Q._L = [V - q(d - \delta_L I)^{-1} W]g_L \tag{13.7.10}$$

13.7.2 Computational Instructions

Equation 13.7.1 gives a vector U as the product of the normative covariance matrix postmultiplied by the ipsatizing vector V. If one has only the ρ matrix to begin with as in the case of ipsative personality measures, then one may be able to hypothesize a U vector, for the computational procedure requires only the U vector and not the R matrix as such.

Equation 13.7.2 gives a W vector as the product of the right orthonormal q' of ρ and the U vector of Eq. 13.7.1.

The next step is the calculation of the scalar α in Eq. 13.7.3. This is the minor product of the U and V vectors.

The outer limits of the first basic diagonal of R, namely, δ_1, are given by Eqs. 13.7.4 and 13.7.5. The $_1Y_1$ value assumes that the normative matrix is actually a correlation matrix so that its trace is n, the order of the matrix. It is well known that this trace is the sum of the basic diagonals, hence, δ_1 must be less than n.

Equations 13.7.6 and 13.7.7 give the outer limits of the remaining δ_L values.

As in the solutions of the previous sections, the kth approximation to δ_L is given by $_kZ_L$ in Eq. 13.7.8.

Equation 13.7.9 gives the iteration equation for the δ_L values. The same procedure is used for narrowing the limits of the δ_L's as in the previous sections.

TABLE 13.7.1 Basic Diagonals δ and Basic Orthonormal Q' as Determined from Basic Structure of ρ and from RV

3.74906	2.04952	1.33080	0.47443	0.38261	0.34741	0.28533	0.21215	0.16870
0.3701	0.3821	0.3991	0.2869	0.2392	0.2673	0.3308	0.3177	0.3693
−0.3442	−0.3340	−0.2066	0.4532	0.5197	0.4845	−0.0556	−0.1159	0.0235
−0.3037	−0.2788	−0.3521	−0.0585	−0.1567	−0.1633	0.5093	0.5385	0.3195
0.0435	0.0812	−0.0129	−0.1486	0.1665	0.1868	0.4181	0.2390	−0.8214
0.0154	0.0765	−0.1403	−0.7818	0.2993	0.4081	−0.1858	0.1134	0.2439
−0.0039	0.0572	−0.0224	0.1555	0.2291	−0.2644	−0.6069	0.6778	−0.1479
−0.1263	−0.0606	0.2330	−0.1740	0.6618	−0.6058	0.2156	−0.2014	0.0626
0.4425	0.3106	−0.7709	0.1371	0.1963	−0.1694	0.0624	−0.1504	0.0307
0.6622	−0.7408	0.0716	−0.0476	0.0431	0.0018	−0.0076	0.0570	−0.0089

It is to be noted, however, that the summation goes only to $n-1$. This equation also differs from the corresponding equation of previous sections in that the right-hand side includes the Z and α terms instead of 1.

Equation 13.7.10 shows the calculations for the $Q_{.L}$ vectors of the basic orthonormal of R. The g_L on the extreme right is a normalizing scalar.

13.7.3   Numerical Example

The first row of Table 13.7.1 gives the basic diagonal elements δ of the correlation matrix R, as calculated from Eqs. 13.7.1–13.7.9. The body of the table gives the basic orthonormal Q' of R as calculated from Eq. 13.7.10. Note that this matrix is the transpose of the one in Table 13.4.5. The values in the two tables agree within limits of decimal accuracy.

13.8   Mathematical Proofs

13.8.1   Basic Structure and Left-Centering

Given the matrix

$$x = \left(I - \frac{1\,1'}{N}\right)X \tag{13.8.1}$$

and

$$x = P\Delta Q' \tag{13.8.2}$$

$$M' = \frac{1'X}{N} \tag{13.8.3}$$

From Eqs. 13.8.1 and 13.8.3,

$$x'x + MM' = X'X \tag{13.8.4}$$

Let

$$C = x'x \tag{13.8.5}$$

$$G = X'X \tag{13.8.6}$$

From Eqs. 13.8.4, 13.8.5 and 13.8.6,

$$C + MM' = G \tag{13.8.7}$$

From Eqs. 13.8.2, 13.8.3, and 13.8.7,

$$Q\Delta^2 Q' + MM' = G \tag{13.8.8}$$

Let us now find the roots of G. Assume Q is vertical. Let $Q = Q_i$ and Q_j be a complement of Q_i. In particular, we may have

$$Q_j Q_j' = I - Q_i Q_i' \tag{13.8.9}$$

where Q_j is the partial triangular factor of the right of Eq. 13.8.9.

From Eq. 13.8.8, we may write

$$\left[(Q_i, Q_j)\begin{bmatrix} \Delta^2 & 0 \\ 0 & 0 \end{bmatrix}\begin{bmatrix} Q_i' \\ Q_j' \end{bmatrix} + MM' - \phi_i I \right] H_{.i} = 0 \qquad (13.8.10)$$

where $H_{.i}$ is a basic vector of G.

From Eq. 13.8.10,

$$\left[\begin{bmatrix} \Delta^2 & 0 \\ 0 & 0 \end{bmatrix} + \begin{bmatrix} Q_i' \\ Q_j' \end{bmatrix} MM'(Q_i, Q_j) - \begin{bmatrix} \phi_i I & 0 \\ 0 & \phi_i I \end{bmatrix} \right] \begin{bmatrix} Q_i' \\ Q_j' \end{bmatrix} H_{.i} = 0 \qquad (13.8.11)$$

Let

$$Q_i' H_{.i} = V_{.i} \qquad (13.8.12)$$

$$Q_j' H_{.i} = V_{.j} \qquad (13.8.13)$$

$$Q_i' M = v_i \qquad (13.8.14)$$

$$Q_j' M = v_j \qquad (13.8.15)$$

Equations 13.8.12–13.8.15 in (13.8.11) give

$$\left[\begin{bmatrix} \Delta^2 - \phi I & 0 \\ 0 & -\phi I \end{bmatrix} + \begin{bmatrix} v_i \\ v_j \end{bmatrix}(v_i', v_j') \right]\begin{bmatrix} V_{.i} \\ V_{.j} \end{bmatrix} = \begin{bmatrix} 0 \\ 0 \end{bmatrix} \qquad (13.8.16)$$

From Eq. 13.8.16,

$$\begin{bmatrix} V_{.i} \\ V_{.j} \end{bmatrix} + \begin{bmatrix} (\Delta^2 - \phi I)^{-1} & 0 \\ 0 & -I\frac{1}{\phi} \end{bmatrix}\begin{bmatrix} v_i \\ v_j \end{bmatrix}(v_i' V_{.i} + v_j' V_{.j}) = \begin{bmatrix} 0 \\ 0 \end{bmatrix} \qquad (13.8.17)$$

From Eq. 13.8.17,

$$1 + v_i'(\Delta^2 - \phi I)^{-1}v_i + \frac{v_j' v_j}{\phi} = 0 \qquad (13.8.18)$$

In particular, if c is basic, then Eq. 13.8.18 becomes

$$1 + v'(\Delta^2 - \phi I)^{-1}v = 0 \qquad (13.8.19)$$

where i is dropped from v_i. Or in scalar notation,

$$1 + \frac{v_1^2}{\delta_1 - \phi} + \frac{v_2^2}{\delta_2 - \phi} + \cdots + \frac{v_n^2}{\delta_n - \phi} = 0 \qquad (13.8.20)$$

where the v's in the numerators of Eq. 13.8.20 are the elements of v in Eq. 13.8.19.

To solve for the kth root ϕ_k in Eq. 13.8.20, we consider

$$F = 1 + \frac{v_1^2}{\delta_1 - Z} + \frac{v_2^2}{\delta_2 - Z} + \cdots + \frac{v_n^2}{\delta_n - Z} \qquad (13.8.21)$$

We can now prove that a root of F lies between δ_{k+1} and δ_k. As Z approaches

δ_{k+1} from above, $F \to -\infty$, and as it approaches δ_k from below, $F \to \infty$. Therefore, a root of F must lie between δ_{k+1} and δ_k. To solve for any ϕ_k lying between δ_{k+1} and δ_k, we may begin by letting

$$Y = \delta_k \tag{13.8.22}$$

$$y = \delta_{k+1} \tag{13.8.23}$$

$$Z = \frac{Y + y}{2} \tag{13.8.24}$$

If now Z in Eq. 13.8.21 gives F positive, Z is too large and we take

$$Y = Z$$

If Z in Eq. 13.8.21 had given F negative, Z would have been too small and we would have taken

$$y = Z$$

and used Eq. 13.8.24 for a new Z. We continue in this manner until F in Eq. 13.8.21 is sufficiently close to 0. We know, however, that

$$\phi_1 \geq \delta_1 \tag{13.8.25}$$

Therefore, we must find an upper bound to ϕ_1. This will in general not be greater than

$$Y = M'M + \delta_1 \tag{13.8.26}$$

To solve for the $H_{.k}$, we have from Eq. 13.8.17,

$$V_{.k} = (\delta - \phi_k I)^{-1} v \tag{13.8.27}$$

From Eq. 13.8.12,

$$U_{.k} = Q V_{.k} \tag{13.8.28}$$

and

$$H_{.k} = \frac{U_{.k}}{\sqrt{U_{.k}' U_{.k}}} \tag{13.8.29}$$

The proof for the left-centered matrix derived from that of the uncentered matrix follows similar lines.

13.8.2   Proof of Basic Structure and Right-Centering Ipsative from Normative Basic Structure Factors

Let R be the basic normative covariance or correlation matrix and ρ the ipsative covariance matrix so that

$$\rho = (I - VV')R(I - VV') \tag{13.8.30}$$

where

$$V'V = 1 \tag{13.8.31}$$

Let the basic structures of R and ρ, respectively, be

$$R = Q\delta Q' \tag{13.8.32}$$

and

$$\rho = qdq' \tag{13.8.33}$$

From Eqs. 13.8.30, 13.8.32 and 13.8.33,

$$qdq' = (I - VV')Q\delta Q'(I - VV') \tag{13.8.34}$$

Because of Eq. 13.8.30,

$$V'q = 0 \tag{13.8.35}$$

From Eqs. 13.8.34 and 13.8.35,

$$qd - (I - VV')Q\delta Q'q = 0 \tag{13.8.36}$$

From Eq. 13.8.36

$$Q'qd - (I - Q'VV'Q)\delta Q'q = 0 \tag{13.8.37}$$

From Eq. 13.8.37,

$$\delta Q'q - Q'qd - Q'VV'Q\delta Q'q = 0 \tag{13.8.38}$$

From Eq. 13.8.38,

$$Q'q_{.i} - (\delta - d_i I)^{-1} Q'VV'Q\delta Q'q_{.i} = 0 \tag{13.8.39}$$

From Eq. 13.8.39,

$$(V'Q\delta)Q'q_{.i} - (V'Q\delta)(\delta - d_i I)^{-1} Q'VV'Q\delta Q'q_{.i} = 0$$

or

$$V'Q\delta^{1/2}(\delta - d_i I)^{-1}\delta^{1/2}Q'V - 1 = 0 \tag{13.8.40}$$

From Eq. 13.8.40, we solve for the d_i as in the case of the raw-normative methods. Having solved for the basic diagonal, we can solve for the basic orthonormal of ρ from Eq. 13.8.39. We have

$$q_{.i} = Q(\delta - d_i I)^{-1} Q'Vg \tag{13.8.41}$$

where g is a normalizing scalar.

13.8.2a NORMATIVE FROM IPSATIVE BASIC STRUCTURE FACTORS

From Eqs. 13.8.34 and 13.8.35, we have

$$dq'Q - q'Q\delta(I - Q'VV'Q) = 0 \tag{13.8.42}$$

From Eqs. 13.8.32 and 13.8.42,

$$dq'Q_{.i} - q'Q_{.i}\delta_i + q'RVV'Q_{.i} = 0 \tag{13.8.43}$$

From Eq. 13.8.43,

$$q'Q_{.i} + (d - \delta_i I)^{-1}q'RVV'Q_{.i} = 0 \tag{13.8.44}$$

From Eq. 13.8.44,

$$qq'Q_{.i} + q(d - \delta_i I)^{-1}q'RVV'Q_{.i} = 0 \qquad (13.8.45)$$

It can be proved that

$$qq' = I - VV' \qquad (13.8.46)$$

From Eqs. 13.8.45 and 13.8.46,

$$Q_{.i} - VV'Q_{.i} + q(d - \delta_i I)^{-1}q'RVV'Q_{.i} = 0 \qquad (13.8.47)$$

Premultiplying Eq. 13.8.47 by $V'R$ gives, because of Eq. 13.8.32,

$$V'Q_{.i}\delta_i - V'RVV'Q_{.i} + V'Rq(d - \delta_i I)^{-1}q'RVV'Q_{.i} = 0$$

or

$$V'Rq(d - \delta_i I)^{-1}q'RV + \delta_i - V'RV = 0 \qquad (13.8.48)$$

If we have the vector RV we can solve Eq. 13.8.48 for the δ_i's by methods analogous to the previous methods since we can readily show that

$$d_i \geq \delta_{i+1} \geq d_{i+1} \qquad (13.8.49)$$

We can solve for the $Q_{.i}$ by rewriting Eq. 13.8.47 as

$$Q_{.i} = (V - q(d - \delta_i I)^{-1}q'RV)g_i \qquad (13.8.50)$$

where g_i is a normalizing scalar.

Chapter 14

Categorical Variations in Factor Analysis

In the previous chapters we have regarded data matrices as consisting essentially of measures for a given number of entities on each of a different number of attributes. This type of data matrix has been the one most commonly used in factor analytic studies. You recall, however, that in several chapters we indicated that in some cases the attributes might have a natural origin of measurement. For example, in the previous chapter we suggested that the entities might be persons practicing typewriting, and the attributes might be successive time intervals.

14.1 Multicategory Sets

We may, however, consider a somewhat more general model. For example, suppose that we have a number of individuals for each of whom a number of physiological and psychological variables were measured on each of a number of successive days or time intervals. For such a set of data we have three, rather than two, categories to consider. In the conventional case we have entities and attributes only. In this more general case we have entities, attributes, and occasions. Let us now consider possible ways of studying data of this type.

14.1.1 The Attribute-Entity Sets. In the case of the three-category set, we may consider a number of matrices of the conventional type consisting of attributes as columns and entities as rows. Each of these matrices would have the same attributes and entities for a number of different occasions. We may call these matrices *slabs* of the three-category data matrix.

The problem of how to handle such a set of data by means of factor analytic technique is one which has not been thoroughly explored. Horst (1963) has recently discussed the general problem of multicategory sets of data and proposed several different ways of analyzing such sets. Tucker (1963) also has considered the general problem of entities, attributes, and occasions in what he calls the three-mode factor analysis mobel. He has presented an ingenious procedure for conceiving of a three-category set of data in terms of what he calls a core matrix, which includes the categories of entities, attributes, and occasions. The method assumes lower orders for each of these categories than are represented in the data matrix, and the problem then is to solve for this lower order, three-category matrix as a basis for reproducing the observed three-category data matrix.

We may consider a simpler way of handling data of this type as a two-category set. Here the analysis of the data would be amenable to the techniques which we have discussed in the previous chapters.

The first of these ways of considering the data is to regard each occasion for each attribute as a distinct attribute. Thus we would regard an attribute measured today for a group of entities as different from the same attribute measured tomorrow on the same entities. For example, the variable of typewriting speed on Monday for individual A, and the variable of typewriting speed on Tuesday for the same individual would be regarded as two different variables. We would then consider a supermatrix in which the entity-attribute slabs would be strung out in such a way that, if we had 4 occasions and 10 attributes, the supermatrix would actually have 10×4, or 40, attributes. We would therefore have a 40-variable matrix. We may then consider a factor analysis of such a matrix along the lines outlined in the previous chapters. This could be solved for principal axis factor loadings for each variable or attribute on each occasion.

Another way of regarding the same set of data would be to consider each occasion as a different set of entities. This would mean that the person whose typewriting speed is recorded today will be considered a different person when his speed is recorded tomorrow, even though he has the same name and is identifiable as the same individual. If we look at the problem in this way, we could then string out the entity-attribute slabs for the various occasions so that, if we had, say, 20 persons and 4 occasions, we would actually now have 80 different persons, since we regard each individual as a different person on each of the 4 different occasions. This would give us a supermatrix, or a column type 3 supervector, in which each of the matric elements is an entity-attribute matrix for a specific occasion. Here we would have 80 entities and 10 attributes. We can now, on a matrix of this type, do a factor analysis according to procedures described in previous chapters. Such an analysis could then yield a set of factor scores for each person on each of the 4 different occasions. It would also yield a set of factor loadings for each of the 10 variables.

It will be seen that the first and the second ways of setting up the matrices of data in the form of type 3 supervectors yield essentially different results. In the first case, we get a factor score matrix for the 20 entities and we get factor loading matrices for the 10 attributes on each of 4 different occasions. In the second case, we get a factor score matrix for the entities on each of the 4 different occasions and a factor loading matrix for the 10 attributes. In the one case we regard the occasions as different variables, and in the second we regard them as different entities.

14.1.2 The Attribute-Occasion Set.

In the previous example we have considered the decomposition of the data cube, as it were, into occasion slabs such that each slab had entities for rows and attributes for columns. We may now consider a different decomposition of this three-dimensional matrix such that each slab represents a person. Each person matrix may be regarded as consisting of occasion rows and attribute columns. We would then have, using the previous example, twenty (4×10) matrices.

We now have two obvious alternatives in treating these slabs of data. In the first of these, we could string out the slabs into a row type 2 supervector so that each person is regarded as a different attribute. Therefore, we would have a supermatrix of 4 occasions and 10×20, or 200, attributes. On such a matrix one could then perform a factor analysis.

On the other hand, we may string the matrices in the other direction, so that each person is considered as a different occasion. We would therefore have a matrix with 80 rows and 10 columns. We recognize at once that this arrangement of the data is the same as the second way of arranging it in the previous method, except that there has been an interchange of rows. In both methods the columns are the 10 attributes, but the entities for a single occasion are grouped together in rows. In the second case we have the same 10 attributes, but the occasion rows are grouped for a specific entity. We see, therefore, that we actually have, so far, three different ways of arranging the data into a row by column data matrix which can be factor analyzed by available methods.

14.1.3 The Entity-Occasion Pair or Set.

Let us now see what happens if we take the third remaining possibility of decomposing the data. In the first case we took slabs such that each slab was a different occasion. In the second case we took slabs such that each slab was a different person or entity, and in the third case we take slabs from the cube so that each slab is a different attribute.

In this latter case, each slab may be regarded as having entities for rows and occasions for columns. Suppose we string these slabs out into a row supervector so that the 20 entities constitute the rows, and the columns are sets of occasions for each of the successive attributes. We recognize at once that this is the first arrangement considered in the attribute-entity slabs, except that occasions are grouped by attributes, while in the first case attributes were grouped by successive occasions.

Obviously then, since a data matrix of this type has simply undergone a right-hand permutation of the former type of data matrix, the factor analysis results would be the same except for the permutation of columns in the data matrix and the corresponding permutation of rows in the factor loading matrix.

Let us see now what happens if we string these entity-occasion slabs in a vertical manner so that in the column supervector we have occasions for columns, and the rows consist of entities grouped by successive attributes. We see that this gives the same result as when the attribute-occasion set is arranged in the vertical supermatrix, except that now the submatrices exhibit grouping of entities according to successive attributes rather than grouping of attributes according to successive entities. It is therefore clear that nothing new has been added by reordering of the data into entity by occasion slabs. The factor analysis of such an ordering of the data would be the same as for the second case involving the attribute-occasion set.

14.1.4 Additional Categories. In the previous section we have considered what may be regarded as the most obvious categories in sets of data to be obtained in real life situations. These are certainly important, and it is probable that a great deal more attention will be given to the three-category type of data matrix and to efficient methods of reproducing such a set of observed data with a smaller number of parameters. This would constitute a generalization of the lower rank approximation to data matrices of the two-category type. However, it is already becoming clear that even the three-category type of data matrix will not cover all meaningful categories encountered in important psychological research.

Let us consider a specific example. Suppose we have a questionnaire with a set of 64 items to which 18 individuals will respond. Let us assume that these entities or individuals are requested to give responses under a number of different conditions or instructions. For example, they may be asked to respond to the items as they apply to themselves, to the average person, to the ideal person, to the respondent as he would like to be, and so on. One may have as many different conditions as he can invent.

Let us assume that there are eight of these conditions. Suppose the respondents are a group of psychiatric residents in a mental hospital. It may be expected that these residents are undergoing training and experience which will modify their responses to the items over a period of time for the varying conditions. Suppose, then, that these individuals are requested to repeat the 8 sets of responses to each of the 64 items on 4 different occasions at six-month intervals.

Let us now review the essential characteristics of this data model. First, we have sets of matrices involving 18 entities and 64 attributes or variables. For each condition on each occasion we have such a matrix. For example, if we have 8 conditions and 4 occasions, this means that we have 32 matrices of order 18 × 64.

We may also conceive of an additional categorical set which would consist of a set of instruments or evaluators. This would involve a number of different ways of evaluating or measuring each attribute for each entity under each condition and on each occasion. It is interesting to note that the instrument and the occasion categories are the basic concepts involved in traditional theories of reliability of measures. The instruments correspond to comparable form or comparable measure reliability, and the occasions correspond to consistency or stability over time.

In most of the measurement models, comparable form reliability usually involves only two instruments. These instruments may be persons, test booklets, hardware, or whatnot. For example, we may have a number of different raters evaluating the same individual on the same attribute for a given occasion. In the case of the occasion category, we have a special case of retest reliability which ordinarily involves only two occasions. The problem of evaluating change, for example, becomes sufficiently complicated from the model point of view even if we have only the four categories of entities, attributes, conditions, and occasions. It becomes even more complex, if we include also the additional category of instruments. In any case, it is reasonable to assume that a general data model which is completely satisfactory should be prepared to handle at least a five-category matrix.

Even though we cannot present a complete analysis of the more general problem, it may be worthwhile to examine the possibilities of arrangements for multicategory sets of data in two-dimensional arrays which would be amenable to the conventional methods of factor analysis.

First we may summarize the possibilities with three-category sets. We indicate these by A, B, and C, respectively.

$$(A), \quad (B,C)$$
$$(B), \quad (A,C)$$
$$(C), \quad (A,B)$$

Fig. 14.1.1

We see in Fig. 14.1.1 how we may arrange this set of data into three different kinds of two-dimensional sets. The first set would have the A category for rows, and the B and C categories for columns. The next set would have the B category for rows, and the A and C categories for columns. The third set would have the C category for rows, and the A and B categories for columns. A review of the previous subsection will show that this constitutes the three independent ways in which the data can be ordered in terms of two-dimensional arrays. Any other arrangement would constitute repetitions of these, except for transposition or permutation of the matrices. Obviously, such operations on a matrix would not affect its basic structure, except for transposition of the basic orthonormals or permutation of rows and columns.

Suppose now we have four sets of categories such as entities, attributes, occasions, and conditions, which we designate A, B, C, and D, respectively. Figure 14.1.2 indicates the ways in which these four categories can be arranged in two-dimensional array matrices.

$$
\begin{aligned}
&(A), \quad (B,C,D) \\
&(B), \quad (A,C,D) \\
&(C), \quad (A,B,D) \\
&(D), \quad (A,B,C)
\end{aligned}
$$

$$
\begin{aligned}
&(A,B) \quad (C,D) \\
&(A,C), \quad (B,D) \\
&(A,D) \quad (B,C)
\end{aligned}
$$

Fig. 14.1.2

It will be noted that Fig. 14.1.2 is divided into two parts. The first part indicates those arrangements involving only one categorical set as rows and three categorical sets as columns. The second part of the figure shows how the two-dimensional submatrices may be arranged into sets so that the rows will consist of two of the categories and the columns of the other two categories.

Note that in the first part of the figure the first arrangement has the members of the A category for rows and the B, C, and D categories for columns. The particular arrangement or permutations of the B, C, and D categories is irrelevant. It must be remembered that the notation used here does *not* mean that first, all of the B-category columns are given, then all of the C categories, and finally the D categories. There would presumably be some hierarchical order of groupings and subgroupings, but these are irrelevant since these various hierarchical arrangements can be produced by permutations of columns.

The second arrangement has the members of the B categories for rows, and members of the A, C, and D categories, respectively, for columns. Here again the order of A, C, and D are irrelevant as far as a factor analytic solution is concerned. The third arrangement has the C category for rows and the A, B, and D categories for columns. Finally, the fourth arrangement has the D category for rows and the A, B, and C categories for columns.

Next we consider the second part of Fig. 14.1.2 in which we have two categories for rows and two categories for columns. Here we see in the first row that the A and B categories are used for rows, and the C and D categories for columns. Again, the ordering of the members of the A and B categories is irrelevant, since they may be permuted at will by a left-hand permutation matrix. The second arrangement has the A and C categories for rows, and the B and D categories for columns. The last arrangement in the second part of Fig. 14.1.2 has the A and D categories for rows, and the B and C categories for columns.

It can be seen that no other arrangements exist involving two categories for rows and two for columns, which are not either transpositions or permutations of the matrices indicated in the lower part of Fig. 14.1.2. Any other combination of two categories, not involving A, which might be used for rows would actually constitute a transposition of those already indicated. For example, if B and C were used for rows, then A and D would be used for columns, and one would have the transpose of the third case in the second part of Fig. 14.1.2.

We see now that there are seven different ways, not involving transpositions or permutations, in which the four-category data model can be arranged into double array matrices. Any of these may have a conventional factor analysis performed upon it so as to get a basic structure solution or some other approximation or transformation of a basic structure solution. Any of these arrangements admits of a lower rank approximation solution.

One relevant and interesting question is which of these arrangements is best from the point of view of providing the most parsimonious approximation to the data. It should be noted, for example, that if we have only three occasions, and we let these be indicated by D, the last arrangement in the first part of Fig. 14.1.2 has only three rows. A lower rank approximation to this matrix could obviously not be greater than two.

One criterion which could be useful in deciding what arrangement would give the greatest possibility for parsimonious description of the data would be to consider which combination of all possible seven indicated in Fig. 14.1.2 would result in a two-array matrix such that its smaller dimension would be a maximum. Let us take, for example, the illustration used in the previous section in which we had 18 persons, 64 attributes, 8 conditions, and 3 occasions. Suppose we designate these as categories A, B, C, and D, respectively. Obviously, the arrangement here whose smallest dimension is a maximum would be A and C as rows and B and D as columns. Then the smaller dimension would be 8×18 or 144. This, however, is only one consideration in deciding what arrangement to use, and the problem of interpreting the results still remains.

Let us now see what happens if we have five categorical sets, say A, B, C, D, and E. These may in particular be the sets of entities, attributes, conditions, evaluations, and occasions discussed in a previous example. Since there are five categorical sets, these can obviously be arranged so that one of the dimensions includes one set, and the other dimension includes the remaining four, as indicated in Fig. 14.1.3.

$(A),\quad (B,C,D,E)$
$(B),\quad (A,C,D,E)$
$(C),\quad (A,B,D,E)$
$(D),\quad (A,B,C,E)$
$(E),\quad (A,B,C,D)$

Fig. 14.1.3

Here again, we can without loss of generality take the row dimension as the one having a single category. The data can also be arranged so that one dimension has two sets and the other has three sets, as in Fig. 14.1.4. It is irrelevant which dimension has the three categories and which has the two, so that without loss of generality we may take the row dimension as having the two categories.

We may now examine in greater detail the case of the one-category row arrangement in Fig. 14.1.3. We take each of the categories in turn as the row dimension and the other four as the column dimension of the two-array matrix. Again, it must be remembered that the sequence of the symbols in parentheses is not relevant, that only the symbols themselves are important. One may have any hierarchical order desired. To adopt a convention, one may assume that the hierarchical order progresses from left to right so that the E category is the final or top hierarchy for the first four arrangements in Fig. 14.1.3. This implies a number of submatrices, each of which may be a supermatrix, such that each successive submatrix corresponds to each successive member of the E category.

Let us now examine the two category by three-category, two-dimensional array matrix arrangements indicated by Fig. 14.1.4.

$(A,B),\quad (C,D,E)$
$(A,C),\quad (B,D,E)$
$(A,D),\quad (B,C,E)$
$(A,E),\quad (B,C,D)$

_____

$(B,C),\quad (A,D,E)$
$(B,D),\quad (A,C,E)$
$(B,E),\quad (A,C,D)$

_____

$(C,D),\quad (A,B,E)$
$(C,E),\quad (A,B,D)$

_____

$(D,E),\quad (A,B,C)$

Fig. 14.1.4

We can very simply set forth the rules for specifying the various arrangements by noting that the dimension having two categories can be made up by considering all possible different pairs of the two categories. This will obviously be 10, as indicated in the figure, because this is the number of five things taken two at a time. The column categories will, of course, be the three categories not represented in the row.

We now have the general problem of deciding which of these arrangements would be best for analyzing the data of three or more categorical sets in terms of a two-dimensional array matrix amenable to the factor analytic techniques set forth in earlier chapters. It would doubtless be of interest to investigate the properties and to attempt interpretations of the various ways in which the data can be laid out in a two-dimensional matrix. It is probable that simplifying or unifying relationships among these various methods may be established.

14.2 Consideration of Origin

In the previous chapter we have given attention to the problem of origin of measurements and have discussed in part the problem of scale. We have seen how the basic structure of a matrix varies as we perform either a right- or left-centering operation. We shall now consider the relationship of the metric problem to the multicategory data model which we have just discussed.

In general, any of the data arrangements considered in Figs. 14.1.1–14.1.4, must face the problem of metric. Whether we should have raw score, deviation, or standard deviation measures and to what extent these separate considerations apply to submatrices within the set, must be decided. Ordinarily, if we have a three-category entity-attribute-occasion matrix, we may assume that the difference in variance and mean for a given attribute over a given number of individuals from one occasion to the next would be of interest in the analysis of the data. Considering, therefore, the entity-attribute matrix for each occasion slab, we would not standardize the measures by columns. Such operations would obviously lose information as to relative changes or variations over time for the entities with respect to each of these attributes.

If we take the second arrangement in Fig. 14.1.1, in which B is the attribute category and A and C are, respectively, entities and occasions, we might well take standard deviation measures with respect to the attributes, since these could be a number of different kinds of things which were not measured in comparable units or from comparable origins. If the centering and scaling were done over all occasions for all the entities, we could see how relative means and variances fluctuated for a single attribute over the various conditions.

It may be that the problem of metric with respect to multicategory data matrices may best be resolved by considering those arrangements which involve only attributes and evaluators as the row categories. For those arrangements one would standardize by rows. This would allow differences in origins and variances to show up with respect to changing conditions and occasions, and would suppress the differences due to the arbitrary metric generally characteristic of attributes and evaluators. Once the data have been standardized for these arrangements, they can be rearranged according to other patterns indicated in Figs. 14.1.1–14.1.4.

14.3 Computational Considerations

One of the problems which frequently arises and which has led to a great deal of confusion is that of determining under what conditions it is desirable to factor entities and under what conditions attributes.

Suppose we have a two-category array, irrespective of what the categories might be. They might be entities and attributes, as in the conventional case; they might be entities and occasions; or they might be attributes and occasions, as in the case of the single individual who now represents a complete population or universe. With any of these two-dimensional matrices we may get either a major or a minor product moment matrix after applying some appropriate operations to achieve a specified metric. This may consist of either right- or left-centering or both; or it may also include scaling the members of a category, whether they are entities, attributes, or conditions, by means of multiplication by a diagonal matrix on either the right or left or both.

It is certainly true that the basic structure of such matrices will be very much a function of the kinds of scaling and origin relocating operations that have been performed on them. However, it does not seem to be generally recognized that for any given set of metricizing operations, that is, for any given set of operations by which we apply additive and scaling constants to rows or columns or both, it does not matter whether we factor one set of categories or the other. If, for example, we have a data matrix which we standardize by persons or by columns, let us say, we may get the minor product moment of this normalized data matrix and perform a basic structure analysis on it. This will give us a factor loading matrix by means of which we can solve for a principal axis or basic structure factor score matrix as indicated in Chapter 4.

On the other hand, we can get a major product moment of this matrix and perform a basic structure analysis on it. The basic structure analysis will give us precisely the factor score matrix that we obtained previously by getting first the factor loading matrix and then solving for the factor score matrix.

Furthermore, if we use this factor score matrix we can then postmultiply the transpose of the standard score matrix by the factor score matrix, and this will yield the factor loading matrix which we obtained directly from the previous method by operating on a minor product moment of the standardized score matrix. It can readily be seen from the definition of the basic structure that this must be the case, because if we premultiply a matrix by the transpose of its left orthonormal, we must by definition have the right orthonormal premultiplied by the basic diagonal. Conversely, if we premultiply the transpose of such a data matrix by its right orthonormal and then premultiply again by the inverse of its basic diagonal, we must get the left orthonormal.

It must be pointed out, however, that these reciprocal relationships hold only if the basic structure analysis is performed without altering the diagonal elements of the product moment matrix, whether this is major or minor. The communalities issue is very much a part of this problem. It should be emphasized that the definition of communalities has not been made sufficiently mathematical so that one can specify the relationship involved in these reciprocal types of solutions if communalities, rather than 1, are used in the diagonals of the correlation matrix. The various methods of approximating the communalities will influence the kinds of relationships obtained. Since any mathematical formulation of the communality model is extremely complex, involving complicated nonlinear relationships, we must conclude that the studies which have been done to compare the results of so-called obverse factor analysis with the conventional methods are not meaningful.

As a matter of fact, it is only for the basic structure solution that we can express precisely this reciprocal type of relationship. From a theoretical point of view, therefore, much of the discussion about the factoring of people versus factoring of tests, or the obverse types of factor analysis, is irrelevant. However, there are some practical implications involved in deciding whether one does a direct factor analysis on the major product moment of the standardized data matrix.

If, for example, one has many more attributes than entities, what we have conventionally called the minor product moment of this data matrix is naturally larger than what we have called the major product moment. This is clear if we regard the natural order of the data matrix as having rows for entities and attributes for columns. We define the minor product moment as the natural order premultiplied by its transpose, and the major product moment as the natural order postmultiplied by its transpose. Then the order of the minor product moment will be the number of attributes, and the order of the major product moment the number of entities.

If, for example, we have given a personality inventory of, say, 250 items to a group of 100 persons, and we wish to have a factor analysis of the individual items in the inventory, the conventional procedure would be to get the intercorrelations of these items and to do a factor analysis by one of the methods outlined in previous chapters. This, of course, would be a 250 × 250 matrix. This is a large matrix for any of the methods. Its analysis would be prohibitive with desk calculators and quite expensive with electronic computers. On the other hand, if we take the product of the data matrix postmultiplied by its transpose, we have a 100th order matrix which can be factor analyzed in perhaps one fifth of the time it takes to factor analyze one which has an order of 250.

We shall see, therefore, how we may proceed computationally with a data matrix having many more variables than entities. We shall assume that the matrix is normalized by columns so that we have means of 0 and standard deviations of 1. If we took the product of this matrix premultiplied by its transpose, and then divided by the number of cases, we would have precisely the intercorrelation matrix of the items.

On the other hand, if we took the product of the standardized data matrix postmultiplied by its transpose, we would not have a correlation matrix. Nevertheless, from such a product we may derive a factor loading matrix by one of the basic structure or principal axis methods. This procedure we shall indicate in the next section.

14.4   Obverse Factor Solution with Standard Metric

14.4.1   Computational Equations

14.1.1a   DEFINITION OF NOTATION

X is the $N \times n$ matrix of raw measures.

M is the vector of means.

D_σ^2 is the diagonal matrix of variances.

G is the major product moment of the standard score matrix.

P is the $N \times m$ matrix of factor scores.

a is the $n \times m$ matrix of factor loadings.

14.4.1b   THE EQUATIONS

$$M = \frac{X'1}{N} \tag{14.4.1}$$

$$\mu = \frac{X^{(2)'}1}{N} \tag{14.4.2}$$

$$D_\sigma^2 = D_\mu - D_M^2 \tag{14.4.3}$$

$$d = D_\sigma^{-2} \tag{14.4.4}$$

$$U = dM \tag{14.4.5}$$

$$V = XU \tag{14.4.6}$$

$$\alpha = U'M \qquad (14.4.7)$$

$$W = V - \tfrac{1}{2}\alpha 1 \qquad (14.4.8)$$

$$Y_{k.}' = X_{k.}'d \qquad (14.4.9)$$

$$G_{kj} = Y_{k.}'X_{j.} - W_k - W_j \qquad (14.4.10)$$

$$G = P\delta P' \qquad (14.4.11)$$

$$a = d^{1/2}(X'P) \qquad (14.4.12)$$

14.4.2 Computational Instructions. We begin with the raw score data matrix. Although the factor loading matrix which we shall proceed to solve for is precisely the same as the solution we would get from the correlation matrix, we never actually calculate the standardized score matrix.

First we calculate the means of the variables as indicated in Eq. 14.4.1. Here we simply get a column vector of the column sums of the raw score matrix X, divided by N, the number of cases.

Next we calculate a vector each element of which is the sum of the squares of the elements of the corresponding column of X, divided by N. This is the μ vector, as indicated in Eq. 14.4.2.

We then calculate the elements of the diagonal matrix, as shown in Eq. 14.4.3. This is obtained by constructing a diagonal matrix of the elements calculated in the vector of Eq. 14.4.2, and subtracting from it a diagonal matrix consisting of the squares of the elements calculated in Eq. 14.4.1. It can readily be shown that this is a diagonal matrix whose diagonal elements are the variances of the variables in the raw score data matrix X.

Next we indicate the elements in a diagonal matrix by Eq. 14.4.4. Here we take the inverse of the diagonal matrix on the left of Eq. 14.4.3.

We next premultiply the column vector calculated in Eq. 14.4.1 by the diagonal matrix calculated in Eq. 14.4.4 to get the vector U indicated in Eq. 14.4.5.

Now we get a vector V, as indicated in Eq. 14.4.6. This is the raw score data matrix postmultiplied by the vector U calculated in Eq. 14.4.5.

We then calculate a scalar quantity α, as indicated in Eq. 14.4.7. This is the minor product of the vectors calculated in Eqs. 14.4.1 and 14.4.5.

Next we calculate the vector W as in Eq. 14.4.8. This is obtained by subtracting from each element of V calculated in Eq. 14.4.6, one half the scalar α calculated in Eq. 14.4.7.

Next we calculate a vector $Y_{k.}$ beginning with $k = 1$, as in Eq. 14.4.9. This vector is obtained by postmultiplying the kth row of the X raw data matrix by the diagonal matrix calculated in Eq. 14.4.4.

This vector is then used to solve in turn for the elements of a matrix G, which is the major product moment of the standard score matrix. Clearly, in this case it is smaller than the minor product moment. Equation 14.4.10

shows how we calculate the elements for the kth row and the jth column. The $Y_{k.}'$ vector calculated in Eq. 14.4.9 is postmultiplied by the jth row of the X matrix in column form, and from this minor product are subtracted the kth and the jth elements of the W vector of Eq. 14.4.8. It is not necessary to calculate the scalar quantities of Eq. 14.4.10 for all values of j. We need calculate them only for values of j equal to or greater than k. This gives us the elements in and above the diagonal of the G matrix indicated in Eq. 14.4.11.

Equation 14.4.11 shows the major product moment of the standardized score matrix as a function of the basic diagonal and basic orthonormals. To this matrix we now apply one of the principal axis solutions indicated in previous chapters. This may be carried to any number of factors desired, according to how much of the variance we want to account for or what other criteria we may have for stopping the factoring.

The factor loading matrix a is indicated in Eq. 14.4.12. Here we see on the right-hand side that first we postmultiply the transpose of the raw score matrix by the P matrix calculated from Eq. 14.4.11. This, it should be recognized, is precisely the principal axis factor score matrix for the normalized score matrix. That is, Eq. 14.4.11 gives us the product moment matrix we would have obtained if we had normalized the X matrix first by columns and then postmultiplied this normalized matrix by its transpose.

The next step in the calculation of the a matrix, as indicated in Eq. 14.4.12, is to premultiply the product in parentheses by the square root of the diagonal matrix calculated in Eq. 14.4.4.

It should be observed that the major saving in computations is achieved when the number of variables is much larger than the number of entities. Actually, as can be seen, the steps involved in Eqs. 14.4.1–14.4.10 are not, in general, more laborious than the calculation of the correlation matrix in which the minor product moment of the standard score matrix is involved. There is, however, an additional multiplication indicated in Eq. 14.4.12, in which the factor score matrix is postmultiplied into the transpose of the raw score data matrix. The computations for this operation ordinarily would not be great, compared with the iterative procedures involved in the solution for the basic orthonormal and the basic diagonals of a very large correlation matrix.

14.4.3 Numerical Example. We illustrate the method with the same data matrix used in Chapter 12, even though it is a vertical matrix, so that we may compare the results with those obtained in Section 12.4.

Table 14.4.1 gives the major product moment of the standardized data matrix. The number 108.0 at the lower left of the table is the sum of the diagonal elements. This should be equal to the product of the orders of the matrix. This is $12 \times 9 = 108$ and serves as a check on the computations.

TABLE 14.4.1 Major Product Moment Matrix of Standardized Score Matrix

23.328	0.057	4.059	-7.228	-9.764	-7.643	-3.918	-4.275	-2.775	2.719	3.560	1.879
0.057	22.494	4.107	-6.720	-7.004	-6.001	-1.449	-0.011	-1.007	-0.551	-0.088	-3.827
4.059	4.107	16.482	-3.170	-4.305	-3.899	-3.951	-5.014	-1.774	-0.363	0.790	-1.962
-7.228	-6.720	-3.170	9.573	5.200	4.282	0.655	0.054	0.899	-1.044	-2.355	-0.147
-9.764	-7.004	-4.305	5.200	10.916	5.283	1.535	1.212	0.990	-1.452	-2.201	-0.410
-7.643	-6.001	-3.899	4.282	5.283	8.155	1.251	0.813	0.827	-1.091	-1.964	-0.013
-3.918	-1.449	-3.951	0.655	1.535	1.251	4.605	1.795	0.752	-0.087	-1.160	-0.027
-4.275	-0.011	-5.014	0.054	1.212	0.813	1.795	5.048	0.831	0.087	-0.827	0.286
-2.775	-1.007	-1.774	0.899	0.990	0.827	0.752	0.831	2.342	-0.208	-0.638	-0.238
2.719	-0.551	-0.363	-1.044	-1.452	-1.091	-0.087	0.087	-0.208	0.858	1.097	1.035
2.560	-0.088	0.790	-2.355	-2.201	-1.964	-1.160	-0.827	-0.638	1.097	2.281	1.506
1.879	-3.827	-1.962	-0.147	-0.410	-0.013	-0.027	0.286	-0.238	1.035	1.506	1.918
108.000											

TABLE 14.4.2 Factor Score Matrix for Three Factors

0.553	0.388	0.327	-0.328	-0.403	-0.326	-0.141	-0.130	-0.088	0.051	0.114	-0.015
-0.572	0.765	0.092	-0.063	0.004	-0.022	0.052	0.107	0.038	-0.098	-0.108	-0.195
0.178	0.206	-0.823	-0.198	-0.147	-0.090	0.202	0.318	0.050	0.143	0.052	0.109

Table 14.4.2 gives the normalized factor score matrix for the first three factors. The rows of this table are proportional to the columns of Table 12.4.2. The proportionality factor is $\sqrt{N}$ or $\sqrt{12}$.

The first row of Table 14.4.3 gives the first three basic diagonals of the correlation matrix corresponding to the data matrix. These results may be seen to agree closely with those of basic structure solutions for the same correlation matrix in previous chapters. The second row gives the number of iterations for each factor. The body of the table gives the first three principal axis factor loading vectors. These also agree closely with those solved for in previous chapters.

TABLE 14.4.3   Basic Diagonals, Number of Iterations, and Factor Loading Matrix for Three Factors

3.748	2.050	1.341
11	7	8
0.717	0.489	0.352
0.740	0.474	0.324
0.773	0.291	0.408
0.553	−0.652	0.070
0.461	−0.747	0.181
0.517	−0.696	0.186
0.643	0.078	−0.589
0.615	0.165	−0.626
0.716	−0.037	−0.367

14.5 Mathematical Proof

We now give the proof that the foregoing computational outline does yield the conventional solution for the principal axis factor loading matrix given in previous chapters.

Given the raw score matrix X, let

$$M = \frac{X'1}{N} \tag{14.5.1}$$

$$\mu = \frac{X^{(2)'}1}{N} \tag{14.5.2}$$

where $X^{(2)}$ means a matrix of the squared elements of X.

$$D_\sigma^2 = D_\mu - D_M^2 \tag{14.5.3}$$

$$d = D_\sigma^{-2} \tag{14.5.4}$$

$$z = \left[I - \frac{11'}{N}\right]Xd^{1/2} \tag{14.5.5}$$

From Eq. 14.5.5,

$$zz' = \left[I - \frac{11'}{N}\right]XdX'\left[I - \frac{11'}{N}\right] \tag{14.5.6}$$

From Eq. 14.5.6,

$$zz' = XdX' - \frac{11'XdX'}{N} - \frac{XdX'11'}{N} + \frac{11'XdX'11'}{N^2} \tag{14.5.7}$$

From Eqs. 14.5.1 and 14.5.7,

$$zz' = XdX' - 1M'dX' - XdM1' + 1M'dM1' \tag{14.5.8}$$

Let

$$U = dM \tag{14.5.9}$$

Substituting Eq. 14.5.9 into Eq. 14.5.8,

$$zz' = XdX' - 1U'X' - XU1' + 1U'M1' \tag{14.5.10}$$

Let

$$\left.\begin{aligned} V &= XU \\ \alpha &= U'M \end{aligned}\right\} \tag{14.5.11}$$

From Eqs. 14.5.11 into Eq. 14.5.10,

$$zz' = XdX' - 1V' - V1' + \alpha 1 1' \tag{14.5.12}$$

Let

$$W = V - \tfrac{1}{2}\alpha 1 \tag{14.5.13}$$

From Eq. 14.5.13 in Eq. 14.5.12,

$$zz' = XdX' - 1W' - W1' \tag{14.5.14}$$

Let

$$G = zz' \tag{14.5.15}$$

From Eqs. 14.5.14 and 14.5.15,

$$G_{kj} = X_{k.}'dX_{j.} - W_k - W_j \tag{14.5.16}$$

Given the basic structure forms

$$G = P\delta P' \tag{14.5.17}$$

$$z = P\delta^{1/2}Q' \tag{14.5.18}$$

From Eqs. 14.5.5 and 14.5.18,

$$Q\delta^{1/2}P' = d^{1/2}X'\left[I - \frac{11'}{N}\right] \tag{14.5.19}$$

From Eq. 14.5.19,

$$Q\delta^{1/2} = d^{1/2} X'P - X'1\,1'P \qquad (14.5.20)$$

From Eq. 14.5.19,

$$P'1 = 0 \qquad (14.5.21)$$

From Eq. 14.5.21 in Eq. 14.5.20,

$$Q\delta^{1/2} = d^{1/2}(X'P) \qquad (14.5.22)$$

Chapter 15

The Problem of Scaling

In Chapter 13 we considered the problem of origin or zero point as it affects factor analytic solutions. We saw that we may work with raw score matrices, deviation score matrices, or a number of combinations of these two methods. We learned that we may factor right-centered and left-centered matrices or both, that is, matrices which have means subtracted from the columns, those which have means subtracted from the rows, and those which have means subtracted from both rows and columns.

We saw also that we may conduct factor analytic solutions based on procedures which may subtract or add constants other than means to the rows and/or columns, and that these solutions vary according to the specific patterns for adding constants to rows or columns. We indicated that there may be rational procedures for determining what constants should be added, for example, in cases where natural zero points are available. We showed in Chapters 4 and 13 that the unit for scaling one attribute may not be comparable to that for scaling another, and that therefore rationales for making such scales comparable may be of interest.

15.1 Kinds of Scaling

It is clear that if we have a large set of measures, such as physiological, psychological, or other types, these may vary widely in comparability. For example, height may be measured in feet, and a test score may be measured in terms of items correct on a 500-item test.

The conventional procedure, as indicated, has been to reduce all these to standard deviation measures. We have in general three types of possibilities for scaling. We may scale by entities, by attributes, or by both. In any case, it is well known that a particular factor analytic solution will depend on the scaling procedure. This is because the basic structure of a data matrix is altered in a very complicated fashion if the data matrix is multiplied by a diagonal matrix.

15.1.1 Scaling by Attributes. We have already considered in some detail the reasons why the problem of scaling by attributes arises. This, of course, means that we postmultiply a data matrix by a diagonal matrix. In the case of a scaling procedure which reduces all variables to unit standard deviations, we simply postmultiply the data matrix by the inverse of a diagonal matrix whose elements are standard deviations of the variables in whatever units they are measured. This has been the traditional method of scaling for factor analytic solutions.

It should be noted, however, that such a scaling procedure is specific to the particular sample to which it is applied. If one used such a scaling procedure on a particular sample and applied the same diagonal scaling matrix to a data matrix obtained from some other sample, he would not expect that the variances for the new sample would be 1. In general, these would depart from 1 to a greater or lesser degree. The fact that the normalizing scaling procedure is specific to a particular sample casts doubts on its validity.

15.1.2   Scaling by Entities.

The problem of scaling by entities has not received much attention or perhaps even been regarded as a relevant problem in factor analysis procedures. Certainly the question of origin by entities is of both theoretical and practical importance in the analysis of behavioral science data. We have seen how it arises in the case of ipsative type measures in personality scales. It also arises in the case of differential prediction problems. This we have discussed in Chapter 13. Obviously, the shifting of origins by entities or rows of the natural order data matrix has its analog in scaling by entities. This implies formally, of course, a multiplication on the left of the natural order data matrix by a diagonal matrix. The question of what sort of diagonal matrix is appropriate for a given problem depends on the particular interest of the investigator.

One may assume, for example, that certain of the entities should receive less weight than others in a factor analytic solution. It may be that because of biased sample selection it might be desirable to weight certain of the entities more and others less, in order to overcome the effects of bias. For example, if one had selected a group of individuals so that in general the higher scoring individuals were believed to be less well represented, compared to some target population, than those in the lower group, then the former might be given higher weightings. Therefore, the diagonal elements of the left scaling matrix would be larger for the higher group than for the lower.

15.1.3   Scaling by Entities and Attributes.

It is now obvious that a more general view of the scaling problem for a data matrix would involve scaling by both entities and attributes. Here the formal model includes both pre- and postmultiplication of the data matrix by diagonal matrices. One may make a rather basic distinction, however, between the types of left and right scaling matrices which might be considered. In the case of right diagonal scaling matrices, one might well have both positive and negative elements in the scaling diagonal. For example, if one wishes to reverse the scale for certain personality item variables in a data matrix to change a negative statement to a positive form, then presumably one would use a negative element. However, in the case of the left diagonal multiplier, it is difficult to see by what rationale one might wish to give a negative weight to a particular entity. In general, any left diagonal multiplier for the data matrix would almost certainly have all positive elements.

Since currently there is very little available on the rationale or technique of scaling data matrices by entities, and since no experimental or computational work has been carried out, we shall not pursue the matter further. We shall direct our attention to problems involved in the scaling of data matrices by attributes.

15.2 Scaling by Attributes

15.2.1 The General Problem of Scale. We have already discussed a number of considerations involved in the scaling of a data matrix by attributes or the postmultiplication of the natural order data matrix by a diagonal matrix. We have pointed out that factor analytic results may vary considerably according to what scaling procedures are used. We have indicated that the Gordian knot is usually cut by using standardized measures. Nevertheless, it would seem desirable to have factor analytic procedures which are relatively independent of the scale. We shall now consider in more detail some of the criteria which suggest themselves in establishing scaling procedures.

15.2.2 Criteria for Scaling. One of the most obvious rationales for scaling has been previously suggested, namely, that of using natural units when they are available. We have indicated that in the case of the three-category matrix in which one of the slabs is an entity-occasion matrix, the occasions regarded as attributes may already be in relative natural units. For example, the measures of a set of entities on typewriting scores for successive weeks are comparable both with respect to origin and scale. The variation in scores from one week to the next for this group of entities is not some artifact of the method of evaluation, but may be of considerable interest in itself. Unfortunately, however, such natural units are not available for much of the data to be subjected to factor analytic solutions.

We have already mentioned the possibility that the factor analytic procedure may be such that the solution is relatively independent of any scaling diagonal matrix. We shall now consider some of these solutions.

15.3 The Communality Problem and Scaling

Throughout the previous chapters dealing with specific methods of factor analysis we have referred to the communality problem without being very specific as to what is meant by the term *communality*. True, it is defined both theoretically and computationally in texts on factor analysis. In general, it is said to be that part of the variance of a system which is common to two or more variables. This is not a very precise definition.

The communality problem has also been discussed from a computational point of view. Here the problem is to determine the diagonal elements of a correlation or covariance matrix so as to reduce the rank of the matrix. To solve this problem we must decide whether we want to reduce the rank of an experimental correlation matrix precisely or whether we want to reduce the rank of another matrix which resembles the original correlation matrix as closely as possible according to some criterion. But in the latter case we have to define "as closely as possible."

The traditional approach has used approximations to the diagonal values which enable one to account more accurately for the nondiagonal elements with a smaller number of factors than is accounted for by using 1 in the diagonals. We have seen that for correlation and residual matrices, one method is to substitute the largest absolute nondiagonal element in a column for the diagonal element.

These procedures, however, do not provide precise or rigorous definitions of communalities nor do they indicate an underlying mathematical model for their determination. They are merely verbal and arithmetic procedures, with little reference to their interpretation or significance for the data matrix from which the correlation matrix is derived. We have indicated in Chapter 4 that one should be able to account completely for the results of a factor analysis in terms of the original data matrix rather than in terms of the correlation matrix.

Perhaps some of the best work on the communality problem has been done by Guttman (1958), Harris (1962), and earlier by Lawley (1940) and Rao (1955). In general, these investigators have been aware of the relationship of the communality problem to the scaling problem. Implicit in their work is the notion that the communality problem is really a scaling problem.

We shall therefore consider certain types of factor analytic solutions which have techniques for solving the scaling problem built into them. These are, in effect, methods which are independent of scale or in which the scaling diagonal cancels out in the mathematical model.

15.4 Characteristics of the Methods

All of the models to be considered have certain characteristics in common. First, they are all special cases of the rank reduction method; second, they are least square or basic structure solutions; third, each solves for a scaling diagonal matrix; and fourth, they are what may be called doubly iterative solutions.

15.4.1 Special Case of Rank Reduction Method. Each of the methods to be considered is a special case of the rank reduction formula in that the removal of each factor results in a residual matrix which is of rank one less than the previous residual matrix. Furthermore, each approximation to a factor matrix is a rank reduction solution.

15.4.2 Least Square Basic Structure Solutions. All of the solutions we shall consider are basic structure or least square solutions, with respect to the scaled matrices. This point will not be elaborated here, since it will be clarified in the computational procedure and the mathematical proofs.

15.4.3 Solution for Scaling Diagonals. As implied by the previous discussion, all of the solutions to be considered solve for a scaling diagonal matrix. It is to be observed, however, that the procedure used to solve for this scaling diagonal matrix varies considerably from one method to another. In two of the models, a single scaling diagonal matrix is solved for. In the other model, the scaling diagonal matrix is different for each factor vector. In this latter model, a scaling diagonal matrix is found for each residual matrix. The solution, however, is again independent of any particular scale that we start with, such as in the normalized data matrix.

15.4.4 Doubly Iterative Type Solutions. All of the methods to be considered might be regarded as doubly iterative, because not only does one iterate to the solution for a factor vector or matrix, but one also iterates to the scaling diagonal. This is because the scaling diagonal matrix is itself a function of the factor loading vectors, which in turn are a function of the scaling diagonal matrix. One of the consequences is that the solution may be very laborious and costly. Even with high-speed computers, the cost and time may be excessive if the number of variables or attributes is large.

15.5 Kinds of Solutions

We shall consider six different kinds of solutions which are independent of scale. These may be divided into two general classes.

The first of these classes we call the *specificity type solutions.* The model on which these solutions are based was first proposed by Lawley (1940), and later developed in essentially the same form, but from a somewhat different set of hypotheses and assumptions, by Rao (1955).

The second class of solutions may be called the *communality type solutions.* These are based on a general model developed by Horst. Beginning in 1950, the method was presented in lecture notes at the University of Washington, but these were not published. More recently, Kaiser, in personal communication and in conference presentations, proposed a related type of procedure.

Both the specificity and the communality types of solutions may be divided into three different variations. The first of these we shall call the *successive factor method*. It requires the solution of a single factor vector at a time. With the solution for each factor vector, a residual matrix is calculated and another factor vector is calculated from the residual matrix. This type of solution is analogous to the single factor residual solution outlined for the centroid and the basic structure or principal axis methods in Chapters 5 and 7, respectively. With the solution for each factor one obtains a scaling diagonal matrix which is a function of the elements of the factor vector itself.

The second type of solution for both the specificity and the communality models may be called the *factor matrix solution*. Here one makes some assumption as to the number of factors in the set, and begins with some crude approximation matrix of this order for the factor matrix. By a process of successive iterations one converges to the factor loading matrix and to the scaling diagonal which is a function of all of the factor vectors.

These two types of solutions do not in general give the same results for a specified number of factors. The scaling varies from one factor vector solution to the next in the residual method, whereas it converges to a single diagonal matrix when one iterates to all the desired factor vectors simultaneously.

There is a variation of the factor matrix method which combines the features of both of the others. This we shall call the *progressive factor matrix method*. Here one begins with the solution for a single factor, and then successively adds factors to the factor loading matrix without ever computing residual matrices.

15.6   Specificity Successive Factor Solution

We shall first take up the specificity scaling method for each of the three variations: the successive factor, the factor matrix, and the progressive factor matrix solutions. First we shall consider the successive factor type solution.

15.6.1   Characteristics of the Solution. This method is characterized by the fact that only one factor at a time is solved for, after which a residual matrix is calculated, the next factor loading vector is calculated from the residual, and so on.

All of the specificity types of solutions are similar with respect to the scaling unit solved for. The scaling unit is such that the variance of the rescaled variables is proportional to the reciprocal square root of their residual variances. That is, we define these residual variances as the original variance of the variables less the amount of variance accounted for by a given factor or set of factors, depending on which type of solution is used. In the successive factor solution, the first scaling constant for each variable is proportional to the reciprocal square root of the difference between the original variance of the variables and the variance accounted for by the first factor. The first factor is then removed from the covariance matrix to yield a residual matrix. This residual matrix is then scaled in the same manner as are subsequent residual matrices.

15.6.2 Computational Equations

15.6.2a DEFINITION OF NOTATION

C is a correlation or covariance matrix.
D_C is a diagonal matrix of the diagonals of C.
$_0a$ is an arbitrary vector.
D_{ia} is a diagonal matrix whose elements are from the vector $_ia$.
$_iP$ is a tolerance limit.

15.6.2b THE EQUATIONS

$$_0a = C1(1'C1)^{-1/2} \tag{15.6.1}$$

$$_0D^2 = (D_C - D_{0a}{}^2)^{-1} \tag{15.6.2}$$

$$_0U = {}_0D^2 {}_0a \tag{15.6.3}$$

$$_0W = C_0U - {}_0a \tag{15.6.4}$$

$$_0\alpha = \frac{1}{\sqrt{{}_0W' {}_0U}} \tag{15.6.5}$$

$$_1a = {}_0W {}_0\alpha \tag{15.6.6}$$

$$_iD^2 = (D_C - D_{ia}{}^2)^{-1} \tag{15.6.7}$$

$$_iU = {}_iD^2 {}_ia \tag{15.6.8}$$

$$_iW = C_iU - {}_ia \tag{15.6.9}$$

$$_i\alpha = \frac{1}{\sqrt{{}_iW' {}_iU}} \tag{15.6.10}$$

$$_{i+1}a = {}_iW {}_i\alpha \tag{15.6.11}$$

$$_{i+1}\alpha - {}_i\alpha = {}_iP \tag{15.6.12}$$

$$_{i+1}a = a_{.1} \tag{15.6.13}$$

$$_2C = C - a_{.1} a_{.1}' \tag{15.6.14}$$

$$_{k+1}C = {}_kC - a_{.k} a_{.k}' \tag{15.6.15}$$

15.6.3 Computational Instructions.
In this procedure, like in all of the methods in this section, one may begin with either a correlation matrix or at

covariance matrix scaled in any convenient fashion. Ordinarily it is probably best to work with correlation matrices. These are familiar to most investigators and are convenient from the point of view of number of digits carried in the elements of the matrix.

All of the diagonals are 1, of course, in the correlation matrix. In any case, for all of the methods to be discussed, 1 is used in the diagonals of correlation matrices, and variances are used in the diagonals of covariance matrices.

We begin with some arbitrary approximation to a first factor loading vector. This can be, for example, a first centroid vector, as indicated in Eq. 15.6.1. It could also be a principal axis factor loading vector.

The next step is indicated in Eq. 15.6.2. Here one gets the difference between the diagonal elements of the covariance or correlation matrix and a diagonal made up of the squared elements of the vector in Eq. 15.6.1. This is indicated on the right-hand side of the equation. This diagonal matrix is then inverted to give the diagonal matrix on the left of the equation. It will be recognized that the matrix on the left is a diagonal matrix of the reciprocal of the difference between two diagonal matrices, the first of which is a diagonal matrix of variances, and the second of which is a diagonal matrix of the variances accounted for by the first approximation factor.

The next step is indicated in Eq. 15.6.3. Here we calculate a vector $_0U$ on the right of the equation. It is obtained by premultiplying the vector of Eq. 15.6.1 by the diagonal matrix of Eq. 15.6.2.

Next we calculate the $_0W$ vector in Eq. 15.6.4. This, as shown on the right of the equation, is obtained by postmultiplying the covariance or correlation matrix by the $_0U$ vector calculated in Eq. 15.6.3, and subtracting from the product the vector $_0a$ calculated in Eq. 15.6.1.

Now we calculate the scalar quantity indicated by Eq. 15.6.5. Here we get the minor product of the vectors calculated in Eqs. 15.6.3 and 15.6.4 and take the reciprocal square root of this product.

Then we get the first rank reduction approximation to the first factor loading vector, as indicated in Eq. 15.6.6 by the vector $_1a$ on the left of the equation. This is seen to be the vector $_0W$ of Eq. 15.6.4 multiplied by the scalar quantity of $_0\alpha$ of Eq. 15.6.5.

Equation 15.6.7 gives the ith approximation to the D^2 matrix as the inverse of a matrix obtained by subtracting from the diagonal of the C matrix the corresponding squared elements of the current approximation to the factor loading vector. As will be seen, therefore, Eq. 15.6.7 gives a diagonal matrix which is an approximation to the inverse of the diagonal of the residual matrix.

The general equation for the U vector is given in Eq. 15.6.8. This is simply the current approximation to the factor loading vector premultiplied by the diagonal matrix of Eq. 15.6.7.

The general equation for the W vector is given by Eq. 15.6.9. This is obtained by postmultiplying the correlation matrix by the U vector of Eq. 15.6.8, and subtracting from the product the previous approximation to the factor vector.

The ith approximation for the scalar quantity α is the reciprocal square root of the minor product of the vectors given by Eqs. 15.6.8 and 15.6.9, as indicated on the right-hand side of Eq. 15.6.10.

The general equation for the $i + 1$ approximation to the first factor loading vector is given by Eq. 15.6.11. This is the W vector of Eq. 15.6.9 multiplied by the scalar of Eq. 15.6.10.

To determine whether we have gone far enough in our approximation, we can compare successive approximations to the a vector given by Eq. 15.6.11. However, it is probably simpler to use the criterion indicated by Eq. 15.6.12. This is the difference between successive α values. These α values should, in general, increase in magnitude or stabilize so that when the P value indicated by Eq. 15.6.12 is sufficiently small, we may stop the iterations for the first factor vector.

When the iterations are sufficiently close, we may regard the $i + 1$ approximation to a as the first factor loading vector, namely, $a_{.1}$, as given in Eq. 15.6.13.

Next we calculate a residual matrix $_2C$ as indicated in Eq. 15.6.14. This is obtained by subtracting the major product moment of the factor loading vector from the covariance or correlation matrix.

We now proceed through the same set of computations outlined in Eqs. 15.6.1–15.6.13, except that these are performed on the residual matrix given by the left side of Eq. 15.6.14, rather than on the original matrix.

Each successive residual matrix is calculated as in Eq. 15.6.15. Then the routine outlined in Eqs. 15.6.1–15.6.14 is applied to each of the residual matrices. The criterion of when to stop factoring may be one of those suggested in previous chapters.

15.6.4 Numerical Example.

A numerical example of the method is given below. We use the same correlation matrix as in previous chapters. This correlation matrix is repeated for convenience in Table 15.6.1. The arbitrary vector for each of the four factors was taken as the unit vector. The solution is doubtless dependent on the arbitrary vectors, and currently no "best" method is available for determining these vectors.

The first row of Table 15.6.2 gives the number of iterations for each of the first four factors. The second row gives the variance accounted for by each factor. The body of the table gives the first four factor loading vectors. As in the methods of previous chapters, only the first three factors appear "significant."

It is interesting to note that the factor loading vectors bear little resemblance to the principal axis factors of Chapters 8–10. As a matter of fact, they resemble more closely the factors given by the group centroid methods of Chapter 6. It is not clear, however, to what extent the factors might change if vastly more iterations were taken.

TABLE 15.6.1   Correlation Matrix

1.000	0.829	0.768	0.108	0.033	0.108	0.298	0.309	0.351
0.829	1.000	0.775	0.115	0.061	0.125	0.323	0.347	0.369
0.768	0.775	1.000	0.272	0.205	0.238	0.296	0.271	0.385
0.108	0.115	0.272	1.000	0.636	0.626	0.249	0.183	0.369
0.033	0.061	0.205	0.636	1.000	0.709	0.138	0.091	0.254
0.108	0.125	0.238	0.626	0.709	1.000	0.190	0.103	0.291
0.298	0.323	0.296	0.249	0.138	0.190	1.000	0.654	0.527
0.309	0.347	0.271	0.183	0.091	0.103	0.654	1.000	0.541
0.351	0.369	0.385	0.369	0.254	0.291	0.527	0.541	1.000

TABLE 15.6.2   Specificity Successive Factor Method.
Number of Iterations, Variance Accounted for, and
First Four Factor Vectors

24	21	30	30
2.9730	2.0250	1.1978	0.0898
0.8910	−0.1076	−0.0480	−0.0116
0.9067	−0.0867	−0.0182	−0.0654
0.8572	0.0914	−0.0932	0.0874
0.2151	0.7438	0.0475	0.2218
0.1389	0.8266	−0.0821	−0.0500
0.2025	0.7968	−0.0680	−0.0587
0.3911	0.1770	0.6572	0.0118
0.3957	0.1012	0.7303	−0.0627
0.4539	0.2908	0.4556	0.1360

15.7   The Specificity Factor Matrix Solution

15.7.1   Characteristics of the Method. In this method the residual variance scaling matrix is based on all of the factors to be solved for, rather than on a single factor as in the method just outlined. Therefore, we do not have a rescaling after each factor vector. The method is different also in that, instead of solving for a single factor at a time and getting a residual matrix for each cycle, we start with a rough approximation to the complete factor matrix in which some specified number of factors is assumed. We then iterate successively to the factor loading matrix and to the scaling diagonal whose elements are the reciprocal square roots of the residual variances.

15.7.2 Computational Equations

15.7.2a DEFINITION OF NOTATION

C is a covariance matrix.

D_C is the diagonal matrix from C.

$_0a$ is an arbitrary factor matrix approximation of specified width.

$_ia$ is the ith approximation to the factor matrix.

$D_{_ia\,_ia'}$ is the diagonal matrix of $_ia\,_ia'$.

$_it$ is a triangular matrix.

P is a tolerance limit.

15.7.2b THE EQUATIONS

$$_0D^2 = (D_C - D_{_0a\,_0a'})^{-1} \tag{15.7.1}$$

$$_0U = {_0D^2}\,_0a \tag{15.7.2}$$

$$_0W = C\,_0U - {_0a} \tag{15.7.3}$$

$$S = {_0W'}\,_0U \tag{15.7.4}$$

$$\begin{bmatrix} _0t \\ _0W\,_0t'^{-1} \end{bmatrix}\,_0t' = \begin{bmatrix} _0S \\ _0W \end{bmatrix} \tag{15.7.5}$$

$$_1a = {_0W}\,_0t'^{-1} \tag{15.7.6}$$

$$_iD^2 = (D_C - D_{_ia\,_ia'})^{-1} \tag{15.7.7}$$

$$_iU = {_iD^2}\,_ia \tag{15.7.8}$$

$$_iW = C\,_iU - {_ia} \tag{15.7.9}$$

$$_iS = {_iW'}\,_iU \tag{15.7.10}$$

$$\begin{bmatrix} _it \\ _iW\,_it'^{-1} \end{bmatrix}\,_it' = \begin{bmatrix} _iS \\ _iW \end{bmatrix} \tag{15.7.11}$$

$$_{i+1}a = {_iW}\,_it'^{-1} \tag{15.7.12}$$

$$H = \left| \frac{tr(_it)}{tr(_{i+1}t)} - P \right| \tag{15.7.13}$$

15.7.3 Computational Instructions.

In this variation of the specificity method we postulate a given number of factors and begin with an arbitrary factor loading matrix including the assumed number of factors. This we may obtain from the methods of previous chapters.

We first calculate a diagonal matrix as in Eq. 15.7.1. This is obtained by subtracting from the diagonal of the covariance matrix the diagonal of the major product moment of the arbitrary factor loading matrix. Then we take the inverse of this difference matrix as indicated on the right of Eq. 15.7.1.

The next step is to calculate the U matrix, as indicated in Eq. 15.7.2. Here we premultiply the arbitrary approximation to the factor loading matrix by the diagonal matrix calculated in Eq. 15.7.1.

We then calculate a W matrix, as in Eq. 15.7.3. This is obtained by postmultiplying the covariance matrix C by the U matrix calculated in Eq. 15.7.2, and subtracting from the product the arbitrary approximation to the factor matrix.

Next we calculate the matrix S in Eq. 15.7.4. This is the minor product of the matrices calculated in Eqs. 15.7.2 and 15.7.3. It can be seen by the definitions of these matrices that the product is symmetric.

We now indicate a supermatrix of the matrices solved for in Eqs. 15.7.3 and 15.7.4. This is given in the right-hand side of Eq. 15.7.5. The left-hand side of Eq. 15.7.5 indicates a partial triangular factoring of the supermatrix.

The lower part of the left partial triangular factor is then the first approximation to the factor loading matrix, as indicated on the right of Eq. 15.7.6.

The general equations are given in Eqs. 15.7.7–15.7.13. Equation 15.7.7 gives the general equation for the D^2 matrix. This, as indicated on the right, is obtained by subtracting from the diagonal of the covariance matrix, the diagonal of the major product moment of the current approximation to the factor loading matrix, and then taking the inverse of this difference diagonal matrix.

Equation 15.7.8 gives the ith approximation to the U matrix, which is the current approximation to the factor loading matrix premultiplied by the diagonal matrix of Eq. 15.7.7.

The ith approximation to the W matrix is given by Eq. 15.7.9. This is the product of the covariance matrix postmultiplied by the U matrix calculated in Eq. 15.7.8, less the current approximation to the factor matrix.

Equation 15.7.10 indicates the ith approximation to the symmetric S matrix, which is the minor product of the U and W matrices calculated, respectively, in Eqs. 15.7.8 and 15.7.9.

We indicate in general the supermatrix made up of the matrices calculated in Eqs. 15.7.9 and 15.7.10, as on the right-hand side of Eq. 15.7.11. We then indicate the partial triangular factoring of this supermatrix, as shown on the left side of Eq. 15.7.11.

The lower matric element of the supermatrix on the left-hand side of Eq. 15.7.11 gives the next approximation to the factor loading matrix, as indicated in Eq. 15.7.12. It can be proved that the triangular matrix indicated in the upper element of the left-hand matrix in Eq. 15.7.11 converges to a diagonal matrix whose elements are the largest roots or basic diagonal elements of the scaled covariance matrix.

We then assume that the traces of successive t matrices or the sums of their diagonal elements will converge to some value. Therefore, as indicated in Eq. 15.7.13, we take the ratios of successive traces to get H values. When these are sufficiently close to 1, the computations cease.

15.7.4 Numerical Example. We use the same correlation matrix as in the previous methods. For the arbitrary matrix we take the first four principal axis factor vectors of this matrix as found in previous solutions.

For convenient reference the first four principal axis row vectors are given in Table 15.7.1.

The first row of Table 15.7.2 gives the variance accounted for by each of the first four factors. The body of the table gives the first four column factor loading vectors. These factor loadings bear little relation to the principal axis factors of Table 15.7.1. However, again it is apparent that the fourth factor may be ignored. While the factor loadings are not the same within decimal error as those of Table 15.6.2, we may compare factors with the three highest loadings. For Tables 15.6.2 and 15.7.2 we have as comparable factors respectively, factors 1 and 2, 2 and 3, 3 and 1. Again, it may be that a great many more iterations would yield a matrix considerably different from that of Table 15.7.2.

TABLE 15.7.1   First Four Principal Axis Row Factor Vectors of Correlation Matrix

0.717	0.740	0.773	0.556	0.463	0.518	0.640	0.615	0.715
0.493	0.478	0.296	−0.649	−0.744	−0.694	0.080	0.166	−0.034
0.350	0.322	0.406	0.068	0.181	0.188	−0.588	−0.621	−0.369
0.030	−0.056	0.009	0.102	−0.115	−0.129	−0.288	−0.165	0.566

TABLE 15.7.2   Specificity Factor Matrix Method.
Variance Accounted for and Column Factor
Vectors for First Four Factors

2.8295	1.6250	1.6337	0.6243
0.5091	0.7508	−0.0229	0.0439
0.5297	0.7447	−0.0087	0.0093
0.5390	0.6577	0.1617	0.0735
0.4148	−0.1135	0.6337	−0.0521
0.3020	−0.1292	0.7893	−0.0128
0.3476	−0.0770	0.7470	−0.0199
0.5858	0.0322	−0.0403	−0.5875
0.5901	0.0384	−0.1302	−0.5152
0.9611	−0.1897	−0.0760	0.0559

15.8 The Specificity Progressive Factor Matrix Method

15.8.1 Characteristics of the Method. This method is essentially a combination of the previous two methods. It uses the same scaling rationale, that is, the reciprocal square roots of the residual variances of the attributes. It starts with a single factor and proceeds by adding successive factors.

It differs essentially from the first method, however, in that no residual matrices are calculated. It is similar to the second method in that only a single scaling of the variables is solved for. It differs in that no assumptions are made as to the number of factors required.

15.8.2 Computational Equations

15.8.2a DEFINITION OF NOTATION
 (k) subscript designates a matrix of width k.
 Other notation is the same as in Section 15.7.2a.

15.8.2b THE EQUATIONS

$$_0a_{(k-1)} = (a_{.1} \ldots a_{.k-1}) \tag{15.8.1}$$

$$_0a_{(k)} = (a_{(k-1)}, {}_0a) \tag{15.8.2}$$

$$_0D_k^2 = (D_C - D_{{}_0a_{(k)}\,{}_0a_{(k)'}})^{-1} \tag{15.8.3}$$

$$_0U_{(k)} = {}_0D_k^2\,{}_0a_{(k)} \tag{15.8.4}$$

$$_0W_{(k)} = C_0U_{(k)} - {}_0a_{(k)} \tag{15.8.5}$$

$$_0t_{(k)}\,{}_0t_{(k)'} = {}_0W_{(k)'}\,{}_0U_{(k)} \tag{15.8.6}$$

$$_1a_{(k)} = {}_0W_{(k)}\,{}_0t_{(k)'}^{\,-1} \tag{15.8.7}$$

$$_iD_k^2 = (D_C - D_{{}_ia_{(k)}\,{}_ia_{(k)'}})^{-1} \tag{15.8.8}$$

$$_iU_{(k)} = {}_iD_k^2\,{}_ia_{(k)} \tag{15.8.9}$$

$$_iW_{(k)} = C_iU_{(k)} - {}_ia_{(k)} \tag{15.8.10}$$

$$_it_{(k)}\,{}_it_{(k)'} = {}_iW_{(k)'}\,{}_iU_{(k)} \tag{15.8.11}$$

$$_{i+1}a_{(k)} = {}_iW_{(k)}\,{}_it_{(k)'}^{\,-1} \tag{15.8.12}$$

15.8.3 Computational Instructions. This method begins with an arbitrary vector as in the first specificity type of solution. The method for getting the first factor vector is the same as in that solution.

We next proceed to indicate a factor loading matrix, as indicated in Eq. 15.8.1, where now $k - 1$ is the number of factors currently solved for.

We then indicate an augmented matrix to which one more factor has been added, as indicated in Eq. 15.8.2. To begin with, the first matrix in the parentheses on the right of Eq. 15.8.2 is simply the first factor loading vector $a_{.1}$. This is augmented now by a second arbitrary vector which may be assumed to be a reasonable approximation to the second factor loading vector.

We then have, as in Eq. 15.8.3, a diagonal matrix which is, as indicated on the right, the reciprocal of the diagonal of the covariance matrix minus the diagonal of the major product moment of the matrix in Eq. 15.8.2.

We indicate in Eq. 15.8.4 the matrix of Eq. 15.8.2 premultiplied by the diagonal matrix of Eq. 15.8.3.

Equation 15.8.5 is obtained by premultiplying the matrix of Eq. 15.8.4 by the covariance matrix and subtracting the arbitrary approximation to the factor matrix from it.

Equation 15.8.6 indicates the minor product moment of the matrices of Eqs. 15.8.4. and 15.8.5 as a major product of a partial triangular matrix. In particular, this could be solved for by means of the partial triangular factoring of the supermatrix indicated in Eq. 15.7.5 of the previous method.

Equation 15.8.7 gives the first approximation to the factor loading matrix of width k as the W matrix of Eq. 15.8.5 postmultiplied by the inverse of the upper triangular matrix of Eq. 15.8.6.

The general iterative type of solution is indicated by Eqs. 15.8.8–15.8.12. Here the equations are, respectively, the same as Eqs. 15.8.3–15.8.7, except that now the prescript becomes i for the ith approximation. In this type of solution we may again iterate to some convergence criterion for the trace of the triangular matrix, indicated on the left of Eq. 15.8.11. If the traces of two successive t matrices are sufficiently close, we may assume that the approximation is sufficiently close for the current number of factors, k.

Once this criterion has been satisfied, we again augment the currently stabilized factor loading matrix by another arbitrary vector, which is presumably reasonably orthogonal to the current factor vectors and which is not too poor an approximation to the next factor vector we wish to obtain.

We then proceed again through Eqs. 15.8.2–15.8.7 to get a first approximation to the factor loading matrix with one more factor added.

Going through Eqs. 15.8.8–15.8.12, we continue to iterate, increasing the value of susbcript i until the solution has stabilized to some specified tolerance with reference to the traces of two successive t matrices.

We proceed to augment the matrix in Eq. 15.8.2 until we have accounted for enough factors, according to some specified criterion. This criterion may well be simply the sums of squares of elements of a currently stabilized a matrix, such as given in Eq. 15.8.12. The sums of squares of these elements are, of course, the amount of variance accounted for by the given number of factors.

15.8.4 Numerical Example. We use the same correlation matrix as in the previous section. In this numerical example we use as the arbitrary vector for each new factor the corresponding principal axis vector of the correlation matrix.

The first row of Table 15.8.1 gives the variance accounted for by each of the first four factors. The body of the table gives the first four factor vectors. Again it appears that the fourth factor may be ignored.

TABLE 15.8.1   Specificity Progressive Factor Matrix Method. Variance Accounted for and First Four Factor Vectors

3.3946	1.8123	1.0936	0.2634
0.8251	−0.3481	−0.1503	−0.0012
0.8444	−0.3236	−0.1332	0.0332
0.8203	−0.1577	−0.2405	−0.0311
0.3659	0.6436	−0.2086	0.0083
0.2814	0.7159	−0.3664	0.0805
0.3410	0.6670	−0.3468	0.0579
0.5341	0.2126	0.4568	0.2343
0.5445	0.1573	0.5665	0.2987
0.6458	0.3463	0.4095	−0.3276

15.9   The Communality Successive Factor Method

We shall now consider the first of the communality class of scaling methods. In these methods we have the three different types of solutions, namely, the successive factor vector solution, the factor matrix solution and the progressive factor matrix solution. These methods are essentially the same as the specificity scaling methods, except that the scaling diagonal is different and no diagonal matrix is subtracted from the correlation matrix.

Here the scaling constants are inversely proportional to the square roots of the variances accounted for by the vectors solved for. This principal of scaling is just the opposite of that used in the specificity method. In the specificity method the scaling is such that the variance unaccounted for by the factors is the same for all variables, while in the communality method the scaling is such that the variance accounted for by the factors is the same for all variables. In this latter procedure it is assumed that more weight should be given to the variables which otherwise would have less of their variance accounted for by the factors.

We begin now with the computational equations for the successive factor method.

15.9.1 Computational Equations

15.9.1a DEFINITION OF NOTATION

C is a correlation or covariance matrix.

V is an arbitrary vector.

$_ia$ is the ith approximation to a factor vector.

D_{ia} is a diagonal matrix of the elements of $_ia$.

H_i is a tolerance limit.

$_{k+1}C$ is the kth residual matrix.

15.9.1b THE EQUATIONS

$$_0a = CV(V'CV)^{-1/2} \tag{15.9.1}$$

$$_0D = D_{0a}^{-1} \tag{15.9.2}$$

$$_0U = {_0}D1 \tag{15.9.3}$$

$$_0W = C_0U \tag{15.9.4}$$

$$_0\alpha = \frac{1}{\sqrt{_0W'\,{_0}U}} \tag{15.9.5}$$

$$_1a = {_0}W_0\alpha \tag{15.9.6}$$

$$_iD = D_{ia}^{-1} \tag{15.9.7}$$

$$_iU = {_i}D1 \tag{15.9.8}$$

$$_iW = C_iU \tag{15.9.9}$$

$$_i\alpha = \frac{1}{\sqrt{_iW'\,{_i}U}} \tag{15.9.10}$$

$$_{i+1}a = {_i}W_i\alpha \tag{15.9.11}$$

$$\left| \frac{_1\alpha}{_{i+1}\alpha} - 1 \right| = H_i \tag{15.9.12}$$

$$a_{.1} = {_{i+1}}a \tag{15.9.13}$$

$$_2C = C - a_{.1}a_{.1}' \tag{15.9.14}$$

$$_{k+1}C = {_k}C - a_{.k}a_{.k}' \tag{15.9.15}$$

15.9.2 Computational Instructions.

The computational procedure for this method is the same as for the corresponding method in the specificity class of solutions, except that the D^2 matrix and the W vector are calculated differently.

By means of an arbitrary vector V we first calculate the rank reduction $_0a$ vector as in Eq. 15.9.1.

Next we take the inverse of the elements of the $_0a$ matrix given in Eq. 15.9.1 to construct the D matrix given in Eq. 15.9.2. This is a diagonal matrix of the inverse of the elements in the vector given by Eq. 15.9.1.

Equation 15.9.3 indicates U as a vector of the elements of the D matrix given by Eq. 15.9.2.

Equation 15.9.4 is the C matrix postmultiplied by the U vector of Eq. 15.9.3.

Equation 15.9.5 is a scalar quantity which is the reciprocal square root of the minor product of the vectors of Eqs. 15.9.3 and 15.9.4.

Equation 15.9.6 gives the W vector of Eq. 15.9.4 multiplied by the scalar of Eq. 15.9.5.

Equations 15.9.7–15.9.11 indicate the iterations as in the analogous specificity method.

Equation 15.9.12 indicates the tolerance limit which is assumed to give a sufficiently close approximation.

The $i + 1$ approximation to a_1 is then taken as the first factor vector, as indicated in Eq. 15.9.13.

Equation 15.9.14 gives the first residual matrix as in the specificity method. Equation 15.9.15 gives a generalization of Eq. 15.9.14.

The procedures for Eqs. 15.9.1–15.9.13 are applied to the successive residual matrices.

15.9.3 Numerical Example.

We use the same correlation matrix as in the three previous examples to illustrate this method. The unit vector is

TABLE 15.9.1   Communality Successive
Factor Solution. Number of Iterations,
Variance Accounted for,
and First Three Factors

5	30	30
3.7106	1.8969	1.3096
0.6398	0.3749	0.4982
0.6639	0.3751	0.4818
0.7117	0.2347	0.5164
0.6326	−0.5577	−0.2927
0.5685	−0.6786	0.0257
0.6087	−0.6347	0.0133
0.6351	0.3527	−0.4426
0.6053	0.4040	−0.4655
0.7002	0.3139	−0.2522

taken for the arbitrary vectors. The computations are a little simpler with respect to the D matrix, since it involves only the factor loading vector and does not involve elements from the covariance matrix.

The first row of Table 15.9.1 gives the number of iterations for each of three factors. The second row gives the variance accounted for by each factor. The body of the table gives the first three factor loading vectors.

15.10   The Communality Factor Matrix Solution

15.10.1   Computational Equations

15.10.1a   DEFINITION OF NOTATION
C is a covariance or residual matrix.
$_ia$ is the ith approximation to the factor matrix.
$D_{_ia\,_ia'}$ is a diagonal matrix of the diagonals of $_ia\,_ia'$.
$_it$ is a triangular matrix.
H_i is a tolerance limit.

15.10.1b   THE EQUATIONS

$$_0D^2 = D_{0a\,0a'}{}^{-1} \tag{15.10.1}$$

$$_0U = {}_0D^2\,{}_0a \tag{15.10.2}$$

$$_0W = C\,{}_0U \tag{15.10.3}$$

$$_0t\,{}_0t' = {}_0W'\,{}_0U \tag{15.10.4}$$

$$_1a = {}_0W\,{}_0t'^{-1} \tag{15.10.5}$$

$$_iD^2 = D_{_ia\,_ia'}{}^{-1} \tag{15.10.6}$$

$$_iU = {}_iD^2\,{}_ia \tag{15.10.7}$$

$$_iW = R\,{}_iU \tag{15.10.8}$$

$$_it\,{}_it' = {}_iW'\,{}_iU \tag{15.10.9}$$

$$_{i+1}a = {}_iW\,{}_it'^{-1} \tag{15.10.10}$$

$$\left| \frac{tr(_it)}{tr(_{i+1}t)} - 1 \right| = H_i \tag{15.10.11}$$

15.10.2   Computational Instructions.
The computational instructions for this method are almost identical to those of the corresponding specificity factor scaling method, except that again the D^2 matrices of Eqs. 15.10.1 and 15.10.6, and the W matrices of Eqs. 15.10.3 and 15.10.8, are calculated differently. It will be seen that the D^2 matrices are obtained by taking the reciprocal of the diagonal of the major product moment of the factor loading matrix,

rather than by subtracting this diagonal from the original diagonal of variances. This difference in the calculation of the D matrices reflects the difference in the underlying rationale of the method. The W matrices are different in that they do not involve the subtraction of the current a matrix.

It will be noted that Eqs. 15.10.4 and 15.10.9 indicate the minor product of the W and the U matrices as the major product moment of partial triangular factors. These equations do not explicitly indicate the partial triangular factoring of a type 3 supervector, as indicated in Eqs. 15.7.5 and 15.7.10. However, the computations may be carried out in the same manner.

15.10.3 Numerical Example. Again we take the same correlation matrix as in the previous illustrations. We also take its first four principal axis vectors as the arbitrary matrix.

Table 15.10.1 gives the first four factor loading vectors for the correlation matrix as determined from the rescaled matrix. These are considerably different from those in Table 15.9.1.

TABLE 15.10.1   Communality Factor Matrix Method.
First Four Factor Vectors

0.6927	0.5144	0.3644	−0.0312
0.7165	0.5022	0.3346	−0.0585
0.7593	0.3215	0.4158	0.0135
0.5903	−0.6276	0.0442	0.1678
0.4992	−0.7235	0.1528	−0.1334
0.5515	−0.6716	0.1633	−0.1568
0.6369	0.1303	−0.5901	−0.2628
0.6078	0.2166	−0.6236	−0.1325
0.7053	0.0158	−0.3522	0.5589

15.11   The Communality Progressive Factor Matrix Method

15.11.1   Computational Equations

15.11.1a   DEFINITION OF NOTATION

C is the covariance or correlation matrix.

$_i a_{(k)}$ is the ith approximation to a factor loading matrix of width k.

$D_{_i a_{(k)}\ _i a_{(k)}'}$ is a matrix of the diagonal of $_i a_{(k)}\ _i a_{(k)}'$.

15.11.1b   THE EQUATIONS

$$_0 a_{(k-1)} = (a_{.1} \ldots a_{.k-1}) \tag{15.11.1}$$

$$_0 a_{(k)} = (a_{(k-1)},\ _0 a) \tag{15.11.2}$$

$$_0D_{(k)}{}^2 = D_{_0a_{(k)}\,_0a_{(k)}'}{}^{-1} \tag{15.11.3}$$

$$_0U_{(k)} = {}_0D_{(k)}{}^2\,_0a_{(k)} \tag{15.11.4}$$

$$_0W_{(k)} = C\,_0U_{(k)} \tag{15.11.5}$$

$$_0t_{(k)}\,_0t_{(k)}' = {}_0W_{(k)}'\,_0U_{(k)} \tag{15.11.6}$$

$$_1a_{(k)} = {}_0W_{(k)}\,_0t_{(k)}'{}^{-1} \tag{15.11.7}$$

$$_iD_{(k)}{}^2 = D_{_ia_{(k)}\,_ia_{(k)}'}{}^{-1} \tag{15.11.8}$$

$$_iU_{(k)} = {}_iD_{(k)}{}^2\,_ia_{(k)} \tag{15.11.9}$$

$$_iW_{(k)} = C\,_iU_{(k)} \tag{15.11.10}$$

$$_it_{(k)}\,_it_{(k)}' = {}_iW_{(k)}'\,_iU_{(k)} \tag{15.11.11}$$

$$_{i+1}a_{(k)} = {}_iW_{(k)}\,_it_{(k)}'{}^{-1} \tag{15.11.12}$$

$$\left|1 - \frac{tr(t_k)}{tr(C)}\right| = P_k \tag{15.11.13}$$

15.11.2 Computational Instructions.

Here the computational procedure is essentially the same as that of the corresponding specificity method, except that again the D matrices are calculated only as the major product moment of the factor loading matrix, and the W matrices do not involve the subtraction of the current approximation to the factor loading matrix.

15.11.3 Numerical Example.

The correlation matrix is the same as in the previous examples.

The first row of Table 15.11.1 gives the variance accounted for by each

TABLE 15.11.1 Communality Progressive
Factor Matrix Method. Variance
Accounted for, and First
Three Factor Vectors

3.7343	2.0508	1.3421
0.6655	0.5042	0.4242
0.6904	0.4932	0.3969
0.7306	0.3105	0.4711
0.5884	−0.6275	0.0621
0.4908	−0.7257	0.1613
0.5429	−0.6746	0.1763
0.6630	0.1528	−0.5376
0.6331	0.2390	−0.5627
0.7476	0.0312	−0.3406

of the first three factors. The body of the table gives the three factor vectors.

Although the three communality scaling methods give different results, the general orders of magnitude of the factor loadings compare favorably with one another. The signs for corresponding elements of all three sets are the same for the first three factors, except for the element in the third column, fourth row of Table 15.9.1.

15.12 Mathematical Proofs

15.12.1 The Specificity Successive Factor Method

Let C be the correlation of the covariance matrix, and consider

$$C - D^{-2} - aa' = {}_1C \tag{15.12.1}$$

where a is a vector or matrix of specified width and

$$D = (D_C - D_{aa'})^{-1/2} \tag{15.12.2}$$

We let

$$Da = \alpha \tag{15.12.3}$$

$$D(C - D^{-2})D\alpha = \alpha\alpha'\alpha \tag{15.12.4}$$

We may begin with some approximation to the first principal axis vector such as the centroid. We let this vector be ${}_0a$, and calculate

$${}_0D^2 = (D_C - D_{{}_0a}{}^2)^{-1} \tag{15.12.5}$$

Then consider

$${}_0D{}_1a = {}_0D(C - {}_0D^{-2}){}_0D^2{}_0a[{}_0a'{}_0D^2(C - {}_0D^{-2}){}_0D^2{}_0a]^{-1/2} \tag{15.12.6}$$

which is a rank reduction form.

We let

$${}_0U = {}_0D^2{}_0a \tag{15.12.7}$$

From Eqs. 15.12.6 and 15.12.7,

$${}_1a = (C - {}_0D^{-2}){}_0U[{}_0U'(C - {}_0D^{-2}){}_0U]^{-1/2} \tag{15.12.8}$$

If we let

$${}_0W = C{}_0U - {}_0a \tag{15.12.9}$$

and

$${}_0b = \frac{1}{\sqrt{{}_0W'{}_0U}} \tag{15.12.10}$$

Then from Eqs. 15.12.8–15.12.10,

$${}_1a = {}_0W{}_0b \tag{15.12.11}$$

In general then, we have

$$_iD^2 = (D_C - D_{_ia}{}^2)^{-1} \tag{15.12.12}$$

$$_iU = {}_iD^2 \,{}_ia \tag{15.12.13}$$

$$_iW = C \,{}_iU - {}_ia \tag{15.12.14}$$

$$_ib = \frac{1}{\sqrt{_iW' \,{}_iU}} \tag{15.12.15}$$

$$_{i+1}a = {}_iW \,{}_ib \tag{15.12.16}$$

We may continue until $_ib$ stabilizes and then calculate the residual

$$_1C = C - a_{.1} \, a_{.1}' \tag{15.12.17}$$

The operations on $_1C$ are the same as for C. Successive residual $_iC$'s may be obtained to a specified number of factors.

We show in Section 15.12.7 that the solution is independent of scale.

15.12.2 The Specificity Factor Matrix Method

Let a be a factor loading matrix of specified width. We may still use Eqs. 15.12.1–15.12.7 without loss of generality. We now, however, introduce

$$_0t \,{}_0t' = {}_0W' \,{}_0U \tag{15.12.18}$$

Analogous to Eq. 15.12.11, we now write

$$_1a = {}_0W \,{}_0t'^{\,-1} \tag{15.12.19}$$

In general then, for a of any width, we have

$$_iD^2 = (D_C - D_{_ia \,{}_ia'})^{-1} \tag{15.12.20}$$

$$_iU = {}_iD^2 \,{}_ia \tag{15.12.21}$$

$$_iW = C \,{}_iU - {}_ia \tag{15.12.22}$$

$$_it \,{}_it' = {}_iW' \,{}_iU \tag{15.12.23}$$

$$_{i+1}a = {}_iW \,{}_it'^{\,-1} \tag{15.12.24}$$

These iterations may continue until

$$tr(_{i+1}t) - tr(_it) = P \tag{15.12.25}$$

for P sufficiently small. Then $_it$ will approach the basic diagonal δ of

$$DCD - I = Q\delta Q' \tag{15.12.26}$$

and

$$Q\delta^{1/2} = Da = \alpha \tag{15.12.27}$$

That this solution is independent of scale is shown in Section 15.12.7.

15.12.3   The Specificity Progressive Factor Matrix Method

Let Eqs. 15.12.20–15.12.24 be the iterative procedure for a of width k. In particular, k may be 1. Continue until Eq. 15.12.25 is satisfied and indicate

$$a_{(k)} = (a_{.1} \ldots a_{.k}) \tag{15.12.28}$$

Let

$$_0a_{(k+1)} = (a_{.1} \ldots a_{.k}, {}_0a) \tag{15.12.29}$$

where $_0a$ is an arbitrary vector distinct from all the preceding $a_{.1}$'s and preferably orthogonal to them.

Then let

$$_0D^2 = (D_C - D_{_0a_{(k+1)}\,_0a_{(k+1)'}})^{-1} \tag{15.12.30}$$

$$_0U = {}_0D^2\,_0a_{(k+1)} \tag{15.12.31}$$

$$_0W = C_0U - {}_0a_{(k+1)} \tag{15.12.32}$$

$$_0t\,_0t' = {}_0W'\,_0U \tag{15.12.33}$$

$$_1a = {}_0W\,_0t'^{-1} \tag{15.12.34}$$

and in general

$$_iD^2 = (D_C - D_{_ia_{(k+1)}\,_ia_{(k+1)'}})^{-1} \tag{15.12.35}$$

$$_iU = {}_iD^2\,_ia_{(k+1)} \tag{15.12.36}$$

$$_iW = C_iU - {}_ia_{(k+1)} \tag{15.12.37}$$

$$_it\,_it' = {}_iW'\,_iU \tag{15.12.38}$$

$$_{i+1}a = {}_iW\,_it'^{-1} \tag{15.12.39}$$

We may continue until

$$_it_{(k+1),(k+1)} < 0 \tag{15.12.40}$$

or sooner.

Here also the solution is independent of scale, as shown in Section 15.12.7.

15.12.4   The Communality Successive Factor Vector Method

Let C be the covariance matrix and consider the rank reduction vector $_0a$ given by

$$_0a = CV(V'CV)^{-1/2} \tag{15.12.41}$$

where V is arbitrary.

We indicate a diagonal of the elements of $_0a$ by

$$_0D = D_{_0a}{}^{-1} \tag{15.12.42}$$

Let

$$_1a = C_0D^2\,_0a({}_0a'\,_0D^2C_0D^2\,_0a)^{-1/2} \tag{15.12.43}$$

In general, let

$$_iD = D_{_ia}{}^{-1} \tag{15.12.44}$$

and

$$_{i+1}a = C_i D^2 {}_i a(_i a' {}_i D^2 C_i D^2 {}_i a)^{-1/2} \qquad (15.12.45)$$

Let

$$_i U = D_{ia}^{-1} 1 \qquad (15.12.46)$$

From Eqs. 15.12.44 and 15.12.46,

$$_i U = {}_i D^2 {}_i a \qquad (15.12.47)$$

From Eq. 15.12.47 in Eq. 15.12.45,

$$_{(i+1)}a = C_i U(_i U' C_i U)^{-1/2} \qquad (15.12.48)$$

From Eqs. 15.12.44 and 15.12.47,

$$_i D = {}_i D_U \qquad (15.12.49)$$

If we let

$$_i W = C_i U \qquad (15.12.50)$$

we have as the computational sequence

$$D_{iU} = D_{ia}^{-1} \qquad (15.12.51)$$

$$_i W = C_i U \qquad (15.12.52)$$

$$_i \alpha = \frac{1}{\sqrt{_i W' {}_i U}} \qquad (15.12.53)$$

$$_{i+1}a = {}_i W {}_i \alpha \qquad (15.12.54)$$

We may continue Eqs. 15.12.51–15.12.54 until α_i stabilizes, at which point

$$_i a = a_{.1} \qquad (15.12.55)$$

That this solution is independent of scale can be readily seen by writing the general form from Eq. 15.12.45 as

$$a = C D_a^{-1} 1 (1' D_a^{-1} C D_a^{-1} 1)^{-1/2} \qquad (15.12.56)$$

Then consider any scaling diagonal Δ such that

$$A = \Delta a \qquad (15.12.57)$$

$$\gamma = \Delta C \Delta \qquad (15.12.58)$$

and

$$A = \gamma D_A^{-1} 1 (1' D_A^{-1} C D_A^{-1} 1)^{-1/2} \qquad (15.12.59)$$

Substituting Eqs. 15.12.57 and 15.12.58 in Eq. 15.12.59,

$$\Delta a = \Delta C \Delta (\Delta^{-1} D_a^{-1} 1)[1' D_a^{-1} \Delta^{-1}(\Delta C \Delta)\Delta^{-1} D_a^{-1} 1]^{-1/2} \qquad (15.12.60)$$

Equation 15.12.60 reduces at once to Eq. 15.12.56.

Once $a_{.1}$ is obtained, we can solve for a residual matrix

$$_1C = C - a_{.1}a_{.1}'$$ (15.12.61)

and operate on $_1C$ as before to obtain $a_{.2}$. The procedure is readily generalized to any number of factors.

15.12.5   The Communality Factor Matrix Method

Let C be the covariance matrix and consider the approximate solution

$$C - aa' = {}_1C$$ (15.12.62)

where the width of a is chosen.

We let

$$D^{-2} = D_{aa'}$$ (15.12.63)

and

$$Da = \alpha$$ (15.12.64)

Consider also

$$DRD\alpha = \alpha\alpha'\alpha$$ (15.12.65)

We assume a of fixed width and start with, say, a principal axis or some other approximation to a. We call this solution $_0a$. We let

$$_0D = D_{_0a\,_0a'}{}^{-1/2}$$ (15.12.66)

and

$$_0\alpha = {}_0D\,_0a$$ (15.12.67)

We then consider the matrix reduction solution

$$_1a_1a' = C\,_0D\,_0\alpha({}_0\alpha'\,_0DC\,_0D\,_0\alpha)^{-1}\,_0\alpha'\,_0DC$$ (15.12.68)

We let

$$_0U = {}_0D^2\,_0a$$ (15.12.69)

From Eqs. 15.12.64, 15.12.68 and 15.12.69,

$$_1a_1a' = R\,_0U({}_0U'R_0\,_0U)^{-1}\,_0U'R$$ (15.12.70)

We let

$$_0W = R\,_0U$$ (15.12.71)

$$_0t\,_0t' = {}_0W'\,_0U$$ (15.12.72)

$$_1a = {}_0W\,_0t'^{-1}$$ (15.12.73)

or in general

$$_iD = D_{_ia\,_ia'}{}^{-1/2}$$ (15.12.74)

$$_iU = {}_iD^2\,_ia$$ (15.12.75)

$$_iW = C\,_iU$$ (15.12.76)

$$_it\,_it' = {}_iW'\,_iU$$ (15.12.77)

$$_{i+1}a = {}_iW\,_it'^{-1}$$ (15.12.78)

Equations 15.12.74–15.12.78 continue until in

$$tr(_{i+1}t) - tr(_it) = P \tag{15.12.79}$$

P is sufficiently small. As i increases, $_it$ will approach a diagonal matrix of the basic structure of $_iDR\ _iD$ or, in general,

$$D_{it} \rightarrow\ _i\alpha'\ _i\alpha \tag{15.12.80}$$

We can show by Section 15.12.7 that this procedure is independent of scale.

15.12.6 The Communality Progressive Factor Matrix Method

Let Eqs. 15.12.74–15.12.78 be the iterative procedure for a of width k where $k \geq 1$. We continue until Eq. 15.12.79 is satisfied and let

$$a_{(k)} = (a_{.1} \ldots a_{.k}) \tag{15.12.81}$$

We then let

$$a_{(k+1)} = (a_{(k)},\ _0a) \tag{15.12.82}$$

where $_0a$ is determined in some suitable manner. In particular, we may consider

$$_{k+1}C = C - a_{(k)}a_{(k)}' \tag{15.12.83}$$

and let

$$_0a =\ _{k+1}C1(1'\ _{k+1}C1)^{-1/2} \tag{15.12.84}$$

where obviously the operations in Eq. 15.12.84 can be performed directly with C and $a_{(k)}$ so that $_{k+1}C$ need not be computed.

We then let

$$_0D^2 = D_{_0a_{(k+1)}\ _0a_{(k+1)}'}^{-1} \tag{15.12.85}$$

$$_0U =\ _0D^2\ _0a_{(k+1)} \tag{15.12.86}$$

$$_0W = C\ _0U \tag{15.12.87}$$

$$_0t\ _0t' =\ _0W'\ _0U \tag{15.12.88}$$

$$_1a =\ _0a +\ _0W\ _0t'^{-1} \tag{15.12.89}$$

and, in general,

$$_iD^2 = D_{_ia_{(k+1)}\ _ia_{(k+1)}'}^{-1} \tag{15.12.90}$$

$$_iU =\ _iD^2\ _ia_{(k+1)} \tag{15.12.91}$$

$$_iW = C\ _iU \tag{15.12.92}$$

$$_it\ _it' =\ _iW'\ _iU \tag{15.12.93}$$

$$_{i+1}a =\ _ia\ _iW\ _it'^{-1} \tag{15.12.94}$$

We continue until

$$\left|1 - \frac{tr(t_k)}{tr(C)}\right| = P \tag{15.12.95}$$

is sufficiently small.

Here also the solution is independent of scale as shown in the following section.

15.12.7   The Generalized Procedure Independent of Scale

Given the $n \times n$ covariance matrix C and the $n \times k$ factor matrix a. Consider

$$E = C - aa' \qquad (15.12.96)$$

Let

$$D = g D_C + f D_{aa'} \qquad (15.12.97)$$

where g and f are scalars. Consider the basic structure rank reduction solution

$$a = CD^{-1}a(a'D^{-1}CD^{-1}a)^{-1/2}h \qquad (15.12.98)$$

where h is a square orthonormal. Let Δ be diagonal and

$$\gamma = \Delta C \Delta \qquad (15.12.99)$$

$$A = \Delta a \qquad (15.12.100)$$

$$\delta = g D_\gamma + f D_{AA'} \qquad (15.12.101)$$

and consider the basic structure rank reduction solution

$$A = \gamma \delta^{-1} A(A'\delta^{-1}\gamma\delta^{-1}A)^{-1/2}h \qquad (15.12.102)$$

From Eqs. 15.12.96, 15.12.99, and 15.12.100 in 15.12.101,

$$\delta = \Delta^2 D \qquad (15.12.103)$$

From Eqs. 15.12.99, 15.12.100 and 15.12.103 in 15.12.102,

$$a = CD^{-1}a(a'D^{-1}CD^{-1}a)^{-1/2}h \qquad (15.12.104)$$

which is the same as Eq. 15.12.98.

Now we let

$$\alpha = \delta^{-1/2}A \qquad (15.12.105)$$

From Eqs. 15.12.100 and 15.12.103 in 15.12.105,

$$\alpha = D^{-1/2}a \qquad (15.12.106)$$

which shows that α is independent of Δ and depends only on g and f in Eq. 15.12.97. If we let $g = 0, f = 1$, we get the communality scaling type solutions. If we let $g = 1, f = 0$, we get the conventional basic structure solution applied to the correlation matrix.

We may now substitute $C - D$ for C and $\gamma - \delta$ for γ, and show that α is independent of Δ and depends only on g and f. Then for $g = 1$ and $f = -1$, we get the specificity scaling type of solutions.

Chapter 16

Image Analysis

In earlier chapters we have referred to the communality problem and have indicated that from a computational point of view we may be concerned with solving for unknown diagonal elements of the correlation or covariance matrix in such a way that the modified matrix is of lower rank than the original. Presumably the original matrix will be basic in most cases.

Whether we can select diagonal elements so that the matrix without alterations in the nondiagonal elements is of lower rank than the original is a question of fact. We know that in some cases this cannot be done except for a rank reduction of 1. It is well known that experimental covariance matrices can in general be reduced to a rank one less than their order by a change in one diagonal element.

There are, of course, as many diagonal elements as the order of the matrix, so that there would be n ways that the matrix could be reduced in rank by at least 1. Actually, in the case of the correlation matrix, we know that this diagonal element, which for any particular variable will reduce the rank of the matrix by 1, is the squared multiple correlation of that variable with all of the others.

The problem of communality and how to solve for the unknown elements has been very troublesome over the years. Many investigators are becoming convinced that the questions have not been properly stated and that the problem has not been properly formulated.

We have seen in the previous chapter that another way of looking at the problem is from the scaling point of view. It should be remembered that the communality problem has its origin and basic motivation from a consideration of hypotheses about the kinds of factors which may exist in a set of variables. These are factors which are common to two or more of the variables, and factors which are specific to each of the variables. This does not, however, suggest specifically a mathematical formulation, because the unique variance must consist of both systematic specific variance and error or unsystematic specific variance.

Another approach to the solution of the issues involved in the communality controversy has in recent years received considerable emphasis under the impetus of Louis Guttman (1953). His work has offered some hope of getting out of some of the dilemmas and contradictions involved in the traditional formulations of the communality problem. This approach is based on what he terms *image analysis*. The notion here is that a factor analysis should be concerned primarily with that part of each variable which can be estimated from all of the other variables in the set, and that as much as possible of the specific variance should be eliminated.

We shall therefore consider in this chapter a group of methods based on Guttman's image analysis which are somewhat different from those considered in the previous chapter. The methods of Chapter 15 operate upon a transformed score matrix in which the transformation consists of multiplication by a scaling diagonal. In the examples here, we also work with the transformed score matrix, in that the matrix is multiplied on the right by another matrix. The matrix in this case, however, is not a diagonal matrix but a more general type of matrix which we shall develop in detail in the following sections.

16.1 Characteristics of the Methods

We shall consider now the characteristics which are common to all of these methods. First, all of the methods are based on the image matrix, which is the matrix consisting of the part of each variable which can be predicted by all the remaining ones. Second, the calculation of the inverse of the correlation matrix is required in all of the solutions. The problem of scaling of the variables is a consideration, but the methods differ essentially in the arbitrary scaling procedures adopted. Third, the correlation matrix should be basic. Finally, the solutions are, in general, basic structure solutions.

16.1.1 The Communality Score Matrix. The basis for all of these methods is a matrix derived from the data matrix by conventional least square procedures. In effect, one gets the best least square estimate of each attribute vector in the data matrix from all of the remaining $n - 1$ vectors. In this way one gets a matrix of least square estimates of the data matrix vectors. Actually, one does not go through the tedious and detailed operations of calculating the regression equations and the estimated vectors. By algebraic short-cuts, one arrives at a matrix which transforms the original data matrix into this so-called image or estimated data matrix. Also, in practice, one does not operate directly on the data matrix, but rather on a correlation or covariance matrix derived from it.

16.1.2 Calculation of the Inverse. The methods considered in this chapter differ essentially from all of those we have considered previously in that the calculation of the inverse of the correlation matrix is required as a basis for the solution. For this reason the computations can be considerably more involved than previous methods we have considered. The computation of the inverse of a very large matrix involving several hundred or more variables is in itself an appreciable computational enterprise. It is therefore only since the advent of the high-speed electronic computers that methods of factor analysis based upon the image analysis approach of Guttman have become feasible.

16.1.3 Scaling Considerations. The essential differences in the methods we shall consider are those involving scaling of the variables after the original data matrix has been converted to an image or estimated matrix. These scaling methods are, however, considerably simpler than those in the previous chapter where, as we recall, elaborate iteration procedures were required to arrive at a scaling matrix for each of the models presented. In this set of methods, one adopts a simple and perhaps arbitrary rationale for the scaling of the variables, and proceeding from this scaling on the covariance matrix of the estimated variables, one does not attempt to alter it by successive approximations as in the previous chapter. It is possible with these models to solve for scaling constants as in Chapter 15. However, the fruitfulness of such approaches has not yet been demonstrated.

16.1.4 The Basic Correlation Matrix. In the methods discussed in this chapter we must have a basic correlation matrix. This, of course, follows from the fact that we work with the inverse of the correlation or covariance matrix as part of the general procedure. In the past it has been true that most of the correlation matrices on which factor analyses were performed were basic and did have a regular inverse. Therefore, this restriction in the method has not been a practical or serious one. However, we may very well encounter correlation matrices which are not basic. The most obvious case is the one in which we have more attributes than entities or persons. An example is the personality inventory for which we wish to consider each item on the inventory as a variable. We may have many hundreds of items in the inventory, and it may be administered to only a hundred persons. Actually, in the experimental situation, one is faced with the problem that the longer the inventory to be administered for research purposes, the more difficult it is to amass cases or entities which have responded to the inventory. Therefore, in practical situations there is a tendency to find an inverse relationship between the number of variables and the number of entities. This is a consequence of the limited time which potential subjects have available for taking the inventory.

In any case, the correlation or covariance matrix cannot have rank greater than the number of entities. The problem of how the concept of the general inverse of the matrix could be used in connection with the image analysis type of factor analytic models has not yet been explored. Whether or not this would be a fruitful approach, even if it were mathematically and computationally feasible, requires further investigation.

16.1.5 Basic Structure Solutions. It is quite possible to apply any of the factor analytic procedures we have discussed in previous chapters to the types of transformed covariance or correlation matrices which we work with in the image analysis models. Even the centroid, the group centroid and the multiple group methods can be applied. However, after going to all the trouble of calculating the inverse of the matrix and considering the advantages of the basic structure solution, one would in general adopt some basic structure type of solution, particularly when high-speed computers are available. The methods based on the image analysis approach would not be feasible for sizable sets of data matrices if only desk computers were available. As a matter of fact, it is only for small demonstrations or fictitious examples that one would be likely to use desk computers for the types of models outlined in the following sections.

16.2 Kinds of Methods

As just indicåted, all of the methods start with a covariance matrix which consists of the variances and covariances of the least square estimated variables. We assume that the data matrix has been reduced to standard or normalized form. This has been done before the symbolic transformation to the estimated or image variables has been accomplished.

On the basis of this assumption, we then have four different variations of the factoring procedure. First, the estimated covariance matrix may be factored. Second, the correlation matrix of the estimated variables may be factored. Third, the covariance matrix of estimated variables may be scaled in such a way that it is independent of the scaling of the original variables. Finally, the inverse of the covariance matrix may be scaled so that it yields the best least square approximation to the identity matrix.

16.2.1 The Estimated Covariance Matrix. As just indicated, the matrix of variances and covariances of the variables estimated by least square regression from the data matrix of normalized variables can be obtained by suitable mathematical transformation of the correlation matrix. After this transformation has been applied to the correlation matrix, the resulting covariance matrix is subjected to a basic structure type solution such as an eigenvalue-eigenvector solution in which the largest roots and corresponding vectors are extracted without further alteration of this covariance matrix.

16.2.2 The Estimated Correlation Matrix. Instead of working with the covariance matrix of estimated variables, one may wish to work with the actual correlation matrix of these estimated variables. This is a simple matter, for one can merely pre- and postmultiply the estimated covariance matrix by the reciprocal square root of its diagonal or, what amounts to the same thing, by the reciprocal square root of the variances of the estimated variables. This correlation matrix with 1 in the diagonal is now factored in the conventional manner by basic structure or eigenvalue procedures.

16.2.3   The Independent Scale Procedure. It will be recognized that both of the variations just considered are arbitrary from the scaling point of view. One may, however, prefer a model which does not depend on the assumption of either a standardized data or an image matrix, but a method which is independent of the scaling of the original or image variables. In other words, one may wish to use a procedure so that for any scaling diagonal one may use on the data matrix, this diagonal cancels out in the covariance matrix which is finally adopted for factoring. The third method achieves this objective.

16.2.4   The Optimal Residual Matrix. In the image analysis approach, each vector of the image matrix is defined as the part of each variable which can be predicted from all of the others. Implicit also is the concept of the anti-image matrix which consists of that part of each variable which cannot be predicted from any of the others. We may therefore also define an anti-image covariance matrix as indicated in Section 16.7. This method proceeds on the assumption that the image covariance matrix should be scaled in such a way that when the anti-image covariance matrix is scaled in the same way, it will be as close to an identity matrix as possible. In other words, the rationale is that the anti-image covariance matrix shall have a scaling such that, compared to the variances, the covariances will be as small as possible in the least square sense.

16.3   The Image Covariance Matrix

16.3.1   Characteristics of the Method. In this method, as just indicated, the analysis is performed directly on the covariance matrix of the variables which have been estimated from the normalized data matrix by the least square method. It can be seen from the mathematical proof of this method in Section 16.7 that a diagonal element of this covariance matrix consists of the squared multiple correlation of a variable with all of the others.

In general, any method of factor analysis based on basic structure procedures or approximations to them tends to give the greatest weight to the variables with the largest variances. That is, if a covariance rather than a correlation matrix is operated upon, other things being equal, the variables with the largest variances have the greatest weight or influence in determining the factor loadings for that matrix. It can be seen, therefore, that since the variances are squared multiple correlation coefficients, those variables which have the highest multiple correlation with all of the other variables receive the greatest weight in the determination of the basic structure factor matrix. Conversely, variables with very low multiple correlations receive very little weight in the solution. In particular, if a variable is entirely independent of the others, that is, if it has zero correlations, it receives no weight whatever, and therefore will not have a loading in any of the factors.

The rationale here can obviously be defended if one takes the position that he is interested only in the factor loadings for those factors which are common to two or more of the variables. This is the traditional Thurstonian approach to the problem. The communality concept appears to make more sense from the mathematical and theoretical point of view via the image analysis approach than via the more traditional approach in which one alters the diagonal elements without altering the correlation coefficients. It would seem that any defensible approach should be based on some transformation of the data matrix, rather than on the data matrix plus something which is not connected in any way with the data matrix. This latter is implicit in the conventional communality approach.

16.3.2   Computational Equations

16.3.2a   DEFINITION OF NOTATION
 R is the correlation matrix.
 ρ is the inverse of R.
 D_ρ is the diagonal of ρ.
 C_{WW} is the estimated covariance matrix.
 a is the factor loading matrix.

16.3.2b   THE EQUATIONS

$$\rho = R^{-1} \tag{16.3.1}$$

$$D = D_\rho^{-1} \tag{16.3.2}$$

$$_c\rho = \rho - D_\rho \tag{16.3.3}$$

$$_f\rho = D_{\,c}\rho D \tag{16.3.4}$$

$$_cR = R - D \tag{16.3.5}$$

$$C_{WW} = {}_cR + {}_f\rho \tag{16.3.6}$$

$$C_{WW} = Q\delta Q' \tag{16.3.7}$$

$$a = Q\delta^{1/2} \tag{16.3.8}$$

16.3.3 Computational Instructions.

We assume that the matrix of correlations of the variables to be factored is available. This matrix we indicate by R. The first step is to calculate its inverse by one of the conventional procedures. Equation 16.3.1 indicates the inverse of the correlation matrix. We designate this by ρ.

Equation 16.3.2 is the diagonal matrix whose elements are the reciprocals of the diagonal elements in the matrix given by Eq. 16.3.1.

We next indicate the inverse of the correlation matrix with the diagonal elements removed or made 0, as in Eq. 16.3.3.

The next step is the pre- and postmultiplication of the matrix given by Eq. 16.3.3, by the diagonal matrix of Eq. 16.3.2. This is indicated by Eq. 16.3.4.

The next step consists of subtracting from the original correlation matrix the diagonal matrix of Eq. 16.3.2. This is indicated in Eq. 16.3.5. It can be shown that the diagonal elements in the matrix on the left-hand side of Eq. 16.3.5 are now the squared multiple correlation coefficients of each variable with the remaining variables.

We next add together the matrices given by Eqs. 16.3.4 and 16.3.5, as indicated in Eq. 16.3.6. This is now the covariance matrix of the estimated variables or the image covariance matrix.

Equation 16.3.7 indicates the basic structure solution of this image covariance matrix.

The analysis may be carried to as many factors as desired. There seems to be no very good rule for this particular model, but a rough rule-of-thumb criterion is that the sum of the currently calculated basic diagonals be approximately 80–85 percent of the trace of the image covariance matrix given by Eq. 16.3.6.

Equation 16.3.8 gives the factor loading matrix as a function of the basic diagonal and the basic orthonormal vectors indicated in Eq. 16.3.7.

16.3.4 Numerical Example.

The correlation matrix used here is the same as in previous chapters.

Table 16.3.1 gives the image covariance matrix of the correlation matrix. The inverse of the correlation matrix is not displayed, although it can be printed out from the appropriate Fortran program if desired. The procedure for calculating the inverse is given in Section 3.5. This is included as *Subroutine Symin* in the Fortran listing.

The first row of Table 16.3.2 gives all the basic diagonal elements of the image covariance matrix. The body of the table gives the column vectors of the left basic orthonormal. These are, of course, proportional to the corresponding factor loading vectors of the image covariance matrix. The basic orthonormal matrix must be postmultiplied by the square root of the basic diagonal matrix to yield the principal axis vectors. These have not been

TABLE 16.3.1   Image Covariance Matrix

0.7331	0.6880	0.6621	0.1204	0.0652	0.1011	0.2936	0.3018	0.3356
0.6880	0.7444	0.6659	0.1472	0.0672	0.1167	0.3163	0.3067	0.3577
0.6621	0.6659	0.6905	0.2146	0.1693	0.2389	0.2877	0.3047	0.3554
0.1204	0.1472	0.2146	0.5114	0.4875	0.4942	0.2182	0.1784	0.2853
0.0652	0.0672	0.1693	0.4875	0.5720	0.4858	0.1611	0.0814	0.2464
0.1011	0.1167	0.2389	0.4942	0.4858	0.5624	0.1602	0.1417	0.2625
0.2936	0.3163	0.2877	0.2182	0.1611	0.1602	0.4808	0.3964	0.4177
0.3018	0.3067	0.3047	0.1784	0.0814	0.1417	0.3964	0.4989	0.3885
0.3356	0.3577	0.3554	0.2853	0.2464	0.2625	0.4177	0.3885	0.4359

TABLE 16.3.2   Basic Diagonal and Basic Orthonormal of Image Covariance Matrix

3.0137	1.3337	0.5792	0.1254	0.0651	0.0508	0.0371	0.0214	0.0029
-0.4108	0.3458	-0.2489	0.0805	-0.4535	0.0380	0.6019	0.2427	-0.1224
-0.4221	0.3318	-0.2246	0.1425	0.4382	-0.4261	-0.3195	0.1327	-0.3261
-0.4310	0.2016	-0.3089	-0.2148	-0.0538	0.3573	-0.2874	-0.4966	0.4149
-0.2587	-0.4596	-0.0780	-0.0329	0.1784	-0.5532	0.3880	-0.1702	0.4442
-0.2172	-0.5232	-0.1902	0.4109	-0.5056	-0.0719	-0.3804	-0.0709	-0.2522
-0.2472	-0.4862	-0.1926	-0.4374	0.3164	0.4173	0.1472	0.1934	-0.3752
-0.3027	-0.0133	0.5306	0.4669	0.2479	0.2779	0.2532	-0.4101	-0.1940
-0.2924	0.0468	0.5653	-0.5696	-0.3283	-0.2947	-0.1488	-0.0951	-0.2063
-0.3391	-0.0765	0.3343	0.1533	0.0352	0.1999	-0.2234	0.6544	0.4739

calculated. The basic structure factors are probably of more interest than the principal axis vectors, although the latter could readily be obtained by several additional statements in the Fortran program.

16.4   The Image Correlation Matrix

16.4.1   Characteristics of the Method. The method is similar to most of the conventional methods of factor analysis we have considered in previous chapters in that we begin with the matrix of the correlations of measures with 1 in the diagonal. Here we make an arbitrary assumption that for the particular sample, each of the estimated variables should have equal variance. The rationale or justification for this assumption is probably no worse or better than such an assumption for the original data matrix. If, however, one assumes that variables which correlate low with others should not, therefore, be weighted less in the factor solution, the procedure of using unit variances for the image variables is justified. In any case, this method does give relatively more weight to the variables which have the greater unique variance than does the previous method.

16.4.2   Computational Equations

16.4.2a   DEFINITION OF NOTATION
C_{WW} is the estimated covariance matrix.
$D_{R^{-1}}$ is the diagonal of R^{-1}.
R_{WW} is the estimated correlation matrix.
$Q\delta Q'$ is the basic structure of R_{WW}.

16.4.2b   THE EQUATIONS
Given the C_{WW} matrix,

$$d = (I - D_{R^{-1}}^{-1})^{1/2} \tag{16.4.1}$$

$$R_{WW} = d^{-1}C_{WW}d^{-1} \tag{16.4.2}$$

$$R_{WW} - Q\delta Q^{-1} = \varepsilon \tag{16.4.3}$$

$$a = Q\delta^{1/2} \tag{16.4.4}$$

16.4.3   Computational Instructions. The computational instructions for this procedure involve only a few more steps than those of the previous method. We begin in the same way by calculating the covariance matrix of the image variables, that is, the C_{WW} matrix. We have seen that the diagonal elements of this covariance matrix are given by the identity less a diagonal matrix which is the inverse of the diagonal elements of the inverse of the correlation matrix. This is indicated in Eq. 16.4.1.

The next set of computational steps is given in Eq. 16.4.2. This consists of pre- and postmultiplying the covariance image matrix by the inverse of the d matrix calculated in Eq. 16.4.1. The resulting matrix is the correlation matrix of the image variables.

The next set of computations consists in finding the basic structure factor vectors for the required number of factors, as indicated in Eq. 16.4.3.

The factor loading matrix is indicated in the conventional manner in Eq. 16.4.4.

16.4.4 Numerical Example. We use the same correlation matrix as in the previous section. Here we begin with the image covariance matrix solved for in the previous section.

Table 16.4.1 gives the correlation matrix obtained from the image covariance matrix. This is obtained by pre- and postmultiplying the image covariance matrix by the reciprocal square root of its diagonal.

The first row of Table 16.4.2 gives the elements of the basic diagonal of the image correlation matrix. The body of the table gives the left basic orthonormal of this matrix. It may be transformed to a factor loading matrix by the usual method indicated in Eq. 16.4.4.

16.5 The Independent Scale Matrix

16.5.1 Characteristics of the Method. The previous two methods which we considered were based on arbitrary scaling procedures. In the first case, we required that the original variables be in standard score form, and in the second case, we required that the image variables be in standard score form. It may be desirable to have a method which does not impose any such arbitrary scaling.

We therefore consider a method which scales the image covariance matrix in such a way as to cancel out any particular scaling which has been applied to the original or image variables.

This method also has some interesting characteristics which are indicated in Section 16.7.3. The particular scaling applied to the data matrix is such that the image covariance matrix is the sum of the covariance matrix of the scaled data matrix and the inverse of this covariance matrix, less twice the identity matrix.

16.5.2 Computational Equations

16.5.2a DEFINITION OF NOTATION

C_{WW} is the estimated covariance matrix.

G is the estimated covariance matrix independent of scale.

$Q\delta Q'$ is the basic structure of G.

TABLE 16.4.1 Image Correlation Matrix

1.0000	0.9314	0.9306	0.1966	0.1008	0.1574	0.4946	0.4990	0.5936
0.9314	1.0000	0.9289	0.2387	0.1029	0.1803	0.5287	0.5033	0.6279
0.9306	0.9289	1.0000	0.3612	0.2695	0.3834	0.4992	0.5192	0.6479
0.1966	0.2387	0.3612	1.0000	0.9015	0.9214	0.4400	0.3532	0.6042
0.1008	0.1029	0.2695	0.9015	1.0000	0.8566	0.3072	0.1524	0.4934
0.1574	0.1803	0.3834	0.9214	0.8566	1.0000	0.3081	0.2674	0.5301
0.4946	0.5287	0.4992	0.4400	0.3072	0.3081	1.0000	0.8093	0.9125
0.4990	0.5033	0.5192	0.3532	0.1524	0.2674	0.8093	1.0000	0.8330
0.5936	0.6279	0.6479	0.6042	0.4934	0.5301	0.9125	0.8330	1.0000

TABLE 16.4.2 Basic Diagonal and Basic Orthonormal Matrix of Image Correlation Matrix

5.1559	2.2350	1.0679	0.2392	0.1099	0.0883	0.0589	0.0397	0.0052
−0.3300	−0.3557	−0.3292	−0.0630	−0.3118	0.0426	−0.6088	−0.4021	−0.1445
−0.3392	−0.3428	−0.3068	−0.1185	0.2553	−0.4410	0.5042	−0.0200	−0.3807
−0.3668	−0.2347	−0.3792	0.1657	0.0189	0.3361	0.0650	0.5459	0.4728
−0.3094	0.4512	−0.0757	0.0589	0.0797	−0.6697	−0.2413	−0.0117	0.4223
−0.2523	0.5038	−0.1594	−0.3643	−0.6019	0.1279	0.2244	0.1799	−0.2512
−0.2814	0.4648	−0.1780	0.3935	0.4708	0.3568	−0.1045	−0.1302	−0.3760
−0.3533	−0.0798	0.4927	−0.4978	0.3183	0.0554	−0.3357	0.3636	−0.1699
−0.3312	−0.1450	0.5081	0.6234	−0.3792	−0.1391	0.0655	0.1355	−0.1914
−0.4104	−0.0036	0.2999	−0.1644	0.0419	0.2760	0.3666	−0.5830	0.4030

16.5.2b   THE EQUATIONS

Given the C_{WW} matrix,

$$d = D_{R^{-1}}^{1/2} \tag{16.5.1}$$

$$G = dC_{WW}d \tag{16.5.2}$$

$$G = Q\delta Q' \tag{16.5.3}$$

$$a = Q\delta^{1/2} \tag{16.5.4}$$

16.5.3   Computational Instructions. This method, like the previous one, begins with the covariance matrix of the image variables. It may or may not be based on an image covariance matrix derived from standard measures. The result is the same whether it is applied to a matrix derived from standard measures or to a matrix derived from arbitrarily scaled measures. For convenience we shall assume that the image covariance matrix is based on standardized measures.

We begin with a diagonal matrix, as indicated in Eq. 16.5.1. This is a diagonal matrix made up of the square roots of the diagonal elements in the inverse of the correlation matrix.

We now pre- and postmultiply the covariance matrix of the image variables by this diagonal matrix, as indicated in Eq. 16.5.2. This we call the G matrix. This matrix now has the interesting property that it is the sum of a matrix and its inverse less twice the identity matrix.

Equation 16.5.3 indicates the basic structure resolution of the G matrix. Equation 16.5.4 gives the principal axis factor loading vectors for the specified number of factors.

16.5.4   Numerical Example. We use the correlation matrix as in the previous sections and begin with the image covariance matrix as calculated in those examples.

The first row in Table 16.5.1 gives the basic diagonal elements of the scale-free, image covariance matrix. The body of the table gives the left basic orthonormal of this matrix. Perhaps the most striking feature of this table, compared with corresponding tables for the two preceding methods, is the large first eigenvalue of 8.9569.

16.6   The Optimal Residual or Anti-Image Matrix

16.6.1   Characteristics of the Method. This method is somewhat different in rationale from the previous methods. It begins, as they do, with a covariance matrix of the image variables, but the rationale for the scaling procedure is less arbitrary than in the first two, although perhaps in a sense more arbitrary than for the third method.

TABLE 16.5.1 Basic Diagonal and Basic Orthonormal of Scale-Free Image Matrix

8.9569	3.2956	1.2383	0.2787	0.2096	0.1196	0.1001	0.0466	0.0066
-0.5144	0.2675	-0.1628	-0.0754	0.6286	0.1830	-0.4206	0.1335	-0.0905
-0.5353	0.2518	-0.1301	-0.2229	-0.6625	0.2269	0.1128	0.1484	-0.2414
-0.4803	0.0791	-0.2376	0.3257	0.0569	-0.4390	0.3673	-0.3991	0.3322
-0.1069	-0.4786	-0.0668	-0.0277	-0.1704	0.4936	-0.3349	-0.3726	0.4650
-0.1329	-0.5571	-0.2088	-0.4379	0.3024	0.0869	0.5231	0.0373	-0.2501
-0.1608	-0.5268	-0.1949	0.4610	-0.1566	-0.3049	-0.3482	0.2665	-0.3692
-0.2160	-0.1096	0.5587	-0.4044	-0.0401	-0.4185	-0.2722	-0.4061	-0.2233
-0.2166	-0.0592	0.6101	0.5023	0.1264	0.4083	0.3018	-0.0429	-0.2225
-0.2348	-0.1624	0.3601	-0.1329	-0.0104	-0.1904	0.0567	0.6503	0.5556

Here the essential consideration is one developed independently by Guttman (1956) and Harris (1962). They were concerned with a scaling rationale for which the scaled anti-image covariance matrix yields the best least square approximation to an identity matrix. The method is of particular interest because of the recent work of Harris (1962), in which he has been concerned with the estimation of diagonal elements in the correlation matrix which will yield the best approximation to a lower rank approximation. This is the conventional communality problem.

16.6.2   Computational Equations

16.6.2a   DEFINITION OF NOTATION

C_{WW} is the estimated covariance matrix.

$\rho^{(2)}$ is a matrix whose elements are the squares of the elements in ρ.

γ is the covariance matrix with optimal residual variance components.

16.6.2b   THE EQUATIONS

$$\rho = R^{-1} \tag{16.6.1}$$

$$P = \rho^{(2)} \tag{16.6.2}$$

$$d1 = P^{-1}D_\rho 1 \tag{16.6.3}$$

$$D = d^{1/2}D_\rho \tag{16.6.4}$$

$$\gamma = DC_{WW}D \tag{16.6.5}$$

$$\gamma = Q\delta Q' \tag{16.6.6}$$

$$a = Q\delta^{1/2} \tag{16.6.7}$$

16.6.3   Computational Instructions.
The computations begin with the image covariance matrix calculated as in the previous methods. However, we must go back now to a solution of the scaling diagonal. We begin with the inverse of the correlation matrix, as indicated in Eq. 16.6.1.

Next we square each of the elements of the inverse calculated in Eq. 16.6.1, as indicated in Eq. 16.6.2. The superscript 2 enclosed in parentheses means that each element of the matrix on the right-hand side of the equation has been squared.

Next we cálculate a vector, as indicated in Eq. 16.6.3. The right-hand side of this equation shows that the vector consists of the diagonal elements of the inverse of the correlation matrix given by Eq. 16.6.1. We then premultiply this vector by the inverse of the matrix calculated in Eq. 16.6.2.

We now define a new diagonal matrix, as in Eq. 16.6.4. This matrix is obtained by taking the diagonal elements of the inverse of the correlation matrix and multiplying these by the square roots of the elements calculated in Eq. 16.6.3. It should be observed that the solution given by Eq. 16.6.3 does not indicate offhand that all elements in the d matrix must be positive. If they are not positive, of course, we cannot have real numbers for their square roots. This is a limitation of the method. Research to date seems to indicate that with most experimental data matrices, Eq. 16.6.3 will give all positive elements.

We next pre- and postmultiply the image covariance matrix by the diagonal matrix of Eq. 16.6.4 to get a γ matrix, as in Eq. 16.6.5. This is the matrix which we now factor.

The basic structure of this matrix is indicated in Eq. 16.6.6.

The factor loading matrix is given in Eq. 16.6.7. This is simply the usual principal axis factors calculated for the desired number of factors.

16.6.4   Numerical Example.   We use the same correlation matrix as in the previous section.

Table 16.6.1 gives the inverse of the correlation matrix.

The body of Table 16.6.2 is the inverse of the matrix obtained by squaring the elements of Table 16.6.1. The row at the bottom of the table contains the elements of the scaling diagonal.

Table 16.6.3 gives the image covariance matrix scaled so that the corresponding anti-image matrix is the best least square approximation to the identity matrix.

The first row of Table 16.6.4 consists of the elements of the basic diagonal of the matrix in Table 16.6.3. The body of the table is the corresponding left basic orthonormal.

16.7   Mathematical Proofs

16.7.1   The Estimated Covariance Matrix

Given the data matrix x in standard measures. We consider another matrix W, such that each vector $W_{.j}$ of W is the least square estimate of $x_{.j}$ calculated from the remaining $n - 1$ vectors of x. We let

$$R = \frac{x'x}{N} \tag{16.7.1}$$

We let β be the matrix of regression coefficients for estimating each variable from the remaining $n - 1$ variables so that

$$W = x\beta \tag{16.7.2}$$

It is well known that β is given by

$$\beta = I - R^{-1}D_{R^{-1}}^{-1} \tag{16.7.3}$$

Table 16.6.1 Inverse of Correlation Matrix or ρ

3.7463	−2.0659	−1.2821	0.0950	0.2822	−0.0594	−0.0314	−0.0542	−0.1026
−2.0659	3.9116	−1.3784	0.2582	0.0563	−0.0744	−0.0506	−0.3145	−0.0787
−1.2821	−1.3784	3.2313	−0.3794	−0.2692	0.0068	−0.0519	0.2176	−0.1694
0.0950	0.2582	−0.3794	2.0465	−0.7099	−0.6166	−0.1215	−0.0187	−0.3038
0.2822	0.0563	−0.2692	−0.7099	2.3365	−1.1916	0.1040	−0.0447	−0.0316
−0.0594	−0.0744	0.0068	−0.6166	−1.1916	2.2853	−0.1310	0.1764	−0.1155
−0.0314	−0.0506	−0.0519	−0.1215	0.1040	−0.1310	1.9261	−0.9902	−0.3731
−0.0542	−0.3145	0.2176	−0.0187	−0.0447	0.1764	−0.9902	1.9958	−0.5397
−0.1026	−0.0787	−0.1694	−0.3038	−0.0316	−0.1155	−0.3731	−0.5397	1.7726

Table 16.6.2 Inverse of P Matrix and Scaling Diagonals for Optimal Error or Anti-Image Matrix

0.0786	−0.0209	−0.0086	0.0006	−0.0011	0.0002	−0.0002	0.0006	−0.0002
−0.0209	0.0724	−0.0099	−0.0008	0.0005	−0.0001	0.0004	−0.0018	0.0002
−0.0086	−0.0099	0.0990	−0.0031	−0.0010	0.0005	0.0002	−0.0009	−0.0007
0.0006	−0.0008	−0.0031	0.2425	−0.0191	−0.0124	−0.0008	0.0009	−0.0071
−0.0011	0.0005	−0.0010	−0.0191	0.1987	−0.0526	−0.0004	0.0004	0.0007
0.0002	−0.0001	0.0005	−0.0124	−0.0526	0.2067	−0.0003	−0.0015	−0.0003
−0.0002	0.0004	0.0002	−0.0008	−0.0004	−0.0003	0.2884	−0.0706	−0.0062
0.0006	−0.0018	−0.0009	0.0009	0.0004	−0.0015	−0.0706	0.2701	−0.0219
−0.0002	0.0002	−0.0007	−0.0071	0.0007	−0.0003	−0.0062	−0.0219	0.3208
1.6103	1.6127	1.5790	1.2936	1.2807	1.2964	1.2215	1.1905	1.2497

TABLE 16.6.3 Image Covariance Matrix Scaled for Optimal Anti-Image Matrix

1.9008	1.7867	1.6834	0.2508	0.1346	0.2110	0.5776	0.5785	0.6752
1.7867	1.9358	1.6957	0.3072	0.1387	0.2439	0.6230	0.5889	0.7208
1.6834	1.6957	1.7216	0.4384	0.3424	0.4891	0.5548	0.5728	0.7013
0.2508	0.3072	0.4384	0.8558	0.8077	0.8287	0.3447	0.2748	0.4611
0.1346	0.1387	0.3424	0.8077	0.9382	0.8066	0.2520	0.1241	0.3943
0.2110	0.2439	0.4891	0.8287	0.8066	0.9452	0.2538	0.2186	0.4252
0.5776	0.6230	0.5548	0.3447	0.2520	0.2538	0.7174	0.5764	0.6376
0.5785	0.5889	0.5728	0.2748	0.1241	0.2186	0.5764	0.7071	0.5779
0.6752	0.7208	0.7013	0.4611	0.3943	0.4252	0.6376	0.5779	0.6807

TABLE 16.6.4 Basic Diagonal and Orthonormal for Scaled Image Covariance Matrix

6.4745	2.4373	0.9357	0.2035	0.1438	0.0915	0.0730	0.0380	0.0052
−0.4973	−0.2864	0.1653	0.1004	0.6053	−0.2447	0.4182	0.1503	−0.0974
−0.5075	−0.2653	0.1303	0.2162	−0.6671	−0.2084	−0.1616	0.1532	−0.2651
−0.4937	−0.1097	0.2564	−0.3168	0.0677	0.4550	−0.2944	−0.4056	0.3395
−0.1804	0.4946	0.0833	0.0303	−0.1885	−0.5371	0.2678	−0.3289	0.4594
−0.1408	0.5336	0.2088	0.4374	0.3220	−0.0198	−0.5343	0.0142	−0.2659
−0.1720	0.5154	0.2087	−0.4509	−0.1466	0.2876	0.3715	0.2610	−0.3842
−0.2281	0.1037	−0.5631	0.3897	−0.0515	0.3584	0.3170	−0.4330	0.2217
−0.2181	0.0494	−0.5767	−0.5284	0.1431	−0.3830	−0.3355	−0.0583	−0.2346
−0.2643	0.1655	−0.3822	0.1272	−0.0054	0.2073	−0.0633	0.6497	0.5120

if the variables are standard measures and $D_{R^{-1}}$ is the diagonal of R^{-1}. We therefore have

$$W = x(I - R^{-1}D_{R^{-1}}{}^{-1}) \tag{16.7.4}$$

The matrix of residuals E is then, from Eq. 16.7.4,

$$E = x - W \tag{16.7.5}$$

From Eqs. 16.7.4 and 16.7.5, we have

$$E = xR^{-1}D_{R^{-1}}{}^{-1} \tag{16.7.6}$$

We shall now consider the covariance matrices involving x, W, and E. We let

$$C_{xW} = \frac{x'W}{N} \tag{16.7.7}$$

$$C_{xE} = \frac{x'E}{N} \tag{16.7.8}$$

$$C_{WW} = \frac{W'W}{N} \tag{16.7.9}$$

$$C_{WE} = \frac{W'E}{N} \tag{16.7.10}$$

$$C_{EE} = \frac{E'E}{N} \tag{16.7.11}$$

These are the formulas developed by Guttman (1953) and discussed by Harris (1962).

From Eqs. 16.7.1, 16.7.4 and 16.7.7,

$$C_{xW} = R - D_{R^{-1}}{}^{-1} \tag{16.7.12}$$

From Eqs. 16.7.1, 16.7.5 and 16.7.8,

$$C_{xE} = D_{R^{-1}}{}^{-1} \tag{16.7.13}$$

From Eqs. 16.7.1, 16.7.4 and 16.7.9,

$$C_{WW} = (I - D_{R^{-1}}{}^{-1}R^{-1})R(I - R^{-1}D_{R^{-1}}{}^{-1}) \tag{16.7.14}$$

or

$$C_{WW} = R - 2D_{R^{-1}}{}^{-1} + D_{R^{-1}}{}^{-1}R^{-1}D_{R^{-1}}{}^{-1} \tag{16.7.15}$$

From Eqs. 16.7.1, 16.7.4, 16.7.6 and 16.7.10,

$$C_{WE} = D_{R^{-1}}{}^{-1} - D_{R^{-1}}{}^{-1}R^{-1}D_{R^{-1}}{}^{-1} \tag{16.7.16}$$

From Eqs. 16.7.1, 16.7.6 and 16.7.11,

$$C_{EE} = D_{R^{-1}}{}^{-1}R^{-1}D_{R^{-1}}{}^{-1} \tag{16.7.17}$$

The relationships among the various covariance matrices are obvious and have been discussed by Guttman (1953) and Harris (1962).

One may now regard the covariance matrix of the "estimated" variables as the logical matrix to factor, since presumably it has removed from each variable that part which does not overlap with the other variables. We therefore let the basic structure of Eq. 16.7.15 be

$$C_{WW} = Q\delta Q' \tag{16.7.18}$$

and factor to the desired number of roots and vectors.

16.7.2 The Estimated Correlation Matrix. Suppose we do not wish to factor the covariance matrix of the estimated variables but rather the actual correlation matrix of this estimated matrix. We have from Section 16.7.1

$$C_{WW} = R - 2D_{R^{-1}}{}^{-1} + D_{R^{-1}}{}^{-1}R^{-1}D_{R^{-1}}{}^{-1} \tag{16.7.19}$$

We let

$$d = D_{C_{WW}} \tag{16.7.20}$$

The matrix we wish to factor is

$$R_{WW} = d^{-1/2}C_{WW}\,d^{-1/2} \tag{16.7.21}$$

From Eqs. 16.7.19 and 16.7.20,

$$d = I - D_{R^{-1}}{}^{-1} \tag{16.7.22}$$

It is well known that Eq. 16.7.22 is a diagonal of the squared multiple correlations between each variable and the remaining $n - 1$ variables of the set. We repeat the covariance matrix of the estimated variables with the observed variables.

$$C_{xW} = R - D_{R^{-1}}{}^{-1} \tag{16.7.23}$$

It is clear from Eqs. 16.7.22 and 16.7.23 that the diagonals of C_{WW} and C_{xW} are the same.

16.7.3 The Solution Independent of Scale. Consider again the covariance matrix of the estimated variables x, namely,

$$C_{WW} = R - 2D_{R^{-1}}{}^{-1} + D_{R^{-1}}{}^{-1}R^{-1}D_{R^{-1}}{}^{-1} \tag{16.7.24}$$

It may be desirable to consider a factoring of, say,

$$G = DC_{WW}D \tag{16.7.25}$$

where G is independent of the scaling of the variables. That is, we remove the assumption of standardized measures in x. Suppose we let

$$C = \frac{x'x}{N} \tag{16.7.26}$$

where now we place no restrictions on the scaling of x. We then rewrite Eq. 16.7.24 as

$$C_{WW} = C - 2D_{C^{-1}}{}^{-1} + D_{C^{-1}}{}^{-1}C^{-1}D_{C^{-1}}{}^{-1} \qquad (16.7.27)$$

We let

$$C = dRd \qquad (16.7.28)$$

where d is an arbitrary scaling diagonal.

Suppose we let D in Eq. 16.7.25 be

$$D = D_{R^{-1}}{}^{1/2} \qquad (16.7.29)$$

From Eqs. 16.7.24, 16.7.25 and 16.7.29, we have

$$G = D_{R^{-1}}{}^{1/2}RD_{R^{-1}}{}^{1/2} - 2I + D_{R^{-1}}{}^{-1/2}R^{-1}D_{R^{-1}}{}^{-1/2} \qquad (16.7.30)$$

Suppose now we write Eq. 16.7.27 in the form of Eq. 16.7.30:

$$G = D_{C^{-1}}{}^{1/2}CD_{C^{-1}}{}^{1/2} - 2I + D_{C^{-1}}{}^{-1/2}C^{-1}D_{C^{-1}}{}^{-1/2} \qquad (16.7.31)$$

From Eqs. 16.7.28 and 16.7.31 we see that the d matrix divides out, and Eq. 16.7.31 becomes precisely Eq. 16.7.30. Therefore G in Eq. 16.7.31 is independent of scale and would seem to be a desirable matrix for factoring. Furthermore, suppose we let

$$g = D_{R^{-1}}{}^{1/2}RD_{R^{-1}}{}^{1/2} \qquad (16.7.32)$$

Then Eq. 16.7.31 can be written

$$G = g + g^{-1} - 2I \qquad (16.7.33)$$

We also know that the basic orthonormals of g, g^{-1} and G are the same and that if the basic structure of g is

$$g = Q\delta Q' \qquad (16.7.34)$$

then

$$g^{-1} = Q\delta^{-1}Q' \qquad (16.7.35)$$

and

$$G = Q(\delta + \delta^{-1} - 2I)Q' \qquad (16.7.36)$$

It should also be noted that g^{-1} is the well-known matrix of $n - 2$ order partial correlation coefficients.

16.7.4 The Optimal Error Covariance Matrix.

Consider again the estimated covariance matrix

$$C_{WW} = R - 2D_{R^{-1}}{}^{-1} + D_{R^{-1}}{}^{-1}R^{-1}D_{R^{-1}}{}^{-1} \qquad (16.7.37)$$

and the estimated error covariance matrix

$$C_{EE} = D_{R^{-1}}^{-1} R^{-1} D_{R^{-1}}^{-1} \tag{16.7.38}$$

We may wish to consider a scaling of C_{WW} in Eq. 16.7.37 and hence the same scaling of C_{EE} in Eq. 16.7.38, which will result in the best least square approximation to the identity matrix. We may then equally well consider the scaling of R^{-1} which is the best least square estimate of the identity matrix. Let

$$dR^{-1}d - I = \varepsilon \tag{16.7.39}$$

and determine d so that

$$tr\varepsilon'\varepsilon = min = \psi \tag{16.7.40}$$

From Eqs. 16.7.39 and 16.7.40,

$$\psi = tr(dR^{-1}d^2R^{-1}d - 2dR^{-1}d + I) \tag{16.7.41}$$

Let

$$R^{-1} = \rho \tag{16.7.42}$$

and from Eqs. 16.7.41 and 16.7.42,

$$\psi = tr(d\rho d^2 \rho d - 2d\rho d + I) \tag{16.7.43}$$

Let

$$V = d1 \tag{16.7.44}$$

From Eq. 16.7.44,

$$tr(d\rho d) = V'D_\rho V \tag{16.7.45}$$

Let $\rho^{(2)}$ be a matrix of the squared elements of ρ. Then it can be shown that

$$tr(d\rho d^2 \rho d) = V'd\rho^{(2)}dV \tag{16.7.46}$$

From Eqs. 16.7.43–16.7.46,

$$\psi = V'd\rho^{(2)}dV - 2V'D_\rho V + n \tag{16.7.47}$$

Differentiating Eq. 16.7.47 symbolically with respect to V',

$$\frac{\partial \psi}{\partial V'} = 4(d\rho^{(2)}dV - D_\rho V) \tag{16.7.48}$$

Equating Eq. 16.7.48 to zero,

$$d\rho^{(2)}dV = D_\rho V \tag{16.7.49}$$

or from Eqs. 16.7.44 and 16.7.49,

$$\rho^{(2)}d^2 1 = D_\rho 1 \tag{16.7.50}$$

From Eq. 16.7.50,

$$d^2 1 = (\rho^{(2)})^{-1} D_\rho 1 \tag{16.7.51}$$

To scale C_{WW} in Eq. 16.7.37, therefore, so that the scaled C_{EE} part is the best least square approximation to an identity matrix, we write first from Eq. 16.7.37,

$$D_{R^{-1}}C_{WW}D_{R^{-1}} = D_{R^{-1}}RD_{R^{-1}} - 2D_{R^{-1}} + R^{-1} \qquad (16.7.52)$$

Then letting γ be the scaled C_{WW} matrix and using d given by Eq. 16.7.51, we have

$$\gamma = d(D_{R^{-1}}RD_{R^{-1}} - 2D_{R^{-1}} + R^{-1})d \qquad (16.7.53)$$

Part V

Transformation Problems and Methods

Chapter 17

Primary Factor Matrices from Hypotheses

We have seen in the previous chapters that we may calculate, in a wide variety of ways, a factor loading matrix whose major product moment gives a lower rank approximation to the correlation or covariance matrix obtained from data matrices. We also know from Chapter 4 that if any of these matrices obtained by a particular computational method were postmultiplied by a square orthonormal matrix, the major product moment of the resulting matrix would be the same as the major product moment of the matrix prior to multiplication by the orthonormal matrix. This, of course, is because in the major product moment the square orthonormal matrix is multiplied by its transpose to yield the identity matrix.

We also saw in Chapter 4 that if we regard the factor loading matrix as one of the factors in the product of the two matrices which purports to approximate the data matrix, the same situation prevails. Suppose we have some approximation to a factor score matrix postmultiplied by the transpose of a factor loading matrix as a lower rank approximation to the data matrix. We may then also have the factor score matrix postmultiplied by an orthonormal matrix to yield another factor score matrix and the transpose of the factor loading matrix premultiplied by the transpose of the same orthonormal matrix. Then the product of these two transformed matrices would be exactly the same as that of the original matrices.

Furthermore, we learned that these transformation matrices need not be square orthonormal but that we may have a more general situation. We may have the factor score matrix postmultiplied by some square basic matrix and the transpose of the factor loading matrix premultiplied by the inverse of this same matrix. Then the major product of the two transformed matrices would be the same as the major product of the two original matrices. This is because the square basic matrix multiplied by its inverse yields the identity matrix.

It is clear then that we may have a multiply infinite number of factor loading matrices whose major product moments give identical results. Similarly, we may have an infinite number of pairs of factor score and factor loading matrices whose major products give identical results. The question then arises as to which of these pairs of factor loading and factor score matrices is best in some defined sense.

In this chapter we shall consider only factor loading matrices. We shall attempt to achieve some transformation of the arbitrary matrix so that the new factor loading matrix will have the following characteristics. First, for each factor loading vector, only a relatively small number of the variables will have high loadings, and the remainder would have small loadings. Second, each variable will have loadings in only a few of the factors. Third, for any given pair of factors, a number of the variables will have small loadings in both factors. Fourth, for any given pair of factors, some of the variables will have high loadings in one factor and low in the other, while other variables will have high loadings in the second factor but not in the first. Fifth, for any given pair of factors, very few of the variables will have high loadings in both.

These are the conditions which Thurstone (1947) has formulated as the *simple structure* criteria. We shall therefore refer to transformations which attempt to achieve these objectives as simple structure transformations, and we shall refer to the transformed factor loading matrix as a simple structure factor loading matrix.

There are, in general, three kinds of methods which have been used for transforming arbitrary factor matrices to simple structure matrices. The first of these is by means of *graphical methods of rotation.* In this method, every vector of factor loadings is plotted against every other vector, and by inspection of the plots, rotations or transformations are made two at a time. This is the oldest of the methods. It was developed by Thurstone (1947) and has been used extensively. The chief disadvantages of the method are that it is extremely time consuming; it is not adapted to objective computational routines; and a great deal of personal judgment is left to the individual who does the plotting and the transformations.

The second procedure is based on *a priori* hypotheses. Here the investigator has some *a priori* hypothesis as to which variables should have high loadings in which factors and which should not. This we may call *the hypothesis method of transformation.*

The third type of method involves analytical or mathematical criteria for transformation. These methods adopt certain mathematical functions of the transformed factor loadings which are to be optimized. They are called *the analytical methods of transformation.*

While the graphical methods have been extensively used in the past, they have been falling more and more into disuse as more objective methods have been developed. Therefore, these methods will not be discussed in this book.

In this chapter, we shall give consideration to those methods which start with some hypothesis as to which factor loading should be sizable in which variables. In the next chapter, we shall consider some analytical methods which do not depend on *a priori* hypotheses.

In any case, it must be emphasized, as Thurstone (1947) has done so frequently, that the extent to which simple structure can be achieved by any of the methods is definitely limited by the nature of the data to be analyzed, and that simple structure must be inherent in the data if any of the methods is to reveal it in the transformed factor matrices.

17.1 Characteristics of the Hypothesis Methods

The hypothesis methods of transformation are similar in several respects. First, they begin with some arbitrary factor loading matrix, that is, with some factor loading matrix computed by one of the various methods outlined in the previous chapters or by other methods. Second, they are based on some hypothesis as to which of the variables have high loadings in which factors. The methods differ essentially in the types of transformation matrices employed.

17.1.1 The Arbitrary Factor Matrices. The methods all begin with some arbitrary factor matrix such as the centroid, the multiple group, the group centroid, or the principal axis solution. In the methods we have discussed, it will be recalled that they are all special cases of the rank reduction method. It is, however, not necessary that the arbitrary factor matrices be special cases of the rank reduction method. They may be based on some clustering or *B*-coefficient methods, such as those described by Holzinger and Harman (1941).

The computational routines of the hypothesis methods differ essentially according to which particular type of arbitrary matrix is used. It should be emphasized at this point that most of the procedures we have outlined have had as their primary objective the finding of a factor loading matrix which, with a minimum number of factors, will give the best approximation to the correlation or covariance matrix. A major concern has been to find the smallest number of factors which, with a satisfactory degree of accuracy, can reproduce the correlation or covariance matrix and, indirectly, the data matrix. This objective recognizes the finding of a lower rank best approximation to a data matrix as fundamental to all scientific investigations.

17.1.2 The Hypothesis Matrix. The group of methods considered in this chapter depend on having some *a priori* hypotheses as to which variables should have high loadings in which factors and which tests should have low loadings. These methods are characterized by the specification of a binary hypothesis matrix. This binary matrix has a 1 in the ijth position if the ith variable has a high loading in the jth factor. Otherwise, it has a 0 in this position.

This binary hypothesis matrix can be made up after the variables are assembled. However, Thurstone (1947), Guttman (1952) and others have emphasized that it is better first to make up an hypothesis matrix and then to attempt to specify variables which will satisfy the hypothesis.

The ideal binary hypothesis matrix would be one in which there is only a single 1 in each row and roughly an equal number of 1's in each column. This would be a nonoverlapping hypothesis matrix. However, there is nothing to prevent one from having a more complex hypothesis so that he may have several 1's in each row for some of the variables, indicating that he believes the variables have loadings on more than one of the factors.

It will be recalled that a binary matrix is also involved in the multiple group method of factor analysis and that binary vectors are involved in the group centroid method. In those methods, however, it was considered desirable, but not mandatory, that these binary matrices or vectors represent plausible hypotheses as to the factor loadings to be found.

17.1.3 The Transformation Matrix. The methods described in this chapter all require a decision as to what particular conditions are to be satisfied by the transformation matrix. Usually it is considered desirable to have a transformation matrix which is normal by columns. That is, the minor product moment of the transformation matrix should have 1 in the diagonals. This restriction is required so that the factor vectors of the new transformed factor matrix will be comparable to one another. More technically, such a transformation provides the basis for finding the correlation among the new reference axes from which the new factor loadings are measured.

This concept, however, involves us with geometric and trigonometric symbolic systems which we wish to avoid in this book. We have attempted to restrict ourselves to algebraic and arithmetic concepts. This has been in the belief that the traditional random mixture of various types of symbolic mathematical systems does not yield a better understanding of the phenomena under study, unless one is already thoroughly familiar with the standard symbolic systems and the interrelationships among them. The assumption in this book is that many readers are not thoroughly familiar with these overlapping and interrelated symbolic systems.

The methods differ with respect to the type of transformation involved. These may be square orthonormal transformations. If the transformations are not orthonormal, they are called *oblique*. Therefore, a choice between orthonormal and oblique transformations is available. Although the term oblique is not particularly appropriate, we shall continue to use it since it is well established in the literature.

The methods differ also in restrictions which may be placed on the transformed simple structure factor loading matrix. For example, one type of transformation is such that for all variables which have zeros in a given column of the hypothesis binary matrix, the sum of their loadings in the simple structure matrix for the corresponding factor vector is 0.

17.2   Kinds of Methods

In this chapter we shall outline three methods which differ with respect to the type of arbitrary matrix on which they are based. A fourth method will yield a zero sum for assumed zero loadings in each factor. A fifth method uses a square orthonormal transformation.

17.2.1   The Multiple Group Matrix. This method begins with an arbitrary factor matrix obtained by the multiple group method. We shall assume that the binary matrix used in the multiple group method was actually an hypothesis matrix and that it is the one which the transformed simple structure matrix is to resemble as closely as possible. This particular type of arbitrary factor loading matrix is regarded as a special case because certain computational simplifications are possible when the binary grouping matrix and the binary hypothesis matrix are the same.

17.2.2   The Principal Axis Arbitrary Matrix. The second method we shall outline uses the principal axis or basic structure factor loading matrix as the arbitrary matrix. In many cases when high-speed computers have been used, the solution will be a principal axis or basic structure factor matrix. The computations for the transformed simple structure matrix are simplified because the principal axis solution yields an orthogonal factor matrix.

17.2.3   The Arbitrary Factor Matrix. This method may be regarded as a generalization of other methods, of which the multiple group and the principal axis arbitrary matrices are special cases. However, the solution does not depend on any peculiar properties of the factor loading matrix, such as orthogonality, or on the identity of the hypothesis and the grouping binary matrix, as in the multiple group method. The method does not depend on how the arbitrary factor matrix was determined and requires only the construction of the binary hypothesis matrix.

17.2.4   The Zero Partial Sum Method. This method is independent of the particular type of arbitrary matrix on which it is based. We may begin with any of the solutions discussed in the previous chapters. In any case, the transformation of the arbitrary matrix yields a simple structure matrix such that those variables which have zeros in an hypothesis vector will yield a 0 sum for the corresponding factor loadings. This does not mean necessarily that the simple structure criteria may be well satisfied or that the binary hypothesis matrix may be reasonably well approximated by the transformed matrix. For example, it is quite possible that even though partial sums are 0, the elements going into the sum may still vary greatly. Furthermore, appreciable or high loadings may not appear in the simple structure matrix to correspond with 1's in the hypothesis matrix. The results yielded by this or any simple structure solution are as much a function of the data themselves as of the particular method used.

17.2.5   The Orthonormal Transformation. In the methods just discussed, the type of transformation—whether orthonormal or oblique—was not mentioned. It will be recalled that only if the transformation of a factor loading matrix is orthonormal, will the major product moment of the original and the transformed factor loading matrix be the same. There is nothing in the computational procedures of the methods just discussed to guarantee that the transformation matrix will be orthonormal. In general, it will be oblique. It should be emphasized here that this is not a serious objection because, as we have indicated in Chapter 4, the main objective is not to reproduce the correlation or covariance matrix with the major product moment of a factor loading matrix, but rather to reproduce the original or rescaled data matrix as closely as possible by the major product of a factor score and a factor loading matrix. Therefore, if we get a given factor loading matrix and transform it with some nonorthonormal or oblique matrix, we can always transform the factor score matrix corresponding to it by the inverse of this transformation, so that the major product of the two will be the same as the major product of the original factor score and factor loading matrices.

However, there has been considerable insistence among some researchers that transformations be orthonormal, and it is of interest to consider a method which will guarantee an orthonormal solution based on the binary hypothesis matrix. The chief advantage of the orthonormal transformation procedures is that in certain cases, for example, the principal axis method, one can be sure that the factor scores are uncorrelated or, what amounts to the same thing, that the factor score matrix is an orthogonal matrix.

17.3   The Multiple Group Factor Matrix

17.3.1   Characteristics of the Method. This method assumes that we have adopted the multiple group method of factoring the correlation matrix. As will be recalled, this method begins with the multiplication of the correlation covariance matrix by a grouping binary matrix. In the technique of this section, the grouping binary matrix is the same as the binary hypothesis matrix.

However, the procedure is such that one does not need to carry out all of the computations for the multiple group factor matrix. Because the grouping and the hypothesis binary matrices are the same, one can omit some of the computations for the multiple group matrix. Distinguishing characteristics of this method are that one begins with only a partial solution of the multiple group matrix, and that the computations are somewhat simpler than for other hypothesis methods discussed in this chapter.

17.3.2   Computational Equations

17.3.2a   DEFINITION OF NOTATION
  R is the correlation matrix.
  f is the binary hypothesis matrix.
  H is the transformation matrix.
  r is the correlation of the reference axes.
  b is the simple structure factor matrix.

17.3.2b   THE EQUATIONS

$$F = Rf \tag{17.3.1}$$

$$S = F'f \tag{17.3.2}$$

$$tt' = S \tag{17.3.3}$$

$$G = F'F \tag{17.3.4}$$

$$C = G^{-1}S \tag{17.3.5}$$

$$g = SC \tag{17.3.6}$$

$$\gamma = gC \tag{17.3.7}$$

$$D = D_\gamma^{-1/2} \tag{17.3.8}$$

$$H = t'CD \tag{17.3.9}$$

$$r = D\gamma D \tag{17.3.10}$$

$$b = F(CD) \tag{17.3.11}$$

17.3.3   Computational Instructions.

We begin the computations with the correlation or covariance matrix, rather than with the multiple group factor matrix, because we shall omit the final steps of the multiple group solution. We assume that the binary matrix f has been constructed. It has 1's for those tests in each factor which are assumed to have high loadings, and zeros for all of the others.

The first step, as in the multiple group method, is indicated in Eq. 17.3.1. Here we postmultiply a correlation matrix by the hypothesis binary matrix f. Obviously, this merely serves to sum those columns of the correlation matrix corresponding to the 1's in the vectors of the f matrix on the right of Eq. 17.3.1.

The next step, as in the multiple group method, is to premultiply the f matrix by the transpose of the F matrix calculated in Eq. 17.3.1. This is indicated in Eq. 17.3.2 by the S matrix on the left of the equation. This, in effect, adds rows of the F matrix from Eq. 17.3.1 corresponding to the 1's in the vectors of the f matrix to give a symmetric matrix S in Eq. 17.3.2.

Equation 17.3.3 indicates a triangular factoring of the matrix S of Eq. 17.3.2. This triangular factoring is not necessary unless one actually wishes to see the transformation matrix which is indicated in Eq. 17.3.9. For most of the parameters of interest in a factor analysis, this transformation matrix, as such, is not required. It is only to make the analysis complete that it might be included.

Equation 17.3.4 is the minor product moment of the F matrix calculated in Eq. 17.3.1. This is indicated on the left by G.

Equation 17.3.5 requires the calculation of the inverse of the G matrix calculated in Eq. 17.3.4. The matrix designated as C in Eq. 17.3.5 is the S matrix of Eq. 17.3.2 premultiplied by the inverse of the G matrix given in Eq. 17.3.4.

The next step is to calculate the product indicated in Eq. 17.3.6. Here we premultiply the C matrix of Eq. 17.3.5 by the S matrix of Eq. 17.3.2. This we designate as g.

We next require the γ matrix indicated in Eq. 17.3.7. This is obtained by premultiplying the C matrix of Eq. 17.3.5 by the g matrix of Eq. 17.3.6.

The computation of a diagonal matrix is indicated by Eq. 17.3.8. This is simply a matrix whose elements are the reciprocal square roots of the diagonal elements of the γ matrix given by Eq. 17.3.7.

The computation of the H matrix, which is the transformation matrix for the multiple group factor matrix, is indicated in Eq. 17.3.9. This is the triple product, from left to right, of the upper triangular factor of the S matrix in Eq. 17.3.3 by the C matrix of Eq. 17.3.5 by the diagonal matrix of Eq. 17.3.8. As just indicated, this matrix is not used in the computation of the simple structure factor loading matrix. It is used in Chapter 21 for the calculation of general factor parameters, but if these are not desired it need not be calculated.

The calculation of a correlation matrix is indicated in Eq. 17.3.10. This matrix is the minor product moment of the H matrix of Eq. 17.3.9. It could be calculated as such from Eq. 17.3.9, but it is simpler to calculate it from Eqs. 17.3.7 and 17.3.8. This matrix is of interest because it shows the extent to which the reference vectors of the transformation matrix are correlated. It is precisely a correlation matrix of the simple structure reference axes. In most factor analyses, both this matrix and its normalized inverse are calculated to indicate the extent to which the transformation departs from orthonormality. More particularly, these matrices are useful for purposes of further analysis, as indicated in Chapter 21. The matrix is of interest also because, while in general simple structure factor matrices on the same variables are supposed to be relatively invariant from one type of sample to another, the correlation matrix of the simple structure reference axes as given in Eq. 17.3.10 may be regarded as characterizing the particular sample on which the analysis is based. It may vary greatly from one sample to another.

The calculation of the simple structure factor loading matrix is given in Eq. 17.3.11. As indicated on the right of this equation, we compute first a matrix which is the product of the C matrix of Eq. 17.3.5 postmultiplied by the diagonal matrix of Eq. 17.3.8. This matrix is then postmultiplied into the F matrix of Eq. 17.3.1.

The characteristic of this b matrix in Eq. 17.3.11 is that it should represent as nearly as possible in the least square sense the simple structure hypothesis matrix f which has been scaled on the left by a diagonal such that the transformation matrix H in Eq. 17.3.9 is normal by columns.

17.3.4 Numerical Example.

We begin this numerical example with the correlation matrix of previous chapters.

We shall solve for only three factors; therefore, the binary matrix consists of only three column vectors. The unit elements in these three vectors are taken, respectively, as the first three, the second three, and the third three.

Table 17.3.1 gives the correlation matrix postmultiplied by the binary matrix f, as indicated by Eq. 17.3.1.

TABLE 17.3.1   Matrix $Rf = F$

2.59700	0.24900	0.95800
2.60400	0.30100	1.03900
2.54300	0.71500	0.95200
0.49500	2.26200	0.80100
0.29900	2.34500	0.48300
0.47100	2.33500	0.58400
0.91700	0.57700	2.18100
0.92700	0.37700	2.19500
1.10500	0.91400	2.06800

TABLE 17.3.2   Matrix $F'f = S$

7.74400	1.26500	2.94900
1.26500	6.94200	1.86800
2.94900	1.86800	6.44400

Table 17.3.2 gives the minor product S of the f and the F matrices, as indicated by Eq. 17.3.2.

Table 17.3.3 gives the minor product moment G of the F matrix, as indicated by Eq. 17.3.4.

Table 17.3.4 gives the inverse of the G matrix shown in Table 17.3.3.

Table 17.3.5 gives the product of the S matrix of Table 17.3.2 premultiplied by the G^{-1} matrix of Table 17.3.4. This product is the C matrix of Eq. 17.3.5.

In the body of Table 17.3.6 is given the product of the C matrix of Table 17.3.5 premultiplied by the S matrix of Table 17.3.2. This product is the g matrix of Eq. 17.3.6. The last line of Table 17.3.6 is obtained by calculating only the diagonal elements of the product $\gamma = gC$ given by Eq. 17.3.7, and taking the reciprocal square roots of these elements as indicated by Eq. 17.3.8.

TABLE 17.3.3   Matrix $F'F = G$

23.46958	8.05789	14.75028
8.05789	18.04217	9.51620
14.75028	9.51620	17.97094

TABLE 17.3.4   Matrix G^{-1}

0.08804	−0.00167	−0.07138
−0.00167	0.07694	−0.03937
−0.07138	−0.03937	0.13508

TABLE 17.3.5   Matrix $G^{-1}S = C$

0.46919	−0.03358	−0.20345
−0.03173	0.45844	−0.11490
−0.20421	−0.11126	0.58641

TABLE 17.3.6   Matrix $SC = g$ and Vector of $D1 = D_{gC}{}^{-1/2}1$

2.99109	−0.00818	0.00847
−0.00818	2.93220	0.04042
0.00847	0.04042	2.96422
0.845	0.864	0.760

Table 17.3.7 is the simple structure factor loading matrix b. This is the triple product of the matrix F given by Table 17.3.1, the matrix C given by Table 17.3.5, and a diagonal matrix D constituted from the elements of the last row of Table 17.3.6. This product is indicated by Eq. 17.3.11.

The computations indicated by Eqs. 17.3.3, 17.3.9 and 17.3.10 are not given in this numerical example.

TABLE 17.3.7   Simple Structure Factor
Loading Matrix $b = F(CD)$

0.857	−0.069	0.004
0.845	−0.056	0.034
0.824	0.118	−0.031
−0.003	0.804	0.083
−0.028	0.874	−0.036
0.023	0.855	−0.016
−0.028	−0.008	0.780
−0.021	−0.089	0.802
0.057	0.131	0.671

17.4   The Principal Axis Factor Matrix

17.4.1   Characteristics of the Method. This method, like the previous one, is a special case of an arbitrary matrix resulting in simplified computations. Here the simplification results because the principal axis factor matrix is orthogonal by columns.

One of the most important characteristics of the method is that the computations do not call for the calculation of the inverse of any matrix except a diagonal matrix. This is far easier to calculate than the inverses of symmetric or other square matrices. The method is of considerable practical importance because, with the increasing availability of high-speed computers, most of the arbitrary factor loading matrices calculated will be of the principal axis or basic structure type.

17.4.2   Computational Equations

17.4.2a   DEFINITION OF NOTATION

a is the principal axis factor matrix.

δ is that part of the basic diagonal matrix of R corresponding to a.

r is the correlation matrix of the reference axes.

b is the simple structure factor loading matrix.

17.4.2b THE EQUATIONS

$$G = a'f \tag{17.4.1}$$

$$C = \delta^{-1}G \tag{17.4.2}$$

$$S = C'C \tag{17.4.3}$$

$$D = D_{C'C}^{-1/2} \tag{17.4.4}$$

$$H = CD \tag{17.4.5}$$

$$r = DSD \tag{17.4.6}$$

$$b = aH \tag{17.4.7}$$

17.4.3 Computational Instructions. We begin with Eq. 17.4.1. This is simply the product of the transposed principal axis factor loading matrix postmultiplied by the binary hypothesis matrix f.

Next we calculate the C matrix in Eq. 17.4.2. This is the G matrix of Eq. 17.4.1 premultiplied by the reciprocal of the basic diagonal corresponding to the largest principal axis factors. In other words, this basic diagonal includes only the basic diagonal elements of the correlation matrix corresponding to the factors which have been solved for previously.

Next we calculate Eq. 17.4.3. This is the minor product moment of the C matrix calculated in Eq. 17.4.2.

We then calculate a diagonal matrix whose elements are the reciprocal square roots of the diagonal elements of S calculated in Eq. 17.4.3. This is indicated in Eq. 17.4.4.

Next we calculate the transformation matrix H as in Eq. 17.4.5. This is the matrix C of Eq. 17.4.2 postmultiplied by the diagonal matrix of Eq. 17.4.4. It will be noted that this computation was optional in the previous method. Here, however, it is required for further calculations, as will be indicated for Eq. 17.4.7.

The next step is to calculate the correlation of the simple structure reference axes, as indicated in Eq. 17.4.6. Here the matrix S of Eq. 17.4.3 is pre- and postmultiplied by the diagonal matrix of Eq. 17.4.4. As seen from Eqs. 17.4.3–17.4.5, r could also have been calculated by taking the minor product moment of the H matrix in Eq. 17.4.5. However, this would have meant the multiplication of square matrices, whereas the computations in Eq. 17.4.6 require only operations on the symmetric matrix S by diagonal matrices.

Equation 17.4.7 gives, finally, the simple structure factor loading matrix. This is the principal axis factor loading matrix postmultiplied by the transformation matrix H of Eq. 17.4.5. This matrix now is the best least square approximation to the scaled binary hypothesis matrix F, in which the scaling is such as to make the column vectors of H in Eq. 17.4.5 normal.

17.4.4   Numerical Example. We take as numerical data for this illustration the principal axis factor loading matrix calculated in Chapter 8. This is repeated for convenience in Table 17.4.1, together with the first three basic diagonals in the top row. The binary hypothesis matrix is the same as given in the previous section. This hypothesis assumes that no variable has factor loadings in more than one factor.

Table 17.4.2 gives the product of the transpose of the matrix in Table 17.4.1 postmultiplied by the binary hypothesis matrix.

Table 17.4.3 is the product C of the matrix of Table 17.4.2 premultiplied by the inverse of a diagonal matrix constituted from the basic diagonal elements at the top of Table 17.4.1. These calculations are indicated by Eq. 17.4.2.

Table 17.4.4 is the minor product moment of the matrix C calculated in Table 17.4.3.

TABLE 17.4.1   First Three Basic Diagonals
and Principal Axis Factor Vectors

3.749		
2.050		
1.331		
0.717	0.493	0.350
0.740	0.478	0.322
0.773	0.296	0.406
0.556	−0.649	0.068
0.463	−0.744	0.181
0.518	−0.694	0.188
0.640	0.080	−0.588
0.615	0.166	−0.621
0.715	−0.034	−0.369

TABLE 17.4.2   Matrix $G = a'f$

2.23000	1.53700	1.97000
1.26700	−2.08700	0.21200
1.07800	0.43700	−1.57800

TABLE 17.4.3   Matrix $C = \delta^{-1}G$

0.59483	0.40998	0.52547
0.61805	−1.01805	0.10341
0.80992	0.32832	−1.18557

Table 17.4.5 is the matrix obtained by postmultiplying the matrix C of Table 17.4.3 by the inverse of a diagonal matrix whose elements are from the diagonal of the matrix in Table 17.4.4. This gives the transformation H indicated by Eq. 17.4.5.

Table 17.4.6 is the simple structure factor loading matrix. It is the product of the principal axis factor matrix of Table 17.4.1 postmultiplied by the matrix H of Table 17.4.5. This product is indicated by Eq. 17.4.7.

The correlation matrix r of Eq. 17.4.6 is not calculated in this numerical example.

TABLE 17.4.4 Matrix $S = C'C$

1.39177	−0.11942	−0.58374
−0.11942	1.31230	−0.27910
−0.58374	−0.27910	1.69240

TABLE 17.4.5 Transformation Matrix
$$H = CD_{C'C}^{-1/2}$$

0.50420	0.35788	0.40392
0.52389	−0.88869	0.07949
0.68653	0.28661	−0.91133

TABLE 17.4.6 Simple Structure Matrix $b = aH$

0.860	−0.081	0.010
0.845	−0.068	0.043
0.824	0.130	−0.034
−0.013	0.795	0.111
−0.032	0.879	−0.037
0.027	0.856	−0.017
−0.039	−0.011	0.801
−0.029	−0.105	0.828
0.089	0.180	0.622

17.5 The Arbitrary Factor Matrix

17.5.1 Characteristics of the Method. This method is more general than the two previous methods in that it applies to any factor matrix, including the principal axis, centroid, grouping, and multiple group matrices as special cases. However, the method includes a slight modification of the previous two methods. This modification is desirable in most transformation solutions, although frequently it makes very little difference, and it has been omitted from the two previous methods in order to simplify computations.

In this method, the arbitrary factor loading matrix is normalized by rows, that is, by variables, before transformation operations begin upon it. The reason for this is that all of the tests will then be given equal weight in the transformation solution. In most of the arbitrary-type solutions which are designed primarily to find the minimum number of factors which can adequately account for a correlation or data matrix, all of the variables do not account for the same amount of variance in the factor matrix. In other words, what have been called the communalities of the variables, or the sums of squares of factor loadings for a given variable, will vary considerably from one variable to another. Therefore, it is considered desirable to normalize the rows, that is, to make all of the test vectors of unit length. The unit length vector will be recognized by some as a geometric concept. We shall not, however, develop this concept further, since it would contribute to a confusion of symbolic systems. From the algebraic or arithmetic point of view we can simply state that we wish each of the tests to carry unit weight in the determination of the transformation. It may be recalled that in Chapter 15, for the communality-type scaling method, the α factor loading matrices satisfy this condition. That is, for any given number of factors, the sums of squares of rows of the α matrix are all equal to 1.

17.5.2   Computational Equations

17.5.2a   DEFINITION OF NOTATION
   a is an arbitrary factor matrix.
   f is the binary hypothesis matrix.
   r is the correlation of the simple structure reference axes.
   H is the simple structure transformation matrix.
   b is the simple structure factor matrix.

17.5.2b   THE EQUATIONS

$$D = D_{aa'}{}^{-1/2} \tag{17.5.1}$$

$$A = Da \tag{17.5.2}$$

$$G = A'f \tag{17.5.3}$$

$$C = A'A \tag{17.5.4}$$

$$M = C^{-1}G \tag{17.5.5}$$

$$g = M'M \tag{17.5.6}$$

$$D = D_g{}^{-1/2} \tag{17.5.7}$$

$$H = MD \tag{17.5.8}$$

$$r = H'H \tag{17.5.9}$$

$$b = AH \tag{17.5.10}$$

17.5.3 Computational Instructions. In this method we assume that all of the computations for an arbitrary factor matrix have been completed and that we start with this arbitrary matrix, however arrived at.

The first step in the calculations is indicated in Eq. 17.5.1. Here we calculate a diagonal matrix whose elements are the reciprocal square root of the diagonal elements of the major product moment of the arbitrary matrix *a*. This means, of course, that we must calculate the sums of squares of row elements for the arbitrary factor matrix *a*. These are what are called the communalities of the variables based on the particular factoring solution.

The second step is to calculate the normalized factor loading matrix *A*, as indicated in Eq. 17.5.2. This is given by premultiplying the arbitrary factor matrix by the diagonal matrix in Eq. 17.5.1.

Equation 17.5.3 is the minor product of the matrix in Eq. 17.5.2 and the hypothesis matrix *f*.

We then calculate, as shown in Eq. 17.5.4, the minor product moment of the matrix *A* given by Eq. 17.5.2. This we call *C*.

Next we calculate a matrix *M* which is the *G* matrix of Eq. 17.5.3 premultiplied by the inverse of the matrix *C* in Eq. 17.5.4.

We then calculate Eq. 17.5.6, which is the minor product moment of the matrix calculated in Eq. 17.5.5. This we call *g*.

Next we calculate the diagonal matrix of Eq. 17.5.7. This is simply a matrix whose diagonal elements are the reciprocal square roots of the diagonal elements of the matrix *g* calculated in Eq. 17.5.6.

We now calculate the transformation matrix *H* indicated in Eq. 17.5.8. This is the matrix *M* of Eq. 17.5.5 postmultiplied by the diagonal matrix of Eq. 17.5.7. The method of computation indicates that the column vectors of the *H* matrix are normal.

Equation 17.5.9 gives the correlation of the primary reference axes as the minor product moment of the transformation matrix *H* given in Eq. 17.5.8.

Finally, Eq. 17.5.10 gives the simple structure factor loading matrix. This is obtained by postmultiplying the matrix of Eq. 17.5.2 by the transformation matrix *H* given in Eq. 17.5.8.

17.5.4 Numerical Example

Table 17.5.1 gives the group centroid factor loading matrix calculated in Section 6.3. The same binary hypothesis matrix is used as in the previous two methods.

Table 17.5.2 gives the group centroid factor matrix normalized by rows, as computed by Eqs. 17.5.1 and 17.5.2.

Table 17.5.3 is the minor product *G* of the normalized factor matrix and the binary hypothesis matrix, as computed by Eq. 17.5.3.

Table 17.5.4 is the minor product moment *C* of the normalized factor matrix, as indicated by Eq. 17.5.4.

Table 17.5.5 is the inverse C^{-1} of the matrix of Table 17.5.4.

Table 17.5.6 is the matrix M calculated from the matrices of Tables 17.5.3 and 17.5.5, as shown in Eq. 17.5.5.

TABLE 17.5.1 Group Centroid Factor Matrix a

0.933	−0.068	0.002
0.936	−0.048	0.033
0.914	0.115	−0.035
0.178	0.840	0.073
0.107	0.885	−0.046
0.169	0.870	−0.027
0.330	0.165	0.777
0.333	0.087	0.800
0.397	0.283	0.667

TABLE 17.5.2 Normalized Factor Matrix A

0.99735	−0.07269	0.00214
0.99807	−0.05118	0.03519
0.99146	0.12475	−0.03797
0.20656	0.97476	0.08471
0.11987	0.99145	−0.05153
0.19060	0.98120	−0.03045
0.38366	0.19183	0.90333
0.38237	0.09990	0.91860
0.48052	0.34254	0.80732

TABLE 17.5.3 Matrix $G = A'f$

2.98688	0.51703	1.24654
0.00087	2.94741	0.63426
−0.00064	0.00273	2.62925

TABLE 17.5.4 Matrix $C = A'A$

3.59151	0.78369	1.09087
0.78369	3.08345	0.53650
1.09087	0.53650	2.32504

Table 17.5.7 is the transformation matrix H obtained by normalizing the columns of M in Table 17.5.6 by means of Eqs. 17.5.7 and 17.5.8.

Table 17.5.8 is the simple structure factor matrix b obtained from the matrices of Tables 17.5.2 and 17.5.7, indicated by Eq. 17.5.10. It is to be noted that the matrix b may be premultiplied by the inverse of the diagonal matrix of Eq. 17.5.1. This procedure is preferred by some factor analysts. The correlation matrix r of Eq. 17.5.9 has not been calculated.

TABLE 17.5.5   Matrix C^{-1}

0.33511	−0.06023	−0.14333
−0.06023	0.34870	−0.05220
−0.14333	−0.05220	0.50939

TABLE 17.5.6   Matrix $M = C^{-1}G$

1.00098	−0.00466	0.00268
−0.17957	0.99649	0.00883
−0.42848	−0.22658	1.12755

TABLE 17.5.7   Transformation Matrix
$$H = MD_{M'M}^{-1/2}$$

0.90706	−0.00456	0.00237
−0.16273	0.97510	0.00783
−0.38828	−0.22171	0.99997

TABLE 17.5.8 Simple Structure Factor Matrix
$$b = AH$$

0.916	−0.076	0.004
0.900	−0.062	0.037
0.894	0.126	−0.035
−0.004	0.931	0.093
−0.033	0.978	−0.043
0.025	0.963	−0.022
−0.034	−0.015	0.906
−0.026	−0.108	0.920
0.067	0.153	0.811

17.6 The Zero Partial Sum Transformation

17.6.1 Characteristics of the Method. As indicated earlier in this chapter, the rationale of this procedure is to find a transformation such that for any given factor vector, the factor loadings in the simple structure matrix corresponding to the zero elements in the corresponding vector of the binary hypothesis matrix will add up to 0. This restriction can be imposed on any oblique solution for any arbitrary factor matrix. It applies equally well to the multiple group, principal axis, and the other methods.

In general, this additional restriction tends to give smaller values for the near-zero elements. However, there might still be considerable dispersion about the mean of 0 for these hypothesized zero elements. In any case, the computations, as will be seen, are somewhat more involved than they are in the methods previously considered.

17.6.2 *Computational Equations*

17.6.2a DEFINITION OF NOTATION
  a is an arbitrary factor matrix.
  f is the binary hypothesis matrix.
  r is the matrix of correlations of the simple structure reference axes.
  H is the simple structure transformation matrix.
  b is the simple structure factor matrix.

17.6.2b THE EQUATIONS

$$S = a'a \tag{17.6.1}$$

$$tt' = S \tag{17.6.2}$$

$$\alpha = at'^{-1} \tag{17.6.3}$$

$$Y = \alpha'1 \tag{17.6.4}$$

$$W = \alpha'f \tag{17.6.5}$$

$$U = Y1' - W \tag{17.6.6}$$

$$V = UD_{U'U}^{-1/2} \tag{17.6.7}$$

$$Z = VD_{V'W} \tag{17.6.8}$$

$$C = W - Z \tag{17.6.9}$$

$$M = t'^{-1}C \tag{17.6.10}$$

$$\gamma = M'M \tag{17.6.11}$$

$$D = D_\gamma^{-1/2} \tag{17.6.12}$$

$$H = MD_\gamma^{-1/2} \tag{17.6.13}$$

$$r = D\gamma D \tag{17.6.14}$$

$$b = aH \tag{17.6.15}$$

17.6.3   Computational Instructions. In this method we may begin with any arbitrary factor loading matrix and operate directly upon it or we may first normalize the rows of the factor loading matrix as we did in the method of Section 17.5. In either case, we have a binary hypothesis matrix *f*, as in the previous three methods.

Equation 17.6.1 gives the initial computations, which consist of the minor product moment of the factor loading matrix. If this happens to be a principal axis matrix, then, of course, the matrix *S* on the left will be a diagonal matrix.

We then indicate the triangular factoring of the *S* matrix of Eq. 17.6.1 by Eq. 17.6.2.

The next step is to postmultiply the factor loading matrix *a* by the inverse of the upper triangular factor of the *S* matrix in Eq. 17.6.2. This is indicated in Eq. 17.6.3.

Next we calculate a vector as indicated in Eq. 17.6.4. This is simply a vector whose elements are the sums of column elements of the α matrix in Eq. 17.6.3. It is, of course, the transpose of the α matrix of Eq. 17.6.3 postmultiplied by a unit vector.

Next we calculate the minor product of the α matrix of Eq. 17.6.3 by the hypothesis binary matrix *f*, as indicated in Eq. 17.6.5. This is the matrix *W* on the left of Eq. 17.6.5.

We then calculate the matrix *U* as indicated in Eq. 17.6.6. Each column of the *U* matrix in Eq. 17.6.6 is obtained by subtracting from the *Y* vector calculated in Eq. 17.6.4, the corresponding *W* vector from the matrix calculated in Eq. 17.6.5. This is given in matrix notation on the right of Eq. 17.6.6 as the major product of the *Y* vector of Eq. 17.6.4 by a unit row vector, less the matrix *W* of Eq. 17.6.5.

We now normalize the column vectors of *U* calculated in Eq. 17.6.6, as indicated in Eq. 17.6.7. We call this the *V* matrix. The right side of Eq. 17.6.7 shows the *U* matrix of Eq. 17.6.6 postmultiplied by the reciprocal square root of the diagonal of the minor product moment of *U*. It is, of course, not necessary to calculate the entire product moment of *U*, but only the sums of squares of column elements, in order to get the *D* matrix used in Eq. 17.6.7.

In Eq. 17.6.8, we calculate the matrix *Z*, which is the *V* matrix of Eq. 17.6.7 postmultiplied by a diagonal matrix. Now the diagonal matrix is made up of the elements of the diagonal of the minor product moment of the *V* matrix of Eq. 17.6.7 and the *W* matrix of Eq. 17.6.5. Here again, it is not necessary to calculate the minor product moment but only the diagonal elements consisting of the minor products of corresponding columns of the *V* and the *W* matrices.

The next step is indicated by Eq. 17.6.9. This is the matrix *W* of Eq. 17.6.5 minus the *Z* matrix of Eq. 17.6.8. This we indicate as the *C* matrix.

Next we calculate the matrix M indicated in Eq. 17.6.10. This is obtained by premultiplying the C matrix of Eq. 17.6.9 by the inverse of the upper triangular factor of the matrix S in Eq. 17.6.2.

We then calculate the minor product moment γ of the matrix M calculated in Eq. 17.6.10, as indicated in Eq. 17.6.11.

The next step is to calculate a diagonal matrix D, whose elements are the reciprocal square roots of the diagonal elements of γ calculated in Eq. 17.6.11.

We calculate the transformation matrix H as indicated in Eq. 17.6.13. This consists in normalizing the elements of the M matrix of Eq. 17.6.10 as shown on the right-hand side of Eq. 17.6.13. The M matrix is postmultiplied by the reciprocal square root of the diagonal elements of its minor product moment.

The calculations for the correlations among the primary reference axes are indicated in Eq. 17.6.14. Here we pre- and postmultiply the γ matrix of Eq. 17.6.11 by the D matrix of Eq. 17.6.12.

Finally, we calculate the simple structure factor loading matrix as in Eq. 17.6.15. As in previous methods, we postmultiply the arbitrary factor loading matrix by the transformation matrix H calculated in Eq. 17.6.13.

17.6.4 Numerical Example

We use the same group centroid factor matrix as in the preceding section.

The tables for this example will not be discussed in detail. We merely give below the table number and the corresponding equation number where such an equation is given.

Table Number	Equation Number
17.6.1	17.6.1
17.6.2	17.6.2
17.6.3	—
17.6.4	17.6.5
17.6.5	17.6.6
17.6.6	17.6.7
17.6.7	17.6.8
17.6.8	17.6.9
17.6.9	17.6.10
17.6.10	17.6.11
17.6.11	17.6.13
17.6.12	17.6.15

TABLE 17.6.1   Matrix $S = a'a$

3.03107	0.58375	0.79188
0.58375	2.38076	0.37794
0.79188	0.37794	1.69911

TABLE 17.6.2 Matrix t

1.74100		
0.33530	1.50610	
0.45484	0.14968	1.21236

TABLE 17.6.3 Matrix t^{-1}

0.57438		
−0.12787	0.66397	
−0.19970	−0.08197	0.82484

TABLE 17.6.4 Matrix $W = \alpha'f$

1.59851	0.26077	0.60885
−0.35654	1.66494	0.21968
−0.55570	−0.30339	1.59539

TABLE 17.6.5 Matrix $U = Y1' - W$

0.86962	2.20735	1.85928
1.88462	−0.13686	1.30840
1.29200	1.03969	−0.85909

TABLE 17.6.6 Matrix $V = UD_{U'U}^{-1/2}$

0.35569	0.90325	0.76501
0.77085	−0.05600	0.53835
0.52846	0.42544	−0.35347

TABLE 17.6.7 Matrix $Z = VD_{V'W}$

0.00003	0.01195	0.01538
0.00006	−0.00074	0.01082
0.00004	0.00563	−0.00711

TABLE 17.6.8 Matrix $C = W - Z$

1.59848	0.24882	0.59346
−0.35660	1.66568	0.20885
−0.55574	−0.30901	1.60250

TABLE 17.6.9   Matrix $M = t'^{-1}C$

1.07472	−0.00836	−0.00586
−0.19121	1.13129	0.00731
−0.45839	−0.25489	1.32180

TABLE 17.6.10   Matrix $\gamma = M'M$

1.40172	−0.10847	−0.61359
−0.10847	1.34485	−0.32859
−0.61359	−0.32859	1.74723

TABLE 17.6.11   Matrix $H = MD_\gamma^{-1/2}$

0.90775	−0.00721	−0.00443
−0.16151	0.97552	0.00553
−0.38718	−0.21979	0.99997

TABLE 17.6.12   Matrix $b = aH$

0.857	−0.074	−0.003
0.845	−0.061	0.029
0.825	0.113	−0.038
−0.002	0.802	0.077
−0.028	0.873	−0.042
0.023	0.853	−0.023
−0.028	−0.012	0.776
−0.022	−0.093	0.799
0.056	0.127	0.667

It is of interest to note that the elements for each vector of Table 17.6.12 corresponding to the zero element in the corresponding binary hypothesis vector, actually do sum to 0.

17.7   The Orthogonal Transformation Matrix

17.7.1   Characteristics of the Method. As indicated earlier in this chapter, it is sometimes desirable to impose the condition of orthonormality on the simple structure transformation matrix. This restriction can be used on any type of arbitrary factor loading matrix which is to be transformed to a simple structure hypothesis matrix. The orthonormal restriction, however, has not been generally used. Nevertheless, it has a clear advantage over oblique methods when applied to the principal axis factor loading matrix for which a simple structure binary hypothesis matrix is available. Then the simple structure factor score matrix whose solution we shall consider in a later chapter is an orthonormal matrix. This means that the factor scores are uncorrelated in both the unrotated and the rotated solutions.

One characteristic of this method is that it is much more laborious computationally, and is therefore not recommended for desk computers. The method requires successive solutions of the basic structure of certain matrices which are required in the repeated approximations to the final orthonormal transformation matrix.

17.7.2 Computational Equations

17.7.2a DEFINITION OF NOTATION
a is an arbitrary factor matrix.
f is the binary hypothesis matrix.
r is the correlations of the simple structure reference axes.
H is the simple structure transformation matrix.
b is the simple structure factor matrix.

17.7.2b THE EQUATIONS

$$\gamma = a'f \tag{17.7.1}$$

$$G = \gamma D_{f'f}^{-1} \tag{17.7.2}$$

$$C_i = a'b_{i-1} - GD_{b_{i-1}'f} \tag{17.7.3}$$

$$C_i'C_i = Q_i \Delta_c^2 Q_i' \tag{17.7.4}$$

$$H_i = C_i Q_i \Delta_i^{-1} Q_i' \tag{17.7.5}$$

$$b_i = aH_i \tag{17.7.6}$$

$$r = H_i'H_i = I \tag{17.7.7}$$

17.7.3 Computational Instructions.
The computational instructions for this method are brief, but the actual computations can be lengthy even on high-speed computers if the number of variables and the number of factors are moderately large, such as those encountered in experimental investigations.

The method consists in a set of successive approximation cycles beginning with any arbitrary factor loading matrix which may or may not be normalized by rows. We have given a binary hypothesis matrix, as in the other methods.

We begin with Eq. 17.7.1, which gives the matrix γ as the product of the binary matrix premultiplied by the transpose of the factor loading matrix.

We then define a scaling of the γ matrix as in Eq. 17.7.2. The scaling diagonal is obtained from the diagonal matrix of the minor product moment of the hypothesis matrix. Each diagonal element is the reciprocal of the number of 1's in the corresponding column of the binary matrix.

We next indicate an iteration cycle by Eq. 17.7.3. Here we have on the right, two terms. The first of these includes the preceding approximation to the simple structure factor loading matrix. This first term is an approximation to the simple structure factor matrix premultiplied by the transpose of the arbitrary matrix. When $i = 1$, the approximation to the simple structure matrix b_0 may be taken as the simple structure matrix arrived at by any one of the four preceding methods. The second term on the right is the G matrix calculated in Eq. 17.7.2, postmultiplied by a diagonal matrix whose elements are the diagonal elements of the minor product of the previous approximation to the simple structure factor matrix and the hypothesis matrix.

We indicate the minor product moment of the matrix calculated in Eq. 17.7.3 by Eq. 17.7.4. Equation 17.7.4 also indicates the basic structure solution for this minor product moment. For each approximation i, we calculate all the vectors of the basic structure factors Δ^2 and Q.

Equation 17.7.5 indicates the ith approximation to the orthonormal transformation matrix. This is obtained, as indicated on the right, by multiplying from left to right as follows: the C matrix by the Q matrix by the inverse of the Δ matrix by the transpose of the Q matrix.

Finally, we indicate the ith approximation to the simple structure factor loading matrix by Eq. 17.7.6. This is the arbitrary factor matrix postmultiplied by the ith approximation to the transformation matrix solved for in Eq. 17.7.5.

This iteration procedure continues until, according to some criterion, the approximations are close enough. Presumably, the trace of the matrix given in Eq. 17.7.4 would provide a satisfactory criterion. When this trace does not change by more than a specified amount from one approximation to another, we may discontinue the computations.

Equation 17.7.7 assumes that the computations have stabilized, and therefore we have the minor product moment of the current H or transformation matrix. This will be a check on the computations and by definition this should be an identity matrix.

17.7.4 Numerical Example.
We begin with the same group centroid matrix and binary hypothesis matrix as in the previous section.

Tables 17.7.1 and 17.7.2 show the computations indicated by Eqs. 17.7.1 and 17.7.2, respectively.

The remaining tables are for the 10th approximation, as follows: Tables 17.7.3 and 17.7.4 give the computation indicated by Eq. 17.7.3. Table 17.7.5 gives the minor product moment of the matrix C in Table 17.7.4. Table

TABLE 17.7.1   Matrix $\gamma = a'f$

2.78300	0.45400	1.06000
−0.00100	2.59500	0.53500
0.00000	0.00000	2.24400

TABLE 17.7.2   Matrix $G = \gamma D_{f'f}^{-1}$

0.92767	0.15133	0.35333
−0.00033	0.86500	0.17833
0.00000	0.00000	0.74800

TABLE 17.7.3   Matrix $a'b_{i-1}$ for $i = 10$

0.62649	2.03184	−2.37365
2.39956	0.37041	−0.50667
0.56197	1.82739	0.04159

TABLE 17.7.4   Vector $D_{b_{i-1}'f}\,1$, and Matrix
$C_i = a'b_{i-1} - GD_{b_{i-1}'f}$ for $i = 10$

−0.043	−0.044	0.040
0.66639	2.03846	−2.38776
2.39955	0.40826	−0.51379
0.56197	1.82739	0.01172

TABLE 17.7.5   Matrix $C_i'C_i$ for $i = 10$

6.51772	3.36497	−2.81748
3.36497	7.66132	−5.05569
−2.81748	−5.05569	5.96551

TABLE 17.7.6   Matrix $Q_i \Delta_i^{-1} Q_i'$ for $i = 10$

0.44064	−0.07679	0.06205
−0.07679	0.50770	0.22263
0.06205	0.22263	0.58089

17.7.6 gives the matrix $(C'C)^{-1/2} = Q\Delta^{-1}Q'$ which is required in Table 17.7.7 and Eq. 17.7.5. Table 17.7.7 gives the approximation to the orthogonal transformation matrix H as indicated by Eq. 17.7.5. Table 17.7.8 is the approximation to the simple structure factor matrix, as indicated by Eq. 17.7.6.

TABLE 17.7.7   Matrix $H_i = C_i Q_i \Delta_i^{-1} Q_i'$ for $i = 10$

-0.01105	0.45218	-0.89184
0.99410	-0.09137	-0.05867
0.10803	0.88723	0.44851

TABLE 17.7.8   Simple Structure Approximation $b_i = aH_i$ for $i = 10$

-0.078	0.430	-0.827
-0.054	0.457	-0.817
0.100	0.372	-0.838
0.841	0.069	-0.175
0.874	-0.073	-0.168
0.860	-0.027	-0.214
0.244	0.824	0.044
0.169	0.852	0.057
0.349	0.745	-0.072

17.8   Mathematical Proofs

17.8.1   The Multiple Group Matrix

Given the correlation matrix R and the binary simple structure hypothesis matrix f, let

$$F = Rf \tag{17.8.1}$$

and

$$S = F'f \tag{17.8.2}$$

$$tt' = S \tag{17.8.3}$$

Then the multiple group factor matrix is well known to be

$$a = Ft'^{-1} \tag{17.8.4}$$

Assume now we wish to find the simple structure matrix b of best fit to f. We consider

$$aH = b \tag{17.8.5}$$

and

$$b - fD = \varepsilon \tag{17.8.6}$$

where D is diagonal, and where for H in Eq. 17.8.5 we have

$$D_{H'H} = I \tag{17.8.7}$$

We wish to minimize

$$tr\varepsilon'\varepsilon = \psi \tag{17.8.8}$$

The solution is well known to be

$$H = (a'a)^{-1}a'fD \tag{17.8.9}$$

From Eqs. 17.8.2–17.8.4 and 17.8.9,

$$H = t'(F'F)^{-1}SD \tag{17.8.10}$$

Let

$$F'F = G \tag{17.8.11}$$

From Eqs. 17.8.3, 17.8.10, and 17.8.11,

$$H'H = DSG^{-1}SG^{-1}SD \tag{17.8.12}$$

Let

$$C = G^{-1}S \tag{17.8.13}$$

and

$$g = SC \tag{17.8.14}$$

From Eqs. 17.8.7 and 17.8.12–17.8.14,

$$H'H = DgCD \tag{17.8.15}$$

From Eq. 17.8.15,

$$D = D_{gC}^{-1/2} \tag{17.8.16}$$

From Eqs. 17.8.4, 17.8.5, 17.8.11, and 17.8.16,

$$b = FCD_{gC}^{-1/2} \tag{17.8.17}$$

17.8.2 The Principal Axis Matrix
Given the principal axis factor matrix

$$a = Q\delta^{1/2} \tag{17.8.18}$$

and the binary hypothesis matrix f, consider the least square transformation

$$aH = b \tag{17.8.19}$$

such that in

$$b - fD = \varepsilon \tag{17.8.20}$$

the trace of $\varepsilon'\varepsilon$ is minimized with a diagonal D such that for H in Eq. 17.8.19, we have

$$D_{H'H} = I \tag{17.8.21}$$

From Eqs. 17.8.19 and 17.8.20,

$$aH - fD = \varepsilon \qquad (17.8.22)$$

The solution for H is obviously

$$H = (a'a)^{-1}a'fD \qquad (17.8.23)$$

From Eq. 17.8.18 in Eq. 17.8.23,

$$H = \delta^{-1}a'fD \qquad (17.8.24)$$

From Eq. 17.8.24,

$$H'H = D(f'a)\delta^{-2}(a'f)D \qquad (17.8.25)$$

Let

$$a'f = G \qquad (17.8.26)$$

$$\delta^{-1}G = C \qquad (17.8.27)$$

From Eqs. 17.8.25, 17.8.26, and 17.8.27,

$$H'H = DC'CD \qquad (17.8.28)$$

From Eqs. 17.8.21 and 17.8.28,

$$D = D_{C'C}^{-1/2} \qquad (17.8.29)$$

From Eqs. 17.8.24, 17.8.26, 17.8.27, and 17.8.29,

$$H = CD \qquad (17.8.30)$$

17.8.3   The Arbitrary Matrix

Let a be any factor loading matrix, f the binary hypothesis matrix, and consider

$$A = D_{aa'}^{-1/2}a \qquad (17.8.31)$$

so that the rows of A are normalized.

Consider

$$AH = b \qquad (17.8.32)$$

and

$$b - fD = \varepsilon \qquad (17.8.33)$$

with H determined so that $tr\varepsilon'\varepsilon$ is minimized and D is a diagonal such that

$$D_{H'H} = I \qquad (17.8.34)$$

Then the solution for H is well known to be

$$H = (A'A)^{-1}A'fD \qquad (17.8.35)$$

Let

$$M = (A'A)^{-1}A'f \qquad (17.8.36)$$

From Eqs. 17.8.34 and 17.8.36,

$$D = D_{M'M}^{-1/2} \qquad (17.8.37)$$

and from Eqs. 17.8.35–17.8.37,

$$H = MD \qquad (17.8.38)$$

17.8.4   The Zero Partial Sum Simple Structure Matrix

Given the arbitrary factor matrix a and the binary hypothesis matrix f, let

$$L = 1\,1' - f \qquad (17.8.39)$$

be called the supplementary matrix to f. Consider

$$aM = b \qquad (17.8.40)$$

and

$$b - f = \varepsilon \qquad (17.8.41)$$

with the restriction that

$$D_{b'L} = 0 \qquad (17.8.42)$$

that is, the hypothesized zeros in f sum to 0 in b for corresponding columns. From Eqs. 17.8.40–17.8.42, we write

$$tr(\varepsilon'\varepsilon - 2D_{b'L}D_\lambda) = \psi \qquad (17.8.43)$$

where D_λ is a diagonal matrix of Lagrangian multipliers.

It will be simpler now to consider Eq. 17.8.43 with respect to each $M_{.i}$ vector separately. From Eqs. 17.8.40, 17.8.41 and 17.8.43,

$$M_{.i}'a'aM_{.i} - 2M_{.i}'a'f_{.i} + f_{.i}'f_{.i} - 2M_{.i}'a'L_{.i}\lambda_i = \psi_i \qquad (17.8.44)$$

Differentiating Eq. 17.8.45 symbolically with respect to $M_{.i}'$ and equating to 0 gives

$$\frac{\partial \psi_i}{\partial M_{.i}'} = 2(a'aM_{.i} - a'f_{.i} - a'L_{.i}\lambda_i) = 0 \qquad (17.8.45)$$

From Eq. 17.8.45,

$$M_{.i} = (a'a)^{-1}a'f_{.i} + (a'a)^{-1}a'L_{.i}\lambda_i \qquad (17.8.46)$$

Premultiplying Eq. 17.8.46 by $L_{.i}'a$ and using Eqs. 17.8.40 and 17.8.42,

$$\lambda_i = -\frac{L_{.i}'a(a'a)^{-1}a'f_{.i}}{L_{.i}'a(a'a)^{-1}a'L_{.i}} \qquad (17.8.47)$$

Let

$$tt' = a'a \qquad (17.8.48)$$

$$\alpha = at'^{-1} \qquad (17.8.49)$$

Using Eqs. 17.8.48 and 17.8.49 in Eqs. 17.8.46 and 17.8.47, we get, respectively,

$$M_{.i} = t'^{-1}(\alpha' f_{.i} - a' L_{.i} \lambda_i) \tag{17.8.50}$$

$$\lambda_i = -\frac{L_{.i}' \alpha \alpha' f_{.i}}{L_{.i}' \alpha \alpha' L_{.i}} \tag{17.8.51}$$

Using Eq. 17.8.51 in Eq. 17.8.50,

$$M_{.i} = t'^{-1}\left(\alpha' f_{.i} - \frac{\alpha' L_{.i} L_{.i}' \alpha \alpha' f_{.i}}{L_{.i}' \alpha \alpha' L_{.i}}\right) \tag{17.8.52}$$

or

$$M_{.i} = t'^{-1}\left(I - \frac{\alpha' L_{.i} L_{.i}' \alpha}{L_{.i}' \alpha \alpha' L_{.i}}\right) \alpha' f_{.i} \tag{17.8.53}$$

Let

$$\alpha' L_{.i} = U_{.i} \tag{17.8.54}$$

$$V_{.i} = \frac{U_i}{\sqrt{U_{.i}' U_{.i}}} \tag{17.8.55}$$

$$\alpha' f_{.i} = W_{.i} \tag{17.8.56}$$

From Eqs. 17.8.54–17.8.56 in Eq. 17.8.53,

$$M_{.i} = t'^{-1}(I - V_{.i} V_{.i}') W_{.i} \tag{17.8.57}$$

Going now to the complete matrix notation, we have from Eqs. 17.8.54–17.8.56, respectively,

$$\alpha' L = U \tag{17.8.58}$$

$$V = U D_{U'U}^{-1/2} \tag{17.8.59}$$

$$\alpha' f = W \tag{17.8.60}$$

From Eqs. 17.8.39 and 17.8.58,

$$U = \alpha'(1\,1' - f) \tag{17.8.61}$$

From Eqs. 17.8.60 and 17.8.61,

$$U = \alpha' 1\,1' - W \tag{17.8.62}$$

Or if we let

$$\alpha' 1 = Y \tag{17.8.63}$$

we have from Eq. 17.8.63 in Eq. 17.8.62,

$$U = Y1' - W \tag{17.8.64}$$

Using Eqs. 17.8.58–17.8.60 in Eq. 17.8.57,

$$M = t'^{-1}(W - V D_{V'W}) \tag{17.8.65}$$

If now we wish to normalize M we have

$$H = MD_{M'M}^{-1/2} \qquad (17.8.66)$$

17.8.5   The Orthogonal Transformation Matrix

Suppose we have a binary hypothesis matrix f and an arbitrary factor matrix a which we wish to transform by a square orthonormal transformation to the best least square approximation to fD, where D is a diagonal to be determined. We let

$$b = aH \qquad (17.8.67)$$

where by hypothesis

$$H'H = I \qquad (17.8.68)$$

The approximation equation is

$$b - fD = \varepsilon \qquad (17.8.69)$$

We write the least square function with the constraint in Eq. 17.8.69 as

$$tr(\varepsilon'\varepsilon - H'H\lambda) = \psi \qquad (17.8.70)$$

where λ is a matrix of Lagrangian multipliers and

$$\lambda = \lambda' \qquad (17.8.71)$$

From Eqs. 17.8.67 and 17.8.69 in Eq. 17.8.70, we have

$$\psi = tr(H'a'aH - 2H'a'fD + Df'fD - H'H\lambda) \qquad (17.8.72)$$

Differentiating Eq. 17.8.72 symbolically with respect to H' and equating to 0 gives

$$\frac{\partial \psi}{\partial H'} = 2(a'aH - a'fD - H\lambda) = 0 \qquad (17.8.73)$$

To differentiate Eq. 17.8.72 with respect to D, we let

$$V_D = D1 \qquad (17.8.74)$$

Using Eqs. 17.8.67 and 17.8.74 in Eq. 17.8.72 gives

$$\psi = tr(b'b - 2V_D'D_{b'f}1 + V_D'D_{f'f}V_D - H'H\lambda) \qquad (17.8.75)$$

Differentiating Eq. 17.8.75 symbolically with respect to V_D' and equating to 0 gives

$$\frac{\partial \psi}{\partial V_D'} = -2(D_{b'f}1 - D_{f'f}V_D) = 0 \qquad (17.8.76)$$

From Eq. 17.8.76,

$$D = D_{f'f}^{-1}D_{b'f} \qquad (17.8.77)$$

Using Eqs. 17.8.67 and 17.8.77 in Eq. 17.8.73,

$$a'b - a'fD_{f'f}^{-1}D_{b'f} - H\lambda = 0 \tag{17.8.78}$$

Let

$$a'fD_{f'f}^{-1} = G \tag{17.8.79}$$

From Eqs. 17.8.78 and 17.8.79,

$$(a'b - GD_{b'f})\lambda^{-1} = H \tag{17.8.80}$$

Let

$$a'b - GD_{b'f} = C \tag{17.8.81}$$

and

$$C = P\Delta Q' \tag{17.8.82}$$

From Eqs. 17.8.81 and 17.8.82 in Eq. 17.8.80,

$$P\Delta Q'\lambda^{-1} = H \tag{17.8.83}$$

Because of Eqs. 17.8.68 and 17.8.72, the only λ^{-1} which will satisfy Eq. 17.8.83 is

$$\lambda^{-1} = Q\Delta^{-1}Q' \tag{17.8.84}$$

Therefore, from Eqs. 17.8.83 and 17.8.84,

$$H = PQ' \tag{17.8.85}$$

From Eq. 17.8.82, we have

$$C'C = Q\Delta^2 Q' \tag{17.8.86}$$

From Eq. 17.8.82,

$$P = CQ\Delta^{-1} \tag{17.8.87}$$

From Eqs. 17.8.85 and 17.8.87,

$$H = CQ\Delta^{-1}Q' \tag{17.8.88}$$

From Eqs. 17.8.67 and 17.8.88, we have

$$b = aCQ\Delta^{-1}Q' \tag{17.8.89}$$

We may start with the approximation

$$b_0 = a \tag{17.8.90}$$

Then

$$C_1 = a'a - GD_{a'f} \tag{17.8.91}$$

$$C_1'C_1 = Q_1 \Delta_1^2 Q_1' \tag{17.8.92}$$

$$H_1 = C_1 Q_1 \Delta_1^{-1}Q_1' \tag{17.8.93}$$

In general,

$$C_i = a'b_{i-1} - GD_{b_{i-1}'f} \tag{17.8.94}$$

$$C_i'C_i = Q_i \Delta_i^2 Q_i' \tag{17.8.95}$$

$$H_i = C_i Q_i \Delta_i^{-1} Q_i' \tag{17.8.96}$$

$$b_i = aH_i \tag{17.8.97}$$

Chapter 18

Analytical Rotations

We saw in Chapter 17 that if we have some hypothesis as to which variables have high loadings and which have low loadings in each factor, we may set up a binary hypothesis matrix and by least square procedures with certain constraints on the transformation get the best approximation to the binary matrix. We saw that the transformation matrices for these procedures are not, in general, square orthonormal unless we impose this additional constraint, as in the last method of that chapter. In many cases, however, a binary matrix may not be available or it may be that the hypotheses are poorly satisfied by the data.

It is therefore desirable to have analytical methods which are independent of the *a priori* hypotheses of the experimenter. These analytical methods presumably should approximate the criteria outlined in the introduction to Chapter 17. These are the criteria formulated by Thurstone (1947).

A great many methods have been proposed for analytical rotations to simple structure factor loading matrices. The earlier methods were proposed by Thurstone (1947), followed by several methods developed by Horst (1941) and Tucker (1944) which were semi-analytical. Later Wrigley and Neuhaus (1952) proposed more completely analytical procedures. Then followed the work of Carroll (1953), Saunders (1953), and several others. Perhaps the best-known methods are based on the work of Kaiser (1958).

In any case, although the mathematical thinking and development which have gone into many of the proposed analytical methods is ingenious, these methods have not resulted in the success which may have been expected for them. The methods in general are very laborious computationally, even with the high-speed computers, and often they do not give results which come close to satisfying the criteria of simple structure.

At least two conditions should be satisfied by analytical methods or by any method of rotation. First, the factor loadings should be relatively invariant with respect to the group of entities on which the data are collected. Second, a subset of factor loadings should be relatively invariant, irrespective of which particular battery of variables includes that subset. This latter criterion is subject to certain further qualifications, but one criterion of a good transformation procedure is that the factor loadings of variables be relatively invariant, both with respect to the sampling of entities and the sampling of attributes.

One of the chief difficulties with most of the analytical methods which have been developed is that they are greatly influenced by the particular selection of variables which go into the correlation matrix. In this book we shall not attempt to give an account of all of the analytical methods which have been proposed. We shall, however, briefly describe the methods of Professor Carroll, whose pioneering and ingenious work may eventually result in more adequate methods.

Carroll (1953) proposed that we have a minimum number of negative factor loadings and that such as were present should be small. His criterion for transformation was based on the squared factor loadings of the transformed matrix. Therefore, the signs would not influence the criterion of goodness of transformation. For this matrix he required in his early model that the minor products of all possible pairs of vectors be a minimum. This meant, in effect, that for any pair there should be a number of very small squared factor loadings; there should be very few factor loadings which were high for both factors; and that for those which were high in one factor, the loadings should be low in the other and vice versa. Here, then, are included three of the Thurstone criteria of simple structure. These conditions would, of course, satisfy the criterion that the minor product moment of the two vectors of squared factor loadings should be small.

Carroll (1953) worked out an ingenious computational procedure for the electronic computer for achieving such a minimum for all pairs of factor loading vectors. The difficulties with the procedure were, first, it was strongly influenced by the particular variables in the set and second, it resulted in too few high factor loadings and too many negative loadings of medium size. The transformation matrix in general was such that the correlations of the reference axes were negative, and the correlation among the primary factors, as discussed in Chapter 21, tended to be positive.

Later, Carroll (1957) changed this criterion by considering, not the minimization of sums of minor products for all pairs of squared element factor loading vectors, but rather the minimization of the covariance of these vectors. This resulted in an overcorrection for the limitations of the previous method.

The earlier of these methods was called the *quartimin method*, and the later one was called the *covarimin method*. Carroll found from empirical investigation that neither of these methods worked very well. The former procedure was biased in favor of reference axes which were too low in correlation among themselves, and the latter method resulted in reference axes which were too highly correlated. For the latter method, the large simple structure factor loadings tended to be too large and the small ones tended to be considerably greater than 0.

Carroll then formulated a combination of the two methods so as to neutralize the undesirable effects of both. This combination of the quartimin and covarimin methods has been called the *oblimin method*. The procedure still left a decision as to just how to combine the two procedures, and a certain amount of arbitrariness remained.

The great advantage of Carroll's approach is that one need not hypothesize as to whether a transformation is orthonormal or oblique. The solution itself purports to solve for the correlations among the simple structure reference axes and the primary factor axes. Unfortunately, even with the ingenious rationale and the extraordinarily elaborate computational procedures which have been worked out, the methods still have not demonstrated their usefulness for some sets of experimental data.

Currently, it appears that the work of Kaiser (1958) has had more practical impact on the work of factor analysts than that of other investigators. The procedures of Kaiser specify an orthonormal transformation. This makes the mathematics and the computational routines considerably more straightforward and amenable to the application of the basic structure concepts. It does impose limitations on the results to be expected. In particular, the possibility of achieving relative invariance of transformed factor loadings with respect to both sample of entities and sample of attributes is more remote than if more general transformation procedures were available. However, since in this book our emphasis is on practical application, we shall give our major attention to the methods developed by Kaiser, and to variations of these.

18.1   Characteristics of the Methods

18.1.1   The Orthonormal Transformation Matrix. The methods we shall consider do not admit of oblique transformations. The mathematical models on which they are based, and the computational routines, have the restriction of orthonormality built into them. While even yet a number of investigators prefer the orthonormal type of transformation as more desirable from a philosophical and scientific point of view, the tendency seems to be gaining ground to prefer the earlier objectives of Thurstone in his relaxed oblique transformations, which he was able to achieve by graphical methods and shrewd subjective judgment. Unfortunately, many of his followers were not able to apply the same ingenious insights and judgments in their efforts to use the nonanalytical graphical methods.

It is probable that the quest to relax the orthonormal transformation by satisfactory objective analytical procedures will eventually triumph. If so, it will probably result in methods for objectively eliminating from the variables contributing to the simple structure determination, those which are most complex in structure and which tend to confuse the transformation attempts.

18.1.2 The Optimizing Function. With the constraint that the transformation shall be orthonormal, the class of solutions we shall discuss all consider a transformed matrix whose elements have been raised to some even power. This means that the new matrix has all positive elements.

In particular, we may consider the matrix of squared elements of transformed factor loadings, as did Carroll. Our attention, however, is directed to only a single factor vector of these positive elements at a time. Specifically, the optimizing criterion which Kaiser (1958) suggested is that the variance of each such vector of positive elements shall be a maximum.

Since the elements are all positive by hypothesis, the maximum for each vector would be achieved if all of its elements were either large or 0. Therefore, in working toward the maximization of this variance criterion, one tends to reduce the intermediate loadings to a minimum and to maximize the number of large and small loadings. This again satisfies one of the criteria of Thurstone for simple structure, that is, that each factor should have a relatively large number of near vanishing elements, a limited number of very large elements, with very few elements of intermediate size.

18.1.3 Iterative Type Solutions. All of the models considered in this chapter differ essentially from most of those in Chapter 17 in that the solution for the orthonormal transformation matrix is arrived at by successive approximations. It will be recalled that in the last chapter only the last model required successive approximations. This is the one in which the restriction of orthonormality of the transformation is imposed.

The varimax solution, as it was called by Kaiser and as developed by him, consists of a large number of orthonormal transformations involving only two factor vectors at a time. The procedure in general is to start with, say, the first two factor vectors, and transform them by an orthonormal transformation so that the variance of their squared elements is a maximum. One then proceeds with the new first and the third vectors, and applies another orthonormal transformation which satisfies the criterion of maximum variance of squared elements for the transformed vectors. This procedure continues for all possible pairs until the criterion of variances of squared factor loadings ceases to improve.

It can be seen that this would be an extremely laborious procedure for desk calculators. Even for the electronic computers it can be expensive and time-consuming if the matrices to be transformed are very large, for example, of the order of 500 attributes by 20 or 30 factors. After the varimax criterion is satisfied, the method of Kaiser requires the product of all of the orthonormal matrices involved in the computational routine. This cumulative product gives the orthonormal transformation which, when applied directly to the arbitrary factor loading matrix, yields a transformed matrix satisfying the varimax criterion.

18.1.4 Accumulation of Decimal Error.

The method of Kaiser, because of the very large number of individual computations going into the procedure, each of which involves rounding errors, is subject to the accumulation of considerable decimal error if the number of variables is large. The methods we shall outline use somewhat different approaches to achieve the varimax criterion. They do not in general accumulate as much decimal error as those of Kaiser. As a matter of fact, they are self-correcting with respect to both decimal and computational error.

18.2 Kinds of Methods

We shall discuss four variations of the methods proposed by Kaiser. These we may call the *successive factor varimax*, the *simultaneous factor varimax*, the *successive factor general varimax*, and the *simultaneous factor general varimax*.

18.2.1 Successive Factor Varimax.

The successive factor varimax method differs essentially from that of Kaiser in that we solve for one factor vector at a time, rather than for all of them simultaneously. As each factor is solved for, it satisfies the varimax criterion in that the variance of the sums of the squared elements for a factor is a maximum. Having found this factor, we find another in which the transformation vector is orthogonal to the first. With this restriction, the variance of the squared elements of the next factor vector is a maximum. We continue in this way until we have found the last factor.

18.2.2 Simultaneous Factor Varimax.

In this model we start with an approximation of some sort to the simple structure matrix of factor loadings. We then solve for a second approximation to the factor loading matrix which will satisfy the varimax criterion. We thus proceed by successive approximations to get factor loading matrices which will yield better and better approximations to the matrix which ultimately best satisfies the varimax criterion.

The restriction for each approximation is always that the transformation matrix for that approximation is orthonormal. The procedure therefore yields all of the final simple structure factor loading vectors simultaneously, rather than one at a time.

18.2.3 Successive Factor General Varimax. This method is like the successive factor varimax, which gets one factor at a time and maximizes the variances of the squared factor loadings, except that we require that some even power of the factor loading elements be positive. This even power may be any value not less than 1. In particular, we can require that the variance of the absolute values of the factor loadings be maximum.

18.2.4 Simultaneous Factor General Varimax. This model is similar to the one discussed in Section 18.2.2 in that, by successive iterations, the simple structure factor loading matrix is solved for by approximations to all of the factor vectors at one time. It is similar to the model discussed in Section 18.2.3 in that the criterion which is maximized is a generalization of the variance of the squared factor loadings. Here again, we maximize the variance of some positive even power of the factor loadings, where the power is not less than 1.

As will be seen in the mathematical proof, Section 18.7.4, one may take a positive even power which in the limiting case approaches the absolute value of the factor loadings. On the other hand, one could maximize the variance of the fourth powers, or the four-thirds powers, or any other powers in which the numerator of the exponent is even and the denominator odd and less than the numerator. It can be seen that if the numerator of the exponent is an even number approaching infinity, and the odd number in the denominator is always one less than the numerator, an element raised to this power would approach the absolute value of the element.

18.3 Successive Factor Varimax Solution

18.3.1 Characteristics of the Method. It has been indicated that the successive factor varimax solution does not give the same answer as the method of Kaiser, in which the transformations are made two vectors at a time. Actually, in the former case, the factor loading vectors for the transformed solution tend to come out in the order of the variance of their squared loadings. This may not always be the case, as the final result may depend somewhat on the approximation one starts with. There is currently no mathematical proof to indicate whether, or under what conditions, this might be true.

Perhaps the chief advantage of this method is that the simple structure factors tend to come out in the order of clarity of interpretation, so that one may neglect the factors which appear later in the solution if they seem to be too obscure or ambiguous. The method is different in this respect from Kaiser's, since the ambiguity of the simple structure factors for his method seems to be spread over all the factors approximately equally.

18.3.2 Computational Equations

18.3.2a DEFINITION OF NOTATION

$_1a$ is the arbitrary factor matrix.

H is the orthogonal transformation matrix.

b is the simple structure factor matrix.

$b^{(2)}$ is a matrix whose elements are the second powers of the elements in b.

$b^{(3)}$ is a matrix whose elements are the third powers of the elements in b.

18.3.2b THE EQUATIONS

$$W = \frac{a'1}{\sqrt{(1'a)(a'1)}} \qquad (18.3.1)$$

$$_1V = _1aW \qquad (18.3.2)$$

$$_1V_{L_1} = \min \qquad (18.3.3)$$

$$_0H_{.1} = _1a_{L_1}. \qquad (18.3.4)$$

$$_1b_{.1} = _1a\,_0H_{.1} \qquad (18.3.5)$$

$$_1\beta_{.1} = _1b_{.1}^{(3)} - _1b_{.1}\frac{1'\,_1b_{.1}^{(2)}}{n} \qquad (18.3.6)$$

$$_1U_{.1} = _1a'\,_1\beta_{.1} \qquad (18.3.7)$$

$$_1\alpha_1 = \sqrt{_1U_{.1}'\,_1U_{.1}} \qquad (18.3.8)$$

$$_1H_{.1} = \frac{_1U_{.1}}{_1\alpha_1} \qquad (18.3.9)$$

$$_2b_{.1} = _1a\,_1H_{.1} \qquad (18.3.10)$$

$$_s\beta_{.1} = _sb_{.1}^{(3)} - _sb_{.1}\frac{1'\,_sb_{.1}^{(2)}}{n} \qquad (18.3.11)$$

$$_sU_{.1} = _1a'\,_s\beta_{.1} \qquad (18.3.12)$$

$$_s\alpha_1 = \sqrt{_sU_{.1}'\,_sU_{.1}} \qquad (18.3.13)$$

$$_sH_{.1} = \frac{_sU_{.1}}{_s\alpha_1} \qquad (18.3.14)$$

$$_{s+1}b_{.1} = _1a\,_sH_{.1} \qquad (18.3.15)$$

$$_2a = _1a - b_{.1}\,H_{.1}' \qquad (18.3.16)$$

$$_iV = _{i-1}V + b_{.i-1} \qquad (18.3.17)$$

$$_iV_{L_i} = \min V \qquad (18.3.18)$$

$$_i a_{L_i.} = {_0}H_{.i} \tag{18.3.19}$$

$$_1 b_{.i} = {_i}a {_0}H_{.i} \tag{18.3.20}$$

$$_s \beta_{.i} = {_s}b_{.i}^{(3)} - {_s}b_{.i} \frac{1' {_s}b_{.i}^{(2)}}{n} \tag{18.3.21}$$

$$_s U_{.i} = {_i}a' {_s}\beta_{.i} \tag{18.3.22}$$

$$_s \alpha_i = \sqrt{{_s}U_{.i}' {_s}U_{.i}} \tag{18.3.23}$$

$$_s H_{.i} = \frac{_s U_{.i}}{_s \alpha_i} \tag{18.3.24}$$

$$_{s+1} b_{.i} = {_i}a {_s}H_{.i} \tag{18.3.25}$$

$$_{i+1} a = {_i}a - b_{.i} H_{.i}' \tag{18.3.26}$$

18.3.3 Computational Instructions.

We begin with an arbitrary factor loading matrix $_1a$. Kaiser has recommended, and the practice seems to be generally desirable, that any arbitrary factor loading matrix, before it is transformed or rotated, should be normalized by rows. We shall therefore assume in this and the succeeding models that the arbitrary factor loading matrices have been normalized by rows.

The rationale for selecting the first approximation to the first transformation vector is as follows. We assume that if there were, in the set of tests or measures, one which measured one of the primary factors rather accurately, it would have a relatively low correlation with the average of all the variables. Therefore we calculate a normalized vector of the average of the factor loadings by columns, as indicated in Eq. 18.3.1. The right-hand side of this equation gives in the numerator a column vector whose elements are the sums of the column elements of the factor loading matrix $_1a$. As can be seen, the denominator scalar of this right-hand term is the square root of the minor product moment of the vector in the numerator. Therefore, the W column vector on the left of Eq. 18.3.1 is a normal vector.

In Eq. 18.3.2, we calculate the vector $_1V$. This is the factor loading matrix $_1a$ postmultiplied by the vector W of Eq. 18.3.1. This now gives a vector of correlations of the average of all the tests with each of the measures. Presumably, that variable which correlates lowest with this average would be a relatively pure measure of a factor.

We therefore look for the lowest element in the vector given by Eq. 18.3.2. This is indicated in Eq. 18.3.3. We use the subscript L_1 to indicate the position of this lowest value.

We then take the L_1 row vector of the $_1a$ factor loading matrix as the zero approximation to the first vector of the transformation matrix H, as indicated in Eq. 18.3.4.

Next we postmultiply the factor loading matrix by the vector indicated in Eq. 18.3.4. This gives the first approximation to the first transformed factor loading vector, as indicated in Eq. 18.3.5.

Then we calculate the first approximation to a β vector, as shown in Eq. 18.3.6. On the right-hand side of the equation, the first term is a vector whose elements are the cubes of the elements of the vector calculated in Eq. 18.3.5. The second term on the right of Eq. 18.3.6 is the vector calculated in Eq. 18.3.5 multiplied by a scalar quantity, which is the average of the sums of squares of the elements of the vector in Eq. 18.3.5. This second vector is subtracted from the first.

Next we calculate the first approximation to the $U_{.1}$ vector, as indicated in Eq. 18.3.7. This is the transpose of the factor loading matrix postmultiplied by the vector calculated in Eq. 18.3.6.

We now calculate a scalar quantity as in Eq. 18.3.8. This is the square root of the minor product moment of the vector calculated in Eq. 18.3.7.

Next we calculate the first approximation to the first transformation vector as in Eq. 18.3.9. The vector calculated in Eq. 18.3.7 is divided by the scalar calculated in Eq. 18.3.8. We see, therefore, that the vector calculated in Eq. 18.3.9 is a normal vector.

We now calculate the second approximation to the transformed factor loading vector $b_{.1}$. As indicated in Eq. 18.3.10, we postmultiply the arbitrary factor loading matrix by the vector calculated in Eq. 18.3.9.

We continue to calculate successive approximations to the first transformation vector $H_{.1}$ and the first simple structure factor vector $b_{.1}$, as indicated in Eqs. 18.3.11–18.3.15. These equations are the same as Eqs. 18.3.6–18.3.10, except that the prescript of 1 has been changed to the general subscript s, which means the s approximation.

The stabilization limit may be based on the scalar α indicated in Eqs. 18.3.8 and 18.3.13. When this scalar has stabilized to a sufficient degree of accuracy, we may assume that the $H_{.1}$ vector is sufficiently accurate, and therefore that the $b_{.1}$ vector is also sufficiently accurate.

We then calculate a residual factor loading matrix, as indicated in Eq. 18.3.16. The first term on the right side is the factor loading matrix a with a prescript 1. We use this prescript to show that it is the original arbitrary factor loading matrix, rather than some residual matrix derived from it. The second term on the right of this equation is the major product moment of the factor loading vector $b_{.1}$ and the transformation vector $H_{.1}$. This major product is subtracted from the factor loading matrix to give a residual matrix $_2a$.

We are now ready to begin the computations for the second simple structure factor vector $b_{.2}$, and the second transformation vector $H_{.2}$. We require a first approximation to the $H_{.2}$ vector. This is accomplished by considering Eq. 18.3.17. Here for the subscript i we substitute 2. On the right-hand side of the equation this gives as the first term $_1V$, which we calculated in Eq.

18.3.2. To this is added $b_{.1}$, calculated in the previous cycle of computations, to give the vector V with a prescript of 2.

We now consider Eq. 18.3.18 in which the i subscript takes the value of 2. This equation means that we find the smallest value in the vector calculated in Eq. 18.3.17 and call this the L_2 position.

Having identified this position, we then take as our zero approximation to the $H_{.2}$ vector the L_2 row of the residual factor loading matrix $_2a$ calculated in Eq. 18.3.16. This is indicated in Eq. 18.3.19.

Next we calculate the first approximation to $b_{.2}$ as indicated in Eq. 18.3.20, in which $i = 2$. The right-hand side of this equation shows that we post-multiply the matrix calculated in Eq. 18.3.16 by the vector for $i = 2$ from Eq. 18.3.19.

For the computation of the s approximation to the ith transformation vector $H_{.i}$, and the $s + 1$ approximation to the ith factor loading vector $b_{.i}$, we now have the series of equations 18.3.21–18.3.25.

Equation 18.3.26 shows the general equation for calculating the $i + 1$ residual factor loading matrix $_{i+1}a$ from the ith residual factor loading matrix $_ia$, the ith factor loading vector $b_{.i}$, and the ith transformation vector $H_{.i}$.

18.3.4 Numerical Example. We shall use the same numerical example throughout to illustrate the various models in this chapter.

We begin with the first three factors of the principal axis factor loading matrix which are given in Table 18.3.1.

Table 18.3.2 gives the final matrix H which transforms the arbitrary matrix a to the varimax simple structure matrix b.

Table 18.3.3 shows the final approximation to the varimax factor loading matrix. It can be verified that the rows of this matrix are normalized. If desired, they may be scaled back to the variances of the rows of the principal axis matrix whose transpose is given in Table 18.3.1.

TABLE 18.3.1　Transpose of Principal Axis Factor Loading Matrix

0.717	0.740	0.773	0.556	0.463	0.518	0.640	0.615	0.715
0.493	0.478	0.296	−0.649	−0.744	−0.694	0.080	0.166	−0.034
0.350	0.322	0.406	0.068	0.181	0.188	−0.588	−0.621	−0.369

TABLE 18.3.2　Final Transformation
Matrix H for
Successive Factor Varimax Solution

0.502	0.702	0.505
−0.842	0.531	0.098
0.199	0.475	−0.857

TABLE 18.3.3 Final Varimax Factor
Matrix b for
Successive Factor Varimax Solution

0.016	0.993	0.118
0.035	0.987	0.154
0.238	0.968	0.077
0.978	0.091	0.185
1.000	0.018	0.006
0.995	0.095	0.036
0.157	0.244	0.957
0.051	0.253	0.966
0.390	0.384	0.837

18.4   Simultaneous Factor Varimax Solution

18.4.1   Characteristics of the Method. The computational procedures in this method are essentially different from those of the method just described. Successive iterations are required, but we iterate simultaneously to all of the factor vectors of the b or varimax matrix, rather than getting one vector at a time. This method of solution should give exactly the same results, within limits of decimal error, as Kaiser's computational procedure (1959). It appears to have the advantage that the computations are self-correcting and that it does not accumulate decimal error. The time required for the computations, as compared with the Kaiser method, has not been accurately determined, but it appears that for small matrices the Kaiser method may be slightly faster, and for larger matrices this method may be slightly faster.

One of the characteristics of the method is that each iteration requires the basic structure solution of the matrix whose order is equal to the number of factors. For high-speed computers, however, this is not a serious restriction, since the number of factors would ordinarily not be over 10 or 15 at most, and available computer programs are extremely rapid for calculating the basic structure factors of matrices of this order.

18.4.2   Computational Equations

18.4.2a   DEFINITION OF NOTATION
$a, H, b, b^{(2)}, b^{(3)}$ are the same as in Section 18.3.2a.

18.4.2b   THE EQUATIONS

$$_1\beta = {}_1b^{(3)} - {}_1b \frac{D_{1b'1b}}{n} \tag{18.4.1}$$

$$_1C = a'_1\beta \tag{18.4.2}$$

$$_1C'\,_1C = {}_1Q\,_1\Delta^2\,_1Q' \tag{18.4.3}$$

$$_1H = ((_1C\,_1Q)_1\Delta^{-1})_1Q' \tag{18.4.4}$$

$$_2b = a\,_1H \tag{18.4.5}$$

$$_i\beta = {}_ib^{(3)} - {}_ib\,\frac{D_{ib'\,ib}}{n} \tag{18.4.6}$$

$$_iC = a'\,_i\beta \tag{18.4.7}$$

$$_iC'\,_iC = {}_iQ_i\Delta^2\,_iQ' \tag{18.4.8}$$

$$_iH = ((_iC\,_iQ)_i\Delta^{-1})_iQ' \tag{18.4.9}$$

$$_{i+1}b = a\,_iH \tag{18.4.10}$$

18.4.3 Computational Instructions. We begin with a first approximation to the simple structure factor loading matrix. This could be the normalized arbitrary factor matrix itself. It may be better to start with a more accurate approximation, such as some binary hypothesis matrix, as discussed in the previous chapter.

The first step in the computational cycles is indicated in Eq. 18.4.1. On the right-hand side of this equation we have as the first term a matrix whose elements are the cubes of the elements of the first approximation to the b matrix. The second term on the right is obtained by postmultiplying the first approximation to the b matrix by a diagonal matrix. This diagonal matrix consists of the diagonal elements of the minor product moment of this approximation to the b matrix, divided by n, the number of variables.

The next step is indicated in Eq. 18.4.2. Here we have the first approximation to a C matrix which is the minor product moment obtained by postmultiplying the transpose of the a factor loading matrix by the β matrix of Eq. 18.4.1.

The next set of computations is indicated by Eq. 18.4.3. We get the minor product moment of the matrix calculated in Eq. 18.4.2 and find its basic structure factors Q and Δ^2, as indicated on the right-hand side of this equation.

We then get the approximation to the transformation matrix, as indicated in Eq. 18.4.4. Here we postmultiply the C matrix of Eq. 18.4.2 successively by the factors Q, Δ^{-1}, and Q'. This approximation to the H matrix is orthonormal.

The second approximation to the b matrix is given in Eq. 18.4.5. This is the factor loading matrix a postmultiplied by the matrix of Eq. 18.4.4.

The general equations for the approximations to the H and the b matrices are given in Eqs. 18.4.6–18.4.10, which are analogous to Eqs. 18.4.1–18.4.5. The subscripts 1 and 2 have been replaced by i and $i+1$.

18.4.4   Numerical Example. We begin with the same factor loading
matrix in this numerical example as in the previous one.

Table 18.4.1 gives the final approximation to the varimax transformation
matrix *H*. Intermediate approximations are not given, although they could
be readily outputted from the corresponding Fortran program in the Appendix.

Table 18.4.2 gives the final approximation to the varimax factor loading
matrix. Here, too, the outputting of intermediate approximations may be
readily inserted in the Fortran program. It can be seen that, aside from the
order of the factors, the loadings do not differ markedly from those in the
previous section. With other data the results may differ more for the two
methods. As in the previous section, the matrix is normal by rows.

TABLE 18.4.1   Final Approximation to
Transformation Matrix *H* for
Simultaneous Factor Varimax Solution

0.664	−0.472	−0.580
0.514	0.851	−0.105
0.543	−0.229	0.808

TABLE 18.4.2   Final Approximation to
Varimax Factor Matrix *b* for
Simultaneous Factor Varimax Solution

0.980	0.001	0.197
0.972	−0.017	0.234
0.961	−0.223	0.164
−0.084	0.969	−0.233
−0.026	0.998	−0.049
−0.100	0.991	−0.085
0.168	−0.114	0.979
0.175	−0.008	0.984
0.318	−0.351	0.881

18.5   Successive Factor General Varimax

18.5.1   Characteristics of the Method. This method is like the one
discussed in Section 18.3, except that now instead of maximizing the variance
of the squared factor vector elements, we solve for one vector at a time so as
to maximize the variance of some power of the elements in which the power
is the ratio of an even number to a smaller odd number. The computations
are essentially the same as for Section 18.3 with the difference that, having
chosen a particular power, we have the problem of finding the required

powers of elements, either by means of tables of logarithmic and exponential functions or by means of computer program statements.

18.5.2 Computational Equations

18.5.2a DEFINITION OF NOTATION

$_1a$, b and H are the same as in Section 18.3.2a.

18.5.2b THE EQUATIONS

$$_s\beta_{.1} = {}_sb_{.1}{}^{(2k-1)} - {}_sb_{.1}{}^{(k-1)} \frac{1'\,{}_sb_{.1}{}^{(k)}}{n} \tag{18.5.1}$$

$$_sU_{.1} = {}_1a'\,{}_s\beta_{.1} \tag{18.5.2}$$

$$_s\alpha_1 = \sqrt{{}_sU_{.1}'\,{}_sU_{.1}} \tag{18.5.3}$$

$$_sH_{.1} = \frac{{}_sU_{.1}}{{}_s\alpha_1} \tag{18.5.4}$$

$$_{s+1}b_{.1} = {}_1a\,{}_sH_{.1} \tag{18.5.5}$$

$$_2a = {}_1a - b_{.1}\,H_{.1}' \tag{18.5.6}$$

$$_{i+1}a = {}_ia - b_{.i}\,H_{.i}' \tag{18.5.7}$$

18.5.3 Computational Instructions. In this model we may let the power of the transformed factor loading elements be any positive number k greater than 1 which may be expressed as the ratio of an even to an odd integer.

We begin with Eq. 18.5.1. Here we indicate the s approximation to a β vector, which is analogous to the β vector which we calculated in Section 18.3. We assume that some approximation to the transformed vector is available. As a matter of fact, we can use the methods of Section 18.3 to get this approximation. We raise the elements to the $2k - 1$ power to get the first term on the right of Eq. 18.5.1, in which the prescript s takes the value 1. The second term on the right consists of the approximation vector with elements raised to the $k - 1$ power and multiplied by a scalar which is the mean of the kth power elements of the vector.

Equation 18.5.2 is obtained by postmultiplying the transpose of the arbitrary factor loading matrix by the s approximation to the $\beta_{.1}$ vector to give an s approximation to a $U_{.1}$ vector.

A scalar quantity is then calculated as in Eq. 18.5.3, which is the square root of the minor product moment of the vector calculated in Eq. 18.5.2.

The vector calculated in Eq. 18.5.2 is divided by the scalar calculated in Eq. 18.5.3 to give the s approximation to the first transformation vector of H, as indicated in Eq. 18.5.4.

The $s + 1$ approximation to the first factor loading b vector is given by Eq. 18.5.5. This is the factor loading matrix postmultiplied by the vector calculated in Eq. 18.5.4. When the iterations stabilize sufficiently, as indicated by some tolerance limit set on the α scalar of Eq. 18.5.3, we may take the resulting $b_{.1}$ approximation as the first simple structure factor vector.

We then calculate a residual matrix as in Eq. 18.5.6. This is obtained by subtracting the major product of the first simple structure factor loading vector and the corresponding transformation vector H from the arbitrary factor matrix a.

We now operate on this new matrix with Eqs. 18.5.1–18.5.5 in exactly the same way as we did on the original matrix. To get a first approximation we may use the method of Section 18.3.

The general equation for the $i + 1$ residual of the arbitrary factor loading matrix a is given by Eq. 18.5.7.

18.5.4 Numerical Example. We begin with the same data as in Section 18.3.4 and take $k = 10/3$. Here we indicate only the results of the method. The intermediate computations are not given.

Table 18.5.1 is the final approximation to the orthonormal transformation matrix.

Table 18.5.2 is the final approximation to the varimax matrix b. It must

TABLE 18.5.1   Final Approximation to Transformation
Matrix H for Successive Factor General Varimax
Method with $k = 10/3$

0.735	0.412	0.538
0.089	−0.846	0.526
−0.672	0.339	0.659

TABLE 18.5.2   Final Approximation to Varimax Factor
Matrix b for Successive Factor General Varimax
Method with $k = 10/3$

0.358	−0.003	0.934
0.395	0.010	0.919
0.349	0.223	0.910
0.356	0.934	0.003
0.171	0.985	−0.026
0.218	0.975	0.042
1.000	−0.004	−0.001
0.994	−0.110	0.010
0.957	0.246	0.154

be remembered that this is the transformation such that the variance of the 10/3 power of the elements in the b matrix is a maximum for each column—with the restriction, of course, that the columns were obtained one at a time. It is of interest to compare this matrix with Table 18.3.3 of Section 18.3.^{t}

18.6 Simultaneous Factor General Varimax

18.6.1 Characteristics of the Method. This method is the same as the one discussed in Section 18.4, except that now we maximize the variance of any even power of the transformed elements we wish, as long as the power is greater than 1. The method, like that of Kaiser (1958), solves simultaneously for all of the transformed simple structure vectors, rather than for one at a time. It has the advantage that decimal error is not accumulated as it is in Kaiser's method.

18.6.2 Computational Equations

18.6.2a DEFINITION OF NOTATION
a, b, and H are the same as in Section 18.3.2a.
$_sb$ is the s approximation to b.
$_sb^{(2k-1)}$ is a matrix whose elements are those of $_sb$ raised to the $2k-1$ power.
$_sH$ is the s approximation to the transformation matrix.

18.6.2b THE EQUATIONS

$$_s\beta = {_sb^{(2k-1)}} - {_sb^{(k-1)}} \frac{D_{1'{_sb^{(k)}}}}{n} \tag{18.6.1}$$

$$_sC = a'\,_s\beta \tag{18.6.2}$$

$$_sC'_sC = {_sQ}\,_s\Delta^2\,_sQ' \tag{18.6.3}$$

$$_sH = ((_sC_sQ)_s\Delta^{-1})_sQ' \tag{18.6.4}$$

$$_{s+1}b = a\,_sH \tag{18.6.5}$$

18.6.3 Computational Instructions. In the example of the model discussed here, we shall again assume that it is the variance of the kth power of the elements in the transformed factor vectors which we wish to maximize.

We may begin with the arbitrary factor loading matrix itself, presumably normalized by rows. We consider Eq. 18.6.1 for the prescript s equal to 1. The first term on the right is a matrix whose elements are the $2k - 1$ powers of the elements in $_1b$. The second term on the right has for the first factor a matrix whose elements are the $k - 1$ powers of the elements in b. This matrix is postmultiplied by a diagonal matrix whose elements are the means of columns of a matrix obtained by raising the elements of b to the kth power.

Equation 18.6.2 indicates the computation of a matrix C. This is the transpose of the arbitrary factor matrix, postmultiplied by the β matrix of Eq. 18.6.1.

Equation 18.6.3 is the minor product moment of the matrix obtained in Eq. 18.6.2, and also indicates the solution for the basic structure factors Q and Δ^2 of this matrix. This involves, as in Section 18.4, basic structure computations outlined in earlier chapters.

The calculation of the s approximation to the H matrix is given in Eq. 18.6.4. This is obtained by postmultiplying in turn the C matrix of Eq. 18.6.2 by the Q matrix shown in Eq. 18.6.3, by the inverse of the Δ matrix of Eq. 18.6.3, by the transpose of the Q matrix of Eq. 18.6.3.

The $s + 1$ approximation to the transformed factor loading matrix is given in Eq. 18.6.5. This is the arbitrary factor loading matrix a multiplied by the matrix of Eq. 18.6.4. A stabilization limit may be set on the sum of the elements of the basic diagonal in Eq. 18.6.3. These will in general increase asymptotically to an upper limit.

18.6.4 Numerical Example. We begin with the same principal axis matrix as in the preceding sections.

TABLE 18.6.1   Final Approximation to Transformation
Matrix H for Simultaneous Factor General Varimax
Solution with $k = 10/3$

0.670	−0.476	−0.569
0.513	0.851	−0.108
0.536	−0.220	0.815

TABLE 18.6.2   Final Approximation to Varimax Factor
Matrix b for Simultaneous Factor General Varimax
Solution with $k = 10/3$

0.982	0.002	0.188
0.974	−0.017	0.224
0.963	−0.223	0.153
−0.089	0.971	−0.223
−0.028	0.999	−0.040
−0.104	0.992	−0.076
0.177	−0.123	0.976
0.185	−0.017	0.983
0.328	−0.358	0.874

Table 18.6.1 gives the final approximation for the transformation matrix H. Table 18.6.2 gives the final approximation for the varimax factor matrix b. The factors can readily be identified with those from previous solutions in this chapter, even though the results expectedly differ by more than decimal accuracy.

18.7 Mathematical Proofs

18.7.1 Successive Factor Varimax
Let

$$b = aH \qquad (18.7.1)$$

and $b^{(2)}$ be a matrix whose elements are the squares of those in b. Consider the function

$$b_{.1}^{(2)\,'}\left(I - \frac{1\,1'}{n}\right)b_{.1}^{(2)} = \phi_1 = \max \qquad (18.7.2)$$

This is the well-known varimax criterion of Kaiser (1958) which maximizes the variance of the squared factor loading vectors in b. We impose the restriction that

$$H_{.1}'H_{.1} = 1 \qquad (18.7.3)$$

We let

$$D_{b_{.1}} 1 = b_{.1} \qquad (18.7.4)$$

From Eqs. 18.7.1–18.7.4, we write

$$\psi_1 = H_{.1}'a'D_{b_{.1}}\left(I - \frac{1\,1'}{n}\right)D_{b_{.1}}aH_{.1} - H_{.1}'H_{.1}\lambda_1 \qquad (18.7.5)$$

where λ_1 is a Lagrangian scalar.

Differentiating Eq. 18.7.5 symbolically with respect to $H_{.1}'$ and equating to 0, we have

$$\frac{\partial \psi_1}{\partial H_{.1}'} = 2\left[a'D_{b_{.1}}\left(I - \frac{1\,1'}{n}\right)D_{b_{.1}}aH_{.1} - H_{.1}\lambda_1\right] = 0 \qquad (18.7.6)$$

From Eqs. 18.7.1 and 18.7.6,

$$a'\left(b_{.1}^{(3)} - b_{.1}\frac{b_{.1}'b_{.1}}{n}\right) = H_{.1}\lambda_1 \qquad (18.7.7)$$

Let

$$\beta_{.1} = b_{.1}^{(3)} - b_{.1}\frac{b_{.1}'b_{.1}}{n} \qquad (18.7.8)$$

From Eqs. 18.7.7 and 18.7.8,

$$a'\beta_{.1} = H_{.1}\lambda_1 \qquad (18.7.9)$$

We start with a first approximation by considering, say,

$$W = \frac{a'1}{\sqrt{1'aa'1}} \tag{18.7.10}$$

$$_1V = aW \tag{18.7.11}$$

and find the smallest element in $_1V$, say $_1V_L$. We may then let

$$_0b_{.1} = aa_L. \tag{18.7.12}$$

We have as the general iteration equations:

$$_s\beta_{.1} = {}_sb_{.1}{}^{(3)} - {}_sb_{.1}\frac{{}_sb_{.1}'\,{}_sb_{.1}}{n} \tag{18.7.13}$$

$$a'\,{}_s\beta_{.1} = {}_sU_{.1} \tag{18.7.14}$$

$$_sH_{.1} = \frac{{}_sU_{.1}}{\sqrt{{}_sU_{.1}'\,{}_sU_{.1}}} \tag{18.7.15}$$

$$_{s+1}b_{.1} = a\,{}_sH_{.1} \tag{18.7.16}$$

To get $H_{.2}$ we require that

$$H_{.2}'H_{.1} = 0 \tag{18.7.17}$$

$$H_{.2}'H_{.2} = 1 \tag{18.7.18}$$

We then write

$$\psi_2 = \phi_2 - 2H_{.2}'H_{.1}\lambda_{12} - H_{.2}'H_{.2}\lambda_2 \tag{18.7.19}$$

where ϕ_2 is analogous to Eq. 18.7.2, and where λ_{12} and λ_2 are Lagrangian multipliers.

Differentiating Eq. 18.7.19 symbolically with respect to $H_{.2}'$ and equating to 0 gives, after solving for λ_{12} by means of Eq. 18.7.17,

$$(I - H_{.1}H_{.1}')a'\beta_{.2} = H_{.2}\lambda_2 \tag{18.7.20}$$

where

$$\beta_{.2} = b_{.2}{}^{(3)} - b_{.2}\frac{b_{.2}'b_{.2}}{n} \tag{18.7.21}$$

But from Eq. 18.7.1,

$$(I - H_{.1}H_{.1}')a' = a' - H_{.1}b_{.1}' \tag{18.7.22}$$

If we let

$$_2a = a - b_{.1}H_{.1}' \tag{18.7.23}$$

we may write Eq. 18.7.20:

$$_2a'\beta_{.2} = H_{.2}\lambda_2 \tag{18.7.24}$$

We may now solve for $H_{.2}$ iteratively as we did for $H_{.1}$, except that we use Eqs. 18.7.21 and 18.7.24. As a first approximation to $H_{.2}$ we consider

$$_2V = {}_1V + b_{.1} \tag{18.7.25}$$

Find the smallest value in $_2V$, say, $_sV_{L_2}$, and let

$$_0H_{.2} = a_{L_2}. \tag{18.7.26}$$

In general, then,

$$_sb_{.i} = {}_ia\ _{s-1}H_{.i} \tag{18.7.27}$$

$$_s\beta_{.i} = {}_sb_{.i}^{(3)} - {}_sb_{.i}\frac{_sb_{.i}'\ _sb_{.i}}{n} \tag{18.7.28}$$

$$_ia'\ _s\beta_{.i} = {}_sU_{.i} \tag{18.7.29}$$

$$_sH_{.i} = \frac{_sU_{.i}}{\sqrt{_sU_{.i}'\ _sU_{.i}}} \tag{18.7.30}$$

$$_{i+1}a = {}_ia - b_{.i}\ H_{.i}' \tag{18.7.31}$$

18.7.2 Simultaneous Factor Varimax
Let

$$b = aH \tag{18.7.32}$$

and $b^{(2)}$ be a matrix whose elements are the squares of those in b. Consider the function

$$b_{.i}^{(2)\,'}\left(I - \frac{1\,1'}{n}\right)b_{.i}^{(2)} = \phi_i = \max \tag{18.7.33}$$

We require that

$$H'H = I \tag{18.7.34}$$

From Eqs. 18.7.32, 18.7.33, and 18.7.34, we write

$$\psi_i = H_{.i}'a'D_{b_{.i}}\left(I - \frac{1\,1'}{n}\right)D_{b_{.i}}\,aH_{.i} - H_{.i}'H_{.i}\lambda_{ii} + \sum_{\substack{j=1\\i\neq j}}^{n} H_{.i}'H_{.j}\lambda_{ij} \tag{18.7.35}$$

where the λ's are Lagrangian multipliers.

Let

$$\beta_{.i} = b_{.i}^{(3)} - b_{.i}\frac{b_{.i}'b_{.i}}{n} \tag{18.7.36}$$

Differentiating Eq. 18.7.35 symbolically with respect to $H_{.1}'$, equating to 0, and using Eq. 18.7.36, we have

$$a'\beta_{.i} - H\lambda_{.i} = 0 \tag{18.7.37}$$

or, setting up the complete matrix,

$$a'\beta - H\lambda = 0 \tag{18.7.38}$$

where now λ is a matrix of Lagrangian multipliers, and where because of Eq. 18.7.35,

$$\lambda' = \lambda \tag{18.7.39}$$

and from Eq. 18.7.36,

$$\beta = b^{(3)} - b\frac{D_{b'b}}{n} \tag{18.7.40}$$

From Eq. 18.7.38,

$$a'\beta\lambda^{-1} = H \tag{18.7.41}$$

Let

$$a'\beta = P\Delta Q' \tag{18.7.42}$$

be the basic structure of $a'\beta$. From Eq. 18.7.42,

$$P\Delta Q'\lambda^{-1} = H \tag{18.7.43}$$

Because of Eqs. 18.7.34 and 18.7.39, the only λ^{-1} which will satisfy Eq. 18.7.43 is

$$\lambda^{-1} = Q\Delta^{-1}Q' \tag{18.7.44}$$

From Eqs. 18.7.43 and 18.7.44,

$$H = PQ' \tag{18.7.45}$$

We let

$$C = a'\beta \tag{18.7.46}$$

From Eqs. 18.7.42 and 18.7.46,

$$Q\Delta^2 Q' = C'C \tag{18.7.47}$$

From Eqs. 18.7.42 and 18.7.46,

$$P = CQ\Delta^{-1} \tag{18.7.48}$$

From Eqs. 18.7.45 and 18.7.48,

$$H = CQ\Delta^{-1}Q' \tag{18.7.49}$$

The iteration procedure is as follows. Given the ith approximation to b, then

$$_i\beta = _ib^{(3)} - _ib\frac{D_{ib'\,ib}}{n} \tag{18.7.50}$$

$$_iC = a'\,_i\beta \tag{18.7.51}$$

$$_iQ\,_i\Delta^2\,_iQ' = _iC'\,_iC \tag{18.7.52}$$

$$_{i+1}H = _iC\,_iQ\,_i\Delta^{-1}\,_iQ' \tag{18.7.53}$$

$$_{i+1}b = a\,_{i+1}H \tag{18.7.54}$$

18.7.3   Successive Factor General Varimax

Let

$$b_{.1} = aH_{.1} \tag{18.7.55}$$

$$k = \frac{2m_1}{2m_2 - 1} \tag{18.7.56}$$

where m_1 and m_2 are integers and $m_2 \lesssim m_1$. Let $b_{.1}^{(k)}$ be the vector whose elements are the kth power of those in $b_{.1}$. Because of Eq. 18.7.56, all elements of $b_{.1}^{(k)}$ are nonnegative.

Consider

$$b_{.1}^{(k)\,\prime}\left(I - \frac{1\,1'}{n}\right)b_{.1}^{(k)} = \phi_1 = \max \tag{18.7.57}$$

with the constraint

$$H_{.1}'H_{.1} = 1 \tag{18.7.58}$$

Let

$$\psi_1 = \phi_1 - kH_{.1}'H_{.1}\lambda_1 \tag{18.7.59}$$

where λ_1 is a Lagrangian scalar. From Eqs. 18.7.55 and 18.7.57,

$$H_{.1}'a'D_{b_{.1}}{}^{k-1}\left(I - \frac{1\,1'}{n}\right)D_{b_{.1}}{}^{k-1}aH_{.1} = \phi_1 \tag{18.7.60}$$

From Eqs. 18.7.59 and 18.7.60, we may write the maximizing equation

$$\frac{\partial\psi}{\partial H_{.1}'} = 2k\left[a'D_{b_{.1}}{}^{k-1}\left(I - \frac{1\,1'}{n}\right)D_{b_{.1}}{}^{k-1}aH_{.1} - H_{.1}\lambda_1\right] = 0 \tag{18.7.61}$$

We let

$$\beta_{.1} = b_{.1}^{(2k-1)} - b_{.1}^{(k-1)}\frac{1'b_{.1}^{(k)}}{n} \tag{18.7.62}$$

From Eqs. 18.7.61 and 18.7.62,

$$a'\beta_{.1} = H_{.1}\lambda_1 \tag{18.7.63}$$

We may begin with some arbitrary $b_{.1}$, say, $_1b_{.1}$, and set up the iterative equations

$$_s\beta_{.1} = {}_sb_{.1}^{(2k-1)} - {}_sb_{.1}^{(k-1)}\frac{1'\,{}_sb_{.1}^{(k)}}{n} \tag{18.7.64}$$

$$a'\,{}_s\beta_{.1} = {}_sU_{.1} \tag{18.7.65}$$

$$_s\alpha_1 = \sqrt{{}_sU_{.1}'\,{}_sU_{.1}} \tag{18.7.66}$$

$$_sH_{.1} = \frac{{}_sU_{.1}}{{}_s\alpha_1} \tag{18.7.67}$$

$$_s b_{.1} = a\,_s H_{.1} \tag{18.7.68}$$

After α_1 stabilizes, we calculate

$$_2 a = a - b_{.1}\,H_{.1}' \tag{18.7.69}$$

This is then substituted for a in Eqs. 18.7.65 and 18.7.68 to get $b_{.2}$. The general equation for Eq. 18.7.69 is, of course,

$$_{i+1}a = {}_i a - b_{.i}\,H_{.i}' \tag{18.7.70}$$

To calculate the elements in $_s b_{.i}$ raised to the respective powers, we proceed as follows. We let B be any element of $_s b_{.i}$. Now because of Eq. 18.7.56,

$$k - 1 = \frac{2(m_1 - m_2) + 1}{2m_2 - 1} \tag{18.7.71}$$

and

$$2k - 1 = \frac{2(2m_1 - m_2) + 1}{2m_2 - 1} \tag{18.7.72}$$

From Eq. 18.7.71, all B^{k-1} and B^{2k-1} have the same sign as B. From Eq. 18.7.56 all B^k are positive. Hence to calculate the several required powers of B we have

$$B^k = \text{antilog}(k \log |B|) \tag{18.7.73}$$

$$B^{k-1} = \text{antilog}[(k - 1)\log |B|\,]\frac{|B|}{B} \tag{18.7.74}$$

$$B^{2k-1} = \text{antilog}[(2k - 1)\log |B|\,]\frac{|B|}{B} \tag{18.7.75}$$

These three powers of B may be readily calculated from tables or from standard library programs for computer installations.

18.7.4   Simultaneous Factor General Varimax
Let

$$b = aH \tag{18.7.76}$$

$$k = \frac{2m_1}{2m_2 - 1} \tag{18.7.77}$$

where m_1 and m_2 are integers and $m_2 \lessgtr m_1$. Consider, then, the generalization of Kaiser's criterion

$$tr\left[b^{(k)\,'}\left(I - \frac{1\,1'}{n}\right)b^{(k)} \right] = \max = \phi \tag{18.7.78}$$

with the constraint

$$H'H = I \tag{18.7.79}$$

From Eqs. 18.7.76, 18.7.77, and 18.7.78,

$$\sum H_{.i}' a' D_{b.i}{}^{k-1}\left(I - \frac{1\,1'}{n}\right)D_{b.i}{}^{k-1} a H_{.i} = \phi \qquad (18.7.80)$$

Consider

$$\psi = \phi - k\,tr(H'H\lambda) \qquad (18.7.81)$$

where λ is a symmetric matrix of Lagrangian multipliers.

From Eqs. 18.7.80 and 18.7.81, we may write

$$\frac{\partial\psi}{\partial H_{.i}'} = 2k\left[a' D_{b.i}{}^{k-1}\left(I - \frac{1\,1'}{n}\right)D_{b.i}{}^{k-1} a H_{.i} - H\lambda_{.i}\right] = 0 \qquad (18.7.82)$$

Let

$$\beta_{.i} = b_{.i}{}^{(2k-1)} - b_{.i}{}^{(k-1)}\frac{1'b_{.i}{}^{(k)}}{n} \qquad (18.7.83)$$

From Eqs. 18.7.82 and 18.7.83,

$$a'\beta_{.i} - H\lambda_{.i} = 0 \qquad (18.7.84)$$

or for the matrix form

$$a'\beta = H\lambda \qquad (18.7.85)$$

By the methods of the previous section, we may let the basic structure of $a'\beta$ be

$$a'\beta = P\Delta Q' \qquad (18.7.86)$$

From Eq. 18.7.85,

$$a'\beta\lambda^{-1} = H \qquad (18.7.87)$$

To satisfy Eqs. 18.7.87 and 18.7.79,

$$H = a'\beta Q\Delta^{-1}Q' \qquad (18.7.88)$$

We may begin with some arbitrary approximation to b in Eq. 18.7.76, say, $_1b$. From $_1b$ and Eq. 18.7.83 we calculate $_1\beta$. Then from Eq. 18.7.86

$$a'_1\beta = {}_1P_1\Delta_1 Q' \qquad (18.7.89)$$

and from Eq. 18.7.88,

$$_1H = {}_1P_1 Q' \qquad (18.7.90)$$

In general, then,

$$_s\beta_{.i} = {}_sb_{.i}{}^{(2k-1)} - {}_sb_{.i}{}^{(k-1)}\frac{1'{}_sb_{.i}{}^{(k)}}{n} \qquad (18.7.91)$$

$$a'_s\beta = {}_sP_s\Delta_s Q' \qquad (18.7.92)$$

$$_sH = a'_s\beta Q_s\Delta^{-1}{}_s Q' \qquad (18.7.93)$$

$$_{s+1}b = a_sH \qquad (18.7.94)$$

The several required powers of the $_sb_{.i}$ in Eq. 18.7.91 can be calculated as in the previous section.

Chapter 19

Direct Varimax Solutions

We saw in Chapter 18 that we may begin with any arbitrary factor loading matrix, and transform it to a simple structure varimax factor loading matrix by means of a square orthonormal transformation. In this chapter, we shall see how we may avoid the intermediate step of first calculating an arbitrary factor loading matrix, such as in the principal axis, multiple group, group centroid, and variations of these methods.

19.1   Characteristics of the Method

19.1.1   No Arbitrary Factor Matrices Required. In the procedures outlined in the following sections, we shall see how we may operate directly on the correlation matrices or the score matrices from which they are derived. Strangely enough, this seems to be a novel approach for factor analysts. The tradition has been to calculate first some arbitrary factor loading matrix, such as the principal axis, centroid, or other type of arbitrary factor loading matrix, whose major product moment gives a reasonable approximation to the correlation matrix. These arbitrary matrices are then transformed by the procedures outlined in the previous chapter or by other analytical, semi-analytical, or graphical methods. Actually, the transition from operations upon the arbitrary matrices to achieve simple structure matrices to that of a direct solution for the simple structure matrices from the correlation or data matrices is perfectly natural, both from a logical and a mathematical point of view.

19.1.2   Analytical Methods. As a matter of fact, however, the methods of direct solution for simple structure factor matrices are applicable primarily to those procedures and rationales which use analytical, rather than graphical or judgmental, methods. It should be pointed out that the method for achieving simple structure by means of a binary hypothesis matrix, such as discussed in Chapter 17 for the special case of the multiple group method, might be regarded as a special case of a direct solution from the correlation matrix. Here, however, the rationale and procedure are essentially different from that of the methods to be discussed in this chapter.

All of the methods discussed in this chapter are based on the analytical procedures of the varimax method and constitute applications of the rationale of this method to the correlation and data matrices. The direct solutions for simple structure matrices need not be limited to the varimax type of solution. However, as in the previous chapter, they will be so restricted in this chapter because of the practical difficulties encountered with other alternatives to the varimax solutions which have been developed and experimented with so far.

19.1.3 Rank Reduction Solutions.

All of the solutions considered in this chapter are of a rank reduction type. This means that the rank of the residual matrix, following the solution of any factor vector, is one less than that of the previous residual matrix or, in the case of a factor matrix, its rank is equal to that of the correlation matrix less the number of factors in the factor matrix.

19.1.4 Iterative Solutions.

All of the solutions outlined below are of an iterative type. In this respect, they differ from the direct solution considered for the multiple group method in Chapter 17, in which a binary hypothesis was used. Here, we recall, no successive approximations were required, except for the orthonormal transformation.

All of the iterative solutions required for the various types of direct solutions outlined below can be shown to be special, though rather complicated, eigenvector or basic structure type solutions in which we have a symmetric matrix, some of whose elements are functions of its own basic orthonormal and basic diagonal elements. Therefore, the iterative procedure may be somewhat more involved than in the case of a straightforward basic structure solution, in which the elements of the symmetric matrix whose basic structure is desired are constant values. As a matter of fact, this type of basic structure solution is characteristic not only of the methods of this chapter, but also of those of the previous chapter, in which the solutions are not applied directly to the correlation or data matrices but to some arbitrary factor matrix.

19.1.5 Utilization of Information.

One of the distinguishing characteristics of the methods outlined in this chapter is that, in a sense, more of the information in the correlation or data matrix is utilized than in the methods of Chapter 18. Implicit in the methods of both Chapters 17 and 18 is the assumption that the factor loading matrix accounts for all of the significant or systematic nonrandom information inherent in the correlation or data matrices. This assumption may not be valid in many cases.

In the methods outlined below, all of the information in the data or correlation matrices is utilized in the determination of the simple structure varimax factor matrices or vectors. This may be regarded as an advantage from the point of view of information utilization, or it may be regarded as a disadvantage if one takes the position that the information left over after the major product moment of the factor loading matrix is subtracted from the correlation matrix essentially represents error or random variation. In this latter case, one may argue that the application of direct varimax methods to the correlation or the data matrices may be spuriously affected by such random variation. A great deal more theoretical and experimental work needs to be done before the relative validity of these alternative points of view can be established. In general, the criterion of invariance from one sample of entities and attributes to another would be a relevant consideration here. Presumably, if the direct methods turn out to yield more consistent results from one sample of entities to another, and from one sample of attributes to another, their superiority would be definitely indicated.

19.1.6   Results Different from Transformation Solutions.   It must become obvious that one cannot expect exactly the same results from the direct methods outlined below as from the transformation solutions indicated in Chapters 17 and 18. Even for the direct methods of Chapter 18, in which we use the same varimax criteria and precisely the same models, one cannot expect to get exactly the same results as when the criteria are applied to the correlation or data matrices. The reason for this is, of course, that we utilize not only the information provided by some arbitrary factor loading matrix, but also information inherent in the data or correlation matrix which has not been reflected in the solution for the arbitrary factor loading matrix.

Only extensive research can tell which of the methods is better from the point of view of factorial invariance. There is, of course, the question of which factor loadings make more sense from the point of view of the particular discipline concerned. But as we have suggested earlier, the determination of whether or not the results make sense for a particular discipline is subjective. Until the concept is more objectively defined than it has been in the past, we cannot use the criterion of how much sense the results make as a basis for comparison of any of the methods of factor analysis.

19.2   Kinds of Methods

For convenience, we may group the various methods into four classes. These are (1) the successive factor varimax solution from the correlation matrix, (2) the simultaneous factor varimax solution from the correlation matrix, (3) the successive factor varimax solution from the data matrix, and (4) the simultaneous factor varimax solution from the data matrix. Each of these classes of solutions may, in the conventional manner, maximize the variance of the squared elements or, more generally, the variance of some other even power, just as in Chapter 18. We shall consider first the conventional type solutions, and then the general type.

19.2.1 Solutions from the Correlation Matrix.

As indicated in the previous section, the direct solutions may proceed either by operations on the correlation matrix or by operations directly on the data matrix. The methods based on operations on the correlation matrix may again be of two kinds, analogous to the two types of varimax rotations for arbitrary factor matrices. One of these is the successive factor vector method which obtains a single factor vector at a time. The other is the simultaneous factor matrix method, which iterates successively to the entire factor loading matrix for the particular number of factors hypothesized to be significant for a set of variables.

19.2.2 Solutions from the Data Matrix.

One may bypass the calculation of the correlation matrix and operate directly upon the data matrix. Solutions of this class obviously cannot achieve a net saving in computations over the number required for the correlation matrix, since, as one may guess, the solutions for the direct varimax from the data matrix involve more computations than solutions based on the correlation matrix itself. The question as to which of the methods is most economical from a computer or cost point of view depends on a number of factors. In general, if the number of cases is not vastly greater than the number of variables, one may save some time operating directly upon the data matrix.

In any case, the methods outlined here assume that the data matrix has been scaled so that the variables have means of 0 and variances of 1. It is possible, of course, to work out computational procedures so that the data matrix need not first be processed to yield a standardized metric. Such a computational procedure would incorporate the vector of means and the diagonal of standard deviations or variances. These methods, like those in Section 19.2.1, include the successive factor varimax model and the simultaneous factor matrix model, but here they are applied directly to the scaled data matrix.

19.2.3 The Successive Factor General Varimax Method.

The conventional or Kaiser varimax method, as we know, maximizes the variance of the squared factor loadings. This rationale, we recall, may be generalized so that the variance of any even power function of the factor loading variable may be maximized. As indicated in Chapter 18, the power should be greater than 1; otherwise, we may get into difficulty with reciprocals of very small values. The successive factor general varimax procedures may again be divided into two models. One of these operates on the correlation matrix, and the other operates directly on the data matrix.

19.2.4   The Simultaneous Factor General Varimax. Just as we have the simultaneous factor general varimax method operating on the arbitrary factor loading matrix, so also we can apply this model directly to either the correlation matrix or the data matrix. In this chapter we shall consider its application to both the correlation matrix and the data matrix. The data matrix is assumed to be scaled so as to give means of 0 and variances of 1.

19.3   The Successive Factor Varimax from the Correlation Matrix

19.3.1   Characteristics of the Method. We are already familiar with some of the characteristics of the successive factor varimax method applied directly to the correlation matrix. It may be of interest to compare this method with others, such as the principal axis or centroid, with respect to the amount of variance accounted for by the successive factors. In the latter methods, we recall that the amount of variance accounted for tends to decrease, in general, with the successive factors calculated.

We cannot, however, assert that each varimax factor calculated from the correlation matrix does account for more of the variance than the subsequent one. We cannot even guarantee that the criterion of maximum variance of the squared factor loadings will be greater for a given factor vector than for one calculated subsequently. The order depends very largely on the characteristics of the matrix and also on what is used as a first approximation for any particular factor loading vector.

A further reason for the uncertainty of the order of the factors, with respect to the amount of variance accounted for and the variance of their squared factor loadings, is the fact that we are dealing with an eigenvector or basic structure problem of a very complicated nature. As we have seen, the model involves symmetric matrices whose elements are functions of its eigenvectors and eigenvalues. We do not yet have available an adequate mathematical substructure for a satisfactory understanding of what determines the order in which the factors will appear.

19.3.2   Computational Equations

19.3.2a   DEFINITION OF NOTATION

$_iR$ is the ith residual correlation matrix where $_1R$ is the correlation matrix itself.

$_sb._i$ is the s approximation to the ith varimax factor vector.

$_s\gamma_i$ is the amount of variance accounted for by the s approximation to the ith varimax factor vector.

$_s\alpha_i$ is the varimax criterion for the s approximation to the ith varimax factor vector.

$_sb._i^{(3)}$ is a factor vector whose elements are the cubes of those in $_sb._i$.

19.3.2b THE EQUATIONS

$$_iR = {}_{i-1}R - b_{.(i-1)} b_{.(i-1)}' \tag{19.3.1}$$

$$_s\gamma_i = {}_sb_{.i}' {}_sb_{.i} \tag{19.3.2}$$

$$_s\beta_{.i} = {}_sb_{.i}{}^{(3)} - {}_sb_{.i}\frac{{}_s\gamma_i}{n} \tag{19.3.3}$$

$$_sW_{.i} = {}_iR {}_s\beta_{.i} \tag{19.3.4}$$

$$_s\alpha_i = \sqrt{{}_sW_{.i}' {}_s\beta_{.i}} \tag{19.3.5}$$

$$_{s+1}b_{.i} = \frac{{}_sW_{.i}}{{}_s\alpha_i} \tag{19.3.6}$$

$$r = {}_1R - I \tag{19.3.7}$$

$$\rho = r^{(2)} \tag{19.3.8}$$

$$U_{.0} = \rho 1 - \frac{(r1)^{(2)}}{n-1} \tag{19.3.9}$$

$$U_{L0} \text{ is largest element in } U \tag{19.3.10}$$

$$_1b_{.1} = {}_1R_{.L} \tag{19.3.11}$$

19.3.3 Computational Instructions. We begin with a correlation matrix. The meaning of Eq. 19.3.1 is as follows. If $i = 1$, we have simply the correlation matrix. The right-hand side of this equation will then be ignored, because the $i - 1$ would be 0 and have no meaning, that is, it would not be defined. It is only for i greater than 1 that Eq. 19.3.1 has meaning.

We assume now that we have a first approximation to a factor loading vector which will be described in detail in Eqs. 19.3.7–19.3.11. Equations 19.3.2–19.3.6 describe the successive cycles for the s approximation to the ith factor loading vector.

Having given any approximation to the ith factor loading vector, its minor product moment is calculated as indicated in Eq. 19.3.2.

Next we calculate a vector as indicated in Eq. 19.3.3. This is the β vector with which we are already familiar. It is obtained by cubing the elements of the b vector, and subtracting from it the b vector multiplied by the scalar in Eq. 19.3.2 divided by n.

The next step is indicated by Eq. 19.3.4, which again is of course a general equation for the s approximation. It is the product of the ith residual correlation matrix postmultiplied by the β vector calculated in Eq. 19.3.3.

Next we calculate the scalar indicated by Eq. 19.3.5. This is the square root of the minor product moment of the vectors of Eqs. 19.3.3 and 19.3.4.

The $s + 1$ approximation to the varimax factor loading vector for the ith factor is calculated in Eq. 19.3.6. This is the vector of Eq. 19.3.4 divided by the scalar of Eq. 19.3.5.

As yet there appears to be no completely satisfactory method for choosing a first approximation to any particular varimax factor loading vector, including the first one. However, the following method is recommended and should give good results in most cases.

Consider the correlation matrix with zeros in the diagonal, as indicated in Eq. 19.3.7.

First we square each element of the matrix r of Eq. 19.3.7, as indicated in Eq. 19.3.8.

We then calculate a U vector as indicated in Eq. 19.3.9. This is obtained by calculating a vector of the sums of the rows of the matrix in Eq. 19.3.8. From this is subtracted a vector of the squares of the sums of rows of the matrix in Eq. 19.3.7 divided by $n-1$, the number of variables less 1. The U vector is therefore $n-1$ times the vector of the variances of the columns of the correlation matrix with the diagonal elements excluded.

In Eq. 19.3.10, we find the largest element in the U vector calculated in Eq. 19.3.9, and call this the L position.

We then take as the first approximation to the first varimax vector the Lth column of the correlation matrix, as indicated in Eq. 19.3.11.

Using Eqs. 19.3.2–19.3.6, we then calculate the first varimax factor loading vector by successive iterations until the α scalar of Eq. 19.3.5 stabilizes to some prespecified degree of accuracy.

Then we calculate the first residual matrix by substituting 2 for the i subscript in Eq. 19.3.1. This residual matrix is simply the original correlation matrix, less the major product moment of the final approximation to the $b_{.1}$ vector.

We now require a first approximation to the second varimax factor vector. We apply the procedures of Eqs. 19.3.7–19.3.11 to the residual matrix.

We continue with Eqs. 19.3.1–19.3.6, and generalizations of Eqs. 19.3.7–19.3.11, until enough factors have been extracted.

19.3.4 Numerical Example. In this and subsequent numerical examples in this chapter, the presentation of the results will not conform to that of the presentation of the methods themselves. Rather it will conform to a computer program sequence which is more efficient for performing the computations included in all of the methods of this chapter. Each numerical example section will include both the conventional case in which the variance of squared elements of the varimax factor vectors are maximized, and a special example of the general case for the 10/3 power.

The same correlation matrix used in previous chapters will be used for all of those methods beginning with the correlation matrix. This is repeated for convenient reference in Table 19.3.1.

The same data matrix will be used for all methods operating directly on the data matrix. This matrix yields the correlation matrix of Table 19.3.1, so that the results obtained from the data matrix may be compared with those obtained from the correlation matrix. Table 19.3.2 gives the data matrix. Table 19.3.3 gives the varimax factor matrix for three factors obtained by the

TABLE 19.3.1   Correlation Matrix

1.000	0.829	0.768	0.108	0.033	0.108	0.298	0.309	0.351
0.829	1.000	0.775	0.115	0.061	0.125	0.323	0.347	0.369
0.768	0.775	1.000	0.272	0.205	0.238	0.296	0.271	0.385
0.108	0.115	0.272	1.000	0.636	0.626	0.249	0.183	0.369
0.033	0.061	0.205	0.636	1.000	0.709	0.138	0.091	0.254
0.108	0.125	0.238	0.626	0.709	1.000	0.190	0.103	0.291
0.298	0.323	0.296	0.249	0.138	0.190	1.000	0.654	0.527
0.309	0.347	0.271	0.183	0.091	0.103	0.654	1.000	0.541
0.351	0.369	0.385	0.369	0.254	0.291	0.527	0.541	1.000

TABLE 19.3.2   Normalized Deviation Data Matrix

0.128	0.181	0.421	0.506	0.857	0.746	0.280	0.178	0.246
0.764	0.740	0.563	−0.387	−0.293	−0.202	0.261	0.281	0.043
−0.030	−0.046	0.014	0.147	−0.109	−0.135	0.640	0.682	0.661
−0.280	−0.351	−0.326	−0.023	−0.109	−0.186	0.083	0.091	−0.654
−0.336	−0.306	−0.429	−0.542	−0.006	−0.153	−0.428	0.056	−0.124
−0.276	−0.324	−0.271	−0.370	−0.225	0.035	0.129	−0.446	−0.124
0.057	−0.070	−0.016	0.006	0.152	−0.441	−0.166	−0.354	−0.033
−0.010	−0.140	0.326	−0.004	−0.258	−0.091	−0.410	−0.200	−0.101
−0.303	0.227	−0.014	0.029	−0.102	−0.125	−0.086	−0.106	−0.074
0.086	0.057	−0.003	0.161	0.073	0.134	−0.082	−0.067	−0.009
0.164	0.106	−0.124	0.234	−0.002	0.227	−0.072	0.025	0.156
0.036	−0.074	−0.142	0.242	0.023	0.192	−0.148	−0.119	0.011

TABLE 19.3.3   Successive Factor
Varimax Matrix from Correlation
Matrix for $k = 2$

0.937	0.003	0.092
0.933	0.023	0.127
0.887	0.175	0.063
0.098	0.782	0.130
0.042	0.921	0.026
0.100	0.894	0.044
0.234	0.129	0.837
0.243	0.058	0.903
0.300	0.247	0.527

successive factor matrix method directly from the correlation matrix, for the conventional case in which the variances of the elements of the squared factor loading vectors are maximized. Table 19.3.4 gives the varimax factor loading matrix for the successive factor general matrix, where the 10/3 power, rather than the square of the elements, is used.

TABLE 19.3.4   Successive Factor
General Varimax Matrix from
Correlation Matrix for $k = 10/3$

0.947	−0.040	0.018
0.946	−0.013	0.057
0.880	0.140	−0.012
0.143	0.663	0.099
0.078	0.991	0.000
0.143	0.769	0.008
0.302	0.123	0.596
0.311	0.067	0.948
0.364	0.235	0.430

19.4   The Simultaneous Factor Varimax from the Correlation Matrix

19.4.1   Characteristics of the Method.   This method is like the preceding one in that we operate directly on the correlation matrix rather than on the arbitrary factor matrix. Here, however, we iterate simultaneously to all of the factor loading vectors which we wish to solve for. It differs also from the previous method in that we have a less objective way for getting a first approximation to the factor loading vectors than we did in that method. It is also essentially different computationally from the previous method in that each iteration involves the solution for the basic structure of a symmetric matrix. The Q orthonormal and Δ^2 basic diagonal of this matrix are required in the successive approximations to the factor loading vectors. In this respect the method is analogous to the simultaneous method of Chapter 18.

19.4.2   Computational Equations

19.4.2a   DEFINITION OF NOTATION

R is the correlation matrix.

$_sb$ is the s approximation to the varimax factor matrix.

$_sb^{(3)}$ is a matrix whose elements are the cubes of those in $_sb$.

$D_{sb's b}$ is a diagonal matrix whose elements are the diagonals of the minor product moment of $_sb$.

$_sQ$ is a basic orthonormal.

$_s\Delta^2$ is a basic diagonal.

19.4.2b   THE EQUATIONS

$$_s\beta = {_s}b^{(3)} - {_s}b\frac{D_{sb's b}}{n} \tag{19.4.1}$$

$$_sM = R {_s}\beta \tag{19.4.2}$$

$$_sG = {_s}\beta' {_s}M \tag{19.4.3}$$

$$_sQ {_s}\Delta^2 {_s}Q' = {_s}G \tag{19.4.4}$$

$$_{s+1}b = (({_s}M {_s}Q){_s}\Delta^{-1}){_s}Q' \tag{19.4.5}$$

19.4.3   Computational Instructions. In this method we start with some arbitrary approximation to the varimax factor loading matrix. This may be simply the first *m* columns of the correlation matrix, where *m* is the number of factors. In any case, one must make an assumption as to the number of significant factors in the data matrix. It is better to overestimate than to underestimate the number, as some of the factors can later be rejected from the final stabilized varimax factor loading matrix if they do not seem interpretable or of sufficient importance.

If one has an hypothesis as to which of the variables represents which factor, he may select a variable to represent each factor. Then the columns of the correlation matrix corresponding to these variables will constitute the vectors of the first approximation to the varimax factor matrix.

We begin then with Eq. 19.4.1 in which the subscript *s* is taken as 1. This equation is similar to those we are already familiar with. The right-hand side has for the first term a matrix whose elements are the cubes of the elements of the corresponding approximation to the factor loading matrix. We subtract from this the factor loading matrix itself, after scaling it by a diagonal matrix. This diagonal matrix is made up of the diagonals of the minor product moment of the current approximation to the factor loading matrix and then divided by *n*, the number of variables.

Next we calculate the product indicated in Eq. 19.4.2. This is the correlation matrix postmultiplied by the matrix calculated in Eq. 19.4.1.

We then calculate the minor product of the matrices calculated in Eqs. 19.4.1 and 19.4.2. This is the matrix *G* indicated in Eq. 19.4.3.

Next we calculate the basic structure factors of the matrix *G*. This is indicated by Eq. 19.4.4.

Finally, for each approximation, we calculate the product of the four factors as indicated in Eq. 19.4.5. This is the product of the matrix of Eq. 19.4.2 postmultiplied first by the right orthonormal of the matrix in Eq. 19.4.4, then by the inverse of the square root of the basic diagonal of the matrix in Eq. 19.4.4, and finally by the left orthonormal of the matrix in Eq. 19.4.4, which is, of course, the transpose of the right orthonormal. This is true because *G* is a product moment matrix. We now have the *s* + 1 approximation to the matrix of varimax factor loadings. These iterations continue until the approximation is sufficiently close.

A good criterion of convergence is the trace of the G matrix given by Eq. 19.4.3. Another criterion may be the trace of the minor product moment of the current approximation to the factor loading matrix. This would be the diagonal matrix in the right term of the right side of Eq. 19.4.1. This trace is simply the total amount of variance accounted for by any particular s approximation to the factor loading matrix. As indicated earlier in this chapter, any approximation is a rank reduction solution, and therefore the larger this trace the greater the amount of variance accounted for.

19.4.4 Numerical Example. This example begins with the same correlation matrix given in Table 19.3.1.

TABLE 19.4.1   Simultaneous Factor
Varimax Matrix from Correlation
Matrix for $k = 2$

0.929	0.007	0.153
0.922	0.025	0.187
0.882	0.179	0.125
0.085	0.781	0.153
0.033	0.917	0.048
0.090	0.896	0.072
0.177	0.112	0.884
0.186	0.040	0.891
0.266	0.238	0.551

TABLE 19.4.2   Simultaneous Factor
General Varimax Matrix from
Correlation Matrix for $k = 10/3$

0.944	0.018	0.121
0.935	0.024	0.148
0.857	0.194	0.112
0.080	0.989	0.116
0.037	0.670	0.049
0.100	0.645	0.092
0.189	0.123	0.974
0.242	0.088	0.633
0.306	0.292	0.442

Table 19.4.1 gives the first three varimax factor vectors for the simultaneous factor method applied to the correlation matrix for the conventional case of the squared elements.

Table 19.4.2 gives the first three varimax factor vectors for the simultaneous factor general method applied to the correlation matrix for the case of the 10/3 power of the varimax factor elements. The results are not markedly different from those in Table 19.4.1.

19.5   The Successive Factor Varimax from the Data Matrix

19.5.1   Characteristics of the Method. This method differs essentially from the preceding methods in that the calculation of the correlation matrix is not required. The computations proceed directly upon the data matrix. It is assumed that it has been previously normalized. This assumption is not imperative, however, since the computations could be modified to operate on a raw data matrix. The method differs also from the successive factor matrix method of Section 19.3 in that it is difficult to select a first approximation to a factor loading vector by objective means. Perhaps the simplest way to get the first approximation to the first factor loading vector is to assume that the first variable is not an extremely poor representation of the first varimax factor.

19.5.2   Computational Equations

19.5.2a   DEFINITION OF NOTATION

$_iZ$ is the ith residual data matrix where $_1Z$ is the scaled data matrix with 0 means and unit variances.

$_s\gamma_i$, $_sb_{.i}$, $_sb_{.i}^{(3)}$, and $_s\alpha_i$ are the same as in Section 19.3.2a.

$_sY_{.i}$ is the s approximation to the ith varimax factor score vector.

19.5.2b   THE EQUATIONS

$$_iZ = {}_{i-1}Z - Y_{.(i-1)}\, b_{.(i-1)}{}' \qquad (19.5.1)$$

$$_1b_{.i} = {}_iZ'\, {}_iZ_{.L_i} \qquad (19.5.2)$$

$$_s\gamma_i = {}_sb_{.i}'\, {}_sb_{.i} \qquad (19.5.3)$$

$$_s\beta_{.i} = {}_sb_{.i}^{(3)} - {}_sb_{.i}\frac{{}_s\gamma_i}{n} \qquad (19.5.4)$$

$$_sU_{.i} = {}_iZ\, {}_s\beta_{.i} \qquad (19.5.5)$$

$$_s\alpha_i = \sqrt{{}_sU_{.i}'\, {}_sU_{.i}} \qquad (19.5.6)$$

$$_sY_{.i} = \frac{{}_sU_{.i}}{{}_s\alpha_i} \qquad (19.5.7)$$

$$_{s+1}b_{.i} = {}_iZ'\, {}_sY_{.i} \qquad (19.5.8)$$

$$U_{.1} = b_{.1} \qquad (19.5.9)$$

$$U_{L1} = \text{smallest } U_{.1} \tag{19.5.10}$$

$$U_{.i} = U_{.i-1} + b_{.i-1} \tag{19.5.11}$$

$$U_{Li} = \text{smallest } U_{.i} \tag{19.5.12}$$

19.5.3 Computational Instructions.

We assume that a normalized data matrix is available. Ordinarily, one would not normalize a complete data matrix with a large number of variables if the computations are done with a desk computer. It is assumed, however, that for this particular model a high-speed computer is available. It is also assumed that a preliminary computer program is available for transforming the raw data matrix to one whose means are 0 and whose variances are 1.

We begin by considering Eq. 19.5.1. If $i = 1$, this is the standardized data matrix and we bypass this equation to get a first approximation to the first factor loading vector.

This is indicated in Eq. 19.5.2. On the basis of some rationale or hypothesis, we may select some particular variable as a satisfactory approximation to one of the factors. If no satisfactory rationale is available, we may arbitrarily begin with the first variable. It is seen, therefore, that the vector given by Eq. 19.5.2 is the correlation of the selected variable L with all of the variables, including itself.

Equations 19.5.3–19.5.8 give the successive cycles required for a particular approximation to the factor loading vector $b_{.i}$. We shall discuss this set of computations before indicating generally how we get the first approximation for any particular factor vector following the first.

Equation 19.5.3 shows the minor product moment of the current approximation to the ith factor vector. This scalar γ indicates the amount of variance accounted for by the s approximation to the ith factor vector.

The β vector is given in Eq. 19.5.4. This is obtained by constructing first a vector of the cubes of the elements in the current approximation to the ith factor vector, and subtracting from it the current approximation multiplied by the scalar of Eq. 19.5.3 divided by n.

Next we compute the product indicated in Eq. 19.5.5, which is the ith residual data matrix postmultiplied by the vector of Eq. 19.5.4.

Then we calculate the scalar indicated by Eq. 19.5.6 which is the square root of the minor product moment of the vector calculated in Eq. 19.5.5.

We next calculate the current approximation to the factor score vector $Y_{.i}$ as indicated in Eq. 19.5.7. This is the vector calculated in Eq. 19.5.5 divided by the scalar calculated in Eq. 19.5.6.

Finally, we calculate the $s + 1$ approximation to the $b_{.i}$ vector by means of Eq. 19.5.8. This is the transpose of the ith residual data matrix postmultiplied by the factor score vector of Eq. 19.5.7.

We then begin again with Eq. 19.5.3 and repeat the cycle. We continue this set of iterations until either the γ scalar of Eq. 19.5.3 or the α scalar of Eq. 19.5.6 is stabilized to some specified degree.

Then we return to Eq. 19.5.1 to calculate a new residual matrix, which is obtained by subtracting the major product of the stabilized Y and b vectors of Eqs. 19.5.7 and 19.5.8, respectively, from the current residual matrix.

To get the first approximation to the second varimax factor vector, we consider Eq. 19.5.9. Here we simply equate the $U_{.1}$ vector to the first stabilized factor loading vector $b_{.1}$.

We then find the algebraically smallest element in the vector of Eq. 19.5.9, as indicated in Eq. 19.5.10.

Next we get the first approximation to the second factor vector by letting $i = 2$ in Eq. 19.5.2.

To get the first approximation to the ith factor loading vector we consider Eq. 19.5.11. To get $U_{.i}$, we add $U_{.i-1}$ to the stabilized $b_{.i-1}$ varimax vector.

Equation 19.5.12 indicates the algebraically smallest element in a vector of Eq. 19.5.11. This we designate as in the L_i position.

Then we return to Eq. 19.5.2 to get the first approximation to the ith varimax factor loading vector. This is the transpose of the ith residual data matrix postmultiplied by the L_i column of this residual matrix.

19.5.4 Numerical Example. This numerical example begins with the data matrix given in Table 19.3.2.

TABLE 19.5.1   Successive Factor
Varimax Matrix from Data
Matrix for $k = 2$

0.934	0.091	−0.010
0.934	0.127	0.016
0.891	0.076	0.169
0.093	0.165	0.726
0.044	0.077	0.932
0.096	0.093	0.839
0.236	0.881	0.081
0.240	0.871	0.012
0.300	0.541	0.212

Table 19.5.1 shows the first three varimax factor vectors obtained by the successive factor method directly from the data matrix for the case of $k = 2$.

Table 19.5.2 gives the varimax factor matrix obtained by the successive factor general method from the data matrix for the case of $k = 10/3$.

TABLE 19.5.2   Successive Factor
General Varimax Matrix from
Data Matrix for $k = 10/3$

0.943	−0.226	−0.052
0.947	0.320	−0.006
0.884	−0.156	0.136
0.136	−0.050	0.606
0.079	−0.019	0.991
0.136	−0.016	0.700
0.304	0.072	0.124
0.307	0.107	0.069
0.363	0.048	0.225

19.6   The Simultaneous Factor Matrix from the Data Matrix

19.6.1   Characteristics of the Method. The characteristics of this method have already been fairly well covered in the previous sections. Except for decimal accuracy, it should give essentially the same results as the method discussed in Section 19.4. The calculation of the correlation matrix as such is bypassed, and the multiplications implied by the correlation matrix, that is, the minor product moment of the data matrix, is accomplished at each iteration by two successive multiplications of a matrix by a vector.

The method avoids the accumulation of decimal error resulting from the calculation of residual matrices, such as in Sections 19.3 and 19.5. However, as in Section 19.4, for each approximation one must calculate the basic orthonormal and basic diagonal of a Gramian matrix whose order is equal to the number of factors. Again, this is not a formidable task for electronic computers, since a number of computer programs, including those in the appendix for Chapter 9, are already available for computing all of the latent roots and vectors of the Gramian matrix.

19.6.2   Computational Equations

19.6.2a   DEFINITION OF NOTATION
Z is the data matrix with means of 0 and variances of 1.
$_sb$, $_sb^{(3)}$, $_sQ$, and $_s\Lambda^2$ are the same as in Section 19.4.2a.
$_sY$ is the s approximation to the varimax factor score matrix.

19.6.2b   THE EQUATIONS

$$_1b = Z'Z_{(m)} \qquad (19.6.1)$$

$$_s\beta = {_sb^{(3)}} - {_sb}\frac{D_{sb's^b}}{n} \qquad (19.6.2)$$

$$_sU = Z_s\beta \tag{19.6.3}$$

$$_sG = {_sU'}_sU \tag{19.6.4}$$

$$_sQ_s\Delta^2{_sQ'} = {_sG} \tag{19.6.5}$$

$$_sG^{-1/2} = {_sQ}_s\Delta^{-1}{_sQ'} \tag{19.6.6}$$

$$_sY = {_sU}_sG^{-1/2} \tag{19.6.7}$$

$$_{s+1}b = Z'_sY \tag{19.6.8}$$

19.6.3 Computational Instructions. In this model we begin with a standardized data matrix.

We must choose some sort of approximation to the first varimax factor loading matrix. If we have some hypothesis as to a single variable which best measures each of the factors, we can use these variables to begin the computations. In any case, whether we have a rational procedure, or whether we select the first m variables where m is the number of factors we expect to solve for, we begin with Eq. 19.6.1. The right side of this equation is the transpose of the data matrix postmultiplied by a submatrix made up of m vectors out of Z. These m vectors may be rationally or arbitrarily selected. Actually, then, this first approximation to the b matrix is simply a matrix of the correlations of the m variables with all the variables, including the correlations among themselves.

The general equations for the computations are then indicated by Eqs. 19.6.2–19.6.7.

Equation 19.6.2 gives the computation for the first approximation to the β matrix, just as in Section 19.4.2. The first term on the right of this equation is a matrix whose elements are the cupes of the corresponding elements of the current approximation to the b or varimax factor loading matrix. From this is subtracted the current approximation to the b matrix, scaled by a diagonal matrix on the right. This diagonal matrix is made up of the diagonal elements of the minor product moment of the current approximation to the b matrix, divided by n, the number of variables.

The next step is given by Eq. 19.6.3. As indicated on the right-hand side of this equation, the data matrix Z is postmultiplied by the β matrix given in Eq. 19.6.2.

The next step is given in Eq. 19.6.4. The matrix G is the minor product moment of the matrix calculated in Eq. 19.6.3.

We then calculate the basic structure factors of the matrix G given in Eq. 19.6.4, as indicated by the left-hand side of Eq. 19.6.5. The computer programs given for Chapter 9 for finding basic structure factors, or eigenvalues and eigenvectors, of symmetric matrices are applicable here.

Next we calculate the $G^{-1/2}$ matrix of Eq. 19.6.6. This is the triple product involving the factors obtained from Eq. 19.6.5.

We then calculate the current approximation to the varimax factor score matrix, as indicated in Eq. 19.6.7. This is the matrix of Eq. 19.6.3 postmultiplied by the matrix of Eq. 19.6.6.

Finally, we calculate the next approximation to the b or varimax factor loading matrix, as indicated in Eq. 19.6.8. This is simply the transpose of the data matrix Z postmultiplied by the factor score matrix given in Eq. 19.6.7.

These computations continue until either the trace of the minor product moment of the current factor loading approximation matrix, or the trace of the G matrix in Eq. 19.6.4, reaches some specified degree of stabilization.

19.6.4   Numerical Example. This numerical example begins with the data matrix given in Table 19.3.2.

TABLE 19.6.1   Simultaneous Factor
Varimax Matrix from Data Matrix
for $k = 2$

0.932	0.000	0.161
0.932	0.026	0.192
0.893	0.180	0.121
0.082	0.755	0.145
0.040	0.961	0.031
0.089	0.874	0.064
0.181	0.091	0.901
0.185	0.021	0.899
0.269	0.227	0.562

TABLE 19.6.2   Simultaneous Factor
General Varimax Matrix from
Data Matrix for $k = 10/3$

0.945	0.018	0.136
0.948	0.034	0.147
0.874	0.224	0.066
0.083	1.036	0.087
0.046	0.694	0.012
0.102	0.630	0.093
0.194	0.118	0.972
0.241	0.081	0.641
0.312	0.302	0.446

Table 19.6.1 gives the first three varimax factor vectors obtained by the simultaneous factor matrix method directly from the data matrix for the case of $k = 2$.

Table 19.6.2 shows the varimax factor matrix obtained by the simultaneous factor general matrix method directly from the data matrix for the case of $k = 10/3$.

19.7 The Successive Factor General Varimax

As we recall, the general varimax method is similar to the Kaiser varimax method, except that it is based on some even fractional power, greater than 1, of the elements whose variance is maximized, rather than on the squares of these elements.

19.7.1 Computational Equations

19.7.1a DEFINITION OF NOTATION

m_1 is an integer not less than 1.

m_2 is an integer not greater than m_1.

$_sb._i$ is the s approximation to the ith varimax factor vector.

$_sb._i^{(2k-1)}$, $_sb._i^{(k-1)}$, $_sb._i^{(k)}$ are vectors whose elements are, respectively, the $2k - 1$, $k - 1$, and k powers of those in $_sb._i$.

19.7.1b THE EQUATIONS

$$k = \frac{2m_1}{2m_2 - 1} \tag{19.7.1}$$

$$_s\beta._i = _sb._i^{(2k-1)} - _sb._i^{(k-1)}\frac{1'\,_sb._i^{(k)}}{n} \tag{19.7.2}$$

19.7.2 Computational Instructions.
The procedures here are precisely the same as in Sections 19.3 and 19.5, respectively, except that the β vectors are calculated in a different manner, since the variance we want to maximize is more general than that of the squares of the factor loadings.

We begin with Eq. 19.7.1. Here we have, instead of the second power, the kth power of the elements of the factor loading vectors whose variance we wish to maximize. This is expressed as the ratio of twice the sum of a positive integer, divided by twice some other positive integer less 1. The positive integer in the denominator of this equation cannot be greater than that in the numerator.

To define the s approximation to the β vector corresponding to the ith varimax factor loading vector, we use Eq. 19.7.2. This is the same as Eq. 18.5.1 of Chapter 18. As indicated in that chapter, either we will require tables of logs and exponentials to calculate the powers of the elements of b indicated on the right-hand side of Eq. 19.7.2, or library functions for the computer program must be available.

19.8 The Simultaneous General Varimax

The simultaneous general varimax procedure is similar to procedures described in Sections 19.4 and 19.6, except for the power of the elements in the simple structure matrices whose variances are to be maximized.

19.8.1 Computational Equations

19.8.1a   DEFINITION OF NOTATION

m_1 and m_2 are the same as in Section 19.7.1a.

$_s b$ is the s approximation to the varimax factor matrix.

$_s b^{(2k-1)}$, $_s b^{(k)}$, $_s b^{(k-1)}$ are matrices whose elements are, respectively, the $2k - 1$, k, and $k - 1$ powers of the corresponding elements in $_s b$.

$D_{1'_s b^{(k)}}$ is a diagonal matrix whose elements are those of $1'_s b^{(k)}$.

19.8.1b   THE EQUATIONS

$$k = \frac{2m_1}{2m^2 - 1} \tag{19.8.1}$$

$$_s \beta = _s b^{(2k-1)} - _s b^{(k-1)} \frac{D_{1'_s b^{(k)}}}{n} \tag{19.8.2}$$

19.8.2 Computational Instructions.
The computational instructions are the same as for the method using the correlation matrix, given in Section 19.4, and the method using the data matrix, given in Section 19.6, except for the calculation of the β matrices.

We shall first consider the general case for both the correlation and the data matrices. Again, as in Section 19.7, we begin with Eq. 19.8.1 which gives the value of k as the power of the elements of the simple structure factor loading vector whose variance we wish to maximize. The restrictions on m_1 and m_2 on the right-hand side of this equation are the same as the previous ones.

The general equation for the β matrix is now given by Eq. 19.8.2, where the exponents in parentheses for the b matrices indicate that the corresponding elements of the current approximation to the b matrix have been raised to the indicated power. The diagonal matrix on the right of the right-hand term of the right side of Eq. 19.8.2 is obtained as follows. We sum the columns of the matrix whose elements are the kth power of the elements in the b matrix, and use the elements of this vector in the diagonal. This diagonal is then divided by n, and the b matrix with elements raised to the $k - 1$ power is scaled accordingly.

19.9   Mathematical Proofs

19.9.1   The Successive Factor Matrix from the Correlation Matrix

From Section 18.3 we have, as the iterative solution for the varimax factor vector $b_{.i}$,

$$_s\beta_{.i} = {_sb_{.i}}^{(3)} - {_sb_{.i}} \frac{1'\,{_sb_{.i}}^{(2)}}{n} \tag{19.9.1}$$

$$_sU_{.i} = {_ia'}\,{_s\beta_{.i}} \tag{19.9.2}$$

$$_s\alpha_i = \sqrt{_sU_{.i}'\,{_sU_{.i}}} \tag{19.9.3}$$

$$_sH_{.i} = \frac{_sU_{.i}}{_s\alpha_i} \tag{19.9.4}$$

$$_{s+1}b_{.i} = {_ia}\,{_sH_{.i}} \tag{19.9.5}$$

where

$$_ia = {_{i-1}a} - b_{.(i-1)}\,H_{.(i-1)}' \tag{19.9.6}$$

From Eq. 19.9.2,

$$_ia\,{_ia'}\,{_s\beta_{.i}} = {_ia}\,{_sU_1} \tag{19.9.7}$$

From Eqs. 19.9.5 and 19.9.6,

$$_ia\,{_ia'} = {_{(i-1)}a}\,{_{(i-1)}a'} - b_{.(i-1)}\,b_{.(i-1)}' \tag{19.9.8}$$

From Eqs. 19.9.4, 19.9.5, and 19.9.7,

$$_ia\,{_ia'}\,{_s\beta_{.i}} = {_sb_{.i}}\,{_s\alpha_i} \tag{19.9.9}$$

From Eq. 19.9.3,

$$_s\alpha_i = \sqrt{_s\beta_{.i}'\,{_ia}\,{_ia'}\,{_s\beta_{.i}}} \tag{19.9.10}$$

We now let

$$_1R = {_1a}\,{_1a'} \tag{19.9.11}$$

where $_1a$ is the factor loading matrix.

From Eqs. 19.9.8 and 19.9.11,

$$_2R = {_1R} - b_{.1}\,b_{.1}' \tag{19.9.12}$$

or, in general,

$$_{i+1}R = {_iR} - b_{.i}\,b_{.i}' \tag{19.9.13}$$

From Eqs. 19.9.8 and 19.9.13,

$$_{i+1}a\,{_{i+1}a'} = {_{i+1}R} \tag{19.9.14}$$

From Eqs. 19.9.9, 19.9.10, and 19.9.14,

$$_{s+1}b_{.i} = \frac{_iR\,{_s\beta_{.i}}}{\sqrt{_s\beta_{.i}'\,{_iR}\,{_s\beta_{.i}}}} \tag{19.9.15}$$

From Eqs. 19.9.1, 19.9.13, and 19.9.15, we can solve iteratively for $b_{.i}$. From Eq. 19.9.15, we see that for any iteration s, $_sb_{.i}$ is a rank reduction solution for Eq. 19.9.13, irrespective of how well the solution has stabilized. We let

$$_s\gamma_i = {}_sb_{.i}'\,{}_sb_{.i} \tag{19.9.16}$$

Then from Eqs. 19.9.1 and 19.9.16,

$$_s\beta_{.i} = {}_sb_{.i}^{(3)} - {}_sb_{.i}\frac{_s\gamma_i}{n} \tag{19.9.17}$$

Let

$$_sW_{.i} = {}_iR\,{}_s\beta_{.i} \tag{19.9.18}$$

From Eqs. 19.9.10, 19.9.14, and 19.9.18,

$$_s\alpha_i = \sqrt{{}_sW_{.i}'\,{}_s\beta_{.i}} \tag{19.9.19}$$

From Eqs. 19.9.15, 19.9.18, and 19.9.19,

$$_{s+1}b_{.i} = \frac{_sW_{.i}}{_s\alpha_i} \tag{19.9.20}$$

The computational equations then for the $b_{.i}$ are given by Eqs. 19.9.16–19.9.20, and the successive $_iR$'s are calculated from Eq. 19.9.13. The variance reduction in the $_iR$ matrix accounted for by the s approximation to $_sb_{.i}$ is obviously given by $_s\gamma_i$ in Eq. 19.9.16.

19.9.2   The Simultaneous Factor Matrix from the Correlation Matrix

From Section 18.4.2 we have, as the s approximation to the simultaneous varimax factor matrix,

$$_s\beta = {}_sb^{(3)} - {}_sb\frac{D_{{}_sb'{}_sb}}{n} \tag{19.9.21}$$

$$a'\,{}_s\beta = {}_sC \tag{19.9.22}$$

$$_sC'\,{}_sC = {}_sQ\,{}_s\Delta^2\,{}_sQ' \tag{19.9.23}$$

$$_sH = {}_sC\,{}_sQ\,{}_s\Delta^{-1}\,{}_sQ' \tag{19.9.24}$$

$$_{s+1}b = a\,{}_sH \tag{19.9.25}$$

From Eqs. 19.9.22 and 19.9.23,

$$_s\beta'aa'\,{}_s\beta = {}_sQ\,{}_s\Delta^2\,{}_sQ' \tag{19.9.26}$$

From Eqs. 19.9.22, 19.9.24, and 19.9.25,

$$_{s+1}b = aa'\,{}_s\beta\,{}_sQ\,{}_s\Delta^{-1}\,{}_sQ' \tag{19.9.27}$$

We let

$$aa' = R \tag{19.9.28}$$

From Eqs. 19.9.26 and 19.9.28,

$$_sQ_s\Delta^2{}_sQ' = {}_s\beta' R_s\beta \tag{19.9.29}$$

From Eqs. 19.9.27 and 19.9.28,

$$_{s+1}b = R_s\beta_sQ_s\Delta^{-1}{}_sQ' \tag{19.9.30}$$

Let

$$_sM = R_s\beta \tag{19.9.31}$$

$$_sG = {}_s\beta'{}_sM \tag{19.9.32}$$

From Eqs. 19.9.29 and 19.9.32,

$$_sQ_s\Delta^2{}_sQ' = {}_sG \tag{19.9.33}$$

From Eqs. 19.9.30 and 19.9.31,

$$_{s+1}b = {}_sM_sQ_s\Delta^{-1}{}_sQ' \tag{19.9.34}$$

Then Eqs. 19.9.21 and 19.9.31–19.9.34 constitute the computational equations for calculating the s approximation to the b matrix. That any approximation $_sb$ of width m is a solution for

$$_mR = R - {}_sb_sb' \tag{19.9.35}$$

such that the rank of $_mR$ is m less than the rank of R, can be readily shown as follows. Dropping the prescripts, we have from Eqs. 19.9.29 and 19.9.30,

$$b = R\beta(\beta' R\beta)^{-1/2} \tag{19.9.36}$$

Substituting Eq. 19.9.36 in Eq. 19.9.35,

$$_mR = R - R\beta(\beta' R\beta)^{-1}\beta' R \tag{19.9.37}$$

which is, of course, the rank reduction form.

The iterations may proceed until tr_sG converges to the desired degree of decimal accuracy.

19.9.3 The Successive Factor Varimax from the Data Matrix

Given the data matrix Z such that

$$R = Z'Z \tag{19.9.38}$$

The successive factor varimax from the correlation matrix, according to Section 19.3.2, is given by the set of equations

$$_s\gamma_i = {}_sb_{.i}'{}_sb_i \tag{19.9.39}$$

$$_s\beta_{.i} = {}_sb_{.i}{}^{(3)} - {}_sb_{.i}\frac{{}_s\gamma_i}{n} \tag{19.9.40}$$

$$_sW_{.i} = {}_iR_s\beta_{.i} \tag{19.9.41}$$

$$_s\alpha_i = \sqrt{{}_sW_{.i}'{}_s\beta_{.i}} \tag{19.9.42}$$

$$_{s+1}b_{.i} = \frac{{}_sW_{.i}}{{}_s\alpha_i} \tag{19.9.43}$$

and

$$_{i+1}R = {}_iR - b_{.i}\,b_{.i}' \tag{19.9.44}$$

From Eqs. 19.9.38 and 19.9.41–19.9.43,

$$_{s+1}b_{.i} = \frac{Z'Z_s\beta_{.i}}{\sqrt{{}_s\beta_{.i}'Z'Z_s\beta_{.i}}} \tag{19.9.45}$$

Let

$$_sU_{.i} = Z_s\beta_{.i} \tag{19.9.46}$$

$$_sY_{.i} = \frac{{}_sU_{.i}}{\sqrt{{}_sU_{.i}'{}_sU_{.i}}} \tag{19.9.47}$$

From Eqs. 19.9.45–19.9.47,

$$_{s+1}b_{.i} = Z'{}_sY_{.i} \tag{19.9.48}$$

Consider now the residual matrix

$$_2Z = {}_1Z - Y_{.1}\,b_{.1}' \tag{19.9.49}$$

From Eqs. 19.9.48 and 19.9.49,

$$_2Z = {}_1Z - Y_{.1}\,Y_{.1}'\,{}_1Z \tag{19.9.50}$$

or

$$_2Z = (I - Y_{.1}\,Y_{.1}')_1Z \tag{19.9.51}$$

From Eqs. 19.9.47 and 19.9.51,

$$_2Z'\,_2Z = {}_1Z'(I - Y_{.1}\,Y_{.1}')_1Z \tag{19.9.52}$$

From Eqs. 19.9.38, 19.9.44, 19.9.48, and 19.9.52,

$$_2Z'\,_2Z = {}_1R - b_{.1}b_{.1}' \tag{19.9.53}$$

or from Eqs. 19.9.38 and 19.9.53,

$$_2Z'\,_2Z = {}_2R \tag{19.9.54}$$

In general, if

$$_{i+1}Z = {}_iZ - Y_{.i}\,b_{.i}' \tag{19.9.55}$$

then

$$_{i+1}Z'\,_{i+1}Z = {}_{i+1}R \tag{19.9.56}$$

Equations 19.9.39, 19.9.40, 19.9.46–19.9.48, and 19.9.55 may therefore be used to calculate the successive varimax factor vectors directly from the standard score matrix. Since Eq. 19.9.44 is a rank reduction form, Eq. 19.9.56 shows that Eq. 19.9.55 is also a rank reduction form for any approximation s to $Y_{.i}$ and $b_{.i}$.

Consider then

$$Y = (Y_{.1} \ldots Y_{.m}) \tag{19.9.57}$$

$$b = (b_{.1} \ldots b_{.m}) \tag{19.9.58}$$

Then in

$$_mZ = Z - Yb' \tag{19.9.59}$$

the rank of $_mZ$ is m less than the rank of Z. Also, it should now be obvious that Y is the factor score matrix corresponding to the factor loading matrix b.

19.9.4 The Simultaneous Varimax from the Data Matrix

Consider again the data matrix Z, such that

$$R = Z'Z \tag{19.9.60}$$

The simultaneous varimax matrix from the correlation matrix, according to Section 19.4, is given by the set of equations

$$_s\beta = _sb^{(3)} - _sb\frac{D_{sb'sb}}{n} \tag{19.9.61}$$

$$_sM = R_s\beta \tag{19.9.62}$$

$$_sG = _s\beta'_sM \tag{19.9.63}$$

$$_{s+1}b = _sM_sG^{-1/2} \tag{19.9.64}$$

From Eqs. 19.9.60 and 19.9.62,

$$_sM = Z'Z_s\beta \tag{19.9.65}$$

From Eqs. 19.9.60, 19.9.62, and 19.9.63,

$$_sG = _s\beta'Z'Z_s\beta \tag{19.9.66}$$

From Eqs. 19.9.62–19.9.66,

$$_{s+1}b = Z'Z_s\beta(_s\beta'Z'Z_s\beta)^{-1/2} \tag{19.9.67}$$

Let

$$Z_s\beta = _sU \tag{19.9.68}$$

Let

$$_sU = _sP_s\Delta'_sQ' \tag{19.9.69}$$

From Eqs. 19.9.66 and 19.9.68,

$$_sG = _sU'_sU \tag{19.9.70}$$

From Eqs. 19.9.69 and 19.9.70,

$$_sG = {}_sQ_s\Delta^2{}_sQ' \tag{19.9.71}$$

Let

$$_sY = {}_sU_sG^{-1/2} \tag{19.9.72}$$

From Eqs. 19.9.71 and 19.9.72,

$$_sY = {}_sU_sQ_s\Delta^{-1}{}_sQ' \tag{19.9.73}$$

From Eqs. 19.9.67–19.9.73,

$$_{s+1}b = Z'_sY \tag{19.9.74}$$

We can then solve for successive approximations to b and Y by Eqs. 19.9.61, 19.9.68, 19.9.70, 19.9.71, and 19.9.73.

From Eqs. 19.9.69 and 19.9.73,

$$_sY = {}_sP_sQ' \tag{19.9.75}$$

hence

$$_sY'_sY = I \tag{19.9.76}$$

Let

$$_mZ = Z - Yb' \tag{19.9.77}$$

From Eqs. 19.9.74 and 19.9.77,

$$_mZ = Z - YY'Z \tag{19.9.78}$$

or

$$_mZ = (I - YY')Z \tag{19.9.79}$$

From Eqs. 19.9.60, 19.9.74, 19.9.76, and 19.9.79,

$$_mZ'_mZ = R - {}_sb_sb' \tag{19.9.80}$$

hence

$$_mR = R - {}_sb_sb' \tag{19.9.81}$$

In Section 19.9.2 we proved the rank of $_mR$ is m less than the rank of R. Hence the rank of $_mZ$ in Eq. 19.9.77 is m less than the rank of Z for any approximation s.

19.9.5 The Successive General Varimax Vectors

The direct solutions for the successive factor general varimax differ from the solutions which maximize the variance of squared factor loadings only in the calculation of the $_s\beta_{\cdot i}$ vectors.

Let

$$k = \frac{2m_1}{2m_2 - 1} \tag{19.9.82}$$

where

$$m_1 \geq m_2 \tag{19.9.83}$$

and m_1 and m_2 are both integers greater than 0.

Then

$$_s\beta_{.i} = {}_sb_{.i}^{(2k-1)} - {}_sb_{.i}^{(k-1)} \frac{1'_sb_{.i}^{(k)}}{n} \tag{19.9.84}$$

From Eq. 19.9.82,

$$2k - 1 = \frac{2(2m_1 - m_2) + 1}{2m_2 - 1} \tag{19.9.85}$$

$$k - 1 = \frac{2(m_1 - m_2) + 1}{2m_2 - 1} \tag{19.9.86}$$

If we wish to calculate the successive general varimax vectors directly from the correlation matrix, we use the same equations as in Section 19.3.2, with the exception of the $_s\beta_{.i}$ vector indicated in Eq. 19.9.84.

If we wish to calculate the successive general varimax vectors directly from the data matrix, we use the same equations as in 19.5.2, with the exception of the $_s\beta_{.i}$ vector which is now given by Eq. 19.9.84.

19.9.6   The Simultaneous General Varimax Factor Matrix

The rationale for the simultaneous general varimax directly from the correlation or data matrices is the same as for the special case of the squared factor loadings, except that the $_s\beta$ matrix is different for values of k other than 2. The general expression for $_s\beta$ is given by

$$_s\beta = {}_sb^{(2k-1)} - {}_sb^{(k-1)} \frac{D_{1'_sb}^{(k)}}{n} \tag{19.9.87}$$

where $D_{1'_sb}$ is a diagonal of the vector of column sums of the $_sb^{(k)}$ matrix.

Chapter 20

Factor Score Matrices

20.1 Introduction

Over the past 40 years a vast amount of attention has been given to the factor analysis of correlation matrices. In this book we have already devoted a large number of chapters to various methods for getting factor loading matrices from correlation matrices. We saw in Chapter 4 how we may view the general factor analysis problem as one of approximating a data matrix by a matrix of lower rank. We saw that the problem viewed in this way is one of finding two basic matrices whose major product is in some sense a satisfactory approximation to the data matrix. The factors of this major product have a common order much less than the smaller order of the data matrix, and therefore the rank of the product is equal to the common order of its factors.

Again in Chapter 4 we saw how we may regard the postfactor of this product as the transpose of the factor loading matrix. We also saw how we may regard the prefactor as the factor score matrix. Therefore, the factor score matrix postmultiplied by the transpose of the factor loading matrix yields the lower rank approximation to the data matrix. In this formulation of the problem, the communality problem does not appear. There seems to be no clear justification for considering the communality concept when we view factor analysis not as a method of factoring the correlation or covariance matrix but rather as one of factoring the data matrix. Guttman (1955) has discussed an interesting exception, which is, however, beyond the scope of this book.

In any case, with all of the attention given to the solutions for factor loading matrices, very little has been devoted to the derivation of factor score matrices. This is especially curious inasmuch as the scientific, logical, and philosophical status of the factor score matrix would appear to be at least as respectable as that of the factor loading matrix. Some would argue, of course, that the factor loading matrix is of more fundamental importance because it enables us to identify or define the fundamental variables of a particular discipline. Certainly there is something to be said for this point of view, if one regards the major objective of the simple structure or transformation technique as one of finding factor loadings which are relatively invariant from one sample of entities and attributes to another.

From a philosophical point of view, these considerations may justify greater interest in the factor loading matrix. However, from a purely formal point of view, considering only the mathematics involved, there is no reason to be more interested in the factor loading matrix than in the factor score matrix. Considering the model in which the major product of these two matrices approximates the data matrix, there is actually nothing in the mathematics of the model which would in some sense give higher status to the postfactor than to the prefactor.

This statement is even more cogent if we recall Chapters 13 and 15 dealing with linear transformations involving both scale and origin, which may be applied to both the right- and left-hand sides of the data matrix. We have seen that these operations can materially affect the results of a factor analysis, and that the traditional practice of metricizing the data matrix by attributes rather than by entities is more or less arbitrary. In any case, the problem of finding the left-hand factor of the matrix product which purports to approximate the data matrix appears to merit considerably more attention than it has received in the past.

But even the attention which the problem has received seems to have caused as much confusion as clarification for the central issues involved. These are actually rather simple, if one does not become unduly involved with the red herrings of the communality and specificity problems. One need only examine the bewildering, even if at times ingenious, traditional discussions of the factor measurement problem to realize that they have often strayed far from the solid ground of the data matrix.

Some investigators have argued that factor scores give no more information than do the measures from which they are derived, and that, therefore, at best these scores are of more theoretical than practical interest. Unfortunately, these investigators have asked the wrong question. Instead of asking whether the factor scores give more information than the original data scores, they should have asked whether the original data scores give more information than the factor scores. If one asks this latter question, he may conclude that the data matrix may yield not only relevant or systematic information but also random or unreliable information.

One may then regard the lower rank data matrix approximation model as a procedure for eliminating from the data matrix random or irrelevant variance. Horst (1941) has utilized the factor score matrix to reduce the effect of this variance. The method has never received wide attention. Leiman (1951) has applied this conception of factor analysis objectives to experimental data. He has found that, by the use of lower rank approximation matrices to data matrices, one may obtain multiple regression parameters which hold up better on cross-validation than when the data matrices are employed directly in the traditional methods. A much more extensive application of factor score matrices and the lower rank approximation model has been made by Burket (1964). In his work it is clear that for prediction purposes the lower rank approximation procedures have a definite advantage over the conventional multiple regression procedures. This application of the factor score concept will be considered in more detail in Chapter 23. Here we will present various types of methods for calculating factor score matrices.

20.2   Kinds of Factor Score Solutions

We may classify the various kinds of solutions for factor score matrices to correspond with the procedures for getting factor loading matrices which we have discussed in the previous chapters. The solutions will be presented under the headings of the centroid factor score matrix, the multiple group factor score matrix, the principal axis factor score matrix, the least square factor score matrix, and the image analysis factor score matrix.

20.2.1   The Centroid Factor Score Matrix. The calculation of a centroid factor score matrix directly from the data matrix has already been explicitly considered in Chapter 12. In this process, we arrive successively at factor loading vectors and factor score vectors. However, in this chapter we shall present the calculation of a factor score matrix based on a previous calculation of the centroid factor loading matrix. This factor loading matrix, together with a matrix of sign vectors, yields a transformation matrix which, when applied to the data matrix, gives the centroid factor score matrix.

20.2.2   The Multiple Group Factor Score Matrix. We shall see that by the use of a binary grouping matrix we can also calculate a multiple group factor score matrix directly from the data matrix. As a matter of fact, it is easier to use the multiple group method directly on the data matrix than it is to use the centroid method, because in the centroid method we must have a matrix of sign vectors, and this ordinarily becomes available only with a successive factor solution. In the centroid method, it will be recalled that residual matrices are calculated, and with each residual matrix one iterates to the optimal sign vector.

On the other hand, in the case of the multiple group method, one presumably has an *a priori* binary grouping matrix. For this reason one need not go through the actual calculation of the multiple group factor loading matrix before calculating the multiple group factor score matrix.

20.2.3   The Principal Axis Factor Score Matrix. Perhaps the simplest and most elegant of all of the methods for getting factor score matrices is the basic structure method. As we have seen in Chapter 4, the principal axis or basic structure type solution yields the least square approximation to the data matrix for any specified rank of the approximation matrix. We have seen that the principal axis or basic structure factor loading matrix is a rank reduction solution and provides a least square approximation to the correlation or covariance matrix. It is easy to show that the first m vectors of the left basic orthonormal matrix of the data matrix yield precisely the principal axis factor score matrix, and that this is an orthogonal matrix.

20.2.4 The Least Square Factor Score Matrix. Having given some arbitrary factor loading matrix, whether centroid, multiple group, or principal axis, we may wish to determine that factor score matrix which, when post-multiplied by the transpose of the factor loading matrix, yields a product which is the least square approximation to the data matrix. This means that the sums of squares of elements of the residual matrix will be a minimum. This will in general be true, as we have seen, for the principal axis method. We can also find factor score matrices for the centroid and the multiple group methods which are least square solutions to the data matrix. As a matter of fact, for any arbitrary basic matrix of width equal to the number of attributes and of height equal to the number of factors, we can find what particular vertical matrix, postmultiplied by the transpose of the arbitrary factor matrix, yields a product which is the best approximation to the data matrix in the least square sense.

20.2.5 The Image Analysis Factor Score Matrix. To our knowledge, no detailed analysis for the calculation of the factor score matrix from the image type factor loading matrix has been previously presented. Harris (1962) has given an interesting theoretical analysis of this problem. The image analysis approach implies a transformation of the data matrix. It is therefore of interest to see what procedures are appropriate in the calculation of factor score matrices based on these image factor loading matrices and the transformed data matrix.

20.3 The Centroid Factor Score Matrix

20.3.1 Characteristics of the Method. We have indicated in the previous section that the centroid factor loading matrix may be used in the solution of a factor score matrix, such that the major product of the two will give the best least square approximation to the data matrix. We shall, however, consider here only a particular type of centroid factor score solution. In this solution the factor score matrix is an orthogonal matrix.

It has been repeatedly said or implied that the centroid solution yields orthogonal factors. But like much of the discussion about orthogonal factors, the definition of orthogonal factors has been vague. We shall insist on using the term orthogonal only with respect to vectors. We shall insist that the term orthogonality is not useful unless considered in this connection. By saying that two vectors are orthogonal, we simply mean that their minor product is 0.

The solution for the centroid factor score matrix which we shall consider does yield factor scores such that the minor product of any pair of factor score vectors taken from the factor score matrix will be 0.

A further characteristic of this method is that the solution is a rank reduction solution. That is, the solution is such that when the major product of the factor score matrix by the factor loading matrix is subtracted from the data matrix, the residual matrix is of rank equal to the rank of the data matrix less the number of factors.

This solution, like all of the solutions for factor score matrices which we shall consider, involves no iterative procedures. In this respect it is relatively simple and straightforward computationally.

The methods outlined in all of the procedures in this chapter are concerned particularly with the calculation of transformation matrices which may be applied to data matrices to convert them to factor score matrices. Therefore, in actual practice it may be desirable to use these transformation matrices on data matrices other than those from which the factor loading matrices were calculated. When this is the case, the resulting factor score matrices cannot be expected to exhibit precisely the same characteristics as when these transformation matrices are applied to the original data matrix.

20.3.2 Computational Equations

20.3.2a DEFINITION OF NOTATION

a is the centroid factor loading matrix.
L is the matrix of sign vectors.
Y is the centroid factor score matrix.
Z is the normalized data matrix.

20.3.2b THE EQUATIONS

$$t' = a'L \tag{20.3.1}$$

$$B = Lt'^{-1} \tag{20.3.2}$$

$$Y = ZB \tag{20.3.3}$$

20.3.3 Computational Instructions.
We begin with the centroid factor loading matrix a. We also have given the matrix of sign vectors used in the calculation of the centroid factor loading matrix, which we designate L.

We calculate the upper triangular matrix as indicated in Eq. 20.3.1. This is the transpose of the factor loading matrix postmultiplied by the sign matrix.

Next we calculate Eq. 20.3.2, which is the matrix of sign vectors post-multiplied by the inverse of the triangular matrix in Eq. 20.3.1.

We now calculate the centroid factor score matrix, as indicated in Eq. 20.3.3. This is the data matrix postmultiplied by the transformation matrix of Eq. 20.3.2.

20.3.4 Numerical Example. We begin with the data matrix used in Chapter 19, whose corresponding correlation matrix is the same used in previous chapters. The data matrix is repeated for convenient reference in Table 20.3.1.

Table 20.3.2 gives the centroid factor loading matrix for three factors, calculated from the correlation matrix.

TABLE 20.3.1 Normalized Deviation Data Matrix

0.128	0.181	0.421	0.506	0.857	0.746	0.280	0.178	0.246
0.764	0.740	0.563	−0.387	−0.293	−0.202	0.261	0.281	0.043
−0.030	−0.046	0.014	0.147	−0.109	−0.135	0.640	0.682	0.661
−0.280	−0.351	−0.326	−0.023	−0.109	−0.186	0.083	0.091	−0.654
−0.336	−0.306	−0.429	−0.542	−0.006	−0.153	−0.428	0.056	−0.124
−0.276	−0.324	−0.271	−0.370	−0.225	0.035	0.129	−0.446	−0.124
0.057	−0.070	−0.016	0.006	0.152	−0.441	−0.166	−0.354	−0.033
−0.010	−0.140	0.326	−0.004	−0.258	−0.091	−0.410	−0.200	−0.101
−0.303	0.227	−0.014	0.029	−0.102	−0.125	−0.086	−0.106	−0.074
0.086	0.057	−0.003	0.161	0.073	0.134	−0.082	−0.067	−0.009
0.164	0.106	−0.124	0.234	−0.002	0.227	−0.072	0.025	0.156
0.036	−0.074	−0.142	0.242	0.023	0.192	−0.148	−0.119	0.011

TABLE 20.3.2 Centroid Factor Loading Matrix by Rows for Three Factors

0.659	0.684	0.730	0.617	0.542	0.588	0.637	0.606	0.708
0.457	0.452	0.283	−0.601	−0.709	−0.663	0.271	0.346	0.164
0.456	0.439	0.451	−0.209	0.094	0.116	−0.479	−0.488	−0.378

TABLE 20.3.3 Sign Matrix by Rows for Three Factors

1.	1.	1.	1.	1.	1.	1.	1.	1.
1.	1.	1.	−1.	−1.	−1.	1.	1.	1.
1.	1.	1.	−1.	1.	1.	−1.	−1.	−1.

Table 20.3.3 gives the matrix of sign vectors by rows, used in calculating the centroid matrix, and subsequently in the calculation of the factor score matrix.

Table 20.3.4 gives the centroid factor score matrix for three factors, calculated by means of Eqs. 20.3.1–20.3.3.

TABLE 20.3.4   Normalized Centroid
Factor Score Matrix by Columns

0.614	−0.525	0.175
0.307	0.719	0.462
0.316	0.329	−0.810
−0.304	−0.108	−0.191
−0.393	0.007	0.019
−0.324	−0.003	−0.015
−0.150	0.011	0.105
−0.154	0.043	0.211
−0.096	0.015	−0.004
0.061	−0.133	0.083
0.124	−0.123	−0.031
0.004	−0.228	−0.011

Table 20.3.5 gives the minor product moment of the factor score matrix. As proved in Section 20.8.1, this should be an identity matrix, which it is within limits of rounding error.

TABLE 20.3.5   Minor Product Moment
of Centroid Factor Score Matrix

0.997	−0.001	0.002
−0.001	0.999	0.000
0.002	0.000	1.001

20.4   The Multiple Group Factor Score Matrix

20.4.1   Characteristics of the Method. The solution for the multiple group factor scores, as already indicated, does not first require the calculation of the multiple group factor loading matrix. If we have the binary grouping matrix, it can be applied directly to the correlation matrix to yield a transformation matrix which, when applied to the data matrix, gives the factor score matrix. As in the case of the centroid method, this solution is not a least square solution in the sense that the major product of the factor score and factor loading matrices gives the best least square fit to the data matrix. However, it does yield a factor score matrix which is orthonormal and of rank reduction form.

20.4.2   Computational Equations

20.4.2a   DEFINITION OF NOTATION

R is the correlation matrix.

f is a binary grouping matrix.

t is a lower triangular matrix.

Y is the multiple group factor score matrix.

Z is the normalized data matrix.

20.4.2b   THE EQUATIONS

$$G = f'Rf \tag{20.4.1}$$

$$tt' = G \tag{20.4.2}$$

$$B = ft'^{-1} \tag{20.4.3}$$

$$Y = ZB \tag{20.4.4}$$

20.4.3   Computational Instructions.
We assume that the correlation matrix R and a binary grouping matrix f are given. We then calculate the matrix in Eq. 20.4.1. This is the correlation matrix postmultiplied by the binary grouping matrix and premultiplied by its transpose.

Next we calculate the triangular factors of the matrix of Eq. 20.4.1, as indicated in Eq. 20.4.2.

In Eq. 20.4.3 we postmultiply the binary grouping matrix by the inverse of the upper triangular factor in Eq. 20.4.2.

The multiple group factor score matrix is indicated in Eq. 20.4.4. This is the data matrix postmultiplied by the transformation matrix of Eq. 20.4.3. The minor product moment of this matrix is shown in Section 20.8.2 to be the identity matrix.

20.4.4   Numerical Example.
We use the same data matrix and correlation matrix as in the previous section.

Table 20.4.1 gives the binary grouping matrix by rows for three factors.

Table 20.4.2 gives the normalized multiple group factor score matrix by columns for three factors. The matrix was calculated by means of Eqs. 20.4.1–20.4.4.

TABLE 20.4.1   Binary Grouping Matrix
by Rows for Three Factors

1.	1.	1.	0.	0.	0.	0.	0.	0.
0.	0.	0.	1.	1.	1.	0.	0.	0.
0.	0.	0.	0.	0.	0.	1.	1.	1.

Table 20.4.3 gives the minor product moment of the multiple group factor score matrix. Within rounding error this is an identity matrix, as it should be according to Section 20.8.2. In this sense the multiple group factors may be

TABLE 20.4.2   Normalized Multiple
Group Factor Score Matrix
for Three Factors

0.262	0.767	0.007
0.743	−0.470	0.022
−0.022	−0.033	0.902
−0.344	−0.062	−0.037
−0.385	−0.203	0.009
−0.313	−0.161	−0.010
−0.010	−0.107	−0.216
0.063	−0.147	−0.312
−0.032	−0.071	−0.086
0.050	0.133	−0.126
0.052	0.168	−0.016
−0.065	0.187	−0.128

said to be orthogonal, but only if the factor scores are calculated in this manner.

The same may also be said for the centroid factors when the factor score matrix is calculated according to Section 20.3.

TABLE 20.4.3   Minor Product Moment of
Multiple Group Factor Score Matrix

1.000	0.000	−0.003
0.000	1.000	−0.001
−0.003	−0.001	1.000

20.5   The Principal Axis Factor Score Matrix

20.5.1   Characteristics of the Method.   As indicated in the previous discussion on kinds of methods, the principal axis solution is the simplest of the methods, if the basic structure or principal axis factor loading matrix is already available. One of the most important advantages of the principal axis method is that it gives, at the same time, a least square, a rank reduction, and an orthogonal solution for the factor score matrix.

20.5.2 Computational Equations

20.5.2a DEFINITION OF NOTATION

a is the principal axis factor loading matrix.
δ is the basic diagonal of the correlation matrix.
Y is the principal axis factor score matrix.
Z is the normalized data matrix.

20.5.2b THE EQUATIONS

$$B = a\delta^{-1} \tag{20.5.1}$$

$$Y = ZB \tag{20.5.2}$$

20.5.3 Computational Instructions. The computational instructions for the principal axis factor score matrix are very simple. We begin with the factor loading matrix a and the basic diagonal δ. Equation 20.5.1, then, directly gives the transformation matrix. This is simply the factor loading matrix postmultiplied by the inverse of the δ diagonal.

The factor score matrix is then calculated in the usual manner, as indicated in Eq. 20.5.2.

Hotelling (1933) published this solution for the factor score matrix. However, it does not seem to be well known and has not been used extensively.

20.5.4 Numerical Example. In this example we use the same data and correlation matrices as in the previous sections.

Table 20.5.1 gives the first three basic diagonals of the correlation matrix, as found in early chapters giving basic structure solutions.

TABLE 20.5.1 First Three Basic
Diagonals of Correlation Matrix

3.749	2.050	1.331

Table 20.5.2 gives the first three principal axis factor vectors by rows, as found in previous chapters, for example, Chapters 7 and 8.

TABLE 20.5.2 Principal Axis Factor Loading Matrix by Rows for Three Factors

0.717	0.740	0.773	0.556	0.463	0.518	0.640	0.615	0.715
0.493	0.478	0.296	−0.649	−0.744	−0.694	0.080	0.166	−0.034
0.350	0.322	0.406	0.068	0.181	0.188	−0.588	−0.621	−0.369

Table 20.5.3 gives the normalized principal axis factor score matrix for three factors, as calculated from Eqs. 20.5.1 and 20.5.2.

Table 20.5.4 gives the minor product moment of the principal axis factor score matrix. This is the identity matrix to within rounding error.

TABLE 20.5.3 Normalized Principal Axis
Factor Score Matrix for Three Factors

0.555	−0.569	0.179
0.386	0.767	0.205
0.325	0.092	−0.825
−0.328	−0.065	−0.198
−0.403	0.001	−0.146
−0.325	−0.023	−0.093
−0.140	0.053	0.200
−0.129	0.107	0.317
−0.088	0.037	0.049
0.052	−0.098	0.143
0.114	−0.107	0.052
−0.014	−0.195	0.109

TABLE 20.5.4 Minor Product Moment of
Principal Axis Factor Score Matrix

0.998	−0.001	0.002
−0.001	1.000	0.000
0.002	0.000	1.002

20.6 The Least Square Factor Score Matrix

20.6.1 Characteristics of the Method. This method is not mutually exclusive of those previously considered. It may be applied to any factor loading matrix such as the centroid, the multiple group, or the principal axis. When applied to the principal axis factor matrix it yields precisely the solution given in the preceding section. The least square solution yields a factor score matrix such that, when the major product of this matrix and the factor loading matrix is subtracted from the data matrix, the sum of squares of elements in the residual matrix is a minimum. This solution, as all least square solutions in general, can be shown to be a rank reduction solution. The left arbitrary multiplier, however, is somewhat more involved than in other methods, as can be seen from Section 20.9.4. In general, also, the computations are somewhat more involved than they are for the solutions we have already discussed.

20.6.2   Computational Equations

20.6.2a   DEFINITION OF NOTATION
a is an arbitrary factor loading matrix.
Z is the normalized data matrix.
Y is the least square factor score matrix.

20.6.2b   THE EQUATIONS

$$G = a'a \tag{20.6.1}$$

$$B = aG^{-1} \tag{20.6.2}$$

$$Y = ZB \tag{20.6.3}$$

20.6.3   Computational Instructions. We begin with any arbitrary factor loading matrix.

Equation 20.6.1 gives the minor product moment of the arbitrary factor loading matrix.

The next step is indicated by Eq. 20.6.2, which is the factor loading matrix postmultiplied by the inverse of the matrix in Eq. 20.6.1. This is the matrix which transforms the data matrix to the factor score matrix.

Equation 20.6.3 shows the least square factor score matrix as the product of the data matrix postmultiplied by the transformation matrix of Eq. 20.6.2.

20.6.4   Numerical Example. We use the same data and correlation matrices as in the previous sections. We also use the centroid factor matrix of Section 20.3.4.

Table 20.6.1 shows the minor product moment matrix of the centroid factor matrix for three factors.

TABLE 20.6.1   Minor Product Moment
of Centroid Factor Loading Matrix
for Three Factors

3.730	0.170	0.052
0.170	2.017	0.156
0.052	0.156	1.280

TABLE 20.6.2   Inverse of Minor Product
Moment of Factor Loading Matrix

0.269	−0.022	−0.008
−0.022	0.502	−0.060
−0.008	−0.060	0.789

Table 20.6.2 gives the inverse of the matrix in Table 20.6.1.

Table 20.6.3 gives the product of the natural order of the matrix in Table 20.6.1 postmultiplied by the matrix of Table 20.6.2. This gives the matrix for transforming the data matrix to the least square factor score matrix.

Table 20.6.4 gives the least square factor score matrix.

Table 20.6.5 gives the minor product moment of the least square factor score matrix. This is not an identity matrix, nor should it be so, unless the factor loading matrix consists of basic structure factors.

TABLE 20.6.3   Matrix for Transforming
Data Matrix to Factor Score Matrix

0.164	0.188	0.327
0.171	0.185	0.313
0.187	0.099	0.333
0.181	−0.303	−0.134
0.161	−0.374	0.112
0.172	−0.353	0.127
0.169	0.151	−0.399
0.160	0.190	−0.411
0.190	0.090	−0.314

TABLE 20.6.4   Least Square Factor
Score Matrix

0.611	−0.540	0.100
0.302	0.731	0.429
0.319	0.316	−0.812
−0.316	−0.065	−0.208
−0.400	−0.007	−0.109
−0.321	−0.031	−0.083
−0.147	−0.002	0.174
−0.143	0 025	0.299
−0.092	0.018	0.037
0.061	−0.123	0.112
0.124	−0.104	0.012
0.005	−0.215	0.040

TABLE 20.6.5   Minor Product Moment
of Least Square Factor Score Matrix

0.998	−0.002	0.004
−0.002	1.004	0.004
0.004	0.004	1.050

20.7 The Image Analysis Factor Score Matrix

20.7.1 Characteristics of the Method. When the image analysis approach to factor analysis is used, we may employ any of the factoring methods discussed so far: the principal axis, the group centroid, the centroid, the multiple group, or other methods. Furthermore, we may also use any of the metricizing methods of Chapters 13 and 15. We shall in our description of computational procedures indicate a scaling diagonal. In particular, this may be an identity matrix.

20.7.2 Computational Equations

20.7.2a DEFINITION OF NOTATION
R is the correlation matrix.
D is an attribute scaling matrix.
t is a triangular matrix.
Y is the image factor score matrix.
Z is the normalized data matrix.

20.7.2b THE EQUATIONS

$$M = (I - R^{-1}D_{R^{-1}}^{-1})D \tag{20.7.1}$$

$$G = D(R - 2D_{R^{-1}}^{-1} + D_{R^{-1}}^{-1}R^{-1}D_{R^{-1}}^{-1})D \tag{20.7.2}$$

$$C = L'GL \tag{20.7.3}$$

$$tt' = C \tag{20.7.4}$$

$$B = M(Lt'^{-1}) \tag{20.7.5}$$

$$Y = ZB \tag{20.7.6}$$

20.7.3 Computational Instructions. We shall assume the correlation matrix given. We then calculate a matrix M as indicated in Eq. 20.7.1. This will be recognized as the matrix which transforms the data matrix to the image of the data matrix. The matrix on the extreme right of the right-hand side of the equation is a scaling diagonal. It may be chosen according to one of the methods suggested in Chapter 16, or it may be determined according to the self-scaling procedures of Chapter 15.

We then calculate the image covariance scaled matrix, as in Eq. 20.7.2. The part in parentheses on the right-hand side of this equation will be recognized as the standard covariance image matrix of Guttman (1953). It is pre- and postmultiplied by the diagonal scaling matrix of Eq. 20.7.1.

Next we calculate the C matrix in Eq. 20.7.3. This is the matrix of Eq. 20.7.2 premultiplied by the transpose of an L matrix and postmultiplied by the natural order of this matrix. This L matrix is of the same order as the factor loading matrix, which presumably has been obtained from the G matrix. In particular, it may be a binary grouping matrix, a matrix of sign vectors for the centroid method, or a principal axis factor loading matrix calculated from the G matrix of Eq. 20.7.2. This depends on which particular type of factor loading matrix one has calculated.

Equation 20.7.4 shows a triangular factoring of the matrix in Eq. 20.7.3.

Next the L matrix is postmultiplied by the inverse of the upper triangular factor of Eq. 20.7.4, and then the matrix of Eq. 20.7.1 is postmultiplied by this product, to give the matrix B of Eq. 20.7.5.

The matrix of Eq. 20.7.5 is the transformation matrix which, when applied to the data matrix as in Eq. 20.7.6, yields the factor score matrix. This factor score matrix is orthonormal and of rank reduction form. It is not a least square solution, unless L in Eq. 20.7.3 happens to be the basic structure or principal axis factor loading matrix for the covariance matrix G in Eq. 20.7.2.

TABLE 20.7.1   Image Covariance Matrix

0.733	0.688	0.662	0.120	0.065	0.101	0.294	0.302	0.336
0.688	0.744	0.666	0.147	0.067	0.117	0.316	0.307	0.358
0.662	0.666	0.691	0.215	0.169	0.239	0.288	0.305	0.355
0.120	0.147	0.215	0.511	0.488	0.494	0.218	0.178	0.285
0.065	0.067	0.169	0.488	0.572	0.486	0.161	0.081	0.246
0.101	0.117	0.239	0.494	0.486	0.562	0.160	0.142	0.262
0.294	0.316	0.288	0.218	0.161	0.160	0.481	0.396	0.418
0.302	0.307	0.305	0.178	0.081	0.142	0.396	0.499	0.388
0.336	0.358	0.355	0.285	0.246	0.262	0.418	0.388	0.436

TABLE 20.7.2   Image Factor Score
Matrix for Three Factors

0.265	0.796	−0.058
0.734	−0.490	0.013
0.018	0.018	0.881
−0.359	−0.112	0.121
−0.383	−0.170	−0.019
−0.316	−0.106	−0.068
−0.025	−0.104	−0.248
0.019	−0.113	−0.331
−0.034	−0.078	−0.051
0.054	0.102	−0.115
0.079	0.111	−0.003
−0.053	0.144	−0.111

20.7.4 Numerical Example. We use the same data and correlation matrices as in the previous sections, and the grouping matrix of Table 20.4.1. The identity matrix is taken as the scaling diagonal.

Table 20.7.1 gives the image covariance matrix.

Table 20.7.2 gives the image factor score matrix for three factors, as calculated by means of Eqs. 20.7.1–20.7.6.

Table 20.7.3 gives the minor product moment of the image factor score matrix. This is an identity matrix to within rounding error, as it should be.

TABLE 20.7.3   Minor Product Moment
of Image Factor Score Matrix

1.000	0.000	−0.004
0.000	1.000	−0.001
−0.004	−0.001	0.999

20.8 Mathematical Proofs

20.8.1   The Centroid Factor Score Matrix

Consider any basic matrix L of order $n \times m$.
Let

$$a_{.i} = \frac{{}_iRL_{.i}}{\sqrt{L_{.i}'RL_{.i}}} \tag{20.8.1}$$

where

$$_{i+1}R = {}_iR - a_{.i}a_{.i}' \tag{20.8.2}$$

Let

$$a = (a_{.1} \cdots a_{.m}) \tag{20.8.3}$$

We can prove, by the methods of Chapter 5, from Eqs. 20.8.1 and 20.8.2 that

$$L'a = t_a \tag{20.8.4}$$

where t_a is lower triangular.

Consider now

$$L'RL = t_b t_b' \tag{20.8.5}$$

and

$$b = {}_1RLt_b'^{-1} \tag{20.8.6}$$

From Eqs. 20.8.5 and 20.8.6,

$$L'b = t_b \tag{20.8.7}$$

From Eqs. 20.8.2 and 20.8.3,

$$_{m+1}R = R - aa' \tag{20.8.8}$$

From Eqs. 20.8.1–20.8.4, it can be shown that

$$_{m+1}RL = 0 \tag{20.8.9}$$

From Eqs. 20.8.8 and 20.8.9,

$$L'RL = L'aa'L \tag{20.8.10}$$

From Eqs. 20.8.5–20.8.7,

$$L'RL = L'bb'L \tag{20.8.11}$$

From Eqs. 20.8.4, 20.8.7, 20.8.10, and 20.8.11,

$$t_a = t_b \tag{20.8.12}$$

From Eqs. 20.8.4, 20.8.7, and 20.8.12,

$$L'a = L'b \tag{20.8.13}$$

If $m = n$ and L is nonsingular, we have from Eq. 20.8.13 that $a = b$. But from Eqs. 20.8.1 and 20.8.2 the solution for any $a_{.i}$ is independent of the solution for any $a_{.i+k}$. Also, from Eq. 20.8.6 the solution for any $b_{.i}$ is independent of the solution for any $b_{.i+k}$. Hence, in general

$$a = b \tag{20.8.14}$$

Consider then the $n \times m$ matrix L of sign vectors for the centroid factor solution such that

$$_{i+1}R = {}_iR - a_{.i}a_{.i}' \tag{20.8.15}$$

where

$$a_{.i} = \frac{{}_iRL_{.i}}{\sqrt{L_{.i}'RL_{.i}}} \tag{20.8.16}$$

From Eqs. 20.8.3 and 20.8.4 we can express the centroid factor matrix as a function directly of the correlation matrix by

$$a = RLt'^{-1} \tag{20.8.17}$$

where

$$tt' = L'RL \tag{20.8.18}$$

We may now let L and $L'Z'$ be the right and left arbitrary multipliers in the rank reduction equation and write

$$E = Z - ZL[(L'Z')ZL]^{-1}(L'Z')Z \tag{20.8.19}$$

If

$$R = Z'Z \tag{20.8.20}$$

we have from Eqs. 20.8.18–20.8.20,

$$E = Z - (ZLt'^{-1})(t^{-1}L'R) \tag{20.8.21}$$

We now consider the general lower rank approximation form to the data matrix

$$E = Z - Ya' \tag{20.8.22}$$

If a is given by Eq. 20.8.17, then from Eq. 20.8.21,

$$Y = ZLt'^{-1} \qquad (20.8.23)$$

and from Eqs. 20.8.18, 20.8.20, and 20.8.23,

$$Y'Y = I \qquad (20.8.24)$$

If now we have an orthonormal transformation

$$b = aH \qquad (20.8.25)$$

we consider W such that

$$Wb' = Ya' \qquad (20.8.26)$$

From Eqs. 20.8.25, and 20.8.26,

$$W = YH \qquad (20.8.27)$$

which is a simple structure factor score matrix. Since H is orthonormal by definition, we have from Eqs. 20.8.24 and 20.8.27,

$$W'W = I \qquad (20.8.28)$$

If the simple structure transformation is not orthonormal, we use h instead of H and show that

$$w = Yh'^{-1} \qquad (20.8.29)$$

and the covariance matrix C_w for w is

$$C_w = (h'h)^{-1} \qquad (20.8.30)$$

or if we let r be the correlation of the simple structure reference axes, then

$$C_w = r^{-1} \qquad (20.8.31)$$

For computational purposes we have from Eq. 20.8.4,

$$t' = a'L \qquad (20.8.32)$$

$$Y = Z(Lt'^{-1}) \qquad (20.8.33)$$

Then

$$W = Z(L(t'^{-1}H)) \qquad (20.8.34)$$

for the orthonormal transformation, and

$$w = Z(L(t'^{-1}h'^{-1})) \qquad (20.8.35)$$

20.8.2   The Multiple Group Factor Score Matrix

Suppose we let f be the binary grouping matrix for the multiple group method of factor analysis. The factor loading matrix given in Chapter 6 is

$$a = Rft'^{-1} \qquad (20.8.36)$$

where

$$tt' = f'Rf \tag{20.8.37}$$

Then by the methods of the preceding section we have for the rank reduction type multiple group factor score matrix

$$Y = Zft'^{-1} \tag{20.8.38}$$

Since

$$R = Z'Z \tag{20.8.39}$$

we can readily see from Eqs. 20.8.37–20.8.39 that

$$Y'Y = I \tag{20.8.40}$$

We also show that Y can be computed directly from the data matrix. We let

$$U = Zf \tag{20.8.41}$$

$$tt' = U'U \tag{20.8.42}$$

From Eqs. 20.8.37–20.8.39, 20.8.41, and 20.8.42,

$$Y = Ut'^{-1} \tag{20.8.43}$$

We may now use Eqs. 20.8.36, 20.8.38, and 20.8.43 to calculate a from the factor score matrix Y, thus

$$a = Z'Y \tag{20.8.44}$$

The same procedure could have been used to calculate the centroid factor score matrix directly from the data matrix, having given the matrix L of sign vectors. It will be recalled that in Chapter 5 the successive residual matrices were required from which to calculate the successive sign vectors, and hence they are not available in advance. It is of interest to note that a in Eq. 20.8.44 is precisely a matrix of the correlations of the factor scores with the variables, since both Z and Y are in standard measures. For the case of orthonormal transformations to simple structure we have

$$W = YH \tag{20.8.45}$$

and for oblique transformations we have

$$w = Yh'^{-1} \tag{20.8.46}$$

For the computational equations we have Eqs. 20.8.41, 20.8.42, and

$$W = U(t'^{-1}H) \tag{20.8.47}$$

and

$$w = U(t'^{-1}h'^{-1}) \tag{20.8.48}$$

for the orthonormal and oblique transformations, respectively.

20.8.3 The Principal Axis Factor Score Matrix

The basic structure or principal axis factor score matrix is well known to be

$$Y = ZQ\Delta^{-1} \tag{20.8.49}$$

or, if the basic structure of Z is

$$Z = P\Delta Q' \tag{20.8.50}$$

then

$$Y = P \tag{20.8.51}$$

For the orthonormal and oblique transformations, respectively, we have

$$W = PH \tag{20.8.52}$$

and

$$w = Ph'^{-1} \tag{20.8.53}$$

For the covariance matrices of Eqs. 20.8.51–20.8.53, we have

$$C_Y = I \tag{20.8.54}$$

$$C_W = I \tag{20.8.55}$$

$$C_w = (h'h)^{-1} = r^{-1} \tag{20.8.56}$$

20.8.4 The Least Square Factor Score Matrix

Given the arbitrary factor loading matrix a and the residual factor score matrix

$$E = Z - Ya' \tag{20.8.57}$$

the solution for Y which minimizes $trE'E$ is well known to be

$$Y = Za(a'a)^{-1} \tag{20.8.58}$$

If

$$a = RLt'^{-1} \tag{20.8.59}$$

where L is arbitrary and

$$R = Z'Z \tag{20.8.60}$$

$$tt' = L'RL \tag{20.8.61}$$

then from Eqs. 20.8.58–20.8.61,

$$C_Y = Y'Y = t'(L'R^2L)^{-1}(L'R^3L)(L'R^2L)^{-1}t \tag{20.8.62}$$

If

$$R = Q\Delta^2Q' \tag{20.8.63}$$

and

$$L = Q\Delta \tag{20.8.64}$$

then it can be shown that

$$t = t' = \Delta^2 \tag{20.8.65}$$

and therefore also that

$$C_Y = I \tag{20.8.66}$$

There appears, however, to be no simple expression for C_Y for other L matrices, such as the centroid sign matrix or the binary grouping matrix f.

If we have the orthonormal or oblique transformations H or h, respectively, then

$$W = YH \tag{20.8.67}$$

and

$$w = Yh'^{-1} \tag{20.8.68}$$

For the case of Eq. 20.8.64, we have

$$C_W = I \tag{20.8.69}$$

$$C_w = r^{-1} \tag{20.8.70}$$

Otherwise,

$$C_W = H'C_Y H \tag{20.8.71}$$

and

$$C_w = h^{-1}C_Y h'^{-1} \tag{20.8.72}$$

as can be seen from Eqs. 20.8.62, 20.8.67, and 20.8.68.

20.8.5   The Image Analysis Factor Score Matrix
Let

$$U = Z(I - R^{-1}D_{R^{-1}}^{-1})D \tag{20.8.73}$$

be the image data matrix scaled with D according to one of the procedures of Chapter 15. We let

$$M = (I - R^{-1}D_{R^{-1}}^{-1})D \tag{20.8.74}$$

and the scaled image covariance matrix be

$$C_U = U'U \tag{20.8.75}$$

Let L be a matrix of the order of the factor matrix. As a special case, it may be a centroid sign matrix, a binary grouping matrix, or the principal axis factor matrix of C_U. In all cases, we know by the previous methods that the rank reduction type factor score matrix is as follows.

$$u = UL \tag{20.8.76}$$

$$tt' = u'u \tag{20.8.77}$$

$$Y = ut'^{-1} \tag{20.8.78}$$

We let

$$U = P\Delta Q' \tag{20.8.79}$$

and

$$L = Q\Delta \tag{20.8.80}$$

that is, L is the principal axis factor matrix of C_U. Then it can readily be shown from Eq. 20.8.76–20.8.80 that

$$Y = P \qquad (20.8.81)$$

$$W = PH \qquad (20.8.82)$$

$$w = Ph'^{-1} \qquad (20.8.83)$$

and

$$C_Y = I \qquad (20.8.84)$$

$$C_W = I \qquad (20.8.85)$$

$$C_w = (h'h)^{-1} = r^{-1} \qquad (20.8.86)$$

For the general case of L we have computationally

$$tt' = L'D(R - 2D_{R^{-1}}{}^{-1} + D_{R^{-1}}{}^{-1}R^{-1}D_{R^{-1}}{}^{-1})DL \qquad (20.8.87)$$

$$B = M(Lt'^{-1}) \qquad (20.8.88)$$

$$Y = ZB \qquad (20.8.89)$$

$$W = Z(BH) \qquad (20.8.90)$$

$$w = Z(Bh'^{-1}) \qquad (20.8.91)$$

For the general case we also have Eqs. 20.8.84–20.8.86.

Part VI

Special Problems

Chapter 21

General Factor Solutions

21.1 Introduction

The history of factor analysis theory and procedures has been marked by a preoccupation with the types of factors to be found in typical sets of experimental data. In the preceding chapters we have not been concerned primarily with an analysis of these various types of factors. However, implicit in the different kinds of solutions we have considered are assumptions about the types of factors which factor analysts have postulated.

The early work of Spearman (1927) assumed two types of factors in mental abilities, specific factors and general factors. A specific factor was postulated for each of the variables. A general factor was assumed to be present to a greater or lesser degree in all of the variables. Psychological measures correlate among themselves, according to Spearman's early theory, because of this general factor of intelligence. The theory is known as the *two-factor theory of intelligence*.

If the two-factor theory of intelligence is valid, it should be possible to express a matrix of correlation coefficients for a set of psychological variables as the sum of a diagonal matrix plus the major product moment of a vector. The diagonal matrix would represent the loadings of specific factors, that is, those which are peculiar to each of the individual tests. According to this hypothesis, each nondiagonal element in the correlation matrix would be the product of two elements of the vector whose major product moment is added to the diagonal matrix. Each element of this vector was regarded as the factor loading of the general factor for the corresponding test.

Spearman argued that if his theory were true, it should be possible to substitute diagonal elements in a correlation matrix so that the rank of the resulting matrix is one, or simply the major product moment of a vector. He did not express it in this simple manner, but this is what his theory amounts to. He formulated it in cumbersome scalar mathematics; however, it can be expressed much more simply in matrix notation. Actually, of course, Spearman recognized that a table of experimental correlation coefficients would not satisfy the model exactly. His objective then was to find the best approximation to a correlation matrix which would satisfy the rank one condition for the nondiagonal elements of the matrix.

492

It will be recognized, of course, that Spearman's hypothesis is very restricted. As is clear from the preceding chapters, factor analysis may be regarded as a general tool for all of the sciences. If Spearman's theory were generalized to all of the scientific disciplines, it would mean that no matter what set of measures one might obtain for a particular discipline on a specified number of entities, the resulting data matrix would be one in which the intercorrelations could all be accounted for in terms of a single vector of factor loadings. It would mean further that each of the variables must contain a certain amount of variance specific to itself. Obviously, this hypothesis would be highly restrictive and could not be expected to describe all natural phenomena in all areas.

As a matter of fact, Spearman soon found that his two-factor theory of intelligence could not be verified in terms of this simple theory of specifics and a single general factor. He found that many correlation matrices derived from psychological measures could not be approximated with even a reasonable degree of accuracy by the sum of a diagonal matrix and a major product moment of a vector. Spearman and some of his followers spent a great deal of time attempting to find the standard error of scalar quantities called *tetrads*. These are functions of the elements of second-order minors of the correlation matrix. The tetrads were supposed to vanish if the two-factor theory of intelligence were correct. The standard errors of these tetrads were used to indicate whether the tetrads differed significantly from 0.

This turned out to be a forlorn pursuit, because natural phenomena are not that simple. Spearman was soon forced to complicate his theory by considering also what he called group factors, that is, factors which are common to some of the variables in a set of data but not to all of them. Both Spearman and Kelley (1928) did considerable work on the identification of group factors. Unfortunately, neither of these investigators utilized the powerful notation and methods of matrix algebra. They struggled with cumbersome scalar equations in an attempt to find solutions for the group factor loadings of subsets of variables in a data matrix.

It was not until some years later that Thurstone (1931) attempted to generalize Spearman's two-factor theory. Thurstone still retained the concept of the specific factor as a particular type of factor which he regarded as necessary for analysis of psychological data. However, he extended and modified the general factor vector of Spearman to a common factor matrix. This common factor matrix then could be considered as a generalization of Spearman's general factor of intelligence. The vectors of the matrix of common factor loadings could include Spearman's hypothesized general factor and also the group factors that Spearman, Kelley, and others were forced to incorporate in their model.

With the Thurstone common-plus-specific factor theory, the correlation matrix was assumed to be expressible as the sum of a diagonal matrix plus the major product moment of a factor loading matrix. This constituted an extension of Spearman's theory, in that Thurstone now substituted the major product moment of a matrix for the special case of the major product moment of the single vector. The problem which Thurstone set for himself was to find the matrix of smallest width, that is, the matrix with the smallest number of common factors, such that the major product moment, when added to some diagonal matrix, would, in some specified sense, give the best approximation to the correlation matrix.

It is here that the notion of communality which we have referred to in previous chapters entered into the picture. The communality of the correlation matrix is simply the diagonal of the major product moment of the matrix of common factor loadings. The specificity is this diagonal subtracted from 1. In terms of matrix notation, the communality of a single test is the minor product moment of the vector from the factor loading matrix corresponding to that test or variable. Here then, we have introduced another type of factor to take the place of the general factor, namely, the common factor.

Thurstone soon recognized an important characteristic of matrix products discussed in Chapter 4. There we saw that if the major product moment of a particular matrix is a good approximation to the correlation matrix, the major product moment of a multiply infinite number of matrices will also yield exactly the same result. The reason for this is, of course, that if we post-multiply a vertical matrix by a square orthonormal matrix to get another matrix, then in the major product moment of this second matrix the ortho-normal drops out, because it is multiplied by its transpose and becomes the identity. Therefore, the major product moment of such an orthonormally transformed matrix is the same as the major product moment of the original matrix.

Thurstone then proceeded to search for some particular transformation of an arbitrary factor loading matrix, such that the transformed factor loading matrix would satisfy certain criteria. These conditions we discussed in Chapters 17 and 18. We saw how the varimax, the quartimax, the oblimax, and other methods of transformation attempt to satisfy the descriptive criteria which Thurstone proposed.

A great deal of time and effort went into the development of the methods of transformation which would satisfy the criteria. In addition to satisfying these criteria, Thurstone insisted that the factor loadings should make psychological sense. He placed a great deal of emphasis on this notion of "psychological sense," and many investigators were impressed with the concept. Others, however, recognized that what might make sense to one person does not to another, and they therefore looked for more scientific criteria of adequate transformation procedures.

As a matter of fact, Thurstone believed that if the factor loadings made psychological sense, one could then expect them to be relatively invariant, irrespective of the particular sample of entities or the particular sample of variables from which they were derived. This invariance is the objective discussed in Chapter 17, in which the concept of simple structure is justified in terms of invariance with respect to samples of entities and samples of variables, rather than with respect to the subjective judgments which people might make about psychological sense.

In any case, both graphical and analytical methods of transformation were developed. These were of two types, the orthonormal transformation and the oblique. Thurstone found that by allowing oblique transformation, rather than imposing orthonormality upon them, the resulting matrices more adequately satisfied the simple structure criteria. The tendency to favor the oblique over the orthonormal transformation has increased over the years.

However, if one applies an oblique transformation to a factor loading matrix, the factor scores corresponding to this transformed factor loading matrix will not in general be uncorrelated. We may then consider a correlation matrix of these factor scores. Curiously enough, the literature resulting from the work of Thurstone and his students has not explicitly emphasized this consequence of the oblique transformation. The traditional treatment has emphasized the correlations of what are called the *simple structure reference axes*. These correlations are given by the minor product moment of the oblique transformation matrix. We can, however, bypass this concept and direct our attention to the factor scores and their correlations.

In essence this is what Thurstone did, although not explicitly. He employed the concept of the correlations among the "primaries." These correlations turn out to be the same mathematically as the correlations among the oblique simple structure factor scores. The interest now centers around this correlation matrix derived from the matrix of oblique simple structure factor scores. However, we need not actually calculate the factor score matrix in order to compute the corresponding correlation matrix.

To pursue further the subject of types of factors, we shall consider in some detail the matrix of correlations of the oblique simple structure factor scores. We ask first whether this correlation matrix can be expressed as the sum of a diagonal matrix and the major product moment of a vector. Here the two-factor model of Spearman emerges in what is called the second-order factor model. If the correlation matrix can be expressed in this manner, one might hypothesize a second-order general factor and second-order specific factor. Therefore, the notion of the general factor again emerges as a by-product of the oblique method of transformation.

But if the correlation matrix of the factor scores cannot be so simply expressed, we may again utilize Thurstone's generalization and see whether it can be adequately approximated by the sum of a diagonal matrix and a major product moment of a matrix. It will be recognized, of course, that typically the correlation matrix of the oblique factor scores will be very much smaller than the correlation matrix of the original variables. Its order will be precisely the same as the number of factors extracted from the correlation matrix.

If, now, we can express the correlation matrix of the oblique factor scores as the sum of a diagonal matrix and the major product moment of a matrix, then we might regard the diagonal elements as specific to the factors we extracted from the original correlation matrix, and the higher-order common factor matrix as accounting for the correlations among these factor scores.

However, we are again confronted with the indeterminacy of the factor matrix whose major product moment accounts for the correlations among the factor scores. We may consider the transformation of this second-order, smaller factor loading matrix to simple structure form by the methods discussed in Chapter 17. We can therefore proceed in this way to successively higher orders of factors. A detailed development of this general model is given by Schmid and Leiman (1957).

We now have three types of factors. These are specific factors, common factors, and a sort of second-order general factor. This general factor emerges from the oblique transformation to simple structure. We shall concern ourselves, then, with the problem of how we may bring this general factor back into the first-order realm, as it may relate both to the factor loading matrix and to the factor score matrix. Since we wish to adhere to the principle of interpreting solutions in terms of the data matrix, we shall see how we may express the data matrix as the major product of a factor score and a factor loading matrix, where in each of them both the general and the common factors are represented. We shall not, however, pursue in detail the concept and computation of specific factor scores. Bartlett (1938) has considered this latter problem, and more recently Guttman (1955) has presented a more fundamental theoretical discussion of specific factor scores.

In the next section we shall direct our attention to the calculation of the correlations of the oblique factor scores, the derivation of second-order specific and common factors, and finally the calculation of first-order general factor loadings and general factor scores.

21.2   General and Specific Simple Structure Factor Scores

The solution for general factors may be divided into three parts. First, we find the covariance matrix of factor scores and the second-order common and specific factors; second, we find the first-order general and rescaled simple structure common factor loadings; and third, we find the general and rescaled simple structure common factor scores.

21.2.1   The Factor Score Covariance Matrix, and the Second-Order Common and Specific Factor Loadings. As indicated previously, we can find the covariance matrix of the oblique factor scores without actually finding the oblique factor scores themselves. This can be done by means of appropriate mathematical formulas. Furthermore, the computations both for rescaled simple structure and general factor loadings, and for rescaled simple structure and general factor scores, do not depend on solving for the correlation matrix, as such. A solution for these two sets of matrices does depend, however, on a factoring of the covariance factor score matrix.

21.2.2   The First-Order General and Common Factor Loading Matrix.
It is not necessary to solve for the general and common factor loading matrix before solving for the corresponding factor score matrix. However, interest usually centers around the factor loading matrices, and in many cases one may not be interested in solving for the factor scores. Therefore, what little work has been done in the calculation of first-order general and rescaled simple structure common factors from simple structure oblique factors has ended with this part of the analysis. The solution for these factor loadings is a function of the arbitrary factor loading matrix, the oblique transformation matrix, and the second-order common and specific factors obtained from the covariance matrix of the oblique factor scores.

21.2.3   The First-Order General and Common Factor Score Matrix.
To our knowledge, no one has been concerned with the solution for the general and rescaled simple structure common factor scores. It is true that Spearman (1927) very early provided a method for estimating general factor scores when there was only one general factor and as many specifics as variables. This is quite a different problem, however, because what Spearman regarded as the general factor is currently interpreted as a common factor. Spearman's solution is a special case which does not generalize readily to the second-order factors. It seems appropriate, however, that if we insist on the derivation of first-order general and rescaled simple structure factor loadings from second-order common and specific factor loadings, we should also recognize the implication of these two types of factor loadings for the corresponding factor scores. Again we emphasize the importance of returning to the data matrix, and assuring ourselves that any of the parameters which we impute to the correlation matrix should also be interpreted in terms of the original data matrix.

21.3   The Factor Score Covariance Matrix, and the Second-Order Common and Specific Factor Loadings

21.3.1   Characteristics of the Method.   One of the essential characteristics of the solution, which distinguishes it from the treatment of Thurstone (1947) and Thomson (1950), for example, is its emphasis and interpretation rather than its computational procedures. The computations start, as they

do traditionally, with a consideration of the oblique transformation matrix. The Thurstonian approach is to emphasize this oblique transformation matrix in terms of geometrical concepts. It places particular emphasis on the reference axes for the new simple structure factors, and shows how the oblique transformation matrix is the algebraic analog of these new simple structure reference axes, from which the coordinates of each of the variables is measured.

We do not, however, concern ourselves with these geometrical representations. We start with the oblique transformation matrix, and calculate its minor product moment. This is then a correlation matrix of hypothetical variables, such that the correlation of each of the observed measures with the hypothetical attributes gives a matrix which we call the simple structure factor matrix. Here the simple structure concept is related to factor scores. We define a set of hypothetical variables in such a way that the correlations of the observed variables with the hypothetical variables constitute a matrix which satisfies the descriptive and analytical simple structure criteria.

Suppose, then, that the minor product moment of the oblique transformation matrix is available. A factor analysis of the inverse of this matrix, to get second-order specific and common factors from it, is required next. Here we have no choice with reference to the communality problem. If the correlation matrix cannot be adequately resolved into the sum of a diagonal matrix and the major product moment of a vertical matrix, the notion of second-order specific and general factors breaks down, and the general factor model is not tenable in connection with these data. Therefore, the communality concept which has caused so much difficulty both theoretically and computationally in the case of correlation and covariance matrices, must be adopted for the correlation matrix of the simple structure factor scores, if we wish to include the general factor in our model.

It must be emphasized that the matrix to be factored is not the minor product moment of the transformation matrix, but rather its inverse. This inverse is the covariance matrix of the oblique simple structure factor scores. Traditionally, this covariance matrix is first normalized so that it becomes the matrix of correlations of factor scores. It is not necessary, however, to normalize the matrix before factoring. The factoring procedures can be applied directly to the covariance matrix. Thus, a shortcut in some of the computational details can be effected. It should be noted, however, that as in the case of factor analyses of the original covariance matrices, the factors one gets are dependent on the particular factoring method.

21.3.2   Computational Equations

21.3.2a   DEFINITION OF NOTATION

h is the oblique transformation matrix.

C is the covariance factor score matrix.

r is the correlation among the simple structure reference axes.
g is a matrix of second-order common factor loadings.
d is a diagonal matrix of second-order specific factor loadings.
$D_{gg'}$ is a diagonal matrix from gg'.

21.3.2b THE EQUATIONS

$$r = h'h \tag{21.3.1}$$

$$C = r^{-1} \tag{21.3.2}$$

$$_0W = C \,_0g \tag{21.3.3}$$

$$_0S = _0g' \,_0W \tag{21.3.4}$$

$$\begin{bmatrix} _0t \\ _1g \end{bmatrix} _0t' = \begin{bmatrix} _0S \\ _0W \end{bmatrix} \tag{21.3.5}$$

$$_1D = D_{_1g \, _1g'} \tag{21.3.6}$$

$$_1C = C - D_C + \,_1D \tag{21.3.7}$$

$$_iD = D_{_ig \, _ig'} \tag{21.3.8}$$

$$_iC = C - D_C + \,_iD \tag{21.3.9}$$

$$_iW = _iC \,_ig \tag{21.3.10}$$

$$_iS = _ig' \,_iW \tag{21.3.11}$$

$$\begin{bmatrix} _it \\ _{i+1}g \end{bmatrix} _it' = \begin{bmatrix} _iS \\ _iW \end{bmatrix} \tag{21.3.12}$$

$$d^2 = D_C - D_{gg'} \tag{21.3.13}$$

21.3.3 Computational Instructions.
One begins with the calculation of the minor product moment of the transformation matrix h, as indicated in Eq. 21.3.1. This we have indicated as r. It is a correlation matrix of the hypothetical variables, defined in such a way that the correlations of the observed variables with these hypothetical variables constitute the simple structure matrix which satisfies the descriptive and analytical criteria discussed in previous chapters.

The next step is to calculate the inverse of the matrix in Eq. 21.3.1 by means of Eq. 21.3.2. This gives the covariance matrix C of the oblique simple structure factor scores. We could proceed now to get a correlation matrix from the matrix of Eq. 21.3.2 by pre- and postmultiplying the resulting matrix C by the reciprocal square root of its diagonals. This will, however, not be necessary in the computational procedure which we outline in the following steps.

Next we require some approximation to the second-order common factor matrix g. This may consist of certain vectors of the matrix in Eq. 21.3.2. In particular, one may start with a single vector and proceed by successive approximations as outlined below. One may begin with the first column of the C matrix of Eq. 21.3.2 or simply a unit vector, and then calculate a vector as in Eq. 21.3.3. This is the C matrix postmultiplied by the $_0g$ vector.

We then calculate the values given by Eq. 21.3.4. This is a general equation for any first approximation involving a single or a specified number of vectors in the g matrix. In any case, the W matrix or vector calculated in Eq. 21.3.3 is premultiplied by the transpose of the g matrix. This then gives a scalar or symmetric matrix, $_0S$, as indicated in Eq. 21.3.4.

Assuming that $_0S$ is a matrix, we next consider Eq. 21.3.5. On the right-hand side of the equation is a type 3 column supervector, as in previous computational procedures. The upper matric element is a symmetric matrix, and the lower matric element is a rectangular matrix. In this case, the upper element is the symmetric matrix calculated in Eq. 21.3.4, and the lower element is the rectangular matrix calculated in Eq. 21.3.3. The left-hand side of this equation is the conventional partial triangular factoring of the matrix. This then gives the lower rectangular element of the supermatrix on the left of Eq. 21.3.5 as the first computed approximation to the g matrix.

If we start with a single vector, we need not go through the partial triangular factoring of Eq. 21.3.5. We would simply have the vector $_0W$ of Eq. 21.3.3 divided by the square root of the scalar quantity $_0S$ in Eq. 21.3.4.

The next step is to calculate a diagonal matrix, as in Eq. 21.3.6, which is a diagonal of the major product moment of the $_1g$ calculated in Eq. 21.3.5.

We then consider Eq. 21.3.7, which is a modification of the C matrix of Eq. 21.3.2 in which its diagonals have been replaced by the diagonal matrix calculated in Eq. 21.3.6.

The general procedure is as indicated in Eqs. 21.3.8–21.3.12.

Equation 21.3.8 indicates a diagonal of the major product moment of the $_ig$ matrix which is the ith approximation to the g matrix or vector.

In Eq. 21.3.9 we substitute in the diagonals of the C matrix the diagonal of Eq. 21.3.8.

We next consider the $_iW$ vector which is the matrix of Eq. 21.3.9 postmultiplied by the current approximation to the g matrix or vector.

We then calculate the minor product of the current g matrix and the matrix or vector calculated in Eq. 21.3.10, as shown in Eq. 21.3.11. This is the ith approximation to the S matrix, comparable to the one in Eq. 21.3.4.

Finally, we calculate the partial triangular factor of the type 3 supervector indicated in the right side of Eq. 21.3.12. This then gives us, as the lower matric element of the type 3 supervector on the left of Eq. 21.3.12, the $i + 1$ approximation to the g matrix. Alternately, we may calculate the $_{i+1}g$ matrix in two stages by first getting the triangular factor $_it'$ of $_iS$, and then postmultiplying the $_iW$ matrix by the inverse of this triangular matrix.

An alternative procedure is to go through a series of iterations for g as a vector, as indicated by Eqs. 21.3.1–21.3.12, until the g vector and the S scalar stabilize. We may then use this g vector as the first approximation to the first vector of a second-order g matrix, and take some vector as the second vector of the zero approximation to the g matrix of width two. We may then continue to go through the cycles indicated by Eqs. 21.3.6–21.3.12 until a g matrix of two vectors stabilizes.

This g matrix is taken as the first two vectors of the zero approximation of a g matrix of width three, and we can then take some third vector as the zero approximation to the third column of the g matrix of width three.

We continue in this fashion until, according to some criterion, a g matrix of sufficient width has been calculated. Then, by means of Eq. 21.3.13, we calculate the diagonal matrix d^2 as the difference between the diagonal of the matrix C in Eq. 21.3.2 and the diagonal of the major product moment of the final g. We have then the g matrix as the matrix of second-order common factors, and the matrix d as the diagonal matrix of specific second-order factors.

It is important before leaving this subject to point out that for a common and specific type of factor analysis to be carried out on the C matrix, the nondiagonal elements of the C matrix of Eq. 21.3.2 must be positive. If we have positive elements in the nondiagonals of this matrix, we cannot, in general, have positive elements in the nondiagonal elements of its inverse, which by definition is the matrix in Eq. 21.3.1.

This means that if the correlations of the simple structure reference axes are positive, then the correlations of the simple structure factor scores must be negative, and vice versa. This fact does not seem to have been pointed out by previous investigators. In many cases, the correlations of the simple structure reference axes tend to be high positive. This is particularly true in the case of personality items, in which the intercorrelations of the items are usually low. Then if one takes the inverse of an oblique matrix which has been used to rotate these to simple structure, this inverse will have appreciable negative factor correlations or covariances in the nondiagonal positions of the matrix C of Eq. 21.3.2. Such a matrix cannot be expressed as the sum of a diagonal matrix and the major product moment of a vector. As a matter of fact, one cannot even express it as the sum of a diagonal and the major product moment of a matrix of real numbers. As Johnson (1958) has pointed out, this leads to a model which must postulate imaginary general factors.

21.3.4 Numerical Example.

The examples in this and the following sections of this chapter are based on the correlation matrix used in previous chapters, and on the corresponding 12×9 data matrix used in Chapters 12 and 19.

The arbitrary factor loading matrix for three factors is the principal axis factor loading matrix calculated in previous chapters. This is repeated for convenient reference in Table 21.3.1.

TABLE 21.3.1   Principal Axis Factor Loading Matrix by Rows for Three Factors

0.717	0.740	0.773	0.556	0.463	0.518	0.640	0.615	0.715
0.493	0.478	0.296	−0.649	−0.744	−0.694	0.080	0.166	−0.034
0.350	0.322	0.406	0.068	0.181	0.188	−0.588	−0.621	−0.369

This matrix was transformed to a simple structure matrix by a matrix h, calculated by the methods of Chapter 17 for oblique transformations. This transformation matrix is given in Table 21.3.2.

TABLE 21.3.2   Simple Structure
Transformation Matrix h

0.504	0.358	0.404
0.524	−0.889	0.079
0.687	0.287	−0.911

Table 21.3.3 gives the minor product moment r of the transformation matrix h.

TABLE 21.3.3   Minor Product Moment r of
Transformation Matrix h

1.0006	−0.0882	−0.3808
−0.0882	1.0009	−0.1871
−0.3808	−0.1871	0.9994

Table 21.3.4 shows the matrix C, which is the inverse of the matrix r and also the covariance matrix of the simple structure factor scores.

TABLE 21.3.4   Matrix $C = r^{-1}$

1.2062	0.1992	0.4969
0.1992	1.0683	0.2759
0.4969	0.2759	1.2416

The second-order common factor vector is given in the first column of Table 21.3.5. For compactness, the second-order specific factor loadings are given in the second column of this table. It is understood, however, that these are the elements of the second-order specific factor diagonal matrix. This table was calculated by means of Eqs. 21.3.3–21.3.13.

TABLE 21.3.5 Second-Order Common
Factor Vector g, and Vector $d1$ of
Second-Order Specific Factor
Diagonal Matrix d

0.604	0.918
0.334	0.978
0.823	0.752

21.4 The First-Order General and Common Factor Loading Matrix

21.4.1 Characteristics of the Method. Having given the factor analysis of the covariance matrix of oblique factor scores, which yields a matrix of second-order common and specific factor loadings, we are now ready to calculate a factor loading matrix which includes both one or more general factors, and rescaled simple structure common factors. We may now obtain a supermatrix in which the one or more vectors in the first submatrix may be interpreted as general factors and those in the second submatrix as common factors. These common simple structure factors, however, will not be quite the same as those in the oblique solution. They will be proportional to them, and the proportionality factors will be precisely the corresponding elements from the specific factor loadings for the second-order analysis. The one or more general factor loading vectors will be linear combinations of the oblique simple structure factor loading vectors, and the matrix of coefficients for these linear combinations will be precisely the g matrix for the second-order common factors calculated in the previous section.

21.4.2 Computational Equations

21.4.2a DEFINITION OF NOTATION

a is the arbitrary factor loading matrix.

h is the oblique transformation matrix.

b is the simple structure factor loading matrix.

g is the second-order factor loading matrix.

d is the diagonal matrix of second-order specific factor loadings.

$_gb$ is the first-order general factor loading submatrix.

$_db$ is the first-order rescaled simple structure factor matrix.

21.4.2b THE EQUATIONS

$$b = ah \qquad (21.4.1)$$

$$_gb = bg \qquad (21.4.2)$$

$$_db = bd \qquad (21.4.3)$$

$$B = (_gb, \; _db) \qquad (21.4.4)$$

21.4.3 Computational Instructions. The procedure for calculating the first-order general and simple structure common factors from the second-order common and specific factors is simple.

We begin with the computations in Eq. 21.4.1. This indicates the product of the arbitrary factor loading matrix a postmultiplied by the oblique transformation matrix h, to give the simple structure oblique factor loading matrix b. As a matter of fact, this matrix will usually be available in the course of the computations for the oblique transformation matrix. If the binary hypothesis matrix procedure of Chapter 17 is used for calculating the oblique transformation matrix, one usually also calculates the oblique factor loading matrix.

Having given the simple structure oblique factor loading matrix, we then calculate the general factor loading submatrix as indicated in Eq. 21.4.2. This is obtained by postmultiplying the simple structure factor loading matrix of Eq. 21.4.1 by the g factor loading matrix or vector as calculated in the previous section.

The procedure for calculating the rescaled simple structure factor submatrix is indicated in Eq. 21.4.3. Here we postmultiply the matrix of Eq. 21.4.1 by the square root of the diagonal matrix of Eq. 21.3.13. This is the simple structure factor loading matrix postmultiplied by a scaling diagonal matrix of the specific factor loadings from the second-order factor analysis.

TABLE 21.4.1   Matrix b of Simple
Structure Factors

0.860	−0.081	0.010
0.845	−0.068	0.043
0.824	0.130	−0.034
−0.013	0.796	0.111
−0.032	0.879	−0.037
0.027	0.856	−0.017
−0.039	−0.011	0.801
−0.030	−0.106	0.827
0.089	0.180	0.622

The complete simple structure factor loading matrix, in terms of the general factor loading vectors and the scaled simple structure factor loading matrix, is indicated in Eq. 21.4.4. Here we use the matrices of Eqs. 21.4.2 and 21.4.3 as the elements of the supermatrix B, to indicate the augmented simple structure factor loading matrix.

21.4.4 Numerical Example. Table 21.4.1 gives the simple structure matrix b obtained by multiplying the factor loading matrix of Table 21.3.1 by the transformation matrix of Table 21.3.2.

The first column in the supermatrix of Table 21.4.2 gives the first-order general factor vector. The remaining three columns give the rescaled simple structure factor vectors. This table was calculated by means of Eqs. 21.4.2. and 21.4.3.

TABLE 21.4.2 Supermatrix of First-Order General
Factor Vector, and First-Order Rescaled
Simple Structure Factors

0.500	0.789	−0.079	0.007
0.523	0.775	−0.066	0.033
0.512	0.756	0.127	−0.026
0.349	−0.012	0.778	0.084
0.244	−0.030	0.860	−0.028
0.288	0.024	0.838	−0.013
0.631	−0.036	−0.011	0.602
0.627	−0.027	−0.103	0.622
0.626	0.082	0.176	0.468

21.5 The First-Order General and Common Factor Score Matrix

21.5.1 Characteristics of the Method. We may now calculate a factor score supermatrix corresponding to the factor loading supermatrix whose computations we have just discussed. The first submatrix of this supermatrix will consist of the general factor scores and the second submatrix of the simple structure common factor scores. When this factor score supermatrix is postmultiplied by the transpose of the factor loading supermatrix of the previous section, it yields the same approximation to the data matrix as the arbitrary factor score matrix postmultiplied by the transpose of the arbitrary factor loading matrix. The transformation matrix which is used to transform the arbitrary factor loading matrix to the factor loading supermatrix is precisely the same as the one used to transform the arbitrary factor score matrix to the factor score supermatrix. Furthermore, this matrix is orthonormal. It should be noted, however, that it is horizontal rather than square.

The number of rows is equal to the number of rows in the arbitrary factor matrix, but the number of columns is equal to the number of general factors plus the number of arbitrary factors.

As indicated previously, it is not necessary to calculate the factor loading supermatrix before calculating the factor score supermatrix. If one has already calculated the g and the diagonal matrices from the covariance matrix of oblique factor scores, one may calculate the factor score supermatrix directly. However, the factor score supermatrix is not a basic matrix, and therefore contains redundant information. This is because it is calculated as a major product of matrices, namely, the arbitrary factor score matrix and the horizontal transformation matrix.

21.5.2   Computational Equations

21.5.2a   DEFINITION OF NOTATION
  R is the correlation matrix.
  L is an arbitrary matrix of the order of the factor loading matrix.
  Z is the data matrix.
  $_gU$ is the general factor score matrix.
  $_dU$ is the simple structure common factor score matrix.

21.5.2b   THE EQUATIONS

$$W = RL \tag{21.5.1}$$

$$S = L'W \tag{21.5.2}$$

$$\begin{bmatrix} t \\ M \end{bmatrix} t' = \begin{bmatrix} S \\ L \end{bmatrix} \tag{21.5.3}$$

$$_gh = hg \tag{21.5.4}$$

$$_dh = hd \tag{21.5.5}$$

$$_gM = M\,_gh \tag{21.5.6}$$

$$_dM = M\,_dh \tag{21.5.7}$$

$$_gU = Z\,_gM \tag{21.5.8}$$

$$_dU = Z\,_dM \tag{21.5.9}$$

21.5.3   Computational Instructions. We begin with the computations indicated in Eq. 21.5.1. Some explanation is required here. We have on the right of Eq. 21.5.1 the correlation matrix postmultiplied by a matrix L. In general, this L matrix is the arbitrary matrix used to calculate an arbitrary factor loading matrix by means of the rank reduction formula. This has been discussed in Chapter 20. In particular, it may be the binary grouping matrix for the multiple group method or the matrix of sign vectors for the centroid method. It may also be the vertical basic orthonormal of the first m eigenvectors of the correlation matrix R.

In any case, the next step is as indicated in Eq. 21.5.2. This is the matrix of Eq. 21.5.1 premultiplied by the transpose of the L matrix to give a symmetric matrix S. It will be recognized as the triple product in the rank reduction equation.

We next consider a type 3 supervector with the symmetric matrix of Eq. 21.5.2 as the upper element and the L matrix as the lower element, as indicated on the right of Eq. 21.5.3. The left side of this equation indicates the now-familiar partial triangular factoring of the second-order column type 3 supervector. We note that the lower element of this type 3 supervector on the left of Eq. 21.5.3 has been designated as a matrix M.

Next we calculate the matrix indicated in Eq. 21.5.4. This is the oblique transformation matrix, postmultiplied by the g matrix obtained as indicated in Section 21.3.

Equation 21.5.5 shows the h matrix, postmultiplied by the d matrix calculated in Section 21.3.

Next we calculate Eq. 21.5.6. This is the matrix M on the left of Eq. 21.5.3, postmultiplied by the matrix calculated in Eq. 21.5.4.

We then calculate the matrix of Eq. 21.5.7 which is the matrix M on the left of Eq. 21.5.3, postmultiplied by the matrix calculated in Eq. 21.5.5.

The two matrices calculated in Eqs. 21.5.6 and 21.5.7 are, respectively, the matrices required to transform the data matrix to the submatrix of general factor scores and the submatrix of simple structure factor scores. These computations are indicated, respectively, in Eqs. 21.5.8 and 21.5.9.

Throughout Eqs. 21.5.4–21.5.9 we have used the prescripts g and d to refer to those matrices which correspond, respectively, to computations involving the general factors, and to computations involving the simple structure common factors.

21.5.4 Numerical Example.
The first column of Table 21.5.1. gives the general factor score vector for the data matrix used in the examples of Chapters 12, 19, and 20. The last three columns give the rescaled simple structure factor score vectors. This table was calculated by Eqs. 21.5.1–21.5.9.

21.6 Mathematical Proofs

21.6.1 The Factor Score Covariance Matrix, and the Second-Order Common and Specific Factor Loadings

Suppose we have given an arbitrary factor loading matrix a, and an oblique transformation matrix h, so that for the simple structure factor loading matrix

TABLE 21.5.1   Supermatrix of First-Order General
Factor Scores, and Rescaled First-Order Simple
Structure Factor Scores

0.328	0.096	0.739	0.012
0.307	0.677	−0.474	0.022
0.451	−0.326	−0.198	0.669
−0.206	−0.308	−0.114	0.032
−0.269	−0.278	−0.183	−0.022
−0.226	−0.220	−0.120	−0.037
−0.149	0.086	−0.039	−0.176
−0.165	0.192	−0.050	−0.250
−0.075	0.008	−0.050	−0.058
−0.003	0.067	0.143	−0.088
0.065	0.034	0.148	−0.007
−0.053	−0.032	0.195	−0.090

we have

$$b = ah \tag{21.6.1}$$

Assume that

$$a = RLt'^{-1} \tag{21.6.2}$$

where

$$tt' = L'RL \tag{21.6.3}$$

and where L is an arbitrary multiplier of the order of a. In particular, it may be a centroid sign matrix, a binary hypothesis matrix, or a basic structure factor loading matrix. In any case, if the factor score matrix is given by

$$Y = ZLt'^{-1} \tag{21.6.4}$$

then, as we have shown in Chapter 20,

$$Y'Y = I \tag{21.6.5}$$

that is, the factor scores are uncorrelated. We consider the approximation equation

$$E = Z - Ya' \tag{21.6.6}$$

where now because of Eqs. 21.6.2–21.6.4, Eq. 21.6.6 is the rank reduction form.

If now we let

$$U = Yh'^{-1} \tag{21.6.7}$$

we see from Eqs. 21.6.1 and 21.6.7 that

$$Ub' = Ya' \tag{21.6.8}$$

or from Eqs. 21.6.6 and 21.6.8,

$$E = Z - Ub'$$ (21.6.9)

so that Ya' and Ub' give the identical approximation to Z. If we let C_U be the covariance of U and

$$r = h'h$$ (21.6.10)

then from Eqs. 21.6.5, 21.6.7, and 21.6.10,

$$C_U = r^{-1}$$ (21.6.11)

21.6.1a FACTORING THE COVARIANCE MATRIX OF FACTOR SCORES

Let us consider now

$$C_U - (gg' + d^2) = \varepsilon$$ (21.6.12)

where d is diagonal, g is a vector or vertical matrix, and $tr\ \varepsilon'\varepsilon$ is sufficiently small. To solve for d and g we may write from Eq. 21.6.12,

$$(C - D_c + D_{gg'})Q = Q\delta$$ (21.6.13)

where Q and δ are the basic structure factors of the expression in parentheses and where

$$g = Q\delta^{1/2}$$ (21.6.14)

and

$$d^2 = D_c - D_{gg'}$$ (21.6.15)

Equation 21.6.14 may be solved for iteratively as follows. Assume the first approximation to d to be 0 and let

$$_1g = C_0 g\ _0t'^{-1}$$ (21.6.16)

where

$$_0t\ _0t' = _0g'C_0g$$ (21.6.17)

and $_0g$ is some approximation to g. Then

$$_1D = D_{_1g\ _1g'}$$ (21.6.18)

and

$$_1C = C - D_c + _1D$$ (21.6.19)

In general,

$$_iC = C - D_c + _iD$$ (21.6.20)

$$_iS = _ig'\ _iC\ _ig$$ (21.6.21)

$$_it\ _it' = _iS$$ (21.6.22)

$$_{i+1}g = _iC\ _ig\ _it'^{-1}$$ (21.6.23)

We may stabilize on $tr\ _iS$.

It should be noted that if, in Eq. 21.6.12, $\varepsilon = 0$, we shall have for r,

$$r = \left[d^{-2} - \frac{d^{-2}gg'd^{-2}}{1 + g'd^{-2}g} \right] \tag{21.6.24}$$

We note that Eq. 21.6.12 implies a communality type factoring. If this can be done from Eq. 21.6.16, we see that r will not yield to the communality factoring. In general, if C_U has positive nondiagonals, r will have negative, and vice versa.

21.6.2   The First-Order General and Common Factor Loading Matrix

Assume that

$$(h'h)^{-1} = gg' + d^2 \tag{21.6.25}$$

where g is a vector or vertical matrix. Let

$$\psi' = h(g, d) \tag{21.6.26}$$

and

$$B = a\psi' \tag{21.6.27}$$

From Eq. 21.6.26,

$$\psi'\psi = h(gg' + d^2)h' \tag{21.6.28}$$

From Eqs. 21.6.25 and 21.6.28,

$$\psi'\psi = h(h'h)^{-1}h' \tag{21.6.29}$$

or

$$\psi'\psi = I \tag{21.6.30}$$

From Eqs. 21.6.27 and 21.6.30,

$$BB' = aa' \tag{21.6.31}$$

Hence the major product moments of B and a yield the same approximation to the correlation matrix.

From Eqs. 21.6.26 and 21.6.27,

$$B = ah(g, d) \tag{21.6.32}$$

If we let

$$b = ah \tag{21.6.33}$$

then

$$B = (bg, bd) \tag{21.6.34}$$

From Eq. 21.6.34,

$$BB' = bgg'b' + bd^2b' \tag{21.6.35}$$

It is interesting to note that the factors of B cannot, in general, be rank reduction factors if those of a are. For if g is of order $m \times s$, and d is of order m, then B will have $m \times s$ factors. Consider

$$E = R - BB' \tag{21.6.36}$$

and assume R of rank and order n. If the vectors of B were of rank reduction form, E would be of rank $n - m - s$. From Eq. 21.6.31, we know that E is of rank $n - m$.

21.6.3 The First-Order General and Common Factor Score Matrix

Given the arbitrary factor score matrix

$$Y = ZLt'^{-1} \tag{21.6.37}$$

where L is an arbitrary matrix as in Eq. 21.6.2, and

$$tt' = L'RL \tag{21.6.38}$$

Assume the factor loading matrix

$$a = RLt'^{-1} \tag{21.6.39}$$

Then

$$E = Z - Ya' \tag{21.6.40}$$

is rank reduction in form.

Let

$$b = ah \tag{21.6.41}$$

$$r = h'h \tag{21.6.42}$$

$$C = r^{-1} \tag{21.6.43}$$

$$gg' + d^2 = C \tag{21.6.44}$$

and

$$\psi' = h(g, d) \tag{21.6.45}$$

Consider now

$$U = Y\psi' \tag{21.6.46}$$

$$B = a\psi' \tag{21.6.47}$$

From Eqs. 21.6.41–21.6.47,

$$UB' = Ya' \tag{21.6.48}$$

From Eqs. 21.6.37, 21.6.45, and 21.6.46,

$$U = ZLt'^{-1}h(g, d) \tag{21.6.49}$$

Let

$$M = Lt'^{-1} \tag{21.6.50}$$

$$_gh = hg \tag{21.6.51}$$

$$_dh = hd \tag{21.6.52}$$

$$U = (_gU, {}_dU) \tag{21.6.53}$$

$$_gM = M {}_gh \tag{21.6.54}$$

$$_dM = M {}_dh \tag{21.6.55}$$

From Eqs. 21.6.49–21.6.55,

$$_gU = Z_g M \tag{21.6.56}$$

$$_dU = Z_d M \tag{21.6.57}$$

Again we see that the factor score vectors of U cannot be rank reduction vectors.

In particular, we note that if

$$L = Q\Delta \tag{21.6.58}$$

then M in Eq. 21.6.50 becomes

$$M = Q\Delta^{-1} \tag{21.6.59}$$

This follows if we indicate the basic structure of R by

$$R = Q\Delta^2 Q' \tag{21.6.60}$$

From Eqs. 21.6.38, 21.6.58, and 21.6.60,

$$tt' = \Delta^4 \tag{21.6.61}$$

and

$$t'^{-1} = \Delta^{-2} \tag{21.6.62}$$

From Eqs. 21.6.58 and 21.6.62 in Eq. 21.6.50, we get Eq. 21.6.59.

Chapter 22

Factor Analysis
and the Binary Data Matrix

22.1 Introduction

In the methods of factor analysis which we have discussed in previous chapters, no particular attention has been given to the types of measures which went into the original data matrix. We did, in the models involving changes in scale and origin, consider the effect of these alterations on the factor analytic solutions. The problem of natural versus arbitrary scale and origin has been discussed in Chapters 13 and 15. In this chapter we shall consider a very special kind of data matrix, frequently used in the social sciences, for which the scale and origin are predetermined. This is the *binary data matrix*, or the data matrix in which each element is either 1 or 0.

Variables for which the measures are in terms of either 1 or 0 are sometimes called *categorical variables*. They have also been called *qualitative variables* and *dichotomous variables*. A more appropriate designation for the type of measures which result in either a 0 or 1 value is probably *binary variable*.

We shall see that the binary variable and the binary data matrix in which it is found present some special problems with respect to factor analysis. The fact that the variables can take only one of two values places certain restrictions on the results we can expect to obtain. Although this type of data matrix can be found in most scientific disciplines, it is probably in the field of psychological measurement that most attention has been given to the properties of binary measures. Over the years, many investigators in the areas of factor analysis and test theory have been interested in the implications of variation in item difficulty or preference for the various models and objectives with which they were concerned.

Item difficulty or preference refers to the number of individuals or entities receiving scores of 1 on a particular binary variable. In the case of psychological tests, we get this kind of matrix when a person is assigned a score of 1 if he answers an item in a prespecified way, and a score of 0 if he does not.

Ferguson (1941) was one of the first to call attention to the fact that the correlations among objective tests are influenced by the dispersions of item preferences. It has long been known that only if two binary variables have equal preference values is it possible to have a correlation of 1 between the two. Some investigators have insisted that the ideal test for most purposes is one in which all of the items are of equal difficulty or preference value. Others have insisted that in order to get adequate discrimination, the dispersion of item difficulty should be large. Some who have been concerned with the effect of item difficulty on correlation have proposed that when matrices of intercorrelations from binary variables are required, tetrachoric correlations should be used to neutralize the influence of item difficulty or preference. This proposal seems to be based on the notion that variation in item difficulty is a sort of experimental nuisance which creeps into our data, and that in some way the data should be purged of this impurity.

Perhaps one of the first developments which explicitly recognized the fundamental role of variation in item preference for measurement theory is the work of Guttman (1950) on scaling theory. His concept of a perfectly scalable set of items was based on the notion that all persons marking an item with a given preference value should also mark all items of greater preference value. He developed his coefficient of reproducibility to indicate to what extent a set of items satsified this condition. From this concept he developed the notion of the simplex, which he extended to more general types of data such as those encountered in learning experiments.

The work of Edwards (1957), which has concerned itself with the concept of social desirability in personality type items, is also intimately concerned with variation in item preference values, and the implications of this variation on attempts to measure distinct personality traits. The general notion is that items should be cast in forced choice format so that items of equal preference value are paired together.

In general, the phenomenon of variation in item preference values, and its implications for measurement theory, have not been given the systematic treatment they deserve. Certainly one may not disregard this variation as a sort of nuisance phenomenon to be done away with by various tricks or gimmicks in the same way that one attempts to eliminate experimental error. If one has a perfectly homogeneous set of items with perfect retest reliability, one such item is of just as much value for measurement purposes as the entire set, if all items are of exactly equal difficulty or preference value. The entire set will separate any particular group into only two parts, since an individual can have only one of two scores.

The notion that all items in a set should be of equal difficulty or preference value is not logically or scientifically sound. A perfectly homogeneous and perfectly reliable set of items, which is also useful for discrimination among members of a group at a number of different levels, must have variation in item preference value. Such a set results in what we may call the *simplex binary matrix.* This is a special case of the binary data matrix. In this case, all persons scoring 1 on an item of a given preference value also score 1 on all items of greater preference value.

We now seem to have a paradox. If we define a perfectly homogeneous, perfectly reliable, and optimally discriminating set of items in this way, the rank of the intercorrelation matrix of the items cannot possibly be 1. As a matter of fact, if we have a binary matrix of the Guttman type, it is fairly easy to show that the rank of this matrix is exactly equal to the number of distinct preference or difficulty values present in the set. That is, its rank must be equal to the number of distinct values in the vector of column sums of this type of binary data matrix.

This point has been made in much of Guttman's work. He seems to have believed that a set of items which has a unique difficulty value for each item will yield a correlation matrix which can have at most a rank two less than its order, no matter how the diagonals are chosen. This ties in the rank of a binary data matrix with the communality concept.

DuBois (1960) has shown that if a correlation matrix is calculated from a Guttman type binary matrix, this correlation matrix can have its diagonal values altered in such a way that the rank of the reduced matrix is not greater than one half the number of attributes. That is, one may select communalities for at least one half of the variables in such a way that the rank of the adjusted matrix is no greater than one half the number of items. The problem of determining diagonal values so as to reduce the rank of the matrix is part of the currently rather ill-defined and controversial communality problem to which we have alluded from time to time in this book. We may choose to formulate a model in which varying levels of difficulty or preference for the variables in the data matrix are regarded as being interpretable as distinct dimensions or factors. However, this leads us into more fundamental philosophical difficulties.

It might be argued that the problems caused by variations in item preferences are due to attempts to measure attributes in terms of binary measures, when ideally we should strive for some sort of continuous measure. It is doubtful that this can be a fruitful point of view. If we press it far enough, we should have to abandon most of the work in both the practice and theory of psychological measurement since the beginning of objective instruments.

Just because much time and money have already been spent on an approach is not, of course, reason enough to preserve it. It is probable, however, that the problem goes much deeper than this, and that we require more adequate models to reconcile the concept of variation in item preference or difficulty, and dimensionality. We cannot resort to tetrachoric correlations for item intercorrelations of unequal preference value when we know that this phenomenon is an essential characteristic of the attributes which we are measuring. We know that for all psychological test scores which are obtained from

0-1 scoring of the constituent items, we are dealing with unweighted sums of binary variables. Therefore, the properties of the binary variables are embedded in all test measures which are sums of binary measures.

It would seem, then, that one useful approach might be to embrace wholeheartedly the preference dispersion phenomenon, and to have some systematic devices for taking it into account in the factor models. One approach to the problem would appear to be the assumption of a latent simplex for a given binary data matrix. By statistical or computational procedures, we might then segregate the simplex from the part of the dimensionality of the set which was not due to dispersion of item preferences.

Let us therefore assume that we have a binary data matrix. We may let the columns of this matrix represent individual items and the rows represent persons. The items may be personality type items, or they may be any kind of objective test items. Or they may be of a much more general nature, and may apply to any particular scientific discipline in which we have a large number of attributes or variables which may be regarded to be either present or absent in the entities involved in the experiment.

Since the advent of high-speed computers, we are now free to conduct factor analyses on matrices of item scores, and to extend the techniques for determining dimensionalities to sets of items themselves. We may now test much more fully the rational and *a priori* approaches which have been used in the past for developing sets of homogeneous items. Since we know that the dimensionality of a system will be accounted for in part by the dispersion of item preferences, we may consider procedures for segregating this part of the dimensionality. We may call the simplex of the system that part which is due to variation in item preferences or, in general, to variation in the number of unit elements in each column of the binary data matrix.

We have indicated that the simplex and the binary data matrix problem are very closely related to the communality problem. In Section 22.7.4 we present a mathematical development of a general case for which the simplex or binary data matrix is a special case. First we consider a symmetric permutation of rows and columns of a covariance matrix. We also consider a symmetric partitioning by rows and columns so that we get a second-order supermatrix. This partitioning and permutation will also apply to the inverse of the matrix. We may then investigate what permutation and partitioning is required to make one of the matric diagonal elements of the inverse a diagonal matrix of maximum order. We show that by appropriate alteration of the corresponding diagonal elements of the covariance matrix, its rank is reduced by exactly the order of this diagonal submatrix. The results of DuBois (1960) for the simplex covariance matrix are a special case.

In what follows we shall consider a solution for eliminating or partialing out that part of the dimensionality which is due to dispersion of item preference from the data matrix.

22.2 Kinds of Solutions for Eliminating or Partialing Out the Simplex

We shall discuss three kinds of approaches to the elimination of the simplex phenomenon from the data matrix in which the elements are binary measures. Only the first of these will be outlined in detail, since insufficient experience is available with the other two.

22.2.1 The Least Square Simplex Data Matrix Solution.

The first method we shall consider assumes that we construct a binary simplex or Guttman type data matrix which will satisfy certain restrictions. These may be that the sums of rows or the sums of columns of the simplex data matrix will be the same as for the experimental binary matrix. In general, we cannot make both sums of rows and sums of columns the same, unless the data matrix itself is precisely a simplex data matrix. This will not, in general, be the case for experimental data.

The general approach, then, is to apply a least square transformation to this hypothetical simplex matrix which in the least square sense best approximates the observed data matrix. From here we proceed to find a residual matrix and then a residual covariance matrix. This residual covariance matrix will presumably be freed from the effects of item dispersion, and therefore, if factors are present other than those due to the dispersion of item preferences, this may be determined by factoring the residual covariance or residual correlation matrix.

22.2.2 The Least Square Simplex Covariance Matrix Solution.

We may not insist that the best least square approximation of a simplex matrix to the observed binary data matrix be obtained. Rather, we may assume that we have the covariance matrix for the observed binary data matrix, and that we wish to find the simplex covariance matrix which is the best least square approximation to the observed covariance matrix. As will be shown, the number of parameters in this simplex covariance matrix will be equal to the order of the covariance matrix. The problem, then, is to determine these parameters in such a way that we get a best least square approximation to the observed covariance matrix.

22.2.3 Computational Short Cut for the Simplex Covariance Matrix Solution.

Instead of getting a least square solution, as in the previous method, we may get a simplex covariance matrix which is a sufficiently close approximation to the observed covariance matrix but which is much simpler to calculate. Again, as in the previous case, this simplex matrix will be a function of only n parameters, where n is the number of variables.

22.3 The Least Square Simplex Data Matrix

22.3.1 Characteristics of the Method. We have already indicated in a general way how we may attempt to find some transformation of a binary simplex matrix which will yield a least square approximation to the observed binary matrix. We have indicated that we might then take the difference between these two matrices and consider that this residual matrix was free from the effects of the dispersion of item preferences. The covariance matrix of the residual matrix would next be factored to indicate dimensions or factors distinct from these difficulty factors.

The model requires the construction of a simplex binary data matrix, and involves the minor product of this matrix with the observed binary data matrix. We must also get the covariance matrix of the data matrix which requires the product moment of a binary matrix.

This type of calculation is simple in that it is essentially a counting operation in which the number of 1's in each column of the data matrix, and the number of 1's common to all pairs of two columns, are determined. However, such calculations are not efficient on the high-speed computers when set up as a standard matrix multiplication routine. Each number consists of either a 0 or a 1, which for the binary type computers uses a single bit in a word. The number of bits in a word for these computers is, of course, from 35 to 45 or more, depending on the particular computer. It is obvious, therefore, that the conventional matrix multiplication procedure does not use efficiently the capacity of the computer.

22.3.2 Computational Equations

22.3.2a DEFINITION OF NOTATION

N is the number of entities.

M is the binary data matrix.

L is the simplex binary matrix.

B is N^2 times the covariance matrix for the binary data matrix.

K is N^2 times the covariance matrix between the data matrix and the simplex binary matrix.

T is a matrix defined in Section 22.7.1, Eq. 22.7.20.

ρ is the correlation matrix of the binary data matrix after removal of the simplex.

22.3.2b THE EQUATIONS

$$B = NM'M - (M'1)(1'M) \tag{22.3.1}$$

$$K = NM'L - (M'1)(1'L) \tag{22.3.2}$$

$$W = KT^{-1} \tag{22.3.3}$$

$$D1 = \left[\frac{L'1}{N}\right] T^{-1} \tag{22.3.4}$$

$$H = (WD^{-1})W' \tag{22.3.5}$$

$$F = H + \left[\frac{K_{.1}}{\sqrt{1 - P_1}}\right] \left[\frac{K_{.1}'}{\sqrt{1 - P_1}}\right] \tag{22.3.6}$$

$$E = N^2 B - F \tag{22.3.7}$$

$$\rho = D_E^{-1/2} E D_E^{-1/2} \tag{22.3.8}$$

22.3.3 Computational Instructions. We begin with the data matrix of binary measures which we call M. In Eq. 22.3.1 we indicate the calculation of N^2 times the covariance matrix. This is indicated by B.

Next we require the covariance matrix of the observed binary data matrix with the hypothetical simplex binary matrix. This is N^2 times the covariance matrix, and is indicated in Eq. 22.3.2. We may regard each column vector of the simplex binary matrix as a type 1 second-order supervector, in which the upper and lower elements are, respectively, null and unit vectors. The unit subvectors are then of successively lower order from left to right. The computations for the minor product would then proceed as follows. The first vector of the L matrix has the effect of isolating that part of the M matrix below the null subvector of the first column of L. The column sums of this isolated submatrix would then be the first column of elements of the minor product in the first term on the right of Eq. 22.3.2. Similarly, for successive columns of this minor product we would have a vector of column sums of the submatrix of M isolated by the corresponding vector of L. It will be noted that the second term on the right of Eq. 22.3.2 is the major product of vectors. The prefactor is simply the vector of column sums of the M matrix, and the postfactor is the row vector of column sums of the L matrix. If, in particular, the L matrix had been selected in such a way that its column sums would satisfy certain prespecified conditions, as indicated in Section 22.7.1, then these would already be available.

The next step is to calculate the W matrix of Eq. 22.3.3. This is the matrix of Eq. 22.3.2 postmultiplied by the inverse of a T matrix as defined in Section 22.7.1, Eq. 22.7.20. This inverse is a lower triangular matrix in which the diagonal elements are all 1's, the elements below and paralleling the diagonal are all -1's, and all remaining elements are 0. It is seen, therefore, that this product is obtained by subtracting each succeeding column of K from the preceding column, except for the last column of W which is the last column of K.

We next calculate the vector indicated in Eq. 22.3.4. This is shown as the vector form of a diagonal matrix. The right-hand side of this equation shows that first we calculate a vector whose elements are the column sums of L divided by N. This is a vector of the proportion of entities scoring 1 on each of the attributes in the hypothetical L matrix. This vector is then post-multiplied by the inverse of the T matrix, which simply amounts to subtracting each element of the vector in brackets from the preceding one, except for the last element of D which is simply the last element of the vector in brackets.

The next computation is indicated in Eq. 22.3.5. Here we first postmultiply the W matrix calculated in Eq. 22.3.3 by the inverse of the diagonal matrix whose elements were calculated in Eq. 22.3.4. This product is then post-multiplied by the transpose of the W matrix of Eq. 22.3.3.

We then calculate the matrix given by Eq. 22.3.6. This is the sum of the matrix of Eq. 22.3.5 and the major product moment of a vector obtained by dividing the first column of the matrix K, calculated in Eq. 22.3.2, by the scalar $\sqrt{1 - P_1}$, where P_1 is the proportion of individuals getting a score of 1 for the first column of the M matrix.

We next calculate the matrix indicated in Eq. 22.3.7, which is designated E. This is obtained by multiplying the B matrix of Eq. 22.3.1 by N^2, and subtracting from this the F matrix of Eq. 22.3.6. The difference matrix is proportional to the residual covariance matrix after the simplex has been partialed out. The proportionality factor is N^4.

The correlation matrix corresponding to the residual matrix is indicated in Eq. 22.3.8. This is obtained in the usual manner by pre- and postmultiplying the matrix E of Eq. 22.3.7 by a diagonal which is the reciprocal square root of the diagonal of E.

22.3.4   Numerical Example.   We begin with a binary data matrix whose transpose is given in Table 22.3.1. We take as suitable ρ values of a three-column simplex, the numbers 0.9, 0.7, and 0.5 (see Eq. 22.7.42).

TABLE 22.3.1   Transpose of Binary Data Matrix

1.	1.	1.	1.	1.	1.	1.	1.	1.	1.
1.	1.	1.	1.	1.	0.	1.	1.	0.	0.
1.	1.	1.	0.	1.	1.	0.	0.	1.	0.
1.	1.	1.	1.	0.	1.	0.	0.	0.	0.

Table 22.3.2 gives the data matrix with rows permuted so that the row sums are in descending order of magnitude from the top down.

Table 22.3.3 shows the covariance matrix of the binary data matrix multiplied by a factor of N, or 10.

Table 22.3.4 gives the covariance matrix of the hypothesized simplex with the data matrix, multiplied by 10.

Table 22.3.5 gives the residual covariance matrix multiplied by 10. This matrix is independent of the simplex.

Table 22.3.6 gives the final correlation matrix of the data matrix freed from the influence of the simplex.

TABLE 22.3.2
Binary Data Matrix
Permuted by Rows

1.	1.	1.	1.
1.	1.	1.	1.
1.	1.	1.	1.
1.	1.	0.	1.
1.	1.	1.	0.
1.	0.	1.	1.
1.	1.	0.	0.
1.	1.	0.	0.
1.	0.	1.	0.
0.	0.	0.	0.

TABLE 22.3.3   Covariance Matrix of Binary Data Matrix
Times N

0.9000	0.7000	0.6000	0.5000
0.7000	2.1000	−0.2000	0.5000
0.6000	−0.2000	2.4000	1.0000
0.5000	0.5000	1.0000	2.5000

TABLE 22.3.4   Covariance Matrix of Simplex with
Binary Data Matrix Times N

0.2000	−0.4000	−0.2000	−1.0000
0.2000	−0.4000	−0.2000	0.0000
0.5000	1.5000	1.0000	1.5000

TABLE 22.3.5   Residual Covariance Matrix Times N

0.9000	0.7000	0.6000	0.5000
0.7000	1.1000	0.8000	1.0000
0.6000	0.8000	0.6000	0.7000
0.5000	1.0000	0.7000	1.2000

TABLE 22.3.6   Correlation Matrix Independent
of Simplex

−1.0000	−0.0002	−0.0001	−0.0002
−0.0002	1.0000	−0.7454	−0.4385
0.0000	−0.7454	1.0000	0.1961
−0.0004	−0.4385	0.1961	1.0000

22.4   The Least Square Simplex Covariance Matrix

22.4.1   Characteristics of the Method.   We have seen in the previous method that we must hypothesize a simplex binary matrix which we wish to partial out of the observed binary data matrix. Then, for the solution we shall now develop, we go directly to the covariance matrix of the data matrix, and find the best-fitting simplex covariance matrix in the least square sense. The solution is somewhat involved computationally, and probably is not practical for an extremely large number of binary variables. It requires some *a priori* ordering of the variables, presumably on the basis of item difficulty or preference, so that the most preferred items come first. This type of solution, as all solutions attempting to partial out the simplex, presents a special problem. The problem arises from the fact that in most practical situations we can arbitrarily reverse the order of the variables so that we may assign 1's to what were zeros, and zeros to what were 1's. In the case of personality or inventory type items, we may reverse the scoring for any dichotomously scored item. For example, we may score a "yes" response either 0 or 1, as we choose.

Because of this arbitrariness, we may require a preliminary type of centroid or principal axis analysis applied to the correlation matrix of the binary variables. This analysis would result in establishing the direction or signs of each of the variables, in that the first centroid or principal axis vector would have negative elements for those variables which should have their signs reversed. As a matter of fact, this is a reasonable method for determining which of two alternative responses should be scored 1, if it is desired to remove the simplex from a binary data matrix.

Assuming that some such preliminary analysis has been conducted, we can then order the variables on the basis of the number of 1 scores for each variable. This simply means that for those variables which had their signs changed, the number of zeros in the original scoring becomes the number of 1's in the new scoring.

In any case, we assume that some preliminary operations have been carried out to establish the direction and ordering of the variables. The computational procedure for getting the best least square approximation to such a matrix could proceed in one of several different ways. We could attempt to find that simplex matrix which is the least square approximation to the experimental covariance matrix. Or we may consider some convenient transformation of the experimental covariance matrix, and find the least square simplex approximation to this transformation. In the method outlined here we shall assume that a transformation has been performed upon the experimental covariance matrix, so that if it were in fact a pure simplex type matrix, this transformation would now yield an identity. The problem is then to solve for certain parameters of the transformation matrix such that the transformed matrix will be the least square approximation to an identity matrix.

22.4.2   Computational Equations

22.4.2a   DEFINITION OF NOTATION

M is the binary data matrix.

σ is the covariance matrix of the binary data matrix.

ρ is the correlation matrix of the data matrix with the simplex removed.

22.4.2b   THE EQUATIONS

$$\gamma = \frac{M'M}{N} \tag{22.4.1}$$

$$P = \frac{M'1}{N} \tag{22.4.2}$$

$$\sigma = \gamma - PP' \tag{22.4.3}$$

$$g = T'^{-1}\gamma T^{-1} \tag{22.4.4}$$

$$D^{-1}1 = (g^{(2)})^{-1} D_g 1 \tag{22.4.5}$$

$$C = T'DT - [T'(D1)][(1'D)T] \tag{22.4.6}$$

$$E = \sigma - C \tag{22.4.7}$$

$$\rho = D_E^{-1/2} E D_E^{-1/2} \tag{22.4.8}$$

22.4.3   Computational Instructions. We begin with the matrix of Eq. 22.4.1. This is simply the minor product moment of the binary data matrix divided by N, the number of cases. This is sometimes called a *joint occurrence matrix*.

Next we calculate the vector in Eq. 22.4.2. From the right-hand side we can see that this is a vector of the proportions of individuals getting a score of 1 on each of the items.

In Eq. 22.4.3 we calculate the difference between the matrix γ of Eq.22.4.1 and the major product moment of the vector calculated in Eq. 22.4.2. This should be recognized as the covariance matrix of the binary data matrix. It is on this matrix that a preliminary analysis might now be performed in order to get an approximation to a first principal axis or a first centroid vector. Such a vector would indicate the variables which should have their signs changed. This means that we would exchange zeros for 1's, and vice versa, for those variables which had negative elements in this first factor vector.

On the basis of this procedure we then assume that appropriate permutations of the γ matrix in Eq. 22.4.1, the P vector in Eq. 22.4.2, and the σ matrix of Eq. 22.4.3, are effected. It is not actually necessary to go through the clerical operations of interchanging these rows and columns, so long as some accounting procedure is carried along to indicate the reversal of signs and the appropriate permutation.

The next step is the computation indicated in Eq. 22.4.4 for the g matrix. Here we have the γ matrix of Eq. 22.4.1, with appropriate row and column interchanges and sign changes, post- and premultiplied by the inverses of the T matrix and its transpose. This means that first, a matrix is calculated by subtracting from each column of γ the following column. The last column is the last column of γ. Second, the same procedures are carried out for the rows of this product.

We next calculate the vector of Eq. 22.4.5. This is obtained by first squaring all of the elements of the g matrix of Eq. 22.4.4. Then we get the inverse of this matrix, and multiply it on the right by a vector which is composed of the diagonal elements of the g matrix. This gives us a vector of the inverses of the elements which we shall use in the next equation.

Equation 22.4.6 utilizes the elements whose inverses were found in Eq. 22.4.5. Here the first term on the right of the equation is a pre- and post-multiplication of the diagonal matrix D, whose elements were calculated in Eq. 22.4.5, by T' and T, respectively. The matrix T has been previously defined as a lower triangular matrix in which all the nonzero elements are 1. The first term on the right of Eq. 22.4.6, therefore, gives the type of matrix indicated in Eq. 22.7.56 of Section 22.7.2. The second term, which is subtracted, consists of the major product moment of a vector which is obtained by taking a row vector of the D elements whose inverses are calculated in Eq. 22.4.5, and postmultiplying this by the T matrix. From the definition it can be seen that the first element of this vector is the sum of all of the D elements, the second is the sum of all but the first, and so on. The matrix C is the estimate of the covariance of the simplex matrix embedded in the experimental covariance matrix, the σ of Eq. 22.4.3.

In Eq. 22.4.7 we take the difference between the covariance matrix of Eq. 22.4.3 and the matrix of Eq. 22.4.6 to get the residual matrix E.

Equation 22.4.8 is the normalization of the matrix in Eq. 22.4.7, and gives the correlation of the measures in the data matrix freed from the effect of the embedded simplex.

22.5   Computational Short Cut for the Simplex Covariance Matrix

22.5.1   Characteristics of the Method. In this model also, we find certain parameters corresponding to distinct preference values which may be regarded as typical of the embedded simplex. As we have seen in the previous method, considerable computational work is required to get the inverse of the matrix of squared elements, required in the solution for the parameters of the simplex. We shall formulate a simple rationale to estimate these parameters, requiring fewer computations than the previous method. This method avoids the calculation of an inverse. It requires mainly the minor product moment of the data matrix for the calculation of the simplex parameters.

22.5.2   Computational Equations

22.5.2a   DEFINITION OF NOTATION

M is the binary data matrix.

σ is the covariance matrix of the binary data matrix.

ρ is the correlation matrix of the data matrix with the simplex removed.

22.5.2b   THE EQUATIONS

$$\gamma = \frac{M'M}{N} \tag{22.5.1}$$

$$P = \frac{M'1}{N} \tag{22.5.2}$$

$$D_{T1}1 = T1 \tag{22.5.3}$$

$$D1 = D_{T1}^{-1}[T'^{-1}(\gamma 1)] \tag{22.5.4}$$

$$C = T'DT - [T'(D1)][(1'D)T] \tag{22.5.5}$$

$$\sigma = \gamma - PP' \tag{22.5.6}$$

$$E = \sigma - C \tag{22.5.7}$$

$$\rho = D_E^{-1/2}E D_E^{-1/2} \tag{22.5.8}$$

22.5.3   Computational Instructions. In this method we require first the minor product moment of the data matrix, as indicated in Eq. 22.5.1, divided by N, the number of cases, to give a joint occurrence matrix.

We also require the vector of means of the data matrix, as indicated in Eq. 22.5.2. This is a vector of the proportion of persons answering each of the items in the keyed manner.

Next we consider the diagonal matrix indicated in Eq. 22.5.3. This is a T matrix postmultiplied by a unit vector. From the definition of the T matrix, then, the diagonal matrix in Eq. 22.5.3 is one in which the elements are successively the numbers from 1 to n, the number of variables.

Now we calculate the vector indicated in Eq. 22.5.4. The right-hand side of this equation is calculated as follows. First we postmultiply the γ matrix by the unit vector, which sums the rows of the matrix. This vector is then premultiplied by the inverse of the transpose of the T matrix. According to the definition of T, this gives a vector of the differences of successive elements in the $\gamma 1$ vector, with the exception of the last element which is the last element of the γ matrix. This vector is then premultiplied by the reciprocal of the diagonal matrix indicated in Eq. 22.5.3. It will be recalled, however, that these elements are simply the numbers from 1 to n.

Next we calculate the estimated simplex matrix C, as indicated in Eq. 22.5.5. The first term on the right-hand side is readily determined because of the definition of T. The vector whose major product moment is indicated in the last term on the right side of Eq. 22.5.5 is the first row or column of the first term on the right of Eq. 22.5.5.

We now calculate the covariance matrix for the binary data matrix, as indicated in Eq. 22.5.6. This is obtained by subtracting from the matrix of Eq. 22.5.1 the major product moment of the vector in Eq. 22.5.2.

Next we calculate the residual matrix E of Eq. 22.5.7. This is the observed covariance matrix calculated in Eq. 22.5.6 less the estimated simplex matrix of Eq. 22.5.5.

Finally, in Eq. 22.5.8, we calculate the correlation of the residual matrix, which is the matrix E of Eq. 22.5.7 pre- and postmultiplied by a diagonal matrix whose elements are the reciprocal square roots of the diagonal elements of E.

22.6 Communality and the Simplex as a Special Case

We have implied that the simplex problem and the communality problem are closely related. We have said that DuBois (1960) was the first to point out that a true simplex covariance or correlation matrix could be reduced in rank to $n/2$, where n is the number of variables, simply by altering the diagonal elements of the odd-numbered variables. If this simplex is a correlation matrix, DuBois has shown in particular that if in the odd-numbered diagonal positions one substitutes the squared multiple correlation of that variable with all of the other variables, then the rank of the resulting matrix will be reduced by the number of odd variables.

This means that if the number of variables is odd, then by diagonal adjustment the rank can be reduced to $n/2 + 1/2$, and if it is even, the rank can be reduced to $n/2$. DuBois proved this by showing that, beginning with the first row and column of a simplex matrix, one can alter the diagonal of the first row so that the first row and column are proportional to the second row and column. This shows that by altering the diagonal in this way, one can reduce the rank of the matrix by 1.

Having reduced its rank by 1 in this fashion, one can get a matrix whose first two rows and columns are 0, by subtracting the appropriate major product moment vector from the matrix. In the same way, one could operate on the remaining $n - 2$ rows to reduce the matrix to one with two less non-zero rows and columns, and so on.

Actually, these computational procedures are not needed for the proof. One can begin with a more general case. If the inverse of a covariance matrix can be permuted in such a way as to yield a diagonal submatrix of order s, then one may reduce the rank of the original matrix by exactly s, by altering the corresponding s diagonal elements.

It is proved in Section 22.7.4 that the simplex type of covariance matrix has as its inverse a tridiagonal matrix in which all elements, except the diagonal and those immediately above and below, are 0. It is easy to see that such a matrix may be permuted by rows and columns so that if the odd-numbered rows and columns are permuted to the top and side, respectively, and if we partition between the odd and the even sets, the diagonal submatrices will both be diagonal. Therefore, this can be seen to be a special case of the general theorem we have stated, and proves directly DuBois' theorem for the simplex.

22.7 Mathematical Proofs

22.7.1 The Least Square Simplex Data Matrix

We begin with an $N \times n$ binary data matrix M of item scores. We let 1 be a vector, all of whose elements are 1. Assuming that a score is the number of items "correctly" marked by a person, the vector S of test scores is given by

$$M1 = S \qquad (22.7.1)$$

We let P' be a row vector of the proportion of individuals answering correctly each of the items. This vector is given by

$$\frac{1'M}{N} = P' \qquad (22.7.2)$$

We shall assume further that the items are so arranged as to satisfy the inequality

$$S_i \gtrless S_{i+1} \qquad (22.7.3)$$

This simply means that the rows of the matrix are arranged so that the lower scores are at the top and the higher scores are at the bottom. We also assume that the columns are arranged in such a way as to satisfy

$$P_i \gtrless P_{i+1} \tag{22.7.4}$$

Here we mean that the items are arranged in descending order of preference, or increasing order of difficulty, from left to right.

We next consider an $N \times m$ binary matrix L such that its width or number of columns is equal to or less than the number of items or width of the M matrix. We indicate a column of row sums of L by

$$U = L1 \tag{22.7.5}$$

We shall assume that, as in the case of the M matrix, the scores from the L matrices are in increasing order of magnitude from top to bottom, as indicated by

$$U_i \gtrless U_{i+1} \tag{22.7.6}$$

We let ρ' be the vector of proportions for the columns of L, as indicated by

$$\rho' = \frac{1'L}{N} \tag{22.7.7}$$

Consider now any two columns $L_{.i}$ and $L_{.j}$ of the L matrix, where i is equal to or less than j. We assume the vectors have been chosen so that their minor product moment is proportional to the jth element of ρ as given in Eq. 22.7.7. This condition is indicated by

$$\frac{L_{.i}'L_{.j}}{N} = \rho_j \qquad \text{where } i \gtrless j \tag{22.7.8}$$

We impose the further restriction that each element of ρ' in Eq. 22.7.7 shall be greater than the one following it. This is indicated by the inequality

$$\rho_i > \rho_{i+1} \tag{22.7.9}$$

The L matrix is what we have called a binary simplex matrix. This is a matrix in which each person who marks the keyed answer to a given item also marks the keyed answers to all previous items. This matrix represents a hypothetical set of data on a perfectly reliable, homogeneous, discriminating set of items.

Let us assume for the moment that the L matrix is a good representation of whatever characteristics or properties of the M matrix are due to a dispersion of item difficulties. Our problem, then, is to find a transformation of the L matrix which will yield the best least square fit to the M matrix. First, we convert the L matrix to deviation form, as indicated in

$$x = \left(I - \frac{11'}{N}\right)L \tag{22.7.10}$$

We also make the transformation of the M matrix to deviation form, indicated by

$$y = \left(I - \frac{1\ 1'}{N}\right) M \tag{22.7.11}$$

We can now write the equation for the regression of the y matrix on the x matrix, as in

$$xB - y = \varepsilon \tag{22.7.12}$$

It is well known that the least square solution for B, or the solution which minimizes the trace of the product moment of ε in Eq. 22.7.12, is given by

$$B = (x'x)^{-1}x'y \tag{22.7.13}$$

From Eqs. 22.7.12 and 22.7.13, we have the solution for ε given by

$$[x(x'x)^{-1}x' - I]y = \varepsilon \tag{22.7.14}$$

Assuming now that the L matrix has been satisfactorily chosen, we may assume that the residual matrix ε is free of the effect of item dispersion. We may therefore proceed to a factoring of the residual covariance matrix as given in Eq. 22.7.15.

$$\frac{\varepsilon'\varepsilon}{N} = \frac{y'[I - x(x'x)^{-1}x']y}{N} \tag{22.7.15}$$

Such a factoring may be assumed to yield the dimensionality of a set of items after they have been freed from the effect of the simplex phenomenon. The removal of the simplex may be regarded as analogous to removal of the first centroid, or first principal axis, from a set of variables which is independent of the simplex phenomenon.

From Eqs. 22.7.10, 22.7.11, and 22.7.15, we get the minor product moment of the residual matrix ε in terms of the original M and L matrices, as given in

$$\varepsilon'\varepsilon = M'\left(I - \frac{1\ 1'}{N}\right)M - M'\left(I - \frac{1\ 1'}{N}\right)L\left[L'\left(I - \frac{1\ 1'}{N}\right)L\right]^{-1}L'\left(I - \frac{1\ 1'}{N}\right)M \tag{22.7.16}$$

We now define the matrix G by

$$\frac{L'L}{N} = G \tag{22.7.17}$$

Because of Eq. 22.7.8, which defines the L matrix as a simplex, we can write G as in

$$G = \begin{bmatrix} \rho_1 & \rho_2 & \cdots & \rho_m \\ \rho_2 & \rho_2 & \cdots & \rho_m \\ \cdots & \cdots & \cdots & \cdots \\ \rho_m & \rho_m & \cdots & \rho_m \end{bmatrix} \tag{22.7.18}$$

Here we see that the first row of G is precisely ρ', given by Eq. 22.7.7. In succeeding rows, all values to the left of the diagonal are equal to the diagonal value, and all values to the right of the diagonal are equal to the corresponding values from Eq. 22.7.7.

It is now useful to define a diagonal matrix, as in

$$D = \begin{bmatrix} \rho_1 - \rho_2 & 0 & \cdots & 0 \\ 0 & \rho_2 - \rho_3 & \cdots & 0 \\ \cdots & \cdots & \cdots & \cdots \\ 0 & 0 & \cdots & \rho_m \end{bmatrix} \qquad (22.7.19)$$

Here it is clear that the first element is obtained by subtracting ρ_2 from ρ_1, the second element by subtracting ρ_3 from ρ_2, and so on. The last element is simply the last element of the ρ' vector in Eq. 22.7.7.

We also define a triangular matrix of the form given in

$$T = \begin{bmatrix} 1 & 0 & 0 & \cdots & 0 & 0 \\ 1 & 1 & 0 & \cdots & 0 & 0 \\ 1 & 1 & 1 & \cdots & 0 & 0 \\ \cdots & \cdots & \cdots & \cdots & \cdots & \cdots \\ 1 & 1 & 1 & \cdots & 1 & 0 \\ 1 & 1 & 1 & \cdots & 1 & 1 \end{bmatrix} \qquad (22.7.20)$$

Here all elements above the diagonal are 0, and all elements in and below the diagonal are 1. It can readily be verified now that G, given by Eq. 22.7.18, can be expressed by

$$G = T'DT \qquad (22.7.21)$$

If next we substitute Eqs. 22.7.2, 22.7.7, and 22.7.21 in Eq. 22.7.16, we get

$$\frac{\varepsilon'\varepsilon}{N} = \frac{M'M}{N} - PP' - \frac{M'}{N}(L - 1\rho')(G - \rho\rho')^{-1}(L' - \rho 1')\frac{M}{N} \qquad (22.7.22)$$

This equation can be simplified by considering the middle parentheses on the right. The inverse of this factor can be verified to be as given in

$$(G - \rho\rho')^{-1} = G^{-1} + \frac{G^{-1}\rho\rho'G^{-1}}{1 - \rho'G^{-1}\rho} \qquad (22.7.23)$$

Using Eq. 22.7.21, we can write the inverse of G as in

$$G^{-1} = T^{-1}D^{-1}T'^{-1} \qquad (22.7.24)$$

It can readily be verified, now, that the inverse of T is of the form given by

$$T^{-1} = \begin{bmatrix} 1 & 0 & 0 & \cdots & 0 & 0 \\ -1 & 1 & 0 & \cdots & 0 & 0 \\ 0 & -1 & 1 & \cdots & 0 & 0 \\ \cdots & \cdots & \cdots & \cdots & \cdots & \cdots \\ 0 & 0 & & \cdots & 1 & 0 \\ 0 & 0 & 0 & \cdots & -1 & 1 \end{bmatrix} \qquad (22.7.25)$$

Here we have simply an identity matrix whose diagonals of 1 are bordered from beneath by -1. It may be recognized that this is a convenient form of matrix for transforming another matrix into one whose columns are the differences between successive columns of the matrix. Also, from Eqs. 22.7.19 and 22.7.25 we have

$$T'^{-1}\rho = D1 \qquad (22.7.26)$$

We proceed now to simplify the right side of Eq. 22.7.23. First, we have from Eq. 22.7.24 the result indicated by

$$G^{-1}\rho = T^{-1}D^{-1}T'^{-1}\rho \qquad (22.7.27)$$

From Eqs. 22.7.26 and 22.7.27, we get

$$G^{-1}\rho = T^{-1}1 \qquad (22.7.28)$$

but from Eqs. 22.7.25 and 22.7.28, we get

$$G^{-1}\rho = e_1 \qquad (22.7.29)$$

where e_1 is a column vector all of whose elements are 0, except the first which is 1.

From Eq. 22.7.29, we get

$$\rho'G^{-1}\rho = \rho_1 \qquad (22.7.30)$$

Now, putting together Eqs. 22.7.23, 22.7.24, 22.7.29, and 22.7.30, we finally have

$$(G - \rho\rho')^{-1} = T^{-1}D^{-1}T'^{-1} + \frac{e_1 e_1'}{1 - \rho_1} \qquad (22.7.31)$$

Substituting Eq. 22.7.31 in Eq. 22.7.22, we get Eq. 22.7.32, the minor product moment or the covariance of the residuals, independent of the simplex due to dispersion of item difficulty.

$$\frac{\varepsilon'\varepsilon}{N} = \frac{M'M}{N} - PP' - \frac{M'}{N}(L - 1\rho')(T^{-1}D^{-1}T'^{-1} + \frac{e_1 e_1'}{1 - \rho_1})(L' - \rho1')\frac{M}{N}$$

$$(22.7.32)$$

For computational purposes, it is convenient to define additional notation. We define the matrix K by

$$K = NM'L - M'1\,1'L \qquad (22.7.33)$$

We indicate N^2 times the covariance matrix for M by

$$N^2 C_M = NM'M - M'1\,1'M \qquad (22.7.34)$$

From Eqs. 22.7.32–22.7.34, we get N times the residual covariance matrix given by

$$N\varepsilon'\varepsilon = N^2 C_M - \frac{K\left(T^{-1}D^{-1}T'^{-1} + \dfrac{e_1 e_1'}{1 - \rho_1}\right)K'}{N^2} \tag{22.7.35}$$

We next define the matrix W by

$$W = KT^{-1} \tag{22.7.36}$$

This equation means that each column vector of W is obtained by subtracting a vector of K from the one immediately preceding, as indicated in

$$W_{.i} = K_{.i} - K_{.(i+1)} \tag{22.7.37}$$

The final vector in the W matrix is the last column of K, as shown in

$$W_{.n} = K_{.n} \tag{22.7.38}$$

We define the matrix H by

$$H = \frac{WD^{-1}W'}{N^2} \tag{22.7.39}$$

and the matrix F by

$$F = H + \frac{K_{.1}K_{.1}'}{N^2(1 - \rho_1)} \tag{22.7.40}$$

Then from Eqs. 22.7.33–22.7.40, we get

$$N\varepsilon'\varepsilon = N^2 C_M - F \tag{22.7.41}$$

Another procedure for determining the L matrix is to require that the ρ_i in Eq. 22.7.7 be the same, respectively, as the distinct P values in Eq. 22.7.2. This means that the experimental P values are taken as the theoretical simplex values in the least square solution. One objection to this procedure is that, although some of the P's may not be exactly equal, they may be very close. Very small values in Eq. 22.7.19 will then occur. These may cause difficulty in solutions involving the inverse of the matrix.

A third method, which gets around this objection, is to construct the L matrix so that the ρ_i in Eq. 22.7.7 are equally spaced, as indicated by

$$\rho_i - c = \rho_{i+1} \tag{22.7.42}$$

In this equation c is an appropriately determined constant. This method has the advantage that no two ρ_i need be very close together, and it thus avoids difficulty in the inverse of the diagonal matrix in Eq. 22.7.19. Ordinarily, c should be determined so that ρ_1 and ρ_m will be close, respectively, to P_1 and P_n. The effect of varying the size of c requires further investigation.

22.7.2   The Least Square Simplex Covariance Matrix

Consider the perfect simplex binary matrix L such that in

$$\frac{1'L}{N} = \rho' \tag{22.7.43}$$

we specify that

$$\rho_i > \rho_{i+1} \tag{22.7.44}$$

Consider also

$$G = \frac{L'L}{N} \tag{22.7.45}$$

Let T be a lower triangular matrix in which all nonzero elements are 1. Let D be a diagonal matrix in which

$$D_n = \rho_n \tag{22.7.46}$$

where n is the width of L in Eq. 22.7.43 and

$$D_i = \rho_i - \rho_{i+1} \tag{22.7.47}$$

It can be proved, then, from Eqs. 22.7.43 and 22.7.45–22.7.47, and the definition of T that

$$G = T'DT \tag{22.7.48}$$

Then the covariance matrix for L, say C, would be, from Eqs. 22.7.43 and 22.7.45,

$$C = G - \rho\rho' \tag{22.7.49}$$

From Eq. 22.7.48, it can be shown that

$$Ge_1 = \rho \tag{22.7.50}$$

and, in general, for $i \gtrless j$,

$$G_{ij} = \rho_j \tag{22.7.51}$$

and for $i \gtrless j$,

$$G_{ij} = \rho_i \tag{22.7.52}$$

Equations 22.7.51 and 22.7.52 must follow from the definition of L or, more precisely, L is defined so that Eqs. 22.7.51 and 22.7.52 hold.

From Eqs. 22.7.49 and 22.7.50,

$$C = G - Ge_1 e_1'G \tag{22.7.53}$$

From Eqs. 22.7.48 and 22.7.53,

$$C = T'(D - DTe_1 e_1'T'D)T \tag{22.7.54}$$

But from the definition of T,

$$Te_1 = 1 \tag{22.7.55}$$

From Eqs. 22.7.54 and 22.7.55,

$$C = T'(D - D1\ 1'D)T \qquad (22.7.56)$$

We could now consider

$$\gamma = \frac{M'M}{N} \qquad (22.7.57)$$

where M is the observed binary matrix, and

$$\sigma = \gamma - PP' \qquad (22.7.58)$$

where

$$P = \frac{M'1}{N} \qquad (22.7.59)$$

and where the columns of M are ordered so that $P_i \gtrless P_{i+1}$. We could then write

$$\sigma - C = E \qquad (22.7.60)$$

and from Eqs. 22.7.56 and 22.7.60,

$$\sigma - T'(D - D1\ 1'D)T = E \qquad (22.7.61)$$

From Eq. 22.7.61, we could write

$$T'^{-1}\sigma T^{-1} - (D - D1\ 1'D) = \varepsilon \qquad (22.7.62)$$

and solve for D so that $tr\ \varepsilon'\varepsilon$ would be minimized. It will be simpler, however, to redefine ε and E and consider

$$G - \gamma = \varepsilon \qquad (22.7.63)$$

and from Eqs. 22.7.48 and 22.7.63,

$$T'DT - \gamma = \varepsilon \qquad (22.7.64)$$

From Eq. 22.7.64, we can write

$$I - D^{-1/2}T'^{-1}\gamma T^{-1}D^{-1/2} = E \qquad (22.7.65)$$

Let

$$T'^{-1}\gamma T^{-1} = g \qquad (22.7.66)$$

From Eqs. 22.7.65 and 22.7.66, we write

$$I - D^{-1/2}gD^{-1/2} = E \qquad (22.7.67)$$

We now determine $D^{-1/2}$ so as to minimize $tr\ E'E$. Let

$$\psi = trE'E \qquad (22.7.68)$$

From Eqs. 22.7.67 and 22.7.68,

$$\psi = tr(D^{-1/2}gD^{-1}gD^{-1/2} - 2D^{-1/2}gD^{-1/2} + I) \qquad (22.7.69)$$

We let

$$V = D^{-1}1 \tag{22.7.70}$$

From Eqs. 22.7.69 and 22.7.70, it can be shown that

$$\psi = V'g^{(2)}V - 2V'D_g1 + n \tag{22.7.71}$$

where $g^{(2)}$ is a matrix whose elements are the squares of those in g. From Eq. 22.7.71, symbolic differentiation gives

$$\frac{\partial \psi}{\partial V'} = g^{(2)}V - D_g1 \tag{22.7.72}$$

Equating Eq. 22.7.72 to 0 and solving for V, we get

$$V = (g^{(2)})^{-1}D_g1 \tag{22.7.73}$$

Perhaps a better way of ordering the columns of M in Eq. 22.7.57 is to consider

$$U = \gamma 1 \tag{22.7.74}$$

Let

$$Y = U\pi \tag{22.7.75}$$

where π is such that

$$Y_i \geqslant Y_{i+1} \tag{22.7.76}$$

We then let

$$_\pi\gamma = \pi'\gamma\pi \tag{22.7.77}$$

and use $_\pi\gamma$ instead of γ in the foregoing equations.

From Eq. 22.7.70, then, we solve for D. We may then solve for C in Eq. 22.7.56, and for E from Eqs. 22.7.58 and 22.7.60. E is the residual covariance matrix after the simplex has been removed. A factor analysis of this would reveal the number of factors in M independent of the P values.

22.7.3   Computational Short Cut for the Simplex Covariance Matrix

Let L be a perfect simplex binary matrix and M be an observed binary data matrix of the same order. Then the raw covariance matrix of L can be expressed as

$$G = T'DT \tag{22.7.78}$$

where D is a positive diagonal, and T is as defined previously. The raw covariance matrix of M will be γ, which will be so ordered that the column sums are in decreasing order of magnitude.

Consider now

$$G - \gamma = \varepsilon \tag{22.7.79}$$

From Eqs. 22.7.78 and 22.7.79,

$$T'DT - \gamma = \varepsilon \tag{22.7.80}$$

We shall consider a simplified solution for D in Eq. 22.7.80, which is not least square. From Eq. 22.7.80,

$$DT - T'^{-1}\gamma = E \tag{22.7.81}$$

From Eq. 22.7.81,

$$DD_{T1}1 - T'^{-1}\gamma 1 = E1 \tag{22.7.82}$$

where

$$D_{T1}1 = T1 \tag{22.7.83}$$

According to the definition of T,

$$D_{T1} = \begin{bmatrix} 1 & 0 & \cdots & 0 \\ 0 & 2 & \cdots & 0 \\ \cdots & \cdots & \cdots & \cdots \\ 0 & 0 & \cdots & n \end{bmatrix} \tag{22.7.84}$$

Assume

$$E1 = 0 \tag{22.7.85}$$

From Eqs. 22.7.82 and 22.7.85,

$$D1 = D_{T1}^{-1}T'^{-1}\gamma 1 \tag{22.7.86}$$

Using Eq. 22.7.56 from the previous section, we have as the deviation covariance matrix of L,

$$C = T'(D - D1\ 1'D)T \tag{22.7.87}$$

If

$$\sigma = \gamma - PP' \tag{22.7.88}$$

where

$$P = \frac{M'1}{N} \tag{22.7.89}$$

we may write

$$\sigma - C = \varepsilon \tag{22.7.90}$$

Equation 22.7.90 gives the residual ε, which is independent of the simplex. This may be factored to find the dimensions independent of the simplex.

22.7.4   Communality and the Simplex as a Special Case
Let G be a Gramian basic matrix, and

$$g = \pi'G\pi \tag{22.7.91}$$

where π is a permutation matrix. Suppose we let

$$g = \begin{bmatrix} g_{aa} & g_{ab} \\ g_{ba} & g_{bb} \end{bmatrix} \tag{22.7.92}$$

where g is symmetrically partitioned, and a and b indicate order. Let

$$M = g_{bb} - g_{ba}g_{aa}^{-1}g_{ab} \tag{22.7.93}$$

and

$$B_{ab} = g_{aa}^{-1} g_{ab} \tag{22.7.94}$$

It is well known that

$$g^{-1} = \begin{bmatrix} g_{aa}^{-1} + B_{ab} M^{-1} B_{ba} & -B_{ab} M^{-1} \\ -M^{-1} B_{ba} & M^{-1} \end{bmatrix} \tag{22.7.95}$$

We let

$$C = g^{-1} \tag{22.7.96}$$

and

$$C = \begin{bmatrix} C_{aa} & C_{ab} \\ C_{ba} & C_{bb} \end{bmatrix} \tag{22.7.97}$$

Suppose that M^{-1} is diagonal. M must also, then, be diagonal. Consider

$$\gamma = \begin{bmatrix} g_{aa} & g_{ab} \\ g_{ba} & g_{ba} g_{aa}^{-1} g_{ab} \end{bmatrix} \tag{22.7.98}$$

From Eq. 22.7.98,

$$\gamma = \begin{bmatrix} g_{aa} \\ g_{ba} \end{bmatrix} g_{aa}^{-1} [g_{aa} \; g_{ab}] \tag{22.7.99}$$

From Eq. 22.7.99, γ is of rank a.

Now from Eq. 22.7.98,

$$\gamma_{bb} = g_{ba} g_{aa}^{-1} g_{ab} \tag{22.7.100}$$

From Eqs. 22.7.93 and 22.7.100,

$$\gamma_{bb} = g_{bb} - M \tag{22.7.101}$$

From Eq. 22.7.99, we have the theorem that if a permutation of the rows and columns of G exists, such that M in Eq. 22.7.93 is diagonal, and if this diagonal matrix is subtracted from g_{bb} in Eq. 22.7.92, the resulting matrix will be γ of Eq. 22.7.99, and hence of rank a.

In particular, suppose that G^{-1} is tridiagonal. Suppose we permute the even-numbered rows and columns to the top and left, respectively, and partition vertically and horizontally between even and odd sets. Then C_{aa} and C_{bb} are diagonal, and the order of C_{aa} is the same or one less than that of C_{bb}, according to whether the order of G is even or odd.

If G is a simplex raw covariance matrix of the form

$$G = T'DT \tag{22.7.102}$$

then the deviation covariance matrix is given by

$$C = G - \rho\rho' \tag{22.7.103}$$

From Eq. 22.7.31, we know that

$$C^{-1} = T^{-1} D^{-1} T'^{-1} + \frac{e_1 e_1'}{1 - \rho_1} \tag{22.7.104}$$

Since T^{-1} is of the form given by Eq. 22.7.25, we know from Eq. 22.7.104 that C^{-1} is tridiagonal, and therefore the rank of G can be reduced by the number of its odd-numbered attributes by adjusting the diagonals corresponding to them. This is the theorem given by DuBois (1960).

Chapter 23

Factor Analysis and Prediction

We have seen in the previous chapters that factor analysis is typically concerned with procedures for approximating a given data matrix with one of lower rank. We learned that this procedure involves the solution for a pair of factors whose common order is much less than the smaller order of the data matrix, and whose major product is a satisfactory approximation to the data matrix. In these discussions we have considered the data matrix from a general point of view, without any particular interest in the types of variables involved. However, a large class of problems is concerned with the types of variables which go to make up the data matrix. This class of problems is sometimes referred to as the model of multiple rectilinear regression.

In this type of problem, we regard the data matrix as consisting of two kinds of variables—one, the predictor variables, and the other, the criterion variables. Another way of designating these two kinds is to call the predictor variables the independent variables, and the criterion variables the dependent variables. In the parlance of mathematical statistics, the independent variables are sometimes called fixed variables, as distinguished from random variables.

From a practical point of view, this is what happens. We ordinarily have given a number of variables which are more or less readily available on a given number of entities at a specified time. In general, these variables are not regarded as of particular importance in themselves. We may also consider a second set of variables with reference to the group of entities which are not, typically, available at the same time as the predictor variables, but which become available somewhat later. For example, if we have a group of individuals for whom we have a set of test scores, we might at a later time obtain for these individuals a set of measures of success in various kinds of course areas in college. This second set of variables is one which in and of itself seems to have some importance to the individual; therefore, we call these *socially significant variables*.

We may then wish to predict from the test scores the probable success of the entities in each of a number of different college course areas. Here the classical methods of multiple regression, or linear least square analysis, are available. It is of some interest, however, to see not only how the classical methods of least square multiple rectilinear prediction can be brought into the general framework of factor analysis, but also how these classical methods can be modified, and perhaps even improved, by formulating the problems in terms of the models and objectives of factor analysis.

With these objectives in view, then, we shall see what different kinds of solutions may be applied to the general model of multiple prediction. We may wish to estimate or predict a set of criterion variables from a set of predictor or independent variables. In general, we start with a data matrix which may be regarded as being partitioned between the set of predictor variables and the set of criterion variables. We regard the data matrix as a type 3 row supervector in which the first matric element is the submatrix of predictor measures and the second matric element is the submatrix of criterion measures.

In the past it has been more common for the submatrix of criterion variables to be simply a vector. In such a case we have only one criterion variable. However, recently, attention has been focused on the more general model in which the criterion submatrix may involve a number of variables. These variables may represent a number of different course areas in college, a number of different job categories in business, a number of different military occupational specialties in the military services, and so on. A more complete discussion of the data matrix as a supermatrix consisting of the two types of submatrices, and the implications of this formulation in terms of the appropriate analyses and in terms of practical applications, has been presented in detail by Horst (1962).

23.1   Kinds of Solutions

The kinds of statistical prediction models which may be formulated as special cases of factor analytic models, and which we shall discuss, are first, the rank reduction solution, second, the basic structure solution, third, the nonbasic solution, fourth, the solution which increases degrees of freedom of the system, and fifth, the solution which enables one to select predictor variables by objective means.

23.1.1   The Rank Reduction Solution. This type of solution is the one which is most commonly known and used, particularly for the case of several or more predictors and one criterion. However, it is also used when several or more criteria are available. This is the conventional least square solution, or what is sometimes, but not too appropriately, called the multiple regression solution. However, the traditional multiple regression approach does not explicitly regard the problem as a special case of a factor analytic solution.

In our treatment we shall regard the multiple regression model as a special case of the rank reduction formula in which certain restrictions are imposed on the residual matrix.

23.1.2 The Basic Structure Solution.

A much less familiar method of considering the multiple prediction problem involves certain sets of compu- tations from which we get a product moment matrix involving both the dependent and the independent variables. From these computations we calcu- late a root and vector, or a basic diagonal element and its corresponding basic orthonormal vector, such that the basic orthonormal vector is readily interpretable in terms of a regression vector.

23.1.3 The Nonbasic Solution.

For some types of data matrices, we encounter a data submatrix which, when standardized and normalized, is not a basic data matrix. This means that when we calculate the minor product moment of this submatrix, one or more of the roots or basic diagonals are 0. A particular example occurs in the case of ipsative matrices. For the solution of this special case of the multiple regression model, it is necessary to use the concept of the general inverse of a matrix in order to calculate the matrix of regression vectors. This concept is discussed in Section 3.5.1.

23.1.4 Increasing the Degrees of Freedom by Factor Analysis.

Another approach to the solution of the multiple regression problem is appropriate when the number of variables is large, compared to the number of entities. It is well known that if we have the same number of independent variables as observations, it is always possible to find a transformation of the submatrix of predictor variables which will yield precisely the submatrix of the criterion measures. This, of course, is a meaningless solution, since such a transformation would be possible even if all of the numbers in the predictor submatrix and the criterion submatrix were chosen from a table of random numbers.

Any transformation matrix obtained in this manner, and applied to a subsequent data matrix of predictor measures for another set of entities, could not be expected to give even a remote approximation to a corresponding submatrix of criterion measures for the same entities. In general, this problem is identified as the degrees of freedom problem. For a scientifically useful solution which can be generalized to other samples and other data, we must have many degrees of freedom. That is, the number of entities, as compared with the number of variables, must be large. The role of factor analysis in achieving this objective will be considered in this chapter.

23.1.5 Predictor Selection and Factor Analysis.

Much attention has been given in the past, not only to the problem of finding or solving for a matrix of regression vectors from a submatrix of predictor and a submatrix of criterion measures, but also to deciding what predictor measures, from a large pool of potential predictor measures, might be most efficiently used.

Several kinds of methods for attacking this problem have been developed by Horst (1954, 1955), and by Horst and MacEwan (1960). One consists in what has been called the *predictor accretion methods*, and another, the *predictor elimination methods*. Both kinds are applicable to the case of a single criterion variable or to multiple criterion variables. Nevertheless, all of these methods break down when, in the particular sample on which the analysis is being made, the number of potential predictors is too large and the number of entities is too small. The method outlined in one of the following sections, therefore, attempts to overcome the limitations imposed when the number of entities is too small compared to the number of variables.

23.2   The Rank Reduction Solution

23.2.1   Characteristics of the Method. The first method we shall consider is the general case of the classical multiple regression procedure in which we have a number of independent variables and a number of dependent variables. The classical least square solution for this case is well known. However, it does not seem to be well known that this solution is a special case of the rank reduction model.

We shall show how we may begin with the supermatrix consisting of the predictor and the criterion submatrices. We then specify the arbitrary right and left multipliers in the rank reduction form, which, when applied in the usual way, result in a residual matrix which is precisely the residual matrix we get in the classical least square solution.

For completeness of presentation we shall outline the computational procedures for the generalized multiple regression model. In the mathematical proofs section we shall show that this model is a special case of the rank reduction model.

23.2.2   Computational Equations

23.2.2a   DEFINITION OF NOTATION

x_p is the standardized matrix of predictor variables.

x_c is the standardized matrix of criterion variables.

R_{pp} is the matrix of correlations among the predictor variables.

R_{pc} is the matrix of correlations of the predictor with the criterion variables.

B is the matrix of regression coefficients.

$\tilde{x}_c$ is the estimated matrix of criterion variables.

23.2.2b THE EQUATIONS

$$x = [x_p, \quad x_c] \tag{23.2.1}$$

$$R_{pp} = \frac{x_p{'}x_p}{N} \tag{23.2.2}$$

$$R_{pc} = \frac{x_p{'}x_c}{N} \tag{23.2.3}$$

$$B = R_{pp}{}^{-1}R_{pc} \tag{23.2.4}$$

$$\tilde{x}_c = x_pB \tag{23.2.5}$$

23.2.3 Computational Instructions. The computational procedures for the general multiple rectilinear least square solutions are well known, and are given in many books and articles. However, they are not, in general, given compactly, or exclusively in matrix notation. It will therefore be convenient to present such an outline below.

We begin with the data supermatrix, as indicated in Eq. 23.2.1. Here we have a type 3 row supervector in which the first submatric element on the right of the equation is the matrix of predictor measures, and the second submatric element is the matrix of criterion measures.

We assume that the variables are in standard form in which the means are 0 and the variances 1. We then indicate the computation for the covariance matrices involving the predictor and criterion variables. The matrix of intercorrelations of the predictor measures is given by Eq. 23.2.2. This is the minor product moment of the standardized predictor measures, divided by N, the number of entities.

The matrix of intercorrelations of the predictor with the criterion variables is shown in Eq. 23.2.3. This is the minor product of the submatrix of predictor variables and the submatrix of criterion variables, divided by N.

The matrix of regression vectors B is given in Eq. 23.2.4. This is the matrix of Eq. 23.2.3 premultiplied by the inverse of the matrix in Eq. 23.2.2.

The matrix of estimated criterion variables is given in Eq. 23.2.5. This, of course, is simply the matrix of predictor variables postmultiplied by the matrix calculated in Eq. 23.2.4.

23.2.4 Numerical Example. We begin with a supermatrix of six predictor measures, x_p, and three criterion measures, x_c, as given in Table 23.2.1.

Table 23.2.2 gives the matrix of intercorrelations of the predictor measures.

Table 23.2.3 gives the matrix of correlations of the three criterion measures with the six predictor measures.

Table 23.2.4 shows the matrix of three regression vectors for estimating the three criterion variables from the six predictor variables. These were calculated by means of Eq. 23.2.4.

TABLE 23.2.1   Supermatrix $x = [x_p, \quad x_c]$ of Predictor and Criterion Measures

0.128	0.181	0.421	0.506	0.857	0.746	0.280	0.178	0.246
0.764	0.740	0.563	−0.387	−0.293	−0.202	0.261	0.281	0.043
−0.030	0.046	−0.014	0.147	−0.109	−0.135	0.640	0.682	0.661
−0.280	−0.351	−0.326	−0.023	−0.109	−0.186	0.083	0.091	−0.654
−0.336	−0.306	−0.429	−0.542	−0.006	−0.153	−0.428	0.056	−0.124
−0.276	−0.324	−0.271	−0.370	−0.225	0.035	0.129	−0.446	−0.124
0.057	−0.070	−0.016	0.006	0.152	−0.441	−0.166	−0.354	−0.003
−0.010	−0.140	0.326	−0.004	−0.258	−0.091	−0.410	−0.200	−0.101
−0.303	0.227	−0.014	0.029	−0.102	−0.125	−0.086	−0.106	−0.074
0.086	0.057	−0.003	0.161	0.073	0.134	−0.082	−0.067	−0.009
0.164	0.106	−0.124	0.234	−0.002	0.227	−0.072	0.025	0.156
0.036	−0.074	−0.142	0.242	0.023	0.192	−0.148	−0.119	0.011

TABLE 23.2.2   Matrix R_{pp} of Predictor Intercorrelations

0.999	0.829	0.768	0.108	0.033	0.108
0.829	1.000	0.775	0.115	0.061	0.125
0.768	0.775	1.000	0.272	0.205	0.239
0.108	0.115	0.272	0.999	0.636	0.625
0.033	0.061	0.205	0.636	1.001	0.709
0.108	0.125	0.239	0.625	0.709	1.000

TABLE 23.2.3   Matrix R_{cp} of Correlations Between Criterion and Predictor Variables

0.298	0.323	0.296	0.249	0.138	0.190
0.304	0.341	0.266	0.176	0.087	0.104
0.350	0.368	0.385	0.369	0.254	0.291

TABLE 23.2.4   Matrix B of Regression Vectors

0.089	0.100	0.106
0.229	0.315	0.190
−0.011	−0.095	0.064
0.215	0.179	0.274
−0.054	−0.010	0.005
0.058	−0.028	0.066

23.3 The Basic Structure Solution

23.3.1 Characteristics of the Method. This method of solving for regression vectors is adapted to the solution for one regression vector at a time. If there are a number of criterion variables, it is probably better to solve for the regression vectors one at a time rather than to attempt to solve for them simultaneously. The method is essentially an iteration procedure, since it solves for the largest root and corresponding vector of a symmetric matrix. The largest roots of the matrix whose largest root and vector are to be solved for are usually very close together; therefore, a large number of iterations may be required.

We begin with the matrix of intercorrelations of the predictor variables, and the vector of intercorrelations of these predictor variables with the criterion variable. We set up a type 3 row supervector with these two submatric elements. We then consider the major product moment matrix of this type 3 supervector. It can readily be shown that this matrix has one zero root. A vector exists such that the product of this matrix and the vector is a null vector. This must be the case, for the matrix cannot be basic, since it is a major product moment of a matrix in which the number of columns is one more than the number of rows.

We may, however, subtract this product moment matrix from a scalar matrix in which the scalar is greater than the largest root of the product moment matrix. The vector corresponding to the largest root of this difference matrix is the same as the vector which is orthogonal to the major product moment matrix. This method of solution is presented by Bodewig (1959). It is probable that basic structure type solutions for regression vectors more convenient than this particular one could be worked out.

23.3.2 Computational Equations

23.3.2a DEFINITION OF NOTATION
R_{pp} is the matrix of correlations among the predictor variables.
R_{pc} is the vector of correlations of the predictors with the criterion.
$_i\beta$ is the *i*th approximation to the regression vector.

23.3.2b THE EQUATIONS

$$K = tr R_{pp}^{2} + R_{pc}' R_{pc} \qquad (23.3.1)$$

$$M' = [R_{pp}, \quad -R_{pc}] \qquad (23.3.2)$$

$$_i b = \begin{bmatrix} _i\beta \\ 1 \end{bmatrix} \qquad (23.3.3)$$

$$V = R_{pp} 1 \qquad (23.3.4)$$

$$g = \frac{1'R_{pc}}{V'1} \tag{23.3.5}$$

$$_1U = gV - R_{pc} \tag{23.3.6}$$

$$_iU = M'_{\ i}b \tag{23.3.7}$$

$$_iW = M_{\ i}U \tag{23.3.8}$$

$$_iY = K_{\ i}b - _iW \tag{23.3.9}$$

$$_{i+1}b = \frac{_iY}{_iY_{n+1}} \tag{23.3.10}$$

23.3.3 Computational Instructions. In this method we begin with the matrix of correlations of the predictor variables, and the vector of correlations of the predictors with the criterion variable. It will be recalled that this procedure is suitable primarily for finding a single regression vector at a time. The first step is to find a scalar quantity which is as large as, or larger than, the largest root of a major product moment matrix. The problem of finding such a scalar quantity can be computationally quite laborious, particularly if we insist that it shall be a close approximation to the largest root. We can always, however, find a value which is equal to the sum of all of the roots simply by finding the trace of the product moment matrix.

The difficulty is that if we use a scalar much larger than the largest root, then the number of iterations required to solve for the regression vector may be large. As shown in the mathematical proofs section, this is because the manner in which the scalar is used in connection with the major product moment yields the matrix whose roots are precisely the roots of the product moment matrix subtracted from the scalar. In general, these product moment matrices can be expected to have a large number of small roots approximately equal in magnitude. When these are subtracted from a large scalar quantity, the ratio of the resulting roots to one another will be close to 1. As we have seen in the earlier sections on the calculation of basic structure factor vectors, the closer the adjacent roots are, the more iterations are needed to solve for a given basic orthonormal vector.

In any case, we shall begin with the scalar to be calculated, as indicated in Eq. 23.3.1. As will be seen, this is the trace of the square of the correlation matrix for the predictor variables, plus the minor product moment of the vector of correlations of the predictors with the criterion. Obviously, the trace of the square of the predictor correlation matrix is simply the sum of the squares of the elements of this matrix.

We then set up the type 3 row supervector, as indicated in Eq. 23.3.2. The first submatric element on the right side of this equation is the matrix of predictor intercorrelations. The second element is the negative of the column vector of correlations of the predictor variables with the criterion.

We next wish to get an approximation to the regression vector β. This vector is augmented at the bottom by a unit element so that we have the type 1 column supervector indicated in Eq. 23.3.3.

First, however, we must define a vector V as in Eq. 23.3.4. This is simply a column vector of row sums of the predictor correlation matrix.

We then calculate a scalar as in Eq. 23.3.5. As indicated on the right side of this equation, the scalar g is the sum of the elements of the vector of criterion correlations, divided by the sum of the elements of the vector calculated in Eq. 23.3.4, which is, of course, the sum of all of the elements in the predictor correlation matrix.

In Eq. 23.3.6, we calculate a $_1U$ vector by multiplying the V vector of Eq. 23.3.4 by the g scalar of Eq. 23.3.5, and subtracting from the product the vector of predictor-criterion correlation coefficients.

The general approximation to the U vector is given in Eq. 23.3.7. This vector is simply the product of the matrix of Eq. 23.3.2 postmultiplied by the vector of Eq. 23.3.3.

Next we calculate the ith approximation to a W vector, as in Eq. 23.3.8. This is the product of the transpose of the matrix in Eq. 23.3.2 postmultiplied by the vector of Eq. 23.3.7.

We then calculate the ith approximation to a Y vector, as indicated in Eq. 23.3.9. This is obtained by multiplying the b vector of Eq. 23.3.3 by the scalar of Eq. 23.3.1, and subtracting from the product the vector of Eq. 23.3.8.

To get the $i + 1$ approximation to the b vector, we use Eq. 23.3.10. This is the Y vector of Eq. 23.3.9 divided by its last element. We assume that there are n predictor variables, and therefore that the last element of the b vector in Eq. 23.3.3 is the $n + 1$ element. This means that the last element of the b vector in Eq. 23.3.10 is simply the unit element, as indicated in the right side of Eq. 23.3.3.

We are then ready to begin again with Eq. 23.3.7 to calculate a new approximation to the U vector. The calculations from Eqs. 23.3.7–23.3.10 proceed, then, until the vector b stabilizes to a sufficient number of decimal places.

23.3.4 Numerical Example. The computations for this method are not shown, although a Fortran program is included in the Appendix for carrying out the necessary computations.

23.4 The Nonbasic Solution

23.4.1 Characteristics of the Method. In this method we assume that the submatrix of predictor measures is not basic. This is the case, for example, in a set of ipsative variables in which the sums of the rows of the data matrix add up to a constant. We have shown in Chapter 13 that, for such a matrix

in deviation form, the sums of rows add up to 0. If then, the columns of this matrix are standardized, the standardized matrix postmultiplied by a vector of the standard deviations of the original variables must give a null vector.

The deviation matrix is therefore orthogonal to the unit vector, and the standardized matrix is orthogonal to the vector of standard deviations. Consequently, the covariance matrix of the predictor measures must also be orthogonal to the unit vector, and the correlation matrix must be orthogonal to the vector of standard deviations.

We get such covariance or correlation matrices from personality inventories in which the forced-choice format has been used as a method of correcting for the social desirability factor. The Edwards Personal Preference Schedule and the Kuder Preference Schedule are of this type. If, then, we want to find a matrix of regression vectors to use in estimating a set of criterion vectors from such a data matrix, we cannot use the conventional procedure in which we premultiply the matrix of predictor-criterion correlations by the inverse of the matrix of predictor correlations. This is because the matrix of predictor correlations is nonbasic and therefore does not have a regular inverse.

We have seen, however, in Chapter 3, that for such cases we may obtain an optimal solution by using the general inverse of the nonbasic covariance or correlation matrix. But the solution for the general inverse implies the solution for the basic structure factors of the covariance or correlation matrix. This, as we know from the principal axis method of factor analysis, is a relatively expensive and time-consuming procedure, since it depends on iterative calculations involving matrix multiplication.

It is desirable, therefore, to have some method of getting an optimal solution which does not actually require the calculation of the basic structure factors in the solution for the general inverse. This can be accomplished without iterative procedures if the vector orthogonal to the covariance or correlation matrix of predictors is known. In the case of ipsative variables, of course, this vector is known, as we have just indicated.

23.4.2 Computational Equations

23.4.2a DEFINITION OF NOTATION

U is the matrix orthogonal to the standardized predictor data matrix.

B is the matrix of regression coefficients.

R_{pc} is the matrix of correlations of the predictor with the criterion variables.

R_{pp} is the matrix of correlations of the predictor variables.

23.4.2b THE EQUATIONS

$$\gamma = U'U \tag{23.4.1}$$

$$tt' = \gamma \tag{23.4.2}$$

$$u = Ut'^{-1} \tag{23.4.3}$$

$$G = R_{pp} + uu' \tag{23.4.4}$$

$$B = G^{-1}R_{pc} \tag{23.4.5}$$

$$W' = \gamma^{-1}U' \tag{23.4.6}$$

$$G = R_{pp} + WU' \tag{23.4.7}$$

23.4.3 Computational Instructions. We begin with a knowledge of the vector or matrix which is orthogonal to the correlation matrix of predictor variables. We then calculate the minor product moment of this matrix or vector, as the case may be, as indicated in Eq. 23.4.1.

In Eq. 23.4.2, we indicate this minor product moment in terms of its triangular factors.

Equation 23.4.3 shows the postmultiplication of the matrix or vector by the inverse of its upper triangular factor. Again, as in previous examples, the computations indicated in Eqs. 23.4.2 and 23.4.3 may be accomplished by the partial triangular factoring of the type 3 supervector, in which the first element is the product moment of the matrix to be orthogonalized and the second element is the matrix itself.

Having calculated the orthogonalized form u of the matrix U, we add its major product moment to the nonbasic correlation matrix of predictor variables, as indicated in Eq. 23.4.4. Since u presumably now includes all of the vectors orthogonal to the correlation matrix, it can be proved that G in Eq. 23.4.4 is a basic matrix having a regular inverse.

We therefore get the matrix of regression vectors, as in Eq. 23.4.5, by premultiplying the matrix of correlations of the predictor variables with the criterion variables by the inverse of the G matrix calculated in Eq. 23.4.4.

Of course, if the orthogonal matrix u is simply a vector, the computations indicated in Eqs. 23.4.1–23.4.3 simplify to the normalization of a vector. In this case, γ in Eq. 23.4.1 is a scalar, and the u vector in Eq. 23.4.3 is obtained by dividing the U vector by the square root of this scalar.

An alternate method of solution is as follows. We may premultiply the transpose of the U matrix by the inverse of the γ matrix calculated in Eq. 23.4.1 to ge the W matrix, as indicated in Eq. 23.4.6. We may then get the G matrix of Eq. 23.4.4 as indicated in Eq. 23.4.7, by adding to the correlation matrix of the predictors the major product of the W matrix calculated in Eq. 23.4.6 and the U matrix. It can readily be seen that the major product WU' is the same as the major product of the u matrix of Eq. 23.4.3.

The method of computation given in Eqs. 23.4.3 and 23.4.4 is particularly appropriate for electronic computers where immediate access storage is often at a premium. In the case of Eqs. 23.4.3 and 23.4.4, it is possible to dimension only a matrix u rather than both the matrices U and W. Of course, if U and

W are only vectors, this is not an important consideration. Even if the matrix U had several vectors, the advantage of the method using Eqs. 23.4.3 and 23.4.4 would not be great.

23.4.4 Numerical Example. We begin with the matrix of intercorrelations given in Table 23.4.1. The last variable in this matrix is the sum of the first five normalized variables. Therefore, the correlation matrix is nonbasic.

Table 23.4.2 gives the matrix of correlations of the six predictor variables with the three criterion variables.

TABLE 23.4.1   Nonbasic Matrix of Correlations Among
Ipsative Predictor Variables

1.000	0.829	0.768	0.108	0.033	0.771
0.829	1.000	0.775	0.115	0.061	0.783
0.768	0.775	1.000	0.272	0.205	0.851
0.108	0.115	0.272	1.000	0.636	0.600
0.033	0.061	0.205	0.636	1.000	0.545
0.771	0.783	0.851	0.600	0.545	1.000

TABLE 23.4.2   Matrix of Correlations
of Ipsative Predictor Variables
with Criterion Variables

0.298	0.304	0.350
0.323	0.341	0.368
0.296	0.266	0.385
0.249	0.176	0.369
0.138	0.087	0.254
0.367	0.330	0.486

TABLE 23.4.3   Optimal Regression
Matrix B for Estimating Criterion
Variables from Ipsative
Predictor Variables

0.061	0.073	0.069
0.201	0.287	0.153
−0.040	−0.121	0.025
0.202	0.145	0.253
−0.053	−0.051	−0.001
0.104	0.094	0.141

Table 23.4.3 shows the matrix of optimal regression vectors calculated by means of Eqs. 23.4.1–23.4.5.

23.5 Increasing the Degrees of Freedom by Factor Analysis

23.5.1 Characteristics of the Method. We have indicated that one of the chief difficulties encountered in the classical multiple regression technique is with reference to the problem of overfitting, or of degrees of freedom. We have seen, for example, that the classical methods break down when, in a particular sample, we have as many or more attributes as entities.

Even though the number of entities may be somewhat greater than the number of attributes, we may still get into difficulty because of not having enough degrees of freedom. A matrix of regression vectors for transforming a data matrix of predictor measures to an estimated matrix of criterion measures may give very poor results on another sample, simply because we have capitalized on random variance and covariance components of the predictor variables.

We have seen, however, in Chapter 20, that we may solve for a matrix of factor scores which gives almost as much information as the original data matrix of predictor measures, and in which the number of factors may be much smaller than the number of attributes or variables in the predictor data matrix.

The rationale of this section has been considered by Horst (1941), Leiman (1950), and Burket (1964). It is based on the assumption that with a small number of factors as compared to the number of predictor variables, one can reproduce the matrix of predictor measures for the sample with sufficient accuracy by the major product of the factor score and factor loading matrices. This, of course, is one of the basic concepts in the factor analytic procedures discussed in Chapter 4.

Suppose now that we begin with a predictor data matrix, and go through the conventional procedures of getting the correlation or covariance matrix of this data matrix and the principal axis factor loading matrix. Assume that we have taken out only the reliable variance. Suppose also that we solve for the factor score matrix by one of the methods of Chapter 20. We may then assume that the factor score matrix represents that part of the predictor scores which is free from error or random variation. In other words, it is free from variance which could not be predicted from one time to another with the same set of measures, or with a set of measures from another comparable set. This random variance may be considered as that part of the predictor variables which is capitalized upon to increase the multiple correlations of the criterion variables with the predictor variables in a particular sample, but which, because it is random, reduces the predictive effectiveness of the resulting regression matrix when it is applied to new samples.

The traditional regression matrix may be regarded as consisting in part of this random variation. But suppose one uses the factor score matrix obtained from the predictor measures as a basis for estimating the criterion measures in the sample. The regression matrix calculated from the factor score matrix may be assumed to be free of the random error in the predictor part of the matrix, and therefore it should be more efficient when applied to other samples. One can, then, solve for such a factor score matrix for a particular sample, and find a regression matrix which, for the sample, gives the best least square estimate of the criterion submatrix. One may also, presumably, solve for the factor score matrices from the predictor data matrices on successive samples, and then apply the regression matrix found on the first sample to the subsequent factor score matrices to estimate the corresponding criterion submatrices.

One difficulty with this approach is that one can not be sure how many factors he needs, to account for the predictor data matrices in the successive samples. He may need more or less than in the original sample. Furthermore, certain problems of transformation of the factor score matrices on the new samples enter in, because one can not be sure that the arbitrary factor scores represent the same factors as in the sample. We must remember, however, that the factor score matrix is obtained by a transformation of the data matrix, as indicated in Section 20.5. Therefore, one may apply a second transformation to this first transformation. We may then consider the product of these two transformation matrices which may be applied directly to the data matrix.

We see, therefore, that one need not go through the two stages of calculating the two transformation matrices. For a given sample, one may calculate a single transformation matrix for transforming the predictor data matrix to the estimated criterion matrix, on the assumption that the system has only a limited number of factors, much smaller than the number of predictors. This will involve a nonbasic transformation.

In any case, this discussion should make clear that the type of solution we are now considering involves factor analytic type computations on the predictor data submatrix, or on the covariance or correlation matrix derived from it. The type of solution required is the basic structure solution for the first m factors of the covariance or correlation matrix, since such a solution for a particular scaling of the variables gives the best least square, lower rank approximation to the data matrix.

The implication of this rationale is that one should use total variances in the diagonal of the correlation or covariance matrix. In the case of the correlation matrix, this means that one must use 1 in the diagonal, and that the traditional cut and try methods for communalities in the diagonal are not appropriate.

23.5.2 Computational Equations

23.5.2a DEFINITION OF NOTATION

R_{pp}, R_{pc}, and B are the same as in the preceding section.
Q and Q' are the basic orthonormals of R_{pp}.
Δ^2 is the basic diagonal of R_{pp}.
$Q_{(m)}$ is the first m vectors of Q.
$\Delta_{(m)}^2$ is the first m elements of Δ^2.

23.5.2b THE EQUATIONS

$$R_{pp} = \frac{x_p' x_p}{N} \tag{23.5.1}$$

$$R_{pc} = \frac{x_p' x_c}{N} \tag{23.5.2}$$

$$Q\Delta^2 Q' = R_{pp} \tag{23.5.3}$$

$$b = Q_{(m)} \Delta_{(m)}^{-1} \tag{23.5.4}$$

$$B = b(b' R_{pc}) \tag{23.5.5}$$

23.5.3 Computational Instructions.
The computational procedure for this method begins with the correlation matrix of predictor variables, as indicated in Eq. 23.5.1.

We also require the correlation of the predictor variables with the criterion variables, as indicated in Eq. 23.5.2.

The first stage in the solution for the regression matrix is given by Eq. 23.5.3. Here we indicate the basic structure solution for the matrix of correlations of the predictor variables calculated in Eq. 23.5.1. One need not, however, calculate all of the vectors of the basic orthonormal and the corresponding elements of the basic diagonal. One of the methods of the preceding chapters may be used to solve for only those vectors and diagonals which account for the proportion of total variance of the predictor set which has been pre-specified. Ordinarily, this would probably be in the neighborhood of 60–80 percent, or perhaps more in some cases.

Equation 23.5.4 gives the matrix $Q_{(m)}$, postmultiplied by the inverse of the reciprocal square roots of the first m elements of Δ^2, given by Eq. 23.5.3.

Equation 23.5.5 shows the solution for the matrix of regression vectors B. Here we first premultiply the matrix of Eq. 23.5.2 by the transpose of the matrix of Eq. 23.5.4. This product is then premultiplied by the natural order of the latter matrix.

It can be seen now that if the number of factors is less than the number of criterion variables, the B matrix of Eq. 23.5.5 is a major product and therefore nonbasic. Nevertheless, the solution does have the optimal properties of a general inverse solution discussed in Section 3.8.

It must be remembered that this regression matrix is to be applied to a set of normalized scores, rather than to a set of deviation or raw measures. If one wishes to apply it to a set of raw or deviation measures, the appropriate linear transformations must be made on the basis of the means and variances of the sample.

23.5.4 Numerical Example. In this example we use the same matrix of predictor intercorrelations as in Table 23.2.2, and the same matrix of correlations of criteria with predictors as in Table 23.2.3.

Table 23.5.1 shows the first two principal axis factor vectors for the correlation matrix of Table 23.2.2.

Table 23.5.2 gives the reduced rank matrix of regression vectors for estimating the three criterion variables from the six predictor variables. This matrix was calculated by means of Eqs. 23.5.3–23.5.5.

TABLE 23.5.1   First Two Principal Axis Factor Loading Vectors by Rows from Correlation Matrix of Predictor Variables

0.753	0.766	0.841	0.597	0.557	0.606
−0.559	−0.542	−0.373	0.610	0.702	0.646

TABLE 23.5.2   Reduced Rank Matrix of Regression Vectors

0.106	0.113	0.119
0.108	0.114	0.122
0.114	0.113	0.136
0.064	0.034	0.108
0.057	0.025	0.103
0.064	0.033	0.110

23.6   Predictor Selection and Factor Analysis

23.6.1   Characteristics of the Method. In the method just discussed we have assumed that we wish to use all of the potential variables for estimating a given set of criterion variables, but that we wish to suppress that part of the variance in the predictor set which may be attributed to random variance. Sometimes many more predictors may be available than it is feasible to use in an administrative or operational situation. One may be able to administer a very large number of potential predictor measures to an experimental group.

It may be, however, that for subsequent administrative purposes, much less time is available for testing. It may also be that facilities and resources for processing the data and estimating criterion measures on new samples are limited, even assuming that regression matrices of the type indicated in the preceding section are available. For this reason it may be desirable, not only to have the advantages of the previous method in suppressing error or random variance in a potential set of predictor variables, but also to select only a limited number of these predictor variables for administrative purposes.

Current and traditional predictor selection techniques have serious limitations, as indicated previously. If the number of potential predictor variables from which a subset is to be selected is large, the selection procedures may capitalize on chance error or, by using statistical tests of the null hypothesis, they may well reject variables which would in practice be useful in prediction. As a matter of fact, the classical types of significance tests do not seem at all appropriate in the predictor selection procedures. In effect, they reject a variable unless one can be almost positive that the addition of the variable will add to the predictive efficiency of the set. In any case, none of these methods takes into account errors of measurement or error variance in the predictor data.

The method we shall now present does take into account errors of measurement. It is similar to the previous method in that one begins with a principal axis factor analysis of the matrix of intercorrelations of the predictor data. One solves for the number of factors which account for the estimated amount of systematic variance in the set, just as in the previous method. Here also, 1's, rather than estimates of communalities, are used in the diagonal of the correlation matrix.

In addition to a solution for the largest principal axis vectors, a simple structure transformation of the principal axis factor loading matrix is also required. A basic assumption underlying this technique is that not only do we wish to eliminate as much unsystematic variance in the set of predictors as possible, but we also wish to identify those variables which are the purest measures of the factors represented by the set. The simple structure transformation may be either orthonormal or oblique, as discussed in Chapter 17. It is probably more convenient to use the orthonormal varimax method, since computer programs are readily available for this method. In general, it has been found to give as good or better results than the other methods.

The simple structure factor loading matrix enables us to identify those variables which are the best measures of the simple structure factors. We assume that these variables are the ones which will be most useful in the prediction of the criterion variables. The method then requires that, from the simple structure transformation of the principal axis factor loading matrix, we select subsets of variables such that each of the simple structure factors will be adequately represented by the subset.

After the subset of variables has been selected on the basis of their loadings in the simple structure factor loading matrix, these variables are now used as a subset to get a regression matrix whose rank is no greater than the number of factors extracted.

23.6.2   Computational Equations

23.6.2a   DEFINITION OF NOTATION

x is the standardized data matrix of predictor variables.

R_{pp} is the matrix of intercorrelations of the potential predictors.

Q and Δ^2 are the basic factors of R.

$Q_{(m)}$ and $\Delta_{(m)}{}^2$ are the first m vectors and elements, respectively, of the basic factors.

a is the m-factor principal axis factor loading matrix of R_{pp}.

H is the simple structure transformation matrix.

b is the simple structure factor loading matrix.

α is the matrix of selected rows from a.

w is the matrix of selected columns from x.

R_{ww} is the matrix of correlations among the selected predictor variables.

R_{wc} is the matrix of correlations of the selected predictor variables with the criterion variables.

23.6.2b   THE EQUATIONS

$$Q_{(m)}\Delta_{(m)}{}^2 Q_{(m)}' = R_{pp} + \varepsilon \qquad (23.6.1)$$

$$a = Q_{(m)}\Delta_{(m)} \qquad (23.6.2)$$

$$b = aH \qquad (23.6.3)$$

$$U = R_{ww}\alpha \qquad (23.6.4)$$

$$G = \alpha' U \qquad (23.6.5)$$

$$M = \alpha' R_{wc} \qquad (23.6.6)$$

$$A = G^{-1}M \qquad (23.6.7)$$

$$B = \alpha A \qquad (23.6.8)$$

23.6.3   Computational Instructions. We begin with the intercorrelation matrix of the total pool of predictor variables. We solve for the first m eigenvectors and eigenvalues of this matrix, as indicated in Eq. 23.6.1. It should be recalled that we may also solve for basic structure factors on the basis of the major product moment of a data matrix. In the type of solution indicated in this subsection, it may well be the case that we have many more variables than entities. This means, therefore, that the major product moment may be much smaller than the minor product moment or correlation matrix. In this case, the methods of Chapter 14 should be used to get the largest principal axis vectors of the correlation matrix without actually calculating the correlation matrix itself.

The principal axis factor loading matrix is given in Eq. 23.6.2. This is simply the matrix of the first m eigenvectors postmultiplied by the square root of the diagonal of the first m eigenvalues.

We then solve for a simple structure transformation of the principal axis factor loading matrix of Eq. 23.6.2 to get the simple structure factor loading matrix indicated in Eq. 23.6.3.

Next we examine the simple structure factor loading matrix b of Eq. 23.6.3. We select variables with the highest loadings in each of the factors. Presumably, we do not select any variables which have high loadings in more than one factor. The total number of variables selected should be no greater than the total number which it is believed would be feasible to use for prediction purposes in applied situations. In any case, on the basis of Eq. 23.6.3 we select a subset, say, w, from the total potential set of predictor variables.

We have now selected from the total potential pool those variables which will be included in the administrative or operational predictor set. We may then operate on this subset of selected predictor variables exactly as in the previous subsection to solve for a matrix of regression vectors. It is possible that, in such an operation, we would find that the number of factors required to account adequately for the systematic variance in the subset w was less than the number required to account adequately for the systematic variance in the total set. This would be a question of experimental fact to be determined computationally. We may, however, assume that the factor loading determination for the simple structure factor loading matrix of Eq. 23.6.3 gives a better indication of the factors represented in the subset than would a new principal axis factor solution for the subset of w variables. On the basis of this assumption we may then proceed as follows.

We lift from the factor loading matrix a of Eq. 23.6.2 those rows representing the selected variables, and call this factor loading matrix for the subset α. We then consider the correlation matrix R_{ww} involving only the selected set of predictors w. This correlation matrix is now postmultiplied by the α matrix, as indicated in Eq. 23.6.4.

Next we calculate the matrix of Eq. 23.6.5. This is the matrix U of Eq. 23.6.4 premultiplied by the transpose of the α matrix.

We also segregate the submatrix R_{wc} of the correlations of the selected predictor variables with the criterion variables. We then calculate Eq. 23.6.6. This is the correlation matrix R_{wc} premultiplied by the transpose of the α matrix.

Next we calculate the matrix A of Eq. 23.6.7. This is the matrix of Eq. 23.6.6 premultiplied by the inverse of the G matrix in Eq. 23.6.5.

Finally, we postmultiply the α matrix by the A matrix of Eq. 23.6.7. This gives the regression matrix B of Eq. 23.6.8.

This solution implies the calculation of a factor score matrix from the subset of w predictors, such that this factor score matrix postmultiplied by the transpose of the α or factor loading matrix for the subset gives the best least square approximation to the subset of predictor measures.

23.7 Mathematical Proofs

23.7.1 Rank Reduction Solution. The multiple regression model as a rank reduction model.

Consider the partitioned data matrix

$$x = [x_p, \quad x_c] \tag{23.7.1}$$

where we let x_p be the predictors and x_c the criteria. Consider the conventional regression form

$$x_p B - x_c = E \tag{23.7.2}$$

Let

$$\psi = trE'E = \min \tag{23.7.3}$$

The solution for B is well known to be

$$B = (x_p'x_p)^{-1}x_p'x_c \tag{23.7.4}$$

From Eqs. 23.7.1 and 23.7.2, we can write

$$[0, \quad E_c] = [x_p, \quad x_c] - x_p[I, \quad B] \tag{23.7.5}$$

where now Eq. 23.7.5 shows how we may regard the conventional least square solution as a rank n_p approximation to the supermatrix x, such that the first submatrix is given exactly by the approximation. The left side of Eq. 23.7.5 shows that the residual is of rank n_p less than that of x, assuming x basic. We may therefore suspect that Eq. 23.7.5 is a rank reduction form, and ask what the arbitrary multipliers are. Suppose we designate the right and left multipliers, respectively, as $\begin{bmatrix} {}_RA_p \\ {}_RA_c \end{bmatrix}$ and ${}_LA$. We have then

$$[E_p, \quad E_c] = [x_p, \quad x_c] - [x_p, \quad x_c]\begin{bmatrix} {}_RA_p \\ {}_RA_c \end{bmatrix}\left[{}_LA[x_p, \quad x_c]\begin{bmatrix} {}_RA_p \\ {}_RA_c \end{bmatrix}\right]^{-1} {}_LA[x_p, \quad x_c] \tag{23.7.6}$$

We shall verify that

$$\begin{bmatrix} {}_RA_p \\ {}_RA_c \end{bmatrix} = \begin{bmatrix} (x_p'x_p)^{-1} \\ 0 \end{bmatrix} \tag{23.7.7}$$

$$_LA = x_p' \tag{23.7.8}$$

satisfy Eq. 23.7.5. Substituting Eqs. 23.7.7 and 23.7.8 in Eq. 23.7.6,

$$[E_p, \quad E_c] = [x_p, \quad x_c] - [x_p, \quad x_c]\begin{bmatrix}(x_p{}'x_p)^{-1} & \\ 0 & \end{bmatrix}\left[x_p{}'[x_p, \quad x_c]\begin{bmatrix}(x_p{}'x_p)^{-1} & \\ 0 & \end{bmatrix}\right]^{-1}$$

$$x_p{}'[x_p, \quad x_c] \tag{23.7.9}$$

From Eq. 23.7.9,

$$[E_p, \quad E_c] = [x_p, \quad x_c] - [x_p, \quad x_c]\begin{bmatrix}(x_p{}'x_p)^{-1} & \\ 0 & \end{bmatrix}x_p{}'[x_p, \quad x_c] \tag{23.7.10}$$

or

$$[E_p, \quad E_c] = [x_p, \quad x_c] - x_p[I, \quad (x_p{}'x_p)^{-1}x_p{}'x_c] \tag{23.7.11}$$

Using Eq. 23.7.4 in Eq. 23.7.11,

$$[0, \quad E_c] = [x_p, \quad x_c] - x_p[I, \quad B] \tag{23.7.12}$$

which is the same as Eq. 23.7.5.

23.7.2 Basic Structure Solution

Consider the conventional regression form

$$R_{pp}\beta = R_{pc} \tag{23.7.13}$$

where R_{pp} is the correlation matrix for the predictor variables, and R_{pc} is the vector of correlations of the predictor variables with the criterion variables. The solution for β is, of course,

$$\beta = R_{pp}{}^{-1}R_{pc} \tag{23.7.14}$$

This solution can be cast in the form of a basic structure solution. From Eq. 23.7.13, we have

$$[R_{pp}, \quad -R_{pc}]\begin{bmatrix}\beta \\ 1\end{bmatrix} = 0 \tag{23.7.15}$$

Premultiplying Eq. 23.7.15 by the transpose of the left factor, we get

$$\begin{bmatrix}R_{pp}{}^2 & -R_{pp}R_{pc} \\ -R_{pc}{}'R_{pp} & R_{pc}{}'R_{pc}\end{bmatrix}\begin{bmatrix}\beta \\ 1\end{bmatrix} = \begin{bmatrix}0 \\ 0\end{bmatrix} \tag{23.7.16}$$

Let M' be the row supermatrix on the left of Eq. 23.7.15, and b the supervector. Then from Eqs. 23.7.15 and 23.7.16,

$$MM'b = 0 \tag{23.7.17}$$

Let L be equal to or greater than the largest root of MM'. Since by Eq. 23.7.17 MM' has a zero root, K is the largest root of $KI - MM'$. Hence we consider

$$(KI - MM')b = Kb \tag{23.7.18}$$

and solve Eq. 23.7.18 iteratively for b, which will be the eigenvector corresponding to the zero root in Eq. 23.7.17.

To avoid squaring R_{pp} we may write

$$\begin{bmatrix} \beta_i K \\ K \end{bmatrix} - \begin{bmatrix} R_{pp} \\ -R_{pc}' \end{bmatrix} \begin{bmatrix} R_{pp}, & -R_{pc} \end{bmatrix} \begin{bmatrix} \beta_i \\ 1 \end{bmatrix} = \begin{bmatrix} \beta_{i+1} K \\ K \end{bmatrix} \qquad (23.7.19)$$

and

$$\beta_{i+1} = \frac{_{i+1}b}{K} \qquad (23.7.20)$$

The constant K may be obtained to a sufficient degree of approximation by iterating several times with

$$b_{i+1} = \frac{MM'_{\,i}b}{\sqrt{_{i}bMM'_{\,i}b}} \qquad (23.7.21)$$

and

$$K_{i+1} = \sqrt{_{i+1}b'_{\,i+1}b} \qquad (23.7.22)$$

or more simply by

$$K = trR_{pp}^{\,2} + R_{pc}'R_{pc} \qquad (23.7.23)$$

23.7.3   The Nonbasic Solution

Consider the nonbasic data matrix x such that

$$xU = 0 \qquad (23.7.24)$$

Suppose we have the least square form

$$xb - y = \varepsilon \qquad (23.7.25)$$

If the basic structure of x is

$$x = P\Delta Q' \qquad (23.7.26)$$

then the general inverse solution for Eq. 23.7.25 is known from Chapter 3 to be

$$B = Q\Delta^{-1}P'y \qquad (23.7.27)$$

We need not, however, solve for the basic structure of x if U is known, as it is for ipsative measures. From Eq. 23.7.24, we write

$$x'xB - x'y = 0 \qquad (23.7.28)$$

but from Eq. 23.7.26,

$$x'x = Q\delta Q' = C \qquad (23.7.29)$$

Suppose we let

$$tt' = U'U \qquad (23.7.30)$$

$$u = Ut'^{-1} \qquad (23.7.31)$$

or, in fact, u may be any orthogonalization of U. We require now the general inverse of $x'x$, namely,

$$Q\delta^{-1}Q' = C^{(-1)} \tag{23.7.32}$$

We let

$$G = C + uu' \tag{23.7.33}$$

From Eqs. 23.7.29 and 23.7.33,

$$G = Q\delta Q' + uu' \tag{23.7.34}$$

We let

$$q = [Q, \quad u] \tag{23.7.35}$$

From Eqs. 23.7.24, 23.7.26, 23.7.31, and 23.7.35, q is square orthonormal. Let

$$D = \begin{bmatrix} \delta & 0 \\ 0 & I \end{bmatrix} \tag{23.7.36}$$

From Eqs. 23.7.34–23.7.36,

$$G = qDq' \tag{23.7.37}$$

so that Eq. 23.7.37 now gives the basic structure of G. From Eq. 23.7.36,

$$G^{-1} = qD^{-1}q' \tag{23.7.38}$$

From Eqs. 23.7.35–23.7.37,

$$G^{-1} = Q\delta^{-1}Q' + uu' \tag{23.7.39}$$

From Eqs. 23.7.32 and 23.7.39,

$$C^{(-1)} = G^{-1} - uu' \tag{23.7.40}$$

From Eqs. 23.7.33 and 23.7.40,

$$C^{(-1)} = (C + uu')^{-1} - uu' \tag{23.7.41}$$

The general inverse solution for B in Eq. 23.7.28 is

$$B = C^{(-1)}x'y \tag{23.7.42}$$

But from Eq. 23.7.41 in Eq. 23.7.42, we have

$$B = [(C + uu')^{-1} - uu']x'y \tag{23.7.43}$$

From Eqs. 23.7.24, 23.7.30, 23.7.31, and 23.7.43,

$$B = (C + uu')^{-1}x'y \tag{23.7.44}$$

If, in particular, we have an ipsative deviation score matrix X such that

$$X1 = g1 \tag{23.7.45}$$

where g is a scalar, then for the standard score matrix x it can be proved that

$$xD_\sigma 1 = 0 \tag{23.7.46}$$

where D_σ is a diagonal of standard deviations of X. In this case, C in Eq. 23.7.29 becomes the correlation matrix R, and U becomes

$$U = D_\sigma 1 \tag{23.7.47}$$

and from Eqs. 23.7.30, 23.7.31, and 23.7.47,

$$u = \frac{D_\sigma 1}{\sqrt{1' D_\sigma^2 1}} \tag{23.7.48}$$

For the regression matrix of such an ipsative set we would have, therefore,

$$B = \left[R_{pp} + \frac{D_\sigma 1\, 1' D_\sigma}{1' D_\sigma^2 1} \right]^{-1} R_{pc} \tag{23.7.49}$$

where R_{pp} is the intercorrelation matrix of the ipsative predictors, D_σ^2 is a diagonal of their variances, and R_{pc} is the matrix of correlations of the predictors with the criteria.

23.7.4   Increasing the Degrees of Freedom by Factor Analysis

Consider the case in which we have many predictors as compared to the number of entities, and the least square form

$$xB - y = \varepsilon \tag{23.7.50}$$

If the ratio of the width to the height is large, the conventional least square solution is not feasible because of insufficient degrees of freedom. Consider the least square approximation matrix

$$U = P_{(m)} \Delta_{(m)} Q_{(m)}' \tag{23.7.51}$$

where (m) means the first m basic structure vectors and diagonals of x.

We substitute U for x in Eq. 23.7.50, thus,

$$UB - y = \varepsilon \tag{23.7.52}$$

and consider the general inverse solution for B, namely,

$$B = Q_{(m)} \Delta_{(m)}^{-1} P_{(m)}' y \tag{23.7.53}$$

But we know the solution for $P_{(m)}$ to be

$$P_{(m)} = x Q_{(m)} \Delta_{(m)}^{-1} \tag{23.7.54}$$

Substituting Eq. 23.7.54 in Eq. 23.7.53,

$$B = Q_{(m)} \Delta_{(m)}^{-2} Q_{(m)}' R_{xy} \tag{23.7.55}$$

where

$$R_{xy} = \frac{x'y}{N} \tag{23.7.56}$$

It is seen from Eq. 23.7.55 that we need compute only the basic structure factors of R_{xx}, where

$$R_{xx} = \frac{x'x}{N} \tag{23.7.57}$$

23.7.5 Predictor Selection and Factor Analysis

Suppose we have calculated the basic structure of

$$R = Q\Delta^2 Q' \tag{23.7.58}$$

and the principal axis factor loading matrix a. We also calculate the simple structure matrix

$$b = aH \tag{23.7.59}$$

We may now use the simple structure matrix to select those variables which have the highest loadings in each factor. Presumably, we would select several or more variables for each factor, but in no case would we select a variable to represent more than one factor. Also, presumably, we would select approximately the same number of variables for each factor. We consider, then, the reduced matrix of factor loadings, say, α, and the reduced matrix of test variables w. We then have the approximation equation

$$w = v\alpha' = \varepsilon \tag{23.7.60}$$

where v is the factor score matrix, and the least square solution is

$$v = w\alpha(\alpha'\alpha)^{-1} \tag{23.7.61}$$

We consider now the regression form

$$vb - y = \varepsilon \tag{23.7.62}$$

The solution for b in Eq. 23.7.62 is

$$b = (v'v)^{-1}v'y \tag{23.7.63}$$

From Eq. 23.7.61 in Eq. 23.7.63,

$$b = [(\alpha'\alpha)^{-1}\alpha'(w'w)\alpha(\alpha'\alpha)^{-1}]^{-1}(\alpha'\alpha)^{-1}\alpha'w'y \tag{23.7.64}$$

or

$$b = (\alpha'\alpha)(\alpha'(w'w)\alpha)^{-1}\alpha'w'y \tag{23.7.65}$$

Substituting Eqs. 23.7.61 and 23.7.65 in Eq. 23.7.62 gives

$$w\alpha(\alpha'(w'w)\alpha)^{-1}\alpha'w'y - y = \varepsilon \tag{23.7.66}$$

or, letting B be the matrix of regression vectors, we have

$$B = w\alpha(\alpha'(w'w)\alpha)^{-1}\alpha' R_{wc} \tag{23.7.67}$$

where R_{wc} is the vector of correlations of the selected predictors with the criteria y.

We may also get the basic structure

$$w'w = q\delta q' \qquad (23.7.68)$$

and let

$$B = q\delta^{-1}q'R_{wc} \qquad (23.7.69)$$

This could retain more of the information in w for the same number of factors than would Eq. 23.7.67, even though more random variation might be retained.

Chapter 24

Multiple Set Factor Analysis

We discussed in Chapter 14 the multicategory type of data matrix. A closely related type of data matrix will be considered in this chapter.

We may have an experimental design which includes several or more sets of measures on the same set of entities, and the problem is to determine to what extent the various sets are essentially the same. Data of this type have been discussed by Campbell and Fisk (1959) in terms of the multitrait-multimethod matrix. Comments on the multitrait-multimethod matrix have also been presented by Humphries (1960). Examples of this general type of problem may be considered briefly.

24.1 Experimental Sources of the Models

Suppose we have two or more sets of tests which we assume measure the same set of abilities. In particular, these may be sets of comparable forms for some specified battery of tests. We administer these sets of comparable forms to a sample of persons. We may wish to determine to what extent the various sets all measure the same set of functions. A similar situation arises when we administer the same set of tests two or more times to the same group of persons. Here we may wish to determine to what extent the same set of functions are being evaluated by the repeated administrations.

Another variation of this general type of design may consist of giving the same sets of measures to the same group under several or more different sets of instructions. For example, suppose the measures were a number of scales in a personality schedule. We may administer the schedule to the same group three different times under three different instructions as follows: (1) answer the items as they apply to you, (2) answer them as you think they apply to most people, (3) answer according to what you regard as the socially desirable form of behavior. We may then be interested in finding to what extent the three different sets of instructions result in the same set of evaluations.

A similar type of problem arises in factor analysis studies. Suppose we have administered the same set of measures to two or more different groups of persons, and have carried out a factor analysis of the variables for each group. The variables may be test scores, personality items, physiological measures, or any combination we wish. The groups may be random subgroups of a larger group, or they may be differentiated on the basis of sex, hospitalization, age, and so on. We may have, for example, only two groups: normals and hospitalized. Or each of these may be subdivided according to sex so that we would have a total of four groups. We might then calculate a factor loading matrix for each of the groups on the same set of variables. The problem now is to determine to what extent these various factor matrices represent the same set of factors. Many more experimental situations can be invented which would be special cases of the general design.

The general problem may be stated as follows. Suppose we have m sets of measures on a group of N entities where the number of measures in set i is n_i. It is not essential that the number of variables in all sets be the same. How can we find for each set of measures a transformation so that the m sets of transformed measures will be maximally congruent, one with another? The extent to which the transformed sets are mutually similar or congruent will indicate to what extent they are all measures of the same set of underlying variables. Or to put it conversely, the extent to which a transformed set deviates from the others is an indication of the extent to which it measures factors not measured by the other sets. While the original sets may not all have the same number of variables, the transformed sets will. Ordinarily, however, the number will not exceed the number for the smallest set of original variables. In the examples given of sets of comparable forms of tests, or of repeated administrations of a set of measures either under the same or successively different instructions or conditions, the original sets will all have the same number of variables. In the case of sets of factor matrices for different groups on the same sets of variables, the factor matrices may have different numbers of factors.

24.2 Characteristics of the Methods

Various criteria of similarity may be specified as a basis for transforming a number of sets and for expressing the degree of similarity. We shall assume that each set of variables has first been subjected to an orthogonalizing transformation. We then consider further transformations such that the new sets of transformed variables shall be as nearly alike from one set to another as possible, according to the specified model. Four different models will be considered. These we shall call (1) the *maximum correlation method*, (2) the *rank one approximation method*, (3) the *oblique maximum variance method*, and (4) the *orthogonal maximum variance method*.

24.2.1 The Maximum Correlation Method. In the first model, we consider a vector transformation for each set of variables such that the sum of the intercorrelations among the transformed variables is a maximum. We then consider a second vector transformation of each set such that the sum of the intercorrelations of these transformed variables is also a maximum, with the restriction that each of this second group of transformed variables shall correlate zero with the first transformed variable from its set. Similarly, a third transformed variable from each set is determined so as to yield a maximum sum of intercorrelations and zero correlations with the first two transformed variables from its own set. This process may continue until the number of transformed variables for each set is equal to the number of variables in the smallest set. The criterion of similarity for each successive group of transformed variables is the sum of their intercorrelations.

24.2.2 The Rank One Approximation Method.

The second model specifies that the intercorrelations of the first transformed variables for the m sets shall give the best least square approximation to a rank one matrix. The intercorrelations of the second transformed variables for the m sets shall also give the best least square approximations to a rank one matrix, and at the same time shall be orthogonal to the first transformed variable from its own set. Similarly, the intercorrelations of the third and following transformed variables for each set shall be best least square approximations to rank one matrices, and at the same time shall be orthogonal to all the previously transformed variables from its own set. For each group of transformed variables, the largest root of the matrix of intercorrelations is a measure of how well the matrix approximates a rank one matrix. If this root were m, the intercorrelations would all be 1. The root can never be greater than the number of sets m.

24.2.3 The Oblique Maximum Variance Method.

The third model begins by considering the best rank n_s approximation to all m sets of variables. The best least square orthonormal factor score matrix of width n_s is determined from the superset of m subsets of measures. A transformation for each subset is then found which gives the best least square fit to the factor score matrix. This method does not in general yield transformed variables which are uncorrelated within sets. The measure of fit to the factor score matrix is the sum of the first m roots of the supermatrix of intercorrelations of the sets of variables prior to transformation. This sum cannot exceed nm, the total number of variables. Although this least square transformation yields transformed variables whose variances cannot exceed 1, in actual practice they are subsequently normalized.

24.2.4 The Orthogonal Maximum Variance Method.

The fourth model is similar to the third, except that the additional constraint of orthonormality is imposed on the transformation matrices. As a consequence, the transformed variables are uncorrelated within sets, and are all of unit variance. With this constraint, however, the transformed sets cannot in general be as good least square approximations to the factor score matrix as in the case of the third model. The measure of fit to the factor score matrix is a little more involved than for the third model. We consider the covariance matrices for each set of transformed variables in model three. We consider further the latent roots of each of these matrices. The sum of the square roots of all these nm roots is the measure of agreement. It cannot be greater than nm.

24.3   The Case of Two Sets

Before beginning an analysis involving any of the four models, it is usually convenient to apply some preliminary transformation to each set of variables so that they will be mutually orthogonal within sets. When this is done, it is interesting that all four models reduce to the same solution for only two sets of variables. In this case, the third model also yields transformed variables which are mutually orthogonal within sets. Furthermore, for all four models, the correlations of noncorresponding variables between sets are all zero. This is not generally true for any of the four models in the case of more than two sets.

For the case of two sets of variables, the solution was first considered by Hotelling (1936). Subsequently, Hotelling's solution has come to be called, not too aptly, the *canonical correlation*. Actually, Hotelling was concerned primarily with a special case of the two-set problem. Here, one set of variables consisted of independent or predictor variables, and the other of criterion or dependent variables. The variables in each set could be selected in any way desired, and were not necessarily regarded as the same for each set. Neither did the two sets necessarily have the same number of variables. Hotelling was concerned with a single vector transformation for each set, such that the correlation between the two sets was a maximum. His technique, however, was capable of yielding additional transformed variables, even though these were not considered a major interest at the time. A more convenient computational procedure than that published by Hotelling has been presented (Horst, 1961b). This consists of a preliminary orthogonalization of each subset.

The technique for the case of two sets has been used to compare the factor structure of the Minnesota Multiphasic Personality Inventory on a group of normal and hospitalized cases (Mees, 1959).

The rationale and computational procedure for the first model have recently been developed by Horst (1961a). The other three models have also been presented by Horst (1961b) in a later publication.

24.4 The Preliminary Orthogonalizations

In this chapter we shall apply all four models to the same set of data so as to provide a comparison of the four methods. The data are taken from Thurstone and Thurstone (1941). They consist of scores on three sets of tests. In each set are three tests, designed to measure verbal, numerical, and spatial ability. For all four models, we start with a supermatrix of inter-correlations in which the ijth matric element is the matrix of intercorrelations of the ith set with the jth set.

If there is reason to believe that the experimental variables in each set may be represented appropriately by a smaller set of factor variables, then the procedures of preceding chapters may be used for transforming the original sets of variables to sets with a reduced number of orthogonal uncorrelated factor scores. If, however, we assume that all of the variables in each of the sets represent systematic unique variance, then we may use a simpler method for orthogonalizing the sets.

24.4.1 Computational Equations

24.4.1a DEFINITION OF NOTATION

r is the supermatrix of correlations involving all sets of variables.

D_r is a diagonal supermatrix of the diagonal submatrices of r.

D_t is a diagonal supermatrix whose matric diagonal elements are the lower triangular factors of the corresponding matric elements in D_r.

R is the supermatrix of correlations involving all sets of orthogonalized variables.

24.4.1b THE EQUATIONS

$$r = \begin{bmatrix} r_{11} & r_{12} & \cdots & r_{1m} \\ r_{21} & r_{22} & \cdots & r_{2m} \\ \cdots & \cdots & \cdots & \cdots \\ r_{m1} & r_{m2} & \cdots & r_{mm} \end{bmatrix} \qquad (24.4.1)$$

$$D_r = \begin{bmatrix} r_{11} & 0 & \cdots & 0 \\ 0 & r_{22} & \cdots & 0 \\ \cdots & \cdots & \cdots & \cdots \\ 0 & 0 & \cdots & r_{mm} \end{bmatrix} \qquad (24.4.2)$$

$$D_t = \begin{bmatrix} t_1 & 0 & \cdots & 0 \\ 0 & t_2 & \cdots & 0 \\ \cdots & \cdots & \cdots & \cdots \\ 0 & 0 & \cdots & t_m \end{bmatrix} \qquad (24.4.3)$$

$$D_t D_t' = D_r \qquad (24.4.4)$$

$$R = D_t^{-1} r D_t'^{-1} \qquad (24.4.5)$$

$$R = \begin{bmatrix} I & R_{12} & \cdots & R_{1m} \\ R_{21} & I & \cdots & R_{2m} \\ \cdots & \cdots & \cdots & \cdots \\ R_{m1} & R_{m2} & \cdots & I \end{bmatrix} \qquad (24.4.6)$$

24.4.2 Computational Instructions. We begin with the supermatrix of correlations indicated in Eq. 24.4.1, where the ijth matric element gives the correlations of the ith set of variables with the jth set.

Equation 24.4.2 is the diagonal supermatrix whose ith element is the ith diagonal matric element from Eq. 24.4.1, namely, r_{ii}. This is the matrix of intercorrelations among the variables in the ith set.

Equation 24.4.3 displays in expanded notation the diagonal supermatrix of lower triangular factors of the diagonal elements of D_r in Eq. 24.4.2.

The first computational equation is actually Eq. 24.4.4. This indicates the triangular factoring of the matrix given by Eq. 24.4.2.

Equation 24.4.5 shows the pre- and postmultiplication of the matrix r in Eq. 24.4.1 by the inverse of the matrix D_t and its transpose, respectively. This gives the supermatrix R of correlations involving all sets of the orthogonalized variables.

Equation 24.4.6 shows the matric elements of the supermatrix R calculated in Eq. 24.4.5. This is now the supermatrix of correlations which will be used as a basis for calculating the sets of transformation matrices for each of the four maximum similarity models.

24.4.3 Numerical Example. Table 24.4.1 gives the supermatrix of correlations among three sets of three variables each. The sets, after appropriate transformations, are assumed to measure the same variables.

TABLE 24.4.1   Supermatrix r of Correlations Among Sets of Variables

1.000	0.249	0.271	0.636	0.183	0.185	0.626	0.369	0.279
0.249	1.000	0.399	0.138	0.654	0.262	0.190	0.527	0.356
0.271	0.399	1.000	0.180	0.407	0.613	0.225	0.471	0.610
0.636	0.138	0.180	1.000	0.091	0.147	0.709	0.254	0.191
0.183	0.654	0.407	0.091	1.000	0.296	0.103	0.541	0.394
0.185	0.262	0.613	0.147	0.296	1.000	0.179	0.437	0.496
0.626	0.190	0.225	0.709	0.103	0.179	1.000	0.291	0.245
0.369	0.527	0.471	0.254	0.541	0.437	0.291	1.000	0.429
0.279	0.356	0.610	0.191	0.394	0.496	0.245	0.429	1.000

Table 24.4.2 gives a type 3 column supervector, each element of which is the inverse of the upper triangular factor of the corresponding diagonal matric element of the supermatrix in Table 24.4.1.

Table 24.4.3 is the supermatrix of correlations of the orthogonalized sets of the variables represented in Table 24.4.1. It is obtained after constructing a diagonal supermatrix whose diagonal elements are the corresponding

TABLE 24.4.2   Supermatrix Of Inverse
Upper Triangular Matrices $_it'$

1.0000	−0.2571	−0.2034
	1.0325	−0.3929
		1.1115
1.0000	−0.0914	−0.1278
	1.0042	−0.3008
		1.0554
1.0000	−0.3042	−0.1468
	1.0452	−0.4369
		1.1179

matric elements of Table 24.4.2. The supermatrix of Table 24.4.1 is postmultiplied by this diagonal supermatrix and premultiplied by its transpose to yield the matrix of Table 24.4.3. These computations are indicated by Eq. 24.4.5.

24.5   The Maximum Correlation Method

24.5.1   Computational Equations

24.5.1a   DEFINITION OF NOTATION

D_t and R have the same meaning as in Section 24.4.1a.

n_i is the number of variables in the ith set.

m is the number of sets.

n_s is the number of variables in the smallest set.

$_i\beta$ is the $n_i \times n_s$ matrix for transforming the ith orthogonalized set to maximum similarity.

$_ib$ is the $n_i \times n_s$ matrix for transforming the ith original set to maximum similarity.

D_β is an mth order diagonal supermatrix of the $_i\beta$ matrices.

ρ is the mth order supermatrix of intercorrelations within and between sets of maximally similar sets.

TABLE 24.4.3   Supermatrix R of Correlations Among Orthogonalized Sets of Variables

1.0000	−0.0000	0.0000	0.6360	0.1256	0.0589	0.6260	0.1953	0.0588
−0.0000	1.0000	0.0000	−0.0210	0.6328	0.0490	0.0352	0.4589	0.1293
0.0000	0.0000	1.0000	0.0165	0.1574	0.5210	0.0481	0.2377	0.4256
0.6360	−0.0210	0.0165	1.0000	0.0000	0.0000	0.7090	0.0498	−0.0015
0.1256	0.6328	0.1574	0.0000	1.0000	0.0000	0.0386	0.5318	0.1899
0.0589	0.0490	0.5210	0.0000	0.0000	1.0000	0.0673	0.2576	0.2993
0.6260	0.0352	0.0481	0.7090	0.0386	0.0673	1.0000	−0.0000	−0.0000
0.1953	0.4589	0.2377	0.0498	0.5318	0.2576	−0.0000	1.0000	0.0000
0.0588	0.1293	0.4256	−0.0015	0.1899	0.2993	−0.0000	0.0000	1.0000

24.5.1b THE EQUATIONS

$$D_{\beta_{.1}} = \begin{bmatrix} _1\beta_{.1} & 0 & \cdots & 0 \\ 0 & _2\beta_{.1} & \cdots & 0 \\ \cdots & \cdots & \cdots & \cdots \\ 0 & 0 & \cdots & _m\beta_{.1} \end{bmatrix} \qquad (24.5.1)$$

$$_1D_{U_{.1}}1 = {_1R}(_1D_{\beta_{.1}}1) \qquad (24.5.2)$$

$$_1D_{1\lambda}{}^2 = {_1D_{U_{.1}}}'{_1D_{U_1}} \qquad (24.5.3)$$

$$_2D_{\beta_{.1}} = {_1D_{U_{.1}}}{_1D_{1\lambda}}^{-1} \qquad (24.5.4)$$

$$_kD_{U_{.1}}1 = {_1R}{_kD_{\beta_{.1}}}1 \qquad (24.5.5)$$

$$_kD_{1\lambda}{}^2 = {_kD_{U_{.1}}}'{_kD_{U_{.1}}} \qquad (24.5.6)$$

$$_{k+1}D_{\beta_{.1}} = {_kD_{U_{.1}}}{_kD_{1\lambda}}^{-1} \qquad (24.5.7)$$

$$_2R = (I - D_{\beta_{.1}}D_{\beta_{.1}}'){_1R}(I - D_{\beta_{.1}}D_{\beta_{.1}}') \qquad (24.5.8)$$

$$_kD_{U_{.L}}1 = {_LR}{_kD_{\beta_{.L}}}1 \qquad (24.5.9)$$

$$_kD_{L\lambda}{}^2 = {_kD_{U_{.L}}}'{_kD_{U_{.L}}} \qquad (24.5.10)$$

$$_{k+1}D_{\beta_{.L}} = {_kD_{U_{.L}}}{_kD_{L\lambda}}^{-1} \qquad (24.5.11)$$

$$_{L+1}R = (I - D_{\beta_{.L}}D_{\beta_L}'){_LR}(I - D_{\beta_{.L}}D_{\beta_{.L}}') \qquad (24.5.12)$$

$$\rho = D_{\beta}'{_1RD_{\beta}} \qquad (24.5.13)$$

$$D_b = D_t'{}^{-1}D_{\beta} \qquad (24.5.14)$$

24.5.2 Computational Instructions. We begin with the supermatrix defined by Eq. 24.4.6. This is the matrix of correlations for the orthogonalized sets of variables.

We then consider a diagonal supermatrix whose diagonal elements are the first vectors respectively from the $_i\beta$ matrices. This matrix is shown in Eq. 24.5.1. It is, of course, not a computational equation.

We take some approximation to the diagonal supermatrix of Eq. 24.5.1. The diagonal vector elements may usually be taken as unit vectors.

The next step is to calculate the vector indicated by Eq. 24.5.2. The product in parentheses on the right simply indicates the collapse of the diagonal supervector of Eq. 24.5.1 into a simple vector. The $_1R$ supermatrix is postmultiplied by this vector to yield the vector on the left. The diagonal factor on the left is a supermatrix of the same simple and super order as the one on the right. The unit vector serves to collapse it into a simple vector. The reason for this notation will be clarified in the subsequent instructions.

Next we calculate the simple diagonal matrix indicated by Eq. 24.5.3. The order of this matrix is of course m, the number of sets. It is the minor product moment of the diagonal supermatrix on the left of Eq. 24.5.2. Obviously therefore, its elements are the minor product moments of the corresponding vector elements of $_1 D_{U_{.1}}$.

We now calculate the second approximation to the $D_{\beta_{.1}}$ matrix, as indicated by Eq. 24.5.4. This is the current $D_{U_{.1}}$ matrix postmultiplied by the reciprocal square root of the diagonal matrix calculated in Eq. 24.5.3. Obviously, the vector elements of $_2 D_{\beta_{.1}}$ are now normalized vectors.

To get the $k + 1$ approximation to the $D_{\beta_{.1}}$ vector, we proceed as in Eqs. 24.5.5–24.5.7. These are analogous, respectively, to Eqs. 24.5.2–24.5.4. The iterations may continue until the sum of the elements in $D_{1\lambda}$ stabilize to some specified tolerance limit, such as .0001.

We are now ready to begin the computations for the second set of vectors out of the $_i\beta$. First we calculate the reduced matrix $_2 R$, as indicated in Eq. 24.5.8 The $_1 R$ matrix is pre- and postmultiplied by the idempotent matrix in parentheses. This latter is obtained by subtracting from an identity matrix the major product moment of the $D_{\beta_{.1}}$ matrix. Actually, the computations can be simplified as indicated by the subroutine RESID in the Fortran programs for this chapter. The simplifications result from the definition of the $D_{\beta_{.1}}$ matrix.

To get the kth approximation to $D_{\beta_{.L}}$, the Lth vectors out of the $_i\beta$, we use Eqs. 24.5.9–24.5.11. The first approximation for $D_{\beta_{.L}}$ may be made up of unit vectors.

The $L + 1$ reduced R matrix is obtained as indicated in Eq. 24.5.12. This is analogous to Eq. 24.5.8. Again, simplifications in the calculations are introduced by the Fortran subroutine RESID.

The matrix ρ gives the intercorrelations for the maximally similar sets as obtained by Eq. 24.5.13. This is simply the $_1 R$ matrix post- and premultiplied by the D_β matrix and its transpose. Finally, to get the diagonal matrix D_b for transforming the sets before orthogonalization to maximum similarity, we use Eq. 24.5.14. Here we simply premultiply the D_β matrix by the transpose of the reciprocal of the D_t matrix.

24.5.3 Numerical Example.
This example begins with the supermatrix R of Table 24.4.3.

Table 24.5.1 gives the supermatrix whose matric elements are the $_i\beta$ transformation matrices. These are the matrices required to transform the orthogonalized sets to maximum similarity. They are calculated by means of Eqs. 24.5.2–24.5.12.

Table 24.5.2 gives the supermatrix ρ of correlations among the maximally similar sets. This matrix is calculated by first constructing a diagonal supermatrix D_β whose diagonal elements are the matric elements of the matrix in Table 24.5.1. The supermatrix R of Table 24.4.3 is then postmultiplied by this

TABLE 24.5.1 Supermatrix of
Transformation Matrices $_tβ$

0.7252	−0.6883	−0.0191
0.5196	0.5652	−0.6408
0.4519	0.4548	0.7675
0.6504	−0.7596	−0.0088
0.6305	0.5462	−0.5515
0.4237	0.3531	0.8341
0.6705	−0.7392	0.0632
0.6450	0.5387	−0.5421
0.3667	0.4042	0.8379

TABLE 24.5.2 Supermatrix ρ of Correlations Among Maximally Similar Sets

1.0000	0.0000	0.0000	0.7359	0.0277	−0.0215	0.7564	0.0195	0.0202
0.0000	1.0000	−0.0000	0.0235	0.6022	0.0018	−0.0277	0.5046	0.0386
0.0000	−0.0000	1.0000	−0.0163	−0.0377	0.4646	0.0162	0.0342	0.2660
0.7359	0.0235	−0.0163	1.0000	−0.0000	0.0000	0.7422	−0.0238	−0.0202
0.0277	0.6022	−0.0377	−0.0000	1.0000	−0.0000	−0.0322	0.6351	−0.0410
−0.0215	0.0018	0.4646	0.0000	−0.0000	1.0000	0.0215	−0.0050	0.1660
0.7564	−0.0277	0.0162	0.7422	−0.0322	0.0215	1.0000	−0.0000	0.0000
0.0195	0.5046	0.0342	−0.0238	0.6351	−0.0050	−0.0000	1.0000	0.0000
0.0202	0.0386	0.2660	−0.0202	−0.0410	0.1660	0.0000	0.0000	1.0000

diagonal matrix and premultiplied by its transpose, to give the supermatrix of Table 24.5.2.

Table 24.5.3 is the supermatrix of the $_ib$ transformation matrices. The matric elements of this supermatrix will transform the original sets of variables

TABLE 24.5.3   Supermatrix
of $_ib$ Submatrices

0.4997	−0.9261	−0.0104
0.3589	0.4049	−0.9632
0.5023	0.5055	0.8531
0.5386	−0.8546	−0.0650
0.5057	0.4423	−0.8047
0.4472	0.3727	0.8803
0.4205	−0.9624	0.1051
0.5140	0.3864	−0.9327
0.4099	0.4519	0.9367

directly to the maximally similar sets without going through the orthogonalization procedure. These $_ib$ matrices are calculated by premultiplying the $_i\beta$ matrices by the corresponding $_it'^{-1}$ matrices of Table 24.4.2.

24.6   The Rank One Approximation Method

24.6.1   Computational Equations

24.6.1a   DEFINITION OF NOTATION
The notation is the same as in the previous section.

24.6.1b   THE EQUATIONS

$$_{k+1}A_{.1} = \frac{_1R_kA_{.1}}{\sqrt{_kA_{.1}'\,_1R_kA_{.1}}} \qquad (24.6.1)$$

$$D_{A_{.1}} = \begin{bmatrix} _1A_{.1} & 0 & \cdots & 0 \\ 0 & _2A_{.1} & \cdots & 0 \\ \cdots & \cdots & \cdots & \cdots \\ 0 & 0 & \cdots & _mA_{.1} \end{bmatrix} \qquad (24.6.2)$$

$$D_{\beta.1} = D_{A_{.1}}(D_{A_{.1}}'D_{A_{.1}})^{-1/2} \qquad (24.6.3)$$

$$_2R = (I - D_{\beta_{.1}}D_{\beta_{.1}}{}')\,_1R(I - D_{\beta_{.1}}D_{\beta_{.1}}{}') \tag{24.6.4}$$

$$_{k+1}A_{.L} = \frac{_LR_kA_{.L}}{\sqrt{_kA_{.L}{}'\,_LR_kA_{.L}}} \tag{24.6.5}$$

$$D_{\beta.L} = D_{A.L}(D_{A.L}{}'D_{A.L})^{-1/2} \tag{24.6.6}$$

$$_{L+1}R = (I - D_{\beta.L}D_{\beta.L}{}')\,_LR(I - D_{\beta.L}D_{\beta.L}{}') \tag{24.6.7}$$

$$\rho = D_{\beta}{}'\,_1RD_{\beta} \tag{24.6.8}$$

$$D_b = D_t{}'^{-1}D_{\beta} \tag{24.6.9}$$

24.6.2 Computational Instructions.

The computations begin by finding the first principal axis factor loading vector $A_{.1}$ of $_1R$, the correlation matrix for the orthogonalized sets of variables. The $k + 1$ approximation is given in Eq. 24.6.1. This procedure will be recognized as the successive factor method of Chapter 7.

Equation 24.6.2 indicates a diagonal supermatrix whose vector elements $_iA_{.1}$ are respectively the subvectors of order n_i from $A_{.1}$.

Equation 24.6.3 indicates the normalization of the subvectors in $A_{.1}$. This gives the first vectors out of the $_i\beta$ matrices.

The next series of operations is indicated by Eq. 24.6.4. This gives $_2R$ which is the first reduction of the correlation matrix $_1R$. It is analogous to Eq. 24.5.8, and the series of computations necessary for the reduction are provided in the Fortran subroutine RESID.

The first principal axis factor vector corresponding to each $_LR$ is given by Eq. 24.6.5. This shows the $k + 1$ approximation to the $A_{.L}$ vector.

Equation 24.6.6 indicates the normalization of the subvectors of $A_{.L}$ to yield the Lth vectors from the $_i\beta$.

The general equation for calculating the $L + 1$ reduced R matrix from the Lth matrix is given by Eq. 24.6.7.

The ρ and b matrices are obtained as in the previous section by means of Eqs. 24.6.8 and 24.6.9.

24.6.3 Numerical Example.

We start with the supermatrix R of Table 24.4.3.

Table 24.6.1 gives the supermatrix of the $_i\beta$ matrices as calculated from Eqs. 24.6.1–24.6.7. These are the matrices for transforming the orthogonalized sets to maximum similarity.

Table 24.6.2 gives the supermatrix ρ of correlations among the maximally similar sets. These are obtained by means of Eq. 24.6.8.

Table 24.6.3 gives the supermatrix of $_ib$ transformation matrices as

TABLE 24.6.1 Supermatrix of Transformation Matrices $_i\beta$

0.7265	−0.6868	−0.0226
0.5184	0.5693	−0.6381
0.4511	0.4518	0.7697
0.6518	−0.7583	−0.0112
0.6294	0.5492	−0.5498
0.4231	0.3513	0.8352
0.6718	−0.7383	0.0597
0.6440	0.5423	−0.5396
0.3660	0.4009	0.8398

Table 24.6.2 Supermatrix ρ of Correlations for Maximally Similar Sets

1.0000	0.0000	0.0000	0.7358	0.0281	−0.0214	0.7564	0.0198	0.0202
0.0000	1.0000	−0.0000	0.0238	0.6025	0.0014	−0.0272	0.5042	0.0397
0.0000	−0.0000	1.0000	−0.0161	−0.0362	0.4645	0.0159	0.0355	0.2664
0.7358	0.0238	−0.0161	1.0000	−0.0000	0.0000	0.7423	−0.0237	−0.0203
0.0281	0.6025	−0.0362	−0.0000	1.0000	−0.0000	−0.0319	0.6352	−0.0386
−0.0214	0.0014	0.4645	0.0000	−0.0000	1.0000	0.0213	−0.0038	0.1659
0.7564	−0.0272	0.0159	0.7423	−0.0319	−0.0203	1.0000	−0.0000	0.0000
0.0198	0.5042	0.0355	−0.0237	0.6352	−0.0038	−0.0000	1.0000	0.0000
0.0202	0.0397	0.2664	0.0213	−0.0386	0.1659	0.0000	0.0000	1.0000

calculated from Eq. 24.6.9. The matrices transform the original sets directly to the maximally similar sets.

TABLE 24.6.3 Supermatrix of
$_ib$ Submatrices

0.5014	−0.9251	−0.0151
0.3580	0.4104	−0.9612
0.5014	0.5022	0.8555
0.5403	−0.8533	−0.0677
0.5047	0.4458	−0.8033
0.4465	0.3708	0.8814
0.4222	−0.9621	0.1006
0.5132	0.3917	−0.9309
0.4092	0.4482	0.9388

24.7 The Oblique Maximum Variance Method

24.7.1 Computational Equations

24.7.1a DEFINITION OF NOTATION

R, β, D_t, ρ, and b have the same meaning as in the previous sections. a is a principal axis factor matrix of the first n_s factors of R.

24.7.1b THE EQUATIONS

$$a = \begin{bmatrix} _1a \\ _2a \\ \vdots \\ _ma \end{bmatrix} \tag{24.7.1}$$

$$D_a = \begin{bmatrix} _1a & 0 & \cdots & 0 \\ 0 & _2a & \cdots & 0 \\ \cdots & \cdots & \cdots & \cdots \\ 0 & 0 & \cdots & _ma \end{bmatrix} \tag{24.7.2}$$

$$D_d = D_{D_a'D_a} \tag{24.7.3}$$

$$D_\beta = D_a D_d^{-1/2} \tag{24.7.4}$$

$$\rho = D_\beta' R D_\beta \tag{24.7.5}$$

$$D_b = D_t'^{-1} D_\beta \tag{24.7.6}$$

TABLE 24.7.1 Supermatrix of $_tβ$ Transformation Matrices

0.7265	−0.6673	−0.0423
0.5184	0.5835	−0.6269
0.4511	0.4628	0.7779
0.6518	−0.7583	0.0121
0.6294	0.5499	−0.5920
0.4231	0.3502	0.8058
0.6718	−0.7589	0.0570
0.6440	0.5220	−0.4927
0.3660	0.3894	0.8683

TABLE 24.7.2 Supermatrix ρ of Correlations for Maximally Similar Sets of Variables

1.0000	0.0265	−0.0048	0.7358	0.0281	−0.0403	0.7564	−0.0037	0.0503
0.0265	1.0000	0.0224	0.0433	0.6030	−0.0316	−0.0071	0.5045	0.0592
−0.0048	0.0224	1.0000	−0.0191	−0.0228	0.4653	0.0117	0.0469	0.2690
0.7358	0.0433	−0.0191	1.0000	−0.0000	−0.0238	0.7423	−0.0467	0.0077
0.0281	0.6030	−0.0228	−0.0000	1.0000	−0.0526	−0.0320	0.6359	−0.0153
−0.0403	−0.0316	0.4653	−0.0238	−0.0526	1.0000	0.0053	−0.0359	0.1666
0.7564	−0.0071	0.0117	0.7423	−0.0320	0.0053	1.0000	−0.0311	0.0389
−0.0037	0.5045	0.0469	−0.0467	0.6359	−0.0359	−0.0311	1.0000	0.0377
0.0503	0.0592	0.2690	0.0077	−0.0153	0.1666	0.0389	0.0377	1.0000

24.7.2   Computational Instructions. The computations for this model begin with a matrix a of the first n_s principal axis factor loading vectors of the matrix R. These may be computed according to one of the methods of Chapters 7 and 8. This matrix is then partitioned into the submatrices $_i a$ of order $n_i \times n_s$, as shown in Eq. 24.7.1.

Equation 24.7.2 indicates a diagonal supermatrix of the $_i a$ in Eq. 24.7.1. Next we calculate the diagonal supermatrix D_d of Eq. 24.7.3. This is a diagonal supermatrix of simple diagonal matrices $_i d$ of order n_s whose elements are the diagonals of the minor product moments of the corresponding $_i a$ matrices.

Equation 24.7.4 gives the calculations for the diagonal supermatrix of the $_i \beta$'s. This will be recognized as a normalizing operation on the column vectors of the $_i \beta$'s.

Equations 24.7.5 and 24.7.6 indicate the computations for ρ and the b matrices as in the previous sections.

24.7.3   Numerical Example. This example begins with the R matrix of Table 24.4.3.

Table 24.7.1 gives the supermatrix of $_i \beta$ transformation matrices, as calculated from the first n_s basic structure factor loading vectors of the matrix R and from Eqs. 24.7.3 and 24.7.4.

TABLE 24.7.3   Supermatrix of $_i b$
Transformation Matrices

0.5014	−0.9115	−0.0393
0.3580	0.4207	−0.9529
0.5014	0.5145	0.8647
0.5403	−0.8533	−0.0367
0.5047	0.4468	−0.8369
0.4465	0.3696	0.8504
0.4222	−0.9748	0.0794
0.5132	0.3755	−0.8943
0.4092	0.4353	0.9707

Table 24.7.2 gives the supermatrix ρ of correlations among the maximally similar sets as calculated from Eq. 24.7.5.

Table 24.7.3 gives the supermatrix of the $_i b$ transformation matrices as calculated by Eq. 24.7.6.

24.8   The Orthogonal Maximum Variance Method

24.8.1   Computational Equations

24.8.1a   DEFINITION OF NOTATION

R, β, D_t, b, and ρ have the same meaning as in previous sections.

D_a has the same meaning as in Eq. 24.7.2.

V_I is a supervector of identity matrices of order n_s.

D_H is a diagonal supermatrix of orthonormal matrices $_iH$ whose orders are $n_i \times n_s$.

D_d is a diagonal supermatrix of simple diagonal matrices whose orders are n_s.

24.8.1b   THE EQUATIONS

$$D_H\, D_d\, V_I = D_a{}'D_a\, D_H\, V_I \tag{24.8.1}$$

$$D_\beta = D_a\, D_H\, D_d^{-1/2} D_H{}' \tag{24.8.2}$$

$$\rho = D_\beta{}'RD_\beta \tag{24.8.3}$$

$$D_b = D_t{}'^{-1}D_\beta \tag{24.8.4}$$

24.8.2   Computational Instructions.   We begin with the same diagonal

supermatrix of $_ia$ submatrices as in Eq. 24.7.2.

The first step is to find the basic orthonormals and diagonals of the minor product moments of the $_ia$ matrices. These solutions are indicated by the supermatrix of Eq. 24.8.1. Here the D_H matrix is a diagonal supermatrix of the left orthonormals of the $_ia'$, and D_d is a diagonal supermatrix whose submatrices are the squares of the basic diagonal matrices of the $_ia$. These basic factors may be solved for by the methods of Chapter 9, since a complete solution for each $_ia$ is required.

Equation 24.8.2 indicates the solution for $_i\beta$ as a function of the $_ia$ and their basic factors. These computations are not spelled out in detail here, as the Fortran statements are provided in the Fortran programs for this chapter. The calculations would not be feasible for a desk computer.

The solutions for the ρ matrix and the b matrices are given by Eqs. 24.8.3 and 24.8.4, respectively, as in the previous sections.

24.8.3   Numerical Example.   Here, too, we begin with the supermatrix

R of Table 24.4.3.

Table 24.8.1 gives the supermatrix of the $_i\beta$ transformation matrices, as calculated from Eqs. 24.8.1 and 24.8.2.

Table 24.8.2 gives the supermatrix ρ of correlations among the maximally similar sets, as calculated from Eq. 24.8.3.

TABLE 24.8.1 Supermatrix of $_i\beta$ Transformation Matrices

0.7350	−0.6773	−0.0328						
0.5096	0.5836	−0.6322						
0.4473	0.4479	0.7741						
0.6518	−0.7584	−0.0008						
0.6232	0.5361	−0.5693						
0.4322	0.3706	0.8221						
0.6598	−0.7492	0.0581						
0.6601	0.5410	−0.5212						
0.3590	0.3822	0.8515						

TABLE 24.8.2 Supermatrix ρ of Correlations for Maximally Similar Sets of Variables

1.0000	0.0000	0.0000	0.7351	0.0198	−0.0288	0.7565	0.0019	0.0319
0.0000	1.0000	−0.0000	0.0331	0.6029	−0.0190	−0.0110	0.5035	0.0443
0.0000	−0.0000	1.0000	−0.0125	−0.0180	0.4652	0.0103	0.0373	0.2676
0.7351	0.0331	−0.0125	1.0000	0.0000	−0.0000	0.7423	−0.0346	−0.0077
0.0198	0.6029	−0.0180	0.0000	1.0000	0.0000	−0.0216	0.6358	−0.0251
−0.0288	−0.0190	0.4652	−0.0000	0.0000	1.0000	0.0111	−0.0211	0.1668
0.7565	−0.0110	0.0103	0.7423	−0.0216	0.0111	1.0000	0.0000	−0.0001
0.0019	0.5035	0.0373	−0.0346	0.6358	−0.0211	0.0000	1.0000	0.0000
0.0319	0.0443	0.2676	−0.0077	−0.0251	0.1668	−0.0001	0.0000	1.0000

Table 24.8.3 gives the supermatrix of the $_ib$ transformation matrices, as calculated from Eq. 24.8.4.

TABLE 24.8.3   Supermatrix of $_ib$
Transformation Matrices

0.5130	−0.9185	−0.0277
0.3505	0.4267	−0.9569
0.4972	0.4979	0.8605
0.5396	−0.8548	−0.0538
0.4958	0.4269	−0.8189
0.4561	0.3911	0.8676
0.4064	−0.9698	0.0916
0.5331	0.3985	−0.9168
0.4013	0.4273	0.9518

24.9   Mathematical Proofs

24.9.1   The Orthogonalization Procedure

Let x_i be an $N \times n_i$ matrix of standard measures for N cases; x be a supermatrix of m matrices x_i. Then

$$x = [x_1, \quad \cdots, \quad x_m] \tag{24.9.1}$$

Let t_i be a lower triangular matrix defined by

$$t_i t_i' = \frac{x_i' x_i}{N} \tag{24.9.2}$$

Let

$$D_t = \begin{bmatrix} t_1 & \cdots & 0 \\ \cdots & \cdots & \cdots \\ 0 & \cdots & t_m \end{bmatrix} \tag{24.9.3}$$

and

$$u = x D_t'^{-1} \tag{24.9.4}$$

Let

$$r = \frac{x'x}{N} \tag{24.9.5}$$

$$R = \frac{u'u}{N} \tag{24.9.6}$$

From Eqs. 25.9.4–24.9.6,

$$R = D_t^{-1} r D_t'^{-1} \tag{24.9.7}$$

Because of Eqs. 24.9.2, 24.9.4, and 24.9.5, the diagonal submatrices of R in Eq. 24.9.7 are all identity matrices which we indicate by

$$D_R = D_I \tag{24.9.8}$$

The proof for all four models proceeds from R in Eq. 24.9.7.

24.9.2   The Maximum Correlation Method
First we consider

$$\phi_1 = 1'{}_1\rho 1 \tag{24.9.9}$$

where ${}_1\rho$ is a matrix of intercorrelations of the first transformed variables. Because of the definitions of R and ${}_1\rho$, Eq. 24.9.9 may be written

$$\phi_1 = 1'D_{\beta_{.1}}'{}_1RD_{\beta_{.1}}1 \tag{24.9.10}$$

We impose the restriction

$$D_{\beta_{.1}}'D_{\beta_{.1}} = I \tag{24.9.11}$$

and set up the function

$$\psi_1 = \phi_1 - 1'D_{\beta_{.1}}'{}_1\lambda \tag{24.9.12}$$

where ${}_1\lambda$ is a vector of Lagrangian multipliers. From Eqs. 24.9.10 and 24.9.12, we get by symbolic differentiation with respect to $1'D_{\beta_{.1}}'$

$$\frac{\partial\psi}{\partial(1'D_{\beta_{.1}}')} = {}_1RD_{\beta_{.1}}1 - D_{\beta_{.1}1}\lambda \tag{24.9.13}$$

or equating Eq. 24.9.13 to zero we get

$$_1RD_{\beta_{.1}}1 = D_{\beta_{.1}1}\lambda \tag{24.9.14}$$

Premultiplying Eq. 24.9.14 by $D_{\beta_{.1}}'$ and using Eq. 24.9.11, we have

$$D_{\beta_{.1}}'{}_1RD_{\beta_{.1}}1 = {}_1\lambda \tag{24.9.15}$$

From Eqs. 24.9.9, 24.9.10, and 24.9.15,

$$_1\rho 1 - 1 = {}_1\lambda \tag{24.9.16}$$

If the variables are in standard units, then ${}_1\lambda_i$ is, according to Eq. 24.9.16, simply the sum of the correlations involving the ith row of ${}_1\rho$.

From Eqs. 24.9.9 and 24.9.16,

$$\phi_1 = 1'{}_1\lambda \tag{24.9.17}$$

Therefore, ϕ_1 is simply twice the sum of all the ${}_1\rho$ intercorrelations plus self correlations.

No rigorous proof has been developed to show that the iterative solutions given by Eqs. 24.5.9–24.5.11 converge for $D_{\beta_{.1}}$, or that the ϕ_1 obtained is a maximum. However, suppose we let $D_{_1\lambda}$ be a diagonal matrix such that

$$D_{_1\lambda}1 = {}_1\lambda \tag{24.9.18}$$

Substituting Eq. 24.9.18 in Eq. 24.9.14,

$$_1RD_{\beta.1}1 = D_{\beta.1}D_{1\lambda}1 \tag{24.9.19}$$

Let

$$D_{1\lambda I} = \begin{bmatrix} _1\lambda_1 I & 0 & \cdots & 0 \\ 0 & _1\lambda_2 I & \cdots & 0 \\ \cdots & \cdots & \cdots & \cdots \\ 0 & 0 & \cdots & _1\lambda_m I \end{bmatrix} \tag{24.9.20}$$

where the identity submatrices in Eq. 24.9.20 have, respectively, the orders $n_1, n_2, \cdots, n_m$. Then it is obvious that

$$D_{\beta.1}D_{1\lambda} = D_{1\lambda I}\, D_{\beta.1} \tag{24.9.21}$$

From Eq. 24.9.21 in Eq. 24.9.19,

$$_1RD_{\beta.1}1 = D_{1\lambda I}\, D_{\beta.1}1 \tag{24.9.22}$$

Now let

$$D_{1\lambda I} = dc \tag{24.9.23}$$

where c is a scalar, and d is a diagonal matrix such that

$$1'd1 = 1 \tag{24.9.24}$$

From Eqs. 24.9.22 and 24.9.23, we may write

$$d^{-1/2}\,_1Rd^{-1/2}d^{1/2}D_{\beta.1}1 = d^{1/2}D_{\beta.1}1c \tag{24.9.25}$$

Suppose now we let

$$d^{1/2}D_{\beta.1} = D_{F.1} \tag{24.9.26}$$

Because of Eqs. 24.9.11, 24.9.23, and 24.9.24,

$$1'D_{F.1}{}'D_{F.1}1 = 1 \tag{24.9.27}$$

$$d = \begin{bmatrix} (_1F_{.1}{}'_1F_{.1})I & 0 & \cdots & 0 \\ 0 & (_2F_{.1}{}'_2F_{.1})I & \cdots & 0 \\ \cdots & \cdots & \cdots & \cdots \\ 0 & 0 & \cdots & (_mF_{.1}{}'_mF_{.1})I \end{bmatrix} \tag{24.9.28}$$

Using Eq. 24.9.26 in Eq. 24.9.25,

$$[d^{-1/2}\,_1Rd^{-1/2} - cI]D_{F.1}1 = 0 \tag{24.9.29}$$

We see from Eq. 24.9.29 that d is determined so that a latent vector of $d^{-1/2}\,_1Rd^{-1/2}$ is precisely $D_{F.1}1$ and Eq. 24.9.28 is also satisfied. Also, c is a latent root of this matrix. The iterative solution indicated by Eqs. 24.5.9–24.5.11, is equivalent to the methods of solution in Chapter 7, with the additional feature that successive approximations are taken to the d matrix.

It can readily be proved that these methods converge to the largest latent root and the corresponding latent vector. It is interesting to note that because of Eqs. 24.9.23 and 24.9.29, each submatrix R_{ij} in R is weighted relatively as the inverse geometric mean of its two corresponding $_1\lambda_i$ and $_1\lambda_j$ values. These $_1\lambda_i$'s, it is recalled, are the sums of the corresponding rows of $_1\rho$.

Although the foregoing development does not constitute a rigorous proof of convergence, it does appear to provide intuitive support. Furthermore, the experimental results so far obtained have converged, thus providing also empirical evidence.

Next we find the solutions for the $_i\beta._2$ vectors under the constraint that

$$D_{\beta._2}'D_{\beta._1} = 0 \qquad (24.9.30)$$

$$D_{\beta._2}'D_{\beta._2} = I \qquad (24.9.31)$$

We let

$$\phi_2 = 1'D_{\beta._2}'_1RD_{\beta._2}1 \qquad (24.9.32)$$

and set up the function

$$\psi_2 = \phi_2 - 1'D_{\beta._2}'D_{\beta._1 21}\gamma - 1'D_{\beta._2}'D_{\beta._2 2}\lambda \qquad (24.9.33)$$

where $_{21}\gamma$ and $_2\lambda$ are vectors of Lagrangian multipliers.

Differentiating Eq. 24.9.33 symbolically with respect to $1'D_{\beta._2}'$ and equating to zero, we get because of Eq. 24.9.32,

$$\frac{\partial \psi_2}{\partial (1'D_{\beta._2}')} = {}_1RD_{\beta._2}1 - D_{\beta._1 21}\gamma - D_{\beta._2 2}\lambda = 0 \qquad (24.9.34)$$

Premultiplying Eq. 24.9.34 by $D_{\beta._1}'$ and using Eqs. 24.9.30 and 24.9.31, we have

$$D_{\beta._1}' {}_1RD_{\beta._2}1 = {}_{21}\gamma \qquad (24.9.35)$$

Substituting Eq. 24.9.35 in Eq. 24.9.34,

$$[I - D_{\beta._1}D_{\beta._1}']_1RD_{\beta._2}1 = D_{\beta._2 2}\lambda \qquad (24.9.36)$$

Because of Eq. 24.9.30, we can write Eq. 24.9.36 as

$$[I - D_{\beta._1}D_{\beta._1}']_1R[I - D_{\beta._1}D_{\beta._1}']D_{\beta._2}1 = D_{\beta._2 2}\lambda \qquad (24.9.37)$$

or if we let

$$_2R = [I - D_{\beta._1}D_{\beta._1}']_1R[I - D_{\beta._1}D_{\beta._1}'] \qquad (24.9.38)$$

we have

$$_2RD_{\beta._2}1 = D_{\beta._2 2}\lambda \qquad (24.9.39)$$

Finally, we prove the solution for any $D_{\beta._h}$ with the constraints that

$$D_{\beta._h}'D_{\beta._h} = I \qquad (24.9.40)$$

and

$$D_{\beta._h}'D_{\beta._k} = 0 \qquad (24.9.41)$$

for every k less than h. We let

$$\phi_h = 1'D_{\beta.h\,1}{'}RD_{\beta.h}1 \tag{24.9.42}$$

and set up the function

$$\psi_h = \phi_h - 1'D_{\beta.h}{'}D_{\beta.1\,h1}\gamma - \cdots - 1'D_{\beta.h}{'}D_{\beta.(h-1)\,h(h-1)}\gamma - 1'D_{\beta.h}{'}D_{\beta.h\,h}\lambda \tag{24.9.43}$$

where the γ's and $_h\lambda$ are vectors of Lagrangian multipliers.

Differentiating Eq. 24.9.43 symbolically with respect to $1'D_{\beta.h}{'}$ and equating to zero, we have

$$\frac{\partial \psi_h}{\partial(1'D_{\beta.h}{'})} = {}_1RD_{\beta.h}1 - D_{\beta.1\,h1}\gamma - \cdots - D_{\beta.(h-1)\,h(h-1)}\gamma - D_{\beta.h\,h}\lambda = 0 \tag{24.9.44}$$

Premultiplying Eq. 24.9.44 successively with the $D_{\beta.k}{'}$ for $k = 1, \cdots, (h-1)$, and using Eqs. 24.9.40 and 24.9.41, we have

$$\left.\begin{array}{c} D_{\beta.1}{'}\,{}_1RD_{\beta.h}1 = {}_{h1}\gamma \\ \cdots \\ D_{\beta.(h-1)}{'}\,{}_1RD_{\beta.h}1 = {}_{h(h-1)}\gamma \end{array}\right\} \tag{24.9.45}$$

Substituting Eq. 24.9.45 in Eq. 24.9.44,

$$[I - D_{\beta.1}D_{\beta.1}{'} - \cdots - D_{\beta.(h-1)}D_{\beta.(h-1)}{'}]_1RD_{\beta.h}1 = D_{\beta.h\,h}\lambda \tag{24.9.46}$$

Because of Eq. 24.9.41, we can write Eq. 24.9.46 as

$$[I - D_{\beta.1}D_{\beta.1}{'} - \cdots - D_{\beta.(h-1)}D_{\beta.(h-1)}{'}]_1R \cdot$$
$$[I - D_{\beta.1}D_{\beta.1}{'} - \cdots - D_{\beta.(h-1)}D_{\beta.(h-1)}{'}]D_{\beta.h}1 = D_{\beta.h\,h}\lambda \tag{24.9.47}$$

But also because of Eq. 24.9.41,

$$[I - D_{\beta.1}D_{\beta.1}{'} - \cdots - D_{\beta.(h-1)}D_{\beta.(h-1)}{'}] =$$
$$[I - D_{\beta.1}D_{\beta.1}{'}] \cdots [I - D_{\beta.(h-1)}D_{\beta.(h-1)}{'}] \tag{24.9.48}$$

Therefore, if we define

$$_hR = [I - D_{\beta.(h-1)}D_{\beta.(h-1)}{'}]_{(h-1)}R[I - D_{\beta.(h-1)}D_{\beta.(h-1)}{'}] \tag{24.9.49}$$

we have because of Eqs. 24.9.48 and 24.9.49,

$$_hR = [I - D_{\beta.1}D_{\beta.1}{'} - \cdots - D_{\beta.(h-1)}D_{\beta.(h-1)}{'}]_1R \cdot$$
$$[I - D_{\beta.1}D_{\beta.1}{'} - \cdots - D_{\beta.(h-1)}D_{\beta.(h-1)}{'}] \tag{24.9.50}$$

Using Eq. 24.9.50 in Eq. 24.9.47,

$$_hRD_{\beta.h}1 = D_{\beta.h\,h}\lambda \tag{24.9.51}$$

24.9.3   The Rank One Approximation Method

We let

$$D_{\beta_{.1}} = \begin{bmatrix} {}_1\beta_{.1} & \cdots & 0 \\ \cdots & \cdots & \cdots \\ 0 & \cdots & {}_m\beta_{.1} \end{bmatrix} \tag{24.9.52}$$

where the ${}_i\beta_{.1}$ are column vectors such that

$$D_{\beta_{.1}}'D_{\beta_{.1}} = I \tag{24.9.53}$$

We consider

$$_{11}\rho = D_{\beta_{.1}}'RD_{\beta_{.1}} \tag{24.9.54}$$

Because of Eqs. 24.9.8 and 24.9.53, Eq. 24.9.54 is a correlation matrix. We wish to determine $D_{\beta_{.1}}$ so that $_{11}\rho$ will be the best least square approximation to a correlation matrix of rank one. We write

$$_{11}\rho\alpha_1 = \alpha_1 k_1 \tag{24.9.55}$$

where k_1 and α_1 are the largest root and corresponding vector of $_{11}\rho$. Without loss of generality

$$\alpha_1'\alpha_1 = 1 \tag{24.9.56}$$

It is well known that $_{11}\rho$ is the best least square approximation to a rank one matrix when k_1 is a maximum. From Eqs. 24.9.54–24.9.56, we have

$$\alpha_1'D_{\beta_{.1}}'RD_{\beta_{.1}}\alpha_1 = k_1 \tag{24.9.57}$$

Let

$$D_{\beta_{.1}}\alpha_1 = Q_{.1} \tag{24.9.58}$$

From Eqs. 24.9.53 and 24.9.56,

$$Q_{.1}'Q_{.1} = 1 \tag{24.9.59}$$

From Eqs. 24.9.57 and 24.9.58,

$$Q_{.1}'RQ_{.1} = k_1 \tag{24.9.60}$$

It is well known that k_1 is a maximum when it is the largest latent root of R, and Q_1 is the corresponding latent vector. From Eqs. 24.9.53 and 24.9.58, therefore, we get

$$D_{\beta_{.1}} = D_{Q_{.1}}(D_{Q_{.1}}'D_{Q_{.1}})^{-1/2} \tag{24.9.61}$$

and

$$\alpha_1 = (D_{Q_{.1}}'D_{Q_{.1}})^{1/2}1 \tag{24.9.62}$$

where 1 is a vector of unit elements, and $D_{Q_{.1}}$ is defined analogous to Eq. 24.9.52. The vector elements of Eq. 24.9.61 are proportional to those given in Eq. 24.6.3.

Next we consider, analogous to Eq. 24.9.54,

$$_{22}\rho = D_{\beta_{.2}}'RD_{\beta_{.2}} \tag{24.9.63}$$

where $D_{\beta.2}$ is defined as in Eq. 24.9.52.
Also

$$_{12}\rho = D_{\beta.1}'RD_{\beta.2} \qquad (24.9.64)$$

Now Eq. 24.9.64 gives the correlations of the first transformed variables of each set with those of the second transformed variables of each set. But the model requires that the correlations of transformed variables within sets be zero. Therefore, the diagonal of $_{12}\rho$ must be zero. Hence, because of Eq. 24.9.8,

$$D_{\beta.1}'D_{\beta.2} = 0 \qquad (24.9.65)$$

Also as in Eq. 24.9.53,

$$D_{\beta.2}'D_{\beta.2} = I \qquad (24.9.66)$$

Following the logic of Eqs. 24.9.54–24.9.60, we write

$$Q_{.2}'RQ_{.2} = k_2 \qquad (24.9.67)$$

where

$$D_{\beta.2}\alpha_2 = Q_{.2} \qquad (24.9.68)$$

and

$$\alpha_2 = (D_{Q.2}'D_{Q.2})^{1/2}1 \qquad (24.9.69)$$

From Eqs. 24.9.65 and 24.9.68, we have

$$D_{\beta.1}'Q_{.2} = 0 \qquad (24.9.70)$$

We then wish to maximize k_2 in Eq. 24.9.67 subject to Eq. 24.9.70. It can be readily verified with the aid of Lagrangian multipliers that in the equation

$$(I - D_{\beta.1}D_{\beta.1}')RQ_{.2} = Q_{.2}k_2 \qquad (24.9.71)$$

$Q_{.2}$ will yield the maximum k_2 in Eq. 24.9.67 subject to Eq. 24.9.70. Therefore, if we let

$$_2R = (I - D_{\beta.1}D_{\beta.1}')R(I - D_{\beta.1}D_{\beta.1}') \qquad (24.9.72)$$

then because of Eq. 24.9.70, k_2 and $Q_{.2}$ are the largest latent root and corresponding vector of $_2R$. To get $D_{\beta.2}$ we have

$$D_{\beta.2} = D_{Q.2}(D_{Q.2}'D_{Q.2})^{-1/2} \qquad (24.9.73)$$

In general, following the logic above, we have

$$Q_{.i}'RQ_{.i} = k_i \qquad (24.9.74)$$

subject to

$$\begin{bmatrix} D_{\beta.1}' \\ \vdots \\ D_{\beta.(i-1)}' \end{bmatrix} Q_{.i} = \begin{bmatrix} 0 \\ \vdots \\ 0 \end{bmatrix} \qquad (24.9.75)$$

with the solution

$$[I - D_{\beta.1}D_{\beta.1}' - \cdots - D_{\beta.(i-1)}D_{\beta.(i-1)}']RQ_{.i} = Q_{.i}k_i \qquad (24.9.76)$$

If we let

$$_iR = [I - D_{\beta.1}D_{\beta.1}' - \cdots - D_{\beta.(i-1)}D_{\beta.(i-1)}']R[I - D_{\beta.1}D_{\beta.1}' - \cdots \\ - D_{\beta.(i-1)}D_{\beta.(i-1)}'] \qquad (24.9.77)$$

then Eqs. 24.9.75 and 24.9.76 show that

$$_iRQ_{.i} = Q_{.i}k_i \qquad (24.9.78)$$

We have also in general, analogous to Eqs. 24.9.61 and 24.9.73,

$$D_{\beta.i} = D_{Q.i}(D_{Q.i}'D_{Q.i})^{-1/2} \qquad (24.9.79)$$

From Eqs. 24.9.75, 24.9.77, and 24.9.79, it can be shown that

$$_{(i+1)}R = (I - D_{\beta.i}D_{\beta.i}')_iR(I - D_{\beta.i}D_{\beta.i}') \qquad (24.9.80)$$

The equations required for the solution of the D_β matrix of transformations are therefore Eqs. 24.9.78–24.9.80. If there are n variables in each subset, the solutions will continue to $i = n$. For each value of i, the measure of degree of approximation to a rank one matrix of transformed variables is k_i/m.

24.9.4   The Oblique Maximum Variance Method

To develop the proof of this model we first need the best least square fit to u in Eq. 24.9.4 of rank n. We consider

$$u = [P, \quad P_\varepsilon]\begin{bmatrix} \Delta & 0 \\ 0 & \Delta_\varepsilon \end{bmatrix}\begin{bmatrix} Q' \\ Q_\varepsilon' \end{bmatrix} \qquad (24.9.81)$$

where the outside matrices are the basic orthonormals of u, the center is the basic diagonal, and the partitioning is immediately after n vectors. The work of Eckhart and Young (1936) shows that the best least square fit to u of rank n is indicated by

$$u - P\Delta Q' = \varepsilon \qquad (24.9.82)$$

where from Eqs. 24.9.81 and 24.9.82,

$$\varepsilon = P_\varepsilon \Delta_\varepsilon Q_\varepsilon' \qquad (24.9.83)$$

and from Eq. 24.9.83,

$$tr\varepsilon'\varepsilon = 1'\Delta_\varepsilon^2 1 \qquad (24.9.84)$$

It can be shown, therefore, that P is the best least square n-factor score matrix from u, based on a principal axis factor solution. From Eqs. 24.9.6 and 24.9.82,

$$RQ = Q\Delta^2 \qquad (24.9.85)$$

Or if we partition Q according to R, and form the diagonal supermatrix

$$D_Q = \begin{bmatrix} Q_1 & \cdots & 0 \\ \cdots & \cdots & \cdots \\ 0 & \cdots & Q_m \end{bmatrix} \qquad (24.9.86)$$

we may write Eq. 24.9.85 as

$$R D_Q V_I = D_Q V_I \Delta^2 \qquad (24.9.87)$$

where V_I is a column supervector of identity matrices. From Eq. 24.9.85 or Eq. 24.9.87, we get D_Q and Δ.

Because of the definition in Eq. 24.9.81, we can show that

$$P = u D_Q V_I \Delta^{-1} \qquad (24.9.88)$$

We consider now a diagonal supermatrix of transformation matrices

$$D_a = \begin{bmatrix} a_1 & \cdots & 0 \\ \cdots & \cdots & \cdots \\ 0 & \cdots & a_m \end{bmatrix} \qquad (24.9.89)$$

such that

$$u D_a - P V_I' = \varepsilon \qquad (24.9.90)$$

We wish to determine D_a so that

$$tr \, \varepsilon' \varepsilon = \phi = \min \qquad (24.9.91)$$

From Eqs. 24.9.90 and 24.9.91, and the definition of Eq. 24.9.81, we have

$$\phi = tr(D_a' u' u D_a - 2 D_a' u' P V_I' + V_I' V_I) \qquad (24.9.92)$$

From Eqs. 24.9.6 and 24.9.8,

$$tr(D_a' u' u D_a) = tr(V_I' D_a' D_a V_I) \qquad (24.9.93)$$

From Eqs. 24.9.6, 24.9.88, and 24.9.81,

$$u' P = D_Q V_I \Delta \qquad (24.9.94)$$

Substituting Eqs. 24.9.93 and 24.9.94 in Eq. 24.9.92, we can get

$$\phi = tr(V_I' D_a' D_a V_I - 2 V_I' D_a' D_Q V_I \Delta + mI) \qquad (24.9.95)$$

Differentiating Eq. 24.9.95 symbolically with respect to $V_I' D_a'$ and equating to zero, we get

$$D_a V_I - D_Q V_I \Delta = 0 \qquad (24.9.96)$$

or

$$D_a = D_Q D_\Delta \qquad (24.9.97)$$

where D_Δ is a diagonal supermatrix constructed from Δ. Since we wish all transformed variables to have unit variance, we get from Eq. 24.9.97,

$$D_\beta = D_a(D_a'D_a)^{-1/2} \tag{24.9.98}$$

Equation 24.9.98 gives the same solution as Eq. 24.8.2.

The value of ϕ is obtained by substituting Eq. 24.9.97 in Eq. 24.9.95. This gives, because of Eq. 24.9.81,

$$\phi = nm - tr\,\Delta^2 \tag{24.9.99}$$

According to Eq. 24.9.85, ϕ is the difference between the total number of variables and the sum of the first n latent roots of R.

24.9.5   The Orthogonal Maximum Variance Method

This model is similar to the previous model, but the restriction is added that the transformed variables within each set are all orthogonal. We let

$$D_\beta = \begin{bmatrix} \beta_1 & \cdots & 0 \\ \cdots & \cdots & \cdots \\ 0 & \cdots & \beta_m \end{bmatrix} \tag{24.9.100}$$

be a diagonal supermatrix of square orthonormal matrices and consider the equation

$$uD_\beta - PV_I' = \varepsilon \tag{24.9.101}$$

We let

$$\phi = tr\,\varepsilon'\varepsilon \tag{24.9.102}$$

We wish to minimize ϕ, subject to the condition

$$D_\beta'D_\beta = D_I \tag{24.9.103}$$

where D_I is a diagonal supermatrix of identity matrices. We let

$$D_\lambda = \begin{bmatrix} \lambda_1 & \cdots & 0 \\ \cdots & \cdots & \cdots \\ 0 & \cdots & \lambda_m \end{bmatrix} \tag{24.9.104}$$

where the λ_i are each n^2 and their elements are Lagrangian multipliers. We set up the function

$$\psi = tr(\phi - D_\beta'D_\beta\,D_\lambda) \tag{24.9.105}$$

Because of Eq. 24.9.103, it can be proved that

$$D_\lambda = D_\lambda' \tag{24.9.106}$$

From Eqs. 24.9.101 and 24.9.102 in Eq. 24.9.105,

$$\psi = tr(D_\beta'u'uD_\beta - 2D_\beta'u'PV_I' + V_I V_I' - D_\beta'D_\beta\,D_\lambda) \tag{24.9.107}$$

Considering Eqs. 24.9.93 and 24.9.94, we have from Eq. 24.9.107,

$$\psi = tr(D_\beta' D_\beta - 2D_\beta' D_Q V_I \Delta V_I' + mI - D_\beta' D_\beta D_\lambda) \quad (24.9.108)$$

or

$$\psi = tr(V_I' D_\beta' D_\beta V_I - 2V_I' D_\beta' D_Q V_I \Delta + mI - V_I' D_\beta' D_\beta D_\lambda V_I) \quad (24.9.109)$$

Differentiating Eq. 24.9.109 symbolically with respect to $V_I' D_\beta'$ and equating to zero, we have

$$D_\beta V_I - D_Q D_\Delta V_I - D_\beta D_\lambda V_I = 0 \quad (24.9.110)$$

From Eq. 24.9.110,

$$D_\beta(D_I - D_\lambda)V_I = D_Q D_\Delta V_I \quad (24.9.111)$$

Let

$$D_I - D_\lambda = D_\gamma^{-1} \quad (24.9.112)$$

From Eqs. 24.9.97, 24.9.111, and 24.9.112,

$$D_\beta = D_a D_\gamma \quad (24.9.113)$$

From Eq. 24.9.106, we know that

$$D_\gamma = D_\gamma' \quad (24.9.114)$$

From Eqs. 24.9.103, 24.9.113, and 24.9.114,

$$D_I = D_\gamma D_a' D_a D_\gamma \quad (24.9.115)$$

From Eq. 24.9.115,

$$D_\gamma = (D_a' D_a)^{-1/2} \quad (24.9.116)$$

If we indicate the basic structure of $D_a' D_a$ by

$$D_a' D_a = D_H D_d D_H' \quad (24.9.117)$$

the solution for D_H and D_d is obtained from

$$D_H D_d V_I = D_a' D_a D_H V_I \quad (24.9.118)$$

which is the same as Eq. 24.8.1. We have from Eqs. 24.9.116 and 24.9.117,

$$D_\gamma = D_H D_d^{-1/2} D_H' \quad (24.9.119)$$

Substituting Eq. 24.9.119 in Eq. 24.9.113,

$$D_\beta = D_a D_H D_d^{-1/2} D_H' \quad (24.9.120)$$

To find ϕ in Eq. 24.9.102, we note first from Eqs. 24.9.97 and 24.9.108 that

$$\phi = tr(D_\beta' D_\beta - 2D_\beta' D_a V_I V_I' + mI) \quad (24.9.121)$$

From Eqs. 24.9.103, 24.9.117, and 24.9.120 in Eq. 24.9.121,

$$\phi = 2mn - tr(V_I'D_H \, D_d^{1/2} D_H'V_I) \qquad (24.9.122)$$

But because of Eq. 24.9.118,

$$D_H'D_H = D_H \, D_H' = D_I \qquad (24.9.123)$$

From Eqs. 24.9.122 and 24.9.123,

$$\phi = 2mn - V_1'D_d^{1/2}V_1 \qquad (24.9.124)$$

where V_1 is a supervector of unit vectors. From Eq. 24.9.118, it is seen that the second term on the right in Eq. 24.9.124 is simply the sum of the square roots of the latent roots of $D_a'D_a$. This sum cannot exceed mn.

Bibliography

Bartlett, M.S. "Methods of Estimating Mental Factors," *Nature*, **141**, 609–610 (1938).

Bodewig, E. *Matrix Calculus*. New York: Interscience Publishers, Inc., 1959. Pp. xi + 452.

Burket, George R. "A Study of Reduced Rank Models for Multiple Prediction," *Psychometric Monographs*, No. 12 (1964).

Campbell, D. L. & Fisk, D.W. "Convergent and Discriminant Validation by the Multitrait-Multimethod Matrix," *Psychological Bulletin*, **56**, 81–105 (1959).

Carroll, John B. "An Analytical Solution for Approximating Simple Structure in Factor Analysis," *Psychometrika*, **18**, 23–38 (1953).

———. "Biquartimin Criterion for Rotation to Oblique Simple Structure in Factor Analysis," *Science*, **126**, 1114–1115 (1957).

Clemans, W. V. "An Analytical and Empirical Examination of Some Properties of Ipsative Measures," Unpublished doctoral dissertation, University of Washington (1956).

DuBois, Philip H. "An Analysis of Guttman's Simplex," *Psychometrika*, **25**, 173–182 (1960).

Edwards, Allen L. *The Social Desirability Variable in Personality Assessment and Research*. New York: Dryden, 1957. 108 pp.

Ferguson, George A. "The Factorial Interpretation of Test Difficulty," *Psychometrika*, **6**, 323–329 (1941).

Guttman, Louis. "The Principal Components of Scale Analysis," in Samuel A. Stouffer, *et al.*, *Measurement and Prediction*. Princeton, N.J.: Princeton University Press, 1950, pp. 312–361.

———. "Multiple Group Methods for Common-Factor Analysis: Their Basis, Computation, and Interpretation," *Psychometrika*, **17**, 209–222 (1952).

———. "Image Theory for the Structure of Quantitative Variates," *Psychometrika*, **18**, 277–296 (1953).

———. "The Determinacy of Factor Score Matrices with Implications for Five Other Basic Problems of Common-Factor Theory," *British Journal of Statistical Psychology*, **8**, 65–81 (1955).

———. " 'Best Possible' Systematic Estimates of Communalities," *Psychometrika*, **21**, 273–285 (1956).

———. "To What Extent Can Communalities Reduce Rank ?", *Psychometrika*, **23**, 297–308 (1958).

Harmon, Harry H. "Factor Analysis," in H. S. Wilf and A. Ralston (eds.), *Mathematical Methods for Digital Computers*. New York: John Wiley & Sons, Inc., 1960, pp. 204–212.

Harris, Chester W. "Some Rao-Guttman Relationships," *Psychometrika*, **27**, 247–264 (1962).

Heywood, H. B. "On Finite Sequences of Real Number," *Proceedings of the Royal Society of London*, Series A, **134**, 486–501 (1931).

Holzinger, Karl J. "A Simple Method of Factor Analysis," *Psychometrika*, **9**, 257–262 (1944).

Holzinger, Karl J., and Harman, Harry H. *Factor Analysis*. Chicago: University of Chicago Press, 1941, pp. xii + 417.

Horst, Paul. "A Method of Factor Analysis by Means of Which All Coordinates of the Factor Matrix Are Given Simultaneously," *Psychometrika*, **2**, 225–236 (1937).

————. "A Non-Graphical Method for Transforming an Arbitrary Factor Matrix Into a Simple Structure Factor Matrix," *Psychometrika*, **6**, 79–99 (1941).

————. "A Technique for the Development of a Differential Prediction Battery," *Psychological Monographs*, No. 380 (1954).

————. "A Technique for the Development of a Multiple Absolute Prediction Battery," *Psychological Monographs*, No. 390 (1955).

————. "Relations Among *m* Sets of Measures," *Psychometrika*, **26**, 129–149 (1961-*a*).

————. "Generalized Canonical Correlations and Their Application to Experimental Data," *Journal of Clinical Psychology*, Monograph Supplement No. 14 (1961-*b*).

————. "Matrix Reduction and Approximation to Principal Axes," *Psychometrika*, **27**, 169–178 (1962).

————. "Multivariate Models for Evaluating Change," in Chester Harris, *et al.*, *Problems in Measuring Change*, Madison, Wis.: University of Wisconsin Press, 1963, pp. 104–121.

Horst, Paul and MacEwan, Charlotte. "Predictor Elimination Techniques for Determining Multiple Prediction Batteries," *Psychological Reports*, Monograph Supplement 1-V7 (1960).

Hotelling, Harold. "Analysis of a Complex of Statistical Variables into Principal Components," *Journal of Educational Psychology*, **24**, 417–441, 498–520 (1933).

————. "The Most Predictable Criterion," *Journal of Educational Psychology*, **26**, 139–142 (1935).

————. "Relations between Two Sets of Variates," *Biometrika*, **28**, 321–377 (1936).

Householder, A. S., and Bauer, F. L. "On Certain Methods for Expanding the Characteristic Polynomial," *Numerische Mathematik* 1 Band, 1 Heft, 1959, p. 29.

Humphries, Lloyd G. "Note on the Multitrait-Multimethod Matrix," *Psychological Bulletin*, **57**, 86–88 (1960).

Johnson, R. M. "Re-analysis of Mosier's Factor Analysis of Neurotic Items." Unpublished master's dissertation, University of Washington (1958).

Kaiser, Henry F. "The Varimax Criterion for Analytic Rotation in Factor Analysis," *Psychometrika*, **23**, 187–200 (1958).

————. "Computer Program for Varimax Rotation in Factor Analysis," *Educational and Psychological Measurement*, **19**, 413–420 (1959).

Kelley, Truman L. *Crossroads in the Mind of Man*. Stanford, Calif.: Stanford University Press, 1928.

————. "Essential Traits of Mental Life," *Harvard Studies in Education*, **26**. Cambridge, Mass.: Harvard University Press, 1935, pp. 146.

Lawley, D. N. "The Estimation of Factor Loadings by the Method of Maximum Likelihood," *Proceedings of the Royal Society of Edinburgh*, A, **60**, 64–82 (1940).

————. "Further Investigations in Factor Estimation," *Proceedings of the Royal Society of Edinburgh*, A, **61**, 176–185 (1942).

Leiman, John. "The Calculation of Regression Weights from Common Factor Loadings." Unpublished doctoral dissertation, University of Washington (1951).

Mees, H. L. "Preliminary Steps in the Construction of Factor Scales for the MMPI." Unpublished doctoral dissertation, University of Washington (1959).

Ortega, James M. and Kaiser, Henry F. "The LL^T and QR Methods for Symmetric Tridiagonal Matrices," *The Computer Journal*, **6**, 99–101 (1963).

Pearson, Karl. "On Lines and Planes of Closest Fit to Systems of Points in Space," *Philosophical Magazine*, **6**, 559–572 (1901).

Rao, C. R. "Estimation and Tests of Significance in Factor Analysis," *Psychometrika*, **20**, 93–111 (1955).

Saunders, D. R. "An Analytic Method for Rotation to Orthogonal Simple Structure," *Research Bulletin* 53-10. Princeton, N.J.: Educational Testing Service (1953).

Schmid, J., and Leiman J. M. "The Development of Hierarchical Factor Solutions," *Psychometrika*, **22**, 53–61 (1957).

Spearman, Charles. *The Abilities of Man*. New York: Macmillan Co., pp. vi + 416 + xxxiv (1927).

Thomson, Godfrey H. *The Factorial Analysis of Human Ability*. Boston: Houghton Mifflin Co., 1950.

Thurstone, L. L. "Multiple Factor Analysis," *Psychological Review*, **38**, 406–427 (1931).

———. *Multiple Factor Analysis*. Chicago: University of Chicago Press, 1947, pp. xix + 535.

Thurstone, L. L. & Thurstone, L. G. "Factorial Studies of Intelligence," *Psychometric Monographs*, No. 2 (1941).

Tucker, Ledyard R. "A Semi-Analytical Method of Factorial Rotation to Simple Structure," *Psychometrika*, **9**, 43–68 (1944).

———. "An Inter-Battery Method of Factor Analysis," *Psychometrika*, **23**, 111–136 (1958).

———. "Implications of Factor Analysis of Three-Way Matrices for Measurement of Change," in Chester Harris, *et al.*, *Problems in Measuring Change*, Madison, Wis.: University of Wisconsin Press, 1963, pp. 122–137.

Wilkinson, H. H. "The Calculation of the Eigenvectors of Codiagonal Matrices," *The Computer Journal*, Vol. **1**, p. 90 (1958).

Wright, C. E. "Relations Between Normative and Ipsative Measures of Personality." Unpublished doctoral dissertation, University of Washington (1957).

Wrigley, Charles, and Neuhaus, Jack O. "A Re-Factorization of the Burt-Pearson Matrix with the ORDVAC Electronic Computer," *British Journal of Psychology, Statistical Section*, **5**, 105–108 (1952).

Young, Gale, and Carl Eckhart. "The Approximation of One Matrix by Another of Lower Rank," *Psychometrika*, **1**, 211–218 (1936).

Fortran Program Listings

```
C CHAPTER 5 - THE CENTROID METHOD                                              001
C    5.3 UNITY IN THE DIAGONAL                                                 002
C                                                                             003
         DIMENSION R(160, 160), W(160), V(160), D(160)                       004
     1F1(12), F2(12), F3(12)                                                 005
         READ INPUT TAPE 5,03,(F1(I),I=1,12),(F2(I),I=1,12),(F3(I),I=1,12)   006
03       FORMAT(12A6)                                                        007
         READ INPUT TAPE 5,F1,N,M                                           008
         DO 05  I = 1,N                                                      009
05       READ INPUT TAPE 5,F2, (R(I,J),J=1,N)                               010
         FN = N                                                              011
         FM = M                                                              012
09       DO 11  I = 1,N                                                      013
         D(I) = R(I,I)                                                       014
11       R(I,I) = 0.                                                         015
C        SIGN VECTOR                                                         016
         DO 21  I = 1,N                                                      017
         W(I) = 0.                                                           018
         V(I) = 1.                                                           019
         DO 21  J = 1,N                                                      020
21       W(I) = W(I) + R(I,J)                                                021
22       J = 1                                                               022
         DO 26  I = 2,N                                                      023
         IF (W(J) * V(J) - W(I) * V(I)) 26, 25, 25                          024
25       J = I                                                               025
26       CONTINUE                                                            026
         IF (W(J) * V(J)) 28, 34, 34                                        027
28       V(J) = -V(J)                                                        028
         DO 30  I = 1,N                                                      029
30       W(I) = W(I) + 2. * R(I,J) * V(J)                                   030
         WRITE OUTPUT TAPE 6,F3, (V(I),I=1,N)                               031
         WRITE OUTPUT TAPE 6,F3, (W(I),I=1,N)                               032
         GO TO 22                                                            033
C        FACTOR VECTOR                                                       034
34       DO 35  I = 1,N                                                      035
35       W(I) = W(I) + D(I) * V(I)                                          036
         S = 0.                                                             037
         DO 38  I = 1,N                                                      038
38       S = S + ABSF(W(I))                                                 039
         S = 1./SQRTF(S)                                                    040
         DO 41  I = 1,N                                                      041
41       W(I) = W(I)*S                                                      042
         S=0.                                                               043
         DO 413 I =1,N                                                      044
413      S = S+W(I)**2                                                      045
         WRITE OUTPUT TAPE 6,F2,S                                          046
         IF(1.-S)42,54,54                                                   047
C        RESIDUAL MATRIX                                                    048
42       DO 45  I=1,N                                                       049
         R(I,I) = D(I)                                                      050
         DO 45  J=1,N                                                       051
45       R(I,J) = R(I,J) - W(I) * W(J)                                     052
         WRITE OUTPUT TAPE 6, 47                                           053
47       FORMAT (1H0)                                                      054
         WRITE OUT PUT TAPE 6,F3, (W(I),I=1,N)                            055
         WRITE OUTPUT TAPE 6, 47                                          056
         DO 51  I=1,N                                                      057
51       WRITE OUTPUT TAPE 6, F3, (R(I,J), J=1,N)                        058
         WRITE OUTPUT TAPE 6, 47                                          059
         GO TO 09                                                          060
54       CALL EXIT                                                         061
         END                                                               062
*        DATA
(I4)
(12F6.3)
(16F7.3)
   9
 700
1.000  .829  .768  .108  .033  .108  .298  .309  .351
 .829 1.000  .775  .115  .061  .125  .323  .347  .369
 .768  .775 1.000  .272  .205  .238  .296  .271  .385
 .108  .115  .272 1.000  .636  .626  .249  .183  .369
 .033  .061  .205  .636 1.000  .709  .138  .091  .254
 .108  .125  .238  .626  .709 1.000  .190  .103  .291
 .298  .323  .296  .249  .138  .190 1.000  .654  .527
 .309  .347  .271  .183  .091  .103  .654 1.000  .541
 .351  .369  .385  .369  .254  .291  .527  .541 1.000
```

```
C CHAPTER 5 - THE CENTROID METHOD                                          001
C    5.4 OPTIMIZING THE DIAGONAL ELEMENTS                                  002
C                                                                          003
      DIMENSION R(160, 160), W(160), V(160), D(160)                        004
      READ INPUT TAPE 5, 03, N, M                                          005
   03 FORMAT (I4)                                                          006
      DO 05  I=1,N                                                         007
   05 READ INPUT TAPE 5, 06, (R(I,J), J=1,N)                               008
   06 FORMAT (12F6.3)                                                      009
      FN = N                                                               010
      FM = M                                                               011
C    TEST SIGNIFICANCE OF CORRELATIONS                                     012
   09 DO 10  I = 1,N                                                       013
   10 R(I,I) = 0.                                                          014
      S = 0.                                                               015
      DO 14  I = 1,N                                                       016
      DO 14  J = 1,N                                                       017
   14 S = S + R(I,J)**2                                                    018
      IF (2. * S/(FN*(FN-1.)) - 1./FM) 56, 56, 16                          019
C    LARGEST OFF DIAGONAL                                                  020
   16 DO 19  J=1,N                                                         021
      D(J) = 0.                                                            022
      DO 19  I=1,N                                                         023
   19 D(J) = MAX1F (D(J), ABSF(R(I,J)))                                    024
C    SIGN VECTOR                                                           025
      DO 24  I=1,N                                                         026
      W(I) = 0.                                                            027
      V(I) = 1.                                                            028
      DO 24  J = 1,N                                                       029
   24 W(I) = W(I) + R(I,J)                                                 030
   25 J = 1                                                                031
      DO 29  I=2,N                                                         032
      IF (W(J) * V(J) - W(I) * V(I)) 29, 28, 28                            033
   28 J=I                                                                  034
   29 CONTINUE                                                             035
      IF (W(J) * V(J)) 31, 37, 37                                          036
   31 V(J) = -V(J)                                                         037
      DO 33  I=1,N                                                         038
   33 W(I) = W(I) + 2. * R(I,J) * V(J)                                     039
      WRITE OUTPUT TAPE 6,35,(V(I),I=1,N)                                  040
      WRITE OUTPUT TAPE 6,35,(W(I),I=1,N)                                  041
   35 FORMAT (15F7.3)                                                      042
      GO TO 25                                                             043
C    FACTOR VECTOR                                                         044
   37 DO 38  I=1,N                                                         045
   38 W(I) = W(I) + D(I) * V(I)                                            046
      S = 0.                                                               047
      DO 41  I=1,N                                                         048
   41 S= S+ ABSF(W(I))                                                     049
      S=1./SQRTF(S)                                                        050
      DO 44  I=1,N                                                         051
   44 W(I) = W(I) * S                                                      052
C    RESIDUAL MATRIX                                                       053
      DO 47  I=1,N                                                         054
      DO 47  J=1,N                                                         055
   47 R(I,J) = R(I,J) - W(I) * W(J)                                        056
      WRITE OUTPUT TAPE 6, 49                                              057
   49 FORMAT (1H )                                                         058
      WRITE OUTPUT TAPE 6, 35, (W(I), I=1,N)                               059
      WRITE OUTPUT TAPE 6, 49                                              060
      DO 53  I=1,N                                                         061
   53 WRITE OUTPUT TAPE 6, 35, (R(I,J), J=1,N)                             062
      WRITE OUTPUT TAPE 6, 49                                              063
      GO TO 09                                                             064
   56 CALL EXIT                                                            065
      END                                                                  066
*     DATA
   9
 200
1.000  .829  .768  .108  .033  .108  .298  .309  .351
 .829 1.000  .775  .115  .061  .125  .323  .347  .369
 .768  .775 1.000  .272  .205  .238  .296  .271  .385
 .108  .115  .272 1.000  .636  .626  .249  .183  .369
 .033  .061  .205  .636 1.000  .709  .138  .091  .254
 .108  .125  .238  .626  .709 1.000  .190  .103  .291
 .298  .323  .296  .249  .138  .190 1.000  .654  .527
 .309  .347  .271  .183  .091  .103  .654 1.000  .541
 .351  .369  .385  .369  .254  .291  .527  .541 1.000
```

```
C CHAPTER 5 - THE CENTROID METHOD                                              001
C    5.5 ITERATIVE SOLUTIONS FOR DIAGONALS                                     002
C                                                                              003
      DIMENSION  R(150,150),W(150),V(150),D(150),U(150)                        004
      READ INPUT TAPE 5, 03, P, N, M, NL                                       005
03    FORMAT (F8.6/I4/I4/I4)                                                    006
      DO 05  I=1,N                                                             007
05    READ INPUT TAPE 5, 06, (R(I,J), J=1,N)                                    008
06    FORMAT (12F6.3)                                                          009
      FN = N                                                                    010
      FM = M                                                                    011
      REWIND 2                                                                  012
      REWIND 3                                                                  013
      DO 11 I=1,N                                                              014
      U(I) = R(I,I)                                                            015
11    WRITE TAPE 2, (R(I,J),J=1,N)                                             016
      REWIND 2                                                                  017
      L = 0                                                                     018
      K = 0                                                                     019
C        TEST SIGNIFICANCE OF RESIDUAL                                          020
15    DO 17  I=1,N                                                             021
      D(I) = R(I,I)                                                            022
17    R(I,I) =0.                                                               023
      S = 0.                                                                    024
      DO 21  I=1,N                                                             025
      DO 21   J=1,N                                                            026
21    S = S + R(I,J)**2                                                        027
      IF ((2.*S*FM) - (FN*(FN-1.))) 24, 24, 25                                 028
24    IF (K-1) 93, 93, 54                                                      029
C        SIGN VECTOR                                                            030
25    DO 29  I=1,N                                                             031
      W(I) = 0.                                                                031
      V(I)=1.                                                                   033
      DO 29   J=1,N                                                            034
29    W(I) = W(I) + R(I,J)                                                     035
30    J = 1                                                                     036
      DO 34   I=2,N                                                            037
      IF (W(J) * V(J) - W(I) * V(I)) 34, 33, 33                                038
33    J = I                                                                     039
34    CONTINUE                                                                  040
      IF (W(J) * V(J)) 36, 40, 40                                              041
36    V(J) = -V(J)                                                             042
      DO 38  I=1,N                                                             043
38    W(I) = W(I) + 2. * R(I,J) * V(J)                                         044
      GO TO 30                                                                  045
C        FACTOR VECTOR                                                          046
40    DO 41  I = 1,N                                                           047
41    W(I) = W(I) + D(I) * V(I)                                                048
      S = 0.                                                                    049
      DO 44  I =1,N                                                            050
44    S = S + ABSF(W(I))                                                       051
      S = 1./SQRTF(S)                                                          052
      DO 47  I=1,N                                                             053
47    W(I) = W(I) * S                                                          054
      WRITE TAPE 3, (W(I), I=1,N)                                              055
      K = K+1                                                                   056
C        RESIDUAL MATRIX                                                        057
      DO 52  I=1,N                                                             058
      R(I,I) = D(I)                                                            059
      DO 52   J=1,N                                                            060
52    R(I,J) = R(I,J) - W(I) * W(J)                                            061
      GO TO 15                                                                  062
C        DIAGONALS OF R                                                         063
54    S = 0.                                                                    064
      DO 542 I = 1,N                                                           065
542   S = MAX1F(S,ABSF(D(I)))                                                  066
      DO 56 I =1,N                                                             067
      D(I) = MIN1F(1.,(U(I) - D(I)))                                           068
56    U(I) = D(I)                                                             069
      WRITE OUTPUT TAPE 6,71, (U(I),I=1,N)                                     070
71    FORMAT (15F7.3)                                                          071
      REWIND 3                                                                  072
      IF (S-P) 83, 83, 73                                                      073
73    L = L+1                                                                   074
      WRITE OUTPUT TAPE 6, 732,K,L                                             075
732   FORMAT (2I4)                                                             076
      IF (L-NL) 75, 75, 83                                                     077
```

```
C     NEW DIAGONALS                                                      078
 75   K = 0                                                              079
      DO 77   I=1,N                                                      080
 77   READ TAPE 2, (R(I,J), J=1,N)                                       081
      REWIND 2                                                           082
      DO 81   I=1,N                                                      083
 81   R(I,I) = 0.                                                        084
      GO TO 25                                                           085
 83   WRITE OUTPUT TAPE 6, 84                                            086
 84   FORMAT (1H )                                                       087
      DO 88   J=1,K                                                      088
      READ TAPE 3, (W(I), I=1,N)                                         089
      WRITE OUTPUT TAPE 6, 71, (W(I), I=1,N)                             090
 88   CONTINUE                                                           091
      REWIND 3                                                           092
      WRITE OUTPUT TAPE 6, 84                                            093
      DO 92   I=1,N                                                      094
 92   WRITE OUTPUT TAPE 6, 71, (R(I,J), J=1,N)                           095
 93   CALL EXIT                                                          096
      END                                                               097
*     DATA
.001
  9
500
 30
1.000  .829  .768  .108  .033  .108  .298  .309  .351
 .829 1.000  .775  .115  .061  .125  .323  .347  .369
 .768  .775 1.000  .272  .205  .238  .296  .271  .385
 .108  .115  .272 1.000  .636  .626  .249  .183  .369
 .033  .061  .205  .636 1.000  .709  .138  .091  .254
 .108  .125  .238  .626  .709 1.000  .190  .103  .291
 .298  .323  .296  .249  .138  .190 1.000  .654  .527
 .309  .347  .271  .183  .091  .103  .654 1.000  .541
 .351  .369  .385  .369  .254  .291  .527  .541 1.000
```

602

```
C CHAPTER 6 - GROUPING METHODS                                          001
C    6.3 GROUP CENTROID WITH BINARY VECTOR                              002
C                                                                       003
      DIMENSION R(160,160), S(160), V(160), IY(160)                    004
      READ INPUT TAPE 5, 03, N, M, P                                   005
03    FORMAT (I4/I4/F5.2)                                              006
      DO 05  I = 1,N                                                   007
05    READ INPUT TAPE 5, 06, (R(I,J), J=1,N)                           008
06    FORMAT (9F6.3)                                                   009
07    DO 12  I = 1,N                                                   010
      S(I) = -R(I,I)                                                   011
      V(I) = -R(I,I)**2                                                012
      DO 12  J = 1,N                                                   013
      S(I) = S(I) + R(I,J)                                             014
12    V(I) = V(I) + R(I,J)**2                                          015
      FM = M                                                           016
      FN = N                                                           017
      DO 22  I = 1,N                                                   018
22    V(I) = SQRTF(V(I)/FN - (S(I)/FN)**2)                             019
      L = 1                                                            020
      DO 27  I = 2,N                                                   021
      IF (V(L) - V(I)) 26, 27, 27                                     022
26    L = I                                                            023
27    CONTINUE                                                         024
      G = S(L)/FN + V(L) * P                                          025
      K = 0                                                            026
      DO 34  I = 1,N                                                   027
      IF (R(I,L) - G) 34, 34, 32                                      028
32    K = K + 1                                                        029
      IY(K) = I                                                        030
34    CONTINUE                                                         031
      DO 39 J=1,N                                                      032
      V(J) = 0.                                                        033
      DO 39  I = 1,K                                                   034
      IV = IY(I)                                                       035
39    V(J) = V(J) + R(J,IV)                                           036
      C = 0.                                                           037
      DO 43  I = 1,K                                                   038
      IV = IY(I)                                                       039
43    C = C + V(IV)                                                    040
      C = 1./SQRTF(C)                                                  041
      DO 56  I = 1,N                                                   042
56    V(I) = V(I) * C                                                  043
      C = 0.                                                           044
      DO 563  I=1,N                                                    045
563   C = C + V(I)**2                                                  046
      WRITE OUTPUT TAPE 6, 63, C                                      047
      IF (1.-C) 57, 69, 69                                            048
57    DO 59  I = 1,N                                                   049
      DO 59  J = 1,N                                                   050
59    R(I,J) = R(I,J) - V(I) * V(J)                                   051
      WRITE OUTPUT TAPE 6, 61, L, (IY(I), I = 1,K)                    052
61    FORMAT (I2/14I3)                                                 053
      WRITE OUTPUT TAPE 6, 997                                        054
997   FORMAT (1H )                                                     055
      WRITE OUTPUT TAPE 6,  63, (V(I), I = 1,N)                       056
      WRITE OUTPUT TAPE 6,997                                         057
63    FORMAT (12F8.3)                                                 058
      DO 65  I = 1,N                                                   059
65    WRITE OUTPUT TAPE 6, 63, (R(I,J), J = 1,N)                      060
      WRITE OUTPUT TAPE 6, 67                                         061
67    FORMAT (1H0/1H0)                                                 062
      GO TO 07                                                         063
69    CALL EXIT                                                        064
      END                                                             065
*     DATA
   9
 500
  .5
1.000  .829  .768  .108  .033  .108  .298  .309  .351
 .829 1.000  .775  .115  .061  .125  .323  .347  .369
 .768  .775 1.000  .272  .205  .238  .296  .271  .385
 .108  .115  .272 1.000  .636  .626  .249  .183  .369
 .033  .061  .205  .636 1.000  .709  .138  .091  .254
 .108  .125  .238  .626  .709 1.000  .190  .103  .291
 .298  .323  .296  .249  .138  .190 1.000  .654  .527
 .309  .347  .271  .183  .091  .103  .654 1.000  .541
 .351  .369  .385  .369  .254  .291  .527  .541 1.000
```

```
C CHAPTER 6 - GROUPING METHODS                                          001
C    6.4 GROUP CENTROID WITH BINARY AND UNIT VECTORS                     002
C                                                                        003
      DIMENSION R(160,160), S(160), V(160), IY(160), U(160), W(160)      004
      READ INPUT TAPE 5, 03, N, M, P                                     005
03    FORMAT (I4/I4/F5.2)                                                006
      DO 05  I = 1,N                                                     007
05    READ INPUT TAPE 5, 06, (R(I,J), J=1,N)                             008
06    FORMAT (9F6.3)                                                     009
      DO 0602 I = 1,N                                                    010
0602  U(I) = 1.                                                          011
      DO 12  I = 1,N                                                     012
      S(I) = -R(I,I)                                                     013
      V(I) = -R(I,I)**2                                                  014
      DO 12  J = 1,N                                                     015
      S(I) = S(I) + R(I,J)                                               016
12    V(I) = V(I) + R(I,J)**2                                           017
      FM = M                                                             018
      FN = N                                                             019
      DO 22  I = 1,N                                                     020
22    W(I) = SQRTF(V(I)/(FN-1.)-(S(I)/(FN-1.))**2)                       021
      DO 6241  IL = 1,5                                                  022
      L = 1                                                              023
      WRITE OUTPUT TAPE 6,63, (U(I),I=1,N)                               024
      DO 27  I = 2,N                                                     025
      IF(W(L)*U(L)-W(I))26,27,27                                         026
26    L = I                                                              027
27    CONTINUE                                                           028
      G = S(L)/(FN-1.)+W(L)*P                                            029
      K = 0                                                              030
      DO 34  I = 1,N                                                     031
      IF (R(I,L)*U(I)-G) 34, 34, 32                                      032
32    K = K + 1                                                          033
      U(I) =0.                                                           034
      IY(K) = I                                                          035
34    CONTINUE                                                           036
      DO 39  J=1,N                                                       
      V(J) = 0.                                                          038
      DO 39  I = 1,K                                                     039
      IV = IY(I)                                                         040
39    V(J) = V(J) + R(J,IV)                                             041
      C = 0.                                                             042
      DO 43  I = 1,K                                                     043
      IV = IY(I)                                                         044
43    C = C + V(IV)                                                      045
      A = 0.                                                             046
      DO 46  I = 1,N                                                     047
46    A = A + S(I) + R(I,I)                                             048
      B = 0.                                                             049
      DO 49  I = 1,N                                                     050
49    B = B + V(I)                                                      051
      G = (B-C)/(A-B)                                                    052
      C = ((G**2)*A) - (2.*G*B) + C                                      053
      DO 53  I = 1,N                                                     054
53    V(I) = V(I) - G * (S(I)+R(I,I))                                   055
      C = 1./SQRTF(C)                                                    056
      DO 56  I = 1,N                                                     057
56    V(I) = V(I) * C                                                   058
      WRITE OUTPUT TAPE 6, 61, L, (IY(I), I=1,K)                         059
61    FORMAT (I2/14I3)                                                   060
      WRITE OUTPUT TAPE 6, 997                                           061
997   FORMAT (1H )                                                       062
      WRITE OUTPUT TAPE 6, 63, (V(I), I=1,N)                             063
      WRITE OUTPUT TAPE 6, 997                                           064
      E =0.                                                              065
      DO 623  I=1,N                                                      066
623   E = MAX1F(E,U(I))                                                 067
      WRITE OUTPUT TAPE 6,63,E                                           068
      IF(.1-E)6241,6241,69                                               069
6241  CONTINUE                                                           070
63    FORMAT (12F8.3)                                                    071
69    CALL EXIT                                                          072
      END                                                                073
*     DATA
   9
 200
 .5
1.000  .829  .768  .108  .033  .108  .298  .309  .351
 .829 1.000  .775  .115  .061  .125  .323  .347  .369
 .768  .775 1.000  .272  .205  .238  .296  .271  .385
 .108  .115  .272 1.000  .636  .626  .249  .183  .369
 .033  .061  .205  .636 1.000  .709  .138  .091  .254
 .108  .125  .238  .626  .709 1.000  .190  .103  .291
```

```
 .298   .323   .296   .249   .138   .190  1.000   .654   .527
 .309   .347   .271   .183   .091   .103   .654  1.000   .541
 .351   .369   .385   .369   .254  -.291   .527   .541  1.000
C CHAPTER 6 - GROUPING METHODS                                            001
C    6.5 MULTIPLE GROUP METHOD                                            002
C                                                                         003
C(FT)R=(AT)                                                               004
      DIMENSION R(100, 100), A(20, 100), IB(2000), S(20, 20), B(20, 100)  005
      READ INPUT TAPE 5, 03, L, N, M                                      006
  03  FORMAT (3I3)                                                        007
      READ INPUT TAPE 5, 401, (IB(I), I = 1,M)                            008
 401  FORMAT (30I3)                                                       009
      DO 06 I=1,L                                                         010
  06  READ INPUT TAPE 5, 07, (R(I,J), J=1,L)                              011
  07  FORMAT(12F6.3)                                                      012
      JB=1                                                                013
      DO 19 I=1,N                                                         014
      JA = JB                                                             015
      DO 19  J=1,L                                                        016
      JB = JA                                                             017
      A(I,J) = 0.                                                         018
  14  K = IB(JB)                                                          019
      JB = JB+1                                                           020
      IF (K) 19, 19, 17                                                   021
  17  A(I,J) = A(I,J) + R(K,J)                                            022
      GO TO 14                                                            023
  19  CONTINUE                                                            024
      DO 21  I=1,N                                                        025
  21  WRITE OUTPUT TAPE 6, 22, (A(I,J),  J=1,L)                           026
      WRITE OUTPUT TAPE 6,997                                            027
  22  FORMAT(12F7.3)                                                      028
C(FT)A = S                                                                029
      JB = 1                                                              030
      DO 34 J=1,N                                                         031
      JA = JB                                                             032
      DO 34 I=1,N                                                         033
      JB = JA                                                             034
      S(I,J) = 0.                                                         035
  29  K = IB(JB)                                                          036
      JB = JB+1                                                           037
      IF (K) 34, 34, 32                                                   038
  32  S(I,J) = S(I,J) + A(I,K)                                            039
      GO TO 29                                                            040
  34  CONTINUE                                                            041
      DO 36 I=1,N                                                         042
  36  WRITE OUTPUT TAPE 6, 22, (S(I,J), J=1,N)                            043
      WRITE OUTPUT TAPE 6,997                                            044
CA=A((TU)(-1))                                                            045
      N1 = N-1                                                            046
      DO 50   K = 1, N1                                                   047
      C = 1./SQRTF(S(K,K))                                                048
      DO 41  J = K,N                                                      049
  41  S(K,J) = S(K,J) * C                                                 050
      DO 43   J = 1, L                                                    051
  43  A(K,J) = A(K,J) * C                                                 052
      K1 = K+1                                                            053
      DO 47   I = K1, N                                                   054
      DO 47   J = I, N                                                    055
  47  S(I,J) = S(I,J) - S(K,I) * S(K,J)                                   056
      DO 50   I = K1, N                                                   057
      DO 50   J = 1, L                                                    058
  50  A(I,J) = A(I,J) - S(K,I) * A(K,J)                                   059
      C = 1./SQRTF (S(N,N))                                               060
      DO 543   J = 1, L                                                   061
 543  A(N,J) = A(N,J) * C                                                 062
      DO 59 I=1,N                                                         063
  59  WRITE OUTPUT TAPE 6, 57, (S(I,J), J=1,N)                            064
      WRITE OUTPUT TAPE 6,997                                            065
      DO 56  J=1,L                                                        066
  56  WRITE OUTPUT TAPE 6, 57, (A(I,J), I=1,N)                            067
      WRITE OUTPUT TAPE 6,997                                            068
  57  FORMAT(9F7.3)                                                       069
 997  FORMAT(1H )                                                         070
      DO 63  I=1,L                                                        071
      DO 63  J=1,L                                                        072
      DO 63  K=1,N                                                        073
```

```
 63    R(I,J) = R(I,J) - A(K,I) * A(K,J)                               074
       DO 65  I=1,L                                                     075
 65    WRITE OUTPUT TAPE 6, 66, (R(I,J), J=1,L)                         076
 66    FORMAT(12F7.3)                                                  077
       CALL EXIT                                                        078
       END                                                             079
*      DATA
  9  3 12
  1  2  3  0  4  5  6  0  7  8  9  0
1.000  .829  .768  .108  .033  .108  .298  .309  .351
 .829 1.000  .775  .115  .061  .125  .323  .347  .369
 .768  .775 1.000  .272  .205  .238  .296  .271  .385
 .108  .115  .272 1.000  .636  .626  .249  .183  .369
 .033  .061  .205  .636 1.000  .709  .138  .091  .254
 .108  .125  .238  .626  .709 1.000  .190  .103  .291
 .298  .323  .296  .249  .138  .190 1.000  .654  .527
 .309  .347  .271  .183  .091  .103  .654 1.000  .541
 .351  .369  .385  .369  .254  .291  .527  .541 1.000
```

```
C CHAPTER 7 - BASIC STRUCTURE SUCCESSIVE FACTOR METHODS                      001
C     7.3 SOLUTION WITH RESIDUAL MATRIX                                       002
C                                                                            003
      DIMENSION R(24000), A(225), U(225), KV(28), EV(28)                     004
      READ INPUT TAPE 5, 03, N, LI, LF, P                                    005
03    FORMAT (I4/I4/I4/F8.5)                                                 006
      M = (N*(N+1))/2                                                        007
      READ INPUT TAPE 5, 12, (R(I), I = 1,M)                                 008
12    FORMAT (9F6.3)                                                         009
      E = 0.                                                                 010
      DO 502 L =1,LF                                                         011
      LK=L
      DO 102 I =1,N                                                          012
      DO 101 J=1,I                                                           013
      IJ = I+((J-1)*(N*2-J))/2                                               014
101   U(J) = R(IJ)                                                           015
102   WRITE OUTPUT TAPE 6, 45, (U(J), J=1,I)                                 016
      WRITE OUTPUT TAPE 6, 97                                                017
97    FORMAT(1H0)                                                            018
      DO 18  I = 1,N                                                         019
18    A(I) = 1.                                                              020
      DO 41  K = 1,LI                                                        021
      DO 28  I = 1,N                                                         022
      I1 = I +1                                                              023
      U(I) = 0.                                                              024
      DO 24  J = 1,I                                                         025
      IJ = I + ((J-1) * (N*2-J))/2                                           026
24    U(I) = U(I) + R(IJ) * A(J)                                             027
      DO 28  J = I1,N                                                        028
      IJ = ((I-1) * (N*2-I))/2 + J                                           029
28    U(I) = U(I) + R(IJ) * A(J)                                             030
      S = 0.                                                                 031
      DO 31  I = 1,N                                                         032
31    S = S + U(I) * A(I)                                                    033
      S = 1./SQRTF(S)                                                        034
      DO 34  I = 1,N                                                         035
34    A(I) = U(I)*S                                                          036
      S=0.                                                                   037
      DO 37  I = 1,N                                                         038
37    S = S + A(I)**2                                                        039
      E1 = E                                                                 040
      E = SQRTF(S)                                                           041
      IF((ABSF(E1/E-1.))-P) 42, 41, 41                                       042
41    CONTINUE                                                               043
42    KV(L) = K                                                              044
      EV(L) = S                                                              045
      WRITE OUTPUT TAPE 6, 45, (A(I), I=1,N)                                 046
45    FORMAT(1H /(14F8.3))                                                   047
      IF (E-1.) 52, 47, 47                                                   048
47    DO 50  I = 1,N                                                         049
      DO 50  J = 1,I                                                         050
      IJ = I + ((J-1)*(N*2-J))/2                                             051
50    R(IJ) = R(IJ) - A(I) * A(J)                                            052
      IF(1.-S)502,52,52                                                      053
502   CONTINUE                                                              054
52    WRITE OUTPUT TAPE 6, 53, (KV(I),I=1,LK)
53    FORMAT(1H0/(14I8))                                                     056
      WRITE OUTPUT TAPE 6,45,(EV(I),I=1,LK)
      CALL EXIT                                                              058
      END                                                                    059
*     DATA
  9
 30
 28
 .00001
1.000  .829  .768  .108  .033  .108  .298  .309  .351
1.000  .775  .115  .061  .125  .323  .347  .369 1.000
 .272  .205  .238  .296  .271  .385 1.000  .636  .626
 .249  .183  .369 1.000  .709  .138  .091  .254 1.000
 .190  .103  .291 1.000  .654  .527 1.000  .541 1.000
```

```
C CHAPTER 7 - BASIC STRUCTURE SUCCESSIVE FACTOR METHODS            001
C    7.4 SOLUTION WITHOUT RESIDUALS                                 002
C                                                                   003
      DIMENSION R(2400), A(215, 28), U(215), W(28), KV(28), EV(28)  004
      READ INPUT TAPE 5, 03, N, LI, LF, P                          005
03    FORMAT(I4/I4/I4/F8.5)                                        006
      M = (N * (N+1))/2                                            007
      READ INPUT TAPE 5, 06, (R(I), I = 1,M)                       008
06    FORMAT (9F6.3)                                               009
      E = 0.                                                       010
      L = 0                                                        011
09    L = L+1                                                      012
      IF (L-LF) 11, 11, 51                                         013
11    DO 12  I = 1,N                                               014
12    A(I,L) = 1.                                                  015
      DO 46   K = 1,LI                                             016
      IF (L-1) 24, 24, 15                                          017
15    L1 = L-1                                                     018
      DO 19  J = 1,L1                                              019
      W(J) = 0.                                                    020
      DO 19  I = 1,N                                               021
19    W(J) = W(J) + A(I,J) * A(I,L)                                022
      DO 23  I = 1,N                                               023
      U(I) = 0.                                                    024
      DO 23  J = 1,L1                                              025
23    U(I) = U(I) - A(I,J) * W(J)                                  026
24    DO 33  I = 1,N                                               027
      IF (L-1) 26, 26, 27                                          028
26    U(I) = 0.                                                    029
27    DO 29  J = 1,I                                               030
      IJ = I+((J-1)*(N*2-J))/2                                     031
29    U(I) = U(I) + R(IJ) * A(J,L)                                 032
      I1 = I + 1                                                   033
      DO 33  J = I1,N                                              034
      IJ = ((I-1) * (N*2-I))/2 + J                                 035
33    U(I) = U(I) + R(IJ) * A(J,L)                                 036
      S = 0.                                                       037
      DO 36  I = 1,N                                               038
36    S = S+U(I)*A(I,L)                                            039
      S = 1./SQRTF(S)                                              040
      DO 39  I = 1,N                                               041
39    A(I,L) = U(I) * S                                            042
      S = 0.                                                       043
      DO 42  I = 1,N                                               044
42    S = S + A(I,L)**2                                            045
      E1 = E                                                       046
      E = SQRTF(S)                                                 047
      IF ((ABSF(E1/E-1.))-P) 47, 46, 46                           048
46    CONTINUE                                                     049
47    KV(L) = K                                                    050
      EV(L) = S                                                    051
      IF (E-1.) 51, 50, 50                                         052
50    GO TO 09                                                     053
51    DO 52  I = 1,N                                               054
52    WRITE OUTPUT TAPE 6, 53, (A(I,J), J=1,L)                     055
53    FORMAT (14F7.3)                                              056
      WRITE OUTPUT TAPE 6, 55, (KV(I), I=1,L)                      057
55    FORMAT (14I7)                                                058
      WRITE OUTPUT TAPE 6, 53, (EV(I), I=1,L)                      059
      CALL EXIT                                                    060
      END                                                          061
*     DATA
  9
 30
 28
 .00001
1.000  .829  .768  .108  .033  .108  .298  .309  .351
1.000  .775  .115  .061  .125  .323  .347  .369 1.000
 .272  .205  .238  .296  .271  .385 1.000  .636  .626
 .249  .183  .369 1.000  .709  .138  .091  .254 1.000
 .190  .103  .291 1.000  .654  .527 1.000  .541 1.000
```

```
C CHAPTER 8 - SIMULTANEOUS BASIC STRUCTURE METHODS                          001
C     8.3 RANK REDUCTION METHOD                                              002
C                                                                           003
      DIMENSION R(100,100),A(100,20),B(20,100),S(20,20),C(10),G(100)       006
      READ INPUT TAPE 5, 103, N, M, LIM                                     007
103   FORMAT (3I4)                                                          008
      DO 105  I = 1,N                                                       009
105   READ INPUT TAPE 5, 106, (R(I,J),   J = 1,N)                          010
106   FORMAT (12F6.3)                                                       011
      DO 03  J = 1,M                                                        012
      DO 03  I = 1,M                                                        013
03    S(I,J) = R(I,J)                                                       014
      DO 06  I = 1,N                                                        015
      DO 06  J = 1,M                                                        016
06    B(J,I) = R(I,J)                                                       017
      DO 25  L = 1,LIM                                                      018
      CALL PARTRI(S, B, N, M)                                               019
      DO 11  J = 1,M                                                        020
      DO 11  I = 1,N                                                        021
11    A(I,J) = B(J,I)                                                       022
      DO 16  J = 1,M                                                        023
      DO 16  I = 1,N                                                        024
      B(J,I) = 0.                                                           025
      DO 16  K = 1,N                                                        026
16    B(J,I) = B(J,I) + R(I,K) * A(K,J)                                     027
      DO 21  J = 1,M                                                        028
      DO 21  I = 1,M                                                        029
      S(I,J) = 0.                                                           030
      DO 21  K = 1,N                                                        031
21    S(I,J) = S(I,J) + A(K,I) * B(J,K)                                     032
      G(L) = 0.                                                             033
      DO 24  I = 1,M                                                        034
24    G(L) = G(L) + S(I,I)                                                  035
25    CONTINUE                                                              036
      DO 27  I = 1,M                                                        037
27    C(I) = SQRTF(S(I,I))                                                  038
      WRITE OUTPUT TAPE 6, 130                                             039
130   FORMAT (12H1G(I) VECTOR)                                             040
      WRITE OUTPUT TAPE 6, 132, (G(I),   I = 1,LIM)                        041
132   FORMAT (10F12.6)                                                      042
      WRITE OUTPUT TAPE 6, 134                                             043
134   FORMAT (13HO C(I) VECTOR)                                            044
      WRITE OUTPUT TAPE 6, 132, (C(I), I=1,M)                             045
      WRITE OUTPUT TAPE 6,997                                             046
997   FORMAT(1HO)                                                          047
      DO 139 I =1,N                                                        048
139   WRITE OUTPUT TAPE 6,132,(A(I,J),J=1,M)                              049
      CALL      EXIT                                                       050
      END                                                                  051
C                                                                           052
      SUBROUTINE PARTRI (S, A, L, N)                                       053
      DIMENSION S(20,20),A(20,100)                                         054
      N1 = N-1                                                             055
      DO 50   K = 1, N1                                                    056
      C = 1./SQRTF(S(K,K))                                                 057
      DO 41  J = K,N                                                       058
41    S(K,J) = S(K,J) * C                                                  059
      DO 43   J = 1, L                                                     060
43    A(K,J) = A(K,J) * C                                                  061
      K1 = K+1                                                             062
      DO 47   I = K1, N                                                    063
      DO 47   J = L, N                                                     064
47    S(I,J) = S(I,J) - S(K,I) * S(K,J)                                    065
      DO 50   I = K1, N                                                    066
      DO 50   J = 1, L                                                     067
50    A(I,J) = A(I,J) - S(K,I) * A(K,J)                                    068
      C = 1./SQRTF (S(N,N))                                                069
      DO 543  J = 1, L                                                     070
543   A(N,J) = A(N,J) * C                                                  071
      RETURN                                                               072
      END                                                                  073
*     DATA
  9   4  30
1.000  .829  .768  .108  .033  .108  .298  .309  .351
 .829 1.000  .775  .115  .061  .125  .323  .347  .369
 .768  .775 1.000  .272  .205  .238  .296  .271  .385
 .108  .115  .272 1.000  .636  .626  .249  .183  .369
 .033  .061  .205  .636 1.000  .709  .138  .091  .254
 .108  .125  .238  .626  .709 1.000  .190  .103  .291
 .298  .323  .296  .249  .138  .190 1.000  .654  .527
 .309  .347  .271  .183  .091  .103  .654 1.000  .541
 .351  .369  .385  .369  .254  .291  .527  .541 1.000
```

```
C CHAPTER 8 - SIMULTANEOUS BASIC STRUCTURE METHODS                        001
C     8.4 ORTHOGONALIZATION METHOD                                        002
C                                                                         003
C     INPUT                                                               004
      DIMENSION R(1990D), B(200,16), W(200), C(16), G(100), U(16)         005
      COMMON C, G                                                         006
      READ INPUT TAPE 5, 03, M, L, LM                                     007
  03  FORMAT (3I4)                                                        008
      N=(M*(M+1))/2                                                       009
      READ INPUT TAPE 5, 06, (R(I),  I = 1, N)                            010
  06  FORMAT(9F6.3)                                                       011
C                                                                         012
C     FIRST APPROXIMATION TO B(I, J)                                      013
      DO 14  I = 1, L                                                     014
      I1 = I + 1                                                          015
      DO 10   J = 1, I                                                    016
      JI = ((J-1) * (M * 2 - J)) / 2 + I                                  017
  10  B(J,I) = R(JI)                                                      018
      DO 14  J = I1, M                                                    019
      IJ = JI + J - I                                                     020
  14  B(J,I) = R(IJ)                                                      021
C                                                                         022
C     ORTHONORMALIZATION OF B(I,J)                                        023
      DO 49   IL = 1, LM                                                  024
      IC = IL                                                             025
      G(IC) = 0.                                                          026
      DO 36  K = 1, L                                                     027
      K1 = K - 1                                                          028
      IF (K-1) 29, 29, 22                                                 029
  22  DO 25 J=1,K1                                                        030
      W(J) = 0.                                                           031
      DO 25   I = 1, M                                                    032
  25  W(J) = W(J) + B(I,J) * B(I,K)                                       033
      DO 28    I = 1, M                                                   034
      DO 28    J = 1, K1                                                  035
  28  B(I,K) = B(I,K) - B(I,J) * W(J)                                     036
  29  C(K) = 0.                                                           037
      DO 31  I = 1, M                                                     038
  31  C(K) = C(K) + B(I,K)**2                                            039
      C(K) = SQRTF (C(K))                                                 040
      DO 34  I = 1, M                                                     041
  34  B(I,K) = B(I,K) / C(K)                                             042
      G(IC) = G(IC) + C(K)                                                043
      IF ((ABSF(G(IC-1) / G(IC)-1.))-.00001) 50, 50, 36                   044
  36  CONTINUE                                                            045
C                                                                         046
C     B = RB                                                              047
      DO 48   K = 1, L                                                    048
      DO 46  I = 1, M                                                     049
      W(I) = 0.                                                           050
      DO 42   J = 1, I                                                    051
      JI = ((J-1) * (M*2-J)) / 2 + I                                      052
  42  W(I) = W(I) + R(JI) * B(J,K)                                        053
      I1 = I + 1                                                          054
      DO 46  J = I1, M                                                    055
      IJ = JI + J - I                                                     056
  46  W(I) = W(I) + R(IJ) * B(J,K)                                        057
      DO 48  J = 1, M                                                     058
  48  B(J,K) = W(J)                                                       059
  49  CONTINUE                                                            060
  50  DO 53   J = 1, L                                                    061
      V = SQRTF(C(J))                                                     062
      DO 53   I = 1, M                                                    063
  53  B(I,J) = B(I,J) * V                                                 064
C                                                                         065
C     OUTPUT                                                              066
      WRITE OUTPUT TAPE 6, 55                                             067
  55  FORMAT (14H1 G(IC) VECTOR)                                          068
      WRITE OUTPUT TAPE 6, 57, (G(I),  I = 1, IC)                         069
  57  FORMAT (10F12.6)                                                    070
      WRITE OUTPUT TAPE 6, 58                                             071
  58  FORMAT (13H0 C(I) VECTOR)                                           072
      WRITE OUTPUT TAPE 6, 57, (C(I),  I = 1, L)                          073
      WRITE OUTPUT TAPE 6,997                                             074
 997  FORMAT(1H0)                                                         075
      DO 63 I =1,M                                                        076
  63  WRITE OUTPUT TAPE 6,57,(B(I,J),J=1,L)                               077
      CALL    EXIT                                                        078
      END                                                                 079
  *   DATA
      9   4  50
  1.000  .829  .768  .108  .033  .108  .298  .309  .351
  1.000  .775  .115  .061  .125  .323  .347  .369 1.000
   .272  .205  .238  .296  .271  .385 1.000  .636  .626
   .249  .183  .369 1.000  .709  .138  .091  .254 1.000
   .190  .103  .291 1.000  .654  .527 1.000  .541 1.000
```

610

```
C CHAPTER 9 - JACOBI TYPE SOLUTIONS                                    001
C    9.3 SIMULTANEOUS METHODS                                          002
C                                                                      003
      DIMENSION R(220,110), D(110)                                     004
      READ INPUT TAPE 5, 03, P, N, NL                                  005
03    FORMAT (F8.6/(I4))                                               006
      DO 05 I=1,N                                                      007
05    READ INPUT TAPE 5, 051, (R(I,J), J=1,N)                          008
051   FORMAT (10F6.3)                                                  009
      N1 = N+1                                                         010
      N11=N-1                                                          011
      N2 = N*2                                                         012
      DO 10 I=N1, N2                                                   013
      DO 10  J = 1,N                                                   014
10    R(I,J) = 0.                                                      015
      DO 12 I=1,N                                                      016
      NI = N + I                                                       017
12    R(NI,I) = 1.                                                     018
      L = 0                                                            019
14    DO 15  I=1,N                                                     020
15    D(I) = R(I,I)                                                    021
      DO 282 I = 1,N11                                                 022
      I1 = I+1                                                         023
      DO 282 J= I1,N                                                   024
      DR = R(I,I) - R(J,J)                                             025
      A = SQRTF(DR**2 + 4.*R(I,J)**2)                                  026
      A = SQRTF((A+DR)/(2.*A))                                         027
      B = SQRTF(1.-A**2)                                               028
      C = SIGNF(1.,R(I,J))                                             029
      DO 252 K = 1,N2                                                  030
      U = R(K,I)*A*C + R(K,J)*B                                        031
      R(K,J) = -R(K,I)*B*C + R(K,J)*A                                  032
252   R(K,I) = U                                                       033
      DO 282 K = 1,N                                                   034
      U = R(I,K)*A*C + R(J,K)*B                                        035
      R(J,K) = -R(I,K)*B*C + R(J,K)*A                                  036
282   R(I,K) = U                                                       037
      DO 30  I=1,N                                                     038
30    D(I) = ABSF(D(I) - R(I,I))                                       039
      S = 0.                                                           040
      DO 33  I=1,N                                                     041
33    S = MAX1F (S, D(I))                                              042
      IF (S-P) 38, 38, 35                                              043
35    L = L+1                                                          044
      IF (L-NL) 37, 38, 38                                             045
37    GO TO 14                                                         046
38    WRITE OUTPUT TAPE 6, 39, L                                       047
39    FORMAT (I2)                                                      048
      WRITE OUTPUT TAPE 6, 392, (R(I,I), I=1,N)                        049
      DO 41  I=1,N                                                     050
41    D(I) = SQRTF (R(I,I))                                            051
      DO 44  J=1,N                                                     052
      DO 44  I=N1, N2                                                  053
44    R(I,J)=R(I,J)*D(J)                                               054
      WRITE OUTPUT TAPE 6, 442                                         055
442   FORMAT (1H )                                                     056
      WRITE OUTPUT TAPE 6, 392, (D(I), I=1,N)                          057
      WRITE OUTPUT TAPE 6, 442                                         058
      DO 48 J=1,N                                                      059
48    WRITE OUTPUT TAPE 6, 392, (R(I,J), I=N1, N2)                     060
      WRITE OUTPUT TAPE 6, 442                                         061
392   FORMAT (15F7.3)                                                  062
      CALL EXIT                                                        063
      END                                                              064
*     DATA
.001000
  9
  7
1.000  .829  .768  .108  .033  .108  .298  .309  .351
 .829 1.000  .775  .115  .061  .125  .323  .347  .369
 .768  .775 1.000  .272  .205  .238  .296  .271  .385
 .108  .115  .272 1.000  .636  .626  .249  .183  .369
 .033  .061  .205  .636 1.000  .709  .138  .091  .254
 .108  .125  .238  .626  .709 1.000  .190  .103  .291
 .298  .323  .296  .249  .138  .190 1.000  .654  .527
 .309  .347  .271  .183  .091  .103  .654 1.000  .541
 .351  .369  .385  .369  .254  .291  .527  .541 1.000
```

611

```
C CHAPTER 9 - JACOBI TYPE SOLUTIONS                              001
C    9.4 SUCCESSIVE METHOD                                       002
C                                                                003
      DIMENSION R(220,110), LI(110)                              004
      READ INPUT TAPE 5, 03, T, P, N, NL                         005
03    FORMAT (F8.6/F8.6/I4/I4)                                   006
      DO  05 I = 1,N                                             007
05    READ INPUT TAPE 5, 051, (R(I,J), J = 1, N)                 008
051   FORMAT (10F6.3)                                            009
      FN = N                                                     010
      N11=N-1                                                    011
      N1 = N+1                                                   012
      N2 = N*2                                                   013
      DO 11  I=N1, N2                                            014
      DO 11  J=1,N                                               015
11    R(I,J) = 0.                                                016
      DO 14  I=1,N                                               017
      NI = N+I                                                   018
14    R(NI,I) = 1.                                               019
      G = 0.                                                     020
      DO 36 I = 1,N11                                            021
      I1 = I+1                                                   022
      L = 0                                                      023
18    S = R(I,I)                                                 024
      DO 282 J = I1,N                                            025
      DR = R(I,I) - R(J,J)                                       026
      A = SQRTF(DR**2 + 4.*R(I,J)**2)                            027
      A = SQRTF((A+DR)/(2.*A))                                   028
      B = SQRTF(1. - A**2)                                       029
      C = SIGNF(1.,R(I,J))                                       030
      DO 252 K = I,N2                                            031
      U = R(K,I)*A*C + R(K,J)*B                                  032
      R(K,J) = -R(K,I)*B*C + R(K,J)*A                            033
252   R(K,I) = U                                                 034
      DO 282 K = 1,N                                             035
      U = R(I,K)*A*C + R(J,K)*B                                  036
      R(J,K) = -R(I,K)*B*C + R(J,K)*A                            037
282   R(I,K) = U                                                 038
      IF(ABSF(R(I,I)/S-1.)-P) 33,33,31                           039
31    L = L+1                                                    040
      IF (L-NL) 18, 18, 33                                       041
33    G = G+R(I,I)                                               042
      IF (G/FN-T) 35, 37, 37                                     043
35    LI(I) = L                                                  044
36    CONTINUE                                                   045
37    WRITE OUTPUT TAPE 6, 44, G                                 046
      WRITE OUTPUT TAPE 6,372, (LI(K), K=1,I)                    047
372   FORMAT (15I7)                                              048
      DO 39  J=1,I                                               049
39    R(J,J) = SQRTF(R(J,J))                                     050
      DO 42  J=1,I                                               051
      DO 42  K=N1, N2                                            052
42    R(K,J) = R(K,J)*R(J,J)                                     053
      WRITE OUTPUT TAPE 6, 997                                   054
997   FORMAT (1H )                                               055
      WRITE OUTPUT TAPE 6, 44, (R(J,J), J=1,I)                   056
44    FORMAT (15F7.3)                                            057
      WRITE OUTPUT TAPE 6, 997                                   058
      DO 46  J=1,I                                               059
46    WRITE OUTPUT TAPE 6, 44, (R(K,J), K=N1, N2)                060
      CALL    EXIT                                               061
      END                                                        062
*     DATA
.750000
.000100
 9
 30
1.000  .829  .768  .108  .033  .108  .298  .309  .351
 .829 1.000  .775  .115  .061  .125  .323  .347  .369
 .768  .775 1.000  .272  .205  .238  .296  .271  .385
 .108  .115  .272 1.000  .636  .626  .249  .183  .369
 .033  .061  .205  .636 1.000  .709  .138  .091  .254
 .108  .125  .238  .626  .709 1.000  .190  .103  .291
 .298  .323  .296  .249  .138  .190 1.000  .654  .527
 .309  .347  .271  .183  .091  .103  .654 1.000  .541
 .351  .369  .385  .369  .254  .291  .527  .541 1.000
```

```
C CHAPTER 10 - ORDER REDUCTION METHODS                                    001
C    10.3 PARTIAL REDUCTION METHOD                                        002
C                                                                         003
      DIMENSION R(24000), Q(225), U(225)                                  004
      READ INPUT TAPE 5, 03, N, NI, NF, P, T                             005
03    FORMAT (I4/I4/I4/F7.5/F7.5)                                         006
      M = (N * (N+1))/2                                                   007
      READ INPUT TAPE 5, 06, (R(I),  I=1,M)                              008
06    FORMAT (9F6.3)                                                      009
      FN = N                                                             010
      G = 0.                                                             011
      DO 77  L=1,NF                                                      012
      E = 0.                                                             013
      L1 = L+1                                                           014
      LF = ((L-1) * (N*2-L))/2                                          015
      LL = LF + L                                                        016
C PRINCIPAL AXIS SOLUTIONS                                                
      DO 15  I=1,N                                                      018
15    Q(I) = 1.                                                          019
      DO 37  K=1,NI                                                      020
      DO 26  I=L,N                                                       021
      U(I) = 0.                                                          022
      DO 21  J=L,I                                                       023
      IJ = I + ((J-1) * (N*2-J))/2                                      024
21    U(I) = U(I) + R(IJ) * Q(J)                                         025
      I1 = I+1                                                          026
      IF = ((I-1) * (N*2-I))/2                                          027
      DO 26  J=I1,N                                                      028
      IJ = IF + J                                                        029
26    U(I) = U(I) + R(IJ) * Q(J)                                         030
C                                                                         031
      S = 0.                                                             032
      DO 29  I=L,N                                                       033
29    S = S + U(I)**2                                                    034
      S = SQRTF(S)                                                       035
      SI = SIGNF (1., Q(L))                                             036
      DO 33  I = L,N                                                     037
33    Q(I) = U(I)/(S*SI)                                                 038
      E1 = E                                                             039
      E = S                                                              040
      IF ((ABSF(E1/E - 1.))-P) 38, 37, 37                               041
37    CONTINUE                                                           042
38    WRITE OUTPUT TAPE 6, 39, K, S                                      043
      WRITE OUTPUT TAPE 6,75, (Q(I), I=L,N)                             044
      WRITE OUTPUT TAPE 6, 997                                           
      DO 391 I=L,N                                                      046
      I1 = I+1                                                          047
      IF = ((I-1)*(N*2-I))/2                                            048
      DO 387 J=L,I                                                       049
      IJ = ((J-1)*(N*2-J))/2  + I                                       050
387   U(J) = R(IJ)                                                       051
      DO 390 J =I1,N                                                     052
      IJ = IF + J                                                        053
390   U(J) = R(IJ)                                                       054
391   WRITE OUTPUT TAPE 6,75, (U(J),J=L,N)                             055
      WRITE OUTPUT TAPE 6, 997                                           
39    FORMAT (I4 / F7.3)                                                 057
      G = G + S                                                          058
C ORDER REDUCTION                                                         
      A = 1. + Q(L)                                                      060
      C = (S - R(LL)) / (2.*A)                                          061
      A = SQRTF(A)                                                       062
      R(LL) = A                                                          063
      DO 50 I = L1,N                                                     064
      LI = LF + I                                                        065
      U(I) = Q(I) / A                                                    066
      Q(I) = (R(LI) + C*Q(I))/A                                         067
50    R(LI) = U(I)                                                       068
      DO 53 I = L1,N                                                     069
      IF = ((I-1) * (N*2-I)) / 2                                        070
      DO 53  J=I,N                                                       071
      IJ = IF + J                                                        072
53    R(IJ) = R(IJ) - U(I) * Q(J) - U(J) * Q(I)                         073
      DO 546 I = 1,N                                                     074
546   Q(I) = 0.                                                          075
      DO 57 I = L,N                                                      076
      LI = LF + I                                                        077
57    Q(I) = R(LI)*R(LL)                                                 078
      Q(L)  = Q(L) - 1.                                                  079
      K = L                                                              080
59    K = K-1                                                            081
      K1 = K-1                                                           082
      IF (K) 71,71,62                                                    083
```

                                   613

```
      62    KF = ((K-1) * (N*2-K)) / 2                                          084
            A = 0.                                                              085
            DO 66  I=K,N                                                        086
            KI = KF + I                                                         087
      66    A = A + R(KI) * Q(I)                                                088
            DO 69 I = K,N                                                       089
            KI = KF + I                                                         090
      69    Q(I) = R(KI)*A-Q(I)                                                 091
            GO TO 59                                                            092
      71    S = SQRTF(S)                                                        093
            DO 73  I=1,N                                                        094
      73    Q(I) = Q(I) * S                                                     095
            WRITE OUTPUT TAPE 6, 75, (Q(I), I=1,N)                              096
      75    FORMAT(12F10.4)                                                     097
            WRITE OUTPUT TAPE 6, 997                                            098
      997   FORMAT (1H )                                                        099
            IF (G/FN-T)  77, 77, 78                                             100
      77    CONTINUE                                                            101
      78    CALL EXIT                                                           102
            END                                                                 103
      C
      *     DATA
        9
       20
        7
      .00010
      .99000
      1.000  .829  .768  .108  .033  .108  .298  .309  .351
      1.000  .775  .115  .061  .125  .323  .347  .369 1.000
      .272  .205  .238  .296  .271  .385 1.000  .636  .626
      .249  .183  .369 1.000  .709  .138  .091  .254 1.000
      .190  .103  .291 1.000  .654  .527 1.000  .541 1.000


C CHAPTER 10 - ORDER REDUCTION METHODS                                         001
C    10.4 TRIDIAGONAL SOLUTION                                                  002
C                                                                              003
*     CHAIN (1, A4)
      DIMENSION R(18000),P(200),A(200),B(200),A1(200),A2(200),Y(200)
      EQUIVALENCE (A1(1), Y(1))                                                005
      REWIND 2                                                                 008
      READ INPUT TAPE 5, 03, N, NF, IL, PP, T                                  009
03    FORMAT (I4/I4/I4/F6.5/F6.5)                                             010
      M = (N * (N+1)) /2                                                       011
      READ INPUT TAPE 5, 06, (R(I), I=1,M)                                    012
06    FORMAT (9F6.3)                                                         013
      N2 = N-2                                                                014
      DO 51  L=1,N2                                                           015
      L1 = L+1                                                                016
      L2 = L+2                                                                017
      LN = ((L-1) * (N*2-L)) /2                                               018
      LL = LN + L                                                             019
      LL1 = LL+1                                                              020
      S = SIGNF(1., R(LL1))                                                   021
      P(L) = 0.                                                              022
      DO 18  I=L1, N                                                          023
      LI = LN+I                                                              024
18    P(L) = P(L) + R(LI)**2                                                 025
      P(L) = SQRTF(P(L))                                                     026
      R(LL1) = SQRTF(1.+R(LL1)*S/P(L))                                       027
      G = S/(P(L)*R(LL1))                                                    028
      DO 24  I=L2,N                                                          029
      LI = LN+I                                                              030
24    R(LI) = R(LI) * G                                                      031
      P(L) = -S * P(L)                                                       032
C RU = P
      DO 35  I=L1,N                                                          034
      IN = ((I-1) * (N*2-I)) /2                                              035
      I1 = I+1                                                               036
      P(I) = 0.                                                              037
      DO 32  J=L1,I                                                          038
      IJ = ((J-1) * (N*2-J)) /2 + I                                          039
      LJ = LN+J                                                              040
32    P(I) = P(I) + R(IJ) * R(LJ)                                            041
      DO 35  J=I1,N                                                          042
      LJ = LN + J                                                            043
      IJ = IN + J                                                            044
35    P(I) = (P(I) + R(IJ) * R(LJ))                                          045
      WRITE OUTPUT TAPE 6,73, (P(I),I=1,N)                                   046
C RU - GU = P
      G = 0.                                                                 048
      DO 39  I=L1,N                                                          049
      LI = LN + I                                                            050
39    G = G + R(LI) * P(I)                                                   051
      G = G/2.                                                               052
```

```
      DO 43  I=L1,N                                            053
      LI = LN + I                                              054
   43 P(I) = P(I) - R(LI) * G                                  055
C R - BU(T) - UB(T) = R
      DO 50  I=L1,N                                            057
      IN = ((I-1) * (N*2-I)) /2                                058
      LI = LN + I                                              059
      DO 50  J = I,N                                           060
      LJ = LN + J                                              061
      IJ = IN + J                                              062
   50 R(IJ) = R(IJ) - P(I) * R(LJ) - R(LI) * P(J)             063
   51 CONTINUE                                                 064
      WRITE TAPE 2, N,NF,IL,PP,T,M,
     1(R(I),I=1,M),(P(I),I=1,N),(A(I),I=1,N),(B(I),I=1,N)     067
   73 FORMAT (9F10 .4)                                         068
      REWIND 2                                                 070
      CALL CHAIN (2,A4)                                        071
      END                                                      072
      CHAIN (2,A4)                                             073
      DIMENSION R(18000),P(200),A(200),B(200),A1(200),A2(200),Y(200),
     1Q(200),P1(200),C(200),R1(200)                            075
      EQUIVALENCE(A2(1),R1(1)),(C(1),Y(1))                     076
      READ TAPE 2, N,NF,IL,PP,T,M,
     1(R(I),I=1,M),(P(I),I=1,N),(A(I),I=1,N),(B(I),I=1,N)     079
      REWIND 2                                                 080
      PP = .00001                                              081
      M1 = M-1                                                 082
      N1 = N-1                                                 083
      FN = N                                                   084
      G = 0.                                                   085
      T = .99                                                  086
      P(N1) = R(M1)                                            087
      B(1) = 0.                                                088
      P(N) = 0.                                                089
      DO 60  I=1,N                                             090
      II = ((I-1) * (N*2-I)) /2 + I                            091
      A(I) = R(II)                                             092
   60 B(I+1) = P(I)                                            093
      DO 602  I=1,N                                            094
  602 P(I) = B(I)                                              095
      P(1) = 0.                                                096
      WRITE OUTPUT TAPE 6, 73, (A(I), I=1,N)                   097
      WRITE OUTPUT TAPE 6, 73, (B(I), I=1,N)                   098
      WRITE OUTPUT TAPE 6, 997                                 099
      A(N+1) = 0.                                              100
C ROOTS OF TRIDIAGONAL
      DO 630  I=1,N                                            102
  630 B(I) = B(I) **2                                          103
      NB = 1                                                   104
  632 IF (B(NB)+B(NB+1)-PP) 633, 633, 635                      105
  633 G = G + A(NB)                                            106
      IF (G/FN-T) 6331, 6331, 7909                             107
 6331 NB = NB + 1                                              108
      IF (NB-N) 632, 790, 790                                  109
  635 NE = NB + 1                                              110
  636 IF (PP-B(NE+1)) 637, 650, 650                            111
  637 NE = NE + 1                                              112
      GO TO 636                                                113
  650 DO 670  I=NB,NE                                          114
      A(I) = A(I) - B(I)                                       115
  670 B(I+1) = B(I+1) / A(I)                                   116
      DO 700  I=NB,NE                                          117
      A(I) = A(I) + B(I+1)                                     118
  700 B(I+1) = A(I+1) * B(I+1)                                 119
      GO TO 632                                                120
  790 WRITE OUTPUT TAPE 6, 73, (A(K), K=1,N)
      WRITE OUTPUT TAPE 6, 73, (B(K), K=1,N)
      WRITE OUTPUT TAPE 6,997                                  125
   73 FORMAT(9F10.5 )                                          126
  997 FORMAT (1H )                                             128
 7909 CALL EXIT
      END                                                      130
C
*     DATA
    9
    5
  100
 .00100
 .75000
 1.000   .829   .768   .108   .033   .108   .298   .309   .351
 1.000   .775   .115   .061   .125   .323   .347   .369 1.000
  .272   .205   .238   .296   .271   .385 1.000   .636   .626
  .249   .183   .369 1.000   .709   .138   .091   .254 1.000
  .190   .103   .291 1.000   .654   .527 1.000   .541 1.000
```

615

```
C CHAPTER 11 - SOLUTIONS FROM INCOMPLETE COVARIANCE MATRICES          001
C     11.3 R(X,Y) MATRIX                                              002
C                                                                    003
      DIMENSION R(120,60), RXY(120,60), LI(15), D(15)                004
      READ INPUT TAPE 5, 03, P, NX, NY, NL                           005
03    FORMAT (F6.5/(I4))                                             006
      DO 051  I=1,NY                                                 007
      READ INPUT TAPE 5, 06, (RXY(I,J), J=1,NX)                      008
051   WRITE OUTPUT TAPE 6, 43, (RXY(I,J), J=1,NX)                    009
      WRITE OUTPUT TAPE 6, 997                                       010
06    FORMAT (10F6.3)                                                011
      P = .0001                                                      012
      FNX = NX                                                       013
      FNY = NY                                                       014
      FN = NX + NY                                                   015
      N = NX + NY                                                    016
      DO 14  I=1,NX                                                  017
      DO 14  J=1,NX                                                  018
      R(I,J) = 0.                                                    019
      DO 14  K=1,NY                                                  020
14    R(I,J) = R(I,J) + RXY(K,I) * RXY(K,J)                          021
      T = 0.                                                         022
      DO 17  I=1,NX                                                  023
17    T = T + R(I,I)                                                 024
      FT = .9999 * T                                                 025
      CALL JACSUC (R, LI, NX, D, NL, T, FT, IM, P)                   026
      DO 23  I=1,NX                                                  027
      INX = I + NX                                                   028
      DO 23  J=1,IM                                                  029
23    R(I,J) = R(INX,J)                                              030
      DO 29  I=1,NY                                                  031
      INX = I + NX                                                   032
      DO 29  J=1,IM                                                  033
      R(INX,J) = 0.                                                  034
      DO 29  K=1,NX                                                  035
29    R(INX,J) = R(INX,J) + RXY(I,K) * R(K,J)                        036
      DO 292  I=1,IM                                                 037
292   D(I) = SQRTF(D(I))                                             038
      PX = SQRTF(SQRTF(FNX/FNY))                                     039
      DO 33  I=1,IM                                                  040
33    D(I) = PX * SQRTF(D(I))                                        041
      DO 36  I=1,NX                                                  042
      DO 36  J=1,IM                                                  043
36    R(I,J) = R(I,J) * D(J)                                         044
      DO 362  I=1,IM                                                 045
362   D(I) = 1./D(I)                                                 046
      DO 40  I=1,NY                                                  047
      INX = I + NX                                                   048
      DO 40  J=1,IM                                                  049
40    R(INX,J) = R(INX,J) * D(J)                                     050
      DO 42  I=1,N                                                   051
42    WRITE OUTPUT TAPE 6, 43, (R(I,J), J=1,IM)                      052
      WRITE OUTPUT TAPE 6, 997                                       053
      DO 426  I=1,N                                                  054
      DO 426  J=1,N                                                  055
      RXY(I,J) = 0.                                                  056
      DO 426  K=1,IM                                                 057
426   RXY(I,J) = RXY(I,J) + R(I,K) * R(J,K)                          058
      DO 428  I=1,N                                                  059
428   WRITE OUTPUT TAPE 6, 43, (RXY(I,J), J=1,N)                     060
43    FORMAT (13F7.3)                                                061
997   FORMAT (1H )                                                   062
      CALL    EXIT                                                   063
      END                                                            064
C
      SUBROUTINE JACSUC (R, LI, N, D, NL, T, FT, IM, P)              001
      DIMENSION R(120,60), D(15), LI(15)                             002
      N11=N-1                                                        003
      N1 = N+1                                                       004
      N2 = N*2                                                       005
      DO 11  I=N1, N2                                                006
      DO 11  J=1,N                                                   007
11    R(I,J) = 0.                                                    008
      DO 14  I=1,N                                                   009
      NI = N+I                                                       010
14    R(NI,I) = 1.                                                   011
      DO 142  I=1,N2                                                 012
142   WRITE OUTPUT TAPE 6, 143, (R(I,J), J=1,N)                      013
143   FORMAT (10F10.5)                                               014
      WRITE OUTPUT TAPE 6. 997
```

```
997    FORMAT (1H )                                                        015
       T = 0.                                                              016
                                                                           017
       DO 36 I = 1,N11                                                     018
       IM = I                                                              019
       I1 = I+1                                                            020
       I2 = I+2                                                            021
       L = 0                                                               022
18     J = I2 - 1                                                          023
       DO 186 K=I2,N                                                       024
       IF (ABSF(R(I,J)) - ABSF(R(I,K))) 185, 185, 186                      025
185    J = K                                                               026
186    CONTINUE                                                            027
       IF (P-ABSF(R(I,J))) 20, 20, 330                                     028
C                                                                          029
20     DR = R(I,I) - R(J,J)                                                030
       A = SQRTF(DR**2 + 4.*R(I,J)**2)                                     031
       A = SQRTF((A+DR)/(2.*A))                                            032
       B = SQRTF(1. - A**2)                                                033
       C = SIGNF(1.,R(I,J))                                                034
C                                                                          035
       DO 252 K = I,N2                                                     036
       U = R(K,I)*A*C + R(K,J)*B                                           037
       R(K,J) = -R(K,I)*B*C + R(K,J)*A                                     038
252    R(K,I) = U                                                          039
       DO 282 K = 1,N                                                      040
       U = R(I,K)*A*C + R(J,K)*B                                           041
       R(J,K) = -R(I,K)*B*C + R(J,K)*A                                     042
282    R(I,K) = U                                                          043
C                                                                          044
       L = L+1                                                             045
       IF (L-NL) 18, 18, 330                                               046
330    D(I) = R(I,I)                                                       047
       T = T + R(I,I)                                                      048
       IF (FT-T) 351, 351, 35                                             049
35     LI(I) = L                                                           050
36     CONTINUE                                                            051
351    DO 352 I1=1,N2                                                      052
352    WRITE OUTPUT TAPE 6, 143, (R(I1,I2), I2=1,N)                        053
       WRITE OUTPUT TAPE 6, 997                                           054
       IF (N11-IM) 354, 354, 37                                           055
354    IF (T-FT) 355, 355, 37                                             056
355    IM = IM + 1                                                         057
       D(IM) = R(IM,IM)                                                    058
37     RETURN                                                             059
       END                                                                060
C
*      DATA
.00100
   4
   7
   9
 .108   .125   .238   .626
 .298   .323   .296   .249
 .309   .347   .271   .183
 .351   .369   .385   .369
 .492   .468   .446   .271
 .555   .525   .523   .185
 .425   .381   .396   .279
```

```
C CHAPTER 11 - SOLUTIONS FROM INCOMPLETE COVARIANCE MATRICES    001
C     11.4 SIMULTANEOUS SOLUTION FOR TWO SUBMATRICES            002
C                                                               003
C
      DIMENSION R(220,110), W(110), U(100), D(30), LI(30)       004
      READ INPUT TAPE 5, 03, P, N, NL, M                        005
03    FORMAT (F6.5 / (I4))                                      006
      DO 05  I=1,N                                              007
05    READ INPUT TAPE 5, 06, (R(I,J),   J=1,M)                  008
06    FORMAT (4F6.3)                                            009
      DO 0602 I = 1,N                                           010
0602  WRITE OUTPUT TAPE 6, 531, (R(I,J), J = 1,M)               011
      REWIND 2                                                  012
      REWIND 3                                                  013
C 11.4.1                                                        014
      DO 17  K=1,M                                              015
      S = 1./SQRTF(R(K,K))                                      016
      DO 12  I=K,N                                              017
12    R(I,K) = R(I,K) * S                                       018
      K1 = K+1                                                  019
      IF (M-K) 18, 18, 15                                       020
15    DO 17  J=K1,M                                             021
      DO 17 I = J,N                                             022
17    R(I,J) = R(I,J) - R(I,K) * R(J,K)                         023
18    DO 19  J=1,M                                              024
19    WRITE TAPE 2, (R(I,J),  I=J,N)                            025
      WRITE OUTPUT TAPE 6, 997                                  026
      DO 202  I=1,M                                             027
202   WRITE OUTPUT TAPE 6, 531, (R(I,J), J=1,M)                 028
      WRITE OUTPUT TAPE 6, 997                                  029
      REWIND 2                                                  030
C 11.4.2                                                        031
      DO 26  I=1,M                                              032
      DO 26  J=I,M                                              033
      S = 0.                                                    034
      DO 25 K = J,N                                             035
25    S = S + R(K,I) * R(K,J)                                   036
26    R(I,J) = S                                                037
      DO 29  I=1,M                                              038
      DO 29  J=I,M                                              039
29    R(J,I) = R(I,J)                                           040
      T = 0.                                                    041
      DO 32  I=1,M                                              042
32    T = T+ R(I,I)                                             043
      FT = .99*T                                                044
C 11.4.3                                                        045
      CALL JACSUC (R, LI, M, D, NL, T, FT, IM, P)               046
C 11.4.4                                                        047
      DO 36  J=1,M                                              048
36    READ TAPE 2, (R(I,J),  I=J,N)                             049
      REWIND 2                                                  050
      DO 54  K=1,IM                                             051
      READ TAPE 3, (W(I),  I=1,M)                               052
      DO 43  I=1,M                                              053
      U(I) = 0.                                                 054
      DO 43  J=1,I                                              055
43    U(I) = U(I) + R(I,J) * W(J)                               056
      M1 = M+1                                                  057
      DO 48  I=M1,N                                             058
      U(I) = 0.                                                 059
      DO 48  J=1,M                                              060
48    U(I) = U(I) + R(I,J) * W(J)                               061
54    WRITE TAPE 2, (U(I), I=1,N)                               062
      REWIND 2                                                  063
      DO 542  J=1,IM                                            064
542   READ TAPE 2, (R(I,J), I=1,N)                              065
      REWIND 2                                                  066
      WRITE OUTPUT TAPE 6, 532, (LI(K), K=1,IM)                 067
      WRITE OUTPUT TAPE 6, 997                                  068
      WRITE OUTPUT TAPE 6, 531, (D(K), K=1,IM)                  069
      WRITE OUTPUT TAPE 6, 997                                  070
      DO 546  I=1,N                                             071
546   WRITE OUTPUT TAPE 6, 531, (R(I,J), J=1,IM)                072
      WRITE OUTPUT TAPE 6, 997                                  073
      DO 552  I=1,IM                                            074
      DO 551  J=1,IM                                            075
      W(J) = 0.                                                 076
      DO 551  K=1,N                                             077
551   W(J) = W(J) + R(K,I) * R(K,J)                             078
552   WRITE OUTPUT TAPE 6, 531, (W(J), J=1,IM)                  079
997   FORMAT (1H )                                              080
531   FORMAT (10F7.3)                                           081
532   FORMAT (10I4)                                             082
```

618

```
       REWIND 3                                                              083
       CALL    EXIT                                                          086
       END                                                                   087
C
       SUBROUTINE JACSUC (R, LI, N, D, NL, T, FT, IM, P)
       DIMENSION R(220,110), D(30), LI(30)
 061   N11=N-1
 07    N1 = N+1
 08    N2 = N*2
 09    DO 11  I=N1, N2
 10    DO 11  J=1,N
 11    R(I,J) = 0.
 12    DO 14  I=1,N
 13    NI = N+I
 14    R(NI,I) = 1.
 141   DO 142  I=1,N2
 142   WRITE OUTPUT TAPE 6, 143, (R(I,J), J=1,N)
 143   FORMAT (10F7.3)
 144   WRITE OUTPUT TAPE 6, 997
 145   T = 0.
 997   FORMAT (1H )
 16    DO 36 I = 1,N11
       IM = I
 181   I1 = I+1
 1811  I2 = I+2
 17    L = 0
 18    J = I2 - 1
 183   DO 186  K=I2,N
 284   IF (ABSF(R(I,J)) - ABSF(R(I,K))) 185, 185, 186
 185   J = K
 186   CONTINUE
       IF (P-R(I,J)) 20, 20, 330
C
 20    DR = R(I,I) - R(J,J)
 21    A = SQRTF(DR**2 + 4.*R(I,J)**2)
 22    A = SQRTF((A+DR)/(2.*A))
 23    B = SQRTF(1. - A**2)
 221   C = SIGNF(1.,R(I,J))
C
 24    DO 252 K = 1,N2
 241   U = R(K,I)*A*C + R(K,J)*B
 25    R(K,J) = -R(K,I)*B*C + R(K,J)*A
 252   R(K,I) = U
 26    DO 282 K = 1,N
 271   U = R(I,K)*A*C + R(J,K)*B
 28    R(J,K) = -R(I,K)*B*C + R(J,K)*A
 282   R(I,K) = U
C
 31    L = L+1
 32    IF (L-NL) 18, 18, 330
 330   D(I) = R(I,I)
 33    T = T + R(I,I)
 34    IF (FT-T) 351, 351, 35
 35    LI(I) = L
 36    CONTINUE
 351   DO 352  I1=1,N2
 352   WRITE OUTPUT TAPE 6, 143, (R(I1,I2), I2=1,N)
       WRITE OUTPUT TAPE 6, 997
 353   IF (T-FT) 354, 354, 37
 354   IF (N11-IM) 355, 355, 37
 355   IM = IM + 1
 356   D(IM) = R(IM,IM)
C
 37    DO 100 J = 1,IM
 100   WRITE TAPE 3, (R(K,J),  K=N1,N2)
       REWIND 3
       RETURN
       END
*      DATA
.00100
 12
 10
 4
1.000  .829  .768  .108
 .829 1.000  .775  .115
 .768  .775 1.000  .272
 .108  .115  .272 1.000
 .033  .061  .205  .636
 .108  .125  .238  .626
 .298  .323  .296  .249
 .309  .347  .271  .183
```

```
 .351  .369  .385  .369
 .492  .468  .446  .271
 .555  .525  .523  .185
 .425  .381  .396  .279


C CHAPTER 11 - SOLUTIONS FROM INCOMPLETE COVARIANCE MATRICES       001
C    11.5 TWO MATRIC ELEMENT TWO STAGE SOLUTION                     002
C                                                                   003
      DIMENSION R(150,150), A(150), W(150), D(150)                  004
      READ INPUT TAPE 5, 03, N, M, NF                               005
 03   FORMAT (I4/I4/I4)                                             006
      READ INPUT TAPE 5, 05, (D(I),  I=1,NF)                        007
 05   FORMAT (10F6.3)                                               008
      REWIND 2                                                      009
      DO 071  I=1,M                                                 010
      READ INPUT TAPE 5, 05, (R(I,J),  J=1,N)                       011
 071  WRITE OUTPUT TAPE 6, 05, (R(I,J), J=1,N)                      012
      WRITE OUTPUT TAPE 6, 997                                      013
      DO 15  K=1,NF                                                 014
      READ INPUT TAPE 5, 05, (A(I),  I=1,N)                         015
      WRITE TAPE 2, (A(I), I=1,N)                                   016
      DO 14  I=1,M                                                  017
      W(I) = 0.                                                     018
      DO 13  J=1,N                                                  019
 13   W(I) = W(I) + R(I,J) * A(J)                                   020
 14   W(I) = W(I) / D(K)                                            021
 15   WRITE TAPE 2, (W(J), J=1,M)                                   022
      REWIND 2                                                      023
      WRITE OUTPUT TAPE 6, 18, (D(I), I=1,NF)                       024
      WRITE OUTPUT TAPE 6, 997                                      025
      NM = N + M                                                    026
      N1 = N+1                                                      027
      DO 1621 J = 1,NF                                              028
      READ TAPE 2, (R(I,J), I=1,N)                                  029
 1621 READ TAPE 2, (R(I,J),I =N1,NM)                                030
      REWIND 2                                                      031
      DO 164  I=1,NM                                                032
 164  WRITE OUTPUT TAPE 6,18,(R(I,J),J=1,NF)                        033
 18   FORMAT (15F7.3)                                               034
      WRITE OUTPUT TAPE 6, 997                                      035
 997  FORMAT (1H )                                                  036
      CALL    EXIT                                                  039
      END                                                          040
C
*     DATA
    9
    3
    3
3.749 2.050 1.331
 .492  .468  .446  .271  .180  .225  .399  .407  .471
 .555  .525  .523  .185  .147  .179  .262  .296  .437
 .425  .381  .396  .279  .191  .245  .356  .394  .429
0.717 0.740 0.773 0.556 0.463 0.518 0.640 0.615 0.715
0.493 0.478 0.296-0.649-0.744-0.694 0.080 0.166-0.034
0.350 0.322 0.406 0.068 0.181 0.188-0.588-0.621-0.369
```

```
C CHAPTER 12 - FACTORING THE DATA MATRIX
C    12.3 CENTROID METHOD
C
      DIMENSION Z(100,100),U(100),V(100),Y(100),W(100)
      READ INPUT TAPE 5, 05, P, NI, NJ, NL
      DO 401  I=1,NI
      READ INPUT TAPE 5, 06, (Z(I,J), J=1,NJ)
401   WRITE OUTPUT TAPE 6, 08, (Z(I,J), J=1,NJ)
      WRITE OUTPUT TAPE 6, 998
      REWIND 2
      REWIND 3
      FNI = NI
      FNJ = NJ
      NL = 9
      DO 20  J=1,NJ
      A = 0.
      S = 0.
      DO 16  I=1,NI
      A = A + Z(I,J)
16    S = S + Z(I,J)**2
      A = A/FNI
      S = 1./SQRTF(S/FNI-A**2)
      DO 20  I=1,NI
20    Z(I,J) = (Z(I,J)-A) * S
      DO 2002  I=1,NI
2002  WRITE OUTPUT TAPE 6, 08, (Z(I,J), J=1,NJ)
      WRITE OUTPUT TAPE 6, 998
      DO 206 J = 1,NJ
      U(J) = 0.
      V(J) = 0.
      DO 206  I=1,NI
      U(J) = U(J) + Z(I,J)
206   V(J) = V(J) + Z(I,J)**2
      WRITE OUTPUT TAPE 6, 08, (U(J), J=1,NJ)
      WRITE OUTPUT TAPE 6, 08, (V(J), J=1,NJ)
      WRITE OUTPUT TAPE 6, 998
      DO 731  L=1,NL
      DO 242 J = 1,NJ
      V(J) = 1.
      U(J) = 0.
      DO 242 I = 1,NI
242   U(J) = U(J) + Z(I,J)
      DO 29  I=1,NI
      W(I) = 1.
      Y(I) = 0.
      DO 29  J=1,NJ
29    Y(I) = Y(I) + Z(I,J)
30    MI = 1
      DO 34  I=2,NI
      IF (W(I)*Y(I)-W(MI)*Y(MI)) 33, 34, 34
33    MI = I
34    CONTINUE
      B = W(MI) * Y(MI)
      IF (B) 37, 40, 40
37    W(MI) = -W(MI)
      DO 39  J=1,NJ
39    U(J) = U(J) + 2. * W(MI) * Z(MI,J)
      WRITE OUTPUT TAPE 6, 08, (W(I), I=1,NI)
      WRITE OUTPUT TAPE 6, 08, (Y(I), I=1,NI)
      WRITE OUTPUT TAPE 6, 997
      WRITE OUTPUT TAPE 6, 08, (V(J), J=1,NJ)
      WRITE OUTPUT TAPE 6, 08, (U(J), J=1,NJ)
      WRITE OUTPUT TAPE 6, 998
40    MJ = 1
      DO 44  J=2,NJ
      IF (V(J)*U(J)-V(MJ)*U(MJ)) 43, 44, 44
43    MJ = J
44    CONTINUE
      C = V(MJ) * U(MJ)
      IF (C) 47, 50, 50
47    V(MJ) = -V(MJ)
      DO 49  I=1,NI
49    Y(I) = Y(I) + 2.* V(MJ)*Z(I,MJ)
50    IF (B) 30, 51, 51
51    B = 0.
      DO 53  I=1,NI
```

001
002
003
005
006
007
008
009
010
018
019
020
021
022
023
024
025
026
027
028
029
030
031
032
033
034
035
036
037
038
039
040
041
042
043
044
045
046
047
048
049
050
051
052
053
054
055
056
057
058
059
060
061
062
063
064
065
066
067
068
069
070
071
072
073
074
075
076
077
078
079
080
081
082
083
084

```
55    B = B + Y(I)**2                                                085
      B = SQRTF(FNI/B)                                               086
      C = O.                                                         087
      DO 57  J=1,NJ                                                  088
57    C = C + V(J) * U(J)                                            089
      E = C/(FNI*FNJ)                                                090
      C = 1./(B*C)                                                   091
      DO 61  I=1,NI                                                  092
61    Y(I) = Y(I) * B                                                093
      WRITE TAPE 2, (Y(I), I=1,NI)                                   094
      DO 63  J=1,NJ                                                  095
63    U(J) = U(J) * C                                                096
      WRITE TAPE 3, (U(J), J=1,NJ)                                   097
      WRITE OUTPUT TAPE 6, 07, E                                     098
      WRITE OUTPUT TAPE 6, 08, (W(I), I=1,NI)                        099
      WRITE OUTPUT TAPE 6, 08, (Y(I), I=1,NI)                        100
      WRITE OUTPUT TAPE 6, 997                                       101
      WRITE OUTPUT TAPE 6, 08, (V(J), J=1,NJ)                        102
      WRITE OUTPUT TAPE 6, 08, (U(J), J=1,NJ)                        103
      IF (E-P) 7301, 7301, 70                                        105
70    DO 72  I=1,NI                                                  106
      DO 72  J=1,NJ                                                  107
72    Z(I,J) = Z(I,J) - Y(I) * U(J)                                  108
      DO 7202 I=1,NI                                                 109
7202  WRITE OUTPUT TAPE 6, 08, (Z(I,J), J=1,NJ)                      110
731   CONTINUE                                                       111
7301  REWIND 2                                                       112
      REWIND 3                                                       113
      DO 733  J=1,NL                                                 114
733   READ TAPE 3, (Z(I,J), I=1,NJ)                                  115
      REWIND 2                                                       116
      DO 735  I=1,NJ                                                 117
735   WRITE OUTPUT TAPE 6, 08, (Z(I,J), J=1,NL)                      118
      WRITE OUTPUT TAPE 6, 997                                       119
      DO 737  J=1,NL                                                 120
737   READ TAPE 2, (Z(I,J), I=1,NI)                                  121
      REWIND 2                                                       122
      DO 739  I=1,NI                                                 123
739   WRITE OUTPUT TAPE 6, 08, (Z(I,J), J=1,NL)                      124
05    FORMAT (F6.4/(I4))                                            011
06    FORMAT (9F7.3)                                                012
07    FORMAT (F7.3)                                                 013
08    FORMAT (13F7.3)                                               014
997   FORMAT (1H )                                                  015
998   FORMAT (1HO)                                                  016
      CALL EXIT                                                     125
      END                                                           126
C
*     DATA
0.0010
  12
   9
   4
 0.128  0.181  0.421  0.506  0.857  0.746  0.280  0.178  0.246
 0.764  0.740  0.563 -0.387 -0.293 -0.202  0.261  0.281  0.043
-0.030 -0.046  0.014  0.147 -0.109 -0.135  0.640  0.682  0.661
-0.280 -0.351 -0.326 -0.023 -0.109 -0.186  0.083  0.091 -0.654
-0.336 -0.306 -0.429 -0.542 -0.006 -0.153 -0.428  0.056 -0.124
-0.276 -0.324 -0.271 -0.370 -0.225  0.035  0.129 -0.446 -0.124
 0.057 -0.070 -0.016  0.006  0.152 -0.441 -0.166 -0.354 -0.033
-0.010 -0.140  0.326 -0.004 -0.258 -0.091 -0.410 -0.200 -0.101
-0.303  0.227 -0.014  0.029 -0.102 -0.125 -0.086 -0.106 -0.074
 0.086  0.057 -0.003  0.161  0.073  0.134 -0.082 -0.067 -0.009
 0.164  0.106 -0.124  0.234 -0.002  0.227 -0.072  0.025  0.156
 0.036 -0.074 -0.142  0.242  0.023  0.192 -0.148 -0.119  0.011
```

```
C CHAPTER 12 - FACTORING THE DATA MATRIX                                    001
C     12.4 BASIC STRUCTURE SINGLE FACTOR METHOD                             002
C                                                                          003
      DIMENSION Z(100,100),Y(100),U(100),A1(100),IL(100)                   005
      READ INPUT TAPE 5, 05, P, PN, NI, NJ, NK, NL                         006
      DO 04  I=1,NI                                                        007
04    READ INPUT TAPE 5, 06, (Z(I,J), J=1,NJ)                             008
      FNI = NI                                                            013
      REWIND 2                                                            014
      REWIND 3                                                            015
C STANDARDIZED SCORE MATRIX                                                016
      DO 17  J=1,NJ                                                        017
      A = 0.                                                              018
      S = 0.                                                              019
      DO 13  I=1,NI                                                        020
      A = A + Z(I,J)                                                       021
13    S = S + Z(I,J)**2                                                    022
      A = A/FNI                                                            023
      S = 1./SQRTF(S/FNI-A**2)                                             024
      DO 17  I=1,NI                                                        025
17    Z(I,J) = (Z(I,J)-A) * S                                              026
      DO 50  K=1,NK                                                        027
      KN = K                                                              028
      A1(K) =0.                                                           029
      DO 21  J=1,NJ                                                        030
21    U(J) = 1.                                                           031
      DO 40  L=1,NL                                                        032
      IL(K) = L                                                           033
      DO 26  I=1,NI                                                        034
      Y(I) = 0.                                                           035
      DO 26  J=1,NJ                                                        036
26    Y(I) = Y(I) + Z(I,J) * U(J)                                          037
      A = 0.                                                              038
      DO 29  I=1,NI                                                        039
29    A = A + Y(I)**2                                                      040
      A = SQRTF(A/FNI)                                                     041
      DO 302  I=1,NI                                                       042
302   Y(I) = Y(I)/A                                                        043
      A2 = A1(K)                                                          044
      A1(K) = A                                                            045
      DO 38  J=1,NJ                                                        046
      U(J) = 0.                                                           047
      DO 38  I=1,NI                                                        048
38    U(J) = U(J) + Y(I) * Z(I,J)                                          049
      DO 3802  J=1,NJ                                                      050
3802  U(J) = U(J)/FNI                                                      051
      IF (ABSF(A2/A1-1.)-P) 41, 41, 40                                     052
40    CONTINUE                                                            053
41    WRITE TAPE 2, (Y(I), I=1,NI)                                         054
      WRITE TAPE 3, (U(J), J=1,NJ)                                         055
      IF (PN-A1) 47, 51, 51                                                056
47    DO 49  I=1,NI                                                        057
      DO 49  J=1,NJ                                                        058
49    Z(I,J) = Z(I,J) - Y(I) * U(J)                                        059
      WRITE OUTPUT TAPE 6, 998                                            060
      DO 502  J=1,NJ                                                       061
      U(J) = 0.                                                           062
      DO 502  I=1,N                                                        063
502   U(J) = U(J) + Y(I) * Z(I,J)                                          064
      WRITE OUTPUT TAPE 6, 06, (U(J), J=1,NJ)                             065
      WRITE OUTPUT TAPE 6, 998                                            066
50    CONTINUE                                                            067
51    WRITE OUTPUT TAPE 6, 900, (IL(K), K=1,KN)                           068
      WRITE OUTPUT TAPE 6, 06, (A1(K), K=1,KN)                            069
      WRITE OUTPUT TAPE 6, 998                                            070
      REWIND 2                                                            071
      REWIND 3                                                            072
      DO 54 J = 1,KN                                                       073
54    READ TAPE 3, (Z(I,J),I=1,NJ)                                         074
      REWIND 3                                                            075
      DO 56  I=1,NJ                                                        076
56    WRITE OUTPUT TAPE 6, 06, (Z(I,J), J=1,KN)                           077
      WRITE OUTPUT TAPE 6, 998                                            078
      DO 58 J= 1,KN                                                        079
58    READ TAPE 2, (Z(I,J),I=1,NI)                                         080
      REWIND 2                                                            081
      DO 60  I=1,NI                                                        082
60    WRITE OUTPUT TAPE 6, 06, (Z(I,J), J=1,KN)                           083
05    FORMAT (F7.5/F7.5/(I4))                                             009
```

623

```
06    FORMAT (13F7.3)                                                010
900   FORMAT (13I7)                                                  084
997   FORMAT (1H )                                                   011
998   FORMAT (1H0)                                                   012
      CALL EXIT                                                      085
      END                                                            086
C
*     DATA
0.00100
1.40000
  12
   9
   4
  20
  0.128  0.181  0.421  0.506  0.857  0.746  0.280  0.178  0.246
  0.764  0.740  0.563 -0.387 -0.293 -0.202  0.261  0.281  0.043
 -0.030 -0.046  0.014  0.147 -0.109 -0.135  0.640  0.682  0.661
 -0.280 -0.351 -0.326 -0.023 -0.109 -0.186  0.083  0.091 -0.654
 -0.336 -0.306 -0.429 -0.542 -0.006 -0.153 -0.428  0.056 -0.124
 -0.276 -0.324 -0.271 -0.370 -0.225  0.035  0.129 -0.446 -0.124
  0.057 -0.070 -0.016  0.006  0.152 -0.441 -0.166 -0.354 -0.033
 -0.010 -0.140  0.326 -0.004 -0.258 -0.091 -0.410 -0.200 -0.101
 -0.303  0.227 -0.014  0.029 -0.102 -0.125 -0.086 -0.106 -0.074
  0.086  0.057 -0.003  0.161  0.073  0.134 -0.082 -0.067 -0.009
  0.164  0.106 -0.124  0.234 -0.002  0.227 -0.072  0.025  0.156
  0.036 -0.074 -0.142  0.242  0.023  0.192 -0.148 -0.119  0.011


C CHAPTER 12 - FACTORING THE DATA MATRIX                            001
C    12.5 BASIC STRUCTURE WITH SIMULTANEOUS FACTOR SOLUTION         002
C                                                                   003
      DIMENSION Z(140,140), W(140,15), U(155,15)                    004
      READ INPUT TAPE 5, 05, P, NI, NJ, NK, NL                      005
      DO 04  I=1,NI                                                 006
04    READ INPUT TAPE 5, 06, (Z(I,J), J=1,NJ)                       007
C                                                                   012
      FNI = NI                                                      013
      DO 17  J=1,NJ                                                 014
      A = 0.                                                        015
      S = 0.                                                        016
      DO 13  I=1,NI                                                 017
      A = A + Z(I,J)                                                018
13    S = S + Z(I,J)**2                                             019
      A = A/FNI                                                     020
      S = 1./SQRTF(S-(A**2)*FNI)                                    021
      DO 17  I=1,NI                                                 022
17    Z(I,J) = (Z(I,J)-A) * S                                       023
      NK1 = NK + 1                                                  024
      NKJ = NK + NJ                                                 025
      G1 = 0.                                                       026
C1                                                                  027
      DO 23  I=1,NI                                                 028
      DO 23  K=1,NK                                                 029
23    W(I,K) = Z(I,K)                                               030
      DO 55  L=1,NL                                                 031
      DO 29  K1=1,NK                                                032
      DO 29  K2=K1,NK                                               033
      U(K2,K1) = 0.                                                 034
      DO 29  I=1,NI                                                 035
29    U(K2,K1) = U(K2,K1) + W(I,K1) * W(I,K2)                       036
C3                                                                  037
      DO 34  K=1,NK                                                 038
      DO 34  J=1,NJ                                                 039
      JNK = J + NK                                                  040
      U(JNK,K) = 0.                                                 041
      DO 34  I=1,NI                                                 042
34    U(JNK,K) = U(JNK,K) + Z(I,J) * W(I,K)                         043
C4                                                                  044
      DO 43  K1=1,NK                                                045
      K11 = K1 + 1                                                  046
      C = 1./SQRTF(U(K1,K1))                                        047
      DO 39  J=K1,NKJ                                               048
39    U(J,K1) = U(J,K1) * C                                         049
      IF (NK-K1) 44, 44, 41                                         050
41    DO 43  K2=K11,NK                                              051
      DO 43  J=K2,NKJ                                               052
43    U(J,K2) = U(J,K2) - U(J,K1) * U(K2,K1)                        053
C5                                                                  054
44    G2 = 0.                                                       055
      WRITE OUTPUT TAPE 6, 06, (U(K,K), K=1,NK)                     056
      WRITE OUTPUT TAPE 6, 997                                      057
      DO 444  J=NK1,NKJ                                             058
```

624

```
444     WRITE OUTPUT TAPE 6, 06, (U(J,K), K=1,NK)         059
        WRITE OUTPUT TAPE 6, 998                          060
        DO 46   K=1,NK                                    061
46      G2 = G2 + U(K,K)                                  062
        G = G1                                            063
        G1 = G2                                           064
        IF (ABSF(G/G1 -1.)-P) 56, 56, 50                  065
50      DO 55   I=1,NI                                    066
        DO 55   K=1,NK                                    067
        W(I,K) = 0.                                       068
        DO 55   J=1,NJ                                    069
        JNK = J + NK                                      070
55      W(I,K) = W(I,K) + Z(I,J) * U(JNK,K)              071
56      WRITE OUTPUT TAPE 6, 06, (U(K,K), K=1,NK)         072
        WRITE OUTPUT TAPE 6, 997                          073
        DO 59   J=NK1,NKJ                                 074
59      WRITE OUTPUT TAPE 6, 06, (U(J,K), K=1,NK)         075
05      FORMAT (F6.5/(I4))                                008
06      FORMAT (13F7.3)                                   009
997     FORMAT (1H )                                      010
998     FORMAT (1H0)                                      011
        CALL EXIT                                         076
        END                                               077
C
*       DATA
.00100
  12
   9
   4
  20
 0.128   0.181   0.421   0.506   0.857   0.746   0.280   0.178   0.246
 0.764   0.740   0.563  -0.387  -0.293  -0.202   0.261   0.281   0.043
-0.030  -0.046   0.014   0.147  -0.109  -0.135   0.640   0.682   0.661
-0.280  -0.351  -0.326  -0.023  -0.109  -0.186   0.083   0.091  -0.654
-0.336  -0.306  -0.429  -0.542  -0.006  -0.153  -0.428   0.056  -0.124
-0.276  -0.324  -0.271  -0.370  -0.225   0.035   0.129  -0.446  -0.124
 0.057  -0.070  -0.016   0.006   0.152  -0.441  -0.166  -0.354  -0.033
-0.010  -0.140   0.326  -0.004  -0.258  -0.091  -0.410  -0.200  -0.101
-0.303   0.227  -0.014   0.029  -0.102  -0.125  -0.086  -0.106  -0.074
 0.086   0.057  -0.003   0.161   0.073   0.134  -0.082  -0.067  -0.009
 0.164   0.106  -0.124   0.234  -0.002   0.227  -0.072   0.025   0.156
 0.036  -0.074  -0.142   0.242   0.023   0.192  -0.148  -0.119   0.011
```

```
C CHAPTER 13 - THE PROBLEM OF ORIGIN                                         001
C    13.4 BASIC STRUCTURE OF RAW COVARIANCE MATRIX FROM CORRELATION MATRIX   002
C                                                                            003
      DIMENSION R(200,100), DR(100), DN(100), DI(100), VM(100), VR(100),     004
     1V(100), U(100), W(100) , Q(200,100),                                   005
     1VRR(100), VN(100), VNN(100), VI(100)                                   006
      EQUIVALENCE (R(1), Q(1))                                               007
      CALL CHORIG
     1(R, DR, DN, DI, VM, VR, V, U, W, VRR, VN, VNN, VI, P, N, NL)
      A =0.                                                                  010
      DO 51  I=1,N                                                           011
51    READ TAPE 3, (Q(I,J), J=1,N)                                           012
      REWIND 3                                                               013
      DO 56  J=1,N                                                           014
      V(J) = 0.                                                              015
      DO 56  I=1,N                                                           016
56    V(J) = V(J) + VM(I) * Q(I,J)                                           017
      DO 570 L=1,N                                                           018
      F = 1.                                                                 019
      IF (L-1) 563, 563, 567                                                 020
563   X = DN(1)                                                              021
      DO 565  I=1,N                                                          022
565   X = X + V(I)**2                                                        023
      Y = DN(1)                                                              024
      GO TO 569                                                              025
567   X = DN(L-1)                                                            026
      Y = DN(L)                                                              027
569   CALL ROOTS (N, NL, L, P, X, Y, F, DN, U,V,VR,A)                        028
570   CONTINUE                                                               029
      WRITE OUTPUT TAPE 6,997                                                030
      WRITE OUTPUT TAPE 6, 400, (U(I), I=1,N)                                031
      CALL VECTOR (N,V,U,DN,DR,Q)                                            032
400   FORMAT (11F11.5)                                                       033
997   FORMAT (1H )                                                           034
      CALL EXIT                                                              035
      END                                                                    036
C
      SUBROUTINE ORIGIN (R, D, P, N, NL, NT)                                 001
      DIMENSION R(200,100), D(100)                                           002
      N1 = N + 1                                                             003
      N2 = N * 2                                                             004
      DO 051  I=1,N                                                          005
      READ TAPE NT, (R(I,J), J=1,N)                                          006
051   WRITE OUTPUT TAPE 6, 17, (R(I,J), J=1,N)                               007
      WRITE OUTPUT TAPE 6, 997                                               008
      REWIND NT                                                              009
      CALL JACSIM (R, D, P, N, NL)                                           010
      DO 09  I=1,N                                                           011
09    D(I) = R(I,I)                                                          012
      WRITE OUTPUT TAPE 6, 17, (D(I), I=1,N)                                 013
      WRITE OUTPUT TAPE 6, 997                                               014
      DO 14  I=N1,N2                                                         015
      WRITE TAPE NT, (R(I,J), J=1,N)                                         016
14    WRITE OUTPUT TAPE 6, 17, (R(I,J), J=1,N)                               017
      WRITE OUTPUT TAPE 6, 998                                               018
      REWIND NT                                                              019
17    FORMAT(11F11.5)                                                        027
997   FORMAT (1H )                                                           028
998   FORMAT (1H0)                                                           029
      RETURN                                                                 030
      END                                                                    031
C
      SUBROUTINE CHORIG                                                      001
     1(R, DR, DN, DI, VM, VR, V, U, W, VRR, VN, VNN, VI, P, N, NL)
      DIMENSION R(200,100), DR(100), DN(100), DI(100), VM(100), VR(100),     003
     1V(100), U(100), W(100), VRR(100), VN(100), VNN(100), VI(100)
      READ INPUT TAPE 5, 04, P, N, NL                                        007
      WRITE OUTPUT TAPE 6, 04, P, N, NL                                      008
04    FORMAT (F8.6/(I4))                                                     009
      READ INPUT TAPE 5, 06, (VM(I), I=1,N)                                  010
      WRITE OUTPUT TAPE 6, 06, (VM(I), I=1,N)                                011
      WRITE OUTPUT TAPE 6, 997                                               012
      WRITE OUTPUT TAPE 6, 997                                               013
06    FORMAT (10F4.1)                                                        014
      DO 08  I=1,N                                                           015
08    READ INPUT TAPE 5, 09, (R(I,J), J=1,N)                                 016
09    FORMAT (10F6.3)                                                        017
      REWIND 2                                                               018
      REWIND 3                                                               019
      REWIND 4                                                               020
      DO 14  I=1,N                                                           021
14    WRITE TAPE 3, (R(I,J), J=1,N)                                          022
      REWIND 3                                                               023
      DO 19  I=1,N                                                           024
```

```
        VR(I) = 0.                                                      025
        DO 19  J=1,N                                                    026
 19     VR(I) = VR(I) + R(I,J)                                          027
        FN = N                                                          028
        DO 202 I =1,N                                                   029
 202    VN(I) = VR(I)                                                   030
        G = 0.                                                          031
        DO 23  I=1,N                                                    032
 23     G = G + VR(I)                                                   033
        G = G / (2.*FN)                                                 034
        DO 26  I=1,N                                                    035
 26     U(I) = (VR(I)-G)/FN                                             036
        DO 30  I=1,N                                                    037
        DO 29  J=1,N                                                    038
 29     R(I,J) = R(I,J) - U(I) - U(J)                                   039
 30     WRITE TAPE 4, (R(I,J), J=1,N)                                   040
        REWIND 4                                                        041
        DO 33  I=1,N                                                    042
 33     READ TAPE 3, (R(I,J), J=1,N)                                    043
        REWIND 3                                                        044
        DO 38  I=1,N                                                    045
        DO 37  J=1,N                                                    046
 37     R(I,J) = R(I,J) + VM(I) * VM(J)                                 047
 38     WRITE TAPE 2, (R(I,J), J=1,N)                                   048
        REWIND 2                                                        049
        NR = 2                                                          050
        CALL ORIGIN (R, DR, P, N, NL, NR)                              051
        NN = 3                                                          052
        CALL ORIGIN (R, DN, P, N, NL, NN)                              053
        NI = 4                                                          054
        CALL ORIGIN (R, DI, P, N, NL, NI)                              055
 997    FORMAT (1H )                                                    056
        RETURN                                                          057
        END                                                            058
C
        SUBROUTINE JACSIM (R, D, P, N, NL)                             001
        DIMENSION R(200,100), D(100)                                   002
        N1 = N+1                                                        003
        N11=N-1                                                         004
        N2 = N*2                                                        005
        DO 10  I=N1, N2                                                 006
        DO 10  J = 1,N                                                  007
 10     R(I,J) = 0.                                                     008
        DO 12  I=1,N                                                    009
        NI = N + I                                                      010
 12     R(NI,I) = 1.                                                    011
        L = 0                                                           012
 14     DO 15  I=1,N                                                    013
 15     D(I) = R(I,I)                                                   014
        DO 282 I = 1,N11                                                015
        I1 = I+1                                                        016
        DO 282 J= I1,N                                                  017
        DR = R(I,I) - R(J,J)                                            018
        A = SQRTF(DR**2 + 4.*R(I,J)**2)                                019
        A = SQRTF((A+DR)/(2.*A))                                        020
        B = SQRTF(1.-A**2)                                              021
        C = SIGNF(1.,R(I,J))                                            022
        DO 252 K = 1,N2                                                 023
        U = R(K,I)*A*C + R(K,J)*B                                       024
        R(K,J) = -R(K,I)*B*C + R(K,J)*A                                025
 252    R(K,I) = U                                                      026
        DO 282 K = 1,N                                                  027
        U = R(I,K)*A*C + R(J,K)*B                                       028
        R(J,K) = -R(I,K)*B*C + R(J,K)*A                                029
 282    R(I,K) = U                                                      030
        DO 30  I=1,N                                                    031
 30     D(I) = ABSF(D(I) - R(I,I))                                      032
        S = 0.                                                          033
        DO 33  I=1,N                                                    034
 33     S = MAX1F (S, D(I))                                             035
        IF (S-P) 38, 38, 35                                            036
 35     L = L+1                                                         037
        IF (L-NL) 37, 38, 38                                            038
 37     GO TO 14                                                        039
 38     RETURN                                                          040
        END                                                            041
C
        SUBROUTINE ROOTS (N,NL,L,P,X,Y,F,D,U,V,VR,A)                   001
        DIMENSION D(100),U(100)  , V(100) , VR(100)                   002
        FN = N                                                         003
        DO 10 K =1,NL                                                  004
        KL = K                                                         005
        Z =(X+Y)/2.                                                    006
        VR(K) = F+A*Z*FN                                               007
```

627

```
        DO 2 I = 1,N
2       VR(K) = VR(K) + V(I)**2/(D(I)-Z)
        IF (P-ABSF(VR(K)))4,12,12
4       IF (VR(K)) 6,8,8
6       Y = Z
        GO TO 10
8       X = Z
10      CONTINUE
12      U(L) = Z
        WRITE OUTPUT TAPE 6,400, (VR(K),K=1,KL)
        WRITE OUTPUT TAPE 6,997
400     FORMAT (11F10.4)
997     FORMAT (1H )
        RETURN
        END
C
        SUBROUTINE VECTOR (N,V,U,D,D1,Q)
        DIMENSION V(100),U(100),D(100),D1(100),Q(200,100)
        WRITE OUTPUT TAPE 6,997
        DO 8 L =1,N
        DO 2 I =1,N
        U(I) =0.
        DO 2 J =1,N
2       U(I) = U(I) + Q(I,J)*V(J)/(D(J) - D1(L))
        IF (Q(N,N))3,9,3
9       DO 10 I = 1,N
10      U(I) = 1. - U(I)
3       G = 0.
        DO 4 I =1,N
4       G = G + U(I)**2
        G = SQRTF(G)
        DO 6 I =1,N
6       U(I) = U(I)/G
8       WRITE OUTPUT TAPE 6,400, (U(I),I=1,N)
        WRITE OUTPUT TAPE 6,997
400     FORMAT (11F10.4)
997     FORMAT (1H )
        RETURN
        END
C
*       DATA
0.000010
   9
  40-
 -.4 -.3 -.2 -.1  .0  .1  .2  .3  .4
1.000  .829  .768  .108  .033  .108  .298  .309  .351
 .829 1.000  .775  .115  .061  .125  .323  .347  .369
 .768  .775 1.000  .272  .205  .238  .296  .271  .385
 .108  .115  .272 1.000  .636  .626  .249  .183  .369
 .033  .061  .205  .636 1.000  .709  .138  .091  .254
 .108  .125  .238  .626  .709 1.000  .190  .103  .291
 .298  .323  .296  .249  .138  .190 1.000  .654  .527
 .309  .347  .271  .183  .091  .103  .654 1.000  .541
 .351  .369  .385  .369  .254  .291  .527  .541 1.000


C CHAPTER 13 - THE PROBLEM OF ORIGIN
C    13.5 NORMATIVE COVARIANCE BASIC STRUCTURE FROM RAW COVARIANCE
C    BASIC STRUCTURE
C
        DIMENSION R(200,100), DR(100), DN(100), DI(100), VM(100), VR(100),
       1V(100), U(100), W(100) , Q(200,100),
       1VRR(100), VN(100), VNN(100), VI(100)
        EQUIVALENCE (R(1), Q(1))
        CALL CHORIG
       1(R, DR, DN, DI, VM, VR, V, U, W, VRR, VN, VNN, VI, P, N, NL)
        A =0.
        DO 94  I=1,N
94      READ TAPE 2, (Q(I,J), J=1,N)
        REWIND 2
        DO 99  J=1,N
        V(J) = 0.
        DO 99  I=1,N
99      V(J) = V(J) + VM(I) * Q(I,J)
        DO 9910 L = 1,N
        F = -1.
        IF (N-L)9903,9903,9907
9903    X = DR(N)
        Y = 0.
        GO TO 9909
9907    X = DR(L)
        Y = DR(L+1)
9909 CALL ROOTS (N, NL, L, P, X, Y, F, DR, U,V,VR,A)
9910 CONTINUE
        WRITE OUTPUT TAPE 6,997
```

628

```
          WRITE OUTPUT TAPE 6,400, (U(I), I =1,N)                    030
          CALL VECTOR (N,V,U,DR,DN,Q)                                031
  997     FORMAT (1H )                                               032
  400     FORMAT (11F11.5)                                           033
          CALL EXIT                                                  034
          END                                                        035
C
          SUBROUTINE CHORIG                                          001
         1(R, DR, DN, DI, VM, VR, V, U, W, VRR, VN, VNN, VI, P, N, NL)
          DIMENSION R(200,100), DR(100), DN(100), DI(100), VM(100), VR(100),  003
         1V(100), U(100), W(100), VRR(100), VN(100), VNN(100), VI(100)
          READ INPUT TAPE 5, 04, P, N, NL                            007
          WRITE OUTPUT TAPE 6, 04, P, N, NL                          008
  04      FORMAT (F8.6/(I4))                                         009
          READ INPUT TAPE 5, 06, (VM(I), I=1,N)                      010
          WRITE OUTPUT TAPE 6, 06, (VM(I), I=1,N)                    011
          WRITE OUTPUT TAPE 6, 997                                   012
          WRITE OUTPUT TAPE 6, 997                                   013
  06      FORMAT (10F4.1)                                            014
          DO 08  I=1,N                                               015
  08      READ INPUT TAPE 5, 09, (R(I,J), J=1,N)                     016
  09      FORMAT (10F6.3)                                            017
          REWIND 2                                                   018
          REWIND 3                                                   019
          REWIND 4                                                   020
          DO 14  I=1,N                                               021
  14      WRITE TAPE 3, (R(I,J), J=1,N)                              022
          REWIND 3                                                   023
          DO 19  I=1,N                                               024
          VR(I) = 0.                                                 025
          DO 19  J=1,N                                               026
  19      VR(I) = VR(I) + R(I,J)                                     027
          FN = N                                                     028
          DO 202 I =1,N                                              029
  202     VN(I) = VR(I)                                              030
          G = 0.                                                     031
          DO 23  I=1,N                                               032
  23      G = G + VR(I)                                              033
          G = G / (2.*FN)                                            034
          DO 26  I=1,N                                               035
  26      U(I) = (VR(I)-G)/FN                                        036
          DO 30  I=1,N                                               037
          DO 29  J=1,N                                               038
  29      R(I,J) = R(I,J) - U(I) - U(J)                              039
  30      WRITE TAPE 4, (R(I,J), J=1,N)                              040
          REWIND 4                                                   041
          DO 33  I=1,N                                               042
  33      READ TAPE 3, (R(I,J), J=1,N)                               043
          REWIND 3                                                   044
          DO 38  I=1,N                                               045
          DO 37  J=1,N                                               046
  37      R(I,J) = R(I,J) + VM(I) * VM(J)                            047
  38      WRITE TAPE 2, (R(I,J), J=1,N)                              048
          REWIND 2                                                   049
          NR = 2                                                     050
          CALL ORIGIN (R, DR, P, N, NL, NR)                          051
          VN = 3                                                     052
          CALL ORIGIN (R, DN, P, N, NL, NN)                          053
          NI = 4                                                     054
          CALL ORIGIN (R, DI, P, N, NL, NI)                          055
  997     FORMAT (1H )                                               056
          RETURN                                                     057
          END                                                        058
C
          SUBROUTINE ORIGIN (R, D, P, N, NL, NT)                     001
          DIMENSION R(200,100), D(100)                               002
          N1 = N + 1                                                 003
          N2 = N * 2                                                 004
          DO 051  I=1,N                                              005
          READ TAPE NT, (R(I,J), J=1,N)                              006
  051     WRITE OUTPUT TAPE 6, 17, (R(I,J), J=1,N)                   007
          WRITE OUTPUT TAPE 6, 997                                   008
          REWIND NT                                                  009
          CALL JACSIM (R, D, P, N, NL)                               010
          DO 09  I=1,N                                               011
  09      D(I) = R(I,I)                                              012
          WRITE OUTPUT TAPE 6, 17, (D(I), I=1,N)                     013
          WRITE OUTPUT TAPE 6, 997                                   014
          DO 14  I=N1,N2                                             015
          WRITE TAPE NT, (R(I,J), J=1,N)                             016
  14      WRITE OUTPUT TAPE 6, 17, (R(I,J), J=1,N)                   017
          WRITE OUTPUT TAPE 6, 998                                   018
          REWIND NT                                                  019
  17      FORMAT(11F11.5)                                            027
  997     FORMAT (1H )                                               028
```

629

```
998   FORMAT (1H0)                                              029
      RETURN                                                    030
       END                                                      031
C
      SUBROUTINE JACSIM (R, D, P, N, NL )                       001
      DIMENSION R(200,100), D(100)                              002
      N1 = N+1                                                  003
      N11=N-1                                                   004
      N2 = N*2                                                  005
      DO 10 I=N1, N2                                            006
      DO 10 J = 1,N                                             007
10    R(I,J) = 0.                                               008
      DO 12 I=1,N                                               009
      NI = N + I                                                010
12    R(NI,I) = 1.                                              011
      L = 0                                                     012
14    DO 15 I=1,N                                               013
15    D(I) = R(I,I)                                             014
      DO 282 I = 1,N11                                          015
      I1 = I+1                                                  016
      DO 282 J= I1,N                                            017
      DR = R(I,I) - R(J,J)                                      018
      A = SQRTF(DR**2 + 4.*R(I,J)**2)                           019
      A = SQRTF((A+DR)/(2.*A))                                  020
      B = SQRTF(1.-A**2)                                        021
      C = SIGNF(1.,R(I,J))                                      022
      DO 252 K = 1,N2                                           023
      U = R(K,I)*A*C + R(K,J)*B                                 024
      R(K,J) = -R(K,I)*B*C + R(K,J)*A                           025
252   R(K,I) = U                                                026
      DO 282 K = 1,N                                            027
      U = R(I,K)*A*C + R(J,K)*B                                 028
      R(J,K) = -R(I,K)*B*C + R(J,K)*A                           029
282   R(I,K) = U                                                030
      DO 30 I=1,N                                               031
30    D(I) = ABSF(D(I) - R(I,I))                                032
      S = 0.                                                    033
      DO 33 I=1,N                                               034
33    S = MAX1F (S, D(I))                                       035
      IF (S-P) 38, 38, 35                                       036
35    L = L+1                                                   037
      IF (L-NL) 37, 38, 38                                      038
37    GO TO 14                                                  039
38    RETURN                                                    040
       END                                                      041
C
      SUBROUTINE ROOTS (N,NL,L,P,X,Y,F,D,U,V,VR,A)
      DIMENSION D(100),U(100)  , V(100) , VR(100)
      FN = N
      DO 10 K =1,NL
      KL = K
      Z =(X+Y)/2.
      VR(K) = F+A*Z*FN
      DO 2 I = 1,N
2     VR(K) = VR(K) + V(I)**2/(D(I)-Z)
      IF (P-ABSF(VR(K)))4,12,12
4     IF (VR(K)) 6,8,8
6     Y = Z
      GO TO 10
8     X = Z
10    CONTINUE
12    U(L) = Z
      WRITE OUTPUT TAPE 6,400, (VR(K),K=1,KL)
      WRITE OUTPUT TAPE 6,997
400   FORMAT (11F10.4)
997   FORMAT (1H )
      RETURN                                                    160
       END
C
      SUBROUTINE VECTOR (N,V,U,D,D1,Q)
      DIMENSION V(100),U(100),D(100),D1(100),Q(200,100)
      WRITE OUTPUT TAPE 6,997
      DO 8 L =1,N
      DO 2 I =1,N
      U(I) =0.
      DO 2 J =1,N
2     U(I) = U(I) + Q(I,J)*V(J)/(D(J) - D1(L))
      IF (Q(N,N))3,9,3
9     DO 10 I = 1,N
10    U(I) = 1. - U(I)
3     G = 0.
      DO 4 I =1,N
4     G = G + U(I)**2
      G = SQRTF(G)
```

630

```
      DO 6 I =1,N
6     U(I) = U(I)/G
8     WRITE OUTPUT TAPE 6,400, (U(I),I=1,N)
      WRITE OUTPUT TAPE 6,997
400   FORMAT (11F10.4)
997   FORMAT (1H )
      RETURN
      END
C
*     DATA
0.000010
  9
  40
-.4 -.3 -.2 -.1  .0  .1  .2  .3  .4
1.000  .829  .768  .108   .033  .108  .298  .309  .351
 .829 1.000  .775  .115   .061  .125  .323  .347  .369
 .768  .775 1.000  .272   .205  .238  .296  .271  .385
 .108  .115  .272 1.000   .636  .626  .249  .183  .369
 .033  .061  .205  .636  1.000  .709  .138  .091  .254
 .108  .125  .238  .626   .709 1.000  .190  .103  .291
 .298  .323  .296  .249   .138  .190 1.000  .654  .527
 .309  .347  .271  .183   .091  .103  .654 1.000  .541
 .351  .369  .385  .369   .254  .291  .527  .541 1.000


C CHAPTER 13 - THE PROBLEM OF ORIGIN                                    001
C     13.6 IPSATIVE COVARIANCE BASIC STRUCTURE FROM NORMATIVE           002
C     COVARIANCE BASIC STRUCTURE                                        003
C                                                                       004
      DIMENSION R(200,100), DR(100), DN(100), DI(100), VM(100), VR(100),005
     1V(100), U(100), W(100) , Q(200,100),                             006
     1VRR(100), VN(100), VNN(100), VI(100)                             007
      EQUIVALENCE (R(1), Q(1))                                          008
      CALL CHORIG                                                       009
     1(R, DR, DN, DI, VM, VR, V, U, W, VRR, VN, VNN, VI, P, N, NL)
      FN=N
      A =0.                                                             011
      DO 102  I=1,N                                                     012
102   READ TAPE 3, (Q(I,J), J=1,N)                                      013
      REWIND 3                                                          014
      DO 106  J=1,N                                                     015
      V(J) = 0.                                                         016
      DO 106  I=1,N                                                     017
106   V(J) = V(J) + Q(I,J)                                              018
      DO 1062 I =1,N                                                    019
1062  W(I) = V(I)                                                       020
      DO 108 J = 1,N                                                    021
108   V(J) = V(J) * SQRTF(DN(J)/FN)                                     022
      DO  1089  L=1,N                                                   023
      F = -1.                                                           024
      IF (N-L) 1084, 1084, 1086                                         025
1084  X = DN(N)                                                         026
      Y = 0.                                                            027
      GO TO 1088                                                        028
1086  X = DN(L)                                                         029
      Y = DN(L+1)                                                       030
1088 CALL ROOTS (N, NL, L, P, X, Y, F, DN, U,V,VR,A)                    031
1089 CONTINUE                                                           032
      WRITE OUTPUT TAPE 6,997                                           033
      WRITE OUTPUT TAPE 6,400,(U(I),I=1,N)                              034
      CALL VECTOR (N,W,U,DN,DI,Q)                                       035
400   FORMAT (11F11.5)                                                  036
997   FORMAT (1H )                                                      037
      CALL    EXIT                                                      038
      END                                                              039
C
      SUBROUTINE CHORIG                                                 001
     1(R, DR, DN, DI, VM, VR, V, U, W, VRR, VN, VNN, VI, P, N, NL)
      DIMENSION R(200,100), DR(100), DN(100), DI(100), VM(100), VR(100),003
     1V(100), U(100), W(100), VRR(100), VN(100), VNN(100), VI(100)
      READ INPUT TAPE 5, 04, P, N, NL                                   007
      WRITE OUTPUT TAPE 6, 04, P, N, NL                                 008
04    FORMAT (F8.6/(I4))                                                009
      READ INPUT TAPE 5, 06, (VM(I), I=1,N)                             010
      WRITE OUTPUT TAPE 6, 06, (VM(I), I=1,N)                           011
      WRITE OUTPUT TAPE 6, 997                                          012
      WRITE OUTPUT TAPE 6, 997                                          013
06    FORMAT (10F4.1)                                                   014
      DO 08  I=1,N                                                      015
08    READ INPUT TAPE 5, 09, (R(I,J), J=1,N)                            016
09    FORMAT (10F6.3)                                                   017
      REWIND 2                                                          018
      REWIND 3                                                          019
      REWIND 4                                                          020
      DO 14 I=1.N                                                       021
```

```
14      WRITE TAPE 3, (R(I,J), J=1,N)                                    022
        REWIND 3                                                        023
        DO 19  I=1,N                                                    024
        VR(I) = 0.                                                      025
        DO 19  J=1,N                                                    026
19      VR(I) = VR(I) + R(I,J)                                          027
        FN = N                                                          028
        DO 202 I =1,N                                                   029
202     VN(I) = VR(I)                                                   030
        G = 0.                                                          031
        DO 23  I=1,N                                                    032
23      G = G + VR(I)                                                   033
        G = G / (2.*FN)                                                 034
        DO 26  I=1,N                                                    035
26      U(I) = (VR(I)-G)/FN                                             036
        DO 30  I=1,N                                                    037
        DO 29  J=1,N                                                    038
29      R(I,J) = R(I,J) - U(I) - U(J)                                   039
30      WRITE TAPE 4, (R(I,J), J=1,N)                                   040
        REWIND 4                                                        041
        DO 33  I=1,N                                                    042
33      READ TAPE 3, (R(I,J), J=1,N)                                    043
        REWIND 3                                                        044
        DO 38  I=1,N                                                    045
        DO 37  J=1,N                                                    046
37      R(I,J) = R(I,J) + VM(I) * VM(J)                                 047
38      WRITE TAPE 2, (R(I,J), J=1,N)                                   048
        REWIND 2                                                        049
        NR = 2                                                          050
        CALL ORIGIN (R, DR, P, N, NL, NR)                               051
        NN = 3                                                          052
        CALL ORIGIN (R, DN, P, N, NL, NN)                               053
        NI = 4                                                          054
        CALL ORIGIN (R, DI, P, N, NL, NI)                               055
997     FORMAT (1H )                                                    056
        RETURN                                                          057
        END                                                             058
C
        SUBROUTINE ORIGIN (R, D, P, N, NL, NT)                          001
        DIMENSION R(200,100), D(100)                                    002
        N1 = N + 1                                                      003
        N2 = N * 2                                                      004
        DO 051  I=1,N                                                   005
        READ TAPE NT, (R(I,J), J=1,N)                                   006
051     WRITE OUTPUT TAPE 6, 17, (R(I,J), J=1,N)                        007
        WRITE OUTPUT TAPE 6, 997                                        008
        REWIND NT                                                       009
        CALL JACSIM (R, D, P, N, NL)                                    010
        DO 09  I=1,N                                                    011
09      D(I) = R(I,I)                                                   012
        WRITE OUTPUT TAPE 6, 17, (D(I), I=1,N)                          013
        WRITE OUTPUT TAPE 6, 997                                        014
        DO 14  I=N1,N2                                                  015
        WRITE TAPE NT, (R(I,J), J=1,N)                                  016
14      WRITE OUTPUT TAPE 6, 17, (R(I,J), J=1,N)                        017
        WRITE OUTPUT TAPE 6, 998                                        018
        REWIND NT                                                       019
17      FORMAT(11F11.5)                                                 027
997     FORMAT (1H )                                                    028
998     FORMAT (1H0)                                                    029
        RETURN                                                          030
        END                                                             031
C
        SUBROUTINE JACSIM (R, D, P, N, NL)                              001
        DIMENSION R(200,100), D(100)                                    002
        N1 = N+1                                                        003
        N11=N-1                                                         004
        N2 = N*2                                                        005
        DO 10  I=N1, N2                                                 006
        DO 10  J = 1,N                                                  007
10      R(I,J) = 0.                                                     008
        DO 12  I=1,N                                                    009
        NI = N + I                                                      010
12      R(NI,I) = 1.                                                    011
        L = 0                                                           012
14      DO 15  I=1,N                                                    013
15      D(I) = R(I,I)                                                   014
        DO 282 I = 1,N11                                                015
        I1 = I+1                                                        016
        DO 282 J= I1,N                                                  017
        DR = R(I,I) - R(J,J)                                            018
        A = SQRTF(DR**2 + 4.*R(I,J)**2)                                 019
        A = SQRTF((A+DR)/(2.*A))                                        020
```

632

```
        B = SQRTF(1.-A**2)                                              021
        C = SIGNF(1.,R(I,J))                                            022
        DO 252 K = 1,N2                                                 023
        U = R(K,I)*A*C + R(K,J)*B                                       024
        R(K,J) = -R(K,I)*B*C + R(K,J)*A                                 025
252     R(K,I) = U                                                      026
        DO 282 K = 1,N                                                  027
        U = R(I,K)*A*C + R(J,K)*B                                       028
        R(J,K) = -R(I,K)*B*C + R(J,K)*A                                 029
282     R(I,K) = U                                                      030
        DO 30  I=1,N                                                    031
30      D(I) = ABSF(D(I) - R(I,I))                                      032
        S = 0.                                                          033
        DO 33  I=1,N                                                    034
33      S = MAX1F (S, D(I))                                             035
        IF (S-P) 38, 38, 35                                             036
35      L = L+1                                                         037
        IF (L-NL) 37, 38, 38                                            038
37      GO TO 14                                                        039
38      RETURN                                                          040
        END                                                             041
C

        SUBROUTINE ROOTS (N,NL,L,P,X,Y,F,D,U,V,VR,A)
        DIMENSION D(100),U(100)  , V(100) , VR(100)
        FN = N
        DO 10 K =1,NL
        KL = K
        Z =(X+Y)/2.
        VR(K) = F+A*Z*FN
        DO 2 I = 1,N
2       VR(K) = VR(K) + V(I)**2/(D(I)-Z)
        IF (P-ABSF(VR(K)))4,12,12
4       IF (VR(K)) 6,8,8
6       Y = Z
        GO TO 10
8       X = Z
10      CONTINUE
12      U(L) = Z
        WRITE OUTPUT TAPE 6,400, (VR(K),K=1,KL)
        WRITE OUTPUT TAPE 6,997
400     FORMAT (11F10.4)
997     FORMAT (1H )
        RETURN
        END                                                             160
C

        SUBROUTINE VECTOR (N,V,U,D,D1,Q)
        DIMENSION V(100),U(100),D(100),D1(100),Q(200,100)
        WRITE OUTPUT TAPE 6,997
        DO 8 L =1,N
        DO 2 I =1,N
        U(I) =0.
        DO 2 J =1,N
2       U(I) = U(I) + Q(I,J)*V(J)/(D(J) - D1(L))
        IF (Q(N,N))3,9,3
9       DO 10 I = 1,N
10      U(I) = 1. - U(I)
3       G = 0.
        DO 4 I =1,N
4       G = G + U(I)**2
        G = SQRTF(G)
        DO 6 I =1,N
6       U(I) = U(I)/G
8       WRITE OUTPUT TAPE 6,400, (U(I),I=1,N)
        WRITE OUTPUT TAPE 6,997
400     FORMAT (11F10.4)
997     FORMAT (1H )
        RETURN
        END                                                             160
C
*       DATA
0.000010
   9
  40
 -.4 -.3 -.2 -.1  .0  .1   .2   .3   .4
1.000  .829  .768  .108  .033  .108   .298   .309   .351
 .829 1.000  .775  .115  .061  .125   .323   .347   .369
 .768  .775 1.000  .272  .205  .238   .296   .271   .385
 .108  .115  .272 1.000  .636  .626   .249   .183   .369
 .033  .061  .205  .636 1.000  .709   .138   .091   .254
 .108  .125  .238  .626  .709 1.000   .190   .103   .291
 .298  .323  .296  .249  .138  .190  1.000   .654   .527
 .309  .347  .271  .183  .091  .103   .654 1.000   .541
 .351  .369  .385  .369  .254  .291   .527   .541 1.000
```

```
C CHAPTER 13 - THE PROBLEM OF ORIGIN                                        001
C   13.7 NORMATIVE COVARIANCE BASIC STRUCTURE FROM IPSATIVE BASIC           002
C   STRUCTURE                                                               003
C                                                                           004
      DIMENSION R(200,100), DR(100), DN(100), DI(100), VM(100), VR(100),    005
     1V(100), U(100), W(100) , Q(200,100),                                  006
     1VRR(100), VN(100), VNN(100), VI(100)                                  007
      EQUIVALENCE (R(1), Q(1))                                              008
      CALL CHORIG                                                           009
     1(R, DR, DN, DI, VM, VR, V, U, W, VRR, VN, VNN, VI, P, N, NL)
      FN=N                                                                  011
      A =1.                                                                 012
      DO 302   I=1,N                                                        013
302   READ TAPE 4, (Q(I,J), J=1,N)                                         014
      REWIND 4                                                              015
      G =0.                                                                 016
      DO 3024 I = 1,N                                                       017
      G = G + VN(I)                                                         018
3024  Q(I,N) = 0.                                                           019
      DO 306   J=1,N                                                        020
      V(J) = 0.                                                             021
      DO 306   I=1,N                                                        022
306   V(J) = V(J) + VN(I) * Q(I,J)                                         023
      DO 3062   I=1,N                                                       024
3062  W(I) = V(I)                                                           025
      DO 319   L=1,N                                                        026
      F = -G                                                                027
      IF (L-1) 312, 312, 316                                               028
312   X = (DI(1) + FN)/2.                                                   029
      Y = DI(1)                                                             030
      GO TO 318                                                             031
316   X = DI(L-1)                                                           032
      Y = DI(L)                                                             033
318   CALL ROOTS (N, NL, L, P, X, Y, F, DI, U, V, VR,A)                    034
319   CONTINUE                                                              035
      WRITE OUTPUT TAPE 6, 997                                             036
      WRITE OUTPUT TAPE 6, 400, (U(I), I=1,N)                              037
      CALL VECTOR (N, W, U, DI, DN, Q)                                     038
400   FORMAT(11F11.5)                                                      039
997   FORMAT(1H )                                                          040
      CALL EXIT                                                            041
      END
C
      SUBROUTINE CHORIG                                                    001
     1(R, DR, DN, DI, VM, VR, V, U, W, VRR, VN, VNN, VI, P, N, NL)
      DIMENSION R(200,100), DR(100), DN(100), DI(100), VM(100), VR(100),   003
     1V(100), U(100), VRR(100), VN(100), VNN(100), VI(100)
      READ INPUT TAPE 5, 04, P, N, NL                                      007
      WRITE OUTPUT TAPE 6, 04, P, N, NL                                    008
04    FORMAT (F8.6/(I4))                                                   009
      READ INPUT TAPE 5, 06, (VM(I), I=1,N)                                010
      WRITE OUTPUT TAPE 6, 06, (VM(I), I=1,N)                              011
      WRITE OUTPUT TAPE 6, 997                                             012
      WRITE OUTPUT TAPE 6, 997                                             013
06    FORMAT (10F4.1)                                                      014
      DO 08   I=1,N                                                        015
08    READ INPUT TAPE 5, 09, (R(I,J), J=1,N)                               016
09    FORMAT (10F6.3)                                                      017
      REWIND 2                                                             018
      REWIND 3                                                             019
      REWIND 4                                                             020
      DO 14   I=1,N                                                        021
14    WRITE TAPE 3, (R(I,J), J=1,N)                                        022
      REWIND 3                                                             023
      DO 19   I=1,N                                                        024
      VR(I) = 0.                                                           025
      DO 19   J=1,N                                                        026
19    VR(I) = VR(I) + R(I,J)                                               027
      FN = N                                                               028
      DO 202 I =1,N                                                        029
202   VN(I) = VR(I)                                                        030
      G = 0.                                                               031
      DO 23   I=1,N                                                        032
23    G = G + VR(I)                                                        033
      G = G / (2.*FN)                                                      034
      DO 26   I=1,N                                                        035
26    U(I) = (VR(I)-G)/FN                                                  036
      DO 30   I=1,N                                                        037
      DO 29   J=1,N                                                        038
29    R(I,J) = R(I,J) - U(I) - U(J)                                        039
30    WRITE TAPE 4, (R(I,J), J=1,N)                                        040
      REWIND 4                                                             041
      DO 33   I=1,N                                                        042
```

```
  33    READ TAPE 3, (R(I,J), J=1,N)                                          043
        REWIND 3                                                              044
        DO 38  I=1,N                                                          045
        DO 37   J=1,N                                                         046
  37    R(I,J) = R(I,J) + VM(I) * VM(J)                                       047
  38    WRITE TAPE 2, (R(I,J), J=1,N)                                         048
        REWIND 2                                                              049
        NR = 2                                                                050
        CALL ORIGIN (R, DR, P, N, NL, NR)                                     051
        NN = 3                                                                052
        CALL ORIGIN (R, DN, P, N, NL, NN)                                     053
        NI = 4                                                                054
        CALL ORIGIN (R, DI, P, N, NL, NI)                                     055
  997   FORMAT (1H )                                                          056
        RETURN                                                                057
         END                                                                  058
C
        SUBROUTINE ORIGIN (R, D, P, N, NL, NT)                                001
        DIMENSION R(200,100), D(100)                                          002
        N1 = N + 1                                                            003
        N2 = N * 2                                                            004
        DO 051  I=1,N                                                         005
        READ TAPE NT, (R(I,J), J=1,N)                                         006
  051   WRITE OUTPUT TAPE 6, 17, (R(I,J), J=1,N)                              007
        WRITE OUTPUT TAPE 6, 997                                              008
        REWIND NT                                                             009
        CALL JACSIM (R, D, P, N, NL)                                          010
        DO 09  I=1,N                                                          011
  09    D(I) = R(I,I)                                                         012
        WRITE OUTPUT TAPE 6, 17, (D(I), I=1,N)                                013
        WRITE OUTPUT TAPE 6, 997                                              014
        DO 14  I=N1,N2                                                        015
        WRITE TAPE NT, (R(I,J), J=1,N)                                        016
  14    WRITE OUTPUT TAPE 6, 17, (R(I,J), J=1,N)                              017
        WRITE OUTPUT TAPE 6, 998                                              018
        REWIND NT                                                             019
  17    FORMAT(11F11.5)                                                       027
  997   FORMAT (1H )                                                          028
  998   FORMAT (1H0)                                                          029
        RETURN                                                                030
         END                                                                  031
C
        SUBROUTINE JACSIM (R, D, P, N, NL)                                    001
        DIMENSION R(200,100), D(100)                                          002
        N1 = N+1                                                              003
        N11=N-1                                                               004
        N2 = N*2                                                              005
        DO 10  I=N1, N2                                                       006
        DO 10  J = 1,N                                                        007
  10    R(I,J) = 0.                                                           008
        DO 12  I=1,N                                                          009
        NI = N + I                                                            010
  12    R(NI,I) = 1.                                                          011
        L = 0                                                                 012
  14    DO 15  I=1,N                                                          013
  15    D(I) = R(I,I)                                                         014
        DO 282 I = 1,N11                                                      015
        I1 = I+1                                                              016
        DO 282 J= I1,N                                                        017
        DR = R(I,I) - R(J,J)                                                  018
        A = SQRTF(DR**2 + 4.*R(I,J)**2)                                       019
        A = SQRTF((A+DR)/(2.*A))                                              020
        B = SQRTF(1.-A**2)                                                    021
        C = SIGNF(1.,R(I,J))                                                  022
        DO 252 K = 1,N2                                                       023
        U = R(K,I)*A*C + R(K,J)*B                                            024
        R(K,J) = -R(K,I)*B*C + R(K,J)*A                                      025
  252   R(K,I) = U                                                            026
        DO 282 K = 1,N                                                        027
        U = R(I,K)*A*C + R(J,K)*B                                            028
        R(J,K) = -R(I,K)*B*C + R(J,K)*A                                      029
  282   R(I,K) = U                                                            030
        DO 30  I=1,N                                                          031
  30    D(I) = ABSF(D(I) - R(I,I))                                            032
        S = 0.                                                                033
        DO 33  I=1,N                                                          034
```

```
33      S = MAXIF (S, D(I))                                          035
        IF (S-P) 38, 38, 35                                          036
35      L = L+1                                                      037
        IF (L-NL) 37, 38, 38                                         038
                                                                     039
37      GO TO 14                                                     040
38      RETURN                                                       041
        END

C
        SUBROUTINE ROOTS (N,NL,L,P,X,Y,F,D,U,V,VR,A)
        DIMENSION D(100),U(100)  , V(100) , VR(100)
        FN = N
        DO 10 K =1,NL
        KL = K
        Z =(X+Y)/2.
        VR(K) = F+A*Z*FN
        DO 2 I = 1,N
2       VR(K) = VR(K) + V(I)**2/(D(I)-Z)
        IF (P-ABSF(VR(K)))4,12,12
4       IF (VR(K)) 6,8,8
6       Y = Z
        GO TO 10
8       X = Z
10      CONTINUE
12      U(L) = Z
        WRITE OUTPUT TAPE 6,400, (VR(K),K=1,KL)
        WRITE OUTPUT TAPE 6,997
400     FORMAT (11F10.4)
997     FORMAT (1H )
        RETURN
        END                                                          160

C
        SUBROUTINE VECTOR (N,V,U,D,D1,Q)
        DIMENSION V(100),U(100),D(100),D1(100),Q(200,100)
        WRITE OUTPUT TAPE 6,997
        DO 8 L =1,N
        DO 2 I =1,N
        U(I) =0.
        DO 2 J =1,N
2       U(I) = U(I) + Q(I,J)*V(J)/(D(J) - D1(L))
        IF (Q(N,N))3,9,3
9       DO 10 I = 1,N
10      U(I) = 1. - U(I)
3       G = 0.
        DO 4 I =1,N
4       G = G + U(I)**2
        G = SQRTF(G)
        DO 6 I =1,N
6       U(I) = U(I)/G
8       WRITE OUTPUT TAPE 6,400, (U(I),I=1,N)
        WRITE OUTPUT TAPE 6,997
400     FORMAT (11F10.4)
997     FORMAT (1H )
        RETURN
        END                                                          160

C
*       DATA
0.000010
   9
  40
-.4 -.3 -.2 -.1  .0  .1  .2  .3  .4
1.000  .829  .768  .108  .033  .108  .298  .309  .351
 .829 1.000  .775  .115  .061  .125  .323  .347  .369
 .768  .775 1.000  .272  .205  .238  .296  .271  .385
 .108  .115  .272 1.000  .636  .626  .249  .183  .369
 .033  .061  .205  .636 1.000  .709  .138  .091  .254
 .108  .125  .238  .626  .709 1.000  .190  .103  .291
 .298  .323  .296  .249  .138  .190 1.000  .654  .527
 .309  .347  .271  .183  .091  .103  .654 1.000  .541
 .351  .369  .385  .369  .254  .291  .527  .541 1.000
```

636

```
C CHAPTER 14 - CATEGORICAL VARIATIONS IN FACTOR ANALYSIS                      001
C    14.4 OBVERSE FACTOR SOLUTION WITH STANDARD METRIC                        002
C                                                                             003
      DIMENSION X(120,200), U(200), V(200), W(120), KV(20), S(200)           004
      READ INPUT TAPE 5, 401, P, PV, N, M, NL, NF                            005
      WRITE OUTPUT TAPE 6, 401, P, PV, N, M, NL, NF                          006
      WRITE OUTPUT TAPE 6, 997                                               007
      DO 04   I=1,N                                                          008
04    READ INPUT TAPE 5, 402, (X(I,J), J=1,M)                                009
      DO 0411  I=1,N                                                         010
0411  WRITE OUTPUT TAPE 6, 402, (X(I,J), J=1,M)                             011
      WRITE OUTPUT TAPE 6, 999                                               012
999   FORMAT (1H1)                                                           013
      REWIND 2                                                               014
      REWIND 3                                                               015
      DO 08   I=1,N                                                          016
08    WRITE TAPE 2, (X(I,J), J=1,M)                                          017
      REWIND 2                                                               018
      DO 15   J=1,M                                                          019
      U(J) = 0.                                                              020
      V(J) = 0.                                                              021
      DO 15   I=1,N                                                          022
      U(J) = U(J) + X(I,J)                                                   023
15    V(J) = V(J) + X(I,J)**2                                                024
      FN = N                                                                 025
      FM = M                                                                 026
      FM = FM * FN                                                           027
      DO 18   J=1,M                                                          028
18    V(J) = 1. / (V(J)/FN - (U(J)/FN)**2)                                   029
      DO 20   J=1,M                                                          030
20    S(J) = SQRTF (V(J)/FN)                                                 031
      A = 0.                                                                 032
      DO 23   J=1,M                                                          033
23    A = A + ((U(J)**2) * V(J))                                             034
      A = A/(FN**2)                                                          035
      DO 26   J=1,M                                                          036
26    U(J) = U(J) * V(J) / FN                                                037
      DO 30   I=1,N                                                          038
      W(I) = -A/2.                                                           039
      DO 30   J=1,M                                                          040
30    W(I) = W(I) + X(I,J) * U(J)                                            041
      DO 37   I=1,N                                                          042
      DO 35   J=I,N                                                          043
      U(J) = -W(I) - W(J)                                                    044
      DO 35   K=1,M                                                          045
35    U(J) = U(J) + X(I,K) * X(J,K) * V(K)                                   046
      DO 37   J=I,N                                                          047
37    X(I,J) = U(J)                                                          048
      DO 40   I=1,N                                                          049
      DO 40   J=I,N                                                          050
40    X(J,I) = X(I,J)                                                        051
      DO 4002 I=1,N                                                          052
4002  WRITE OUTPUT TAPE 6,400, (X(I,J),J=1,N)                               053
      A=0.                                                                   054
      DO 4005 I=1,N                                                          055
4005  A = A+X(I,I)                                                           056
      WRITE OUTPUT TAPE 6,400,A                                             057
      G = 0.                                                                 058
      DO 75   L=1,NF                                                         059
      LF = L                                                                 060
      DO 45   I=1,N                                                          061
45    V(I) = 1.                                                              062
      WRITE OUTPUT TAPE 6,400, (V(I),I=1,N)                                 063
      E = 0.                                                                 064
      DO 62   K=1,NL                                                         065
      KV(L) = K                                                              066
      DO 52   I=1,N                                                          067
      U(I) = 0.                                                              068
      DO 52   J=1,N                                                          069
52    U(I) = U(I) + X(I,J) * V(J)                                            070
      W(L) = 0.                                                              071
      DO 55   I=1,N                                                          072
55    W(L) = W(L) + V(I) * U(I)                                              073
      W(L) = SQRTF (W(L))                                                    074
      DO 58   I=1,N                                                          075
58    V(I) = U(I) / W(L)                                                     076
      WRITE OUTPUT TAPE 6,400, (V(I),I=1,N)                                 077
      E1 = E                                                                 078
      E = W(L)                                                               079
      IF ((ABSF(E1/E-1.))-P) 68, 68, 62                                      080
```

637

```
 62    CONTINUE                                               081
 68    A = 0.                                                 082
       DO 70  I=1,N                                           083
 70    A = A + V(I)**2                                        084
       A = SQRTF (A)                                          085
       DO 73  I=1,N                                           086
 73    V(I) = V(I) / A                                        087
       WRITE OUTPUT TAPE 6, 997                               088
       WRITE OUTPUT TAPE 6,400,(V(I),I=1,N)                   089
       WRITE TAPE 3, (V(I), I=1,N)                            090
       G = G + W(L)                                           091
       IF (G-PV*FM) 65, 65, 76                                092
 65    DO 67   I=1,N                                          093
       DO 67   J=1,N                                          094
 67    X(I,J) = X(I,J) - V(I) * V(J) * W(L)                   095
 75    CONTINUE                                               096
 76    REWIND 3                                               097
       DO 78  I=1,N                                           098
 78    READ TAPE 2, (X(I,J), J=1,M)                           099
       REWIND 2                                               100
       DO 88  L=1,LF                                          101
       READ TAPE 3, (V(I), I=1,N)                             102
       WRITE OUTPUT TAPE 6,400,(V(I),I=1,N)                   103
       DO 85  J=1,M                                           104
       U(J) = 0.                                              105
       DO 85   I=1,N                                          106
 85    U(J) = U(J) + X(I,J) * V(I)                            107
       DO 87   J=1,M                                          108
 87    U(J) = U(J) * S(J)                                     109
 88    WRITE TAPE 2, (U(J), J=1,M)                            110
       REWIND 3                                               111
       REWIND 2                                               112
       DO 92   J=1,LF                                         113
 92    READ TAPE 2, (X(I,J), I=1,M)                           114
       DO 922 L = 1,LF                                        115
 922   W(L) = W(L)/FN                                         116
       WRITE OUTPUT TAPE 6, 400, (W(L), L=1,LF)               117
       WRITE OUTPUT TAPE 6, 403, (KV(L), L=1,LF)              118
       WRITE OUTPUT TAPE 6, 997                               119
       DO 97  I=1,M                                           120
 97    WRITE OUTPUT TAPE 6, 400, (X(I,J), J=1,LF)             121
 400   FORMAT (12F9.3)                                        122
 401   FORMAT (F7.6/F3.2/(I4))                                123
 402   FORMAT (9F7.3)                                         124
 403   FORMAT (10I7)                                          125
 997   FORMAT (1H )                                           126
       CALL    EXIT                                           170
       END                                                    160
*      DATA
.000100
.75
  12
   9
  50
   4
  0.128  0.181  0.421  0.506  0.857  0.746  0.280  0.178  0.246
  0.764  0.740  0.563 -0.387 -0.293 -0.202  0.261  0.281  0.043
 -0.030 -0.046  0.014  0.147 -0.109 -0.135  0.640  0.682  0.661
 -0.280 -0.351 -0.326 -0.023 -0.109 -0.186  0.083  0.091 -0.654
 -0.336 -0.306 -0.429 -0.542 -0.006 -0.153 -0.428  0.056 -0.124
 -0.276 -0.324 -0.271 -0.370 -0.225  0.035  0.129 -0.446 -0.124
  0.057 -0.070 -0.016  0.006  0.152 -0.441 -0.166 -0.354 -0.033
 -0.010 -0.140  0.326 -0.004 -0.258 -0.091 -0.410 -0.200 -0.101
 -0.303  0.227 -0.014  0.029 -0.102 -0.125 -0.086 -0.106 -0.074
  0.086  0.057 -0.003  0.161  0.073  0.134 -0.082 -0.067 -0.009
  0.164  0.106 -0.124  0.234 -0.002  0.227 -0.072  0.025  0.156
  0.036 -0.074 -0.142  0.242  0.023  0.192 -0.148 -0.119  0.011
```

```
C CHAPTER 15 - THE PROBLEM OF SCALING                                        001
C     15.6 SPECIFICITY SUCCESSIVE FACTOR SOLUTION                            002
C                                                                           003
      DIMENSION R(100,100), AM(100,15), UM(100,15), WM(115,15),             004
     1A(100), U(100), W(100), KV(15), GF(15), D(100)                        005
      READ INPUT TAPE 5, 902, P, PV, N, NF, NL, M                           006
      REWIND 2                                                              007
      DO 05  I=1,N                                                          008
 05   READ INPUT TAPE 5, 903, (R(I,J), J=1,N)                               009
      DO 081  J=1,M                                                         010
 081  READ INPUT TAPE 5, 903, (AM(I,J), I=1,N)                              011
      FN = N                                                                012
      NL = 30                                                               013
      G = 0.                                                                014
      DO 52  L=1,NF                                                         015
      LF = L                                                                016
      DO 15  I=1,N                                                          017
      A(I) = 0.                                                             018
      DO 15  J=1,N                                                          019
 15   A(I) = A(I) + R(I,J)                                                  020
      AL = 0.                                                               021
      DO 18  I=1,N                                                          022
 18   AL = AL + A(I)                                                        023
      AL = 1./SQRTF(AL)                                                     024
      DO 21  I=1,N                                                          025
 21   A(I) = A(I) * AL                                                      026
      E = 0.                                                                027
      DO 43  K=1,NL                                                         028
      KV(L) = K                                                             029
      DO 29  I=1,N                                                          030
 29   U(I) = A(I) / (R(I,I)-A(I)**2)                                        031
      DO 33  I=1,N                                                          032
      W(I) = -A(I)                                                          033
      DO 33  J=1,N                                                          034
 33   W(I) = W(I) + R(I,J) * U(J)                                           035
      AL = 0.                                                               036
      DO 36  I=1,N                                                          037
 36   AL = AL + W(I) * U(I)                                                 038
      AL = SQRTF (AL)                                                       039
      DO 39  I=1,N                                                          040
 39   A(I) = W(I)/AL                                                        042
      E1 = E                                                                043
      E = AL                                                                044
      IF ((ABSF(E1/E-1.))-P) 44, 44, 43                                     045
 43   CONTINUE                                                              046
 44   WRITE TAPE 2, (A(I), I=1,N)                                           047
      WRITE OUTPUT TAPE 6, 997                                             048
      GF(L) = 0.                                                            049
      DO 47  I=1,N                                                          050
 47   GF(L) = GF(L) + A(I)**2                                               051
      G = G + GF(L)                                                         052
      IF (G-PV*FN) 50, 50, 53                                               053
 50   DO 52  I=1,N                                                          054
      DO 52  J=1,N                                                          055
 52   R(I,J) = R(I,J) - A(I) * A(J)                                         056
 53   REWIND 2                                                              057
      DO 55  J=1,LF                                                         058
 55   READ TAPE 2, (R(I,J), I=1,N)                                          059
      REWIND 2                                                              060
      WRITE OUTPUT TAPE 6, 901, (KV(L), L=1,LF)                             061
      WRITE OUTPUT TAPE 6, 900, (GF(L), L=1,LF)                             062
      WRITE OUTPUT TAPE 6, 997                                             063
      DO 61  I=1,N                                                          064
 61   WRITE OUTPUT TAPE 6, 900, (R(I,J), J=1,LF)                            065
 900  FORMAT (13F9.4)                                                       066
 901  FORMAT (10I7)                                                         067
 902  FORMAT (F7.6/F3.2/(I4))                                               068
 903  FORMAT (10F6.3)                                                       069
 997  FORMAT (1H )                                                          070
 998  FORMAT (1H0)                                                          071
      CALL EXIT                                                             072
      END
C
*     DATA
.000100
.75
  9
  4
 50
  4
1.000  .829  .768  .108  .033  .108  .298  .309  .351
 .829 1.000  .775  .115  .061  .125  .323  .347  .369
 .768  .775 1.000  .272  .205  .238  .296  .271  .385
```

639

```
     .108   .115   .272 1.000   .636   .626   .249   .183   .369
     .033   .061   .205   .636 1.000   .709   .138   .091   .254
     .108   .125   .238   .626   .709 1.000   .190   .103   .291
     .298   .323   .296   .249   .138   .190 1.000   .654   .527
     .309   .347   .271   .183   .091   .103   .654 1.000   .541
     .351   .369   .385   .369   .254   .291   .527   .541 1.000
   0.717 0.740 0.773 0.556 0.463 0.518 0.640 0.615 0.715
   0.493 0.478 0.296-0.649-0.744-0.694 0.080 0.166-0.034
   0.350 0.322 0.406 0.068 0.181 0.188-0.588-0.621-0.369
  -0.030-0.056 0.009 0.102-0.115-0.129-0.288-0.165 0.566
```

```
C CHAPTER 15 - THE PROBLEM OF SCALING                                001
C   15.7 SPECIFICITY FACTOR MATRIX SOLUTION                           002
C                                                                     003
      DIMENSION R(100,100), AM(100,15), UM(100,15), WM(115,15),       004
     1A(100), U(100), W(100), KV(15), GF(15), D(100)                  005
      READ INPUT TAPE 5, 902, P, PV, N, NF, NL, M                     006
      REWIND 2                                                        007
      DO 05  I=1,N                                                    008
 05   READ INPUT TAPE 5, 903, (R(I,J), J=1,N)                         009
      DO 081  J=1,M                                                   010
 081  READ INPUT TAPE 5, 903, (AM(I,J), I=1,N)                        011
      FN = N                                                          012
      NL = 30                                                         013
      E = 0.                                                          014
      DO 2451  L=1,NL                                                 015
      LF = L                                                          016
      DO 210  I=1,N                                                   017
      D(I) = R(I,I)                                                   018
      DO 210  J=1,M                                                   019
 210  D(I) = D(I) - AM(I,J)**2                                        020
      S = D(1)                                                        021
      DO 700  I=2,N                                                   022
 700  S = MIN1F (S,D(I))                                              023
      S = 1.                                                          024
      DO 213  I=1,N                                                   025
      DO 213  J=1,M                                                   026
 213  UM(I,J) = (AM(I,J) / D(I)) * S                                  027
      DO 219  I=1,N                                                   028
      IM = I + M                                                      029
      DO 219  J=1,M                                                   030
      WM(IM,J) = -AM(I,J)                                             031
      DO 219  K=1,N                                                   032
 219  WM(IM,J) = WM(IM,J) + R(I,K) * UM(K,J)                          033
      DO 225  I=1,M                                                   034
      DO 225  J=1,M                                                   035
      WM(I,J) = 0.                                                    036
      DO 225  K=1,N                                                   037
      KM = K + M                                                      039
 225  WM(I,J) = WM(I,J) + WM(KM,I) * UM(K,J)                          040
      DO 241  K=1,M                                                   041
      S = 1./SQRTF(WM(K,K))                                           042
      NM = N + M                                                      043
      DO 236  I=K,NM                                                  044
 236  WM(I,K) = WM(I,K) * S                                           045
      K1 = K + 1                                                      046
      IF (M-K) 242, 242, 239                                          047
 239  DO 241  J=K1,M                                                  048
      DO 241  I=J,NM                                                  049
 241  WM(I,J) = WM(I,J) - WM(I,K) * WM(J,K)                           050
 242  DO 245  I=1,N                                                   051
      IM = I + M                                                      052
      DO 245  J=1,M                                                   053
 245  AM(I,J) = WM(IM,J)                                              054
      GF(L) = 0.                                                      055
      DO 228  I=1,M                                                   056
 228  GF(L) = GF(L) + WM(I,I)                                         057
      E1 = E                                                          058
      E = GF(L)                                                       059
      IF ((ABSF(E1/E-1.))-P) 247, 247, 2451                          060
 2451 CONTINUE                                                        061
 247  WRITE OUTPUT TAPE 6, 900, (GF(L), L=1,LF)                       062
      WRITE OUTPUT TAPE 6,997                                         063
      DO 2473 J= 1,M                                                  064
      GF(J) =0.                                                       065
      DO 2473 I = 1,N                                                 066
 2473 GF(J) = GF(J) + AM(I,J)**2                                      067
      WRITE OUTPUT TAPE 6, 997                                        068
      WRITE OUTPUT TAPE 6,900, (GF(J),J=1,M)                          069
      DO 250  I=1,N                                                   070
 250  WRITE OUTPUT TAPE 6, 900, (AM(I,J), J=1,M)                      071
 900  FORMAT (13F9.4)                                                 072
 902  FORMAT (F7.6/F3.2/(I4))
 903  FORMAT (10F6.3)
```

```
 997   FORMAT (1H )                                                         073
       CALL EXIT                                                            074
       END                                                                  075
C
*      DATA
.000100
.75
    9
    4
   50
    4
1.000   .829   .768   .108   .033   .108   .298   .309   .351
 .829  1.000   .775   .115   .061   .125   .323   .347   .369
 .768   .775  1.000   .272   .205   .238   .296   .271   .385
 .108   .115   .272  1.000   .636   .626   .249   .183   .369
 .033   .061   .205   .636  1.000   .709   .138   .091   .254
 .108   .125   .238   .626   .709  1.000   .190   .103   .291
 .298   .323   .296   .249   .138   .190  1.000   .654   .527
 .309   .347   .271   .183   .091   .103   .654  1.000   .541
 .251   .369   .385   .369   .254   .291   .527   .541  1.000
 0.717 0.740 0.773 0.556 0.463 0.518 0.640 0.615 0.715
 0.493 0.478 0.296-0.649-0.744-0.694 0.080 0.166-0.034
 0.350 0.322 0.406 0.068 0.181 0.188-0.588-0.621-0.369
-0.030-0.056 0.009 0.102-0.115-0.129-0.288-0.165 0.566
C CHAPTER 15 - THE PROBLEM OF SCALING                                       001
C    15.8 SPECIFICITY PROGRESSIVE FACTOR MATRIX METHOD                      002
C                                                                           003
       DIMENSION R(100,100), AM(100,15), UM(100,15), WM(115,15),            004
      1A(100), U(100), W(100), KV(15), GF(15), D(100)                       005
       READ INPUT TAPE 5, 902, P, PV, N, NF, NL, M                          006
       REWIND 2                                                             007
       DO 05  I=1,N                                                         008
05     READ INPUT TAPE 5, 903, (R(I,J), J=1,N)                              009
       DO 081  J=1,M                                                        010
081    READ INPUT TAPE 5, 903, (AM(I,J), I=1,N)                             011
       FN = N
       NL = 30
       DO 351  L=1,NF                                                       012
       LF = L                                                               013
       LN = L + N                                                           014
       E = 0.                                                               015
       DO 346  KI=1,NL                                                      016
       DO 312  I=1,N                                                        017
       D(I) = R(I,I)                                                        018
       DO 312  J=1,L                                                        019
312    D(I) = D(I) - AM(I,J)**2                                            020
       S = D(1)                                                             021
       DO 701  I=2,N                                                        022
701    S = MIN1F(S, D(I))                                                   023
       S = 1.                                                               024
       DO 315  I=1,N                                                        025
       DO 315  J=1,L                                                        026
315    UM(I,J) = (AM(I,J) / D(I)) * S                                       027
       DO 321  I=1,N                                                        028
       IL = I + L                                                           029
       DO 321  J=1,L                                                        030
       WM(IL,J) = -AM(I,J)                                                  031
       DO 321  K=1,N                                                        032
321    WM(IL,J) = WM(IL,J) + R(I,K) * UM(K,J)                              033
       DO 327  I=1,L                                                        034
       DO 327  J=1,L                                                        035
       WM(I,J) = 0.                                                         036
       DO 327  K=1,N                                                        037
       KL = K + L                                                           038
327    WM(I,J) = WM(I,J) + WM(KL,I) * UM(K,J)                              039
       DO 336  K=1,L                                                        041
       S = 1./SQRTF(WM(K,K))                                                042
       DO 331  I=K,LN                                                       043
331    WM(I,K) = WM(I,K) * S                                                044
       K1 = K + 1                                                           045
       IF (L-K) 343, 343, 334                                               046
334    DO 336  J=K1,L                                                       047
       DO 336  I=J,LN                                                       048
336    WM(I,J) = WM(I,J) - WM(I,K) * WM(J,K)                               049
       C = 0.                                                               050
       DO 339  J=1,L                                                        051
339    C = C + WM(J,J)                                                      052
       E1 = E                                                               053
       E = C                                                                054
       IF ((ABSF(E1/E-1.))-P) 347, 347, 343                                055
343    DO 346  I=1,N                                                        056
       IL = I + L                                                           057
       DO 346  J=1,L                                                        058
```

641

```
 346   AM(I,J) = WM(IL,J)                                             059
 347   WRITE OUTPUT TAPE 6, 998                                       060
       G = 0.                                                         062
       DO 349  I=1,N                                                  063
 349   G = G + R(I,I) - D(I)                                          064
       IF (G-PV*FN) 351, 351, 352                                     065
 351   CONTINUE                                                       066
 352   DO 355  J=1,LF                                                 067
       GF(J) = 0.                                                     068
       DO 355  I=1,N                                                  069
 355   GF(J) = GF(J) + AM(I,J)**2                                     070
       WRITE OUTPUT TAPE 6, 998                                       071
       WRITE OUTPUT TAPE 6, 900, (GF(J), J=1,LF)                      072
       WRITE OUTPUT TAPE 6, 997                                       073
       C = 0.
       DO 3601  I=1,N
3601   C = C + AM(I,1)
       S = SIGNF(1., C)
       DO 3602  I=1,N
       DO 3602  J=1,LF
3602   AM(I,J) = S * AM(I,J)
       DO 360  I=1,N                                                  074
 360   WRITE OUTPUT TAPE 6, 900, (AM(I,J), J=1,LF)                    075
 900   FORMAT (13F9.4)                                                076
 902   FORMAT (F7.6/F3.2/(I4))
 903   FORMAT (10F6.3)
 997   FORMAT (1H )                                                   079
 998   FORMAT (1H0)                                                   080
       CALL EXIT                                                      081
       END                                                           082
C
*      DATA
.000100
.75
    9
    4
   50
    4
 1.000  .829  .768  .108  .033  .108  .298  .309  .351
  .829 1.000  .775  .115  .061  .125  .323  .347  .369
  .768  .775 1.000  .272  .205  .238  .296  .271  .385
  .108  .115  .272 1.000  .636  .626  .249  .183  .369
  .033  .061  .205  .636 1.000  .709  .138  .091  .254
  .108  .125  .238  .626  .709 1.000  .190  .103  .291
  .298  .323  .296  .249  .138  .190 1.000  .654  .527
  .309  .347  .271  .183  .091  .103  .654 1.000  .541
  .351  .369  .385  .369  .254  .291  .527  .541 1.000
 0.717 0.740 0.773 0.556 0.463 0.518 0.640 0.615 0.715
 0.493 0.478 0.296-0.649-0.744-0.694 0.080 0.166-0.034
 0.350 0.322 0.406 0.068 0.181 0.188-0.588-0.621-0.369
-0.030-0.056 0.009 0.102-0.115-0.129-0.288-0.165 0.566
C CHAPTER 15 - THE PROBLEM OF SCALING                                 001
C    15.9 COMMUNALITY SUCCESSIVE FACTOR METHOD                        002
C                                                                     003
       DIMENSION R(100,100), AM(100,15), UM(100,15), WM(115,15),      004
      1A(100), U(100), W(100), KV(15), GF(15), D(100)                 005
       READ INPUT TAPE 5, 902, P, PV, N, NF, NL, M                    006
       REWIND 2                                                       007
       DO 05  I=1,N                                                   008
 05    READ INPUT TAPE 5, 903, (R(I,J), J=1,N)                        009
       DO 081  J=1,M                                                  010
 081   READ INPUT TAPE 5, 903, (AM(I,J), I=1,N)                       011
       FN = N
       NL = 30
       G = 0.                                                         013
       DO 444  L=1,NL                                                 014
       LF = L                                                         015
       DO 410  I=1,N                                                  016
       A(I) = 0.                                                      017
       DO 410  J=1,N                                                  018
 410   A(I) = A(I) + R(I,J)                                           019
       AL = 0.                                                        020
       DO 413  I=1,N                                                  021
 413   AL = AL + A(I)                                                 022
       AL = 1./SQRTF(AL)                                              023
       DO 416  I=1,N                                                  024
 416   A(I) = A(I) * AL                                               025
       E = 0.                                                         026
       DO 435  K=1,NL                                                 027
       KV(L) = K                                                      028
       DO 421  I=1,N                                                  029
 421   U(I) = 1./A(I)                                                 030
       DO 425  I=1,N                                                  031
```

642

```
      W(I) = 0.                                                        032
      DO 425   J=1,N                                                   033
425   W(I) = W(I) + R(I,J) * U(J)                                      034
      AL = 0.                                                          035
      DO 428   I=1,N                                                   036
428   AL = AL + U(I) * W(I)                                            037
      AL = SQRTF(AL)                                                   038
      DO 431   I=1,N                                                   039
431   A(I) = W(I)/AL                                                   040
      E1 = E                                                           042
      E = AL                                                           043
      IF ((ABSF(E1/E-1.))-P) 436, 436, 435                            044
435   CONTINUE                                                         045
436   WRITE TAPE 2, (A(I), I=1,N)                                      046
      GF(L) = 0.                                                       048
      DO 439   I=1,N                                                   049
439   GF(L) = GF(L) + A(I)**2                                          050
      G = G + GF(L)                                                    051
      IF (G-PV*FN) 442, 442, 445                                       052
442   DO 444   I=1,N                                                   053
      DO 444   J=1,N                                                   054
444   R(I,J) = R(I,J) - A(I) * A(J)                                    055
445   REWIND 2                                                         056
      DO 447   J=1,LF                                                  057
447   READ TAPE 2, (R(I,J), I=1,N)                                     058
      REWIND 2                                                         059
      WRITE OUTPUT TAPE 6, 901, (KV(L), L=1,LF)                        060
      WRITE OUTPUT TAPE 6, 900, (GF(L), L=1,LF)                        061
      WRITE OUTPUT TAPE 6, 997                                         062
      DO 454   I=1,N                                                   063
454   WRITE OUTPUT TAPE 6, 900, (R(I,J), J=1,LF)                       064
900   FORMAT (13F9.4)                                                  065
901   FORMAT (10I7)                                                    066
902   FORMAT (F7.6/F3.2/(I4))
903   FORMAT (10F6.3)
997   FORMAT (1H )                                                     067
      CALL EXIT                                                        068
      END                                                              069
C
*     DATA
.000100
.75
   9
   4
  50
   4
 1.000  .829  .768  .108  .033  .108  .298  .309  .351
  .829 1.000  .775  .115  .061  .125  .323  .347  .369
  .768  .775 1.000  .272  .205  .238  .296  .271  .385
  .108  .115  .272 1.000  .636  .626  .249  .183  .369
  .033  .061  .205  .636 1.000  .709  .138  .091  .254
  .108  .125  .238  .626  .709 1.000  .190  .103  .291
  .298  .323  .296  .249  .138  .190 1.000  .654  .527
  .309  .347  .271  .183  .091  .103  .654 1.000  .541
  .351  .369  .385  .369  .254  .291  .527  .541 1.000
 0.717 0.740 0.773 0.556 0.463 0.518 0.640 0.615 0.715
 0.493 0.478 0.296-0.649-0.744-0.694 0.080 0.166-0.034
 0.350 0.322 0.406 0.068 0.181 0.188-0.588-0.621-0.369
-0.030-0.056 0.009 0.102-0.115-0.129-0.288-0.165 0.566
C CHAPTER 15 - THE PROBLEM OF SCALING                                  001
C    15.10 COMMUNALITY FACTOR MATRIX SOLUTION                          002
C                                                                      003
      DIMENSION R(100,100), AM(100,15), UM(100,15), WM(115,15),        004
     1A(100), U(100), W(100), KV(15), GF(15), D(100)                   005
      READ INPUT TAPE 5, 902, P, PV, N, NF, NL, M                      006
      REWIND 2                                                         007
      DO 05   I=1,N                                                    008
05    READ INPUT TAPE 5, 903, (R(I,J), J=1,N)                          009
      DO 081   J=1,M                                                   010
081   READ INPUT TAPE 5, 903, (AM(I,J), I=1,N)                         011
      FN = N
      NL = 30
      E = 0.                                                           012
      DO 548   L=1,NL                                                  013
      LF = L                                                           014
      DO 510   I=1,N                                                   015
      D(I) = 0.                                                        016
      DO 510   J=1,M                                                   017
510   D(I) = D(I) + AM(I,J)**2                                         018
      DO 513   I=1,N                                                   019
      DO 513   J=1,N                                                   020
513   UM(I,J) = AM(I,J) / D(I)                                         021
      DO 519   I=1,N                                                   022
      IM = I + M                                                       023
```

```
            DO 519  J=1,M                                                024
            WM(IM,J) = 0.                                                025
            DO 519  K=1,N                                                026
  519       WM(IM,J) = WM(IM,J) + R(I,K) * UM(K,J)                       027
            DO 526  I=1,M                                                
            DO 526  J=1,M                                                029
            WM(I,J) = 0.                                                 030
            DO 526   K=1,N                                               031
            KM = K + M                                                   032
  526       WM(I,J) = WM(I,J) + WM(KM,I) * UM(K,J)                       033
            NM = N + M                                                   034
            DO 537  K=1,M                                                035
            S = 1./SQRTF(WM(K,K))                                        036
            DO 531  I=K,NM                                               037
  531       WM(I,K) = WM(I,K) * S                                        038
            K1 = K + 1                                                   039
            IF (M-K) 538, 538, 534                                       040
  534       DO 537  J=K1,M                                               041
            DO 537  I=J,NM                                               042
  537       WM(I,J) = WM(I,J) - WM(I,K) * WM(J,K)                        043
  538       CALL OUTPUB (WM, N, M, NM)                                   044
            WRITE OUTPUT TAPE 6, 997                                     045
            DO 541  I=1,N                                                046
            IM = I + M                                                   047
            DO 541  J=1,M                                                048
  541       AM(I,J) = WM(IM,J)                                           049
            GF(L) = 0.                                                   050
            DO 544  J=1,M                                                051
  544       GF(L) = GF(L) + WM(J,J)                                      052
            E1 = E                                                       053
            E = GF(L)                                                    054
            IF ((ABSF(E1/E-1.))-P) 549, 549, 548                         055
  548       CONTINUE                                                     056
  549       WRITE OUTPUT TAPE 6,900, (WM(I,I),I=1,LF)                    057
            WRITE OUTPUT TAPE 6, 997                                     058
            DO 553  I=1,N                                                059
  553       WRITE OUTPUT TAPE 6, 900, (AM(I,J), J=1,M)                   060
  900       FORMAT (13F9.4)                                              061
  902       FORMAT (F7.6/F3.2/(I4))                                      
  903       FORMAT (10F6.3)                                              
  997       FORMAT (1H )                                                 062
            CALL EXIT                                                    063
            END                                                         064
            SUBROUTINE OUTPUB (WM, N, M, NM)                             
            DIMENSION WM(115, 15)                                        
            DO 1  J=1,M                                                  
  1         WRITE OUTPUT TAPE 6, 900, (WM(I,J), I=1,NM)                  
            WRITE OUTPUT TAPE 6, 997                                     
  900       FORMAT (13F9.3)                                              
  997       FORMAT (1H )                                                 
            RETURN                                                       
            END                                                         
C                                                                       
*        DATA                                                           
.000100                                                                 
.75                                                                     
  9                                                                     
  4                                                                     
 50                                                                     
  4                                                                     
1.000  .829  .768  .108  .033  .108  .298  .309  .351
 .829 1.000  .775  .115  .061  .125  .323  .347  .369
 .768  .775 1.000  .272  .205  .238  .296  .271  .385
 .108  .115  .272 1.000  .636  .626  .249  .183  .369
 .033  .061  .205  .636 1.000  .709  .138  .091  .254
 .108  .125  .238  .626  .709 1.000  .190  .103  .291
 .298  .323  .296  .249  .138  .190 1.000  .654  .527
 .309  .347  .271  .183  .091  .103  .654 1.000  .541
 .351  .369  .385  .369  .254  .291  .527  .541 1.000
0.717 0.740 0.773 0.556 0.463 0.518 0.640 0.615 0.715
0.493 0.478 0.296-0.649-0.744-0.694 0.080 0.166-0.034
0.350 0.322 0.406 0.068 0.181 0.188-0.588-0.621-0.369
-0.030-0.056 0.009 0.102-0.115-0.129-0.288-0.165 0.566
C CHAPTER 15 - THE PROBLEM OF SCALING                                   001
C    15.11 COMMUNALITY PROGRESSIVE FACTOR MATRIX METHOD                 002
C                                                                       003
            DIMENSION R(100,100), AM(100,15), UM(100,15), WM(115,15),   004
           1A(100), U(100), W(100), KV(15), GF(15), D(100)              005
            READ INPUT TAPE 5, 902, P, PV, N, NF, NL, M                 006
            REWIND 2                                                    007
            DO 05  I=1,N                                                008
  05        READ INPUT TAPE 5, 903, (R(I,J), J=1,N)                     009
            DO 081  J=1,M                                               010
  081       READ INPUT TAPE 5, 903, (AM(I,J), I=1,N)                    011
            FN = N                                                      
```

644

```
        NL = 30                                                    012
        DO 652   L=1,NF                                            013
        LF = L                                                     014
        LN = L + N                                                 015
        E = 0.                                                     016
        DO 647   KI=1,NL                                           017
        DO 612   I=1,N                                             018
        D(I) = 0.                                                  019
        DO 612   J=1,L                                             020
612     D(I) = D(I) + AM(I,J)**2                                   021
        DO 615   I=1,N                                             022
        DO 615   J=1,L                                             023
615     UM(I,J) = AM(I,J) / D(I)                                   024
        DO 621   I=1,N                                             025
        IL = I + L                                                 026
        DO 621   J=1,L                                             027
        WM(IL,J) = 0.                                              028
        DO 621   K=1,N                                             029
621     WM(IL,J) = WM(IL,J) + R(I,K) * UM(K,J)                     030
622     DO 627   I = 1,L                                           031
623     DO 627   J=1,L                                             032
624     WM(I,J) = 0.                                               033
625     DO 627   K=1,N                                             034
        KL = K + L                                                 035
627     WM(I,J) = WM(I,J) + WM(KL,I) * UM(K,J)                     037
        DO 636   K=1,L                                             038
        S = 1./SQRTF(WM(K,K))                                      039
        DO 631   I=K,LN                                            040
631     WM(I,K) = WM(I,K) * S                                      041
        K1 = K + 1                                                 042
        IF (L-K) 637, 637, 634                                     043
634     DO 636   J=K1,L                                            044
        DO 636   I=J,LN                                            045
636     WM(I,J) = WM(I,J) - WM(I,K) * WM(J,K)                      046
637     DO 640   I=1,N                                             047
        IL = I + L                                                 048
        DO 640   J=1,L                                             049
640     AM(I,J) = WM(IL,J)                                         050
        C = 0.                                                     051
        DO 643   J=1,L                                             052
643     C = C + WM(J,J)                                            053
        E1 = E                                                     054
        E = C                                                      055
        IF ((ABSF(E1/E-1.))-P) 648, 648, 647                       056
647     CONTINUE                                                   057
648     WRITE OUTPUT TAPE 6, 998                                   059
        G = 0.                                                     060
        DO 650   I=1,N                                             061
650     G = G + D(I)                                               062
        IF (G-PV*FN) 652, 652, 653                                 063
652     CONTINUE                                                   064
653     DO 656   J=1,LF                                            065
        GF(J) = 0.                                                 066
        DO 656   I=1,N                                             067
656     GF(J) = GF(J) + AM(I,J)**2                                 068
        WRITE OUTPUT TAPE 6, 900, (GF(J), J=1,LF)                  069
        WRITE OUTPUT TAPE 6, 997
        DO 661   I=1,N
661     WRITE OUTPUT TAPE 6, 900, (AM(I,J), J=1,LF)                071
900     FORMAT (13F9.4)                                            072
902     FORMAT (F7.6/F3.2/(I4))                                    077
903     FORMAT (10F6.3)                                            078
997     FORMAT (1H )                                               073
998     FORMAT (1H0)                                               074
        CALL EXIT                                                  075
        END                                                        076
C
*       DATA
.000100
.75
  9
  4
 50
  4
1.000  .829  .768  .108  .033  .108  .298  .309  .351
 .829 1.000  .775  .115  .061  .125  .323  .347  .369
 .768  .775 1.000  .272  .205  .238  .296  .271  .385
 .108  .115  .272 1.000  .636  .626  .249  .183  .369
 .033  .061  .205  .636 1.000  .709  .138  .091  .254
 .108  .125  .238  .626  .709 1.000  .190  .103  .291
 .298  .323  .296  .249  .138  .190 1.000  .654  .527
 .309  .347  .271  .183  .091  .103  .654 1.000  .541
 .351  .369  .385  .369  .254  .291  .527  .541 1.000
0.717 0.740 0.773 0.556 0.463 0.518 0.640 0.615 0.715
0.493 0.478 0.296-0.649-0.744-0.694 0.080 0.166-0.034
0.350 0.322 0.406 0.068 0.181 0.188-0.588-0.621-0.369
-0.030-0.056 0.009 0.102-0.115-0.129-0.288-0.165 0.566
```

```
C CHAPTER 16 - IMAGE ANALYSIS                                              001
C    16.3 IMAGE COVARIANCE MATRIX                                          002
C                                                                          003
      DIMENSION C(160,80), S(80,80), D(80), U(80)                          004
      READ INPUT TAPE 5, 901, P, N, NL                                     005
901   FORMAT (F7.6/(I4))                                                   006
      DO 04  I=1,N                                                         007
04    READ INPUT TAPE 5, 902, (C(I,J), J=1,N)                              008
902   FORMAT (10F6.3)                                                      009
      REWIND 2                                                             010
      DO 09  I=1,N                                                         011
09    WRITE TAPE 2, (C(I,J), J=1,N)                                        012
      REWIND 2                                                             013
      DO 14  I=1,N                                                         014
      DO 14  J=I,N                                                         015
14    S(I,J) = C(I,J)                                                      016
      CALL SYMIN (S,N)                                                     017
      DO 19  I=1,N                                                         018
      DO 18  J=1,N                                                         019
18    C(I,J) = C(I,J) + S(I,J) / (S(I,I)*S(J,J))                           020
19    C(I,I) = C(I,I) - 2. / S(I,I)                                        021
      DO 21  I=1,N                                                         022
21    WRITE OUTPUT TAPE 6, 900, (C(I,J), J=1,N)                            023
      WRITE OUTPUT TAPE 6, 998                                             024
      CALL JACSIM (C, D, P, N, NL)                                         025
      N2 = N * 2                                                           026
      WRITE OUTPUT TAPE 6, 900, (D(I), I=1,N)                              027
      WRITE OUTPUT TAPE 6, 997                                             028
      DO 29  I=1,N2                                                        029
29    WRITE OUTPUT TAPE 6, 900, (C(I,J), J=1,N)                            030
900   FORMAT (10F8.4)                                                      031
997   FORMAT (1H )                                                         032
998   FORMAT (1H0)                                                         
      CALL EXIT                                                            033
      END                                                                 034
C
      SUBROUTINE JACSIM (R, D, P, N, NL)                                   001
      DIMENSION R(160,80), D(80)                                          002
      N1 = N+1                                                            003
      N11=N-1                                                             004
      N2 = N*2                                                            005
      DO 10  I=N1, N2                                                     006
      DO 10  J = 1,N                                                      007
10    R(I,J) = 0.                                                         008
      DO 12  I=1,N                                                        009
      NI = N + I                                                          010
12    R(NI,I) = 1.                                                        011
      L = 0                                                               012
14    DO 15  I=1,N                                                        013
15    D(I) = R(I,I)                                                       014
      DO 282 I = 1,N11                                                    015
      I1 = I+1                                                            016
      DO 282 J= I1,N                                                      017
      DR = R(I,I) - R(J,J)                                                018
      A = SQRTF(DR**2 + 4.*R(I,J)**2)                                     019
      A = SQRTF((A+DR)/(2.*A))                                            020
      B = SQRTF(1.-A**2)                                                  021
      C = SIGNF(1.,R(I,J))                                                022
      DO 252 K = 1,N2                                                     023
      U = R(K,I)*A*C + R(K,J)*B                                           024
      R(K,J) = -R(K,I)*B*C + R(K,J)*A                                     025
252   R(K,I) = U                                                          026
      DO 282 K = 1,N                                                      027
      U = R(I,K)*A*C + R(J,K)*B                                           028
      R(J,K) = -R(I,K)*B*C + R(J,K)*A                                     029
282   R(I,K) = U                                                          030
      DO 30  I=1,N                                                        031
30    D(I) = ABSF(D(I) - R(I,I))                                          032
      S = 0.                                                              033
      DO 33  I=1,N                                                        034
33    S = MAX1F (S, D(I))                                                 035
      DO 332 I =1,N                                                       036
332   D(I) = R(I,I)                                                       037
      IF (S-P) 38, 38, 35                                                 038
35    L = L+1                                                             039
      IF (L-NL) 37, 38, 38                                                040
37    GO TO 14                                                            041
38    RETURN                                                              042
      END                                                                043
C
      SUBROUTINE SYMIN (S, N)                                             001
      DIMENSION S(80,80)                                                  002
```

```
      DO 04 I = 2,N                                                    003
      I1 = I-1                                                         004
      DO 04 J = 1,I1                                                   005
 04   S(I,J) = 0.                                                      006
      C = 1./SQRTF(S(1,1))                                             007
      S(1,1) = 1.                                                      008
      DO 13  J=1,N                                                     009
 13   S(1,J) = S(1,J) * C                                              010
      DO 21  K=2,N                                                     011
      DO 17  J=1,N                                                     012
      K1 = K-1                                                         013
      DO 17  I=1,K1                                                    014
 17   S(K,J) = S(K,J) - S(I,K) * S(I,J)                               015
      C = 1./SQRTF(S(K,K))                                             016
      DO 191  I=1,K1                                                   017
191   S(I,K) = 0.                                                      018
      S(K,K) = 1.                                                      019
      DO 21  J=1,N                                                     020
 21   S(K,J) = S(K,J) * C                                              021
      DO 30  J=2,N                                                     022
      J1 = J-1                                                         023
      DO 30  I=1,J1                                                    024
      DO 30  K=J,N                                                     025
 30   S(I,J) = S(I,J) + S(K,I) * S(K,J)                               026
      DO 35  J=1,N                                                     027
      S(J,J) = S(J,J) **2                                              028
      J2 = J+1                                                         029
      DO 35  I=J2,N                                                    030
 35   S(J,J) = S(J,J) + S(I,J)**2                                     031
      N1 = N-1                                                         032
      DO 42  I=1,N1                                                    033
      I2 = I+1                                                         034
      DO 42  J=I2,N                                                    035
 42   S(J,I) = S(I,J)                                                  036
      RETURN                                                           037
      END                                                              038
C
*     DATA
.000100
   9
  40
1.000   .829   .768   .108   .033   .108   .298   .309   .351
 .829  1.000   .775   .115   .061   .125   .323   .347   .369
 .768   .775  1.000   .272   .205   .238   .296   .271   .385
 .108   .115   .272  1.000   .636   .626   .249   .183   .369
 .033   .061   .205   .636  1.000   .709   .138   .091   .254
 .108   .125   .238   .626   .709  1.000   .190   .103   .291
 .298   .323   .296   .249   .138   .190  1.000   .654   .527
 .309   .347   .271   .183   .091   .103   .654  1.000   .541
 .351   .369   .385   .369   .254   .291   .527   .541  1.000

C CHAPTER 16 - IMAGE ANALYSIS                                          001
C    16.4 IMAGE CORRELATION MATRIX
C                                                                      003
      DIMENSION C(160,80), S(80,80), D(80), U(80)                      004
      READ INPUT TAPE 5, 901, P, N, NL                                 005
901   FORMAT (F7.6/(I4))                                               006
      DO 04  I=1,N                                                     007
 04   READ INPUT TAPE 5, 902, (C(I,J), J=1,N)                          008
902   FORMAT (10F6.3)                                                  009
      REWIND 2                                                         010
      DO 09  I=1,N                                                     011
 09   WRITE TAPE 2, (C(I,J), J=1,N)                                    012
      REWIND 2                                                         013
      DO 404  I=1,N                                                    015
404   READ TAPE 2, (C(I,J), J=1,N)                                     016
      REWIND 2                                                         017
      DO 409  I=1,N                                                    018
      DO 409  J=I,N                                                    019
      S(J,I) = 0.                                                      020
409   S(I,J) = C(I,J)                                                  021
      CALL SYMIN (S, N)                                                022
      DO 414  I=1,N                                                    023
      DO 413  J=1,N                                                    024
413   C(I,J)  = C(I,J) + S(I,J) / (S(I,I)*S(J,J))                      025
414   C(I,I) = C(I,I) - 2. / S(I,I)                                    026
      DO 4142  I=1,N                                                   027
4142  D(I) = 1./SQRTF(C(I,I))                                          028
      DO 417  I=1,N                                                    029
      DO 417  J=1,N                                                    030
417   C(I,J) = C(I,J) * D(I) * D(J)                                    031
      WRITE OUTPUT TAPE 6, 997                                         032
      DO 419  I=1,N                                                    033
```

647

```
 419    WRITE OUTPUT TAPE 6, 900, (C(I,J), J=1,N)              034
        WRITE OUTPUT TAPE 6, 997                              035
        DO 422  I=1,N                                         036
 422    WRITE TAPE 2, (C(I,J), J=1,N)                         037
        REWIND 2                                              038
        CALL JACSIM (C, D, P, N, NL)                          039
        N2 = N * 2                                            040
        WRITE OUTPUT TAPE 6, 900, (D(I), I=1,N)               041
        WRITE OUTPUT TAPE 6, 997                              042
        DO 429  I=1,N2                                        043
 429    WRITE OUTPUT TAPE 6, 900, (C(I,J), J=1,N)             044
 900    FORMAT (10F8.4)                                       045
 997    FORMAT (1H )                                          046
        CALL EXIT                                             047
        END                                                  048
C
        SUBROUTINE JACSIM (R, D, P, N, NL)
 01     DIMENSION R(160,80), D(80)
 06     N1 = N+1
 061    N11=N-1
 07     N2 = N*2
 08     DO 10   I=N1, N2
 09     DO 10   J = 1,N
 10     R(I,J) = 0.
 11     DO 12   I=1,N
 111    NI = N + I
 12     R(NI,I) = 1.
 13     L = 0
 14     DO 15   I=1,N
 15     D(I) = R(I,I)
 17     DO 282 I = 1,N11
 16     I1 = I+1
 18     DO 282 J= I1,N
 19     DR = R(I,I) - R(J,J)
 20     A = SQRTF(DR**2 + 4.*R(I,J)**2)
 21     A = SQRTF((A+DR)/(2.*A))
 22     B = SQRTF(1.-A**2)
 221    C = SIGNF(1.,R(I,J))
 23     DO 252 K = 1,N2
 241    U = R(K,I)*A*C + R(K,J)*B
 25     R(K,J) = -R(K,I)*B*C + R(K,J)*A
 252    R(K,I) = U
 26     DO 282 K = 1,N
 271    U = R(I,K)*A*C + R(J,K)*B
 28     R(J,K) = -R(I,K)*B*C + R(J,K)*A
 282    R(I,K) = U
 29     DO 30   I=1,N
 30     D(I) = ABSF(D(I) - R(I,I))
 31     S = 0.
 32     DO 33   I=1,N
 33     S = MAX1F (S, D(I))
 331    DO 332 I =1,N
 332    D(I) = R(I,I)
 34     IF (S-P) 38, 38, 35
 35     L = L+1
 36     IF (L-NL) 37, 38, 38
 37     GO TO 14
 38     RETURN
        END
C
        SUBROUTINE SYMIN (S, N)
        DIMENSION S(80,80)
 01     DO 04 I = 2,N
 02     I1 = I-1
 03     DO 04 J = 1,I1
 04     S(I,J) = 0.
 10     C = 1./SQRTF(S(1,1))
 11     S(1,1) = 1.
 12     DO 13   J=1,N
 13     S(1,J) = S(1,J) * C
 14     DO 21   K=2,N
 15     DO 17   J=1,N
 151    K1 = K-1
 16     DO 17   I=1,K1
 17     S(K,J) = S(K,J) - S(I,K) * S(I,J)
 18     C = 1./SQRTF(S(K,K))
 19     DO 191  I=1,K1
 191    S(I,K) = 0.
 192    S(K,K) = 1.
 20     DO 21   J=1,N
 21     S(K,J) = S(K,J) * C
 25     DO 30   J=2,N
 26     J1 = J-1
 27     DO 30   I=1,J1
```

648

```
29    DO 30  K=J,N
30    S(I,J) = S(I,J) + S(K,I) * S(K,J)
31    DO 35  J=1,N
32    S(J,J) = S(J,J) **2
33    J2 = J+1
34    DO 35  I=J2,N
35    S(J,J) = S(J,J) + S(I,J)**2
38    N1 = N-1
39    DO 42  I=1,N1
40    I2 = I+1
41    DO 42  J=I2,N
42    S(J,I) = S(I,J)
      RETURN
      END
C
*     DATA
.000100
    9
   40
1.000  .829  .768  .108  .033  .108  .298  .309  .351
 .829 1.000  .775  .115  .061  .125  .323  .347  .369
 .768  .775 1.000  .272  .205  .238  .296  .271  .385
 .108  .115  .272 1.000  .636  .626  .249  .183  .369
 .033  .061  .205  .636 1.000  .709  .138  .091  .254
 .108  .125  .238  .626  .709 1.000  .190  .103  .291
 .298  .323  .296  .249  .138  .190 1.000  .654  .527
 .309  .347  .271  .183  .091  .103  .654 1.000  .541
 .351  .369  .385  .369  .254  .291  .527  .541 1.000


C CHAPTER 16 - IMAGE ANALYSIS                                      001
C     16.5 INDEPENDENT SCALE MATRIX
C                                                                  003
      DIMENSION C(160,80), S(80,80), D(80), U(80)                  005
      READ INPUT TAPE 5, 901, P, N, NL                            006
901   FORMAT (F7.6/(I4))                                          007
      DO 04  I=1,N                                                008
04    READ INPUT TAPE 5, 902, (C(I,J), J=1,N)                     009
902   FORMAT (10F6.3)                                             010
      REWIND 2                                                    011
      DO 09  I=1,N                                                012
09    WRITE TAPE 2, (C(I,J), J=1,N)                               013
      REWIND 2                                                    014
      DO 14  I=1,N                                                015
      DO 14  J=I,N                                                016
14    S(I,J) = C(I,J)                                             017
      CALL SYMIN (S,N)                                            018
      DO 19  I=1,N                                                019
      DO 18  J=1,N                                                020
18    C(I,J) = C(I,J) + S(I,J) / (S(I,I)*S(J,J))                  021
19    C(I,I) = C(I,I) - 2. / S(I,I)                               022
      DO 21  I=1,N                                                023
21    WRITE OUTPUT TAPE 6, 900, (C(I,J), J=1,N)                   024
      WRITE OUTPUT TAPE 6, 998                                    025
      DO 205  I=1,N                                               026
205   U(I) = SQRTF(S(I,I))                                        027
      DO 208  I=1,N                                               028
      DO 208  J=1,N                                               029
208   C(I,J) = C(I,J) * U(I) * U(J)                               030
      CALL JACSIM (C, D, P, N, NL)                                031
      N2 = N * 2                                                  032
      WRITE OUTPUT TAPE 6, 900, (D(I), I=1,N)                     033
      WRITE OUTPUT TAPE 6, 997                                    034
      DO 215  I=1,N2                                              035
215   WRITE OUTPUT TAPE 6, 900, (C(I,J), J=1,N)                   036
900   FORMAT (10F8.4)                                             037
997   FORMAT (1H )                                                038
998   FORMAT (1H0)                                                039
      CALL EXIT                                                   040
      END                                                         041
C
      SUBROUTINE JACSIM (R, D, P, N, NL)
01    DIMENSION R(160,80), D(80)
06    N1 = N+1
061   N11=N-1
07    N2 = N*2
08    DO 10  I=N1, N2
09    DO 10  J = 1,N
10    R(I,J) = 0.
11    DO 12  I=1,N
111   NI = N + I
12    R(NI,I) = 1.
13    L = 0
14    DO 15  I=1,N
```

649

```
 15    D(I) = R(I,I)
 17    DO 282 I = 1,N11
 16    I1 = I+1
 18    DO 282 J= I1,N
 19    DR = R(I,I) - R(J,J)
 20    A = SQRTF(DR**2 + 4.*R(I,J)**2)
 21    A = SQRTF((A+DR)/(2.*A))
 22    B = SQRTF(1.-A**2)
221    C = SIGNF(1.,R(I,J))
 23    DO 252 K = 1,N2
241    U = R(K,I)*A*C + R(K,J)*B
 25    R(K,J) = -R(K,I)*B*C + R(K,J)*A
252    R(K,I) = U
 26    DO 282 K = 1,N
271    U = R(I,K)*A*C + R(J,K)*B
 28    R(J,K) = -R(I,K)*B*C + R(J,K)*A
282    R(I,K) = U
 29    DO 30  I=1,N
 30    D(I) = ABSF(D(I) - R(I,I))
 31    S = 0.
 32    DO 33  I=1,N
 33    S = MAXIF (S, D(I))
331    DO 332 I =1,N
332    D(I) = R(I,I)
 34    IF (S-P) 38, 38, 35
 35    L = L+1
 36    IF (L-NL) 37, 38, 38
 37    GO TO 14
 38    RETURN
       END
C
       SUBROUTINE SYMIN (S, N)
       DIMENSION S(80,80)
01     DO 04 I = 2,N
02     I1 = I-1
03     DO 04 J = 1,I1
04     S(I,J) = 0.
10     C = 1./SQRTF(S(1,1))
11     S(1,1) = 1.
12     DO 13  J=1,N
13     S(1,J) = S(1,J) * C
14     DO 21  K=2,N
15     DO 17  J=1,N
151    K1 = K-1
16     DO 17  I=1,K1
17     S(K,J) = S(K,J) - S(I,K) * S(I,J)
18     C = 1./SQRTF(S(K,K))
19     DO 191  I=1,K1
191    S(I,K) = 0.
192    S(K,K) = 1.
20     DO 21  J=1,N
21     S(K,J) = S(K,J) * C
25     DO 30  J=2,N
26     J1 = J-1
27     DO 30  I=1,J1
29     DO 30  K=J,N
30     S(I,J) = S(I,J) + S(K,I) * S(K,J)
31     DO 35  J=1,N
32     S(J,J) = S(J,J) **2
33     J2 = J+1
34     DO 35  I=J2,N
35     S(J,J) = S(J,J) + S(I,J)**2
38     N1 = N-1
39     DO 42  I=1,N1
40     I2 = I+1
41     DO 42  J=I2,N
42     S(J,I)= S(I,J)
       RETURN
       END
C
*      DATA
.000100
   9
  40
1.000   .829   .768   .108   .033   .108   .298   .309   .351
 .829  1.000   .775   .115   .061   .125   .323   .347   .369
 .768   .775  1.000   .272   .205   .238   .296   .271   .385
 .108   .115   .272  1.000   .636   .626   .249   .183   .369
 .033   .061   .205   .636  1.000   .709   .138   .091   .254
 .108   .125   .238   .626   .709  1.000   .190   .103   .291
 .298   .323   .296   .249   .138   .190  1.000   .654   .527
 .309   .347   .271   .183   .091   .103   .654  1.000   .541
 .351   .369   .385   .369   .254   .291   .527   .541  1.000
```

650

```
C CHAPTER 16 - IMAGE ANALYSIS                                              001
C    16.6 OPTIMAL RESIDUAL OR ANTI-IMAGE MATRIX                            002
C                                                                          003
      DIMENSION C(160,80), S(80,80), D(80), U(80)                          004
      READ INPUT TAPE 5, 901, P, N, NL                                     005
901   FORMAT (F7.6/(I4))                                                   006
      DO 04  I=1,N                                                         007
04    READ INPUT TAPE 5, 902, (C(I,J), J=1,N)                              008
902   FORMAT (10F6.3)                                                      009
      REWIND 2                                                             010
      DO 09  I=1,N                                                         011
09    WRITE TAPE 2, (C(I,J), J=1,N)                                        012
      REWIND 2                                                             013
      DO 14  I=1,N                                                         014
      DO 14  J=I,N                                                         015
14    S(I,J) = C(I,J)                                                      016
      CALL SYMIN (S,N)                                                     017
      DO 19  I=1,N                                                         018
      DO 18  J=1,N                                                         019
18    C(I,J) = C(I,J) + S(I,J) / (S(I,I)*S(J,J))                           020
19    C(I,I) = C(I,I) - 2. / S(I,I)                                        021
      DO 21  I=1,N                                                         022
21    WRITE OUTPUT TAPE 6, 900, (C(I,J), J=1,N)                            023
      WRITE OUTPUT TAPE 6, 998                                             024
      DO 305 I=1,N                                                         025
305   D(I) = S(I,I)                                                        026
      DO 3053  I=1,N                                                       027
      WRITE OUTPUT TAPE 6, 900, (S(I,J), J=1,N)                            028
      DO 3053  J=1,N                                                       029
3053  S(I,J) = S(I,J)**2                                                   030
      CALL SYMIN (S, N)                                                    031
      WRITE OUTPUT TAPE 6, 997                                             032
      DO 309  I=1,N                                                        033
      WRITE OUTPUT TAPE 6, 900, (S(I,J), J=1,N)                            034
      U(I) = 0.                                                            035
      DO 309  J=1,N                                                        036
309   U(I) = U(I) + S(I,J) * D(J)                                          037
      WRITE OUTPUT TAPE 6, 900, (U(I), I=1,N)                              038
      DO 311  I=1,N                                                        039
311   D(I) = SQRTF(U(I)) * D(I)                                           040
      WRITE OUTPUT TAPE 6, 900, (D(I), I=1,N)                              041
      WRITE OUTPUT TAPE 6, 997                                             042
      DO 3141  I=1,N                                                       043
      DO 314  J=1,N                                                        044
314   C(I,J) = D(I) * C(I,J) * D(J)                                        045
3141  WRITE OUTPUT TAPE 6, 900, (C(I,J), J=1,N)                            046
      WRITE OUTPUT TAPE 6, 997                                             047
      CALL JACSIM (C, D, P, N, NL)                                         048
      N2 = N * 2                                                           049
      WRITE OUTPUT TAPE 6, 900, (D(I), I=1,N)                              050
      WRITE OUTPUT TAPE 6, 997                                             051
      DO 321  I=1,N2                                                       052
321   WRITE OUTPUT TAPE 6, 900, (C(I,J), J=1,N)                            053
900   FORMAT (10F8.4)                                                      054
997   FORMAT (1H )                                                         055
998   FORMAT (1H0)                                                         056
      CALL EXIT                                                            057
      END                                                                  058
C
      SUBROUTINE JACSIM (R, D, P, N, NL)
01    DIMENSION R(160,80), D(80)
06    N1 = N+1
061   N11=N-1
07    N2 = N*2
08    DO 10  I=N1, N2
09    DO 10  J = 1,N
10    R(I,J) = 0.
11    DO 12  I=1,N
111   NI = N + I
12    R(NI,I) = 1.
13    L = 0
14    DO 15  I=1,N
15    D(I) = R(I,I)
17    DO 282 I = 1,N11
16    I1 = I+1
18    DO 282 J= I1,N
19    DR = R(I,I) - R(J,J)
20    A = SQRTF(DR**2 + 4.*R(I,J)**2)
21    A = SQRTF((A+DR)/(2.*A))
22    B = SQRTF(1.-A**2)
```

651

```
221   C = SIGNF(1.,R(I,J))
23    DO 252 K = 1,N2
241   U = R(K,I)*A*C + R(K,J)*B
25    R(K,J) = -R(K,I)*B*C + R(K,J)*A
252   R(K,I) = U
26    DO 282 K = 1,N
271   U = R(I,K)*A*C + R(J,K)*B
28    R(J,K) = -R(I,K)*B*C + R(J,K)*A
282   R(I,K) = U
29    DO 30  I=1,N
30    D(I) = ABSF(D(I) - R(I,I))
31    S = 0.
32    DO 33  I=1,N
33    S = MAX1F (S, D(I))
331   DO 332 I =1,N
332   D(I) = R(I,I)
34    IF (S-P) 38, 38, 35
35    L = L+1
36    IF (L-NL) 37, 38, 38
37    GO TO 14
38    RETURN
      END
C
      SUBROUTINE SYMIN (S, N)
      DIMENSION S(80,80)
01    DO 04 I = 2,N
02    I1 = I-1
03    DO 04 J = 1,I1
04    S(I,J) = 0.
10    C = 1./SQRTF(S(1,1))
11    S(1,1) = 1.
12    DO 13  J=1,N
13    S(1,J) = S(1,J) * C
14    DO 21  K=2,N
15    DO 17  J=1,N
151   K1 = K-1
16    DO 17  I=1,K1
17    S(K,J) = S(K,J) - S(I,K) * S(I,J)
18    C = 1./SQRTF(S(K,K))
19    DO 191  I=1,K1
191   S(I,K) = 0.
192   S(K,K) = 1.
20    DO 21  J=1,N
21    S(K,J) = S(K,J) * C
25    DO 30  J=2,N
26    J1 = J-1
27    DO 30  I=1,J1
29    DO 30  K=J,N
30    S(I,J) = S(I,J) + S(K,I) * S(K,J)
31    DO 35  J=1,N
32    S(J,J) = S(J,J) **2
33    J2 = J+1
34    DO 35  I=J2,N
35    S(J,J) = S(J,J) + S(I,J)**2
38    N1 = N-1
39    DO 42  I=1,N1
40    I2 = I+1
41    DO 42  J=I2,N
42    S(J,I) = S(I,J)
      RETURN
      END
C
*     DATA
.000100
   9
  40
1.000  .829  .768  .108  .033  .108  .298  .309  .351
 .829 1.000  .775  .115  .061  .125  .323  .347  .369
 .768  .775 1.000  .272  .205  .238  .296  .271  .385
 .108  .115  .272 1.000  .636  .626  .249  .183  .369
 .033  .061  .205  .636 1.000  .709  .138  .091  .254
 .108  .125  .238  .626  .709 1.000  .190  .103  .291
 .298  .323  .296  .249  .138  .190 1.000  .654  .527
 .309  .347  .271  .183  .091  .103  .654 1.000  .541
 .351  .369  .385  .369  .254  .291  .527  .541 1.000
```

```
C CHAPTER 17 - PRIMARY FACTOR MATRICES FROM HYPOTHESES          001
C     17.3 MULTIPLE GROUP FACTOR MATRIX                         002
C                                                               003
      DIMENSION R(120,120), F(140,15), S(15,15), C(15,15), IH(300),   004
     1JV(70), NJ(15), D(140), DP(15), G(15,15)                  005
      READ INPUT TAPE 5, 903, P                                 006
      READ INPUT TAPE 5, 901, N, M, NL                          007
      READ INPUT TAPE 5, 904, (IH(I), I=1,N)                    008
      READ INPUT TAPE 5, 904, (NJ(J), J=1,M)                    009
      DO 106  I=1,N                                             010
 106  READ INPUT TAPE 5, 900, (R(I,J), J=1,N)                   011
C 1.
      DO 1093  I=1,N                                            015
      DO 1093  J=1,N                                            016
 1093 G(I,J) = R(I,J)                                           017
      CALL SYMIN (R, N)                                         018
      DO 1098  I=1,N                                            019
      DO 1098  J=1,N                                            020
      S(I,J) = 0.                                               021
      DO 1098  K=1,N                                            022
 1098 S(I,J) = S(I,J) + G(I,K) * R(K,J)                         023
      DO 1100  I=1,N                                            024
 1100 WRITE OUTPUT TAPE 6, 902, (S(I,J), J=1,N)                 025
      WRITE OUTPUT TAPE 6, 997                                  026
      DO 1103  I=1,N                                            027
      DO 1103  J=1,N                                            028
 1103 R(I,J) = G(I,J)                                           029
      NN = 0                                                    030
      DO 122  J=1,M                                             031
      N1 = NN + 1                                               032
      NN = NN + NJ(J)                                           033
      JN = NJ(J)                                                034
      DO 117  K=N1,NN                                           035
      K1 = K - N1 + 1                                           036
 117  JV(K1) = IH(K)                                            037
      DO 122  I=1,N                                             038
      F(I,J) = 0.                                               039
      DO 122  K=1,JN                                            040
      KJ = JV(K)                                                041
 122  F(I,J) = F(I,J) + R(KJ,I)                                 042
      CALL OUTPU1 (F, N, M)                                     043
C 2.
      CALL BIMUL (F, S, IH, NJ, JV, M)                          047
      CALL OUTPU3 (S, M)                                        048
C 4.
      DO 128  I=1,M                                             052
      DO 128  J=1,M                                             053
      R(I,J) = 0.                                               054
      DO 128  K=1,N                                             055
 128  R(I,J) = R(I,J) + F(K,I) * F(K,J)                         056
      CALL OUTPU2 (R,M)                                         057
      DO 1283  I=1,M                                            058
      DO 1283  J=1,M                                            059
 1283 G(I,J) = R(I,J)                                           060
C 5.
      CALL SYMIN (R, M)                                         064
      CALL OUTPU2 (R,M)                                         065
      DO 134  I=1,M                                             066
      DO 134  J=1,M                                             067
      C(I,J) = 0.                                               068
      DO 134  K=1,M                                             069
 134  C(I,J) = C(I,J) + R(I,K) * S(K,J)                         070
      CALL OUTPU3 (C, M)                                        071
C 6.
      DO 139  I=1,M                                             075
      DO 139  J=1,M                                             076
      R(I,J) = 0.                                               077
      DO 139  K=1,M                                             078
 139  R(I,J) = R(I,J) + S(I,K) * C(K,J)                         079
      CALL OUTPU2 (R,M)                                         080
C 8.
      DO 143  I=1,M                                             084
      D(I) = 0.                                                 085
      DO 143  J=1,M                                             086
 143  D(I) = D(I) + R(I,J) * C(J,I)                             087
      DO 145  I=1,M                                             088
 145  D(I) = 1./SQRTF(D(I))                                     089
      WRITE OUTPUT TAPE 6, 997                                  090
      WRITE OUTPUT TAPE 6, 900, (D(I), I=1,M)                   091
      WRITE OUTPUT TAPE 6, 997                                  092
C 11.
      DO 150  I=1,N                                             096
```

653

```
      DO 150  J=1,M                                              097
      R(I,J) = 0.                                               098
      DO 150  K=1,M                                             099
150   R(I,J) = R(I,J) + F(I,K) * C(K,J)                        100
      DO 1502  I=1,N                                            101
1502  WRITE OUTPUT TAPE 6, 900, (R(I,J), J=1,M)                 102
      WRITE OUTPUT TAPE 6, 997                                  103
      DO 1507  I=1,M                                            104
      DO 1507  J=1,M                                            105
      C(I,J) = 0.                                               106
      DO 1507  K=1,N                                            107
1507  C(I,J) = C(I,J) + R(K,I) * R(K,J)                        108
      DO 1509  I=1,M                                            109
1509  WRITE OUTPUT TAPE 6, 900, (C(I,J), J=1,M)                 110
      WRITE OUTPUT TAPE 6, 997                                  111
      DO 153  I=1,N                                             112
      DO 153  J=1,M                                             113
153   R(I,J) = R(I,J) * D(J)                                   114
      DO 1535  I=1,M                                            115
      DO 1535  J=1,M                                            116
      C(I,J) = 0.                                               117
      DO 1535  K=1,N                                            118
1535  C(I,J) = C(I,J) + R(K,I) * R(K,J)                        119
      DO 1538  I=1,M                                            120
      DO 1538  J=1,M                                            121
1538  G(I,J) = C(I,J) / (D(I)*D(J))                            122
      DO 1540  I=1,M                                            123
1540  WRITE OUTPUT TAPE 6, 902, (G(I,J), J=1,M)                 124
      WRITE OUTPUT TAPE 6, 997                                  125
      DO 155  I=1,N                                             126
155   WRITE OUTPUT TAPE 6, 902,  (R(I,J), J =1,M)              127
900   FORMAT (10F6.3)                                          128
901   FORMAT (I4)                                              129
902   FORMAT (10F7.3)                                          130
903   FORMAT (F7.5)                                            131
904   FORMAT (10I2)                                            132
997   FORMAT (1H )                                             133
      CALL EXIT                                                 134
      END                                                       135
C
      SUBROUTINE SYMIN (S, N)                                   001
      DIMENSION S(120,120)                                      002
      N1 = N-1                                                  003
      DO 04 I = 2,N                                             004
      I1 = I-1                                                  005
      DO 04 J = 1,I1                                            006
04    S(I,J) = 0.                                               007
      C = 1./SQRTF(S(1,1))                                      008
      S(1,1) = 1.                                               009
      DO 13  J=1,N                                              010
13    S(1,J) = S(1,J) * C                                      011
      DO 21  K=2,N                                              012
      DO 17  J=1,N                                              013
      K1 = K-1                                                  014
      DO 17  I=1,K1                                             015
17    S(K,J) = S(K,J) - S(I,K) * S(I,J)                        016
      C = 1./SQRTF(S(K,K))                                     017
      DO 191  I=1,K1                                            018
191   S(I,K) = 0.                                               019
      S(K,K) = 1.                                               020
      DO 21  J=1,N                                              021
21    S(K,J) = S(K,J) * C                                      022
      DO 30  J=2,N                                              023
      J1 = J-1                                                  024
      DO 30  I=1,J1                                             025
      DO 30  K=J,N                                              026
30    S(I,J) = S(I,J) + S(K,I) * S(K,J)                        027
      DO 35  J=1,N1                                             028
      S(J,J) = S(J,J) **2                                      029
      J2 = J+1                                                  030
      DO 35  I=J2,N                                             031
35    S(J,J) = S(J,J) + S(I,J)**2                              032
      S(N,N) = S(N,N)**2                                       033
      DO 42  I=1,N1                                             034
      I2 = I+1                                                  035
      DO 42  J=I2,N                                             036
42    S(J,I) = S(I,J)                                          037
      RETURN                                                    038
      END                                                       039
C
      SUBROUTINE OUTPU1 (F, N, M)                               001
      DIMENSION F(140,15)                                       002
      DO 1  I=1,N                                               003
```

654

```
      1    WRITE OUTPUT TAPE 6, 902, (F(I,J), J=1,M)                          004
           WRITE OUTPUT TAPE 6, 997                                           005
    902    FORMAT (10F9.5)                                                    006
    997    FORMAT (1H )                                                       007
           RETURN                                                             008
           END                                                                009
C
           SUBROUTINE OUTPU2 (R, M)                                           001
           DIMENSION R(120,120)                                               002
           DO 1  I=1,M                                                        003
      1    WRITE OUTPUT TAPE 6, 902, (R(I,J), J=1,M)                          004
           WRITE OUTPUT TAPE 6, 997                                           005
    902    FORMAT (10F9.5)                                                    006
    997    FORMAT (1H )                                                       007
           RETURN                                                             008
           END                                                                009
C
           SUBROUTINE OUTPU3 (C, M)                                           001
           DIMENSION C(15,15)                                                 002
           DO 1  I=1,M                                                        003
      1    WRITE OUTPUT TAPE 6, 902, (C(I,J), J=1,M)                          004
           WRITE OUTPUT TAPE 6, 997                                           005
    902    FORMAT (10F9.5)                                                    006
    997    FORMAT (1H )                                                       007
           RETURN                                                             008
           END                                                                009
C
           SUBROUTINE BIMUL (A, B, IH, NJ, JV, M)                             001
           DIMENSION A(140,15), B(15,15), IH(300), NJ(15), JV(70)            002
           NN = 0                                                             003
           DO 14  J=1,M                                                       004
           N1 = NN + 1                                                        005
           NN = NN + NJ(J)                                                    006
           JN = NJ(J)                                                         007
           DO 09  K=N1,NN                                                     008
           K1 = K - N1 + 1                                                    009
    09     JV(K1) = IH(K)                                                     010
           DO 14  I=1,M                                                       011
           B(I,J) = 0.                                                        012
           DO 14  K=1,JN                                                      013
           KJ = JV(K)                                                         014
    14     B(I,J) = B(I,J) + A(KJ,I)                                          015
           RETURN                                                             016
           END                                                                017
C
*     DATA
 .00010
      9
      3
     40
   1 2 3 4 5 6 7 8 9
   3 3 3
 1.000  .829  .768  .108  .033  .108  .298  .309  .351
  .829 1.000  .775  .115  .061  .125  .323  .347  .369
  .768  .775 1.000  .272  .205  .238  .296  .271  .385
  .108  .115  .272 1.000  .636  .626  .249  .183  .369
  .033  .061  .205  .636 1.000  .709  .138  .091  .254
  .108  .125  .238  .626  .709 1.000  .190  .103  .291
  .298  .323  .296  .249  .138  .190 1.000  .654  .527
  .309  .347  .271  .183  .091  .103  .654 1.000  .541
  .351  .369  .385  .369  .254  .291  .527  .541 1.000


C CHAPTER 17 - PRIMARY FACTOR MATRICES FROM HYPOTHESES               001
C     17.4 PRINCIPAL AXIS FACTOR MATRIX                               002
C                                                                     003
      DIMENSION R(120,120), F(140,15), S(15,15), C(15,15), IH(300),   004
     1JV(70), NJ(15), D(140), DP(15), G(15,15)                        005
      READ INPUT TAPE 5, 903, P                                       006
      READ INPUT TAPE 5, 901, N, M, NL                                007
      READ INPUT TAPE 5, 904, (IH(I), I=1,N)                          008
      READ INPUT TAPE 5, 904, (NJ(J), J=1,M)                          009
      READ INPUT TAPE 5, 900, (DP(I), I=1,M)                          010
      DO 205  J=1,M                                                   011
  205 READ INPUT TAPE 5, 900, (F(I,J), I=1,N)                         012
C 1.
      CALL BIMUL (F, C, IH, NJ, JV, M)                                016
      CALL OUTPU3 (C, M)                                              017
C 2.
      DO 212  I=1,M                                                   021
      DO 212  J=1,M                                                   022
  212 C(I,J) = C(I,J) / DP(I)                                         023
```

```
                CALL OUTPU3 (C, M)                                              024
      C 3.
                DO 217  I=1,M                                                    028
                DO 217  J=1,M                                                    029
                S(I,J) = 0.                                                      030
                DO 217  K=1,M                                                    031
        217     S(I,J) = S(I,J) + C(K,I) * C(K,J)                               032
                CALL OUTPU3 (S, M)                                              033
      C 4.
                DO 219  I=1,M                                                    037
        219     D(I) = 1./SQRTF(S(I,I))                                         038
      C 5.
                DO 222  I=1,M                                                    042
                DO 222  J=1,M                                                    043
        222     C(I,J) = C(I,J) * D(J)                                          044
                CALL OUTPU3 (C, M)                                              045
      C 7.
                DO 227  I=1,N                                                    049
                DO 227  J=1,N                                                    050
                R(I,J) = 0.                                                      051
                DO 227  K=1,M                                                    052
        227     R(I,J) = R(I,J) + F(I,K) * C(K,J)                              053
                DO 229  I=1,N                                                    054
        229     WRITE OUTPUT TAPE 6, 902, (R(I,J), J=1,M)                      055
        900     FORMAT (10F6.3)                                                 056
        901     FORMAT (I4)                                                     057
        902     FORMAT (10F7.3)                                                 058
        903     FORMAT (F7.5)                                                   059
        904     FORMAT (10I2)                                                   060
        997     FORMAT (1H )                                                    061
                CALL EXIT                                                       062
                END                                                             063
      C
                SUBROUTINE BIMUL (A, B, IH, NJ, JV, M)
        01      DIMENSION A(140,15), B(15,15), IH(300), NJ(15), JV(70)
        02      NN = 0
        03      DO 14  J=1,M
        04      N1 = NN + 1
        05      NN = NN + NJ(J)
        06      JN = NJ(J)
        07      DO 09  K=N1,NN
        08      K1 = K - N1 + 1
        09      JV(K1) = IH(K)
        10      DO 14  I=1,M
        11      B(I,J) = 0.
        12      DO 14  K=1,JN
        13      KJ = JV(K)
        14      B(I,J) = B(I,J) + A(KJ,I)
                RETURN
                END
      C
                SUBROUTINE OUTPU3 (C, M)
                DIMENSION C(15,15)
                DO 1  I=1,M
        1       WRITE OUTPUT TAPE 6, 902, (C(I,J), J=1,M)
                WRITE OUTPUT TAPE 6, 997
        902     FORMAT (10F9.5)
        997     FORMAT (1H )
                RETURN
                END
      C
      *         DATA
       .00010
          9
          3
         40
       1 2 3 4 5 6 7 8 9
       3 3 3
       3.749 2.050 1.331
       0.717 0.740 0.773 0.556 0.463 0.518 0.640 0.615 0.715
       0.493 0.478 0.296-0.649-0.744-0.694 0.080 0.166-0.034
       0.350 0.322 0.406 0.068 0.181 0.188-0.588-0.621-0.369


      C CHAPTER 17 - PRIMARY FACTOR MATRICES FROM HYPOTHESES                     001
      C    17.5 ARBITRARY FACTOR MATRIX                                         002
      C                                                                         003
                DIMENSION R(120,120), F(140,15), S(15,15), C(15,15), IH(300),   004
               1JV(70), NJ(15), D(140), DP(15), G(15,15)                        005
                READ INPUT TAPE 5, 903, P                                       006
                READ INPUT TAPE 5, 901, N, M, NL                               007
```

```
        READ INPUT TAPE 5, 904, (IH(I), I=1,N)                        008
        READ INPUT TAPE 5, 904, (NJ(J), J=1,M)                        009
        DO 302  J=1,M                                                 010
  302   READ INPUT TAPE 5, 902, (F(I,J), I=1,N)                       011
C 1.
        DO 308  I=1,N                                                 015
        D(I) = 0.                                                     016
        DO 308  J=1,M                                                 017
  308   D(I) = D(I) + F(I,J)**2                                       018
        DO 310  I=1,N                                                 019
  310   D(I) = 1./SQRTF(D(I))                                         020
C 2.
        DO 313  I=1,N                                                 024
        DO 313  J=1,M                                                 025
  313   F(I,J) = D(I) * F(I,J)                                        026
        CALL OUTPU1 (F, N, M)                                         027
C 3.
        CALL BIMUL (F, C, IH, NJ, JV, M)                              031
        CALL OUTPU3 (C, M)                                            032
C 4.
        DO 319  I=1,M                                                 036
        DO 319  J=1,M                                                 037
        R(I,J) = 0.                                                   038
        DO 319  K=1,N                                                 039
  319   R(I,J) = R(I,J) + F(K,I) * F(K,J)                             040
        CALL OUTPU2 (R,M)                                             041
C 5.
        CALL SYMIN (R, M)                                             045
        CALL OUTPU2 (R,M)                                             046
        DO 325  I=1,M                                                 047
        DO 325  J=1,M                                                 048
        S(I,J) = 0.                                                   049
        DO 325  K=1,M                                                 050
  325   S(I,J) = S(I,J) + R(I,K) * C(K,J)                             051
        CALL OUTPU3 (S, M)                                            052
C 6.
        DO 331  J=1,M                                                 056
        D(J) = 0.                                                     057
        DO 329  I=1,M                                                 058
  329   D(J) = D(J) + S(I,J)**2                                       059
C 7.
  331   D(J) = 1./SQRTF(D(J))                                         063
C 8.
        DO 334  I=1,M                                                 067
        DO 334  J=1,M                                                 068
  334   S(I,J) = S(I,J) * D(J)                                        069
        CALL OUTPU3 (S, M)                                            070
C 10.
        DO 339  I=1,N                                                 074
        DO 339  J=1,M                                                 075
        R(I,J) = 0.                                                   076
        DO 339  K=1,M                                                 077
  339   R(I,J) = R(I,J) + F(I,K) * S(K,J)                             078
        DO 341  I=1,N                                                 079
  341   WRITE OUTPUT TAPE 6, 902, (R(I,J), J=1,M)                     080
  901   FORMAT (I4)                                                   081
  902   FORMAT (10F7.3)                                               082
  903   FORMAT (F7.5)                                                 083
  904   FORMAT (10I2)                                                 084
        CALL EXIT                                                     085
        END                                                          086
C
        SUBROUTINE OUTPU1 (F, N, M)
        DIMENSION F(140,15)
        DO 1  I=1,N
    1   WRITE OUTPUT TAPE 6, 902, (F(I,J), J=1,M)
        WRITE OUTPUT TAPE 6, 997
  902   FORMAT (10F9.5)
  997   FORMAT (1H )
        RETURN
        END
C
        SUBROUTINE OUTPU2 (R, M)
```

657

```
      DIMENSION R(120,120)
      DO 1 I=1,M
    1 WRITE OUTPUT TAPE 6, 902, (R(I,J), J=1,M)
      WRITE OUTPUT TAPE 6, 997
  902 FORMAT (10F9.5)
  997 FORMAT (1H )
      RETURN
      END
C
      SUBROUTINE OUTPU3 (C, M)
      DIMENSION C(15,15)
      DO 1 I=1,M
    1 WRITE OUTPUT TAPE 6, 902, (C(I,J), J=1,M)
      WRITE OUTPUT TAPE 6, 997
  902 FORMAT (10F9.5)
  997 FORMAT (1H )
      RETURN
      END
C
      SUBROUTINE BIMUL (A, B, IH, NJ, JV, M)
   01 DIMENSION A(140,15), B(15,15), IH(300), NJ(15), JV(70)
   02 NN = 0
   03 DO 14  J=1,M
   04 N1 = NN + 1
   05 NN = NN + NJ(J)
   06 JN = NJ(J)
   07 DO 09  K=N1,NN
   08 K1 = K - N1 + 1
   09 JV(K1) = IH(K)
   10 DO 14  I=1,M
   11 B(I,J) = 0.
   12 DO 14  K=1,JN
   13 KJ = JV(K)
   14 B(I,J) = B(I,J) + A(KJ,I)
      RETURN
      END
C
      SUBROUTINE SYMIN (S, N)
      DIMENSION S(120,120)
   38 N1 = N-1
   01 DO 04 I = 2,N
   02 I1 = I-1
   03 DO 04 J = 1,I1
   04 S(I,J) = 0.
   10 C = 1./SQRTF(S(1,1))
   11 S(1,1) = 1.
   12 DO 13  J=1,N
   13 S(1,J) = S(1,J) * C
   14 DO 21  K=2,N
   15 DO 17  J=1,N
  151 K1 = K-1
   16 DO 17  I=1,K1
   17 S(K,J) = S(K,J) - S(I,K) * S(I,J)
   18 C = 1./SQRTF(S(K,K))
   19 DO 191  I=1,K1
  191 S(I,K) = 0.
  192 S(K,K) = 1.
   20 DO 21  J=1,N
   21 S(K,J) = S(K,J) * C
   25 DO 30  J=2,N
   26 J1 = J-1
   27 DO 30  I=1,J1
   29 DO 30  K=J,N
   30 S(I,J) = S(I,J) + S(K,I) * S(K,J)
   31 DO 35  J=1,N1
   32 S(J,J) = S(J,J) **2
   33 J2 = J+1
   34 DO 35  I=J2,N
   35 S(J,J) = S(J,J) + S(I,J)**2
  351 S(N,N) = S(N,N)**2
   39 DO 42  I=1,N1
   40 I2 = I+1
   41 DO 42  J=I2,N
   42 S(J,I) = S(I,J)
      RETURN
      END
C
*     DATA
 .00010
    9
    3
   40
  1 2 3 4 5 6 7 8 9
  3 3 3
   0.933  0.936  0.914  0.178  0.107  0.169  0.330  0.333  0.397
  -0.068 -0.048  0.115  0.840  0.885  0.870  0.165  0.087  0.283
   0.002  0.033 -0.035  0.073 -0.046 -0.027  0.777  0.800  0.667
```

```
C CHAPTER 17 - PRIMARY FACTOR MATRICES FROM HYPOTHESES          001
C    17.6 ZERO PARTIAL SUM TRANSFORMATION                       002
C                                                               003
      DIMENSION R(120,120), F(140,15), S(15,15), C(15,15), IH(300),   004
     1JV(70), NJ(15), D(140), DP(15), G(15,15)                  005
      READ INPUT TAPE 5, 903, P                                 006
      READ INPUT TAPE 5, 901, N, M, NL                          007
      READ INPUT TAPE 5, 904, (IH(I), I=1,N)                    008
      READ INPUT TAPE 5, 904, (NJ(J), J=1,M)                    009
      DO 402  J=1,M                                             010
  402 READ INPUT TAPE 5, 902, (F(I,J), I=1,N)                   011
C 1.
      DO 407  I=1,M                                             015
      DO 407  J=1,M                                             016
      S(I,J) = 0.                                               017
      DO 407  K=1,N                                             018
  407 S(I,J) = S(I,J) + F(K,I) * F(K,J)                         019
      CALL OUTPU3 (S, M)                                        020
C 2.
      CALL TRIANG (S, M)                                        024
      CALL OUTPU3 (S, M)                                        025
      CALL TRIN (S, C, M)                                       026
      CALL OUTPU3 (C, M)                                        027
C 3.
      DO 417  I=1,N                                             031
      DO 417  J=1,M                                             032
      R(I,J) = 0.                                               033
      DO 417  K=1,J                                             034
  417 R(I,J) = R(I,J) + F(I,K) * C(J,K)                         035
      DO 4175  I=1,M                                            036
      DO 4175  J=1,M                                            037
      S(I,J) = 0.                                               038
      DO 4175  K=1,N                                            039
 4175 S(I,J) = S(I,J) + R(K,I) * R(K,J)                         040
      CALL OUTPU3 (S,M)                                         041
      REWIND 2                                                  042
      DO 4178  I=1,N                                            043
 4178 WRITE TAPE 2, (F(I,J), J=1,M)                             044
      REWIND 2                                                  045
      DO 4181  I=1,N                                            046
      DO 4181  J=1,M                                            047
 4181 F(I,J) = R(I,J)                                           048
C 4.
      DO 421  J=1,M                                             052
      D(J) = 0.                                                 053
      DO 421  I=1,N                                             054
  421 D(J) = D(J) + R(I,J)                                      055
C 5.
      CALL BIMUL (F, S, IH, NJ, JV, M)                          059
      CALL OUTPU3 (S, M)                                        060
      DO 4222  I=1,N                                            061
 4222 READ TAPE 2, (F(I,J), J=1,M)                              062
      REWIND 2                                                  063
C 6.
      DO 425  I=1,M                                             067
      DO 425  J=1,M                                             068
  425 R(I,J) = D(I) - S(I,J)                                    069
      CALL OUTPU2 (R,M)                                         070
C 7.
      DO 429  J=1,M                                             074
      D(J) = 0.                                                 075
      DO 429  I=1,M                                             076
  429 D(J) = D(J) + R(I,J) * R(I,J)                             077
      DO 431  I=1,M                                             078
  431 D(I) = 1./SQRTF(D(I))                                     079
      DO 434  I=1,M                                             080
      DO 434  J=1,M                                             081
  434 R(I,J) = R(I,J) * D(J)                                    082
      CALL OUTPU2 (R,M)                                         083
C 8.
      DO 438  J=1,M                                             087
      D(J) = 0.                                                 088
      DO 438  I=1,M                                             089
  438 D(J) = D(J) + R(I,J) * S(I,J)                             090
      DO 440  I=1,M                                             091
      DO 440  J=1,M                                             092
  440 R(I,J) = R(I,J) * D(J)                                    093
      CALL OUTPU2 (R,M)                                         094
C 9.
      DO 443  I=1,M                                             097
      DO 443  J=1,M                                             098
  443 S(I,J) = S(I,J) - R(I,J)                                  099
      CALL OUTPU3 (S, M)                                        100
```

```
C 10.
      DO 448   I=1,M                                              104
      DO 448   J=1,M                                              105
      R(I,J) = 0.                                                 106
      DO 448   K=I,M                                              107
 448  R(I,J) = R(I,J) + C(K,I) * S(K,J)                           108
      CALL OUTPU2 (R,M)                                           109
C 11.
      DO 453   I=1,M                                              113
      DO 453   J=1,M                                              114
      C(I,J) = 0.                                                 115
      DO 453   K=1,M                                              116
 453  C(I,J) = C(I,J) + R(K,I) * R(K,J)                           117
      CALL OUTPU3 (C, M)                                          118
C 12.
      DO 455   I=1,M                                              122
 455  D(I) = 1./SQRTF(C(I,I))                                     123
C 13.
      DO 458   I=1,M                                              127
      DO 458   J=1,M                                              128
 458  S(I,J) = R(I,J) * D(J)                                      129
      CALL OUTPU3 (S, M)                                          130
C 15.
      DO 463   I=1,N                                              134
      DO 463   J=1,M                                              135
      R(I,J) = 0.                                                 136
      DO 463   K=1,M                                              137
 463  R(I,J) = R(I,J) + F(I,K) * S(K,J)                           138
      DO 465   I=1,N                                              139
 465  WRITE OUTPUT TAPE 6, 902, (R(I,J), J=1,M)                   140
 901  FORMAT (I4)                                                 141
 902  FORMAT (10F7.3)                                             142
 903  FORMAT (F7.5)                                               143
 904  FORMAT (10I2)                                               144
      CALL EXIT                                                   145
      END                                                         146
C
      SUBROUTINE OUTPU2 (R, M)
      DIMENSION R(120,120)
      DO 1   I=1,M
 1    WRITE OUTPUT TAPE 6, 902, (R(I,J), J=1,M)
      WRITE OUTPUT TAPE 6, 997
 902  FORMAT (10F9.5)
 997  FORMAT (1H )
      RETURN
      END
C
      SUBROUTINE OUTPU3 (C, M)
      DIMENSION C(15,15)
      DO 1   I=1,M
 1    WRITE OUTPUT TAPE 6, 902, (C(I,J), J=1,M)
      WRITE OUTPUT TAPE 6, 997
 902  FORMAT (10F9.5)
 997  FORMAT (1H )
      RETURN
      END
C
      SUBROUTINE TRIANG (A,N)                                     001
C TRIANGULAR FACTOR                                               003
      DIMENSION A(15,15)                                          004
      NN = N-1                                                    005
      DO 14 K=1,NN                                                006
      C=1./SQRTF(A(K,K))                                          007
      DO 10   I = K,N                                             008
 10   A(I,K) = A(I,K) * C                                         009
      KK = K + 1                                                  010
      DO 14 J = KK,N                                              011
      DO 14 I = J,N                                               012
 14   A(I,J) = A(I,J) - A(I,K)*A(J,K)                             013
      A(N,N) = SQRTF(A(N,N))                                      014
      RETURN                                                      015
      END
C
      SUBROUTINE TRIN (A,B,N)                                     001
C INVERSE OF TRIANGULAR MATRIX                                    003
      DIMENSION A(15,15), B(15,15)                                004
      DO 10   J=1,N                                               005
      B(J,J) = 1./A(J,J)                                          006
      DO 10   I=J,N                                               007
 10   A(I,J) = A(I,J) * B(J,J)                                    008
      DO 16   I=2,N                                               009
      DO 16   IJ=2,I                                              010
      J=I+1-IJ                                                    011
      B(I,J) = 0.0                                                012
      J1 = J+1
```

```
          DO 16  K=J1, I                                           013
 16       B(I,J) = B(I,J) - B(I,K) * A(K,J)                         014
          RETURN                                                   015
          END                                                      016
C
          SUBROUTINE BIMUL (A, B, IH, NJ, JV, M)
 01       DIMENSION A(140,15), B(15,15), IH(300), NJ(15), JV(70)
 02       NN = 0
 03       DO 14  J=1,M
 04       N1 = NN + 1
 05       NN = NN + NJ(J)
 06       JN = NJ(J)
 07       DO 09  K=N1,NN
 08       K1 = K - N1 + 1
 09       JV(K1) = IH(K)
 10       DO 14  I=1,M
 11       B(I,J) = 0.
 12       DO 14  K=1,JN
 13       KJ = JV(K)
 14       B(I,J) = B(I,J) + A(KJ,I)
          RETURN
          END
C
*         DATA
 .00010
      9
      3
     40
  1 2 3 4 5 6 7 8 9
  3 3 3
   0.933  0.936  0.914  0.178  0.107  0.169  0.330  0.333  0.397
  -0.068 -0.048  0.115  0.840  0.885  0.870  0.165  0.087  0.283
   0.002  0.033 -0.035  0.073 -0.046 -0.027  0.777  0.800  0.667


C CHAPTER 17 - PRIMARY FACTOR MATRICES FROM HYPOTHESES            001
C     17.7 ORTHOGONAL TRANSFORMATION MATRIX                        002
C                                                                  003
      DIMENSION R(120,120), F(140,15), S(15,15), C(15,15), IH(300),  004
     1JV(70), NJ(15), D(140), DP(15), G(15,15)                     005
      READ INPUT TAPE 5, 903, P                                    006
      READ INPUT TAPE 5, 901, N, M, NL                             007
      READ INPUT TAPE 5, 904, (IH(I), I=1,N)                       008
      READ INPUT TAPE 5, 904, (NJ(J), J=1,M)                       009
      DO 402  J=1,M                                                010
 402  READ INPUT TAPE 5, 902, (F(I,J), I=1,N)                      011
      DO 5003  I=1,N                                               012
      DO 5003  J=1,N                                               013
 5003 R(I,J) = F(I,J)                                              014
C 1.
      CALL BIMUL (F, S, IH, NJ, JV, M)                             018
      CALL OUTPU3 (S, M)                                           019
C 2.
      DO 507  I=1,M                                                023
      DO 507  J=1,M                                                024
      FNJ = NJ(J)                                                  025
 507  G(I,J) = S(I,J) / FNJ                                        026
      CALL OUTPU3 (G, M)                                           027
C 3.
      E = 0.                                                       031
      DO 562  L=1,10                                               032
      LF = L                                                       033
      DO 512  I=1,M                                                034
      DO 512  J=1,M                                                035
      C(I,J) = 0.                                                  036
      DO 512  K=1,N                                                037
 512  C(I,J) = C(I,J) + F(K,I) * R(K,J)                            038
      CALL OUTPU3 (C, M)                                           039
      NN = 0                                                       040
      DO 524  J=1,M                                                041
      N1 = NN + 1                                                  042
      NN = NN + NJ(J)                                              043
      JN = NJ(J)                                                   044
      DO 520  K=N1,NN                                              045
      K1 = K - N1 + 1                                              046
 520  JV(K1) = IH(K)                                               047
      D(J) = 0.                                                    048
      DO 524  K=1,JN                                               049
      KJ = JV(K)                                                   050
 524  D(J) = D(J) + R(KJ,J)                                        051
      WRITE OUTPUT TAPE 6, 902, (D(J), J=1,M)                      052
      WRITE OUTPUT TAPE 6, 997                                     053
      DO 527  I=1,M                                                054
                                                                   055
```

```
            DO 527  J=1,M                                           056
  527   C(I,J) = C(I,J) - G(I,J) * D(J)                             057
        CALL OUTPU3 (C, M)
C 4.
            DO 532  I=1,M                                           061
            DO 532  J=1,M                                           062
        R(I,J) = 0.                                                 063
            DO 532  K=1,M                                           064
  532   R(I,J) = R(I,J) + C(K,I) * C(K,J)                           065
        CALL OUTPU2 (R,M)                                           066
        IF ((ABSF(E1/E-1.))-P) 563, 563, 538                        067
  538   CALL JACSIM (R, D, P, M, NL)                                068
        EE = 0.                                                     069
            DO 5382  I=1,M                                          070
 5382   EE = EE + R(I,I)                                            071
C 5.
            DO 540  I=1,M                                           075
  540   D(I) = 1./SQRTF(D(I))                                       076
            DO 547  I=1,M                                           077
        IM = I + M                                                  078
            DO 547  J=1,M                                           079
        JM = J + M                                                  080
        S(I,J) = 0.                                                 081
            DO 547  K=1,M                                           082
  547   S(I,J) = S(I,J) + R(IM,K) * D(K) * R(JM,K)                  083
        CALL OUTPU 3(S,M)                                           084
            DO 552  I=1,M                                           085
            DO 552  J=1,M                                           086
        R(I,J) = 0.                                                 087
            DO 552  K=1,M                                           088
  552   R(I,J) = R(I,J) + C(I,K) * S(K,J)                           089
        CALL OUTPU2 (R,M)                                           090
            DO 556  I=1,M                                           091
            DO 556  J=1,M                                           092
  556   S(I,J) = R(I,J)                                             093
C 6.
            DO 561  I=1,N                                           097
            DO 561  J=1,M                                           098
        R(I,J) = 0.                                                 099
            DO 561  K=1,M                                           100
  561   R(I,J) = R(I,J) + F(I,K) * S(K,J)                           101
        WRITE OUTPUT TAPE 6, 998                                    102
        E1 = E                                                      103
        E = EE                                                      104
        IF (P-ABSF(E1/E-1.)) 562, 5621,5621                         105
  562   CONTINUE                                                    106
 5621   DO 5625  I=1,M                                              107
            DO 5625  J=1,M                                          108
        C(I,J) = 0.                                                 109
            DO 5625  K=1,M                                          110
 5625   C(I,J) = C(I,J) + S(K,I) * S(K,J)                           111
        CALL OUTPU3 (C,M)                                           112
  563   WRITE OUTPUT TAPE 6, 901, LF                                113
            DO 565  I=1,N                                           114
  565   WRITE OUTPUT TAPE 6, 902, (R(I,J), J=1,M)                   115
  901   FORMAT (I4)                                                 116
  902   FORMAT (10F7.3)                                             117
  903   FORMAT (F7.5)                                               118
  904   FORMAT (10I2)                                               119
  997   FORMAT (1H )                                                120
  998   FORMAT (1H0)                                                121
        CALL EXIT                                                   122
        END                                                         123
C
        SUBROUTINE OUTPU2 (R, M)
        DIMENSION R(120,120)
            DO 1  I=1,M
    1   WRITE OUTPUT TAPE 6, 902, (R(I,J), J=1,M)
        WRITE OUTPUT TAPE 6, 997
  902   FORMAT (10F9.5)
  997   FORMAT (1H )
```

662

```
      RETURN
      END
C
      SUBROUTINE OUTPU3 (C, M)
      DIMENSION C(15,15)
      DO 1  I=1,M
   1  WRITE OUTPUT TAPE 6, 902, (C(I,J), J=1,M)
      WRITE OUTPUT TAPE 6, 997
 902  FORMAT (10F9.5)
 997  FORMAT (1H )
      RETURN
      END
C
      SUBROUTINE BIMUL (A, B, IH, NJ, JV, M)
01    DIMENSION A(140,15), B(15,15), IH(300), NJ(15), JV(70)
02    NN = 0
03    DO 14  J=1,M
04    N1 = NN + 1
05    NN = NN + NJ(J)
06    JN = NJ(J)
07    DO 09  K=N1,NN
08    K1 = K - N1 + 1
09    JV(K1) = IH(K)
10    DO 14  I=1,M
11    B(I,J) = 0.
12    DO 14  K=1,JN
13    KJ = JV(K)
14    B(I,J) = B(I,J) + A(KJ,I)
      RETURN
      END
C
      SUBROUTINE JACSIM (R, D, P, N, NL)                              001
      DIMENSION R(120,120), D(140)                                   002
      N1 = N+1                                                       003
      N11=N-1                                                        004
      N2 = N*2                                                       005
      DO 10  I=N1, N2                                                006
      DO 10  J = 1,N                                                 007
   10 R(I,J) = 0.                                                    008
      DO 12  I=1,N                                                   009
      NI = N + I                                                     010
   12 R(NI,I) = 1.                                                   011
      DO 35 L=1,NL                                                   012
      DO 15  I=1,N                                                   013
   15 D(I) = R(I,I)                                                  014
      DO 282 I = 1,N11                                               015
      I1 = I+1                                                       016
      DO 282 J= I1,N                                                 017
      DR = R(I,I) - R(J,J)                                           018
      A = SQRTF(DR**2 + 4.*R(I,J)**2)                                019
      A = SQRTF((A+DR)/(2.*A))                                       020
      B = SQRTF(1.-A**2)                                             021
      C = SIGNF(1.,R(I,J))                                           022
      DO 252 K = 1,N2                                                023
      U = R(K,I)*A*C + R(K,J)*B                                      024
      R(K,J) = -R(K,I)*B*C + R(K,J)*A                                025
  252 R(K,I) = U                                                     026
      DO 282 K = 1,N                                                 027
      U = R(I,K)*A*C + R(J,K)*B                                      028
      R(J,K) = -R(I,K)*B*C + R(J,K)*A                                029
  282 R(I,K) = U                                                     030
      DO 30 I=1,N                                                    031
   30 D(I) = ABSF(D(I) - R(I,I))                                     032
      S = 0.                                                         033
      DO 33  I=1,N                                                   034
   33 S = MAX1F (S, D(I))                                            035
      DO 332 I =1,N                                                  036
  332 D(I) = R(I,I)                                                  037
      IF (S-P) 38, 38, 35                                            038
   35 CONTINUE                                                       039
   38 RETURN                                                         040
      END                                                            041
C
*     DATA
.00010
   9
   3
  40
1 2 3 4 5 6 7 8 9
3 3 3
 0.933  0.936  0.914  0.178  0.107  0.169  0.330  0.333  0.397
-0.068 -0.048  0.115  0.840  0.885  0.870  0.165  0.087  0.283
 0.002  0.033 -0.035  0.073 -0.046 -0.027  0.777  0.800  0.667
```

```
C CHAPTER 18 - ANALYTICAL ROTATIONS                                          001
C    18.3 SUCCESSIVE FACTOR VARIMAX SOLUTION                                  002
C                                                                            003
      DIMENSION A(200,10), B(200,10), H(20,10), S(10,10), C(200),           004
     1V(500), KV(20), BS(20), W(20) , U(20)                                  005
      READ INPUT TAPE 5, 902, P, N, M, NL                                    006
      DO 106  J=1,M                                                          007
  106 READ INPUT TAPE 5, 901, (A(I,J), I=1,N)                                008
C ROW NORMALIZATION                                                          009
      DO 115  I=1,N                                                          010
      C(I) = 0.                                                              011
      DO 115  J=1,M                                                          012
  115 C(I) = C(I) + A(I,J)**2                                                013
      DO 117  I=1,N                                                          014
  117 C(I) = 1./SQRTF(C(I))                                                  015
      DO 120  I=1,N                                                          016
      DO 120  J=1,M                                                          017
  120 A(I,J) = C(I) * A(I,J)                                                 018
C 1.                                                                         
      DO 127  J=1,M                                                          022
      W(J) = 0.                                                              023
      DO 127  I=1,N                                                          024
  127 W(J) = W(J) + A(I,J)                                                   025
      FN = N                                                                 026
      AL = 0.                                                                027
      DO 131  J=1,M                                                          028
  131 AL = AL + W(J)**2                                                      029
      AL = 1./SQRTF(AL)                                                      030
      DO 134  J=1,M                                                          031
  134 W(J) = W(J) * AL                                                       032
C 2.                                                                         
      DO 138  I=1,N                                                          036
      V(I) = 0.                                                              037
      DO 138  J=1,M                                                          038
  138 V(I) = V(I) + A(I,J) * W(J)                                            039
C 3.                                                                         
      DO 178  L=1,M                                                          043
      LA = 1                                                                 044
      DO 144  I=2,N                                                          045
      IF (V(LA)-V(I)) 144, 144, 143                                          046
  143 LA = I                                                                 047
  144 CONTINUE                                                               048
C 4.                                                                         
      DO 146  J=1,M                                                          052
  146 H(J,L) = A(LA,J)                                                       053
      E = 0.                                                                 054
      DO 173  K=1,NL                                                         055
      KV(L) = K                                                              056
C 5.                                                                         
      DO 153  I=1,N                                                          060
      B(I,L) = 0.                                                            061
      DO 153  J=1,M                                                          062
  153 B(I,L) = B(I,L) + A(I,J) * H(J,L)                                      063
C 6.                                                                         
      BS(L) = 0.                                                             067
      DO 156  I=1,N                                                          068
  156 BS(L) = BS(L) + B(I,L)**2                                              069
      BS(L) = BS(L) / FN                                                     070
      E1 = E                                                                 071
      E = AL                                                                 072
      IF (P-ABSF(E1/E-1.)) 158, 158, 174                                     073
  158 DO 159  I=1,N                                                          074
  159 B(I,L) = B(I,L) **3 - B(I,L) * BS(L)                                   075
C 7.                                                                         
      DO 163  J=1,M                                                          079
      U(J) = 0.                                                              080
      DO 163  I=1,N                                                          081
  163 U(J) = U(J) + B(I,L) * A(I,J)                                          082
C 8.                                                                         
      AL = 0.                                                                086
      DO 166  J=1,M                                                          087
  166 AL = AL + U(J)**2                                                      088
      AL = SQRTF(AL)                                                         089
C 9.                                                                         
      DO 169  J=1,M                                                          093
  169 H(J,L) = U(J) / AL                                                     094
  173 CONTINUE                                                               095
C 16.                                                                        
  174 DO 176  I=1,N                                                          099
```

```
        DO 176   J=1,M                                              100
  176   A(I,J) = A(I,J) - B(I,L) * H(J,L)                           101
        WRITE OUTPUT TAPE 6, 900, AL                                102
C 17.
        DO 178  I=1,N                                               106
  178   V(I) = V(I) + B(I,L)                                        107
        WRITE OUTPUT TAPE 6, 903, (KV(L), L=1,M)                    108
        WRITE OUTPUT TAPE 6, 997                                    109
        WRITE OUTPUT TAPE 6, 900, (BS(L), L=1,M)                    110
        WRITE OUTPUT TAPE 6, 998                                    111
        DO 184  I=1,M                                               112
  184   WRITE OUTPUT TAPE 6, 900, (H(I,J), J=1,M)                   113
        WRITE OUTPUT TAPE 6, 997                                    114
        CALL SINCHA (A, B, V, C, N, M, NL, P)
  900   FORMAT (10F7.3)                                             116
  901   FORMAT (10F6.3)                                             117
  902   FORMAT (F7.5/(I4))                                          118
  903   FORMAT (10I7)                                               119
  997   FORMAT (1H )                                                120
  998   FORMAT (1H0)                                                121
        CALL EXIT                                                   122
        END                                                         123
C
        SUBROUTINE SINCHA (A, B, W, V, N, M, NL, P)
        DIMENSION A(200,1), B(200,1), W(1), V(1)
        DO 6   I=1,M
        DO 4   J=I,M
        A(I,J) = 0.
        DO 2   K=1,N
    2   A(I,J) = A(I,J) + B(K,I) * B(K,J)
    4   A(J,I) = A(I,J)
    6   V(I) = 1.
        E = 0.
        DO 14  L=1,NL
        DO 8   I=1,M
        W(I) = 0.
        DO 8   J=1,M
    8   W(I) = W(I) + A(I,J) * V(J)
        AL = 0.
        DO 10  I=1,M
   10   AL = AL + W(I) * V(I)
        AL = SQRTF(AL)
        E1 = E
        E = AL
        IF (P - ABSF(E1/E-1.)) 12, 12, 15
   12   DO 13  I=1,M
   13   V(I) = W(I)/AL
   14   CONTINUE
   15   DO 16  I=1,N
        W(I) = 0.
        DO 16  J=1,M
   16   W(I) = W(I) + B(I,J) * V(J)
        DO 18  I=1,N
        DO 18  J=1,M
        S = SIGNF(1., W(I)) * SIGNF(1., V(J))
   18   B(I,J) = B(I,J) * S
        DO 20  I=1,N
   20   WRITE OUTPUT TAPE 6, 22, (B(I,J), J=1,M)
   22   FORMAT (12F7.3)
        RETURN
        END
C
*       DATA
 .00010
    9
    3
   40
 0.717 0.740 0.773 0.556 0.463 0.518 0.640 0.615 0.715
 0.493 0.478 0.296-0.649-0.744-0.694 0.080 0.166-0.034
 0.350 0.322 0.406 0.068 0.181 0.188-0.588-0.621-0.369

C CHAPTER 18 - ANALYTICAL ROTATIONS                                001
C    18.4 SIMULTANEOUS FACTOR VARIMAX SOLUTION                      002
C                                                                   003
        DIMENSION A(200,10), B(200,10), H(20,10), S(10,10), C(200), 004
       1V(500), KV(20), BS(20), W(20) , U(20)                       005
        READ INPUT TAPE 5, 902, P, N, M, NL                         006
        DO 106  J=1,M                                               007
  106   READ INPUT TAPE 5, 901, (A(I,J), I=1,N)                     008
        FN = N
```

665

```
C ROW NORMALIZATION                                               009
      DO 115  I=1,N                                               010
      C(I) = 0.                                                   011
      DO 115  J=1,M                                               012
115   C(I) = C(I) + A(I,J)**2                                     013
      DO 117  I=1,N                                               014
117   C(I) = 1./SQRTF(C(I))                                       015
      DO 120  I=1,N                                               016
      DO 120  J=1,M                                               017
120   A(I,J) = C(I) * A(I,J)                                      018
      DO 206  I=1,N                                               019
      DO 206  J=1,M                                               020
206   B(I,J) = A(I,J)                                             021
      E = 0.                                                      022
      DO 257  L=1,NL                                              023
      LF = L                                                      024
C 1.
      DO 213  J=1,M                                               028
      BS(J) = 0.                                                  029
      DO 213  I=1,N                                               030
213   BS(J) = BS(J) + B(I,J)**2                                   031
      DO 215  J=1,M                                               032
215   BS(J) = BS(J) / FN                                          033
      DO 218  I=1,N                                               034
      DO 218  J=1,M                                               035
218   B(I,J) = B(I,J) **3 - B(I,J) * BS(J)                        036
C 2.
      DO 223  I=1,M                                               040
      DO 223  J=1,M                                               041
      S(I,J) = 0.                                                 042
      DO 223  K=1,N                                               043
223   S(I,J) = S(I,J) + A(K,I) * B(K,J)                           044
C 3.
      DO 228  I=1,M                                               048
      DO 228  J=1,M                                               049
      H(I,J) = 0.                                                 050
      DO 228  K=1,M                                               051
228   H(I,J) = H(I,J) + S(K,I) * S(K,J)                           052
      CALL JACSIM (H, W, P, M, NL)                                053
      G = 0.                                                      054
      DO 232  J=1,M                                               055
232   G = G + W(J)                                                056
C 4.
      DO 234  J=1,M                                               060
234   W(J) = 1. / SQRTF(W(J))                                     061
      DO 241  I=1,M                                               062
      IM = I + M                                                  063
      DO 241  J=1,M                                               064
      JM = J + M                                                  065
      H(I,J) = 0.                                                 066
      DO 241  K=1,M                                               067
241   H(I,J) = H(I,J) + H(IM,K) * W(K) * H(JM,K)                  068
      DO 247  I=1,M                                               069
      IM = I + M                                                  070
      DO 247  J=1,M                                               071
      H(IM,J) = 0.                                                072
      DO 247  K=1,M                                               073
247   H(IM,J) = H(IM,J) + S(I,K) * H(K,J)                         074
C 5.
      DO 253  I=1,N                                               078
      DO 253  J=1,M                                               079
      B(I,J) = 0.                                                 080
      DO 253  K=1,M                                               081
      KM = K + M                                                  082
253   B(I,J) = B(I,J) + A(I,K) * H(KM,J)                          083
      E1 = E                                                      084
      E = G                                                       085
      IF ((ABSF(E1/E-1.))-P) 258, 258, 257                        086
257   CONTINUE                                                    087
258   WRITE OUTPUT TAPE 6, 903, LF                                088
      WRITE OUTPUT TAPE 6, 997                                    089
      WRITE OUTPUT TAPE 6, 900, (BS(J), J=1,M)                    090
      WRITE OUTPUT TAPE 6, 997                                    091
      DO 264  I=1,M                                               092
      IM = I + M                                                  093
264   WRITE OUTPUT TAPE 6, 900, (H(IM,J), J=1,M)                  094
      WRITE OUTPUT TAPE 6, 997                                    095
      CALL SINCHA (A,B, V, C, N, M, NL, P)
900   FORMAT (10F7.3)                                             097
901   FORMAT (10F6.3)                                             098
902   FORMAT (F7.5/(I4))                                          099
903   FORMAT (10I7)                                               100
```

```
997   FORMAT (1H )                                                    101
      CALL EXIT                                                       102
      END                                                            103
C
      SUBROUTINE JACSIM (R, D, P, N, NL)
      DIMENSION R(20,10), D(20)
06    N1 = N+1
061   N11=N-1
07    N2 = N*2
08    DO 10  I=N1, N2
09    DO 10   J = 1,N
10    R(I,J) = 0.
11    DO 12  I=1,N
111   NI = N + I
12    R(NI,I) = 1.
13    DO 35 L=1,NL
14    DO 15   I=1,N
15    D(I) = R(I,I)
17    DO 282 I = 1,N11
16    I1 = I+1
18    DO 282 J= I1,N
19    DR = R(I,I) - R(J,J)
20    A = SQRTF(DR**2 + 4.*R(I,J)**2)
21    A = SQRTF((A+DR)/(2.*A))
22    B = SQRTF(1.-A**2)
221   C = SIGNF(1.,R(I,J))
23    DO 252 K = 1,N2
241   U = R(K,I)*A*C + R(K,J)*B
25    R(K,J) = -R(K,I)*B*C + R(K,J)*A
252   R(K,I) = U
26    DO 282 K = 1,N
271   U = R(I,K)*A*C + R(J,K)*B
28    R(J,K) = -R(I,K)*B*C + R(J,K)*A
282   R(I,K) = U
29    DO 30  I=1,N
30    D(I) = ABSF(D(I) - R(I,I))
31    S = 0.
32    DO 33  I=1,N
33    S = MAX1F (S, D(I))
331   DO 332 I =1,N
332   D(I) = R(I,I)
34    IF (S-P) 38, 38, 35
35    CONTINUE
38    RETURN
      END
C
      SUBROUTINE SINCHA (A, B, W, V, N, M, NL, P)
      DIMENSION A(200,1), B(200,1), W(1), V(1)
      DO 6  I=1,M
      DO 4   J=I,M
      A(I,J) = 0.
      DO 2  K=1,N
2     A(I,J) = A(I,J) + B(K,I) * B(K,J)
4     A(J,I) = A(I,J)
6     V(I) = 1.
      E = 0.
      DO 14  L=1,NL
      DO 8  I=1,M
      W(I) = 0.
      DO 8   J=1,M
8     W(I) = W(I) + A(I,J) * V(J)
      AL = 0.
      DO 10  I=1,M
10    AL = AL + W(I) * V(I)
      AL = SQRTF(AL)
      E1 = E
      E = AL
      IF (P - ABSF(E1/E-1.)) 12, 12, 15
12    DO 13  I=1,M
13    V(I) = W(I)/AL
14    CONTINUE
15    DO 16  I=1,N
      W(I) = 0.
      DO 16   J=1,M
16    W(I) = W(I) + B(I,J) * V(J)
      DO 18  I=1,N
      DO 18   J=1,M
      S = SIGNF(1., W(I)) * SIGNF(1., V(J))
18    B(I,J) = B(I,J) * S
      DO 20  I=1,N
20    WRITE OUTPUT TAPE 6, 22, (B(I,J), J=1,M)
22    FORMAT (12F7.3)
      RETURN
```

```
       END
C
*      DATA
 .00010
    9
    3
   40
 0.717 0.740 0.773 0.556 0.463 0.518 0.640 0.615 0.715
 0.493 0.478 0.296-0.649-0.744-0.694 0.080 0.166-0.034
 0.350 0.322 0.406 0.068 0.181 0.188-0.588-0.621-0.369
```

```
C CHAPTER 18 - ANALYTICAL ROTATIONS                                        001
C     18.5 SUCCESSIVE FACTOR GENERAL VARIMAX                               002
C                                                                          003
      DIMENSION A(200,10), B(200,10), H(20,10), S(10,10), C(200),          004
     1V(500), KV(20), BS(20), W(20) , U(20)                                005
      READ INPUT TAPE 5, 902, P, N, M, NL                                  006
      DO 106  J=1,M                                                        007
  106 READ INPUT TAPE 5, 901, (A(I,J), I=1,N)                              008
      FN = N
C ROW NORMALIZATION
      DO 115  I=1,N                                                        010
      C(I) = 0.                                                            011
      DO 115  J=1,M                                                        012
  115 C(I) = C(I) + A(I,J)**2                                              013
      DO 117  I=1,N                                                        014
  117 C(I) = 1./SQRTF(C(I))                                                015
      DO 120  I=1,N                                                        016
      DO 120  J=1,M                                                        017
  120 A(I,J) = C(I) * A(I,J)                                               018
      M1 = 5                                                               020
      M2 = 2                                                               021
      FM1 = M1                                                             022
      FM2 = M2                                                             023
      F = (2.*FM1) / (2.*FM2-1.)                                           024
      F1 = F - 1.                                                          025
      F2 = 2. * F - 1.                                                     026
C 1.
      DO 314  J=1,M                                                        030
      W(J) = 0.                                                            031
      DO 314  I=1,N                                                        032
  314 W(J) = W(J) + A(I,J)                                                 033
      FN = N                                                               034
      AL = 0.                                                              035
      DO 318  J=1,M                                                        036
  318 AL = AL + W(J)**2                                                    037
      AL = 1./SQRTF(AL)                                                    038
      DO 321  J=1,M                                                        039
  321 W(J) = W(J) * AL                                                     040
C 2.
      DO 325  I=1,N                                                        044
      V(I) = 0.                                                            045
      DO 325  J=1,M                                                        046
  325 V(I) = V(I) + A(I,J) * W(J)                                          047
C 3.
      DO 367  L=1,M                                                        051
      LA = 1                                                               052
      DO 331  I=2,N                                                        053
      IF (V(LA)-V(I)) 331, 331, 330                                        054
  330 LA = I                                                               055
  331 CONTINUE                                                             056
C 4.
      DO 333  J=1,M                                                        060
  333 H(J,L) = A(LA,J)                                                     061
      E = 0.                                                               062
      DO 362  K=1,NL                                                       063
      KV(L) = K                                                            064
C 5.
      DO 340  I=1,N                                                        068
      B(I,L) = 0.                                                          069
      DO 340  J=1,M                                                        070
  340 B(I,L) = B(I,L) + A(I,J) * H(J,L)                                    071
      DO 3404  I=1,N                                                       072
      C(I) = (B(I,L) + C(I)) / 2.                                          073
 3404 B(I,L) = C(I)                                                        074
      WRITE OUTPUT TAPE 6, 900, (B(I,L), I=1,N)                            075
      BS(L) = 0.                                                           076
      DO 344  I=1,N                                                        077
  344 BS(L) = BS(L) + EXPF(F*LOGF(B(I,L)))                                 078
      BS(L) = BS(L) / FN                                                   079
```

668

```
          E1 = E                                                       080
          E = AL                                                       081
          IF (P-ABSF(E1/E-1.)) 346, 346, 3621                          082
    346   DO 348  I=1,N                                                083
          SI = SIGNF(1., B(I,L))                                       084
    348   B(I,L) = SI * (EXPF(F2*LOGF(B(I,L)))- (EXPF(F1*LOGF(B(I,L))))*BS  085
         1(L))                                                         086
          WRITE OUTPUT TAPE 6, 900, (B(I,L), I=1,N)                    087
          WRITE OUTPUT TAPE 6, 997                                     088
C 7.
          DO 352  J=1,M                                                092
          U(J) = 0.                                                    093
          DO 352  I=1,N                                                094
    352   U(J) = U(J) + B(I,L) * A(I,J)                                095
C 8.
          AL = 0.                                                      099
          DO 355  J=1,M                                                100
    355   AL = AL + U(J)**2                                            101
          AL = SQRTF(AL)                                               102
C 9.
          DO 358  J=1,M                                                106
    358   H(J,L) = U(J) / AL                                           107
    362   CONTINUE                                                     108
C 16.
   3621   DO 3622  I=1,N                                               112
   3622   B(I,L) = C(I)                                                113
          DO 365  I=1,N                                                114
          DO 365  J=1,M                                                115
    365   A(I,J) = A(I,J) - B(I,L) * H(J,L)                            116
          DO 3654  I=1,N                                               117
          U(I) = 0.                                                    118
          DO 3654  J=1,M                                               119
   3654   U(I) = U(I) + A(I,J) * H(J,L)                                120
          WRITE OUTPUT TAPE 6, 900, (U(I), I=1,N)                      121
          WRITE OUTPUT TAPE 6, 997                                     122
C 17.
          DO 367  I=1,N                                                126
    367   V(I) = V(I) + B(I,L)                                         127
          WRITE OUTPUT TAPE 6, 903, (KV(L), L=1,M)                     128
          WRITE OUTPUT TAPE 6, 997                                     129
          WRITE OUTPUT TAPE 6, 900, (BS(L), L=1,M)                     130
          WRITE OUTPUT TAPE 6, 998                                     131
          DO 373  I=1,M                                                132
    373   WRITE OUTPUT TAPE 6, 900, (H(I,J), J=1,M)                    133
          WRITE OUTPUT TAPE 6, 997                                     134
          CALL SINCHA (A,B, V, C, N, M, NL, P)
    900   FORMAT (10F7.3)                                              136
    901   FORMAT (10F6.3)                                              137
    902   FORMAT (F7.5/(I4))                                           138
    903   FORMAT (10I7)                                                139
    905   FORMAT (I7)                                                  140
    997   FORMAT (1H )                                                 141
    998   FORMAT (1H0)                                                 142
          CALL EXIT                                                    143
          END                                                          144
C
          SUBROUTINE SINCHA (A, B, W, V, N, M, NL, P)
          DIMENSION A(200,1), B(200,1), W(1), V(1)
          DO 6  I=1,M
          DO 4  J=I,M
          A(I,J) = 0.
          DO 2  K=1,N
    2     A(I,J) = A(I,J) + B(K,I) * B(K,J)
    4     A(J,I) = A(I,J)
    6     V(I) = 1.
          E = 0.
          DO 14  L=1,NL
          DO 8  I=1,M
          W(I) = 0.
          DO 8  J=1,M
    8     W(I) = W(I) + A(I,J) * V(J)
          AL = 0.
          DO 10  I=1,M
    10    AL = AL + W(I) * V(I)
          AL = SQRTF(AL)
          E1 = E
          E = AL
          IF (P - ABSF(E1/E-1.)) 12, 12, 15
    12    DO 13  I=1,M
    13    V(I) = W(I)/AL
    14    CONTINUE
    15    DO 16  I=1,N
```

```
          W(I) = 0.
          DO 16  J=1,M
 16       W(I) = W(I) + B(I,J) * V(J)
          DO 18  I=1,N
          DO 18  J=1,M
          S = SIGNF(1., W(I)) * SIGNF(1., V(J))
 18       B(I,J) = B(I,J) * S
          DO 20  I=1,N
 20       WRITE OUTPUT TAPE 6, 22, (B(I,J), J=1,M)
 22       FORMAT (12F7.3)
          RETURN
          END
C
*         DATA
 .00010
    9
    3
   40
 0.717 0.740 0.773 0.556 0.463 0.518 0.640 0.615 0.715
 0.493 0.478 0.296-0.649-0.744-0.694 0.080 0.166-0.034
 0.350 0.322 0.406 0.068 0.181 0.188-0.588-0.621-0.369
```

```
C CHAPTER 18 - ANALYTICAL ROTATIONS                                      001
C     18.6 SIMULTANEOUS FACTOR GENERAL VARIMAX                           002
C                                                                        003
      DIMENSION A(200,10), B(200,10), H(20,10), S(10,10), C(200),        004
     1V(500), KV(20), BS(20), W(20) , U(20)                              005
      READ INPUT TAPE 5, 902, P, N, M, NL                                006
      DO 106  J=1,M                                                      007
 106  READ INPUT TAPE 5, 901, (A(I,J), I=1,N)                            008
      FN = N
C ROW NORMALIZATION                                                      009
      DO 115  I=1,N                                                      010
      C(I) = 0.                                                          011
      DO 115  J=1,M                                                      012
 115  C(I) = C(I) + A(I,J)**2                                            013
      DO 117  I=1,N                                                      014
 117  C(I) = 1./SQRTF(C(I))                                              015
      DO 120  I=1,N                                                      016
      DO 120  J=1,M                                                      017
 120  A(I,J) = C(I) * A(I,J)                                             018
      M1 = 5                                                             020
      M2 = 2                                                             021
      FM1 = M1                                                           022
      FM2 = M2                                                           023
      F = (2.*FM1) / (2.*FM2-1.)                                         024
      F1 = F - 1.                                                        025
      F2 = 2. * F - 1.                                                   026
      DO 406  I=1,N                                                      019
      DO 406  J=1,M                                                      020
 406  B(I,J) = A(I,J)                                                    021
      E = 0.                                                             022
      DO 458  L=1,NL                                                     023
      LF = L                                                             024
      DO 413  J=1,M                                                      025
      BS(J) = 0.                                                         026
      DO 413  I=1,N                                                      027
 413  BS(J) = BS(J) + EXPF(F*LOGF(B(I,J)))                              028
      DO 415  J=1,M                                                      029
 415  BS(J) = BS(J) / FN                                                 030
      DO 419  I=1,N                                                      031
      DO 419  J=1,N                                                      032
      SI = SIGNF(1.,B(I,J))                                              033
 419  B(I,J) = SI * (EXPF(F2 * LOGF(B(I,J))) -                          034
     1(EXPF(F1 * LOGF(B(I,J)))) * BS(J))                                 035
C 2.
      DO 424  I=1,M                                                      039
      DO 424  J=1,M                                                      040
      S(I,J) = 0.                                                        041
      DO 424  K=1,N                                                      042
 424  S(I,J) = S(I,J) + A(K,I) * B(K,J)                                 043
C 3.
      DO 429  I=1,M                                                      047
      DO 429  J=1,M                                                      048
      H(I,J) = 0.                                                        049
      DO 429  K=1,M                                                      050
 429  H(I,J) = H(I,J) + S(K,I) * S(K,J)                                 051
      CALL JACSIM (H, W, P, M, NL)                                       052
      G = 0.                                                             053
```

670

```
         DO 433  J=1,M                                        054
  433    G = G + W(J)                                         055
C 4.
         DO 435  J=1,M                                        059
  435    W(J) = 1./SQRTF(W(J))                                060
         DO 442  I=1,M                                        061
         IM = I + M                                           062
         DO 442  J=1,M                                        063
         JM = J + M                                           064
         H(I,J) = 0.                                          065
         DO 442  K=1,M                                        066
  442    H(I,J) = H(I,J) + H(IM,K) * W(K) * H(JM,K)           067
         DO 448  I=1,M                                        068
         IM = I + M                                           069
         DO 448  J=1,M                                        070
         H(IM,J) = 0.                                         071
         DO 448  K=1,M                                        072
  448    H(IM,J) = H(IM,J) + S(I,K) * H(K,J)                  073
C 5.
         DO 454  I=1,N                                        077
         DO 454  J=1,M                                        078
         B(I,J) = 0.                                          079
         DO 454  K=1,M                                        080
         KM = K + M                                           081
  454    B(I,J) = B(I,J) + A(I,K) * H(KM,J)                   082
         DO 4542  J=1,M                                       083
 4542    WRITE OUTPUT TAPE 6, 900, (B(I,J), I=1,N)            084
         WRITE OUTPUT TAPE 6, 997                             085
         E1 = E                                               086
         E = G                                                087
         IF ((ABSF(E1/E-1.))-P) 459, 459, 458                 088
  458    CONTINUE                                             089
  459    WRITE OUTPUT TAPE 6, 903, LF                         090
         WRITE OUTPUT TAPE 6, 997                             091
         WRITE OUTPUT TAPE 6, 900, (W(J), J=1,M)              092
         WRITE OUTPUT TAPE 6, 997                             093
         DO 465  I=1,M                                        094
         IM = I + M                                           095
  465    WRITE OUTPUT TAPE 6, 900, (H(IM,J), J=1,M)           096
         WRITE OUTPUT TAPE 6, 997                             097
         CALL SINCHA (A,B, V, C, N, M, NL, P)
  900    FORMAT (10F7.3)                                      099
  901    FORMAT (10F6.3)                                      100
  902    FORMAT (F7.5/(I4))                                   101
  903    FORMAT (10I7)                                        102
  905    FORMAT (I7)
  997    FORMAT (1H )                                         104
  998    FORMAT (1H0)                                         103
         CALL EXIT                                            105
         END                                                 106
C
         SUBROUTINE JACSIM (R, D, P, N, NL)
         DIMENSION R(20,10), D(20)
  06     N1 = N+1
  061    N11=N-1
  07     N2 = N*2
  08     DO 10  I=N1, N2
  09     DO 10  J = 1,N
  10     R(I,J) = 0.
  11     DO 12  I=1,N
  111    NI = N + I
  12     R(NI,I) = 1.
  13     DO 35 L=1,NL
  14     DO 15  I=1,N
  15     D(I) = R(I,I)
  17     DO 282 I = 1,N11
  16     I1 = I+1
  18     DO 282 J= I1,N
  19     DR = R(I,I) - R(J,J)
  20     A = SQRTF(DR**2 + 4.*R(I,J)**2)
  21     A = SQRTF((A+DR)/(2.*A))
  22     B = SQRTF(1.-A**2)
  221    C = SIGNF(1.,R(I,J))
  23     DO 252 K = 1,N2
  241    U = R(K,I)*A*C + R(K,J)*B
  25     R(K,J) = -R(K,I)*B*C + R(K,J)*A
  252    R(K,I) = U
  26     DO 282 K = 1,N
  271    U = R(I,K)*A*C + R(J,K)*B
  28     R(J,K) = -R(I,K)*B*C + R(J,K)*A
  282    R(I,K) = U
  29     DO 30  I=1,N
```

```
30    D(I) = ABSF(D(I) - R(I,I))
31    S = 0.
32    DO 33  I=1,N
33    S = MAX1F (S, D(I))
331   DO 332 I =1,N
332   D(I) = R(I,I)
34    IF (S-P) 38, 38, 35
35    CONTINUE
38    RETURN
      END
C
      SUBROUTINE SINCHA (A, B, W, V, N, M, NL, P)
      DIMENSION A(200,1), B(200,1), W(1), V(1)
      DO 6  I=1,M
      DO 4  J=I,M
      A(I,J) = 0.
      DO 2  K=1,N
2     A(I,J) = A(I,J) + B(K,I) * B(K,J)
4     A(J,I) = A(I,J)
6     V(I) = 1.
      E = 0.
      DO 14 L=1,NL
      DO 8  I=1,M
      W(I) = 0.
      DO 8  J=1,M
8     W(I) = W(I) + A(I,J) * V(J)
      AL = 0.
      DO 10 I=1,M
10    AL = AL + W(I) * V(I)
      AL = SQRTF(AL)
      E1 = E
      E = AL
      IF (P - ABSF(E1/E-1.)) 12, 12, 15
12    DO 13 I=1,M
13    V(I) = W(I)/AL
14    CONTINUE
15    DO 16 I=1,N
      W(I) = 0.
      DO 16 J=1,M
16    W(I) = W(I) + B(I,J) * V(J)
      DO 18 I=1,N
      DO 18 J=1,M
      S = SIGNF(1., W(I)) * SIGNF(1., V(J))
18    B(I,J) = B(I,J) * S
      DO 20 I=1,N
20    WRITE OUTPUT TAPE 6, 22, (B(I,J), J=1,M)
22    FORMAT (12F7.3)
      RETURN
      END
C
*     DATA
.00010
   9
   3
  40
0.717 0.740 0.773 0.556 0.463 0.518 0.640 0.615 0.715
0.493 0.478 0.296-0.649-0.744-0.694 0.080 0.166-0.034
0.350 0.322 0.406 0.068 0.181 0.188-0.588-0.621-0.369
```

```
C CHAPTER 19 - DIRECT VARIMAX SOLUTIONS                                 001
C    19.3 SUCCESSIVE VARIMAX FACTOR FROM CORRELATION MATRIX             002
C                                                                       003
      DIMENSION R(100,100), A(100,15), B(100,15), C(30,15), V(100),     004
     1U(100), W(100), BS(15), KV(15), Y(100), JV(15)                    005
      REWIND 2                                                          006
      REWIND 3                                                          007
      READ INPUT TAPE 5, 902, P, PV, NI, NJ, NK, IL                     008
      DO 13  I=1,NJ                                                     010
      READ INPUT TAPE 5, 901, (R(I,J), J=1,NJ)                          011
   13 WRITE TAPE 2, (R(I,J), J=1,NJ)                                    012
      REWIND 2                                                          013
      M1 = 5                                                            014
      M2 = 2
      FNI = NI                                                          016
      FNJ = NJ                                                          017
      FM1 = M1                                                          018
      FM2 = M2                                                          019
      F = (2.*FM1) / (2.*FM2-1.)                                        020
      F1 = F - 1.                                                       021
      F2 = 2. * F - 1.                                                  022
      FNJ1 = FNJ - 1.                                                   023
      DO 162  NS =1,2                                                   024
      G = 0.                                                            025
      DO 106  I=1,NJ
  106 READ TAPE 2, (R(I,J), J=1,NJ)
      REWIND 2
      DO 151  L=1,NK                                                    026
      LF = L                                                            027
      DO 116  I=1,NJ                                                    028
      U(I) = -R(I,I)                                                    029
      V(I) = -R(I,I)**2                                                 030
      DO 113  J=1,NJ                                                    031
      U(I) = U(I) + R(I,J)                                              032
  113 V(I) = V(I) + R(I,J)**2                                           033
      U(I) = U(I) / FNJ1                                                034
      V(I) = V(I) / FNJ1                                                035
  116 V(I) = V(I) - U(I)**2                                             036
C 10.
      LV = 1                                                            042
      DO 121  I=2,NJ                                                    043
      IF (V(LV)-V(I)) 120,120,121                                       044
  120 LV = I                                                            045
  121 CONTINUE                                                          046
      DO 123  I=1,NJ                                                    047
      Y(I) = R(I,LV)                                                    048
  123 B(I,L) = R(I,LV)                                                  049
      E = 0.                                                            050
      DO 145  KI=1,IL                                                   051
      KV(L) = KI                                                        052
      CALL VARMOD (B, BS, NJ, L, NS, F, F1, F2, FNJ)                    053
C 4.
      DO 136  I=1,NJ                                                    057
      W(I) = 0.                                                         058
      DO 136  J=1,NJ                                                    059
  136 W(I) = W(I) + R(I,J) * B(J,L)                                     060
C 5.
      AL = 0.                                                           064
      DO 138  I=1,NJ                                                    065
  138 AL = AL + W(I) * B(I,L)                                           066
      AL = SQRTF(AL)                                                    067
C 6.
      DO 141  I=1,NJ                                                    071
  141 B(I,L) = (W(I)/AL+Y(I)) / 2.                                      072
      DO 1412  I=1,NJ                                                   073
 1412 Y(I) = B(I,L)                                                     074
      E1 = E                                                            075
      E = AL                                                            076
      IF ((ABSF(E1/E-1.))-P) 146, 146, 145                             077
  145 CONTINUE                                                          078
  146 G = G + BS(L)                                                     079
      IF (G-PV*FNJ) 148, 148, 152                                       080
  148 DO 150  I=1,NJ                                                    081
      DO 150  J=1,NJ                                                    082
  150 R(I,J) = R(I,J) - B(I,L) * B(J,L)                                 083
  151 CONTINUE                                                          084
  152 WRITE OUTPUT TAPE 6, 903, (KV(L), L=1,LF)                         085
      WRITE OUTPUT TAPE 6, 997                                          086
      WRITE OUTPUT TAPE 6, 900, (BS(L), L=1,LF)                         087
      WRITE OUTPUT TAPE 6, 997                                          088
      CALL SINCHA (A, B, W, V, NJ, NK, IL, P)
      WRITE OUTPUT TAPE 6, 998                                         090
  162 CONTINUE                                                         091
```

```
900   FORMAT (10F7.3)                                                092
901   FORMAT (10F6.3)                                                093
902   FORMAT (F7.5/F4.2/(I4))                                        094
903   FORMAT (10I7)                                                  095
905   FORMAT (I7)                                                    096
997   FORMAT (1H )                                                   097
998   FORMAT (1H0)                                                   098
      CALL EXIT                                                      099
      END                                                            100
C
      SUBROUTINE VARMOD (B, BS, NJ, L, NS, F, F1, F2, FNJ)           001
      DIMENSION B(100,15), BS(15)                                    002
      IF (NS-2) 1, 2, 2                                              003
1     CALL SQUARE (B, BS, NJ, L, FNJ)                                004
      GO TO 4                                                        005
2     CALL GENERA (B, BS, NJ, L, F, F1, F2, FNJ)                     006
4     RETURN                                                         007
      END                                                            008
C
      SUBROUTINE SQUARE (B, BS, NJ, L, FNJ)
      DIMENSION B(100,15), BS(15)
      BS(L) = 0.
      DO 04  I=1,NJ
04    BS(L) = BS(L) + B(I,L)**2
      BS(L) = BS(L)/FNJ
      DO 07  I=1,NJ
07    B(I,L) = B(I,L)**3 - B(I,L) * BS(L)
      RETURN
      END
C
      SUBROUTINE GENERA (B, BS, NJ, L, F, F1, F2, FNJ)               001
      DIMENSION B(100,15), BS(15)                                    002
      BS(L)=0.                                                       003
      DO 04 I =1,NJ                                                  004
04    BS(L) = BS(L) + EXPF(F*LOGF(B(I,L)))                           005
      BS(L) = BS(L)/FNJ                                              006
      DO 07 I =1,NJ                                                  007
07    B(I,L) = SIGNF(1.,B(I,L)) * (EXPF(F2*LOGF(B(I,L)))             008
     1-(EXPF(F1*LOGF(B(I,L))))*BS(L))                                009
      RETURN                                                         010
      END                                                            011
C
      SUBROUTINE SINCHA (A, B, W, V, N, M, NL, P)
      DIMENSION A(100,1), B(100,1), W(1), V(1)
      DO 6  I=1,M
      DO 4  J=I,M
      A(I,J) = 0.
      DO 2  K=1,N
2     A(I,J) = A(I,J) + B(K,I) * B(K,J)
4     A(J,I) = A(I,J)
6     V(I) = 1.
      E = 0.
      DO 14  L=1,NL
      DO 8  I=1,M
      W(I) = 0.
      DO 8  J=1,M
8     W(I) = W(I) + A(I,J) * V(J)
      AL = 0.
      DO 10  I=1,M
10    AL = AL + W(I) * V(I)
      AL = SQRTF(AL)
      E1 = E
      E = AL
      IF (P - ABSF(E1/E-1.)) 12, 12, 15
12    DO 13  I=1,M
13    V(I) = W(I)/AL
14    CONTINUE
15    DO 16  I=1,N
      W(I) = 0.
      DO 16  J=1,M
16    W(I) = W(I) + B(I,J) * V(J)
      DO 18  I=1,N
      DO 18  J=1,M
      S = SIGNF(1., W(I)) * SIGNF(1., V(J))
18    B(I,J) = B(I,J) * S
      DO 20  I=1,N
20    WRITE OUTPUT TAPE 6, 22, (B(I,J), J=1,M)
22    FORMAT (12F7.3)
      RETURN
      END
C
*     DATA
 .00010
 .75
 12
```

674

```
   9
   3
  40
1.000   .829   .768   .108   .033   .108   .298   .309   .351
 .829  1.000   .775   .115   .061   .125   .323   .347   .369
 .768   .775  1.000   .272   .205   .238   .296   .271   .385
 .108   .115   .272  1.000   .636   .626   .249   .183   .369
 .033   .061   .205   .636  1.000   .709   .138   .091   .254
 .108   .125   .238   .626   .709  1.000   .190   .103   .291
 .298   .323   .296   .249   .138   .190  1.000   .654   .527
 .309   .347   .271   .183   .091   .103   .654  1.000   .541
 .351   .369   .385   .369   .254   .291   .527   .541  1.000
C CHAPTER 19 - DIRECT VARIMAX SOLUTIONS
C    19.4 SIMULTANEOUS VARIMAX FACTOR FROM CORRELATION MATRIX
C
      DIMENSION R(100,100), A(100,15), B(100,15), C(30,15), V(100),
     1U(100), W(100), BS(15), KV(15), Y(100), JV(15)
      REWIND 2
      REWIND 3
      READ INPUT TAPE 5, 902, P, PV, NI, NJ, NK, IL
      DO 13  I=1,NJ
      READ INPUT TAPE 5, 901, (R(I,J), J=1,NJ)
 13   WRITE TAPE 2, (R(I,J), J=1,NJ)
      REWIND 2
      READ INPUT TAPE 5, 903, (JV(J), J=1,NK)
      M1 = 5
      M2 = 2
      FNI = NI
      FNJ = NJ
      FM1 = M1
      FM2 = M2
      F = (2.*FM1) / (2.*FM2-1.)
      F1 = F - 1.
      F2 = 2. * F - 1.
      FNJ1 = FNJ - 1.
      DO 261  NS=1,2
      DO 206  I=1,NJ
 206  READ TAPE 2, (R(I,J), J=1,NJ)
      REWIND 2
      DO 207  J=1,NK
      JJ = JV(J)
      DO 207  I=1,NJ
 207  B(I,J) = R(I,JJ)
      E = 0.
      DO 250  KI=1,IL
C 1.
      KIL = KI
      DO 8042  L=1,NK
      CALL VARMOD (B, BS, NJ, L, NS, F, F1, F2, FNJ)
 8042 CONTINUE
C 2.
      DO 223  I=1,NJ
      DO 223  J=1,NK
      A(I,J) = 0.
      DO 223  K=1,NJ
 223  A(I,J) = A(I,J) + R(I,K) * B(K,J)
C 3.
      DO 228  I=1,NK
      DO 228  J=1,NK
      C(I,J) = 0.
      DO 228  K=1,NJ
 228  C(I,J) = C(I,J) + B(K,I) * A(K,J)
C 4.
      CALL JACSIM (C, W, P, NK, IL)
C 5.
      DO 231  I=1,NK
 231  W(I) = SQRTF(W(I))
      G = 0.
      DO 234  I=1,NK
 234  G = G + W(I)
      DO 241  I=1,NK
      INK = I + NK
      DO 241  J=1,NK
      JNK = J + NK
      C(I,J) = 0.
      DO 241  K=1,NK
 241  C(I,J) = C(I,J) + C(INK,K) * C(JNK,K) / W(K)
      DO 246  I=1,NJ
      DO 246  J=1,NK
      B(I,J) = 0.
      DO 246  K=1,NK
 246  B(I,J) = B(I,J) + A(I,K) * C(K,J)
```

675

```
      EI = E                                                              079
      E = G                                                               080
      IF ((ABSF(EI/E-1.))-P) 251, 251, 250                                081
250   CONTINUE                                                            082
251   WRITE OUTPUT TAPE 6, 903, KIL                                       083
      WRITE OUTPUT TAPE 6, 997                                            084
      WRITE OUTPUT TAPE 6, 900, (BS(L), L=1,NK)                           085
      WRITE OUTPUT TAPE 6, 998                                            086
      CALL SINCHA (A, B, W, V, NJ, NK, IL, P)
      WRITE OUTPUT TAPE 6, 998                                            088
261   CONTINUE                                                            089
900   FORMAT (10F7.3)                                                     090
901   FORMAT (10F6.3)                                                     091
902   FORMAT (F7.5/F4.2/(I4))                                             092
903   FORMAT (10I7)                                                       093
905   FORMAT (I7)                                                         094
997   FORMAT (1H )                                                        095
998   FORMAT (1H0)                                                        096
      CALL EXIT                                                           097
      END                                                                 098
C
      SUBROUTINE VARMOD (B, BS, NJ, L, NS, F, F1, F2, FNJ)
      DIMENSION B(100,15), BS(15)
      IF (NS-2) 1, 2, 2
1     CALL SQUARE (B, BS, NJ, L, FNJ)
      GO TO 4
2     CALL GENERA (B, BS, NJ, L, F, F1, F2, FNJ)
4     RETURN
      END
C
      SUBROUTINE SQUARE (B, BS, NJ, L, FNJ)
01    DIMENSION B(100,15), BS(15)
02    BS(L)=0.
03    DO 04 I =1,NJ
04    BS(L) = BS(L) + B(I,L)**2
05    BS(L) = BS(L)/FNJ
06    DO 07 I =1,NJ
07    B(I,L) = B(I,L)**3 - B(I,L) * BS(L)
      RETURN
      END
C
      SUBROUTINE GENERA (B, BS, NJ, L, F, F1, F2, FNJ)
01    DIMENSION B(100,15), BS(15)
02    BS(L)=0.
03    DO 04 I =1,NJ
04    BS(L) = BS(L) + EXPF(F*LOGF(B(I,L)))
05    BS(L) = BS(L)/FNJ
06    DO 07 I =1,NJ
07    B(I,L) = SIGNF(1.,B(I,L)) * (EXPF(F2*LOGF(B(I,L)))
     1-(EXPF(F1*LOGF(B(I,L))))*BS(L))
      RETURN
      END
C
      SUBROUTINE JACSIM (R, D, P, N, NL)
01    DIMENSION R(30,15), D(100)
06    N1 = N+1
061   N11=N-1
07    N2 = N*2
08    DO 10  I=N1, N2
09    DO 10  J = 1,N
10    R(I,J) = 0.
11    DO 12  I=1,N
111   NI = N + I
12    R(NI,I) = 1.
13    DO 35 L=1,NL
14    DO 15  I=1,N
15    D(I) = R(I,I)
17    DO 282 I = 1,N11
16    I1 = I+1
18    DO 282 J= I1,N
19    DR = R(I,I) - R(J,J)
20    A = SQRTF(DR**2 + 4.*R(I,J)**2)
21    A = SQRTF((A+DR)/(2.*A))
22    B = SQRTF(1.-A**2)
221   C = SIGNF(1.,R(I,J))
23    DO 252 K = 1,N2
241   U = R(K,I)*A*C + R(K,J)*B
25    R(K,J) = -R(K,I)*B*C + R(K,J)*A
252   R(K,I) = U
26    DO 282 K = 1,N
271   U = R(I,K)*A*C + R(J,K)*B
28    R(J,K) = -R(I,K)*B*C + R(J,K)*A
282   R(I,K) = U
29    DO 30  I=1,N
```

676

```
30    D(I) = ABSF(D(I) - R(I,1))
31    S = 0.
32    DO 33  I=1,N
33    S = MAX1F (S, D(I))
331   DO 332 I =1,N
332   D(I) = R(I,I)
34    IF (S-P) 38, 38, 35
35    CONTINUE
38    RETURN
      END
C
      SUBROUTINE SINCHA (A, B, W, V, N, M, NL, P)
      DIMENSION A(100,1), B(100,1), W(1), V(1)
      DO 6  I=1,M
      DO 4  J=I,M
      A(I,J) = 0.
      DO 2  K=1,N
2     A(I,J) = A(I,J) + B(K,I) * B(K,J)
4     A(J,I) = A(I,J)
6     V(I) = 1.
      E = 0.
      DO 14  L=1,NL
      DO 8  I=1,M
      W(I) = 0.
      DO 8  J=1,M
8     W(I) = W(I) + A(I,J) * V(J)
      AL = 0.
      DO 10  I=1,M
10    AL = AL + W(I) * V(I)
      AL = SQRTF(AL)
      E1 = E
      E = AL
      IF (P - ABSF(E1/E-1.)) 12, 12, 15
12    DO 13  I=1,M
13    V(I) = W(I)/AL
14    CONTINUE
15    DO 16  I=1,N
      W(I) = 0.
      DO 16  J=1,M
16    W(I) = W(I) + B(I,J) * V(J)
      DO 18  I=1,N
      DO 18  J=1,M
      S = SIGNF(1., W(I)) * SIGNF(1., V(J))
18    B(I,J) = B(I,J) * S
      DO 20  I=1,N
20    WRITE OUTPUT TAPE 6, 22, (B(I,J), J=1,M)
22    FORMAT (12F7.3)
      RETURN
      END
C
*     DATA
 .00010
 .75
  12
   9
   3
  40
1.000  .829  .768  .108  .033  .108  .298  .309  .351
 .829 1.000  .775  .115  .061  .125  .323  .347  .369
 .768  .775 1.000  .272  .205  .238  .296  .271  .385
 .108  .115  .272 1.000  .636  .626  .249  .183  .369
 .033  .061  .205  .636 1.000  .709  .138  .091  .254
 .108  .125  .238  .626  .709 1.000  .190  .103  .291
 .298  .323  .296  .249  .138  .190 1.000  .654  .527
 .309  .347  .271  .183  .091  .103  .654 1.000  .541
 .351  .369  .385  .369  .254  .291  .527  .541 1.000
        1        4        7
```

```
C CHAPTER 19 - DIRECT VARIMAX SOLUTIONS                                    001
C    19.5 SUCCESSIVE FACTOR VECTOR FROM DATA MATRIX                        002
C                                                                          003
      DIMENSION R(100,100), A(100,15), B(100,15), C(30,15), V(100),       004
     1U(100), W(100), BS(15), KV(15), Y(100), JV(15)                      005
      REWIND 2                                                            006
      REWIND 3                                                            007
      READ INPUT TAPE 5, 902, P, PV, NI, NJ, NK, IL                       008
      DO 18  I=1,NI                                                       010
      READ INPUT TAPE 5, 900, (R(I,J), J=1,NJ)                            011
      WRITE OUTPUT TAPE 6, 900, (R(I,J), J=1,NJ)                          012
18    WRITE TAPE 3, (R(I,J), J=1,NJ)                                      013
      REWIND 3                                                            014
      M1 = 5                                                              015
      M2 = 2
      FNI = NI                                                            017
      FNJ = NJ                                                            018
      FM1 = M1                                                            019
      FM2 = M2                                                            020
      F = (2.*FM1) / (2.*FM2-1.)                                          021
```

677

```
        F1 = F - 1.                                          022
        F2 = 2. * F - 1.                                     023
        FNJ1 = FNJ - 1.                                      024
        DO 314  J=1,NJ                                       025
        U(J) = 0.                                            026
        V(J) = 0.                                            027
        DO 312  I=1,NI                                       028
        U(J) = U(J) + R(I,J)                                 029
        V(J) = V(J) + R(I,J)**2                              030
        U(J) = U(J) / FNI                                    031
        V(J) = V(J) / FNI                                    032
312     V(J) = SQRTF((V(J)-U(J)**2) * FNI)                   033
        DO 314  I=1,N                                        034
314     R(I,J) = (R(I,J) - U(J)) / V(J)                      035
        DO 316  I=1,NI                                       036
316     WRITE TAPE 3, (R(I,J), J=1,NJ)                       037
        REWIND 3                                             038
        DO 369  NS=1,2                                       039
        DO 320  I=1,NI                                       040
320     READ TAPE 3, (R(I,J), J=1,NJ)                        041
        REWIND 3                                             042
        G = 0.                                               043
        DO 359  L=1,NK                                       044
        LF = L                                               045
C 2.
        DO 328  J=1,NJ                                       049
        B(J,L) = 0.                                          050
        DO 328  I=1,NI                                       051
328     B(J,L) = B(J,L) + R(I,J) * R(I,L)                    052
        DO 3282  J=1,NJ                                      053
3282    Y(J) = B(J,L)                                        054
        E = 0.                                               055
        DO 353  KI=1,IL                                      056
        KV(L) = KI                                           057
        CALL VARMOD (B, BS, NJ, L, NS, F, F1, F2, FNJ)       058
C 5.
        DO 339  I=1,NI                                       062
        U(I) = 0.                                            063
        DO 339  J=1,NJ                                       064
339     U(I) = U(I) + R(I,J) * B(J,L)                        065
C 6.
        AL = 0.                                              069
        DO 342  I=1,NI                                       070
342     AL = AL + U(I)**2                                    071
        AL = SQRTF(AL)                                       072
        DO 345  I=1,NI                                       073
345     U(I) = U(I) / AL                                     074
C 7.
        DO 349  J=1,NJ                                       078
        B(J,L) = 0.                                          079
        DO 349  I=1,NI                                       080
349     B(J,L) = B(J,L) + R(I,J) * U(I)                      081
        DO 3493  J=1,NJ                                      082
        B(J,L) = (B(J,L)+Y(J)) / 2.                          083
3493    Y(J) = B(J,L)                                        084
        E1 = E                                               085
        E = AL                                               086
        IF ((ABSF(E1/E-1.))-P) 354, 354, 353                087
353     CONTINUE                                             088
354     G = G + BS(L)                                        089
        IF (G-PV*FNJ) 356, 356, 360                          090
356     DO 358  I=1,NI                                       091
        DO 358  J=1,NJ                                       092
358     R(I,J) = R(I,J) - U(I) * B(J,L)                      093
359     CONTINUE                                             094
360     WRITE OUTPUT TAPE 6, 903, (KV(L), L=1,LF)            095
        WRITE OUTPUT TAPE 6, 997                             096
        WRITE OUTPUT TAPE 6, 900, (BS(L), L=1,LF)            097
        WRITE OUTPUT TAPE 6, 998                             098
        CALL SINCHA (A, B, W, V, NJ, NK, IL, P)
        WRITE OUTPUT TAPE 6, 998                             100
369     CONTINUE                                             101
900     FORMAT (10F7.3)                                      102
902     FORMAT (F7.5/F4.2/(I4))                              103
903     FORMAT (10I7)                                        104
905     FORMAT (I7)                                          105
997     FORMAT (1H )                                         106
998     FORMAT (1H0)                                         107
        CALL EXIT                                            108
        END                                                  109
C
        SUBROUTINE VARMOD (B, BS, NJ, L, NS, F, F1, F2, FNJ)
        DIMENSION B(100,15), BS(15)
```

```
        IF (NS-2) 1, 2, 2
1       CALL SQUARE (B, BS, NJ, L, FNJ)
        GO TO 4
2       CALL GENERA (B, BS, NJ, L, F, F1, F2, FNJ)
4       RETURN
        END
C
        SUBROUTINE SQUARE (B, BS, NJ, L, FNJ)
01      DIMENSION B(100,15), BS(15)
02      BS(L)=0.
03      DO 04 I =1,NJ
04      BS(L) = BS(L) + B(I,L)**2
05      BS(L) = BS(L)/FNJ
06      DO 07 I =1,NJ
07      B(I,L) = B(I,L)**3 - B(I,L) * BS(L)
        RETURN
        END
C
        SUBROUTINE GENERA (B, BS, NJ, L, F, F1, F2, FNJ)
01      DIMENSION B(100,15), BS(15)
02      BS(L)=0.
03      DO 04 I =1,NJ
04      BS(L) = BS(L) + EXPF(F*LOGF(B(I,L)))
05      BS(L) = BS(L)/FNJ
06      DO 07 I =1,NJ
07      B(I,L) = SIGNF(1.,B(I,L)) * (EXPF(F2*LOGF(B(I,L)))
       1-(EXPF(F1*LOGF(B(I,L))))*BS(L))
        RETURN
        END
C
        SUBROUTINE SINCHA (A, B, W, V, N, M, NL, P)
        DIMENSION A(100,1), B(100,1), W(1), V(1)
        DO 6   I=1,M
        DO 4   J=I,M
        A(I,J) = 0.
        DO 2   K=1,N
2       A(I,J) = A(I,J) + B(K,I) * B(K,J)
4       A(J,I) = A(I,J)
6       V(I) = 1.
        E = 0.
        DO 14   L=1,NL
        DO 8   I=1,M
        W(I) = 0.
        DO 8   J=1,M
8       W(I) = W(I) + A(I,J) * V(J)
        AL = 0.
        DO 10   I=1,M
10      AL = AL + W(I) * V(I)
        AL = SQRTF(AL)
        E1 = E
        E = AL
        IF (P - ABSF(E1/E-1.)) 12, 12, 15
12      DO 13   I=1,M
13      V(I) = W(I)/AL
14      CONTINUE
15      DO 16   I=1,N
        W(I) = 0.
        DO 16   J=1,M
16      W(I) = W(I) + B(I,J) * V(J)
        DO 18   I=1,N
        DO 18   J=1,M
        S = SIGNF(1., W(I)) * SIGNF(1., V(J))
18      B(I,J) = B(I,J) * S
        DO 20   I=1,N
20      WRITE OUTPUT TAPE 6, 22, (B(I,J), J=1,M)
22      FORMAT (12F7.3)
        RETURN
        END
C
*       DATA
.00010
.75
 12
  9
  3
 40
  0.128   0.181   0.421   0.506   0.857   0.746   0.280   0.178   0.246
  0.764   0.740   0.563 -0.387 -0.293 -0.202   0.261   0.281   0.043
 -0.030 -0.046   0.014   0.147 -0.109 -0.135   0.640   0.682   0.661
 -0.280 -0.351 -0.326 -0.023 -0.109 -0.186   0.083   0.091 -0.654
 -0.336 -0.306 -0.429 -0.542 -0.006 -0.153 -0.428   0.056 -0.124
 -0.276 -0.324 -0.271 -0.370 -0.225   0.035   0.129 -0.446 -0.124
  0.057 -0.070 -0.016   0.006   0.152 -0.441 -0.166 -0.354 -0.033
 -0.010 -0.140   0.326 -0.004 -0.258 -0.091 -0.410 -0.200 -0.101
```

```
 -0.303   0.227 -0.014   0.029 -0.102 -0.125 -0.086 -0.106 -0.074
  0.086   0.057 -0.003   0.161   0.073   0.134 -0.082 -0.067 -0.009
  0.164   0.106 -0.124   0.234 -0.002   0.227 -0.072   0.025   0.156
  0.036 -0.074 -0.142   0.242   0.023   0.192 -0.148 -0.119   0.011
C CHAPTER 19 - DIRECT VARIMAX SOLUTIONS                                   001
C    19.6 SIMULTANEOUS FACTOR MATRIX FROM DATA MATRIX                     002
C                                                                         003
      DIMENSION R(100,100), A(100,15), B(100,15), C(30,15), V(100),       004
     1U(100), W(100), BS(15), KV(15), Y(100), JV(15)                      005
      REWIND 2                                                            006
      REWIND 3                                                            007
      READ INPUT TAPE 5, 902, P, PV, NI, NJ, NK, IL                       008
      DO 18  I=1,NI                                                       010
      READ INPUT TAPE 5, 900, (R(I,J), J=1,NJ)                            011
      WRITE OUTPUT TAPE 6, 900, (R(I,J), J=1,NJ)                          012
   18 WRITE TAPE 3, (R(I,J), J=1,NJ)                                      013
      REWIND 3                                                            014
      READ INPUT TAPE 5, 903, (JV(J), J=1,NK)                             015
      M1 = 5                                                              016
      M2 = 2
      FNI = NI                                                            018
      FNJ = NJ                                                            019
      FM1 = M1                                                            020
      FM2 = M2                                                            021
      F = (2.*FM1) / (2.*FM2-1.)                                          022
      F1 = F - 1.                                                         023
      F2 = 2. * F - 1.                                                    024
      FNJ1 = FNJ - 1.                                                     025
      DO 314  J=1,NJ                                                      026
      U(J) = 0.                                                          027
      V(J) = 0.                                                          028
      DO 312  I=1,NI                                                      029
      U(J) = U(J) + R(I,J)                                               030
      V(J) = V(J) + R(I,J)**2                                            031
      U(J) = U(J) / FNI                                                  032
      V(J) = V(J) / FNI                                                  033
  312 V(J) = SQRTF((V(J)-U(J)**2) * FNI)                                 034
      DO 314  I=1,N                                                      035
  314 R(I,J) = (R(I,J) - U(J)) / V(J)                                    036
C 1.                                                                     040
      DO 471  NS=1,2
      DO 316  I=1,NI
  316 WRITE TAPE 3, (R(I,J), J=1,NJ)
      REWIND 3                                                           041
      DO 408  J=1,NJ                                                     042
      DO 408  K=1,NK                                                     043
      KK = JV(K)                                                         044
      B(J,K) = 0.                                                        045
      DO 408  I=1,NI                                                     046
  408 B(J,K) = B(J,K) + R(I,J) * R(I,KK)                                 047
      E = 0.                                                             048
      DO 460  KI =1,IL                                                   049
      KIL = KI                                                           050
      DO 413  L=1,NK                                                     051
      CALL VARMOD (B, BS, NJ, L, NS, F, F1, F2, FNJ)                     052
  413 CONTINUE                                                           056
C 3.
      DO 425  I=1,NI                                                     057
      DO 425  K=1,NK                                                     058
      A(I,K) = 0.                                                        059
      DO 425  J=1,NJ                                                     060
  425 A(I,K) = A(I,K) + R(I,J) * B(J,K)
C 4.                                                                     064
      DO 430  K1=1,NK                                                    065
      DO 430  K2=1,NK                                                    066
      C(K1,K2) = 0.                                                      067
      DO 430  I=1,NJ                                                     068
  430 C(K1,K2) = C(K1,K2) + A(I,K1) * A(I,K2)
C 5.                                                                     072
      CALL JACSIM (C, W, P, NK, IL)                                      073
      DO 433  K=1,NK                                                     074
  433 W(K) = SQRTF(W(K))                                                 075
      G = 0.                                                             076
      DO 436  K=1,NK                                                     077
  436 G = G + W(K)
C 6.                                                                     081
      DO 443  I=1,NK                                                     082
      INK = I + NK                                                       083
      DO 443  J=1,NK                                                     084
      JNK = J + NK                                                       085
      C(I,J) = 0.                                                        086
      DO 443  K=1,NK                                                     087
  443 C(I,J) = C(I,J) + C(INK,K) * C(JNK,K) / W(K)
```

```
        DO 448   I=1,NI                                          088
        DO 448   J=1,NK                                          089
        B(I,J) = 0.                                             090
        DO 448   K=1,NK                                          091
448     B(I,J) = B(I,J) + A(I,K) * C(K,J)                       092
        DO 451   J=1,NJ                                          093
        DO 451   K=1,NK                                          094
451     A(J,K) = B(J,K)                                         095
C 7.
        DO 456   J=1,NJ                                          099
        DO 456   K=1,NK                                          100
        B(J,K) = 0.                                             101
        DO 456   I=1,NI                                          102
456     B(J,K) = B(J,K) + R(I,J) * A(I,K)                       103
        E1 = E                                                  104
        E = G                                                   105
        IF ((ABSF(E1/E-1.))-P) 461, 461, 460                    106
460     CONTINUE                                                107
461     WRITE OUTPUT TAPE 6, 903, KIL                           108
        WRITE OUTPUT TAPE 6, 997                                109
        WRITE OUTPUT TAPE 6, 900, (BS(L), L=1,NK)               110
        WRITE OUTPUT TAPE 6, 998                                111
        CALL SINCHA (A, B, W, V, NJ, NK, IL, P)
        WRITE OUTPUT TAPE 6, 998                                113
471     CONTINUE                                                114
900     FORMAT (10F7.3)                                         116
902     FORMAT (F7.5/F4.2/(I4))                                 118
903     FORMAT (10I7)                                           119
905     FORMAT (I7)                                             120
997     FORMAT (1H )                                            121
998     FORMAT (1H0)                                            122
        CALL EXIT                                               123
        END                                                     124
C
        SUBROUTINE VARMOD (B, BS, NJ, L, NS, F, F1, F2, FNJ)
        DIMENSION B(100,15), BS(15)
        IF (NS-2) 1, 2, 2
1       CALL SQUARE (B, BS, NJ, L, FNJ)
        GO TO 4
2       CALL GENERA (B, BS, NJ, L, F, F1, F2, FNJ)
4       RETURN
        END
C
        SUBROUTINE SQUARE (B, BS, NJ, L, FNJ)
01      DIMENSION B(100,15), BS(15)
02      BS(L)=0.
03      DO 04 I =1,NJ
04      BS(L) = BS(L) + B(I,L)**2
05      BS(L) = BS(L)/FNJ
06      DO 07 I =1,NJ
07      B(I,L) = B(I,L)**3 - B(I,L) * BS(L)
        RETURN
        END
C
        SUBROUTINE GENERA (B, BS, NJ, L, F, F1, F2, FNJ)
01      DIMENSION B(100,15), BS(15)
02      BS(L)=0.
03      DO 04 I =1,NJ
04      BS(L) = BS(L) + EXPF(F*LOGF(B(I,L)))
05      BS(L) = BS(L)/FNJ
06      DO 07 I =1,NJ
07      B(I,L) = SIGNF(1.,B(I,L)) * (EXPF(F2*LOGF(B(I,L)))
       1-(EXPF(F1*LOGF(B(I,L))))*BS(L))
        RETURN
        END
C
        SUBROUTINE JACSIM (R, J, P, N, NL)
01      DIMENSION R(30,15), D(100)
06      N1 = N+1
061     N11=N-1
07      N2 = N*2
08      DO 10  I=N1, N2
09      DO 10  J = 1,N
10      R(I,J) = 0.
11      DO 12  I=1,N
111     NI = N + I
12      R(NI,I) = 1.
13      DO 35 L=1,NL
14      DO 15  I=1,N
15      D(I) = R(I,I)
17      DO 282 I = 1,N11
16      I1 = I+1
18      DO 282 J= I1,N
```

681

```
19      DR = R(I,I) - R(J,J)
20      A = SQRTF(DR**2 + 4.*R(I,J)**2)
21      A = SQRTF((A+DR)/(2.*A))
22      B = SQRTF(1.-A**2)
221     C = SIGNF(1.,R(I,J))
23      DO 252 K = 1,N2
241     U = R(K,I)*A*C + R(K,J)*B
25      R(K,J) = -R(K,I)*B*C + R(K,J)*A
252     R(K,I) = U
26      DO 282 K = 1,N
271     U = R(I,K)*A*C + R(J,K)*B
28      R(J,K) = -R(I,K)*B*C + R(J,K)*A
282     R(I,K) = U
29      DO 30   I=1,N
30      D(I) = ABSF(D(I) - R(I,I))
31      S = 0.
32      DO 33   I=1,N
33      S = MAX1F (S, D(I))
331     DO 332 I =1,N
332     D(I) = R(I,I)
34      IF (S-P) 38, 38, 35
35      CONTINUE
38      RETURN
        END
C
        SUBROUTINE SINCHA (A, B, W, V, N, M, NL, P)
        DIMENSION A(100,1), B(100,1), W(1), V(1)
        DO 6   I=1,M
        DO 4   J=1,M
        A(I,J) = 0.
        DO 2   K=1,N
2       A(I,J) = A(I,J) + B(K,I) * B(K,J)
4       A(J,I) = A(I,J)
6       V(I) = 1.
        E = 0.
        DO 14   L=1,NL
        DO 8   I=1,M
        W(I) = 0.
        DO 8   J=1,M
8       W(I) = W(I) + A(I,J) * V(J)
        AL = 0.
        DO 10   I=1,M
10      AL = AL + W(I) * V(I)
        AL = SQRTF(AL)
        E1 = E
        E = AL
        IF (P - ABSF(E1/E-1.)) 12, 12, 15
12      DO 13   I=1,M
13      V(I) = W(I)/AL
14      CONTINUE
15      DO 16   I=1,N
        W(I) = 0.
        DO 16   J=1,M
16      W(I) = W(I) + B(I,J) * V(J)
        DO 18   I=1,N
        DO 18   J=1,M
        S = SIGNF(1., W(I)) * SIGNF(1., V(J))
18      B(I,J) = B(I,J) * S
        DO 20   I=1,N
20      WRITE OUTPUT TAPE 6, 22, (B(I,J), J=1,M)
22      FORMAT (12F7.3)
        RETURN
        END
C
*       DATA
.00010
.75
 12
  9
  3
 40
 0.128  0.181  0.421  0.506  0.857  0.746  0.280  0.178  0.246
 0.764  0.740  0.563 -0.387 -0.293 -0.202  0.261  0.281  0.043
-0.030 -0.046  0.014  0.147 -0.109 -0.135  0.640  0.682  0.661
-0.280 -0.351 -0.326 -0.023 -0.109 -0.186  0.083  0.091 -0.654
-0.336 -0.306 -0.429 -0.542 -0.006 -0.153 -0.428  0.056 -0.124
-0.276 -0.324 -0.271 -0.370 -0.225  0.035  0.129 -0.446 -0.124
 0.057 -0.070 -0.016  0.006  0.152 -0.441 -0.166 -0.354 -0.033
-0.010 -0.140  0.326 -0.004 -0.258 -0.091 -0.410 -0.200 -0.101
-0.303  0.227 -0.314  0.029 -0.102 -0.125 -0.086 -0.106 -0.074
 0.086  0.057 -0.003  0.161  0.073  0.134 -0.082 -0.067 -0.009
 0.164  0.106 -0.124  0.234 -0.002  0.227 -0.072  0.025  0.156
 0.036 -0.074 -0.142  0.242  0.023  0.192 -0.148 -0.119  0.011
    1        4        7
```

```
C CHAPTER 20 - FACTOR SCORE MATRICES                                          001
C    20.3 CENTROID FACTOR SCORE MATRIX                                        002
C                                                                             003
      DIMENSION Z(90,90), A(90,10 ), B(90,10), F(90,10), Y(90,10),            004
     1T(90,90), G(10,10 ), D(10)                                              005
      READ INPUT TAPE 5, 903, NI, NJ, NK                                      009
      DO 07  I=1,NI                                                           010
07    READ INPUT TAPE 5, 900, (Z(I,J), J=1,NJ)                                011
      DO 102  K=1,NK                                                          013
102   READ INPUT TAPE 5, 900, (A(J,K), J=1,NJ)                                014
      DO 106  K=1,NK                                                          015
106   READ INPUT TAPE 5, 905, (F(J,K), J=1,NJ)                                016
C 1.                                                                          021
      DO 116  K=1,NK                                                          023
      DO 116  J=1,K                                                           024
      T(K,J) = 0.                                                             025
      DO 116  I=1,NI                                                          026
116   T(K,J) = T(K,J) + F(I,K) * A(I,J)                                       027
      CALL TRIN (T, G, NK)                                                    028
C 2.                                                                          032
      DO 122  I=1,NJ                                                          032
      DO 122  J=1,NK                                                          033
      B(I,J) = 0.                                                             034
      DO 122  K=1,J                                                           035
122   B(I,J) = B(I,J) + F(I,K) * G(J,K)                                       036
C 3.                                                                          040
      DO 127  I=1,NI                                                          040
      DO 127  K=1,NK                                                          041
      Y(I,K) = 0.                                                             042
      DO 127  J=1,NJ                                                          043
127   Y(I,K) = Y(I,K) + Z(I,J) * B(J,K)                                       044
      DO 132  J=1,NK                                                          045
      DO 132  K=1,NK                                                          046
      T(J,K) = 0.                                                             047
      DO 132  I=1,NI                                                          048
132   T(J,K) = T(J,K) + Y(I,J) * Y(I,K)                                       049
      DO 134  I=1,NI                                                          050
134   WRITE OUTPUT TAPE 6, 900, (Y(I,K), K=1,NK)                              051
      WRITE OUTPUT TAPE 6, 997                                                052
      DO 137  I=1,NK                                                          053
137   WRITE OUTPUT TAPE 6, 900, (T(I,J), J=1,NK)                              054
900   FORMAT (10F7.3)                                                         055
903   FORMAT (I4)                                                             056
905   FORMAT (10F4.0)                                                         057
997   FORMAT (1H )                                                            058
      CALL EXIT                                                               059
      END                                                                     060
C
      SUBROUTINE TRIN (A,B,N)                                                  001
C INVERSE OF TRIANGULAR MATRIX
      DIMENSION A(90,90), B(10,10)                                            003
      DO 10  J=1,N                                                            004
      B(J,J) = 1./A(J,J)                                                      005
      DO 10  I=J,N                                                            006
10    A(I,J) = A(I,J) * B(J,J)                                                007
      DO 16  I=2,N                                                            008
      DO 16  IJ=2,I                                                           009
      J=I+1-IJ                                                                010
      B(I,J) = 0.0                                                            011
      J1 = J+1                                                                012
      DO 16  K=J1, I                                                          013
16    B(I,J) = B(I,J) - B(I,K) * A(K,J)                                       014
      DO 164  J=2,N                                                           015
      J1 = J - 1                                                              016
      DO 164  I=1,J1                                                          017
164   B(I,J) = 0.                                                             018
      RETURN                                                                  019
      END                                                                     020
C
*     DATA
  12
   9
   3
 0.128  0.181  0.421  0.506  0.857  0.746  0.280  0.178  0.246
 0.764  0.740  0.563 -0.387 -0.293 -0.202  0.261  0.281  0.043
-0.030 -0.046  0.014  0.147 -0.109 -0.135  0.640  0.682  0.661
-0.280 -0.351 -0.326 -0.023 -0.109 -0.186  0.083  0.091 -0.654
-0.336 -0.306 -0.429 -0.542 -0.006 -0.153 -0.428  0.056 -0.124
-0.276 -0.324 -0.271 -0.370 -0.225  0.035  0.129 -0.446 -0.124
 0.057 -0.070 -0.016  0.006  0.152 -0.441 -0.166 -0.354 -0.033
-0.010 -0.140  0.326 -0.004 -0.258 -0.091 -0.410 -0.200 -0.101
```

683

```
-0.303   0.227  -0.014   0.029  -0.102  -0.125  -0.086  -0.106  -0.074
 0.086   0.057  -0.003   0.161   0.073   0.134  -0.082  -0.067  -0.009
 0.164   0.106  -0.124   0.234  -0.002   0.227  -0.072   0.025   0.156
 0.036  -0.074  -0.142   0.242   0.023   0.192  -0.148  -0.119   0.011
 0.659   0.684   0.730   0.617   0.542   0.588   0.637   0.606   0.708
 0.457   0.452   0.283  -0.601  -0.709  -0.663   0.271   0.346   0.164
 0.456   0.439   0.451  -0.209   0.094   0.116  -0.479  -0.488  -0.378
 1.  1.  1.  1.  1.  1.  1.  1.
 1.  1.  1. -1. -1. -1.  1.  1.  1.
 1.  1.  1. -1.  1.  1. -1. -1. -1.
```

```
C CHAPTER 20 - FACTOR SCORE MATRICES                                      001
C    20.4 MULTIPLE GROUP FACTOR SCORE MATRIX                              002
C                                                                         003
      DIMENSION Z(90,90), A(90,10 ), B(90,10), F(90,10), Y(90,10),        004
     1T(90,90), G(10,10 ), D(10)                                          005
      REWIND 2                                                            006
      READ INPUT TAPE 5, 903, NI, NJ, NK                                  009
      DO 07  I=1,NI                                                       010
      READ INPUT TAPE 5, 900, (Z(I,J), J=1,NJ)                            011
07    WRITE TAPE 2, (Z(I,J), J=1,NJ)                                      012
      REWIND 2                                                            015
      DO 205 I=1,NJ                                                       016
205   READ INPUT TAPE 5, 901, (Z(I,J), J=1,NJ)                           017
      DO 211  K=1,NK                                                      018
211   READ INPUT TAPE 5, 902, (F(J,K), J=1,NJ)                           019
C 1.
      DO 218  I=1,NJ                                                      025
      DO 218  K=1,NK                                                      026
      A(I,K) = 0.                                                         027
      DO 218  J=1,NJ                                                      028
218   A(I,K) = A(I,K) + Z(I,J) * F(J,K)                                   029
      DO 2182  I=1,NJ                                                     030
2182  WRITE OUTPUT TAPE 6, 900, (A(I,K), K=1,NK)                          031
      WRITE OUTPUT TAPE 6, 997                                            032
      WRITE OUTPUT TAPE 6, 997                                            033
      DO 223  J=1,NK                                                      034
      DO 223  K=1,NK                                                      035
      T(J,K) = 0.                                                         036
      DO 223  I=1,NJ                                                      037
223   T(J,K) = T(J,K) + A(I,J) * F(I,K)                                   038
      DO 2232  I=1,NK                                                     039
2232  WRITE OUTPUT TAPE 6, 900, (T(I,J), J=1,NK)                          040
      WRITE OUTPUT TAPE 6, 997                                            041
C 2.
      CALL TRIANG (T, NK)                                                 045
      DO 2242  I=1,NK                                                     046
2242  WRITE OUTPUT TAPE 6, 900, (T(I,J), J=1,NK)                          047
      WRITE OUTPUT TAPE 6, 997                                            048
C 3.
      CALL TRIN (T, G, NK)                                                052
      DO 2252  I=1,NK                                                     053
2252  WRITE OUTPUT TAPE 6, 900, (G(I,J), J=1,NK)                          054
      WRITE OUTPUT TAPE 6, 998                                            055
      DO 230  I=1,NJ                                                      056
      DO 230  J=1,NK                                                      057
      B(I,J) = 0.                                                         058
      DO 230  K=1,J                                                       059
230   B(I,J) = B(I,J) + F(I,K) * G(J,K)                                   060
      DO 232  I=1,NI                                                      061
232   READ TAPE 2, (Z(I,J), J=1,NJ)                                       062
      REWIND 2                                                            063
      DO 2322  I=1,NJ                                                     064
2322  WRITE OUTPUT TAPE 6, 900, (B(I,J), J=1,NK)                          065
      WRITE OUTPUT TAPE 6, 997                                            066
      DO 2324  I=1,NI                                                     067
2324  WRITE OUTPUT TAPE 6, 900, (Z(I,J), J=1,NJ)                          068
      WRITE OUTPUT TAPE 6, 997                                            069
C 4.
      DO 237  I=1,NI                                                      073
      DO 237  K=1,NK                                                      074
      Y(I,K) = 0.                                                         075
      DO 237  J=1,NJ                                                      076
237   Y(I,K) = Y(I,K) + Z(I,J) * B(J,K)                                   077
      DO 242  J=1,NK                                                      078
      DO 242  K=1,NK                                                      079
      T(J,K) = 0.                                                         080
      DO 242  I=1,NI                                                      081
242   T(J,K) = T(J,K) + Y(I,J) * Y(I,K)                                   082
      DO 244  I=1,NI                                                      083
```

```
244   WRITE OUTPUT TAPE 6, 900, (Y(I,J), J=1,NK)                        084
      WRITE OUTPUT TAPE 6, 997                                          085
      DO 247  I=1,NK                                                    086
247   WRITE OUTPUT TAPE 6, 900, (T(I,J), J=1,NK)                        087
900   FORMAT (10F7.3)                                                   088
901   FORMAT (10F6.3)                                                   089
902   FORMAT (10F2.0)                                                   090
903   FORMAT (I4)                                                       091
997   FORMAT (1H )                                                      092
998   FORMAT (1H0)                                                      093
      CALL EXIT                                                         094
      END                                                              095
C
      SUBROUTINE TRIANG (A,N)
C TRIANGULAR FACTOR
      DIMENSION A (90,90)
07    NN = N-1
08    DO 14 K=1,NN
      C=1./SQRTF(A(K,K))
09    DO 10  I = K,N
10    A(I,K) = A(I,K) * C
11    KK = K + 1
12    DO 14 J = KK,N
13    DO 14 I = J,N
14    A(I,J) = A(I,J) - A(I,K)*A(J,K)
15    A(N,N) = SQRTF(A(N,N))
161   DO 164  J=2,N
162   J1 = J - 1
163   DO 164  I=1,J1
164   A(I,J) = 0.
      RETURN
      END
C
      SUBROUTINE TRIN (A,B,N)
C INVERSE OF TRIANGULAR MATRIX
      DIMENSION A(90,90), B(10,10)
07    DO 10  J=1,N
08    B(J,J) = 1./A(J,J)
09    DO 10  I=J,N
10    A(I,J) = A(I,J) * B(J,J)
11    DO 16  I=2,N
12    DO 16  IJ=2,I
13    J=I+1-IJ
      B(I,J) = 0.0
14    J1 = J+1
15    DO 16  K=J1, I
16    B(I,J) = B(I,J) - B(I,K) * A(K,J)
161   DO 164  J=2,N
162   J1 = J - 1
163   DO 164  I=1,J1
164   B(I,J) = 0.
      RETURN
      END
C
*     DATA
  12
   9
   3
 0.128  0.181  0.421  0.506  0.857  0.746  0.280  0.178  0.246
 0.764  0.740  0.563 -0.387 -0.293 -0.202  0.261  0.281  0.043
-0.030 -0.046  0.014  0.147 -0.109 -0.135  0.640  0.682  0.661
-0.280 -0.351 -0.326 -0.023 -0.109 -0.186  0.083  0.091 -0.654
-0.336 -0.306 -0.429 -0.542 -0.006 -0.153 -0.428  0.056 -0.124
-0.276 -0.324 -0.271 -0.370 -0.225  0.035  0.129 -0.446 -0.124
 0.057 -0.070 -0.016  0.006  0.152 -0.441 -0.166 -0.354 -0.033
-0.010 -0.140  0.326 -0.004 -0.258 -0.091 -0.410 -0.200 -0.101
-0.303  0.227 -0.014  0.029 -0.102 -0.125 -0.086 -0.106 -0.074
 0.086  0.057 -0.003  0.161  0.073  0.134 -0.082 -0.067 -0.009
 0.164  0.106 -0.124  0.234 -0.002  0.227 -0.072  0.025  0.156
 0.036 -0.074 -0.142  0.242  0.023  0.192 -0.148 -0.119  0.011
1.000   .829   .768   .108   .033   .108   .298   .309   .351
 .829  1.000   .775   .115   .061   .125   .323   .347   .369
 .768   .775  1.000   .272   .205   .238   .296   .271   .385
 .108   .115   .272  1.000   .636   .626   .249   .183   .369
 .033   .061   .205   .636  1.000   .709   .138   .091   .254
 .108   .125   .238   .626   .709  1.000   .190   .103   .291
 .298   .323   .296   .249   .138   .190  1.000   .654   .527
 .309   .347   .271   .183   .091   .103   .654  1.000   .541
 .351   .369   .385   .369   .254   .291   .527   .541  1.000
1 1 1 0 0 0 0 0 0
0 0 0 1 1 1 0 0 0
0 0 0 0 0 0 1 1 1
```

685

```
C CHAPTER 20 - FACTOR SCORE MATRICES                                          001
C    20.5 PRINCIPAL AXIS FACTOR SCORE MATRIX                                   002
C                                                                             003
      DIMENSION Z(90,90), A(90,10 ), B(90,10), F(90,10), Y(90,10),           004
     1T(90,90), G(10,10 ), D(10)                                              005
      READ INPUT TAPE 5, 903, NI, NJ, NK                                      009
      DO 07  I=1,NI                                                           010
   07 READ INPUT TAPE 5, 900, (Z(I,J), J=1,NJ)                                011
      READ INPUT TAPE 5, 901, (D(K), K=1,NK)                                  013
      DO 305  K=1,NK                                                          015
  305 READ INPUT TAPE 5, 901, (A(J,K), J=1,NJ)                                016
C 1.
      DO 310  J=1,NJ                                                          020
      DO 310  K=1,NK                                                          021
  310 A(J,K) = A(J,K) / D(K)                                                  022
      DO 3102  J=1,NJ                                                         023
 3102 WRITE OUTPUT TAPE 6, 900, (A(J,K), K=1,NK)                              024
      WRITE OUTPUT TAPE 6, 997                                               025
      DO 3104  I=1,NI                                                         026
 3104 WRITE OUTPUT TAPE 6, 900, (Z(I,J), J=1,NJ)                              027
      WRITE OUTPUT TAPE 6, 997                                               028
C 2.
      DO 315  I=1,NI                                                          032
      DO 315  K=1,NK                                                          033
      Y(I,K) = 0.                                                            034
      DO 315  J=1,NJ                                                          035
  315 Y(I,K) = Y(I,K) + Z(I,J) * A(J,K)                                       036
      DO 320  J=1,NK                                                          037
      DO 320  K=1,NK                                                          038
      T(J,K) = 0.                                                            039
      DO 320  I=1,NI                                                          040
  320 T(J,K) = T(J,K) + Y(I,J) * Y(I,K)                                       041
      DO 322  I=1,NI                                                          042
  322 WRITE OUTPUT TAPE 6, 900, (Y(I,K), K=1,NK)                              043
      WRITE OUTPUT TAPE 6, 997                                               044
      DO 325  I=1,NK                                                          045
  325 WRITE OUTPUT TAPE 6, 900, (T(I,J), J=1,NK)                              046
  900 FORMAT (10F7.3)                                                         047
  901 FORMAT (10F6.3)                                                         048
  903 FORMAT (I4)                                                             049
  997 FORMAT (1H )                                                            050
      CALL EXIT                                                              051
      END                                                                    052
C
*     DATA
  12
   9
   3
  0.128  0.181  0.421  0.506  0.857  0.746  0.280  0.178  0.246
  0.764  0.740  0.563 -0.387 -0.293 -0.202  0.261  0.281  0.043
 -0.030 -0.046  0.014  0.147 -0.109 -0.135  0.640  0.682  0.661
 -0.280 -0.351 -0.326 -0.023 -0.109 -0.186  0.083  0.091 -0.654
 -0.336 -0.306 -0.429 -0.542 -0.006 -0.153 -0.428  0.056 -0.124
 -0.276 -0.324 -0.271 -0.370 -0.225  0.035  0.129 -0.446 -0.124
  0.057 -0.070 -0.016  0.006  0.152 -0.441 -0.166 -0.354 -0.033
 -0.010 -0.140  0.326 -0.004 -0.258 -0.091 -0.410 -0.200 -0.101
 -0.303  0.227 -0.014  0.029 -0.102 -0.125 -0.086 -0.106 -0.074
  0.086  0.057 -0.003  0.161  0.073  0.134 -0.082 -0.067 -0.009
  0.164  0.106 -0.124  0.234 -0.002  0.227 -0.072  0.025  0.156
  0.036 -0.074 -0.142  0.242  0.023  0.192 -0.148 -0.119  0.011
 3.749 2.050 1.331
 0.717 0.740 0.773 0.556 0.463 0.518 0.640 0.615 0.715
 0.493 0.478 0.296-0.649-0.744-0.694 0.080 0.166-0.034
 0.350 0.322 0.406 0.068 0.181 0.188-0.588-0.621-0.369

C CHAPTER 20 - FACTOR SCORE MATRICES                                          001
C    20.6 LEAST SQUARE FACTOR SCORE MATRIX                                    002
C                                                                             003
      DIMENSION Z(90,90), A(90,10 ), B(90,10), F(90,10), Y(90,10),           004
     1T(90,90), G(10,10 ), D(10)                                              005
      READ INPUT TAPE 5, 903, NI, NJ, NK                                      009
      DO 07  I=1,NI                                                           010
   07 READ INPUT TAPE 5, 900, (Z(I,J), J=1,NJ)                                011
      DO 4021  K=1,NK                                                         013
 4021 READ INPUT TAPE 5, 900, (A(J,K), J=1,NJ)
C 1.
      DO 408  K1=1,NK                                                         020
      DO 408  K2=1,NK                                                         021
      T(K1,K2) = 0.                                                          022
      DO 408  J=1,NJ                                                          023
  408 T(K1,K2) = T(K1,K2) + A(J,K1) * A(J,K2)                                 024
      DO 4083  K=1,NK                                                         025
      DO 4083  J=1,NK                                                         026
 4083 B(J,K) = T(J,K)                                                         027
```

686

```
         DO 4085  J=1,NK                                              028
 4085 WRITE OUTPUT TAPE 6, 900, (B(J,K), K=1,NK)                      029
      WRITE OUTPUT TAPE 6, 997                                        030
      CALL SYMIN (T, NK)                                              031
      DO 411  J=1,NK                                                  032
  411 WRITE OUTPUT TAPE 6, 900, (T(J,K), K=1,NK)                      033
      WRITE OUTPUT TAPE 6, 997                                        034
      DO 4136  I=1,NK                                                 035
      DO 4136  J=1,NK                                                 036
      G(I,J) = 0.                                                     037
      DO 4136  K=1,NK                                                 038
 4136 G(I,J) = G(I,J) + B(I,K) * T(K,J)                              039
      DO 4138  I=1,NK                                                 040
 4138 WRITE OUTPUT TAPE 6, 900, (G(I,J), J=1,NK)                      041
      WRITE OUTPUT TAPE 6, 997                                        042
C 2.
      DO 418   J=1,NJ                                                 046
      DO 418   K1=1,NK                                                047
      B(J,K1) = 0.                                                    048
      DO 418   K2=1,NK                                                049
  418 B(J,K1) = B(J,K1) + A(J,K2) * T(K2,K1)                          050
      DO 4185  I=1,NK                                                 051
      DO 4185  J=1,NK                                                 052
      G(I,J) = 0.                                                     053
      DO 4185  K=1,NJ                                                 054
 4185 G(I,J) = G(I,J) + B(K,I) * A(K,J)                              055
      DO 4187  I=1,NK                                                 056
 4187 WRITE OUTPUT TAPE 6, 900, (G(I,J), J=1,NK)                      057
      WRITE OUTPUT TAPE 6, 997                                        058
      DO 4190  I=1,NJ                                                 059
 4190 WRITE OUTPUT TAPE 6, 900, (B(I,J), J=1,NK)                      060
      WRITE OUTPUT TAPE 6, 997                                        061
C 3.
      DO 423   I=1,NI                                                 065
      DO 423   K=1,NK                                                 066
      Y(I,K) = 0.                                                     067
      DO 423   J=1,NJ                                                 068
  423 Y(I,K) = Y(I,K) + Z(I,J) * B(J,K)                              069
      DO 428   K1=1,NK                                                070
      DO 428   K2=1,NK                                                071
      T(K1,K2) = 0.                                                   072
      DO 428   I=1,NI                                                 073
  428 T(K1,K2) = T(K1,K2) + Y(I,K1) * Y(I,K2)                        074
      DO 430   I=1,NI                                                 075
  430 WRITE OUTPUT TAPE 6, 900, (Y(I,K), K=1,NK)                      076
      WRITE OUTPUT TAPE 6, 997                                        077
      DO 433   I=1,NK                                                 078
  433 WRITE OUTPUT TAPE 6, 900, (T(I,J), J=1,NK)                      079
  900 FORMAT (10F7.3)                                                 080
  901 FORMAT (10F6.3)                                                 081
  903 FORMAT (I4)                                                     082
  997 FORMAT (1H )                                                    083
      CALL EXIT                                                       084
      END                                                            085
C
      SUBROUTINE SYMIN (S, N)
      DIMENSION S(90,90)
 01   DO 04  I=2,N
 02   I1 = I-1
 03   DO 04  J = 1,I1
 04   S(I,J) = 0.
 10   C = 1./SQRTF(S(1,1))
 11   S(1,1) = 1.
 12   DO 13  J=1,N
 13   S(1,J) = S(1,J) * C
 14   DO 21  K=2,N
 15   DO 17  J=1,N
 151  K1 = K-1
 16   DO 17  I=1,K1
 17   S(K,J) = S(K,J) - S(I,K) * S(I,J)
 18   C = 1./SQRTF(S(K,K))
 19   DO 191  I=1,K1
 191  S(I,K) = 0.
 192  S(K,K) = 1.
 20   DO 21  J=1,N
 21   S(K,J) = S(K,J) * C
 25   DO 30  J=2,N
 26   J1 = J-1
 27   DO 30  I=1,J1
 29   DO 30  K=J,N
 30   S(I,J) = S(I,J) + S(K,I) * S(K,J)
 31   DO 35  J=1,N
```

```
32    S(J,J) = S(J,J) **2
33    J2 =  J+1
34    DO 35   I=J2,N
35    S(J,J) = S(J,J) + S(I,J)**2
38    N1 = N-1
39    DO 42  I=1,N1
40    I2 = I+1
41    DO 42   J=I2,N
42    S(J,I) = S(I,J)
      RETURN
      END
C
*     DATA
  12
   9
   3
  0.128   0.181   0.421   0.506   0.857   0.746   0.280   0.178   0.246
  0.764   0.740   0.563  -0.387  -0.293  -0.202   0.261   0.281   0.043
 -0.030  -0.046   0.014   0.147  -0.109  -0.135   0.640   0.682   0.661
 -0.280  -0.351  -0.326  -0.023  -0.109  -0.186   0.083   0.091  -0.654
 -0.336  -0.306  -0.429  -0.542  -0.006  -0.153  -0.428   0.056  -0.124
 -0.276  -0.324  -0.271  -0.370  -0.225   0.035   0.129  -0.446  -0.124
  0.057  -0.070  -0.016   0.006   0.152  -0.441  -0.166  -0.354  -0.033
 -0.010  -0.140   0.326  -0.004  -0.258  -0.091  -0.410  -0.200  -0.101
 -0.303   0.227  -0.014   0.029  -0.102  -0.125  -0.086  -0.106  -0.074
  0.086   0.057  -0.003   0.161   0.073   0.134  -0.082  -0.067  -0.009
  0.164   0.106  -0.124   0.234  -0.002   0.227  -0.072   0.025   0.156
  0.036  -0.074  -0.142   0.242   0.023   0.192  -0.148  -0.119   0.011
  0.659   0.684   0.730   0.617   0.542   0.588   0.637   0.606   0.708
  0.457   0.452   0.283  -0.601  -0.709  -0.663   0.271   0.346   0.164
  0.456   0.439   0.451  -0.209   0.094   0.116  -0.479  -0.488  -0.378
```

```
C CHAPTER 20 - FACTOR SCORE MATRICES                                        001
C    20.7 IMAGE ANALYSIS FACTOR SCORE MATRIX                                 002
C                                                                           003
      DIMENSION Z(90,90), A(90,10 ), B(90,10), F(90,10), Y(90,10),          004
     1T(90,90), G(10,10 ), D(10)                                            005
      REWIND 2                                                              006
      READ INPUT TAPE 5, 903, NI, NJ, NK                                    009
      DO 07  I=1,NI                                                         010
      READ INPUT TAPE 5, 900, (Z(I,J), J=1,NJ)                              011
07    WRITE TAPE 2, (Z(I,J), J=1,NJ)                                        012
      REWIND 2                                                              006
      DO 504  I=1,NJ                                                        013
      READ INPUT TAPE 5, 901, (T(I,J), J=1,NJ)                              014
      DO 504   J=1,NJ                                                       015
504   Z(I,J) = T(I,J)                                                       016
      DO 5071   K=1,NK                                                      017
5071  READ INPUT TAPE 5, 902, (F(J,K), J=1,NJ)                              018
C 2.                                                                        025
      DO 512  I=1,NJ                                                        026
      I1 = I + 1                                                            027
      DO 512   J=I1,NJ                                                      028
512   T(J,I) = 0.                                                          029
      CALL SYMIN (T, NJ)                                                    030
      DO 516  I=1,NJ                                                        031
      DO 516   J=1,NJ                                                       032
516   Z(I,J) = Z(I,J) + T(I,J) / (T(I,I)*T(J,J))                           033
      DO 518   J=1,NJ                                                       034
518   Z(J,J) = Z(J,J) - 2. / (T(J,J))                                      035
      DO 5182  I=1,NJ                                                       036
5182  WRITE OUTPUT TAPE 6, 900, (Z(I,J), J=1,NJ)                           037
      WRITE OUTPUT TAPE 6, 997
C 3.                                                                        041
      DO 523  I=1,NJ                                                        042
      DO 523  J=1,NK                                                        043
      B(I,J) = 0.                                                          044
      DO 523   K=1,NJ                                                       045
523   B(I,J) = B(I,J) + Z(I,K) * F(K,J)                                    046
      DO 528  I=1,NK                                                        047
      DO 528   J=1,NK                                                       048
      G(I,J) = 0.                                                          049
      DO 528   K=1,NJ                                                       050
528   G(I,J) = G(I,J) + F(K,I) * B(K,J)                                    051
      DO 5282  I=1,NK                                                       052
5282  WRITE OUTPUT TAPE 6, 900, (G(I,J), J=1,NK)                           053
      WRITE OUTPUT TAPE 6, 997
C 1.                                                                        057
      DO 531  I=1,NJ                                                        058
      DO 531   J=1,NJ                                                       059
531   Z(I,J) = -T(I,J) / T(J,J)                                            060
      DO 533  I=1,NJ                                                        061
533   Z(I,I) = 1. + Z(I,I)                                                 062
      DO 5333  I=1,NK
```

688

```
        DO 5333   J=1,NK                                              063
 5333  T(I,J) = G(I,J)                                               064
C 4.
        CALL TRIANG (T, NK)                                           068
        DO 5342   I=1,NK                                             069
 5342  WRITE OUTPUT TAPE 6, 900, (T(I,J), J=1,NK)                    070
        WRITE OUTPUT TAPE 6, 997                                      071
C 5.
        CALL TRIN (T, G, NK)                                          075
        DO 5362   I=1,NK                                             076
 5362  WRITE OUTPUT TAPE 6, 900, (G(I,J), J=1,NK)                    077
        WRITE OUTPUT TAPE 6, 997                                      078
        DO 5367   I=1,NK                                             079
        DO 5367   J=1,NK                                             080
        B(I,J) = 0.                                                   081
        DO 5366   K=1,NK                                             082
 5366  B(I,J) = B(I,J) + T(I,K) * G(K,I)                            083
 5367  WRITE OUTPUT TAPE 6, 900, (B(I,J), J=1,NK)                    084
        WRITE OUTPUT TAPE 6, 997                                      085
        DO 541   I=1,NJ                                              086
        DO 541   J=1,NK                                              087
        A(I,J) = 0.                                                   088
        DO 541   K=1,J                                               089
  541  A(I,J) = A(I,J) + F(I,K) * G(J,K)                            090
        DO 546   I=1,NJ                                              091
        DO 546   J=1,NK                                              092
        B(I,J) = 0.                                                   093
        DO 546   K=1,NJ                                              094
  546  B(I,J) = B(I,J) + Z(I,K) * A(K,J)                            095
C 6.
        DO 548   I=1,NI                                              099
  548  READ TAPE 2, (Z(I,J), J=1,NJ)                                100
        REWIND 2                                                      101
        DO 554   I=1,NI                                              102
        DO 554   J=1,NK                                              103
        Y(I,J) = 0.                                                   104
        DO 554   K=1,NJ                                              105
  554  Y(I,J) = Y(I,J) + Z(I,K) * B(K,J)                            106
        DO 559   I=1,NK                                              107
        DO 559   J=1,NK                                              108
        T(I,J) = 0.                                                   109
        DO 559   K=1,NI                                              110
  559  T(I,J) = T(I,J) + Y(K,I) * Y(K,J)                            111
        DO 561   I=1,NI                                              112
  561  WRITE OUTPUT TAPE 6, 900, (Y(I,J), J=1,NK)                    113
        WRITE OUTPUT TAPE 6, 997                                      114
        DO 564   I=1,NK                                              115
  564  WRITE OUTPUT TAPE 6, 900, (T(I,J), J=1,NK)                    116
  900  FORMAT (10F7.3)                                               117
  901  FORMAT (10F6.3)                                               118
  902  FORMAT (10F2.0)                                               119
  903  FORMAT (I4)                                                   120
  997  FORMAT (1H )                                                  121
        CALL     EXIT                                                 122
        END                                                          123
C
        SUBROUTINE SYMIN (S, N)
        DIMENSION S(90,90)
 01    DO 04   I=2,N
 02    I1 = I-1
 03    DO 04 J = 1,I1
 04    S(I,J) = 0.
 10    C = 1./SQRTF(S(1,1))
 11    S(1,1) = 1.
 12    DO 13   J=1,N
 13    S(1,J) = S(1,J) * C
 14    DO 21   K=2,N
 15    DO 17   J=1,N
 151   K1 = K-1
 16    DO 17   I=1,K1
 17    S(K,J) = S(K,J) - S(I,K) * S(I,J)
 18    C = 1./SQRTF(S(K,K))
 19    DO 191   I=1,K1
 191   S(I,K) = 0.
 192   S(K,K) = 1.
 20    DO 21   J=1,N
 21    S(K,J) = S(K,J) * C
 25    DO 30   J=2,N
 26    J1 = J-1
 27    DO 30   I=1,J1
 29    DO 30   K=J,N
 30    S(I,J) = S(I,J) + S(K,I) * S(K,J)
```

689

```
31      DO 35   J=1,N
32      S(J,J) = S(J,J) **2
33      J2 = J+1
34      DO 35   I=J2,N
35      S(J,J) = S(J,J) + S(I,J)**2
38      N1 = N-1
39      DO 42   I=1,N1
40      I2 = I+1
41      DO 42   J=I2,N
42      S(J,I) = S(I,J)
        RETURN
        END
C
        SUBROUTINE TRIANG (A,N)
C TRIANGULAR FACTOR
        DIMENSION A (90,90)
07      NN = N-1
08      DO 14 K=1,NN
        C=1./SQRTF(A(K,K))
09      DO 10  I = K,N
10      A(I,K) = A(I,K) * C
11      KK = K + 1
12      DO 14 J = KK,N
13      DO 14 I = J,N
14      A(I,J) = A(I,J) - A(I,K)*A(J,K)
15      A(N,N) = SQRTF(A(N,N))
161     DO 164   J=2,N
162     J1 = J - 1
163     DO 164   I=1,J1
164     A(I,J) = 0.
        RETURN
        END
C
        SUBROUTINE TRIN (A,B,N)
C INVERSE OF TRIANGULAR MATRIX
        DIMENSION A(90,90), B(10,10)
07      DO 10   J=1,N
08      B(J,J) = 1./A(J,J)
09      DO 10   I=J,N
10      A(I,J) = A(I,J) * B(J,J)
11      DO 16   I=2,N
12      DO 16   IJ=2,I
13      J=I+1-IJ
        B(I,J) = 0.0
14      J1 = J+1
15      DO 16   K=J1, I
16      B(I,J) = B(I,J) - B(I,K) * A(K,J)
161     DO 164   J=2,N
162     J1 = J - 1
163     DO 164   I=1,J1
164     B(I,J) = 0.
        RETURN
        END
*       DATA
C
  12
   9
   3
  0.128   0.181   0.421   0.506   0.857   0.746   0.280   0.178   0.246
  0.764   0.740   0.563  -0.387  -0.293  -0.202   0.261   0.281   0.043
 -0.030  -0.046   0.014   0.147  -0.109  -0.135   0.640   0.682   0.661
 -0.280  -0.351  -0.326  -0.023  -0.109  -0.186   0.083   0.091  -0.654
 -0.336  -0.306  -0.429  -0.542  -0.006  -0.153  -0.428   0.056  -0.124
 -0.276  -0.324  -0.271  -0.370  -0.225   0.035   0.129  -0.446  -0.124
  0.057  -0.070  -0.016   0.006   0.152  -0.441  -0.166  -0.354  -0.033
 -0.010  -0.140   0.326  -0.004  -0.258  -0.091  -0.410  -0.200  -0.101
 -0.303   0.227  -0.014   0.029  -0.102  -0.125  -0.086  -0.106  -0.074
  0.086   0.057  -0.003   0.161   0.073   0.134  -0.082  -0.067  -0.009
  0.164   0.106  -0.124   0.234  -0.002   0.227  -0.072   0.025   0.156
  0.036  -0.074  -0.142   0.242   0.023   0.192  -0.148  -0.119   0.011
 1.000    .829    .768    .108    .033    .108    .298    .309    .351
  .829   1.000    .775    .115    .061    .125    .323    .347    .369
  .768    .775   1.000    .272    .205    .238    .296    .271    .385
  .108    .115    .272   1.000    .636    .626    .249    .183    .369
  .033    .061    .205    .636   1.000    .709    .138    .091    .254
  .108    .125    .238    .626    .709   1.000    .190    .103    .291
  .298    .323    .296    .249    .138    .190   1.000    .654    .527
  .309    .347    .271    .183    .091    .103    .654   1.000    .541
  .351    .369    .385    .369    .254    .291    .527    .541   1.000
 1 1 1 0 0 0 0 0 0
 0 0 0 1 1 1 0 0 0
 0 0 0 0 0 0 1 1 1
```

```
C CHAPTER 21 - GENERAL FACTOR SOLUTIONS                                     001
C                                                                           002
      DIMENSION R(150,100), W(100,10), F(100,10), B(100,10), A(10,10),      003
     1H(10,10), T(10,10), D1(10), D(10), V(10), S(10,10), GS(10)            004
      REWIND 2                                                              005
      REWIND 3                                                              006
      READ INPUT TAPE 5, 902, P, PV, NI, NJ, NK, IL, NG                     007
      WRITE OUTPUT TAPE 6, 902, P, PV, NI, NJ, NK, IL, NG                   008
      WRITE OUTPUT TAPE 6, 997                                              009
      DO 10  I=1,NI                                                         010
      READ INPUT TAPE 5, 900, (R(I,J), J=1,NJ)                              011
      WRITE OUTPUT TAPE 6, 900, (R(I,J), J=1,NJ)                            012
   10 WRITE TAPE 2, (R(I,J), J=1,NJ)                                        013
      WRITE OUTPUT TAPE 6, 997                                              014
      REWIND 2                                                              015
      DO 16  I=1,NJ                                                         016
      READ INPUT TAPE 5, 901, (R(I,J), J=1,NJ)                              017
      WRITE OUTPUT TAPE 6, 901, (R(I,J), J=1,NJ)                            018
   16 WRITE TAPE 3, (R(I,J), J=1,NJ)                                        019
      WRITE OUTPUT TAPE 6, 997                                              020
      REWIND 3                                                              021
      DO 21  K=1,NK                                                         022
      READ INPUT TAPE 5,903, (F(J,K),J=1,NJ)                                023
   21 WRITE OUTPUT TAPE 6,903, (F(J,K), J=1,NJ)                             024
      WRITE OUTPUT TAPE 6, 997                                              025
      DO 25  K=1,NK                                                         026
      READ INPUT TAPE 5,901, (B(J,K), J=1,NJ)                               027
   25 WRITE OUTPUT TAPE 6,900, (B(J,K), J=1,NJ)                             028
      WRITE OUTPUT TAPE 6, 997                                              029
      DO 29  J=1,NK                                                         030
      READ INPUT TAPE 5, 900, (H(J,K), K=1,NK)                              031
   29 WRITE OUTPUT TAPE 6, 900, (H(J,K), K=1,NK)                            032
      WRITE OUTPUT TAPE 6, 999                                              033
C                                                                           034
C 21.3 FACTOR SCORE COVARIANCE MATRIX, AND SECOND ORDER COMMON AND
C SPECIFIC FACTOR LOADINGS
C 1.
      P = .001                                                              040
      DO 105 I=1,NK                                                         041
      DO 105  J=1,NK                                                        042
      R(I,J) = 0.                                                           043
      DO 105  K=1,NK                                                        044
  105 R(I,J) = R(I,J) + H(K,I) * H(K,J)                                     045
      DO 1052  I=1,NK                                                       046
 1052 WRITE OUTPUT TAPE 6, 905, (R(I,J), J=1,NK)                            047
      WRITE OUTPUT TAPE 6, 997                                              048
C 2.
      CALL SYMIN (R, NK)                                                    052
      DO 1062  I=1,NK                                                       053
 1062 WRITE OUTPUT TAPE 6, 905, (R(I,J), J=1,NK)                            054
      WRITE OUTPUT TAPE 6,997                                               055
C 3.
      FNK = NK                                                              061
      DO 111  I=1,NK                                                        062
  111 V(I) = R(I,I)                                                         063
      G = 0.                                                                064
      NK1 = NK-1                                                            065
      DO 118  I=1,NK1                                                       066
      I1 = I+1                                                              067
      DO 118  J=I1,NK                                                       068
  118 G = G + R(I,J)**2                                                     069
      G = G*2.                                                              070
      WRITE OUTPUT TAPE 6,900,G                                             071
      WRITE OUTPUT TAPE 6,997                                               072
C 4.
      DO 161  L=1,NG                                                        077
      DO 1212 I = 1,NK                                                      078
 1212 A(I,L) = 1.                                                           079
      LG = L                                                                080
      DO 124  I=1,NK                                                        081
      R(I,I) = V(I)                                                         082
      WRITE OUTPUT TAPE 6,997                                               083
  124 D(I) = R(I,I)                                                         084
      DO 156  M=1,IL                                                        085
      MI = M                                                                086
C 5.
      DO 131  I=1,NK                                                        090
      DO 131  J=1,LG                                                        091
```

```
            W(I,J) = 0.                                                 092
            DO 131  K=1,NK                                               093
 131    W(I,J) = W(I,J) + R(I,K) * A(K,J)                                094
            DO 1312 J = 1,LG                                             095
1312    WRITE OUTPUT TAPE 6,900,(W(I,J),I=1,NK)                          096
            WRITE OUTPUT TAPE 6,997                                      097
            DO 136  I=1,LG                                               098
            DO 136  J=1,LG                                               099
            S(I,J) = 0.                                                  100
            DO 136  K=1,NK                                               101
 136    S(I,J) = S(I,J) + A(K,I) * W(K,J)                                102
            DO 1362 I =1,LG                                              103
1362    GS(I) = S(I,I)                                                   104
            CALL TRIANG (S, LG)                                          105
            DO 1372 I = 1,LG                                             106
1372    WRITE OUTPUT TAPE 6,900,(S(I,J),J =1,LG)                         107
            WRITE OUTPUT TAPE 6,997                                      108
            CALL TRIN (S, T, LG)                                         109
            DO 143  I=1,NK                                               110
            DO 143  J=1,LG                                               111
            A(I,J) = 0.                                                  112
            DO 143  K=1,J                                                113
 143    A(I,J) = A(I,J) + W(I,K) * T(J,K)                                114
            DO 1432 J = 1,LG                                             115
1432    WRITE OUTPUT TAPE 6,900, (A(I,J),I =1,NK)                        116
            WRITE OUTPUT TAPE 6,997                                      117
C 6.
            DO 147  I=1,NK                                               121
            D1(I) = 0.                                                   122
            DO 147  J=1,LG                                               123
 147    D1(I) = D1(I) + A(I,J)**2                                       124
            DO 149  I=1,NK                                               125
 149    R(I,I) = MIN1F(D1(I), V(I))                                      126
            C = 0.                                                       127
            DO 152  I=1,NK                                               128
 152    C = MAX1F(C, ABSF(R(I,I)-D(I)))                                  129
            DO 154  I=1,NK                                               130
 154    D(I) = R(I,I)                                                    131
            WRITE OUTPUT TAPE 6,900, (D(I),I=1,NK)                       132
            WRITE OUTPUT TAPE 6,997                                      133
            IF (P-C) 156, 156, 1561                                      136
 156    CONTINUE                                                         137
C 7.
1561    DO 1562 I=1,LG                                                   141
1562    G = G - GS(I)                                                    142
            WRITE OUTPUT TAPE 6,999                                      143
            DO 158  I=1,NK                                               144
 158    G = G + D(I)**2                                                 145
            WRITE OUTPUT TAPE 6,900,G                                    146
            G = G/(FNK*(FNK-1.))                                         147
            WRITE OUTPUT TAPE 6,900,G                                    148
            WRITE OUTPUT TAPE 6,906,MI                                   149
            WRITE OUTPUT TAPE 6,997                                      150
            DO 159  J=1,LG                                               151
 159    WRITE OUTPUT TAPE 6, 900, (A(I,J), I=1,NK)                       152
            WRITE OUTPUT TAPE 6,997                                      153
            IF (P-G) 161, 161, 162                                       154
 161    CONTINUE                                                         155
 162    DO 163  I=1,NK                                                   156
 163    D(I) = SQRTF(V(I)-D(I))                                          157
            WRITE OUTPUT TAPE 6,900, (GS(I),I =1,LG)                     158
            WRITE OUTPUT TAPE 6, 997                                     159
            DO 169  I=1,NK                                               160
 169    WRITE OUTPUT TAPE 6, 900, (A(I,J), J=1,LG), D(I)                 161
            WRITE OUTPUT TAPE 6, 999                                     162
C                                                                       163
C 21.4 FIRST ORDER GENERAL AND COMMON FACTOR LOADING MATRIX             164
C 2.
            DO 805  I=1,NJ                                               168
            DO 805  J=1,NK                                               169
            W(I,J) = 0.                                                  170
            DO 805  K=1,NK                                               171
 805    W(I,J) = W(I,J) + B(I,K) * H(K,J)                                172
            DO 807  I=1,NJ                                               173
 807    WRITE OUTPUT TAPE 6, 900, (W(I,J), J=1,NK)                       174
            WRITE OUTPUT TAPE 6, 997                                     175
            DO 205  I=1,NJ                                               176
            DO 205  J=1,LG                                               177
            F(I,J) = 0.                                                  178
```

692

```
            DO 205  K=1,NK                                                    179
  205  F(I,J) = F(I,J) + W(I,K) * A(K,J)                                      180
C 3.
            DO 208  I=1,NJ                                                    184
            DO 208  J=1,NK                                                    185
  208  W(I,J) = W(I,J)*D(J)                                                   186
            DO 210  I=1,NJ                                                    187
  210  WRITE OUTPUT TAPE 6, 900, (F(I,J), J=1,LG), (W(I,J), J=1,NK)           188
            WRITE OUTPUT TAPE 6,997                                          189
            DO 2110 I=1,NJ                                                    190
            DO 2109  J=1,NJ                                                   191
            S(I,J) = 0.                                                       192
            DO 2105  K=1,LG                                                   193
 2105  S(I,J) = S(I,J) + F(I,K) * F(J,K)                                      194
            DO 2107  K=1,NK                                                   195
 2107  S(I,J) = S(I,J) + W(I,K) * W(J,K)                                      196
            DO 2109  K=1,NK                                                   197
 2109  S(I,J) = S(I,J) - B(I,K) * B(J,K)                                      198
 2110  WRITE OUTPUT TAPE 6, 900, (S(I,J), J=1,NJ)                             199
            WRITE OUTPUT TAPE 6, 999                                          201
C                                                                            202
C 21.5 FIRST ORDER GENERAL AND COMMON FACTOR SCORE MATRIX
            DO 302  I=1,NJ                                                    205
  302  READ TAPE 3, (R(I,J), J=1,NJ)                                          206
            REWIND 3                                                          207
C 1.
            DO 309  I=1,NJ                                                    211
            DO 309  J=1,NK                                                    212
            W(I,J) = 0.                                                       213
            DO 309  K=1,NJ                                                    214
  309  W(I,J) = W(I,J) + R(I,K) * B(K,J)                                      215
C 2.
            DO 314  I=1,NK                                                    219
            DO 314  J=1,NK                                                    220
            S(I,J) = 0.                                                       221
            DO 314  K=1,NJ                                                    222
  314  S(I,J) = S(I,J) + B(K,I) * W(K,J)                                      223
            DO 3142  I=1,NK                                                   224
 3142  WRITE OUTPUT TAPE 6, 905, (S(I,J), J=1,NK)                             225
            WRITE OUTPUT TAPE 6, 997                                          226
C 3.
            CALL TRIANG (S, NK)                                               230
            CALL TRIN (S, T, NK)                                              231
            DO 321  I=1,NJ                                                    232
            DO 321  J=1,NK                                                    233
            W(I,J) = 0.                                                       234
            DO 321  K=1,J                                                     235
  321  W(I,J) = W(I,J) + B(I,K) * T(J,K)                                      236
            DO 3212  I=1,NJ                                                   237
 3212  WRITE OUTPUT TAPE 6, 905, (W(I,J), J=1,NK)                             238
            WRITE OUTPUT TAPE 6, 997                                          239
C 4.
            DO 326  I=1,NK                                                    243
            DO 326  J=1,LG                                                    244
            B(I,J) = 0.                                                       245
            DO 326  K=1,NK                                                    246
  326  B(I,J) = B(I,J) + H(I,K) * A(K,J)                                      247
            DO 3262  I=1,NK                                                   248
 3262  WRITE OUTPUT TAPE 6, 905, (B(I,J), J=1,LG)                             249
            WRITE OUTPUT TAPE 6, 997                                          250
C 5.
            DO 329  I=1,NK                                                    254
            DO 329  J=1,NK                                                    255
  329  H(I,J) = H(I,J) * D(J)                                                 256
            DO 3292  I=1,NK                                                   257
 3292  WRITE OUTPUT TAPE 6, 905, (H(I,J), J=1,NK)                             258
            WRITE OUTPUT TAPE 6, 997                                          259
C 6.
            DO 334  I=1,NJ                                                    263
            DO 334  J=1,LG                                                    264
            F(I,J) = 0.                                                       265
            DO 334  K=1,NK                                                    266
  334  F(I,J) = F(I,J) + W(I,K) * B(K,J)                                      267
            DO 3342  I=1,NJ                                                   268
 3342  WRITE OUTPUT TAPE 6, 905, (F(I,J), J=1,LG)                             269
            WRITE OUTPUT TAPE 6, 997                                          270
C 7.
            DO 339  I=1,NJ                                                    274
            DO 339  J=1,NK                                                    275
            B(I,J) = 0.                                                       276
            DO 339  K=1,NK                                                    277
```

```
  339  B(I,J) = B(I,J) + W(I,K) * H(K,J)                              278
       DO 3392  I=1,NJ                                                279
 3392  WRITE OUTPUT TAPE 6, 905, (B(I,J), J=1,NK)                     280
       WRITE OUTPUT TAPE 6, 997                                       281
C 8.
       DO 341  I=1,NI                                                 285
  341  READ TAPE 2, (R(I,J), J=1,NJ)                                  286
       REWIND 2                                                       287
       DO 347  I=1,NI                                                 288
       DO 347  J=1,LG                                                 289
       W(I,J) = 0.                                                    290
       DO 347  K=1,NJ                                                 291
  347  W(I,J) = W(I,J) + R(I,K) * F(K,J)                              292
C 9.
       DO 352  I=1,NI                                                 296
       DO 352  J=1,NK                                                 297
       F(I,J) = 0.                                                    298
       DO 352  K=1,NJ                                                 299
  352  F(I,J) = F(I,J) + R(I,K) * B(K,J)                              300
       DO 354  I=1,NI                                                 301
  354  WRITE OUTPUT TAPE 6, 900, (W(I,J), J=1,LG), (F(I,J), J=1,NK)   302
       DO 3545 I = 1,NJ                                               303
       DO 3545 J = 1,LG                                               304
       B(I,J) = 0.                                                    305
       DO 3545 K = 1,NI                                               306
 3545  B(I,J) = B(I,J) + R(K,I)*W(K,J)                                307
       DO 3550 I = 1,NJ                                               308
       DO 3550 J = 1,NK                                               309
       W(I,J) =0.                                                     310
       DO 3550 K = 1,NI                                               311
 3550  W(I,J) = W(I,J) + R(K,I)*F(K,J)                                312
       WRITE OUTPUT TAPE 6,997                                        313
       DO 3552 I = 1,NJ                                               314
 3552  WRITE OUTPUT TAPE 6,900,(B(I,J),J =1,LG),(W(I,J),J =1,NK)      315
  900  FORMAT (10F7.3)                                                316
  901  FORMAT (10F6.3)                                                317
  902  FORMAT (F7.5/F4.2/(I4))                                        318
  903  FORMAT (10F2.0)                                                319
  905  FORMAT (10F10.4)                                               320
  906  FORMAT (I5)                                                    321
  997  FORMAT (1H )                                                   322
  999  FORMAT (1H1)                                                   323
       CALL    EXIT                                                   324
       END                                                            325
C
       SUBROUTINE SYMIN (S, N)                                        001
       DIMENSION S(150,100)                                           002
       N1 = N-1                                                       003
       DO 04  I=2,N                                                   004
       I1 = I - 1                                                     005
       DO 04  J=1,I1                                                  006
   04  S(I,J) = 0.                                                    007
       C = 1./SQRTF(S(1,1))                                           008
       S(1,1) = 1.                                                    009
       DO 13  J=1,N                                                   010
   13  S(1,J) = S(1,J) * C                                            011
       DO 21  K=2,N                                                   012
       DO 17  J=1,N                                                   013
       K1 = K-1                                                       014
       DO 17  I=1,K1                                                  015
   17  S(K,J) = S(K,J) - S(I,K) * S(I,J)                              016
       C = 1./SQRTF(S(K,K))                                           017
       DO 191  I=1,K1                                                 018
  191  S(I,K) = 0.                                                    019
       S(K,K) = 1.                                                    020
       DO 21  J=1,N                                                   021
   21  S(K,J) = S(K,J) * C                                            022
       DO 30  J=2,N                                                   023
       J1 = J-1                                                       024
       DO 30  I=1,J1                                                  025
       DO 30  K=J,N                                                   026
   30  S(I,J) = S(I,J) + S(K,I) * S(K,J)                              027
       DO 35 J = 1,N1                                                 028
       S(J,J) = S(J,J) **2                                            029
       J2 = J+1                                                       030
       DO 35  I=J2,N                                                  031
   35  S(J,J) = S(J,J) + S(I,J)**2                                    032
       S(N,N) = S(N,N)**2                                             033
       DO 42  I=1,N1                                                  034
       I2 = I+1                                                       035
       DO 42  J=I2,N                                                  036
                                                                      037
```

694

```
 42   S(J,I) = S(I,J)
      RETURN                                                        038
      END                                                           039
C
      SUBROUTINE TRIANG (A,N)                                       001
C TRIANGULAR FACTOR
      DIMENSION A(10,10)                                            003
      NN = N-1                                                      004
      DO 14 K=1,NN                                                  005
      C=1./SQRTF(A(K,K))                                            006
      DO 10  I = K,N                                                007
 10   A(I,K) = A(I,K) * C                                           008
      IF(I-N)11,16,16                                               009
 11   KK = K + 1                                                    010
      DO 14 J = KK,N                                                011
      DO 14 I = J,N                                                 012
 14   A(I,J) = A(I,J) - A(I,K)*A(J,K)                               013
      A(N,N) = SQRTF(A(N,N))                                        014
 16   RETURN                                                        015
      END                                                           016
C
      SUBROUTINE TRIN (A,B,N)                                       001
C INVERSE OF TRIANGULAR MATRIX
      DIMENSION A(10,10), B(10,10)                                  003
      DO 10   J=1,N                                                 004
      B(J,J) = 1./A(J,J)                                            005
      DO 10   I=J,N                                                 006
 10   A(I,J) = A(I,J) * B(J,J)                                      007
      DO 16   I=2,N                                                 008
      DO 16   IJ=2,I                                                009
      J=I+1-IJ                                                      010
      B(I,J) = 0.0                                                  011
      J1 = J+1                                                      012
      DO 16   K=J1, I                                               013
 16   B(I,J) = B(I,J) - B(I,K) * A(K,J)                             014
      RETURN                                                        015
      END                                                           016
C
 *    DATA
 .00010
 .80
   12
    9
    3
   40
    2
  0.128   0.181   0.421   0.506   0.857   0.746   0.280   0.178   0.246
  0.764   0.740   0.563  -0.387  -0.293  -0.202   0.261   0.281   0.043
 -0.030  -0.046   0.014   0.147  -0.109  -0.135   0.640   0.682   0.661
 -0.280  -0.351  -0.326  -0.023  -0.109  -0.186   0.083   0.091  -0.654
 -0.336  -0.306  -0.429  -0.542  -0.006  -0.153  -0.428   0.056  -0.124
 -0.276  -0.324  -0.271  -0.370  -0.225   0.035   0.129  -0.446  -0.124
  0.057  -0.070  -0.016   0.006   0.152  -0.441  -0.166  -0.354  -0.033
 -0.010  -0.140   0.326  -0.004  -0.258  -0.091  -0.410  -0.200  -0.101
 -0.303   0.227  -0.014   0.029  -0.102  -0.125  -0.086  -0.106  -0.074
  0.086   0.057  -0.003   0.161   0.073   0.134  -0.082  -0.067  -0.009
  0.164   0.106  -0.124   0.234  -0.002   0.227  -0.072   0.025   0.156
  0.036  -0.074  -0.142   0.242   0.023   0.192  -0.148  -0.119   0.011
 1.000    .829    .768    .108    .033    .108    .298    .309    .351
  .829   1.000    .775    .115    .061    .125    .323    .347    .369
  .768    .775   1.000    .272    .205    .238    .296    .271    .385
  .108    .115    .272   1.000    .636    .626    .249    .183    .369
  .033    .061    .205    .636   1.000    .709    .138    .091    .254
  .108    .125    .238    .626    .709   1.000    .190    .103    .291
  .298    .323    .296    .249    .138    .190   1.000    .654    .527
  .309    .347    .271    .183    .091    .103    .654   1.000    .541
  .351    .369    .385    .369    .254    .291    .527    .541   1.000
 1 1 1 0 0 0 0 0 0
 0 0 0 1 1 1 0 0 0
 0 0 0 0 0 0 1 1 1
 0.717 0.740 0.773 0.556 0.463 0.518 0.640 0.615 0.715
 0.493 0.478 0.296-0.649-0.744-0.694 0.080 0.166-0.034
 0.350 0.322 0.406 0.068 0.181 0.188-0.588-0.621-0.369
  0.504   0.358   0.404
  0.524  -0.889   0.079
  0.687   0.287  -0.911
```

695

```
C CHAPTER 22 - FACTOR ANALYSIS AND THE BINARY DATA MATRIX                    001
C    22.3 LEAST SQUARE SIMPLEX DATA MATRIX
C                                                                            002
      DIMENSION X(70,70), B(70,70), BL(70,70), H(70,70), S(70), IV(70),      003
     1VM(70), D(70), P(70), V(70)                                            004
      READ INPUT TAPE 5, 903, NI, NJ, NL                                     005
      WRITE OUTPUT TAPE 6, 903, NI, NJ, NL                                   006
      WRITE OUTPUT TAPE 6, 997                                               007
      READ INPUT TAPE 5, 904, (P(I), I=1,NL)                                 008
      WRITE OUTPUT TAPE 6, 904, (P(I), I=1,NL)                               009
      WRITE OUTPUT TAPE 6, 997                                               010
      DO 10   J=1,NJ                                                         011
      READ INPUT TAPE 5, 902, (X(I,J), I=1,NI)                               012
   10 WRITE OUTPUT TAPE 6, 905, (X(I,J), I=1,NI)                             013
      FNI = NI                                                               014
      REWIND 2                                                               018
C SUM OF ROWS                                                                020
      DO 107 I=1,NI                                                          022
      S(I) = 0.                                                              023
      DO 106 J=1,NJ                                                          024
  106 S(I) = S(I) + X(I,J)                                                   025
  107 WRITE TAPE 2, (X(I,J), J=1,NJ)                                         026
      REWIND 2                                                               027
C RANK ORDER OF ROWS                                                         029
      DO 115 I=1,NI                                                          031
      IL = 0                                                                 032
      DO 114  J=1,NI                                                         033
      IF (S(I)-S(J)) 113, 113, 114                                           034
  113 IL = IL + 1                                                            035
  114 CONTINUE                                                               036
  115 IV(I) = IL                                                             037
      DO 118  I=1,NI                                                         038
      IL = IV(I)                                                             039
  118 READ TAPE 2, (X(IL,J), J=1,NJ)                                         040
      REWIND 2                                                               041
C RANK ORDER OF COLUMNS                                                      043
      DO 123  J=1,NJ                                                         045
      VM(J) = 0.                                                             046
      DO 123  I=1,NI                                                         047
  123 VM(J) = VM(J) + X(I,J)                                                 048
      DO 125  J=1,NJ                                                         049
  125 WRITE TAPE 2, (X(I,J), I=1,NI)                                         050
      REWIND 2                                                               051
      DO 133  I=1,NJ                                                         052
      IL = 0                                                                 053
      DO 132  J=1,NJ                                                         054
      IF (VM(I)-VM(J)) 131, 131, 132                                         055
  131 IL = IL + 1                                                            056
  132 CONTINUE                                                               057
  133 IV(I) = IL                                                             058
      DO 137  J=1,NJ                                                         059
      JL = IV(J)                                                             060
      READ TAPE 2, (X(I,JL), I=1,NI)                                         061
  137 V(JL) = VM(J)                                                          062
      REWIND 2
      DO 1372  J=1,NJ                                                        063
 1372 VM(J) = V(J)                                                           064
      WRITE OUTPUT TAPE 6, 998                                               065
      DO 1374  I=1,NI                                                        066
 1374 WRITE OUTPUT TAPE 6, 905, (X(I,J), J=1,NJ)                             067
      WRITE OUTPUT TAPE 6, 997                                               068
      WRITE OUTPUT TAPE 6, 905, (VM(J), J=1,NJ)                             069
C 1.
      DO 142  I=1,NJ                                                         073
      DO 142  J=1,NJ                                                         074
      B(I,J) = -VM(I) * VM(J) / FNI                                          075
      DO 142  K=1,NI                                                         076
  142 B(I,J) = B(I,J) + X(K,I) * X(K,J)                                      077
      DO 1422  I=1,NJ                                                        078
 1422 WRITE OUTPUT TAPE 6, 900, (B(I,J), J=1,NJ)                             079
      WRITE OUTPUT TAPE 6, 997                                               080
      NL1 = NL - 1                                                           081
      DO 144  I=1,NL1                                                        082
  144 D(I) = P(I) - P(I+1)                                                   083
      D(NL) = P(NL)                                                          084
      WRITE OUTPUT TAPE 6, 900, (D(I), I=1,NL)                               085
      WRITE OUTPUT TAPE 6, 997                                               086
```

```
C 2., 3.
      P(NL+1) = 0.                                              090
      DO 153  L=1,NL                                            091
      LL = FNI * P(L+1) + 1.1                                   092
      LU = FNI * P(L) + .1                                      093
      WRITE OUTPUT TAPE 6, 1492, LL, LU                        094
 1492 FORMAT (2I2)                                              095
      WRITE OUTPUT TAPE 6, 997                                  096
      DO 153  J=1,NJ                                            097
      BL(J,L) = -VM(J) * D(L)                                   098
      DO 153  K=LL,LU                                           099
  153 BL(J,L) = BL(J,L) + X(K,J)                                100
      WRITE OUTPUT TAPE 6, 998                                  101
      DO 1572  I=1,NL                                           102
 1572 WRITE OUTPUT TAPE 6, 900, (BL(J,I), J=1,NJ)              103
      WRITE OUTPUT TAPE 6, 997                                  104
C 5.
      DO 162  I=1,NJ                                            108
      DO 162  J=1,NJ                                            109
      H(I,J) = 0.                                               110
      DO 162  K=1,NL                                            111
  162 H(I,J) = H(I,J) + BL(I,K) * BL(J,K) / D(K)               112
      DO 801  I=1,NJ                                            113
  801 WRITE OUTPUT TAPE 6, 900, (H (I,J), J=1,NJ)              114
      WRITE OUTPUT TAPE 6, 997                                  115
      NP1 = FNI * P(1) + .1                                     116
      DO 1626  J=1,NJ                                           117
      S(J) = -VM(J) * P(1)                                      118
      DO 1626  I=1,NP1                                          119
 1626 S(J) = S(J) + X(I,J)                                      120
      SQ = 1. / SQRTF(1.-P(1))                                  121
      DO 1629  I=1,NJ                                           122
 1629 S(J) = S(J) * SQ                                          123
      DO 1632  I=1,NJ                                           124
      DO 1632  J=1,NJ                                           125
 1632 H(I,J) = H(I,J) / FNI + S(I) * S(J)                      126
      WRITE OUTPUT TAPE 6, 998                                  127
      DO 1634  I=1,NJ                                           128
 1634 WRITE OUTPUT TAPE 6, 900, (H(I,J), J=1,NJ)               129
      WRITE OUTPUT TAPE 6, 998                                  130
C 7.
      DO 166  I=1,NJ                                            134
      DO 165  J=1,NJ                                            135
  165 H(I,J) = B(I,J) - H(I,J)                                  136
  166 D(I) = 1. / SQRTF(H(I,I))                                 137
C 8.
      DO 169  I=1,NJ                                            141
      DO 169  J=1,NJ                                            142
  169 H(I,J) = D(I) * H(I,J) * D(J)                             143
      DO 171  I=1,NJ                                            144
  171 WRITE OUTPUT TAPE 6, 900, (H(I,J), J=1,NJ)               145
  900 FORMAT (10F11.4)                                          146
  902 FORMAT (20F2.0)                                           147
  903 FORMAT (I4)                                               148
  904 FORMAT (15F4.2)                                           149
  905 FORMAT (20F3.0)                                           150
  997 FORMAT (1H )                                              151
  998 FORMAT (1H0)                                              152
      CALL    EXIT                                              154
      END                                                       155
C
*     DATA
   10
    4
    3
  .90 .70 .50
  1 1 1 1 1 1 1 1 1 0
  1 1 1 1 0 1 1 0 0
  1 1 1 0 1 1 0 0 1 0
  1 1 1 1 0 1 0 0 0 0
```

697

```
C CHAPTER 23 - FACTOR ANALYSIS AND PREDICTION                        001
C    23.2 RANK REDUCTION SOLUTION                                     002
C                                                                     003
      DIMENSION X(100,50), XP(100,30), XC(100,20), RPP(30,30),        004
     1RPC(30,20), B(30,20), Y(30), W(30), D(10), KV(10), R(30,30)     005
      EQUIVALENCE (X(1),XP(1)), (X(3001),XC(1)), (R(1),RPP(1))  ,     006
     1(R(1501),RPC(1))                                                007
      REWIND 2                                                        008
      REWIND 3                                                        009
      READ INPUT TAPE 5, 902, P, PV, NI, NJ, NP, NC, IL, NF           011
      DO 12  I=1,NI                                                   014
      READ INPUT TAPE 5, 900, (X(I,J), J=1,NJ)                        015
   12 WRITE TAPE 2, (X(I,J), J=1,NJ)                                  016
      REWIND 2                                                        019
      FNI = NI                                                        017
      FNP = NP                                                        018
C 2.
      DO 53  J=1,NC                                                   023
      JNC = J + NP                                                    024
      DO 53  I=1,NI                                                   025
   53 XC(I,J) = X(I,JNC)                                              026
      DO 105  I=1,NP                                                  027
      DO 105  J=1,NP                                                  028
      RPP(I,J) = 0.                                                   029
      DO 105  K=1,NI                                                  030
  105 RPP(I,J) = RPP(I,J) + XP(K,I) * XP(K,J)                         031
      DO 1082  I=1,NP                                                 032
 1082 WRITE OUTPUT TAPE 6, 900, (RPP(I,J), J=1,NP)                    033
      WRITE OUTPUT TAPE 6, 997                                        034
C 3.
      DO 113  I=1,NP                                                  038
      DO 113  J=1,NC                                                  039
      RPC(I,J) = 0.                                                   040
      DO 113  K=1,NI                                                  041
  113 RPC(I,J) = RPC(I,J) + XP(K,I) * XC(K,J)                         042
      DO 1162  J=1,NC                                                 043
 1162 WRITE OUTPUT TAPE 6, 900, (RPC(I,J), I=1,NP)                    044
      WRITE OUTPUT TAPE 6, 998                                        045
      DO 118  I=1,NP                                                  046
      WRITE TAPE 3, (RPP(I,J), J=1,NP)                                047
  118 WRITE TAPE 3, (RPC(I,J), J=1,NC)                                048
      REWIND 3                                                        049
C 4.
      CALL SYMIN (RPP, NP)                                            053
C 5.
      DO 125  I=1,NP                                                  057
      DO 125  J=1,NC                                                  058
      B(I,J) = 0.                                                     059
      DO 125  K=1,NP                                                  060
  125 B(I,J) = B(I,J) + RPP(I,K) * RPC(K,J)                           061
      DO 127  I=1,NP                                                  062
  127 WRITE OUTPUT TAPE 6, 900, (B(I,J), J=1,NC)                      063
      WRITE OUTPUT TAPE 6, 997                                        064
      DO 802  I=1,NP                                                  065
      READ TAPE 3, (R(I,J), J=1,NP)                                   066
  802 READ TAPE 3, (RPC(I,J), J=1,NC)                                 067
      REWIND 3                                                        068
      DO 1275  I=1,NP                                                 069
      DO 1275  J=1,NC                                                 070
      X(I,J) = 0.                                                     071
      DO 1275  K=1,NP                                                 072
 1275 X(I,J) = X(I,J) + R(I,K) * B(K,J)                               073
      DO 1277  J=1,NC                                                 074
 1277 WRITE OUTPUT TAPE 6, 900, (X(I,J), I=1,NP)                      075
  900 FORMAT (10F7.3)                                                 076
  902 FORMAT (F7.5/F4.2/(I4))                                         077
  997 FORMAT (1H )                                                    078
  998 FORMAT (1H0)                                                    079
      CALL EXIT                                                       080
      END                                                             081
C
      SUBROUTINE SYMIN (S, N)                                         001
      DIMENSION S(30,30)                                              002
      DO 04 I = 2,N                                                   003
      I1 = I-1                                                        004
      DO 04 J = 1,I1                                                  005
   04 S(I,J) = 0.                                                     006
      C = 1./SQRTF(S(1,1))                                            007
      S(1,1) = 1.                                                     008
      DO 13  J=1,N                                                    009
```

698

```
13      S(1,J) = S(1,J) * C                                      010
        DO 21   K=2,N                                            011
        DO 17   J=1,N                                            012
        K1 = K-1                                                 013
        DO 17   I=1,K1                                           014
17      S(K,J) = S(K,J) - S(I,K) * S(I,J)                        015
        C = 1./SQRTF(S(K,K))                                     016
        DO 191  I=1,K1                                           017
191     S(I,K) = 0.                                              018
        S(K,K) = 1.                                              019
        DO 21   J=1,N                                            020
21      S(K,J) = S(K,J) * C                                      021
        DO 30   J=2,N                                            022
        J1 = J-1                                                 023
        DO 30   I=1,J1                                           024
        DO 30   K=J,N                                            025
30      S(I,J) = S(I,J) + S(K,I) * S(K,J)                        026
        DO 35   J=1,N                                            027
        S(J,J) = S(J,J) **2                                      028
        J2 = J+1                                                 029
        DO 35   I=J2,N                                           030
35      S(J,J) = S(J,J) + S(I,J)**2                              031
        N1 = N-1                                                 032
        DO 42   I=1,N1                                           033
        I2 = I+1                                                 034
        DO 42   J=I2,N                                           035
42      S(J,I) = S(I,J)                                          036
        RETURN                                                   037
        END                                                      038
C
*       DATA
.00010
.75
 12
  9
  6
  3
 40
  2
  0.128  0.181  0.421  0.506  0.857  0.746  0.280  0.178  0.246
  0.764  0.740  0.563 -0.387 -0.293 -0.202  0.261  0.281  0.043
 -0.030 -0.046  0.014  0.147 -0.109 -0.135  0.640  0.682  0.661
 -0.280 -0.351 -0.326 -0.023 -0.109 -0.186  0.083  0.091 -0.654
 -0.336 -0.306 -0.429 -0.542 -0.006 -0.153 -0.428  0.056 -0.124
 -0.276 -0.324 -0.271 -0.370 -0.225  0.035  0.129 -0.446 -0.124
  0.057 -0.070 -0.016  0.006  0.152 -0.441 -0.166 -0.354 -0.033
 -0.010 -0.140  0.326 -0.004 -0.258 -0.091 -0.410 -0.200 -0.101
 -0.303  0.227 -0.014  0.029 -0.102 -0.125 -0.086 -0.106 -0.074
  0.086  0.057 -0.003  0.161  0.073  0.134 -0.082 -0.067 -0.009
  0.164  0.106 -0.124  0.234 -0.002  0.227 -0.072  0.025  0.156
  0.036 -0.074 -0.142  0.242  0.023  0.192 -0.148 -0.119  0.011

C CHAPTER 23 - FACTOR ANALYSIS AND PREDICTION                    001
C    23.3 BASIC STRUCTURE SOLUTION                               002
C                                                                003
        DIMENSION X(100,50), XP(100,30), XC(100,20), RPP(30,30), 004
       1RPC(30,20), B(30,20), Y(30), W(30), D(10), KV(10), R(30,30) 005
        EQUIVALENCE (X(1),XP(1)), (X(3001),XC(1)), (R(1),RPP(1)) 006
       1(R(1501),RPC(1))                                         007
        REWIND 2                                                 008
        REWIND 3                                                 009
        READ INPUT TAPE 5, 902, P, PV, NI, NJ, NP, NC, IL, NF    011
        DO 12   I=1,NI                                           014
        READ INPUT TAPE 5, 900, (X(I,J), J=1,NJ)                 015
12      WRITE TAPE 2, (X(I,J), J=1,NJ)                           016
        REWIND 2                                                 019
        FNI = NI                                                 017
        FNP = NP                                                 018
C 2.
        DO 53   J=1,NC                                           023
        JNC = J + NP                                             024
        DO 53   I=1,NI                                           025
53      XC(I,J) = X(I,JNC)                                       026
        DO 105  I=1,NP                                           027
        DO 105  J=1,NP                                           028
        RPP(I,J) = 0.                                            029
        DO 105  K=1,NI                                           030
105     RPP(I,J) = RPP(I,J) + XP(K,I) * XP(K,J)                  031
C 3.
        DO 113  I=1,NP                                           038
```

699

```
          DO 113  J=1,NC                                              039
          RPC(I,J) = 0.                                              040
          DO 113  K=1,NI                                             041
  113     RPC(I,J) = RPC(I,J) + XP(K,I) * XC(K,J)                    042
          DO 118  I=1,NP                                             046
          WRITE TAPE 3, (RPP(I,J), J=1,NP)                           047
  118     WRITE TAPE 3, (RPC(I,J), J=1,NC)                           048
          REWIND 3                                                   049
          IL = 2000                                                  050
          P = .00001                                                 051
          DO 202  I=1,NP                                             052
          READ TAPE 3, (RPP(I,J), J=1,NP)                            053
  202     READ TAPE 3, (RPC(I,J), J=1,NC)                            054
          REWIND 3                                                   055
C 1.
          G = 0.                                                     065
          P = .00001                                                 066
          NP1 = NP + 1                                               067
          DO 2052  I=1,NP                                            068
 2052     RPP(I,NP1) = RPC(I,1)                                      069
          DO 209  J=1,NP1                                            070
          DO 209  I=1,NP                                             071
          G = G + R(I,J)**2                                          072
  209     Y(J) = 1. / FNP                                            073
          Y(NP1) = -1.                                               074
          E = 0.                                                     075
          DO 227  K=1,IL                                             076
          KI = K                                                     077
C 2.
  214     DO 217  I=1,NP                                             081
  215     W(I) = 0.                                                  082
  216     DO 217  J=1,NP1                                            083
  217     W(I) = W(I) + R(I,J) * Y(J)                               084
          S = 0.                                                     085
          DO 218  I=1,NP                                             086
  218     S = MAX1F(S,ABSF(W(I)))                                    087
C 3.
          DO 221  I=1,NP1                                            091
          Y(I) = Y(I)*G                                              092
          DO 221  J=1,NP                                             093
  221     Y(I) = Y(I) - W(J) * R(J,I)                               094
          E1 = E                                                     095
          E = Y(NP1)                                                 096
          DO 226  I=1,NP1                                            097
  226     Y(I) = -Y(I) / Y(NP1)                                     098
          IF(P-S)227,229,229                                         099
  227     CONTINUE                                                   100
  229     WRITE OUTPUT TAPE 6, 903, KI                               101
          WRITE OUTPUT TAPE 6, 900, E                                102
          WRITE OUTPUT TAPE 6, 900, (Y(I), I=1,NP1)                  103
          DO 2294  I=1,NP                                            104
          W(I) = -RPC(I,1)                                           105
          DO 2294  J=1,NP                                            106
 2294     W(I) = W(I) + R(I,J) * Y(J)                               107
          WRITE OUTPUT TAPE 6, 900, (W(I), I=1,NP)                   108
  900     FORMAT (10F7.3)                                            109
  902     FORMAT (F7.5/F4.2/(I4))                                    110
  903     FORMAT (I4)                                                111
  997     FORMAT (1H )                                               112
  998     FORMAT (1HO)                                               113
          CALL EXIT                                                  114
          END                                                        115
C
*     DATA
.00010
.75
 12
  9
  6
  3
 40
  2
 0.128  0.181  0.421  0.506  0.857  0.746  0.280  0.178  0.246
 0.764  0.740  0.563 -0.387 -0.293 -0.202  0.261  0.281  0.043
-0.030 -0.046  0.014  0.147 -0.109 -0.135  0.640  0.682  0.661
-0.280 -0.351 -0.326 -0.023 -0.109 -0.186  0.083  0.091 -0.654
-0.336 -0.306 -0.429 -0.542 -0.006 -0.153 -0.428  0.056 -0.124
-0.276 -0.324 -0.271 -0.370 -0.225  0.035  0.129 -0.446 -0.124
```

```
 0.057 -0.070 -0.016  0.006  0.152 -0.441 -0.166 -0.354 -0.033
-0.010 -0.140  0.326 -0.004 -0.258 -0.091 -0.410 -0.200 -0.101
-0.303  0.227 -0.014  0.029 -0.102 -0.125 -0.086 -0.106 -0.074
 0.086  0.057 -0.003  0.161  0.073  0.134 -0.082 -0.067 -0.009
 0.164  0.106 -0.124  0.234 -0.002  0.227 -0.072  0.025  0.156
 0.036 -0.074 -0.142  0.242  0.023  0.192 -0.148 -0.119  0.011


C CHAPTER 23 - FACTOR ANALYSIS AND PREDICTION                              001
C    23.4 NONBASIC SOLUTION                                                002
C                                                                         003
      DIMENSION X(100,50), XP(100,30), XC(100,20), RPP(30,30),            004
     1RPC(30,20), B(30,20), Y(30), W(30), D(10), KV(10), R(30,30)         005
      EQUIVALENCE (X(1),XP(1)), (X(3001),XC(1)), (R(1),RPP(1))            006
     1(R(1501),RPC(1))                                                    007
      REWIND 2                                                            008
      REWIND 3                                                            009
      READ INPUT TAPE 5, 902, P, PV, NI, NJ, NP, NC, IL, NF              011
      WRITE OUTPUT TAPE 6, 902, P, PV, NI, NJ, NP, NC, IL, NF            012
      WRITE OUTPUT TAPE 6, 997                                            013
      DO 12  I=1,NI                                                       014
      READ INPUT TAPE 5, 900, (X(I,J), J=1,NJ)                            015
   12 WRITE TAPE 2, (X(I,J), J=1,NJ)                                      016
      REWIND 2                                                            019
      FNI = NI                                                            017
      FNP = NP                                                            018
C 2.
      DO 53  J=1,NC                                                       023
      JNC = J + NP                                                        024
      DO 53  I=1,NI                                                       025
   53 XC(I,J) = X(I,JNC)                                                  026
      DO 105  I=1,NP                                                      027
      DO 105  J=1,NP                                                      028
      RPP(I,J) = 0.                                                       029
      DO 105  K=1,NI                                                      030
  105 RPP(I,J) = RPP(I,J) + XP(K,I) * XP(K,J)                            031
      DO 1082  I=1,NP                                                     032
 1082 WRITE OUTPUT TAPE 6, 900, (RPP(I,J), J=1,NP)                        033
      WRITE OUTPUT TAPE 6, 997                                            034
C 3.
      DO 113  I=1,NP                                                      038
      DO 113  J=1,NC                                                      039
      RPC(I,J) = 0.                                                       040
      DO 113  K=1,NI                                                      041
  113 RPC(I,J) = RPC(I,J) + XP(K,I) * XC(K,J)                            042
      DO 1162  J=1,NC                                                     043
 1162 WRITE OUTPUT TAPE 6, 900, (RPC(I,J), I=1,NP)                        044
      WRITE OUTPUT TAPE 6, 998                                            045
      DO 118  I=1,NP                                                      046
      WRITE TAPE 3, (RPP(I,J), J=1,NP)                                    047
  118 WRITE TAPE 3, (RPC(I,J), J=1,NC)                                    048
      REWIND 3                                                            049
      DO 302  I=1,NP                                                      050
      READ TAPE 3, (RPP(I,J), J=1,NP)                                     051
  302 READ TAPE 3, (RPC(I,J), J=1,NC)                                     052
      REWIND 3                                                            053
C 1.
      N1 = NP - 1                                                         057
      DO 308  I=1,N1                                                      058
      R(I,NP) = 0.                                                        059
      DO 308  J=1,N1                                                      060
  308 R(I,NP) = R(I,NP) + R(I,J)                                          061
      C = 0.                                                              062
      DO 311  I=1,N1                                                      063
  311 C = C + R(I,NP)                                                     064
      C = SQRTF(C)                                                        065
      DO 314  I=1,N1                                                      066
  314 R(I,NP) = R(I,NP) / C                                               067
      DO 318  J=1,NC                                                      068
      RPC(NP,J) = 0.                                                      069
      DO 317  I=1,N1                                                      070
  317 RPC(NP,J) = RPC(NP,J) + RPC(I,J)                                    071
  318 RPC(NP,J) = RPC(NP,J) / C                                           072
      DO 322  J=1,N1                                                      073
  322 R(NP,J) = R(J,NP)                                                   074
      R(NP,NP) = 1.                                                       075
      WRITE OUTPUT TAPE 6, 997                                            076
      DO 3232  I=1,NP                                                     077
 3232 WRITE OUTPUT TAPE 6, 900, (R(I,J), J=1,NP)                          078
      WRITE OUTPUT TAPE 6, 998                                            079
      DO 3234  I=1,NP                                                     080
                                                                          081
```

```
3234 WRITE OUTPUT TAPE 6, 900, (RPC(I,J), J=1,NC)
     WRITE OUTPUT TAPE 6, 998                          082
C 2.
     FN1 = N1                                          086
     Y(NP) = -C / SQRTF(FN1 + C**2)                    087
     C1 = 1. / SQRTF(FN1+C**2)                         088
C 4.
     DO 328  I=1,N1                                    092
328  Y(I) = C1                                         093
C 5.
     DO 331  I=1,NP                                    097
     DO 331  J=1,NP                                    098
331  R(I,J) = R(I,J) + Y(I) * Y(J)                     099
     CALL SYMIN (RPP, NP)                              100
C 6.
     DO 337   I=1,NP                                   104
     DO 337   J=1,NC                                   105
     B(I,J) = 0.                                       106
     DO 337   K=1,NP                                   107
337  B(I,J) = B(I,J) + RPP(I,K) * RPC(K,J)             108
     DO 339  I=1,NP                                    109
339  WRITE OUTPUT TAPE 6, 900, (B(I,J), J=1,NC)        110
     WRITE OUTPUT TAPE 6, 998                          111
     DO 3394  J=1,NC                                   112
     W(J) = 0.                                         113
     DO 3394  I=1,NP                                   114
3394 W(J) = W(J) + Y(I) * (B(I,J)-RPC(I,J))            115
     WRITE OUTPUT TAPE 6, 900, (W(J), J=1,NC)          116
900  FORMAT (10F7.3)                                   117
902  FORMAT (F7.5/F4.2/(I4))                           118
997  FORMAT (1H )                                      119
998  FORMAT (1H0)                                      120
     CALL EXIT                                         121
     END                                               122
C
     SUBROUTINE SYMIN (S, N)
     DIMENSION S(30,30)
01   DO 04 I = 2,N
02   I1 = I-1
03   DO 04 J = 1,I1
04   S(I,J) = 0.
10   C = 1./SQRTF(S(1,1))
11   S(1,1) = 1.
12   DO 13  J=1,N
13   S(1,J) = S(1,J) * C
14   DO 21  K=2,N
15   DO 17  J=1,N
151  K1 = K-1
16   DO 17  I=1,K1
17   S(K,J) = S(K,J) - S(I,K) * S(I,J)
18   C = 1./SQRTF(S(K,K))
19   DO 191  I=1,K1
191  S(I,K) = 0.
192  S(K,K) = 1.
20   DO 21  J=1,N
21   S(K,J) = S(K,J) * C
25   DO 30  J=2,N
26   J1 = J-1
27   DO 30  I=1,J1
29   DO 30  K=J,N
30   S(I,J) = S(I,J) + S(K,I) * S(K,J)
31   DO 35  J=1,N
32   S(J,J) = S(J,J) **2
33   J2 = J+1
34   DO 35  I=J2,N
35   S(J,J) = S(J,J) + S(I,J)**2
38   N1 = N-1
39   DO 42  I=1,N1
40   I2 = I+1
41   DO 42  J=I2,N
42   S(J,I) = S(I,J)
     RETURN
     END
C
*    DATA
.00010
.75
 12
  9
  6
  3
 40
  2
```

702

```
 0.128   0.181   0.421   0.506   0.857   0.746   0.280   0.178   0.246
 0.764   0.740   0.563  -0.387  -0.293  -0.202   0.261   0.281   0.043
-0.030  -0.046   0.014   0.147  -0.109  -0.135   0.640   0.682   0.661
-0.280  -0.351  -0.326  -0.023  -0.109  -0.186   0.083   0.091  -0.654
-0.336  -0.306  -0.429  -0.542  -0.006  -0.153  -0.428   0.056  -0.124
-0.276  -0.324  -0.271  -0.370  -0.225   0.035   0.129  -0.446  -0.124
 0.057  -0.070  -0.016   0.006   0.152  -0.441  -0.166  -0.354  -0.033
-0.010  -0.140   0.326  -0.004  -0.258  -0.091  -0.410  -0.200  -0.101
-0.303   0.227  -0.014   0.029  -0.102  -0.125  -0.086  -0.106  -0.074
 0.086   0.057  -0.003   0.161   0.073   0.134  -0.082  -0.067  -0.009
 0.164   0.106  -0.124   0.234  -0.002   0.227  -0.072   0.025   0.156
 0.036  -0.074  -0.142   0.242   0.023   0.192  -0.148  -0.119   0.011
```

```
C CHAPTER 23 - FACTOR ANALYSIS AND PREDICTION                           001
C    23.5 INCREASING DEGREES OF FREEDOM BY FACTOR ANALYSIS              002
C                                                                       003
      DIMENSION X(100,50), XP(100,30), XC(100,20), RPP(30,30),          004
     1RPC(30,20), B(30,20), Y(30), W(30), D(10), KV(10), R(30,30)       005
      EQUIVALENCE (X(1),XP(1)), (X(3001),XC(1)), (R(1),RPP(1))  ,       006
     1(R(1501),RPC(1))                                                  007
      REWIND 2                                                          008
      REWIND 3                                                          009
      READ INPUT TAPE 5, 902, P, PV, NI, NJ, NP, NC, IL, NF             011
      WRITE OUTPUT TAPE 6, 902, P, PV, NI, NJ, NP, NC, IL, NF           012
      WRITE OUTPUT TAPE 6, 997                                          013
      DO 12  I=1,NI                                                     014
      READ INPUT TAPE 5, 900, (X(I,J), J=1,NJ)                          015
   12 WRITE TAPE 2, (X(I,J), J=1,NJ)                                    016
      REWIND 2                                                          019
      FNI = NI                                                          017
      FNP = NP                                                          018
      IL = 2000
      P = .00001
C 2.
C 3.
      DO 53  J=1,NC                                                     023
      JNC = J + NP                                                      024
      DO 53  I=1,NI                                                     025
   53 XC(I,J) = X(I,JNC)                                                026
      DO 105  I=1,NP                                                    027
      DO 105  J=1,NP                                                    028
      RPP(I,J) = 0.                                                     029
      DO 105  K=1,NI                                                    030
  105 RPP(I,J) = RPP(I,J) + XP(K,I) * XP(K,J)                           031
      DO 1082  I=1,NP                                                   032
 1082 WRITE OUTPUT TAPE 6, 900, (RPP(I,J), J=1,NP)                      033
      WRITE OUTPUT TAPE 6, 997                                          034
C 3.
      DO 113  I=1,NP                                                    038
      DO 113  J=1,NC                                                    039
      RPC(I,J) = 0.                                                     040
      DO 113  K=1,NI                                                    041
  113 RPC(I,J) = RPC(I,J) + XP(K,I) * XC(K,J)                           042
      DO 1162  J=1,NC                                                   043
 1162 WRITE OUTPUT TAPE 6, 900, (RPC(I,J), I=1,NP)                      044
      WRITE OUTPUT TAPE 6, 998                                          045
      DO 118  I=1,NP                                                    046
      WRITE TAPE 3, (RPP(I,J), J=1,NP)                                  047
  118 WRITE TAPE 3, (RPC(I,J), J=1,NC)                                  048
      REWIND 3                                                          049
      DO 402  I=1,NP                                                    050
      READ TAPE 3, (RPP(I,J), J=1,NP)                                   051
  402 READ TAPE 3, (RPC(I,J), J=1,NC)                                   052
      REWIND 3                                                          053
C 3.
      G = 0.                                                            057
      DO 430 L=1,NF                                                     058
      DO 4052  I=1,NP                                                   059
 4052 WRITE OUTPUT TAPE 6, 900, (R(I,J), J=1,NP)                        060
      WRITE OUTPUT TAPE 6, 997                                          061
      LF = L                                                            062
      E = 0.                                                            063
      DO 409  I=1,NP                                                    064
  409 B(I,L) = 1.                                                       065
      DO 425  K=1,IL                                                    066
      KV(L) = K                                                         067
      DO 415  I=1,NP                                                    068
      W(I) = 0.                                                         069
```

```
          DO 415  J=1,NP
415   W(I) = W(I) + R(I,J) * B(J,L)
          D(L) = 0.
          DO 418  I=1,NP
418   D(L) = D(L) + W(I) * B(I,L)
          D(L) = SQRTF(D(L))
          WRITE OUTPUT TAPE 6, 900, (W(I), I=1,NP)
          WRITE OUTPUT TAPE 6, 900, D(L)
          DO 424  I=1,NP
424   B(I,L) = W(I) / D(L)
          WRITE OUTPUT TAPE 6, 900, (B(I,L), I=1,NP)
          WRITE OUTPUT TAPE 6, 997
          E1 = E
          E = D(L)
          IF ((ABSF(E1/E-1.))-P) 426, 426, 425
425   CONTINUE
426   G = G + D(L)
          IF (G-PV*FNP) 428, 428, 431
428   DO 430  I=1,NP
          DO 430  J=1,NP
430   R(I,J) = R(I,J) - B(I,L) * B(J,L)
C 4.
431   DO 432  J=1,LF
432   WRITE OUTPUT TAPE 6, 900, (B(I,J), I=1,NP)
          WRITE OUTPUT TAPE 6, 997
          DO 435  I=1,NP
          DO 435  J=1,LF
435   B(I,J) = B(I,J) / D(J)
C 5.
          DO 440  I=1,LF
          DO 440  J=1,NC
          R(I,J) = 0.
          DO 440  K=1,NP
440   R(I,J) = R(I,J) + B(K,I) * RPC(K,J)
          DO 445  I=1,NP
          DO 445  J=1,NC
          X(I,J) = 0.
          DO 445  K=1,LF
445   X(I,J) = X(I,J) + B(I,K) * R(K,J)
          DO 4465  I=1,NC
          DO 4465  J=1,NC
          R(I,J) = 0.
          DO 4465  K=1,NP
4465  R(I,J) = R(I,J) + RPC(K,I) * X(K,J)
          DO 4467  I=1,NC
4467  WRITE OUTPUT TAPE 6, 900, (R(I,J), J=1,NC)
          WRITE OUTPUT TAPE 6, 997
          DO 447  I=1,NP
447   WRITE OUTPUT TAPE 6, 900, (X(I,J), J=1,NC)
          WRITE OUTPUT TAPE 6, 997
          WRITE OUTPUT TAPE 6, 900, (D(L), L=1,LF)
          WRITE OUTPUT TAPE 6, 997
          WRITE OUTPUT TAPE 6, 904, (KV(L), L=1,LF)
900   FORMAT (10F7.3)
902   FORMAT (F7.5/F4.2/(I4))
904   FORMAT (10I7)
997   FORMAT (1H )
998   FORMAT (1H0)
          CALL EXIT
          END
C
*     DATA
 .00010
 .75
  12
   9
   6
   3
  40
   2
  0.128   0.181   0.421   0.506   0.857   0.746   0.280   0.178   0.246
  0.764   0.740   0.563  -0.387  -0.293  -0.202   0.261   0.281   0.043
 -0.030  -0.046   0.014   0.147  -0.109  -0.135   0.640   0.682   0.661
 -0.280  -0.351  -0.326  -0.023  -0.109  -0.186   0.083   0.091  -0.654
 -0.336  -0.306  -0.429  -0.542  -0.006  -0.153  -0.428   0.056  -0.124
 -0.276  -0.324  -0.271  -0.370  -0.225   0.035   0.129  -0.446  -0.124
  0.057  -0.070  -0.016   0.006   0.152  -0.441  -0.166  -0.354  -0.033
 -0.010  -0.140   0.326  -0.004  -0.258  -0.091  -0.410  -0.200  -0.101
 -0.303   0.227  -0.014   0.029  -0.102  -0.125  -0.086  -0.106  -0.074
  0.086   0.057  -0.003   0.161   0.073   0.134  -0.082  -0.067  -0.009
  0.164   0.106  -0.124   0.234  -0.002   0.227  -0.072   0.025   0.156
  0.036  -0.074  -0.142   0.242   0.023   0.192  -0.148  -0.119   0.011
```

```
C CHAPTER 24 - MULTIPLE SET FACTOR ANALYSIS                                    001
C    24.4 PRELIMINARY ORTHOGONALIZATIONS, AND
C    24.5 MAXIMUM CORRELATION METHOD                                           002
C                                                                              003
*      CHAIN (99,A4)                                                           001
       DIMENSION R(100,100), B(100,10), S(20,10), A(10,10),                    005
      1U(100), UK(10), UL(10), N(10), NN(10)                                   006
       EQUIVALENCE (U(1), UK(1)), (U(15), UL(1))                               007
       COMMON P, NS, NSS, NI, NM, N, NN                                        008
       REWIND 2                                                                009
       REWIND 3                                                                010
       READ INPUT TAPE 5, 900, P, NS, NSS, NI                                  011
       READ INPUT TAPE 5, 901, (N(I), I=1,NS)                                  012
       WRITE OUTPUT TAPE 6, 901, (N(I), I=1,NS)                                013
       WRITE OUTPUT TAPE 6, 997                                                014
       P = .00001                                                             015
       NI = 100                                                               016
       NM = 0                                                                 017
       DO 1  I=1,NS                                                           018
 1     NM = NM + N(I)                                                         019
       DO 201 I = 1,NM                                                        020
       READ INPUT TAPE 5, 903, (R(I,J),J=1,NM)                                021
 201   WRITE OUTPUT TAPE 6,903,(R(I,J),J=1,NM)                                022
       WRITE OUTPUT TAPE 6, 997                                               024
       NN(1) = 0                                                              025
       DO 3  K=2,NS                                                           026
 3     NN(K) = NN(K-1) + N(K-1)                                               027
C INVERSE TRIANGULAR                                                          028
       DO 8  K=1,NS                                                           029
       NK = N(K)                                                              030
       DO 4  I=1,NK                                                           031
       IK = NN(K) + I                                                         032
       DO 4  J=1,NK                                                           033
       JK = NN(K) + J                                                         034
 4     S(I,J) = R(IK,JK)                                                      035
       CALL TRYIN (NK,S)                                                      036
       DO 5  I=1,NK                                                           037
       WRITE TAPE 2, (S(I,J), J=1,NK)                                         038
 5     WRITE OUTPUT TAPE 6, 904, (S(I,J), J=1,NK)                             039
       WRITE OUTPUT TAPE 6, 997                                               040
C PREMULTIPLICATION BY INVERSE TRIANGULAR                                     041
       DO 8  I=1,NM                                                           042
       DO 6  J=1,NK                                                           043
       U(J) = 0.                                                              044
       DO 6  M=1,J                                                            045
       MK = NN(K) + M                                                         046
 6     U(J) = U(J) + R(I,MK) * S(M,J)                                         047
       DO 8  J=1,NK                                                           048
       JK = NN(K) + J                                                         049
 8     R(I,JK) = U(J)                                                         050
       REWIND 2                                                               051
       DO 13  I=1,NM                                                          052
 13    WRITE OUTPUT TAPE 6, 904, (R(I,J), J=1,NM)                             053
       WRITE OUTPUT TAPE 6, 997                                               054
C POSTMULTIPLICATION BY INVERSE TRIANGULAR                                    055
       DO 18  K=1,NS                                                          056
       NK = N(K)                                                              057
       DO 14  I=1,NK                                                          058
 14    READ TAPE 2, (S(I,J), J=1,NK)                                          059
       DO 18  J=1,NM                                                          060
       DO 16  I=1,NK                                                          061
       U(I) = 0.                                                              062
       DO 16  M=1,I                                                           063
       MK = NN(K) + M                                                         064
 16    U(I) = U(I) + S(M,I)*R(MK,J)                                           065
       DO 18  I=1,NK                                                          066
       IK = NN(K) + I                                                         067
 18    R(IK,J) = U(I)                                                         068
       REWIND 2                                                               069
       DO 19  I=1,NM                                                          070
       WRITE TAPE 3, (R(I,J), J=1,NM)                                         071
 19    WRITE OUTPUT TAPE 6, 904, (R(I,J), J=1,NM)                             072
       WRITE OUTPUT TAPE 6, 997                                               073
       REWIND 3                                                               074
       WRITE OUTPUT TAPE 6,999                                                075
 900   FORMAT (F7.5/(I3))                                                     076
 901   FORMAT (12I3)                                                          077
 903   FORMAT (12F6.3)                                                        078
 904   FORMAT (12F9.4)                                                        079
 997   FORMAT (1H )                                                           080
 999   FORMAT (1H1)                                                           081
       CALL CHAIN (1, A4)                                                     082
       END                                                                    083
C
       SUBROUTINE TRYIN (N,A)                    705                          001
```

```
       DIMENSION A(20,1)                                        002
       N1 = N - 1                                               003
       DO 141  K=1,N1                                           004
       C = 1./SQRTF(A(K,K))                                     005
       DO 101  I=K,N                                            006
101    A(I,K) = A(I,K) * C                                      007
       KK = K + 1                                               008
       DO 141  J =KK,N                                          009
       DO 141  I=J,N                                            010
141    A(I,J) = A(I,J) - A(I,K) * A(J,K)                        011
       A(N,N) = SQRTF(A(N,N))                                   012
       A(1,1) = 1./A(1,1)                                       013
       DO 07 I = 2,N                                            014
       I1 = I-1                                                 015
       DO 065 J = 1,I1                                          016
065    A(I,J) = A(I,J)/A(I,I)                                   017
07     A(I,I) = 1./A(I,I)                                       018
       DO 14 I = 1,N1                                           019
       I2 = I+1                                                 020
       DO 14 J = I2,N                                           021
       J1 = J-1                                                 022
       A(I,J) =0.                                               023
       DO 14 K = I,J1                                           024
14     A(I,J) = A(I,J)- A(J,K)*A(I,K)                           025
       RETURN                                                   026
       END                                                      027
C
*      CHAIN (1,A4)                                             004
       DIMENSION R(100,100), B(100,10), S(20,10), A(10,10),     005
      1U(100), UK(10), UL(10), N(10), NN(10)                    006
       EQUIVALENCE (U(1), UK(1)), (U(15), UL(1))                007
       COMMON P, NS, NSS, NI, NM, N, NN                         008
       REWIND 3                                                 007
       DO 2  I=1,NM                                             009
2      READ TAPE 3, (R(I,J), J=1,NM)                            010
       REWIND 3                                                 011
C ITERATIONS FOR SUCCESSIVE VECTORS OF BETAS                   012
       DO 43 M = 1,NSS                                          013
       DO 10 I =1,NM                                            014
10     B(I,M) =1.                                               015
       F = 0.                                                   016
       DO 40  KK=1,NI                                           017
       DO 30  I=1,NM                                            018
       U(I) = 0.                                                019
       DO 30  J=1,NM                                            020
30     U(I) = U(I) + R(I,J) * B(J,M)                            021
       DO 36  K=1,NS                                            022
       NK = N(K)                                                023
       A(K,M) = 0.                                              024
       DO 34  I=1,NK                                            025
       IK = NN(K) + I                                           026
34     A(K,M) = A(K,M) + U(IK)**2                               027
       A(K,M) = SQRTF(A(K,M))                                   028
       DO 36  I=1,NK                                            029
       IK = NN(K) + I                                           030
36     B(IK,M) = U(IK)/A(K,M)                                   031
       E = 0.                                                   032
       DO 38  K=1,NS                                            033
38     E = E + A(K,M)                                           034
       F1 = F                                                   035
       F = E                                                    036
       IF (P-ABSF(F1/F-1.)) 40, 40, 42                          037
40     CONTINUE                                                 038
       WRITE OUTPUT TAPE 6,997                                  039
42     CALL RESID (NS,N,NN,U,UL,UK,B,R,NM,M)                    040
43     CONTINUE                                                 041
       DO 44 I = 1,NS                                           042
44     WRITEOUTPUT TAPE 6,904,(A(I,J),J=1,NSS)                  043
       WRITE OUTPUT TAPE 6,997                                  044
       DO 59  I=1,NM                                            045
59     WRITE OUTPUT TAPE 6, 904, (B(I,J), J=1,NSS)              046
       WRITE OUTPUT TAPE 6, 997                                 047
       CALL RHO (NS, NSS, NM, N, NN, U, B, R)                   048
       CALL BEE (NS, NSS, NM, N, NN, U, S, B)                   049
       WRITE OUTPUT TAPE 6, 999                                 050
904    FORMAT (12F9.4)                                          051
997    FORMAT (1H )                                             052
999    FORMAT (1H1)                                             053
       CALL EXIT                                                054
       END                                                      055
C
       SUBROUTINE RESID (NS,N,NN,U,UL,UK,B,R,NM,M)              001
       DIMENSION N(1),NN(1),U(1),UL(1),UK(1),B(100,1),R(100,1)  002
C RESIDUAL SUPER MATRIX                                         003
42     DO 56  K=1,NS                                            004
```

706

```
      NK = N(K)                                                          005
      DO 56 L = K,NS                                                     006
      NL = N(L)                                                          007
      DO 44   J=1,NL                                                     008
      JL = NN(L) + J                                                     009
      UL(J) = 0.                                                         010
      DO 44   I=1,NK                                                     011
      IK = NN(K) + I                                                     012
  44  UL(J) = UL(J) + B(IK,M) * R(IK,JL)                                 013
      G = 0.                                                             014
      DO 46   J=1,NL                                                     015
      JL = NN(L) + J                                                     016
  46  G = G + UL(J) * B(JL,M)                                            017
      G = G / 2.                                                         018
      DO 48   J=1,NL                                                     019
      JL = NN(L) + J                                                     020
  48  UL(J) = UL(J) - G * B(JL,M)                                        021
      DO 50   I=1,NK                                                     022
      IK = NN(K) + I                                                     023
      UK(I) = 0.                                                         024
      DO 50   J=1,NL                                                     025
      JL = NN(L) + J                                                     026
  50  UK(I) = UK(I) + R(IK,JL) * B(JL,M)                                 027
      DO 52   I=1,NK                                                     028
      IK = NN(K) + I                                                     029
  52  UK(I) = UK(I) - G * B(IK,M)                                        030
      DO 54   I=1,NK                                                     031
      IK = NN(K)+I                                                       032
      DO 54   J=1,NL                                                     033
      JL = NN(L) + J                                                     034
  54  R(IK,JL) = R(IK,JL) - B(IK,M) * UL(J) - UK(I) * B(JL,M)            035
      DO 56   I=1,NK                                                     036
      IK = NN(K) + I                                                     037
      DO 56   J=1,NL                                                     038
      JL = NN(L) + J                                                     039
  56  R(JL,IK) = R(IK,JL)                                                040
      DO 57   I=1,NM                                                     041
  57  WRITE OUTPUT TAPE 6, 904, (R(I,J), J=1,NM)                         042
      WRITE OUTPUT TAPE 6, 997                                          043
 904  FORMAT (12F9.4)                                                   044
 997  FORMAT (1H )                                                      045
      RETURN                                                            046
      END                                                               047
C
      SUBROUTINE RHO (NS,NSS,NM,N,NN,U,B,R)                             001
      DIMENSION N(1),NN(1),U(1),B(100,1),R(100,1)                       002
C POSTMULTIPLICATION OF SUPERMATRIX BY DIAGONALS OF BETAS
      DO 71   I=1,NM                                                    004
  71  READ TAPE 3, (R(I,J), J=1,NM)                                     005
      REWIND 3                                                          006
      DO 80   K=1,NS                                                    007
      NK = N(K)                                                         008
      DO 80   L=K,NS                                                    009
      NL = N(L)                                                         010
      DO 73   I=1,NK                                                    011
      IK = NN(K) + I                                                    012
      DO 72   J=1,NS                                                    013
      JL = NN(L) + J                                                    014
      U(J) = 0.                                                         015
      DO 72   M=1,NL                                                    016
      ML = NN(L) + M                                                    017
  72  U(J) = U(J) + R(IK,ML) * B(ML,J)                                  018
      DO 73   J=1,NS                                                    019
      JL = NN(L) + J                                                    020
  73  R(IK,JL) = U(J)                                                   021
C PREMULTIPLICATION OF SUPERMATRIX BY DIAGONALS OF BETAS
      DO 76   J=1,NL                                                    023
      JL = NN(L) + J                                                    024
      DO 75   I=1,NS                                                    025
      U(I) = 0.                                                         026
      DO 75   M=1,NK                                                    027
      MK = NN(K) + M                                                    028
  75  U(I) = U(I) + B(MK,I) * R(MK,JL)                                  029
      DO 76   I=1,NS                                                    030
      IK = NN(K) + I                                                    031
  76  R(IK,JL) = U(I)                                                   032
      DO 80   I=1,NK                                                    033
      IK = NN(K) + I                                                    034
      DO 80   J=1,NL                                                    035
      JL = NN(L) + J                                                    036
  80  R(JL,IK) = R(IK,JL)                                               037
      DO 82   I=1,NM                                                    038
  82  WRITE OUTPUT TAPE 6, 904, (R(I,J), J=1,NM)                        039
      WRITE OUTPUT TAPE 6, 997                                          043
```

```
904    FORMAT (12F9.4)                                                  040
997    FORMAT(1H )                                                      041
       RETURN                                                           042
       END                                                              043
C
       SUBROUTINE BEE (NS,NSS,NM,N,NN,U,S,B)                            001
       DIMENSION N(1),NN(1),U(1),S(20,1),B(100,1)                       002
C PREMULTIPLICATION OF BETAS BY INVERSE OF TRIANGULAR                   003
       DO 62  K=1,NS                                                    004
       NK = N(K)                                                        005
       DO 60  I=1,NK                                                    006
60     READ TAPE 2, (S(I,J), J=1,NK)                                    007
       DO 62 J=1,NSS                                                    008
       DO 61  I=1,NK                                                    009
       U(I) = 0.                                                        010
       DO 61  M=I,NK                                                    011
       MK = NN(K) + M                                                   012
61     U(I) = U(I) + S(I,M) * B(MK,J)                                   013
       DO 62  I=1,NK                                                    014
       IK = NN(K) + I                                                   015
62     B(IK,J) = U(I)                                                   016
       REWIND 2                                                         017
       WRITE OUTPUT TAPE 6,997                                          018
       DO 70 I =1,NM                                                    019
70     WRITE OUTPUT TAPE 6,904, (B(I,J),J=1,NSS)                        020
       WRITE OUTPUT TAPE 6, 997                                         021
904    FORMAT (12F9.4)                                                  022
997    FORMAT (1H )                                                     023
       RETURN                                                           024
       END                                                              025
C
*      DATA
.00010
  3
  3
 40
  3  3  3
1.000  .249  .271  .636  .183  .185  .626  .369  .279
 .249 1.000  .399  .138  .654  .262  .190  .527  .356
 .271  .399 1.000  .180  .407  .613  .225  .471  .610
 .636  .138  .180 1.000  .091  .147  .709  .254  .191
 .183  .654  .407  .091 1.000  .296  .103  .541  .394
 .185  .262  .613  .147  .296 1.000  .179  .437  .496
 .626  .190  .225  .709  .103  .179 1.000  .291  .245
 .369  .527  .471  .254  .541  .437  .291 1.000  .429
 .279  .356  .610  .191  .394  .496  .245  .429 1.000
*      DATA
.00010
  3
  3
 40
  3  3  3
1.000  .249  .271  .636  .183  .185  .626  .369  .279
 .249 1.000  .399  .138  .654  .262  .190  .527  .356
 .271  .399 1.000  .180  .407  .613  .225  .471  .610
 .636  .138  .180 1.000  .091  .147  .709  .254  .191
 .183  .654  .407  .091 1.000  .296  .103  .541  .394
 .185  .262  .613  .147  .296 1.000  .179  .437  .496
 .626  .190  .225  .709  .103  .179 1.000  .291  .245
 .369  .527  .471  .254  .541  .437  .291 1.000  .429
 .279  .356  .610  .191  .394  .496  .245  .429 1.000
C CHAPTER 24 - MULTIPLE SET FACTOR ANALYSIS                            001
C    24.6 RANK ONE APPROXIMATION METHOD                                002
C                                                                      003
*      CHAIN (99,A4)                                                   001
       DIMENSION R(100,100), B(100,10), S(20,10), A(10,10),            005
      1U(100), UK(10), UL(10), N(10), NN(10)                           006
       EQUIVALENCE (U(1), UK(1)), (U(15), UL(1))                       007
       COMMON P, NS, NSS, NI, NM, N, NN                                008
       REWIND 2                                                        009
       REWIND 3                                                        010
       READ INPUT TAPE 5, 900, P, NS, NSS, NI                         011
       READ INPUT TAPE 5, 901, (N(I), I=1,NS)                         012
       WRITE OUTPUT TAPE 6, 901, (N(I), I=1,NS)                       013
       WRITE OUTPUT TAPE 6, 997                                        014
       P = .00001                                                      015
       NI = 100                                                        016
       NM = 0                                                          017
       DO 1  I=1,NS                                                    018
       NM = NM + N(I)                                                  019
       DO 201 I = 1,NM                                                 020
       READ INPUT TAPE 5, 903, (R(I,J),J=1,NM)                        021
201    WRITE OUTPUT TAPE 6,903,(R(I,J),J=1,NM)                        022
       WRITE OUTPUT TAPE 6, 997                                        024
       NN(1) = 0                                                       025
```

708

```
          DO 3   K=2,NS                                          026
    3     NN(K) = NN(K-1) + N(K-1)                               027
C INVERSE TRIANGULAR                                             028
          DO 8   K=1,NS                                          029
          NK = N(K)                                              030
          DO 4   I=1,NK                                          031
          IK = NN(K) + I                                         032
          DO 4   J=1,NK                                          033
          JK = NN(K) + J                                         034
    4     S(I,J) = R(IK,JK)                                      035
          CALL TRYIN (NK,S)                                      036
          DO 5   I=1,NK                                          037
          WRITE TAPE 2, (S(I,J), J=1,NK)                         038
    5     WRITE OUTPUT TAPE 6, 904, (S(I,J), J=1,NK)             039
          WRITE OUTPUT TAPE 6, 997                               040
C PREMULTIPLICATION BY INVERSE TRIANGULAR                        041
          DO 8   I=1,NM                                          042
          DO 6   J=1,NK                                          043
          U(J) = 0.                                              044
          DO 6   M=1,J                                           045
          MK = NN(K) + M                                         046
    6     U(J) = U(J) + R(I,MK) * S(M,J)                         047
          DO 8   J=1,NK                                          048
          JK = NN(K) + J                                         049
    8     R(I,JK) = U(J)                                         050
          REWIND 2                                               051
          DO 13   I=1,NM                                         052
   13     WRITE OUTPUT TAPE 6, 904, (R(I,J), J=1,NM)             053
          WRITE OUTPUT TAPE 6, 997                               054
C POSTMULTIPLICATION BY INVERSE TRIANGULAR                       055
          DO 18   K=1,NS                                         056
          NK = N(K)                                              057
          DO 14   I=1,NK                                         058
   14     READ TAPE 2, (S(I,J), J=1,NK)                          059
          DO 18   J=1,NM                                         060
          DO 16   I=1,NK                                         061
          U(I) = 0.                                              062
          DO 16   M=1,I                                          063
          MK = NN(K) + M                                         064
   16     U(I) = U(I) + S(M,I)*R(MK,J)                           065
          DO 18   I=1,NK                                         066
          IK = NN(K) + I                                         067
   18     R(IK,J) = U(I)                                         068
          REWIND 2                                               069
          DO 19   I=1,NM                                         070
          WRITE TAPE 3, (R(I,J), J=1,NM)                         071
   19     WRITE OUTPUT TAPE 6, 904, (R(I,J), J=1,NM)             072
          WRITE OUTPUT TAPE 6, 997                               073
          REWIND 3                                               074
          WRITE OUTPUT TAPE 6,999                                075
  900     FORMAT (F7.5/(I3))                                     076
  901     FORMAT (12I3)                                          077
  903     FORMAT (12F6.3)                                        078
  904     FORMAT (12F9.4)                                        079
  997     FORMAT (1H )                                           080
  999     FORMAT (1H1)                                           081
          CALL CHAIN (1, A4)                                     082
          END                                                    083
C
          SUBROUTINE TRYIN (N,A)                                 001
          DIMENSION A(20,1)                                      002
          N1 = N - 1                                             003
          DO 141   K=1,N1                                        004
          C = 1./SQRTF(A(K,K))                                   005
          DO 101   I=K,N                                         006
  101     A(I,K) = A(I,K) * C                                    007
          KK = K + 1                                             008
          DO 141   J =KK,N                                       009
          DO 141   I=J,N                                         010
  141     A(I,J) = A(I,J) - A(I,K) * A(J,K)                      011
          A(N,N) = SQRTF(A(N,N))                                 012
          A(1,1) = 1./A(1,1)                                     013
          DO 07 I = 2,N                                          014
          I1 = I-1                                               015
          DO 065 J = 1,I1                                        016
  065     A(I,J) = A(I,J)/A(I,I)                                 017
  07      A(I,I) = 1./A(I,I)                                     018
          DO 14 I = 1,N1                                         019
          I2 = I+1                                               020
          DO 14 J = I2,N                                         021
          J1 = J-1                                               022
          A(I,J) =0.                                             023
          DO 14 K = I,J1                                         024
  14      A(I,J) = A(I,J)- A(J,K)*A(I,K)                         025
          RETURN                                                 026
          END                                                    027
```

```
C
*       CHAIN (1,A4)                                                    004
        DIMENSION R(100,100), B(100,10), S(20,10), A(10,10),            005
       1U(100), UK(10), UL(10), N(10), NN(10)                           006
        EQUIVALENCE (U(1), UK(1)), (U(15), UL(1))                       007
        COMMON P, NS, NSS, NI, NM, N, NN                                008
        REWIND 3                                                        023
        DO 2  I=1,NM                                                    009
2       READ TAPE 3, (R(I,J), J=1,NM)                                   010
        REWIND 3                                                        011
        DO 22  M=1,NSS                                                  012
        F = 0.                                                          013
        DO 6  I=1,NM                                                    014
6       B(I,M) = 1.                                                     015
        DO 14 KK=1,NI                                                   016
        DO 8  I=1,NM                                                    017
        U(I) = 0.                                                       018
        DO 8  J=1,NM                                                    019
8       U(I) = U(I) + R(I,J) * B(J,M)                                   020
        D = 0.                                                          021
        DO 10  I=1,NM                                                   022
10      D = D + U(I) * B(I,M)                                           023
        D = SQRTF(D)                                                    024
        DO 12  I=1,NM                                                   025
12      B(I,M) = U(I) / D                                               026
        F1 = F                                                          027
        F = D                                                           028
        IF (P-ABSF(F1/F-1.)) 14, 14, 16                                 029
14      CONTINUE                                                        030
16      DO 20  K=1,NS                                                   031
        NK = N(K)                                                       032
        C = 0.                                                          033
        DO 18  I=1,NK                                                   034
        IK = NN(K) + I                                                  035
18      C = C + B(IK,M)**2                                              036
        C = SQRTF(C)                                                    037
        DO 20  I=1,NK                                                   038
        IK = NN(K) + I                                                  039
20      B(IK,M) = B(IK,M) / C                                           040
        CALL RESID (NS, N, NN, U, UL, UK, B, R, NM, M)                  041
22      CONTINUE                                                        042
        DO 100 I = 1,NM                                                 043
100     WRITE OUTPUT TAPE 6,904,(B(I,J),J=1,NSS)                        044
        WRITE OUTPUT TAPE 6,997                                         045
        CALL RHO (NS, NSS, NM, N, NN, U, B, R)                          046
        CALL BEE (NS, NSS, NM, N, NN, U, S, B)                          047
        WRITE OUTPUT TAPE 6, 999                                        048
904     FORMAT (12F9.4)                                                049
997     FORMAT (1H )                                                    050
999     FORMAT (1H1)                                                    051
        CALL EXIT                                                       052
        END                                                            053
C
        SUBROUTINE RESID (NS,N,NN,U,UL,UK,B,R,NM,M)
        DIMENSION N(1),NN(1),U(1),UL(1),UK(1),B(100,1),R(100,1)
C RESIDUAL SUPER MATRIX
42      DO 56  K=1,NS
        NK = N(K)
        DO 56 L = K,NS
        NL = N(L)
        DO 44  J=1,NL
        JL = NN(L) + J
        UL(J) = 0.
        DO 44  I=1,NK
        IK = NN(K) + I
44      UL(J) = UL(J) + B(IK,M) * R(IK,JL)
        G = 0.
        DO 46  J=1,NL
        JL = NN(L) + J
46      G = G + UL(J) * B(JL,M)
        G = G / 2.
        DO 48  J=1,NL
        JL = NN(L) + J
48      UL(J) = UL(J) - G * B(JL,M)
        DO 50  I=1,NK
        IK = NN(K) + I
        UK(I) = 0.
        DO 50  J=1,NL
        JL = NN(L) + J
50      UK(I) = UK(I) + R(IK,JL) * B(JL,M)
        DO 52  I=1,NK
        IK = NN(K) + I
52      UK(I) = UK(I) - G * B(IK,M)
        DO 54  I=1,NK
        IK = NN(K)+I
        DO 54  J=1,NL
        JL = NN(L) + J
```

710

```
 54    R(IK,JL) = R(IK,JL) - B(IK,M) * UL(J) - UK(I) * B(JL,M)
       DO 56  I=1,NK
       IK = NN(K) + I
       DO 56  J=1,NL
       JL = NN(L) + J
 56    R(JL,IK) = R(IK,JL)
       DO 57  I=1,NM
 57    WRITE OUTPUT TAPE 6, 904, (R(I,J), J=1,NM)
 58    WRITE OUTPUT TAPE 6, 997
904    FORMAT (12F9.4)
997    FORMAT (1H )
       RETURN
       END
C
       SUBROUTINE RHO (NS,NSS,NM,N,NN,U,B,R)
       DIMENSION N(1),NN(1),U(1),B(100,1),R(100,1)
C POSTMULTIPLICATION OF SUPER MATRIX BY DIAGONAL OF BETA,S
       DO 71  I=1,NM
 71    READ TAPE 3, (R(I,J), J=1,NM)
       REWIND 3
       DO 80  K=1,NS
       NK = N(K)
       DO 80  L=K,NS
       NL = N(L)
       DO 73  I=1,NK
       IK = NN(K) + I
       DO 72  J=1,NS
       JL = NN(L) + J
       U(J) = 0.
       DO 72  M=1,NL
       ML = NN(L) + M
 72    U(J) = U(J) + R(IK,ML) * B(ML,J)
       DO 73  J=1,NS
       JL = NN(L) + J
 73    R(IK,JL) = U(J)
C PREMULTIPLICATION OF SUPERMATRIX BY DIAGONAL OF BETA'S
       DO 76  J=1,NL
       JL = NN(L) + J
       DO 75  I=1,NS
       U(I) = 0.
       DO 75  M=1,NK
       MK = NN(K) + M
 75    U(I) = U(I) + B(MK,I) * R(MK,JL)
       DO 76  I=1,NS
       IK = NN(K) + I
 76    R(IK,JL) = U(I)
       DO 80  I=1,NK
       IK = NN(K) + I
       DO 80  J=1,NL
       JL = NN(L) + J
 80    R(JL,IK) = R(IK,JL)
       DO 82  I=1,NM
 82    WRITE OUTPUT TAPE 6, 904, (R(I,J), J=1,NM)
904    FORMAT (12F9.4)
997    FORMAT(1H )
       RETURN
       END
C
       SUBROUTINE BEE (NS,NSS,NM,N,NN,U,S,B)
       DIMENSION N(1),NN(1),U(1),S(20,1),B(100,1)
C PREMULTIPLICATION OF BETAS BY INVERSE OF TRIANGULAR
       DO 62  K=1,NS
       NK = N(K)
       DO 60  I=1,NK
 60    READ TAPE 2, (S(I,J), J=1,NK)
       DO 62  J=1,NSS
       DO 61  I=1,NK
       U(I) = 0.
       DO 61  M=I,NK
       MK = NN(K) + M
 61    U(I) = U(I) + S(I,M) * B(MK,J)
       DO 62  I=1,NK
       IK = NN(K) + I
 62    B(IK,J) = U(I)
       REWIND 2
       WRITE OUTPUT TAPE 6,997
       DO 70 I =1,NM
 70    WRITE OUTPUT TAPE 6,904, (B(I,J),J=1,NSS)
       WRITE OUTPUT TAPE 6, 997
904    FORMAT (12F9.4)
997    FORMAT (1H )
       RETURN
       END
C
*_    DATA
```

711

```
 .00010
  3
  3
 40
  3   3   3
1.000   .249   .271   .636   .183   .185   .626   .369   .279
 .249  1.000   .399   .138   .654   .262   .190   .527   .356
 .271   .399  1.000   .180   .407   .613   .225   .471   .610
 .636   .138   .180  1.000   .091   .147   .709   .254   .191
 .183   .654   .407   .091  1.000   .296   .103   .541   .394
 .185   .262   .613   .147   .296  1.000   .179   .437   .496
 .626   .190   .225   .709   .103   .179  1.000   .291   .245
 .369   .527   .471   .254   .541   .437   .291  1.000   .429
 .279   .356   .610   .191   .394   .496   .245   .429  1.000
```

```
C CHAPTER 24 - MULTIPLE SET FACTOR ANALYSIS                               001
C    24.7 OBLIQUE MAXIMUM VARIANCE METHOD                                 002
C                                                                         003
*     CHAIN (99,A4)                                                       001
      DIMENSION R(100,100), B(100,10), S(20,10), A(10,10),                005
     1U(100), UK(10), UL(10), N(10), NN(10)                               006
      EQUIVALENCE (U(1), UK(1)), (U(15), UL(1))                           007
      COMMON P, NS, NSS, NI, NM, N, NN                                    008
      REWIND 2                                                            009
      REWIND 3                                                            010
      READ INPUT TAPE 5, 900, P, NS, NSS, NI                             011
      READ INPUT TAPE 5, 901, (N(I), I=1,NS)                              012
      WRITE OUTPUT TAPE 6, 901, (N(I), I=1,NS)                            013
      WRITE OUTPUT TAPE 6, 997                                            014
      P = .00001                                                          015
      NI = 100                                                            016
      NM = 0                                                              017
      DO 1  I=1,NS                                                        018
 1    NM = NM + N(I)                                                      019
      DO 201 I = 1,NM                                                     020
      READ INPUT TAPE 5, 903, (R(I,J),J=1,NM)                             021
 201  WRITE OUTPUT TAPE 6,903,(R(I,J),J=1,NM)                             022
      WRITE OUTPUT TAPE 6, 997                                            024
      NN(1) = 0                                                           025
      DO 3  K=2,NS                                                        026
 3    NN(K) = NN(K-1) + N(K-1)                                            027
C INVERSE TRIANGULAR                                                      028
      DO 8  K=1,NS                                                        029
      NK = N(K)                                                           030
      DO 4  I=1,NK                                                        031
      IK = NN(K) + I                                                      032
      DO 4  J=1,NK                                                        033
      JK = NN(K) + J                                                      034
 4    S(I,J) = R(IK,JK)                                                   035
      CALL TRYIN (NK,S)                                                   036
      DO 5  I=1,NK                                                        037
      WRITE TAPE 2, (S(I,J), J=1,NK)                                      038
 5    WRITE OUTPUT TAPE 6, 904, (S(I,J), J=1,NK)                          039
      WRITE OUTPUT TAPE 6, 997                                            040
C PREMULTIPLICATION BY INVERSE TRIANGULAR                                 041
      DO 8  I=1,NM                                                        042
      DO 6  J=1,NK                                                        043
      U(J) = 0.                                                           044
      DO 6  M=1,J                                                         045
      MK = NN(K) + M                                                      046
 6    U(J) = U(J) + R(I,MK) * S(M,J)                                      047
      DO 8  J=1,NK                                                        048
      JK = NN(K) + J                                                      049
 8    R(I,JK) = U(J)                                                      050
      REWIND 2                                                            051
      DO 13  I=1,NM                                                       052
 13   WRITE OUTPUT TAPE 6, 904, (R(I,J), J=1,NM)                          053
      WRITE OUTPUT TAPE 6, 997                                            054
C POSTMULTIPLICATION BY INVERSE TRIANGULAR                                055
      DO 18  K=1,NS                                                       056
      NK = N(K)                                                           057
      DO 14  I=1,NK                                                       058
 14   READ TAPE 2, (S(I,J), J=1,NK)                                       059
      DO 18  J=1,NM                                                       060
      DO 16  I=1,NK                                                       061
      U(I) = 0.                                                           062
      DO 16  M=1,I                                                        063
      MK = NN(K) + M                                                      064
 16   U(I) = U(I) + S(M,I)*R(MK,J)                                        065
      DO 18  I=1,NK                                                       066
      IK = NN(K) + I                                                      067
 18   R(IK,J) = U(I)                                                      068
      REWIND 2                                                            069
      DO 19  I=1,NM                                                       070
      WRITE TAPE 3, (R(I,J), J=1,NM)                                      071
```

712

```
 19     WRITE OUTPUT TAPE 6, 904, (R(I,J), J=1,NM)          072
        WRITE OUTPUT TAPE 6, 997                            073
        REWIND 3                                            074
        WRITE OUTPUT TAPE 6,999                             075
 900    FORMAT (F7.5/(I3))                                  076
 901    FORMAT (12I3)                                       077
 903    FORMAT (12F6.3)                                     078
 904    FORMAT (12F9.4)                                     079
 997    FORMAT (1H )                                        080
 999    FORMAT (1H1)                                        081
        CALL CHAIN (1, A4)                                  082
         END                                                083
C
        SUBROUTINE TRYIN (N,A)                              001
        DIMENSION A(20,1)                                   002
        N1 = N - 1                                          003
        DO 141   K=1,N1                                     004
        C = 1./SQRTF(A(K,K))                                005
        DO 101   I=K,N                                      006
 101    A(I,K) = A(I,K) * C                                 007
        KK = K + 1                                          008
        DO 141   J =KK,N                                    009
        DO 141   I=J,N                                      010
 141    A(I,J) = A(I,J) - A(I,K) * A(J,K)                   011
        A(N,N) = SQRTF(A(N,N))                              012
        A(1,1) = 1./A(1,1)                                  013
        DO 07 I = 2,N                                       014
        I1 = I-1                                            015
        DO 065 J = 1,I1                                     016
 065    A(I,J) = A(I,J)/A(I,I)                              017
 07     A(I,I) = 1./A(I,I)                                  018
        DO 14 I = 1,N1                                      019
        I2 = I+1                                            020
        DO 14 J = I2,N                                      021
        J1 = J-1.                                           022
        A(I,J) =0.                                          023
        DO 14 K = I,J1                                      024
 14     A(I,J) = A(I,J)- A(J,K)*A(I,K)                      025
        RETURN                                              026
         END                                                027
C
 *      CHAIN (1,A4)                                        004
        DIMENSION R(100,100), B(100,10), S(20,10), A(10,10),  005
       1U(100), UK(10), UL(10), N(10), NN(10)               006
        EQUIVALENCE (U(1), UK(1)), (U(15), UL(1))           007
        COMMON P, NS, NSS, NI, NM, N, NN                    008
        REWIND 3                                            009
        DO 2   I=1,NM                                       010
 2      READ TAPE 3, (R(I,J), J=1,NM)                       011
        REWIND 3                                            012
        DO 16   M=1,NSS                                     013
        F = 0.                                              014
        DO 6   I=1,NM                                       015
 6      B(I,M) = 1.                                         016
        DO 12 KK=1,NI                                       017
        DO 8   I=1,NM                                       018
        U(I) = 0.                                           019
        DO 8   J=1,NM                                       020
 8      U(I) = U(I) + R(I,J) * B(J,M)                       021
        D = 0.                                              022
        DO 10   I=1,NM                                      023
 10     D = D + U(I) * B(I,M)                               024
        D = SQRTF(D)                                        025
        DO 11   I=1,NM                                      026
 11     B(I,M) = U(I) / D                                   027
        F1 = F                                              028
        F = D                                               029
        IF (P-ABSF(F1/F-1.)) 12, 12, 13                     030
 12     CONTINUE                                            031
 13     DO 16   I=1,NM                                      032
        DO 16 J =I,NM                                       033
 14     R(I,J) = R(I,J) - B(I,M) * B(J,M)                   034
 16     R(J,I) = R(I,J)                                     035
        DO 20   M=1,NSS                                     036
        DO 20   K=1,NS                                      037
        NK = N(K)                                           038
        C = 0.                                              039
        DO 18   I=1,NK                                      040
        IK = NN(K) + I                                      041
 18     C = C + B(IK,M)**2                                  042
        C = SQRTF(C)                                        043
        DO 20   I=1,NK                                      044
        IK = NN(K) + I                                      045
 20     B(IK,M) = B(IK,M) / C                               046
        DO 22   I=1,NM
```

713

```
22     WRITE OUTPUT TAPE 6, 904, (B(I,M), M=1,NSS)                    047
       WRITE OUTPUT TAPE 6, 997                                       048
       CALL RHO (NS, NSS, NM, N, NN, U, B, R)                         049
       CALL BEE (NS, NSS, NM, N, NN, U, S, B)                         050
       WRITE OUTPUT TAPE 6, 999                                       051
904    FORMAT (12F9.4)                                                052
997    FORMAT (1H )                                                   053
999    FORMAT (1H1)                                                   054
       CALL EXIT                                                      055
       END                                                            056
C
       SUBROUTINE RHO (NS,NSS,NM,N,NN,U,B,R)
       DIMENSION N(1),NN(1),U(1),B(100,1),R(100,1)
C POSTMULTIPLICATION OF SUPER MATRIX BY DIAGONAL OF BETA,S
       DO 71  I=1,NM
71     READ TAPE 3, (R(I,J), J=1,NM)
       REWIND 3
       DO 80  K=1,NS
       NK = N(K)
       DO 80  L=K,NS
       NL = N(L)
       DO 73  I=1,NK
       IK = NN(K) + I
       DO 72  J=1,NS
       JL = NN(L) + J
       U(J) = 0.
       DO 72  M=1,NL
       ML = NN(L) + M
72     U(J) = U(J) + R(IK,ML) * B(ML,J)
       DO 73  J=1,NS
       JL = NN(L) + J
73     R(IK,JL) = U(J)
C PREMULTIPLICATION OF SUPERMATRIX BY DIAGONAL OF BETA'S
       DO 76  J=1,NL
       JL = NN(L) + J
       DO 75  I=1,NS
       U(I) = 0.
       DO 75  M=1,NK
       MK = NN(K) + M
75     U(I) = U(I) + B(MK,I) * R(MK,JL)
       DO 76  I=1,NS
       IK = NN(K) + I
76     R(IK,JL) = U(I)
       DO 80  I=1,NK
       IK = NN(K) + I
       DO 80  J=1,NL
       JL = NN(L) + J
80     R(JL,IK) = R(IK,JL)
       DO 82  I=1,NM
82     WRITE OUTPUT TAPE 6, 904, (R(I,J), J=1,NM)
904    FORMAT (12F9.4)
997    FORMAT(1H )
       RETURN
       END
C
       SUBROUTINE BEE (NS,NSS,NM,N,NN,U,S,B)
       DIMENSION N(1),NN(1),U(1),S(20,1),B(100,1)
C PREMULTIPLICATION OF BETAS BY INVERSE OF TRIANGULAR
       DO 62  K=1,NS
       NK = N(K)
       DO 60  I=1,NK
60     READ TAPE 2, (S(I,J), J=1,NK)
       DO 62  J=1,NSS
       DO 61  I=1,NK
       U(I) = 0.
       DO 61  M=I,NK
       MK = NN(K) + M
61     U(I) = U(I) + S(I,M) * B(MK,J)
       DO 62  I=1,NK
       IK = NN(K) + I
62     B(IK,J) = U(I)
       REWIND 2
       WRITE OUTPUT TAPE 6,997
       DO 70 I =1,NM
70     WRITE OUTPUT TAPE 6,904, (B(I,J),J=1,NSS)
       WRITE OUTPUT TAPE 6, 997
904    FORMAT (12F9.4)
997    FORMAT (1H )
       RETURN
       END
C
*      DATA
.00010
3
3
```

714

```
40
3  3  3
1.000  .249  .271  .636  .183  .185  .626  .369  .279
.249 1.000  .399  .138  .654  .262  .190  .527  .356
.271  .399 1.000  .180  .407  .613  .225  .471  .610
.636  .138  .180 1.000  .091  .147  .709  .254  .191
.183  .654  .407  .091 1.000  .296  .103  .541  .394
.185  .262  .613  .147  .296 1.000  .179  .437  .496
.626  .190  .225  .709  .103  .179 1.000  .291  .245
.369  .527  .471  .254  .541  .437  .291 1.000  .429
.279  .356  .610  .191  .394  .496  .245  .429 1.000
```

```
C CHAPTER 24 - MULTIPLE SET FACTOR ANALYSIS                          001
C    24.8 ORTHOGONAL MAXIMUM VARIANCE METHOD                         002
C                                                                    003
*     CHAIN (99,A4)                                                  001
      DIMENSION R(100,100), B(100,10), S(20,10), A(10,10),           005
     1U(100), UK(10), UL(10), N(10), NN(10)                          006
      EQUIVALENCE (U(1), UK(1)), (U(15), UL(1))                      007
      COMMON P, NS, NSS, NI, NM, N, NN                               008
      REWIND 2                                                       009
      REWIND 3                                                       010
      READ INPUT TAPE 5, 900, P, NS, NSS, NI                        011
      READ INPUT TAPE 5, 901, (N(I), I=1,NS)                        012
      WRITE OUTPUT TAPE 6, 901, (N(I), I=1,NS)                      013
      WRITE OUTPUT TAPE 6, 997                                      014
      P = .00001                                                    015
      NI = 100                                                      016
      NM = 0                                                        017
      DO 1  I=1,NS                                                  018
1     NM = NM + N(I)                                                019
      DO 201 I = 1,NM                                               020
      READ INPUT TAPE 5, 903, (R(I,J),J=1,NM)                      021
201   WRITE OUTPUT TAPE 6,903,(R(I,J),J=1,NM)                      022
      WRITE OUTPUT TAPE 6, 997                                      024
      NN(1) = 0                                                     025
      DO 3  K=2,NS                                                  026
3     NN(K) = NN(K-1) + N(K-1)                                      027
C INVERSE TRIANGULAR                                                028
      DO 8  K=1,NS                                                  029
      NK = N(K)                                                     030
      DO 4  I=1,NK                                                  031
      IK = NN(K) + I                                                032
      DO 4  J=1,NK                                                  033
      JK = NN(K) + J                                                034
4     S(I,J) = R(IK,JK)                                             035
      CALL TRYIN (NK,S)                                             036
      DO 5  I=1,NK                                                  037
      WRITE TAPE 2, (S(I,J), J=1,NK)                                038
5     WRITE OUTPUT TAPE 6, 904, (S(I,J), J=1,NK)                   039
      WRITE OUTPUT TAPE 6, 997                                      040
C PREMULTIPLICATION BY INVERSE TRIANGULAR                           041
      DO 8  I=1,NM                                                  042
      DO 6  J=1,NK                                                  043
      U(J) = 0.                                                     044
      DO 6  M=1,J                                                   045
      MK = NN(K) + M                                                046
6     U(J) = U(J) + R(I,MK) * S(M,J)                               047
      DO 8  J=1,NK                                                  048
      JK = NN(K) + J                                                049
8     R(I,JK) = U(J)                                                050
      REWIND 2                                                      051
      DO 13  I=1,NM                                                 052
13    WRITE OUTPUT TAPE 6, 904, (R(I,J), J=1,NM)                   053
      WRITE OUTPUT TAPE 6, 997                                      054
C POSTMULTIPLICATION BY INVERSE TRIANGULAR                          055
      DO 18  K=1,NS                                                 056
      NK = N(K)                                                     057
      DO 14  I=1,NK                                                 058
14    READ TAPE 2, (S(I,J), J=1,NK)                                059
      DO 18  J=1,NM                                                 060
      DO 16  I=1,NK                                                 061
      U(I) = 0.                                                     062
      DO 16  M=1,I                                                  063
      MK = NN(K) + M                                                064
16    U(I) = U(I) + S(M,I)*R(MK,J)                                 065
      DO 18  I=1,NK                                                 066
      IK = NN(K) + I                                                067
18    R(IK,J) = U(I)                                                068
      REWIND 2                                                      069
      DO 19  I=1,NM                                                 070
      WRITE TAPE 3, (R(I,J), J=1,NM)                                071
19    WRITE OUTPUT TAPE 6, 904, (R(I,J), J=1,NM)                   072
      WRITE OUTPUT TAPE 6, 997                                      073
      REWIND 3                                                      074
      WRITE OUTPUT TAPE 6,999                                       075
```

715

```
900   FORMAT (F7.5/(I3))                                          076
901   FORMAT (12I3)                                               077
903   FORMAT (12F6.3)                                             078
904   FORMAT (12F9.4)                                             079
997   FORMAT (1H )                                                080
999   FORMAT (1H1)                                                081
      CALL CHAIN (1, A4)                                          082
      END                                                        083
C
      SUBROUTINE TRYIN (N,A)                                      001
      DIMENSION A(20,1)                                           002
      N1 = N - 1                                                  003
      DO 141  K=1,N1                                              004
      C = 1./SQRTF(A(K,K))                                        005
      DO 101  I=K,N                                               006
101   A(I,K) = A(I,K) * C                                         007
      KK = K + 1                                                  008
      DO 141  J =KK,N                                             009
      DO 141  I=J,N                                               010
141   A(I,J) = A(I,J) - A(I,K) * A(J,K)                           011
      A(N,N) = SQRTF(A(N,N))                                      012
      A(1,1) = 1./A(1,1)                                          013
      DO 07 I = 2,N                                               014
      I1 = I-1                                                    015
      DO 065 J = 1,I1                                             016
065   A(I,J) = A(I,J)/A(I,I)                                      017
07    A(I,I) = 1./A(I,I)                                          018
      DO 14 I = 1,N1                                              019
      I2 = I+1                                                    020
      DO 14 J = I2,N                                              021
      J1 = J-1                                                    022
      A(I,J) =0.                                                  023
      DO 14 K = I,J1                                              024
14    A(I,J) = A(I,J)- A(J,K)*A(I,K)                              025
      RETURN                                                      026
      END                                                        027
C
*     CHAIN (1,A4)                                                004
      DIMENSION R(100,100), B(100,10), S(20,10), A(10,10),        005
     1U(100), UK(10), UL(10), N(10), NN(10)                       006
      EQUIVALENCE (U(1), UK(1)), (U(15), UL(1))                   007
      COMMON P, NS, NSS, NI, NM, N, NN                            008
      DO 2  I=1,NM                                                009
2     READ TAPE 3, (R(I,J), J=1,NM)                               010
      REWIND 3                                                    011
      DO 16  M=1,NSS                                              012
      F = 0.                                                      013
      DO 6  I=1,NM                                                014
6     B(I,M) = 1.                                                 015
      DO 12 KK=1,NI                                               016
      DO 8  I=1,NM                                                017
      U(I) = 0.                                                   018
      DO 8  J=1,NM                                                019
8     U(I) = U(I) + R(I,J) * B(J,M)                               020
      D = 0.                                                      021
      DO 10  I=1,NM                                               022
10    D = D + U(I) * B(I,M)                                       023
      D = SQRTF(D)                                                024
      DO 11 I=1,NM                                                025
11    B(I,M) = U(I) / D                                           026
      F1 = F                                                      027
      F = D                                                       028
      IF (P-ABSF(F1/F-1.)) 12, 12, 13                             029
12    CONTINUE                                                    030
13    DO 16  I=1,NM                                               031
      DO 16 J =I,NM                                               032
14    R(I,J) = R(I,J) - B(I,M) * B(J,M)                           033
16    R(J,I) = R(I,J)                                             034
      WRITE OUTPUT TAPE 6,997                                     035
      DO 101 I =1,NM                                              036
101   WRITE OUTPUT TAPE 6,904,(B(I,J),J=1,NSS)                    037
      WRITE OUTPUT TAPE 6,997                                     038
      DO 23 K=1,NS                                                039
      NK = N(K)                                                   040
      DO 162 I = 1,NSS                                            041
      DO 162 J=I,NSS                                              042
      S(I,J) = 0.                                                 043
      DO 161 M = 1,NK                                             044
      MK = NN(K) + M                                              045
161   S(I,J) = S(I,J) + B(MK,I) * B(MK,J)                         046
162   S(J,I) = S(I,J)                                             047
      WRITE OUTPUT TAPE 6,997                                     048
      DO 102 I =1,NSS                                             049
102   WRITE OUTPUT TAPE 6,904,(S(I,J),J=1,NSS)                    050
      CALL JACSIM (S, U, P, NSS, NI)                              051
```

716

```
       WRITE OUTPUT TAPE 6,997                                        052
       N2 = NSS*2                                                     053
       DO 103 I=1,N2                                                  054
103    WRITE OUTPUT TAPE 6,904,(S(I,J),J=1,NSS)                       055
       WRITE OUTPUT TAPE 6,997                                        056
       DO 17  I=1,NSS                                                 057
17     U(I) = 1./SQRTF(U(I))                                         058
       DO 19 I =1,NSS                                                 059
       IS = I + NSS                                                  060
       DO 19 J=I,NSS                                                  061
       JS = J + NSS                                                  062
       S(I,J) = 0.                                                    063
       DO 18  M=1,NSS                                                 064
18     S(I,J) = S(I,J) + S(IS,M) * U(M) * S(JS,M)                    065
19     S(J,I) = S(I,J)                                                066
       WRITE OUTPUT TAPE 6,997                                        067
       DO 104 I=1,NSS                                                 068
104    WRITE OUTPUT TAPE 6,904,(S(I,J),J=1,NSS)                       069
       WRITE OUTPUT TAPE 6,997                                        070
       DO 22  I=1,NK                                                  071
       IK = NN(K) + I                                                 072
       DO 20  J=1,NSS                                                 073
       U(J) = 0.                                                      074
       DO 20  M=1,NSS                                                 075
20     U(J) = U(J) + B(IK,M) * S(M,J)                                 076
       DO 22  J=1,NSS                                                 077
22     B(IK,J) = U(J)                                                 078
23     CONTINUE                                                       079
       DO 24  I=1,NM                                                  080
24     WRITE OUTPUT TAPE 6, 904, (B(I,J), J=1,NSS)                    081
       WRITE OUTPUT TAPE 6,997                                        082
       CALL RHO (NS, NSS, NM, N, NN, U, B, R)                         083
       CALL BEE (NS, NSS, NM, N, NN, U, S, B)                         084
       WRITE OUTPUT TAPE 6, 999                                       085
904    FORMAT (12F9.4)                                                086
997    FORMAT (1H )                                                   087
999    FORMAT (1H1)                                                   088
       CALL    EXIT                                                   089
       END                                                            090
C
       SUBROUTINE RHO (NS,NSS,NM,N,NN,U,B,R)
       DIMENSION N(1),NN(1),U(1),B(100,1),R(100,1)
C POSTMULTIPLICATION OF SUPER MATRIX BY DIAGONAL OF BETA,S
       DO 71  I=1,NM
71     READ TAPE 3, (R(I,J), J=1,NM)
       REWIND 3
       DO 80  K=1,NS
       NK = N(K)
       DO 80  L=K,NS
       NL = N(L)
       DO 73  I=1,NK
       IK = NN(K) + I
       DO 72  J=1,NS
       JL = NN(L) + J
       U(J) = 0.
       DO 72  M=1,NL
       ML = NN(L) + M
72     U(J) = U(J) + R(IK,ML) * B(ML,J)
       DO 73  J=1,NS
       JL = NN(L) + J
73     R(IK,JL) = U(J)
C PREMULTIPLICATION OF SUPERMATRIX BY DIAGONAL OF BETA'S
       DO 76  J=1,NL
       JL = NN(L) + J
       DO 75  I=1,NS
       U(I) = 0.
       DO 75  M=1,NK
       MK = NN(K) + M
75     U(I) = U(I) + B(MK,I) * R(MK,JL)
       DO 76  I=1,NS
       IK = NN(K) + I
76     R(IK,JL) = U(I)
       DO 80  I=1,NK
       IK = NN(K) + I
       DO 80  J=1,NL
       JL = NN(L) + J
80     R(JL,IK) = R(IK,JL)
       DO 82  I=1,NM
82     WRITE OUTPUT TAPE 6, 904, (R(I,J), J=1,NM)
904    FORMAT (12F9.4)
997    FORMAT(1H )
       RETURN
       END
```

```
C
      SUBROUTINE BEE (NS,NSS,NM,N,NN,U,S,B)
      DIMENSION N(1),NN(1),U(1),S(20,1),B(100,1)
C PREMULTIPLICATION OF BETAS BY INVERSE OF TRIANGULAR
      DO 62  K=1,NS
      NK = N(K)
      DO 60  I=1,NK
 60   READ TAPE 2, (S(I,J), J=1,NK)
      DO 62 J=1,NSS
      DO 61 I=1,NK
      U(I) = 0.
      DO 61  M=I,NK
      MK = NN(K) + M
 61   U(I) = U(I) + S(I,M) * B(MK,J)
      DO 62 I=1,NK
      IK = NN(K) + I
 62   B(IK,J) = U(I)
      REWIND 2
      WRITE OUTPUT TAPE 6,997
      DO 70 I =1,NM
 70   WRITE OUTPUT TAPE 6,904, (B(I,J),J=1,NSS)
      WRITE OUTPUT TAPE 6, 997
 904  FORMAT (12F9.4)
 997  FORMAT (1H )
      RETURN
      END
C
      SUBROUTINE JACSIM (R, D, P, N, NL)            001
      DIMENSION R(20,1), D(1)                       002
      N1 = N+1                                      003
      N11=N-1                                       004
      N2 = N*2                                      005
      DO 10  I=N1, N2                               006
      DO 10  J = 1,N                                007
 10   R(I,J) = 0.                                   008
      DO 12  I=1,N                                  009
      NI = N + I                                    010
 12   R(NI,I) = 1.                                  011
      DO 35 L=1,NL                                  012
      DO 15  I=1,N                                  013
 15   D(I) = R(I,I)                                 014
      DO 282 I = 1,N11                              015
      I1 = I+1                                      016
      DO 282 J= I1,N                                017
      DR = R(I,I) - R(J,J)                          018
      A = SQRTF(DR**2 + 4.*R(I,J)**2)              019
      A = SQRTF((A+DR)/(2.*A))                     020
      B = SQRTF(1.-A**2)                            021
      C = SIGNF(1.,R(I,J))                          022
      DO 252 K = 1,N2                               023
      U = R(K,I)*A*C + R(K,J)*B                    024
      R(K,J) = -R(K,I)*B*C + R(K,J)*A              025
 252  R(K,I) = U                                    026
      DO 282 K = 1,N                                027
      U = R(I,K)*A*C + R(J,K)*B                    028
      R(J,K) = -R(I,K)*B*C + R(J,K)*A              029
 282  R(I,K) = U                                    030
      DO 30  I=1,N                                  031
 30   D(I) = ABSF(D(I) - R(I,I))                   032
      S = 0.                                        033
      DO 33  I=1,N                                  034
 33   S = MAX1F (S, D(I))                          035
      DO 332 I =1,N                                 036
 332  D(I) = R(I,I)                                 037
      IF (S-P) 38, 38, 35                          038
 35   CONTINUE                                      039
 38   RETURN                                        040
      END                                           041
C
*     DATA
.00010
 3
 3
40
 3   3   3
1.000  .249  .271  .636  .183  .185  .626  .369  .279
 .249 1.000  .399  .138  .654  .262  .190  .527  .356
 .271  .399 1.000  .180  .407  .613  .225  .471  .610
 .636  .138  .180 1.000  .091  .147  .709  .254  .191
 .183  .654  .407  .091 1.000  .296  .103  .541  .394
 .185  .262  .613  .147  .296 1.000  .179  .437  .496
 .626  .190  .225  .709  .103  .179 1.000  .291  .245
 .369  .527  .471  .254  .541  .437  .291 1.000  .429
 .279  .356  .610  .191  .394  .496  .245  .429 1.000
```

718

Index

Addition, associative law of, 49
  commutative law of, 50
  distributive law as check for, 62
  of matrices, 49–50.
  of supermatrices, 50
Analytical rotations, 385, 420–422
Anthropology, applications of factor analysis in, 25
Anti-image matrix, 365
Approximation to basic structure, 115–116
Approximation matrix, 95–96
Arbitrary factor matrix, 386
Arbitrary matrix, 99, 102, 442
  and grouping methods, 137–138
  primary factor matrix from, 388, 397–401
    proof of, 412–413
Associative law, of addition, 49
  as check for matrix multiplication, 61
  of matrix multiplication, 61
Attribute, -entity sets, 315–317
  -occasion sets, 317
Attributes, 8, 12, 15–16
  criterion, 22, 30, 539
  and entities, reciprocal nature of, 29–30
  predictor, 22, 30, 539
  scaling by, 333–334, 335
  in two-category sets, 15–16
  See also Variables

Bartlett, M. S., 496
Basic diagonal, 82, 83
Basic matrices, 79
  rank of, 81
  vertical, general inverse of, 87
Basic structure, 105, 156
  approximation to, 115–116
  from data matrix, 259–260, 266–273, 273–278
    proof of, 280–283
  and image covariance, 364
  ipsative from normative, 305–307
    proof of, 312–314

Basic structure (*Continued*)
  and iterative solution, 158
  and least square solution, 157
  and left centering, 296–307, 310–312
  of a matrix, 81–84
    definition of, 81–82
  of a nonbasic matrix, 82
  normative from ipsative, 307–310
  normative from raw covariance, 303–305
  and order reduction, 211
  and origin, 295
  of a product moment matrix, 82–83
  and raw covariance matrix, 296–303
  and right centering, proof of, 312–314
  and successive factors, 157
  See also Principal axis method
Basic structure solution, 102–106
  and prediction, 541, 545–547
    proof of, 559–560
  with residual matrix, 159–160, 160–167
    proof of, 173–176
  without residual matrix, 160, 167–173
    proof of, 176–177
  and scaling, 336, 337
Bauer, F. L., 224
B-coefficient methods, 386
Bifactor method, 137, 139
Binary data matrix, 513, 515
Binary matrix, 38
Binary vector, 39
  and group centroid, 138–143
    proof of, 152–153
Bodewig, E., 545
Burket, G. R., 470, 551
Business, applications of factor analysis in, 25

Campbell, D. L., 565
Carroll, John, 418, 419, 420, 421
Categories, 9, 10
  See also Sets